The Individual IN SOCIETY

Guillermo J. Grenier

Fabiana Brunetta

Kendall Hunt
publishing company

Kendall Hunt
publishing company

www.kendallhunt.com
Send all inquiries to:
4050 Westmark Drive
Dubuque, IA 52004-1840

Copyright © 2014, 2015 by Kendall Hunt Publishing Company

ISBN 978-1-4652-8099-2

Printed in the United States of America

Contents

How do Sociologists look at the Individual and Society?

In the movie, the Matrix, the main character, Neo, has a special power. He can see the true dynamics of the world around him. He can see how everything in his world, even the objects that seem solid and material, are made of endless strings of computer code. Most of the people inhabiting the world are not aware of this. Indeed, Neo was not aware of this until he made a conscious choice to begin training his ability to see the Matrix. He was offered a choice by Morpheus, the leader of the group compelled to know the secrets of the Matrix. Morpheus offer Neo a choice in the form of two pills in his outstretched hands. If Neo chose to take the Blue Pill, he would be sent back to his bed and remain unaware of the true nature of the Matrix. If he takes the Red Pill, he agrees that he will embrace the sometime painful task of trying to understand the true nature of the Matrix. Neo chose the Red Pill. By taking this course, you have chosen the Red Pill. In the readings ahead, you will learn to see the world as how a sociologist sees the world. You will see how the sometimes invisible forces of society shape our everyday lives as individuals. A well trained sociologist will look at the invisible forces of society much like Neo was able to look at the workings of the Matrix. Sociologist attempt to understand how society "really" works: how we are shaped by social forces that are invisible to our eyes and how we can, sometimes, influence those forces ourselves. All sociologists are interested in the experiences of individuals and how those experiences are shaped by interactions with social groups and society as a whole. To a sociologist, the personal decisions an individual makes do not exist in a vacuum. Cultural patterns and social forces put pressure on people to select one choice over another. Sociologists try to identify these general patterns by examining the behavior of large groups of people living in the same society and experiencing the same societal pressures.

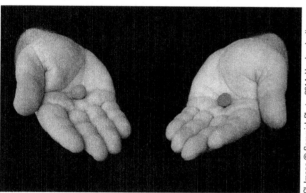

CL Image © Semmick Photo, 2014. Used under license from Shutterstock, Inc.

Social forces are mostly invisible. The gun that the policeman wears is a visible sign of his authority. But where does she get her authority? To understand that we have to learn a bit about social power, social solidarity, cultural deviance and the dynamics of bureaucracy. Most of these social forces are invisible to

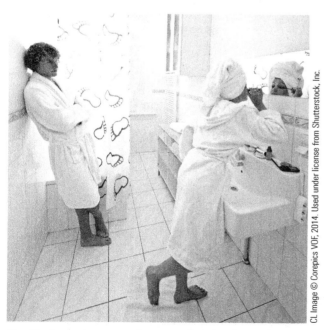

CL Image © Corepics VOF, 2014. Used under license from Shutterstock, Inc.

The Nacirema have peculiar grooming rituals conducted with specific tools in designated geographical locations.

Masai warriors performing the traditional Jump Dance. To be a Masai male is to be a member of one of the world's last great warrior cultures. Those who jump higher are considered to be more manly and more sought after as partners by women. To non-Masai's this ritual might be considered strange but to them, it is a valuable element of their culture which allows for individual differentiation from the group.

the senses, unless you are trained to look for their manifestation in social life. Social forces areas real as the invisible digital waves that work their way through the atmosphere between the cell phone of your friends or your "friends" list on Facebook; or the music that you download through the internet to hear on your mobile device.

Sociology is the systematic study of society and social interaction. The word "sociology" is derived from the Latin word *socius* (companion) and the Greek word *logos* (study of), meaning "the study of companionship." This is a starting point for the discipline, but, of course, sociology is actually much more complex. It uses many different methods to study a wide range of subject matter and to apply these studies to the real world.

Sociologists study all aspects and levels of society. We study the individual and society. But primarily we study the interaction between individuals and society. What is an individual? The Merriam-Webster Dictionary defines the individual as "of, relating to, or existing as just one member or part of a larger group." And what is a "society?" A society is a group of people whose members interact, reside in a definable area, and share a culture. A culture includes the group's shared practices, values, and beliefs. So individuals are part of groups within a society. This set of readings will introduce you to some of the influences that individuals have on society and, more importantly, how individuals are shaped by society.

Anti-government demonstration during the pro-European protest on December 1, 2013 in the center of Kiev, Ukraine. Social forces have an impact on individual lives every day.

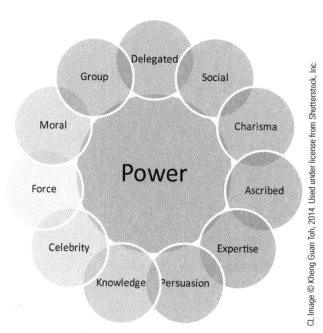

Power is a social force that is sometimes exerted through visible means but mostly it is an invisible dimension of social interaction. How do you feel the force of social power in your life? Who has power over you? When?

The Nepalese cremation ceremony puts the remains of a loved one into the holy river Bagmati. How would they view an open casket ritual at the local funeral home?

While sociology still focuses on how society creates the individual and the world that we live in, we now recognize that we are a species that has created and used society, and its structures, to survive. We managed to survive and develop as humans by creating the "social facts" that have given us an adaptive edge in a largely indifferent universe. Sociologists are interested in the lives of individuals and how individual lives are shaped by social forces independent of the individual. To a sociologist, the personal decisions that we all make are established by the cultural patterns and social forces that shape our lives. Sociologists try to identify these general patterns by examining the behavior of individuals in groups living in the same society and experiencing the same social forces.

What we consider to be individualism, the autonomous control of ourself, can be best understood as a point in a continuum. Some societies value individualism while others place more value on collectivist behavior. Similarly, in sociology and anthropology, we try to establish the relationship between Agency (the individual's ability to exist as an autonomous being) and Structure (the social forces/structures which shape individual ideas and behaviors). Society is a system; all parts are interrelated and when you alter one part, the other parts respond. All societies, from the hunting and gathering societies to our modern industrial society, share these systemic characteristics. We, as individuals, also form part of the system; we are part of the social organization of society.

As a species of organisms we survive by adapting to the specific environments to which we are exposed. We develop adaptive responses (thumbs, brains, language, culture, etc.) which give us a chance at survival. In this way, certain patterns of manifested by biology and behaviors are established which secure survival. In the human species, these patterns take the shape of social systems that include both specific and universal characteristics. We humans then live in those systems and, in turn, continue having an impact on the environment. We are products of our society and, in turn, our society is a product of social forces that have been at work for much longer than our individual lives. There is elegance and beauty to this relationship that I hope you will begin to recognize as you advance through the readings.

When we use the sociological imagination, as your readings will attest, we see that the individual and society are inseparable. It is impossible to study one without the other. German sociologist Norbert Elias called the process of simultaneously analyzing the behavior of individuals and the society that shapes that behavior **figuration**. He described it through a metaphor of dancing.

ENTRADA A LA HABANA 8 DE ENERO DE 1959

Some social forces shape entire regions. The Cuban Revolution not only reshaped the lives of Cubans on the island but created a huge Cuban diaspora which reshaped a major urban center of the United States—Miami, Florida.

There can be no dance without the dancers, but there can be no dancers without the dance. Without the dancers, a dance is just an idea about motions in a choreographer's head. Without a dance, there is just a group of people moving around a floor.

Similarly, there is no society without the individuals that make it up, and there are also no individuals who are not shaped by the society in which they live. Society is the "natural environment" of humans. There really is no social history of an "individual" human. We are herd animals. We survive and develop thanks to the protection provided by social structures and cultural adaptations.

Take the case of religious faith. Individuals experience religious faith in a distinctly personal manner yet religion exists in a social context. Religious practices are influenced by government policies towards holidays, by specific rituals and places of worship. Even the gods that are available for us to worship are influenced by historical and social forces. How many shrines representing the god Thor have you seen lately?

THE SOCIOLOGICAL IMAGINATION
Chapter One: The Promise

C. Wright Mills

Nowadays people often feel that their private lives are a series of traps. They sense that within their everyday worlds, they cannot overcome their troubles, and in this feeling, they are often quite correct. What ordinary people are directly aware of and what they try to do are bounded by the private orbits in which they live; their visions and their powers are limited to the close-up scenes of job, family, neighborhood; in other milieux, they move vicariously and remain spectators. And the more aware they become, however vaguely, of ambitions and of threats which transcend their immediate locales, the more trapped they seem to feel.

Underlying this sense of being trapped are seemingly impersonal changes in the very structure of continent-wide societies. The facts of contemporary history are also facts about the success and the failure of individual men and women. When a society is industrialized, a peasant becomes a worker; a feudal lord is liquidated or becomes a businessman. When classes rise or fall, a person is employed or unemployed; when the rate of investment goes up or down, a person takes new heart or goes broke. When wars happen, an insurance salesperson becomes a rocket launcher; a store clerk, a radar operator; a wife or husband lives alone; a child grows up without a parent. Neither the life of an individual nor the history of a society can be understood without understanding both.

Yet people do not usually define the troubles they endure in terms of historical change and institutional contradiction. The well-being they enjoy, they do not usually impute to the big ups and downs of the societies in which they live. Seldom aware of the intricate connection between the patterns of their own lives and the course of world history, ordinary people do not usually know what this connection means for the kinds of people they are becoming and for the kinds of history-making in which they might take part. They do not possess the quality of mind essential to grasp the interplay of individuals and society, of biography and history, of self and world.

They cannot cope with their personal troubles in such ways as to control the structural transformations that usually lie behind them.

Surely it is no wonder. In what period have so many people been so totally exposed at so fast a pace to such earthquakes of change? That Americans have not known such catastrophic changes as have the men and women of other societies is due to historical facts that are now quickly becoming 'merely history.' The history that now affects every individual is world history. Within this scene and this period, in the course of a single generation, one sixth of humankind is transformed from all that is feudal and backward into all that is modern, advanced, and fearful. Political colonies are freed; new and less visible forms of imperialism installed. Revolutions occur; people feel the intimate grip of new kinds of authority. Totalitarian societies rise, and are smashed to bits - or succeed fabulously. After two centuries of ascendancy, capitalism is shown up as only one way to make society into an industrial apparatus. After two centuries of hope, even formal democracy is restricted to a quite small portion of mankind. Everywhere in the underdeveloped world, ancient ways of life are broken up and vague expectations become urgent demands. Everywhere in the overdeveloped world, the means of authority and of violence become total in scope and bureaucratic in form. Humanity itself now lies before us, the supernation at either pole concentrating its most coordinated and massive efforts upon the preparation of World War Three.

The very shaping of history now outpaces the ability of people to orient themselves in accordance with cherished values. And which values? Even when they do not panic, people often sense that older ways of feeling and thinking have collapsed and that newer beginnings are ambiguous to the point of moral stasis. Is it any wonder that ordinary people feel they cannot cope with the larger worlds with which they are so suddenly confronted? That they cannot understand the meaning of their epoch for their own lives? That - in defense of selfhood - they become morally insensible, trying to remain altogether private individuals? Is it any wonder that they come to be possessed by a sense of the trap?

It is not only information that they need - in this Age of Fact, information often dominates their attention and overwhelms their capacities to assimilate it. It is not only the skills of reason that they need - although their struggles to acquire these often exhaust their limited moral energy.

What they need, and what they feel they need, is a quality of mind that will help them to use information and to develop reason in order to achieve lucid summations of what is going on in the world and of what may be happening within themselves. It is this quality, I am going to contend, that journalists and scholars, artists and publics, scientists and editors are coming to expect of what may be called the sociological imagination.

The sociological imagination enables its possessor to understand the larger historical scene in terms of its meaning for the inner life and the external career of a variety of individuals. It enables him to take into account how individuals, in the welter of their daily experience, often become falsely conscious of their social positions. Within that welter, the framework of modern society is sought, and within that framework the psychologies of a variety of men and women are formulated. By such means the personal uneasiness of individuals is focused upon explicit troubles and the indifference of publics is transformed into involvement with public issues.

The first fruit of this imagination - and the first lesson of the social science that embodies it - is the idea that the individual can understand her own experience and gauge her own fate only by locating herself within her period, that she can know her own chances in life only by becoming aware of those of all individuals in her circumstances. In many ways it is a terrible lesson; in many ways a magnificent one. We do not know the limits of humans capacities for supreme effort or willing degradation, for agony or glee, for pleasurable brutality or the sweetness of reason. But in our time we have come to know that the limits of 'human nature' are frighteningly broad. We have come to know that every individual lives, from one generation to the next, in some society; that he lives out a biography, and lives it out within some historical sequence. By the fact of this living, he contributes, however minutely, to the shaping of this society and to the course of its history, even as he is made by society and by its historical push and shove.

The sociological imagination enables us to grasp history and biography and the relations between the two within society. That is its task and its promise. To recognize this task and this promise is the mark of the classic social analyst. It is characteristic of Herbert Spencer - turgid, polysyllabic, comprehensive; of E. A. Ross - graceful, muckraking, upright; of Auguste Comte and Emile Durkheim; of the intricate and subtle Karl Mannheim. It is the quality of all that is intellectually excellent in Karl Marx; it is the clue to Thorstein Veblen's brilliant and ironic insight, to Joseph Schumpeter's many-sided constructions of reality; it is the basis of the psychological sweep of W. E. H. Lecky no less than of the profundity and clarity of Max Weber. And it is the signal of what is best in contemporary studies of people and society.

No social study that does not come back to the problems of biography, of history and of their intersections within a society has completed its intellectual journey. Whatever the specific problems of the classic social analysts, however limited or however broad the features of social reality they have examined, those who have been imaginatively aware of the promise of their work have consistently asked three sorts of questions:

1. What is the structure of this particular society as a whole? What are its essential components, and how are they related to one another? How does it differ from other varieties of social order? Within it, what is the meaning of any particular feature for its continuance and for its change?

2. Where does this society stand in human history? What are the mechanics by which it is changing? What is its place within and its meaning for the development of humanity as a whole? How does any particular feature we are examining affect, and how is it affected by, the historical period in which it moves? And this period - what are its essential features? How does it differ from other periods? What are its characteristic ways of history-making?

3. What varieties of men and women now prevail in this society and in this period? And what varieties are coming to prevail? In what ways are they selected and formed, liberated and repressed, made sensitive and blunted? What kinds of 'human nature' are revealed in the conduct and character we observe in this society in this period? And what is the meaning for 'human nature' of each and every feature of the society we are examining?

Whether the point of interest is a great power state or a minor literary mood, a family, a prison, a creed - these are the kinds of questions the best social analysts have asked. They are the intellectual pivots of classic studies of individuals in society - and they are the questions inevitably raised by any mind possessing the sociological imagination. For that imagination is the capacity to shift from one perspective to another - from the political to the psychological; from examination of a single family to comparative assessment of the national budgets of the world; from the theological school to the military establishment; from considerations of an oil industry to studies of contemporary poetry. It is the capacity to range from the most impersonal and remote transformations to the most intimate features of the human self - and to see the relations between the two. Back of its use there is always the urge to know the social and historical meaning of the individual in the society and in the period in which she has her quality and her being.

That, in brief, is why it is by means of the sociological imagination that men and women now hope to grasp what is going on in the world, and to understand what is happening in themselves as minute points of the intersections of biography and history within society. In large part, contemporary humanity's self-conscious view of itself as at least an outsider, if not a permanent stranger, rests upon an absorbed realization of social relativity and of the transformative power of history. The sociological imagination is the most fruitful form of this self-consciousness. By its use people whose mentalities have swept only a series of limited orbits often come to feel as if suddenly awakened in a house with which they had only supposed themselves to be familiar. Correctly or incorrectly, they often come to feel that they can now provide themselves with adequate summations, cohesive assessments, comprehensive orientations. Older decisions that once appeared sound now seem to them products of a mind unaccountably dense. Their capacity for astonishment is made lively again. They acquire a new way of thinking, they experience a transvaluation of values: in a word, by their reflection and by their sensibility, they realize the cultural meaning of the social sciences.

Perhaps the most fruitful distinction with which the sociological imagination works is between 'the personal troubles of milieu' and 'the public issues of social structure.' This distinction is an essential tool of the sociological imagination and a feature of all classic work in social science.

Troubles occur within the character of the individual and within the range of his or her immediate relations with others; they have to do with one's self and with those limited areas of social life of which one is directly and personally aware. Accordingly, the statement and the resolution of troubles properly lie within the individual as a biographical entity and within the scope of one's immediate milieu - the social setting that is directly open to her personal experience and to some extent her willful activity. A trouble is a private matter: values cherished by an individual are felt by her to be threatened.

Issues have to do with matters that transcend these local environments of the individual and the range of her inner life. They have to do with the organization of many such milieu into the institutions of an historical society as a whole, with the ways in which various milieux overlap and interpenetrate to form the larger structure of social and historical life. An issue is a public matter: some value cherished by publics is felt to be threatened. Often there is a debate about what that value really is and about what it is that really threatens it. This debate is often without focus if only because it is the very nature of an issue, unlike even widespread trouble, that it cannot very well be defined in terms of the immediate and everyday environments of ordinary people. An issue, in fact, often involves a crisis in institutional arrangements, and often too it involves what Marxists call 'contradictions' or 'antagonisms.'

In these terms, consider unemployment. When, in a city of 100,000, only one is unemployed, that is his personal trouble, and for its relief we properly look to the character of the individual, his skills and his immediate opportunities. But when in a nation of 50 million employees, 15 million people are unemployed, that is an issue, and we may not hope to find its solution within the range of opportunities open to any one individual. The very structure of opportunities has collapsed. Both the correct statement of the problem and the range of possible solutions require us to consider the economic and political institutions of the society, and not merely the personal situation and character of a scatter of individuals.

Consider war. The personal problem of war, when it occurs, may be how to survive it or how to die in it with honor; how to make money out of it; how to climb into the higher safety of the military apparatus; or how to contribute to the war's termination. In short, according to one's values, to find a set of milieux and within it to survive the war or make one's death in it meaningful. But the structural issues of war have to do with its causes; with what types of people it throws up into command; with its effects upon economic and political, family and religious institutions, with the unorganized irresponsibility of a world of nation-states.

Consider marriage. Inside a marriage a man and a woman may experience personal troubles, but when the divorce rate during the first four years of marriage is 250 out of every 1,000 attempts, this is an indication of a structural issue having to do with the institutions of marriage and the family and other institutions that bear upon them.

Or consider the metropolis - the horrible, beautiful, ugly, magnificent sprawl of the great city. For many members of the upperclass the personal solution to 'the problem of the city' is to have an apartment with private garage under it in the heart of the city and forty miles out, a house by Henry Hill, garden by Garrett Eckbo, on a hundred acres of private land. In these two controlled environments - with a small staff at each end and a private helicopter connection - most people could solve many of the problems of personal milieux caused by the facts of the city. But all this, however splendid, does not solve the public issues that the structural fact of the city poses. What should be done with this wonderful monstrosity? Break it all up into scattered units, combining residence and work? Refurbish it as it stands? Or, after evacuation, dynamite it and build new cities according to new plans in new places? What should those plans be? And who is to decide and to accomplish whatever choice is made? These are structural issues; to confront them and to solve them requires us to consider political and economic issues that affect innumerable milieux.

In so far as an economy is so arranged that slumps occur, the problem of unemployment becomes incapable of personal solution. In so far as war is inherent in the nation-state system and in the uneven industrialization of the world, the ordinary individual in her restricted milieu will be powerless - with or without psychiatric aid—to solve the troubles this system or lack of system imposes upon him. In so far as the family as an institution turns women into darling little slaves and men into their chief providers and unweaned dependents, the problem of a satisfactory marriage remains incapable of purely private solution. In so far as the overdeveloped megalopolis and the overdeveloped automobile are built-in features of the overdeveloped society, the issues of urban living will not be solved by personal ingenuity and private wealth.

What we experience in various and specific milieux, I have noted, is often caused by structural changes. Accordingly, to understand the changes of many personal milieux we are required to look beyond them. And the number and variety of such structural changes increase as the institutions within which we live become more embracing and more intricately connected with one another. To be aware of the idea of social structure and to use it with sensibility is to be capable of tracing such linkages among a great variety of milieux. To be able to do that is to possess the sociological imagination.

Body Ritual among the Nacirema

Horace Miner

The anthropologist has become so familiar with the diversity of ways in which different peoples behave in similar situations that he is not apt to be surprised by even the most exotic customs. In fact, if all of the logically possible combinations of behavior have not been found somewhere in the world, he is apt to suspect that they must be present in some yet undescribed tribe. This point has, in fact, been expressed with respect to clan organization by Murdock (1949:71). In this light, the magical beliefs and practices of the Nacirema present such unusual aspects that it seems desirable to describe them as an example of the extremes to which human behavior can go.

Professor Linton first brought the ritual of the Nacirema to the attention of anthropologists twenty years ago (1936:326), but the culture of this people is still very poorly understood. They are a North American group living in the territory between the Canadian Cree, the Yaqui and Tarahumare of Mexico, and the Carib and Arawak of the Antilles. Little is known of their origin, although tradition states that they came from the east. According to Nacirema mythology, their nation was originated by a culture hero, Notgnihsaw, who is otherwise known for two great feats of strength—the throwing of a piece of wampum across the river Pa-To-Mac and the chopping down of a cherry tree in which the Spirit of Truth resided. Nacirema culture is characterized by a highly developed market economy which has evolved in a rich natural habitat. While much of the people's time is devoted to economic pursuits, a large part of the fruits of these labors and a considerable portion of the day are spent in ritual activity. The focus of this activity is the human body, the appearance and health of which loom as a dominant concern in the ethos of the people. While such a concern is certainly not unusual, its ceremonial aspects and associated philosophy are unique.

The fundamental belief underlying the whole system appears to be that the human body is ugly and that its natural tendency is to debility and disease. Incarcerated in such a body, man's only hope is to avert these characteristics through the use of the powerful influences of ritual and ceremony. Every household has one or more shrines devoted to this purpose. The more powerful individuals in the society have several shrines in their houses and, in fact, the opulence of a house is often referred to in terms of the number of such ritual centers it possesses. Most houses are of wattle and daub construction, but the shrine rooms of the more wealthy are walled with stone. Poorer families imitate the rich by applying pottery plaques to their shrine walls.

While each family has at least one such shrine, the rituals associated with it are not family ceremonies but are private and secret. The rites are normally only discussed with children, and then only during the period when they are being initiated into these mysteries. I was able, however, to establish sufficient rapport with the natives to examine these shrines and to have the rituals described to me.

The focal point of the shrine is a box or chest which is built into the wall. In this chest are kept the many charms and magical potions without which no native believes he could live. These preparations are secured from a variety of specialized practitioners. The most powerful of these are the medicine men, whose assistance must be rewarded with substantial gifts. However, the medicine men do not provide the curative potions for their clients, but decide what the ingredients should be and then write them down in an ancient and secret language. This writing is understood only by the medicine men and by the herbalists who, for another gift, provide the required charm.

The charm is not disposed of after it has served its purpose, but is placed in the charm-box of the household shrine. As these magical materials are specific for certain ills, and the real or imagined maladies of the people are many, the charm-box is usually full to overflowing. The magical packets are so numerous that people forget what their purposes were and fear to use them again. While the natives are very vague on this point, we can only assume that the idea in retaining all the old magical materials is

"Body Ritual Among the Nacirema," by Horace Miner, *American Anthropologist*, 1956, Vol. 58, No. 3. pp. 503–507.

that their presence in the charm-box, before which the body rituals are conducted, will in some way protect the worshipper.

Beneath the charm-box is a small font. Each day every member of the family, in succession, enters the shrine room, bows his head before the charm-box, mingles different sorts of holy water in the font, and proceeds with a brief rite of ablution. The holy waters are secured from the Water Temple of the community, where the priests conduct elaborate ceremonies to make the liquid ritually pure.

In the hierarchy of magical practitioners, and below the medicine men in prestige, are specialists whose designation is best translated "holy-mouth-men." The Nacirema have an almost pathological horror of and fascination with the mouth, the condition of which is believed to have a supernatural influence on all social relationships. Were it not for the rituals of the mouth, they believe that their teeth would fall out, their gums bleed, their jaws shrink, their friends desert them, and their lovers reject them. They also believe that a strong relationship exists between oral and moral characteristics. For example, there is a ritual ablution of the mouth for children which is supposed to improve their moral fiber.

The daily body ritual performed by everyone includes a mouth-rite. Despite the fact that these people are so punctilious about care of the mouth, this rite involves a practice which strikes the uninitiated stranger as revolting. It was reported to me that the ritual consists of inserting a small bundle of hog hairs into the mouth, along with certain magical powders, and then moving the bundle in a highly formalized series of gestures.

In addition to the private mouth-rite, the people seek out a holy-mouth-man once or twice a year. These practitioners have an impressive set of paraphernalia, consisting of a variety of augers, awls, probes, and prods. The use of these objects in the exorcism of the evils of the mouth involves almost unbelievable ritual torture of the client. The holy-mouth-man opens the client's mouth and, using the above mentioned tools, enlarges any holes which decay may have created in the teeth. Magical materials are put into these holes. If there are no naturally occurring holes in the teeth, large sections of one or more teeth are gouged out so that the supernatural substance can be applied. In the client's view, the purpose of these ministrations is to arrest decay and to draw friends. The extremely sacred and traditional character of the rite is evident in the fact that the natives return to the holy-mouth-men year after year, despite the fact that their teeth continue to decay.

It is to be hoped that, when a thorough study of the Nacirema is made, there will be careful inquiry into the personality structure of these people. One has but to watch the gleam in the eye of a holy-mouth-man, as he jabs an awl into an exposed nerve, to suspect that a certain amount of sadism is involved. If this can be established, a very interesting pattern emerges, for most of the population shows definite masochistic tendencies. It was to these that Professor Linton referred in discussing a distinctive part of the daily body ritual which is performed only by men. This part of the rite involves scraping and lacerating the surface of the face with a sharp instrument. Special women's rites are performed only four times during each lunar month, but what they lack in frequency is made up in barbarity. As part of this ceremony, women bake their heads in small ovens for about an hour. The theoretically interesting point is that what seems to be a preponderantly masochistic people have developed sadistic specialists.

The medicine men have an imposing temple, or *latipso*, in every community of any size. The more elaborate ceremonies required to treat very sick patients can only be performed at this temple. These ceremonies involve not only the thaumaturge but a permanent group of vestal maidens who move sedately about the temple chambers in distinctive costume and headdress.

The *latipso* ceremonies are so harsh that it is phenomenal that a fair proportion of the really sick natives who enter the temple ever recover. Small children whose indoctrination is still incomplete have been known to resist attempts to take them to the temple because "that is where you go to die." Despite this fact, sick adults are not only willing but eager to undergo the protracted ritual purification, if they can afford to do so. No matter how ill the supplicant or how grave the emergency, the guardians of many temples will not admit a client if he cannot give a rich gift to the custodian. Even after one has gained admission and survived the ceremonies, the guardians will not permit the neophyte to leave until he makes still another gift.

The supplicant entering the temple is first stripped of all his or her clothes. In every-day life the Nacirema avoids exposure of his body and its natural functions. Bathing and excretory acts are performed only in the secrecy of the household shrine, where they are ritualized as part of the body-rites. Psychological shock results from the fact that body secrecy is suddenly lost upon entry into the *latipso*. A man, whose own wife has never seen him in an excretory act, suddenly finds himself naked and assisted by a vestal maiden while he performs his natural functions into a sacred vessel. This sort of ceremonial treatment is necessitated by the fact that the excreta are used by a diviner to ascertain the course and nature of the client's sickness. Female clients, on the other hand, find their naked bodies are subjected to the scrutiny, manipulation and prodding of the medicine men.

Few supplicants in the temple are well enough to do anything but lie on their hard beds. The daily ceremonies, like the rites of the holy-mouth-men, involve discomfort and torture. With ritual precision, the vestals awaken their miserable charges each dawn and roll them about on their beds of pain while performing ablutions, in the formal movements of which the maidens are highly trained. At other times they insert magic wands in the supplicant's mouth or force him to eat substances which are supposed to be healing. From time to time the medicine men come to their clients and jab magically treated needles into their flesh. The fact that these temple ceremonies may not cure, and may even kill the neophyte, in no way decreases the people's faith in the medicine men.

There remains one other kind of practitioner, known as a "listener." This witch-doctor has the power to exorcise the devils that lodge in the heads of people who have been bewitched. The Nacirema believe that parents bewitch their own children. Mothers are particularly suspected of putting a curse on children while teaching them the secret body rituals. The counter-magic of the witch-doctor is unusual in its lack of ritual. The patient simply tells the "listener" all his troubles and fears, beginning with the earliest difficulties he can remember. The memory displayed by the Nacirema in these exorcism sessions is truly remarkable. It is not uncommon for the patient to bemoan the rejection he felt upon being weaned as a babe, and a few individuals even see their troubles going back to the traumatic effects of their own birth.

In conclusion, mention must be made of certain practices which have their base in native esthetics but which depend upon the pervasive aversion to the natural body and its functions. There are ritual fasts to make fat people thin and ceremonial feasts to make thin people fat. Still other rites are used to make women's breasts larger if they are small, and smaller if they are large. General dissatisfaction with breast shape is symbolized in the fact that the ideal form is virtually outside the range of human variation. A few women afflicted with almost inhuman hyper-mammary development are so idolized that they make a handsome living by simply going from village to village and permitting the natives to stare at them for a fee.

Reference has already been made to the fact that excretory functions are ritualized, routinized, and relegated to secrecy. Natural reproductive functions are similarly distorted. Intercourse is taboo as a topic and scheduled as an act. Efforts are made to avoid pregnancy by the use of magical materials or by limiting intercourse to certain phases of the moon. Conception is actually very infrequent. When pregnant, women dress so as to hide their condition. Parturition takes place in secret, without friends or relatives to assist, and the majority of women do not nurse their infants.

Our review of the ritual life of the Nacirema has certainly shown them to be a magic-ridden people. It is hard to understand how they have managed to exist so long under the burdens which they have imposed upon themselves. But even such exotic customs as these take on real meaning when they are viewed with the insight provided by Malinowski when he wrote (1948:70):

Looking from far and above, from our high places of safety in the developed civilization, it is easy to see all the crudity and irrelevance of magic. But without its power and guidance early man could not have mastered his practical difficulties as he has done, nor could man have advanced to the higher stages of civilization.

Reference

Linton, Ralph 1936 The Study of Man. New York, D. Appleton-Century Co.

Malinowski, Bronislaw 1948 Magic, Science, and Religion. Glencoe, The Free Press.

Murdock, George P. 1949 Social Structure. New York, The Macmillan Co.

Society as a System—The Nurture of Nature and the Nature of Nurture

Week 4

We are animals. We are one of the many results of hundreds of millions of years of evolutionary change in multi-cell organisms. We are, in other words, part of nature. And nature, in all of its carbon based, protoplasmic beauty, is an important element of our individuality. Some researchers attempting to highlight the importance of nature in our personal development do so by studying twins. Rarely situations arise where identical twins are separated at birth and their similarities and differences are analyzed in the process of development. These are important studies to conduct because identical twins share the same genetic makeup thus making the impact of the social environment more evident. In 1968, for example, twin girls born to a mentally ill mother were put up for adoption and raised in different households. Years later, in 2003, when they were 35, they were reunited and discovered the similarity of their temperament, gestures and facial expressions. However, they were also separated from each other and raised in different households. The parents, and certainly the babies, did not realize they were one of five pairs of twins who were made subjects of a scientific study. Studies like these point to the important role that genetics and hormones play in human behavior.

Twin studies have provides some information on the limits of nature and the importance of nurture.

Some experts assert that our personalities and who we are in the world is a result of **nurture**; that is, of the web of relationships and interactions that make up our lives as social beings. Others argue that who we are is based entirely on our genetic makeup; the biological dimensions of our humanity. According to this view point, our temperaments, interests, and talents are pretty much set before birth and are dependent on **nature**.

New innovations in neuroscience are giving us an insight into the biological expression of our cultural environment. For example, when we are in love or when we pray to our gods, all of our brains respond similarly. As we will see in the module on religion, our brains seem to be "wired for god." For sociologists, this is an important finding which serves to emphasize the importance of the social environment for our individual as well as communal well-being. So while our biology might "wire us" for

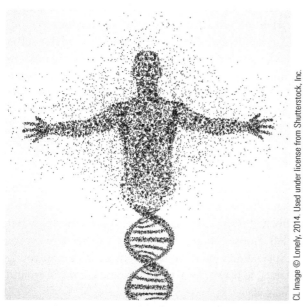

We are organic as well as social beings. Biology is not fate but biology does set the parameters for our species as well as our individual social behavior.

faith, which gods are the object of our attention are culturally established. Similarly, although we all want to fall in love, society establishes who can be the object of our hard wired need to love.

On a similar but less inspiring note is the new research which suggests that prejudices and even racism might have an adaptive root which has hardwired the social tendency into our species. Some of the most compelling evidence for a hard-wired racial divide concerns a brain region called the amygdala, which plays a central role in processing fear and aggression. If you put on a brain scanner and are shown a picture of something scary, your amygdala would leap into action, telling your heart to race and helping you decide what to do? Run? Fight? Wet your pants? Numerous studies have found that if you put someone in a brain scanner and show him brief flashes (1/20th of a second) of emotionally neutral faces, the amygdala activates if the face is someone of a different race, as defined by our culture. But there is good news. These brain responses can be fairly easily overridden if the "other" is viewed as a person rather than a category.

For example, Robert Kurzban at the University of Pennsylvania, conducted an experiment in which subjects were shown a film clip of a mixed-race crowd of people. The "hardwired" response was to unconsciously categorize people in the crowd by race. But if people in that crowd were wearing one of two different sports jerseys, subjects categorized them by team affiliation instead of by race. In other words, if the brain evolved to make automatic racial distinctions, it evolved even more strongly to differentiate between Dodgers fans and Giants fans. Similarly, work by Susan Fiske at Princeton found something else that can override the amygdala response to another race. Subjects were asked to decide whether people in the pictures they were shown would like a particular vegetable. In other words, they were asked to imagine the tastes of the people, to think about what they would buy in a market, and to imagine them relishing a favorite vegetable over dinner. In that exercise, even if the face a subject saw was of another race, the amygdala was not activated. In other words, simply thinking about someone as a person rather than a category makes that supposedly brain-based automatic xenophobia toward other races evaporate in an instant. Nature is important, yes. But the nurture of culture might be the determining factor in prejudice and racism. Maybe there is hope for our multi-cultural species after all.

All this by way of saying that the "social" is part of a system of interaction. There are interactions that occur at the biological level that shape our behavior at the social level. So there is an aspect of nature in our system of nurture. Social analysts, however, focus on the social system and its interaction. And its power to shape the world and how we view it.

CL Image © Maksim Kabakou, 2014. Used under license from Shutterstock, Inc.

Nature gives us a unique identifier to our individuality—our finger prints. But what social characteristics do each of us have that we can truly call unique?

The (Sometimes Invisible) Power of Society—The Nature of Nurture

In the summer of 2005, the police followed a lead from the Department of Children and Families to a home in Plant City, Florida. The police investigated and found a little girl, living in house infested with cockroaches, smeared with feces and urine from both people and pets, and filled with dilapidated furniture and ragged window coverings. Her name was Danielle. Social workers concluded that she had been left almost entirely alone for most of her seven years. Without regular interaction—the holding, hugging, talking, the explanations and demonstrations given to most young children—she had not learned to walk or to speak, to eat or to interact, to play or even to understand the world around her. From a sociological point of view, Danielle had not been socialized.

The process of **socialization** is the way individuals within society are taught how to behave as members of that society. Individuals come to understand and perform societal norms and expectations, to accept society's beliefs, and to be aware of societal values. Socialization is the process that puts in our head the idea that whatever "we" do is "normal"

CL Image © mario.bono, 2014. Used under license from Shutterstock, Inc.

Our species handle survival in a different way than this cheetah. Do you think that the violence that our species exhibit is determined by our needs to survive?

and some of the things that "they" do (members of different cultures or groups) Most importantly, through socialization we learn to use the symbols that make up language and through language we learn about who we are, how we fit with other people, and the natural and social worlds in which we live. Adaptation strategies would be unsuccessful unless a way to pass it on is developed as part of the operations of society.

Agents of Socialization

How does the process of socialization work? Socialization takes place as individuals interact with various agents of socialization. There are two general types of socializing agents: agents of (a) primary socialization and (b) secondary socialization. The most intimate and personal groups that influence us are responsible for what we call primary socialization. Less intimate groups carry on the process of secondary socialization.

Families are the main agents associated with primary socialization. Mothers and fathers, siblings and grandparents, plus members of an extended family, teach a child how to use objects (such as clothes, computers, eating utensils, books, bikes); how to relate to others (some as "family," others as "friends," still others as "strangers" or "teachers" or "neighbors"); and how the world works (what is "real" and what is "imagined").

A **peer group** is another agent of primary socialization. A peer group is made up of people who are similar in age and social status and who have similar interests. The socialization process becomes influence by peers during the earliest years. Even when the family maintains its dominance as primary socialization agent, playground rules are communicated to the new arrivals. How to take turns, how to shoot a basket, how games are played are all instances involving peer group socialization. This process continues into the teenage years indifferent.

Institutional Agents of Socialization

The social institutions of our culture also have an important role in socializing us to function in our society. These are Secondary Agent of Socialization. Formal institutions such as schools, workplaces, and the government teach people how to behave in and navigate important arenas of our social environment. Other institutions, like the media, contribute to socialization by constantly reminding us about social norms and expectations.

The school system is the first bureaucracy that children meet once they leave the intimate predictability of the household. How does the school socialize children? Students are in school to study math, reading, science, and other subjects. These are the **manifest functions** of the school system; to inculcate the skills necessary to become productive members of society. But schools also socialize children to respect authority, follow a schedule, value discipline, work in groups and passively learn from texts and other symbol-intense media. These are the **latent functions** of the school system. School and classroom rituals, led by teachers serving as role models and leaders, regularly reinforce what society expects from children. Sociologists describe this aspect of schools as the **hidden curriculum**; the informal teaching done by schools.

Just as children spend much of their day at school, most adults invest a significant amount of time and energy at a **workplace**. As workers, we need to be socialized into the "culture" of a place of employment, both in terms of material culture (such as how to operate the copy machine) and nonmaterial culture (such as the chain of command or how the refrigerator is shared). Different jobs require different types of socialization and at this time in history the trend is to switch jobs at least once a decade. Between the ages of 18 and 44, the average baby boomer of the younger set held 11 different jobs (U.S. Bureau of Labor Statistics, 2010). This means that people must become socialized into and by a variety of work environments.

Religions can work formally or informally. Some of us disengage the feelings of "faith" or "belief" in God from specific religion traditions. Some of us express faith through specific religious rituals strongly linked to formal institutions.

Like other institutions , places of worship teach participants how to interact with the religion's material culture (like a mezuzah, a prayer rug, or a communion wafer) and nonmaterial culture (faith systems and rituals). From ceremonial rites of passage that reinforce the family unit, to power dynamics which reinforce gender roles, religion fosters a shared set of socialized values that are passed on through society.

Many of the rites of passage that we go through in life are based on age norms established by the **government**. To be defined as an "adult" usually means being 18 years old, the age at which a person becomes legally responsible. American males must register with the Selective Service System within 30 days of turning 18 to be entered into a database for possible military service. And 65 is the start of "old age" since most people become eligible for senior benefits. These government dictates mark the points at which we require socialization into a new category of social interaction.

Mass media refers to the distribution of impersonal information to a wide audience, such as what happens via television, newspapers, radio, and the Internet. With the average person spending over four hours a day in front of the TV (and children averaging even more screen time), media greatly influences social norms. People learn about objects of material culture (like new technology and transportation options), as well as nonmaterial culture—what is true (beliefs), what is important (values), and what is expected (norms).

Socialization throughout the Life Course

Socialization is not a one-shot deal. We are not "stamped" by some socialization machine as we move along a conveyor belt and thereby socialized forever. Socialization is a lifelong process. As we grow older, we encounter age-related transition points that require socialization into a new role, such as becoming school age, entering the workforce, or retiring. Age related norms vary across societies.

Just as young children pretend to be doctors or lawyers, play house, and dress up, adults also engage in **anticipatory socialization**, the preparation for future life roles. Examples would include a couple who cohabitate before marriage or soon-to-be parents who read infant care books and prepare their home for the new arrival.

Nurturing is necessary for survival of all individuals in all species. Ducks seem to do fine growing up in under the guidance of a single mother. Why do we consider a dual parent household to be so important?

CL Image © TSpider, 2014. Used under license from Shutterstock, Inc.

In the process of **resocialization**, behaviors that were helpful in a previous role are removed because they are no longer of use. Resocialization is necessary when a person moves, for example, to a senior care center, or serves time in jail. In the new environment, the old rules no longer apply. The process of resocialization is typically more stressful than normal socialization because people have to unlearn behaviors that have become customary to them. The most common way resocialization occurs is in a total institution where people are isolated from society and are forced to follow someone else's rules. The millions of Americans who live in prisons or penitentiaries are also members of this type of institution as are members of every branch of the military.

Learning to deal with life after having lived in a total institution requires yet another process of resocialization. In the U.S. military, soldiers learn discipline and a capacity for hard work. They set aside personal goals to achieve a mission, and they take pride in the accomplishments of their units. Many soldiers who leave the military transition these skills into excellent careers. Others find themselves lost upon leaving, uncertain about the outside world, and what to do next. The process of resocialization to civilian life is not a simple one for many individuals.

Why Did Human History Unfold Differently on Different Continents For The Last 13,000 Years?

A Talk by Jared Diamond

I've set myself the modest task of trying to explain the broad pattern of human history, on all the continents, for the last 13,000 years. Why did history take such different evolutionary courses for peoples of different continents? This problem has fascinated me for a long time, but it's now ripe for a new synthesis because of recent advances in many fields seemingly remote from history, including molecular biology, plant and animal genetics and biogeography, archaeology, and linguistics.

As we all know, Eurasians, especially peoples of Europe and eastern Asia, have spread around the globe, to dominate the modern world in wealth and power. Other peoples, including most Africans, survived, and have thrown off European domination but remain behind in wealth and power. Still other peoples, including the original inhabitants of Australia, the Americas, and southern Africa, are no longer even masters of their own lands but have been decimated, subjugated, or exterminated by European colonialists. Why did history turn out that way, instead of the opposite way? Why weren't Native Americans, Africans, and Aboriginal Australians the ones who conquered or exterminated Europeans and Asians?

This big question can easily be pushed back one step further. By the year A.D. 1500, the approximate year when Europe's overseas expansion was just beginning, peoples of the different continents already differed greatly in technology and political organization. Much of Eurasia and North Africa was occupied then by Iron Age states and empires, some of them on the verge of industrialization. Two Native American peoples, the Incas and Aztecs, ruled over empires with stone tools and were just starting to experiment with bronze. Parts of sub-Saharan Africa were divided among small indigenous Iron Age states or chiefdoms. But all peoples of Australia, New Guinea, and the Pacific islands, and many peoples of the Americas and sub-Saharan Africa, were still living as farmers or even still as hunter/gatherers with stone tools.

Obviously, those differences as of A.D. 1500 were the immediate cause of the modern world's inequalities.

Empires with iron tools conquered or exterminated tribes with stone tools. But how did the world evolve to be the way that it was in the year A.D. 1500?

This question, too can be easily pushed back a further step, with the help of written histories and archaeological discoveries. Until the end of the last Ice Age around 11,000 B.C., all humans on all continents were still living as Stone Age hunter/gatherers. Different rates of development on different continents, from 11,000 B.C. to A.D. 1500, were what produced the inequalities of A.D. 1500. While Aboriginal Australians and many Native American peoples remained Stone Age hunter/gatherers, most Eurasian peoples, and many peoples of the Americas and sub-Saharan Africa, gradually developed agriculture, herding, metallurgy, and complex political organization. Parts of Eurasia, and one small area of the Americas, developed indigenous writing as well. But each of these new developments appeared earlier in Eurasia than elsewhere.

So, we can finally rephrase our question about the evolution of the modern world's inequalities as follows. Why did human development proceed at such different rates on different continents for the last 13,000 years? Those differing rates constitute the broadest pattern of history, the biggest unsolved problem of history, and my subject today.

Historians tend to avoid this subject like the plague, because of its apparently racist overtones. Many people, or even most people, assume that the answer involves biological differences in average IQ among the world's populations, despite the fact that there is no evidence for the existence of such IQ differences. Even to ask the question why different peoples had different histories strikes some of us as evil, because it appears to be justifying what happened in history. In fact, we study the injustices of history for the same reason that we study genocide, and for the same reason that psychologists study the minds of murderers and rapists: not in order to justify history, genocide, murder, and rape, but instead to understand how those evil things came about, and then to use that understanding so as to prevent their happening again. In case the stink of racism still makes you feel uncomfortable about exploring this subject, just reflect on the underlying reason why so many people accept racist explanations of history's broad pattern: we don't have a convincing alternative explanation. Until we do, people will continue to gravitate by default to racist theories. That leaves us with a huge moral gap, which constitutes the strongest reason for tackling this uncomfortable subject.

Let's proceed continent-by-continent. As our first continental comparison, let's consider the collision of the Old World and the New World that began with Christopher Columbus's voyage in A.D. 1492, because the proximate factors involved in that outcome are well understood. I'll now give you a summary and interpretation of the histories of North America, South America, Europe, and Asia from my perspective as a biogeographer and evolutionary biologist ÷ all that in ten minutes; 2_ minutes per continent. Here we go:

Most of us are familiar with the stories of how a few hundred Spaniards under CortŽs and Pizarro overthrew the Aztec and Inca Empires. The populations of each of those empires numbered tens of millions. We're also familiar with the gruesome details of how other Europeans conquered other parts of the New World. The result is that Europeans came to settle and dominate most of the New World, while the Native American population declined drastically from its level as of A.D. 1492. Why did it happen that way? Why didn't it instead happen that the Emperors Montezuma or Atahuallpa led the Aztecs or Incas to conquer Europe?

The proximate reasons are obvious. Invading Europeans had steel swords, guns, and horses, while Native Americans had only stone and wooden weapons and no animals that could be ridden. Those military advantages repeatedly enabled troops of a few dozen mounted Spaniards to defeat Indian armies numbering in the thousands.

Nevertheless, steel swords, guns, and horses weren't the sole proximate factors behind the European conquest of the New World. Infectious diseases introduced with Europeans, like smallpox and measles, spread from one Indian tribe to another, far in advance of Europeans themselves, and killed an estimated 95% of the New World's Indian population. Those diseases were endemic in Europe, and Europeans had had time to develop both genetic and immune resistance to them, but Indians initially had no such resistance. That role played by infectious diseases in the European conquest of the New World was duplicated in many other parts of the world, including

Aboriginal Australia, southern Africa, and many Pacific islands.

Finally, there is still another set of proximate factors to consider. How is it that Pizarro and CortŽs reached the New World at all, before Aztec and Inca conquistadors could reach Europe? That outcome depended partly on technology in the form of oceangoing ships. Europeans had such ships, while the Aztecs and Incas did not. Also, those European ships were backed by the centralized political organization that enabled Spain and other European countries to build and staff the ships. Equally crucial was the role of European writing in permitting the quick spread of accurate detailed information, including maps, sailing directions, and accounts by earlier explorers, back to Europe, to motivate later explorers.

So far, we've identified a series of proximate factors behind European colonization of the New World: namely, ships, political organization, and writing that brought Europeans to the New World; European germs that killed most Indians before they could reach the battlefield; and guns, steel swords, and horses that gave Europeans a big advantage on the battlefield. Now, let's try to push the chain of causation back further. Why did these proximate advantages go to the Old World rather than to the New World? Theoretically, Native Americans might have been the ones to develop steel swords and guns first, to develop oceangoing ships and empires and writing first, to be mounted on domestic animals more terrifying than horses, and to bear germs worse than smallpox.

The part of that question that's easiest to answer concerns the reasons why Eurasia evolved the nastiest germs. It's striking that Native Americans evolved no devastating epidemic diseases to give to Europeans, in return for the many devastating epidemic diseases that Indians received from the Old World. There are two straightforward reasons for this gross imbalance. First, most of our familiar epidemic diseases can sustain themselves only in large dense human populations concentrated into villages and cities, which arose much earlier in the Old World than in the New World. Second, recent studies of microbes, by molecular biologists, have shown that most human epidemic diseases evolved from similar epidemic diseases of the dense populations of Old World domestic animals with which we came into close contact. For example, measles and TB evolved from diseases of our cattle, influenza from a disease of pigs, and smallpox possibly from a disease of camels. The Americas had very few native domesticated animal species from which humans could acquire such diseases.

Let's now push the chain of reasoning back one step further. Why were there far more species of domesticated animals in Eurasia than in the Americas? The Americas harbor over a thousand native wild mammal species, so you might initially suppose that the Americas offered plenty of starting material for domestication.

In fact, only a tiny fraction of wild mammal species has been successfully domesticated, because domestication requires that a wild animal fulfill many prerequisites: the animal has to have a diet that humans can supply; a rapid growth rate; a willingness to breed in captivity; a tractable disposition; a social structure involving submissive behavior towards dominant animals and humans; and lack of a tendency to panic when fenced in. Thousands of years ago, humans domesticated every possible large wild mammal species fulfilling all those criteria and worth domesticating, with the result that there have been no valuable additions of domestic animals in recent times, despite the efforts of modern science.

Eurasia ended up with the most domesticated animal species in part because it's the world's largest land mass and offered the most wild species to begin with. That preexisting difference was magnified 13,000 years ago at the end of the last Ice Age, when most of the large mammal species of North and South America became extinct, perhaps exterminated by the first arriving Indians. As a result, Native Americans inherited far fewer species of big wild mammals than did Eurasians, leaving them only with the llama and alpaca as a domesticate. Differences between the Old and New Worlds in domesticated plants, especially in large-seeded cereals, are qualitatively similar to these differences in domesticated mammals, though the difference is not so extreme.

Another reason for the higher local diversity of domesticated plants and animals in Eurasia than in the Americas is that Eurasia's main axis is east/west, whereas the main axis of the Americas is north/south. Eurasia's east/west axis meant that species domesticated in one part of Eurasia could easily spread thousands of miles at the same latitude, encountering the same day-length and climate to which they were already adapted. As a result, chickens and citrus fruit domesticated in Southeast Asia quickly spread westward to Europe; horses domesticated in the Ukraine quickly spread eastward to China; and the sheep, goats, cattle, wheat, and barley of the Fertile Crescent quickly spread both west and east.

In contrast, the north/south axis of the Americas meant that species domesticated in one area couldn't spread far without encountering day-lengths and climates to which they were not adapted. As a result, the turkey never spread from its site of domestication in Mexico to the Andes; llamas and alpacas never spread from the Andes to Mexico, so that the Indian civilizations of Central and North America remained entirely without

pack animals; and it took thousands of years for the corn that evolved in Mexico's climate to become modified into a corn adapted to the short growing season and seasonally changing day-length of North America.

Eurasia's domesticated plants and animals were important for several other reasons besides letting Europeans develop nasty germs. Domesticated plants and animals yield far more calories per acre than do wild habitats, in which most species are inedible to humans. As a result, population densities of farmers and herders are typically ten to a hundred times greater than those of hunter/gatherers. That fact alone explains why farmers and herders everywhere in the world have been able to push hunter/gatherers out of land suitable for farming and herding. Domestic animals revolutionized land transport. They also revolutionized agriculture, by letting one farmer plough and manure much more land than the farmer could till or manure by the farmer's own efforts. Also, hunter/gatherer societies tend to be egalitarian and to have no political organization beyond the level of the band or tribe, whereas the food surpluses and storage made possible by agriculture permitted the development of stratified, politically centralized societies with governing elites. Those food surpluses also accelerated the development of technology, by supporting craftspeople who didn't raise their own food and who could instead devote themselves to developing metallurgy, writing, swords, and guns.

Thus, we began by identifying a series of proximate explanations ÷ guns, germs, and so on ÷ for the conquest of the Americas by Europeans. Those proximate factors seem to me ultimately traceable in large part to the Old World's greater number of domesticated plants, much greater number of domesticated animals, and east/west axis. The chain of causation is most direct in explaining the Old World's advantages of horses and nasty germs. But domesticated plants and animals also led more indirectly to Eurasia's advantage in guns, swords, oceangoing ships, political organization, and writing, all of which were products of the large, dense, sedentary, stratified societies made possible by agriculture.

Let's next examine whether this scheme, derived from the collision of Europeans with Native Americans, helps us understand the broadest pattern of African history, which I'll summarize in five minutes. I'll concentrate on the history of sub-Saharan Africa, because it was much more isolated from Eurasia by distance and climate than was North Africa, whose history is closely linked to Eurasia's history. Here we go again:

Just as we asked why CortŽs invaded Mexico before Montezuma could invade Europe, we can similarly ask why Europeans colonized sub-Saharan Africa before sub-Saharans could colonize Europe. The proximate factors were the same familiar ones of guns, steel, oceangoing ships, political organization, and writing. But again, we can ask why guns and ships and so on ended up being developed in Europe rather than in sub-Saharan Africa. To the student of human evolution, that question is particularly puzzling, because humans have been evolving for millions of years longer in Africa than in Europe, and even anatomically modern Homo sapiens may have reached Europe from Africa only within the last 50,000 years. If time were a critical factor in the development of human societies, Africa should have enjoyed an enormous head start and advantage over Europe.

Again, that outcome largely reflects biogeographic differences in the availability of domesticable wild animal and plant species. Taking first domestic animals, it's striking that the sole animal domesticated within sub-Saharan Africa was [you guess] a bird, the Guinea fowl. All of Africa's mammalian domesticates ÷ cattle, sheep, goats, horses, even dogs ÷ entered sub-Saharan Africa from the north, from Eurasia or North Africa. At first that sounds astonishing, since we now think of Africa as the continent of big wild mammals. In fact, none of those famous big wild mammal species of Africa proved domesticable. They were all disqualified by one or another problem such as: unsuitable social organization; intractable behavior; slow growth rate, and so on. Just think what the course of world history might have been like if Africa's rhinos and hippos had lent themselves to domestication! If that had been possible, African cavalry mounted on rhinos or hippos would have made mincemeat of European cavalry mounted on horses. But it couldn't happen.

Instead, as I mentioned, the livestock adopted in Africa were Eurasian species that came in from the north. Africa's long axis, like that of the Americas, is north/south rather than east/west. Those Eurasian domestic mammals spread southward very slowly in Africa, because they had to adapt to different climate zones and different animal diseases.

The difficulties posed by a north/south axis to the spread of domesticated species are even more striking for African crops than they are for livestock. Remember that the food staples of ancient Egypt were Fertile Crescent and Mediterranean crops like wheat and barley, which require winter rains and seasonal variation in day length for their germination. Those crops couldn't spread south in Africa beyond Ethiopia, beyond which the rains come in the summer and there's little or no seasonal variation in day length. Instead, the development of agriculture in the sub-Sahara

had to await the domestication of native African plant species like sorghum and millet, adapted to Central Africa's summer rains and relatively constant day length.

Ironically, those crops of Central Africa were for the same reason then unable to spread south to the Mediterranean zone of South Africa, where once again winter rains and big seasonal variations in day length prevailed. The southward advance of native African farmers with Central African crops halted in Natal, beyond which Central African crops couldn't grow ÷ with enormous consequences for the recent history of South Africa.

In short, a north/south axis, and a paucity of wild plant and animal species suitable for domestication, were decisive in African history, just as they were in Native American history. Although native Africans domesticated some plants in the Sahel and in Ethiopia and in tropical West Africa, they acquired valuable domestic animals only later, from the north. The resulting advantages of Europeans in guns, ships, political organization, and writing permitted Europeans to colonize Africa, rather than Africans to colonize Europe.

Let's now conclude our whirlwind tour around the globe by devoting five minutes to the last continent, Australia. Here we go again, for the last time.

In modern times, Australia was the sole continent still inhabited only by hunter/gatherers. That makes Australia a critical test of any theory about continental differences in the evolution of human societies. Native Australia had no farmers or herders, no writing, no metal tools, and no political organization beyond the level of the tribe or band. Those, of course, are the reasons why European guns and germs destroyed Aboriginal Australian society. But why had all Native Australians remained hunter/gatherers?

There are three obvious reasons. First, even to this day no native Australian animal species and only one plant species (the macadamia nut) have proved suitable for domestication. There still are no domestic kangaroos.

Second, Australia is the smallest continent, and most of it can support only small human populations because of low rainfall and productivity. Hence the total number of Australian hunter/gatherers was only about 300,000.

Finally, Australia is the most isolated continent. The sole outside contacts of Aboriginal Australians were tenuous overwater contacts with New Guineans and Indonesians.

To get an idea of the significance of that small population size and isolation for the pace of development in Australia, consider the Australian island of Tasmania, which had the most extraordinary human society in the modern world. Tasmania is just an island of modest size, but it was the most extreme outpost of the most extreme continent, and it illuminates a big issue in the evolution of all human societies. Tasmania lies 130 miles southeast of Australia. When it was first visited by Europeans in 1642, Tasmania was occupied by 4,000 hunter/gatherers related to mainland Australians, but with the simplest technology of any recent people on Earth. Unlike mainland Aboriginal Australians, Tasmanians couldn't start a fire; they had no boomerangs, spear throwers, or shields; they had no bone tools, no specialized stone tools, and no compound tools like an axe head mounted on a handle; they couldn't cut down a tree or hollow out a canoe; they lacked sewing to make sewn clothing, despite Tasmania's cold winter climate with snow; and, incredibly, though they lived mostly on the sea coast, the Tasmanians didn't catch or eat fish. How did those enormous gaps in Tasmanian material culture arise?

The answer stems from the fact that Tasmania used to be joined to the southern Australian mainland at Pleistocene times of low sea level, until that land bridge was severed by rising sea level 10,000 years ago. People walked out to Tasmania tens of thousands of years ago, when it was still part of Australia. Once that land bridge was severed, though, there was absolutely no further contact of Tasmanians with mainland Australians or with any other people on Earth until European arrival in 1642, because both Tasmanians and mainland Australians lacked watercraft capable of crossing those 130-mile straits between Tasmania and Australia. Tasmanian history is thus a study of human isolation unprecedented except in science fiction ÷ namely, complete isolation from other humans for 10,000 years. Tasmania had the smallest and most isolated human population in the world. If population size and isolation have any effect on accumulation of inventions, we should expect to see that effect in Tasmania.

If all those technologies that I mentioned, absent from Tasmania but present on the opposite Australian mainland, were invented by Australians within the last 10,000 years, we can surely conclude at least that Tasmania's tiny population didn't invent them independently. Astonishingly, the archaeological record demonstrates something further: Tasmanians actually abandoned some technologies that they brought with them from Australia and that persisted on the Australian mainland. For example, bone tools and the practice of fishing were both present in Tasmania at the time that the land bridge was severed, and both disappeared from Tasmania by around 1500 B.C. That represents the loss of valuable technologies: fish could have been smoked to provide a winter food supply, and bone needles could have been used to sew warm clothes.

What sense can we make of these cultural losses?

The only interpretation that makes sense to me goes as follows. First, technology has to be invented or adopted. Human societies vary in lots of independent factors affecting their openness to innovation. Hence the higher the human population and the more societies there are on an island or continent, the greater the chance of any given invention being conceived and adopted somewhere there.

Second, for all human societies except those of totally-isolated Tasmania, most technological innovations diffuse in from the outside, instead of being invented locally, so one expects the evolution of technology to proceed most rapidly in societies most closely connected with outside societies.

Finally, technology not only has to be adopted; it also has to be maintained. All human societies go through fads in which they temporarily either adopt practices of little use or else abandon practices of considerable use. Whenever such economically senseless taboos arise in an area with many competing human societies, only some societies will adopt the taboo at a given time. Other societies will retain the useful practice, and will either outcompete the societies that lost it, or else will be there as a model for the societies with the taboos to repent their error and reacquire the practice. If Tasmanians had remained in contact with mainland Australians, they could have rediscovered the value and techniques of fishing and making bone tools that they had lost. But that couldn't happen in the complete isolation of Tasmania, where cultural losses became irreversible.

In short, the message of the differences between Tasmanian and mainland Australian societies seems to be the following. All other things being equal, the rate of human invention is faster, and the rate of cultural loss is slower, i n areas occupied by many competing societies with many individuals and in contact with societies elsewhere. If this interpretation is correct, then it's likely to be of much broader significance. It probably provides part of the explanation why native Australians, on the world's smallest and most isolated continent, remained Stone Age hunter/ gatherers, while people of other continents were adopting agriculture and metal. It's also likely to contribute to the differences that I already discussed between the farmers of sub-Saharan Africa, the farmers of the much larger Americas, and the farmers of the still larger Eurasia.

Naturally, there are many important factors in world history that I haven't had time to discuss in 40 minutes, and that I do discuss in my book. For example, I've said little or nothing about the distribution of domesticable plants (3 chapters); about the precise way in which complex political institutions and the development of writing and technology and organized religion depend on agriculture and herding; about the fascinating reasons for the differences within Eurasia between China, India, the Near East, and Europe; and about the effects of individuals, and of cultural differences unrelated to the environment, on history. But it's now time to summarize the overall meaning of this whirlwind tour through human history, with its unequally distributed guns and germs.

The broadest pattern of history ÷ namely, the differences between human societies on different continents ÷ seems to me to be attributable to differences among continental environments, and not to biological differences among peoples themselves. In particular, the availability of wild plant and animal species suitable for domestication, and the ease with which those species could spread without encountering unsuitable climates, contributed decisively to the varying rates of rise of agriculture and herding, which in turn contributed decisively to the rise of human population numbers, population densities, and food surpluses, which in turn contributed decisively to the development of epidemic infectious diseases, writing, technology, and political organization. In addition, the histories of Tasmania and Australia warn us that the differing areas and isolations of the continents, by determining the number of competing societies, may have been another important factor in human development.

As a biologist practicing laboratory experimental science, I'm aware that some scientists may be inclined to dismiss these historical interpretations as unprovable speculation, because they're not founded on replicated laboratory experiments. The same objection can be raised against any of the historical sciences, including astronomy, evolutionary biology, geology, and paleontology. The objection can of course be raised against the whole field of history, and most of the other social sciences. That's the reason why we're uncomfortable about considering history as a science. It's classified as a social science, which is considered not quite scientific.

But remember that the word "science" isn't derived from the Latin word for "replicated laboratory experiment," but instead from the Latin word "scientia" for "knowledge." In science, we seek knowledge by whatever methodologies are available and appropriate. There are many fields that no one hesitates to consider sciences even though replicated laboratory experiments in those fields would be immoral, illegal, or impossible. We can't manipulate some stars while maintaining other stars as controls; we can't start and stop ice ages, and we can't experiment with designing and evolving dinosaurs. Nevertheless, we can still gain considerable insight into these historical fields by other means. Then we should surely be able to understand human history, because introspection and preserved writings give us far more insight into the ways of past humans than we have into the ways of past dinosaurs. For that reason I'm optimistic that we can eventually arrive at convincing explanations for these broadest patterns of human history.

India's Sacred Cow

Marvin Harris

Other people's religious practices and beliefs may often appear to be wasteful. They seem to involve a large expenditure of scarce resources on ritual; they contain taboos that restrict the use of apparently useful materials. Their existence seems irrational in the face of ecological needs. One example that many cite in support of this viewpoint is the religious proscription on the slaughter of cattle in India. How can people permit millions of cattle to roam about eating, but uneaten, in a land so continuously threatened by food shortages and starvation? In this article, Marvin Harris challenges the view that religious value is ecologically irrational. Dealing with the Indian case, he argues that Indian cattle, far from being useless, are an essential part of India's productive base. Religious restrictions on killing cattle are ecologically sensible; they have developed and persisted to insure a continuous supply of these valuable animals.

News photographs that came out of India during the famine of the late 1960s showed starving people stretching out bony hands to beg for food while sacred cattle strolled behind them undisturbed. The Hindu, it seems, would rather starve to death than eat his cow or even deprive it of food. The cattle appear to browse unhindered through urban markets eating an orange here, a mango there, competing with people for meager supplies of food.

By Western standards, spiritual values seem more important to Indians than life itself. Specialists in food habits around the world like Fred Simoons at the University of California at Davis consider Hinduism an irrational ideology that compels people to overlook abundant, nutritious foods for scarcer, less healthful foods.

What seems to be an absurd devotion to the mother cow pervades Indian life. Indian wall calendars portray beautiful young women with bodies of fat white cows, often with milk jetting from their teats into sacred shrines.

Cow worship even carries over into politics. In 1966 a crowd of 120,000 people, led by holy men, demonstrated in front of the Indian House of Parliament in support of the All-Party Cow Protection Campaign Committee. In Nepal, the only contemporary Hindu kingdom, cow slaughter is severely punished. As one story goes, the car driven by an official of a United States agency struck and killed a cow. In order to avoid the international incident that would have occurred when the official was arrested for murder, the Nepalese magistrate concluded that the cow had committed suicide.

Many Indians agree with Western assessments of the Hindu reverence for their cattle, the zebu, or *Bos indicus*, a large-humped species prevalent in Asia and Africa. M. N. Srinivas, an Indian anthropologist states: "Orthodox Hindu opinion regards the killing of cattle with abhorrence, even though the refusal to kill the vast number of useless cattle which exists in India today is detrimental to the nation." Even the Indian Ministry of Information formerly maintained that "the large animal population is more a liability than an asset in view of our land resources." Accounts from many different sources point to the same conclusion: India, one of the world's great civilizations, is being strangled by its love for the cow.

The easy explanation for India's devotion to the cow, the one most Westerners and Indians would offer, is that cow worship is an integral part of Hinduism. Religion is somehow good for the soul, even if it sometimes fails the body. Religion orders the cosmos and explains our place in the universe. Religious beliefs, many would claim, have existed for thousands of years and have a life of their own. They are not understandable in scientific terms.

But all this ignores history. There is more to be said for cow worship than is immediately apparent. The earliest Vedas, the Hindu sacred texts from the Second Millennium B.C., do not prohibit the slaughter of cattle. Instead, they ordain it as a part of sacrificial rites. The early Hindus did not avoid the flesh of cows and bulls; they ate it at ceremonial feasts presided over by Brahman priests. Cow worship is a relatively recent development in India; it evolved as the Hindu religion developed and changed.

"India's Sacred Cow" by Marvin Harris, *Human Nature*, February, 1978. Reprinted by permission from Springer.

This evolution is recorded in royal edicts and religious texts written during the last 3,000 years of Indian history. The Vedas from the First Millennium B.C. contain contradictory passages, some referring to ritual slaughter and others to a strict taboo on beef consumption. A. N. Bose, in *Social and Rural Economy of Northern India, 600 B.C.–200 A.D.*, concludes that many of the sacred-cow passages were incorporated into the texts by priests of a later period.

By 200 A.D. the status of Indian cattle had undergone a spiritual transformation. The Brahman priesthood exhorted the population to venerate the cow and forbade them to abuse it or to feed on it. Religious feasts involving the ritual slaughter and consumption of livestock were eliminated and meat eating was restricted to the nobility.

By 1000 A.D., all Hindus were forbidden to eat beef. Ahimsa, the Hindu belief in the unity of all life, was the spiritual justification for this restriction. But it is difficult to ascertain exactly when this change occurred. An important event that helped to shape the modern complex was the Islamic invasion, which took place in the Eighth Century A.D. Hindus may have found it politically expedient to set themselves off from the invaders, who were beefeaters, by emphasizing the need to prevent the slaughter of their sacred animals. Thereafter, the cow taboo assumed its modern form and began to function much as it does today.

The place of the cow in modern India is every place—on posters, in the movies, in brass figures, in stone and wood carvings, on the streets, in the fields. The cow is a symbol of health and abundance. It provides the milk that Indians consume in the form of yogurt and ghee (clarified butter), which contribute subtle flavors to much spicy Indian food.

This, perhaps, is the practical role of the cow, but cows provide less than half the milk produced in India. Most cows in India are not dairy breeds. In most regions, when an Indian farmer wants a steady, high-quality source of milk he usually invests in a female water buffalo. In India the water buffalo is the specialized dairy breed because its milk has a higher butterfat content than zebu milk. Although the farmer milks his zebu cows, the milk is merely a by-product.

More vital than zebu milk to South Asian farmers are zebu calves. Male calves are especially valued because from bulls come oxen, which are the mainstay of the Indian agricultural system.

Small, fast oxen drag wooden plows through late-spring fields when monsoons have dampened the dry, cracked earth. After harvest, the oxen break the grain from the stalk by stomping through mounds of cut wheat and rice. For rice cultivation in irrigated fields, the male water buffalo is preferred (it pulls better in deep mud), but for most other crops, including rainfall rice, wheat, sorghum, and millet, and for transporting goods and people to and from town, a team of oxen is preferred. The ox is the Indian peasant's tractor, thresher and family car combined; the cow is the factory that produces the ox.

If draft animals instead of cows are counted, India appears to have too few domesticated ruminants, not too many. Since each of the 70 million farms in India requires a draft team, it follows that Indian peasants should use 140 million animals in the fields. But there are only 83 million oxen and male water buffalo on the subcontinent, a shortage of 30 million draft teams.

In other regions of the world, joint ownership of draft animals might overcome a shortage, but Indian agriculture is closely tied to the monsoon rains of late spring and summer. Field preparation and planting must coincide with the rain, and a farmer must have his animals ready to plow when the weather is right. When the farmer without a draft team needs bullocks most, his neighbors are all using theirs. Any delay in turning the soil drastically lowers production.

Because of this dependence on draft animals, loss of the family oxen is devastating. If a beast dies, the farmer must borrow money to buy or rent an ox at interest rates so high that he ultimately loses his land. Every year foreclosures force thousands of poverty-stricken peasants to abandon the countryside for the overcrowded cities.

If a family is fortunate enough to own a fertile cow, it will be able to rear replacements for a lost team and thus survive until life returns to normal. If, as sometimes happens, famine leads a family to sell its cow and ox team, all ties to agriculture are cut. Even if the family survives, it has no way to farm the land, no oxen to work the land, and no cows to produce oxen.

The prohibition against eating meat applies to the flesh of cows, bulls, and oxen, but the cow is the most sacred because it can produce the other two. The peasant whose cow dies is not only crying over a spiritual loss but over the loss of his farm as well.

Religious laws that forbid the slaughter of cattle promote the recovery of the agricultural system from the dry Indian winter and from periods of drought. The monsoon, on which all agriculture depends, is erratic. Sometimes it arrives early, sometimes late, sometimes not at all. Drought has struck large portions of India time and again in this century, and Indian farmers and the zebus are accustomed to these natural disasters. Zebus can pass weeks on end with little or no food and water. Like camels, they store both in their humps and recuperate quickly with only a little nourishment.

During droughts the cows often stop lactating and become barren. In some cases the condition is permanent but often it is only temporary. If barren animals were summarily eliminated, as Western experts in animal husbandry have suggested, cows capable of recovery would be lost along with those entirely debilitated. By keeping alive the cows that can later produce oxen, religious laws against cow slaughter assure the recovery of the agricultural system from the greatest challenge it faces—the failure of the monsoon.

The local Indian governments aid the process of recovery by maintaining homes for barren cows. Farmers reclaim any animal that calves or begins to lactate. One police station in Madras collects strays and pastures them in a field adjacent to the station. After a small fine is paid, a cow is returned to its rightful owner when the owner thinks the cow shows signs of being able to reproduce.

During the hot, dry spring months most of India is like a desert. Indian farmers often complain they cannot feed their livestock during this period. They maintain the cattle by letting them scavenge on the sparse grass along the roads. In the cities cattle are encouraged to scavenge near food stalls to supplement their scant diet. These are the wandering cattle tourists report seeing throughout India.

Westerners expect shopkeepers to respond to these intrusions with the deference due a sacred animal; instead, their response is a string of curses and the crack of a long bamboo pole across the beast's back or a poke at its genitals. Mahatma Gandhi was well aware of the treatment sacred cows (and bulls and oxen) received in India. "How we bleed her to take the last drop of milk from her. How we starve her to emaciation, how we ill-treat the calves, how we deprive them of their portion of milk, how cruelly we treat the oxen, how we castrate them, how we beat them, how we overload them."

Oxen generally receive better treatment than cows. When food is in short supply, thrifty Indian peasants feed their working bullocks and ignore their cows, but rarely do they abandon the cows to die. When cows are sick, farmers worry over them as they would over members of the family and nurse them as if they were children. When the rains return and when the fields are harvested, the farmers again feed their cows regularly and reclaim their abandoned animals. The prohibition against beef consumption is a form of disaster insurance for all India.

Western agronomists and economists are quick to protest that all the functions of the zebu cattle can be improved with organized breeding programs, cultivated pastures, and silage. Because stronger oxen would pull the plow faster, they could work multiple plots of land, allowing farmers to share their animals. Fewer healthy, well-fed cows could provide Indians with more milk. But pastures and silage require arable land, land needed to produce wheat and rice.

A look at Western cattle farming makes plain the cost of adopting advanced technology in Indian agriculture. In a study of livestock production in the United States, David Pimentel of the College of Agriculture and Life Sciences at Cornell University found that 91 percent of the cereal, legume, and vegetable protein suitable for human consumption is consumed by livestock. Approximately three quarters of the arable land in the United States is devoted to growing food for livestock. In the production of meat and milk, American ranchers use enough fossil fuel to equal more than 82 million barrels of oil annually. (See Figure I.)

Indian cattle do not drain the system in the same way. In a 1971 study of livestock in West Bengal, Stewart Odend'hal of the University of Missouri found that Bengalese cattle ate only the inedible remains of subsistence crops—rice straw, rice hulls, the tops of sugar cane, and mustard-oil cake. Cattle graze in the fields after harvest and eat the remains of crops left on the ground; they forage for grass and weeds on the roadsides. The food for zebu cattle costs the human population virtually nothing. "Basically," Odend'hal says, "the cattle convert items of little direct human value into products of immediate utility." (See Figure II.)

In addition to plowing the fields and producing milk, the zebus produce dung, which fires the hearths and fertilizes the fields of India. Much of the estimated 800 million tons of manure produced annually is collected by the farmers' children as they follow the family cows and bullocks from place to place. And when the children see the droppings of another farmer's cattle along the road, they pick those up also. Odend'hal reports that the system operates with such high efficiency that the children of West Bengal recover nearly 100 percent of the dung produced by their livestock.

From 40 to 70 percent of all manure produced by Indian cattle is used as fuel for cooking; the rest is returned to the fields as fertilizer. Dried dung burns slowly, cleanly, and with low heat—characteristics that satisfy the household needs of Indian women. Staples like curry and rice can simmer for hours. While the meal slowly cooks over an unattended fire, the women of the household can do other chores. Cow chips, unlike firewood, do not scorch as they burn.

It is estimated that the dung used for cooking fuel provides the energy-equivalent of 43 million tons of coal. At current prices, it would cost India an extra 1.5 billion dollars in foreign exchange to replace the dung with coal. And if the 350 million tons of manure that are being used as fertilizer were replaced with commercial fertilizers, the expense would be even greater. Roger Revelle of the University of California at San Diego has calculated that

89 percent of the energy used in Indian agriculture (the equivalent of about 140 million tons of coal) is provided by local sources. Even if foreign loans were to provide the money, the capital outlay necessary to replace the Indian cow with tractors and fertilizers for the fields, coal for the fires, and transportation for the family would probably warp international financial institutions for years.

Instead of asking the Indians to learn from the American model of industrial agriculture, American farmers might learn energy conservation from the Indians. Every step in an energy cycle results in a loss of energy to the system. Like a pendulum that slows a bit with each swing, each transfer of energy from sun to plants, plants to animals, and animals to human beings involves energy losses. Some systems are more efficient than others; they provide a higher percentage of the energy inputs in a final, useful form. Seventeen percent of all energy zebus consume is returned in the form of milk, traction and dung. American cattle raised on Western range land return only 4 percent of the energy they consume.

But the American system is improving. Based on techniques pioneered by Indian scientists, at least one commercial firm in the United States is reported to be building plants that will turn manure from cattle feedlots into combustible gas. When organic matter is broken down by anaerobic bacteria, methane gas and carbon dioxide are produced. After the methane is cleansed of the carbon dioxide, it is available for the same purposes as natural gas—cooking, heating, electricity generation. The company constructing the biogasification plant plans to sell its product to a gas-supply company, to be piped through the existing distribution system. Schemes similar to this one could make cattle ranches almost independent of utility and gasoline companies, for methane can be used to run trucks, tractors, and cars as well as to supply heat and electricity. The relative energy self-sufficiency that the Indian peasant has achieved is a goal American farmers and industry are now striving for.

Studies like Odend'hal's understate the efficiency of the Indian cow, because dead cows are used for purposes that Hindus prefer not to acknowledge. When a cow dies, an Untouchable, a member of one of the lowest ranking castes in India, is summoned to haul away the carcass. Higher castes consider the body of the dead cow polluting; if they do handle it, they must go through a rite of purification.

Untouchables first skin the dead animal and either tan the skin themselves or sell it to a leather factory. In the privacy of their homes, contrary to the teachings of Hinduism, untouchable castes cook the meat and eat it. Indians of all castes rarely acknowledge the existence of these practices to non-Hindus, but more are aware that beefeating takes place. The prohibition against beefeating restricts

consumption by the higher castes and helps distribute animal protein to the poorest sectors of the population that otherwise would have no source of these vital nutrients.

Untouchables are not the only Indians who consume beef. Indian Muslims and Christians are under no restriction that forbids them beef, and its consumption is legal in many places. The Indian ban on cow slaughter is state, not national, law and not all states restrict it. In many cities, such as New Delhi, Calcutta, and Bombay, legal slaughterhouses sell beef to retail customers and to the restaurants that serve steak.

If the caloric value of beef and the energy costs involved in the manufacture of synthetic leather were included in the estimates of energy, the calculated efficiency of Indian livestock would rise considerably.

As well as the system works, experts often claim that its efficiency can be further improved. Alan Heston, an economist at the University of Pennsylvania, believes that Indians suffer from an overabundance of cows simply because they refuse to slaughter the excess cattle. India could produce at least the same number of oxen and the same quantities of milk and manure with 30 million fewer cows. Heston calculates that only 40 cows are necessary to maintain a population of 100 bulls and oxen. Since India averages 70 cows for every 100 bullocks, the difference, 30 million cows, is expendable.

What Heston fails to note is that sex ratios among cattle in different regions of India vary tremendously, indicating that adjustments in the cow population do take place. Along the Ganges River, one of the holiest shrines of Hinduism, the ratio drops to 47 cows for every 100 male animals. This ratio reflects the preference for dairy buffalo in the irrigated sectors of the Gangetic Plains. In nearby Pakistan, in contrast, where cow slaughter is permitted, the sex ratio is 60 cows to 100 oxen.

Since the sex ratios among cattle differ greatly from region to region and do not even approximate the balance that would be expected if no females were killed, we can assume that some culling of herds does take place; Indians do adjust their religious restrictions to accommodate ecological realities.

They cannot kill a cow but they can tether an old or unhealthy animal until it has starved to death. They cannot slaughter a calf but they can yoke it with a large wooden triangle so that when it nurses it irritates the mother's udder and gets kicked to death. They cannot ship their animals to the slaughterhouse but they can sell them to Muslims, closing their eyes to the fact that the Muslims will take the cattle to the slaughterhouse.

These violations of the prohibition against cattle slaughter strengthen the premise that cow worship is a vital part of Indian culture. The practice arose to prevent the population from consuming the animal on which Indian agriculture depends. During the First Millennium B.C., the Ganges Valley became one of the most densely populated regions of the world.

Where previously there had been only scattered villages, many towns and cities arose and peasants farmed every available acre of land. Kingsley Davis, a population expert at the University of California at Berkeley, estimates that by 300 B.C. between 50 million and 100 million people were living in India. The forested Ganges Valley became a windswept semidesert and signs of ecological collapse appeared; droughts and floods became commonplace, erosion took away the rich topsoil, farms shrank as population increased, and domesticated animals became harder and harder to maintain.

It is probable that the elimination of meat eating came about in a slow, practical manner. The farmers who decided not to eat their cows, who saved them for procreation to produce oxen, were the ones who survived the natural disasters. Those who ate beef lost the tools with which to farm. Over a period of centuries, more and more farmers probably avoided beef until an unwritten taboo came into existence.

Only later was the practice codified by the priesthood. While Indian peasants were probably aware of the role of cattle in their society, strong sanctions were necessary to protect zebus from a population faced with starvation. To remove temptation, the flesh of cattle became taboo and the cow became sacred.

The sacredness of the cow is not just an ignorant belief that stands in the way of progress. Like all concepts of the sacred and the profane, this one affects the physical world; it defines the relationships that are important for the maintenance of Indian society.

Indians have the sacred cow; we have the "sacred" car and the "sacred" dog. It would not occur to us to propose the elimination of automobiles and dogs from our society without carefully considering the consequences, and we should not propose the elimination of zebu cattle without first understanding their place in the social order of India.

Human society is neither random nor capricious. The regularities of thought and behavior called culture are the principal mechanisms by which we human beings adapt to the world around us. Practices and beliefs can be rational or irrational, but a society that fails to adapt to its environment is doomed to extinction. Only those societies that draw the necessities of life from their surroundings without destroying those surroundings, inherit the earth. The West has much to learn from the great antiquity of Indian civilization, and the sacred cow is an important part of that lesson.

Large-Scale Psychological Differences Within China Explained by Rice Versus Wheat Agriculture

T. Talhelm,[1]* X. Zhang,[2,3] S. Oishi,[1] C. Shimin,[4] D. Duan,[2] X. Lan,[5] S. Kitayama[5]

Cross-cultural psychologists have mostly contrasted East Asia with the West. However, this study shows that there are major psychological differences within China. We propose that a history of farming rice makes cultures more interdependent, whereas farming wheat makes cultures more independent, and these agricultural legacies continue to affect people in the modern world. We tested 1162 Han Chinese participants in six sites and found that rice-growing southern China is more interdependent and holistic-thinking than the wheat-growing north. To control for confounds like climate, we tested people from neighboring counties along the rice-wheat border and found differences that were just as large. We also find that modernization and pathogen prevalence theories do not fit the data.

Over the past 20 years, psychologists have cataloged a long list of differences between East and West (*1–3*). Western culture is more individualistic and analytic-thinking, whereas East Asian culture is more interdependent and holistic-thinking. Analytic thought uses abstract categories and formal reasoning, such as logical laws of noncontradiction—if A is true, then "not A" is false. Holistic thought is more intuitive and sometimes even embraces contradiction—both A and "not A" can be true.

Even though psychology has cataloged a long list of East-West differences, it still lacks an accepted explanation of what causes these differences. Building on subsistence style theory (*1, 4*), we offer the rice theory of culture and compare it with the modernization hypothesis (*5*) and the more recent pathogen prevalence theory (*6*).

The modernization hypothesis argues that, as societies become wealthier, more educated, and capitalistic, they become more individualistic and analytical. World Values Surveys (*7*) and studies on indigenous Mayans' transition to a market economy (*5*) have given some support to the modernization hypothesis. But this theory has difficulty explaining why Japan, Korea, and Hong Kong are persistently collectivistic despite per-capita gross domestic products (GDPs) higher than that of the European Union.

The pathogen prevalence theory argues that a high prevalence of communicable diseases in some countries made it more dangerous to deal with strangers, making those cultures more insular and collectivistic (*6*). Studies have found that historical pathogen prevalence correlates with collectivism and lower openness to experience (*6*). However, pathogens are strongly correlated with heat (*8*). Because rice grows in hot areas, pathogens may be confounded with rice—a possibility that prior research did not control for.

The Rice Theory

The rice theory is an extension of subsistence style theory, which argues that some forms of subsistence (such as farming) require more functional interdependence than other forms (such as herding). At the same time, ecology narrows the types of subsistence that are possible. For example, paddy rice requires a significant amount of water. Over time, societies that have to cooperate intensely become more interdependent, whereas societies that do not have to depend on each other as much become more individualistic.

In the past, most subsistence research has compared herders and farmers, arguing that the independence and

* Corresponding author. E-mail: tat8dc@virginia.edu

[1] Department of Psychology, University of Virginia, Charlottesville, VA 22904, USA.

[2] Department of Psychology, Beijing Normal University, Beijing, China.

[3] State Key Lab of Cognitive Neuroscience and Learning, Beijing Normal University, Beijing 100875, China.

[4] Department of Psychology, South China Normal University, Guangzhou, China.

[5] Department of Psychology, University of Michigan, Ann Arbor, MI 48109, USA.

mobility of herding make herding cultures individualistic and that the stability and high labor demands of farming make farming cultures collectivistic (1). We argue that subsistence theory is incomplete because it lumps all farming together. Two of the most common subsistence crops—rice and wheat—are very different, and we argue that they lead to different cultures.

The two biggest differences between farming rice and wheat are irrigation and labor. Because rice paddies need standing water, people in rice regions build elaborate irrigation systems that require farmers to cooperate. In irrigation networks, one family's water use can affect their neighbors, so rice farmers have to coordinate their water use. Irrigation networks also require many hours each year to build, dredge, and drain—a burden that often falls on villages, not isolated individuals.

Paddy rice also requires an extraordinary amount of work. Agricultural anthropologists visiting premodern China observed the number of hours farmers worked and found that growing paddy rice required at least twice the number of hours as wheat (9). The difference in man-hours was not a difference only noticeable to scientists. Medieval Chinese people grew both wheat and rice, and they were aware of the huge labor difference between the two. A Chinese farming guide in the 1600s advised people, "If one is short of labor power, it is best to grow wheat" [quoted in (10)]. A Chinese anthropologist in the 1930s concluded that a husband and wife would not be able to farm a large enough plot of rice to support the family if they relied on only their own labor (11). Strict self-reliance might have meant starvation.

To deal with the massive labor requirements, farmers in rice villages from India to Malaysia and Japan form cooperative labor exchanges (12). Farmers also coordinate their planting dates so that different families harvest at different times, allowing them to help in each others' fields (12). These labor exchanges are most common during transplanting and harvesting, which need to be done in a short window of time, creating an urgent need for labor. In economic terms, paddy rice makes cooperation more valuable. This encourages rice farmers to cooperate intensely, form tight relationships based on reciprocity, and avoid behaviors that create conflict.

In comparison, wheat is easier to grow. Wheat does not need to be irrigated, so wheat farmers can rely on rainfall, which they do not coordinate with their neighbors. Planting and harvesting wheat certainly takes work, but only half as much as rice (9). The lighter burden means farmers can look after their own plots without relying as much on their neighbors.

One point of clarification about the rice theory is that it applies to rice regions, not just the people farming rice. It is a safe bet that none of our thousand participants have actually farmed rice or wheat for a living. Instead, the theory is that cultures that farm rice and wheat over thousands of years pass on rice or wheat cultures, even after most people put down their plows. Simply put, you do not need to farm rice yourself to inherit rice culture.

We propose that the rice theory can partly explain East-West differences. Prior subsistence theory cannot fully explain East-West differences because it focuses on herding versus farming (1), which is not the main East-West difference. Several Western regions herd, such as parts of Scotland and Switzerland, but the bulk of Europe historically farmed wheat (and similarly grown crops, such as barley). Instead, rice-wheat is the main East-West difference, and psychologists have not studied it.

The easiest way to test whether rice and wheat lead to different cultures is to show that rice areas (East Asia) are interdependent and that wheat areas (the West) are independent. But that logic is obviously flawed. We cannot just compare East and West because they differ on many factors besides rice and wheat—religion, politics, and technology, to name a few. A more convincing test case would be a country that has a shared history, government, language, and religion, but farms rice in some areas and wheat in other areas.

China as a Natural Test Case

Han China is a fitting natural test case because it has traditionally grown both rice and wheat but is more ethnically and politically unified than, say, Europe or sub-Saharan Africa. China is over 90% Han Chinese, and the same dynasties have ruled over the wheat and rice cores for most of the past few thousands of years, which controls for some of the major variables that confound East-West comparisons.

Within China, the Yangtze River splits the wheat-growing north from the rice-growing south (Fig. 1). For generations, northern China has grown wheat, and southern China has grown rice. Of course, two regions can never be 100% equivalent. There are differences such as climate and spoken dialect between north and south. To rule out these smaller differences, we report additional analyses that compare people from neighboring counties along the rice-wheat border.

Three Predictions

The three theories make different predictions about which parts of China should be the most interdependent. First, the modernization hypothesis predicts that the least-developed provinces should be the most interdependent. Development has been uneven in China partly because in the late 1970s Deng Xiaoping made several areas along the southeast coast "special economic zones" open to foreign trade. This policy has given southeastern provinces like Guangdong a GDP per capita about 3.5 times that of interior provinces like Guizhou (*13*). That is roughly the ratio difference between the United States and Kazakhstan. Thus, modernization would predict the highest collectivism in China's least-developed interior provinces.

Second, pathogen prevalence theory predicts a gradual rise in interdependence from north to south because pathogens rise gradually along with temperatures (*8*). Among Chinese provinces, overall pathogen rates and latitude are correlated: $r(20) = -0.49, P = 0.02$ (*14*). Furthermore, pathogen theory would predict the highest interdependence in the southwest, which has the highest rates of infectious disease death.

Third, the rice theory predicts the highest interdependence in the south and east. Unlike pathogens, rice is not the highest in the southernmost provinces. Instead, rice is concentrated in the east around Shanghai, which has flat floodplains ideal for growing rice. The rice theory also predicts a sharp divide along the rice-wheat border, which is different from the gradual rise of pathogens with climate.

To measure the prevalence of rice farming, we used statistical yearbook data on the percentage of cultivated land in each province devoted to rice paddies (*13*). Because some rice is grown with less labor on dry land (without paddies), we used statistics on rice paddies, rather than rice output. Because we wanted to assess the crop that different regions farmed traditionally, rather than figures affected by recent advances in irrigation and mechanization, we used rice statistics from 1996, the earliest available on the Bureau of Statistics Web site.

To test the modernization hypothesis, we collected GDP per capita for each province from the same year. To measure precontemporary disease prevalence, we used the earliest study we could find with disease rates in different provinces, from 1976 (*15*). Because the 1976 study did not cover 10 provinces, we also collected recent statistics (*13*). This increased the sample by four provinces. Both sources gave similar pictures: higher disease in the south and the highest in the southwest.

Samples

We tested 1162 Han Chinese students from six sites: Beijing (north), Fujian (southeast), Guangdong (south), Yunnan (southwest), Sichuan (west central), and Liaoning (northeast). We used three measures: a measure of cultural thought, implicit individualism, and loyalty/nepotism (described below). We chose these tasks because they are not self-report scales, avoiding the documented problems with use of self-report scales to measure cultural differences (*16*).

Results from these different sites show that rice-wheat differences held regardless of testing site (*14*). For all tasks, we analyzed only ethnic Han Chinese and excluded Han participants from the provinces of Tibet, Inner Mongolia, and Xinjiang. These areas are historically herding areas and have different ethnicities, cultures, languages, and religions that would confound our comparisons of rice and wheat.

We tested the hypotheses with multilevel models because participants (level 1) were nested within provinces (level 2). We report correlations as an effect size at the province level that can be compared across variables. We calculated this by comparing the province-level variance of the models with and without the key predictor (Tables 1 to 3 report regression output).

Our main dependent variable was a common measure of cultural thought, the triad task (*17*). The triad task shows participants lists of three items, such as train, bus, and tracks. Participants decide which two items should be paired together. Two of the items can be paired because they belong to the same abstract category (train and bus

Table 1 Holistic thought hierarchical linear models for rice (28 provinces, 1019 participants), GDP per capita (28 provinces, 1019 participants), and pathogens (21 provinces, 725 participants). See supplementary materials for detailed information on site effects and regressions with GDP, rice, and pathogens in a single model. Gender is coded as 0 = male and 1 = female.

	B	*SE*	*z*	*P*	*B*	*SE*	*z*	*P*	*B*	*SE*	*z*	*P*
Gender	0.20	0.06	3.55	<0.001	0.20	0.06	3.53	<0.001	0.13	0.07	1.97	0.05
Site$_{Fujian}$	−0.34	0.11	−3.21	0.001	−0.33	0.11	−3.07	0.002	−0.36	0.12	−3.09	0.002
Rice	0.56	0.21	2.72	0.007								
Per-capita GDP					0.52[1]	0.23[1]	2.24[1]	0.03[1]				
Pathogens									−0.22[1]	0.10[1]	−2.08[1]	0.04[1]

[1]Predictor correlates in the opposite direction from what theory predicts.

Table 2 Implicit individualism and loyalty/nepotism hierarchical linear models for rice, GDP per capita, and pathogens. Implicit individualism N equals 28 provinces, 515 participants for rice and GDP. N equals 21 provinces and 452 participants for pathogens. Loyalty/nepotism N equals 27 provinces, 166 participants for rice and GDP. N equals 21 provinces and 146 participants for pathogens.

	B	SE	t	P	B	SE	t	P	B	SE	t	P
					Implicit individualism							
Gender	−0.06	0.02	−2.51	0.01	−0.05	0.02	−2.34	0.02	−0.05	0.02	−2.04	0.04
Site$_{BeijingW2011}$	−0.27	0.05	−5.18	<0.001	−0.25	0.06	−4.40	<0.001	−0.18	0.05	−3.44	0.001
Rice	−0.20	0.08	−2.57	0.016								
Per-capita GDP					0.01	0.15	0.07	0.95				
Pathogens									0.011	0.041	0.331	0.741
					Loyalty/Nepotism							
Site$_{Sichuan}$	2.04	0.83	2.47	0.01	1.63	0.87	1.88	0.06	1.91	0.85	2.25	0.03
Rice	2.45	1.16	2.12	0.04								
Per-capita GDP					1.66[1]	1.69[1]	0.98[1]	0.34[1]				
Pathogens									−0.13	0.62	−0.21	0.84

[1]Predictor correlates in the opposite direction from what theory predicts.

Table 3 Divorce and invention regression models for rice, GDP per capita, and pathogens. Divorces are calculated as divorces per marriage, with 27 provinces for rice and per-capita GDP models and 21 provinces for pathogens. Inventions are the log number of successful patents per capita. Inventions N equals 27 provinces for rice and GDP; N equals 21 for pathogens.

	B	SE	β	t	P	B	SE	β	t	P	B	SE	β	t	P
						Divorces									
Per-capita GDP	0.10	0.04	0.48	2.71	0.01	0.13	0.03	0.61	3.89	0.001	0.11	0.05	0.52	2.04	0.06
Rice						−0.11	0.04	−0.49	−3.11	0.005					
Pathogens											−0.01	0.03	−0.07	−0.26	0.80
						Inventions									
Per-capita GDP	2.22	0.41	0.73	5.37	<0.001	2.55	0.37	0.84	6.98	<0.001	1.78	0.59	0.60	3.00	0.008
Rice						−1.27	0.39	−0.39	−3.28	0.003					
Pathogens											−0.34	0.31	−0.22	−1.10	0.29

belong to the category vehicles), and two because they share a functional relationship (trains run on tracks). People from Western and individualistic cultures choose more abstract (analytic) pairings, whereas East Asians and people from other collectivistic cultures choose more relational (holistic) pairings (1, 17). We report scores as a percentage of holistic choices, where 100% is completely holistic and 0% is completely analytic.

We first tested the modernization hypothesis by testing whether people from provinces with lower GDP per capita thought more holistically. People from richer provinces actually thought more holistically: $\gamma(25) = 0.52$, $P = 0.03$, $r = 0.46$. (γ represents province-level HLM regression coefficients.)

We then tested the pathogen prevalence theory by testing whether provinces with higher rates of disease thought more holistically. Provinces with higher disease rates actually thought less holistically: $\gamma(18) = -0.22$, $P = 0.04$, $r = -0.44$.

The large-scale disease study from 1976 included statistics for 31 counties across China (15), which let us test the pathogen theory more precisely. Thus, we tested whether the 198 people in our sample who came from these 31 counties had different thought styles based on the historical disease prevalence in their county. Even with this finer precision, pathogen prevalence predicted thought style marginally in the wrong direction: $\gamma(28) = -0.43$, $P = 0.08$, $r = -0.33$.

The rice theory was the only model that fit the data (Fig. 2). People from provinces with a higher percentage of farmland devoted to rice paddies thought more holistically: $\gamma(25) = 0.56$, $P = 0.007$, $r = 0.51$. [Controlling for GDP per capita made little difference (table S1).]

Northern and southern China also differ in several factors other than rice, such as climate, dialect, and contact with herding cultures. Therefore, we analyzed differences among neighboring counties along in the five central provinces along the rice-wheat border (Sichuan, Chongqing, Hubei, Anhui, and Jiangsu). Differences between neighboring counties are less likely to be due to climate or other third variables.

We gathered the rice cultivation statistics for each county in these provinces and split counties into rice and wheat counties. We defined rice counties as more than 50% of farmland devoted to rice paddies. Figure 1 depicts an example of the county split in the province of Anhui. The rice-wheat difference between neighboring counties can be stark. For example, in Anhui, Bozhou county farms only 2% rice, whereas neighboring Huainan county farms 67%. We tested for differences in cultural thought style, which had the largest sample, including 224 participants from the rice-wheat border.

People from the rice side of the border thought more holistically than people from the wheat side of the border: $B(221) = 0.54$, $P < 0.001$ (table S5). To compare the border effect size with the effect size for rice and wheat in all of China, we compared effect of a categorical rice-wheat variable. The effect sizes were similar (rice-wheat border, $B = 0.53$; all China, $B = 0.43$). (For group comparisons, wheat provinces are defined throughout as <50% farmland devoted to rice paddies; rice provinces as >50%.)

To test whether the findings generalize beyond thought style, we tested subsamples on two measures previously used for East-West cultural differences. The first was the sociogram task ($n = 515$), which has participants draw a diagram of their social network, with circles to represent the self and friends (18). Researchers measure how large participants draw the self versus how large they draw their friends to get an implicit measure of individualism (or self-inflation). A prior study found that Americans draw themselves about 6 mm bigger than they draw others, Europeans draw themselves 3.5 mm bigger, and Japanese draw themselves slightly smaller (18).

People from rice provinces were more likely than people from wheat provinces to draw themselves smaller than they drew their friends: $\gamma(24) = -0.20$, $P = 0.03$, $r = -0.17$ (fig. S2). On average, people from wheat provinces self-inflated 1.5 mm (closer to Europeans), and people from rice provinces self-inflated −0.03 mm (similar to Japanese).

Pathogen prevalence did not predict self-inflation on the sociogram task: $\gamma(17) = 0.003$, $P = 0.95$, $r = 0$. GDP per capita also failed to predict self-inflation: $\gamma(24) = 0.04$, $P = 0.81$, $r = 0$.

The second measure was the loyalty and nepotism task, which measures whether people draw a sharp distinction between how they treat friends versus strangers ($n = 166$). One defining feature of collectivistic cultures is that they draw a sharp distinction between friends and strangers (3). A previous study measured this by having people imagine going into a business deal with (i) an honest friend, (ii) a dishonest friend, (iii) an honest stranger, and (iv) a dishonest stranger (19). In the stories, the friend or stranger's lies cause the participant to lose money in a business deal, and the honesty causes the participant to make more money. In each case, the participants have a chance to use their own money to reward or punish the other person.

The original study found that Singaporeans rewarded their friends much more than they punished them, which could be seen positively as loyalty or negatively as nepotism (19). Americans were much more likely than Singaporeans to punish their friends for bad behavior. We predicted that people from rice areas would be less likely to punish their friends than people from wheat areas.

We computed loyalty/nepotism as the amount they rewarded their friend minus the amount they punished their friend. People from rice provinces were more likely to show loyalty/nepotism: $\gamma(25) = 2.45$, $P = 0.04$, $r = 0.49$. In their treatment of strangers, people from rice and wheat provinces did not differ: $\gamma(24) = -0.09$, $P = 0.90$, $r = 0$.

Pathogen prevalence was not related to loyalty/nepotism: $\gamma(19) = -0.13$, $P = 0.84$, $r = -0.08$. GDP per capita did not predict loyalty/nepotism: $\gamma(25) = 1.66$, $P = 0.36$, $r = 0.33$.

In short, the results consistently showed that participants from rice provinces are more holistic-thinking, interdependent, and loyal/nepotistic than participants from the wheat provinces. However, one weakness of these studies is that the participants were all college students. To test whether the cultural differences extend beyond college students, we gathered provincial statistics on variables that have been linked to collectivism and analytic thought: divorce rates and patents for new inventions.

A prior study showed that individualistic countries have higher divorce rates, even controlling for gross national product per capita (20). Rice culture's emphasis on avoiding conflict and preserving relationships may make people from rice cultures less willing to get divorced. We collected divorce statistics from the same statistical year-book as the farming statistics, 1996. We also collected statistics from the 2000 and the 2010 yearbooks to track the differences over the past 15 years.

In China, modernization did predict divorce: wealthier provinces had more divorce: $B(26) = 0.10$, $P = 0.01$, $\beta = 0.48$. Adding rice to the model explained even more variation in divorce rates, with rice provinces having lower divorce rates: $B(25) = -0.11$, $P = 0.005$, $\beta = -0.49$. Pathogen prevalence did not predict divorce: $B(20) = -0.01$, $P = 0.80$, $\beta = -0.07$ (controlling for GDP). In 1996, wheat provinces had a 50% higher divorce rate than rice provinces. Although divorce rates have almost doubled in the past 15 years, the raw divorce rate gap between the wheat and rice provinces remained the same in the 2000 and 2010 statistics.

We also analyzed the number of successful patents for new inventions in each province because research has shown that analytic thinkers are better at measures of creativity and thinking of novel uses for ordinary objects (21). Within the United States, immigrants from individualistic cultures hold more patents for inventions (22).

We controlled for GDP per capita because wealthier provinces had more patents: $B(26) = 2.22$, $P < 0.001$, $\beta = 0.73$. Rice provinces had fewer successful patents for new inventions than wheat provinces: $B(25) = -1.27$, $P = 0.003$, $\beta = -0.39$. Pathogen prevalence did not predict patents: $B(19) = -0.34$, $P = 0.29$, $\beta = -0.22$. Wheat provinces had 30% more patents for inventions than rice provinces. This difference persisted through the 2000 statistics but not the 2010 statistics.

This study shows that China's wheat and rice regions have different cultures. China's rice regions have several markers of East Asian culture: more holistic thought, more interdependent self-construals, and lower divorce rates. The wheat-growing north looked more culturally similar to the West, with more analytic thought, individualism, and divorce. Furthermore, Table 4 presents an instrumental variable regression showing that climatic suitability for rice significantly predicts all of the cultural variables in this study, which suggests that reverse causality is unlikely.

How large are these differences compared with East-West differences? We compared results on our main task (cultural thought style) in our China sample to a prior U.S. sample. An East-West categorical variable had an effect of $B = 0.78$. In the China data, a categorical rice-wheat variable had an effect of $B = 0.38$ (table S2). This suggests that rice versus wheat can explain a portion of the variance in thought style between East and West but not all of it. It should also be noted that psychologists have found holistic thought in parts of the world beyond East Asia, which suggests holistic thought is not just an East-West difference (23).

Modernization predicted divorce and patents, but why did it fail to predict the other differences? In China, modernization seems to have changed customs such as divorce, but perhaps the parts of culture and thought style we measured are more resistant to change. Or perhaps modernization simply takes more generations to change cultural interdependence and thought style. However, most of our participants were born after China's reform and opening, which started in 1978. Furthermore, Japan, South Korea, and Hong Kong modernized much earlier than China, but they still score less individualistic on international studies of culture than their wealth would predict (fig. S2).

The rice theory can explain wealthy East Asia's strangely persistent interdependence. China has a rice-wheat split, but Japan and South Korea are complete rice cultures. Most of China's wheat provinces devote less than 20% of farmland to rice paddies. None of Japan's 9 regions or South Korea's 16 regions has that little rice (except for two outlying islands). Japan and Korea's rice legacies could explain why they are still much less individualistic than similarly wealthy countries.

This study focuses on East Asia, but the rice theory also makes predictions about other parts of the world. For example, India has a large rice-wheat split. Indonesia and parts of West Africa have also traditionally farmed rice. If the rice theory is correct, we should find similar cultural differences there.

There are still unresolved questions with the rice theory. For example, studies can test whether irrigation is central to the effect of rice by comparing paddy rice with dryland rice cultures, which grow rice without irrigation. Studies can also explore how rice differences persist in the modern world, whether through values, institutions, or other mechanisms.

There is also the question of how long rice culture will persist after the majority of people stop farming rice. There is evidence that U.S. regions settled by Scottish and Irish herders have higher rates of violence, even though most locals stopped herding long ago (24). This is one example of how subsistence style can shape culture long after people have stopped relying on that subsistence style. In the case of China, only time will tell.

Psychologists, economists, and anthropologists have studied the effects of subsistence style and irrigation (1, 4, 25, 26). This study extends that work by using psychological measures to test differences resulting from rice and wheat agriculture. The rice theory provides a theoretical framework that might explain why East Asia is so much less individualistic than it "should be" based

Table 4   Instrumental variable regressions. Instrumental variable regressions help test whether reverse causality is a problem in the data set—whether regions that were already more collectivistic chose to grow rice. In the topmost regression, "rice suitability" is a z score of the environmental suitability of each province for growing wetland rice based on the United Nations Food and Agriculture Organization's Global Agro-ecological Zones database (*27*). In the five other regressions, "rice suitability" is the predicted rice from the topmost regression with rice suitability. Dash entries indicate not applicable.

	B	*SE*	β	*t/z*	*P*
Actual rice farming					
Rice suitability	0.27	0.03	0.85	8.31	<0.001
28 provinces					
Holistic thought					
Gender	0.20	0.06	–	3.56	<0.001
Site$_{Fujian}$	–0.34	0.11	–	–3.16	0.002
Rice suitability	0.66	0.25	–	2.66	0.008
28 provinces, 1019 participants					
Implicit individualism					
Gender	–0.05	0.02	–	–2.35	0.02
Site$_{BeijingW2011}$	–0.24	0.05	–	–4.87	<0.001
Rice suitability	–0.24	0.10	–	–2.47	0.02
28 provinces, 510 participants					
Loyalty/nepotism					
Site$_{Sichuan}$	1.64	0.80	–	2.05	0.04
Rice suitability	3.73	1.40	–	2.67	0.009
27 provinces, 176 participants					
Divorces					
Per-capita GDP	0.11	0.03	0.51	3.65	0.001
Rice suitability	–0.15	0.04	–0.56	–4.04	<0.001
27 provinces					
Inventions					
Per-capita GDP	2.30	0.34	0.76	6.68	<0.001
Rice suitability	–1.50	0.43	–0.40	–3.50	<0.002
27 provinces					

on its wealth. Finally, the rice theory can explain the large cultural differences within China, advancing a more nuanced picture of East Asian cultural diversity.

Acknowledgments

We thank Z. Xia, N. Qingyun, Y. Wu, Y. Wang, Y. Ma, and A Jiao for collecting data; A. Leung and C. Wang for making the loyalty/nepotism task available; L. Jun Ji for the Chinese version of the triad task; M. Hunter for statistical guidance; and J. P. Seder, A. Putnam, Y. Wang, T. Wilson, and E. Gilbert for comments on earlier versions of this paper. The data are available at the Inter-University Consortium for Political and Social Research (ICPSR no. 35027) or by request to the first author. This research was supported by a Fulbright Scholarship, a NSF Graduate Research Fellowship, and a NSF East Asian and Pacific Summer Institute Fellowship. The Beijing Key Lab of Applied Experimental Psychology supplied laboratory space for the study.

References and Notes

1. R. E. Nisbett, K. Peng, I. Choi, A. Norenzayan, *Psychol. Rev.* **108**, 291–310 (2001).
2. H. R. Markus, S. Kitayama, *Psychol. Rev.* **98**, 224–253 (1991).
3. H. C. Triandis, *Individualism and Collectivism* (Westview, Boulder, CO, 1995).
4. J. W. Berry, *J. Pers. Soc. Psychol.* **7**, 415–418 (1967).
5. P. M. Greenfield, *Dev. Psychol.* **45**, 401–418 (2009).
6. C. L. Fincher, R. Thornhill, D. R. Murray, M. Schaller, *Proc. Biol. Sci.* **275**, 1279–1285 (2008).
7. R. Inglehart, *Wash. Q.* **23**, 215–228 (2000).
8. V. Guernier, M. E. Hochberg, J.-F. Guégan, *PLOS Biol.* **2**, e141 (2004).
9. J. L. Buck, *Land Utilization in China* (Univ. Chicago Press, Chicago, IL, 1935).
10. M. Elvin, in *The Chinese Agricultural Economy*, R. Barker, R. Sinha, B. Rose, Eds. (Westview, Boulder, CO, 1982), pp. 13–35.
11. F. Xiaotong, *Earthbound China: A Study of Rural Economy in Yunnan* (Univ. Chicago Press, Chicago, IL, 1945).
12. F. Bray, *The Rice Economies: Technology and Development in Asian Societies* (Blackwell, New York, 1986).
13. State Statistical Bureau of the People's Republic of China, *China Statistical Yearbook* (1996 and 2005).
14. Materials and methods are available on *Science* Online.
15. C. Junshi, T. C. Campbell, J. Li, R. Peto, *Diet, Life-Style, and Mortality in China: A Study of the Characteristics of 65 Chinese Counties* (Oxford Univ. Press, Oxford, 1990).
16. K. Peng, R. E. Nisbett, N. Y. C. Wong, *Psychol. Methods* **2**, 329–344 (1997).
17. L. J. Ji, Z. Zhang, R. E. Nisbett, *J. Pers. Soc. Psychol.* **87**, 57–65 (2004).
18. S. Kitayama, H. Park, A. T. Sevincer, M. Karasawa, A. K. Uskul, *J. Pers. Soc. Psychol.* **97**, 236–255 (2009).
19. C. S. Wang, A. K.-Y. Leung, Y. H. M. See, X. Y. Gao, *J. Exp. Psychol.* **47**, 1295–1299 (2011).
20. D. Lester, *Psychol. Rep.* **76**, 258 (1995).
21. H. A. Witkin, C. A. Moore, D. R. Goodenough, P. W. Cox, *Rev. Educ. Res.* **47**, 1–64 (1977).
22. S. A. Shane, *J. Bus. Venturing* **7**, 29–46 (1992).
23. J. Henrich, S. J. Heine, A. Norenzayan, *Behav. Brain Sci.* **33**, 61–83, discussion 83–135 (2010).
24. D. Cohen, R. E. Nisbett, *Culture of Honor* (Westview, Boulder, CO, 1997).
25. M. Harris, *Cannibals and Kings* (Random House, New York, 1977).
26. M. Aoki, *Toward a Comparative Institutional Analysis* (MIT Press, Cambridge, MA, 2001).
27. Food and Agricultural Organization (FAO)/International Institute for Applied Systems Analysis (IIASA), Global Agro-ecological Zones (GAEZ v3.0) (2010).

Supplementary Materials

www.sciencemag.org/content/344/6184/603/suppl/DC1
Materials and Methods
Figs. S1 and S2
Tables S1 to S12
References (28–49)

4 October 2013; accepted 25 March 2014
10.1126/science.1246850

The Creation of the Individual in the West: Individualism and Modernity

The process of socialization, as we have seen, passes down the societal blueprints for behavior to individuals and this facilitates the continuation of the society as a system. But social change does occur. Although we live in a "Western" society, the specific values, beliefs and norms of our society vary greatly from the Medieval "Western" society. Through all historical periods, individuals lived their entire lives being socialized into societies that are totally different than ours but which served as the foundation for our own. The content of the culture changed but the dynamics of culture remained the same. So what are the elements of culture that differ from era to era and society to society?

Traditions persist even as modernity expands its reach.

Crucial elements of culture are values and beliefs. **Values** are a culture's standard for discerning what is good and just in society. Values are deeply embedded and critical for transmitting and teaching a culture's beliefs and maintaining continuity in a society over time. **Beliefs** are the tenets or convictions that people hold to be true. Individuals in a society have specific beliefs, but they also share collective values. Values and beliefs change over time as populations and institutions change. Individuals in the middle ages did not hold the same values and beliefs as we do. Indeed, they lived in an entirely different world of knowledge.

Consider the value the culture the United States places upon youth. Children represent innocence and purity, while a youthful adult appearance signifies sexuality. Shaped by this value, individuals spend millions of dollars each year on cosmetic products and surgeries to look young and beautiful. The United States also has an individualistic culture, meaning people place a high value on individuality and independence. In contrast, many other cultures are collectivist, meaning the welfare of the group and group relationships are a primary value.

Norms are the invisible rules of conduct through which societies are structured. **Norms** define how to behave in accordance with what a society has defined as good, right, and important, and most members of the society adhere to them. **Formal norms** are established, written rules. Laws are formal norms, but so are employee manuals, college entrance exam requirements, and "no shirt, no shoes, no service" signs at local restaurants. There are plenty of formal norms, but the list of **informal norms**—casual behaviors that are generally and widely conformed to—is longer. People learn informal norms by observation, imitation, and general socialization.

These elements of the social system have changed over time because, well, change happens. Yet there is a distinctive Western European tradition in our society that has developed through unique historical processes. All of the world did not follow the traditions of Western European societies but the rise of the individual as an autonomous, self controlling part of the social system has very strong roots in the Western European tradition.

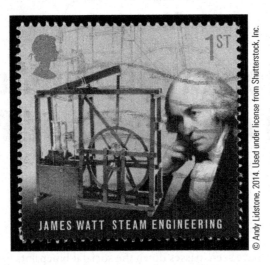

That is not to say that thinking about society or how individuals fit into it is a Western invention. Since ancient times, people have been fascinated by the relationship between individuals and the societies to which they belong. In the 13th century, Ma Tuan-Lin, a Chinese historian, first recognized social dynamics as an underlying component of historical development in his seminal encyclopedia, *General Study of Literary Remains*. The next century saw the emergence of the historian some consider to be the world's first sociologist: Ibn Khaldun (1332–1406) of Tunisia. He wrote about many topics of interest today, setting a foundation for both modern sociology and economics, including a theory of social conflict, a comparison of nomadic and sedentary life, a description of political economy, and a study connecting a tribe's social cohesion to its capacity for power.

Our story of the rise of individualism and the social sciences begins in the 18th century, however. During the Age of Enlightenment philosophers began to develop general principles that could be used to explain social life. Thinkers such as John Locke, Voltaire, Immanuel Kant, and Thomas Hobbes responded to what they saw as social problems by writing on topics that they hoped would lead to social reform.

By the early 19th century, the Industrial Revolution had initiated major changes in the social environments of most European countries. Increased mobility, expansive colonization and new kinds of employment combined with great social and political upheaval to expose many people, for the first time, to societies and cultures other than their own. Millions of people were moving into cities and many people were turning away from their traditional religious beliefs. Society was changing and social thinkers were developing methods of understanding the nature of the changes.

W.E.B. Dubois was a major force in the development of sociology in the United States. He conducted the first studies of urban life of African-Americans in the United States.

The term sociology was first coined in 1780 by the French essayist Emmanuel-Joseph Sieyes (1748–1836) in an unpublished manuscript. In 1838, the term was reinvented by Auguste Comte (1798–1857). Comte thought that society could be studied using the same scientific methods utilized in natural sciences. Comte also believed in the potential of social scientists to work toward the betterment of society. He believed that once scholars identified the laws that governed society, sociologists could address problems such as poor education and poverty. Comte named the scientific study of social patterns **positivism**. He believed that using scientific methods to reveal the laws by which societies and individuals interact would usher in a new "positivist" age of history.

© Lefteris Papaulakis, 2014. Used under license from Shutterstock, Inc.

Karl Marx (1818–1883) was a German philosopher and economist. Marx was the most incisive analysts of the emerging system called Capitalism. He studied Capitalism, wrote extensively about it and developed a theory of society that emphasized the impact of inequality in social development. At the time he was developing his theories, the Industrial Revolution and the rise of capitalism led to great disparities in wealth between the owners of the factories and workers. Capitalism, a dynamic and extremely creative economic system, according to Marx, was characterized by private or corporate ownership of goods. Capitalism needed to constantly expand and grow to be effective. Expansions could occur geographically, though economic or military conquest, or through technological innovations. Marx predicted that inequalities of capitalism eventually would become so extreme that workers would revolt. The collapse of capitalism would lead to a more egalitarian systems; first socialism and then communism. Although he wrote very little about either of the successor systems, he did predict that the collapse of Capitalism would occur only after capitalism as an economic and social system, could expand no more, either through global expansion or technological innovations. The collapse would occur in the most advanced capitalist societies and spread to the least advanced. While his economic predictions may not have come true in the time frame he predicted, Marx's idea that social conflict leads to change in society is still one of the major insights used in modern sociology.

In 1873, the English philosopher Herbert Spencer (1820–1903) published *The Study of Sociology*, the first book with the term "sociology" in the title. Spencer rejected much of Comte's philosophy as well as Marx's theory of class struggle. Instead, he favored a form of analysis which emphasized the role of market forces to control the injustices of capitalism. His work influenced many early sociologists including Emile Durkheim (1858–1917).

Durkheim helped establish sociology as a formal academic discipline by establishing the first European department of sociology at the University of Bordeaux in 1895 and by publishing his *Rules of the Sociological Method* in 1895. In 1897, Durkheim attempted to demonstrate the effectiveness of his rules of social research and the power of sociology to explain behavior that seemed individualistic, but was really driven by broader social forces, when he examined suicide statistics in different police districts throughout Europe. He found patterns to suicide rates that could not be explained simply by individual psychological causes. In his major work *Suicide*, Dukheim argued for the importance of social integration in the establishing patterns to the suicide rates among different communities. For example, single men committed suicide more often than married men; individuals integrated into religious organizations committed fewer suicide than those less integrated and Catholics less than Protestants. Durkheim always tried to research the question: what creates social order? And his answers always tended to support a view of society as being similar to a living organism with many parts. Each part served a function that had to be fulfilled to keep the organism healthy.

Sociologist Max Weber (1864–1920) established a sociology department in Germany at the Ludwig Maximilians University of Munich in 1919. Weber wrote on many topics, including political change in Russia and social forces that affect factory workers. He is known best for his 1904 book, *The Protestant Ethic and the Spirit of Capitalism* in which he argued that the beliefs of many Protestants, especially Calvinists, contributed to the creation of capitalism.

Weber also made a major contribution to the methodology of sociological research. Weber believed that it was difficult if not impossible to use standard scientific methods to accurately predict the behavior of people. He argued that the influence of culture on human behavior had to be taken into account. This even applied to the researchers themselves, who, he believed, should be aware of how their own cultural biases could influence their research. To deal with this problem, Weber introduced the concept of *verstehen*, a German word that means to understand in a deep way. In striving for verstehen, sociologists should attempt to understand any research environment—an entire culture or a small group setting—from an insider's point of view. In his book *The Nature of Social Action* (1922), Weber described sociology as striving to "interpret the meaning of social action and thereby give a causal explanation of the way in which action proceeds and the effects it produces."

Auguste Comte, Max Weber and Emile Durkheim, along with Karl Marx, laid the groundwork for the development of the science of society: Sociology.

It is interesting to note that the term "individualism" was first used in the English language in 1823 by Alexis de Tocqueville in the second volume of *Democracy in America*. De Tocqueville was a French social scientists who studied the American society of the early 19th century by taking a road trip from New York to New Orleans. On the way, he wrote about the social practices of the Americans that he met. He noticed that in the United States the individual was held in higher esteem than institutions, at least by European standards.

Theorizing in Sociology and Social Science: Turning to the Context of Discovery

Richard Swedberg

Abstract

Since World War II methods have advanced very quickly in sociology and social science, while this has not been the case with theory. In this article I suggest that one way of beginning to close the gap between the two is to focus on theorizing rather than on theory. The place where theorizing can be used in the most effective way, I suggest, is in the context of discovery. What needs to be discussed are especially ways for how to develop theory before hypotheses are formulated and tested. To be successful in this, we need to assign an independent place to theorizing and also to develop some basic rules for how to theorize. An attempt is made to formulate such rules; it is also argued that theorizing can only be successful if it is done in close unison with observation in what is called a prestudy. Theorizing has turned into a skill when it is iterative, draws on intuitive ways of thinking, and goes beyond the basic rules for theorizing.

Keywords

Theorizing · Theory · Context of discovery · Context of justification · Abduction

> Looking out my window this lovely spring morning I see an azalea in full bloom. No, no! I do not see that; though that is the only way I can describe what I see. That is a proposition, a sentence, a fact; but what I perceive is not proposition, sentence, fact, but only an image, which I make intelligible in part by means of a statement of fact. This statement is abstract; but what I see is concrete. I perform an abduction when I so much as express in a sentence anything I see. The truth is that the whole fabric of our knowledge is one matted felt of pure hypothesis confirmed and refined by induction. Not the smallest advance can be made in knowledge beyond the stage of vacant staring, without making an abduction at every step.
> —Charles S. Peirce (1901; unpublished manuscript)[1]

During the last half century sociology as well as the other social sciences have made great advances in the kind of methods that they use, while the situation is quite different in the area of theory.[2] The development since World War II has been uneven in this respect: sociologists and other social scientists are today very competent when it comes to methods, but considerably less skillful in the way that they handle theory. The major journals contain many solidly executed articles, while theoretically interesting articles are less common.

Why is this the case? And can the situation be changed? Can the theory part be brought up to par with the methods part in today's social science? In this article I argue that we may want to explore the option of placing more emphasis on *theorizing* rather than on *theory*; and in this way start to close the gap.

The expression "to theorize" roughly means what you do to produce a theory. While theorizing is primarily a process, theory is the end product. The two obviously belong together and complement each other. But to focus mainly on theory, which is what is done today, means that the ways in which a theory is actually produced are being neglected.

If I had chosen a different subtitle for this article, it might have been something like "a Peircean and personal perspective"; and there are several reasons for this. Charles Peirce has been an important source of inspiration in this enterprise and he deserves more of a presence in today's social science. As to the term "personal," I often draw on my own personal experience of theorizing and how to teach theorizing in this article. More importantly, however, the act of theorizing is deeply personal in the sense that you can only theorize well by doing it yourself and drawing on your own experiences and resources.

Emphasizing the role of theorizing also has important consequences for the way that theory is taught,

R. Swedberg (✉)

Department of Sociology, Cornell University, Uris hall 328, Ithaca, NY 14853-7601, USA e-mail: rs328@cornell.edu

Published online: 12 November 2011

something that is discussed in a separate section in this article. The way that theory is typically taught today, the student gets to know what Durkheim-Weber-Bourdieu and so on have said. This knowledge will supposedly come in handy once future research projects are undertaken. To teach theorizing is very different; and here the goal is for the student to learn to theorize on his or her own. The point is to learn to theorize one's own empirical work, not to use somebody else's ideas.

There exist many ways of theorizing, such as induction, deduction, generalizing, model-building, using analogies, and so on. Some of these, I argue, are especially useful for theorizing in sociology and social science. In doing so, I will often use the work of Peirce as my guide. The writings by Peirce, such as "How to Theorize," "Training in Reasoning," and many others, are extremely suggestive when it comes to theorizing (e.g., Peirce 1934, [1992a] 1998).

But there also exists a need to know more about theorizing, something that is very difficult today since there does not really exist a body of work on this topic. There do exist some relevant writings and also many interesting comments and asides, which are scattered throughout the enormous literature in social science.[3]

Finally, throughout this article, I emphasize the many obstacles that exist to creative theorizing. These epistemological obstacles, as I call them here (following Gaston Bachelard), are of many different kinds (e.g., Bachelard 1934 [1984]). Some of them make it hard to deal effectively with data in the process of theorizing. Others encourage the social scientist to rely far too much on existing theory, and thereby skip the element of theorizing and reduce it to a minimum.

Starting From the Distinction Between the Context of Discovery and the Context of Justification

In approaching the topic of theorizing in social science, it is convenient to take one's point of departure in the well-known distinction between the context of discovery and the context of justification. In doing so, it is possible to show that the current neglect of theorizing, and the related overemphasis on theory, has much to do with the tendency in today's social science to ignore the context of discovery for the most part and instead focus nearly all attention on the context of justification.

The distinction between the context of discovery and the context of justification received its most influential formulation in the 1930s through the work of Hans Reichenbach and Karl Popper. Today the distinction is still around, even if it has been much criticized over the years and is far from generally accepted (e.g., Hoyningen-Huene 1987, Schickore and Steinle 2006). The argument in this article does not rest on the notion that these two concepts are each others' opposites or somehow summarize the most relevant features of the research process. Nonetheless, it represents a useful point of departure for the discussion.

Both Reichenbach and Popper were working on ways to improve empiricism as a philosophy of science. Reichenbach coined the two terms "context of discovery" and "context of justification," while Popper helped to diffuse them by giving them a central place in his seminal work *The Logic of Scientific Discovery* (Popper 1935, pp. 4–6; 1959, pp. 31–32, 315; Reichenbach 1938, pp. 6–7, 281; 1951, p. 231).

Reichenbach defined the context of discovery as "the form in which [thinking processes] are subjectively performed," and the context of justification as "the form in which thinking processes are communicated to other persons" (Reichenbach 1938, p. 6). While science can address issues in the context of justification, this is not the case in the context of discovery." The act of discovery escapes logical analysis" (Reichenbach 1951, p. 231).

Popper similarly argued that everything that precedes the testing of a theory is of no interest to science and logic; it belongs to "empirical psychology" (Popper 1935, pp. 4–5; 1959, pp. 31–32). This means in practice that what accounts for the emergence of new theories cannot be studied. In his influential work Popper kept hammering away at this message: it is impossible to study theoretical creativity; the only place for science is in the context of justification (e.g., Popper 1982, pp. 47–48).[4]

In terms of theorizing, what is important with Reichenbach and Popper's distinction is that attention was now directed away from the context of discovery and toward the context of justification. A theory that cannot be verified (Reichenbach) or falsified (Popper) is not scientific; and it therefore becomes imperative to establish the link between theory and facts according to scientific logic. This was mainly done in social science through an emphasis on testable hypotheses: on creating a close link between theory and facts. An idea that could not be formulated as a testable hypothesis was not scientific.

Since the context of discovery was seen as impossible to study with scientific rigor, it fell to the side. If we for the moment view the scientific enterprise as consisting of three elements—you go from (1) *theorizing*, to (2) *theory*, to (3) *the testing of theory*—only the second and the third elements were properly attended to. The first element was largely ignored. Since there exist good reasons for believing that you draw on different ways of thinking when you theorize, and when you test and present your ideas to an audience, this neglect has had serious consequences for social scientists' capacity to theorize.

The strong focus on verification and falsifiability after World War II can be illustrated by Robert K. Merton's influential work in the 1950s and 1960s. Merton looked at theory mainly from the perspective of testability, as his well-known definition of theory illustrates: "The term *sociological theory* refers to logically interconnected sets of propositions from which empirical uniformities can be derived" (Merton 1967, pp. 39, 66, 70). These uniformities should be established via "empirically testable hypotheses" (Merton 1967, p. 66).

Hans Zetterberg, who together with Merton was the main theoretician in sociology at Columbia University during this period, developed a similar set of arguments in his aptly named *Theory and Verification* (1954, 1963, 1965). In Zetterberg's formulation, "theories summarize and inspire, not descriptive studies, but *verificational studies*—studies construed to test specific hypotheses" (Zetterberg 1963, p. 9).

To show how one can improve the situation today, I deal here mainly with the first of the three elements I have mentioned (*theorizing-theory-the testing of theory*). In doing so, I will have little to say about the other two. This should not be interpreted as an argument that they are not of crucial importance, only that theorizing is in need of extra attention today because it has been so neglected.

The General Structure of the Process of Theorizing

> The scientific worker has to take into his bargain the risk that enters into all scientific work: Does an 'idea' occur or does it not?
> —Max Weber, "Science as a Vocation"[5]

Both Merton and Zetterberg were well aware that good theory was the result of inspiration and creativity, as well as rigorous and systematic work with data. Zetterberg noted, for example, the "painstaking triviality" of much sociology, and suggested that social scientists turn to Shakespeare, Dante, and Mark Twain for insight and inspiration (Zetterberg 1963, p. 36).[6] Merton pointed out that method books are full of "tidy normative patterns," but do not describe how sociologists actually "think, feel and act" (Merton 1967, p. 4). As a result of this neglect, Merton continued, their studies have "an immaculate appearance which reproduces nothing of the intuitive leaps, false starts, mistakes, loose ends and happy accidents that actually cluttered up the inquiry" (Merton 1967, p. 4).

But neither Merton nor Zetterberg, both of whom were first class theorists, seem to have felt that theory could be advanced very much by focusing directly on the context of discovery. Merton's main contribution to an understanding of discovery underscores this very point: he singled out discoveries that happen by accident or "serendipity" (e.g., Merton 1967, pp. 158–162; Merton and Barber 2004).

A similar attitude was present among the sociologists who were engaged in what became known as "theory construction" in the mid-1960s to the mid-1970s. According to a historian of this approach, this type of work essentially continued the "verification approach" of Merton and Zetterberg (Zhao 1996, p. 307; see also Hage 1994; Willer 1996; Markovsky 2008). Studies that did not develop a satisfactory way of dealing with verification were labeled "verbal" or otherwise pushed to the side as pre-scientific and passé (e.g., Blalock 1969). The classics were sometimes mentioned as an example of a failure to properly "formalize" (e.g., Freese 1980, p. 63).

While the advocates of theory construction did look at the theorizing process, they were primarily interested in the context of justification, not the context of discovery. Their main concern was with the way you develop hypotheses and test these, not with what precedes these two stages. They focused on formal and cognitive elements, and had little to say on such topics as intuition, imagination, and abduction. This also goes for the best works in the genre, which are still interesting to read, such as *Scientific Sociology* by David Willer, *Constructing Social Theories* by Arthur Stinchcombe, and *An Introduction to Models in the Social Sciences* by Charles Lave and Jim March (Willer 1967; Stinchcombe 1968; Lave and March [1975] 1993).

How then is one to proceed in order to bring the context of discovery into the theorizing process in an effective way? Can one, for example, produce rules for how to theorize, and can these be developed into a solid skill in theorizing that can match the skill in methods that exists today? This is the main question that I address in the rest of this article. The first part of my answer, drawing on Peirce and others, is that some preliminary rules of this type can be devised. The second part of my answer is that one needs to proceed beyond knowing rules, to developing a skill in theorizing.

It deserves to be repeated that to succeed in this enterprise, we also need to get rid of some of the epistemological obstacles that currently exist when it comes to theorizing. One of these is the idea that to theorize one has to proceed in a scientific or logical manner. This is not the case. To theorize well, one needs inspiration, and to get inspiration one can proceed in whatever way that leads to something interesting—and that means *any way*. The reason why this is permissible is that the goal, at this stage of the process, is simply to produce something interesting and novel, and to theorize it. It is first at the stage when the theory is being tested, or otherwise confronted with data in a deliberate manner, that scientific and rigorous rules must be followed. To use a metaphor from the area of law: the context of discovery is where you have to figure out who the murderer is, while the context of justification is where you have to prove your case in court.

In brief, creativity is primarily what matters when a theory is devised; and scientific logic and rigor is primarily what matters in the context of justification. This, of course, is precisely what Reichenbach and Popper had argued. But what to them and their followers became a reason to ignore the context of discovery—it only takes you away from rigor, logic, and proof—can also be seen as an opportunity, an opportunity to make full use of one's imagination, intuition, and capacity for abduction (see also, e.g., Weick 1989; Luker 2008).

Another epistemological obstacle to theorizing is the view in sociology and many other social sciences that empirical data should enter the research process first in the context of justification. According to this view, the social scientist should start the study with a distinct problem or a distinct theoretical point in mind, then construct hypotheses, and finally confront these with data.

This approach can be found in middle-range sociology and to an even stronger extent in so-called theory-driven research. In the former, you typically start with a problem and then try to solve it (e.g., Merton 1959). In theory-driven research you begin with some theoretical point in mind, and then proceed to the empirical phase to confirm or to develop further the initial theory.

Just as middle-range theory, theory-driven research represents an attempt to steer free from "mindless empiricism" or the production of facts without any theory. In mindless empiricism you begin by collecting data, and then summarize the result without linking it to a theory; or you test hypotheses that are not directly related to some theoretical tradition. According to advocates of theory-driven research, social problem-driven research also proceeds in this manner (e.g., Hedström 2007).

The way in which theory has been overtaken by the rapid development of methods after World War II is also reflected in the fact that quite a bit of theorizing is presented these days as being part of methods. This is, for example, the case with some qualitative methods, including participant observation. There is similarly a tendency among the proponents of theory construction to talk about "theoretical methods" (e.g., Willer 1967; Stinchcombe 1978; Freese 1980).

The problem with looking at things in this way is that it feeds into the current tendency to focus primarily on the role of methods in social science research rather than on creativity and originality. The result, especially when it comes to qualitative methods, is a failure to realize that theorizing represents an independent element in the research process and can best be developed if it is realized that theory is not the same as methods.

The types of research that so far have been discussed leave very little room for creative theorizing, except for those rare individuals who happen to have a natural talent for this. For the average social scientist the situation is very different. He or she will typically have been taught methods as a graduate student but not theorizing, since this is not a topic that is currently being taught (e.g., Markovsky 2008). As a result, all too often an awkward attempt is made to force the research findings into some existing theory or just stick some theoretical label on them.

The dilemma for much of contemporary social science is that you are damned if you do and damned if you don't. It is hard to produce good theory if you start from the facts; and it is hard to produce good theory if you start from theory. In the former case, there will be no theory; and in the latter case, the theory already exists.

How then to proceed? First, the general strategy I outline in this article is that empirical data should ultimately drive the theorizing process. This should not be seen as an advocacy of mindless empiricism; and on this point I refer to the sociological tradition. Weber, Durkheim, and many others who are part of what C. Wright Mills called "the classic tradition" all advocate *starting with the facts*. In *Rules of Sociological Method*, Durkheim says that the researcher should proceed "from things to ideas," not "from ideas to things" (Durkheim [1895] 1964, p. 15). According to Weber, "theory must follow the facts, not vice versa" (Weber 2001, p. 36). In *Democracy in America*, Tocqueville writes, "I never gave in to the temptation to tailor facts to ideas rather than adapt ideas to facts" (Tocqueville [1835–1840] (2004, p. 15).[7]

None of the classics, however, has showed us how to go from facts to theory in the creative manner in which they excelled. I suggest that one way of doing this—and this is the move that firmly separates the approach I advocate from mindless empiricism, theory construction, and theory-driven research—is to let the data enter the research process *at two different stages*. One should start the research process by exploring data, and one should at a later stage formulate hypotheses (or their equivalents) and systematically confront these with data.

Just as some researchers advocate the use of a pilot study before the main study is carried out, I suggest that an early empirical phase is necessary. But its purpose is very different from that of a pilot study, namely to develop creative research ideas through theorizing. The first part of the research process may be called a *prestudy*;

and it is characterized by theorizing based on empirical material, with the aim of making a discovery.[8]

At the first stage of the research process (the prestudy), one should deal with the data in whatever way that is conducive to creativity—and *then* try to theorize with their help. Once some interesting theoretical idea has been formulated and worked through to a tentative full theory, one can proceed to the second stage, which is the context of justification or the main study. This is where the research design is drawn up and executed. From this point on, rigor and logic are crucial since the data to be used have to be collected in reliable ways and also presented in this way to the scholarly community.

Two points must immediately be added to this account of the two stages of the research process. First, this is a very general description of how new ideas may be developed and later tested. It is well known, for example, that when hypotheses are tested there may be unexpected findings that lead to the formulation of new theory. Many researchers also work for decades on some problem, hoping to solve it. In brief, while the beginner may want to carefully distinguish between the two stages in conducting research, for the skilled researcher they often become mixed and merge with one another. The process also tends to be is iterative; and its beginning, middle, and end do not necessarily follow in this order.

The second point is that for successful theorizing in social science, you need to be thoroughly grounded in the core ideas of social science. This is a version of Pasteur's dictum that "chance only favors the prepared mind" or, to use a more recent version of the same idea, the 10,000-Hour Rule of Malcolm Gladwell (you need to do something for 10,000 h to become really good at it; Gladwell 2008, pp. 35–68).

This does not mean that, say, the sociologist has to master all the works of Weber-Durkheim-Simmel-Parsons-Merton-Goffman-Coleman-Bourdieu and everyone else who has made a substantial contribution to sociology. What it does mean is that the researcher should have penetrated to the very core and foundation of the social science enterprise. A sociologist should, for example, know intimately what constitutes a social fact (Durkheim), a social action (Weber), and a social form (Simmel).[9]

Those who put in the 10,000 h in sociology or some other social science often do this because they are obsessed with what they are doing. Weber speaks in "Science as a Vocation" of the "strange intoxication" that drives the serious scholar and how this way of acting is "ridiculed by every outsider" (Weber 1946, p. 135).

Weber elevates his point about the strange intoxication to a general rule and states that "nothing is worthy of man as man unless he can pursue it with passionate devotion." There is an existential dimension to this statement; and one can find the same idea in the work of many scientists and philosophers. Kierkegaard, for example, argues that passion should be part of everything one does in life, including thinking and theorizing (e.g., Kierkegaard [1846] 1992).[10]

The research process, to summarize the argument so far, consists of two phases: an early and imaginative phase of theorizing and a later phase in which the major research task is carried out according to the rules of the profession. I call the former the theorizing or discovery phase (or the prestudy) and the latter the phase of major research and justification (or the major study; see Fig. 1). To develop a competence in the first phase or that of theorizing, one does well to follow initially some basic rules and then go from there. In the next two sections I suggest what some of these rules may look like.

Phase # 1: The Prestudy or The Theorizing and Early Discovery Phase

- Observe—and Choose Something Interesting
- Name and Formulate the Central Concept
- Build Out the Theory
- Complete the Tentative Theory, including the Explanation

Phase # 2: The Main Study or The Phase of Major Research and Justification

- Draw up the Research Design
- Execute the Research Design
- Write up the Results

Comment: Theorizing constitutes an independent element of the research process; and it is mainly of importance in the prestudy. The purpose of constructing concepts, typologies, and so on is essentially heuristic at this stage. Theorizing plays a more formal role in the phase in which the major research is carried out and where the full force of methods comes into the picture. Concepts, typologies, and so on have now to be justified primarily on empirical grounds.

Depending on what form the major research takes—a survey, a historical study, an ethnographic case study—there will be changes and shifts in the scheme above, including the theorizing phase. For the skilled researcher, it should be emphasized very strongly, the two phases of research—the prestudy and the main study—tend to meld, be iterative, and take a deeply individual expression.

Figure 1   The two parts of the research process in social science: the prestudy and the main study.

The Basic Rules of Theorizing, Part I: Observation

Dr. Watson: "This is indeed a mystery," I remarked. "What do you imagine that it means?"

Sherlock Holmes: "I have no data yet. It is a capital mistake to theorize before one has data. Insensibly one begins to twist facts to suit theories, instead of theories to suit facts."

—Sir Arthur Conan Doyle, "A Scandal in Bohemia" (1891)[11]

Theorizing is often seen as an activity that is different from observation, but this is not the way that the term was originally understood. The word "theorize" comes from the Greek and means *to see, to observe* and *to contemplate*. It is a mixture, in other words, of several activities: observing something, penetrating something, and finding something out. A philosopher has suggested that theorizing according to the Greeks means that you concentrate on a phenomenon and stay with it, trying in this way to understand it (Heidegger 1977, p. 163).[12]

Theorizing, it is also important to realize, is not conducted in the same way as someone who reasons according to logic. It draws on a very different way of thinking. This is an important point that I return to later in this article. For now, I focus on the element of observation in theorizing. How can observation be part of theorizing? The short answer is that you cannot theorize without having something to theorize about; and this something you have to acquire through observation if it is to be solid. Reasoning and observation are closely and organically related.

Peirce's discussion of this issue is instructive. Observation, as he said in a lecture course from 1898, is one of the three "mental operations" that make up "reasoning" (the others are "experimentation" and "habituation"; Peirce 1992b, 182). There is a logical part to the mental operation of making observations ("upper consciousness") as well as a more intuitive part ("subconscious"). The conscious part of observation is used to get a structural sense of a phenomenon; and one proceeds with this purpose in mind till one's idea corresponds to the phenomenon. This type of observation is described by Peirce as an act "moulding . . . a more or less skeletonized idea until it is felt to respond to the object of observation" (Peirce 1992b, p. 182).

The less conscious part means to take off from some phenomenon, and in this way get a better grip on it. What matters here is "associational potency" or "a magnified tendency to call up ideas" rather than logical thought (Peirce 1992b, p. 182). As an illustration Peirce gives the example of himself looking very closely at an impressionist painting of the sea. "As I gaze upon it I detect myself sniffing the salt-air and holding up my cheek to the sea breeze" (Peirce 1992b, p. 182). The two types of observation do not mix well, according to Peirce; and the theorizer has to be careful so that the conscious part does not suffocate the unconscious part.

Effective theorizing is closely linked to observation; and observation should in my view be interpreted in the very broad sense that it has been understood throughout the history of science (e.g., Daston and Lunbeck 2011). It should not only include, for example, Peirce's conscious type of observation but also his subconscious version. It should include what we ordinarily mean by observation as well as experiments; it should include observations of others as well as observation of oneself (introspection). It should include meaning (thick description) and not exclude it (thin description). Since the main idea is to say something *new* when one theorizes, it is crucial to get as much and as varied information as possible.

Sources should be numerous and of all types: newspapers, archives, books, dreams, daydreams, illusions, speculations, interviews, details, statistical tables, anecdotes, conversations, what is on the web, what one has overheard and much, much more. All of one's senses should ideally be used: sight, hearing, smell, touch, and taste (Simmel [1907] 1997). Anything that provides knowledge, information, associations, and ideas for what something is like is acceptable at this stage of the inquiry. The first rule for observation at the stage of discovery is: *Anything goes!*

Similarly, any objects that can be of help in making interesting observations should be used, from tape recorders and cameras to equipment for neuro-imaging and spectrum analyzers that measure the pitch of the human voice (e.g., Law 2004). There is, to repeat, no need to be overly scientific at this stage. The main point is to get to know some phenomenon in some novel way—and for this imagination is more important than logic.

Everett C. Hughes, who was very interested in the process of theorizing, touches on some of these issues in "The Place of Field Work in Social Science" (Hughes 1984, pp. 496–508). He refers, for example, to "the many arts of observation" and discusses not only the role of the observer, but also those of the participant and the reporter (Hughes 1984, p. 502).

Central to penetrating observation in social science, Hughes says, is what he calls "observation on the hoof" (Hughes 1984, pp. 504–505). By this expression he means the capacity to see what happens in society in terms of "going concerns" or institutional patterns. A good social scientist is deeply tuned in to the social dimension of things, in other words. According to dictionaries, doing something "on the hoof" also means to do it while one is doing something else, and doing something that one does not have the time to think about. In brief, the capacity for observation has to reach deep down into the personality of the researcher and bypass his or her more rational faculties, to be truly successful.

The best information is the one that one acquires oneself. Primary material is untheorized material and much to be preferred to what other social scientists have produced, even if it can be very hard to get. Tocqueville said that he would much rather create his own data than use that of others, even if it took him several times longer to do so. "I take incredible pains to find the facts for myself [and] I thus obtain, with immense labor, what I could have found easily by following another route" (Tocqueville 2003, p. 1200). Observation, as Hughes sums it up, is first of all about the importance "*to see for oneself*" (Hughes 1984, p. 497; emphasis added).

It is imperative to hold off on theorizing one's observations until one knows quite a bit about the topic to be theorized. Unless this is done, one will theorize on the basis of scant information or on the basis of the ideas that float around in society and have little grounding in what actually goes on. The second rule for observation is: "*Don't think but look!*" (Wittgenstein 1953, 66e).

The classical place where this attitude toward observation is explained is *The Rules of Sociological Method* by Durkheim. He calls the popular notions that we all have of what things are like "preconceptions" (*prénotions*); and he contrasts these to the "social facts" that the sociologist wants to map out and explain (Durkheim [1895] 1964, p. 17). According to one of Durkheim's most important rules for how to conduct research, "*all preconceptions [prénotions] have to be eradictated*" (Durkheim [1895] 1964, p. 31; emphasis in text). To do so, the researcher has to enter the research with an understanding of his or her "complete ignorance" of what the situation is really like (Durkheim [1895] 1982, p. 246).

To prevent the popular notions or preconceptions from taking the upper hand, when one engages in observation, one can draw on some of the ideas in Peirce's semiotics. A sign, according to Peirce, does not only stand for something else; it also has a relation to the interpretant or the actor (e.g., Peirce 1991). More precisely, a sign refers to some object, but it also *determines* the actor's perception of the object.[13] The direction of causality, when it comes to the individual in his or her everyday life, is in other words the very opposite from what is claimed in much of social science. According to the latter perspective, a social object/sign is collectively created by a group or society as a whole. The causal arrow goes from the actors to the sign.

According to Peirce, the sign and the object also meld together in the mind of the interpretant; and this means that he or she does not distinguish between the two. An example may illustrate the point. If someone makes, say, the sign of thumbs up, other actors will not pay attention to the person's hand with the thumb pointing upwards, but just think that something has been given an okay or a positive evaluation.

Or to use the example from the quote with which this article begins: when we see an azalea, we do not see something green and something pink in a special configuration. We simply see an azalea—the concept of a specific flower with a specific history *and* the physical image of the flower itself, both simultaneously. How thumbs up and an azalea have turned into a concept, and the whole thing into a kind of mental *Gestalt*, is precisely what interests the theorizer.

To do science, according to Peirce, means among other things to challenge existing signs and concepts, and show how these have come into being; how some elements of reality have come to be cast as this particular concept rather than as some other concept. To be effective in undoing and picking apart existing signs, Peirce also argues, presupposes that the scientist experiences personal doubt. But as opposed to Descartes, he is emphatic that that the scientist cannot conjure up this doubt at will. We grow up with certain notions, and these cannot simply be set aside through an act of will. "Let us not pretend to doubt in philosophy what we do not doubt in our heart" (Peirce 1955, p. 229).

But where there is doubt, Peirce continues, there will be thinking and theorizing. And this thinking will go on till a new stage of certainty ("belief") has been established. "However the doubt may originate, it stimulates the mind to an activity which may be slight or energetic, calm or turbulent. Images pass rapidly through consciousness, one incessantly melting into another" (Peirce 1955, p. 27). The struggle to free ourselves from existing ideas and habits is central to science; and it takes place through a process that Peirce calls inquiry (e.g., Goudge 1969, pp. 13–18; Bertilsson 2009).

Durkheim states firmly that one should avoid introspection and only focus on outer signs or facts that can be observed in a reliable manner. This, I argue, mixes up what is appropriate in the context of discovery with what is appropriate in the context of justification. At the initial stage of the research—the theorizing and creative stage—one may want to do precisely the opposite of what Durkheim recommends, namely to penetrate as deeply as possible into the social facts. You do not only want to know what happens at the surface of some phenomenon, but also in its most fluid and intangible parts—and one way to do this, is for example through introspection. The reason for proceeding in this manner, to repeat, is to get as fine and close information as possible about some phenomenon, before one begins to theorize it.

The researcher should be aware that in observing something, you also pick up quite a bit that you are not conscious of. This means that one should not only try to train one's cognitive skills of observation but also one's general sensibility, and in this way pick up as much as possible of what is going on. By opening oneself up in this manner, one will become aware of some of the tacit knowledge and insignificant details that come with all observation (e.g., Collins 2010). C. Wright Mills, who was very interested in the process of theorizing, writes in *The Sociological Imagination* that "social observation requires high skill and acute sensibility" (Mills 1959, p. 70).

Michael Polanyi, who coined the notion of tacit knowledge, speaks in one of his works of something called "subception" (Polanyi 1966, pp. 7–8). Subception is contrasted to perception, which is an activity one is typically aware of. Polanyi gives the following example of subception. In an experiment, the subjects were given an electric shock each time they failed to recognize some random combination of syllables ("nonsense syllables"). They soon learned to avoid these combinations—but without being aware that they were doing this.

The key idea, once again, is to get as fine and close information as possible about some phenomenon before one starts to theorize. If not, one is likely to theorize on the basis of meager and faulty information, and produce an empty form of theory. When students once asked Everett C. Hughes to teach a course in theory, he is said to have muttered, "theory of what?" (Becker 1998, p. 1). The danger of producing an empty and premature kind of theory naturally also exists if one theorizes *after* having immersed oneself in the data. But when this is the case, we hope it will be corrected at the stage of justification or in the major study.

It can finally be noted that if one wants to be a creative observer, it may be useful to avoid reading too many secondary works early on. Most sociologists smile when they recall Auguste Comte's doctrine of "mental hygiene" or his decision not to read any works on the topic he was studying, on the ground that this would block his creativity. While this no doubt is the wrong strategy to follow, an argument can be made for trying to formulate one's own view, based on primary material, well ahead of reading what other social scientists have written on the topic.

One may view this approach as the intellectual equivalent of the infant industry-argument. Tocqueville, for example, took this stance when he worked on *Democracy in America*. He also devised a strategy for how both

to avoid reading what others have written *and* to get the benefit of their analyses. He did this by asking his friend Gustave de Beaumont to read some literature on the United States that he thought might compete with his own views, and then tell him if they contained anything of importance (e.g., Swedberg 2009b, 101).

The Rules of Theorizing, Part II: Naming, Conceptualizing, Using Analogies, Metaphors, and Types, Developing a Tentative Theory, Including an Explanation

> Theory cannot be improved until we improve the theorizing process, and we cannot improve the theorizing process until we describe it more explicitly, operate it more self-consciously, and de-couple it from validation more deliberately. A more explicit description [of the process of theorizing] is necessary so we can see more clearly where the process can be modified and what the consequences of these modifications are.
> —Karl Weick, "Theory Construction as Disciplined Imagination" (1989)[14]

Before proceeding any further and outlining some of the other rules of theorizing, it may be useful to stop for a moment and define more closely two of the key terms in this article: *theory* and *theorizing*. The emphasis, to repeat, in todays' social science is typically on theory, while theorizing is discussed very little, if at all. In this article, in contrast, the emphasis is on theorizing; and I suggest we may want to view theory as an instance of theorizing rather than the other way around. The reason for this is that theorizing contains the seed of theory, which can also be seen as the final instance of the theorizing process.

But even if we grant this, neither theorizing nor theory should be understood and defined exclusively in words. Both also include actions and interactions, with people as well as objects. In *Philosophical Investigations* Wittgenstein cites the "forming and testing a hypothesis" as an example of a language game; and we may want to do the same with theorizing (Wittgenstein 1953, 12e). Theorizing in social science means an attempt to understand and explain something that happens in society; and it includes everything that precedes the final formulation that is set down on paper or fixed in some other way ("theory"). This means interaction with people and texts such as books and articles, among other things. What is called theory is essentially the end product of the process of theorizing, the final formulation of an attempt to understand

and to explain something that happens. By final formulation is roughly meant its clothing in language (words or symbols) that is made public or made available publicly.

Theorizing includes what I have called observation as well as the activities to be discussed in this section, such as naming, conceptualizing, constructing typologies, providing an explanation, and so on. When these activities are carried out at the stage of discovery or in the prestudy, it should be emphasized, this is done first and foremost for heuristic reasons. This means that they are to be used primarily for purposes of discovery and not to summarize the result of systematic empirical research.[15] And it is very much by becoming aware of precisely this dimension, I argue, that it becomes possible to produce successful theorizing. Intuition, imagination, and abduction are also all indispensable to successful theorizing; and they belong primarily to the stage of discovery.

And so does a certain playfulness or a capacity to let go of logic and rigor, and just let one's mind enjoy itself. Peirce described this as "Pure Play" and called it "Play of Musement" (e.g., Peirce 1935, pp. 458–459). One may begin by having some impression, he says, which will be followed by some observation; and then drift off into playfulness and reverie. . . .

Peirce's thoughts on this topic were deeply inspired by Friedrich Schiller's idea that people are born with an instinct to play (*Spieltrieb*), not unlike Peirce's own view of abduction or the instinct to guess right (Schiller [1794] 2004, pp. 73–81, pp. 133–140; cf. Huizinga 1950). This instinct, according to the German poet and philosopher, was closely linked to aesthetics; and I suggest that we read Peirce's ideas on this topic as a plea for introducing not only play but also art into theorizing (see also March 1970). Art and theorizing belong closely together, even if the precise links between the two still remain to be better understood (for the deep affinity between theorizing and poetry, see, e.g., Heidegger 2011).

While theorizing, then, can be playful and full of movement, theory signifies the freezing of a set of thoughts. Theory is frozen into written language or a symbolic language such as mathematics. While theorizing never ends, theory is stuck forever in its formulation.

Theory is also qualitatively different to its originator and to those who use it but did not create it. For the originator, the link between theory and theorizing is very much alive and obvious. For those who are interested in a theory but did not produce it, things are very different. For them, the whole process that preceded the freezing into the end product is hidden. Theory appears as something that only exists as a text to be read, as mainly cognitive in nature, and as the result of a series of logical moves. The activity of reading an argument or working

through a mathematical model, it can be added, is also a very special kind of cognitive activity. The argument and the way it is presented have been locked into place once and for all. If theorizing is fundamentally alive, theory is dead theorizing.

The fact that theory is typically someone else's theory also means that it is exterior and alien to one's own thinking or, to phrase it differently, that it lacks a certain organic quality. Incorporating someone else's theory into one's own set of thought is also a difficult process that can easily go wrong ("organ rejection").

C. Wright Mills speaks inspiringly in *The Sociological Imagination* about the craft of sociology consisting of two parts: method and theory (Mills 1959, p. 228). A sociologist, he says, should be his or her own theorist as well as methodologist. I am very sympathetic to Mills's idea of speaking about theorizing as a craft (or as a part of a craft), rather than, say, as a job or a profession. One reason for this has to do with the important role that tacit knowledge plays in a craft. It is well understood that the hand of the craftsman knows more than his or her mind; and being aware of this, helps the craftsman do a better job.

A craftsman needs to develop a special relationship to the material he or she works with. A carpenter, for example, must know how the different kinds of wood feel and act. Similarly a social scientist has to develop an intimate sense for what actors feel and think, well beyond what is recorded in standard interviews or surveys. Weber, for example, argues that the easiest way for a sociologist to enter into the mind of another person, to find out what meaning he or she has invested some action with, is if the person is using some rational method of thinking, such as adding 2+2 (Weber [1922] 1978, pp. 5–6). Empathy, according to Weber, represents another option for the sociologist to enter someone else's mind.

But Weber also says that there exists a specific artistic intuition that can be drawn on when we try to understand how others feel and think for sociological purposes (Weber [1922] 1978, p. 5). Authors seem to be able to read the way that people behave, and somehow guess what is behind their actions. That this intuitive capacity differs from logical reasoning is clear from a number of facts. Authors often say, for example, that the characters in their books do not obey them, but tend to behave as the characters want (for a similar "emergent" phenomenon when you improvise in jazz, see, e.g., Sudnow 2001).

While the expression "the craft of theorizing" is appealing, one should warn against the idea that theorizing can be reduced to a set of explicit rules, especially cognitive rules that should always be followed. Rules are typically helpful for the beginner, but they can also prevent a person's development once a certain stage of competence has been reached. The reason for this is that they exclude all that differentiates the mechanical and early following of a rule from what it means to have a skill or the capacity to handle nearly automatically a series of concrete situations in an independent and creative manner (e.g., Dreyfus and Dreyfus 1986). To try to unlock creativity through a set of handy rules that should always be followed, something that is not uncommon in the literature on heuristics, represents another of those epistemological obstacles that Bachelard talks about.

But rules that should be followed only until a skill has been developed is something very different. And the ones that I propose as basic to theorizing in social science are the following: naming, conceptualizing, broadening the concept into a theory, and completing the tentative theory through an explanation. I have roughly listed them in the order in which they are usually carried out, even if the actual process, to repeat, is typically iterative and more complex at a later stage (see Fig. 2).

One becomes good at theorizing through practice; to theorize is also a reflexive activity. One gradually teaches oneself how to theorize by repeatedly doing it, and thinking about what one does. One theorizes and reflects on what one does right and what one does wrong. Engaging in this type of auto-ethnographic analysis helps to increase one's skill as a theorizer.

While the full cycle of theorizing goes from observation to explanation, it is not uncommon to a stop at some stage in the middle, use already existing concepts, categories, explanations, and so on. While it constitutes a contribution to establish a new and interesting phenomenon or a new and interesting concept, to provide an explanation for the phenomenon constitutes the natural end point of the theorizing process.

The general goal of theorizing is to come up with a new idea or what Peirce famously calls abduction, and a few words need to be said about this important but vague concept. "Abduction [means] observing a fact and then professing to say what idea it was that gave rise to that fact," we read at one point (Peirce 1957, p. 244). Here is another central passage:

> The first starting of a hypothesis and the entertaining of it, whether as a simple interrogation or with any degree of confidence, is an inferential step which I propose to call *abduction*. This will include a preference for any one hypothesis over others which would equally explain the facts, so long as this preference is not based upon any previous knowledge bearing upon the truth of the hypotheses, nor on any testing of the hypotheses, after having admitted them on probabtion. I call all such inference by the peculiar name, *abduction*, because its legitimacy depends upon altogether different principles from those of other kinds of inference (Peirce 1957, pp. 236–237).

Abduction essentially comes about by "guessing right." While Peirce disliked the term intuition, it is possible to describe abduction as a kind of scientific intuition, that is, as the kind of intuition that a scientist or scholar is partly born with and partly develops through hard work and the cultivation of one's imagination.

To be good at abduction essentially means going into oneself and trying to locate, and possibly also train, something that is exceedingly fleeting and hard to get

---

Rule # 1 Observe and Choose Something Interesting

You can only theorize on the basis of observation. Anything that can stimulate to a full view of the phenomenon should be used, from sturdy scientific facts to art in various forms. *"Don't think but look!"* (Wittgenstein)

Rule # 2 Name and Formulate the Central Concept

Give a name to what you observe and try to formulate a central concept based on it. Here as elsewhere abduction (Peirce) is the key.

Rule # 3 Build Out the Theory

Give body to the central concept by outlining the structure, pattern or organization of the phenomenon. Use analogies, metaphors, comparisons—and all in a heuristic way to get a better grip on the phenomenon under study.

Rule # 4 Complete the Tentative Theory, including the Explanation

Formulate or model a full tentative theory of the phenomenon, with special emphasis on the explanation that constitutes the natural end of the theorizing process.

Comment: The most important part of theorizing takes place in the context of discovery or what is here called the prestudy, and that includes an early immersion in the empirical material. The way of thinking characteristic at this stage differs from the traditional and logical mode of thinking that is to be used when the result of the research is presented and that also infuses most methods. The rules of theorizing should only be followed initially and abandoned as soon as a skill in theorizing develops. This skill makes room for the iterative and often idiosyncratic way in which advanced and creative research is conducted. The skill in theorizing complements the mainly methodological skills that are in existence today. The different social sciences all have different traditions when it comes to methods and theory, something that means that one can expect many different strands of good theorizing.

Figure 2   The basic rules of theorizing in social science.

hold of, namely one's capacity for scientific intuition. Most of us have at some point experienced creative moments of the type that Peirce describes and the euphoria that comes with them. Some of us also feel that whatever the reason may be, when this happens you have to put everything to the side and just go with the flow. To cite Weber, "when I 'receive' ideas or contemplatively allow them to form *inside* me, everything flows—no matter whether it is a lot or a little, valuable or valueless, it flows in abundance" (Radkau 2009, p. 98).

But can one also train one's capacity for abduction? Weber, for example, notes in "Science as a Vocation" that "ideas occur to us when they please, not when it pleases us" (Weber 1946, p. 136). Many artists have, for example, tried to get their ideas going, using everything from alcohol and drugs to the company of friends and muses.

Peirce himself argued that abduction is a kind of biological quality that human beings as a species are born with. Just like chickens have the capacity of "guessing right," when it picks something up from the ground and start to eat it, human beings have the mental capacity to select somehow the right hypothesis among a myriad of possible ones.

But does Peirce also think that one can train this capacity or, less strongly, to learn to activate it at will? As far as I know, he never addressed these issues in his work. It would seem clear, however, from looking at Peirce's life, that he believed that this was possible. Why else would he train himself in such an austere fashion, in every conceivable science including economics and sociology (e.g., Swedberg 2011)?

It is also true that Peirce believed very strongly in the idea that one can train one's general capacity to reason and to theorize—a position that I also take in this article. This subject is discussed in one of his most important articles when it comes to theorizing, "Training in Reasoning" from 1898. According to Peirce, it is self-evident that one should try to develop one's capacity for reason. "I do not know why a man should not devote himself to the training of his reasoning powers with as much assiduity as to corporeal athletics" (Peirce 1992b, p. 181).

The way to go about this is to focus systematically on the three mental operations that make up reasoning: *observation, experimentation,* and *habituation* (Peirce 1992b, pp. 182–192). I have already mentioned how Peirce thought that observation consists of two parts, one that is conscious and logical, and another that is unconscious and creative. Experimentation means to intervene actively in what one studies; it involves will-power as well as "creative imagination" (Peirce 1992b, p. 188). Habituation has to do with one's capacity to break old mental habits and create new ones. Mental habits, according

to Peirce, mainly have to do with the way that ideas are linked to each other.

Still, what Peirce discusses in "Training in Reasoning" is not abduction or at least not in its pure and characteristic form. And even if it is clear that there exists a distinction between the capacity to theorize and to theorize in a deeply creative manner, something should also be said about the possibility of training one's capacity for abduction.

As those who are familiar with Peirce know, there does exist one intriguing example of how Peirce put his capacity for abduction to an empirical test in a deliberate fashion. It is a peculiar story and I will retell it in some detail (see Sebeok and Umiker-Sebeok 1981 for the full version).

During a boat trip in 1879 Peirce had his coat and a valuable Tiffany watch stolen. He had reason to believe that one of the waiters on the boat was the thief, since only they had had access to his belongings. He therefore had them lined up so he could question them. The interrogation, however, did not result in anything; and Peirce later wrote:

> When I had gone through the row [of waiters] I turned and walked from them, though not away, and said to myself, "Not the least scintilla of truth have I got to go upon." But thereupon my other self (for our communings are always in dialogues), said to me, "But you simply must put your finger on the man. No matter if you have no reason, you must say whom you will think to be the thief." I made a little loop in my walk, which had not taken a minute, and as I turned toward them, all shadow of doubt had vanished (Sebeok and Umiker-Sebeok 1981, pp. 11–12).

Peirce took the person he suspected to be the thief aside and interrogated him. The individual denied that he was guilty, and Peirce had to let him go. Peirce, however, was convinced that he was right and he had the man followed, to find out where he lived. He later entered the apartment of the suspect and guessed exactly where the watch had been hidden. He also guessed that his coat had been removed to a neighbor's apartment, and again he was right.

The story of how Peirce retrieved his stolen items illustrates, among other things, how eccentric and willful he was. He himself described the episode in a letter to William James as an instance of the "theory why it is so that people so often guess right" (Sebeok and Umiker-Sebeok 1981, p. 16). It is hard to disagree with this assessment—and that Peirce had somehow taught himself to become very good at this guessing game.

But even if human beings have guessed right throughout history more often than if only chance was involved, it should also be pointed out that according to Peirce, most scientific abductions are either impossible to test or turn out to be outright wrong, once they have been tested (e.g., Peirce 1957, pp. 242–243). The centrality of abduction to Peirce's theory of how an inquiry should be conducted does not mean that science should consist of fantasy and imagination. A theory, Peirce insisted, has its origin in an abduction but it must be testable as well. And it must be tested.

Naming, to leave abduction now and proceed to what comes after observation, represents a difficult philosophical concept (e.g., Kripke 1980). Here, in contrast, it will simply be used to refer to the following two related elements of theorizing: locating a novel phenomenon and giving it a name. It is clear that one may also want to name new concepts, new models of explanation, and so on.[16]

Discovering a new phenomenon constitutes one of the most important tasks in social science, and finding the right word(s) to describe it, and in this way really capture it, often represents a frustrating task. But if this is not done, the phenomenon can slip between one's fingers. It can similarly be hard to find a new name that fits the new phenomenon and provides it with a distinct identity.

The prevalent view in any society is that most phenomena are well understood (Durkheim's "preconceptions"). To the sharp-eyed observer, however, phenomena are typically different from their common perception; things also constantly change in modern society. But to see something novel and to go beyond habitual categories is very difficult; it can also be unsettling.

It sometimes happens that one locates a totally new phenomenon, but this is not common. What one observes is typically often covered, but not completely so, by some existing concept. In this situation it is important not to dismiss the difference, and to squeeze one's observations into some existing category. Instead one should zoom in on the difference, magnify it, and explore if the phenomenon does not merit a new name or at least a new description or definition.

There exist different attitudes about what name is appropriate for a new phenomenon. One can, for example, use a term that already exists in everyday language, and just introduce it into the social science vocabulary. According to Durkheim, this is the best way to proceed. But he also mentions one exception; and this is when a lay term covers "a plurality of distinct ideas" (Durkheim [1895] 1964, p. 37, n. 12). In this case, he says, it is preferable to create "new and distinctive terms."

One can also select a totally new name and in this way draw attention to some phenomenon and symbolically mark it off from other phenomena. One way of doing this is to choose some forgotten or rarely used name,

such as anomie (Durkheim), *habitus* (Bourdieu) or serendipity (Merton). One can also create a new name, such as sociodicy (Aron), catnet (Harrison White) or gloriometer (Tarde). And one can elaborate on some already existing name or concept, as exemplified by such terms as status contradictions (Hughes), greedy institutions (Coser), and role-set (Merton).

Weber argues that it does not matter very much if one uses a new term or an already existing one, as long as its meaning is clear (Weber 2001, pp. 63, 77). He also notes that many academics get irritated when a new term is introduced, unless they have coined it themselves. His own preference, when no term already existed, was to use "the nearest and most descriptive words from traditional language" (Weber 2001, p. 63).

My own view is that one should avoid introducing too many names and also to give a new phenomenon some odd new name. It is rare to discover something really novel; and forcing the reader to remember new terms, without getting much for it, only creates irritation. The rule should be that if one has something major to say, a new name is warranted. And just as we think highly of "Marx" and "Weber," we have a high regard for such plain concepts as "capital" and "social action." In brief, in the end it is the idea and force behind the word that counts, not the term. The audience one is writing for should also be kept in mind when a new term is chosen (e.g., Hughes and Hughes 1952).

In discussing naming I have a few times crossed the line between a name and a concept. There exist several differences between the two; a scientific concept is in particular more analytical and abstract than a name. Peirce defines a concept as "the rational purport of a word or a conception"; and the reference to rationality is important (Peirce 1998, p. 332). It is precisely this quality, one can argue, that has made the concept "one of the great tools of all scientific knowledge" (Weber 1946, p. 141).

One of the rational qualities of a scientific concept is that it makes it possible for some phenomena to be clearly identified as belonging to a general category. A second rational quality of the scientific concept has to do with its important role in the scientific enterprise as a whole. To cite Carl Hempel: "to be scientifically useful a concept must lend itself to the formulation of general laws or theoretical principles which reflect uniformities in the subject matter under study, and which thus provide a basis for explanation, prediction, and generally scientific understanding" (Hempel 1965, p. 146).

To link up the central concept in the prestudy to a classification, a typology, or an explanation is something I refer to as "building out the theory." It can be described as going beyond the definition of a concept and outlining the full structure of the way that some phenomenon operates. What causes a phenomenon, and what consequences it has, also belong to this phase of theorizing.

One can either develop a new central concept or use an existing one. It is also possible to improve an existing concept by adding to it. In developing a new concept, one can either create a totally new concept or, more commonly, turn a rudimentary one into a full-fledged concept. The former is sometimes called a proto-concept, and the transition from a proto-concept to a full-fledged concept has been discussed in an illuminating way by Merton (1948; see also Fleck [1935] 1979).

"A proto-concept," Merton says, "is an early, rudimentary, particularized and largely unexplicated idea" (Merton 1984, p. 267). "A concept," in contrast, "is a general idea which, once having been tagged, substantially generalized, and explicated can effectively guide inquiry into seemingly diverse phenomena." While proto-concepts "make for early discontinuities in scientific development," fully developed concepts "make for continuities by directing our attention to similarities among substantively quite unconnected phenomena" (Merton 1984, p. 267).

One example of a proto-concept would be the notion of "theorizing," as currently used in sociology. Ever since its first appearance in a sociological journal (in 1896), this term has been much less popular among sociologists than "theory" (Small 1896, p. 306). Through a search on JSTOR one can follow its sporadic appearance in sociological journals since the 1890s until today. Such a search also shows that while the term "theorizing" has been used now and then, it has never been properly defined, discussed, and expounded upon.[17] As a result—and as Merton would predict—little progress has been made in understanding the process of theorizing.

It is also possible, as mentioned earlier, to take an existing concept and improve on it. This can be done in several ways. Weber, for example, sometimes took a concept and split it into two, in this way making it more useful for some particular purpose (interests became "ideal and material interests"; rationality became "formal and substantive rationality," and so on). According to Weber, the value of a concept should be judged from the viewpoint of how useful it is for the concrete task at hand; in itself a concept cannot be said to be good or bad (e.g., Weber 1976, p. 47).

It is sometimes necessary to clarify an existing concept; and also this means that it is changed in some respect. Merton regarded conceptual clarification as a particularly important task in social science. "A good part of the work called 'theorizing,'" he once wrote, "is taken up with the clarification of concepts—and rightly so" (Merton 1948, p. 513). It has also been suggested that

the really important scientific concepts are not suddenly invented, but evolve over time (e.g., Nersessian 2008). In sociology one can perhaps use class as an example of an evolving concept of this type: from Marx over Weber to modern stratification experts.

As earlier mentioned, concepts should primarily be used as heuristic tools at the stage of theorizing, that is, to discover something new, and not to block the discovery process by forcing some interesting observation into some bland category. Insisting on exact operational definitions is usually not helpful at this stage. According to a well-known formulation, concepts should at this stage be seen as sensitizing and not as definitive (Blumer 1955).

Knowledge about the past of a concept can sometimes help and inspire the redefinition of a concept in some novel and interesting way (e.g., Somers 1995). While it is laborious to establish the history of a concept, one can minimally check its use over time in the Oxford English Dictionary. A social science dictionary that not only includes the current meaning of various concepts, but also their earlier ones, can be helpful as well.

A discussion of concepts would be incomplete without a mention of Wittgenstein's work. It was Wittgenstein who first questioned the age-old notion that a concept can be clearly and unambiguously defined, and that the items it covers are all similar in some respect. He concluded that at the most there may exist a certain resemblance between some of the items that a concept covers ("family resemblance"; Wittgenstein 1953). This critique of the classical notion of a concept is today commonplace in cognitive psychology.

Wittgenstein also warned that words and concepts in philosophy can lead you astray; and his ideas on this score can be extended to the social sciences. One solution when there exists a concept that blocks insight, Wittgenstein suggested, is simply to restate the phenomenon without using the concept. This is what Heinrich Hertz did, according to Wittgenstein, when he suggested that Newtonian physics should be recast without using "force" as the central concept (Monk 1990, p. 446).

Another example of how to proceed in this type of situation comes from World War II, when Wittgenstein worked as a volunteer at a hospital in London. Since World War I it had been known among medical doctors that soldiers and civilians who had suffered acute traumatic injuries would experience so-called "wound shock" (Monk 1990, pp. 445–47, 452–53). The doctors whom Wittgenstein worked with, however, were unable to establish clinically the symptoms associated with wound shock. Finally, and to Wittgenstein's great satisfaction, they decided to simply abolish the concept, and instead focus on studying what happens when traumatic injuries take place.

Wittgenstein suggested that the word "shock" should be printed upside down, to indicate how useless it was.

The element of generalizing plays an important role not only when concepts are formed but throughout the process of theorizing. According to Peirce, "the most important operation of the mind is that of generalization" (Peirce 1957, p. 211). He also notes that while the process of generalizing and making abstractions are closely related, they are not identical (Peirce 1957, pp. 211–212). Concepts can be more or less general, and it is crucial to know at what level they should be established. Very general concepts, for example, may be uninteresting and so may very specific concepts.

Once the central concept is in place, the next step (or rule) in theorizing is to try to build the theory out. This can be done in a variety of ways—through the help of metaphors and analogies, by constructing types and typologies, and more. Metaphors are related to concepts, and while they are important to sociology their role in theorizing has rarely been discussed. According to Ilana Silber, who has looked at the use of spatial metaphors in sociology, "little has been done to analyze the metaphorical dimension of sociological theorizing in general" (Silber 1995, p. 326). This is a pity, she notes, since a metaphor can be very useful "as a thinking tool" (Silber 1995, p. 335).

Metaphors, according to Silber, are useful as heuristic devices. The key idea is to compare what is being researched to something else; and in doing so, open up the topic to new perspectives. Well-known examples of master metaphors in social science include society as a contract (Rousseau), social life as a theater (Goffman), and the city as an ecology (Park-Burgess).

Exactly how metaphors operate is not clear; and, again, there exist a number of studies in cognitive science on this topic. Philosopher Max Black has also developed an influential theory of metaphors that is worth mentioning, the so-called interaction view of metaphors. According to Black,

> A memorable metaphor has the power to bring two separate domains into cognitive and emotional relation by using language directly appropriate to the one as a lens for seeing the other; the implications, suggestions, and supporting values entwined with the literal use of the metaphorical expression enable us to see a new subject matter in a new way. The extended meaning that results, the relations between initially disparate realms created, can neither be antecedently predicted nor subsequently paraphrased in prose. . . . Metaphorical thought is a distinctive mode of achieving insight, not to be construed as an ornamental substitute for plain thought (Black 1962, pp. 236–237; cf. pp. 28–47).

An analogy is similar to a metaphor, but less radical. According to Peirce, "*analogy* is the inference that a not very large collection of objects which agree in various respects may very likely agree also in other respects" (Peirce 1957, p. 206). Some helpful attempts to explore the use of analogies in theorizing have been made by sociologists (see, e.g., Abbott 2004, pp. 113–118; Vaughan 2004). Analogies also play an important role in legal reasoning, especially in legal systems based on custom. The key idea is that you go from one particular case to another particular case, often following the logic of syllogism (Weber [1922] 1978, pp. 407, 787; see also Levi 1949; Sunstein 1993).

The study of analogies has proceeded the furthest in cognitive science (e.g., Gentner 2003, Nercessian 2008). According to cognitive scientists, human beings use analogies in a variety of situations and especially when they need to understand something new. While reasoning by logic is traditionally seen in Western thought as the one and only way to advance to a solution, analogies represents another and many times superior way of dealing with a problem. Analogies, cognitive scientists also argue, are often used together with other non-traditional ways of reasoning, such as the use of images and simulation.

Research in cognitive science on the use of analogies, patterns, and other non-traditional ways of reasoning is of much interest to the project of theorizing in social science; and there are several reasons for this. For one thing, it is clear that analogies and similar non-logical ways of thinking play much more of a role in the context of discovery than in the context of justification.

There is also the case, according to various experiments in cognitive science, that one can train oneself in becoming better at these non-traditional ways of reasoning. So far cognitive science has mainly focused on the use of these types of reasoning in everyday life. But once the research on their use by scientists has become more common, there may be useful insights also for social science theorizing.

To create types and categories represents another way of building out a theory. Categories may be created for heuristic purposes and are essentially used to differentiate facts from each other and in this way order them. A taxonomy or a classification can be very useful, but should not be mistaken for an explanation or seen as the substitute for one. Ever since the heydays of Linnean botany, it has also been realized that a classification must not be constructed in such a way that it blocks further research. Ideally there should be a link between a classification and an explanation.

Particularly as a first attempt to order data, categories can nonetheless be very helpful. When I was a graduate student I worked as a research assistant for Everett C.

Hughes, and the task he assigned to me was to locate and categorize studies of a certain type. As I did this, I slowly began to understand that creating categories also means making a number of theoretical assumptions that I had not been aware of.

Types may be further developed than categories, but are usually less comprehensive. A type may be part of a conceptual pair (such as *Gemeinschaft/Gesellschaft*) or of a full typology (such as Weber's three types of authority). Some argue that a typology can only be justified on empirical grounds (e.g., Lazarsfeld 1962; Bailey 1973). This, however, is only true at the stage of justification. At the stage of discovery a type can be used for heuristic purposes as a way of discovering something new.

Arguments in favor of using the type as a heuristic tool go far back in sociology. They can be found in what Weber says on the ideal type, and in what Durkheim says on typology in *Rules of Sociological Method*. Indeed, Weber uses precisely the word heuristic (*heuristisch*) to describe the reason why we may want to use ideal types in the first hand (e.g., Weber [1922] 1972, p. 10; 1988, p. 190; cf. Bruun 2007, pp. 225–231).

At a general level, Weber's ideal type can be described as a special type of concept, more precisely a concept that has been specifically adapted for social science purposes. It is created through an "analytical accentuation" of certain elements in a phenomenon and can be described as a "conceptual construct" (*Gedankenbild*; Weber 1949, p. 90, p. 93). Weber also makes clear that an ideal type is not a hypothesis to be verified, but serves a different purpose. "It [the ideal type] is no 'hypothesis' but it offers guidance to the construction of hypotheses" (Weber 1949, p. 90).

An ideal type can be heuristic in several ways according to Weber. It may, for example, be helpful to start out the analysis by constructing an ideal type. The reason for this is that having an ideal type makes it easier to handle the bewildering amount of facts. In this case the ideal type "serves as a harbor before you have learned to navigate safely in the vast sea of empirical facts" (Weber 1949, p. 104).

An ideal type can also be of help in another way. You construct an ideal type and then compare it to the empirical situation. In this way you will find out that either you are on the right track or there is too much of a gap between the two—in which case you need to account for the difference (e.g., Weber [1922] 1978, p. 21).

A handy tool for theorizing, which is related to the idea of typology, is the 2 × 2. By constructing a 2 × 2 one can sometimes go from an intuition to a more precise idea (e.g., Collier et al. 2008). Stinchcombe describes the fourfold table as "a standard tool of sociological theorizing"; and it is clear that quite a few sociologists use it to develop their ideas (Stinchcombe 1968, p. 46).

Thomas Schelling, another scholar who excels in theorizing, has pointed out that if one uses a 2 × 2 for two actors, one has the rudiments of a simple game of strategy. The example he uses to show this, is two persons who are travelling on a train and want to meet up in the dining car (or who alternatively want to avoid each other when it is time to eat). There are two dining cars, one that is first-class and another that is second-class; and this means that a choice has to be made. This choice can be depicted in 2 × 2 matrices, which are similar to the ones used in game theory (see also, e.g., Rapoport et al. 1976).

Schelling's argument can be found in an article called "What Is Game Theory?" and his analysis is a far cry from the complex models that are common in today's game theory. According to Schelling however, "what may be of most interest to a social scientist is these rudiments" (Schelling 1984, p. 221). "The rudiments can help him to make his own theory, and make it in relation to the particular problems that interest him. . . . Whether the theory that he builds with [these rudiments] is then called game theory, sociology, economics, conflict theory, strategy or anything else is a jurisdictional question of minor importance" (Schelling 1984, pp. 221–222).

The line between a fully built out theory and a model is not very clear. Nonetheless, a fully built out theory includes an explanation and often takes the form of a model. If Basic Rule Number 1 in theorizing is to observe; if Number 2 is to name the phenomenon and develop a central concept; if Number 3 is to build the theory out; then Number 4 is to complete the tentative theory, including an explanation (see Fig. 2 again).

The use of abduction is important throughout the process of theorizing, including the stage at which an explanation is produced. An explanation should ideally be analytically stringent and economical; and the theorizing process is not over till an explanation has been produced. There exist many different kinds of explanation that one can play around with for heuristic reasons: teleological explanations, functional explanations, explanations based on comparisons, counterfactuals, and so on.

Words are used for many explanations and mathematics for many models. Diagrams may be used at several stages in the discovery process and also as a heuristic tool for explanation (e.g., Peirce 1933; Larkin and Simon 1987; Podolny 2003; Edling 2004). As an example of a heuristic use of a diagram, one can mention Thomas Schelling's model for residential segregation, which he developed while he was travelling on an airplane and later finished at his kitchen table (Schelling 1990, p. 191). Decision trees and network figures can be used to make ideas flow and to come up with explanations. In all of these cases, it deserves to be mentioned once more, that what is involved is a non-traditional kind of thinking, typically thinking in some form of patterns.

Can material objects be used for heuristic-explanatory purposes in social science, a bit like Linus Pauling's wooden model of a triple-strained DNA helped Cricks and Watson to discover the correct molecular structure of DNA? I do not know of any examples, even if the idea of using objects to construct an explanation in social science seems plausible enough. It was, for example, a miniature model of a car accident, used in a trial in Paris, that supposedly triggered Wittgenstein's so-called picture theory of meaning.

If one on the other hand takes a broad view of how an explanation comes into being, at the stage of discovery, one might cite many examples of how objects may be of help. One of these would be the paper files and index cards that were used by an earlier generation of social scientists for taking notes, and which today have been replaced by computer files and special programs for taking notes. Many readers of *The Sociological Imagination* will remember Mills's playful suggestion for how to discover some new connections in the material you have collected: "you simply dump out heretofore disconnected folders, mixing up their contents, and then re-sort them" (Mills 1959, p. 212).

Robert K. Merton and Niklas Luhmann both had enormous card files and their own ways of interacting with them. Both used indices and alphabetization, two indispensable means for keeping order among one's notes. Merton seems to have used his files mainly as an extended memory, while Luhmann said that his files helped him to enter into a dialogue with himself (Evans 1961, pp. 39–40; Luhmann 1981).

Also Peirce was an avid advocate of keeping records on slips of papers. His motto was that "everything worth notice is worth recording"; and he gave the advice that "records should be so made that they can readily be arranged, and particularly so that [they] can be *rearranged*" (Peirce 1992b, p. 188). Peirce was very particular about the kind of paper that should be used for note taking; he also had very firm ideas about how many of these one should write every day:

> I recommend slips of stiff smooth paper of this exact size. By ordering 20000 at a time, you get them cheap; and 20000 will last an industrious student a year. For you won't average more than 60 a day and there will be, one way or another a month of idleness in the year. Upon these slips you will note every disconnected fact that you see or read that is worth recording. . . . After thirty years of systematic study, you have every fact at your fingers' ends. Think what a treasure you will have accumulated (Peirce 1992b, p. 188).

In a similarly extended manner as files, one can perhaps say that objects are used for explanation also in experiments. Besides the idea of the concept, Weber considered the experiment to be "the second great tool of scientific work" (Weber 1946, p. 141). The type of experiments that social scientists do, are very different from the ones that are common in the natural sciences (e.g., Knorr Cetina 2002). They also exist in a bewildering amount of variation (e.g., Morton and Williams 2008). Still, objects of different kinds are often part of what produces the explanation; and this also goes for so-called thought experiments.

Explanation is one of the most difficult topics in the philosophy of science; and I limit myself here to some elementary remarks on its role at the stage of discovery. Counterfactuals can, for example, be useful as a heuristic devise to construct an explanation. Weber's description of how the strategy of counterfactuals can be used to determine the importance of the Battle of Marathon for Western culture is an early illustration of this ("objective possibility"; Weber 1949, pp. 164–188; [1922] 1978, p. 10–11).

One may argue that the very notion of explanation is closely linked to the idea of counterfactuals, since there can be no explanation without the existence of a change to some initial stage, be it actual or theoretical (e.g., Lewis 1973; Morgan and Winship 2007). One version of this approach to causality is known as the manipulationist or interventionist account of causality. The key idea is that causal relations can potentially be manipulated and controlled (Woodward 2003).

That explanations at the stage of the discovery process are to be used for heuristic purposes is of special relevance for functionalist explanations. These are currently not considered legitimate in social science, but can nonetheless be useful in generating new ideas. Weber makes precisely this point in *Economy and Society*. While emphasizing that a functionalist analysis can be "highly dangerous," he also says that it is not only helpful but "indispensable" at an early stage of the analysis (Weber [1922] 1978, p. 15).

It deserves to be repeated that the link between explanation and facts is crucial at the stage of discovery. To theorize, as illustrated by the following example, means essentially to produce an explanation of something you have observed. In an interview from some years ago Albert O. Hirschman explained what he meant by theorizing, precisely by linking the explanation to an artful observation. Like Schelling, Hirschman has developed a kind of theorizing style that is very instructive:

> It was when I looked at Colombian economic development—how certain functions are carried out or are not carried out or poorly carried out—that I

made one of my first or most basic observations. It concerned the difference in performance of the airlines and the highways. Airlines perform better than highways for the reason I explained in *The Strategy of Economic Development* (1958), that the penalty for not maintaining planes is far more serious than that for not maintaining highways. It was a very simple observation, but I think that the talent I have is not just to come up with an interesting observation, it is more a question of going to the bottom of such an observation and then generalize to much broader categories. I suppose that this is the nature of theorizing (Hirschman 1990, p. 156)

Before leaving the Hirschman example it should be noted that the capacity to generalize plays an important role in Hirschman's view of "the nature of theorizing." This also seems to have been the case with Everett C. Hughes, who encouraged his students to move up and down the ladder of generalization. According to one of his colleagues, "I do not recall a single doctoral examination in which Hughes did not close by asking the candidate: 'under what other conditions and in what other situations would you expect phenomena similar to those that you have written about to occur'" (Coser 1994, p. 13).

Models are crucial to certain types of explanations, be it at the stage of discovery or justification; and they are often formulated in mathematical language (e.g., Rapaport 1959; Schelling 1978; Simon 1991; Varian 1998). Models are more intuitive and less worked out at the stage of discovery than at the stage of justification. Still, one advantage of using a model when you theorize is that all assumptions are made explicit. Another is that models are economical; and a third that they show all the consequences of making certain assumptions—including novel and unexpected ones.

Models essentially reconstruct something *as if* it had happened in a specific way (cf. Vaihinger [1911] 2009). According to one philosopher, they are "speculative instruments" (Black 1962, p. 237). As does a wedding, they bring together "disparate subjects." They also "reveal new relationships" and, "as with other weddings, their outcomes are unpredictable" (Black 1962, p. 237).

Stephen Toulmin, another philosopher, describes the virtues of a model as follows: "it is in fact a great virtue of a good model that it does suggest further questions, taking us beyond the phenomenon from which we began, and tempts us to formulate hypotheses which turn out to be experimentally fertile . . . Certainly it is this suggestiveness, and systematic deployability, that makes a good model something more than a simple metaphor" (Black 1962, p. 239).

Recently the metaphor of social mechanisms has become popular in sociology (e.g., Hedström and Swedberg 1998). While it is hard to explain exactly what a social mechanism is, one does not have to be overly concerned with this issue at the stage of discovery. What is more important is to try to figure out new social mechanisms, that is, ways of explaining what happens in a highly transparent manner. With the help of a mechanism you practically can see how C leads to D leads to E (e.g., Elster 2007, pp. 32–51). The general goal in science of creating *clarity* is closely related to the idea of social mechanisms (e.g., Peirce 1992, pp. 124–141; Weber 1946, p. 151).

Teaching Theorizing: Exercises in Theorizing

theorizer n. one who theorizes
—*Oxford English Dictionary*[18]

The project of theorizing includes ideas about the way that theorizing can be taught. These ideas, in the version of theorizing that is presented in this article, constitute a crucial part of the project of theorizing. In teaching theory the teacher is essentially an enlightened and knowledgeable guide. The students read important works by important sociologists, and learn to critically comment on these and explicate them (e.g., Markovsky 2008). Exactly how the ideas in these works are later to be used in the students' own research is not very clear (e.g., Rueschemeyer 2009).

In theorizing, in contrast, the students learn to theorize themselves. The goal here is for each student to become a skillful and imaginative theorizer. This is to be accomplished by getting the students to learn for themselves how to observe phenomena, how to create concepts, how to build out the theory, and so on. They do so by drawing on their knowledge of sociology and by learning to locate the capacity to theorize within themselves. The role of the teacher, when it comes to theorizing, is truly Socratic, namely to help the students give birth to their own children/theories.

Theorizing is deeply democratic in that it is built on the assumption that everyone can theorize. "To think at all is to theorize," as Coleridge put it (Coleridge 1812, p. 132). To think about the way that something takes place is to theorize. To learn how to theorize efficiently is to raise this capacity to a conscious level through exercises. The way to do this is to learn how to locate the theorist within oneself. The goal is for every social scientist to be his or her own theorist (Mills 1959, p. 324).

While traditional lecturing, in combination with classroom discussion, is the way that theory is usually taught, something different is needed when theorizing is on the agenda. Learning to theorize is similar to learning methods: you do not do this by reading about them but by using them. Similarly, theorizing demands learning by doing.

There exists no agreement on how to teach students how to theorize on their own. The most natural way, perhaps, would be to let each student develop a research topic during the course of a term and, as part of this, to theorize. This is similar to the way that field work, participant observation, and qualitative methods are often taught; and this means that there exists plenty of experience to draw from.

There also exists another way of teaching theorizing, as advocated by Charles Lave and Jim March in *An Introduction to Models in the Social Sciences*. In this textbook, students are presented with problems to theorize and solve. Hints are given, interspersed with statements in bold, such as the following:

> **STOP AND THINK. Devote a moment's time to thinking of a possible process that might produce the observed result** (Lave and March [1975] 1993, p. 11).

Here is one example that Lave and March use: why are football players considered dumb in college? One possible explanation, they suggest, is that football players spend so much time on practice that they have little time to study. Another is that students who are successful in one area of life are satisfied with this and do not care to exert themselves in a second area. A third is that students are jealous of those who are successful, and therefore call them dumb. Lave and March then encourage the reader to try to figure out a way to discriminate among the various explanations.

The book by Lave and March can be described as an attempt to teach students to theorize primarily by developing their capacity to invent a number of different explanations, each of which could explain some phenomenon. In doing so their general approach is similar to that of Stinchcombe in *Constructing Social Theories*, where one can read that "a student who has difficulty thinking of at least three sensible explanations for any correlation that he is really interested in should probably choose another profession" (Stinchcombe 1968, p. 13).

I have taught a few classes in theorizing, but I have proceeded in a different way from what so far has been discussed: letting the students conduct empirical research during the course of a term, and letting them do exercises that aim at developing their capacity to invent explanations for some existing phenomenon. I have so far resisted the former approach because I think that the students need to theorize repeatedly, not just once, in order to get the hang of it.

The idea of having the students confront problems and invent explanations for these, along the lines of Lave and March, strikes me as being a bit too cognitive in nature. The fact that the problems are prepackaged or predefined, in the sense that the students have not created them themselves, may also make it hard for them to feel inspired to theorize on their own (for the type of problems that inspire scientists, see, e.g., Merton 1959; Kuhn 1970, pp. 35–42; Simon 1991).

The way I myself proceed when I try to teach theorizing is as follows. For each class the students are told to read a social science article that is full of ideas and imaginative. Here is a sample of articles I have used and that work well: "Sociology of the Senses" by Georg Simmel; "Body Techniques" by Marcel Mauss; and "Lyrical Sociology" by Andy Abbott (Simmel [1907] 1997; Mauss [1934] 1973; Abbott 2007). I have also used philosophical texts and poetry, to make the students aware of the central role that language plays in theorizing (excerpts from *Philosophical Investigations* by Wittgenstein and poems by Emily Dickinson).

The students are told that in reading these texts they should be on the outlook for something they find truly *interesting*; and that once they have finished the article, they should try to theorize, using whatever they found interesting as their point of departure. The idea is not to deepen further the thought of the author of the text or to comment on the text, but to theorize on your own with the help of something in the text.

To move along and to set free their theoretical imagination, the students are then encouraged to make free associations from whatever they found interesting in the article until they find a topic they want to work with. They should also try to assign a new name to whatever they end up with, develop new concepts, build out the theory, and finally produce a full tentative theory with an explanation. This is of course a tall order, and more of a goal to strive for than a description of what is usually accomplished. To counter this to some extent, one can let the students work twice or three times on the same topic.

Let me give an example. A student studying negotiations at IMF may, in reading Simmel on the senses, find some remark about the role of the senses in initiating or breaking off social relations that is especially interesting—and then take off on his or her own. The student may develop some ideas about, say, the role of the senses in important negotiations. Negotiators who are able to read honest signals (say, involuntary smell or the movement of certain facial muscles) might do better than those who are not. One can try to name this capacity to read signals, and explain what role it plays in negotiations and perhaps also in other activities.

Here is another example. A student doing no particular research at the time may find something else that is interesting in Simmel's text on the senses. Thinking about smell, he or she may reflect on the fact that air fresheners do not actually eliminate bad smell; they simply stop you from smelling it. This is similar to the way that quarrels often end: the issue remains unresolved, but people decide to agree for the moment. Perhaps this is also typical for behavior in other areas of society?

The two central elements in the type of exercises that I use have to do with (1) locating something *interesting*; and (2) using this to get somewhere else, with the help of *free associations*. Both of these elements need some explication. What is interesting or fascinating is what catches your attention; and this means that it is *you* who decide what is interesting (e.g., Davis 1971). The decision is intuitive, which also means that it goes quicker than you can think and draws on something else than formal reasoning.

That X is seen as interesting—that it awakens someone's interest—also means that the person will want to go further and penetrate things until his or her interest or curiosity is satisfied. According to *The Oxford English Dictionary*, "being in interesting circumstances" means to be pregnant; and the whole process of theorizing can perhaps be described in Socratic terms as going from getting pregnant to giving birth.

The idea of using free association in theorizing was, as we know, mentioned by Peirce when he spoke of observation ("associational potency"). In sociology it has been advocated primarily by Everett C. Hughes, who writes as follows in *The Sociological Eye*:

> In my work I have relied a great deal on free association, sometimes on a freedom of association that could seem outrageous to the defenders of some established interest or cherished sentiment. Wright Mills must be given credit for the phrase *the sociological imagination*. The essence of the social imagination is free association, guided but not hampered by a frame of reference internalized not quite into the unconscious. It must work even in one's dreams but be where it can be called up at will. When people say of my work, as they often do, that it shows insight, I cannot think what they could mean other than whatever quality may have been produced by intensity of observation and the turning of the wheels to find a new combination of the old concepts, or even a new concept. I think I even do my reading by free association: "Didn't Simmel, or Durkheim, Weber, Mead, Marshall, or someone say something on that point?" I do a good deal of my reading by starting with the index" (Hughes 1984, xvi).

While most people associate the expression of free association with Freud, it should be clear from the quote by Hughes that it covers considerably more than verbal associations. The same, it turns out, is perhaps also true for Freud himself. "Free association" is a term used by Freud's English translators, not only for "*freier Assoziation*" but also for "*freier Einfall*"; and these latter can be described as ideas that just pop up in one's mind (Macmillan 2001, p. 115). In brief, the category of free associations also covers a bit of what Peirce calls abduction.

What made Freud choose the technique of free association was that it allowed him to get closer to what actually upset his patients. What in contrast made me decide on using this technique in teaching theorizing was simply that it mirrored the way I sometimes thought. When I tried to explain to students how I go about theorizing from a text, I came to realize that I engaged in a way of thinking that was very close to what is called free association.

It can be added that it is also important to point out to the students that to fail in theorizing exercises is very common and an important part of learning how to do it right. One has to fail in order to become confident and conquer once fear of being stupid; and this means that one has to learn to be comfortable with failing or, to phrase it differently, learn to fail in the right way. There exist many different types of failure; and to fail in theorizing is much more useful when it is reflexive and done in private (for attempts to theorize failure, see, e.g., Gladwell 2009; Schulz 2010).

To leave the students plenty of room to fail, and to be able to do so in private, I tell them to write up their theorizing exercises, and that I will not read them. This makes things easier for the teacher—but also, and more to the point, it both softens the fall and to some extent removes the teacher from inside the mind of the student. Writing exclusively for oneself, and not for the teacher, makes the effort to theorize as natural and personal as possible. To find your own theoretical voice is closely linked to the way that you write; and one should in my view also refrain from telling the students how to write up their exercises. Creative theorizing is a personal enterprise and everybody needs to find his or her own way of doing it.

As the exercises proceed, the students will, one hopes, begin to think about what is interesting, not only from their own perspective but also from other perspectives. What is interesting from the perspective of social science and what is interesting from the viewpoint of oneself may be two different things; and it is important to try to move the two closer together.

What one finds interesting from a social science view also depends on what one knows in social science, which means that learning to theorize needs to be combined with learning theory. Whether one can teach both of these in the very same class or if it should be done in two separate classes, one may discuss. I have done both but prefer at the moment to separate the two.

It is my experience that one cannot have more than something like fifteen students in the class, when doing exercises of the type that I recommend. This way of teaching theorizing also presupposes that the students already know quite a bit of social science, which is true for graduate students but less so for undergraduates. I especially see the teaching of large undergraduate classes as a big challenge; and I have not been able to figure out how this can be done (for a suggestion that involves group exercises, see Rinehart 1999).

Something should also be said about the use of heuristics (e.g., Pólya 1945; Abbott 2004; see also Becker 1998). As already mentioned, heuristics tends to focus on teaching short-cuts and rules for solving problems and not on the general skill of theorizing, as in this article. Heuristic devises have in my view a tendency to become mechanical; and one can easily end up running through a number of tricks in the hope of stumbling on something interesting. This is usually not very helpful; and it reminds me of going through name after name, in a desperate effort to remember somebody's name. It is much easier, in my view, to theorize directly from the facts, and to use such ways of thinking as free association, using analogies, and so on.

Having said this, I have a few heuristic tricks that I myself have used many times and that I tell the students about. One of these comes from Everett C. Hughes and is as useful as it is common. In social science, Hughes said, you may want to look for *"likeness inside the shell of variety"* (Hughes 1984, p. 503; emphasis added). This means that phenomena that may seem different nonetheless are similar in some important analytical or structural respect. One can also turn Hughes's advice around, and look for "variety inside the shell of likeness."

My other heuristic tricks are the following: pluralize; transform nouns into verbs; and transform nouns into social relationships. Instead of analyzing a certain phenomenon (say capitalism), one pluralizes (and gets, say, different kinds of capitalism). One can also transform a noun into a verb in order to make it more dynamic, along the lines of Max Weber. The state, for example, becomes the coming together as a state or, more precisely, the probability of this happening. And one can transform the phenomenon from an entity into a social relationship. According to Marx, capital is not an object but a social relationship; and according to Simmel, the stranger is not a person who is different from other people but someone who is in a very special relationship to them.

Concluding Remarks

Above all seek to develop and to use the sociological imagination . . . Let every man be his own methodologist; let every man be his own theorist; let theory and method again become part of the practice of a craft. Stand for the primacy of the individual scholar.
—C. Wright Mill, *The Sociological Imagination* (1959), 224

Work on philosophy—like work in architecture in many respects—is really more work on oneself. On one's own conception. On how one sees things. (And what one expects of them).
—Wittgenstein, *Culture and Value*, 24e

The main message of this article is that given the current lopsided development in sociology and the other social sciences, with methods being highly developed and theory highly underdeveloped, we may want to focus our energy on theorizing rather than on theory. The way to do this, I also suggest, is to turn to the context of discovery—and then proceed to the context of justification. What needs to be devised, to be more precise, are ways for how to navigate in the context of discovery, not rush to the testing of hypotheses. Theorizing is a form of practical knowledge and not to be equated with social science studies of discoveries and creativity. It is a kind of knowledge that is aimed at helping the individual to act competently and creatively in theory; studies of creativity, on the other hand, tend to explain why some individuals and social structures tend to be more creative than others.

To work exclusively with theories, rather than to think in terms of theorizing, often translates into an awkward struggle of trying to get theory and facts together. When you theorize, in contrast, these two come together in a natural way. You begin with the facts, and an organic link between theory and facts is established from the very beginning.

If carried through with consistency, the enterprise of theorizing might help to usher in a new period of interesting and creative theory in social science. One reason for hoping this is that there is no reason to believe that only a small number of gifted scholars can produce theory. Everyone who can think, can ultimately also theorize; and the project of theorizing is therefore inherently democratic (Kant [1784] 1970). The goal of developing the project of theorizing would be to create a culture of theorizing in the social sciences.

In exploring theorizing, I also argue, social scientists can learn much from Peirce whose ideas on this topic are very helpful and suggestive. Theorizing also necessitates a personal exploration or a personalist exploration, to invent a word that is too ugly to kidnap, as Peirce happily noted about his term "pragmaticism."[19] To theorize well you need to open yourself up, to observe yourself, and to listen carefully to yourself. One's imagination, intuition, and capacity for abduction all need to be observed, reflected upon, and developed by each individual, in his or her own unique and personal way.

We may also want to consult some other scholars than those we rely on when theory is discussed. Besides Peirce, I especially recommend Bachelard, Kierkegaard, Heidegger, and Wittgenstein as very suggestive and helpful when it comes to theorizing. All of these have also proposed ideas that so far have not been incorporated into mainstream social science. In sociology and social science, I have found Everett C. Hughes, Jim March, C. Wright Mills, and Karl Weick to be very instructive when it comes to theorizing. There also exist a number of social scientists who have developed a theorizing style, as exemplified by Thomas Schelling and Albert O. Hirschman.

To this can be added that it is possible to do research from a theorizing perspective on the major social scientists and see what can be learned from approaching them from this angle. This would constitute a kind of reverse engineering, applied to theory. How did the classics come up with the ideas in *The Prince, The General Theory of Employment, Interest and Money*, and so on?

To make the project of theorizing into a coherent whole, much more is needed than what can be found in this article. Imagination, intuition, and improvisation are three important topics that all deserve a long and thorough discussion. One would also want to get a better understanding of how one goes from the context of discovery (the prestudy) to the context of justification (the major study). The notion that one can just introduce the former and then hook it up to the latter, hoping that the two will neatly fit together, may well be illusory. Changes in the one presumably entail changes in the other; and so far all attention has been directed towards the main study, something that has led to distortions. There may also exist a gray zone between the the prestudy and the major study that needs to be better understood.

One should also be aware that before a theory has been properly tested, the data gathered at the stage of observation in the prestudy may lead one wrong. While it is possible to speak positively of "theoretical sampling" and "the testing of ideas" at the stage of discovery, it is also clear that there exists a good chance of making errors at this stage (e.g., Glaser and Strauss 1967; Coslor 2011). Some of these errors have been discussed by behavioral scientists, such as anchoring error, availability error, and attribution error (e.g., Tversky and Kahneman 1982;

Groopman 2007; see also Peirce 1992b, pp. 193–196). There may be other errors as well, which are specific to the process of theorizing.

Throughout this article, I often refer to social science, while most of my examples come from sociology. This reflects the fact that I am a sociologist, but it is clear that good theorizing is something that all of the social sciences are in need of. Economics, political science, psychology, anthropology, and history also have their own ways of theorizing. This means that all of them could benefit from a dialogue across disciplinary boundaries on how to theorize—how to construct concepts, use analogies, build models, and so on. Social scientists would also do well to follow what philosophers have said on these topics; it is their ideas that still form the foundation for most of what is happening in this area.

Another topic that needs to be discussed has to do with the way that theorizing is presented. So far in social science, theory is typically presented in a way that hides the way in which it has come into being. But the value of proceeding in this way may well be limited in the long run, since we not only want a good analysis but also to learn how to make a good analysis. The good theorizer wants a verdict of the type that John Stuart Mill gave to Tocqueville's *Democracy in America*: "the value of his work is less in the conclusions, than in the mode of arriving at them" (Mill 1977, p. 168).

What we come back to, time and time again, is that theorizing means something different from theory, both in terms of content and style. Theorizing is never finished once and for all. It is truly impermanent, imperfect, and incomplete. It is also part of what Peirce calls fallibilism or "the doctrine that our knowledge is never absolute but always swims, as it were, in a continuum of uncertainty and indeterminism" (Peirce 1931, p. 171).

Does it not make sense that the notion of fallibilism should also come through in the presentation of a work that draws in a conscious way on theorizing? Currently social scientists have only two options when they want to publish and present their work: the standard article and the standard monograph. Both of these forms are difficult to work with since they are surrounded by fairly rigid norms for how to write and how to present the data and the argument.

New alternatives are needed; and some suggestions for what these may look like already exist. One can, for example, choose to use an emotionally rich style (Abbott). One can experiment with inserts of various types in the text (e.g., Bourdieu in *Actes de la recherche*). One can also use a more fragmented way of writing (e.g., Wittgenstein) or in some other way try to express the playfulness and free associations that the mind goes through when you theorize (e.g., Simmel, Bachelard).

When theorizers read a piece of theorizing, they do not only want to learn; they also want to participate in the work. In the arts there is today a tendency that those who perform a piece of music, read a poem, and the like, can do so in a way that allows for them to express their own creativity. This is known as an "open work," and it stands for an approach that might also suit those in social science who are interested in theorizing (Eco 1989).

And last, the project of theorizing can truly flourish only if theorizing becomes a communal and co-operative enterprise among all kinds of social scientists, linked to each other as well as to people around the world. Peirce liked to point out that scientific inquiry is profoundly communal in nature, and that new ways of theorizing and analyzing will only succeed if they are deeply rooted in a universal community of scholars. Inquiry and community, he said, must come together in a true community of inquiry—or into *a general culture of theorizing*, as one could also put it.

Notes

1. The quote comes from one of Peirce's unpublished manuscripts at the Houghton Library, Harvard University (MS 692; Brent 1993, p. 72).

2. For encouragement, help, and suggestions I first of all would like to thank Mabel Berezin. I am also grateful to two anonymous reviewers for *Theory and Society* and to Margareta Bertilsson, Angie Boyce, Mikael Carleheden, Nicolas Eilbaum, Laura Ford, Omar Lizardo, Darcy Pan, Roland Paulsen, Jennifer Platt, Eric Schwartz, and Hans Zetterberg. I have learned a lot from the students who have participated in my classes in theorizing at Cornell University, Copenhagen University, and Stockholm University. The key ideas in my approach to theorizing were first presented in 2009 and 2010 in *Perspectives*, the newsletter of the Theory Section at the American Sociological Association (Swedberg 2009a, 2010). For a fuller version of how I view theorizing, see my forthcoming book *Discovery: Learning the Art of Theorizing in the Social Sciences* (Princeton University Press).

3. As a sign of how little attention has been paid to theorizing, compared to theory, it can be mentioned that while references to "theory" were made 120,502 times in sociological journals from the 1890 s to 2010, according to JSTOR, the equivalent number for "theorizing" and "theorize" is 16,087 (based on a search in JSTOR in April 2011). But even if there does not exist a distinct body of literature on theorizing, there do exist some writings that are very suggestive and helpful in this context. Among these I especially recommend the works by the following authors (all of whom are referred to in this article): Karl Weick, C. Wright Mills, Everett C. Hughes, Jim March, Andrew Abbott, and Howard Becker. There also exist a small number of very suggestive social scientists who write in what can

be called a theorizing style, such as Thomas Schelling and Albert O. Hirschman. Philosopher Herbert Dreyfus has also much interesting to say on the topic of theorizing.

4. It should be mentioned at this point that there is an important difference between producing social science studies of theoretical creativity and developing rules for how an individual can theorize in a creative way. This difference is not clear from the statements of Reichenbach and Popper but is crucial to their argument.

5. The quote comes from Weber 1946, p. 136.

6. For an example of Zetterberg's imaginative take on social science, see his recent muti-volume work *The Many-Splendored Society* (2009).

7. The classical foothold of theory-driven research in the social sciences can be found in mainstream economics. During the last few years, however, an empirical type of economics has begun to emerge. As an example of this, see, e.g., the following comment by Paul Krugman: "The profession has shifted towards nitty-gritty empirical investigation using lots of data. Unless you have a brand-new insight, the best you can do is to find evidence that hasn't been exploited. Maybe that will suggest new theoretical insights, *but the starting point is the data*" (Busso 2010, p. 132; emphasis added).

8. A pilot study can be described as a small-scale try-out, executed before the main study. Its general task is to ensure that the research design is sound and to make changes in it before it is too late. It is also common that questions in a questionnaire are tried out in advance, again so they can be changed before the main study is carried out. This means that what primarily distinguishes a prestudy from a pilot study is that while a prestudy is focused on the context of discovery, a pilot study is not. Theorizing has no more of a place in a research design that includes a pilot study than it does in one that does not. The literature on pilot studies is meager, perhaps because they tend not to be reported (e.g., van Teijlingen and Hundley 2001). I am grateful to Jennifer Platt for her thoughts on the topic of pilot studies.

9. Is not old-fashioned "theory" smuggled in through the back door, so to speak, by referring in this manner to certain core ideas in social science? My answer is "no"; there is still a need for theorizing to complement theory. While acknowledging that more discussion deserves to be devoted to this question than is done in this article, I suggest that theorizing can either involve the core ideas of social science or one can accept these ideas as valid when engaging in research. Since the latter case is clearly the most common, this article is devoted to it. When theorizing in contrast is directed at the core ideas in social science, it is mainly done without reference to empirical facts, a bit like theorizing is traditionally done in philosophy. For a discussion of some of the theoretical presuppositions of social science, see, e.g., *Sociology as a Craft: Epistemological Preliminaries* by Bourdieu et al. (1991).

10. Kierkegaard writes, for example, in *Concluding Unscientific Postscript*: "It is impossible to exist without passion, unless

existing means just any sort of so-called existence. For this reason every Greek thinker was essentially a passionate thinker. I have often wondered how one might bring a man to passion. So I have thought I might seat him on a horse and frighten the horse into a wild gallop, or still better, in order to bring out the passion properly, I might take a man who wants to go somewhere as quickly as possible (and so was already in a sort of passion) and seat him on a horse that can barely walk" (Kierkegaard [1846] 1941, p. 276).

11. The quote comes from Doyle [1891] 2001, p. 14.

12. Heidegger describes theorizing in the following way: "Thus it follows that *theōrein* is *thean horan*, to look attentively on the outward appearance wherein what presences becomes visible and, through such sight—seeing—to linger with it" (Heidegger 1977, p. 163). According to Lawrence Scaff, the Greek word *theōrein* is "a compound of *thea*, the view or look of something; *horan*, to see a thing attentively; and the name *theoros*, the attentive observer or the emissary sent to observe foreign practices and to 'theorize' about them—that is, to construct rational explanations of the strange and unexpected" (Scaff 2011, p. 11). The theorizer, in short, goes away to study and observe, and then thinks about it and explains it. For an attempt at a sociology of knowledge explanation of the Greek version of theorizing, see Sandywell (2000).

13. In a well-known letter to Lady Welby from December 23, 1908, Peirce wrote, "I define a Sign as anything which is so determined by anything else, called its Object, and so determines an effect upon a person, which effect I call its Interpretant, that the latter is thereby mediately determined by the former" (Peirce 1963, p. 29).

14. The quote comes from Karl Weick 1989, p. 516. See also Weick's article "What Theory is *Not*, Theorizing *Is*" (Weick 1995).

15. While the purpose of having concepts, typologies, explanations, and so on in the context of discovery or prestudy is essentially heuristic, in the context of justification or the main study they often need to be justified on empirical grounds.

16. Montesquieu writes in *The Spirit of the Laws*, "I have had new ideas; new words have had to be found or new meanings given to old ones" (Montesquieu [1748] 1989, p. xi).

17. See note 3. While JSTOR allows you to track whether a certain word appears in the title, the abstract, or the text of an article, it only covers certain journals and not books at all. I have been unable to find a full book on theorizing in sociology or any other social science. What literature there does exist typically focuses on a special and very cognitive version of theorizing, either bypassing the initial phase of empirical fact gathering or being primarily interested in constructing hypotheses and how these can be falsified.

18. *Oxford English Dictionary* Second edition, 1989; online version November 2010. http://www.oed.com:80/Entry/200430; accessed on February 13, 2011.

19. Peirce 1998, p. 335. The term "personalism" was popularized by Emanuel Mounier during the interwar period in France and became part of the Catholic Worker movement. For the manifesto of the personalist movement, in which the dignity and responsibility of the individual person is at the center, see, e.g., Mounier's *Be Not Afraid: Studies in Personalist Sociology* (Mounier 1954).

References

Abbott, A. (2004). *Methods of discovery: Heuristics for the social sciences.* New York: W.W. Norton.

Abbott, A. (2007). Against narrative: a preface to lyrical sociology. *Sociological Theory, 25*(1), 67–99.

Bachelard, G. (1934 [1984]). *The new scientific spirit.* Boston: Beacon Press.

Bailey, K. (1973). Constructing monothetic and polythetic typologies by the heuristic method. *Sociological Inquiry, 14,* 291–308.

Becker, H. (1998). *Tricks of the trade: How to think about your research while doing it.* Chicago: University of Chicago Press.

Bertilsson, T. M. (2009). *Peirce's theory of inquiry and beyond.* Frankfurt am Main: Peter Lang.

Black, M. (1962). *Models and metaphors: Studies in language and philosophy.* Ithaca: Cornell University Press.

Blalock, H. (1969). *Theory construction: From verbal to mathematical formulations.* Englewood: Prentice-Hall.

Blumer, H. (1955). What's wrong with social theory? *American Sociological Review, 19,* 3–10.

Bourdieu, P., Chamboredon, J.-C., & Passeron, J.-C. (1991). *Sociology as a craft: Epistemological preliminaries.* New York: Walter de Gruyter.

Brent, J. (1993). *Charles Sanders Peirce: A life.* Bloomington: Bloomington University Press.

Bruun, H. H. (2007). *Science, values and politics in Max Weber's Methodology.* New expanded ed. Aldershot, England: Ashgate.

Busso, M. (2010). Not so dismal [Interview with Paul Krugman]. *Bloomberg Markets,* October 2010, 132.

Coleridge, S. T. (1812). *The friend: A series of essays.* London: Gale and Curtis.

Collier, D., Laporte, J., & Seawright, J. (2008). Typologies: Forming concepts and creating categorical variables. In J. Box-Stefensmeier, H. Brady, & D. Collier (Eds.), *The Oxford handbook of political methodology* (pp. 152–173). New York: Oxford University Press.

Collins, H. (2010). *Tacit and explicit knowledge.* Chicago: University of Chicago Press.

Coser, L. (1994). Introduction. In E. C. Hughes (Ed.), *On work, race, and the sociological imagination* (pp. 1–17). Chicago: University of Chicago Press.

Coslor, E. (2011). *Wall Streeting art: The construction of artwork as an alternative investment and the strange rules of the art market.* Unpublished doctoral dissertation. Department of Sociology. Chicago: University of Chicago.

Daston, L., & Lunbeck, E. (Eds.). (2011). *Histories of scientific observation.* Chicago: University of Chicago Press.

Doyle, Sir A. C. ([1891] 2001). *The Adventures of Sherlock Holmes.* London: The Electronic Book Company.

Davis, M. (1971). That's interesting! Towards a phenomenology of sociology and a sociology of phenomenology. *Philosophy of the Social Sciences, 1,* 309–344.

Dreyfus, H., & Dreyfus, S. (1986). *Mind over machine: The power of human intuition and expertise in the era of the computer.* New York: The Free Press.

Durkheim, E. ([1895] 1964). *The rules of sociological method.* Trans. S. Solvay, J. Mueller. New York: The Free Press.

Durkheim, E. ([1895] 1982). *The rules of sociological method.* Trans. W.D. Halls. New York: The Free Press.

Eco, U. (1989). *The open work.* Cambridge: Harvard University Press.

Edling, C. (2004). Visualisering i samhällsvetenskapen. In P. Aspers, P. Fuehrer, & Á. Sverrisson (Eds.), *Bild och samhälle* (pp. 165–193). Lund: Studentlitteratur.

Elster, J. (2007). *Explaining social behavior: More nuts and bolts for the social sciences.* Cambridge: Cambridge University Press.

Evans, M. (1961). A biographical profile of Robert K. Merton. *The New Yorker, 28,* 39–63.

Fleck, L. ([1935] 1979). *Genesis and development of a scientific fact.* Chicago: University of Chicago Press.

Freese, L. (Ed.). (1980). *Theoretical methods in sociology: Seven essays.* Pittsburgh: University of Pittsburgh Press.

Genmer, D. (2003). Analogical Reasoning, Psychology of. In Vol. 1 of *Encyclopedia of Cognitive Science* (pp. 106–112). London: Nature Publishing Company.

Gladwell, M. (2008). *Outliers: The story of success.* New York: Little, Brown and Company.

Gladwell, M. (2009). The art of failure: Why some people choke and others panic. In *What the Dog Saw and Other Adventures* (pp. 263–179). New York: Little, Brown and Company.

Glaser, B., & Strauss, A. (1967). *The discovery of grounded theory.* Chicago: Aldine Press.

Goudge, T. (1969). *The thought of C.S. Peirce.* New York: Dover Publications.

Groopman, J. (2007). *How doctors think.* Boston: Houghton Mifflin.

Hage, J. (Ed.). (1994). *Formal theory in sociology: Opportunity or pitfall?* Albany: State University of New York Press.

Hedström, P. (2007). Sociology that Really Matters . . . to Me. *Sociologica,* July 9. Downloaded from the web on January 25 from http://www.sociologica.mulino.it/news/newsitem/index/Item/News:NEWS_ITEM:54.

Hedström, P., & Swedberg, R. (Eds.). (1998). *Social mechanisms: An analytical approach to social theory.* Cambridge: Cambridge University Press.

Heidegger, M. (2011). *Introduction to philosophy—Thinking and poetizing.* Bloomington: Indiana University Press.

Heidegger, M. (1977). Science and reflection. In *The question concerning technology and other essays* (pp. 154–182). New York: Harper

Hempel, C. G. (1965). *Aspects of scientific explanation and other essays in the philosophy of science.* New York: Free Press.

Hirschman, A. O. (1990). Interview. In R. Swedberg (Ed.), *Economics and sociology* (pp. 146–158). Princeton: Princeton University Press.

Hoyningen-Huene, P. (1987). Context of discovery and context of justification. *Studies in History and Philosophy of Science, 18*(4), 501–515.

Hughes, E. C. (1984). *The sociological eye: Selected papers.* New Brunswick: Transaction Press.

Hughes, E. C., & H. Hughes. (1952). What's in a name? In *Where Peoples Meet* (pp. 130–144). Glencoe, IL: The Free Press.

Huizinga, J. (1950). *Homo Ludens: A study of the play element in culture* (p. 1950). New York: Roy.

Kant, I. ([1784] 1970). An Answer to the Question: 'What is Enlightenment?'. In H. Reiss (ed.), *Kant's Political Writings* (pp. 54–60). New York: Cambridge University Press.

Kierkegaard, S. ([1846] 1941). *Concluding unscientific postscript.* Princeton: Princeton University Press.

Knorr Cetina, K. (2002). The couch, the cathedral, and the laboratory: On the relationship between experiment and laboratory in science. In A. Pickering (Ed.), *Science as practice and culture* (pp. 113–138). Chicago: University of Chicago Press.

Kripke, S. (1980). *Naming and necessity.* Cambridge: Harvard University Press.

Kuhn, T. (1970). *The structure of scientific revolutions.* 2nd enlarged ed. Chicago: University of Chicago Press.

Larkin, J., & Simon, H. (1987). Why a diagram is (Sometimes) worth 10,000 words. *Cognitive Science, 11,* 65–99.

Law, J. (2004). *After method: Mess in social science research.* London: Routledge.

Lazarsfeld, P. (1962). The Sociology of Empirical Research. *American Sociological Review, 27,* 757–767.

Lave, C., J. March. ([1975] 1993). *An introduction to models in the social sciences.* New York: University Press of America.

Levi, E. (1949). *An introduction to legal reasoning.* Chicago: University of Chicago Press.

Lewis, D. (1973). *Counterfactuals.* Cambridge: Harvard University Press.

Luhmann, N. (1981). Kommunikation mit Zettelkästen. Ein Erfahrungsbericht. In H. Baier (Ed.), Öffentliche Meinung und sozialer Wandel. Für Elisabeth Noelle-Neumann (pp. 222–228). Opladen: Westdeutscher Verlag.

Luker, K. (2008). *Salsa dancing in the social sciences: Research in an age of info-glut.* Cambridge: Harvard University Press.

Macmillan, M. (2001). Limitations to free association and interpretation. *Psychological Inquiry, 12*(3), 113–128.

March, J. (1970). Making artists out of pedants. In R. Stogdill (Ed.), *The process of model-building in the behavioral sciences* (pp. 54–75). New York: Norton.

Markovsky, B. (2008). Graduate training in sociological theory and theory construction. *Sociological Perspectives, 51*(2), 423–445.

Mauss, M. ([1934] 1973). Techniques of the body. *Economy and Society, 2*(1), 70–88.

Merton, R. K., & Barber, E. (2004). *The travels and adventures of serendipity.* Princeton: Princeton University Press.

Merton, R. K. (1948). The bearing of empirical research upon the development of social theory. *American Sociological Review, 13*, 505–515.

Merton, R. K. (1959). Introduction: Notes on problem-finding in sociology. In R. K. Merton, L. Broom, & L. Cottrell (Eds.), *Sociology today* (pp. ix–xxxiv). New York: Basic Books.

Merton, R. K. (1967). *On theoretical sociology.* New York: The Free Press.

Merton, R. K. (1984). Socio-economic duration: A case study of concept formation in sociology. In W. Powell & R. Robbins (Eds.), *Conflict and consensus: A Festschrift in honor of Lewis A. Coser* (pp. 262–285). New York: The Free Press.

Mills, C. W. (1959). *The sociological imagination.* New York: Oxford University Press.

Mill, J. S. (1977). *Essays on politics and society, vol. 1 of collected works of John Stuart Mill.* London: Routledge and Kegan Paul.

Monk, R. (1990). *Ludwig Wittgenstein: The duty of genius.* New York: The Free Press.

Montesquieu, Charles de Secondat, Baron de. ([1748] 1989). *The Spirit of the Laws.* Cambridge: Cambridge University Press.

Morgan, S., & Winship, C. (2007). *Counterfactuals and causal inference: Methods and principles for social research.* Cambridge: Cambridge University Press.

Morton, R., & Williams, K. (2008). Experimentation in political science. In J. Box-Stefensmeier, H. Brady, & D. Collier (Eds.), *The Oxford handbook of political methodology* (pp. 339–356). New York: Oxford University Press.

Mounier, E. (1954). *Be not afraid: Studies in personalist sociology.* New York: Harper.

Nersessian, N. (2008). *Creating scientific concepts.* Cambridge: The MIT Press.

Peirce, C. (1931). *Collected papers of Charles Sanders Peirce, vol. 1.* Cambridge: Harvard University Press.

Peirce, C. (1933). *Collected papers of Charles Sanders Peirce, vol. 4.* Cambridge: Harvard University Press.

Peirce, C. (1934). How to theorize. In *Collected papers of Charles Sanders Peirce, vol. 5* (pp. 413–422). Cambridge: Harvard University Press.

Peirce, C. (1935). *Collected papers of Charles Sanders Peirce, vol. 6.* Cambridge: Harvard University Press.

Peirce, C. (1955). *Philosophical writings of Peirce.* New York: Dover Publications.

Peirce, C. (1957). *Essays in the philosophy of science.* New York: Bobbs-Merrill.

Peirce, C. (1963). *Letters to Lady Welby.* New Haven: Whitlock's, Inc.

Peirce, C. (1991). In J. Hoppes (Ed.), *Peirce on signs.* Bloomington: Indiana University Press.

Peirce, C. (1992a, 1998). *The essential Peirce, 2 vols.* Bloomington: Indiana University Press.

Peirce, C. (1992b). Training in reasoning. In *Reasoning and the logic of things* (pp. 181–196). Cambridge: Harvard University Press.

Podolny, J. (2003). A picture is worth a thousand symbols: a sociologist's view of the economic pursuit of truth. *American Economic Review, 93*(2), 169–174.

Polanyi, M. (1966). *The tacit dimension.* Chicago: University of Chicago Press.

Pólya, G. (1945). *How to solve it: A new aspect of mathematical method.* Princeton: Princeton University Press.

Popper, K. (1935). *Logik der Forschung.* Vienna: Julius Springer.

Popper, K. (1959). *The logic of scientific discovery.* London: Hutchinson & Co.

Popper, K. (1982). *Unended quest: An intellectual autobiography.* La Salle: Open Court.

Radkau, J. (2009). *Max Weber: A biography.* Cambridge: Polity Press.

Rapaport, A. (1959). Uses and limitations of mathematical models in social science. In L. Gross (Ed.), *Symposium on sociological theory* (pp. 348–72). Evanston: Row, Peterson and Company.

Rapoport, A., Guyer, M., & Gordon, D. (1976). *The 2 × 2 game.* Ann Arbor: University of Michigan Press.

Reichenbach, H. (1938). *Experience and prediction: An analysis of the foundations and the structure of knowledge.* Chicago: University of Chicago Press.

Reichenbach, H. (1951). *The rise of scientific philosophy.* Berkeley: University of California Press.

Rinehart, J. (1999). Turning theory into theorizing: collaborative learning in a sociological theory course. *Teaching Sociology, 27*, 216–232.

Rueschemeyer, D. (2009). *Usable theory: Analytical tools for social and political research.* Princeton: Princeton University Press.

Sandywell, B. (2000). The agonistic ethic and the spirit of inquiry: On the Greek origin of theorizing. In M. Kusch (Ed.), *The sociology of philosophical knowledge* (pp. 93–124). Dordrecht: Kluwer.

Scaff, L. (2011). *Max Weber in America.* Princeton: Princeton University Press.

Schelling, T. (1978). Thermostats, lemons, and other families of models. In *Micromotives and Macrobehavior* (pp. 81–134). New York: W.W. Norton & Company.

Schelling, T. (1984). "What is game theory?" In *Choice and Consequence* (pp. 213–142). Cambridge: Harvard University Press.

Schelling, T. (1990). Interview. In R. Swedberg (Ed.), *Economics and sociology* (pp. 186–99). Princeton: Princeton University Press.

Schickore, J., & Steinle, F. (Eds.). (2006). *Revisiting discovery and justification: Historical and philosophical perspectives on the context distinction.* Dordrecht: Springer.

Schiller, F. ([1794] 2004). *On the esthetic education of man.* New York: Dover Publications.

Schulz, K. (2010). *Being wrong: Adventures in the margin of error.* New York: HarperCollins.

Sebeok, T., & Umiker-Sebeok, J. (1981). 'You know my method': A juxtaposition of Charles S. Peirce and Sherlock Holmes. In U. Eco & T. Sebeok (Eds.), *The sign of* three: *Dupin, Holmes, Peirce* (pp. 11–51). Bloomington: Indiana University Press.

Silber, I. (1995). Space, fields, boundaries: the rise of spatial metaphors in contemporary sociological theory. *Social Research, 62*(2), 323–356.

Simmel, G. ([1907] 1997). Sociology of the Senses. In D. Frisby, & M. Featherstone (eds.), *Simmel on culture* (pp. 109–119). London: Sage, 1997.

Simon, H. (1991). The scientist as problem solver. In *Models of My Life* (pp. 368–387). New York: Basic Books.

Small, A. (1896). Review of Arthur Fairbanks, An introduction to sociology. *American Journal of Sociology, 2*(2), 305–310.

Somers, M. (1995). What's political or cultural about political culture and the public sphere? Toward an historical sociology of concept formation. *Sociological Theory, 13*(2), 113–144.

Stinchcombe, A. (1968). *Constructing social theories.* Chicago: University of Chicago Press.

Stinchcombe, A. (1978). *Theoretical methods in social history.* New York: Academic.

Sudnow, D. (2001). *Ways of the hand: A rewritten account.* Cambridge: The MIT Press.

Sunstein, C. (1993). On analogical reasoning. *Harvard Law Review, 106,* 741–791.

Swedberg, R. (2009a). The craft of theorizing. *Perspectives: Newsletter of the ASA Theory Section, 31*(2), 1, 7. On the website of the theory section.

Swedberg, R. (2009b). *Tocqueville's political economy.* Princeton: Princeton University Press.

Swedberg, R. (2010). From theory to theorizing. *Perspectives: Newsletter of the ASA Theory Section, 32*(2), 1, 8–9. On the website of the theory section.

Swedberg, R. (2011). Charles Peirce and the sociology of thinking. In C. Edling & J. Rydgren (Eds.), *Sociological insights of great thinkers* (pp. 299–306). New York: Praeger.

Tocqueville, A. de. ([1835–1840] 2004). *Democracy in America.* New York: The Library of America.

Tocqueville, A. (2003). *Lettres choisies, souvenirs, 1814–1859.* In F. Mélonio & L. Guellec (eds.). Paris: Gallimard.

Tversky, A., & Kahneman, D. (1982). *Judgment under uncertainty: Heuristics and biases.* Cambridge: Cambridge University Press.

van Teijlingen, E. & V. Hundley. (2001). The importance of pilot studies. *Social Research Update* (University of Surrey), issue 35. Downloaded on July 31, 2011 from http://sru.soc.surrey.ac.uk/SRU35.html.

Vaihinger, H. ([1911] 2009). *The philosophy 'As If.'* Mansfield Centre: Martino Publishing.

Varian, H. (1998). How to build an economic model in your spare time. In M. Szenberg (Ed.), *Passion and craft: Economists at work* (pp. 256–271). Ann Arbor: University of Michigan Press.

Vaughan, D. (2004). Theorizing disaster: Analogy, historical ethnography, and the challenger accident. *Ethnography, S,* 315–347.

Weber, M. ([1922] 1972). *Wirtschaft und Gesellschaft. Grundriss der verstehenden Soziologie.* 5th ed. Tübingen: J.C.B. Mohr.

Weber, M. ([1922] 1978). *Economy and society, 2 vols.* Berkeley: University of California Press.

Weber, M. (1946). In H. Gerth & C. Wright Mills (Eds.), *From Max Weber.* New York: Oxford University Press.

Weber, M. (1949). *Essays in the methodology of the social sciences.* New York: The Free Press.

Weber, M. (1976). *The protestant ethic and the spirit of capitalism.* Trans. Talcott Parsons. London: George Allen & Unwin.

Weber, M. (1988). *Gesammelte Aufsätze zur Wissenschaftslehre.* Tubingen: J.C.B. Mohr.

Weber, M. (2001). In D. Chalcraft & A. Harrington (Eds.), *The protestant ethic debate: Max Weber's replies to his critics, 1907–1910.* Liverpool: Liverpool University Press.

Weick, K. (1989). Theory construction as disciplined imagination. *Academy of Management Review, 14* (4), 516–531.

Weick, K. (1995). What theory is *not,* theorizing *is. Administrative Science Quarterly, 40*(3), 385–390.

Willer, D. (1967). *Scientific sociology: Theory and method.* Englewood Cliffs: Prentice-Hall.

Willer, D. (1996). The prominence of formal theory in sociology. *Sociological Forum, 11*(2), 319–331.

Wittgenstein, L. (1953). *Philosophical investigations.* New York: Macmillan.

Woodward, J. (2003). *Making things happen: A theory of causal explanation.* New York: Oxford University Press.

Zetterberg, H. (1954). *On theory and verification in sociology.* New York: The Tressler Press.

Zetterberg, H. (1963). *On theory and verification in sociology* (2nd ed.). New York: Bedminster Press.

Zetterberg, H. (1965). *On theory and verification in sociology.* 3rd enlarged ed. New York: Bedminster Press.

Zetterberg, H. (2009). *The many-splendored society.* 4 planned vols. Scotts Valley, CA: CreateSpace.

Zhao, S. (1996). The beginning of the end or the end of the beginning? The theory construction movement revisited. *Sociological Forum, 11*(2), 305–318.

Richard Swedberg is Professor of Sociology at Cornell University since 2002. His two specialties are economic sociology and social theory. He is the author of, among other things, *Max Weber and the Idea of Economic Sociology* (1998) and *Tocqueville's Political Economy* (2009). He is currently working on the financial crisis and on a book on theorizing, *Discovery: Learning the Art of Theorizing in the Social Sciences.*

Sport, Modernity, and the Body

Niko Besnier[1] and Susan Brownell[2]

Keywords

performance, colonialism, mobility, globalization, gender

Abstract

Over the past three decades, the important role that anthropological theory has bestowed on the body, modernity, nationalism, the state, citizenship, transnationalism,
globalization, gender, and sexuality has placed sports at
the center of questions central to the discipline. New
approaches to the body, based on practice theory, view
the sporting body as more than just a biological entity,
allowing us to observe sports as they "travel" transnationally and illuminating issues relevant to such dynamics as
colonialism, globalization, sport mega-events, and labor
migration. A distinctly anthropological approach, with
its unique research methods, approaches to theory, and
holistic thinking, can utilize insights from the constitution of sport as human action to illuminate important
social issues in a way that no other discipline can. On this
foundation, the anthropology of sport is now poised to
make significant contributions to our understanding of
central problems in anthropology.

Introduction

Sport is a human activity in which the body is the object
of most intense scrutiny: trained, disciplined, modified,
displayed, evaluated, and commodified, the sporting
body is the focus of not only the person who inhabits
it but also spectators, trainers, and "owners." Before the
postmodern turn in the 1980s, treatments of sport in
British and American anthropology centered on the
body as a primarily biological entity. Concurrently, an interest in "traditional" sports and games, primarily based
in folklore and in continental Europe, remained wedded
to a unilinear modernization paradigm. Both approaches
had limitations. The postmodern turn foregrounded the
body as a cultural construction, overcoming the limitations of the biological paradigm. It generated a more
complex understanding of representation, turning away
from essentializing sports and games as the embodiment
of a national or ethnic character and replacing modernization paradigms with more complex theories of social
development. Although sports are boundary crossers in
ways that few realms of social life are, exploring this quality became possible only when sports were unleashed
from essentialized concepts of national character anchored in biologized bodies.

By "rescuing sport from the nation" (to paraphrase
Duara 1995), new approaches located sports in transnationalism and observed them as they "traveled" across
boundaries, drawing attention to colonialism, globalization, sport mega-events, labor migration, and so on. Furthermore, over the past three decades, the important role
that anthropological theory has bestowed on the body, nationalism, modernity, globalization, transnationalism, the
state, citizenship, gender, and sexuality has placed sports at
the core of questions central to the discipline. A distinctly
anthropological approach, with its unique research methods, approaches to theory, and holistic thinking, can utilize
insights from the constitution of sport as human action to
illuminate important social issues in a way that no other
discipline can. On this foundation, the anthropology of
sport is now poised to make significant contributions to
our understanding of our increasingly global society.

This article, which highlights ethnographically informed works, focuses on the conceptual gains that have
accumulated since the late 1980s and aims to provide
a research agenda that will further centralize the anthropology of sport. Prior research overviews and attempts
to define the field have surveyed what an anthropological

[1] Department of Sociology and Anthropology, University of
Amsterdam, 1012 DK Amsterdam, Netherlands;
email: n.besnier@uva.nl

[2] Department of Anthropology, Sociology, and Languages,
University of Missouri, St. Louis, Missouri 63121;
email: sbrownell@umsl.edu

approach adds to an understanding of sports (Blanchard & Cheska 1985; Carter 2002; Dyck 2000; Harris & Park 1983; Jonsson & Holthuysen 2011; Palmer 2002; Sands 1999, 2001; Sands & Sands 2010). Here we are equally concerned with what a focus on sports contributes to an understanding of broader anthropological concerns.

Limits of the Biological Paradigm

In the early days of the discipline of anthropology, play, games, and sport were located along an evolutionary continuum from "savage" to "civilized" (see Games and Sport in Exhibition Anthropology, sidebar below). "Salvage anthropology" endeavored to record games and sports along with other cultural practices before they disappeared. Native Americans received particular attention: such practices as Mesoamerican ball games (Whittington 2001), the ritual running race of the Tarahumara (McDougall 2009), and Cherokee stickball (Zogry 2010) still capture anthropological imaginations.

As the twentieth century progressed, increasing numbers of studies were located within a structural-functional framework, answering to the functionalist imperative to explain human activities that seemed non-purposeful. Play became a source of significant theoretical insights in anthropology and in other disciplines (Avedon & Sutton-Smith 1971, Caillois 1979, Csikszentmihalyi 1975, Huizinga 1970, Roberts et al. 1959, Turner 1982). The Association for the Anthropological Study of Play was founded by Cheska in 1974; it led to the publication of *The Anthropology of Sport* (Blanchard & Cheska 1985), the first attempt to define the field. These works tended to identify the purpose of play in biological models of "adaptation," an approach that increasingly became the province of scholars in education and human development. It never found a central place in anthropology, which turned to more cultural approaches (e.g., McMahon 2009).

The Interpretive Paradigm

Arising out of the same period, work by Geertz and Turner on the cultural meaning of play had a more enduring legacy. Geertz's (1972) analysis of Balinese cockfighting as "deep play"—play in which the stakes (in this case, gambling bets) are so high as to seem irrational—remains the classic essay of the era. Explaining that what is at stake in Balinese gambling is not money, but status, Geertz (1972, p. 26) turns functionalism on its head by arguing that the cockfight's primary function is interpretive: It is "a story [the Balinese] tell themselves about themselves."

Thinking of sports as a story that people tell themselves is thought provoking. One version of this insight, often echoed in popular sports media, is that distinctive playing styles represent "national character" (Archetti 1999; Bellos 2002; Lever 1984; Whiting 1977, 1989). In popular discourse, it is inscribed in fans' identification with local teams and in global marketing, as illustrated by the New Zealand All Blacks' performance before each rugby game of a haka, a spectacularly masculine dance borrowed (not without strident controversy) from indigenous Māori people (Jackson & Hokowhitu 2002). But this version of the interpretive approach also magnifies

---

Games and Sport in Exhibition Anthropology

An exhibition of world games at the 1893 World's Fair in Chicago, organized by Stewart Culin, one of the founders of the American Anthropological Association (established in 1902), was very popular. W.J. McGee, the association's first president, co-organized "Anthropology Days" at the 1904 St. Louis World's Fair, a "scientific" experiment in which the athletic performances of "savages" on display at the fair were recorded for comparison with those of "civilized men" in the Olympic Games (Brownell 2008a). Parezo (2008) has argued that the folly of the "experiment" helped to push American anthropology away from McGee's evolutionary paradigm and toward the cultural anthropology advocated by his rival, Franz Boas.

In the twenty-first century, traditional sports and games are regarded as "cultural heritage." To preserve "ludodiversity" in Flanders, Roland Renson (one of the early members of the Association for the Anthropological Study of Play) led the movement to create the "Sportimonium," a museum that combines Belgian Olympic history with folk games (which can be played on the grounds or for which the equipment can be checked out). In 2011, it became the first sports-related program to be inscribed in the UNESCO register of best practices for safeguarding intangible cultural heritage.

its deficiencies—its lack of attention to the power structures that silence some stories in favor of others, eliding the fact that stories arise out of the interplay between interested actors (Kelly 1998, 2009). In fact, the comparison of playing styles with dominant ideologies can offer surprising results: In Samoa, a society that places high value on communalism, young men play the national sport, rugby, with a movement style that foregrounds individualism (Clément 2009).

Turner (1969, 1982) developed his theory of liminality and communitas to characterize the different phases of a rite of passage. Liminality, the state of being "betwixt and between," is characterized by freedom from the constraints of social structure, opening up creative possibilities; this "antistructure" enables initiates to form an egalitarian social bond, "communitas." He argued that liminality and communitas also characterize modern "performance genres" like theater, art, music, games—and sports; however, he stopped short of characterizing sport as a liminal genre and instead developed an evolutionary schema in which traditional rituals evolved into multiple "liminoid" genres in modern societies. Although liminality and communitas remain influential concepts, the evolutionary schema did not survive the test of time (Brownell 2001, pp. 30–33).

Turner's student MacAloon (1984, 2006) cautioned against invoking the concept of ritual too indiscriminately. Distinguishing ritual from other types of cultural performance, he melded Turner's concept of performance genres with Bateson's (1972) concept of the "meta-communicative frame" to create "ramified (or nested) performance theory." It distinguishes four interpretive frames that, if not universal, are at least commonly employed cross culturally to give meaning to different performance genres: spectacle, festival, ritual, and game. They embrace each other in a series of concentric frames, with spectacle as the most inclusive and game at the center. The Olympic Games can be understood as a neatly ordered system of nested frames constituting a "performance system." MacAloon's theory has been influential in sport studies, but it never gained widespread traction in anthropology.

The Problems of Tradition and Modernity

The unilinear modernization paradigm maintained a fundamental separation between "traditional" (or "folk") and "modern" sports, raising the question of whether athletic contests could be lumped together under a single label. Comparative works typically observed that the English word "sport" did not acquire its contemporary meaning until the late-eighteenth century and that, everywhere in the world, the word "sport" had come to refer to Western sports upon their adoption.

It turned out that even characteristics that at first glance appear central to what a sport is, such as a focus on winning, are not always present in activities that are otherwise sport-like: For the Waiwai on the Guyana-Brazil border, what is primordial in archery is the framing of the masculine body as a social being (Mentore 2005, pp. 211–18); kinship relations figure prominently in the way in which Navajos played basketball (Blanchard 1974); and the Gahuku-Gama of the Papua New Guinea Highlands reconfigured rugby football as a substitute for intertribal feuding, with competitions ending when elders of the opposing groups agreed that a tie has been reached (Read 1965, pp. 150–51). Lévi-Strauss (1962, p. 44) used this last example to distinguish a ritual—an activity in which the goal is to bring participants together—from a game.

One result of the modernization paradigm was that anthropologists ignored sports considered to be "modern" inventions until the shift of the 1980s ended the disciplinary convention of focusing exclusively on cultural practices regarded as premodern. An anthropologically minded historian, Guttmann (1978, 1990), came up with an evolutionary schema that resembled Turner's, arguing that premodern sports had a ritual character that disappeared with the emergence of industrial society, replaced by an emphasis on achievement, as seen in sports records and economic productivity. The "from ritual to record" theory has been a topic of heated debate (Carter & Krüger 1990, Hum. Kinet. 2001) but still has its adherents.

Anthropologists contributed to this debate by relativizing both "tradition" and "modernity" as cultural constructions, prompting researchers to examine the ways in which Western sports in many parts of the world occupy a privileged position in the imagination precisely because of their identification with modernity. As a result, "traditional" sports sometimes become emblems in struggles against Westernizing modernization. In this vein, Eichberg (1990, 1998) argued that modern sports have made record-setting itself into a ritual so that what Guttmann considered to be a "tradition" displaced by modernization, in fact, continues to flourish.

The sport forms that emerged in nineteenth-century Europe radiated out from two European centers, each of which linked sports with masculinity, nationalism, and colonial aspirations. Using gymnastics and calisthenics, the Continental European tradition (the

German Turner movement was most influential world-wide) linked physical education to national strength and racial purity. The British tradition showcased ball games and racing and was imbued with the doctrine of muscular Christianity. Proponents of this doctrine saw the cultivation of the body as a means to an end that consisted of not only Christian faith, but also moral rectitude; racial purity; masculinity; and action in the service of God, country, and empire (MacAloon 2007, Mangan 1981). Many British public schools were run by devotees of muscular Christianity, hence the particular association of sports with public schools and the elite universities into which the latter fed. The British model was exported to North America, where sports found a home in elite universities; the American version evolved and spread along with U.S. imperialist expansion (Dyreson & Mangan 2007, Gems 2006).

In the encounter with "modern" sports, "folk" sports met various fates: They died out, as did Tutsi high jumping (Bale & Sang 1996); they were rationalized as modern sports, as were Chinese martial arts (Brownell 2008b, pp. 49–72); or they became the ground of fierce resistance to colonial hegemony, as did wrestling in India (Alter 1992). Some folk sports have had a complex history of successive disappearance and revival, appropriation and reappropriation, as is the case with surfing, which survived proscription by Calvinist missionaries in nineteenth-century Hawai'i to eventually become an international competition sport, one of the most exalted symbols of the culture of leisure, and, back in its birthplace, the locus of political struggle over indigenous rights (Finney & Houston 1996, Walker 2008).

The threat to the survival of sporting activities outside of the Western-dominated international performance system has continued to be a concern of scholars since the days of salvage anthropology. This concern linked up with the multicultural movement in Canada to create the Arctic Winter Games in 1970 and the North American Indigenous Games in 1990, both of which feature traditional as well as Olympic sports (Paraschak 1997). The National Games of Ethnic Minorities of China has been a showcase of ethnic policy since 1952; but at the twelfth installment in 2007, they had fallen into disrepair as a result of the attention paid to the upcoming Beijing Olympics, and most of the participants in the sports were Han students from sports institutes recently recruited to learn the sports just for the Games (Brownell 2011, p. 186). The end of state-supported sport after the fall of socialism produced a backlash in Europe, where sport festivals celebrating alternative local and ethnic identities multiplied rapidly (Eichberg 2008, pp. 360–69).

Supporting the reaction in anthropology of the past two decades against totalizing characterizations of modernity, sport has served as a perfect illustration of the fact that modernity is not a monolithic entity disseminated around the world in a one-way flow. Some sports, such as Gaelic football and hurling, remain deeply local; others, such as soccer football, have become spectacularly global; while yet others, such as baseball, are very important in some regions of the world but not others (Eriksen 2007, Kelly 2007, Klein 2006). The "ownership" of particular sports brings to the fore complex questions of authenticity and appropriation (Kohn 2010). Sport displays an extraordinary malleability as it "travels" across the world and within societies. People readily hybridize sports with different origins, appropriate and reinvent the history of particular sports, and utilize sports to challenge their former colonial masters (Appadurai 1995, Armstrong & Giulianotti 1997, Carter 2008, James 1963). In the annals of anthropology, the most celebrated example—owing to the enduring popularity of the documentary film about it—is the Trobriand Islanders' appropriation of cricket, originally introduced to them by Methodist missionaries (Leach & Kildea 1975; but also Foster 2006 for a critique). People everywhere actively engage with the new possibilities and new constraints of globalization and configure the modern in accord with the local—a view captured in the coined term "glocalization" (Giulianotti & Robertson 2004, 2007a,b).

Sport in Postcolonialism

Meanwhile, an increasing number of historical works on sport in colonialism and imperialism resolved the conundrum of the definition of "sport" by exposing the complex array of material and ideological factors that underpin the making of categories and boundaries. The endeavor to merely define "traditional" and "modern" sports masked the reality that the "tradition" in traditional sports was made into a problem by the onslaught of different sports backed by powerful interests, and so "tradition" is more usefully viewed, not as an unchanging quality, but as a product of globalization. An exploration of the classification of "sport" amounts to an exploration of the nature of modernity. Indeed, the emergence of modernity, the emergence of the modern state as a regulatory entity, the ascendance and naturalization of capitalism, and the concomitant ideological transformations of the body and self all figured centrally in the colonial project. Everywhere, the spread of organized, competitive, and team sports was tied to these processes (Bale & Cronin 2003; Besnier 2011, pp. 160–204).

Although the rules of sport may stay constant, meanings diverge. MacAloon (1996, 2006) called sport an "empty form"—a form that has been deracinated and decontextualized through the active suppression (or, minimally, the passive forgetting) of history and context, enabling "refilling" with local meanings. MacAloon's optimism echoes that of Guttmann (1994) and Maguire (1999) in asserting the potential for the creation of cultural differences through standardized sports. However, it is an open question whether the optimism of Western-based scholars is shared outside the developed West; the Chinese critic Lu (2010, p. 82) argues that Western sport culture has, "like a lawnmower, mowed down the cultural diversity of world sport into neat and tidy rows" (Brownell 2010, p. 72–74).

In fact, closer examination reveals that the struggle to be defined as a legitimate "sport" belongs not only to "traditional" sports, but to "modern" sports as well. Is bodybuilding a "legitimate" sport or simply the obsession of a small coterie of insecure narcissists (Klein 1993, Linder 2007, Rapport 2010, Stokvis 2006)? Are cockfighting and fox-hunting sports or the barbarous pastimes of Balinese villagers and English aristocrats, respectively (Geertz 1972, Marvin 2010)? Are the sports popular with women that do not conform to the masculine archetype, such as figure skating and gymnastics, truly "sports" (Adams 2011, Kestnbaum 2003)? Where do we place Brazilian capoeira: a martial art, a dance form, or a sport (Aceti 2010, Downey 2008)?

Nowhere are the economic and political interests vested in these questions more exposed than in the political maneuverings surrounding the introduction of new sports into the Olympic Games, which have become increasingly fierce due to the media coverage and financial revenues that the Olympics bring: Advocates of the inclusion of different sports are organizations backed by sporting-goods companies and event sponsors or governments that want their "national" sport to take its place on the world stage, as in the case of Chinese wushu (Brownell 2008b, pp. 49–72) and Indian kabbadi (Alter 2000).

The Turning Point

Mired in questions about definitions, essentialized ethnic and national characteristics, and biological imperatives, the anthropology of sport remained peripheral to the discipline as a whole. A little-recognized turning point occurred in 1988, when Korean anthropologist Kang, together with the American MacAloon, garnered considerable support from the Seoul Olympic organizing committee to organize a large international conference (Kang et al. 1988). Many prominent theorists in different

disciplines were invited, including the anthropologists Edith Turner, Sahlins, Bourdieu, Hannerz, and Appadurai. These theorists seemed to benefit from first-hand observation of a sport mega-event in progress, as they produced influential articles out of the papers first presented there (Appadurai 1995, Bourdieu 1988, Hannerz 1990). The anthropology of sport benefited from finally receiving the attention of leading thinkers, but it was not until two decades later that the disciplinary mainstream, aided by developments in sports history, caught up with the approaches outlined by these scholars. A general approach to sport that was grounded in a cultural theory of the body and performance finally cohered, taking into account transnationalism, colonialism, and globalization. This multifaceted approach had moved the study of sport to the center of the discipline.

The Sporting Body

Both Mauss (1934) and Elias (1939) utilized the concept "habitus" in their work, but it was its hardly acknowledged borrowing by Bourdieu (1978, 1988, 1999) that finally placed the sporting body at the center of social scientific interest. Habitus refers to a system of enduring dispositions, a habitual way of being, that becomes inculcated in the body as a result of the objective conditions of daily life; it is the "history incarnate in the body" (Bourdieu 1990, p. 190). Bourdieu approached sport as part of his larger quest, synthesizing the work of Mauss and Merleau-Ponty for an understanding of how the body and its practices articulate agents' embeddedness in structures.

Bourdieu's practice theory is a deeply politicized analytic program and, as a result, is almost diametrically opposed to the symbolic approaches of Geertz or Turner, in that it posits sporting activities as divisive rather than integrative. Bourdieu's interest in ongoing social structures meant that he had little to say about the periodic sports events that punctuate them. By contrast, Turner felt that one-off events such as ritual practices, theater performances, and sporting events were more important for the anthropologist than "habits," because these are the ways in which participants in a culture try to articulate its meaning (Bruner 1986, p. 13).

In his writing on sport and class, Bourdieu sought to understand the way in which different sports inscribed social class onto the body. Even though agents perceive recreational interests as a matter of "personal taste," these interests are deeply structural in nature (Laberge & Kay 2002). Although he denied that there is an "objective realism" at work, he explicitly linked the physical attributes of particular sport activities with class habitus. Thus sports such as boxing, football, and rugby express the "instrumental relation to the body itself which the working classes express in all the practices centred on the body" (Bourdieu 1999, p. 438). By contrast, middle-class sports (e.g., walking, jogging, gym work) treat the body as an end in itself and generate a "body-for-others."

However, the relationship of specific sports (and associated body practices) to specific class locations is historically and spatially unstable. Amateur boxing, for example, was a gentlemanly sport in nineteenth-century Britain (Boddy 2008), whereas in urban North America it is today strongly associated with race and underprivilege (Wacquant 2003). In 1895, rugby fissioned along class lines into two separate sports in Britain, rugby union and rugby league, ostensibly over disagreements about whether players could receive money for playing (Collins 2006). Where they are both practiced, the two sports continue to connote different class positions to this day.

Sport reinforces not only social-class hierarchies but also other forms of social inequality. Sport has played an important role in maintaining the sex-gender system in the West, bolstered by muscular Christianity and its legacy. Although sport's relation to sex and gender may be configured differently outside the West (Brownell 1995, pp. 213–17; Joo 2012), engagement with the Western-dominated global sports system is inevitably shaped by the fact that the lion's share of sport industries is marketed as a hypermasculine spectacle for global consumption (Bolin & Granskog 2003, Burstyn 1999, Hartmann-Tews & Pfister 2003). This has the effect of muffling expressions of non-normative genders and sexualities. The veritable obsession in international sports with gender dimorphism, in the form of stringent "sex verification" to ensure a clear separation of the sexes, is well-known (despite the presence of several mixed-sex sports on the Olympic program). Whether recreational or professional, sports tend to be deeply hostile to lesbian and gay participants (Anderson 2005). This homophobia motivated US decathlon Olympian Tom Waddell to found the Gay Games in 1982, but the organization was successfully sued by the U.S. Olympic Committee in the 1980s to prevent it from using the trademarked word "Olympics," which it had granted permission to some other groups to use, such as the Special Olympics (Symons 2010, pp. 55–58).

The structure of sports often has the effect of circumscribing racial and other minority identities. The exclusion of nonwhite players from rugby football in Apartheid South Africa is well-known (Nauright 2010), but discrimination generally takes more subtle forms, particularly if members of these minorities are essential to the business of the sport. Even when minority identities dominate a particular sport, which is the case in most professional sports today, they are problematized. For example, the stereotypical hypervirility of Polynesian rugby players, on which New Zealand rugby depends (along with the enormous economic interests tied to it), is also yoked in the eyes of the white public with savagery, a lack of discipline, and a propensity to "show off" (Hokowhitu 2004, Teaiwa & Mallon 2005). Politicians and the media in France transformed its multiracial national soccer team, winner of the 1998 World Cup, from a symbol of the success of integrationist republicanism (Dubois 2010), into a pack of arrogant and unpatriotic racialized hoodlums in the 2010 World Cup.

Yet, sport also creates arenas for displays of resistance against social hierarchies, sometimes spectacularly, as illustrated by the memorable Black Power raised fists by US sprinters Tommie Smith and John Carlos at the 1968 Mexico City Olympics in the midst of the Civil Rights movement (Bale & Cronin 2003, Hartmann 2004). More subtly, sport can contradict, if not quite subvert, power dynamics in the society in which it is embedded, as illustrated in Rabinowitz's (1997, pp. 119–45) ethnography of the dynamics between Israeli athletes and a Palestinian coach on an Israeli basketball team.

One of the deficiencies of practice theory for an anthropology of sport is that it lacks a well-developed concept of culture that can account for the ways in which practice is culturally organized by cultural schemas, myths, symbols, rituals, and so on (Ortner 2006, pp. 11–12). For this reason, "body culture" is a better tool than habitus, because it draws on the anthropological concept of culture to contextualize the body within the local meanings that are significant to the people whose bodies are in question. Brownell (1995, pp. 17–21) built on Eichberg's (1998) formulation to define body culture as everything that people do with their bodies (recalling Mauss's "body techniques"), together with the cultural context that shapes the nature of their actions and gives them meaning. Body culture reflects the internalization and incorporation of culture; it is "embodied culture."

Sport as Cultural Performance

Sport involves both ongoing practices and periodic performative events in a complementary relationship, and the performance of sport presumes an audience. Spectatorship can take different forms, from cheering a school game to watching broadcasts of the Olympic Games alongside billions of others, but it invariably involves a strong emotional component (Cash & Damousi 2009). It also includes being witness to the scandals that befall celebrity athletes with particular frequency, particularly if they have crossed racial or other kinds of social boundaries (Baughman 1995, Krause 1998, Starn 2011).

Although practice theory and postcolonial theory opened up new perspectives on everyday body practices, they had less to say about sport events as a performance genre. Recuperating the fact that sport continues to be ritual, symbol, and play, designed to create liminal spaces in which power and inequality are (at least temporarily) sidelined, allows us to create a more well-rounded theory, which is ignorant of neither power nor the fact that human beings can still transcend difference and inequality, and strive for communitas—the best example of which include the Olympics, the FIFA (International Federation of Association Football) World Cup in soccer, and comparable events.

Although anthropological theories of ritual have been influential among communications and media scholars studying the Olympic Games and major sports events, anthropologists have been slow on the uptake. One reason is the undertheorization of the "event" in ritual theory: Since the 1980s, ritual theory has been increasingly expanded to the point that even the everyday habits that Turner once disdained are now labeled as "rituals." For inspiration, we need to turn to communications scholarship, such as Rothenbuhler's (1988) ethnography of American television viewers' "living room celebration" of the Los Angeles 1984 Olympic Games. Similarly, the "media event"—a live broadcast of an historic occasion that transfixes a national or worldwide audience, which does not merely watch the event, but celebrates it—draws heavily on Turner's ritual theory (Dayan & Katz 1992, pp. 1–24). Roche (2000, pp. 1–5) used the term "mega-events" to describe large-scale cultural events that have a dramatic character, mass popular appeal, and international significance.

In short, anthropological theory combined with empirical cases drawn from the world of sport has made important contributions to communications and media studies, yet anthropologists have not taken up media events and mega-events as topics for study (exceptions are Horne & Manzenreiter 2002, 2006; Manzenreiter & Spitaler 2011). Because they are not based in ethnography, the existing theories lack concrete analytical categories derived from the actual experiences of the participants, and the labels "spectacle" and "mega-event" are overused as a "loose, imperial trope for everything dubious about the contemporary world" (MacAloon 2006, p. 15). It is the performance quality of sport, and sport mega-events in particular, that gives it such powerful popular impact, and the anthropology of sport still awaits the development and systematic application of a fully articulated theory of cultural performance.

Sport, Transnationalism, and Labor

We live in an ever more densely connected world in which growing numbers of problems have global impact, such as financial crises, climate change, and social unrest. The scale of these issues requires social scientists to develop better frameworks for analyzing systems and processes on a global scale. International sport provides a valuable lens into globalization because the webs that constitute world sport are a microcosm of those that constitute transnational society as a whole. The threads of this web are composed of sport-governing bodies (typically nongovernmental organizations), nongovernmental organizations concerned with issues other than sport, national governments, corporations, and other institutions; the production chains of sport-merchandise companies and the migration routes of athletes and coaches; the dissemination of television images and media reports of major sport events; and the grassroots networks of fans.

Because these are transnational actors in a world system of sovereign nation-states, sport provides insight into the national structures that still limit transnational action. For example, do supranational bodies such as FIFA and the International Olympic Committee "see like a [territorially bounded] state" (Scott 1998), or do they operate in a completely different paradigm? The European Court of Justice's landmark 1995 "Bosman ruling" against the bodies that regulate professional soccer football in Belgium and Europe—which ended clubs' monetary demands in the transfer of players as well as some citizenship restrictions on team compositions—demonstrated that in some ways the sport system was more restrictive of transnational mobility than the labor law of the European Union (Lanfranchi & Taylor 2001, pp. 213–29).

Klein's meticulous ethnographies of baseball in Dominican Republic academies (Klein 1991) and on the US-Mexico border (Klein 1997) provide rich material about the interplay of nationalism and transnationalism, but owing to sport's marginality in the discipline, his work did not gain the attention that it merited. The theoretical explication of transnationalism and globalization in sport has been largely undertaken by sociologists (most notably, Giulianotti & Robertson 2004, 2007b, 2009; Maguire 1999, 2005), but the development of theory has been hampered by a lack of areal expertise and on-the-ground fieldwork in non-Western and developing societies. The anthropology of sport still awaits a truly global synthesis of theories of transnationalism and globalization with ethnographic case studies.

Athletes and trainers form an increasingly mobile category of migrant labor facilitated by a transnational network of agents in multiple locations, including team-mates, recruiters, managers, trainers, and other brokers, as well as relatives, friends, covillagers, religious and secular leaders, state agents, other institutional authorities, and members of the public. In the last decades of the twentieth century, universities, clubs, and teams began searching for athletic talent across a much broader swath of the planet. This expansion of the talent pool coincided with the much-heralded emergence of globalization, but it was also motivated by the increasing corporatization and commodification of sport, which had gradually turned the competition for athletes into a matter of money and often lots of it (Bale 1991, Bale & Maguire 1994, Kelly 2006, Lanfranchi & Taylor 2001, Taylor 2006).

Many of the resulting migrations reversed former colonial linkages by drawing athletes from the global South to the global North (Magee & Sugden 2002). European clubs run "football farms" in West Africa, and North American teams run "baseball farms" in the Dominican Republic. However, there were also some spectacular indicators of the shift in the global balance of power from East to West, such as the increasing prominence in Japanese sumo of wrestlers from Mongolia, countries of the former Soviet Union, and the Pacific Islands (Tierney 2007).

Unlike other forms of migration, sport migrations invoke dreams of sudden success and wealth, which the migration of laborers or domestic workers never invokes, but which articulates with the millenarianism of "casino capitalism" (Comaroff & Comaroff 2000, Strange 1986). The resulting politics of hope has a number of distinctive characteristics: It is grounded in the very physicality of the athlete's body; it targets material rewards of millenarian proportions; and it is fueled by the possibility of popular recognition on an "even field" by citizens of the industrial world, who in some cases are the symbolic heirs of former colonizers. In many cases, this politics of hope rubs shoulders with the reality of disappointment and exploitation. Young hopefuls are exposed to exploitation in the form of human trafficking, including clandestine border crossing, procurement of faked documents, and deceitful promises of employment (Alegi 2010; Carter 2007, 2011; Darby 2000).

The migration of athletes can represent different things for different agents: West African soccer national teams' decrying of what Bale (1991) memorably termed the "brawn drain" contrasts sharply with the Tongan state's enthusiastic investment in the production and export of rugby talent (see Andreff 2006, Besnier 2012, Hoberman 2007). These different positions refract different ways of conceptualizing citizenship, migration, and development.

Sport, Nationalism, and Citizenship

More than in any other field, sport as spectacle is a means through which the state displays its legitimacy to other states and other societies as well as to its own citizenry. Theorists such as Foucault (1977, 1978) can further extend our understanding of the global ethnoscapes of sport with their insight that the state is more than just national governments. State projects to "integrate," "modernize," and "empower" ethnic minorities, poor people, and other "embarrassing" groups through sports segue into the complicated questions of citizenship and national belonging that surround professional athletes and star athletes who "represent" nations in the Olympics and other global competitions. Some scholars have hailed the power of sports as a vehicle for the integration of immigrant and other minorities into dominant society (Henry 2005, Inst. Sport Leis. Policy 2004, Kennett 2004), although others have also demonstrated the limitations of this position (Cronin & Mayall 2003, MacClancy 1996, Shor & Yonay 2011, Sorek 2010). The assumption is that partaking in sport activities is a matter of the individual rights of citizenship that should be guaranteed to members of minority groups (and which they are supposed to embrace enthusiastically). Conceptualizing access to sport as a matter of rights emerged out of the anti-Apartheid movement (Nauright 2010), and it was later extended from issues of race to issues of gender and, in the context of mega-events such as the Olympics, to the rights of all those whose lives were affected by these events.

The European Union's view of sport as a means of assimilating immigrants by extending this individual right of citizenship to them is in direct opposition to the original North American conception of multiculturalism, which was a reaction against the traditional "melting-pot" approach to assimilation. Thus, the Arctic Winter Games and North American Indigenous Games manifested the Canadian use of sport as an expression of ethnic self-determination.

Nowhere is the intertwining of nationalism (and localism) with masculinity rendered more visible than in sport, the site of what Billig (1995) terms "banal nationalism" and a prime instrument for the socialization of children to both nationalism and gender (Dyck 2010). It is seen in the convergence of extreme forms of masculinity, nationalism, and xenophobia in football hooliganism (Armstrong 1998, Buford 1993); martial sporting events in the service of the nation in Nazi Germany, the USSR, and China; or Western European efforts to promote recreational sports as an integrative mechanism to defuse the youthful masculinity of "problematic" minorities (Silverstein 2000).

At the same time, the configuration of professional sports in late capitalism poses two thorny contradictions for masculinity, nationalism (or localism), and sport. The first is the purchase of local teams by corporations or owners with no particular attachment to local contexts; these teams may then be transformed into products to be consumed transnationally, their ties to their country or city of origin having become only a minor aspect of this consumption (Miller et al. 1999). Thus Manchester United, the Chicago Bulls, and the New Zealand All Blacks, while ostensibly representing particular locations, are primarily products that can be purchased in the form of fan-club memberships anywhere in the world or through clothing-label franchises. The second is the contradiction embedded in the fact that teams are now staffed by large numbers of migrants (or the off-spring of migrants), yet they symbolize a deeply local masculinized identity that continues to be central to their marketing due to fans' identification with local teams, which translates into sales of tickets and licensed products, fan-club subscriptions, and TV ratings.

Both contradictions have important implications for our understanding of the relationships among transnationalism, nationalism, and localism as well as masculinity and belonging in the contemporary world. These issues are rarely tackled in a sustained fashion and have never been posed from the perspectives of migrant team-sport athletes who embody the pride of local and national communities that are not necessarily benign to them. The tense politics of autochthony and belonging that dominates the public sphere in France, Great Britain, and the Netherlands, among others, easily rears its aggressive head when a racialized foreign player misses a goal on the soccer football field, for example.

Centralizing Sport in Anthropology

The institutions that govern sport crosscut local, national, regional, international, and global structures in ways that highlight important theoretical issues. Sport is an important realm of anthropological inquiry because it provides a nexus of body, multiplex identities, and multi-layered governance structures, combined with a performance genre that possesses qualities of play, liminality, and storytelling, that enables us to explore the connections among these dynamics in a unique way. Recent works have been concerned with what anthropology can bring to sport, but this essay draws attention to what sport can bring to anthropology. Reconceptualizing the body as a cultural construction makes it possible to look at how sport "travels" across boundaries and opens up a space for examining how sport creates connections between peoples at the same time that it strengthens local and national identities.

Sport provides a novel angle for the investigation of fundamental questions in contemporary anthropology. A synthesis of the two approaches to sport represented in the history of anthropology—sport as play and sport as the serious life, sport as cultural performance and sport as everyday practice—provides the key to unlock the study of sport and allow it to move to the center of the discipline in this global era.

Future Issues

1. Much work currently exists on the body within the nation-state, but the body in structures beyond the state remains to be explored.
2. We need more ethnography exploring the dynamic in which bodies and capitalism mutually construct each other: How do commodification and corporatization shape the bodies that are valued, and how does the valuation of bodies shape commodification?
3. We also need a more truly "global" synthesis of theories of transnationalism and globalization with ethnographic research on non-Western and developing societies to complement the primarily historical, Western, and macrosociological focus of existing work.
4. The anthropology of sport still awaits the development and systematic application of a fully articulated theory of cultural performance. Ethnography has much to contribute to the understanding not only of the organization of sport mega-events, but also of their "legacy" (to use the current jargon word) for everyday people in host cities and countries.
5. What is the place of play and pleasure in this lucrative, competitive field?
6. As a research method, ethnography could contribute to understanding the social problems in sport, such as doping, homophobia, sexism, exploitation of migrant and child labor, the loss of "traditional" games and sports, and so on.

Disclosure Statement

The authors are not aware of any affiliations, memberships, funding, or financial holdings that might be perceived as affecting the objectivity of this review.

Literature Cited

Aceti M. 2010. Ethnographie multi-située de la capoeira: de la diffusion d'une pratique "sportive" afrobrésilienne à un rituel d'énergie interculturel. *ethnographiques.org* 20; **http://www.ethnographiques.org/2010/Aceti**

Adams ML. 2011. *Artistic Impressions: Figure Skating, Masculinity, and the Limits of Sport.* Toronto: Univ. Tor. Press

Alegi P. 2010. *African Soccerscapes: How a Continent Changed the World's Game.* Athens, OH: Ohio Univ. Press

Alter JS. 1992. *The Wrestler's Body: Identity and Ideology in North India.* Berkeley: Univ. Calif. Press

Alter JS. 2000. Kabbadi, a national sport of India: the internationalism of nationalism and the foreignness of Indianness. See Dyck 2000, pp. 81–116

Anderson E. 2005. *In The Game: Gay Athletes and the Cult of Masculinity.* Albany, NY: SUNY Press

Andreff W. 2006. Sport in developing countries. In *Handbook on the Economics of Sport,* ed. W Andreff, S Szymanski, pp. 308–15. Cheltenham, UK: Edward Elgar

Appadurai A. 1995. Playing with modernity: the decolonization of Indian cricket. In *Consuming Modernity: Public Culture in a South Asian World,* ed. CA Breckenridge, pp. 23–48. Minneapolis: Univ. Minn. Press

Archetti E. 1999. *Masculinities: Football, Polo and the Tango in Argentina.* Oxford: Berg

Armstrong G. 1998. *Football Hooligans: Knowing the Score.* Oxford: Berg

Armstrong G, Giulianotti R. 1997. Introduction: reclaiming the game—an introduction to the anthropology of football. In *Entering the Field: New Perspectives on World Football,* ed. G Armstrong, R Giulianotti, pp. 1–30. Oxford: Berg

Avedon EM, Sutton-Smith B. 1971. *The Study of Games.* New York: John Wiley

Bale J. 1991. *The Brawn Drain: Foreign Student-Athletes in American Universities.* Urbana, IL: Univ. Ill. Press

Bale J, Cronin M. 2003. *Sport and Postcolonialism.* Oxford: Berg

Bale J, Maguire J, eds. 1994. *The Global Sports Arena: Athletic Talent Migration in an Interdependent World.* London: Frank Cass

Bale J, Sang J. 1996. *Kenyan Running: Movement Culture, Geography, and Global Change.* London: Frank Cass

Bateson G. 1972. *Steps to an Ecology of Mind: Collected Essays in Anthropology, Psychiatry, Evolution, and Epistemology.* Chicago: Univ. Chicago Press

Baughman C, ed. 1995. *Women On Ice: Feminist Responses to the Tonya Harding/Nancy Kerrigan Spectacle.* London: Routledge

Bellos A. 2002. *Futebol: The Brazilian Way.* New York: Bloomsbury

Besnier N. 2011. *On the Edge of the Global: Modern Anxieties in a Pacific Island Nation.* Stanford, CA: Stanford Univ. Press

Besnier N. 2012. The athlete's body and the global condition: Tongan rugby players in Japan. *Am. Ethnol.* 39:491–510

Billig M. 1995. *Banal Nationalism.* London: Sage

Blanchard K. 1974. Basketball and the culture-change process: the Rimrock Navajo case. *Counc. Anthropol. Educ. Q.* 5(4):8–13

Blanchard K, Cheska A. 1985. *The Anthropology of Sport: An Introduction.* South Hadley, MA: Bergin & Garvey

Boddy K. 2008. *Boxing: A Cultural History.* London: Reaktion

Bolin A, Granskog J. 2003. *Athletic Intruders: Ethnographic Research on Women, Culture, and Exercise.* Albany, NY: SUNY Press

Bourdieu P. 1978. Sport and social class. *Soc. Sci. Inf.* 17:819–40

Bourdieu P. 1988. Program for a sociology of sport. *Sociol. Sport J.* 5:153–61

Bourdieu P. 1990. *In Other Words: Essays for a Reflexive Sociology.* Stanford, CA: Stanford Univ. Press

Bourdieu P. 1999. How can one be a sports fan? In *The Cultural Studies Reader,* ed. S During, pp. 427–40. London: Routledge. 2nd ed.

Brownell S. 1995. *Training the Body for China: Sports in the Moral Order of the People's Republic.* Chicago: Univ. Chicago Press

Brownell S. 2001. The problems with ritual and modernization theory, and why we need Marx: a commentary on *From Ritual to Record. Sport Hist. Rev.* 32(1):28–41

Brownell S, ed. 2008a. *The 1904 Anthropology Days and Olympic Games.* Lincoln: Univ. Neb. Press

Brownell S. 2008b. *Beijing's Games: What the Olympics Mean to China.* Lanham, MD: Rowman & Littlefield

Brownell S. 2010. Multiculturalism in the Olympic movement. See Ren et al. 2010, pp. 61–80

Brownell S. 2011. The Beijing Olympics as a turning point? China's first Olympics in East Asian perspective. In *The Olympics in East Asia: The Crucible of Localism, Nationalism, Regionalism, and Globalism,* ed. W Kelly, S Brownell, pp. 185–203. New Haven, CT: Yale Counc. East Asian Stud. Monogr. Ser.

Bruner EM. 1986. Experience and its expressions. In *The Anthropology of Experience,* ed. V Turner, EM Bruner, pp. 3–30. Urbana: Univ. Ill. Press

Buford B. 1993. *Among the Thugs.* New York: Vintage

Burstyn V. 1999. *The Rites of Men: Manhood, Politics, and the Culture of Sport.* Toronto: Univ. Tor. Press

Caillois R. *Man, Play and Games.* Champaign: Univ. Ill. Press

Carter A, Krüger R, eds. 1990. *Ritual and Record: Sports Records and Quantification in Pre-Modern Societies.* Westport, CT: Greenwood

Carter TF. 2002. On the need for an anthropological approach to sport. *Identities Glob. Stud. Cult. Power* 9:405–22

Carter TF. 2007. Family networks, state interventions and the experience of Cuban transnational sport migration. *Int. Rev. Social. Sport* 42:371–89

Carter TF. 2008. *The Quality of Home Runs: The Passion, Politics, and Language of Cuban Baseball.* Durham, NC: Duke Univ. Press

Carter TF. 2011. *In Foreign Fields: The Politics and Experiences of Transnational Sport Migration.* London: Pluto

Cash J, Damousi J. 2009. *Footie Passions.* Sydney: Univ. N. S. W. Press

Clément J. 2009. *Le rugby de Samoa: les techniques du corps entre Fa'a Sāmoa et mondialisation du sport.* PhD thesis. Univ. Provence, Aix-Marseille

Coleman S, Kohn T, eds. 2010. *The Discipline of Leisure: Embodying Culture of "Recreation."* Oxford: Berghahn

Collins T. 2006. *Rugby's Great Split: Class, Culture and the Origins of Rugby League Football.* London: Routledge. 2nd ed.

Comaroff J, Comaroff JL. 2000. Millennial capitalism: first thoughts on a second coming. *Public Cult.* 12:291–343

Cronin M, Mayall D, eds. 2003. *Sporting Nationalisms: Identity, Ethnicity, Immigration and Assimilation.* London: Routledge

Csikszentmihalyi M. 1975. *Beyond Boredom and Anxiety: Experiencing Flow in Work and Play.* San Francisco: Jossey-Bass

Darby P. 2000. The new scramble for Africa: African football labour migration to Europe. *Eur. Sports Hist. Rev.* 3:217–44

Dayan D, Katz E. 1992. *Media Events: The Live Broadcasting of History.* Cambridge, MA: Harvard Univ. Press

Downey G. 2008. Scaffolding imitation in capoeira: physical education and enculturation in an Afro-Brazilian Art. *Am. Anthropol.* 110:204–13

Duara P. 1995. *Rescuing History from the Nation: Questioning Narratives of Modern China.* Chicago: Univ. Chicago Press

Dubois L. 2010. *Soccer Empire: The World Cup and the Future of France.* Berkeley: Univ. Calif. Press

Dyck N, ed. 2000. *Games, Sports and Cultures.* Oxford: Berg

Dyck N. 2010. Remembering and the ethnography of children's sports. In *The Ethnographic Self As Resource: Writing Memory and Experience Into Ethnography,* ed. P Collins, A Gallinat, pp. 150–64. Oxford: Berghahn

Dyreson M, Mangan JA, eds. 2007. *Sport and American Society: Exceptionalism, Insularity and "Imperialism."* London: Routledge

Eichberg H. 1990. Stronger, funnier, deadlier: track and field on the way to the ritual of the record. See Carter & Krüger 1990, pp. 123–34

Eichberg H. 1998. *Body Cultures: Essays on Sport, Space and Identity.* London: Routledge

Eichberg H. 2008. Olympic anthropology days and the progress of exclusion: toward an anthropology of democracy. See Brownell 2008a, pp. 343–82

Elias N. 1939. *Über den Prozeß der Zivilisation. Soziogenetische und psychogenetische Untersuchungen.* Basel: Verlag Haus Falken (2000. *The Civilizing Process: Sociogenetic and Psychogenetic Investigations.* Oxford: Blackwell. Rev. transl.)

Eriksen TH. 2007. Steps to an ecology of transnational sports. *Glob. Netw.* 7:132–65

Finney BR, Houston JD. 1996. *Surfing: A History of the Ancient Hawaiian Sport.* Petaluma, CA: Pomegranate. 2nd ed.

Foster RJ. 2006. From Trobriand cricket to rugby nation: the mission of sport in Papua New Guinea. *Int. J. Hist. Sport* 23:739–58

Foucault M. 1977. *Discipline and Punish: The Birth of the Prison.* Transl. A Sheridan. New York: Vintage

Foucault M. 1978. *The History of Sexuality. Volume I: An Introduction.* Transl. R Hurley. New York: Vintage

Geertz C. 1972. Deep play: notes on the Balinese cockfight. *Dædalus* 101(1):1–37

Gems GR. 2006. *The Athletic Crusade: Sport and American Cultural Imperialism.* Lincoln: Univ. Neb. Press

Giulianotti R, Robertson R. 2004. The globalization of football: a study in the glocalization of the "serious life." *Br. J. Sociol.* 55(4):545–68

Giulianotti R, Robertson R. 2007a. Forms of glocalization: globalization and the migration strategies of Scottish football fans in North America. *Sociology* 41(1):133–52

Giulianotti R, Robertson R, eds. 2007b. *Globalization and Sport.* Malden, MA: Blackwell

Giulianotti R, Robertson R. 2009. *Globalization and Football.* London: Sage

Guttmann A. 1978. *From Ritual to Record: The Nature of Modern Sports.* New York: Columbia Univ. Press

Guttmann A. 1990. Rituals, records, responses. See Carter & Krüger 1990, pp. 153–60

Guttmann A. 1994. *Games and Empires: Modern Sports and Cultural Imperialism.* New York: Columbia Univ. Press

Hannerz U. 1990. Cosmopolitans and locals in world culture. *Theory Cult. Soc.* 7(2):237–51

Harris JC, Park RJ, eds. 1983. *Play, Games and Sports in Cultural Contexts.* Champaign, IL: Hum. Kinet.

Hartmann D. 2004. *Race, Culture, and the Revolt of the Black Athlete: The 1968 Olympic Protests and Their Aftermath.* Chicago: Univ. Chicago Press

Hartmann-Tews I, Pfister G, eds. 2003. *Sport and Women: Social Issues in International Perspective.* London: Routledge

Henry I. 2005. *Playing along: sport as a means for social integration.* Presented at Conf. Sport Dev., 2nd, 4–6 Dec., Magglingen, Switz.

Hoberman J. 2007. Race and athletics in the twenty-first century. In *Physical Culture, Power, and the Body,* ed. J Hargreaves, P Vertinsky, pp. 208–31. London: Routledge

Hokowhitu B. 2004. Tackling Māori masculinity: genealogy of savagery and sport. *Contemp. Pac.* 16:259–84

Horne J, Manzenreiter W. 2002. *Japan, Korea and the 2002 World Cup.* New York: Routledge

Horne J, Manzenreiter W. 2006. *Sports Mega-Events: Social Scientific Analyses of a Global Phenomenon.* Oxford: Wiley-Blackwell

Huizinga J. 1970. *Homo Ludens: A Study of the Play Element in Culture.* New York: Harper & Row

Hum. Kinet. 2001. Special issue: re-examination of *From Ritual to Record: A Retrospective Critique. Sport Hist. Rev.* 32(1):1–57

Inst. Sport Leis. Policy. 2004. Studies on education and sport: sport and multiculturalism (lot 3), final report. *Rep. Eur.*

Comm. DG Educ. Cult., Loughborough Univ., Leicestershire, UK

Jackson SJ, Hokowhitu B. 2002. Sport, tribes, and technology: the New Zealand All Blacks haka and the politics of identity. *J. Sport Soc. Issues* 26:125–39

James CLR. 1963. *Beyond a Boundary.* London: Stanley Paul

Jonsson H, Holthuysen J, eds. 2011. *Contests in Context: Readings in the Anthropology of Sports.* Dubuque, IA: Kendall/Hunt

Joo RM. 2012. *Transnational Sport: Gender, Media, and Global Korea.* Durham, NC: Duke Univ. Press

Kang SP, MacAloon J, DaMatta R, eds. 1988. *The Olympics and Cultural Exchange: The Papers of the First International Conference on the Olympics and East/West and South/North Cultural Exchange in the World System.* Seoul: Hanyang Univ. Press

Kelly JD. 2006. *The American Game: Capitalism, Decolonization, World Domination, and Baseball.* Chicago: Prickly Paradigm

Kelly WW. 1998. Blood and guts in Japanese professional baseball. In *The Culture of Japan as Seen Through Its Leisure,* ed. S Linhard, S Frühstück, pp. 95–111. Albany, NY: SUNY Press

Kelly WW. 2007. Is baseball a global sport? America's "national pastime" as global field and international sport. *Glob. Netw.* 7:187–201

Kelly WW. 2009. Samurai baseball: the vicissitudes of a national sporting style. *Int. J. Hist. Sport* 26:429–41

Kennett C. 2004. *Sport, immigration and multiculturality: a conceptual.* Presented at Foro Eur. Cult. Deporte Prox., Ameria, May 5; **http://olympicstudies.uab.es/pdf/wp103_eng.pdf**

Kestnbaum E. 2003. *Culture on Ice: Figure Skating and Cultural Meaning.* Middletown, CT: Wesleyan Univ. Press

Klein AM. 1991. *Sugarball: The American Game, the Dominican Dream.* New Haven, CT: Yale Univ. Press

Klein AM. 1993. *Little Big Men: Bodybuilding Subculture and Gender Construction.* Albany, NY: SUNY Press

Klein AM. 1997. *Baseball on the Border: A Tale of Two Laredos.* Princeton, NJ: Princeton Univ. Press

Klein AM. 2006. *Growing the Game: The Globalization of Major League Baseball.* New Haven, CT: Yale Univ. Press

Kohn T. 2010. Appropriating an authentic bodily practice from Japan: on "being there," "having been there" and "virtually being there." In *Ownership and Appropriation,* ed. V Strang, M Busse, pp. 65–86. Oxford: Berg

Krause EL. 1998. "The bead of raw sweat in a field of dainty perspirers": nationalism, whiteness, and the Olympic-class ordeal of Tonya Harding. *Transform. Anthropol.* 7:33–52

Laberge S, Kay J. 2002. Pierre Bourdieu's sociocultural theory and sport practice. In *Theory, Sport and Society,* ed. J Maguire, K Young, pp. 239–66. Oxford: JAI

Lanfranchi P, Taylor M. 2001. *Moving with the Ball: The Migration of Professional Footballers.* Oxford: Berg

Leach JW, Kildea G. 1975. *Trobriand cricket: an ingenious response to colonialism.* Video rec., produced by Off. Inf. Gov. Papua New Guinea

Lever J. 1984. *Soccer Madness: Brazil's Passion for the World's Most Popular Sport.* Chicago: Univ. Chicago Press

Lévi-Strauss C. 1962. *La Pensée Sauvage.* Paris: Plon

Linder F. 2007. Life as art, and seeing the promise of big bodies. *Am. Ethnol.* 34:451–72

Lu YZ. 2010. Hope lies in the revival of Eastern sport culture. See Ren et al. 2010, pp. 81–92

MacAloon JJ. 1984. Olympic Games and the theory of spectacle in modern societies. In *Rite, Drama, Festival, Spectacle: Rehearsals Toward a Theory of Cultural Performance,* ed. JJ MacAloon, pp. 241–80. Philadelphia: Inst. Study Hum. Issues

MacAloon JJ. 1996. Humanism as political necessity? Reflections on the pathos of anthropological science in Olympic contexts. *Quest* 48:67–81

MacAloon JJ. 2006. The theory of spectacle: reviewing Olympic ethnography. In *National Identity and Global Sports Events,* ed. A Tomlinson, C Young, pp. 15–39. Albany, NY: SUNY Press

MacAloon JJ, ed. 2007. *Muscular Christianity in Colonial and Post-Colonial Worlds.* London: Routledge

MacClancy J, ed. 1996. *Sport, Identity and Ethnicity.* Oxford: Berg

Magee J, Sugden J. 2002. The world at their feet: professional football and international labor migration. *J. Sport Soc. Issues* 26:421–37

Maguire J. 1999. *Global Sport: Identities, Societies, Civilizations.* Cambridge: Polity

Maguire J. 2005. *Power and Global Sport: Zones of Prestige, Emulation and Resistance.* Abingdon: Routledge

Mangan JA. 1981. *Athleticism in the Victorian and Edwardian Public School: The Emergence and Consolidation of an Educational Ideology.* Cambridge, UK: Cambridge Univ. Press

Manzenreiter W, Spitaler G. 2011. *Governance, Citizenship and the New European Football Championships: The European Spectacle.* New York: Routledge

Marvin G. 2010. Animal and human bodies in the landscapes of English foxhunting. See Coleman & Kohn 2010, pp. 91–108

Mauss M. 1934. Les techniques du corps. In *Marcel Mauss: Sociologie et Anthropologie,* pp. 363–86. Paris: Press. Univ. France

McDougall C. 2009. *Born to Run: A Hidden Tribe, Superathletes, and the Greatest Race the World Has Never Seen.* New York: Vintage

McMahon FR. 2009. *Not Just Child's Play: Emerging Tradition and the Lost Boys of Sudan.* Jackson: Univ. Press Miss.

Mentore GP. 2005. *Of Passionate Curves and Desirable Cadences: Themes on Waiwai Social Being.* Lincoln: Univ. Neb. Press

Miller T, Lawrence G, McKay J, Rowe D. 1999. Modifying the sign: sport and globalization. *Soc. Text* 17:15–33

Nauright J. 2010. *The Long Run to Freedom: Sport, Cultures, and Identities in South Africa.* Morgantown, WV: Fit. Inf. Technol.

Ortner SB. 2006. *Anthropology and Social Theory: Culture, Power, and the Acting Subject.* Durham, NC: Duke Univ. Press

Palmer C, ed. 2002. Special issue on anthropology and sport. *Austr. J. Anthropol.* 13(3):253–377

Paraschak V. 1997. Variations in race relations: sporting events for native peoples in Canada. *Sociol. Sport J.* 14(1):1–21

Parezo N. 2008. A "Special Olympics" testing racial strength and endurance at the 1904 Louisiana Purchase Exposition. See Brownell 2008a, pp. 59–126

Rabinowitz D. 1997. *Overlooking Nazareth: The Ethnography of Exclusion in Galilee.* Cambridge, UK: Cambridge Univ. Press

Rapport N. 2010. Bob, hospital bodybuilder: the integrity of the body, the transitiveness of "work" and "leisure." See Coleman & Kohn 2010, pp. 23–37

Read KE. 1965. *The High Valley: An Autobiographical Account of Two Years Spent in the Central Highlands of New Guinea.* New York: Scribner

Ren H, DaCosta L, Miragaya A, eds. 2010. *Olympic Studies Reader: A Multidisciplinary and Multicultural Research Guide.* Beijing: Beijing Sport Univ. Press

Roberts JM, Arth MJ, Bush RR. 1959. Games in culture. *Am. Anthropol.* 61:597–605

Roche M. 2000. *Mega-Events and Modernity: Olympics and Expos in the Growth of Global Culture.* London: Routledge

Rothenbuhler E. 1988. The living room celebration of the Olympic Games. *J. Commun.* 38(4): 61–81

Sands RR, ed. 1999. *Anthropology, Sport, and Culture.* New York: Bergin & Garvey

Sands RR. 2001. *Sport Ethnography.* Champaign, IL: Hum. Kinet.

Sands RR, Sands LR, eds. 2010. *The Anthropology of Sport and Human Movement: A Biocultural Perspective.* Lanham, MD: Lexington Books

Scott JC. 1998. *Seeing Like a State: How Certain Schemes to Improve the Human Condition Have Failed.* New Haven, CT: Yale Univ. Press

Shor E, Yonay Y. 2011. "Play and shut up": the silencing of Palestinian athletes in Israeli media. *Ethnic Racial Stud.* 34:229–47

Silverstein PA. 2000. Sporting faith: Islam, soccer, and the French nation-state. *Soc. Text* 18:25–53

Sorek T. 2010. *Arab Soccer in a Jewish State: The Integrative Enclave.* Cambridge, UK: Cambridge Univ. Press

Starn O. 2011. *The Passion of Tiger Woods: An Anthropologist Reports on Golf, Race, and Celebrity Scandal.* Durham, NC: Duke Univ. Press

Stokvis R. 2006. The emancipation of bodybuilding. *Sport Soc.* 9:463–79

Strange S. 1986. *Casino Capitalism.* London: Blackwell

Symons C. 2010. *The Gay Games: A History.* London: Routledge

Taylor M. 2006. Global players? Football, migration and globalization, c. 1930–2000. *Hist. Soc. Res.* 31:7–30

Teaiwa TK, Mallon S. 2005. Ambivalent kinships? Pacific people in New Zealand. In *New Zealand Identities: Departures and Destinations,* ed. J Liu, T McCreanor, T McIntosh, T Teaiwa, pp. 207–29. Wellington: Victoria Univ. Press

Tierney RK. 2007. From popular performance to national sport: the nationalization of Sumo. In *This Sporting Life: Sports and Body Culture in Modern Japan,* ed. WW Kelly, pp. 67–89. New Haven, CT: Cent. East Asian Stud., Yale Univ.

Turner V. 1969. *The Ritual Process: Structure and Anti-Structure.* Ithaca, NY: Cornell Univ. Press

Turner V. 1982. *From Ritual to Theatre: The Human Seriousness of Play.* New York: Perform. Arts J. Publ.

Wacquant L. 2003. *Body and Soul: Notebooks of an Apprentice Boxer.* New York: Oxford Univ. Press

Walker IH. 2008. Hui Nalu, beachboys, and the surfing boarder-lands of Hawai'i. *Contemp. Pac.* 20:89–113

Whiting R. 1977. *The Chrysanthemum and the Bat: Baseball Samurai Style.* New York: Dodd Mead

Whiting R. 1989. *You Gotta Have Wa.* New York: Vintage

Whittington EM. 2001. *The Sport of Life and Death: The Mesoamerican Ballgame.* London: Thames & Hudson

Zogry MJ. 2010. *Anetso, the Cherokee Ball Game: At the Center of Ceremony and Identity.* Chapel Hill: Univ. N. C. Press

The Individual and Virtual Identity

How many friends do you have? Do you meet up to hang out with them frequently? How many of them would you call in case of an emergency or to invite for a special event? Ok. Now, how many friends do you have on Facebook? How many of them do you know in the flesh? How many of them do you think that you know pretty well even though you have never met them? How sure are you that you know the "real them" and not their virtual identity? Is the virtual identity so different that the real, protoplasmic identity?

Most of us take this plunge every day in a myriad of ways. How many "selves" do you have in how many virtual worlds?

© Andrea Danti, 2014. Used under license from Shutterstock, Inc.

Technology has changed how we interact with each other. It has turned "friend" into a verb and it has allowed us to control and expand interactions across time and space to a degree that was unimaginable just a few decades ago. According to researchers, all Facebook users are separated by only 3.74 degrees of separation. That is, only 3.74 "friends" and "friends of friends" link you to any other Facebook user. A friend of mine in Thailand, for example, is four "hops" away from you through your friends list. Amazing, huh? We live in a brave new world of interactions.

I have a friend whose son met a girl while playing the wildly popular online game World of Warcraft. He lives in a New Mexico and she lives in Australia. Through their avatars (the pixilated representation of the self online, named after the incarnations of the Vishnu, the Hindu god), he became friendly with her and eventually developed a virtual relationship outside the game, through Facebook, Skype and other virtual communication channels. To make a long story short, he quit school and flew to Australia to marry his girlfriend. A truly intense relationship had developed between two separated by a large distance but yet sharing an intimate interaction. That is the nature of the world in which we live today; a world where we can be isolated in our room and simultaneously be extremely "social" with others at various levels of intimacy. We can share mundane news ("My dog just threw up under the bed! Ugh!") with hundreds or even thousands of people who might know you only slightly, if at all. Through the magic of Facebook, you might know about an old elementary school friend's new job before her mother does. Technology is expanding the boundaries of our social interactions.

Much of the social dynamics made possible by new virtual technologies disembed time and space, as Giddens has pointed out. Specifically this means that we can have real time relationships with individuals and organizations that are

Actress Ina Tempel with her Avatar "Alice" at a presentation of the performance "Wunderland" (after "Alice in Wonderland") which took place entirely in "Second Life".

not occupying the same geographic space. Virtual identities can interact instantaneously through time and space. This type of virtuality is flattening our world, as Thomas Friendman posited in his book, *The World is Flat* (2005). Virtual relationships, facilitated by new technologies, are a key element to our stage of modernity. They are changing our economy, our politics, our culture and our social relationships.

New Media

New media encompasses all interactive forms of information exchange. These include social networking sites, blogs, podcasts, wikis, and, my personal favorite, virtual worlds. "Old" media includes all types of print media, television and radio as well as film. In general, new media tends to level the playing field in terms of who is constructing it, that is, creating, publishing, distributing, and accessing information as well as offering alternative forums to groups unable to gain access to traditional political platforms, such as groups associated with the Arab Spring protests.

Cyborgs in our future? Virtual worlds are a new frontier that is allowing us to explore our social selves unencumbered by our material world.

Virtual worlds, worlds that exist via pixelated interactions, create frontiers which exist in a new media platform and they are drawing a great deal of attention from sociologist and psychologists. We can create any virtual self that we wish in many of these virtual frontiers. How much of our "real" self is recreated in the virtual environment? How do we interact with others? Do we carry our biases into the virtual world and/or do we create new ones?

One of the most interesting category of the new media platforms are video games. Video games immerse us in a totally disembedded world.; a world where time and space are pulled apart yet manage to create a dimension where intense interactions can occur. Virtual worlds are important frontiers for social scientists . In these worlds, hundreds of thousands of people create avatars that interact in virtually created environments. If you have not been exposed to these games (World of Warcraft is the largest with over 11 million players) or to other virtual worlds, such as Second Life (where there are universities, dance clubs, and art galleries, etc.), I encourage you to explore them. And when you are there, think like a sociologist.

© Kostyantyn Ivanyshen, 2014. Used under license from Shutterstock, Inc.

What kind of armor is THIS?! Video games hyper sexualize the female form hoping to appeal to what companies consider to be the target audience of video games—the young male gamer. And many of these male games chose to create female avatars because they are treated better in games. They receive more attention and benefits from other players.

Play Money

Or, How I Quit My Day Job and Made Millions Trading Virtual Loot

Julian Dibbell

Not long after I got home from Tijuana, a 43-year-old Wonder Bread delivery man in Stillwater, Oklahoma, logged on to eBay and, as people sometimes do these days, bought himself a house there. Not a shabby one, either. Nine rooms, three stories, rooftop patio, walls of solid stonework—it wasn't quite a castle, but in most respects it put to shame the modest red-brick ranch house the man came home to every weeknight after a long day stocking the supermarket shelves of Stillwater. Excellent location, too; a long, long way from Oklahoma and nestled at the foot of a quiet coastal hillside, the house was just a hike away from a quaint seaside village and a quick commute from two bustling cosmopolitan cities. In short, the house could only have been better if it had actually existed, and even that might have been no great improvement in the buyer's eyes. He wasn't in the market for a real house, after all. He wanted his own small piece of the vast computer database that was Britannia, the mythical world in which the venerable MMO Ultima Online unfolds. And for $750, he got it.

The buyer's name was John Dugger, and I spoke to him by telephone a few weeks after his purchase. By then, it no longer surprised me that people spent real money on this sort of thing. But that's not to say I understood why they did. Dugger had given up a week's wages to own what was at best a digital doll-house, and I grasped only dimly what had inspired him to do that. I suppose I could have simply asked him, and eventually, I would. But the real question, I sensed, was at once more specifically economic and more broadly social: How exactly does a seven-kilobyte piece of digital make-believe turn into a $750 piece of upmarket real estate? And the real answer, I suspected, was a bigger one than Dugger alone could have given me.

So I got into my car and set out to find it.

At a construction site in Indianapolis, Indiana, Troy Stolle sat in the passenger seat of my car, hard hat in his lap and a Big Mac in his hands. "Whoa, A/C at lunchtime," he observed, "that's a rarity." Outside, the temperature was ninety-one degrees; the air was thick with humidity, dust, and the rumble of bulldozers. A hundred yards away, the outline of a future Costco megastore shimmered in the heat, slowly taking shape as workers set rebar and poured concrete. Stolle's job, as a form carpenter, was to build the wooden molds the concrete got poured into and then rip them down after it dried. It was not a cushy gig even in the nicest weather, and in heat like this it could kill you if you didn't drink water constantly. Stolle's arms and hands were flecked with cuts and bruises, and at the moment he had a pounding headache from the early stages of dehydration. Or maybe from the two-by-four that had smacked him in the head earlier that morning. He wasn't certain which.

He was sure of this much, though: This job was a cakewalk compared to the work he'd put into raising a virtual tower in Britannia two years before. "That was a lot more stressful."

A lanky, bespectacled 29-year-old, Stolle looked less like the third-generation construction worker he was than like the second-generation sword-and-sorcery geek he had become. When Stolle was 10, his father, a union electrician, died of a heart attack, leaving behind a cherished 1967 paperback edition of *The Lord of the Rings* and a copy of the Dungeons & Dragons rule set. All through high school, on through his four-year union apprenticeship, and well into his first years as a journeyman carpenter, Stolle spent vast stretches of his free time immersed in the intricacies of D&D, Warhammer, Battletech, and other tabletop role-playing and strategy games.

Then came Ultima Online. The first successful MMO, UO went live in September 1997, and by December Stolle had a character, a blacksmith he called Nils Hansen. The business of bettering Nils's lot in life quickly came to absorb him more intensely than any game ever had. In short order, he added two other characters: an archer, who went out hunting when Nils needed hides, and a mage, who cooked up potions to make the archer a better hunter. "I had everybody interlocked so that they totally supported one another," Stolle said. And to give this little team a base of operations—a place to store equipment, basically—he paid about 40,000 gold pieces for a deed permitting him to build a small house. He found a nice, secluded spot in northern Britannia, placed his cursor there, and double-clicked the building into existence.

The house worked out fine for a while, but in a game whose essence is accumulation, no house stays big enough for long. Stolle's trio needed new digs, and soon. The hitch at this point in Britannia's history, however, was that real estate was acutely hard to come by. Deeds were still available, but there was nowhere left to build. The number of homeless was rising, the prices of existing houses were rising even faster, and the natives were getting restless. At last, the game designers announced a solution—a whole new continent was being added to the map.

Stolle started preparing for the inevitable land rush months before it happened. He scrimped and saved, sold his house for 180,000 gold pieces, and finally had enough to buy a deed for the third-largest class of house in the game, the so-called large tower.

On the night the new continent's housing market was set to open, Stolle showed up early at a spot he had scouted out previously, and found twelve players already there. No one knew exactly when the zero hour was, so Stolle and the others just kept clicking on the site, each hoping to be the first to hit it when the time came.

"It was so stressful," Stolle recalled. "You're sitting there, you double-click the deed once and then click on the spot. And so I did this for four hours, standing in one place." Finally, at about one in the morning, the housing option switched on, and as a couple thousand build commands went through at once, the machine that was processing it all swooned under the load. "The server message pops up, and everything just freezes. And I'm still clicking. Even though nothing's happening, I'm still clicking—boom, boom, boom. For like ten minutes, everything's frozen. You see people kind of disappearing here and there. And then it starts to let up. And a tower appears! Nobody knows for sure whose it is. Guys are like, 'Whose is it? Did I get it?' I double-clicked on it, and I couldn't tell. And so then I double-clicked again—and there was my key to the tower."

Just like that. In a single clock cycle and a double mouse-click, Stolle had built himself a real nice spread.

But of course there was more to it than that. In addition to the four hours of premature clicking, Stolle had had to come up with the money for the deed. To get the money, he had had to sell his old house. To get that house in the first place, he'd had to spend hours crafting virtual broadswords and plate mail and the like to sell to a steady clientele of about three dozen fellow players. To attract and keep that clientele, he'd had to bring Nils Hansen's blacksmithing skills up to the highest level possible. To reach that level, Stolle had spent six solid months doing nothing but smithing: He had clicked on hillsides to mine metal ore, he had headed to a forge to click the ore into ingots, he had clicked again to turn the ingots into

weapons and armor, and then he had headed back to the hills to start the process all over again, each time raising Nils's skill level some tiny fraction of a percentage point, inching him just slightly closer to the distant goal of one hundred points and the illustrious title of Grandmaster Blacksmith.

Take a moment now to pause, step back, and consider just what was going on here: Every day, month after month, a man was coming home from a full day of bone-jarringly repetitive work with hammer and nails to put in a full night of finger-numbingly repetitive work with "hammer" and "anvil"—and paying for the privilege. When I asked Stolle to make sense of this, he had a ready answer: "Well, it's not work if you enjoy it."

Which of course begs the question: Why would anyone enjoy it?

The psychologist Mihaly Csikszentmihalyi has done thousands of interviews over several decades in an effort to understand how people achieve and maintain what is sometimes called happiness. One of the people he interviewed is an assembly-line worker whose job requires him to repeat one simple task all day long, taking no longer than forty-three seconds each time he performs it, for a total of almost six hundred times a day. "Most people would grow tired of such work very soon," Csikszentmihalyi writes, with some understatement. "But [this man] has been at this job for over five years, and he still enjoys it." Why? Because when he is on the job, he thinks of only one thing: how to get better at it. He watches his performance times like a sprinter training for an Olympic match, analyzing his moves, his tools, shaving a few seconds off his record whenever he can. After five years on the job, his best day's average is down to twenty-eight seconds per operation, and whenever he performs close to that, his work becomes, in Csikszentmihalyi's description, "so enthralling it is almost painful for him to slow down."

"It's better than anything else," the worker himself reports. "It's a whole lot better than watching TV."

In Csikszentmihalyi's analysis, what this man regularly experiences at work is a condition called "flow"—an exhilarating and uniquely fulfilling convergence of attention and purpose. "An activity that produces such experiences is so gratifying that people are willing to do it for its own sake," he writes, "with little concern for what they will get out of it, even when it is difficult, or dangerous." And no wonder. Flow, as described by Csikszentmihalyi and his informants, is a trip: "Concentration is so intense that there is no attention left over to think about anything irrelevant, or to worry about problems. Self-consciousness disappears, and the sense of time becomes distorted." There's a touch of mysticism in the concept—Csikszentmihalyi himself suggests that Zen monks were onto it before he was—but in fact, he insists, nearly everyone experiences it to greater or lesser degrees at various points in life, and it's not too hard to isolate the conditions that give rise to it. Above all, flow depends on "a sense that one's skills are adequate to the challenges at hand"—assuring we are neither overwhelmed nor under-stimulated by the tasks we face—and on the context of "a goal-directed, rule-bound action system that provides clear clues as to how well one is performing."

Given how closely these conditions match the description of a well-designed game, it's no surprise Csikszentmihalyi focused initially on players of one sort or another—chess masters, mountain climbers, music makers—as the paradigm of human consciousness in flow. The surprise came later, when he discovered that *workers*, too, in almost every sort of occupation, are just as often in flow's grip. In fact, one study, in which he asked more than one hundred people to record the quality and circumstances of their everyday experience at randomly scheduled intervals, found that the respondents were "in flow" *more* frequently at work than at leisure. Three times more frequently, to be precise. "So much for the dichotomy of play and work," Csikszentmihalyi remarked.

And yet, there is another, equally curious aspect of his findings that points in a somewhat different direction. For though the research finds flow happening more often on the job than anywhere else, it turns out also to be true that workers, even in the very moment of reporting themselves immersed in every known condition and symptom of flow, will also typically say that they would rather—in that same moment—be away from work than at it. Flow alone, in other words, does not suffice to turn work into play. And while it may be true, as Csikszentmihalyi seems to suggest, that flow's indifference to the border between what we call work and play confirms that the border is in fact a fiction, that hardly renders the fiction meaningless. Nor does it cancel the seductive, motivating power that the category of play derives from that fiction—a power work somehow can't duplicate and flow, all by itself, can't quite account for.

And finally, if we really want to understand what made Troy Stolle do it—what drove him through the long, mouse-clicking nights of his career as a Britannian blacksmith—then we will definitely have to look beyond the Zen placidities of flow. As sociologist T. L. Taylor argues in *Play Between Worlds*, her illuminating ethnographic study of EverQuest players, "flow" only partially captures the range of mindstates typical of MMO play, not all of them especially pretty. Even "play" itself comes in for a nearly fatal stretching of its definition here, particularly among that class of MMO aficionados known as power players, the geeks among the geeks, whose obsessions with game statistics and maximally efficient skill gains lead fellow players to deride them as humorless drones who couldn't possibly be enjoying themselves.

Not that anyone in MMO-land gets away clean from the embrace of joyless "fun." Even the most purely social players, for whom the game is all about camaraderie and chitchat, will at some point or another feel themselves more obliged than eager to show up and put in an appearance. The hardcore role-players will wake up one day feeling, like a dead weight on their chest, the strain of endless texting in stilted Renaissance Faire English—yet dutifully go on theeing and thouing all the same. And everyone, of course, must make a separate peace with the profound ambivalence of the "grind": the tantalizing, enervating treadmill of monster bashing, which promises a never-ending daily burst of experience points, gold, loot, and other tokens of self improvement but all too often leaves you feeling sick, unhinged, and inexplicably compelled, at the end of a long, late night, to try for just one more mongbat or ogre lord or lizardman when every rational fiber in your body is cringing at the sound of dawn's first songbirds tweeting outside the window.

"Well, it's not work if you enjoy it."

True enough. The part that Stolle apparently forgot to mention, though, is that somehow, through some obscure mutation of postindustrial human consciousness, it's still play even when you sort of hate it.

And if that sounds plain nuts to you, don't worry: When even a sophisticated conceptual framework like flow theory can't entirely make sense of it, how should you?

Perhaps a slight adjustment of the framework, though, might help. The perspective of psychology, after all—flow theory's disciplinary home base—is not the only angle we could approach the question from. And while it's true no other human science is as centrally preoccupied with the questions of personal desire, motivation, and evaluation that concern us here, there is one that comes close: economics.

Modern economics, according to its textbook definition, studies the allocation of resources under conditions of scarcity. More colloquially, you could say it's about the ways people try to get what they need in a world where they can't always get what they want. Either way, it's not called the dismal science for nothing: Deprivation, solidly embedded in the discipline's founding assumptions, literally defines it.

In this, contemporary economics echoes a founding assumption of Western culture itself, as ancient and as rooted as the book of Genesis, which defines the human condition as a fall from leisure and plenty into scarcity and work. We've been dreaming of the garden ever since. Throughout the rich Western tradition of utopian thought, the most desirable of all possible worlds has typically been imagined as a realm devoid of scarcity. Pie in the sky, manna from heaven, the land of milk and honey: All are shorthand for places or moments of limitless abundance and ease. And though the occasional long-haired visionary has insisted that these utopias might be found or built on planet Earth, the rest of us have by and large accepted that their only place is in our wishful thoughts.

Recently, however, a loose conspiracy of visionaries (mostly long-haired, as it happens, albeit unusually well-funded) created an earthly environment that fits the bill more closely than most. With its effortlessly reproducible wealth of data and light-speed transcendence of geography and time, the Internet, from the start, was rumored to be a place where scarcity had no place. And as anybody in the record business or otherwise dependent on certain scarcities of information for a living can tell you, this rumor has proved in a bewildering variety of ways to be true.

But in certain realms of the emerging online universe—and in some ways just as bewilderingly—scarcity has thrived. In particular, when people have used the Internet not just to document and reflect on the world we live in, but to re-create and redesign it, they've discovered that worlds of limitless abundance and ease aren't necessarily as attractive in fact as they are in dreams. Given the endless malleability of the digital medium, a virtual world can in principle simulate any improvement on the real one imaginable, and not surprisingly, many of the Internet's earliest virtual worlds tried hard to do just that. In commercial, graphics-intensive spaces like World Inc.'s Worlds Away and Time Warner's The Palace, designers erased constraints long considered to be among the real world's most regrettable flaws: Users could fly, could duplicate objects at will, could generally get whatever they needed from the world without having to do much more than hang out socializing. And sure, people liked these places—who wouldn't? But in the end, the worlds they actually wanted to be in—badly enough to pay an entrance fee—were the ones that made the digital necessities almost maddeningly difficult to come by. All else being equal, in other words, the addictive, highly profitable appeal of MMOs suggests that people will choose the world that constrains them over the one that sets them free.

And economically speaking, that too is plain nuts. It was Edward Castronova, the Adam Smith of Ever-Quest, who first arrived at this conclusion. As the first economist to look seriously at virtual worlds, he was naturally puzzled by their mute refusal to take his discipline's most cherished truth very seriously at all. Scarcity, in traditional economics, is a necessary evil, but it is above all an evil. Whatever stands between people and the things they want, whatever constrains them, is a bad thing. Conversely, whatever minimizes that constraint is a good thing—and typically worth paying good money for. So why were so many people now doing exactly the opposite, paying fifteen bucks a month to plow through the infinite constraints of MMOs?

Castronova identified this question as a special case—a peculiarly suggestive one, it turns out—of a broader problem he called the "puzzle of puzzles." The puzzle of puzzles, he wrote, is the first challenge facing any economic theory of games, which arises "primarily because economics is constructed from a model of human behaviour that asserts a universal conflict between our ends and our means." Consider, on the one hand, a jigsaw puzzle with 900 billion pieces, which proposes an end beyond any person's means, and on the other, a puzzle with only two pieces, which annihilates any distance whatsoever from means to end. In the world according to economic theory, the two-piece puzzle always gives better bang for buck—beating any other kind of puzzle, in fact, since none can claim more thoroughly to resolve the conflict between ends and means. Yet in the real world, as it shouldn't take a Milton Bradley executive to explain, both the two-piece and the 900-billion-piece are equally unmarketable.

As a technical matter, this riddle isn't hard to solve. Conventional economics can be tweaked to recognize the entertainment value in a certain degree of constraint; equations can even be written to compute that value (let $S = aR - b[C - W]^2$, Castronova helpfully suggests). But on a more philosophical level, the puzzle of puzzles can't really be unraveled without also tugging hard, finally, on the thread that holds mainstream economic thought together. As long as games remain closed and relatively simple systems, as they have throughout most of history, it's easy to dismiss their curious embrace of constraint as a mere exception to the economic rule. But once games start to take on the complex shape of worlds and yet maintain their power to amuse and obsess us, you have to wonder: Could it be that scarcity is not so much a necessary evil as an economic good? Could it be that the real world's never-ending abundance of scarcity has prevented us from recognizing, until now, that we've actually developed a taste for the stuff?

Well, why not? In an atmosphere of oxygen, our bodies learned to breathe; in a world of scarcity, the soul might just as likely learn to need the universal obstacle to its desires—just maybe not, you know, so damn much of it. This, at any rate, is the lesson Castronova derives from the puzzle of puzzles, and more specifically, from the puzzle of virtual scarcity. "What we're learning is that scarcity itself is an essential variable," he writes. "We just haven't needed to worry about it before. Thanks to God, the Man, or whoever's running this show, we're used to taking scarcity for granted. The emergence of virtual communities means that we have to make it explicit."

And whether or not this lesson ultimately makes Troy Stolle's nightly reenactments of his daily grind seem any less perverse, it should at least make the fact that I can log on to eBay this minute and buy 100,000 imaginary iron ingots for $7.99 seem not only a little less improbable but just about inevitable. Economic theory tells us, after all, that scarcity breeds markets. And markets will seep like gas through any boundary that gives them the slightest opening—never mind a line as porous as the one between real and make-believe.

Or as Castronova had explained to me the day I met him, months before I'd even heard of Stolle's tower: "The minute you hardwire constraints into a virtual world, the economy emerges. One-trillionth of a second later is when that economy starts interacting with ours."

The Proteus Effect: The Effect of Transformed Self-Representation on Behavior

Nick Yee

Jeremy Bailenson

The notion of transforming our appearances permeates our culture. On the one hand, minor alterations such as haircuts, make-up, and dressing up are seen as socially acceptable, if not socially desirable. On the other hand, the ability to truly transform oneself has been regarded in myths and legends as both dangerous and powerful. Consider for example werewolves and vampires from Europe, the kitsune (foxes that can take on human form) from Japan, the god Loki from Norse mythology, and the god Proteus from Greek mythology. The Greek god Proteus is notable for being the origin of the adjective "protean" - the ability to take on many different self representations. And while extreme self-transformations are expensive (e.g., cosmetic surgery) or difficult to perform (e.g., gender reassignment surgery) in real life, nowhere is self-representation more flexible and simple to transform than in virtual environments where users can choose or customize their own *avatars* - digital representations of themselves. For example, the documentation for the online social world *Second Life* notes that "using over 150 unique sliders, they can change everything from their foot size to their eye color to the cut of their shirt" (Labs, 2006). In other words, the mutability of our self-representations in online environments is a fundamental aspect of what it means to have a virtual identity (Turkle, 1995).

Even though the plasticity of our self-representations is an important part of our online identities, the quantitative research in computer-mediated communication (CMC) has tended to focus instead on the impact of technical affordances on social interaction in online environments. For example, it has been argued that lack of social presence (Hiltz, Johnson, & Turoff, 1986; Short, Williams, & Christie, 1976) or the lack of social cues (Culnan & Markus, 1987; Kiesler, Siegel, & McGuire, 1984) creates an impoverished social environment, while others have shown that relationships develop slower in CMC but are not impoverished in the long term (Walther, 1996; Walther, Anderson, & Park, 1994). Other research has looked at how the narrow communication channels in CMC impacts impression formation (Hancock & Dunham, 2001; Jacobson, 1999; Trevino & Webster, 1992; Walther, Slovacek, & Tidwell, 2001). And while there has been research on self-representation in online environments, the focus has been on the impact of anonymity and authenticity (Anonymous, 1998; Flanagin, Tiyaamornwong, O'Connor, & Seibold, 2002; Jarvenpaa & Leidner, 1998; Postmes & Spears, 2002) - in other words, the gap between the real and virtual self and how that difference changes social interactions. In the current work, we were instead interested in exploring how our avatars change how we behave online. As we change our self-representations, do our self-representations change our behaviors in turn? As we choose or create our avatars online and use them in a social context, how might our new self-representations change how we interact with others? Thus, we were interested in the impact of our actual self-representations on our behaviors in virtual environments rather than the effects of anonymity or authenticity.

Behavioral Confirmation

There is good reason to believe that our avatars change how we interact with others. Behavioral confirmation offers one potential pathway for this change. Behavioral confirmation is the process whereby the expectations of one person (typically referred to as the *perceiver*) cause another person (typically referred to as the *target*) to behave in ways that confirm the perceiver's expectations (Snyder, Tanke, & Berscheid, 1977). In the seminal study by Snyder and colleagues (1977), male and female undergraduate students interacted over a telephone. Male perceivers who believed that a female target was attractive caused her to behave in a more charming and friendly manner regardless of how attractive the target actually was. Thus, in an online environment, a perceiver interacting with a target who is using an attractive avatar may cause the target to behave in a more friendly and charming manner. In fact, the study by Snyder and colleagues itself occurred in a mediated context (i.e., over the telephone). It is important to note that the source of behavioral change from the effects of behavioral confirmation stem from the perceiver rather than the target. It is the perceiver's behavior that in turn causes a change in the target's behavior.

Self-Perception Theory and Deindividuation Theory

Behavioral confirmation provides one potential pathway for avatars to change how a person behaves online, but might our avatars change how we behave independent of how others perceive us? When given an attractive avatar, does a user become more friendly and sociable regardless of how others interact with them? Another line of research suggests a potential explanation for why this might occur. Bem (1972) has argued that people observe their own behaviors to understand what attitudes may have caused them (i.e., self-perception theory). For example, people given extrinsic rewards to do something they already enjoy doing are more likely to view the behavior as less intrinsically appealing (i.e., the overjustification effect) because this is what an impartial observer would have concluded as well. Other researchers have shown the far-reaching implications of this theory. In Valins' study (1966), when participants were made to believe their heartbeat had increased while viewing a photograph of a person, they came to believe the person in the photograph was more attractive. In Frank and Gilovich's study (1988), subjects that wore black uniforms behaved more aggressively than subjects in white uniforms. According to Frank and Gilovich, wearing a black uniform is a behavior that the subjects used to infer their own dispositions - "Just as observers see those in black uniforms as tough, mean, and aggressive, so too does the person wearing that uniform" (pg. 83). The subjects then adhere to this new identity by behaving more aggressively. And finally, this effect has been replicated more recently in a digital environment, where users given avatars in a black robe expressed a higher desire to commit anti-social behaviors than users given avatars in a white robe (Merola, Penas, & Hancock, 2006).

Another line of research has shown that the impact of identity cues is particularly strong when people are deindividuated. Zimbardo (1969) originally used deindividuation theory to argue that urban or crowded areas cause deindividuation which leads to antisocial behavior, however it has also been shown that deindividuation can lead to affiliative behavior as well (Gergen, Gergen, & Barton, 1973). When dyads were placed in a darkened room for an hour, many deliberately touched or hugged the other person. On the other hand, dyads in the fully-lit room talked politely and did not engage in physical contact. Thus, the effects of deindividuation are not necessarily anti-social. The argument that deindividuation can lead to both pro-social and anti-social behavior has also been demonstrated in another well-known study. In a teacher- learner paradigm with electric shock as punishment, subjects in costumes that resembled Ku Klux Klan robes delivered significantly longer shocks than subjects in nurse uniforms (Johnson & Downing, 1979). It was also found that these effects were stronger when subjects were made anonymous in the study. Thus, deindividuation does not necessarily always lead to anti-social behavior as Zimbardo originally argued, but may in fact cause a greater reliance on identity cues whether they are anti-social or pro-social.

In the computer-mediated communication literature, the Social Identity Model of Deindividuation Effects (Postmes, Spears, & Lea, 1998; Spears & Lea, 1994) argued that factors that lead to deindividuation, such as anonymity, might thus reinforce group salience and conformity to group norms. In this light, deindividuation does not, in and of itself, always lead to anti-normative behavior, but rather, behavioral changes depend on the local group norms (Postmes, Spears, & Lea, 2000). More importantly, behavior that is typically seen as anti- normative, such as flaming on message boards (Lea, O'Shea, & Spears, 1992), may in fact turn out to be normative and expected in particular contexts (Postmes et al., 1998).

The Proteus Effect

Online environments that afford anonymity are like digital versions of a darkened room where deindividuation might occur, and indeed, many researchers have suggested that deindividuation occurs online due to anonymity or reduced social cues (Kiesler et al., 1984; McKenna & Rargh, 2000). And in online environments, the avatar is not simply a uniform that is worn, the avatar is our entire self-representation. Whereas the uniform is one of many identity cues in the studies mentioned earlier, the avatar is the primary identity cue in online environments. Thus, we might expect that our avatars have a significant impact on how we behave online. Users who are deindividuated in online environments may adhere to a new identity that is inferred from their avatars. And in the same way that subjects in black uniforms conform to a more aggressive identity, users in online environments may conform to the expectations and stereotypes of the identity of their avatars. Or more precisely, in line with self-perception theory, they conform to the behavior that they believe others would expect them to have. We term this the Proteus Effect.

While the Proteus Effect is similar to SIDE theory, there are several important theoretical differences. Most importantly, SIDE theory emphasizes conformity to local group norms (e.g., becoming more hostile on a hostile message board). On the other hand, the Proteus Effect emphasizes conformity to individual identity cues (e.g., becoming friendlier in an attractive avatar). Thus, theoretically, it would also be possible to pit one against the other - i.e., having an attractive avatar on a hostile message board. We would also argue that having an attribute (e.g., "being attractive") is conceptually different from being amongst a group of individuals who have that attribute (e.g., "being in a group of attractive people"), while SIDE theory literature tends to conflate the two. Thus, in a situation where person A in a black uniform interacts with person B in a white uniform, SIDE theory might predict that the social identity of person A would default to the black uniform (i.e., become more aggressive) or the combined colors of the group in question– in other words, gray (i.e., remain neutral). The Proteus Effect would only predict the former. Another point of differentiation is that while the SIDE theory operates on the basis of an existing local group and its social norms, the Proteus Effect should operate even when the user is alone. This is because self-perception theory isn't predicated on the actual presence of other people, but simply that a person evaluates him or herself from a third-person perspective (i.e., an imagined third party).

Collaborative Virtual Environments and Transformed Social Interaction

In designing of our studies, it was crucial that we isolate the impact of the Proteus Effect from that of behavioral confirmation. If participants were perceived to be attractive and believed themselves to be attractive at the same time, it would be impossible for us to claim that the Proteus Effect occurred independent of behavioral confirmation. To isolate the potential effect of the Proteus Effect, we employed a novel methodological paradigm. In the current set of studies, we utilized Collaborative Virtual Environments (CVEs, see Normand et al., 1999) to study the effects of the Proteus Effect. CVEs are communication systems in which multiple interactants share the same three-dimensional digital space despite occupying remote physical locations. In a CVE, immersive virtual environment technology monitors the movements and behaviors of individual interactants and renders those behaviors within the CVE via avatars. These digital representations are tracked naturalistically by optical sensors, mechanical devices, and cameras. Because these avatars are constantly redrawn for each user during interaction, unique possibilities for social interaction emerge (Loomis, Blascovich, & Beall, 1999; Blascovich et al., 2002).

Unlike telephone conversations and videoconferences, the physical appearance and behavioral actions of avatars can be systematically filtered in immersive CVEs idiosyncratically for other interactants, amplifying or suppressing features and nonverbal signals in real-time for strategic purposes. Theoretically, these transformations should impact interactants' persuasive and instructional abilities. Previously, we outlined a theoretical framework for such strategic filtering of communicative behaviors called *Transformed Social Interaction* (Bailenson, Beall, Blascovich, Loomis, & Turk, 2005). In a CVE, every user perceives their own digital rendering of the world and each other and these renderings need not be congruent. In other words, the target may perceive his or her own avatar as being attractive while the perceiver sees the target as being unattractive.

Previous work on transformed social interaction has demonstrated quite resoundingly that changing one's representation has large implications on other's in terms of social influence (Bailenson, 2006). In other words, transforming Avatar A strategically causes Avatar B to behave consistently with the representation of Avatar A (as opposed to the actual representation of Avatar A). In the current set of studies, this decoupling of representation allowed us to test a separate question relating to transforming a representation. Instead of seeing the strategic outcome of a transformation, we examined whether our changes in self-representations - independent of how others perceive us - cause the people behind the avatars to behave differently.

Overview of Studies and Hypotheses

In the current work, we conducted two experimental studies to explore the Proteus Effect. Participants interacted with a confederate's avatar in a virtual reality (VR) environment. In the first study, we manipulated the attractiveness of the participant's avatar while the confederate was blind to condition. Studies have shown that attractive individuals are perceived to possess a constellation of positive traits (Dion, Rerscheid, & Walster, 1972), and are evaluated more favorably by jurors in courtrooms (Friend & Vinson, 1974).

Interpersonal Distance

According to nonverbal expectancy violations theory (Burgoon, 1978), when attractive individuals violate nonverbal expectancies, such as moving too close to someone, the positive valence that is created can be socially advantageous (Burgoon & Walther, 1990; Burgoon, Walther, & Raesler, 1992). Given that attractive individuals have higher confidence (Langlois et al., 2000), we hypothesized that:

H1: Participants in the attractive condition walk closer to the confederate than the participants in the unattractive condition.

Self-Disclosure

Friendliness was one of the measures used in Snyder, Tanke, and Berscheid's original study (1977), and in this study we used self-disclosure as a behavioral operationalization. Because attractive individuals tend to be more extraverted and more friendly (Langlois et al., 2000), we hypothesized that.

H2 Participants in the attractive condition would exhibit higher self-disclosure and present more pieces of information about themselves than participants in the unattractive condition.

In the second study, we manipulated the height of the participant's avatar again with the confederate blind to the condition. Similar to the attractiveness literature, taller people are perceived to be more competent (Young & French, 1996), more desirable as romantic partners (Freedman, 1979; Harrison & Saeed, 1977), and more likely to emerge as leaders (Stogdill, 1948). In this study, we implemented a negotiation task to best gauge confidence.

H2 Participants in taller avatars would behave in a more confident manner and negotiate more aggressively than participants in shorter avatars.

Experiment One

Design

In a between-subjects design, participants were randomly assigned to have an avatar with an attractive or unattractive face of his or her own gender and then interact with a confederate. We followed the paradigm in the study by Snyder and colleagues (1977) and always used a confederate of the opposite gender. The confederate was blind to the attractiveness condition such that the participant's avatar appeared to the confederate with an untextured face - one which was structurally human but left uncolored.

Participants

Thirty-two undergraduate students (16 men and 16 women) participated in the study for course credit.

Materials
Facial Attractiveness Pretest

We ran a pretest to get subjective determinations of attractive and unattractive faces (for the participants), and also average-attractiveness faces (for the confederates). To minimize the chances that our findings would be driven by idiosyncrasies of a particular face, we chose two faces in each of these three attractiveness conditions. Thus, there were two attractive faces, two unattractive faces, and two average faces for each gender. In total, we used 12 faces in the study.

To generate these 12 faces, digital photographs of 34 undergraduate students (17 male and 17 female) from a different academic institution from the main study were used in a pretest. The chances of participant recognition of these faces were thus minimized. To reduce other variations in facial features, only Caucasians were used in the pretest[1]. Frontal and profile photographs of these 34 undergraduate students were converted into digital, three-dimensional head busts using 3DMeNow software. These three-dimensional head busts were then converted into Vizard 2.17 models, our CVE platform, and attached to generic male and female bodies. Finally, a frontal and three-quarter screenshot of every face was taken (see Figure 1). Thus, altogether, 68 screenshots were generated.

Fourteen undergraduates from a separate subject population from the main study used a web-based survey to rate the attractiveness of every screenshot's face on a unipolar 7-point fully-labeled construct-specific scale (from "Not Attractive At All" to "Extremely Attractive"). The frontal and three-quarter screenshot of every face were thus rated separately. Each screenshot was shown by itself and the order of faces was uniquely randomized for every rater.

The ratings of the frontal and three-quarter image of every face were averaged. Then six faces were selected for each gender, where the two attractive faces were each rated as significantly more attractive than the two average faces, and the two average faces were each rated as significantly more attractive than the two unattractive faces. All pair-wise t-tests had a p-value less than .05 (dfs = 26). The 12 faces used in the study are shown in Figure 1. The means and standard deviations of their attractiveness ratings are shown in Table 7.1. In the entire sample of faces we pretested, the mean attractiveness was

Table 7.1 Means and Standard Deviations of Attractiveness Ratings for Avatar Faces.

Attractiveness	Female		Male	
	Face 1 *M (SD)*	Face 2 *M (SD)*	Face 1 *M (SD)*	Face 2 *M (SD)*
High	5.50 (1.35)	4.32 (1.25)	4.64 (1.19)	4.04 (1.10)
Medium	3.39 (1.47)	3.50 (1.40)	3.11 (1.34)	2.93 (1.65)
Low	2.29 (1.15)	1.18 (0.55)	1.75 (1.11)	1.21 (0.50)

3.09 with a standard deviation of 1.30. The faces we chose for the high attractiveness condition had a mean of 4.63 and a standard deviation of 1.22, while the faces in the low attractiveness condition had a mean of 1.61 and a standard deviation of 0.83. Thus, our faces in the high and low attractiveness conditions varied from the average by about one standard deviation.

The Physical Lab Setting

The lab consisted of two rooms with an open doorway. In the room where the study took place, a black curtain divided the room. To ensure that confederates and participants were not biased by the attractiveness each other's real faces, confederates stayed behind this black curtain until the virtual reality interaction began and thus never saw the participant's real face and vice versa.

The Virtual Setting

The virtual setting was a white room that had the same exact dimensions as the physical room participants were in (see Figure 2). Two meters behind the participant was a *virtual mirror* that reflected the head orientation (rotations along pitch, yaw, and roll) and body translation (translation on X, Y, and Z) of the participant with the designated face (See Figure 2). Thus, the mirror image tracked and reflected six degrees of freedom such that when the participant moved in physical space, his or her avatar moved in perfect synchrony in the mirror. The confederate's avatar was located 5 meters in front of the participant, facing the participant, and remained invisible until the conversational portion of the experiment began. The confederate's avatar also had an automated blink animation based on human blinking behavior and lip movement that matched the volume of the confederate's speech.

Apparatus

Perspectively-correct stereoscopic images were rendered at an average frame rate of 60 Hz. The simulated viewpoint was continually updated as a function of the participants' head movements, which were tracked by a three-axis orientation sensing system. The position of the participant along the x, y, and z planes were tracked via an optical tracking system. Participants wore an nVisor SX head-mounted display (HMD) that featured dual 1280 horizontal by 1024 vertical pixel resolution panels that refreshed at 60 Hz. See Figure 2 for equipment setup.

Procedure

Three researcher assistants were present during each trial - the lead research assistant, the male confederate and the female confederate. The confederate in the trial was always the opposite gender of the participant and remained blind to condition. Participants were told that the goal of the experiment was to study social interaction in virtual environments and that they would be having a conversation with another person in a virtual environment. Once the virtual world was loaded, participants saw themselves in a room that was exactly the same dimensions as the physical lab room, as depicted in Figure 2.

Participants were then asked by the lead research assistant to turn around 180 degrees and asked to verify that they saw a mirror in front of them. After verbal affirmation, participants were then told that this is how they appeared to others in the virtual room. Several exercises (head-tilting and nodding in front of the mirror) were used to make sure participants had enough time to observe their avatars' faces. Every participant was thus exposed to the designated face for between 60 to 75 seconds.

Participants were then asked to turn back around to face the front (i.e., their original orientation). Slightly ahead of time, the lead research assistant had triggered the program to make the confederate's avatar visible to the participant in the virtual world. The lead research assistant then introduced the confederate to the participant. The confederate followed a strict script that was displayed in their HMD so they could follow the specific verbal procedures while interacting with the participant inside the CVE. Their behaviors were not scripted and they were instructed to use natural head movements when interacting with the participant. First, participants were greeted and asked to walk closer to the confederate. When the participant stopped or asked whether the distance was close enough, the confederate would then ask them to move a little closer. The confederate then asked the participants to introduce themselves. When the participants stopped or asked whether what they said was enough, the confederate asked the participants to say a little more. If the participants ever asked the confederate any other question, the confederate would reply with "I'm sorry. I can't answer that question. Let's continue".

Measures

Interpersonal Distance

The distance between the participant and the confederate was automatically tracked by the VR system. Previous research has validated the interpersonal distance measure inside CVEs (Railenson, Rlascovich, Reall, & Loomis, 2003).

Self-Disclosure

The amount of self-disclosure was measured by counting the number of pieces of information that participants gave during the two introduction prompts near the beginning of the conversational portion of the study (e.g., "Tell me a little bit about yourself' and "Tell me a little more"). Two blind coders were asked to count the number of pieces of information given by the participants. Every tape recording was coded by two blind coders and the coder inter-reliability was .84.

Results and Discussion

To ensure that our attractiveness manipulation was not so obvious as to elicit strong demand characteristics, we asked all participants to write a paragraph and guess the intent of the experiment. Two coders blind to experimental condition read through these responses. Most participants guessed that the goal was to study conversational dynamics in VR as compared with face-to-face interactions. According to both coders, no participant mentioned attractiveness or mentioned that they thought the avatar's attractiveness was manipulated in the study.

Interpersonal Distance

We ran a t-test with attractiveness as the between-subject variable[2] and the final distance as the dependent variable. Participants in the attractive condition walked significantly closer to the confederate ($M = 0.98$, $SD = 0.36$) than participants in the unattractive condition ($M = 1.74$, $SD = 1.20$), $t[30] = -2.42$, $p = .02$, $d = .40$.

Self-Disclosure

We performed a t-test using attractiveness as the between-subject variable and the self-disclosure count as the dependent variable. Participants in the attractive condition revealed significantly more pieces of information ($M = 7.19$, $SD = 2.77$) than participants in the unattractive condition ($M = 5.42$, $SD = 1.56$), $t[30] = 2.23$, $p = .03$, $d = .38$.

The results from the first experiment provided support for the Proteus Effect - that our self-representations shape our behaviors in turn. Participants in the attractive condition were willing to move closer to the confederate and disclosed more information to the confederate than participants in the unattractive condition. More importantly, this effect was measurable and significant immediately after only a brief exposure to the mirror task. The effect size in the current study—interpersonal distances changes of almost a meter—are quite large, much more so than effects found in previous studies on interpersonal distance (Bailenson, Blascovich, Beall, & Loomis, 2003) which were less than 15 centimeters. The reason the current manipulation produced such a drastic effect is most likely due to the personal nature of the social interaction.

Experiment Two

In the second experiment, we replicated the Proteus Effect with another manipulation - height. Because height is more often associated with self-esteem and competence rather than friendliness (Young & French, 1996), we employed a different behavioral measure. Instead of a proximity and self-disclosure task, a negotiation task - the "ultimatum game" (Forsythe, Horowitz, Savin, & Sefton, 1994) - was used as a behavioral measure of confidence. In the ultimatum game, two individuals take turns to decide how a pool of money should be split between the two of them. One individual makes the split and the other must choose to either accept or reject the split. If the split is accepted, the money is shared accordingly. If the split is rejected, neither of them gets the money. We hypothesized that participants with taller avatars would be more confident and be more willing to make unfair splits than participants in shorter avatars.

Design

In a between-subjects design, participants were randomly assigned to have an avatar that was shorter, taller or the same height as a confederate who was of the opposite gender. We relied on demographic data to assign the base height and height differences in the study. From the NHANES 2003-2004 data set (NCHS, 2004), we calculated the mean and standard deviation of height among Caucasians aged 18 to 22 in the US population. The mean height was 171.5 cm (or 5 feet and 7.5 inches) with a standard deviation of 10.2 cm. While men and women have different average heights, we decided to use the same base height across all conditions to avoid confounding height with gender in the experimental design. In our study, the confederate had a base height of 172 cm. In the short condition, participants were 10 cm shorter than the confederate. In the tall condition, participants were 10 cm taller than the confederate. In the same height condition, participants were the same height as the confederate. Thus the size of our manipulations in the short and tall conditions were about one standard deviation in height. In our study, the confederate was blind to the height condition and the participant's avatar always appeared to the confederate as the same height[3]. In other words, confederates did not know the experimental condition and always perceived the participant as the same height as themselves.

Participants

Participants were 50 undergraduate students who were paid ten dollars for their participation.

Materials

The physical lab and the virtual setting of Experiment Two were identical to the ones described in Experiment One except there was no mirror in the virtual room.

Apparatus

The apparatus used in Experiment Two was identical to the apparatus described in Experiment One.

Procedure

Three researcher assistants were present during each trial - the lead research assistant, the male confederate and the female confederate. The confederate was always the opposite gender of the participant and was blind to condition. Participants were told that the goal of the experiment was to study social interaction in VR environments and that they would be having a conversation with another person in VR. Once the VR world was loaded, participants saw themselves in a room that was exactly the same dimensions as the physical lab room they were in. The confederate's avatar was visible across the virtual room.

The confederate followed a strict verbal script that was displayed in their HMD. Their behaviors were not scripted and they were instructed to use natural head movements when interacting with the participant. First, participants were greeted by the confederate. The confederate then asked the participants to introduce themselves. After the introductory phase, the lead research assistant explained the money sharing task. A hypothetical pool of $100 was to be split between the confederate and the participant. One of the two would designate a split. The other would either accept or reject the split. If the split was accepted, the money would be shared accordingly. If the split was rejected, neither would receive any money. The participant was told there would be four rounds of this game and that the lead research assistant would alternate as to who would be making the split for each round.

The participant always designated the split in the first and third rounds. The confederate was instructed to always accept a split as long as it did not exceed $90 in favor of the participant. The confederate always designated a split of 50/50 in the second round and 75/25 (in the confederate's favor) in the fourth round. These two ratios were chosen to represent a fair and unfair split. After the money sharing task, the participant was taken out of the virtual setting.

Measures
Monetary Splits

The split offers were recorded by the research assistant during the negotiation task.

Results and Discussion

To ensure that our height manipulation was not so obvious as to elicit strong demand characteristics, we asked all participants to guess the intent of the experiment. Two coders blind to condition read through the responses. Most participants guessed that the goal was to study conversational dynamics in virtual reality as compared with face-to-face interactions. According to both coders, no participant mentioned height or guessed that height was manipulated in the study.

Negotiation Behavior

There were three measures of interest: amount offered by participant in the first round (from hereon referred to as *split one*), amount offered by participant in the third round (from hereon referred to as *split two*), and whether the participant accepted the unfair split by the confederate in the final round (from hereon referred to as *final split*). Three outliers (more than 3 standard deviations from the mean) in split one and split 3 were excluded from analysis. The cutoffs were 88.5 and 84.2 respectively.

We ran an ANOVA with height as the between-subject factor and split one as the dependent variable. The effect of height was not significant ($F[2, 47] = 0.63$, $p = .53$, $\eta^2 = .03$), see Table 7.2.

We then ran an ANOVA with height as the between-subject factor and split 3 as the dependent variable. There was a main effect of height ($F[2, 46] = 5.64$, $p = .006$, $\eta^2 = .20$). A post-hoc test using Tukey's HSD showed that participants in the tall condition split the money significantly more in their own favor ($M = 60.63$, $SD = 6.55$) than participants in the short condition ($M = 52.06$, $SD = 7.30$), $p = .004$. See Table 7.2 for all means and standard deviations of the splits by condition.

Finally, to test the effect of height on the acceptance rate of the final unfair offer, we ran a logistic regression using acceptance rate as the dependent variable and height (recoded short as 1, normal as 2, and tall as 3) as the independent variable. height was a significant predictor of acceptance rate, $X^2(1, N = 50) = 4.41$, $p = .04$. Prediction success for acceptance of the unfair offer was 54% and it was 80% for rejection of the unfair offer. Participants in the short condition were about twice as likely to accept the unfair offer (72%) as participants in the normal (31%) and tall condition (38%).

We were surprised that the effect of height on negotiation did not emerge until the second split. Informal discussion with the research assistants and review of the recordings suggest that many participants were "testing the waters" in the first split, but became more bold in the second split. In any case, the effect of height on the second split was highly significant and suggests that the manipulation of height does affect negotiation behavior, but that these effects may emerge over time.

In summary, our findings from Experiment Two extended the Proteus Effect with a different manipulation. Participants in the tall condition were significantly more likely to offer an unfair split than participants in the normal and short conditions. At the same time, participants in the short condition were significantly more likely to accept an unfair split than participants in the normal and tall condition. Thus, our findings from the negotiation task support the Proteus Effect.

General Discussion

Across different behavioral measures and different representational manipulations, we observed the effect of an altered self-representation on behavior. Participants who had more attractive avatars exhibited increased self-disclosure and were more willing to approach opposite gendered strangers after less than one minute of exposure to their altered avatar. In other words, the attractiveness of their avatars impacted how intimate participants were willing to be with a stranger. In our second study, participants who had taller avatars were more willing to make unfair splits in negotiation tasks than those who had shorter avatars, whereas participants with shorter avatars were more willing to accept unfair offers than those who had taller avatars. Thus, the height of their avatars impacted how confident participants became. These two studies show the dramatic and almost instantaneous effect that avatars have on behavior in digital environments.

In our experimental studies, we purposefully excluded the effect of behavioral confirmation even though it too clearly plays a crucial role in social interactions - both online and offline. The advantage of this exclusion was that it enabled us to isolate the effect of changing an individual's self-representation. The disadvantage is the inability to understand how these changes may unfold in an actual situation where the Proteus Effect interacts with behavioral confirmation. What is striking about the current data is that we demonstrated drastic changes in behavior even though there was absolutely no way for behavioral conformation to occur, as the confederates always were blind to experimental condition. Another limitation was that we were unable to explore the role of choice in the Proteus Effect. In our studies, participants were given avatars rather than being able to choose their own avatar - the typical situation in online environments. However, it bears pointing out that the range of avatar choice in many online environments is not truly diverse. For example, in the social online world *There.com*, users can only create youthful avatars. Old people do not exist in *There*. In other words, there may be many features of our avatars that we actually don't have control over in online environments.

Another limitation in our studies was the lack of a direct manipulation check. Since our theoretical claim is

Table 7.2   The Means and Standard Deviations of Interpersonal Distance and Split One across Height Conditions.

Height	Split One	Split Two	Final Split
Short	54.99 (12.47)	52.06 (7.30)	0.72 (0.46)
Normal	58.69 (15.85)	55.69 (8.10)	0.31 (0.48)
Tall	53.75 (10.25)	60.63 (6.55)	0.38 (0.50)

based partly on self-perception theory, our results would have been more convincing if participants in the attractive condition rated their avatar as indeed more attractive than participants in the unattractive condition. And finally, our reliance on the opposite-gender paradigm may have limited our studies to a certain class of interactional behavior (e.g., with a romantic or sexual tone). It would be interesting to carry out additional studies in same-gender pairings to examine this potential bias.

Future research in this area might focus on several other things. First, the Proteus Effect may generalize to other fundamental aspects of self-representation, such as gender or race. For example, when male participants employ female avatars, they may behave in a more gender-stereotypical manner. Secondly, examining whether or not there are long-term consequences of the Proteus Effect which carry over into the physical world is obviously an important research agenda. Do users who frequently use tall and attractive avatars become more confident and friendly in real life? If so, virtual environments may be an excellent venue for therapeutic purposes. Thirdly, examining the role of choice in the Proteus Effect might reveal that choice either augments or diminishes the effect. Also, while we argued in the theoretical framing that the Proteus Effect could occur even if participants were alone and not in a group setting, this was something we did not directly test for in our experimental designs. It would be interesting to devise similar experiments where participants were not in a group setting.

And finally, we suggest that the most interesting area of research lies in the mismatch of self-representation and how others perceive us. In the traditional behavioral confirmation paradigm, the false assumptions of the perceiver are unknown to the target. Unlike the target-centric paradigm that denies the target of their awareness of how others may stereotype them, we have shown that an individual's false self-concept (i.e., self-stereotyping) has a significant impact on their behavior. More importantly, the false self-concept may override behavioral confirmation. In our studies, participants using attractive avatars became more intimate and friendly with strangers. This initial friendliness may elicit more positive responses from the interactant and lead to a more positive interaction overall. Thus, we hypothesize that the precise reverse of behavioral confirmation - a target's false self-concept causes them to interact with the perceiver in a way such that the perceiver behaves in a way that confirms the target's false self-concept - can occur. The most interesting test of this hypothesis may be to pit the Proteus Effect against behavioral confirmation. In other words, future work should examine an experimental paradigm in which participants believe that they are attractive while other interactants

perceive them as unattractive. A similar research agenda has been proposed by Blascovich and colleagues (Blascovich et al., 2002).

The Proteus Effect is a particularly important theoretical framework in understanding behavior in virtual environments where users are able to choose or customize their avatar's appearances. In our experimental studies, dyads interacted after one interactant had their self-representation manipulated. In virtual communities, thousands of users interact with altered self-representations. In many of these environments, the only avatar choices are youthful, in-shape, and attractive. If having an attractive avatar can increase a person's confidence and their degree of self-disclosure within minutes, then this has substantial implications for users in virtual environments. First, the Proteus Effect may impact behavior on the community level. When thousands of users interact, most of whom have chosen attractive avatars, the virtual community may become more friendly and intimate. This may impact the likelihood of relationship formation online (Parks & Floyd, 1996). As graphical avatars become the dominant mode of self-representation in virtual environments, the Proteus Effect may play a substantial role in encouraging hyper-personal interaction (see Walther, 1996). And second, these behavioral changes may carry over to the physical world. If users spend over 20 hours a week in these environments (Yee, 2006), in an avatar that is tall and attractive, is an equilibrium state reached or do two separate behavioral repertoires emerge?

The set of studies presented in this paper makes clear that our self-representations have a significant and instantaneous impact on our behavior. The appearances of our avatars shape how we interact with others. As we choose our self-representations in virtual environments, our self-representations shape our behaviors in turn. These changes happen not over hours or weeks, but within minutes. Every day, millions of users interact with each other via graphical avatars in real time in online games (Chan & Vorderer, 2006). All of them are using an avatar that differs from their physical appearance. In fact, most of them are using avatars that are attractive, powerful, youthful, and athletic. While most research in CMC has focused on the technical affordances of the medium (lack of social cues, social presence, anonymity, etc.), we argue that theoretical frameworks of self-representation cannot be ignored because choosing who we are is a fundamental aspect of virtual environments. More importantly, who we choose to be in turn shapes how we behave. While avatars are usually construed as something of our own choosing - a one-way process - the fact is that our avatars come to change how we behave.

Notes

1. In the analysis of Experiment One, there was no significant interaction effect with the race of the participant. In Experiment Two, participants do not see their own avatar so this was not an issue.

2. In both studies, the effect of subject gender was not significant, and including this factor in the ANOVA did not change the reported significance of the results.

3. In the cases where this caused a mismatch between the perceived and actual height of the participant's avatar, real-time algorithms using trigonometry were used to correct the eye-gaze angle between the participant and the confederate to preserve the possibility of making eye- contact.

References

Anonymous. (1998). To reveal of not to reveal. A theoretical model of anonymous communication. *Communication Theory, 8,* 381–407.

Bailenson, J. (2006). Transformed Social Interaction in Collaborative Virtual Environments. In P. Messaris & L. Humphreys (Eds.), *Digital Media: Transformations in Human Communication* (pp. 255–264). New York. Peter Lang.

Bailenson, J., Beall., A., Blascovich, J., Loomis, J., & Turk, M. (2005). Transformed Social Interaction, Augmented Gaze, and Social Influence in Immersive Virtual Environments. *Human Communication Research, 31,* 511–537.

Bailenson, J., Blascovich, J., Beall, A., & Loomis, J. (2003). Interpersonal distance in immersive virtual environments. *Personality and Social Psychology Bulletin, 29,* 1–15.

Bem, D. (1972). Self perception theory. In L. Berkowitz (Ed.), *Advances in experimental social psychology (Vol. 6).* New York. Academic Press.

Blascovich, J., Loomis, J., Beall, A., Swinth, K., Hoyt, C., & Bailenson, J. (2002). Immersive virtual environment technology as a methodological tool for social psychology. *Psychological Inquiry,* 13(2), 103–124.

Burgoon, J. (1978). A communication model of personal space violation. Explication and an initial test. *Human Communication Research, 4,* 129–142.

Burgoon, J., & Walther, J. (1990). Nonverbal expectancies and the evaluative consequences of violations. *Human Communication Research, 17,* 232–265.

Burgoon, J., Walther, J., & Baesler, E. (1992). Interpretations, evaluations, and consequences of interpersonal touch. *Human Communication Research,* 19(237–263).

Chan, E., & Vorderer, P. (2006). Massively Multiplayer Online Games. In P. Vorderer & J. Bryant (Eds.), *Playing computer games - Motives, responses, and consequences.* Mahwah, NJ: Lawrence Erlbaum.

Culnan, M. J., & Markus, M. L. (1987). Information technologies. In F. M. Jablin & L. L. Putnam (Eds.), *Handbook of organizational communication: An interdisciplinary perspective* (pp. 420–443). Thousand Oaks, CA: Sage Publications, Inc, 1987, 781.

Dion, K., Berscheid, E., & Walster, E. (1972). What is beautiful is good. *Journal of Personality and Social Psychology, 24,* 285–290.

Flanagin, A. J., Tiyaamornwong, V., O'Connor, J., & Seibold, D. R. (2002). Computer-mediated group work: The interaction of member sex and anonymity. *Communication Research,* 29(66–93).

Forsythe, R., Horowitz, J., Savin, N., & Sefton, M. (1994). Fairness in simple bargaining experiments. *Games and Economic Behavior, 6,* 347–369.

Frank, M., & Gilovich, T. (1988). The dark side of self and social perception: Black uniforms and aggression in professional sports. *Journal of Personality and Social Psychology, 54,* 74–85.

Freedman, D. G. (1979). *Human sociobiology.* New York: Free Press.

Friend, R. M., & Vinson, M. (1974). Leaning over backward: Jurors responses to defendants' attractiveness. *Journal of Communication, 24,* 124–129.

Gergen, K., Gergen, M., & Barton, W. H. (1973). Deviance in the dark. *Psychology Today, 11,* 129–130.

Hancock, J., & Dunham, P. (2001). Impression Formation in Computer-Mediated Communication Revisited: An Analysis of the Breadth and Intensity of Impressions. *Communication Research, 28,* 325–347.

Harrison, A. A., & Saeed, L. (1977). Let's make a deal: An analysis of revelations and stipulations in lonely hearts advertisements. *Journal of Personality and Social Psychology, 35,* 257–264.

Hiltz, S., Johnson, K., & Turoff, M. (1986). Experiments in group decision making: Communication processes and outcome in face-to-face versus computerized conferences. *Human Communication Research, 13,* 225–252.

Jacobson, D. (1999). Impression formation in cyberspace: Online expectations and offline experiences in text-based virtual communities. *Journal of Computer-Mediated Communication, 5.*

Jarvenpaa, S., & Leidner, D. (1998). Communication and trust in global virtual teams. *Journal of Computer-Mediated Communication, 3.*

Johnson, R., & Downing, L. (1979). Deindividuation and valence of cues: Effects on prosocial and antisocial behavior. *Journal of Personality and Social Psychology, 37,* 1532–1538.

Kiesler, S., Siegel, J., & McGuire, T. W. (1984). Social psychological aspects of computer-mediated communication. *American Psychologist,* 39(10), 1123–1134.

Langlois, J., Kalakanis, L., Rubenstein, A., Larson, A., Hallam, M., & Smoot, M. (2000). Maxims or myths of beauty?: A meta-analytic and theoretical review. *Psychological Bulletin, 126,* 390–423.

Lea, M., O'Shea, T., & Spears, R. (1992). "Flaming" in computer-mediated communication. In M. Lea (Ed.), *Contexts of Computer-Mediated Communication* (pp. 89–112). New York. Harvester Wheatsheaf.

Linden Labs (2006). *What is Second Life?* Retrieved on 5th May, 2006 from lindenlab.com/ProductFactSheet.pdf

Loomis, J., Blascovich, J., & Beall, A. (1999). Immersive virtual environments as a basic research tool in psychology. *Behavior Research Methods, Instruments, and Computers, 31,* 557–564.

McKenna, K., & Rargh, J. (2000). Plan 9 from cyberspace: The implications of the Internet for personality and social psychology. *Personality and Social Psychology Review, 4,* 57–75.

Merola, N., Penas, J., & Hancock, J. (2006). *Avatar color and social identity effects: On attitudes and group dynamics in virtual realities.* Paper presented at the ICA 2006, Dresden, Germany.

NCHS (2004). National health and nutrition examination survey 2003–2004. Retrieved on 5th September, 2006 from http.//www.cdc.gov/nchs/about/major/nhanes/nhanes2003- 2004/nhanes03_04.htm

Normand, V., Babski, C., Benford, S., Bullock, A., Carion, S., Chrysanthou, Y., et al. (1999). The COVEN Project: Exploring Applicative, Technical, and Usage Dimensions of Collaborative Virtual Environment. *Presence: Teleoperators and Virtual Environments, 8,* 1999.

Parks, M. R., & Floyd, K. (1996). Making friends in cyberspace. *Journal of Communication, 46,* 80–96.

Postmes, T., & Spears, R. (2002). Behavior online: Does anonymous computer communication reduce gender inequality? *Personality & Social Psychology Bulletin, 28,* 1073–1083.

Postmes, T., Spears, R., & Lea, M. (1998). Breaching or building social boundaries? *Communication Research, 25,* 689–699.

Postmes, T., Spears, R., & Lea, M. (2000). The formation of group norms in computer-mediated communication. *Human Communication Research, 26,* 341–371.

Short, J., Williams, E., & Christie, B. (1976). *The social psychology of telecommunications.* London: Wiley.

Snyder, M., Tanke, E. D., & Berscheid, E. (1977). Social perception and interpersonal behavior: On the self-fulfilling nature of social stereotypes. *Journal of Personality & Social Psychology, 35*(9), 656–666.

Spears, R., & Lea, M. (1994). Panacea or panopticon? The hidden power in computer-mediated communication. *Communication Research, 21,* 427–459.

Stogdill, R. M. (1948). Personal factors associated with leadership: A survey of the literature. *Journal of Psychology, 25,* 35–71.

Trevino, L., & Webster, J. (1992). Flow in Computer-Mediated Communication: Electronic Mail and Voice Mail Evaluation and Impacts. *Communication Research, 19,* 539–573.

Turkle, S. (1995). *Life on the Screen: Identity in the Age of the Internet:* New York: Simon and Schuster.

Valins, S. (1966). Cognitive Effects of False Heart-Rate Feedback. *Journal of Personality and Social Psychology, 4,* 400–408.

Walther, J. (1996). Computer-mediated communication: Impersonal, interpersonal, and hyperpersonal interaction. *Communication Research, 23(1),* 3–43.

Walther, J., Anderson, J., & Park, D. (1994). Interpersonal effects in computer-mediated interaction: A meta-analysis of social and anti-social communication. *Communication Research, 21,* 460–487.

Walther, J., Slovacek, C., & Tidwell, L. (2001). Is a Picture Worth a Thousand Words?: Photographic Images in Long-Term and Short-Term Computer-Mediated Communication. *Communication Research, 28,* 105–134.

Yee, N. (2006). The Demographics, Motivations, and Derived Experiences of Users of Massively Multi-User Online Graphical Environments. *Presence: Teleoperators and Virtual Environments, 15,* 309–329.

Young, T. J., & French, L. A. (1996). Height and perceived competence of U. S. Presidents. *Perceptual and Motor Skills, 82,* 1002.

Zimbardo, P. (1969). The human choice: Individuation, reason, and order vs. deindividuation, impulse and chaos. In W. J. Arnold & D. Levine (Eds.), (Vol. 17, pp. 237–307). In W. Arnold & D. Levine (Eds.), *Nebraska Symposium on Motivation* (Vol. 17, pp. 237–307). Lincoln, NE: University of Nebraska Press.

The Individual and Religion

Why do sociologists study religion? Religion is an intricate part of the human experience. From the Latin *religio* (respect for what is sacred) and *religare* (to bind, in the sense of an obligation), the term religion describes various systems of belief and practice associated with what people define as sacred or spiritual. Throughout history, and in societies across the world, religious narratives, symbols and traditions have been used to give meaning to life and understand the universe. Religion, in one form or another, has been found in all human societies since they first appeared and some form of religion, usually practiced in public by a group, is found in every known culture today. Our brains seem to be wired for faith. To understand individuals in society, sociologists must study its religion.

What is religion? Pioneer sociologist Emile Durkheim described it as "a unified system of beliefs and practices relative to sacred things, that is to say set apart and forbidden, beliefs and practices which unite into one single moral community, called a church, all those who adhere to them" (1915). Some people associate religion with places of worship (a synagogue or church), others with a practice (confession or meditation), and still others with a concept that guides their daily lives (like dharma or sin). All of these people can agree that **religion** is a system of beliefs, values, and practices concerning what a person holds sacred or considers to be spiritually significant.

Graffiti on Callejon de Hamel alley, Havana, Cuba. Callejon de Hamel is considered a public temple to Lukumi (Santeria) religion and Afrocuban culture.

Table 5. 1

Religious Classification	What/Who is Divine	Example
Polytheism	Multiple gods	Ancient Greeks and Romans
Monotheism	Single god	Judaism, Islam, Christianity
Atheism	No deities	Atheism
Animism	Non-human beings (animals, plants, natural world)	Indigenous nature worship (Shinto)
Totemism	Human-natural being connection	Ojibwa (Native American)

Types of Religions

Scholars from a variety of disciplines have strived to classify religions. One widely accepted categorization considers what or who people worship (if anything). Using this method of classification, religions might fall into one of these basic categories, as shown in Table 5. 1.

Some religions may occupy various categories. The Christian notion of the Holy Trinity (God, Jesus, Holy Spirit), for example, defies the definition of monotheism to some scholars. Similarly, many Westerners view the multiple manifestations of Hinduism's godhead as polytheistic, while most Hindus describe those manifestations are a monotheistic parallel to the Christian Trinity.

It is also important to note that every society has nonbelievers, such as atheists, who do not believe in a divine being or entity, and agnostics, who hold that ultimate reality (such as God) is unknowable. Atheists and agnostics represent a significant portion of the population. It is important to recognize that being a nonbeliever in a divine entity does not mean that the individual subscribes to no morality.

The World's Religions

Religions have emerged and developed across the world. Some have been short-lived, while others have persisted and grown.

Hindu Brahmin blessing a pilgrim to Meenakshi Temple in Madurai, India. Do you believe in this blessing? Does that make you an atheist?

Hinduism, the oldest major religion in the world, originated in the Indus River Valley about 4,500 years ago in what is now modern-day northwest India and Pakistan. With roughly 1 billion followers, Hinduism is the third-largest of the world's religions. Hindus believe in a divine power that can manifest as different entities. Three main incarnations—Brahma, Vishnu, and Shiva—are sometimes compared to the manifestations of the divine in the Christian Trinity. The deities manifest themselves on earth as avatars. Although the avatars are usually related to Vishnu, other deities also manifest themselves on earth. Multiple sacred texts, collectively called the Vedas, contain hymns and rituals from ancient India and are mostly written in Sanskrit. Hindus generally believe in a set of principles called dharma, which refer to one's duty in the world that corresponds with "right" actions. Hindus also believe in karma, or the notion that spiritual ramifications of one's actions are balanced cyclically in this life or a future life.

Buddhism was founded by Siddhartha Gautama around 500 B.C.E. Siddhartha was said to have given up a comfortable, upper-class life to follow one of poverty and spiritual devotion. At the age of 35, he famously meditated under a sacred fig tree and vowed not to rise before he achieved enlightenment (*bodhi*). After this experience, he became known as Buddha, or "enlightened one." Buddha's teachings encourage Buddhists to lead a moral life by accepting the four Noble Truths: (1) life is suffering, (2) suffering arises from attachment to desires, (3) suffering ceases when attachment to desires ceases, and (4) freedom from suffering is possible by following the "middle way." The concept of "middle way" encourages people to live in the present and to practice acceptance of others. Buddhism also tends to deemphasize the role of a godhead but stress the importance of personal responsibility.

Confucianism was the official religion of China from 200 B.C.E. until it was officially abolished when communist leadership discouraged religious practice in 1949. The religion was developed by Kung Fu-Tzu (Confucius), an extraordinary teacher who lived in the sixth and fifth centuries B.C.E. His lessons—which were about self-discipline, respect for authority and tradition, and *jen* (the kind treatment of every person)—were collected in a book called the . *Analects*. Some religious scholars consider Confucianism more of a social system than a religion because it focuses on sharing wisdom about moral practices but does not involve any type of specific worship; nor does it have formal objects. In fact, its teachings were developed in context of problems of social anarchy and a near-complete deterioration of social cohesion.

In **Taoism**, the purpose of life is inner peace and harmony. Tao is usually translated as "way" or "path." The founder of the religion is recognized to be a man named Laozi, who lived sometime in the sixth century B.C.E. in China. Taoist beliefs emphasize the virtues of compassion and moderation. The central concept of *tao* describes a spiritual reality, the order of the universe, or the way of modern life in harmony. The ying-yang symbol and the concept of polar forces are central Taoist ideas. Some scholars have compared this Chinese tradition to its Confucian counterpart by saying that "whereas Confucianism is concerned with day-to-day rules of conduct, Taoism is concerned with a more spiritual level of being" (Feng and English, 1972).

Judaism is an ancient monotheistic religion. After their Exodus from Egypt in the 13th century B.C.E. Jews became monotheistic, worshipping only one God, the God of Abraham. The Jews covenant, or promise of a special relationship with Yahweh (God), is an important element of Judaism, and their sacred text is the Torah, which Christians also follow as the first five books of the Bible. Talmud refers to a collection of sacred Jewish oral interpretation of the Torah. Jews emphasize moral behavior and action in this world as opposed to beliefs or personal salvation in the next world.

Islam is monotheistic religion and it follows the teaching of the prophet Muhammad, born in Mecca, Saudi Arabia, in 570 C.E. Muhammad is seen only as a prophet, not as a divine being, and he is believed to be the messenger of Allah (God), who is divine. The followers of Islam, whose U.S. population is projected to double in the next 20 years, are called Muslims. Islam means "peace" and "submission." The sacred text for Muslims is the Qur'an (or Koran), the word of God revealed to Mohammed by the Archangel Gabriel, beginning in the month of Ramadan 620 C.E. As with Christianity's Old Testament, many of the Qur'an stories are shared with the Jewish faith. Divisions exist within Islam, but all Muslims are guided by five beliefs or practices, often called "pillars": 1) Allah is the only god and Muhammad is his prophet, 2) daily prayer, 3) helping those in poverty, 4) fasting as a spiritual practice, and 5) pilgrimage to the holy center of Mecca.

© antkevyv, 2014. Used under license from Shutterstock, Inc.

Painted symbols of Christianity, Islam, Judaism and Hinduism. Followers of three of these religions worship the same God—the God of Abraham. Which religion does not come from the same faith tree?

Christianity, the largest religion in the world, began 2,000 years ago in Palestine, with Jesus of Nazareth, a charismatic leader who taught his followers about *caritas* (charity) or treating others as you would like to be treated yourself. The sacred text for Christians is the Bible. While Jews, Christians, and Muslims share many of same historical religious stories, and trace their belief system to the same God, the God of Abraham, their beliefs diverge. In

Pope Francis in his Popemobile on Easter Sunday 2013, greeting the crowds in St Peter's Square, the Vatican, after Mass—31st March 2013.

their shared sacred stories, it is suggested that the son of God—a messiah—will return to save God's followers. While Christians believe that he already appeared in the person of Jesus Christ, Jews, and Muslims disagree. While they recognize Christ as an important historical figure, their traditions do not believe he's the son of God, and their faiths see the prophecy of the messiah's arrival as not yet fulfilled.

A stained glass image of Saint James. His tomb in Santiago de Compostela in Spain is the end point of the Camino de Santiago (The Way of St. James), an ancient pilgrimage trail that still is used by hundreds of thousands of pilgrims yearly.

PRINCIPLES OF NEUROTHEOLOGY
The Case for a Principia Neurotheologica

Andrew B. Newberg

"Neurotheology" is a unique field of scholarship and investigation that seeks to understand the relationship specifically between the brain and theology, and more broadly between the mind and religion. As a topic, neurotheology has garnered substantial attention in the academic and lay communities in recent years. Several books have been written addressing the relationship between the brain and religious experience and numerous scholarly articles have been published on the topic. The scientific and religious communities have been very interested in obtaining more information regarding neurotheology, how to approach this topic, and whether science and religion can be integrated in some manner that preserves, and perhaps enhances, both. However, as would be expected, there have been both positive and negative responses to purported neurotheological studies and perspectives.

If neurotheology is to be considered a viable field going forward, it requires a set of clear principles that can be generally agreed upon and supported by both the theological or religious perspective and the scientific one as well. The overall purpose of this book is to set forth the necessary principles of neurotheology which can be used as a foundation for future neurotheological discourse and scholarship. In time, it would be highly valuable to have added input from a wide range of scholars with regard to these principles so that the field of neurotheology remains dynamic in its scope and process. Thus, it is likely that as this field proceeds, the guiding principles will require some welcome modifications. Also, it should be clearly stated that rather than specifically try to answer major theological or scientific questions, this book intends to espouse a program of scholarship and a methodological basis for future inquiry, thereby laying the groundwork for a new synthesis of scientific and theological discourse. In the end, neurotheology, a term fraught with potential problems, might nevertheless, be a highly useful and important voice in the greater study of religious and theological ideas and their intersection with science.

The relationship between the mind and human spirituality has been considered for at least several thousand years. For example, this intersection was described in the ancient Hindu scriptures of the Upanishads in which it was realized that something within us, particularly within the head, enables us to explore and experience the universe via our cognitive and sensory processes and also to discover our own sense of spirituality:

> Between the two palates there hangs the uvula, like a nipple—that is the starting—point of Indra (the lord). Where the root of the hair divides, there he opens the two sides of the head, and saying Bhu, he enters Agni (the fire); saying Bhuvas, he enters Vayu (air); Saying Suvas, he enters Aditya (sun); saying Mahas, he enters Brahman. He there obtains lordship, he reaches the lord of the mind. He becomes lord of speech, lord of sight, lord of hearing, lord of knowledge. Nay, more than this. There is the Brahman whose body is ether, whose nature is true, rejoicing in the senses (prana), delighted in the mind, perfect in peace, and immortal. (Taittiriya Upanishad)

This section from the Upanishads reveals the importance of the body and the brain in achieving spiritual enlightenment. Neurotheology is a more recent attempt at discerning how the study of the human mind and brain (terms we will define later) relates to the pursuit of religions and religious experience. While a growing number of scholars have written a variety of papers and books about this topic, it is still in its nascent stages. One of the greatest shortcomings of neurotheology so far has been the lack of clear principles by which such scholarship should proceed. Thus, in order to establish more thoroughly neurotheology as an academic discipline, it is vital to consider the primary principles necessary for such an endeavor.

It is important to infuse throughout the principles of neurotheology the notion that neurotheology requires an openness to both the scientific as well as the spiritual perspectives. It is also important to preserve the essential elements of both perspectives. The scientific side must progress utilizing adequate definitions, measures, methodology, and interpretations of data. The religious side must maintain a subjective sense of spirituality, a phenomenological assessment of the sense of ultimate reality that may or may not include a divine presence, a notion of the meaning and purpose in life, an adherence to various doctrinal processes, and a careful analysis of religion from the theological perspective.

In short, for neurotheology to be successful, science must be kept rigorous and religion must be kept religious. This book will also have the purpose of facilitating a sharing of ideas and concepts across the boundary between science and religion. Such a dialogue can be considered a constructive approach that informs both perspectives by enriching the understanding of both science and religion.

But it is not an easy task to combine theological and scientific concepts. A primary problem with neurotheology is the need to reach a common starting ground between these two perspectives. This is something that will be attempted in this book. But, by necessity, sometimes one side or the other will have to be oversimplified. After all, there are not many neuroscientists familiar with the most recent theological debates and there are not many theologians who have a detailed understanding of functional neuroanatomy. Thus, another purpose of this book is to provide some starting points for dialogue between neuroscience and religion. Certainly for the theologian or religious scholar, some statements will seem superficial or incomplete. For the neuroscientist, the material may appear "dumbed down," to use a common phrase among scientists. But neurotheology represents a beginning such that from two disparate fields a new multidisciplinary field can emerge. As an example for future scholarship, one might hope that the neuroscientist attempting to study morality will be well versed in the ancient texts and the writings of theologians such as Aquinas and Luther who were important in shaping our understanding of the topics of free will and ethics. Conversely, the theologian studying the writings of Aquinas or Luther might consider what was happening in their frontal lobes and limbic system while pondering their influential ideas. It would also be hoped that any of these approaches would not diminish, defame, debunk, or decry one perspective for another. Rather, the new synthesis would ultimately help human beings to relate better to the world around them and to engage both their biological and spiritual dimensions.

Before proceeding with the principles of neurotheology, it is first necessary to review the foundations upon which neurotheology rests. The foundations of neurotheology include a historical analysis of related concepts, a description of the contributions of theology and science to neurotheology, and an elaboration of the goals that such scholarship should aspire to. Following a description of the foundations of neurotheology, a number of definitions are necessary to review, and from there, the principles of neurotheology can be elaborated.

Historical Foundations of Neurotheology

To evaluate the historical background of neurotheology requires us to delve several thousand years back into history to see how religious traditions have considered the relationship between the mind and the person's attempt to interact with some higher level of reality. It is also of interest to observe how the variety of philosophical and theological concepts regarding the universe and God may be recapitulated in a variety of brain processes. In this way, we can see more directly how various concepts considered throughout history connect to our current understanding of the brain. As will be discussed later in the book, the ability to relate theological concepts to mental and brain processes does not mean in any way to imply that these concepts have been reduced to brain chemistry, but rather may provide at the very least, a new perspective, and at most, an important method for further evaluating the true basis of those concepts.

In Eastern traditions there is significant historical development of the psychological analysis of the human being in relationship to both Buddhist as well as Hindu conceptions of the world and of spirituality.[1] The lines of the Upanishads above certainly indicate a strong interest not only in the functioning of the mind itself, but in the psychological and possibly biological correlates of mental activity that can be utilized to achieve the highest spiritual state.

Buddhist and Hindu writings have made extensive evaluations of the human mind and psychology focusing on human consciousness of the "self," the emotional attachment human beings have to that "self," and how human consciousness can be altered through various spiritual practices such as meditation. Buddhism elaborates the important elements of human consciousness which it organizes into the "four seals" of belief.[2] The first seal, "dukkha," refers to suffering and is considered a universal aspect of the human condition. The second seal, "anatta," refers to no-self and in particular that there is no separate existing self in the universe, but everything is interconnected. The third seal, "annicca," refers to impermanence such that nothing in this world lasts and thus, personal achievement, success, and happiness should never be associated with transitory phenomena. The fourth seal is that "nirvana," a release from suffering, does exist through the surrendering of attachment to the false sense of self that the mind usually holds.

Each of these seals can also be considered from a neurotheological perspective. For example, one can relate these important ideological concepts to various aspects of the human brain and psyche. Suffering plays a significant role in depression and stress, two topics which are central to current psychiatric research. It is also known that areas of the brain that are involved in the stress response and other negative emotions likely play a role in suffering and ultimately have a long-term effect on the health of the body.[3] Studies have also revealed that emotional suffering may be felt in the brain similarly to physical pain.[4] The second seal of no-self also may have physiological correlates since there are specific areas of the brain and body that contribute to our sense of self.[5] The third seal of impermanence is interesting in the context of the brain since there are specific brain structures that support our sense of change and permanence. Furthermore, the brain itself appears built for change via the process of neuroplasticity which refers to the ability of the brain to change its structure and function.[6] While the neurophysiological correlates of nirvana have yet to be evaluated, various components of letting go and the loss of the sense of self have been associated with specific brain functions.[7] However, understanding the four seals can also help us to understand the human mind. Thus, understanding the relationship between suffering, the self, and change bears directly on how we might strive to understand the workings of the mind and brain.

It is fascinating that without any of the modern methodologies, Buddhist thought captured so well the intricate inner workings of the mind. Buddhist thought also focused substantial attention on consciousness as an energy that is deeply interconnected with the brain, body, and physical world.[8] This has set up, in some sense, a separate biomedical paradigm in Eastern thought which is based on how "energy" moves through the body. While not using the same concept of "energy," current scientific fields such as psychoneuroimmunology and psychoneuroendocrinology have identified many ways in which the interconnection between the brain and body are expressed. These fields might help bridge the gap between Eastern and Western biomedical paradigms, and of course, neurotheology might provide an excellent source for future research.

Another related concept with potential for reconciling differences between Eastern and Western paradigms is that of the *yin* and *yang* that describes the opposing forces that interact within human beings. A corresponding scientific concept of "tone" has been applied to many physiological and neurophysiological systems. Tone refers to the balance between two opposing physiological processes. For example, the autonomic nervous system that governs arousal and calming responses in the body

typically rests in a tonal state such that the body is maintained within a certain balance. When one side of the autonomic nervous system is called upon, such as when we need to respond quickly to a threatening situation, the arousal system is activated while the calming system is suppressed. Thus, the notion of opposing forces that govern the mind and body are similar to those found in ancient Buddhist texts.

Similar concepts of the body's "energy" or "Qi" (pronounced Chi) can also be found in Ayurvedic medical practices that developed in india.[9] These practices also consider the human body, health, and psychological well being, from the perspective of the balance of energy flow in the body. By manipulating the energy, the appropriate health—physical, mental, and spiritual—can be restored. Ultimately a balancing of energy can allow the person to strive towards an enlightened state in which the mind has the ability to contact a more fundamental level of reality.

While Eastern traditions approached the notion of the mind and consciousness more directly, Western conceptions of religion typically did not focus specifically on the relationship between the mind and religious phenomena. For example, the Bible itself speaks very little about particular mental or physiological processes. However, the description of human beings, human frailties, and the "evil" actions that are perpetrated by human beings, clearly signifies a deep interest in the human psyche. For example, the story of the creation of human beings in the Book of Genesis appears to relate how God infused humanity with a certain intellect and psychological prowess which differentiates human beings from the rest of the world.[10] From the beginning, "the tree of the knowledge of good and evil"[11] plays a critical role in the development of human beings. We see throughout the biblical stories how human beings have tried to come to grips with the various intrapsychic forces that compel them to various actions both good and evil, "When I looked for good, then evil came unto me: and when I waited for light, there came darkness."[12] The Bible itself provides the rules and guidelines by which human beings should live their lives. The Commandments and covenants with God are based on an understanding of human behavior and human morality. With the advent of Christianity, the focus was shifted somewhat to other aspects of the human psyche including issues pertaining to love, devotion, forgiveness, and redemption. For example, the Bible states in Acts, "Be it known unto you therefore, men and brethren, that through this man is preached unto you the forgiveness of sins"[13] and also in Ephesians I:

> According as he hath chosen us in him before the foundation of the world, that we should be holy and without blame before him in love: Having

predestinated us unto the adoption of children by Jesus Christ to himself, according to the good pleasure of his will, To the praise of the glory of his grace, wherein he hath made us accepted in the beloved. In whom we have redemption through his blood, the forgiveness of sins, according to the riches of his grace; Wherein he hath abounded toward us in all wisdom and prudence.[14]

However, the Bible does not usually specify precisely how forgiveness, love, devotion, and redemption come about other than through religion and religious adherence. Nonetheless, there is clearly an important relationship between the mind that allows human beings to be human, and the spirit or soul that allows human beings to connect to a higher, divine realm of existence.

Of course the ancient texts did not have the advantage of more modern scientific analyses of the human psyche and the human central nervous system that can allow for a deeper and richer elaboration of such concepts. Regardless, their rudimentary, and in many ways, highly accurate intuitive analysis of the human being and the human mind clearly demonstrate that psychology and religion were some day going to be integrated in a more profound way.

St. Thomas Aquinas provided an important perspective on the human mind in that he considered all healthy, rational action to proceed from the desire to achieve a good or to pursue an end.[15] Man's end is ultimately for a union with God and thus, a person finds his true perfection in life, only in an everlasting friendship with the God who created him. The evil mind then results from an individual who pursues ends that do not lead toward God. But Aquinas engages the issue of human biology and the mind more directly by distinguishing between the *actus hominis* and the *actus humanus*.[16] The former refers to acts of the body while the latter falls under the domain of reflective, deliberate intelligence. The realization via modern cognitive neuroscience that there is an intricate interrelationship between the body and the mind reveals the difficulty in making the distinction that Aquinas makes and this might lead to a new understanding of how the different aspects of the human being interact.

The Protestant Reformation and the work of Martin Luther (1483–1546) had a significant impact on much of religious as well as philosophical thought over the following several hundred years. The reformation brought about a different perspective on religious thinking and religious doctrine, particularly as it pertains to the individual and the authority of the Christian church. Luther's original conception was intended to restore in each individual the power and authority to hear God's guidance without needing to go through a church authority.[17] In practice, however, he ended up replacing the Pope with a new source of external authority. For Luther would not allow believers to be completely free before God; they could only be guided in ways that were consistent with the Bible. Here again, there are limitations placed on the human mind that constrain how it can help us to be religious.

Luther also had several important interactions with philosophers that resulted in somewhat new perspectives on human psychology. For example, Desiderius Erasmus (ca. 1469–1536) argued that the human being is the center of creation and that the measure of God's goodness is that God created a world in which to unfold the nature of the human being.[18] Erasmus' heated debate with Luther was triggered by Luther's critique of Erasmus' essay *On Free Will*. Erasmus insisted on a role for the human will and personal responsibility, as well as God's grace, in achieving salvation while Luther argued that grace alone provided salvation for human beings.[19] Interestingly, this debate also centers around the functions of the human mind as they pertain to human salvation since the issue of human free will, which would clearly be a mental process, is of crucial importance in determining the basis for salvation. It would be most interesting to consider how Luther and Erasmus might have responded to current cognitive neuroscience research regarding the nature of the moral reasoning and the identification of parts of the brain that appear to function as the "seat of the will."[20]

The relationship between the mind and experience extends beyond simply religious and theological issues. Several philosophical movements in the last 500 years had a profound influence on the integration of spirituality and the human mind. This begins most notably with the work of René Descartes (1596–1650) whose meditations were designed to evaluate the world and that which can be known from a rational, contemplative perspective. His analysis went to great lengths to try to exclude erroneous assumptions and to develop concepts in a logical manner.[21] The result of Descartes' meditations led him to the famous notion that, ironically, lies at the heart of modern cognitive neuroscience—"cogito ergo sum." The fundamental concept of modern cognitive neuroscience is that our thoughts and feelings make us who we are, make up our existence, and can be correlated directly to the functions of the brain.[22] This, of course, was not the ultimate goal or conclusion achieved by Descartes, but clearly his meditations led him to ideas that support the development of modern cognitive neuroscience. The notion that thoughts were occurring and that he could identify these thoughts as being related to existence had a clear import into the relationship between human experience and ultimately human understanding of the world.

Descartes also set up an important dualism between the mind and body that would pervade Western philosophy and science for at least 400 years. Antonio Damasio, a Professor of Neurology at the University of Iowa School of Medicine, has argued that Descartes erred by assuming that the mind and body were independent of one another and that human emotions and rationality were basically opposed to each other.[23] Descartes argued in favor of reason over emotion, but Damasio contends that our emotions are fundamental to our ability to make decisions and interface with the world, a view that is now widely accepted in the field of cognitive neuroscience. Regardless, the philosophical works of Descartes provided an important impetus for understanding the integration between science and religion, and particularly between religion and the human mind.

Another philosopher whose work should be considered an important contribution to neurotheology was Baruch Spinoza (1632–1677), the Dutch Jew who heavily based his theological and philosophical ideas on mathematics and science. In fact, his conception of God as being attributed to the beauty and clarity of design in mathematics fostered a unique integration of science and religion. While this did not specifically relate to the neurosciences, Spinoza had an understanding that the laws of nature were reflected in the divine presence in the universe, "the universal laws of nature according to which all things happen and are determined are nothing but God's eternal decrees, which always involve eternal truth and necessity."[24] Furthermore, it was believed by Spinoza that through human thought and philosophical and scientific endeavors, human beings could come to know the order of the world and the nature of God. Although Spinoza's work emphasized the physical sciences, it might be argued that his perspective is highly supportive of neurotheology as a way of understanding the human being and the human perspective of the universe via the brain. For example, Spinoza describes the *conatus*: "Each thing, as far as it can by its own power, strives to persevere in its being." Damasio describes the underlying neurobiological correlates of this process by which human beings persevere in relation to the sensory and cognitive systems that aid in adaptability and survival.[25] In this way, Spinoza might have argued that understanding the mind does help understand the divine presence in the universe, or at least in the human being.

In the eighteenth Century, Immanuel Kant (1724–1804) greatly elaborated the rational perspective in human philosophy. His *Critique of Pure Reason* as well as his other works implied that all the universe, both spiritual and non-spiritual, could be understood through a human rational approach separated from sensorial experience.[26] For Kant, there was something inherent in the human mind that allowed it access to ultimate reality. Thus, "pure reason" was something that could be attainable. However, this rational approach had to be measured and carefully considered. Kant argued that no theoretical argument could prove the existence of God. Kant considered human reason to overreach its powers, and thus in need of self-limitation. The brain itself has its limitations in terms of its cognitive capabilities and capacities. Kant also argued that reason seeks to know what lies beyond the range of "experience"—that is, the apprehension of objects as they are related to one another in a spatio-temporal framework of causal laws.[27] But Kant considered any attempt to claim knowledge outside the limits of human experience to be problematic. This, of course, is commensurate with current neurotheological analysis in that the perceptions of the human brain are considered crucial for knowledge. It is also the tendency of human beings, and human reason, to go beyond the limits of experience and this ultimately results in the representation of ideas of the soul, the world, and God.

In spite of the philosophical consideration of the importance of human experience, until the late eighteenth century, there was practically no attempt at considering religion from the perspective of human experience. Religion until that point was evaluated primarily from the perspective of religion itself. Consequently religions, particularly in the West, were defined by their dogmatic formulations and teachings. It was only with Friedrich schleiermacher (1768–1834) in the late eighteenth century that an attempt was made to define "religion" as such by switching from a doctrinal emphasis to a more cognitive, visceral, or intuitive one. Schleiermacher, in his book *The Christian Faith*, defined religion as a "feeling of absolute dependence."[28] Since his day, more recent attempts at a general conception of religion have emphasized the intuitive, emotional, or visceral aspects of religion. This shift has important implications for bringing a cognitive neuroscientific approach to the study of religion since feelings and emotions can be shown to be associated with specific brain structures and their function.

Another major step in terms of the understanding of the experience of religion came from the work of William James (1842–1910) at the turn of the last century. In *Varieties of Religious Experience*[29] James considers the different forms that religion takes in terms of how human beings experience the spiritual. This includes aspects of traditional religious practices such as through liturgy and ritual, through deeply personal experiences, and via practices such as those associated with prayer or meditation. James certainly placed an emphasis on subjective experiences and considered the assortment of such experiences ranging from the more traditional to the more exotic and mystical. In this regard, James discussed the phenomenology and the mental processes related to healthy-mindedness, conversion experiences, saintliness, and mystical experiences. In addition, James considered the potentially negative experiences associated with religion and their consequences on the mind.

While James' analysis did not specifically relate religious experience to particular brain functions, this most likely was due to the lack of general knowledge that existed within the scientific community of how the brain actually worked. However, the analysis offered by James can be thought of as providing the initial theoretical bases from which a neuroscientific analysis of religious experiences can proceed. Hence, by observing the particular characteristics and experiences associated with religion and spirituality one might then be able to ascertain the neurobiological correlates of such experiences. This would have to wait until a clearer understanding of overall brain function, particularly as it relates to thoughts, feelings, and experiences was developed. Such development would not occur until the latter part of the twentieth century.

A major step forward in the attempt at formulating a general conception of religion was the rise of anthropological and sociological theory. This approach asserted that religion is always embedded in a cultural matrix and that religious beliefs, customs, and rituals must be understood in a radical relationship to the cultures in which they arise. Emile Durkheim (1858–1917), in his *The Elementary Forms of the Religious Life*,[30] described religion as nothing more than an expression of society and he is attributed the quote, "Religion is society, writ large." On the other hand, many psychologists, beginning with Sigmund Freud (1856–1939), have seen religion as a projection of various intrapsychic dynamics or of hopes and expectations based on previous experience.[31] Thus, religion was nothing more than a creation of the human mind, a mind striving for understanding and purpose in a world that appeared to offer little.

Since the turn of the twentieth century, scholars began to devote themselves to the phenomenology of religion on its own terms. They believed that there were phenomena that needed to be explained which eluded both sociological and psychological determinism. An example of such an approach has been to analyze religion in terms of an awareness of the "sacred" and the "holy." Rudolf Otto, in *The Idea of the Holy*,[32] defined the essence of religious awareness as awe, described as a mixture of fear and fascination before the divine and referred to as a *mysterium tremendum et fascinans*. Such an approach began to get at a dominant form of Western mysticism but

was not so applicable to Eastern religions or to primitive ones. A reworking of Otto's concept of the "sacred" as the central core of all religious experience has been espoused by Mircea Eliade.[33] For Eliade, no longer is the sacred to be found almost exclusively in Otto's god-encounter type of experience. Rather, every culture exemplifies the existential sense of the sacred in its rituals and symbols, especially primitive and Asian cultures. However, many anthropologists, linguists, and psychologists question whether the concept of the "sacred" is identifiable in the language, experience, and thought of most primitive societies. Such scholars assert that religious experience is not *sui generis*, but is rather an amalgam of diverse cultural phenomena and experiences.

Paul Tillich should also be considered to have had a substantial impact on neurotheological scholarship. Tillich begins his *Systematic Theology*[34] by discussing the definition of religion as pertaining to "ultimate concerns." He also describes the sources of systematic theology as being ancient texts, church history, and the history of religion and culture. Religious experience is considered a conduit through which the sources of theology are presented to individuals. But this recognition of the experiential aspect as critical to the understanding of theology and the development of the norm of theology[35] underscores the importance of evaluating how religious experience comes about. For Tillich, the cognitive neurosciences were not yet available for incorporation into his analysis of the interrelationship between the sources of theology and the experience of religion. However, neurotheology might be capable of providing not only a subjective assessment of religious experience, but a biological one as well.

As far as the specific development of neurotheology, several scholars are worth mentioning in this regard who developed and helped to advance this emerging field. Some of the earliest scholars to explore these issues were Eugene d'Aquili (1941–1998) and James Ashbrook (1925–1999),[36] whose pioneering work in the 1970s and 1980s ultimately laid the foundation for the work of more recent scholars such as James Austin, Rhawn Joseph, Mario Beauregard, Patrick McNamara, Gregory Peterson, and others.[37] The work of all of these scholars has sought to integrate a neuroscientific analysis with a spiritual perspective without losing too much sight of one or the other. These scholars have worked hard to evaluate current neuroscientific knowledge as well as neuroscientific methods and brought these to bear on a wide variety of religious experiences as well as religious concepts. Initial analyses by Eugene d'Aquili, with his colleagues Charles Laughlin and John McManus, frequently focused on human ritual and its effects on both the mind and body, as well as how ritual was deeply tied to religious experience.[38] Early work also focused on the physiological basis of specific practices such as meditation and prayer. Such analyses were based in part on the existing neuroscientific literature, but also on the growing amount of scientific data obtained by other groups that measured the effects of such practices on various physiological parameters. Researchers such as Gellhorn and Kiely explored the autonomic nervous system effects of meditation.[39] Research conducted at institutions as far ranging as Harvard and the work of Dr. Herbert Benson to the Maharishi Institute and the work of B. Alan Wallace have contributed to the understanding of the relationship between the brain and various religious and spiritual practices. The most recent work has included brain imaging studies of a variety of religious and spiritual practices in addition to studies exploring subjective experiential components of religious and spiritual phenomena.[40]

This brief, and by no means exhaustive, review of the historical foundations of neurotheology was meant to show how and when many philosophical and theological concepts arose that pertain either directly or indirectly to how the mind and brain work. While it clearly was not the intent of many of these early scholars to link philosophical and theological concepts to the brain, now that cognitive neuroscientific techniques exist, we can return to these early developments and review them through a new lens of analysis. Therefore, neurotheology may be capable of creating new avenues for scholarship in the future, but may also allow for a reexamining of prior philosophical and theological ideas from a new perspective.

Scientific and Theological Foundations of Neurotheology

The approach to neurotheological scholarship requires an understanding of the contemporary state of scientific and theological inquiry as well as acknowledging the current science and religion debate. Historically, particularly in the ancient world, the rudiments of science and religion were frequently viewed in a unified manner. Most people practicing a religion also relied heavily on science or technology in order to help with the expression of that religion. Structures such as the pyramids of Egypt or Stonehenge in England were built with great engineering and technological detail, all for the purpose of facilitating religious beliefs. Much of the field of astronomy also developed as a way of monitoring the heavens and evaluating the times for specific holidays of religious importance. With the development of the Reformation and ultimately the Renaissance, history began to witness

a more antagonistic role between science and religion. In many ways this began with the Copernican Revolution which, with Galileo's help, shattered the Catholic church's view of an earth-centered, perfectly designed universe. This set up an antagonism that would last for hundreds of years up to the present day. Of course, Charles Darwin's elaboration of the theory of evolution was, and continues to be, a significant battleground for science and religion. As such, science and religion have typically gone their separate ways over the last hundred years, at times, the intersection being highly contentious. It remains to be seen what will be the ultimate outcome of the science and religion debate, but it may be that neurotheology as a field can offer an alternative to any hostile relationship between science and religion.

Various categories of interaction between science and religion have been expounded with the most elaborate being that of Ian Barbour who identified four types of interactions.[41] The first type of interaction is one of conflict in which it is perceived that only science or religion can present a correct analysis of the world, exclusive of each other. Examples of this conflict include those supporting scientific materialism such as biologists Jacques Monod or Richard Dawkins.[42] In their view, religion became part of human behavior as part of evolutionary forces, or even as an epiphenomenon, and does not represent objective reality as does science. The religious counterpart in this conflict involves those who believe in biblical literalism. Here the Bible is considered to be literally true, and thus it supersedes any scientific data that conflict with the statements of the Bible. This has led to great debate in many scientific and religious arenas. Most notable has been the argument between supporters of the theory of evolution and the adherents of Creationism. In this argument, either science is absolutely accurate or the Bible is absolutely accurate. Because of the vast differences between their descriptions of the origins of life and of the universe, both systems seem to be mutually exclusive.

A second interaction between science and theology is a mutual independence from each other. In this way, religion and science function in totally distinct domains. This second approach, which many naturalists have embraced, is that of the type described by Stephen J. Gould as "non-overlapping magisteria."[43] The notion here is that religion and science are in some sense both allowable, only that they refer to domains that are completely distinct. In this view, religion should have nothing to say about the scientific world and science nothing to say about the religious. However, they are not viewed to be mutually exclusive only providing information about two separate "dimensions" of human existence. Thus, science and religion do not conflict because science interprets human understanding of the world while religion interprets God's activity in the world. This notion does preserve both science and religion; however, it does not foster any dialogue between the two, which would at least provide for the possibility of a mutually beneficial interaction. Thus, the domain of each is essentially off-limits to the other.

Barbour defines the final two relationships between science and religion as dialogue and integration. The dialogue consists of boundary questions that exist in both science and religion. Examples include the Big Bang cosmology and quantum mechanics. In these scientific fields, research eventually results in questions that are unanswerable by scientific analysis. Questions such as what existed before the Big Bang, why did the Big Bang occur, and why is the universe here at all, all appear at the edge of present day scientific inquiry. Some of these "why" questions may never be answerable from a scientific perspective, but may be addressed by religion. David Tracy suggested that there are also more subtle examples of boundary questions that occur in everyday human experience.[44] Examples of such experiences include anxiety, joy, basic trust, and death. Science and religion also share certain methodological principles that are not identical, but similar enough to allow for meaningful dialogue. Holmes Rolston suggested that religion interprets and correlates human experience while science does the same with experimental data.[45] Science and religion both function within certain paradigms that form the basis of the accepted practice and can only be changed with great upheavals. Again, while science and religion are certainly not isomorphic, they are similar enough that there can exist a beneficial dialogue between the two.

The final relationship that may exist between science and religion is integration in which the two come together to help explain each other and the world. As noted above, natural theology (such as that described in the work of Thomas Aquinas and other scholastics) attempts to explain the existence of God and religion entirely by human reasoning. A classic approach of natural theology is the design argument which proposes that the inherent order of the universe implies the existence of God. The anthropic principle suggests that the conditions of the universe are too perfectly tuned for the development of human life, and that there must have been divine intervention, if only to get things started.[46] Another attempt at integrating science and theology is the development of a "theology of nature." This differs from natural theology in that it begins with a firm religious basis which is then modified in order to accommodate the influx of new scientifically derived information.[47] Science and religion

are integrated in "process philosophy" as developed by Alfred North Whitehead.[48] This philosophy was formulated with both scientific and religious concepts in an attempt to create an overarching developmental metaphysics that is applicable to the universe as a whole. More recently, Alan Wallace has suggested that a contemplative science be utilized that incorporates meditation and contemplation as an experimental paradigm to support scientific investigation.[49]

Of course, these four relationships between science and religion—conflict, independence, dialogue, and integration—each has its own advantages and shortcomings. It is also likely that the four possible interactions between science and religion as described by Barbour represent nodal points in the relationship so that there may actually be many variations on these themes and even mixtures to one degree or another. For the purposes of this book, it is important to recognize how each of these possible interactions may eventually be manifested in a neurotheological discourse. It may be the case that sometimes there will be direct conflicts between scientific data on one hand and religious belief on the other. However, there will also be times of dialogue and integration depending on the specific issues being addressed. Either way, it is important to begin the neurotheological pursuit with a framework in which an analysis of theology from the perspective of the mind and brain is considered possible as well as an analysis of science from a religious or theological perspective. This will help clarify and interpret how a synthesis of neuroscience and religion may be useful in the evaluation of epistemological as well as ontological problems.

It is at the neurotheological juncture that the science and religion interaction may be most valuable and help establish a more fundamental link between the spiritual and biological dimensions of the human being. Therefore, neurotheology, which should provide an openness to a number of different perspectives, might also be viewed as a nexus in which those from the religious as well as scientific side can come together to explore deep issues about humanity in a constructive and complementary manner. There, no doubt, will be differing viewpoints that will be raised throughout this process, some of which may be more exclusive of one perspective or the other. However, it should be stressed that for neurotheology to grow as a field, it is imperative that one remains open, at least somewhat, to all of the different perspectives including those that are religious or spiritual, cultural, or scientific.

In addition to the complex interrelationship between science and religion over the years, neurotheological research must draw upon the current state of modern scientific methods and existing theological debates. Science has advanced significantly in the past several decades with regard to the study of the human brain. Neurotheology should be prepared to take full advantage of the advances in fields of science such as functional brain imaging, cognitive neuroscience, psychology, and genetics. On the other hand, neurotheological scholarship should also be prepared to engage the full range of theological issues. That theology continues to evolve and change from the more dogmatic perspectives of the past, through natural theology and systematic theology, neurotheology must acknowledge that there are many fascinating theological issues that face each religious tradition. Neurotheology should therefore strive to engage current theological debate to determine where and how this new perspective might provide some additional value. Neurotheological investigations must also clearly acknowledge neurotheology's own limitations as well as the limitations involved with scientific and theological disciplines.

Foundational Goals of Neurotheology

Now that the historical, scientific, and theological foundations have been considered, there is one more aspect of neurotheology that must be reviewed before discussing the principles of neurotheology. The foundational goals of neurotheology should help provide a compelling case for the pursuit of such topics. These goals are critical to establish how we are going to develop neurotheology and provide a defense for its existence as a field of scholarship. There are many important questions that neurotheology may help address that pertain to the nature of subjective experience, consciousness, the mind, and the soul. Neurotheology will hopefully bring new perspectives to the fields of neuroscience and theology. Neurotheology will also likely enhance many of the fields that contribute to its cross-disciplinary nature including, but not limited to, anthropology, sociology, neurobiology, cognitive neuroscience, medicine, genetics, physics, philosophy, religious studies, and theology. These fields will no doubt bring a richness and depth to the study of neurotheology in that each will provide an important perspective on the various issues that arise. Additionally, trying to integrate neuroscientific and religious or theological perspectives will also help to enhance reciprocally our understanding of the other contributing fields. This will hopefully provide an impetus for future studies and investigations not only in the realm of neurotheology but in all of the other contributing fields as well. The methods that are developed as part of neurotheology also may have broader applications with regard to health and possibly global sociopolitical problems.

When considering the *raison d'être* for developing neurotheology as a field, we can consider four foundational goals for scholarship in this area. These are:

1. to improve our understanding of the human mind and brain;
2. to improve our understanding of religion and theology;
3. to improve the human condition, particularly in the context of health and well being;
4. to improve the human condition, particularly in the context of religion and spirituality.

These four goals are reciprocal in that they suggest that both religious and scientific pursuits might benefit from neurotheological research. The first two are meant to be both esoteric as well as pragmatic regarding scientific and theological disciplines. The second two goals refer to the importance of providing practical applications of neurotheological findings towards improving human life both individually and globally.

Let us explore these goals in more detail. The first is one that many critics of neurotheology often forget. Namely, that neurotheological research, especially studies that utilize cognitive neuroscience techniques, actually challenges science to develop strong methodologies. As a field of study, cognitive neuroscience links various aspects of human thoughts, feelings, and perceptions to their underlying biological correlates. Techniques developed through the study of cognitive neuroscience have already advanced tremendously over the past several decades with the advent of many types of brain imaging abilities and other techniques to measure how the brain functions during various mental tasks and perceptions. The development of these techniques, specifically in the study of religious and spiritual phenomena, will undoubtedly be a cornerstone for neurotheology in the future. But neurotheological research will also have a potentially strong impact on the methods of cognitive neuroscience. The reason for this is that religious, spiritual, mystical, and theological phenomena are notoriously difficult to evaluate from any kind of scientific perspective. Determining which subjects to study, what to measure biologically, what to measure phenomenologically or subjectively, when to make measurements, and what type of approach is needed to actually make the measurements, are substantial problems for any empirically-based neurotheological research. To perform such studies in a manner that provides useful results will require an advancement or even reworking of cognitive neuroscience methodology which will hopefully lead to a better overall understanding of the human brain.

In addition to helping improve cognitive neuroscience methods, neurotheological research also provides new perspectives regarding the human mind itself. With so many new studies exploring a range of human mental processes including those relating to morality, love, honesty, and complex behaviors,[50] a thorough study of one of the most important and pervasive dimensions of human beings—the religious and spiritual—should significantly augment our understanding of the human person. Religion and spirituality has had, and will continue to have, a tremendous impact on behavioral, emotional, and cognitive processes within individuals. Religious rituals are highly complex behaviors that affect the brain on multiple sensory, cognitive, and emotional levels. Similarly, theological analysis requires many different elements of human cognition. Causal, teleological, and epistemological arguments challenge the mind at every turn, and understanding that relationship can only help us to understand better how the human brain works.

The second goal, to improve our understanding of religion and theology, is intriguing since the implication is that theology has something to gain through its interaction with cognitive neuroscientific research. This point was partially made above in the description of the historical foundations of neurotheology. Reflecting upon the neurophysiological correlates of theological ideas and their implications, from the Upanishads to Aquinas to Tillich, has the potential to provide an entirely new perspective on theology itself. Of course, the goal of using neurotheological research to improve theology is often met with trepidation from the religious perspective. The concern is not so much that the understanding of religion and theology will be *improved*, but rather that it will be *replaced* by a reductive, impersonal, and unspiritual version using science.[51] Several attempts at providing such an interpretation of the human soul appear to be antithetical to more traditional views of theology and religion. However, while this concern should be maintained during any neurotheological research program, an *a priori* attempt at reducing religion and spirituality to science would be highly biased and flawed and would not result in a fruitful result in the end.

The third goal of neurotheology is to improve the human condition, particularly in the context of health and well being. This goal derives from the first in that improving our understanding of the relationship between religion and the mind should ultimately yield information that will have practical applications. We will explore this in detail later, but here we might at least consider the range of possibilities by which this goal might be achieved. For example, there is a strong and growing literature regarding the relationship between religion and both physical and mental health. Studies revealing how religion might contribute to improved physical health by reducing stress, helping with coping, and improving compliance with medical interventions might improve the overall health of our population. We might also find that specific practices such as meditation or prayer yield improvements in a variety of physical processes including those related to the cardiovascular system, digestive system, and immune system. Neurotheological research might also identify potentially negative consequences of religious and spiritual beliefs.[52] Some of this research might evaluate attitudes of specific traditions regarding the avoidance of medical interventions, while other studies might reveal how individuals develop a negative perspective of religion or God. These negative perspectives can lead to personal strife, anxiety, and depression. However, at the present time, there is not much known about what factors lead to these negative perspectives.

Another area that would lend itself well to neurotheological study is the growing problem with terrorism and the mind of the terrorist. It is not clear how and why some individuals follow extreme religious or spiritual views.[53] Neurotheological research has the opportunity to evaluate thoroughly which type of individual is most likely to follow such a path and perhaps offer methods for appropriately redirecting them. The ability to determine why hatred and exclusivity are fostered and accepted by an individual or group of individuals is information that could have important consequences for global health.

The fourth foundational goal suggests that through neurotheology, it might be possible to improve the religious and spiritual well being of individuals and of humanity in general. Neurotheology might provide a setting in which the improved understanding of religious and theological phenomena lead to practical applications in the ways in which individuals pursue their own spiritual goals. While it is not clear precisely by what mechanism such a goal might be achieved, it could be argued that whenever there is improved knowledge, especially if a new perspective is offered, there is the opportunity to grow. In the context of theology and religion, spiritual growth is always encouraged and neurotheology should be supported as another mechanism by which such growth might occur.

Critics often raise the concern that neurotheology might offer a way of "taking a pill" to become more spiritual. However, human beings have perpetually utilized different techniques from ritual, prayer, and meditation, to starvation, sustained intense physical activity, and pharmacological substances to help induce spiritual or religious states.[54] Thus, the notion of trying to bring about a spiritual or religious experience via some specified mechanism has existed for thousands of years. It should be no surprise, nor a problem therefore, if neurotheology uncovers better approaches than those that already exist. The important issue will be how to incorporate these approaches appropriately into a specific religious or spiritual paradigm. This, then, is one of the true challenges of neurotheological research.

We might consider one additional, overarching goal of neurotheology which pertains to the nature of reality. In order to address the four foundational goals described above, we must realize that all of them ultimately rest upon one fundamental question: How do we know the true nature of reality? And the corollary question is: Is the reality that we perceive and are conscious of really the real reality? After all, if we are going to try to advance our understanding about ourselves and the world around us, we must try to address better these fundamental epistemological questions.

With these foundational goals in mind, we are close to elaborating the principles of neurotheology. As might be expected, definitions are a crucial step. And this is particularly the case with neurotheology. Neurotheology itself must be defined in addition to many other concepts that can be assessed in this field of research. An exploration of definitions of a variety of religious and scientific concepts will then provide a starting point for delineating the principles of neurotheology.

Before we engage the definitions and, ultimately, the principles of neurotheology, permit me one additional comment regarding an often undervalued, but incredibly important concept in philosophy, theology, and science—humor. Neurotheology must admit the crucial importance of humor in understanding the human mind and its ability to deal with an ever changing and confusing world. In fact, it may be human kind's greatest legacy to be able to look upon an incredibly short life span, often filled with anxiety, fears, loss, suffering, and death and still find some way of laughing at ourselves and at the very world which causes us so much angst. Neurotheology would certainly make sure to include the neurological and theological basis of humor in any final analysis of the human person. And I cannot help but employ a line from the great comedian Groucho Marx with regard to the principles of neurotheology—"These are my principles, and if you don't like them, I have others!" This is a most well taken point since whatever principles we consider in the following pages, we must keep in mind that these principles can and should change as the scholarship, both scientific and theological, that drives neurotheology develops and advances.

Finally, I would like to add that I truly hope that my representation of scholarship in the disparate fields that may contribute to neurotheology is adequate enough to provide a starting point. I certainly look forward to being advised and corrected by other scholars from fields that are different than my own. And this is perhaps the greatest gift of neurotheology, the ability to foster a rich multidisciplinary dialogue in which we help others "get it right" so that we can advance the human person and human thought as it pertains to our mental, biological, and spiritual selves.

Notes

1. Austin, J.H. *Zen and the Brain: Toward an Understanding of Meditation and Consciousness.* Cambridge, MA: MIT Press, 1999; Austin, J.H. *Zen-Brain Reflections.* Cambridge, MA: MIT Press, 2006; Kelly, B.D. "Buddhist psychology, psychotherapy and the brain: a critical introduction." *Transcultural Psychiatr.* 2008;45:5–30; Davids, R. *A Buddhist Manual of Psychological Ethics or Buddhist Psychology.* Columbia, MO: South Asia Books, 1996; McGraw, J.J. *Brain and Belief: An Exploration of the Human Soul.* Del Mar, CA: Aegis Press, 2004.

2. Gyatso, T (fourteenth Dalai Lama). *The World of Tibetan Buddhism: An Overview of Its Philosophy and Practice.* Translated by Thupten Jinpa. Somerville, MA: Wisdom Publications, 1995.

3. Liston., C., McEwen, B.S., and Casey, B.J. "Psychosocial stress reversibly disrupts prefrontal processing and attentional control." *Proc Natl Acad Sci USA.* 2009;106: 912–917; Wang, J., Rao, H., Wetmore, G.S., Furlan, P.M., Korczykowski, M., Dinges, D.F., and Detre, J.A. "Perfusion functional MRI reveals cerebral blood flow pattern under psychological stress." *Proc Natl Acad Sci USA.* 2005;102:17804–17809.

4. Eisenberger, N.I., Lieberman, M.D., and Williams, K.D. "Does rejection hurt? An FMRI study of social exclusion." *Science.* 2003;302:290–292.

5. Newberg, A.B., Alavi, A., Baime, M., Pourdehnad, M., Santanna, J., and d'Aquili, E.G. "The measurement of regional cerebral blood flow during the complex cognitive task of meditation: a preliminary SPECT study." *Psychiatr Res Neuroimaging.* 2001;106:113–122; Newberg, A.B. and Iiversen, J. 'The neural basis of the complex mental task of meditation: neurotransmitter and neurochemical considerations." *Med Hypothesis.* 2003;61:282–291.

6. Schwartz, J.M., Begley, S. *The Mind and the Brain: Neuroplasticity and the Power of Mental Force.* New York, NY: Harper Perennial, 2003.

7. Newberg, A.B., Alavi, A., Baime, M., Pourdehnad, M., Santanna, J., and d'Aquili, E.G. "The measurement of regional cerebral blood flow during the complex cognitive task of meditation: a preliminary SPECT study." *Psychiatr Res Neuroimaging.* 2001; Lou, H.C., Nowak, M., and Kjaer, TW. 'The mental self." *Prog Brain Res.* 2005;150:197–204.

8. Scotton, B.W. "Treating Buddhist patients." in Koenig, H.G. (ed.), *Handbook of Religion and Mental Health.* San Diego, CA: Academic Press, 1998.

9. Micozzi, M. *Fundamentals of Complementary and Alternative Medicine.* New York, NY: Churchill Livingstone, 1996.

10. Meshberger, F.L. "An interpretation of Michelangelo's *Creation of Adam* based on neuroanatomy." *JAMA.* 1990;264:1837–1841.

11. Genesis 2:9. *King James Bible.*

12. Job 30:26. *King James Bible.*

13. Acts 13:38. *King James Bible.*

14. Ephesians I 4–8. *King James Bible.*

15. Thompson, C.J. "Preliminary remarks toward a constructive encounter between St. Thomas and clinical psychology." *Catholic Soc Sci Rev.* 2005;10:41–52.

16. Aquinas, T. *Summa Theologica.* Notre Dame, IN: Christian classics, 1981.

17. Plass, E.W. *What Luther Says* (3 volumes). St. Louis, MO: Concordia Publishing House, 1959.

18. Rupp, E.G., Watson, P.S., and Baillie, J. *Luther and Erasmus: Free Will and Salvation* (Library of Christian Classics; Paperback Westminster). Louisville, KY: Westminster John Knox Press, 1995.

19. Moss, D. "The roots and genealogy of humanistic psychology." in Schneider, K., Bugental, J., and Pierson, J. (ed.), *Handbook of Humanistic Psychology.* Thousand Oaks, CA: Sage, 2001.

20. Ingvar, D.H. 'The will of the brain: cerebral correlates of willful acts." *J Theor Biol.* 1994;171:7–12; Frith, C.D., Friston, K., Liddle, P.F., and Frackowiak, R.S. "Willed action and the prefrontal cortex in man: a study with PET" *Proc R Soc Lond.* 1991;244:241–246.

21. Descartes, R. *Meditations on First Philosophy: With Selections from the Objections and Replies.* translated by Michael Moriarty. Oxford: Oxford University Press, 2008.

22. Gazzaniga, M.S. *The New Cognitive Neurosciences,* 2nd Edition. Cambridge, MA: Mit Press, 2000.

23. Damasio, A. *Descartes Error: Emotion, Reason, and the Human Brain.* New York, NY: Avon Books, 1994.

24. Spinoza, B. *Theological-Political Treatise: Gebhardt Edition.* Translated by Samuel Shirley. Indianapolis, In: Hackett Publishing Company, 2001.

25. Damasio, A. *Looking for Spinoza: Joy, Sorrow, and the Feeling Brain.* New York, NY: Harcourt, 2003.

26. Guyer, P. and Wood, A.W. *Critique of Pure Reason by Immanuel Kant.* Cambridge: Cambridge University Press, 1999.

27. *Stanford Encyclopedia of Philosophy* on line.

28. Gerrish, B.A., MacKintosh, H.R., and stewart, J.S. *The Christian Faith by Friedrich Schleiermacher.* Edinburgh: T. & T. clark Publishers, 1999.

29. James, W. *Varieties of Religious Experience.* London: Routledge, 2002.

30. Durkheim, E. *The Elementary Forms of Religious Life.* Edited by Mark S. Cladis, Translated by Carol Cosman. New York, NY: Oxford University Press, 2008.

31. Freud, S., with Strachey, J. and Gay, P. *The Future of an Illusion.* New York, NY: W.W. Norton & Company, 1989.

32. Otto, R. *Idea of the Holy.* Oxford: Oxford University Press, 1958.

33. Eliade, M. *The Sacred and the Profane.* New York, NY: Harcourt, Brace, and Jovanovich, 1959.

34. Tillich, P. *Systematic Theology* (3 volumes). Chicago, IL: University of Chicago Press, 1951–1963.

35. McKelway, A.J. *The Systematic Theology of Paul Tillich: A Review and Analysis.* Richmond, VA: John Knox Press, 1964.

36. d'Aquili, E.G. "The neurological basis of myth and concepts of diety." *Zygon.* 1978;13:257–275; d'Aquili, E.G. "Senses of reality in science and religion: a neuroepistemological perspective." *Zygon.* 1982;17:361–384; Ashbrook, J.B. and Albright, C.R. *The Humanizing Brain: Where Religion and Neuroscience Meet.* Cleveland, OH: Pilgrim Press, 1997.

37. Joseph, R. (ed.). *Neurotheology: Brain, Science, Spirituality, Religious Experience.* San Jose, CA: University Press, California. 2002; Austin, J.H. *Zen and the Brain: Toward an Understanding of Meditation and Consciousness.* Cambridge, MA: MIT Press, 1999. Beauregard, M. and O'Leary, D. *The Spiritual Brain.* New York, NY: Harper Collins, 2007; Alston, B.C. *What is Neurotheology?* Charleston, SC: BookSurge Publishing, 2007; McNamara, P. *The Neuroscience of Religious Experience.* Cambridge: Cambridge University Press, 2009; McKinney, L. *Neurotheology: Virtual Religion in the 21st Century.* Cambridge, MA: American Institute for Mindfulness, 1994; Peterson, G.R. *Minding God.* Minneapolis, MN: Augsburg Fortress Press, 2003.

38. d'Aquili, E.G. and Laughlin, C. "The biopsychological determinants of religious ritual behavior." *Zygon.* 1975; 10:32–58; d'Aquili, E.G., Laughlin, C., and McManus, J. *The Spectrum of Ritual: A Biogenetic Structural Analysis.* New York, NY: columbia University Press, 1979.

39. Gellhorn, E., Kiely, W.F. "Mystical states of consciousness: neurophysiological and clinical aspects." *J Nerv Ment Dis.* 1972;154:399–405.

40. Newberg, A.B., d'Aquili, E.G., and Rause, V.P. *Why God Won't Go Away: Brain Science and the Biology of Belief.* New York, NY: Ballantine Publishing Group, 2001; Newberg, A.B. and Waldman, M.R. *Why We Believe What We Believe: Uncovering Our Biological Need for Meaning, Spirituality, and Truth.* New York, NY: Free Press, 2006; Beauregard, M. and O'Leary, D. *The Spiritual Brain.* New York, NY: Harper collins, 2007.

41. Barbour, I.G. *Religion in an Age of Science.* New York, NY: Harper & Row, 1990.

42. Monod, J. *Chance and Necessity.* New York, NY: Vintage Books, 1972; Dawkins, R. *The God Delusion.* New York, NY: Houghton Mifflin, 2006.

43. Gould, S.J. *Rocks of Ages.* New York, NY: Ballantine, 1999.

44. Tracy, D. *Blessed Rage for Order.* New York, NY: Seabury, 1975; Tracy, D. *Plurality and Ambiguity.* San Francisco, CA: Harper & Row, 1987.

45. Rolston, H. *Science and Religion: A Critical Survey.* New York, NY: Random House, 1987.

46. Carter, B. "Large number coincidences and the anthropic principle in cosmology." *IAU Symposium 63: Confrontation of Cosmological Theories with Observational Data:* 291–298, Dordrecht: Reidel, 1974; Barrow, J.D. and Tipler, F.J. *The Anthropic Cosmological Principle.* Oxford: Oxford University Press, 1986.

47. Barbour, I.G. *Religion in an Age of Science.* New York, NY: Harper & Row, 1990.

48. Whitehead, A.N. *Process and Reality.* New York, NY: Macmillan, 1929.

49. Wallace, B.A. *Contemplative Science.* New York, NY: Columbia University Press, 2007.

50. d'Aquili, E.G. and Newberg, A.B. *The Mystical Mind: Probing the Biology of Religious Experience.* Minneapolis, MN: Fortress Press, 1999; Moll, J. and de Oliveira- souza, R. "Moral judgments, emotions and the utilitarian brain." *Trends Cogn Sci.* 2007;11:319–321; Gazzaniga, M.S. *The Ethical Brain.* New York, NY: Dana Press, 2005; Talbot, M. "Duped: can brain scans uncover lies?" *New Yorker.* July 2, 2007:52–61; Fisher, H.E., Aron, A., Mashek, D., Li, H., and Brown, L.L. "Defining the brain systems of lust, romantic attraction, and attachment." *Arch Sex Behav.* 2002;31:413–419; Bartels, A. and Zeki, S. 'The neural basis of romantic love." *Neuroreport.* 2000;11:3829–3834.

51. Brown, W.S., Murphy, N., and Malony, H.N. *Whatever Happened to the Soul.* Minneapolis, MN: Fortress Press, 1998.

52. Lee, B. and Newberg, A. "Religion and health: a review and critical analysis." *Zygon.* 2005;40:443–468.

53. Juergensmeyer, M. *Terror in the Mind of God: The Global Rise of Religious Violence.* Berkeley, CA: University of California Press, 2000.

54. Roberts, T.B. (ed.). *Psychoactive Sacramentals: Essays on Entheogens and Religion.* San Francisco, CA: Council on Spiritual Practices, 2001.

Religiosity as an Identity: Young Arab Muslim Women in the United States and France

Danielle Dunand Zimmerman, PhD

School of Social Work, Loyola University Chicago, Chicago, Illinois

Young Arab Muslim women who are religious are particularly challenged by hostility toward Muslims in the United States' and France's secular societies. They feel Muslim first but are not recognized as religious citizens and their personal quest for religious identity faces both stereotypical assumptions from non-Muslims and expectations from their own community. The current study, conducted in the United States and France, shows that as religion is central to their identity negotiation process, young Arab women who are religious Muslims struggle to express who they feel they are, as citizens of their country of residence as well as members of an ethnic and religious minority.

KEYWORDS religiosity, identity, Arab Muslim women, United States, France

Introduction

The United States and France handle integration issues differently, each referring to opposite theoretical models. France remains an example of the assimilation model, where maintaining exterior signs of cultural background and beliefs is perceived as resistance toward integration (House, 2006). The United States gives preference to multiculturalism initiatives since the implementation of the Immigration and Nationality Act of 1965, which abolished the national-origin quotas that favored European immigration, and encouraged a massive immigration of Asian and Latin American nationals to the United States. In the United States, the prevalent initiatives regarding integration of diverse groups are developed by communities (Sundar, 2009). Koser (2007) states, "the hands-off approach by the federal government . . . has fostered self-reliance and leadership among immigrant communities" (p. 12). Wearing the hijab or the burqa is identified in the United States as belonging to a community with specific religious beliefs and cultural traditions. The right to express religious beliefs is protected by the United States Constitution. In contrast, France perceives wearing the hijab or the burqa as signs of defiance to fundamental French values, as expressed by the legal bans of 2004 and 2010. The former prevents Muslim girls from wearing the hijab in public schools and the latter bans the burqa and niqab (full veil covering the face) in all public spaces. In both the United States and France, the 9/11 terrorist attacks have led to a strongly negative focus on Arab Muslims. Caincar (2009) argues that hijabs represent to those opposed to it an evidence of foreignness and disloyalty to American values. For Scott (2007), veiled Muslim women are seen as a more serious threat than Muslim men in France. In both countries, young Arab Muslim women are specifically targeted.

Context of the Study

Secularism in the United States and France

Historically, both the United States and France have established a strong separation between Church and State: this principle is stated in the first amendment of the United States' Constitution, as well as in a French law of 1905 that guaranties the freedom of religion (Scott, 2007). The two countries view the notion of secularism differently. America has a history of welcoming religious minorities fleeing persecution from European countries, and the separation between church and state was meant to protect those groups from government intervention, as well as to prevent any single religion to interfere with the affairs of the State. In France, separation was meant to break the power of the Catholic Church and to ensure allegiance of individuals to the Republic (Scott, 2007).

McClay (2001) calls "negative" secularism the approach promoted by the United States in which the state may neither favor a particular religion nor interfere with religion, while he calls "positive" secularism the French

Received November 8, 2013; accepted March 5, 2014.

Address correspondence to Danielle Dunand Zimmerman, PhD, School of Social Work, Loyola University Chicago, 1032 W. Sheridan Road, Chicago, IL 60660. E-mail: dzimmerman2@luc.edu interdiction of religion and religious symbols in public institutions. While negative secularism is an opponent of established beliefs and a protector of free association, positive secularism is a proponent of established unbelief and a protector of individual rights, including that of religious expression.

Muslim Identity in the United States and France

The 9/11 events have led to an increased consciousness of "Muslimness" among the Muslim Diaspora, and young Muslims in North America and Europe experience a heightened awareness of their Muslim identities (Mishra & Shirazi, 2010). Peek (2005) states that for both Muslims and non-Muslims, religious identity in the United States has become more central to an individual sense of self since the events of 9/11. Young Muslim women attending college in the United States negotiate their identity at the intersection of religion, race, and gender (Mir, 2009; Naber, 2005). In addition, Mir (2009) states, "peer culture . . . exercises the most powerful normative influence upon [Muslim] students" (p. 71). Schmidt (2004) shows that the wearing of Islamic clothing such as the veil helps nurture a sense of community among Muslim students attending college.

Bowen (2007) states, that in France, second-generation Muslim girls who wear the hijab while their mothers would not wear it and would merely follow tradition achieve "an Islamic legitimacy and familial authority by adopting the veil" (p. 72). Keaton (2006) asserts that as they are living in an environment of opposing forces such as Eastern tradition and Western freedom, Muslim teenage girls may manage internal and external constraints by rearticulating an "idealized national identity" (p. 158). As young Muslim women's decision to wear or not to wear the hijab is being scrutinized, their choice has implications beyond their own individual desire. In a college environment, young Arab Muslim women may experience conflicts between the image they end up giving of themselves and their actual sense of self.

Literature Review

Perceived Oppression and Stigmatization and Accelerated Islamization of Young Arab Muslims

Peek (2005) emphasizes the importance of the first college years in further constructing a Muslim religious identity among Muslim students, which she describes as a three-step process: religion as ascribed identity, religion as chosen identity, and religion as declared identity. Right after the events of 9/11, from September 2001 to October

2003, she conducted 23 focus groups, which ranged in size from three to 15 participants. In addition, she used 83 one-on-one, semistructured and unstructured interviews. The study took place in New York and Colorado, among college students recruited through the Muslim Student Associations (MSAs). Her research shows a strong relationship between the crisis generated by the events and aftermath of 9/11 and the increase of Muslim students practicing religion as a declared identity.

Haddad's (2007) findings are described by the author as the result of years of research and in-depth interviews, as well as two focus groups with 30 young American Muslim women attending college in several locations in the United States. She states that the process of re-Islamization among second-generation adolescent and young adult Muslims has accelerated in the United States as a consequence of the oppression sensed following 9/11. An increasing number of young Muslim women are taking on a public Islamic identity by wearing the hijab despite the fact that their mother have never followed Islamic dress requirement. This study shows how young American Muslim women appropriate the hijab as a "symbol of solidarity and resistance to efforts to eradicate the religion of Islam" (p. 253) as well as a symbol of American Islamic identity.

Santelli (2008) refers to three studies that she conducted in France between 2005 and 2007 with second-generation Arab immigrants, to analyze the effects of stigmatization in the construction of citizenship for young Arab Muslims. She links the efforts to overcome stigma to the process of affirming a new Muslim identity. The first study involves 30 participants, men and women, from 25 to 55 years old, and focuses on discrimination encountered at work. The second study, with 50 interviews of young Muslim couples, emphasizes the discrimination against young Arab Muslims in everyday life. The third study involves 30 interviews and 200 surveys of young Arab Muslim men and women between the ages of 20 and 30, living in segregated suburbs of Paris. Santelli (2008) shows how rampant racism and exclusion, reinforced by the negative focus of the media (e.g., while covering the attacks of 9/11 or the 2005 riots in France, they questioned and in some cases rejected the legitimacy of young Arab Muslims' citizenship), leads to a process of Islamization at both the individual and national level. At the individual level, Islam is perceived by some young Arab Muslims, especially those from the segregated suburbs, as a means to fight against social exclusion: defining oneself as Muslim provides feelings of belonging to a group that offers support and resources to fight those who oppress and stigmatize. At the national level, affirming a Muslim identity in French society helps its legitimization.

Beski-Chafiq, Birmant, Benmerzoug, Taibi, and Coignard (2010) conducted a study on youth and Islamist radicalization in Lille, a large city of Northern France, as part of a collective and comparative study with other European cities in Denmark, the United Kingdom, and Italy. Lille has a history of immigration linked to industrial activity, and there is a strong presence of immigrant population in the city, mostly Arab Muslims. The authors performed interviews with 32 young Muslims, 23 men and 9 women between the ages of 15 and 33; 7 parents, 20 social workers, 5 local elected politicians, and 3 religious leaders. Their aim was "to know to what extent the global process of re-Islamization involves youths in Islamism or, rather, makes them stop" (p. 12). Beski-Chafiq et al. (2010) stressed the fundamental difference between "individual and secular Islam experienced by a significant part of young people" (p. 10) and Islamism that is "a doctrine that projects Islam as an ideology governing all spheres of individual and collective life and aims at mobilizing people of Muslim affiliation in building a society or community based on religious values and laws" (p. 12). They emphasized that communicating on the subject of Islamism with religious, political, and social actors was particularly challenging as most of them feared that the study would feed stigmatization of Islam and Muslims. Before beginning the interviews, the researchers were often asked if they were "for or against Muslims" and interviewees expressed distrust when the notion of radicalization was mentioned, "for fear of slipping into racism and becoming an accomplice of the media that would stigmatize Muslims" (p. 16).

The study results show two ideologies of re-Islamization among young Muslim participants: an attempt to apply the Islamic teachings to the letter, as a means to reclaim a learned Islam, different from that of their parents, which provides guidance and support for living within the religion; the desire to build an Islamic identity in France through the promotion of Islamic law that can preserve them from an individualistic modernity. In contrast, parents describe Islam with a pragmatic sense, as a set of values that is transmitted naturally, through family rituals. Social workers point to feelings of social and economic exclusion, confinement, withdrawal, group effects, and the internalization of victimization as major factors of radicalization of some Muslim youth. They also strongly denounce the media as promoters of racism and stigmatization. Local political actors emphasize that Islamic radicalization remained a minority among the Muslim population of Lille and they denounce the lack of a clear and coherent national policy with respect to secularism and its application, as well as the socioeconomic exclusion and the stigmatization of Islam. Finally, the Imam participating in the study emphasizes the need to separate worship and politics and mentions that he considers himself as a secular citizen. Two other religious leaders, both women, promote the fusion of worship and politics which includes the duty to respect Islamic order and to wear the veil, or the fusion of worship and culture, which moves away from Islam as a source of order.

In both countries, accelerated Islamization of young Arab Muslims is linked to oppression and stigmatization. While in the United States the oppression of Muslims is mostly related to the aftermath of the 9/11 attacks, socioeconomic exclusion is identified as another major factor of re-Islamization in France.

Generational Differences in the Experience of Islam Between First and Second-Generation Arab Muslim Women

Williams and Vashi (2007) assert that second-generation Muslim American women negotiate social and religious identities as a reaction both to stereotypical assumptions from non-Muslims and to their immigrant families. They emphasize the implications of wearing the hijab for young Muslim women in the United States in terms of context, meanings for the young women, and consequences on their lives. The authors gathered data in a Midwestern metropolitan area from two sources: one in-depth interview and one focus group interview of eight young Muslim women at a Muslim religious organization; interviews of 40 young Muslim women ages 18–25 attending college. Most women were from South-East Asia and half of them were wearing hijabs. The study shows how young American Muslim attending college perceive two distinct cultural messages: America is a country of equal rights; America is a country of cultural decadence. These conflicted messages produce "a contested space for ethnic, religious, and gender identity development" (p. 273). The authors stress that even though contested cultural space is not a new issue for immigrant populations or religious minorities, Islam's controversial place in the West and the focus on hijab makes this dilemma particularly acute for young American Muslim women in college.

Ali (2005) worked with three sets of data gathered in 1999 to study second-generation Muslim women's religiosity in the United States. She used 22 open-ended e-mail interviews with second generation Muslim women nationally wearing the hijab, whose age ranged from 13 to 29; ethnographic field research in New York City among Indian Muslim women; and observations and interviews of second generation Muslim women wearing the hijab at the Islamic Society of North America in 1999. She notes that the move toward wearing the hijab has only happened in the recent years and to answer the question "why hijab now?" she identifies four main reasons: the rise of multiculturalism has legitimized the public expression of ethnicity; the Muslim population in the United States has grown and second generation Muslims are becoming more politically involved locally and nationally; the events of 9/11 and subsequent stigmatization lead Muslims to self-evaluate and ask themselves what it means to be Muslim; and there is a new trend among young American Muslims to seek out "true" Islamic knowledge on their own, moving away from what their parents taught them.

Killian (2007) conducted audiotaped in-depth, semi-istructured interviews with 45 first-generation Muslim women in Paris and surrounding suburbs in 1999. She identified, even before the events of 9/11, a tendency for these women's daughters to seek visible symbols of religious identity such as the veil, suggesting "the emergence of generational differences in the experience of Islam in France" (p. 305). Based on her original study, she elaborated on the aftermaths of the terrorist attacks and subsequent Islamophobia in France, to confirm a link between feelings of rejection due to racism and discrimination and identity crisis of second-generation Arab Muslims: Young Arab Muslims often feel that despite their best efforts to integrate, they are perceived as Maghrebian rather than French, because of their appearance. Some young Arab Muslim women choose to fight rejection by asserting a non-French appearance as they wear the hijab. Killian asserts that the generational differences between first- and second-generation Muslim women in France occurred before the events of 9/11 and may find their roots in the French context of social exclusion.

In both countries, second generation Muslim women seek to appropriate and assert a new form of identity that is a reaction to both Western stigmatization of Muslim women and their upbringing in families that blended cultural traditions and religion. Daughters of Muslim immigrants to the United States and France may wish to experience "true" Islam as a means to create space for personal and collective emancipation.

Conceptual Framework

The Argument of Secularism Contested

The concept of secularism is contested by critical political philosophy, particularly since the events of September 11, 2001. For example, as a core element of liberal democracy, secularism led to legitimizing France's legal ban of the Muslim headscarf (Jansen, 2006). Critics assert that state's religious neutrality in Western societies should not be presented as absolute, since Christian churches are sometimes financially supported by or incorporated to public institutions; in fact, historically dominant religions may generate religious dogmatism and oppression (Jansen, 2006). Bader (1999) suggests that states may give "priority to democracy" over secularism.

Religious pluralism is presented as an alternative to secularism. Eck (2006) describes religious pluralism as follows: First, pluralism is not diversity itself, but the engagement with diversity; in contemporary democratic societies, religious diversity is a given but pluralism is not. Second, pluralism implies more than tolerance; it involves "the active seeking of understanding across lines of difference" (p. 1). Third, pluralism is not about giving up controversial differences, but rather it promotes holding to one's religious commitments and embracing the encounter of others' commitments. Fourth, in order to create encounters of commitment, pluralism needs dialogue.

Scholars suggest that the concept of separation between church and state does not adequately describe Western liberal states' current approach to secularism, and that instead continuous regulation of religious life expresses a much more blurry delimitation (Mahmood, 2006). In the United States, since the events of 9/11, multiple court decisions have regulated when and how religion may be practiced and expressed in public. Similarly in France, the legal ban on religious symbols and the veil in public schools is another example of how states define what religious and nonreligious attire is in the public domain (Mahmood, 2006). Mahmood argues that the state's interference in the religious sphere is becoming a norm in Western democracies, with the intention of reshaping the form religion takes and the subjectivities it expresses. National cultures privilege historically majoritarian and religious norms. He also calls attention to the "civilizing and disciplinary aspects" of the United States' approach to secularism in its discourse regarding the Muslim world. Asad (2003) argues that even though mutual independence of state and religion is a fundamental notion of secularism, it is the state that has the power to affect religious practices, unilaterally. Secularism in France and the United States is more an argument leading to state's regulation than a value of religious neutrality.

Citizenship and Secularism

Calhoun (2011) state, "the tacit understanding of citizenship in the modern West has been secular" (p. 75). They argue that the distinction between public and private sphere with respect to religious expression leads to impairing participation to the public debate as citizens of religious citizens such as Muslims. They make a parallel with past restrictions of women's political participation as justified by the same public/private sphere argument. Bhargava (2009) criticizes Western societies for ignoring attempts to develop contextual secularisms, as practiced in India, which may allow for depoliticizing of religion and active recognition of multiple religions simultaneously. In both the United States and France, dominant secularism—that does not recognize the specificity of religious citizens such as Muslims—has been strengthened yet since the aftermath of the events of 9/11.

Religion as an Identity

Modood (2010) advocates for a moderate secularism that takes into account religion as a minority identity. He argues that the current hostility to Muslims in Western societies calls for protection from the state: if oppressed minorities value their religious identity more than it is the norm in the dominant society, religion becomes an ethnic feature with personal, social, and political salience. Therefore, the state needs to develop antidiscrimination policies in relation to religious groups, as well as even-handed allocation of resources. The United States and France do not recognize religion as a minority identity that grants specific rights.

Feminist Identity Politics

Feminist concept of intersectionality of identity for women (Crenshaw, 1991) affirms that gender needs to be understood in relation to other social identities such as race, class, ethnicity, and sexual orientation. In contrast to models that suggest for each minority group a given accumulation of disadvantages, intersectionality emphasizes the qualitative differences among intersectional positions; intersectional identities are defined in relation to one another (Shields, 2008). Macey and Carling (2010) call attention to a "communal identity" that incorporates the intersectionality of race *and* ethnicity *and* religion. Weir (2008) advocates for feminist identity politics that move from a static to a relational model, in which the questions of category such as that of "woman" are replaced with the notion of identification with: common identity is based on "desires, relationships, commitments, ideals" (p. 111). Young Arab Muslim women in the United States and France negotiate their identity at the intersection of gender, religion, race, and ethnicity.

Methodology

I conducted the current qualitative study in 2012 with the objective of exploring how young Arab Muslim women attending college in France and the United States negotiated their identity. I used descriptive phenomenology to proceed with data collection and analysis. I interviewed eight French participants in Paris, France, and eight American participants in Chicago, United States. All participants were self-declared as religious; half of the participants in each sample wore the hijab.

Sampling and Recruitment
Sample Description and Access

All participants to this study are college students. The sample is ideally constructed to discuss secularism: from an in-group perspective, the participants are members of a Muslim family living in a secular world and experiencing cultural adjustments; from an out-group perspective, going to college represents being away from Muslim values that may be at odd with dominant values.

I used a combination of purposive and snowball sampling in order to build a sample that would represent both veiling and nonveiling women. After contacting one participant who introduced me to some of her friends, I asked the first participants to help me recruit both veiling and nonveiling friends willing to participate to the study. Snowball sampling led to participant recruitment in four public universities in Paris; one private university, and two public universities in Chicago.

French Sample

The French sample consisted of eight second-generation Muslim women aged 19 to 25. All participants were born in France and were therefore French nationals. In France, the vast majority of Muslim immigrants are working-class laborers, originally from French colonized Maghreb countries of Algeria, Tunisia, and Morocco (Read, 2007). Participants' parents were of Arab origins and were born in Northern Africa; in every case both parents were from the same country. Four of them were of Algerian ancestry, three of Moroccan, and one of Tunisian ancestry. Four participants did not wear the veil, two of them wore the hijab, and two wore the long veil (veil prolonged by a long-sleeved dress; the face is not covered). Among the four who did not veil, one tried wearing the veil during the summer between high school and college but chose to remove it after she entered college. Among the two who wore the hijab (but not the long veil), one started wearing it during the summer between high school and college after visiting the United States, and one was wearing a turban that she called "hijab."

American Sample

The attempt to match the French sample's diversity led to building an American sample that was also very diverse in terms of culture of origins—with five different countries of ancestry—age, and religiosity. As in the French sample, four women were veiling and four were not. The American sample included eight second-generation American Muslim women aged 19 to 23. All participants were born in the United States and were American citizens. Their parents were of Arab origins. Four of them were of Palestinian decent, with both parents being Palestinians. Two of them were of Syrian decent and both their parents were Syrian. One participant was of Egyptian decent from both parents, and one participant had a Moroccan mother and a European American father who converted to Islam. Four participants wore the hijab, and four did not veil. Among the four who did not veil, one tried wearing the hijab in eighth grade and took it off during her freshman year in high school, and one wore it from eighth grade to her sophomore year in college. There were two sisters in the sample: one wore the veil and the other did not.

Sample Size

The sampling size of this study is small, as it is comprised of eight participants in each country. In phenomenological studies, data saturation is a key factor for sample decisions. Authors (Groenewald, 2004; Guest, Bunce, & Johnson, 2006; Wertz, 2005) suggest that the nature and number of participants in phenomenological studies depend on when saturation of data has been reached; meaning that redundancy of findings that fulfill the research goal is achieved. This objective may be reached at an early stage, after a few interviews are conducted, or the researcher may choose to continue recruiting participants whose experience will complete the data. Predetermined sample and sample size are difficult to achieve, as the researcher has to assess themes emerging during data collection as well as quality of data with respect to research goals. In this study, interviews were first conducted in Paris, France, and preliminary analysis indicated that data saturation had been reached with eight interviews, four of veiling women and four of nonveiling women. Subsequently, eight interviews were conducted in Chicago, while building a sample comparable to the French one. Data saturation was also reached in the American sample.

Data Collection and Analysis

I conducted audiorecorded open-ended interviews in person with each participant. Questions were kept broad in scope. There were four main questions: (a) What is it like to be a college student in the United States/France? (b) What five words would you use to describe yourself? (c) How do you make the choice to veil or not to veil? (d) What are your goals and how do you see working towards them? No translator was needed for the French interviews, as I, the researcher/interviewer, am French and bilingual in English. I subsequently translated into English the content of the French interviews. Translation accuracy was ensured by checking for comprehension and testing for naturalness and readability. Trustworthiness of all interviews was ensured by member checking: each participant had the opportunity to view their own interview and to comment on its accuracy.

Following the methodology of descriptive phenomenology, I allowed for themes to emerge from data and used the computer program NVivo 10 to proceed through theme analysis and description of common experience among participants, independently of their history and context.

Assessment of Religiosity

Assessing each participant's level of religiosity allowed comparisons between samples in the United States and France. Religiosity was not part of inclusion criteria. The samples' level of religiosity was assessed with three items from Read's (2003) scale that is specific to Arab American women. Participants were asked to complete the following questionnaire: (a) Attend services: never, a few times a year, once or more a month; (b) Religiosity over the life cycle: low in childhood and adulthood, decreased since childhood, increased since childhood, high in childhood and adulthood; and (c) Religious conservatism: "Holy book of my religion is the literal word of God": Strongly disagree or disagree, neither agree nor disagree, strongly agree or agree.

Religiosity of Sample

Completing three items from Read's (2003) scale, six participants out of eight reported attending service a few times a year; one, once or more a month; one, never. Six participants reported an increased level of religiosity since childhood, one reported a level of religiosity as high in adulthood as in childhood, and one reported a decreased level of religiosity since childhood. Six participants also supported religious conservatism, and two chose the item "neither agreed nor disagree." Seven participants expressed a high level of religiosity and one participant expressed a low level of religiosity.

Findings

One major finding of this study was that, for all participants across sample, being Muslim meant much more than being of Muslim faith; it was an identity. Differences appeared between French and American samples in the manner in which participants were able to express their religious identity.

Across Sample, Being Muslim Is an Identity

All participants to this study, veiling and nonveiling, stated that being Muslim was an essential part of their identity.

Muslim First

When asked to describe themselves in the context of a young Arab Muslim woman in college, eight participants identify as Muslim first, five as Muslim women, two as Muslim citizens of their country of residence, and one as citizen of her country of residence first. In all cases, being Muslim means more to them than being of Muslim faith. As a Muslim, "There's that reference to Islam in every world, every gesture, every behavior . . . I think today if you say you're Muslim, you can't live without it, it's the basis of your existence, at home, at work, in the street." As one participant explains, "My life is actually based around it."

Several participants describe Islam as "a way of life." Islam is not "just a religion, it's not a world religion; it's a world way of life." Islam is "the basis of everything, including my behavior with people in everyday life, it's a bit like my civil code, an instrument that escorts me." One participant who identifies as Muslim first explains, "I see myself as Muslim before any ethnicity or the fact that I'm a woman, just because being Muslim is not just a religion but it's a way of being."

Religiosity is a Personal Process

All participants mention that they have developed their own understanding and practice of religion and they make a distinction between their family's traditions and their own religious process. Most participants emphasize that being Muslim in college gives them the responsibility to fight stereotypes and educate other students.

Seeking Islamic knowledge on one's own. Even as they acknowledge being committed to their parents' values and traditions, all participants mention that they pursue their own approach to religion, beyond the culture of origin carried by their family. One participant explains,

> In college, I got the impression that people were becoming more observant, they engaged in an identity quest, mostly religious. Having parents of different geographical origin, their benchmark was more religion. For example, the people I know come from very different backgrounds . . . and I had the feeling of knowing these people even though we have totally different customs and practices . . . but we were united by religion . . . They had explored their identity and what they wanted to convey beyond their origin, and it was religion.

Another interviewee summarizes her quest: "A word that is very important to me is legacy. This idea has kept my mind very busy; what did I receive and what do I want to pass on and share?" Some participants across sample mention that they developed a personal interest in religion, beyond or despite their parents' own religiosity during their high school years. One states,

> Parents when they tell certain principles, they don't explain . . . The prayers for example . . . I took the initiative in my late teens . . . It's clear that my parents haven't given me as much as what I got later, I learnt by myself.

Another participant adds, "I grew up with Islam and once I reached adolescence, I made the decision on my own to learn more about my religion . . . Parents may be ignorant on some points of religion while I'm going to go deeper." One participant who veils but mentions that she often does not relate to other veiling girls' perspective states, "there's a point when we must think by ourselves . . . Some Muslims believe that the Quran should be interpreted literally . . . I prefer to criticize and eventually realize that I was wrong . . . rather than following it stupidly." Some interviewees mention that it was in college that they started shaping their own approach to religion. In particular, one participant says,

> Until I got to college it was more about what culture dictates . . . Then, when I got to college I was introduced more to what the Quran says . . . We're actually going to the source directly. So, at home it was more about this is what my parents say . . . what I learnt was more by example . . . Then I came to college and sort of become more conscious of my religiosity and I became more curious and wanted to learn more about my religion. So, I've done my own research.

Fighting stereotypes and educating others. Participants across sample express a feeling of responsibility toward their religion, to make Islam better understood and respected around them. Reacting to stereotypes against Arab Muslims, one interviewee declares, "Our job in college is to teach people that it's not all like that . . . To be a Muslim girl going into education shows everyone that we're not all the same." Another participant states, "What I aim to do is be a Muslim woman, a Muslima, I advocate for my faith basically, to show that what's in the media isn't completely true . . . It's an obligation on me to show how Islam is." One participant points that Muslim women are also greatly responsible toward their community: "Ultimately, we have to use our reasoning, not just for ourselves but for the community. In Islam, you're not just yourself; you have to consider everyone else." Veiling women are described as particularly accountable: "the veil gives them a responsibility, duties, they are supposed to be careful about what they say, what they do, because they carry a symbol." One hijabi declares "I'm not afraid to approach professors, I want to break down the perception that non-Muslim people have of hijabi Muslims." Another hijabi told me:

> I try to show a different image than the one we see in the media reports with fairly low intellectual level and an outdated discourse. Opening up to you is a way for me to . . . show an Islam that fits its time.

Differences in College Experience Between French and American Samples

French participants describe a much less positive college experience than their American counterparts who report benefitting from a strong and supportive Muslim community in college.

French Sample

French participants believe that being religious is associated with refusal to integrate French society. Some of them do endorse secular arguments against the veil.

Being religious is associated with refusal to integrate French society. All French participants express feelings that they have to make a choice between being openly religious and being French. Both veiling and nonveiling interviewees report that they feel more themselves at home than in college: One participant says, "I'm not myself in university, I can't practice my religion . . . people don't know my religious or political views, sometimes I slip away without telling where I'm going . . . because I have my prayers." Another interviewee states, "It's a shame there is no allocated space . . . It's a pity we don't have a room anywhere that is not only for Muslims, but also for those who want to meditate or anyone who wants to do yoga." One interviewee spent several months in the United States after high school, before going back to France to enter college. She started wearing hijab in the United States. Regarding the French ban on the veil, she states,

> At first I was thinking, "it's normal, we're not in our country, we're of Arab origin and France is not a Muslim country so it's normal to have this ban on wearing the veil" . . . We were told especially about the influence of parents, friends, etc., and when I left France for the U.S., I completely changed my mind. Because I realized that . . . kids were wearing it in the U.S. . . . and they told me, first, this is not something that our parents forced us to do, we grew up in Islam so for us it's normal to wear it. Second, it's not because

we're wearing it that we're ever going to influence our friends . . . Then I realized I had a false image of France. Especially since when I came back to France and I went to university, I thought, but what's the difference between the veil that is allowed in college and the veil that is prohibited in middle or high school? . . . My views on secularism have evolved after my trip to the United States . . . When I returned to France, I realized that French secularism was everything but neutral. France wants Muslims to be invisible.

The internalization of secular arguments. Four participants in the French sample express their support toward French argument that religion should remain private, without any public display. Two of them reject French bans on the veil and the burqa though. One participant says, "Allowing the veil would be in conflict with French tradition." Another adds, "faith is inside . . . it does not need any clothing or any accessory." Another interviewee refers to being "civilized" and explains,

> I was born in an environment where no one wore the veil, neither my grandmother nor my mother nor my aunt; they are all very civilized . . . I remember that my grandfather was a very civilized man, who did drink, who enjoyed good living while trying to practice some traditions or religious rites, certain holidays . . . I think that in order to integrate and live more discreetly, you must be more civilized rather than less.

American Sample

In contrast with their French counterparts, American participants report that even though hijab does create a unique context within which to negotiate their integration, college provides a space with strong opportunities for constructive social life and personal development. They experience more freedom in college than they do at home. They identify the presence of MSA on campus and the support for religious diversity in universities as important factors that contribute to a positive experience in college.

A strong and supportive Muslim community in college. All American participants are members of MSA. Most report feeling supported by the Muslim community in college. Others, to the contrary, are critical of it. "Kids from MSA, they stick together, they have that community to retain their values, because there are those pressures but they don't really feel them because they are surrounded by like-minded Muslims" and "you have people supporting you . . . I've gotten more religious since I've got to college, because it's a bigger Muslim community there, there are more people who influence you." In contrast, three interviewees are very critical of their college's Muslim community. They state, "I don't relate with the majority of the Muslim students. I just wished that there was a wider variety of thinking . . . A lot of Arab Muslims were raised judgmental . . . and I think I've grown out of that."

Support for religious diversity from religious and public universities. Five participants attend a private religious university. One of them states, "I ended up in a Catholic university! But I like it a lot . . . The prayer spaces we have, it's perfect." One interviewee who attends a public university also states,

> My college is actually very pro-Muslim you know, they have a Muslim Student Association there, so it's very nice because you get to meet a lot of people that are Muslim and attend college. My school actually has its own hall where people can pray, so a lot of the time, between classes I just go up over there and I pray.

Discussion

In both countries, secular society urges young Arab Muslim women who are religious to define their identity at a young age, as their decision toward wearing or not the hijab and following Islamic rules is scrutinized and made highly visible. I found participants across sample very articulate with respect to their identity negotiation process and all of them demonstrated a high level of reflexivity. In this study, all participants across sample state that being Muslim influences all aspects of their life. They negotiate a Muslim identity at the intersection of religion and citizenship in secular state, gender, and culture of origin. As much as they refer to a common identity shared by all their Muslim friends in college, they insist on the personal dimension of their own identity. This finding illustrates the feminist concept of communal identity that is a relational model in which common identity is based on what individuals identify with such as commitments, ideals, and relationships (Macey & Carling, 2010; Weir, 2008). From a feminist perspective, young Arab Muslim women affirming an identity as Muslim first articulate the interaction of race and gender in the identity negotiation process. Naber (2005) refers to strategic politics: being Muslim first allows women to remain faithful to their Muslim community while simultaneously fighting dominant racialized-gendered discourse.

All participants explain that they feel Muslim first, and some also define themselves as a Muslim woman or a Muslim citizen. In any case, being Muslim means more to them than being of Muslim faith. This finding is consistent with studies on increased Islamization of second-generation Muslims (Haddad, 2007; Peek, 2005). As all participants insist that they have been developing an Islamic knowledge of their own, they make a distinction between the cultural heritage of their family and their own religiosity. Without rejecting their parents' values and tradition, they have elaborated their own understanding and practice of Islam. This is consistent with Williams and Vashi's (2007): second-generation Muslim women negotiate social and religious identities as a reaction to both stereotypical assumptions from non-Muslims and their own family's teaching of religious traditions. They seek out "true" Islamic knowledge of their own (Ali, 2005).

In this study, several veiling participants mentioned that their mother was either not veiling or veiling in a more casual manner than they did themselves. As Killian (2007) and Ali (2005) note, the move toward wearing hijab has only happened in recent years. Second-generation Muslim girls feel more legitimate than their mothers to publicly express their ethnicity and religion, and they are becoming more politically involved locally and nationally. In addition, recent stigmatization of Arab Muslims led the second generation to self-evaluate and to appropriate religious teachings independently from that of their parents. This study supports the observation that there are generational differences in the experience of Islam between first-and second-generation Arab Muslims. Participants express feelings of responsibility toward their religion. They want to fight stereotypes and advocate for their faith, help non-Muslims understand and respect their beliefs. They also mention that hijabis are particularly accountable as they promote a symbol of faith. Gender plays an important role in the effects of stigmatization on second-generation Arab Muslims.

As they affirm a "Muslim first" identity, young Arab Muslim women are challenged by hostility to Muslims in western societies. Alternative models such as Modood's (2010) would allow them to express themselves as religious citizens. Modood (2010) calls for a moderate secularism that takes into account religion as a minority identity: If minorities value their religious identity more than is the norm in the dominant society, religion becomes an ethnic feature that is entitled to specific rights and protection. Neither the United States nor France currently recognize religion as a minority identity that grants specific rights. Citizenship in western liberal societies is tacitly understood as being secular and therefore young Arab Muslim women's participation to the public debate as religious citizens is impaired (Calhoun, 2011). In both the United States and France, young Arab Muslim women experience strong tensions between who they wish to be and how they are expected to behave.

As the United States and France handle integration issues differently, young French Arab Muslim women are not able to express their negotiated identities as openly as their American counterparts. The French laws banning hijab in schools and the burqa in all public places single out all women wearing the veil, even in settings where it is allowed, such as in college. French Muslim women wearing hijab are categorized as victims and submissive to their community's violence (Scott, 2007). French participants experience internal conflicts that are imposed on them by French society's attempt to make them choose between being Arab and Muslim and French: the notion of French citizenship is linked to Whiteness and therefore only White skin color provides true citizenship. In effect, the French state endorses colonial racism, and cultural difference in France means racial difference (Jugé & Perez, 2006).

Half of the French participants have internalized and support French secular argument that religion is private and may not be displayed in public. They legitimize secularism in the name of French tradition. The comparison between French and American models is striking when one of the French participants explains that spending the summer of her high school senior year in the United States permanently transformed her understanding of secularism and convinced her that French secularism was aiming at "making Muslims invisible."

American participants do feel stigmatized and do experience racism; they are aware that hijab is a challenge to social life in secular society. Nevertheless, their college experience is globally much more positive than that of their French counterparts. All American participants are members of MSA. As they are categorized by a dominant group, young Arab Muslim women find support in identifying with a minority group that helps them achieve a positive sense of distinctiveness (Mishra & Shirazi, 2010). It is common for American universities, private or public, to host religious student associations, including Muslim associations such as MSA. In France, universities also welcome religious associations, but in practice they are essentially Catholic or Jewish. As I was unable to identify local offices of Muslim student associations in the four Parisian universities represented in my sample, I asked some of the participants how they felt about not having access to a Muslim association on campus. They answered that implementing a Muslim student association on campus would reinforce the current image of a community that does not open up to others.

American participants attend either a private religious or a public university. They report similar experiences in terms of how college campuses facilitate their religious practice by providing a private space for prayers, as well as space for MSA meetings. French and American approaches to religiosity in college and in public settings are very different. American participants benefit from equal religious opportunities on campus, while French participants do not and are discouraged from bringing religious beliefs into their everyday life in college. Several participants from the French sample mention that they wished they could have access to a quiet place to pray on campus and that such lack of private space is particularly disruptive for them as their religion requires that they pray five times a day.

Suggestions For Further Research

In this study, all 16 participants were self-declared as religious or moderately religious. Therefore, their perspective on the veil and on most issues relating to their life in college was influenced by their belief. It would be interesting to explore the experience of young Arab Muslim women who do not follow Islamic religious requirements—and therefore are at odds with their own community. In addition, this study is focused exclusively on college students. Further research on young religious Arab women who are not college students may provide rich data on how participants experience religion in the workplace, or at home, as a single or a married woman, with or without children. The studies could focus on either group (French or American) or be implemented in a comparative setting between the two countries. Separately, comparing young Arab Muslim women's civic engagement in the United States and France would bring light to their specific positioning as citizens in countries that have different approaches to secularism. Both qualitative and quantitative studies would be useful contributions.

References

Ali, S. (2005). Why here, why now? Young Muslim women wearing hijab. *The Muslim World, 95,* 515–528.

Asad, T. (2003). *Formation of the secular: Christianity, Islam, modernity.* Pablo Alto, CA: Stanford University Press.

Bader, V. (1999). Religious pluralism: Secularism or priority for democracy? *Political theory, 27*(5), 597–633.

Beski-Chafiq, C., Birmant, J., Benmerzoug, H., Taibi, A., & Coignard, A. (2010). *Youth and Islamist radicalization, Lille, France.* Center for Studies in Islamism and Radicalization (CIR), Aarhus University, Denmark.

Bhargava, R. (2009). Contextual secularism. In G. B. Levey, & T. Modood (Eds.), *Secularism, religion and multicultural citizenship.* Cambridge, MA: Cambridge University Press.

Bowen, J. R. (2007). *Why the French don't like headscarves.* Princeton, NJ: Princeton University Press.

Caincar, L. A. (2009). *Homeland insecurity*. New York, NY: Russell Sage Foundation.

Calhoun, C. (2011). Secularism, citizenship, and the public sphere. In C. Calhoun, M. Juergensmeyer, & J. Van Antwerpen (Eds.), *Rethinking secularism* (pp. 75–91). New York, NY: Oxford University Press.

Crenshaw, K. (1991). Mapping the margins: Intersectionality, identity politics and violence against women of Color. *Stanford Law Review, 43*(6), 1241–1299.

Eck, D. L. (2006). *What is pluralism? The Pluralism Project at Harvard University*. Retrieved from http://pluralism.org/pages/pluralism/what_is_pluralism

Groenewald, T. (2004). A phenomenological research design illustrated. *International Journal of Qualitative Methods, 3*(1), 1–26.

Guest, G., Bunce, A., & Johnson, L. (2006). How many interviews are enough? *Field Methods, 18*(1), 59–82.

Haddad, Y. (2007). The post 9/11 hijab as icon. *Sociology of Religion, 68*(3), 253–267.

House, J. (2006). *The colonial and post-colonial dimensions of Algerian migration to France*. Institute of Historical Research, University of Leeds, Leeds, UK. Retrieved from http://www.history.ac.uk/ihr/Focus/Migration/articles/house.html

Jansen, Y. (2006). *Stuck in a revolving door: Secularism, assimilation and democratic pluralism* (Published dissertation). Amsterdam University Press, Amsterdam, Netherlands.

Jugé, T. S., & Perez, M. P. (2006). The modern colonial politics of citizenship and whiteness in France. *Social Identities, 12*(2), 187–212.

Keaton, T. D. (2006). *Muslim girls and the other France: Race, identity politics, and social exclusion*. Bloomington, IN: Indiana University Press.

Killian, C. (2007). From a community of believers to an Islam of the heart: "Conspicuous" symbols, Muslim practices, and the privatization of religion in France. *Sociology of Religion, 68*(3), 305–320.

Koser, K. (2007). *International migration: A very short introduction*. New York, NY: Oxford University Press.

Macey, M., & Carling, A. (2010). *Ethnic, racial and religious inequalities: The perils of subjectivity*. Basingstoke, UK: Palgrave Macmillan.

Mahmood, S. (2006). Secularism, hermeneutics, and empire: The politics of Islamic reformation. *Public Culture, 18*(2), 323–347.

McClay, W. M. (2001). Two concepts of secularism. *Journal of Policy History, 13*, 47–72.

Mir, S. (2009). Not too "college-like," not too normal: American Muslim undergraduate women's gendered discourses. *Anthropology and Education Quarterly, 40*(3), 237–256.

Mishra, S., & Shirazi, F. (2010). Hybrid identities: American Muslim women speak. *Gender, Place and Culture, 17*(2), 191–209.

Modood, T. (2010). Moderate secularism, religion as identity and respect for religion. *The Political Quarterly, 81*(1), 4–14.

Naber, N. (2005). Muslim first, Arab second: A strategic politics of race and gender. *Muslim World, 95*(4), 479–495.

Peek, L. (2005). Becoming Muslim: The development of a religious identity. *Sociology of Religion, 66*(3), 215–242.

Read, J. G. (2003). The sources of gender role attitudes among Christian and Muslim Arab-American women. *Sociology of Religion, 64*(2), 207–222.

Read, J. G. (2007). Introduction: The politics of veiling in comparative perspective. *Sociology of Religion, 68*(3), 231–236.

Santelli, E. (2008). Etre musulman après le 11 septembre: l'expérience des descendants d'immigrés maghrébins en France [Being Muslim after 9/11: The experience of second generation Arab Muslims in France.]. *Diversité Urbaine, 8*(2), 135–162.

Schmidt, G. (2004). *Islam in urban America: Sunni Muslims in Chicago*. Philadelphia, PA: Temple University Press.

Scott, W. J. (2007). *The politics of the veil*. Princeton, NJ: Princeton University Press.

Shields, S. A. (2008). Gender: An intersectionality perspective. *Sex Roles, 59*, 301–311.

Sundar, P. (2009). Multiculturalism. In M. Gray & S. A. Webb (Eds.), *Social work theory and methods* (pp. 98–108). Thousand Oaks, CA: Sage Publications.

Weir, A. (2008). Global feminism and transformative identity politics. *Hypatia, 23*(4), 110.

Wertz, F. J. (2005). Phenomenological research methods for counseling psychology. *Journal of Counseling Psychology, 52*(2), 167–177.

Williams, R. H., & Vashi, G. (2007). Hijab and American Muslim women: Creating the space for autonomous selves. *Sociology of Religion, 68*(3), 269–287.

RELIGION EXPLAINED THE EVOLUTIONARY ORIGINS OF RELIGIOUS THOUGHT

What Is the Origin?

Pascal Boyer

A neighbor in the village tells me that I should protect myself against witches. Otherwise they could hit me with invisible darts that will get inside my veins and poison my blood.

A shaman burns tobacco leaves in front of a row of statuettes and starts talking to them. He says he must send them on a journey to distant villages in the sky. The point of all this is to cure someone whose mind is held hostage by invisible spirits.

A group of believers goes around, warning everyone that the end is nigh. Judgement Day is scheduled for October 2. This day passes and nothing happens. The group carries on, telling everyone the end is nigh (the date has been changed).

Villagers organize a ceremony to tell a goddess she is not wanted in their village anymore. She failed to protect them from epidemics, so they decided to "drop" her and find a more efficient replacement.

An assembly of priests finds offensive what some people say about what happened several centuries ago in a distant place, where a virgin is said to have given birth to a child. So these people must be massacred.

Members of a cult on an island decide to slaughter all their live-stock and burn their crops. All these will be useless now, they say, because a ship full of goods and money will reach their shores very shortly in recognition of their good deeds.

My friends are told to go to church or some other quiet place and talk to an invisible person who is everywhere in the world. That invisible listener already knows what they will say, because He knows everything.

I am told that if I want to please powerful dead people—who could help me in times of need—I should pour the blood of a live white goat on the right hand side of a particular rock. But if I use a goat of a different color or another rock, it will not work at all.

You may be tempted to dismiss these vignettes as just so many examples of the rich tapestry of human folly. Or perhaps you think that these illustrations, however succinct (one could fill volumes with such accounts), bear witness to an admirable human capacity to comprehend life and the universe. Both reactions leave questions unanswered. Why do people have such thoughts? What prompts them to do such things? Why do they have such different beliefs? Why are they so strongly committed to them? These questions used to be *mysteries* (we did not even know how to proceed) and are now becoming *problems* (we have some idea of a possible solution), to use Noam Chomsky's distinction. Indeed, we actually have the first elements of that solution. In case this sounds hubristic or self-aggrandizing, let me add immediately that this "we" really refers to a community of people. It is not an insidious way of suggesting that *I* have a new theory and find it of universal significance. In the rest of this book I mention a number of findings and models in cognitive psychology, anthropology, linguistics and evolutionary biology. All of these were discovered by other people, most of whom did not work on religion and had no idea that their findings could help explain religion. This is why, although bookshelves may be overflowing with treatises on religion, histories of religion, religious people's accounts of their ideas, and so on, it makes sense to add to this and show how the intractable mystery that was religion is now just another set of difficult but manageable problems.

Giving Airy Nothing a Local Habitation

The explanation for religious beliefs and behaviors is to be found in the way all human minds work. I really mean all human minds, not just the minds of religious people or of some of them. I am talking about human minds, because what matters here are properties of minds that are found in all members of our species with normal brains. The discoveries I will mention here are about the ways minds in general (men's or women's, British or Brazilian, young or old) function.

This may seem a rather strange point of departure if we want to explain something as diverse as religion. Beliefs are different in different people; some are religious and some are not. Also, obviously, beliefs are different in different places. Japanese Buddhists do not seem to share much, in terms of religious notions, with Amazonian shamans or American Southern Baptists. How could we explain a phenomenon (religion) that is so *variable* in terms of something (the brain) that is *the same* everywhere? This is what I describe in this book. The diversity of religion, far from being an obstacle to general explanations, in fact gives us some keys. But to understand why this is so, we need a precise description of how brains receive and organize information.

For a long time, people used to think that the brain was a rather simple organ. Apart from the bits that control the body machinery, there seemed to be a vast empty space in the young child's mind destined to be filled with whatever education, culture and personal experience provided. This view of the mind was never too plausible, since after all the liver and the gut are much more complex than that. But we did not know much about the way minds develop, so there were no facts to get in the way of this fantasy of a "blank slate" where experience could leave its imprint. The mind was like those vast expanses of unexplored Africa that old maps used to fill with palm trees and crocodiles. Now we know more about minds. We do not know everything, but one fact is clear: the more we discover about how minds work, the less we believe in this notion of a blank slate. Every further discovery in cognitive science makes it less plausible as an explanation.

In particular, it is clear that our minds are not really prepared to acquire just about any kind of notion that is "in the culture." We do not *just* "learn what is in the environment," as people sometimes say. That is not the case, because no mind in the world—this is true all the way from the cockroach to the giraffe to you or me—could ever learn anything without having very sophisticated mental equipment that is *prepared* to identify relevant information in the environment and to treat that information in a special way. Our minds are prepared because natural selection gave us particular mental predispositions. Being prepared for some concepts, human minds are also prepared for certain variations of these concepts. As I will show, this means, among other things, that all human beings can easily acquire a certain *range* of religious notions and communicate them to others.

Does this mean religion is "innate" and "in the genes"? I—and most people interested in the evolution of the human mind—think that the question is in fact meaningless and that it is important to understand why. Consider other examples of human capacities. All human beings can catch colds and remember different melodies. We can catch colds because we have respiratory organs and these provide a hospitable site for all sorts of pathogens, including those of the common cold. We can remember tunes because a part of our brain can easily store a series of sounds with their relative pitch and duration. There are no common colds in our genes and no melodies either. What is in the genes is a tremendously complex set of chemical recipes for the building of normal organisms with respiratory organs and a complex set of connections between brain areas. Normal genes in normal milieu will give you a pair of lungs and an organized auditory cortex, and with these the dispositions to acquire both colds and tunes. Obviously, if we were all brought up in a sterile and nonmusical environment, we would catch neither. We would still have the disposition to catch them but no opportunity to do so.

Having a normal human brain does not imply that you have religion. All it implies is that you can acquire it, which is very different. The reason why psychologists and anthropologists are so concerned with *acquisition* and *transmission* is that evolution by natural selection gave us a particular kind of mind so that only particular kinds of religious notions can be acquired. Not all possible concepts are equally good. The ones we acquire easily are the ones we find widespread the world over; indeed, that is *why* we find them widespread the world over. It has been said of poetry that it gives to airy nothing a local habitation and a name. This description is even more aptly applied to the supernatural imagination. But, as we will see, not all kinds of "airy nothing" will find a local habitation in the minds of people.

Origin Scenarios

What is the origin of religious ideas? Why is it that we can find them wherever we go and, it would seem, as far back in the past as we can see? The best place to start is with our spontaneous, commonsense answers to the question of origins. Everybody seems to have some intuition about the origins of religion. Indeed, psychologists and anthropologists who like me study how mental processes create religion face the minor occupational hazard of constantly running into people who think that they already have a perfectly adequate solution to the problem. They are often quite willing to impart their wisdom and sometimes imply that further work on this question is, if not altogether futile, at least certainly undemanding. If you say "I use genetic algorithms to produce computationally efficient cellular automata," people see quite clearly that doing that kind of thing probably requires some effort. But if you tell them that you are in the business of "explaining religion," they often do not see what is so complicated or difficult about it. Most people have some idea of why there is religion, what religion gives people, why they are sometimes so strongly attached to their religious beliefs, and so on. These common intuitions offer a real challenge. Obviously, if they are sufficient, there is no point in having a complex theory of religion. If, as I am afraid is more likely, they are less than perfect, then our new account should be at least as good as the intuitions it is supposed to replace.

Most accounts of the origins of religion emphasize one of the following suggestions: human minds demand explanations, human hearts seek comfort, human society requires order, human intellect is illusionprone. To express this in more detail, here are some possible scenarios:

Religion Provides Explanations:

- People created religion to explain puzzling natural phenomena.
- Religion explains puzzling experiences: dreams, prescience, etc.
- Religion explains the origins of things.
- Religion explains why there is evil and suffering.

Religion Provides Comfort:

- Religious explanations make mortality less unbearable.
- Religion allays anxiety and makes for a comfortable world.

Religion Provides Social Order:

- Religion holds society together.
- Religion perpetuates a particular social order.
- Religion supports morality.

Religion is a Cognitive Illusion:

- People are superstitious; they will believe anything.
- Religious concepts are irrefutable.
- Refutation is more difficult than belief.

Though this list probably is not exhaustive, it is fairly representative. Discussing each of these common intuitions in more detail, we will see that they all fail to tell us why we have religion and why it is the way it is. So why bother with them? It is not my intent here to ridicule other people's ideas or show that anthropologists and cognitive scientists are more clever than common folk. I discuss these spontaneous explanations because they are widespread, because they are often rediscovered by people when they reflect on religion, and more importantly

because they are *not that bad.* Each of these "scenarios" for the origin of religion points to a real and important phenomenon that any theory worth its salt should explain. Also, taking these scenarios seriously opens up new perspectives on how religious notions and beliefs appear in human minds.

Unfamiliar Diversity

Let it not be said that anthropology is not useful. Religion is found the world over, but it is found in very different forms. It is an unfortunate and all too frequent mistake to explain all religion by one of its characteristics that is in fact special to the religion we are familiar with. Anthropologists are professionally interested in cultural differences, and they generally study a milieu other than their own to avoid this mistake. In the past century or so, they have documented extremely diverse religious notions, beliefs and practices. To illustrate why this knowledge is useful, consider the inadequate information found in many atlases. At the same time as they tell you that the Arctic is all ice and the Sahara mostly sand and rock, they often provide information about religious affiliation. You will read, for instance, that Ulster has a *Protestant* majority and a *Catholic* minority, that Italy, is overwhelmingly *Catholic* and Saudi Arabia *Muslim.* So far, so good. But other countries are more difficult to describe in these terms. Take India or Indonesia, for example. Most of the population belongs to one of the familiar "great religions" (Hinduism, Islam); but in both countries there are large, so-called tribal groups that will have no truck with these established denominations. Such groups are often described as having *animistic* or *tribal* religion—two terms that (anthropologists will tell you) mean virtually nothing. They just stand for "stuff we cannot put in any other category"; we might as well call these people's religions "miscellaneous." Also, what about Congo and Angola? The atlas says that most people in these places are *Christian,* and this is true in the sense that many are baptized and go to church. However, people in Congo and Angola constantly talk about ancestors and witches and perform rituals to placate the former and restrain the latter. This does not happen in *Christian* Northern Ireland. If the atlas says anything about religion, it is using a very confusing notion of religion.

The diversity of religion is not just the fact that some people are called or call themselves Buddhist and others Baptist. It goes deeper, in how people conceive of supernatural agents and what they think these agents are like or what they can do, in the morality that is derived from religious beliefs, in the rituals performed and in many other ways. Consider the following findings of anthropology.:

Supernatural agents can be very different. Religion is about the existence and causal powers of nonobservable entities and agencies. These may be one unique God or many different gods or spirits or ancestors, or a combination of these different kinds. Some people have one "supreme" god, but this does not always mean that he or she is terribly important. In many places in Africa there are two supreme gods. One is a very abstract supreme deity and the other is more down-to-earth, as it were, since he created all things cultural: tools and domesticated animals, villages and society. But neither of them is really involved in people's everyday affairs, where ancestors, spirits and witches are much more important.

Some gods die. It may seem obvious that gods are always thought to be eternal. We might even think that this must be part of the definition of "god." However, many Buddhists think that gods, just like humans, are caught in a never-ending cycle of births and reincarnations. So gods will die like all other creatures. This, however, takes a long time and that is why humans since times immemorial pray to the same gods. If anything, gods are disadvantaged in comparison with humans. Unlike gods, we could, at least in principle, escape from the cycle of life and suffering. Gods must first be reincarnated as humans to do that.

Many spirits are really stupid. To a Christian it seems quite obvious that you cannot fool God, but in many places, fooling superhuman agents is possible and in fact even necessary. In Siberia, for instance, people are careful to use metaphorical language when talking about important matters. This is because nasty spirits often eavesdrop on humans and try to foil their plans. Now spirits, despite their superhuman powers, just cannot understand metaphors. They are powerful but stupid. In many places in Africa it is quite polite when visiting friends or relatives to express one's sympathy with them for having such "ugly" or "unpleasant" children. The idea is that witches, always on the lookout for nice children to "eat," will be fooled by this naive stratagem. It is also common in such places to give children names that suggest disgrace or misfortune, for the same reason. In Haiti one of the worries of people who have just lost a relative is that the corpse might be stolen by a witch. To avoid this, people sometimes buried their dead with a length of thread and an eyeless needle. The idea was that witches would find the needle and try to thread it, which would keep them busy for centuries so that they would forget all about the corpse. People can think that supernatural agents have extraordinary powers and yet are rather easily fooled.

Salvation is not always a central preoccupation. To people familiar with Christianity or Islam or Buddhism, it seems clear that the main point of religion is the salvation or deliverance of the soul. Different religions are thought to offer different perspectives on why souls need to be saved and different routes to salvation. Now, in many parts of the world, religion does not really promise that the soul will be saved or liberated and in fact does not have much to say about its destiny. In such places, people just do not assume that moral reckoning determines the fate of the soul. Dead people become ghosts or ancestors. This is general and does not involve a special moral judgement.

Official religion is not the whole of religion. Wherever we go, we will find that religious concepts are much more numerous and diverse than "official" religion would admit. In many places in Europe people suspect that there are witches around trying to attack them. In official Islam there is no God but God; but many Muslims are terrified of *jinn* and *afreet*—spirits, ghosts and witches. In the United States religion is officially a matter of denomination: Christians of various shades, Jews, Hindus, etc. But many people are seriously engaged in interaction with aliens or ghosts. This is also among the religious concepts to consider and explain.

You can have religion without having "a" religion. For Christians, Jews or Muslims it is quite clear that one belongs to *a* religion and that there is a choice, as it were, between alternative views on the creation of the universe, the destiny of the soul and the kind of morality one should adhere to. This results from a very special kind of situation, where people live in large states with competing Churches and doctrines. Many people throughout history and many people these days live in rather different circumstances, where their religious activity is the only one that is conceivable. Also, many religious notions are tied to specific places and persons. People for instance pray to their ancestors and offer sacrifices to the forest to catch lots of game. It would not make sense to them to pray to other people's ancestors or to be grateful for food that you will not receive. The idea of a universal religion that anyone could adopt—or that everyone should adopt—is not a universal idea.

You can also have religion without having "religion." We have a word for religion. This is a convenient label that we use to put together all the ideas, actions, rules and objects that have to do with the existence and properties of superhuman agents such as God. Not everyone has this explicit concept or the idea that religious stuff is different from the profane or everyday domain. In general, you will find that people begin to have an explicit concept of "religion" when they live in places with several "religions"; but that is a special kind of place, as I said above. That people do not have a special term for religion does not mean they actually have no religion. In many places people have no word for "syntax" but their language has a syntax all the same. You do not need the special term in order to have the thing.

You can have religion without "faith." Many people in the world would find it strange if you told them that they "believe in" witches and ghosts or that they have "faith" in their ancestors. Indeed, it would be very difficult in most languages to translate these sentences. It takes us Westerners some effort to realize that this notion of "believing in something" is peculiar. Imagine a Martian telling you how interesting it is that you "believe" in mountains and rivers and cars and telephones. You would think the alien has got it wrong. We don't "believe in" these things, we just notice and accept that they are around. Many people in the world would say the same about witches and ghosts. They are around like trees and animals—though they are far more difficult to understand and control—so it does not require a particular commitment or faith to notice their existence and act accordingly. In the course of my anthropological fieldwork in Africa, I lived and worked with Fang people, who say that nasty spirits roam the bush and the villages, attack people, make them fall ill and ruin their crops. My Fang acquaintances also knew that I was not too worried about this and that most Europeans were remarkably indifferent to the powers of spirits and witches. This, for me, could be expressed as the difference between believing in spirits and not believing. But that was not the way people saw it over there. For them, the spirits were indeed around but white people were immune to their influence, perhaps because God cast them from a different mold or because Western people could avail themselves of efficient anti-witchcraft medicine. So what we often call faith others may well call knowledge.[1]

The conclusion from all this is straightforward. If people tell you "Religion is faith in a doctrine that teaches us how to save our souls by obeying a wise and eternal Creator of the universe," these people probably have not traveled or read widely enough. In many cultures people think that the dead come back to haunt the living, but this is not universal. In some places people think that some special individuals can communicate with gods or dead people, but that idea is not found everywhere. In some places people assume that people have a soul that survives after death, but that assumption also is not universal. When we put forward general explanations of religion, we had better make sure that they apply outside our parish.

Intellectual Scenarios: The Mind Demands an Explanation

Explanations of religion are scenarios. They describe a sequence of events in people's minds or in human societies, possibly over an immense span of historical time, that led to religion as we know it. But narratives are also misleading. In a good story one thing leads to another with such obvious logic that we may forget to check that each episode really occurred as described. So a good scenario may put us on the right track but also leave us stuck in a rut, oblivious to an easier or more interesting path that was just a few steps aside. This, as we will see, is precisely what happens with each general explanation of religion—which is why I will first describe their valuable points and then suggest that we step back a little and take a different path.

The most familiar scenario assumes that humans in general have certain general intellectual concerns. People want to understand events and processes—that is, to explain, predict and perhaps control them. These very general, indeed universal intellectual needs gave rise to religious concepts at some point during human cultural evolution. This was not necessarily a single event, a sudden invention that took place once and for all. It might be a constant re-creation as the need to explain phenomena periodically suggests concepts that could work as good explanations. Here are some variations on this theme:

- *People created religion to explain puzzling natural phenomena.* People are surrounded with all sorts of phenomena that seem to challenge their everyday concepts. That a window pane breaks if you throw a brick at it poses no problem. But what about the causes of storms, thunder, massive drought, floods? What pushes the sun across the sky and moves the stars and planets? Gods and spirits fulfil this explanatory function. In many places the planets *are* gods, and in Roman mythology the thunder was the sound of Vulcan's hammer striking the anvil. More generally, gods and spirits make rains fall and fields yield good crops. They explain what is beyond the ken of ordinary notions.

- *Religion was created to explain puzzling mental phenomena.* Dreams, precognition, and the feeling that dead persons are still around in some form (and frequently "appear" to the living) are all phenomena that receive no satisfactory explanation in our everyday concepts. The notion of a spirit seems to correspond to such phenomena. Spirits are disembodied persons, and their characteristics make them very similar to persons seen in dreams or hallucinations.

Gods and a unique God are further versions of this projection of mental phenomena.

- *Religion explains the origins of things.* We all know that plants come from seeds, that animals and humans reproduce, and so on. But where did the whole lot come from? That is, we all have commonsense explanations for the origin of each particular aspect of our environment, but all these explanations do is "pass the buck" to some other process or agent. However, people feel that the buck has to stop somewhere . . . and uncreated creators like God or the first ancestors or some cultural heroes fulfil this function.

- *Religion explains evil and suffering.* It is a common human characteristic that misfortune cries out for explanation. Why is there misfortune or evil in general? This is where the concepts of Fate, God, devils and ancestors are handy. They tell you why and how evil originated in the world (and sometimes provide recipes for a better world).

What is wrong with these accounts? There are several problems with them. We say that the origin of religious concepts is the urge to provide certain general aspects of human experience with a satisfactory explanation. Now anthropologists have shown that (i) explaining such general facts is not equally pressing in all cultures and that (ii) the explanations provided by religion are not at all like ordinary explanations.

Consider the idea that everybody wants to identify the general cause of evil and misfortune. This is not as straightforward as we may think. The world over, people are concerned with the causes of *particular* evils and calamities. These are considered in great detail but the existence of evil *in general* is not the object of much reflection. Let me use an example that is familiar to all anthropologists from their Introductory courses. British anthropologist E. E. Evans-Pritchard is famous for his classic account of the religious notions and beliefs of the Zande people of Sudan. His book became a model for all anthropologists because it did not stop at cataloguing strange beliefs. It showed you, with the help of innumerable details, how *sensible* these beliefs were, once you understood the particular standpoint of the people who expressed them and the particular questions those beliefs were supposed to answer. For instance, one day the roof of a mud house collapses in the village where Evans-Pritchard is working. People promptly explain the incident in terms of witchcraft. The people who were under that roof at the time must have powerful enemies. With typical English good sense, Evans-Pritchard points out to his interlocutors that termites had undermined the mud house and that there was nothing particularly mysterious

in its collapse. But people are not interested in this aspect of the situation. As they point out to the anthropologist, they know perfectly well that termites gnaw through the pillars of mud houses and that decrepit structures are bound to cave in at some point. What they want to find out is why the roof collapsed *at the precise time* when so-and-so was sitting underneath it rather than before or after that. This is where witchcraft provides a good explanation. But what explains the existence of witchcraft? No one seems to find *that* a pertinent or interesting question. This is in fact a common situation in places where people have beliefs about spirits or witches. These agents' behavior is an explanation of particular cases, but no one bothers to explain the existence of misfortune in general.

The origin of things *in general* is not always the obvious source of puzzlement that we may imagine. As anthropologist Roger Keesing points out in describing myths of the Kwaio people in the Solomon Islands: "Ultimate human origins are not viewed as problematic. [The myths] assume a world where humans gave feasts, raised pigs, grew taro, and fought blood feuds." What matters to people are *particular* cases in which these activities are disrupted, often by the ancestors or by witchcraft.[2]

But how does religion account for these particular occurrences? The explanations one finds in religion are often more puzzling than illuminating. Consider the explanation of thunderstorms as the booming voice of ancestors venting their anger at some human misdemeanor. To explain a limited aspect of the natural world (loud, rolling, thumping sounds during storms), we have to assume a whole imaginary world with superhuman agents (Where did they come from? Where are they?) that cannot be seen (Why not?), in a distant place that cannot be reached (How does the noise come through all the way?), whose voices produce thunder (How is that possible? Do they have a special mouth? Are they gigantic?). Obviously, if you live in a place where this kind of belief is widespread, people may have an answer to all these questions. But each answer requires a specific narrative, which more often than not presents us with yet more superhuman agents or extraordinary occurrences—that is, with more questions to answer.

As another illustration, here is a short account of shamanistic ritual among the Cuna of Panama by anthropologist Carlo Severi:

> The [shaman's] song is chanted in front of two rows of statuettes facing each other, beside the hammock where the patient is lying. These auxiliary spirits drink up the smoke whose intoxicating effect opens their minds to the invisible aspect of reality and gives them the power to heal. In this way [the statuettes] are believed to become themselves diviners.[3]

The patient in this ritual has been identified by the community as mentally disturbed, which is explained in religious terms. The soul of the person was taken away by evil spirits and it is now held hostage. A shaman is a specialist who can enlist auxiliary spirits to help him deliver the imprisoned soul and thereby restore the patient's health. Note that this goes well beyond a straightforward explanation for aberrant behavior. True, there is direct evidence of the patient's condition; but the evil spirits, the auxiliary spirits, the shaman's ability to journey through the spirits' world, the efficacy of the shaman's songs in his negotiation with the evil spirits—all this has to be postulated. To add to these baroque complications, the auxiliary spirits are in fact wood statuettes; these objects not only hear and understand the shaman, but they actually become diviners for the time of the ritual, perceiving what ordinary people cannot see.

An "explanation" like that does not work in the same way as our ordinary accounts of events in our environment. We routinely produce explanations that (i) use the information available and (ii) rearrange it in a way that yields a more satisfactory view of what happened. Explaining something does not consist in producing one thought after another in a freewheeling sort of way. The point of an explanation is to provide a context that makes a phenomenon less surprising than before and more in agreement with the general order of things. Religious explanations often seem to work the other way around, producing more complication instead of less. As anthropologist Dan Sperber points out, religion creates "relevant mysteries" rather than simple accounts of events.

This leads to a paradox familiar to all anthropologists. If we say that people use religious notions to *explain* the world, this seems to suggest that they do not know what a proper explanation is. But that is absurd. We have ample evidence that they do know. People use the ordinary "getting most of the relevant facts under a simpler heading" strategy all the time. So what people do with their religious concepts is not so much explain the universe as . . . well, this is where we need to step back and consider in more general terms what makes mysteries relevant.[4]

The Mind as a Bundle of Explanation Machines

Is it really true that human ideas are spurred by a general urge to understand the universe? Philosopher Immanuel Kant opened his *Critique of Pure Reason*—an examination of what we can know beyond experience—with the statement that human reason is forever troubled by questions it can neither solve nor disregard. Later, the theme of religion-as-an-explanation was developed by a school

of anthropology called *intellectualism*, which was initiated by 19th-century scholars such as Edward Burnett Tylor and James Frazer and remains quite influential to this day. A central assumption of intellectualism is this: if a phenomenon is common in human experience and people do not have the conceptual means to understand it, then they will try and find some speculative explanation.[5]

Now, expressed in this blunt and general manner, the statement is plainly false. Many phenomena are both familiar to all of us from the youngest age and difficult to comprehend using our everyday concepts, yet nobody tries to find an explanation for them. For instance, we all know that our bodily movements are not caused by external forces that push or pull us but by our *thoughts*. That is, if I extend my arm and open my hand to shake hands with you, it's precisely because I want to do that. Also, we all assume that thoughts have no weight or size or other such material qualities (the idea of an apple is not the size of the apple, the idea of water does not flow, the idea of a rock is no more solid than the idea of butter). If I have the intention to lift my arm, to take a classic example, this intention itself has no weight or solidity. Yet it manages to move parts of my body. . . . How can this occur? How could things without substance have effects in the material world? Or, to put it in less metaphysical terms, how on earth do these mental words and images pull my muscles? This is a difficult problem for philosophers and cognitive scientists . . . but surprisingly enough, it is a problem for nobody else in the entire world. Wherever you go, you will find that people are satisfied with the idea that thoughts and desires have effects on bodies and that's that. (Having raised such questions in English pubs and Fang villages in Cameroon I have good evidence that in both places people see nothing mysterious in the way their minds control their bodies. Why should they? It requires very long training in a special tradition to find the question interesting or puzzling.)

The mistake of intellectualism was to assume that a human mind is driven by a *general* urge to explain. That assumption is no more plausible than the idea that animals, as opposed to plants, feel a general "urge to move around." Animals never move about for the sake of changing places. They are in search of food or safety or sex; their movements in these different situations are caused by different processes. The same goes for explanations. From a distance, as it were, you may think that the general point of having a mind is to explain.and understand. But if you look closer, you see that what happens in a mind is far more complex; this is crucial to understanding religion.

Our minds are not general explanation machines. Rather, minds consist of many different, specialized explanatory engines. Consider this: It is almost impossible to see a scene without seeing it in three dimensions, because our brains cannot help *explaining* the flat images projected onto the retina as the effect of real volumes out there. If you are brought up among English speakers you just cannot help understanding what people say in that language, that is, *explaining* complex patterns of sound frequencies as strings of words. People spontaneously *explain* the properties of animals in terms of some inner properties that are common to their species; if tigers are aggressive predators and yaks quiet grazers, this must be because of their essential nature. We spontaneously assume that the shape of particular tools is *explained* by their designers' intentions rather than as an accidental combination of parts; the hammer has a sturdy handle and a heavy head because that is the best way to drive nails into hard materials. We find that it is impossible to see a tennis ball flying about without spontaneously *explaining* its trajectory as a result of a force originally imposed on it. If we see someone's facial expression suddenly change we immediately speculate on what may have upset or surprised them, which would be the *explanation* of the change we observed. When we see an animal suddenly freeze and leap up we assume it must have detected a predator, which would *explain* why it stopped and ran away. If our houseplants wither away and die we suspect the neighbors did not water them as promised—that is the *explanation*. It seems that our minds constantly produce such spontaneous explanations.

Note that all these explanation-producing processes are "choosy" (for want of a better term). The mind does not go around trying to explain everything and it does not use just any information available to explain something. We don't try to decipher emotional states on the tennis ball's surface. We do not spontaneously assume that the plants died because they were distressed. We don't think that the animal leaped up because it was pushed by a gust of wind. We reserve our physical causes for mechanical events, biological causes for growth and decay and psychological causes for emotions and behavior.

So the mind does not work like one general "let's-review-the-facts-and-get-an-explanation" device. Rather, it comprises lots of specialized explanatory devices, more properly called *inference systems,* each of which is adapted to particular kinds of events and automatically suggests explanations for these events. Whenever we produce an explanation of any event ("the window broke because the tennis ball hit it"; "Mrs. Jones is angry that the kids broke her window"; etc.), we make use of these special inference systems, although they run so smoothly in the mind that we are not aware of their operation. Indeed, spelling out how they contribute to our everyday explanations would

be tedious (e.g., "Mrs. Jones is angry *and* anger is caused by unpleasant events caused by other people *and* anger is directed at those people *and* Mrs. Jones knows the children were playing next to her house *and* she suspects the children knew that tennis balls could break a window *and . . .*"). This is tedious because our minds run all these chains of inferences automatically, and only their results are spelled out for conscious inspection.

By discussing and taking seriously the "religion-as-explanation" scenario, we open up a new perspective on how religious notions work in human minds. Religious concepts may seem out of the ordinary, but they too make use of the inference systems I just described. Indeed, everything I just said about Mrs. Jones and the tennis ball would apply to the ancestors or witches. Returning to Evans-Pritchard's anecdote of the collapsed roof, note how some aspects of the situation were so obvious that no one—neither the anthropologist nor his interlocutors—bothered to make them explicit: for instance, that the witches, if they were involved, probably had a reason to make the roof collapse, that they expected some revenge or profit from it, that they were angry with the persons sitting underneath, that they directed the attack to hurt *those* people, not others, that the witches could see their victims sitting there, that they will attack again if their reasons for striking in the first place are still relevant or if their attack failed, and so on. No one need say all this—no one even *thinks* about it in a conscious, deliberate manner—because it is all self-evident.

Which leads me to two major themes I will expand on in the following chapters. The way our banal inference systems work explains a great deal about human thinking, including religious thoughts. But—this is the most important point—the workings of inference systems are not something we can observe by introspection. Philosopher Daniel Dennett uses the phrase "Cartesian theater" to describe the inevitable illusion that all that happens in our minds consists of conscious, deliberate thoughts and reasoning about these thoughts. But a lot happens beneath that Cartesian stage, in a mental basement that we can describe only with the tools of cognitive science. This point is obvious when we think about processes such as motor control: the fact that my arm indeed goes up when I consciously try to lift it shows that a complicated system in the brain monitors what various muscles are doing. It is far more difficult to realize that similarly complicated systems are doing a lot of underground work to produce such deceptively simple thoughts as "Mrs. Jones is angry because the kids broke her window" or "The ancestors will punish you if you defile their shrine." But the systems are there. Their undetected work explains a lot about religion. It explains

PROGRESS BOX 1: Religion as Explanation

- The urge to explain the universe is not the origin of religion.
- The need to explain particular occurrences seems to lead to strangely baroque constructions.
- You cannot explain religious concepts if you do not describe how they are used by individual minds.
- A different angle: Religious concepts are probably influenced by the way the brain's inference systems produce explanations without our being aware of it.

why *some* concepts, like that of invisible persons with a great interest in our behavior, are widespread the world over, and other possible religious concepts are very rare. It also explains why the concepts are so persuasive, as we will see presently.[6]

Emotive Scenarios: Religion Provides Comfort

Many people think there is a simple explanation for religion: we need it for emotional reasons. The human psyche is thus built that it longs for the reassurance or comfort that supernatural ideas seem to provide. Here are two versions of this widespread account:

- *Religious explanations make mortality less unbearable.* Humans are all aware that they are all destined to die. Like most animals they have developed various ways of reacting to life-threatening situations: fleeing, freezing, fighting. However, they may be unique in being able to reflect on the fact that come what may, they will die. This is one concern for which most religious systems propose some palliative, however feeble. People's notions of gods and ancestors and ghosts stem from this need to explain mortality and make it more palatable.
- *Religion allays anxiety and makes for a comfortable world.* It is in the nature of things that life is for most people nasty, brutish and short. It certainly was so in those Dark Ages when religious concepts were first created by human beings. Religious concepts allay anxiety by providing a context in which these conditions are either explained or offset by the promise of a better life or of salvation.

Like the intellectualist scenarios, these suggestions may well seem plausible enough as they stand, but we must go a bit further. Do they do the intended job? That is, do they explain why we have religious concepts and why we have the ones we have?

There are several serious problems with accounts based on emotions. First, as anthropologists have pointed out for some time, some facts of life are mysterious or awe-inspiring only in places where a local theory provides a solution to the mystery or a cure for the angst. For instance, there are places in Melanesia where people perform an extraordinary number of rituals to protect themselves from witchcraft. Indeed, people think they live under a permanent threat from these invisible enemies. So we might think that in such societies magical rituals, prescriptions and precautions are essentially comforting devices, giving people some imaginary control over these processes. However, in other places people have no such rituals and feel no such threats to their existence. From the anthropologist's viewpoint it seems plausible that the rituals create the need they are supposed to fulfil, and probable that each reinforces the other.

Also, religious concepts, if they are solutions to particular emotional needs, are not doing a very good job. A religious world is often every bit as terrifying as a world without supernatural presence, and many religions create not so much reassurance as a thick pall of gloom. The Christian philosopher Kierkegaard wrote books with titles like *The Concept of Anguish* and *Fear and Trembling,* which for him described the true psychological tenor of the Christian revelation. Also, consider the widespread beliefs about witches, ghouls, ghosts and evil spirits allegedly responsible for illness and misfortune. For the Fang people with whom I worked in Cameroon the world is full of witches, that is, nasty individuals whose mysterious powers allow them to "eat" other people, which in most cases means depriving them of health or good fortune. Fang people also have concepts of anti-witchcraft powers. Some are said to be good at detecting and counteracting the witches' ploys, and one can take protective measures against witches; all such efforts, however, are pitiful in the face of the witches' powers. Most Fang admit that the balance of powers is tipped the wrong way. Indeed, they see evidence of this all the time, in crops that fail, cars that crash and people who die unexpectedly. If religion allays anxiety, it cures only a small part of the disease it creates.

Reassuring religion, insofar as it exists, is not found in places where life is significantly dangerous or unpleasant; quite the opposite. One of the few religious systems obviously designed to provide a comforting worldview is New Age mysticism. It says that people, *all* people, have enormous "power," that all sorts of intellectual and physical feats are within their reach. It claims that we are all connected to mysterious but basically benevolent forces in the universe. Good health can be secured by inner spiritual strength. Human nature is fundamentally good. Most of us lived very interesting lives before this one. Note that these reassuring, ego-boosting notions appeared and spread in one of the most secure and affluent societies in history. People who hold these beliefs are not faced with war, famine, infant mortality, incurable endemic diseases and arbitrary oppression to the same extent as Middle Age Europeans or present-day Third World peasants.

So much for religion as comfort. But what about mortality? Religion the world over has something to say about what happens after death, and what it says is crucial to belief and behavior. To understand this, however, we must first discard the parochial notion that religion everywhere promises salvation, for that is clearly not the case. Second, we must also remember that in most places people are not really motivated by a metaphysical urge to explain or mitigate the *general* fact of mortality. That mortality is unbearable or makes human existence intrinsically pointless is a culture-specific speculation and by no means provides universal motivation. But the prospect of one's own death and the thoughts triggered are certainly more to the point. How do they participate in building people's religious thoughts, how do they make such thoughts plausible and intensely emotional?

The common shoot-from-the-hip explanation—people fear death, and religion makes them believe that it is not the end—is certainly insufficient because the human mind does not produce adequate comforting delusions against all situations of stress or fear. Indeed, any organism that was prone to such delusions would not survive long. Also, inasmuch as some religious thoughts do allay anxiety, our problem is to explain how they become plausible enough that they can play this role. To entertain a comforting fantasy seems simple enough, but to act on it requires that it be taken as more than a fantasy. The experience of comfort alone could not create the necessary level of plausibility.

Before we accept emotion-oriented scenarios of religion's origins, we should probe their assumptions. Human minds may well have death-related anxiety, but what is it about? The question may seem as strange as the prospect of death seems simple and clear enough to focus the mind, as Dr. Johnson pointed out. But human emotions are not that simple. They happen because the mind is a bundle of complicated systems working in the mental basement and solving very complex problems. Consider a simple emotion like the fear induced by the lurking presence of a predator. In many animals, including humans, this results in dramatic somatic events—most noticeably, a quickened heartbeat and increased perspiration. But other systems also are doing complex work. For instance, we have to choose among several behaviors in such situations—freeze or flee or fight—a choice that is made by *computation,* that is, by mentally going through a variety of aspects of the situation and evaluating the least dangerous option. So fear is not just what we experience about it; it is also a *program,* in some ways comparable to a computer program. It governs the resources of the brain in a special way, quite different from what happens in other circumstances. Fear increases the sensitivity of some perceptual mechanisms and leads reasoning through complicated sets of possible outcomes. So Dr. Johnson was right after all.[7]

This leads to other important questions: Why do we have such programs, and why do they work in this way? In the case of fear triggered by predators, it seems quite clear that natural selection designed our brains in such a way that they comprise this specific program. We would not be around if we did not have fairly efficient predator-avoidance mechanisms. But this also suggests that the mental programs are sensitive to the relevant context. You do not survive long if your brain fails to start this program when wolves surround you, or if you activate it every time you run into a sheep. Mortality anxiety may not be as simple as we thought. It is probably true that

---

PROGRESS BOX 2: Emotion in Religion

- Religious concepts do not always provide reassurance or comfort.
- Deliverance from mortality is not quite the universal longing we often assume.
- Religious concepts are indeed connected to human emotional systems, which are connected to life-threatening circumstances.
- A different angle: Our emotional programs are an aspect of our evolutionary heritage, which may explain how they affect religious concepts.

religious concepts gain their great salience and emotional load in the human psyche because they are connected to thoughts about various life-threatening circumstances. So we will not understand religion if we do not understand the various emotional programs in the mind, which are more complex than a diffuse angst.

Social Scenarios: Religion as a Good Thing for Society

Scenarios that focus on *social* needs all start from a commonsense (true) observation. Religion is not just something that is added to social life, it very often organizes social life. People's behavior toward each other, in most places, is strongly influenced by their notions about the existence and powers of ancestors, gods or spirits. So there must be some connection between living in society and having religious concepts. Here are some examples of the connections we may think of:

- *Religion holds society together.* In Voltaire's cynical formulation, "If God did not exist, he would have to be invented." That is, society would not hold together if people did not have some central set of beliefs that bind them together and make social groups work as organic wholes rather than aggregates of self-interested individuals.
- *Religion was invented to perpetuate a particular social order.* Churches and other such religious institutions are notorious for their active participation in and support of political authority. This is particularly the case in oppressive regimes, which often seek support in religious justifications. Religious beliefs are there to convince oppressed people that they can do nothing to better their lot except wait for promised retribution in another world.
- *Religion supports morality.* No society could work without moral prescriptions that bind people together and thwart crime, theft, treachery, etc. Now moral rules cannot be enforced merely by fear of immediate punishment, which all know to be uncertain. The fear of God is a better incentive to moral behavior since it assumes that the monitoring is constant and the sanctions eternal. In most societies some religious agency (spirits, ancestors) is there to guarantee that people behave.

Again, these scenarios point to real issues, and a good account of religion should have something to say about them. For instance, whatever we want to say about religious concepts, we must take into account that they are deeply associated with moral beliefs. Indeed, we cannot ignore the point, because that is precisely what many schools of religion insist on. The connection between religious concepts and political systems is likewise impossible to ignore because it is loudly proclaimed by many religious believers and religious doctrines.

However, here too we find some difficult problems. Consider this: In no human society is it considered all right, morally defensible to kill your siblings in order to have exclusive access to your parents' attention and resources. In no society is it all right to see other members of the group in great danger without offering some help. Yet the societies in question may have vastly different religious concepts. So there is some suspicion that perhaps the link between religion and morality is what psychologists and anthropologists call a rationalization, an ad hoc explanation of moral imperatives that we would have regardless of religion. The same goes for connections between social order and religion. All societies have some prescriptive rules that underpin social organization; but their religious concepts are very diverse. So the connection may not be quite as obvious as it seems. We could brush these doubts aside and say that what matters is that social groups have *some* religion in order to have morality and social order. What matters then is a set of common premises that we find in most religious notions and that support social life and morality. But then, what are those common premises?

The connection between religion and oppression may be more familiar to Europeans than to other people because the history of Europe is also the history of long and intense struggles between Churches and civil societies. But we must be wary of ethnocentric bias. It is simply not the case that every place on earth has an oppressive social order sanctioned by an official Church. (Indeed, even in Europe at some points people have found no other resort than the Church against some oppressive regimes.) More generally, the connection between religious concepts, Church, and State cannot account for concepts that are found in strikingly similar forms in places where there are neither States nor Churches. Such concepts have a long antiquity, dating from periods when such institutions were simply not there. So, again, we have important suggestions that we must integrate into a proper account of religion. But we do not have the easy solution we may have anticipated.

Religion and the Social Mind

Social accounts are examples of what anthropologists call *functionalism.* A functionalist explanation starts with the idea that certain beliefs or practices or concepts make it possible for certain social relations to operate. Imagine for instance a group of hunters who have to plan and coordinate their next expedition. This depends on all sorts of variables; different people have different views on where to go and when, leading to intractable disputes. In some groups people perform a divination ritual to decide where to go. They kill a chicken; the hunters are to follow in the direction of the headless body running away. The functionalist would say that since such beliefs and norms and practices contribute to the solution of a problem, this is probably why they were invented or why people reinvent and accept them. More generally: social institutions are around and people comply with them because they serve some *function*. Concepts too have functions and that is why we have them. If you can identify the function, you have the explanation. Societies have religion because social cohesion requires something like religion. Social groups would fall apart if ritual did not periodically reestablish that all members are part of a greater whole.

Functionalism of this kind fell out of favor with anthropologists sometime in the 1960s. One criticism was that functionalism seemed to ignore many counterexamples of social institutions with no clear function at all. It is all very well to say that having central authority is a good way of managing conflict resolution, but what about the many places where chiefs are warmongers who constantly provoke new conflicts? Naturally, functionalist anthropologists thought of clever explanations for that too but then were vulnerable to a different attack. Functionalism was accused of peddling ad hoc stories. Anyone with enough ingenuity could find some sort of social function for any cultural institution. A third criticism was that functionalism tended to depict societies as harmonious organic wholes where every part plays some useful function. But we know that most human societies are rife with factions, feuds, diverging interests and so on.[8]

As a student, I always found these criticisms less than perfectly convincing. True, extant functionalist explanations were not very good, but that was not sufficient reason to reject the general logic. Functionalism is a tried and tested method of explanation in evolutionary biology. Consider this: When faced with a newly discovered organ or behavior, the first questions biologists will ask are, What does it do for the organism? How does the organ or behavior confer an advantage in terms of spreading whatever genes are responsible for its appearance? How did it gradually evolve from other organs and behaviors? This strategy is now commonly called "reverse engineering." Imagine you are given a complicated contraption you have never seen before. The only way to make sense of what the parts are and how they

are assembled is to try and guess what they are for, what function they are supposed to fulfil. Obviously, this may sometimes lead you down a garden path. The little statue on the bonnet of some luxury cars serves no function as far as locomotion is concerned. The point is not that reverse engineering is always *sufficient* to deliver the right solution but that it is always *necessary*. So there may be some benefit in a functionalist strategy at least as a starting point in the explanation of religion. If people the world over hold religious concepts and perform religious rituals, if so many social groups are organized around common beliefs, it makes sense to ask, How does the belief contribute to the group's functioning? How does it create or change or disrupt social relations?

These questions highlight the great weakness of classical functionalism and the real reason it did not survive in anthropology. It assumed that institutions were around so that society could function but it did not explain how or why individuals would participate in making society function. For instance, imagine that performing communal religious rituals really provided a glue that kept the social group together. Why would that lead people to perform rituals? They may have better things to do. Naturally, one is tempted to think that other members of the group would coerce the reluctant ones into participating. But this only pushes the problem one step further. Why would these others be inclined to enforce conformity? Accepting that conformity is advantageous to the group, they too might guess that free riding—accepting the benefits without doing anything in return—would be even more advantageous to themselves. Classical functionalist accounts had no way of explaining how or why people would adopt representations that were good for social cohesion.

There were no solutions to these puzzles until anthropologists started taking more seriously the fact that humans are *by nature* a social species. What this means is that we are not just individuals thrown together in social groups, trying to cope with the problems this creates. We have sophisticated mental equipment, in the form of special emotions and special ways of thinking, that is designed for social life. And not just for social life in general but for the particular kind of social interaction that humans create. Many animal species have complex social arrangements, but each species has specific dispositions that make its particular arrangements possible. You will not make gregarious chimpanzees out of naturally solitary orangutans, or turn philandering chimpanzees into monogamous gibbons. Obviously, the social life of humans is more complex than the apes', but that is because human social dispositions are more complex too. A human brain is so designed that it includes what

---

PROGRESS BOX 3: Religion, Morality and Society

- Religion cannot be explained by the need to keep society together or to preserve morality, because these needs do not create institutions.
- Social interaction and morality are indeed crucial to how we acquire religion and how it influences people's behavior.
- A different angle: The study of the social mind can show us why people have particular expectations about social life and morality and how these expectations are connected to their supernatural concepts.

---

evolutionary biologists call a particular form of "social intelligence" or a "social mind."

The study of the social mind by anthropologists, evolutionary biologists and psychologists gives us a new perspective on the connections between religion and social life. Consider morality. In some places people say that the gods laid down the rules people live by. In other places the gods or ancestors simply watch people and sanction their misdemeanors. In both cases people make a connection between moral understandings (intuitions, feelings and reasoning about what is ethical and what is not) and supernatural agents (gods, ancestors, spirits). It now seems clear that Voltaire's account—a god is convenient: people will fear him and behave—got things diametrically wrong. Having concepts of gods and spirits does not really make moral rules more *compelling* but it sometimes makes them more *intelligible*. So we do not have gods because that makes society function. We have gods in part because we have the mental equipment that makes society possible but we cannot always understand how society functions.

The Sleep of Reason: Religion as an Illusion

Turning to the last kind of scenario: There is a long and respectable tradition of explaining religion as the consequence of a flaw in mental functioning. Because people do not think much or do not think very well, the argument goes, they let all sorts of unwarranted beliefs clutter their mental furniture. In other words, religion is around because people *fail* to take prophylactic measures against beliefs.

- *People are superstitious; they will believe anything.* People are naturally prepared to believe all sorts of accounts of strange or counterintuitive phenomena. Witness their enthusiasm for UFOs as opposed to scientific cosmology, for alchemy instead of chemistry, for urban legends instead of hard news. Religious concepts are both cheap and sensational; they are easy to understand and rather exciting to entertain.
- *Religious concepts are irrefutable.* Most incorrect or incoherent claims are easily refuted by experience or logic but religious concepts are different. They invariably describe processes and agents whose existence could never be verified, and consequently they are never refuted. As there is no evidence against most religious claims, people have no obvious reason to stop believing them.
- *Refutation is more difficult than belief.* It takes greater effort to challenge and rethink established notions than just to accept them. Besides, in most domains of culture we just absorb other people's notions. Religion is no exception. If everyone around you says that there are invisible dead people around, and everyone acts accordingly, it would take a much greater effort to try and verify such claims than it takes to accept them, if only provisionally.

I find all these arguments unsatisfactory. Not that they are false. Religious claims are indeed beyond verification; people do like sensational supernatural tales better than banal stories and generally spend little time rethinking every bit of cultural information they acquire. But this cannot be a sufficient explanation of why people have the concepts they have, the beliefs they have, the emotions they have. The idea that we are often gullible or superstitious is certainly true . . . but we are not gullible in every possible way. People do not generally manage to believe six impossible things before breakfast, as does the White Queen in Lewis Carroll's *Through the Looking Glass*. Religious claims are irrefutable, but so are all sorts of other baroque notions that we do not find in religion. Take for instance the claim that my right hand is made of green cheese except when people examine it, that God ceases to exist every Wednesday afternoon, that cars feel thirsty when their tanks run low or that cats think in German. We can make up hundreds of such interesting and irrefutable beliefs. There is no clear limit to imagination in this domain. The credulity arguments would explain not just actual religious beliefs but also a whole variety of beliefs that no one ever had.

Religion is *not* a domain where anything goes, where any strange belief could appear and get transmitted from generation to generation. On the contrary, there is only a limited catalogue of possible supernatural beliefs, which I present in Chapter 2. Even without knowing the details of religious systems in other cultures, we all know that some notions are far more widespread than others. The idea that there are invisible souls of dead people lurking around is a very common one; the notion that people's organs change position during the night is very rare. But both are equally irrefutable. . . . So the problem, surely, is not just to explain how people can accept supernatural claims for which there is no strong evidence but also why they tend to represent and accept *these* supernatural claims rather than other possible ones. We should explain also why they are so *selective* in the claims they adhere to.

Indeed, we should go even further and abandon the credulity scenario altogether. Here is why. In this scenario, people relax ordinary standards of evidence for some reason. If you are against religion, you will say that this is because they are naturally credulous, or respectful of received authority, or too lazy to think for themselves, etc. If you are more sympathetic to religious beliefs, you will say that they open up their minds to wondrous truths beyond the reach of reason. But the point is that if you accept this account, you assume that people *first* open up their minds, as it were, and *then* let their minds be filled by whatever religious beliefs are held by the people who influence them at that particular time. This is often the way we think of religious adhesion. There is a gatekeeper in the mind that either allows or rejects visitors—that is, other people's concepts and beliefs. When the gatekeeper allows them in, these concepts and

beliefs find a home in the mind and become the person's own beliefs and concepts.

Our present knowledge of mental processes suggests that this scenario is highly misleading. People receive all sorts of information from all sorts of sources. *All* this information has some effect on the mind. Whatever you hear and whatever you see is perceived, interpreted, explained, recorded by the various inference systems I described above. Every bit of information is fodder for the mental machinery. But then some pieces of information produce the effects that we identify as "belief." That is, the person starts to recall them and use them to explain or interpret particular events; they may trigger specific emotions; they may strongly influence the person's behavior. Note that I said *some* pieces of information, not all. This is where the selection occurs. In ways that a good psychology of religion should describe, it so happens that only some pieces of information trigger these effects, and not others; it also happens that the same piece of information will have these effects in some people but not others. So people do not have beliefs because they somehow made their minds receptive to belief and then acquired the material for belief. They have some beliefs because, among all the material they acquired, some of it triggered these particular effects.

This is important because it changes the whole perspective on explaining religion. As long as you think that people first open up the gates and then let visitors in, as it were, you cannot understand why religion invariably returns to the same recurrent themes. If the process of transmission only consists of *acceptance,* why do we find only a handful of recurrent themes? But if you see things the other way around, you can start describing the effects of concepts in the mind and understand why some of them may well become persuasive enough that people "believe" them. I do not think that people have religion because they relax their usually strict criteria for evidence and accept extraordinary claims; I think they are led to relax these criteria because some extraordinary claims have become quite plausible to them.

PROGRESS BOX 4: Religion and Reasoning

- The sleep of reason is no explanation for religion as it is. There are many possible unsupported claims and only a few religious themes.
- Belief is not just passive acceptance of what others say. People relax their standards because some thoughts become plausible, not the other way around.
- A different angle: We should understand what makes human minds so selective in what supernatural claims they find plausible.

Turning the Question Upside Down

At this point we should perhaps close this survey. We could in principle carry on for quite some time, as philosophers, historians and psychologists have come up with many more suggestions. However, there is a diminishing return for this kind of discussion, as most origin scenarios suffer from similar flaws. If religion is reassuring, why does it create much of the anxiety it cures? If it explains the world, why does it do it with such baroque complication? Why does it have these common, recurrent themes rather than a great variety of irrefutable ideas? Why is it so closely connected to morality, whereas it cannot really create morality? As I said several times, we cannot hope to explain religion if we just fantasize about the way human minds work. We cannot just decide that religion fulfils some particular intellectual or emotional needs, when there is no real evidence for these needs. We cannot just decide that religion is around because it promises this or that, when there are many human groups where religion makes no such promise. We cannot just ignore the anthropological evidence about different religions and the psychological evidence about mental processes. (Or rather, we *should* not; we actually do it quite often.) So the prospect may seem rather dim for a general explanation of religion. However, this survey of possible scenarios also suggests that there is another way to proceed, as I have suggested in reviewing each scenario.

The main problem with our spontaneous explanations of religion lies in the very assumption that we can explain the origin of religion by selecting one particular problem or idea or feeling and deriving the variety of things we now call religion from that unique point. Our spontaneous explanations are meant to lead us from the *One* (religion's origin) to the *Many* (the current diversity of religious ideas). This may seem natural in that this is the usual way we think of origins. The origin of geometry lies in land-tenure and surveying problems. The origin of arithmetic and number theory is in accounting problems encountered by centralized agricultural states. So it seems sensible to assume that a "one thing led to many things" scenario is apposite for cultural phenomena.

But we can approach the question from another angle. Indeed, we can and should turn the whole "origin" explanation upside down, as it were, and realize that the many forms of religion we know are not the outcome of a historical *diversification* but of a constant *reduction*. The religious concepts we observe are relatively successful ones selected among many other variants. Anthropologists explain the origins of many cultural phenomena, including religion, not by going from the *One* to the *Many* but by going from the *Very Many* to the

Many Fewer, the many variants that our minds constantly produce and the many fewer variants that can be actually transmitted to other people and become stable in a human group. To explain religion we must explain how human minds, constantly faced with lots of potential "religious stuff," constantly reduce it to much less stuff.

Concepts in the mind are constructed as a result of being exposed to other people's behavior and utterances. But this acquisition process is not a simple process of "downloading" notions from one brain to another. People's minds are constantly busy reconstructing, distorting, changing and developing the information communicated by others. This process naturally creates all sorts of variants of religious concepts, as it creates variants of all other concepts. But then not all of these variants have the same fate. Most of them are not entertained by the mind for more than an instant. A small number have more staying power but are not easily formulated or communicated to others. An even smaller number of variants remain in memory, are communicated to other people, but then these people do not recall them very well. An extremely small number remain in memory, are communicated to other people, are recalled by these people and communicated to others in a way that more or less preserves the original concepts. These are the ones we can observe in human cultures.

So we should abandon the search for a *historical* origin of religion in the sense of a point in time (however long ago) when people created religion where there was none. All scenarios that describe people sitting around and inventing religion are dubious. Even the ones that see religion as slowly emerging out of confused thoughts have this problem. In the following chapters I will show how religion emerges (has its origins, if you want) in the selection of concepts and the selection of memories. Does this mean that at some point in history people had lots of possible versions of religion and that somehow one of them proved more successful? Not at all. What it means is that, *at all times and all the time,* indefinitely many variants of religious notions were and are created inside individual minds. Not all these variants are equally successful in cultural transmission. What we call a cultural phenomenon is the result of a selection that is taking place all the time and everywhere.

This may seem a bit counterintuitive. After all, if you are a Protestant you went to Sunday school and that was your main source of formal religious education. Similarly, the teachings of the *madrasa* for Muslims and the Talmud-Torah for Jews seem to provide people with *one* version of religion. It does not seem to us that we are shopping in a religious supermarket where the shelves are bursting with alternative religious concepts. But the selection I am talking about happens mostly inside each individual mind. In the following chapters I describe how variants of religious concepts are created and constantly eliminated. This process goes on, completely unnoticed, in parts of our mind that conscious introspection will not reach. This cannot be observed or explained without the experimental resources of cognitive science.

Culture as Memes

The notion that what we find in cultures is a residue or a precipitate of many episodes of individual transmission is not new. But it became very powerful with the development of formal mathematical tools to describe cultural transmission. This happened because anthropologists were faced with a difficult problem. They often described human cultures in terms of "big" objects, like "American fundamentalism," "Jewish religion," "Chinese morality," and so on. Anthropology and history could make all sorts of meaningful statements about these big objects (e.g., "In the 18th century, the progress of science and technology in Europe challenged Christian religion as a source of authority.") However, this is a very remote description of what happens on the ground, in the actual lives of individuals. After all, people do not interact with such abstract objects as scientific progress or Christian authority. They only interact with individual people and material objects. The difficulty was to connect these two levels and to describe how what happened at the bottom, as it were, produced stability and change at the level of populations.

A number of anthropologists and biologists (including C. Lumsden and E.O. Wilson, R. Boyd and P. Richerson, L.L. Cavalli-Sforza and M. Feldman, W. Durham) more or less at the same time proposed that cultural transmission could be to some extent described in the same way as genetic inheritance. Evolutionary biology has put together an impressive set of mathematical tools to describe the way a certain gene can spread in a population, under what conditions it is likely to be "crowded out" by other versions, to what extent genes that are detrimental to one organism can still be transmitted in a population, and so forth. The idea was to adapt these tools to the transmission of cultural notions or behaviors.[9]

Tool Kit 1: Culture as Memes

The equations of population genetics are abstract tools that can be applied to genes but also to any other domain where you have (i) a set of units, (ii) changes that produce different variants of those units, (iii) a

mechanism of transmission that chooses between variants. In cultural transmission we find a certain set of notions and values (these would be the analogue of the genes). They come in different versions. These variants are communicated to people who grow up in a particular group (this is the analogue of reproduction). These internal states have external effects because people act on the basis of their notions and values (in the same way as genes produce phenotypic effects). Over many cycles of communication, certain trends can appear because of accumulated distortions—people do not transmit exactly what they received—and biased transmission—people may acquire or store some material better than the rest.

Biologist Richard Dawkins summarized all this by describing culture as a population of *memes*, which are just "copy-me" programs, like genes. Genes produce organisms that behave in such a way that the genes are replicated—otherwise the genes in question would not be around. Memes are units of culture: notions, values, stories, etc. that get people to speak or act in certain ways that make other people store a replicated version of these mental units. A joke and a popular tune are simple illustrations of such copy-me programs. You hear them once, they get stored in memory, they lead to behaviors (telling the joke, humming the tune) that will implant copies of the joke or tune in other people's memories, and so on. Now describing most cultural phenomena in terms of memes and meme-transmission may seem rather straightforward and innocuous. But it has important consequences that I must mention here because they go against some deeply entrenched ideas about culture.

First, meme-models undermine the idea of culture as some abstract object, independent from individual concepts and norms, that we somehow "share." A comparison with genes shows why this is misguided. I have blue eyes, like other people. Now I do not have their genes and they do not have mine. Our genes are all safely packed inside our individual cells. It would be a misleading metaphor to say that we "share" anything. All we can say is that the genes I inherited are similar to theirs from the point of view of their effects on eye color. In the same way, *culture is the name of a similarity*. What we mean when we say that something is "cultural" is that it is roughly similar to what we find in other members of the particular group we are considering, and unlike what we would find in members of a contrast group. This is why it is confusing to say that people share a culture, as if culture were common property. We may have strictly identical amounts of money in our respective wallets without sharing any of it!

Second, since culture is a similarity between people's ideas, it is very confusing to say things like "American culture places great emphasis on individual achievement" or "Chinese culture is more concerned with harmony within a group." Saying this, we conclude that, for instance, "Many Americans would like to relax but their culture tells them to be competitive" or "Many Chinese people would enjoy competition but their culture incites them to be more group-oriented." So we describe culture as some kind of external force that pushes people one way or another. But this is rather mysterious. How could a similarity *cause* anything? There is no external force here. If people feel a conflict between their inclinations and a norm that is followed by everybody else, it is a conflict *within their heads*. If an American child has a hard time coping with the requirement that "an American child should be competitive," it is because the requirement has been implanted in the child's mind, maybe to his chagrin. But all this is happening inside a mind.

Third, knowing that culture is a similarity between people is helpful because it forces you to remember that two objects are similar only *from a certain point of view*. My blue eyes may make me similar to some other people, but then my shortsightedness makes me similar to others. Apply this to culture. We routinely talk about whole cultures as distinct units, as in "Chinese culture," "Yoruba culture," "British culture" and so forth. What is wrong here? The term *cultural* labels a certain similarity between the representations we find in members of a group. So, it would seem, we can do anthropological fieldwork and surveys among different human groups, say the Americans and the Yoruba, and then describe representations that we find in only one of them as being the American and Yoruba cultures respectively. But why do we assume that "the Americans" or "the Yoruba" constitute a group? Compare this with natural species. We feel justified, to some extent, in comparing the eggplant with the zucchini or the donkey with the zebra. These labels correspond to natural groupings of plants and animals. Now the problem is that *there are no natural groupings for human beings*. We may think that it makes sense to compare the Americans and the Yoruba because there is a Yoruba polity and an American (U.S.) nation. But note that these are historical, purposeful constructions. They are not the effect of some natural similarity. Indeed, if we look at people's actual behavior and representations in either group, we will find that quite a lot of what they do and think can be observed outside these groups. Many norms and ideas of American farmers are more common to farmers than to Americans; many norms and ideas of Yoruba businessmen are more common among businesspeople than among the Yoruba. This confirmed what anthropologists had long suspected, that the choice of human groupings for cultural comparisons is not a natural or scientific choice, but a *political* one.

Finally, quantitative models of cultural transmission replaced mythical notions like "absorbing what's in the air" with a concrete, measurable process of transmission. People communicate with other people, they meet individuals with similar or different notions or values, they change or maintain or discard their ways of thinking because of these encounters, and so forth. What we call their "culture" is the outcome of all these particular encounters. If you find that a particular concept is very stable in a human group (you can come back later and find it more or less unchanged) it is because it has a particular *advantage* inside individual minds. If you want to explain cultural trends, this is far more important than tracing the actual historical origin of this or that particular notion. A few pages back, I described the way a Cuna shaman talks to statuettes. This seems a stable concept among the Cuna. If we want to explain that, we have to explain how this concept is represented in individual minds, in such a way that they can recall it and transmit it better than other concepts. If we want to explain why the Cuna maintain this notion of intelligent statuettes, it does not matter if what happened was that one creative Cuna thought of that a century ago, or that someone had a dream about that, or that someone told a story with intelligent statuettes. What matters is what happened afterward in the many cycles of acquisition, memory and communication.[10]

In this account, familiar religious concepts and associated beliefs, norms, emotions, are just better-replicating memes than others, in the sense that their copy-me instructions work better. This would be why so many people in different cultures think that invisible spirits lurk around and so few imagine that their internal organs change location during the night, why the notion of moralistic ancestors watching your behavior is more frequent than that of immoral ghosts who want you to steal from your neighbors. Human minds exposed to these concepts end up replicating them and passing them on to other people. On the whole, this may seem the right way to understand diffusion and transmission. However. . .

Distortion is of the Essence

The notion of human culture as a huge set of copy-me programs is very seductive and it is certainly on the right track, but it is only a starting point. Why are some memes better than others? Why is singing *Land of Hope and Glory* after hearing it once much easier than humming a tune from Schoenberg's *Pierrot lunaire*? What exactly makes moralistic ancestors better for transmission than immoral ghosts? This is not the only problem. A much more difficult one is that if we look a bit more closely at cultural transmission between human beings, what we see does not look at all like replication of identical memes. On the contrary, the process of transmission seems guaranteed to create an extraordinary profusion of baroque variations. This is where the analogy with genes is more hindrance than help. Consider this. You (and I) carry genes that come from a unique source (a meiotic combination of our parents' genes) and we will transmit them unchanged (though combined with a partner's set) to our offspring. In the meantime, nothing happens; however much you may work out at the gym, you will not have more muscular children. But in mental representations the opposite is true. The denizens of our minds have many parents (in those thousands of renditions of *Land of Hope and Glory*, which one is being replicated when I whistle the tune?) and we constantly modify them.[11]

As we all know, some memes may be faithfully transmitted while others are hugely distorted in the process. Consider for instance the contrasting fortunes of two cultural memes created by Richard Dawkins, one of which replicated very well while the other one underwent a bizarre mutation. The idea of "meme" itself is an example of a meme that replicated rather well. A few years after Dawkins had introduced the notion, virtually everybody in the social sciences and in evolutionary biology or psychology knew about it and for the most part had an essentially correct notion of the original meaning. Now compare this with another of Dawkins's ideas, that of "selfish genes." What Dawkins meant was that genes are DNA strings whose sole achievement is to replicate. The explanation for this is simply that the ones that do not have this functionality (the ones that build organisms that cannot pass on the genes) just disappear from the gene pool. So far, so simple. However, once the phrase *selfish gene* diffused out into the wide world its meaning changed beyond recognition, to become in many people's usage "a gene that makes us selfish." An editorial in the British *Spectator* once urged the Conservative Party to acquire more of that selfish gene that Professor Dawkins talked about. . . . But one does not "acquire" a gene, it makes little sense to say that someone has "more" of a gene than someone else, there is probably no such thing as a gene that makes people selfish, and Dawkins never meant that anyway. This distortion is not too surprising. It confirms the popular perception that biology is all about the struggle for survival, Nature red in tooth and claw, the Hobbesian fight of all against all, etc. (that this is in fact largely false is neither here nor there). So the distortion happened, in this case, because people had a prior notion that the phrase "selfish gene" seemed to match. The original explanation (the original meme) was completely ignored, the better to fit that prior conception.

Cultural memes undergo mutation, recombination and selection *inside* the individual mind every bit as much and as often as (in fact probably more so and more often than) during transmission between minds. We do not just transmit the information we received. We process it and use it to create new information, some of which we do communicate to other people. To some anthropologists this seemed to spell the doom of meme-explanations of culture. What we call culture is the similarity between some people's mental representations in some domains. But how come there *is* similarity at all, if representations come from so many sources and undergo so many changes?

It is tempting to think that there is an obvious solution: some memes are so infectious and hardy that our minds just swallow them whole, as it were, and then regurgitate them in pristine form for others to acquire. They would be transmitted between minds in the same way as an E-mail message is routed via a network of different computers. Each machine stores it for a while and passes it on to another machine via reliable channels. For instance, the idea of a moralistic ancestor, communicated by your elders, might be so "good" that you just store it in your memory and then deliver it intact to your children. But that is not the solution, for the following reason: When an idea gets distorted beyond recognition—as happened to the "selfish gene"—it seems obvious that this occurs because the minds that received the original information added to it, in other words *worked* on it. So far, so good. But this leads us to think that when an idea gets transmitted in a roughly faithful way, this occurs because the receiving minds did *not* rework it, as it were. Now that is a great mistake. The main difference between minds that communicate and computers that route E-mail is this: minds *never* swallow raw information to serve it to others in the same raw state. Minds invariably do a lot of work on available information, *especially so* when transmission is faithful. For instance, I can sing *Land of Hope and Glory* in (roughly) the same way as others before me. This is because hugely complex mental processes shaped my memories of the different versions I heard. In human communication, *good transmission requires as much work as does distortion*.

This is why the notion of "memes," although a good starting point, is only that. The idea of "replication" is very misleading. People's ideas are sometimes roughly similar to those of other people around them, not because ideas can be downloaded from mind to mind but because they are reconstructed in a similar way. Some ideas are good enough that you will entertain them even though your elders did not give you much material to work with, and so good again that your cultural offspring will probably hone in on them even though you too are an incompetent transmitter! Against our intuitions, there is nothing miraculous in the fact that many machines have similar text in memory although the connections between them are terrible, when the machines in question are human minds and the channel is human communication.

How to Catch Concepts with Templates

People have religious notions and beliefs because they acquired them from other people. Naturally, nothing in principle prevents an ingenious Sicilian Catholic from reinventing the Hindu pantheon or imaginative Chinese from re-creating Amazonian mythology. On the whole, however, people get their religion from other members of their social group. But how does that occur? Our spontaneous explanation of transmission is quite simple. People behave in certain ways around a child and the child assimilates what is around until it becomes second nature. In this picture, acquiring culture is a passive process. The developing mind is gradually filled with information provided by cultural elders and peers. This is why Hindus have many gods and Jews only one; this is why the Japanese like raw fish and the Americans toast marshmallows. Now this picture of transmission has a great advantage—it is simple—and a major flaw—it is clearly false. It is mistaken on two counts. First, children do not assimilate the information around them; they actively filter it and use it to go well beyond what is provided. Second, they do not acquire all information in the same way.

To get a feel for the complexity of transmission, compare the ways in which you acquired different bits of your cultural equipment. How did you learn the syntax of your native tongue? It is a very complex system, as any foreigner struggling with the rules will tell you. But the learning process all happened unconsciously, or so it seems, and certainly without any effort, just by virtue of being around native speakers. Compare with etiquette and politeness. These are different from one culture to another and they have to be learned at some point. Again, this seems to be rather easily done, but there is a difference. In this case you learned by being told what to do and not do and by observing examples of people interacting. You were aware, to a certain extent, that you were acquiring ways of behaving in order to have certain effects on other people. Now consider mathematics. In this case you were certainly aware that you were learning something. You had to put some effort into it. Understanding the truth of $(a + b)^2 = a^2 + 2ab + b^2$ does not come very

easily. Most people never acquire this kind of knowledge unless they are guided step by step by competent adults. I could multiply the examples but the point is really simple. There is no single way of acquiring the stuff that makes you a competent member of a culture.

There are different ways of acquiring cultural information because a human brain has dispositions for learning and they are not the same in all domains. For instance, acquiring the right syntax and pronunciation for a natural language is trivially easy for all normal brains at the right age, between about one and six. The dispositions for social interaction develop at a different rhythm. But in all these domains learning is possible because there is a disposition to learn, which means, a disposition to go *beyond* the information that is available. This is quite clear in language. Children gradually build their syntax on the basis of what they hear because their brains have definite biases about how language works. But it is true also in many conceptual domains. Consider our everyday knowledge of animals. Children learn that different animal species reproduce in different ways. Cats deliver live kittens and hens lay eggs. A child can learn that by observing actual animals or by being given explicit information. But there are things you do not have to tell children because they know them already. For example, it is not necessary to tell them that if one hen lays eggs, then it is probably true that hens *in general* lay eggs. In the same way, a five-year-old will guess that if one walrus gives birth to live cubs then all other walruses probably reproduce in that way too. This illustrates another simple point: Minds that acquire knowledge are not empty containers into which experience and teaching pour predigested information. A mind needs and generally has some way of organizing information to make sense of what is observed and learned. This allows the mind to go beyond the information given, or in the jargon, to produce *inferences* on the basis of information given.

Complex inferences allow children and adults to build concepts out of fragmentary information, but inferences are not random. They are governed by special principles in the mind, so that their result is in fact predictable. Even though cultural material is constantly distorted and reshuffled inside the head, the mind is not a free-for-all of random associations. One major reason is the presence of mental dispositions for arranging conceptual material in certain ways rather than others. Crucial to this explanation is the distinction between *concepts* and *templates*.

To illustrate this: A child is shown a new animal, say a walrus, and told the name for the species. What the child does—unconsciously of course—is add a new entry to her mental "encyclopedia," an entry marked "walrus" that probably includes a description of a shape. Over the years this entry may become richer as new facts and experiences provide more information about walruses. As I said above, we also know that the child spontaneously adds some information to that entry, whether we tell her or not. For instance, if she sees a walrus give birth to live cubs, she will conclude that this is the way all walruses have babies. You do not need to tell her that "all walruses reproduce that way." Why is that so? The child has created a "walrus" concept by using the ANIMAL *template*.

Think of the ANIMAL template as one of those official forms that provide boxes to fill out. You can fill out the same form in different ways. What stays the same are the boxes and the rules on what should be put in them. The child has identified that the thing you called "walrus" was an animal, not a heap of minerals or a machine or a person. To put it metaphorically, all she had to do then was to take a new sheet of the form called ANIMAL and fill out the relevant boxes. These include a box for the name of the new kind of animal, a box for its appearance (shape, size, color, etc.), a box for where it lives, a box for how it gets a progeny, and so on. In the figure below I give a *very simplified* illustration of this idea of filling out templates for new animals.

Now the information in each of these boxes has to be filled out according to certain principles. You are not allowed to specify that an animal has sometimes four legs and sometimes two wings and two legs. You have to decide which is true or leave the box empty. In the same way, the box for "reproduces" will be filled out with either one answer or none. This is why I compared templates to official forms. These ask you to give your one given name, not a choice of nicknames your friends call you. This is very important because it means that some generalizations are produced automatically when you learn a new concept. The move from "this one has live cubs" (a particular fact) to "they all have live cubs" (a generalization) is made automatically because the animal template does not allow several different values in the "reproduces" box. So the child does not have to learn how an animal reproduces more than once for each animal kind.

The child is told: "This is a walrus. See how big her belly is! She'll probably give birth to cubs very soon." A few days later this child may well tell a friend that walruses do not lay eggs; they get pregnant and deliver live babies. This is not a *replication* of information she received but an *inference* from that information. Even very young children can produce such inferences because they connect the information received about a particular animal to an abstract template ANIMAL. This template works like a recipe and could be called "recipe for producing new animal-concepts."

There are, obviously, *fewer* templates than concepts. Templates are more abstract than concepts and organize them. You need only one ANIMAL template for the many, many different animal concepts you will acquire. You need one Tool template although you may have concepts for many different tools. Concepts depend on your experience, your environment, but templates are much more stable. For instance, people from Greenland and Congo share very few animal concepts, simply because very few species are encountered in both places. Also, a fishmonger certainly has a richer repertoire of fish concepts than an insurance salesman. But the ANIMAL template does not vary much with differences in culture or expertise. For instance, everyone from Congo to Greenland and from fishmongers to insurance salesmen expects all members of a species to reproduce in the same way. Everyone expects that an animal belongs to a species and only one. Everyone expects that if an animal of a particular species breathes in a particular way this is true of all other members of the species.

The distinction between templates and concepts applies to many other domains. Here is a familiar example: In every place in the world there are very precise notions about which substances are disgusting and which are not. But the concepts are really different. To many in the West the idea of eating cockroaches is rather off-putting, but they would not find anything especially disgusting in having dinner with a blacksmith. The opposite would be true in other places. So we might conclude that there is nothing in common between human cultures in this domain. However, there is a general template of POLLUTING SUBSTANCE that seems to work in the same way in most places. For example, whenever people think that a particular substance is disgusting, they also think that it remains so however much you dilute it: Who (in the West) would want to drink a glass of water if they are told it contains only a tiny drop of cow urine? In the same way, some people in West Africa would think that the mere presence of a blacksmith in their home is enough to spoil the food. Take another example, from the domain of politeness. We know etiquette really differs from place to place. In the West it would be rude to sit in your host's lap; in Cameroon, where I did fieldwork, it shows great respect on some occasions. Concepts are different, but there is a general template of FACE and actions that can make people lose it. You have to learn the local rules, but note how easy it is to produce inferences once you are given the rules. For instance, once told that sitting in a person's lap is a mark of respect, you can infer that it cannot be all the time, that it is probably absurd to do it with small children, that you will offend people if you fail to do it when it is expected, and so forth. Such inferences are easy because you already have a template for such concepts.

Epidemics of Culture

Templates are one of the devices that allow minds to reach similar representations without having a perfect channel to "download" information from one mind to another. The child now thinks that walruses deliver live cubs. I happen to think so too, and you probably have the same idea, and so does, say, Mrs. Jones. But it is very unlikely that we all received precisely the same information about walruses in the same way. What is far more likely is that we extracted this similar information by inference from very different situations and from different statements made by people in different ways. We nonetheless converged on similar inferences because the animal template is the same in the child, you, me and Mrs. Jones (I will show in another chapter how we know this to be the case). In fact we might all converge on this same notion even if the information the child, you, I and Mrs. Jones had received was totally different.

As I said above, the fact that individual minds constantly recombine and modify information would suggest that people's concepts are in constant flux. But then why do we find similar representations among members of a particular social group? The mystery is not so difficult to solve once we realize not just that *all* mental representations are the products of complex inferences—so there is indeed a vast flux and myriad modifications—but also that *some* changes and inferences tend to go in particular directions, no matter where you start from. Inferences in the mind are in many cases a centrifugal force, as it were, that makes different people's representations diverge in unpredictable ways. If I spend a whole day with my friends, going through the same experiences for hours on end, our memories of that day will probably diverge in a million subtle ways. But in some domains inferences do the opposite. Acting as a centripetal force, inferences and memories lead to roughly similar constructions even though the input may be quite different. This is why we can observe similarities between concepts both within a group—my notions about animals are quite similar to those of my relatives—and also between groups—there are important similarities in animal concepts from Congo to Greenland, because of a similar template.

At about the same time as meme-accounts were devised to describe cultural transmission, Dan Sperber and some colleagues put together an *epidemiological* framework to describe the mechanisms of cultural transmission. The substance of this framework is what I just explained in terms of information and inference. An epidemic occurs when a group of individuals display similar symptoms—when for instance people in a whole region of Africa get high fevers. This is explained as an epidemic of malaria, caused by the presence of mosquitoes carrying the *Plasmodium* pathogen. But note that what we call the epidemic is the occurrence of fevers and assorted symptoms, not the presence of mosquitoes or even *Plasmodium*. That is, to explain what happened you must understand the particular ways in which the human body reacts to the presence of this particular agent. If you do not know any physiology, you will have a hard time explaining why only some animals catch malaria, why fewer people with adequate preventive treatment catch it than do others, or indeed how the disease spreads at all. We may well study the structure of *Plasmodium* forever; this will tell us nothing about its effects unless we also learn a lot about human physiology. Mental representations are the effects of external vectors, mostly of communications with other people. But then the structure of the messages exchanged does not by itself tell us how the mind will react to them. To understand that, we must know a lot about human psychology, about the way minds produce inferences that modify and complete the information exchanged.[12]

Tool Kit 2: Cultural Epidemics

Human minds are inhabited by a large population of mental representations. Most representations are found only in one individual but some are present in roughly similar forms in various members of a group. To account for this is to explain the statistical fact that a similar condition affects a number of organisms, as in epidemics. Different people have inferred similar representations from publicly accessible representations: other people's behavior, gestures, utterances, man-made objects, etc. The diffusion of particular representations in a group, as well as similarities across groups, can be predicted if we have a good description of what mental resources people bring to understanding what others offer as cultural material—in particular, what inferential processes they apply to that material.

To explain religion is to explain a particular kind of mental epidemic whereby people develop (on the basis of variable information) rather similar forms of religious concepts and norms. I used the example of animal concepts to show how our minds build inferences in such a way that concepts within a group can be very similar and the concepts of different groups, despite differences, can be shaped by the same templates. This applies to religious notions too. There are templates for religious concepts. That is, there are some "recipes" contained in my mind, and yours, and that of any other normal human being, that build religious concepts by producing inferences on the basis of some information provided by other people and by experience. In the same way as for animal concepts, religious concepts may converge (be roughly similar) even though the particular information from which they were built is in fact very different from one individual to another.

Religion is cultural. People get it from other people, as they get food preferences, musical tastes, politeness and a dress sense. We often tend to think that if something is cultural then it is hugely variable. But then it turns out that food preferences and other such cultural things are not so variable after all. Food preferences revolve around certain recurrent flavors, musical tastes in various cultures vary within strict constraints, and so do politeness codes and standards of elegance.

For anthropologists, the fact that something is cultural is the very *reason* it does not vary that much. Not everything is equally likely to be transmitted, because the templates in the mind filter information from other people and build predictable structures out of that information.

A Puzzlement of Questions

When I started studying anthropology, theories of religion were thoroughly confusing. People in my discipline used to think that the very question, Why is religion the way it is? was naive, ill-formulated or perhaps just intractable. Most people thought this kind of speculation was better left to theologians or retired scientists. What we lacked at the time was a good description of those aspects of human nature that lead people to adopt certain ideas or beliefs rather than others. Convergent developments in evolutionary biology and cognitive psychology have since helped us understand why human cultures display similarities and differences too.

When I say that we now have a better account of religion, I of course mean a better one compared to previous *scientific* accounts. In this kind of theory, we describe phenomena that can be observed and even measured. We explain them in terms of other phenomena that are also detectable. When we say that *a* implies *b*, our account is vulnerable to counterexamples where *a* occurs without *b*. I do not know if this is enough to define scientific explanations but I am sure it excludes quite a few theories of religion. Some people say that the origin of religion is a long-forgotten visit from wise extraterrestrial aliens who were compassionate enough to leave us with fragments of their knowledge. These people will not be interested in the kind of discoveries I discuss here. In a less flamboyant vein, people who think that we have religion because religion is *true* (or their version of it is, or perhaps another,

still-to-be-discovered version is) will find little here to support their views and in fact no discussion of these views.

But we can do much better. We can now address as *problems* rather than *mysteries* a collection of questions that used to be intractable, such as:

- Why do people have religion, more or less everywhere?
- Why does it come in different forms? Are there any common features?
- Why does religion matter so much to people's lives?
- Why are there several religions rather than just one?
- Why does religion prescribe rituals? Why are rituals the way they are?
- Why do most religions have religious specialists?
- Why does religion seem to provide "truth"?
- Why are there Churches and religious institutions?
- Why does religion trigger strong emotions? Why do people kill for religion?
- Why does religion persist in the face of apparently more efficient ways of thinking about the world?
- Why does it lead to so much intolerance and so many atrocities? Or, if you prefer, Why is it sometimes conducive to heroism and self-sacrifice?

There remains one big question that most people would think is the crucial one: *Why do some people believe?* The question is often the *first* one people ask when they consider scientific accounts of religion, yet it will be treated in the *last* chapter of this book. This is not for the sake of creating a spurious suspense. It turns out that you cannot deal with this question unless you have a very precise description of *what* it is that people actually believe. And that is far from obvious.

This may seem a strange thing to say, as religious people are in general all too eager to let us know what they believe. They tell us that an unseen presence is watching our every step, or that the souls of dead people are still around, or that we will reincarnate in some form commensurate with our moral achievements. So all we have to do, or so it seems, is consider these diverse notions and ask ourselves, again: Why do people believe in all this?

But this does not really work. What makes anthropology difficult—and fascinating—is that religious representations are not all *transparent* to the mind. When people have thoughts about gods or spirits or ancestors, a whole machinery of complex mental devices is engaged, most of which is completely outside conscious access. This, obviously, is not special to religion. Speaking a natural language or playing tennis or understanding a joke also engage this complex machinery (though in different ways). If you want to explain how human minds acquire religious concepts, why these concepts become plausible and why they trigger such strong emotions, you will have to describe all the invisible processes that create such thoughts, make it possible to communicate them, and trigger all sorts of associated mental effects such as emotion and commitment.

Explaining Airy Nothing: Magic Bullets vs. Aggregate Relevance

All scenarios for the origin of religion assume that there must be a single factor that will explain why there is religion in all human groups and why it triggers such important social, cognitive, emotional effects. This belief in a "magic bullet" is, unfortunately, exceedingly stubborn. It has hampered our understanding of the phenomenon for a long time. Progress in anthropology and psychology tells us why the belief was naive. Some concepts happen to connect with inference systems in the brain in a way

that makes recall and communication very easy. Some concepts happen to trigger our emotional programs in particular ways. Some concepts happen to connect to our social mind. Some of them are represented in such a way that they soon become plausible and direct behavior. The ones that do *all* this are the religious ones we actually observe in human societies. They are most successful because they combine features relevant to a variety of mental systems.

This is precisely why religion cannot be explained by a single magic bullet. Since cultural concepts are the objects of constant selection in minds, through acquisition and communication, the ones that we find widespread in many different cultures and at different times probably have some transmission advantage, relative to *several* different mental dispositions. They are relevant to different systems in the mind. This is why it takes several chapters to approach a question that many people, in my experience, can solve to their entire satisfaction in a few seconds of dinner-table conversation.

Race, Ethnicity, Identity and Creating the "Other"

Unit 9 (CH# 17, 21, 22)

As we have seen, socialization is the process through which we learn the rules of society. One of the most important rules that we learn is how to define groups and how to locate ourselves in the plethora of groups that make up societies. That is, we learn "us;" what group "we" belong to, and "them;" the groups in which we do not belong. We might belong to many different groups in society. We are members of a family, a geographic space which usually has a name (Hialeah, Orlando), organizations which we willingly join (fraternities/sororities/activist groups), and groups into which we are born (Cuban, Jamaican, African-American). Some groups are more closely tied to what we consider our "identity." As we develop a sense of identity (or more like "senses" of identity, for example, American, Cuban, Nicaraguan, Black, White, Latino, liberal, conservative, smart, not so much, etc.), we also develop a sense of the "other;" those that do not share our identities. Sometimes we identify them as "deviants" but more often we just identify them as "them." We might not know much about them but we sure know that "they" are not like "us."

We are always in the "in-group;" even if you consider yourself some sorts of outsider or rebel, your in-group are other outsiders and rebels. As it turns out, it does not take much to make us identify with a group. The "minimal group" studies associated with social identity theory show that when kids are randomly assigned to groups, they will figure out some way to develop a group identity and that identity will include feeling superior to the individuals in the other randomly assigned groups. Social identity theory posits that we have a variety of identities shaped by our social contexts and we always try to develop identities that will boost our self-image. That is, we want to feel good about ourselves so we assign the best possible value to the groups that we belong to or identify with.

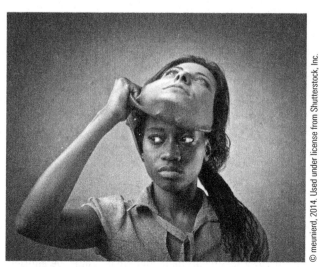

Identity is not ornamental. It is a part of the self.

White privilege cannot be so easily put on or removed.

Race and Ethnicity ✓

The terms "race," "ethnicity," and "minority group," have distinct meanings for sociologists. The idea of race refers to superficial physical differences that a particular society considers significant, while ethnicity is a term that describes shared culture. And minority groups describe groups that are subordinate, or lacking power in society regardless of skin color or country of origin.

Few social categories are as misunderstood as race. The idea that there are different human races leads some of folks to think that the superficial differences that our societies categorize as "race" point to significant biological differences. This is not the case, as research is bearing out. We are one race…the human race. The color of your skin signals the environmental adaptation that the bodies of your ancestors had to make to survive and reproduce in specific places on the earth where the sun was either very bright or not so much. Similarly, some of the biological differences that remain among us reflect adaptations that long ago lost their significance, for example, sickle cell anemia as a prophylactic against malaria. Race, in other words, is a social construct. Consider the "one-drop rule," a legislative measure of blackness adopted by some states in the early part of the 20th century in the United States and not overturned until 1967. Under this definition, anyone with one-drop (or one sixteenth ancestry in some measures) of black blood was considered black. Clearly this is a social categorization. Why not the other way around? Why cannot one drop of "white" ancestry make someone white? This is what sociologist mean when we say that race is a social construct?

Muslim veiled women in the heart of downtown Istanbul. The Turkish government banned women who wear headscarves from working in the public sector. Is this an attack on religious freedom or a benign attempt to westernize a society? or both?

Historically, the concept of race has changed across cultures and eras, eventually becoming less connected with ancestral and familial ties, and more concerned with superficial physical characteristics. In the past, theorists have posited categories of race based on various geographic regions, ethnicities, skin colors, and more. Their labels for racial groups have connoted regions (e.g., Mongolia, Finland and the Caucus Mountains) or denoted skin tones (e.g., black, white, yellow, and red). However, this typology of race developed during previous centuries has fallen into disuse. We now view the concept of race as being a social rather than a biological construct. Advances in the biological sciences have shown that race is not biologically identifiable. When considering skin color, for example, we recognize that the relative darkness or fairness of skin is an evolutionary adaptation to the available sunlight in different regions of the world.

Pigmentation is not a racial signifier, then, but the way that societies categorize pigmentation constitutes our modern understanding of racial categories. Growing research in evolutionary biology and evolutionary psychology is providing evidence that once-upon-a-time, when we were first developing as a species; it was very useful to identify the "other" quickly and effectively since that often meant the difference between survival and death or between eating a fresh kill and getting to pick over the bones. But just like sickle cell anemia has long expired as a protection against malaria, so has the protective identification of the "other" outlasted its adaptation function. Or has it?

According to the 2010 Census, people who reported a background of mixed race grew by 32% to 9 million between 2000 and 2010. In comparison, single-race population increased only 9.2%. How will the archaic concept of "race" be altered as the population changes?

Subordinate & Dominant

In some countries, such as Brazil, class is more important than skin color in determining racial categorization. People with high levels of melanin in their skin may consider themselves "white" if they enjoy a middle-class lifestyle. On the other hand, someone with low levels of melanin in their skin might be assigned the identity of "black" if they have little education or money.

Ethnicity is a term that describes shared culture—the practices, values, and beliefs of a group. This might include shared language, religion, and traditions, among other commonalities. Like race, the term ethnicity is difficult to describe and its meaning has changed over time. And like race, individuals may be identified or self-identify to ethnicities in complex, even contradictory, ways. For example, ethnic groups such as Irish, Italian American, Russian, Jewish, and Serbian might all be groups whose members are predominantly included in the racial category "white." Conversely, the ethnic group British includes citizens from a multiplicity of racial backgrounds: black, white, Asian, and more, plus a variety of race combinations. These examples illustrate the complexity and overlap of these identifying terms. Ethnicity, like race, continues to be an identification method that individuals and institutions use

Louis Wirth (1945)
Minority Groups !! Discussion
10

This woman in Havana has a fine cigar. The African culture and religions have a huge influence in Cuba where a large portion of population is of African descent. A 1995 genetic analysis of the population in the western province of Pinar del Rio found that 46% of the maternal lineages could be traced to Africa. Yet, when one examines the Cuban census, which is conducted by census takers visiting every home and visually registering "race," we find that sixty percent of the population more or less is registered as "white." Racial lines are drawn differently in Cuba and other places in Latin America.

today—whether through the census, affirmative action initiatives, non-discrimination laws, or simply in personal day-to-day relations.

Sociologist Louis Wirth (1945) defined a **minority group** as "any group of people who, because of their physical or cultural characteristics, are singled out from the others in the society in which they live for differential and unequal treatment, and who therefore regard themselves as objects of collective discrimination." The term minority connotes discrimination, and in its sociological use, the term **subordinate** can be used interchangeably with the term minority, while the term **dominant** is often substituted for the group that is in the majority. These definitions correlate to the concept that the dominant group is that which holds the most power in a given society, while subordinate groups are those who lack power compared to the dominant group. Note that being a numerical minority is not a characteristic of being a minority group; sometimes larger groups can be considered minority groups due to their lack of power. It is the lack of power that is the predominant characteristic of a minority, or subordinate group. For example, consider Apartheid in South Africa, in which a numerical majority (the black inhabitants of the country) were exploited and oppressed by the white minority.

Important

According to Charles Wagley and Marvin Harris (1958), a minority group is distinguished by five characteristics: (1) unequal treatment and less power over their lives, (2) distinguishing physical or cultural traits like skin color or language, (3) involuntary membership in the group, (4) awareness of subordination, and (5) high rate of in-group marriage. Additional examples of minority groups might include the LBGT community, religious practitioners whose faith is not widely practiced where they live, and people with disabilities.

SOCIOLOGY COMPASS

The Persistent Problem of Colorism: Skin Tone, Status, and Inequality

Margaret Hunter*
Department of Sociology and Anthropology, Mills College

Abstract

Colorism is a persistent problem for people of color in the USA. Colorism, or skin color stratification, is a process that privileges light-skinned people of color over dark in areas such as income, education, housing, and the marriage market. This essay describes the experiences of African Americans, Latinos, and Asian Americans with regard to skin color. Research demonstrates that light-skinned people have clear advantages in these areas, even when controlling for other background variables. However, dark-skinned people of color are typically regarded as more ethnically authentic or legitimate than light-skinned people. Colorism is directly related to the larger system of racism in the USA and around the world. The color complex is also exported around the globe, in part through US media images, and helps to sustain the multibillion-dollar skin bleaching and cosmetic surgery industries.

Racial discrimination is a pervasive problem in the USA. African Americans, Latinos, Asian Americans, and other people of color are routinely denied access to resources and fair competition for jobs and schooling. Despite this pattern of exclusion, people of color have made great progress in combating persistent discrimination in housing, the labor market, and education. However, hidden within the process of racial discrimination is the often overlooked issue of colorism. Colorism is the process of discrimination that privileges light-skinned people of color over their dark-skinned counterparts (Hunter 2005). Colorism is concerned with actual skin tone, as opposed to racial or ethnic identity. This is an important distinction because race is a social concept, not significantly tied to biology (Hirschman 2004). Lighter-skinned people of color enjoy substantial privileges that are still unattainable to their darker-skinned brothers and sisters. In fact, light-skinned people earn more money, complete more years of schooling, live in better neighborhoods, and marry higher-status people than darker-skinned people of the same race or ethnicity (Arce et al. 1987; Espino and Franz 2002; Hill 2000; Hughes and Hertel 1990; Hunter 1998, 2005; Keith and Herring 1991; Murguia and Telles 1996; Rondilla and Spickard 2007).

How does colorism operate? Systems of racial discrimination operate on at least two levels: race and color. The first system of discrimination is the level of racial category, (i.e. black, Asian, Latino, etc.). Regardless of physical appearance, African Americans of all skin tones are subject to certain kinds of discrimination, denigration, and second-class citizenship, simply because they are African American. Racism in this form is systemic and has both ideological and material consequences (Bonilla-Silva 2006; Feagin 2000). The second system of discrimination, what I am calling colorism, is at the level of skin tone: darker skin or lighter skin. Although all blacks experience discrimination as blacks, the intensity of that discrimination, the frequency, and the outcomes of that discrimination will differ dramatically by skin tone. Darker-skinned African Americans may earn less money that lighter-skinned African Americans, although both earn less than whites. These two systems of discrimination (race and color) work in concert. The two systems are distinct, but inextricably connected. For example, a light-skinned Mexican American may still experience racism, despite her light skin, and a dark-skinned Mexican American may experience racism and colorism simultaneously. Racism is a larger, systemic, social process and colorism is one manifestation of it.

Although many people believe that colorism is strictly a 'black or Latino problem', colorism is actually practiced by whites and people of color alike. Given the opportunity, many people will hire a light-skinned person before a dark-skinned person of the same race (Espino and Franz 2002; Hill 2000; Hughes and Hertel

*Correspondence address: Mills College, Department of Sociology and Anthropology, 5000 MacArthur Blvd., Oakland, CA 94613, USA. Email: mhunter@lmu.edu or mlhunter2000@yahoo.com.

1990; Mason 2004; Telles and Murguia 1990), or choose to marry a lighter-skinned woman rather than a darker-skinned woman (Hunter 1998; Rondilla and Spickard 2007; Udry et al. 1971). Many people are unaware of their preferences for lighter skin because that dominant aesthetic is so deeply ingrained in our culture. In the USA, for example, we are bombarded with images of white and light skin and Anglo facial features. White beauty is the standard and the ideal (Kilbourne 1999).

Historical origins of colorism

Colorism has roots in the European colonial project (Jordan 1968), plantation life for enslaved African Americans (Stevenson 1996), and the early class hierarchies of Asia (Rondilla and Spickard 2007). Despite its disparate roots, today, colorism in the USA is broadly maintained by a system of white racism (Feagin et al. 2001). The maintenance of white supremacy (aesthetic, ideological, and material) is predicated on the notion that dark skin represents savagery, irrationality, ugliness, and inferiority. White skin, and, thus, whiteness itself, is defined by the opposite: civility, rationality, beauty, and superiority. These contrasting definitions are the foundation for colorism.

Colorism for Latinos and African Americans has its roots in European colonialism and slavery in the Americas. Both systems operated as forms of white domination that rewarded those who emulated whiteness culturally, ideologically, economically, and even aesthetically. Light-skinned people received privileges and resources that were otherwise unattainable to their darker-skinned counterparts. White elites ruling the colonies maintained white superiority and domination by enlisting the assistance of the 'colonial elite', often a small light-skinned class of colonized people (Fanon 1967). Although Mexico experienced a high degree of racial miscegenation, the color-caste system was firmly in place. Light-skinned Spaniards culled the most power and resources, while darker-skinned Indians were routinely oppressed, dispossessed of their land, and rendered powerless in the early colony. Vestiges of this history are still visible today in Mexico's color-class system.

A similar color hierarchy developed in the USA during slavery and afterward. Slave owners typically used skin tone as a dimension of hierarchy on the plantation (Horowitz 1973). White slave owners sometimes gave lighter-skinned African slaves some additional privileges, such as working in the house as opposed to the fields, the occasional opportunity to learn to read, and the rare chance for manumission (Davis 1991). During slavery, a small, but elite class of freedmen was established. These disproportionately light-skinned men and women were early business leaders, clergy, teachers, and artisans, who

became economic and community leaders in the early African American community (Edwards 1959; Frazier 1957; Gatewood 1990).

Colorism for Asian Americans seems to have a more varied history. For Asian Americans with a European colonial history, like Indians, Vietnamese, or Filipinos, light skin tone is valued because of the European values enforced by the colonial regime (Karnow 1989; Rafael 2000). Europeans themselves were regarded as high status, as were white skin, Anglo facial features, and the English, French, and Spanish languages, respectively. For other Asian American groups with an indirect relationship to Western culture, light skin tone was associated with the leisure class (Jones 2004; Rondilla and Spickard 2007). Only poor or working people would be dark because they had to work outside as manual laborers. Dark skin tone is therefore associated with poverty and 'backwardness' for many Asian immigrants and Asian Americans (Rondilla and Spickard 2007).

Ronald Hall (1994, 1995, 1997) suggests that 'the bleaching syndrome' the internalization of a white aesthetic ideal, is the result of the historic legacy of slavery and colonialism around the globe. He argues that many African Americans, Latinos, and Asian Americans have internalized the colonial and slavery value systems and learned to valorize light skin tones and Anglo facial features. He understands this deeply rooted cultural value as a cause of psychological distress and socioeconomic stratification.

In many former European colonies, there remains an overt legacy of Eurocentrism and white racism in the culture (Memmi 1965). Whites or light-skinned elites continue to hold powerful positions in the economy, government, and educational sectors. Embedded in the leftover colonial structure is a strong and enduring value of white aesthetics (e.g. light hair, straight hair, light eyes, narrow noses, and light skin). This is evident in Latin American popular culture, for example, in the *telenovelas*, where almost all of the actors look white, unless they are the maids and are then light brown (Jones 2004). Movie stars and popular singers in the Philippines are often *mestizos*, half white, or extremely light-skinned with round eyes (Choy 2005; Rafael 2000). African American celebrities are typically light-skinned with Anglo features (Milkie 1999). They reinforce a beauty ideal based on white bodies (Kilbourne 1999).

Colorism is not just relevant to media images, however. A rising number of discrimination cases based on skin tone have found their way to the courts. In 2002, the EEOC sued the owners of a Mexican restaurant in San Antonio, Texas, for color-based discrimination. A white manager at the restaurant claimed that the owners directed him to hire only light-skinned staff to work in the dining room. The EEOC won the case and the restaurant was forced to pay $100,000 in fines (Valbrun 2003). In 2003, a dark-skinned African American won $40,000 from a national restaurant chain for color-based discrimination from a fellow black employee. The plaintiff argued that he suffered constant taunting and color-based epithets about his dark skin from lighter-skinned African American coworkers (Valbrun 2003). These are just two examples of how colorism affects people of color on a daily basis. Most people of color will not end up in court over color bias, but nearly all people of color have experienced or witnessed unfair treatment of others based on skin tone. Although both of these cases highlight co-ethnic perpetrators of skin-tone bias, whites are also engaged in discrimination by skin tone.

The economics of light skin privilege

The vast majority of social science research on skin-tone discrimination focuses on the employment experiences of African Americans and Latinos (Allen et al. 2000; Arce et al. 1987; Espino and Franz 2002; Gomez 2000; Hill 2000; Hughes and Hertel 1990; Hunter 2002; Keith and Herring 1991; Mason 2004; Murguia and Telles 1996; Telles and Murguia 1990). Latinos are a particularly interesting case to study because social scientists typically treat 'Latino' or 'Hispanic' as a separate category from race. Consequently there are Latinos who identify as white, black, Indian, and others. There are strong variations by national group as to which of those options Latinos choose (Mexicans are most likely to choose 'other race' and Cubans are most likely to choose 'white', for example) (Rodriguez 2000). Some researchers use the racial self-designations of Latinos as proxies for skin color when an actual skin-tone variable is not available (Alba et al. 2000).

In 2003, social science researchers found that Latinos who identified as white earned about $5000 more per year than Latinos who identified as black, and about $2500 more per year than Latinos who identified as 'some other race' (Fears 2003). A clear hierarchy is evident among Latinos with white Latinos at the top, 'others' in the middle, and black Latinos at the bottom. White Latinos also had lower unemployment rates and lower poverty rates than black Latinos (Fears 2003). Their findings are consistent with other work in this area (Montalvo 1987). Dark skin costs for Latinos, in terms of income (Telles and Murguia 1990) and occupational prestige (Espino and Franz 2002).

Other researchers found that lighter-skinned Mexican Americans and African Americans earn more money than their darker-skinned counterparts (Allen et al. 2000; Arce et al. 1987). Even when researchers account for differences in family background, occupation, and education levels, skin-color differences persist. This shows that skin-color stratification cannot be explained away with other variables such as class or family history. In addition to being a historical system, color bias is also a contemporary system that can result in differences of thousands of dollars in yearly income for darker and lighter people that are otherwise similar. Most darker-skinned people would not willingly give up thousands of dollars in income every year, and most light-skinned people would not want to admit that a part of their income may be attributed to skin-color status and not merit. Keith and Herring (1991) suggest that color discrimination operates after the civil rights movement much the way it did before the movement. 'Virtually all of our findings parallel those that occurred before the civil rights movement. These facts suggest that the effects of skin tone are not only historical curiosities from a legacy of slavery and racism, but present-day mechanisms that influence who gets what in America' (Keith and Herring 1991, 777).

It can be difficult to imagine how colorism operates on a day-to-day basis. Colorism, like racism, consists of both overt and covert actions, outright acts of discrimination and subtle cues of disfavor. In employment, negotiations over salary and benefits may be tainted by colorism (Etcoff 2000; Webster and Driskell 1983). How much a new employee is 'worth' and the assessed value of her skills may be affected by her appearance (Thompson and Keith 2001). We know from research on physical attractiveness that people who are considered more attractive are also viewed as smarter and friendlier (Etcoff 2000; Hatfield and Sprecher 1986; Wade and Bielitz 2005). 'Attractiveness' is a cultural construct influenced by racial aesthetics (Hill 2002), among other things, so lighter-skinned job applicants will likely benefit from a halo effect of physical attractiveness (Dion et al. 1972; Mulford et al. 1998).

The relationship between skin color and perceptions of attractiveness may be particularly important for women on the job (Hunter 2002). Many feminist scholars have argued that beauty matters for women in much the same way that 'brains' matter for men (Freedman 1986; Lakoff and Scherr 1984; Wolf 1991). Of course, women's job-related skills are crucial for a successful career, but cultural critic Naomi Wolf (1991) has suggested that 'beauty' has become an additional, unspoken job requirement for women in many professions, even when physical attractiveness is irrelevant for job performance. If this is the case, then in 'front office appearance jobs', like restaurant hostess or office receptionist, beauty, and therefore skin color, must matter even more.

In 2002, Rodolfo Espino and Michael Franz compared the employment experiences of Mexicans, Puerto Ricans, and Cubans in the USA. They found, 'that darker-skinned Mexicans and Cubans face significantly lower occupational prestige scores than their lighter-skinned counterparts even when controlling for factors that influence performance in the labor market' (2002, 612). Dark-skinned Puerto Ricans did not face this disadvantage in the labor market. This means that lighter-skinned Mexicans and Cubans have a better chance at attaining a high status occupation than their darker counterparts who are similar in other ways.

In this same vein, Mark Hill (2000), in his study of African American men, found that light-skinned black men retained a significant advantage in the labor market and that skin tone accounted for more differences in social status than family background did. Hill developed a very creative research methodology that clarified the *ongoing* nature of skin-color bias and challenged the oft-made assertion that light skin benefits are simply remnants of a historical color-caste system. In the labor market, dark skin tone is consistently penalized in terms of income (Allen et al. 2000; Keith and Herring 1991; Mason 2004), unemployment rates, and even occupational prestige (Espino and Franz 2002; Hill 2000).

Light-skinned or white Latinos have clear and significant advantages in income and wealth relative to their darker or black-identified counterparts (Telles and Murguia 1990). Richard Alba, John Logan, and Brian Stults studied housing access, ownership, and segregation. They found that, 'Hispanics who describe themselves as black are in substantially poorer and less white neighborhoods than their compatriots who describe themselves as white. The penalty they absorb in neighborhood affluence varies between $3500 and $6000 and thus places them in neighborhoods comparable to those occupied by African Americans' (2000, 9). Alba, Logan, and Stults' study of immigrant adaptation and spatial-assimilation theory reveals that despite their immigrant status and identity as Latinos, black Latinos' housing experience more closely resembles that of native-born African Americans than that of other Latinos. That is, black Latinos live in more racially segregated neighborhoods with less exposure to non-Hispanic whites and lower property values (Relethford et al. 1983; South et al. 2005). This not only socially isolates, but also stunts the opportunity for accumulation of wealth through home ownership (Oliver and Shapiro 1995).

Colorism in schools

Do schools practice skin-color stratification? Schools do not exist in a vacuum and researchers find the same patterns of inequalities inside schools that exist outside schools (Anderson and Cromwell 1977; Murguia and Telles 1996; Robinson and Ward 1995). In fact, in their groundbreaking study, Hughes and Hertel (1990) found that the education gap between whites and blacks was nearly identical to the education gap between light-skinned blacks and dark-skinned blacks. Consequently, they suggest that colorism plays as significant a role in the lives of African Americans as race does.

The skin-color effect on education has also been shown for Mexican Americans. Murguia and Telles (1996) demonstrated that lighter-skinned Mexican Americans complete more years of schooling than darker-skinned Mexican Americans even when their family backgrounds are similar. This is a particularly important finding in relation to the steady stream of immigration from Mexico. New immigrants who come here face not only racial/ethnic discrimination, but discrimination by phenotype or skin color (Alba et al. 2000). Arce et al. (1987) even included a variable on facial features in their analysis of skin color and education. They found that dark skin color coupled with Indian facial features (as opposed to Anglo) produced a significant depression of educational attainment.

How does skin-color stratification operate in schools? Skin-color hierarchies reflect deeply held cultural beliefs about civility, modernity, sophistication, backwardness, beauty, and virtue (Ernst 1980; Morrison 1992; Smedley 2007). In Western culture, light skin and European facial features have been equated with the positive characteristics mentioned above (Drake 1987). In English and in Spanish, the terms 'fair' and 'la güera' mean both 'light' and 'pretty'. The conflation of these meanings is just one example of a deeply held cultural value that European or white bodies are superior to others (Feagin and McKinney 2002). This gets translated in the classroom in particular ways. Teacher expectations exert a powerful influence on student achievement. If teachers, of any race, expect their light-skinned students of color to be smarter, more academically prepared, from better families, and better behaved than their darker-skinned classmates, the students may rise and fall to meet those racialized expectations (Murguia and Telles 1996). Teachers and principals may respond more positively to light-skinned or white parents of children in their classrooms. We know that school counselors encourage white students to attend college more often than equally talented African American students (Oakes 1987). It is possible that school counselors may also encourage lighter-skinned students of color to go to college more often than they encourage darker-skinned students. Students in the classroom also express these cultural values.

Students of color often valorize their lighter-skinned peers in terms of beauty, brains, and social status, even if they also shun them in terms of ethnic authenticity (Craig 2002; Leeds 1994; Robinson and Ward 1995; Torres 2006). There are many ways that skin-color bias may operate in schools, but the bottom line is that the lighter kids benefit and the darker kids pay the price.

Skin color and ethnic identity

The economic and social advantages of light skin are clear. In societies where resources are divided by race and color, light-skinned people get a disproportionate amount of the benefits. However, light skin may be viewed as a disadvantage with regard to ethnic legitimacy or authenticity. In many ethnic communities, people view darker-skin tones as more ethnically authentic. For example, light-skinned and biracial people often report feeling left out or pushed out of co-ethnic groups. They report other people's perceptions of their racial identity as a common source of conflict or discomfort (Brunsma and Rockquemore 2001).

The task of 'proving' oneself to be a legitimate or authentic member of an ethnic community is a significant burden for the light-skinned in Latino, African American, and Asian American communities. For some people of color, authenticity is the vehicle through which darker-skinned people take back their power from lighter-skinned people (Hunter 2005). For example, a dark-skinned African American woman remarked,

> In terms of female–female relationships, I think color affects how we treat each other. Like if you're lighter and I think you're better, and I think the guys want you, then I won't treat you nicely. I'll take every opportunity to ignore you, or not tell you something, or keep you out of my little group of friends, because really I feel threatened, so I want to punish you because you have it better than me. (Hunter 2005, 72)

In this example, the darker-skinned interviewee describes feeling 'threatened' by the high status of light-skinned African American women. She responded by using her social power and friendship networks.

Light-skinned Mexican Americans are often viewed as more assimilated and less identified with the Mexican American community (Mason 2004). Mexicans report using Spanish language ability as a way to re-establish their Mexican identity when light skin casts doubt on it (Jimenez 2004). Suggestions of not being black enough, or authentically ethnic enough, in any ethnic community, is a serious insult to many. This tactic has particular power against those lighter-skinned people who are from racially mixed backgrounds (Rockquemore 2002). It implies that they do not identify with their fellow ethnics, that they do not care about them, that they think they are better than their co-ethnics, or, in extreme cases, that they wish they were white (Bowman et al. 2004; Ono 2002; Vazquez et al. 1997).

Charges of ethnic illegitimacy are already at work in the 2008 US presidential campaign. Political commentators have charged both Barack Obama and Bill Richardson of not being 'ethnic enough'. These charges may seem inconsequential to the casual observer, but accusations of ethnic illegitimacy can be quite significant. Major media outlets, such as *Time* magazine and the *Los Angeles Times,* ran stories titled, 'Is Obama Black Enough?' (Coates 2007) and 'Obama Not "Black Enough"?' (Huston 2007). Richardson must simultaneously remind people that he is Latino, and downplay his Latino identity in order to navigate the dangerous waters of race, immigration, and assimilation. Researchers have found that voters pay close attention to racial cues and framing in election campaigns. A candidate's skin tone and ethnic identity can be crucial determinants in many elections (Caliendo and Mcilwain 2006; Terkildsen 1993).

Darker skin color, as evidenced in the above example, is associated with more race-conscious views and higher levels of perceived discrimination (Allen et al. 2000; Edwards 1973; Hughes and Hertel 1990; Ono 2002; Ransford 1970). Among Latinos, skin color is also closely associated with language, where dark skin and Spanish language ability are key identifiers of Chicano and Mexican identity (Lopez 1982). Conversely, light skin and English monolingualism are typically identified with Anglo assimilation and thus devalued by some in Mexican American communities (Ortiz and Arce 1984). Herein lies the contradiction: on one hand, dark skin is associated with being Indian or African and therefore backward, ugly, and low status. On the other hand, dark skin is evidence of being Indian or African and therefore, of being truly or authentically Mexican American or African American (Hunter 2005). This contradiction is exemplified in the previous example of Obama and Richardson's presidential candidacies. Their light skin tones, among other factors, are a source of trouble because they represent Anglo assimilation and ethnic illegitimacy, but their political success is also attributable in part to their light skin tones and their perceived high levels of Anglo assimilation. This is the conundrum of colorism.

Research on Asian Americans revealed a similar ambivalence about skin tone (Rondilla and Spickard 2007). In one study, most Asian American respondents agreed that their communities demonstrated strong preferences for light skin, but there were notable exceptions

(Rondilla and Spickard 2007). The researchers asked people to look at three different pictures of Asian American young women, one light skinned, one medium, and one dark and to create a story of each of their lives. This very creative process yielded fascinating results. Participants wrote the most positive narratives about the woman with the medium complexion. Respondents characterized the lightest-skinned woman as 'troubled', 'torn between one culture to the next', and 'she wants to shed her Oriental roots by becoming blond' (Rondilla and Spickard, 2007, 67–68). In contrast, when describing the darkest-skinned woman, respondents created stories that centered on her ethnic authenticity. They described her as a recent immigrant, close to her family, responsible for younger brothers and sisters, with limited English skills, and as the least 'American' of the three women pictured (Rondilla and Spickard 2007). The woman of medium skin tone was described as 'all-American', as a good student, good friend, smart, successful, and as an ideal choice for a daughter-in-law. Rondilla and Spickard's (2007) research reveals the complexity of skin color, status, and identity.

It is tempting to characterize the problem of colorism as equally difficult for both light-skinned people and dark. Dark-skinned people lack the social and economic capital that light skin provides, and are therefore disadvantaged in education, employment, and housing (Alba et al. 2000; Arce et al. 1987; Keith and Herring 1991). Additionally, dark skin is generally not regarded as beautiful, so dark-skinned women often lose out in the dating and marriage markets (Hunter 1998; Sahay and Piran 1997). On the other side, light-skinned men and women are typically not regarded as legitimate members of their ethnic communities. They may be excluded from, or made to feel unwelcome in, community events and organizations (Hunter 2005). At first glance, it may seem that there are equal advantages and disadvantages to both sides of the color line. Upon closer examination, this proves to be untrue. Although exclusion from some community organizations may be uncomfortable psychologically or emotionally for light-skinned people of color, it rarely has significant material effects. More specifically, emotional turmoil about ethnic identity does not have significant economic consequences. However, the systematic discrimination against dark-skinned people of color in the labor market, educational institutions, and marriage market create marked economic disadvantages (Allen et al. 2000; Hill 2000; Hughes and Hertel 1990; Mason 2004). Without minimizing the psychological trauma of exclusion from ethnic communities, it is important to clarify that the disadvantages of dark skin still far outweigh the disadvantages of light.

When compared in this way, it is not simply a case of 'the grass is always greener on the other side'. Although there are downsides to both ends of the color spectrum, the penalties are more common and more severe for dark skin than for light. This is evidenced in Hunter's (2005) interviews with Mexican American and African American women. Nearly all of the dark-skinned women interviewed wanted to be lighter at some time in their lives in order to accrue some of the privileges of light skin. In contrast, despite their painful stories of exclusion, none of the light-skinned women interviewed ever reported wanting to be dark (Hunter 2005). This significant difference points to the enduring and substantial privilege of light skin.

Gender, beauty, and the global color complex

Although colorism affects both men and women, women experience discrimination based on skin tone in particular ways. Skin tone is an important characteristic in defining beauty and beauty is an important resource for women (Hunter 2002; Wolf 1991). Beauty provides women with status that can lead to advances in employment, education, and even the marriage market (Hunter 2005). Light skin color, as an indicator of beauty, can operate as a form of social capital for women (Hunter 2002). This social capital can be transformed into other forms of capital and used to gain status in jobs, housing, schools, and social networks. Social networks can increase capital in a wide variety of ways, and one of the most important is through one's spouse. Light-skinned people of color are not more likely to be married than their darker-skinned counterparts, but light-skinned women, particularly African Americans, are likely to marry higher status spouses (Hunter 1998; Udry et al. 1971). Study after study has shown that light-skinned African American women marry spouses with higher levels of education, higher incomes, or higher levels of occupational prestige, than their darker-skinned counterparts (Hughes and Hertel 1990; Hunter 1998; Keith and Herring 1991; Udry et al. 1971). This phenomenon allows light-skinned people to 'marry up' and essentially exchange the high status of their skin tone for the high status of education, income, or occupation in their spouse (Elder 1969; Webster and Driskell 1983).

Interviews published by Rondilla and Spickard (2007) reveal this social exchange theory or 'marrying up' practice at work. A Filipina interviewee said, 'My father suggested I have children with my White ex-boyfriend so he could have mestizo grandchildren. I think years of this colonial way of thinking and all the American propaganda has made it so that my father (and most other Filipinos) think that everything "American"—White American—is superior' (Rondilla and Spickard 2007, 55). This example illustrates that marrying a lighter-skinned partner is not just a practice that gives the spouse access to more social and economic capital, but it is also a practice that could allow one's children to have a higher status by being lighter-skinned themselves.

The Philippines is a good example of the intersection of internalized colonial values and the cult of the new global beauty. Like many other former European or American colonies, the Philippines' contemporary culture valorizes American culture and white beauty (Rafael 2000). Through globalization, multinational media conglomerates export US cultural products and cultural imperialism. Part of this structure of domination is the exportation of cultural images, including images of race (Choy 2005). The USA exports images of the good life, of white beauty, white affluence, white heroes, and brown and black entertainers/criminals. As many people in other countries yearn for the 'good life' offered in the USA, they also yearn for the dominant aesthetic of the USA: light skin, blond hair, and Anglo facial features (Fraser 2003). Women in Korea, surrounded by other Koreans, pay high sums of money to have double eyelid surgery that Westernizes their eyes. 'In Asian countries like South Korea, Japan and China, double eyelid surgery is a way of life. In fact, because so many people in South Korea have undergone eyelid surgery, the country has the highest percentage of people with plastic surgery in the world' (King and Yun 2005). Women in Saudi Arabia, Uganda, and Brazil are using toxic skin bleaching creams to try and achieve a lighter complexion (Chisholm 2002; Mire 2001; Siyachitema 2002). One of the most common high school graduation presents among the elite in Mexico City is a nose job with the plastic surgeon (Taylor 2002). Each of these choices may sound extreme or pathological, but it is actually quite rational in a context of global racism and US domination. Unfortunately new eyelids, lighter skin, and new noses are likely to offer their owners better opportunities in a competitive global marketplace (Davis 1995; Kaw 1998; Morgan 1998; Sullivan 2001).

The new global racism transcends national borders and infiltrates cultures and families all over the world. It draws on historical ideologies of colonialism and internalized racism buttressed with visions of a new world order. Images associated with white America are highly valued and emulated in the global marketplace. This is part of what makes colorism and racism so hard to battle: the images supporting these systems are everywhere and the rewards for whiteness are real. In addition to wrestling with the values of their colonial pasts, many Third World nations are also contending with the onslaught of US-produced cultural images valorizing whiteness and especially white femininity (and the occasional version of light brown femininity). Television, film, Internet, and print ads all feature white women with blond hair as not only the cultural ideal, but the cultural imperative. White and light-skinned people are rewarded accordingly.

Women and men of color have ever-increasing opportunities to alter their bodies toward whiteness. They can purchase lighter-colored contact lenses for their eyes; they can straighten kinky or curly hair; they can have cosmetic surgeries on their lips, noses, or eyes. But one of the oldest traditions of this sort is skin bleaching. There are lots of old wives' tales recipes for skin bleaching, including baking soda, bleach, toothpaste, or even lye. In the USA, overt skin bleaching with the stated intention of whitening one's skin fell out of favor in many communities after the Civil Rights movements and cultural pride movements of the 1960s and 1970s. However, outside of the USA and in many postcolonial nations of the Global South, skin bleaching is reaching new heights.

Skin-bleaching creams go by many names: skin lighteners, skin whiteners, skin-toning creams, skin evening creams, skin-fading gels, etc. Essentially, they are creams regularly applied to the face or body that purport to 'lighten', 'brighten', or 'whiten' the skin. They are marketed as beauty products available to women to increase their beauty, by increasing their whiteness. The skin bleaching industry is thriving around the globe, particularly in Third World, postcolonial countries (Mire 2001). Skin lighteners are commonly used in places including Mexico, Pakistan, Saudi Arabia, Jamaica, the Philippines, Japan, India, Tanzania, Senegal, Nigeria, Uganda, Kenya, Ghana, and less so, but also USA (Charles 2003; Chisholm 2002; Easton 1998; Kovaleski 1999; Mahe et al. 2004; Schuler 1999). These products are everywhere and easy to get, from the Asian market on the corner, to major cosmetic retailers online. Drugstore.com, an online beauty and drugstore retailer, offers links to categories of products including 'skin lighteners' and 'skin whiteners'. Here, the consumer may purchase 'pH Advantage' a 'pigmentation fader', which sells for $55 for one ounce, or 'Skin Doctor's Dermabrite Brightening Crème', which retails for $35 for 1.7 ounces (see www.drugstore.com and www.beauty.com). There are dozens of products available with prices to match any budget.

For many people around the world, skin bleaching seems like one of the few ways to get a piece of the pie in a highly racialized society. Skin-lightening products constitute a multibillion dollar industry. These products usually contain one of three harmful ingredients: mercury, hydroquinone, or corticosteroids (sometimes used in combination). Many skin-bleaching products are made outside of North America and Europe, in Mexico and

Nigeria, but often under the auspices of larger US and European cosmetics firms (Mire 2001). The products may not be made in the USA, but US women also use them.

In fact, the pursuit of light skin color can be so important it can prove fatal. A Harvard medical school researcher found outbreaks of mercury poisoning in countries such as Saudi Arabia, Pakistan, and Tanzania. He came to learn that the mercury poisoning, found almost exclusively in women, was caused by the widespread use of skin-bleaching creams containing toxic levels of mercury (Counter 2003). Even children were suffering the effects of mercury poisoning, either from *in utero* absorption during pregnancy, or from mothers who put the bleaching cream on their children eager for them to have the benefits of light skin. These stories may seem to be only far away, but they also happen in the USA. The same team of Harvard researchers found outbreaks of mercury poisoning in the southwestern USA where thousands of Mexican American women use skin-bleaching creams to try to achieve a lighter and more valued complexion. In Latin America, Africa, and many parts of Asia, whiteness is such an important commodity that many women overlook what they perceive to be minor risks in order to attain for themselves or their children the benefits of light skin. Skin whiteners are increasingly used by men, as well. India's best-selling 'Fair and Lovely' lightening soaps and creams launched a new line for men in 2005, appropriately branded, 'Fair and Handsome' (Perry 2005).

Skin color continues to shape our lives in powerful ways in the USA and around the globe. The cultural messages that give meaning and value to different skin tones are both deeply historical and actively contemporary. People of color with dark skin tones continue to pay a price for their color, and the light skinned continue to benefit from their association with whiteness. Only a slow dismantling of the larger system of white racism, in the USA and around the globe, will initiate a change in the color hierarchy it has created. But this is not to say it will be easy. Talking about colorism and internalized racism can be challenging. Most white Americans believe that racism is on the wane, and that any talk about racial discrimination does more harm than good (Bonilla-Silva 1999; Brown et al. 2003). This phenomenon is referred to by many social scientists as 'colorblind racism'. Colorblind racism makes racism invisible while actively perpetuating it. But white Americans are not the only ones who do not want to talk about colorism. Many African Americans feel that discussions of colorism 'air our dirty laundry' for all to see and judge (Breland 1997). Others feel that talking about colorism distracts from the larger and more significant problem of racism in the USA. Most

people of color agree that colorism is an 'in house' issue, a personal one that is a tragedy within communities of color (Russell, Wilson, and Hall 1992). It is at minimum, embarrassing, and at its worst, a sign of racial self-hatred (Hall 2006).

Discussing colorism is not a 'distraction' from the important issue of racial discrimination. In fact, understanding colorism helps us better understand how racism works in our contemporary society. Colorism is one manifestation of a larger 'racial project' that communicates meaning and status about race in the USA (Omi and Winant 1994). Studies on skin-color stratification support the contention that racial discrimination is alive and well (Keith and Herring 1991; Mason 2004), and so insidious that communities of color themselves are divided into quasi-racial hierarchies (Alba et al. 2000; Hunter 2005; Seltzer and Smith 1991). As long as the structure of white racism remains intact, colorism will continue to operate.

Short Biography

Margaret Hunter is an assistant professor in the Department of Sociology and Anthropology at Mills College in Oakland, California. Her research areas include comparative racial and ethnic relations, skin color politics, feminist theory, and the sociology of gender. Her recent book, *Race, Gender, and the Politics of Skin Tone* (Routledge, 2005) compares the experiences of African American and Mexican American women with skin color discrimination. Her research on skin tone has been published in several journals including *Gender & Society* (2002) and *Sociological Inquiry* (1998). 'Rethinking Epistemology, Methodology, and Racism: or, Is White Sociology Really Dead?' (*Race & Society* 5 (2002)) is Hunter's contribution to the debate about racism and knowledge construction in the discipline of sociology. She is currently working on an interview study analyzing the public use of colorblind racial discourse.

Note

References

Alba, Richard D., John R. Logan and Brian J. Stults 2000. 'The Changing Neighborhood Contexts of the Immigrant Metropolis.' *Social Forces* **79**: 587–621.

Allen, Walter, Edward Telles and Margaret Hunter 2000. 'Skin Color, Income, and Education: A Comparison of African Americans and Mexican Americans.' *National Journal of Sociology* **12**: 129–80.

Anderson, Claud and Rue Cromwell 1977. '"Black is beautiful" and the Color Preferences of Afro-American Youth.' *Journal of Negro Education* **46**: 76–88.

Arce, Carlos, Edward Murguia and W. Parker Frisbie 1987. 'Phenotype and Life Chances Among Chicanos.' *Hispanic Journal of Behavioral Sciences* **9**: 19–32.

Bonilla-Silva, Eduardo 1999. *Racism and White Supremacy in the Post-Civil Rights Era*. New York: Lynne Reiner Publishers.

Bonilla-Silva, Eduardo 2006. *Racism Without Racists*. Lanham, MD: Rowman and Littlefield.

Bowman, Phillip J., Ray Muhammad and Mosi Ifatunji 2004. 'Skin Tone, Class, and Racial Attitudes Among African Americans.' Pp. 128–58 in *Skin/Deep: How Race and Complexion Matter in the 'Color-Blind' Era*, edited by Cedric Herring, Verna M. Keith and Hayward Derrick Horton. Urbana, IL: University of Illinois Press.

Breland, Alfiee M. 1997. 'Airing Dirty Laundry: Reasons and Processes by which Skin Tone Stratification Continues to Be a Pervasive Aspect of the African American Community.' University of Wisconsin-Madison, Dissertation Abstracts International.

Brown, Michael, Martin Carnoy, Elliott Currie, Troy Duster, David Oppenheimer, Marjorie Schultz and David Wellman 2003. *White-Washing Race: The Myth of the Colorblind Society*. Berkeley, CA: University of California Press.

Brunsma, David L. and Kerry A. Rockquemore 2001. 'The New Color Complex: Appearances and Biracial Identity.' *Identity* **1**: 225–46.

Caliendo, Stephen M. and Charlton D. Mcilwain 2006. 'Minority Candidates, Media Framing, and Racial Cues in the 2004 Election.' *The Harvard International Journal of Press/politics* **11**: 45–69.

Charles, Christopher 2003. 'Skin Bleaching, Self-Hate, and Black Identity in Jamaica.' *Journal of Black Studies* **33**: 711–28.

Chisholm, N. Jamiyla 2002. 'Fade to White: Skin Bleaching and the Rejection of Blackness.' *Village Voice* January 23–29, 2002.

Choy, Catherine 2005. 'Asian American History: Reflections on Imperialism, Immigration, and the Body.' Pp. 81–98 in *Pinay Power: Peminist Critical Theory*, edited by Melinda De Jesus. New York: Routledge.

Coates, Ta-Nehisi Paul 2007. 'Is Obama Black Enough?' *Time* February 1, 2007.

Counter, S. Allen 2003. 'Whitening Skin Can Be Deadly.' *Boston Globe* December 16, 2003.

Craig, Maxine Leeds 2002. *Ain't I a Beauty Queen: Black Women, Beauty, and the Politics of Race*. New York: Oxford University Press.

Davis, F. James 1991. *Who Is Black? One Nation's Definition*. University Park, PA: Pennsylvania State University Press.

Davis, Kathy 1995. *Reshaping the Female Body*. New York: Routledge.

Dion, Karen, Ellen Berscheid and Elaine Walster 1972. 'What Is Beautiful Is Good.' *Journal of Personality and Social Psychology* **24**: 285–90.

Drake, St. Clair 1987. *Black Folk Here and There, Volume One*. Los Angeles, CA: University of California Press.

Easton, A. 1998. 'Women Have Deadly Desire for Paler Skin in the Philippines.' *Lancet* **352**: 355.

Edwards, G. F. 1959. *The Negro Professional Class*. Glencoe, IL: The Free Press.

Edwards, Ozzie 1973. 'Skin Color as a Variable in Racial Attitudes of Black Urbanites.' *Journal of Black Studies* **3**: 473–83.

Elder, Glen 1969. 'Appearance and Education in Marriage Mobility.' *American Sociological Review* **34**: 519–33.

Ernst, Klaus 1980. 'Racialism, Racialist Ideology, and Colonialism, Past and Present.' In *Sociological Theories: Race and Colonialism*. Paris: UNESCO.

Espino, Rodolfo and Michael Franz 2002. 'Latino Phenotypic Discrimination Revisited: The Impact of Skin Color on Occupational Status.' *Social Science Quarterly* **83**: 612–23.

Etcoff, Nancy 2000. *Survival of the Prettiest: The Science of Beauty*. New York: Anchor Books.

Fanon, Frantz 1967. *Black Skin White Masks*. New York: Grove Weidenfeld.

Feagin, Joe R. 2000. *Racist America: Roots, Current Realities, and Future Reparations*. New York: Routledge.

Feagin, Joe R. and Karyn McKinney 2002. *The Many Costs of Racism*. Lanham, MD: Rowman and Littlefield.

Feagin, Joe R., Hernan Vera and Pinar Batur 2001. *White Racism: The Basics*, 2nd edn. New York: Routledge.

Fears, Darryl 2003. 'Race Divides Hispanics, Report Says; Integration and Income Vary With Skin Color.' *Washington Post* July 14, 2003.

Fraser, Suzanne 2003. *Cosmetic Surgery, Gender, and Culture*. New York: Palgrave Macmillan.

Frazier, E. Franklin 1957. *Black Bourgeoisie*. New York: Collier Books.

Freedman, Rita 1986. *Beauty Bound*. Lexington, MA: Lexington Books.

Gatewood, Willard B. 1990. *Aristocrats of Color: The Black Elite 1880-1920*. Bloomington, IN: Indiana University Press.

Gomez, Christina 2000. 'The Continual Significance of Skin Color: An Exploratory Study of Latinos in the Northeast.' *Hispanic Journal of Behavioral Sciences* **22**: 94–103.

Hall, Ronald E. 2006. 'The Bleaching Syndrome Among People of Color: Implications of Skin Color for Human Behavior in the Social Environment.' *Journal of Human Behavior in the Social Environment* **13**: 19–31.

Hall, Ronald 1994. '"The Bleaching Syndrome": Implications of Light Skin for Hispanic American Assimilation.' *Hispanic Journal of Behavioral Sciences* **16**: 307–14.

Hall, Ronald 1995. 'The Bleaching Syndrome: African Americans' Response to Cultural Domination Vis-à-vis Skin Color.' *Journal of Black Studies* **26**: 172–84.

Hall, Ronald 1997. 'Eurogamy Among Asian Americans: A Note on Western Assimilation.' *The Social Science Journal* **34**: 403–8.

Hatfield, Elaine and Susan Sprecher 1986. *Mirror, Mirror: The Importance of Looks in Everyday Life*. Albany, NY: State University of New York Press.

Hill, Mark E. 2000. 'Color Differences in the Socioeconomic Status of African American Men: Results of a Longitudinal Study.' *Social Forces* **78**: 1437–60.

Hill, Mark E. 2002. 'Skin Color and the Perception of Attractiveness Among African Americans: Does Gender Make a Difference?' *Social Psychology Quarterly* **65**: 77–91.

Hirschman, Charles 2004. 'The Origins and Demise of the Concept of Race.' *Population and Development Review* **30**: 385–415.

Horowitz, Donald L. 1973. 'Color Differentiation in the American System of Slavery.' *Journal of Interdisciplinary History* **3**: 509–41.

Hughes, Bradley and Michael Hertel 1990. 'The Significance of Color Remains: A Study of Life Chances, Mate Selection, and Ethnic Consciousness among Black Americans.' *Social Forces* **68**: 1105–20.

Hunter, Margaret 1998. 'Colorstruck: Skin Color Stratification in the Lives of African American Women.' *Sociological Inquiry* **68**: 517–35.

Hunter, Margaret 2002. '"If You're Light, You're Alright": Light Skin Color as Social Capital for Women of Color.' *Gender & Society* **16**: 175–93.

Hunter, Margaret 2005. *Race, Gender, and the Politics of Skin Tone.* New York: Routledge.

Huston, Warner Todd 2007. 'Obama: Not "Black Enough"?' *Los Angeles Times* February 19, 2007.

Jimenez, Tomas R. 2004. 'Negotiating Ethnic Boundaries: Multiethnic Mexican Americans and Ethnic Identity in the United States.' *Ethnicities* **4**: 75–97.

Jones, Vanessa 2004. 'Pride or Prejudice? A Formally Taboo Topic Among Asian-Americans and Latinos Comes Out Into the Open as Skin Tone Consciousness Sparks a Backlash.' *Boston Globe* August 19, 2004.

Jordan, Winthrop 1968. *White Over Black.* Chapel Hill, NC: University of North Carolina Press.

Karnow, Stanley 1989. *In Our Image: America's Empire in the Philippines.* New York: Ballantine.

Kaw, Eugenia 1998. 'Medicalization of Racial Features: Asian American Women and Cosmetic Surgery.' Pp. 167–83 in *The Politics of Women's Bodies: Sexuality, Appearance, and Behavior,* ed. Rose Weitz. New York: Oxford University Press.

Keith, Verna and Cedric Herring 1991. 'Skin Tone and Stratification in the Black Community.' *American Journal of Sociology* **97**: 760–78.

Kilbourne, Jean 1999. *Deadly Persuasion: Why Women and Girls Must Fight the Addictive Power of Advertising.* New York: Free Press.

King, Elizabeth and Jinna Yun 2005. 'Plastic Surgery for Eyelids Popular Among Asian Women.' Medill News Service: Medill School of Journalism, Northwestern University, June 8.

Kovaleski, Serge 1999. 'In Jamaica, Shades of an Identity Crisis: Ignoring Health Risks, Blacks Increase use of Skin Lighteners.' *The Washington Post* August 5, 1999.

Lakoff, Robin and Racquel Scherr 1984. *Face Value: The Politics of Beauty.* Boston, MA: Routledge.

Leeds, Maxine 1994. 'Young African-American Women and the Language of Beauty.' Pp. 147–60 in *Ideals of Feminine Beauty: Philosophical, Social, and Cultural Dimensions,* edited by Karen Callaghan. London: Greenwood Press.

Lopez, David 1982. *Language Maintenance and Shift in the U.S. Today: The Basic Patterns and Their Implications.* Los Alamitos, CA: National Center for Bilingual Research.

Mahe, Antoine, Fatimata Ly and Ari Gounongbe 2004. 'The Cosmetic Use of Bleaching Products in Dakar, Senegal.' *Sciences Sociales et Sante* **22**: 5–33.

Mason, Patrick L. 2004. 'Annual Income, Hourly Wages, and Identity Among Mexican-Americans and Other Latinos.' *Industrial Relations* **43**: 817–34.

Memmi, Albert 1965. *The Colonizer and the Colonized.* Boston, MA: Beacon Press.

Milkie, Melissa 1999. 'Social Comparisons, Reflected Appraisals, and Mass Media: The Impact of Pervasive Beauty Images on White and Black Girls' Self-Concepts.' *Social Psychology Quarterly* **62**: 190–210.

Mire, Amina 2001. 'Skin-Bleaching: Poison, Beauty, Power, and the Politics of the Colour Line.' *Resources for Feminist Research* **28**: 13–38.

Montalvo, F. 1987. *Skin Color and Latinos: The Origins and Contemporary Patterns of Ethnoracial Ambiguity Among Mexican Americans and Puerto Ricans* (monograph). San Antonio, TX: Our Lady of the Lake University.

Morgan, Kathryn Pauly 1998. 'Women and the Knife: Cosmetic Surgery and the Colonization of Women's Bodies.' Pp. 147–66 in *The Politics of Women's Bodies: Sexuality, Appearance, and Behavior,* edited by Rose Weitz. New York: Oxford University Press.

Morrison, Toni 1992. *Playing in the Dark: Whiteness and the Literary Imagination.* New York: Vintage Books.

Mulford, Matthew, John Orbell, Catherine Shatto and Jean Stockard 1998. 'Physical Attractiveness, Opportunity, and Success in Everyday Exchange.' *American Journal of Sociology* **103**: 1565–92.

Murguia, Edward and Edward Telles 1996. 'Phenotype and Schooling Among Mexican Americans.' *Sociology of Education* **69**: 276–89.

Oakes, Jeannie 1985. *Keeping Track: How Schools Structure Inequality.* New Haven, CT: Yale University Press.

Oliver, Melvin and Thomas Shapiro 1995. *Black Wealth White Wealth.* New York: Russell Sage.

Omi, Michael and Howard Winant 1994. *Racial Formation in the United States.* New York: Routledge.

Ono, Hiromi 2002. 'Assimilation, Ethnic Competition, and Ethnic Identities of U.S.-Born Persons of Mexican Origin.' *The International Migration Review* **36**: 726–45.

Ortiz, Vilma and Carlos Arce 1984. 'Language Orientation and Mental Health Status Among Persons of Mexican Descent.' *Hispanic Journal of Behavioral Sciences* **6**: 127–43.

Perry, Alex 2005. 'Could You Please Make Me a Shade Lighter?' *Time* Monday, November 28, 2005.

Rafael, Vicente 2000. *White Love and Other Events in Filipino History.* Durham, NC: Duke University Press.

Ransford, H. E. 1970. 'Skin Color, Life Chances, and Anti-White Attitude.' *Social Problems* **18**: 164–78.

Relethford, J., P. Stern, S. P. Catskill and H. P. Hazuda 1983. 'Social Class, Admixture, and Skin Color Variation in Mexican Americans and Anglo Americans Living in San Antonio, Texas.' *American Journal of Physical Anthropology* **61**: 97–102.

Robinson, Tracy L. and Janie V. Ward 1995. 'African American Adolescents and Skin Color.' *Journal of Black Psychology* **21**: 256–74.

Rockquemore, Kerry A. 2002. 'Negotiating the Color Line: The Gendered Process of Racial Identity Construction Among Black/White Biracial Women.' *Gender & Society* **16**: 485–503.

Rodriguez, Clara 2000. *Changing Race: Latinos, the Census, and the History of Ethnicity in the United States.* New York: NYU Press.

Rondilla, Joanne and Paul Spickard 2007. *Is Lighter Better?* Lanham, MD: Rowman & Littlefield.

Russell, Kathy, Midge Wilson and Ronald Hall 1992. *The Color Complex.* New York: Doubleday.

Sahay, Sarita and Niva Piran 1997. 'Skin-Color Preferences and Body Satisfaction Among South Asian-Canadian and European-Canadian Female University Students.' *Journal of Social Psychology* **137**: 161–71.

Schuler, Corina 1999. 'Africans Look for Beauty in Western Mirror: Black Women Turn to Risky Bleaching Creams and Cosmetic Surgery.' *Christian Science Monitor* December 23, 1999.

Seltzer, Richard and Robert C. Smith 1991. 'Color Differences in the Afro-American Community and the Differences They Make.' *Journal of Black Studies* **21**: 279–86.

Siyachitema, Hilary 2002. 'Health-Zimbabwe: Banned Skin Bleaching Creams Still Easy to Buy.' *Interpress Service* April 25, 2002.

Smedley, Audrey 2007. *Race in North America.* 3rd edn. Boulder, CO: Westview.

South, Scott J., Kyle Crowder and Erick Chavez 2005. 'Migration and Spatial Assimilation Among U.S. Latinos: Classical Versus Segmented Trajectories.' *Demography* **42**: 497–521.

Stevenson, Brenda 1996. *Life in Black and White: Family and Community in the Slave South.* New York: Oxford University Press.

Sullivan, Deborah A. 2001. *Cosmetic Surgery: The Cutting Edge of Commercial Medicine in America.* New Brunswick, NJ: Rutgers University Press.

Taylor, Diane 2002. 'Stitched Up: Where Plastic Surgeons Profit From Teenage Dreams.' *The Mirror* December 7, 2002.

Telles, Edward and Edward Murguia 1990. 'Phenotypic Discrimination and Income Differences among Mexican Americans.' *Social Science Quarterly* **71**: 682–96.

Terkildsen, Nayda 1993. 'When White Voters Evaluate Black Candidates: The processing Implications of Candidate Skin Color, Prejudice, and Self-Monitoring.' *American Journal of Political Science* **37**: 1032–53.

Thompson, Maxine S. and Verna Keith 2001. 'The Blacker the Berry: Gender, Skin Tone, Self-Esteem, and Self-Efficacy.' *Gender & Society* **15**: 336–57.

Torres, Kimberly C. 2006. 'Manufacturing Blackness: Skin Color Necessary But Not Sufficient. Race Relations and Racial Identity at an Ivy League University (Pennsylvania).' Dissertation Abstracts International, University of Pennsylvania.

Udry, Richard, Karl Baumann and Charles Chase 1971. 'Skin Color, Status, and Mate Selection.' *American Journal of Sociology* **76**: 722–33.

Valbrun Marjorie 2003. 'EEOC Sees Rise in Intrarace Complaints of Color Bias.' *Wall Street Journal* August 7, 2003.

Vazquez, Luis A., Enedina Garcia-Vazquez, Sheri A. Bauman and Arturo S. Sierra 1997. 'Skin Color, Acculturation, and Community Interest among Mexican American Students: A Research Note.' *Hispanic Journal of Behavioral Sciences* **19**: 377–86.

Wade, T. J. and Sara Bielitz 2005. *The Differential Effect of Skin Color on Attractiveness, Personality Evaluations, and Perceived Life Success of African Americans.* Thousand Oaks, CA: Sage Publications.

Webster, Murray Jr. and James Driskell Jr. 1983. 'Beauty as Status.' *American Journal of Sociology* **89**: 140–65.

Wolf, Naomi 1991. *The Beauty Myth: How Images of Beauty are Used Against Women.* New York: Doubleday Books.

The Construction of Southern Identity through Reality TV: A Content Analysis of Here Comes Honey Boo Boo, Duck Dynasty and Buckwild

Ariel Miller

Abstract

The reality television genre has been increasingly at the forefront of media and cultural studies and a subject of critique across the disciplines of communications, anthropology and visual studies. While reality television programs have been analyzed for elements of racism and sexism, quantitative research to date has rarely been done to explore whether the portrayal of the American southerner was distorted. Using a data-driven approach, the frequency of commonly held southern stereotypes within three shows across three networks were evaluated through content analysis. The researcher observed 100 minutes of each program, marking incidents of visibly unintelligent, crude, violent and unhealthy behavior. Results showed high frequencies of the "unintelligent," "crude" and "violent" stereotypes.

Introduction

Candid Camera, an American television comedy series that premiered in 1948, is often credited as the first reality television program.[1] Since that time, and particularly within the past decade, reality TV has exploded into mainstream popular culture. Reality-based shows are no longer a rare occurrence on television; they are now ubiquitous in television programming across networks ranging from MTV to The History Channel. Viewers are not just watching these shows, but they are discussing them long after the segment ends. According to an article from the New York Times, 15 of the top 20 highest-rated programs among those between ages 18 and 29 were reality or unscripted shows.[2]

In recent years, reality TV programs featuring redneck culture in particular have seen increased popularity, showing southerners doing everything from fishing with their bare hands, eating triple-fried foods at county fairs, making up words not found within the traditional English dictionary, and often times just acting downright ignorant and crude. The issue here is that while these shows may be watched solely for their entertainment value and while they seem harmless and even fun, they are constructing a distinct southern identity and it is not a flattering one at that. Shows like *Here Comes Honey Boo Boo* (TLC), *Hillbilly Handfishin'* (Animal Planet), *Duck Dynasty* (A&E), and *Swamp People* (History Channel) are beginning to dominate programming across multiple stations. It is interesting to note that these shows are appearing on a variety of networks. They are not limited to the less serious stations and are beginning to be featured on networks heavily trusted for disseminating accurate information through documentary-style production.

One must ask the question, as with any reality TV program, are the subjects of these shows really being represented as they actually exist when the camera is not present? To what extent may they be simply performing constructed cultural identities that have already been, in some sense, assigned to them? Related to this, one must also consider what role both subject and filmmaker play in the production of these programs. Critical analysis from disciplines ranging from anthropology to visual studies may be applied to explore these issues.

This paper will place the study of popular culture, specifically the exploration of issues within reality television, at academic level. The analysis will be approached using theoretical frameworks from sociology and anthropology along with media studies. The intention of this paper is to explore issues of representation of reality television subjects from the American South. Secondary research will explore the impact of reality television on viewers' perception of reality and reference studies on stereotypes seen in other areas of reality television. Primary research will include a content analysis of *Here Comes Honey Boo Boo* (TLC), *Buckwild* (MTV), and *Duck Dynasty* (A&E).

Background

Some might argue that studying popular culture, which is sometimes referred to as "low culture," is essentially frivolous and therefore not worthy of scholarly study. After all, how could studying a genre where absurdity is heightened, where storylines are deliberately constructed, possibly be considered worthy of an intellectual analysis? How could material that is so mass-produced be on the same level as studying high culture?

Filoteo argues that it is precisely because this popular culture is mass-produced and mass consumed that it is worthy of study. Examining popular culture through a critical lens helps us learn about our society. It helps us hold the "dominant class" (i.e. those in control of editing and producing reality television and other forms of popular culture) accountable for the messages that are being communicated through various media. It is thus imperative for us to study these messages and try to uncover meaning from them.

Quoting Friedman (2002), Filoteo explains the possible reason that reality television has been studied minimally. The lack of scholarship is not due to "a lack of an interest in the subject, but rather to an inherent difficulty in describing and containing the ideological, economic, cultural, technological, and political influences that impact televisual representations of real events."[3]

If these reality television shows are deliberately being constructed in a way that expresses overt or perhaps more subtle messages about the subjects in the shows, it is imperative that we study these messages through a critical lens as they may be indicative of larger societal issues. While attention has been brought to the unfair representation of particular ethnic groups as well as women in reality television, little to no academic work has been written on the representation of the American southerner through these shows. Why has this group been neglected? In a 2011 article from NPR, Eric Deggans argues that these shows have emerged to make "a new generation laugh at the expense of real understanding." He writes, "Despite reality TV's tendency to stupefy everything it touches, perhaps it's time for these programs to actually get real and give us a vision of Southern culture that reaches beyond the fun-loving redneck."[4]

In an article from the *Washington Post*, Ted Ownby, the director of the Center for the Study of Southern Culture, is quoted saying that people from the South get frustrated at the "narrow range of representations" on these shows. According to this article, it has become increasingly apparent that individuals from the American South are the last cultural group to be openly mocked and stereotyped without penalty.[5]

Literature Review

Since introduction of reality shows, scholars have been studying the genre. Previous research has explored the psychological appeal of reality television for viewers, issues of performance and authenticity of reality TV subjects, as well as the many ethical issues that arise with the production of these shows. While previous studies have addressed everything from substance abuse in the popular reality show, *The Osbournes*, to issues of racism in *The Real World*, no studies to date have examined the recent explosion of "redneck" reality shows. While scholars and critics have written articles expressing their opinions on the representation of subjects in these shows, there is currently no quantitative research on the actual frequency of southern stereotypes in reality television. For this reason, the findings of this study may be vital in providing some of the first concrete data to support or contradict the claims that these reality shows play a role in emphasizing existing southern stereotypes.

Emergence of Reality TV: Explaining the Phenomenon

Several scholars have written about the emergence of reality television as a popular TV genre. Many have written about how reality television has been born out of earlier styles of observational filmmaking, and now can be considered a part of post-documentary culture, where documentary realism blends with celebrity and constructed scenes.[6] Many have compared earlier observational documentary films with reality television, suggesting the latter is now more relevant in our study of modern culture.

One author who provides some historical background on why reality TV came into existence is journalist Richard Huff. According to Huff, during a time when networks were struggling to fill programming gaps, reality TV served as an inexpensive alternative to bring in the audiences that these networks were specifically trying to reach: young adults.[7] Some of the earliest shows, including MTV's longest running reality series, *The Real World*, and Fox Broadcasting Company's *American Idol*, started to become some of the most watched, most talked about shows on television.

Performance and Authenticity

Several scholars have also explored issues of performance and authenticity in reality television, specifically looking at underlying motivations for reality TV subjects to perform an assigned role despite reality TV's claims of depicting subjects as they really are in everyday life. In her text, Rachel Dubrofsky suggests that participants in reality shows do not actually have complete autonomy in how to present themselves, suggesting that editing techniques in particular play a massive role in constructing reality on these programs.[8]

Other scholars, including those who studied earlier modes of documentary filmmaking, have suggested that subjects are not represented as they really are because the presence of a camera inevitably causes a behavioral change in the subject. Some scholars have suggested that when subjects know they are being filmed, they have a greater tendency to "perform," exaggerating certain personal characteristics or at the other end of the spectrum, changing their persona altogether. Annette Hill, a leader in reality television research, found that many viewers have the common-sense belief that in order to create entertaining television, there is a basic need for participants to be entertaining.[9] Needless to say, this is problematic when considering the supposed authenticity of reality TV subjects.

The Impact of Reality Television on Viewers' Perceptions of Reality

As stated earlier, Annette Hill has been one of the leading researchers of reality television's impact on viewers' perceptions of reality. Hill has studied this topic over the past decade and has published research from in-depth interviews and focus groups that has shed insight on how reality television influences viewers' feelings and attitudes towards subjects, along with their overall trust or mistrust in the programming. Hill's research has shown that most audience members are not naive to the fact that reality television is often "set up" and at least partially scripted. In fact, Hill's research has shown that viewers often discuss and even gossip about how subjects "perform" their roles and to what extent they are acting or being true to their identity.

Ethical Issues of Representation in Reality Television

Especially within the past few years, scholars have given heightened attention to ethical issues within reality TV production, viewing, and participation. As mentioned earlier, the editing process involved with reality television production leads to some ethical problems.

Producers have the opportunity to include or exclude scenes often from many hours or days of filming. They are able to piece together scenes and show participants in a way that is most appealing or entertaining to viewers, inevitably contributing to the "construction" of the representation of reality television subjects.

Jonathan Kraszewski wrote a chapter -"Country Hicks and Urban Cliques: Mediating Race, Reality, and Liberalism on MTV's *The Real World*" -in a book, *Reality TV: Remaking Television Culture*. There he discusses the ethical issues of representation in the MTV show, suggesting that the series is laden with racist elements that reinforce dangerous stereotypes. Kraszewski suggests that MTV producers in one season of the show have actually looked for racist participants, and when they were unable to find a participant who was "racist enough," they encouraged one participant to act as if he were, even though he claimed he "did not have a racist bone in [his] body."[10] Another scholar has similarly noted that it is an ethical issue that viewers may be naive when it comes to casting decisions in that often, someone may be cast solely because that individual embodies and satisfies a stereotype.[11]

The Explosion of Southern Stereotypes

Many scholars and journalists have published highly opinionated articles on the recent popularity of reality television programs showcasing "redneck" culture in the American South. As mentioned earlier, Roger Catlin of the *Washington Post* recently covered both sides of the issue, interviewing experts in the field and finding mixed reactions: While some fervently believed that these shows build upon and proliferate existing negative stereotypes, others felt that the shows are not derogatory because subjects are shown in an affectionate way that lets viewers connect to something both raw and real. Eric Deggans' recent article on NPR, on the other hand, argues that these shows are both disappointing and completely unacceptable and should not be universally embraced and celebrated.

While scholars and journalists have expressed their views by publishing a number of articles on the topic, to date, no quantitative research has been done to explore the issue. Therefore, this paper will serve to provide key, data-driven insights in a specific subject area that has not yet been given this attention.

The thesis statement of this study is that the proliferation of reality television shows featuring subjects from the American South exacerbates the existing stereotypes associated with these communities. The following research questions were derived from the thesis.

- **RQ1**. What have previous scholars discovered about the potential problems with reality television and its representation of "reality"?
- **RQ2**. What are the dominant stereotypes for southerners that exist within reality TV shows and to what extent and frequency do these stereotypes appear? Looking specifically at the stereotypes of southerners as unintelligent, crude, violent and unhealthy, which stereotypes are most prevalent?

- **RQ3**. To what extent does television have the power to influence viewers' perceptions of the subjects within reality television shows?

Methodology

Content analysis was used to quantitatively measure the exploration of this topic. Three reality television shows were selected for the analysis: *Here Comes Honey Boo Boo* (TLC), *Duck Dynasty* (A&E), and *Buckwild* (MTV). These shows were selected as they all contain subjects from and take place in the American South. These shows were also chosen because of their range in network, geographic location, and age of the subjects.

Here Comes Honey Boo Boo airs on TLC and takes place in the rural town of McIntyre, Georgia. It follows the daily activities of 7-year-old Alana "Honey Boo Boo" Thompson and her mother, father, and three teenage sisters. The show was born out of TLC's *Toddler's and Tiaras*, a child pageant reality show where Alana and her entire family proved to be entertaining, larger than life characters apparently deserving of a television show dedicated to chronicling their daily lives. The popularity of the young star and her family is undeniable; according to an article from *Parade* magazine, Honey Boo Boo was one of the ten most Internet-searched reality stars of 2012.

Duck Dynasty, which airs on A&E, follows the lives of the Roberston family in West Monroe, Louisiana. The series primarily follows Willie Robertson, the company's current CEO, while he tries to keep his family, who all work for the company, away from distractions. The family became extremely wealthy from their business, Duck Commander, which makes products for various duck hunting activities. The network's website for the show states, "They may be living the rags-to riches American dream, but they're just as busy staying true to their rugged outdoorsman lifestyle and southern roots." According to A&E, it is the network's most watched series and is in its third season.

Buckwild is a recently cancelled reality show on MTV that follows the lives of several young adults in both Sissonville and Charleston, West Virginia. The show features a group of young adults who have just graduated high school and are either taking classes at local colleges, working at businesses in the area, or not working at all. The show mainly follows the group as they engage in dangerous stunts, go out drinking, or get into fights with each other, neighbors, family members and friends. Following the death of main character Shain Gandee due to a carbon monoxide poisoning incident, the show was cancelled in early April 2013.

Each show was evaluated for four stereotypes sometimes associated with the South. Those elements included unintelligent, crude, violent or unhealthy actions. After reviewing literature identifying southern stereotypes, these four factors were chosen for the study.

Many authors have published articles on what they argue to be southern stereotypes proliferated through both politics and the mainstream media. Kristin Rawls of political journalism site *Salon.com* published an article last year arguing that the "white trash" representation of southern culture makes it seem as if the entire community is uneducated. While underfunded education remains a problem throughout the South, Rawls asserted that the representation of Southerners as universally unintelligent is inaccurate and leads to a dangerous misunderstanding of the entire community.[12]

The crude and violent stereotypes surrounding Southern culture may stem from films like *Deliverance*, which came out over 40 years ago. The influence of this film, according to University of Tulsa professor Robert Jackson, was both "powerful and pernicious." In an interview with CNN he said, "It's had a tenacious hold on people's imaginations, establishing the hillbilly as a kind of menacing, premodern, medieval kind of figure."[13]

The study included the unhealthy stereotype as the final factor for evaluation primarily because of the association of the South with high obesity rates. In 2011, a study from the nonprofit organization Trust for America's Health in conjunction with the Robert Wood Johnson Foundation found that nine of the ten states with the highest obesity rates were in the South. Mississippi, Alabama and West Virginia were at the top of the list, with obesity rates of 34.4%, 32.3%, and 32.3% of the state's population, respectively. This information was based on data from the CDC. According to Jeff Levi, executive director of the Trust for America's Health, this may be due to high rates of poverty in the South and a traditional diet that is unhealthy.[14]

The researcher fully acknowledges that selection of these stereotypes may be a limitation to the study. By narrowing the subject matter to four stereotypes for analysis, some stereotypes are neglected. In addition, no stereotypes with positive connotations have been included, limiting the results of this study so as to provide only insight into the prevalence of negative stereotypes. Additionally, the interpretation of the representation of the frequency of these stereotypes is, of course, personal;, therefore, the results of the study may be largely dependent upon who is conducting the research.

These four factors, unintelligent, crude, violent and unhealthy, must be defined in more specific terms in order to explain the data collection. Any behavior that could be deemed "unintelligent" was included in the analysis. This included any time a character mispronounced or struggled over a word, used words like y'all or ain't, or any time a character expressed an obvious lack of awareness in a topic and it was brought to attention either by other characters or by the producers. It also included any instances of subjects making ignorant comments about other cultures or current events.

Crude behavior was another factor for evaluation. This included any time a subject swore or used vulgar language, any time focus was brought to bodily functions, or any occasions of heightened sexuality, specifically promiscuous behavior. Crude behavior also included any occasions of nudity, regardless of whether this nudity was sexual in nature.

Violent behavior included all physical violence ranging from pushing (even in a joking and not necessarily aggressive way) and general roughhousing to full fledged physical assault. Violent behavior also included verbal violence, where attention was brought to characters that were verbally berating or assaulting other characters or strangers on the show. Violent behavior also included any dangerous stunts, certainly capable of causing serious harm and possibly even death, performed by characters on the show.

Unhealthy behavior included any emphasis on subjects eating heavily processed or fried foods, particularly in excess of what could be considered nutritionally healthy. Unhealthy behavior also included any kind of emphasis brought to characters being excessively overweight or obese.

The process involved a careful watching of five full episodes of each of the three shows, marking tallies for each occasion of a particular stereotype, along with

Table 1 Instances of four stereotype actions in *Here Comes Honey Boo Boo (TLC)*

	Episode #1	Episode #2	Episode #3	Episode #4	Episode #5	Total	Average/ Episode
Unintelligent	26	28	38	49	42	183	36.6
Crude	11	19	12	13	20	65	13
Violent	5	2	6	1	6	20	4
Unhealthy	5	5	6	3	2	21	4.2

Table 2 Instances of four stereotype actions in *Duck Dynasty (A&E)*

	Episode #1	Episode #2	Episode #3	Episode #4	Episode #5	Total	Average/ Episode
Unintelligent	20	21	18	22	20	101	20.2
Crude	1	3	5	5	5	19	3.8
Violent	11	2	3	7	8	31	6.2
Unhealthy	1	1	2	0	0	4	0.8

Table 3 Instances of four stereotype actions in *Buckwild (MTV)*

	Episode #1	Episode #2	Episode #3	Episode #4	Episode #5	Total	Average/ Episode
Unintelligent	28	27	29	28	38	150	30
Crude	39	36	46	47	62	230	46
Violent	15	13	8	4	15	55	11
Unhealthy	1	3	1	1	0	6	1.2

taking detailed notes to with the goal of drawing more qualitative thematic conclusions across the shows.

Based on analysis of the five episodes (roughly 100 minutes) for each show, the author tallied the instances of each stereotype and calculated their means as shown in the following three tables.

Primary Research Findings

Overall, *Here Comes Honey Boo Boo* demonstrated the highest frequency of subjects being portrayed as unintelligent at an average of 36.6 occurrences per episode, followed by MTV's *Buckwild* (30 occurrences per episode) and *Duck Dynasty* (20.2 demonstrations). It is important to note the implications of even this lowest value: it still means that on average at least one unintelligent behavior per minute was shown on screen during the 20-minute segment.

Buckwild had the most frequent demonstrations of crude behavior at an average of 46 instances per episode. *Here Comes Honey Boo Boo* and *Duck Dynasty* had considerably lower numbers of crude behavior at 15 and 3.8 instances, respectively. Much of the crude behavior in *Buckwild* had to do with subjects swearing, using otherwise vulgar language, and engaging in overtly promiscuous sexual behavior throughout the show.

Buckwild also appeared to be the most violent show, with an average of 11 incidents of violence in comparison to *Duck Dynasty* which had 6.2 instances, and *Here Comes Honey Boo Boo* with four. Violence in *Buckwild* included reckless and dangerous stunts performed by the characters as well as several incidents of physical violence. This physical violence ranged from subjects pushing each other around perhaps in a less serious way to full-fledged physical assault.

The unhealthy stereotype was the least frequent stereotype present in all of the shows observed. *Here Comes Honey Boo Boo* had the highest frequency of unhealthy behavior with an average of 4.2 incidents per episode, followed by *Buckwild* (1.2 occasions) and *Duck Dynasty* (0.8 occasions). The unhealthy behavior in *Here Comes Honey Boo Boo* largely had to do with the consumption of fried or heavily processed foods in excess. There was also a heightened attention brought to the weight of the characters as they intermittently competed against each other to lose weight. As the camera zoomed in on the scale reading, it was clear that every character, even young Alana, could be classified as overweight and some even obese or morbidly obese. In one episode, June, otherwise known as "Mama," clocked in at over 300 pounds. Rather than seeming concerned for their health, the characters made minimal efforts to change their eating and lifestyle habits. The camera frequently zoomed in on the subjects continuing to binge eat from huge bags of food.

Discussion of Primary Research Findings

Southern Dialects: Translation, please?

The abundance of unintelligent behavior in *Here Comes Honey Bo Boo* largely consists of subjects struggling with the English language. Frequently, subjects struggle over words, use expressions like "y'all" and "ain't," and have accents so thick that what they say on camera is almost unintelligible. One character in particular who struggles with speaking is Mike Thompson, or as he is called on the show, "Sugar Bear." When Mike is in front of the camera, subtitles are used to help the viewer understand what he is saying. Subtitles are used intermittently for multiple characters throughout the show, which differentiate it from any of the other shows that were observed. It seems there is a heightened attention brought to the struggle with language by the inclusion of these subtitles. For the viewer, it almost implies these subjects are so backwards, so uneducated, that they are unable to communicate in the ways in which we are able to communicate. We need the producers to "decode" what these people are trying to say. It seems that this "language barrier" is one of the most basic ways to emphasize the southern stereotype and to create a distancing sense of "other" for the subjects of these shows. In other words, their struggle with language creates in the viewers' mind a sense of "other": They are different from us; therefore, we are not the same.

Fist Pounds for Fist Fights: Celebrating Violence in Buckwild

As stated earlier, *Buckwild* stood as the most violent show. Through observing several episodes of *Buckwild*, the author found that violence did not just occur on the show, but it was celebrated. In a particularly gruesome scene, Tyler, a character on the show, physically assaults an unwelcome guest at a party to the point where the victim is bleeding profusely from his mouth, unable to stand, and seemingly left unconscious. The viewer feels as though they are thoroughly involved in this fight, as the camera wobbles and shakes while trying to capture all of the action. When Tyler returns to the kitchen where his other friends are congregating, he is met with high fives and one girl even exclaims, while beaming at Tyler, "Oh my god Tyler, that was so hot."

Violence was ever-present throughout all of the *Buckwild* episodes observed. Each episode even starts with a warning, read aloud by a female character of the show: "The following show features wild and crazy behavior that could result in serious personal injury or property damage. MTV and the producers insist that no one attempt to recreate or reenact any activity performed on this show."

Also in the introduction to the show, which is included in every episode, several of the subjects exclaim that living in West Virginia, a place "founded on freedom," gives them the freedom to do "whatever the f*** [they] want." A female subject of Bangladeshi origin is introduced in the second episode of the series. In her first interaction with the camera she exclaims, "I may look exotic, but I'm as country as it gets." This emphasis on identification with the South, and West Virginia in particular, makes it difficult to separate the outrageous violent and crude behavior from this location. By the subjects' constant communication of pride in their home of "wild and crazy" West Virginia, the viewer may be left feeling as though this is representative of the American South as a whole, which is, of course, problematic.

This reality show became tragically real when 21-year-old cast member Shain Gandee was found dead in early April 2013 after an off-roading trip with his uncle and a family friend who were also found dead. Shain's name was synonymous with crazy stunts and daredevil activities through the series. In one episode, he rides a four-wheeler recklessly up a hill and is later yelled at by an adult (presumably a parent) for not wearing a helmet. Shain, along with his friends, laugh off the stern warning from the adult and continue riding up the hill without any kind of protection. This incident, along with countless others where Shain is clearly the ringleader of dangerous activity, seem to eerily foreshadow his death.

Camo versus Cappuccino: Cultural Differences Reach a Boiling Point in Duck Dynasty

In one episode of Duck Dynasty titled, "Duck Be a Lady," several characters from the show express their frustration that the company coffee machine has broken. Jase Robertson, one of the brothers on the show, even goes so far as to say that he cannot survive without a cup of coffee. The men decide to travel to a nearby coffee shop and as they enter the door, immediately provide a stark visual contrast: a sea of camouflage, long untamed beards, and bandanas juxtaposed with the academic types who are reading, typing on their laptops, and sipping their complicated drinks in the shop. Every difference between the worlds of these two groups is emphasized for the next several minutes of the episode. Jase expresses his confusion over the menu, claiming that there is not a single option that is just "coffee." A well-groomed man in front of the group orders a complicated mocha drink and Jase compares it to being as complex as building a bomb.

French sociologist Pierre Bourdieu's theoretical frameworks of habitus and cultural capital may be applied to *Duck Dynasty* and especially to this scene in particular. Bourdieu theorized that the way in which we see the world and our own identities is inextricably bound to our gender, class, and the environment in which we are raised. For Bourdieu, "the culture of modern society is a class culture, characterized by socially ranked symbolic differences that mark out classes and make some seem superior to others."[15] When the men of *Duck Dynasty* enter the coffee shop, they are forced to depart from their habitus, a term used by Bourdieu to describe the personal ideological frameworks by which we all operate. They are forced to interact with people vastly different from themselves in terms of education and what Bourdieu would call "cultural capital." While they reject the high culture of the coffee shop by making mocking remarks and generally putting down the lifestyle of these individuals, this world also in a sense, rejects them. This is visible from the barista's patronizing tone as she, in the close-up shots, explains the different types of coffees to the men, appearing seemingly disgusted by them as they clearly do not regularly inhabit this space.

Something very interesting to note is that although the men of *Duck Dynasty* have acquired a small fortune through the success of their family business, they refuse to adopt certain "high class" behaviors. They all have large, beautiful homes, but continue to wear camouflage outfits and sport unkempt beards. Despite the family's commercial success, it seems clear that they still are holding on to what the eldest family member, Si, would consider "honorable" things, like knowing how to "live off the land." In one notable scene in the episode, "Tickets to the Fun Show," Si teaches the younger sons of the family how to kill and prepare bullfrogs. When giving the boys advice on how to find what he considers to be the perfect woman, he says, "If she knows how to cook, carries her bible, and loves to eat bullfrogs, that's a woman." This "lesson" reinforces a number of southern stereotypes just in one sentence.

Throughout the episodes, it seems that Willie is the bossiest member of the family, but also the smartest and most responsible. While on vacation in Hawaii, Willie plans a complete itinerary for the entire family. When things do not go according to plan and the family essentially rejects Willie's planned programming, the men in particular choose to get into some potentially dangerous adventures. They all find a small cliff and jump into the water, and Willie, who has tagged along, says, "I'm starting to see a link between Jase's definition of manhood and poor judgment." Despite looking down on his family's actions and the entire situation, Willie eventually decides to jump off as well, claiming that he does not want his "manhood" to be challenged any longer. This theme linking masculinity to recklessness seems to be consistent throughout all of the episodes.

While there is a heightened attention brought to the clothes these characters wear and occasionally the way in which they mispronounce words and exhibit reckless behavior, overall, these traits do not seem to come across in a completely derogatory way. The viewer can see that when, for example, Willie is faced with the daunting task of taking his teenage daughter dress shopping, universal family issues are apparent. It is also important to note that each episode concludes with the family at the dinner table, showing that despite their bickering, at the end of the day they come together as a family and share a meal. There is typically also some sort of universal lesson communicated by the end of the episode and the lesson typically ties back in some way to the idea of family and togetherness. As Willie says in one episode, "Nobody drives us crazy like our families. They are the source of our biggest frustrations but also our biggest joys."

Discussion of Secondary Research Findings

Surveillance and "The Gaze"

One issue, briefly mentioned in the review of literature, is how issues of surveillance along with power relations play into reality television. Montemurro suggests that subjects who are placed in front of the camera are perhaps deliberately placed in a position of subordination. Montemurro mentions one of the first examinations of this idea: sociologist Michel Foucault's discussion of prisons and more specifically, Bentham's Panopticon, which was designed so that prisoners knew that they could be watched at any moment, yet were not allowed to know when this was happening. Montemurro argues that this is one of the first examples of technology being used to aid in surveillance of subjects and draws the parallel to present-day reality television production as the modern form of surveillance. Montemurro's piece, which focuses on examining the technology that contributes to surveillance in the popular show *Big Brother*, notes that contestants are not in control over their representation. She states, "Contestants are usually required to wear microphones and sign contracts that dictate that they may be filmed at any time or all of the time. However, they do not know how much of what they do or which specific interactions will actually become a part of the television show."[16] Ultimately, Montemurro suggests it is the producers that have the

power over contestants or subjects in reality television because they choose what is shown.

Media scholar Mark Andrejevic also mentions the concept of the "omnipresent gaze of the camera and audience" in his *Reality TV: The Work of Being Watched*. Looking at reality shows such as *Temptation Island*, which aired in the early 2000s, Andrejevic mentions the idea of voyeurism and the power and control associated with this "voyeuristic fetish" tied to reality television viewing. He argues that viewers are part of this "omnipresent gaze" as they are invited into the private relationships unfolding on these shows.[17]

Dubrofsky, who as mentioned earlier, completed a case study on *The Bachelor*, argues that participants in reality television shows do not have "complete autonomy" in how they present their selves under surveillance. She argues that the mediated presentation (i.e., the construction of montage sequences and the overall editing process involved in reality television filmmaking) plays an important role in the construction of participant identity. These deliberate editing decisions are not communicated to viewers, and they are often not communicated to participants, thus taking their own representation out of their hands. Hill (2004) argues, "All too often ordinary people have little recourse to complain about the way they have been treated or represented in reality programs."[18]

Reality TV & Artistic Sacrifice

One issue inextricably bound to reality television is the criticism that it has departed from "quality" programming or earlier modes of observational documentary. It has been widely argued that reality television is representative of "trash" culture and some have even gone so far as to say that it is playing an active role in making Americans as a whole, less intelligent.

Scholar Junhow Wei conducted an ethnographic study at a reality television production company called Sunshine productions. Through fieldwork, which included observation but also in-depth interviews with employees, Wei uncovered the struggle that workers in this industry face when producing these shows. Wei found that workers struggle to maintain and often have to sacrifice their "artistic integrity" when producing these shows, which ultimately do not meet their standards of artistic quality. Wei spent time with workers, was included in several planning meetings and parties, and also conducted several personal interviews where workers openly expressed frustrations. In one interview, a worker stated:

Well, I think that every single shot is based on will it have an impact on the buyer. Will it make—every single thing is based on is the buyer going to look at it and think, "Cool, I like that." It has nothing to do with my emotions or anybody's emotions. It has everything to do with is the buyer going to sit there and have a reaction to it, because otherwise you're wasting your time.[19]

Many employees expressed that "heightened drama" along with "larger than life characters" are more appealing to buyers and viewers, thus producers and editors are pressured to manipulate situations to heighten entertainment value, even at the perhaps ethical cost of skewing reality. From a wealth of footage, producers and editors are forced to construct a kind of narrative or storyline. Because of the market pressures to create "sellable" entertainment, these decision-makers are likely to position footage in a way that creates the most entertainment value.

While Wei was on location filming a sizzle reel for a reality show called *Riders*, a show about a traveling carnival company, he had an interesting interaction with one of the junior level development associates who was clearly reluctant to focus on the dirty, ramshackle living quarters of the carnival workers. When Wei asked the employee why he felt this way, his grave response was "Well, that's not really the truth." He explained to Wei that he did not want to continue to perpetuate negative, inaccurate stereotypes about the carnival workers.

Viewer Involvement and Feelings of Identification

Several scholars argue that the nature of reality television causes viewers to feel as though they are thoroughly involved in the lives of reality TV subjects. Some scholars have argued that because these programs invite viewers to become involved in the lives of ordinary people, there is an increased level of identification with the subjects in both mental and emotional ways.[20] The danger in this, of course, is that with the increase in feelings of identification, there may also be an increase in viewers' perceptions of reality. If viewers assume that they know the characters, they may potentially forget what could be staged events. They may also forget the good possibility that subjects may be acting a certain way because producers have encouraged them to act in this way or "play up" certain behaviors. Quoting Jaffe (2005), who wrote, "It is a significant issue for viewers to be lulled into a belief in something so artificially constructed, " Coyne, Robinson and Nelson note in their article on relational aggression in reality television.[21]

Conclusion

As the findings of this study suggest, our persistent and curious infatuation with reality television is dangerous because it continues to perpetuate the negative stereotypes associated with the people of the American South. Unintelligent, crude and violent behavior manifested itself across all shows under observation in this study. Through industry pressures to create entertainment, producers are forced to construct individual and cultural identities that are perhaps not representative of reality. The nature of reality television allows an artificial sense of closeness to the characters. This prevents a critical and analytical study of the show and thereby allows stereotypes to proliferate unchallenged. We are consuming without thinking. We are laughing without reflecting. We are exploiting a segment of society at the expense of real understanding and in the process, relegating an entire cultural community to a singular distorted vision.

Acknowledgments

This author is thankful to Dr. David Copeland at Elon University for his guidance and supervision, without which the article could not be published.

References

Andrejevic, Mark. *Reality TV: The Work of Being Watched.* Lanham, Maryland: Rownman & Littlefield Publishers, Inc., 2004.

Carter, Bill. "Reality TV Once Again Dominates Summer Ratings," *New York Times,* Last modified September 13, 2010, http://www.nytimes.com/2010/09/13/business/media/13reality.

Catlin, Roger. "Reality TV's explosion of Southern stereotypes." *The Washington Post.* Last modified June 7, 2012. http://articles.washingtonpost.com/2012-06-07/entertainment/35460112_1_american-hoggersturtleman-swamp-people.

Coyne, Sarah, Simon Robinson and David Nelson. "Does Reality Backbite? Physical, Verbal, and Relational Aggression in Reality Television Programs." *Journal of Broadcasting & Electronic Media* 54 (2010): 282–298.

Deggans, Eric. "Disappointing 'Redneck' TV Shortchanges The American South." *National Public Radio.* Last modified December 7, 2011. http://www.npr.org/blogs/monkeysee/2011/12/07/142861568/disappointing-redneck-tv-shortchanges-the-american-south.

Denham, Brian and Richelle Jones. "Survival of the Stereotypical: A Study of Personal Characteristics and Order of Elimination on Reality Television." *Studies in Popular Culture* 30 (2008): 79–113.

Dubrofsky, Rachel. *The Surveillance of Women on Reality Television: Watching The Bachelor and The Bachelorette.* Lanham, Maryland: Lexington Books, 2011.

Filoteo, Janie. "Placing Reality TV in the Cultural Spectrum: Making a Case for Studying the World of Reality Television," (paper presented at the annual meeting of the

American Sociological Association, Philadelphia, Pennsylvania, August 13–16, 2005), 1–18.

Gartman, David. "Bourdieu and Adorno: Converging theories of culture and inequality." *Theory & Society* 41 (2012): 41–72.

Godlewski, Lisa and Elizabeth Perse. "Audience Activity and Reality Television: Identification, Online Activity, and Satisfaction." *Communication Quarterly* 58 (2010): 148–169.

Hellmich, Nanci. "Southerners, poor have highest rates of obesity." *USA Today*. Last modified July 8, 2011. http://yourlife.usatoday.com/fitness-food/diet-nutrition/story/2011/07/Southerners-poor-have-highestrates-of-obesity/49173468/1

Hill, Annette. *Reality TV Audiences and Popular Factual Television*. London: Routledge, 2005. Huff, Richard. *Reality Television*. Westport, Conn.: Praeger Publishers, 2006.

Kraszewski, Jon. "Country Hicks and Urban Cliques: Mediating Race, Reality, and Liberalism on MTV's *The Real World*." In *Reality TV: Remaking Television Culture*, ed. Susan Murray and Laurie Ouellette. New York: New York University Press, 2004.

Leopold, Todd. "The South: Not all Bubbas and banjos." *CNN*. Last modified April 14, 2012, http://edition.cnn.com/2012/04/14/us/bubba-southern-stereotypes

Lewis, Justin. "The Meaning of Real Life." In *Reality TV: Remaking Television Culture*, ed. Susan Murray and Laurie Ouellette. New York: New York University Press, 2004.

Montemurro, Beth. "Surveillance and Power: The Impact of New Technologies on Reality Television Audiences." (paper presented at the annual meeting of the American Sociological Association, New York, New York, August 11-14, 2007): 1–22.

Rawls, Kristin. "The Media's Southern Stereotypes." *Salon.com*. Last modified April 4, 2012, http://www.salon.com/2012/04/04/the_medias_southern_stereotypes/.

Slocum, Charles. "The Real History of Reality TV Or, How Alan Funt Won the Cold War." *Writers Guild of America*, n.d. http://www.wga.org/organizesub.aspx?id=1099.

Wei, Junhow. "Dealing With Reality: Market demands, artistic integrity, and identity work in reality television production." *Poetics* 40 (2012): 444–466.

Notes

1. Charles Slocum, "The Real History of Reality TV Or, How Alan Funt Won the Cold War," Writers Guild of America, n.d, http://www.wga.org/organizesub.aspx?id=1099 (15 March 2013).

2. Bill Carter, "Reality TV Once Again Dominates Summer Ratings," New York Times, last modified September 13, 2010, http://www.nytimes.com/2010/09/13/business/media/13reality.html?_r=0 (15 March 2013).

3. Janie Filoteo, "Placing Reality TV in the Cultural Spectrum: Making a Case for Studying the World of Reality Television," (paper presented at the annual meeting of the American Sociological Association, Philadelphia, Pennsylvania, August 13-16, 2005), 6.

4. Eric Deggans, "Disappointing 'Redneck' TV Shortchanges The American South," National Public Radio, last modified December 7, 2011, http://www.npr.org/blogs/monkeysee/2011/12/07/142861568/disappointing-redneck-tv-shortchanges-the-american-south (4 April 2013).

5. Roger Catlin, "Reality TV's explosion of Southern stereotypes," The Washington Post, last modified June 7, 2012, http://articles.washingtonpost.com/2012-06-07/entertainment/35460112_1_american-hoggersturtleman-swamp-people (6 April 2013).

6. Justin Lewis "The Meaning of Real Life" In Reality TV: Remaking Television Culture, ed. Susan Murray and Laurie Ouellette (New York: New York University Press, 2004), 288.

7. Richard Huff, Reality Television (Westport, Conn.: Praeger Publishers, 2006), 20.

8. Rachel Dubrofsky, The Surveillance of Women on Reality Television: Watching The Bachelor and The Bachelorette (Lanham, Md.: Lexington Books, 2011), 100.

9. Annette Hill, Reality TV Audiences and Popular Factual Television (London: Routledge, 2005), 75.

10. Jon Krasewski, "Country Hicks and Urban Cliques: Mediating Race, Reality, and Liberalism on MTV's The Real World." In Reality TV: Remaking Television Culture, ed. Susan Murray and Laurie Ouellette (New York: New York University Press, 2004), 179.

11. Brian Denham and Richelle Jones, "Survival of the Stereotypical: A Study of Personal Characteristics and Order of Elimination on Reality Television," Studies in Popular Culture 30, no. 2 (2008): 81.

12. Kristin Rawls, "The media's southern stereotypes," Salon.com, last modified April 4, 2012, http:// www.salon.com/2012/04/04/the_medias_southern_stereotypes/ (24 June 2013).

13. Todd Leopold, "The South: Not all Bubbas and banjos," CNN, last modified April 14, 2012, http://edition.cnn.com/2012/04/14/us/bubba-southern-stereotypes (24 June 2013).

14. Nanci Hellmich, "Southerners, poor have highest rates of obesity," USA Today, last modified July 8, 2011, http://yourlife.usatoday.com/fitness-food/diet-nutrition/story/2011/07/Southerners-poor-have-highestrates-of-obesity/49173468/1 (24 June 2013).

15. David Gartman,"Bourdieu and Adorno: Converging theories of culture and inequality," Theory & Society 41, no.1 (2012): 42.

16. Beth Montemurro, "Surveillance and Power: The Impact of New Technologies on Reality Television Audiences," (paper presented at the annual meeting of the American

Sociological Association, New York, New York, August 11-14, 2007), 6-8.

17. Mark Andrejevic, Reality TV: The Work of Being Watched (Lanham, Maryland: Rownman & Littlefield Publishers, Inc., 2004), 173-175.

18. Annette Hill, Reality TV Audiences and Popular Factual Television (London: Routledge, 2005), 108.

19. Junhow Wei, "Dealing With Reality: Market demands, artistic integrity, and identity work in reality

20. Lisa Godlewski and Elizabeth Perse, "Audience Activity and Reality Television: Identification, Online Activity, and Satisfaction," Communication Quarterly 58 no. 2 (2010), 150-151.

21. Sarah Coyne, Simon Robinson and David Nelson, "Does Reality Backbite? Physical, Verbal, and Relational Aggression in Reality Television Programs," Journal of Broadcasting & Electronic Media 54 no. 2 (2010), 283.

Race in Latin America

Peter Wade

Since the Second World War, most biologists have agreed that race is not an analytic category to understand human biological diversity. Humans vary to some extent in their DNA and their outward physical appearance or phenotype, but this diversity cannot be organized into "racial groups" or "races," even if some genetic and phenotypical variation seems to correlate very broadly with continental geography. Humans are too similar genetically and intracontinental genetic variation is too great to be able to categorize humans into races. So race is a set of *ideas* about human similarity and difference. But what kind of ideas?

Scholars hold different views (Wade 2002b:ch. 1). This is partly because, as Goldberg says, "Race is not a static concept with a single sedimented meaning"; in fact as a signifier it is "almost, but not quite empty" (1993:80–81). While the word "race" began to appear in European languages from about the 14th century, its meaning has changed greatly since then. Banton (1987) traces how the concept first referred to genealogical linkages between a related set of people (or animals). This was "race as lineage": all the descendants of a single ancestor or group of ancestors were connected genealogically and thus of the same lineage or race; physical appearance was not a key feature. Before the 19th century, European representations of Andean people did not show them as physically different from Europeans (D. Poole 1997:ch.2). From the late 18th century, there was a shift to the idea of race as "type," in which humans were categorized into a few racial types (African, European, Mongol, etc.), seen as primordial and relatively fixed; physical appearance was key to identifying racial type. This was the era of so-called scientific racism, when scientists developed "race" as a key biological category for understanding human physical variation and behavior; they legitimated racial hierarchies in which Europeans were at the top. During the 20th century, scientific racism was slowly dismantled, being mainly replaced, among scholars, by the concept of race as a "social construction," a set of ideas about humans which can have very powerful social consequences such as racial discrimination and racial violence. At the same time, so-called cultural racism has been identified, in which categories of people familiar from the older conceptions of race - such as "whites," "blacks," "Indians" and "Asians" - continue to be identified and to discriminate or be discriminated against, but now on the basis of their "culture" rather than their biology (Stolcke 1995).

The question remains: What kind of ideas are racial ideas? First, many social scientists say that racial ideas refer to human physical variation: bodily appearance, biology, genealogy, heredity, "blood" or genes. This is true but needs specifying further: These aspects of human biology are too general. People are fat and thin, tall and short, male and female. Any of these traits could be talked about in terms that included reference to such aspects.

Second, then, racial thinking also refers to human physical variation in relation to *particular kinds* of perceived human difference, which began to be perceived when Europeans started to colonize the globe and encounter different continents. Racial thinking is, typically, a way of thinking about historical categories such as "black," "white," "Indian," "African," "Asian," and so on. The qualifier, "and so on," is important because racial thinking can proliferate beyond such key categories John Beddoe's *The Races of Britain* (published in 1885) divided up the population of Britain into racial subtypes. Also, it is important that the key categories are not stable: the definition, meaning and perception of them has changed over time and place.

Third, racial thinking is not just about dividing people into physical categories, but also about explaining their behavior. Race is about nature, but also about culture. Culture is explained through naturalization, that is by rooting observed behavior in something taken to be "natural"–although what is taken to be natural has varied over time and can include the realms of environment and cosmology as well as biology. Human nature can be thought to be shaped by the environment, the supernatural (including God) and biology (MacCormack and Strathern 1980; Wade 2002b). This third point is important in understanding "cultural racism." Although explicit reference to biology and indeed to race itself may be absent or muted in this discourse, there may still be a sense in which culture is naturalized, seen as part of a person's or a group's "nature" or perhaps seen as heritable in a quasi-biological way.

In sum, racial ideas are about human physical difference of various kinds, refer typically but not exclusively to key historical categories of colonial origin, and produce naturalizing explanations of culture. This is a fairly broad view of race. Some scholars prefer to limit the concept of race to a "worldview" that was typified by Europe and the US during the era of scientific racial typologies and when systematic, institutional racial discrimination was practiced in many colonial regimes and in the US (Smedley 1993). One can then trace the rise and fall of this worldview – and the way it influenced other areas of the globe – to construct a history of race. I think that this approach is not the best when looking at Latin America: It tends to measure the region against a US or European benchmark which establishes a norm for understanding race.

Historical Background

Spanish and Portuguese colonists exploited local indigenous peoples and African slaves to fulfill labor demands. African slaves were widespread in the Iberian Americas, but tended to concentrate where indigenous peoples suffered the worst decimation and/or were difficult to exploit as labor: the Caribbean islands, Brazil, the circum-Caribbean mainland and some areas of the Pacific littoral of South America (see Arocha and Maya, this volume). African slaves attained freedom in many areas and a free black population developed. Sexual relations between Europeans, Africans and indigenous people led to "mixed" people, *mestizos*, who were recognized as socially distinct from their parents and were enumerated using specific categories by colonial censuses. This mixed population became numerically dominant in some areas by the late 18 th century. A broad contrast existed here with the US where, although such mixtures occurred, they were less recognized socially - especially during the 19th century - and the mixed children were placed socially, and often in censuses, into the racial category of the subordinate parent.

In Iberian colonies, a socially stratified pyramid emerged, with Europeans at the apex, black slaves and *indios* (indigenous people) at the bottom and an ambiguous and contestable set of intermediate categories in the middle in which ancestry, appearance (including dress), occupation and wealth all influenced social standing. In the Spanish colonies, this was sometimes known as a *sociedad de castas,* a society of "castes" (or breeds, or stocks). In New Spain (Mexico), this was illustrated by the 18th century *casta* paintings which depicted parents of different racial categories and their mixed offspring - a caption might read "Spaniard and Mestiza produce a Castiza" (Katzew 2004). The exact role "race" played in this system is the subject of debate. "Racial" status – for example, whether a person was classified in a census as castizo or mestizo - was not fixed, could change between censuses and could be influenced by occupation (Cope 1994). But there was a strong interest in genealogy and inherited blood as markers of status in a hierarchy which was structured in part by whiteness, African blackness and indigeneity. Legal disputes could ensue if a person who considered himself white was called a mestizo by another person. Some legislation in the late 1700s tried to control marriages between whites, indigenous people and blacks, while "sumptuary" legislation attempted to prevent black and mulatto people from using high-status clothes and accoutrements (Mörner 1967; Wade 1997:29–30).

Spanish notions of *limpieza de sangre* (cleanliness of blood) also worked in the colonies. In Spain, these ideas had been used from the mid 15 th century to discriminate against "New Christians" - Jews and Muslims who had converted to Christianity. New legislation required people to prove the "purity" of their Old Christian genealogy to gain admittance to certain administrative positions. Although this was mainly a religious measure, there was an intense concern with genealogy and the perceived inherited "contamination" that came from Jewish or Muslim "blood" (S. Poole 1999). Limpieza de sangre was a manifestation of what Banton calls race as lineage (see above). In the colonies, limpieza de sangre was recast to discriminate also against African and indigenous heritage (Manrique 1993; Martínez 2004). This recasting was fueled by the numerous rebellions organized by indigenous people and slaves and by the perceived religious heterodoxy of indigenous, slave and free black people, many of whom retained aspects of indigenous and African religious systems alongside their avowed Catholicism (Harding 2000; Stern 1987). Colonial persecution of those seen as rebellious, heretical or religiously suspect was linked to perceptions of racial status.

In the postcolonial period, there were radical changes. The category *indio*, which had been a key colonial administrative status, defined by residence in a community and the payment of tribute, began to be dismantled in the context of influential European ideologies of liberalism which envisaged new republics comprising equal citizens. Slavery was mainly abolished by the mid-1800s, although later in Brazil (1888), Cuba (1886) and Puerto Rico (1873). During the colonial period, indigenous people had always filtered out of the status of *indio* and into the mestizo population, while African slaves and their offspring had continuously entered the ranks of the free and the mixed. Now the very categories of *indio* and slave which had helped define the colonial racial hierarchy were being undermined or abolished. At the same time, countries such as Cuba, Peru, Brazil and Mexico received large numbers of migrants from China, Japan and the Middle East who complicated the situation (Bonfil Batalla 1993; Wilson 2004).

However, ideologies of race took on more important and, to the observer of today, more familiar patterns. Intellectual and political elites in the newly independent countries were very concerned with issues of race and the building of nations. In Europe and the US, scientists, medics and intellectuals were developing theories about race which gave it huge significance. The British physician Robert Knox (1850) affirmed: "Race is everything: literature, science, art - in a word, civilization depends on it." In the late 19th century, eugenics became fashionable with its progressive agenda of creating fitter and more morally upstanding populations through controlling sexual reproduction and improving the family environment. In these raciological theories, black and indigenous people were ranked as racially inferior and race mixture was seen as degenerative.

Latin American elites had an ambivalent relationship to these theories (Appelbaum, Macpherson and Rosemblatt 2003; Graham 1990). On the one hand, they saw their black and indigenous populations as inferior and their large mestizo populations as a burden. It was up to the whiter populations to lead nations into modernity. Many countries began to enact immigration legislation that sought to restrict the entry of black people, while European immigration was encouraged. While Asian immigration was significant in many countries, Chinese migrants in northern Mexico, and elsewhere, were seen as racially inferior (Rénique 2003). Deborah Poole (1997:chs 5, 6) shows how images of Andean people, created by Europeans and by Peruvians, began to focus on the physical appearance of the body as a key to classification. Throughout Latin America, typological theories which saw each body as analytically reducible to a racial "type" went hand in hand with new technologies of visual imaging which allowed the serial reproduction and circulation of multiple photographic images as instances of racial types: photographic portraits of black and indigenous peoples circulated widely in Latin America and Europe.

On the other hand, elites could not escape the mixedness of their populations—although this varied markedly from one country to another, being more prominent in Mexico than Argentina or Chile. Mixture could however be defined as a process of whitening. The perceived superiority of whites would tip the nation's biological and cultural balance in their favor, helped by European immigration (Stepan 1991). In the early decades of the 20th century, some nations began to take a more positive attitude to mixture: *mestizaje* or *mestigagem* (racial and cultural mixture) was the basis for national identity. The mixture of African, indigenous and European peoples was the founding origin myth of the nation. Mestizaje was something to be celebrated as a distinctive feature; indigenous and African people had, it was said, made useful contributions to the cultures of, for example, Mexico or Brazil. There was, in short, some resistance to European ideologies that simply condemned Latin American nations as mixed and inferior. In postrevolutionary Mexico, in 1925, writer and education minister José Vasconcelos celebrated the "cosmic race" as a superior mixed race which was in the process of evolving, particularly on Latin American soil, and which would undermine US ideologies about the superiority of "pure" segregated races (Vasconcelos 1997). Ironically, in Mexico, this ideology was consolidated by anti-Chinese racism, which pitted a national mestizo identity against an Asian presence seen as alien (Rénique 2003). In 1930s Brazil, intellectual Gilberto Freyre was very influential in promoting the idea of a distinctive mixed nation, with indigenous and African contributions, which avoided the notorious problems of racism and segregation seen to affect the US. The image of the mestizo nation was also influential in Colombia, Central America and, to a lesser extent, Peru (de la Cadena 2000; Gould 1998; Hale 1996; Wade 1993).

However, mestizaje was still seen by many Latin Americans as a progressive process in which black and indigenous people would be integrated into a mestizo nation that was moving toward whiteness. Ideologies of *indigenismo* (indigenism) were prominent in countries such as Peru and Mexico, which had large indigenous populations (see chapters by Nahmad Sitton and Seligmann, this volume). But while indigenismo celebrated the nation's indigenous populations, it tended to extol indigenous history, rather than contemporary indigenous populations (de la Cadena 2000; Knight 1990). In Mexico, prominent indigenista Manuel Gamio studied indigenous populations, but focused on archaeology and overall took an integrationist perspective, envisaging the assimilation of indigenous populations into the mestizo nation (see Walsh, this volume). With the partial exception of Brazil and Cuba, black populations were much less subject to glorification as national ancestors.

Race and Culture in Latin America

De la Cadena (2000) argues that from about the 1920s in Peru, intellectuals began to abandon notions of race and to talk of indigenous peoples in terms of "spirit" or soul rather than biology. This can be seen to mark a shift toward the cultural explanations of human difference that became more commonplace in the later 20th century. The indigenous spirit was seen as largely a product of the environment, but was also seen as deeply ingrained and in some sense innate, even if the language of racial biology was eschewed. "Culture" was thus understood in quite a determinist–one could say naturalized - way. Nevertheless, it could be argued that this shift sets the scene for a specifically Latin American approach to race, which is distinct from that in North America and Europe. This is a key point because scholarly and popular views of race in Latin America have frequently made explicit or implicit use of a comparison with the US.

This comparison has a long history and entered into the way intellectuals such as Freyre in Brazil or Vasconcelos in Mexico defined their countries as relatively free from racial prejudice in comparison with the US (Graham 1990; Wade 2004). Tannenbaum (1948) initiated a historical debate by arguing that slavery had been more benign and colonial society more open to the assimilation of slaves in Iberian colonies than Anglo-Saxon ones. He was wrong about the benevolence of Latin American slavery, but there was no doubt that slaves found it easier to become free in this region than in North America, that mixture between racial categories was more frequent, and that the offspring of such unions were, in the long term, recognized more fully as a mestizo social category, intermediate between black, white and indigenous.

The nature of Latin American societies as mestizo - with the variations that run from Argentina, where the image of mixture is downplayed in favor of whiteness, to Brazil or Mexico, where mixture is foregrounded in discourse on the nation - has powerfully shaped ideas about race in the region. One view is that race is not important: there is little racism and little sense of racial identity for most people. Indigenous people may have their particular ethnic identities, based on local cultures, and people in general may recognize phenotypical differences that are linked to skin color and other typically "racial" features, but none of this creates a society in which racial identities are the basis for significant social divisions and exclusions - the subtext here is usually, "in comparison with the USA" (Wade 1997:51–57). This view is most explicit in the claim that Latin America enjoys "a racial democracy." The opposing view holds that, while Latin American racism is different from that in the US, it still operates to create significant disadvantage for indigenous and black people as collective categories.

Debates on this theme have focused mainly on comparisons of Brazil and the US (Sant'Anna and Souza 1997). In the 1950s, in the wake of Nazism, UNESCO began a series of studies of Brazil designed to explore a racial democracy. In fact, few scholars unequivocally supported the idea of a racial democracy, but many saw race as much less significant than in the US and becoming more insignificant. It was widely argued that class was the key division in Brazil, while race was secondary (Winant 1992). A key factor was mixture itself. First, according to censuses, over a third of Brazilians identify themselves as *pardo* (brown), indicating some kind of mixedness. Second, the prevalence of mixture has created vagueness about who is who in racial terms (Sansone 2003:ch. 1; Telles 2002). Much was made then, and still is now, of the fact that, rather than using a small number of terms such as black, white and indigenous, Brazilians use dozens of descriptive terms, which often try to describe actual shade of skin color. A photograph of a person will elicit different terms depending on how the person is dressed and who is doing the classifying. Racial categorization is shifting and contextual, influenced by appearance, dress, behavior, and, especially, class status: blackness is strongly associated with lower class position. Terms that indicate some degree of mixedness are very common: *moreno* (brown) is common in Brazil and elsewhere, but can include a light-skinned person with dark hair and a person with quite dark skin and of clear African ancestry. If there is little agreement on who is black (or white or indigenous), how can discrimination take place in any systematic way? In contrast, in the US, there is generally a much clearer definition of racial identity, based on a few key categories: black, white, Native American (and Asian and Pacific Islander). This clarity was fundamental both to the institutionalized "Jim Crow" racial segregation that operated for decades until after the Second World War and to the informal discrimination and segregation that still persist. There needs to be general agreement about who is black and white for such systems to operate.

Contrasting views argue that, despite the apparent plethora of racial terms, a few key terms and categories are salient, focused on black, white, indigenous and two or three basic mixed categories. Most importantly, shifting and contextual terminologies lead to shifting and contextual discriminations, rather than the simple absence of them. Sansone shows that racial terminology in Salvador, Brazil, shifts according to context–"a son can be *preto* [black] to his mother and *moreno* [brown] to his father" - and is characterized by a "pragmatic relativism" (2003:46, 50). He also traces recent shifts in terminological usage, with younger, dark-skinned people more prepared to identify as *negro* (black), a term that was previously rather pejorative, but now signifies a more self-conscious, and globalized, political identity based on race. Yet in his view all this does not indicate an absence of racism.

A person can still discriminate against someone she or he *perceives* as "black" or "brown" or "indigenous" and if there is some kind of overlap in perceptions among people who racially discriminate and also control access to valued resources, then this will result in ongoing racial inequalities. Statistical evidence for Brazil shows that racial inequalities do exist which are not just the legacy of slavery or an effect of the fact that many dark-skinned people are in the lower classes and tend to remain there through "normal" processes of class stratification (Hasenbalg and Silva 1999). Lovell (1994) shows that average income difference between white and black men is partly due to the impact of educational background on ability to compete in the job market (which may itself be due to patterns of racial discrimination outside that market), but that 24 percent of the difference is due to processes of discrimination within the job market. The figure is 51 percent when comparing white men with black women. Data on Afro-Colombians reinforce this overall picture (Barbary and Urrea 2004; Wade 1993). Data on indigenous people in Latin America show generalized poverty for indigenous people. Up to 50 percent of income differentials between indigenous and non-indigenous workers may be due to discrimination in the Guatemalan, Peruvian and Mexican labor markets (Psacharopoulos and Patrinos 1994:xxi).

The key to race in Latin America, then, is that racism and mixture coexist and interweave (Wade 1993). There is great demographic and social variety across the region, yet some broad generalizations can be made. The coexistence of racism and mixture creates societies in which categories such as "black" and "indigenous" exist and occupy important places in the national imaginary. There are also often subregions associated with blackness or indigenousness - for blackness, the northeast of Brazil, the Pacific coastal region of Colombia and of Ecuador and Peru, and much of the Caribbean coastline of Central America (see Arocha and Maya, this volume); for indigenousness, the Amazon basin, the Andes, and the highlands of Central America (see Varese, Delgado and Meyer, this volume). These categories and subregions are generally low down in national hierarchies of value, although they may enjoy high symbolic status in particular stereotyped domains (e.g. black people may be seen as superior musicians, dancers and sportspeople; indigenous people as ecologically minded and powerful healers). People identified as black or indigenous do suffer racial

discrimination to some degree. Modernity, development and high status are often associated with whiteness or at least mixedness. Race and gender often intersect in ways that give lighter-skinned men access to both lighter- and darker-skinned women, with their unions with the latter often being informal. Darker-skinned men are more constrained by class and color, while women are constrained by moral codes of honor. Darker women may have informal unions, but run the risk of being labeled as loose (Caulfield 2003; Smith 1996).

However, "black" and "indigenous" are often vaguely defined and there is an indecisive, subjective distinction between them and "mixed" people and between the latter and "whites" (hence the problems of enumerating these populations). There is often not a clear socio-racial hierarchy. In Brazil and Colombia, although many black people are poor, the lower classes are mixed and include many whites; people with evident African ancestry are also found in the middle classes. In Peru and Central America, although the elite is fairly white, people with indigenous physical features are not confined to the lower classes. Racial discrimination does occur but it is often unsystematic, individualistic, silent and masked. Racial identities are often not very important to people: for Brazil, Sansone (2003) calls this blackness without ethnicity (i.e. without a collective, self-conscious sense of identity). Racial identities are rarely key factors in electoral politics (although some Andean countries provide recent partial counterexamples here).

Few would contest nowadays that racism as a practice and race as an idea are significant in Latin America, but there is disagreement about how to analyze them. Twine (1998), Hanchard (1994) and Winant (1994) tend to see mixture as a problem for Brazil. The absence of clear racial identities, the existence of hegemonic ideologies which purvey the myth of racial democracy, together with the devaluation of blackness and the actual practice of racism, create a system in which black political consciousness is hampered and people are encouraged to "whiten" (to identify with whiteness and to actually marry whiter partners). For Winant (1994:156), "The public articulation and exploration of *racial dualism* [a clear black-white distinction] would itself be a major advance" in Brazil. Scholars such as Ferreira da Silva (1998), Sansone (2003) and Fry (2000) see such analyses as ethnocentric, using the US history of black political organization as a benchmark to evaluate the black Brazilian experience and judge it lacking (for a similar approach to Cuba, see also de la Fuente 2001:6–9). For them, Brazil has to be judged on its own terms: black consciousness, for example, might look more class oriented than in the US; antiracism might not depend on clear racial identities, but be based on a more inclusive, universalist project. Hanchard (1999:11) responds by emphasizing that the US and Brazil are variants on a common theme and are linked by transnational connections which undo a binary comparison between them. It is not a question of benchmarking one against the other.

In analyses of race in the Andes and Central America, something similar emerges. In this context, race has been seen by scholars as less relevant than ethnicity. Key distinctions between indigenous and mestizo people were analyzed as ethnic because they seemed to involve "cultural" distinctions of language, dress and behavior rather than "racial" distinctions of physical appearance and ancestry. I argue that this conceptual split is inadequate because (1) it denies the clearly racial discourse that surrounded ideas about indigenous peoples, alongside black people, during the colonial period and especially in the 19th and early 20th centuries (D. Poole 1997; Stepan 1991); (2) it assumes that culture (changeable, malleable) and race (permanent, fixed) are necessarily separate, when we know that identification of blackness also depends – and not only in Latin America–on cultural factors such as clothing, speech and class status; and (3) it ignores the discrimination that indigenous-looking people can suffer, for example in urban contexts (Wade 1997:37–39).

More recently, scholars both inside and outside Latin America have been willing to apply the concept of race to the Andes and Meso-America (Callirgos 1993; de la Torre 1996). The ethnocidal wars in Guatemala and Peru, which targeted these countries' indigenous populations, made public difficult issues of racism (Arenas Bianchi, Hale and Palma Murga 1999; Casaús Arzú 1992; Nelson 1999). Famously, in 2005, indigenous activist Rigoberta Menchú brought several politicians to court in the country's first racism case; and in Peru the Truth and Reconciliation Commission pointed to racism in their analysis of counterinsurgency violence in the 1980s war (Comisión de la Verdad 2004). In Mexico, the war in Chiapas and the explicit denunciation of racism by the EZLN (Zapatista National Liberation Army) have also forced issues of race onto the agenda, while Mexico's black population is getting increasing recognition (Castellanos Guerrero 2003; Nash 2001; Vaughn 2005). For Peru, de la Cadena argues that biological notions of race began to disappear from discourse about the Peruvian Andes, but "racialized notions of cultural heritage" were retained (2000:155). De la Cadena contends that the notions of mestizo and mestizaje are themselves hybrid concepts, mixing pre-Enlightenment, colonial notions of limpieza de sangre, genealogy and purity of lineage with Enlightenment notions of scientific racial typologies: "the new scientific

taxonomies continued to evoke language, faith and morality" (2005:268). More than a hybridization between 19th century concepts of biology and culture–which was not unique to Latin America–this was an epistemological mixing of "two regimes of knowledge, faith and science" which enabled "a conceptual politics where the pull to define race tilted towards culture" (2005:268–269).

Weismantel also deploys a culturalized notion of race, arguing that Andean people talk about race as a physical reality but also changeable: a person's race can alter over time. In the Andes, race can be part of the body and yet be changeable because race accumulates in the body over time; it is the embodied product of history:

> in the interactions between bodies and the substances they ingest, the possessions they accumulate, and the tools they use to act on the world, we can really see race being made, and making the society around it. This kind of race is neither genetic nor symbolic, but organic: a constant, physical process of interaction between living things. (Weismantel 2001:266)

Indigenous and white people's bodies accumulate things–both in the body (hard skin, soft skin; gnarled feet, smooth feet), in/on the body (smells) and on the body (clothes)–that mark them as racially distinct. Gose objects that Weismantel "simply assumes that 'race matters' in the Andes" and that she, speaking from an "omnipotent American standpoint," "accentuates the racism in Andean social life and presents it as absolute and unqualified" (Gose 2003:194). As with the debate on Brazil, we find scholars divided over whether North American understandings of race are being imposed onto a Latin American reality. In this case, however, Weismantel (and de la Cadena) are putting forward very Latin American notions of race as naturalized but still malleable culture and it is hard to accuse either of using US notions of race as a benchmark. As in the debate about Brazil, accusations of ethnocentrism, while potentially valid, can gloss over the way Euro-American notions of race both influenced and were fed by Latin American realities (D. Poole 1997).

In my view, Latin America concepts of race are sui generis, but not therefore the polar opposites of things North American or European. The culturalized versions of race that are particularly prominent in Latin America are not unique to the region: race always involves an interweaving between notions of nature and culture (Wade 2002b) and even in the heyday of scientific, biological theories of race, there were very powerful discourses of morality and what we would now call culture (Stoler 1995). The emergence of "cultural racism" is another case in point (see above). But in Latin America, the coexistence of mestizaje and racism gives a particular twist to the natural-cultural construct of race, making Latin American notions of race particularly culturalized and open to be thought and experienced through, say, class, region and gendered sexuality. Streicker (1995), for example, explored ideas of race among working class black people in Cartagena, Colombia. For them, race was not an everyday way of talking about and identifying people. Most people in the neighborhood he studied were varying shades of black and brown; there was a strong notion that everyone was equal and that racism did not loom large. Ideas about race, however, formed a discourse of the moral evaluation of behavior and status. Perceptions of class status, racial identity and sex/gender behavior all evoked each other. Being *negro* meant being of low class status and also being a father/husband or mother/wife who was sexually promiscuous and did not fulfill family obligations. This worked in reverse too, so that to impute sexual looseness to a woman evoked images of blackness and low class status. Race was not prominent, but it worked through other culturalizing-naturalizing perceptions.

Mestizaje, Difference, Multiculturalism, and Globalization

If the coexistence of mestizaje and racism is the key to Latin American concepts of race, then it is also true that mestizaje has many different dynamics within it. It can be the very manifestation of racism when it takes the form of a nation-building ideology that devalues blackness and indigenousness, consigns them to the past and straitjackets them into stereotyped molds. But it can also be a space – always ambiguous and often ambivalent – in which to reaffirm blackness and indigenousness in practical everyday ways. Postcolonial theorists have recently made much of the potentially subversive nature of hybridity, a process of mixture which can be seen as linked to mestizaje and which can create a "third space" that unsettles colonial binaries of power and racial categorization (Bhabha 1994). Some Latin Americanist scholars have been cautious, well aware of the history of mestizaje and its potential to be the regional face of racism (Hale 1999; Wade 2004). Analyzing Guatemala, Hale (2002:524) recognizes the problems of romanticizing mestizaje, but still holds out the possibility that "some notion of 'mestizaje from below' could emerge as an articulating principle" decentering dominant ideas of mestizo society and the "acceptable" face of indigenous identity. In a related way, de la Cadena (2000) argues for a concept of "de-Indianization" which results in the

formation of "indigenous mestizos." These are Andean people who self-identify as mestizos, but also claim indigenous heritage and culture as their own. They are indigenous and mestizo at the same time; being mestizo means having gained respect through hard work and economic success, rather than having sloughed off indigenous culture. But these indigenous mestizos also hand out racist insults to those they classify as simply *indio*. French (2004) also sees mestizaje as a "supple analytical tool" which allows us to conceptualize how people who are part of northeast Brazilian peasant culture and who look as African-descended as neighbors identifying as descendants of black slaves can nevertheless make land claims as indigenous people. These people are mestizos and indigenous at the same time, but through a process of "re-Indianization" (see also Warren 2001). I have also analyzed everyday notions of mestizaje in Colombia as involving the living out of cultural-racial elements through the physical body, with blackness felt to express itself through music, dance and heat, or through affective ties with family members, or through possession by racialized spirits in religious contexts. Being mestizo allows an inclusive space for difference as well as exclusive definitions of sameness (Wade 2005).

This is important when we come to consider recent moves toward official multiculturalism in Latin America, with the emergence of legal and constitutional measures which, in regionally uneven ways, recognize black and indigenous minorities in more explicit fashion and in some cases give them land and other cultural rights (see Arocha and Maya, this volume). In Brazil, there have been heated debates about affirmative action programs for Afro-Brazilians, with quotas for places in some universities and government entities (Htun 2004). This is not the place for an analysis of these changes and the black and indigenous movements involved in them (see Arocha and Maya, and Varese, Delgado and Meyer, this volume; see also Hale 2002; Sieder 2002; Van Cott 2000; Wade 1997). The question is how they have shaped Latin American concepts of race. One view is that such changes represent a radical departure from previous Latin American nationalisms based on mestizaje understood as homogenization. My view is that, when mestizaje is understood to encompass difference, these official multiculturalisms are not quite such a seismic shift. Still, blackness and indigenousness are beginning to occupy places on a different-looking terrain.

This terrain, at once new and familiar, is defined by struggles between local social movements and national states, but also by transnational and globalizing dynamics. First, nation-states are responding to new global notions of democracy as multicultural and neoliberal governance as creating and operating through self-reliant, self-organizing communities (including ethnically defined ones). Second, black and indigenous social movements are linked into transnational concepts of, and movements for, human and indigenous rights, and into globalizing images of blackness, Africa and indigenousness which also circulate in a world commodity market and a global NGO network. Third, the migration of black and indigenous people to North America and Europe (but also to Africa) has created stronger interactions between differing, but not opposing, conceptions of race and identity.

Latin American states were pushed into legal and constitutional reform by black and indigenous protest, but in some cases, they also took up the torch with a certain alacrity. Some have argued that it suited particular state interests to recognize black and indigenous minorities and thus control them more effectively while also promoting new forms of neoliberal governance (Hale 2002; Laurie, Andolina and Radcliffe 2003). In Colombia, for example, it has been argued that the state was interested in combining defense (and commercial exploitation) of biodiverse forest zones with the creation of Afro-Colombian and indigenous community land rights in those areas: the communities would be cast as stewards of the environment, thus tapping into images of a "natural" predisposition toward ecological sensitivity among indigenous and, to a lesser extent, black people (Escobar 1997; Gros 1997; Wade 2002a). By linking these populations to "nature"–in a way not necessarily challenged and even endorsed by ethnic social movements–there may be subtle processes of the renaturalization and essentialization of racial identities (see Hayden, this volume).

Black and indigenous social movements have from an early date been linked into transnational networks. This is not necessarily new: for example, Afro-Brazilian leaders have since the late 19th century been involved in interactions and dialogues about racism, religion and Africa with both North Americans and Africans, in a Latin American version of Gilroy's "Black Atlantic" (Gilroy 1993; Matory 1999; Sansone 2003:ch. 2). Sansone shows how objects of black culture (e.g. dance and religious forms) have been commodified for some time, but that recent globalization and the growth of the black movement has led new objects (notably the black body itself and its fashion accessories) to become more conspicuous and commodified (2003: 76–79). This links with an increasing willingness among some black people to identify explicitly with the political and self-consciously ethnic category *negro*. In Colombia, too, black icons such as Martin Luther King, Nelson Mandela and Bob Marley have served as inspiration for black activists alongside homegrown heroes of slave resistance (Wade 1999).

Indigenous and black organizations frequently have close links to the Church and other international entities that provide them with support and advice. Radcliffe, Laurie and Andolina (2000) found that transnational institutions and actors have influential effects on how indigenous people represent their identity, starting with the fact that defining oneself as indigenous in the first place enhances access to resources and leads people to emphasize indigenous social capital in ways that reify "tradition." However, these transnational networks open up spaces for contestation, in which, for example, indigenous women can challenge dominant ideas of "gender and development." Interestingly, indigenous people have generally had greater success than black people in establishing themselves as distinct cultures, deserving of special rights. Black people in Latin America tend to be seen as culturally closer to the mainstream and it has been harder to carve out a distinctive legal space, based on cultural difference. One strategy for Afro-Latins – which some states have encouraged – has been to make themselves look more like indigenous groups (Hooker 2005; Wade 1997, 2002a).

Indigenous and black people are also involved in important transnational migrations. Kearney (2000) shows how Mixtecs from Oaxaca (southern Mexico) migrate to California and create a cultural space called "Oaxacalifornia" in which Mixtec identity becomes more self-conscious and explicit, creating the basis for organizations which defend Mixtec rights in the US and in Mexico. Various studies trace how migrants who do not see themselves as "black" are redefined as such in the US context. Duany (1998) shows how Dominican migrants resist this classification and try to retain the concept of an intermediate mixed identity, based on being Latino or Hispanic. Ramos–Zayas (2003:ch. 6) also shows how Puerto Rican nationalists in Chicago sometimes use images of Puerto Rican blackness in a critique of US racism and segregation This blackness is presented, however, in a specifically Latin American discourse, as inclusive and based on mestizaje, rather than exclusive and divisively segregated.

In sum, the effect of globalizing ethnic movements on Latin American concepts of race is uncertain. On the one hand, ideas of race may be taking on more North American dimensions (with globalized imagery): definitions of blackness and indigenousness become clearer and perhaps more polarized; and they include the use of commodified images of indigenous Greenness and spiritual healing alongside a collage of transnational black imagery (reggae, rap, "African" motifs, US black hero figures); in some countries, affirmative action programs are implemented which target black and indigenous people.

On the other hand, there is something resilient about Latin American notions of mestizaje and its irreducibility to a set of US-style racial classifications. The resistance of some US based Latinos to black–white racial binaries is a case in point. Also, it is not yet clear that affirmative action programs for Afro-Colombians and Afro-Brazilians – which so far seem to be progressing in the absence of a clear social consensus on who is black–will necessarily lead to US-style racial categories. In Colombia, university places reserved for Afro-Colombians have been allocated in flexible ways that retain typically Latin American contextual definitions of blackness.

It is perhaps the resilience of mestizaje that leads some commentators to see it as a critique of US notions of race, a way to shatter their sharp boundaries and exclusive definitions of identity (Saldaña-Portillo 2001; Wade 2004). I think great caution is needed with this idea – after all, racism and mestizaje coexist in Latin America. But it may be that Latin American notions of race are colonizing North America as much as the other way round. The sheer number of Latinos in the US has been complicating the traditional racial categories of the US for some time now: the category "Hispanic" is not meant to be a racial category for the census (Hispanics can belong to any census racial category), but it tends to act as one when it is routinely deployed alongside other racial categories in reporting data. One of the keys to understanding race in Latin America is to grasp that it has always been defined in opposition to the US – this was the concern of intellectuals such as Freyre and Vasconcelos in the 1920s. In fact, both regions are variants on a theme and have been in a constant process of mutual racial formation. If globalizing US concepts of race and identity are clarifying racial categories for some Latin Americans, it may be that Latin American concepts of race are blurring the clarity of racial definitions for some North Americans – without this implying that racism is therefore ameliorated.

References

Appelbaum, Nancy P., Macpherson, Anne S., and Rosemblatt, Karin A. (eds) (2003) *Race and Nation in Modern Latin America*. Chapel Hill: University of North Carolina Press.

Arenas Bianchi, Clara, Hale, Charles R., and Palma Murga, Gustavo (eds) (1999) *Racismo en Guatemala? Abriendo debate sobre un tema tabù*. Guatemala: Asociación para el Avance de las Ciencias Sociales en Guatemala.

Banton, Michael (1987) *Racial Theories*. Cambridge: Cambridge University Press.

Barbary, Olivier, and Urrea, Fernando (eds) (2004) *Gente negra en Colombia. Dinámicas sociopolíticas en Cali y el Pacífico*. Paris, Cali: IRD, Colciencias, Univalle.

Bhabha, Homi (1994) *The Location of Culture*. London: Routledge.

Bonfil Batalla, Guillermo (ed.) (1993) *Simbiosis de culturas. Los inmigrantes y su cultura en México*. Mexico City: Fondo de Cultura Económica.

Callirgos, Juan Carlos (1993) *El racismo. La cuestión del otro (y de uno)*. Lima: DESCO.

Casaús Arzú, Marta (1992) *Guatemala. Linaje y racismo*. San José, Costa Rica: FLACSO. Castellanos Guerrero, Alicia (ed.) (2003) *Imágenes del racismo en México*. Mexico City: Universidad Autónoma Metropolitana, Plaza y Valdés.

Caulfield, Sueann (2003) Interracial Courtship in the Rio de Janeiro Courts, 1918–1940. In N. P. Appelbaum, A. S. Macpherson, and K. A. Rosemblatt (eds), *Race and Nation in Modern Latin America* (pp. 163–186). Chapel Hill: University of North Carolina Press.

Comisión de la Verdad y Reconciliación (2004) *Informe final. Peru: 1980–2000*. Lima: Univ. Nacl Mayor de San Marcos y Pont. Univ. Católica del Perú.

Cope, R. Douglas (1994) *The Limits of Racial Domination: Plebeian Society in Colonial Mexico City, 1660–1720*. Madison: University of Wisconsin Press.

de la Cadena, Marisol (2000) Indigenous Mestizos: The Politics of Race and Culture in Cuzco, 1919–1991. Durham, NC: Duke University Press.

de la Cadena, Marisol (2005) Are *Mestizo* Hybrids? The Conceptual Politics of Andean Identities. *Journal of Latin American Studies* 37:259–284.

de la Fuente, Alejandro (2001) *A Nation for All: Race, Inequality, and Politics in Twentieth Century Cuba*. Chapel Hill: University of North Carolina Press.

de la Torre Espinosa, Carlos (1996) *El racismo en Ecuador*. Quito: Centro de Acción Popular-CAAP.

Duany, Jorge (1998) Reconstructing Racial Identity: Ethnicity, Color and Class among Dominicans in the United States and Puerto Rico. *Latin American Perspectives* 25(3):147–172.

Escobar, Arturo (1997) Cultural Politics and Biological Diversity: State, Capital and Social Movements in the Pacific Coast of Colombia. In R. G. Fox and O. Starn (eds), *Between Resistance and Revolution: Cultural Politics and Social Protest* (pp. 40–64). New Brunswick, NJ: Rutgers University Press.

Ferreira da Silva, Denise (1998) Facts of Blackness: Brazil Is Not (Quite) the United States . . . and Racial Politics in Brazil? *Social Identities* 4(2):201–234.

French, Jan Hoffman (2004) *Mestizaje* and Law-Making in Indigenous Identity Formation in Northeastern Brazil: "After the Conflict Came History." *American Anthropologist* 106(4): 663–674.

Fry, Peter (2000) Politics, Nationality, and the Meanings of "Race" in Brazil. *Daedalus* 129(2):83–118.

Gilroy, Paul (1993) *The Black Atlantic: Modernity and Double Consciousness*. London: Verso.

Goldberg, David (1993) *Racist Culture: Philosophy and the Politics of Meaning*. Oxford: Blackwell.

Gose, Peter (2003) Review of Cholas and Pishtacos: Stories of Race and Sex in the Andes by Mary Weismantel. *Journal of the Royal Anthropological Institute* 9(1):193–194.

Gould, Jeffrey L. (1998) *To Die in This Way: Nicaraguan Indians and the Myth of the Mestizaje, 1880–1960.* Durham, NC: Duke University Press.

Graham, Richard (ed.) (1990) *The Idea of Race in Latin America, 1870–1940.* Austin: University of Texas Press.

Gros, Christian (1997) Indigenismo y Etnicidad: el Desafío Neoliberal. In M. V. Uribe and E. Restrepo (eds), *Antropología en la modernidad. Identidades, etnicidades y movimientos sociales en Colombia* (pp. 15–60). Bogotá: Instituto Colombiano de Antropología.

Hale, Charles R. (1996) *Mestizaje,* Hybridity and the Cultural Politics of Difference in Post-Revolutionary Central America. *Journal of Latin American Anthropology* 2(1): 34–61.

Hale, Charles R. (1999) Travel Warning: Elite Appropriations of Hybridity, Mestizaje, Antiracism, Equality, and Other Progressive-Sounding Discourses in Highland Guatemala. *Journal of American Folklore* 112(445):297–315.

Hale, Charles R. (2002) Does Multiculturalism Menace? Governance, Cultural Rights and the Politics of Identity in Guatemala. *Journal of Latin American Studies* 34:485–524.

Hanchard, Michael (1994) *Orpheus and Power: The Movimento Negro ofRio de Janeiro and São Paulo, Brazil, 1945–1988.* Princeton: Princeton University Press.

Hanchard, Michael (1999) Introduction. In M. Hanchard (ed.), *Racial Politics in Contemporary Brazil* (pp. 1–29). Durham, NC: Duke University Press.

Harding, Rachel E. (2000) *A Refuge in Thunder: Candomblé and Alternative Spaces of Blackness.* Bloomington: Indiana University Press.

Hasenbalg, Carlos and Silva, Nelson do Valle (1999) Notes on Racial and Political Inequality in Brazil. In M. Hanchard (ed.), *Racial Politics in Contemporary Brazil* (pp. 154–178). Durham, NC: Duke University Press.

Hooker, Juliet (2005) Indigenous Inclusion/Black Exclusion: Race, Ethnicity and Multicultural Citizenship in Contemporary Latin America. *Journal of Latin American Studies* 37(2):285–310.

Htun, Mala (2004) From "Racial Democracy" to Affirmative Action: Changing State Policy on Race in Brazil. *Latin American Research Review* 39(1):60–89.

Katzew, Ilona (2004) *Casta Painting: Images of Race in Eighteenth-Century Mexico.* New Haven: Yale University Press.

Kearney, Michael (2000) Transnational Oaxacan Indigenous Identity: The Case of Mixtecs and Zapotecs. *Identities: Global Studies in Culture and Power* 7(2):173–195.

Knight, Alan (1990) Racism, Revolution and Indigenismo in Mexico, 1910–1940. In R. Graham (ed.), *The Idea of Race in Latin America* (pp. 71–113). Austin: University of Texas Press.

Knox, Robert (1850) *The Races of Men: A Fragment.* London: Henry Renshaw.

Laurie, Nina, Andolina, Robert, and Radcliffe, Sarah (2003) Indigenous Professionalization: Transnational Social Reproduction in the Andes. *Antipode* 35(3):463–491.

Lovell, Peggy (1994) Race, Gender and Development in Brazil. *Latin American Research Review* 29(3):7–35.

MacCormack, Carol and Strathern, Marilyn (eds) (1980) *Nature, Culture and Gender.* Cambridge: Cambridge University Press.

Manrique, Nelson (1993) *Vinieron los Sarracenos. El universo mental de la conquista de América.* Lima: DESCO.

Martínez, María Elena (2004) The Black Blood of New Spain: Limpieza-de-Sangre, Racial Violence, and Gendered Power in Early Colonial Mexico. *William and Mary Quarterly* 61(3):479–520.

Matory, J. Lorand (1999) The English Professors of Brazil: On the Diasporic Roots of the Yorúbá Nation. *Comparative Studies in Society and History* 41(1):72–103.

Mörner, Magnus (1967) *Race Mixture in the History of Latin America.* Boston: Little, Brown.

Nash, June C. (2001) *Mayan Visions: The Quest for Autonomy in an Age of Globalization.* London: Routledge.

Nelson, Diane M. (1999) *A Finger in the Wound: Body Politics in Quincentennial Guatemala.* Berkeley: California University Press.

Poole, Deborah (1997) *Vision, Race and Modernity: A Visual Economy of the Andean Image World.* Princeton: Princeton University Press.

Poole, Stafford (1999) The Politics of Limpieza de Sangre: Juan de Ovando and His Circle in the Reign of Philip II. *Americas* 55(3):359–389.

Psacharopoulos, George, and Patrinos, Harry A. (1994) Executive Summary. In G. Psacharo-poulos and H. A. Patrinos (eds), *Indigenous People and Poverty in Latin America: An Empirical Analysis* (pp. xvii–xxiii). Washington, DC: World Bank.

Radcliffe, Sarah, Laurie, Nina, and Andolina, Robert (2000) Transnationalism, Indigenous People and Development in Ecuador and Bolivia. Research Briefing 6. ESRC Transnational Communities Programme, Oxford. At www.transcomm.ox.ac.uk/briefings.htm.

Ramos-Zayas, Ana Y. (2003) *National Performances: The Politics of Class, Race and Space in Puerto Rican Chicago.* Chicago: University of Chicago Press.

Rénique, Gerardo (2003) Race, Region and Nation: Sonora's Anti-Chinese Racism and Mexico's Postrevolutionary Nationalism, 1920s–1930s. In N. Appelbaum, A. S. Macpherson, and K. A. Rosemblatt (eds), *Race and Nation in Modern Latin America* (pp. 211–236). Chapel Hill: University of North Carolina Press.

Saldaña-Portillo, Josefina (2001) Who's the Indian in Aztlán? Re-writing Mestizaje, Indianism and Chicanismo from the Lacandón. In I. Rodríguez (ed.), *The Latin American Subaltern Studies Reader* (pp. 402–423). Durham, NC: Duke University Press.

Sansone, Livio (2003) *Blackness without Ethnicity: Constructing Race in Brazil.* Houndmills: Palgrave Macmillan.

Sant'Anna, Alayde, and Souza, Jessé (eds) (1997) *Multiculturalismo e racismo. Una comparação Brasil-Estados Unidos.* Brasilia: Paralelo 15.

Sieder, Rachel (ed.) (2002) *Multiculturalism in Latin America: Indigenous Rights, Diversity and Democracy.* Houndmills: Palgrave Macmillan.

Smedley, Audrey (1993) *Race in North America: Origin and Evolution of a Worldview.* Boulder: Westview Press.

Smith, Carol A. (1996) Race/Class/Gender Ideology in Guatemala: Modern and Anti-Modern Forms. In B. Williams (ed.), *Women Out of Place: The Gender of Agency and the Race of Nationality* (pp. 50–78). New York: Routledge.

Stepan, Nancy Leys (1991) *"The Hour of Eugenics": Race, Gender and Nation in Latin America.* Ithaca: Cornell University Press.

Stern, Steve J. (ed.) (1987) *Resistance, Rebellion and Consciousness in the Andean Peasant World, 18th to 20th Centuries.* Madison: University of Wisconsin Press.

Stolcke, Verena (1995) Talking Culture: New Boundaries, New Rhetorics of Exclusion in Europe. *Current Anthropology* 36(1):1–23.

Stoler, Ann Laura (1995) *Race and the Education of Desire: Foucault's "History of Sexuality" and the Colonial Order of Things.* Durham, NC: Duke University Press.

Streicker, Joel (1995) Policing Boundaries: Race, Class, and Gender in Cartagena, Colombia. *American Ethnologist* 22(1):54–74.

Tannenbaum, Frank (1948) *Slave and Citizen: The Negro in the Americas.* New York: Vintage.

Telles, Edward E. (2002) Racial Ambiguity among the Brazilian Population. *Ethnic and Racial Studies* 25(3):415–441.

Twine, France W. (1998) *Racism in a Racial Democracy: The Maintenance of White Supremacy in Brazil.* New Brunswick: Rutgers University Press.

Van Cott, Donna Lee (2000) *The Friendly Liquidation of the Past: The Politics of Diversity in Latin America.* Pittsburgh: University of Pittsburgh Press.

Vasconcelos, José (1997[1925]) *The Cosmic Race.* Bilingual edn, trans. D. T. Jaén. Baltimore: Johns Hopkins University Press.

Vaughn, Bobby (2005) Afro-Mexico: Blacks, Indians, Politics, and the Greater Diaspora. In A. Dzidzienyo and S. Oboler (eds), *Neither Enemies nor Friends: Latinos, Blacks, Afro-Latinos* (pp. 117–136). New York: Palgrave Macmillan.

Wade, Peter (1993) *Blackness and Race Mixture: The Dynamics of Racial Identity in Colombia.* Baltimore: Johns Hopkins University Press.

Wade, Peter (1997) *Race and Ethnicity in Latin America.* London: Pluto Press.

Wade, Peter (1999) Working Culture: Making Cultural Identities in Cali, Colombia. *Current Anthropology* 40(4): 449–471.

Wade, Peter (2002a) The Colombian Pacific in Perspective. *Journal of Latin American Anthropology* 7(2):2–33.

Wade, Peter (2002b) *Race, Nature and Culture: An Anthropological Perspective.* London: Pluto Press.

Wade, Peter (2004) Images of Latin American Mestizaje and the Politics of Comparison. *Bulletin of Latin American Research* 23(1):355–366.

Wade, Peter (2005) Rethinking Mestizaje: Ideology and Lived Experience. *Journal of Latin American Studies* 37:1–19.

Warren, Jonathan W. (2001) *Racial Revolutions: Antiracism and Indian Resurgence in Brazil.* Durham, NC: Duke University Press.

Weismantel, Mary (2001) *Cholas and Pishtacos: Stories of Race and Sex in the Andes.* Chicago: University of Chicago Press.

Wilson, Tamar Diana (2004) East Asian Migrations to Latin America: Introduction. *Latin American Perspectives* 31(3): 3–17.

Winant, Howard (1992) Rethinking Race in Brazil. *Journal of Latin American Studies* 24: 173–192.

Winant, Howard (1994) *Racial Conditions: Politics, Theory, Comparisons.* Minneapolis: University of Minnesota Press.

Gender Identities and Individualism

When filling out a document such as a job application or school registration form you are often asked to provide your name, address, phone number, birth date, and sex or gender. But have you ever been asked to provide your sex *and* your gender? Sex and gender are not the same; they are conceptually distinct. **Sex** refers to physical or physiological differences between males and females, including both primary sex characteristics (the reproductive system) and secondary characteristics such as height and muscularity. **Gender** is a term that refers to social or cultural distinctions associated with being male or female. **Gender identity** is the extent to which one identifies as being either masculine or feminine.

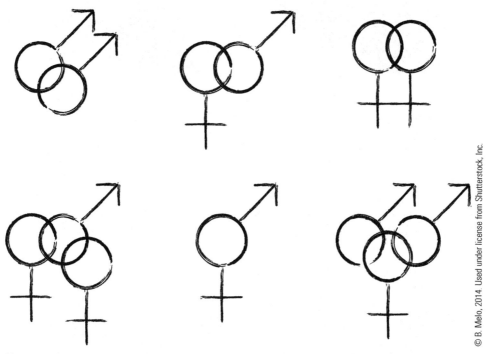

© B. Melo, 2014. Used under license from Shutterstock, Inc.

If you use the symbols assigned to our simplistic binary sexual typologies to arrive at a more realistic representation of individual sexuality, you might come up with something like this.

Since the term *sex* refers to biological or physical distinctions, characteristics of sex will not vary significantly between different human societies. For example, all persons of the female sex, in general, regardless of culture, will eventually menstruate and develop breasts that can lactate.

Characteristics of gender, on the other hand, may vary greatly between different societies. For example, in American culture, it is considered feminine (or a trait of the female gender) to wear a dress or skirt. However, in many Middle Eastern, Asian, and African cultures, dresses or skirts (often referred to assarongs, robes, or gowns) can be considered masculine. The kilt worn by a Scottish male does not make him appear feminine in his culture.

191

The dichotomous view of gender (the notion that one is either male or female) is specific to certain cultures and is not universal. In some cultures and in pre-modern western societies, gender often is viewed as fluid. In the past, some anthropologists used the term *berdache* to refer to individuals who occasionally or permanently dressed and lived as the opposite gender. The practice has been noted among certain Native American tribes. Samoan culture accepts what they refer to as a "third gender." *Fa'afafine*, which translates as "the way of the woman," is a term used to describe individuals who are born biologically male but embody both masculine and feminine traits.

A person's **sexual orientation** is their emotional and sexual attraction to a particular sex (male or female). Sexual orientation is typically divided into four categories: *heterosexuality*, the attraction to individuals of the opposite sex; *homosexuality*, the attraction to individuals of one's own sex; *bisexuality*, the attraction to individuals of either sex; or *asexuality*, no attraction to either sex.

These two shadows are confused about their sexuality. They want to hook up. Does it matter what sign they decide to accept as their identity?

Alfred Kinsey was among the first to conceptualize sexuality as a continuum rather than a strict dichotomy of gay or straight. To classify this continuum of heterosexuality and homosexuality, Kinsey created a six-point rating scale that ranges from exclusively heterosexual to exclusively homosexual. Kinsey and his colleagues felt that sexuality was more complex than the simplistic representation of the heterosexual/homosexual binary. Rather, sexuality, like most aspects of the living world, is a continuum. His research established the foundation for much of the recasting of sexual norms during the last decades of the 20th century.

800,000 people attended the annual Chicago Gay Pride parade June 24, 2012. The annual Helsinki, Finland gay pride parade draws smaller but equally enthusiastic crowds.

The binary of male/female sexuality was a creation of the modern era. We have become our sex, as Foucault famously said.

It is reported that in the workplace discrimination based on sexual orientation is extremely prevalent. Much of this discrimination is based on stereotypes, misinformation, and **homophobia**, an extreme or irrational aversion to homosexuals. Major policies to prevent discrimination based on sexual orientation have not come into effect until the last few years. In 2011, President Obama overturned "don't ask, don't tell," a controversial policy that required homosexuals in the U.S. military to keep their sexuality undisclosed. Between 2004 and 2013, seventeen states and the District of Columbia legalized gay marriage. In 2015, the Supreme Court ruled that the U.S. Constitution guarantees a right for same-sex couples to marry.

Gender identity is an individual's self-conception of being male or female based on his or her association with masculine or feminine gender roles. Individuals who identify with the role that is the opposite of their biological sex are called **transgender**. It is estimated that two to five percent of the U.S. population is transgendered (Transgender Law and Policy Institute, 2007). Transgendered individuals who wish to alter their bodies through medical interventions such as surgery and hormonal therapy—so that their physical being is better aligned with gender identity—are called **transsexuals**.

The term **gender role** refers to society's concept of how men and women are expected to act and how they should behave. These roles are based on norms created by a specific society. In American culture, masculine roles are stereotypically associated with strength, aggression, and dominance, while feminine roles are associated with passivity, nurturing, and subordination. Role learning starts with socialization at birth. Even after all of our social emphasis on gender equality, our society is quick to outfit male infants in blue and girls in pink.

A WIFE OF NOBLE CHARACTER IS HER HUSBAND'S CROWN, BUT A DISGRACEFUL WIFE IS LIKE DECAY IN HIS BONES

PROVERBS 12:4

Religion often sets the standards for gender roles in many societies.

Cross-cultural studies reveal that children are aware of gender roles by age two or three. At four or five, most children are firmly entrenched in culturally appropriate gender roles. Children acquire these roles through the process of socialization. Gender socialization occurs through four major agents of socialization: family, education, peer groups, and mass media. Each agent reinforces gender roles by creating and maintaining normative expectations for gender-specific behavior. Exposure also occurs through secondary agents such as religion and the workplace. Repeated exposure to these agents over time leads men and women into a false sense that they are acting naturally rather than following a socially constructed role.

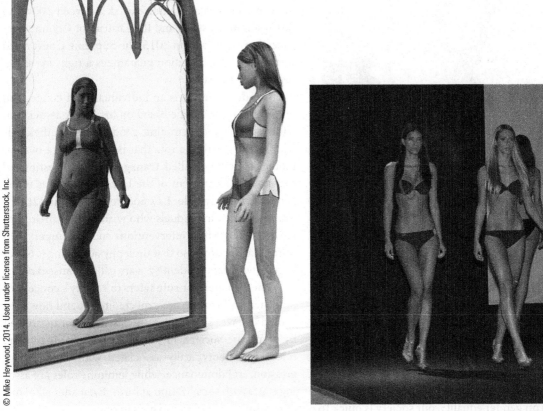

Young women are particularly vulnerable to eating disorders associated with negative body image. Are men also susceptible to such pressures?

Transgender People, Gender Panics, and the Maintenance of the Sex/Gender/ Sexuality System

Laurel Westbrook
Grand Valley State University, USA

Kristen Schilt
University of Chicago, USA

This article explores "determining gender," the umbrella term for social practices of placing others in gender categories. We draw on three case studies showcasing moments of conflict over who counts as a man and who counts as a woman: public debates over the expansion of transgender employment rights, policies determining eligibility of transgender people for competitive sports, and proposals to remove the genital surgery requirement for a change of sex marker on birth certificates. We show that criteria for determining gender differ across social spaces. Gender-integrated spaces are more likely to use identity-based criteria, while gender-segregated spaces, like the sexual spaces we have previously examined (Schilt and Westbrook 2009), are more likely to use biology-based criteria. In addition, because of beliefs that women are inherently vulnerable and men are dangerous, "men's" and "women's" spaces are not policed equally—making access to women's spaces central to debates over transgender rights.

Keywords: gender; sexuality; transgender; doing gender; sports; heteronormativity

In 1989, Christie Lee Cavazos married Jonathon Littleton, a marriage that lasted until Jonathon's untimely death in 1996. Christie filed a medical malpractice suit against the Texas doctor she alleged had misdiagnosed her husband. What might have been an open-and-shut case, however, was complicated by her biography: In the 1970s she had undergone what was then termed a surgical "sex change" operation. Before considering her case, the court first examined the validity of her marriage as a transgender woman to a cis-gender man. At the center of this case was the determination of her gender. Christie had undergone genital surgery, legally amended all of her government documents to categorize her as "female," had a legal marriage, lived as a woman for 20 years, and had medical experts who testified that she was, physically and psychologically, a woman. Yet, the court ruled that she was, and would always be, chromosomally male and, therefore, could not file a malpractice suit as a spouse. Musing about the nature of gender in his ruling, Chief Justice Hardberger wrote, "There are some things you cannot will into being. They just are" (*Littleton v. Prange* 1999).

The Littleton case illustrates two competing cultural ideologies about how a person's gender[1] is to be authenticated by other people. The judge's ruling that gender is an unchangeable, innate fact illustrates what we term a "biology-based determination of gender." In contrast, the validation of Littleton's identity as a woman by others highlights what we term an "identity-based determination of gender." Such a premise does not mean seeing gender identity as fluid, or as an "anything goes" proposition. Rather, under an identity-based gender ideology, people can be recognized as a member of the gender category with which they identify if their identity claim is accepted as legitimate by other people determining their gender—in the Littleton case, her husband, friends, and medical experts.

AUTHORS' NOTE: As with our previous article, all work was shared equally between the two authors. We are extremely grateful to Joya Misra and the anonymous reviewers for the detailed and thoughtful feedback that they provided. Correspondence concerning this article should be addressed to Laurel Westbrook, Grand Valley State University, 1 N. Campus Dr, Allendale, MI 49401, USA; e-mail: westbrol@gvsu.edu.

Laurel Westbrook, Kristen Schilt, *Gender & Society*, Vol. 28, No. 1, February 2014, pp 32-57, Copyright © 2014 by Sociologists for Women in Society. Reprinted by permission of SAGE Publications.

We term this social process of authenticating another person's gender identity "determining gender." In face-to-face interactions, determining gender is the response to doing gender. When people do gender in interactions, they present information about their gender. Others then interpret this information, placing them in gender categories and determining their gender. Yet, the process of gender determination does not always rely on visual and behavioral cues. Expanding upon interactional theories of gender attribution (Kessler and McKenna 1978; West and Zimmerman 1987), we examine gender determination criteria in policy and court cases, where a great deal of biographical and bodily knowledge is known about the person whose gender is in question, as well as how gender is determined in imagined interactions—namely, cis-people's imagined interactions with trans-people, where the knowledge about the person's body and identity are hypothetical. We use "determining gender" as an umbrella term for these diverse practices of placing a person in a gender category. Additionally, we explore the consequences of gender determination, an exploration that goes beyond "How is gender socially attributed?" to an analysis of "How does gender attribution challenge or maintain the sex/gender/sexuality system?"

We examine the criteria for gender determination in moments of ideological collision. As we have previously argued (Schilt and Westbrook 2009; Westbrook 2009), many people use genitalia (biological criteria) to determine another person's gender in (hetero)sexual[2] and sexualized interactions. Yet, since the advent of the "liberal moment" (Meyerowitz 2002), a cultural turn in the 1960s toward values of autonomy and equality, there has been more acceptance of a person's gender self-identity in spaces defined as nonsexual,[3] such as many workplaces (Schilt 2010). When questions of access to gender-segregated locations arise, however, identity-based and biology-based determinations clash. We center our analysis on three such moments: (1) federal and state proposals made between 2009 and 2011 to prohibit discrimination based on gender identity and expression in the arena of employment, housing, and public accommodations (often called "transgender rights bills"); (2) a 2006 proposed policy in New York City to remove the genital surgery requirement for a change of sex marker on birth certificates; and (3) controversies over trans-people participating in competitive sports.

Our cases address different social milieu: sports, employment, and government documents. Yet, each case is, at its core, about upholding the logic of gender segregation. In these ideological collisions, social actors struggle with where actual and imagined trans-people fit in gender-segregated spaces, such as public restrooms. These struggles provoke what we term "gender panics," situations where people react to disruptions to biology-based

gender ideology by frantically reasserting the naturalness of a male–female binary. When successful, this labor, which we term "gender naturalization work," quells the panics. In our cases, enacting policies requiring surgical and hormonal criteria for admission into gender-segregated spaces ends the panic. As in sexual and sexualized interactions, genitals determine gender in gender-segregated spaces, as it is often fears of unwanted (hetero) sexuality that motivates gender identity policing.

These cases demonstrate that criteria for determining gender vary across social situations. In gender-integrated public settings, such as the workplace, identity-based criteria can suffice to determine a person's gender. However, in interactional situations that derive their form and logic from gender oppositeness, such as heterosexual acts and gender-segregated sports competitions, social actors tend to enforce more rigid, biology-based criteria. Yet, gender-segregated spaces are not evenly policed, as the criteria for access are heavily interrogated only for women's spaces. Exploring the implications of this difference, we posit that bodies (mainly the presence or absence of the penis) matter for determining gender in women's spaces because of cultural ideologies of women as inherently vulnerable and in need of protection (Hollander 2001) that reproduce gender inequality under the guise of protecting women. We argue that, in the liberal moment of gender, access to gender-segregated spaces is not determined by unchangeable measures such as chromosomes but, instead, by genitals—a move that suggests a greater acceptance of an identity-based determination of gender. However, as we show, by using changeable bodily aspects to determine gender, the basic premises of the "sex/gender/sexuality system" (Seidman 1995) are maintained, as the system repatriates those whose existence potentially calls it into question, thereby naturalizing gender difference and gender inequality.

Conceptual Framework

Sociologists of gender emphasize the social, rather than biological, processes that produce a person's gender. Focused on the interactional level, such theories illustrate how people sort each other into the category of "male" or "female" in social situations on the basis of visual information cues (such as facial hair) and implicit rules for assigning characteristics to particular genders (women wear skirts; men do not). Such visual cues act as proxies for biological criteria invisible in many interactions. This categorization process, termed "gender attribution" (Kessler and McKenna 1978, 2) or "sex categorization" (West and Zimmerman 1987, 127), is theorized as an inescapable but typically unremarkable hallmark of everyday social interactions—except in instances of ambiguity, which can create an interactional breakdown, generating anxiety, concern, and even anger (Schilt 2010; West and Zimmerman 1987).

This theory is a useful counterpoint to essentialism. Yet, the focus on face-to-face interactions can be analytically limiting. Kessler and McKenna note, "The only physical characteristics that can play a role in gender attribution in everyday life are those that are visible" (Kessler and McKenna 1978, 76). West and Zimmerman, too, see characteristics that are visible in interaction as paramount to sex categorization, arguing, "Neither initial sex assignment (pronouncement at birth as female or male) nor the actual existence of essential criteria for that assignment (possession of a clitoris and vagina or penis and testicles) has much—if anything—to do with the identification of sex category in everyday life" (West and Zimmerman 1987, 132). While such propositions may hold in many nonsexual interactions, genitals play a much more key role in gender determination in sexual and sexualized interactions (Schilt and Westbrook 2009). In addition, as the Littleton case demonstrates, invisible characteristics, such as chromosomes, can override visual cues as the appropriate criteria for determining gender when legal rights are at stake.

We seek to expand these theories beyond face-to-face interactions by proposing a broader conceptualization, offering "determining gender" as an umbrella term for the different subprocesses of attributing or, in some cases, officially deciding another person's gender. Gender determination does occur at the level of *everyday interaction*, a process already well documented in the literature. Both cis- and transwomen, for instance, may find their biological claim to use a public women's restroom challenged by other women if they do not present the expected visual cues warranted for access (Cavanagh 2010), while both groups may have their gender self-identity affirmed in gender-integrated interactions. Gender determination also occurs at the level of *legal cases* and *policy decisions*, where social actors with organizational power devise criteria for who counts as a man or a woman (and therefore who gains or is denied access to gender-specific rights and social settings) (Meadow 2010). In addition, gender determinations occur at the level of the *imaginary*. Illustrating this point, as trans-inclusive policies and laws are discussed in the media, opponents and supporters often draw on hypothetical interactions with trans-people in gender-segregated spaces, such as bathrooms. In these imagined interactions, hypothetical knowledge of the person's genitals or their self-identity, rather than visible gender cues, is used to determine their gender.

When social actors officially or unofficially determine another person's gender, accepted criteria differ across contexts. Face-to-face interactions rely mostly on implicit, culturally agreed on criteria. Imagined interactions and legal or policy decisions, in contrast, often demand more explicit, officially defined criteria. Such a focus on developing explicit criteria for determining gender has grown alongside new surgical possibilities for gender transitions (Meyerowitz 2002). To receive legal and medical gender validation, trans-people have had to follow particular protocols, such as genital reconstructive surgery, that symbolically repatriate them from one side of the gender binary to the other. These criteria, which reflect dominant understandings of sex/gender/ sexuality, allowed liberal values of self-determination to co-exist with beliefs about the innateness of the gender binary (Meyerowitz 2002).

This co-existence faced greater challenges in the 1990s when the hegemony of the "stealth model" of transitioning (Schilt 2010) began to dissipate, and transsexual, intersex, and transgender groups organized in an effort to gain greater cultural recognition and civil rights (Stryker 2008). With this push came wider coverage of trans-people in the media, including debates about where transmen and transwomen fit in institutions, such as legal marriage, and in public gender-segregated spaces, such as bathrooms, prisons, and sports competitions. Policy and lawmakers began to grapple with how to balance trans-inclusivity in a social system predicated on clear, fixed distinctions between men and women, and how to address some cis-gender concerns that the cultural validation of trans-people was a direct challenge to a biologically-determined and/or God-given gender binary.

Cultural beliefs about the sanctity of gender binarism naturalize a sex/gender/sexuality system in which heterosexuality is positioned as the only natural and desirable sexual form. Showing the interrelatedness of ideas about (hetero)sexuality and gender difference, men and women's assumed psychological and embodied distinctions are widely held to be complementary and to require particular relationships with one another (Connell 1995). In nonsexual interactions, in contrast, men and women sometimes are physically segregated on the basis of those same assumed differences in their bodies, capabilities, and interests (Fausto-Sterling 2000; Goffman 1977; Lorber 1993), as well as widely shared beliefs about what activities are normal and appropriate for each gender. While men and women freely interact in many social settings, such as the workplace, the creation of "men's space" and "women's space" "ensure[s] that subcultural differences can be reaffirmed and reestablished in the face of contact between the sexes" (Goffman 1977, 314). In these spaces, gender differences are highlighted, though the same differences are minimized in other settings.

Media coverage of transgender people in the late 2000s provides a useful case study for how gender is determined in various social spaces, what larger cultural beliefs motivate deployment of biology-based and identity-based criteria, and how such criteria are forged in moments of gender ideology collision. We develop the concept of gender determination beyond face-to-face interactions through an analysis of policy and law debates and imagined interactions, situations that often display a call for explicit criteria for deciding who counts as a man or as a woman. At stake in such determinations are the criteria by which trans-people's gender identities are recognized and their rights defined and protected.

Methods

Our data come from a textual analysis of newspaper coverage gathered from LexisNexis. Such a focus is warranted, as the media tend to both reflect and shape prevailing understandings (Gamson et al. 1992; Macdonald 2003). Investigating beliefs about an issue presented in the news media allows researchers to map out the existing dominant viewpoints within the marketplace of ideas, as news is a commodity for attracting audiences who can then be sold to advertisers (Gamson et al. 1992), and, as such, it has to make cultural sense to its audience (Best 2008). Mainstream journalists write stories that reflect commonsense understandings held by (college educated, middle-class, usually white and heterosexual) journalists and their similarly socially situated audience. While there is no single understanding of gender in our society, the dominant views are visible in the mainstream news.

Media scholars have demonstrated that the media do not only represent reality, they also participate in constructing it (Berns 2004; Gamson et al. 1992; Jansen 2002; Macdonald 2003). The mainstream news media do this by providing audiences with narratives, frames, and belief systems that shape interpretations of the world as well as actions within it. While media do not determine the audience viewpoint (Gamson et al. 1992), they greatly influence it, particularly for people with little pre-existing knowledge of an issue (Berns 2004). Examining news coverage allows us to see what ideas might be disseminated to readers who had never before thought about transgender people changing their birth certificates, competing in sports, or seeking protection from employment discrimination.

To explore the criteria for determining gender in nonsexual contexts, we sought out instances in which biology-based and identity-based gender ideologies collided. As the visibility of transgender lives increased broadly in the 2000s, we centered our search in that decade. We looked for moments where who counts as a man or a woman was openly discussed, thus making the process of determining gender more visible. We identified five possible moments of ideological collision surrounding trans-people: sports inclusion, prison housing, inclusion of transgender children in schools, employment rights, and altering of government documents. All of these cases provided instances of cis-people grappling with how trans-people "fit" into previously unquestioned systems and locations. We chose not to examine schools or prisons because we wanted, respectively, all cases to have a comparative focus on adults and to not involve penal settings. Our three remaining cases generated substantial public debate and represented, on our initial selection, different issues: employment nondiscrimination laws, birth certificate alteration policies, and sports participation. We did not focus solely on cases of gender-segregated spaces; however, it is these locales that emerged as salient points of focus.

Birth certificate laws usually get amended with little fanfare. By contrast, a New York City proposal allowing people to change sex markers on their birth certificates without requiring genital surgery generated extensive media coverage. We gathered all the available stories that mentioned "New York" and "birth certificate" and included coverage of the proposed change in policy during 2006–2007, the time period when the amendment was proposed, discussed, and abandoned (a total of 42 articles).

Transgender employment nondiscrimination laws have been debated since the 1990s. Because we were interested in analyzing current criteria for determining gender, we limited our focus to a two-year period (January 1, 2009, to December 31, 2010). We searched for articles that mentioned "transgender" and "nondiscrimination" and were about trans-rights legislation. After a preliminary analysis of the articles, we also searched "bathroom bills," an often applied moniker. We compiled all news stories on the three bills proposed during this time: a federal bill and state-level bills in New Hampshire and Massachusetts (a total of 57 articles).

Since scholars have extensively analyzed most of the major controversies over trans-people in sports, we employ this literature in our analysis. Because this scholarship focuses almost exclusively on transwomen, we supplemented it with media coverage of two cases about transmen from 2009 to 2011: Kye Allums, a transman who played women's basketball, and "Will," a transman who played Australian men's football (a combined total of 92 articles).

We thematically coded each of the 191 articles for beliefs about gender, with a focus on gender determination criteria (such as chromosomes, genitals, or self-identity), and the types of spaces that generated panic (gender-integrated or gender-segregated). We each coded articles from all three of the cases, ensuring intercoder reliability through extensive discussions about themes. Through this preliminary analysis, we recognized the importance of gender-segregated social spaces to each of our three cases. Upon this analytic shift, we further coded the rationales offered in these moments of gender panic for blocking trans-people's access to gender-segregated spaces (such as safety, privacy, and fairness), the final criteria adopted for determining gender (biology-based, identity-based, none), and the gender of the trans-people at the center of these panics. This second wave of analysis revealed the greater policing of transwomen's access to women-only spaces, and the greater ability of biology-based criteria, rather than identity-based criteria, to quell gender panics.

Findings

Messages in news stories are rarely homogeneous (Gamson et al. 1992). To avoid accusations of biased coverage, journalists typically try to provide at least two sides to a story (Best 2008) that typically represent dominant understandings of a particular topic. In our cases, reporters regularly presented the perspectives of people who supported identity-based determination of gender as well as the views of people who positioned biological criteria as essential for determining gender. These inclusions suggest that, in the late 2000s, the identity-based model and the biology-based model represent the two most dominant and competing understandings of gender. An examination of these ideologies provides a deeper understanding of the sex/gender/sexuality system in the liberal moment of gender, the criteria for determining gender, and how gender determination (re)produces inequality.

Ideology Collision, Gender Panics, and Gender Naturalization Work

Modern athletic competition, like all gender-segregated spaces, rests on and reproduces an idea of two opposite genders (Lorber 1993). Because of its influence on other athletic organizations, we focus here on policies enacted by the International Olympic Committee (IOC) that determine under what circumstances and in what categories transgender and intersex athletes can compete. In the modern Olympics, almost all events are gender-segregated (Tucker and Collins 2009). To maintain this segregation, IOC officials have devised policies on coping with athletes who do not fit easily into this binary.

This question of where to place transgender athletes first gained national attention in 1977, when the New York Supreme Court ruled that Dr. Renee Richards, a postoperative transsexual woman, could participate in the U.S. Women's Open Tennis Tournament because her testes had been removed and her body was physically "weakened" by the resulting loss of testosterone (Birrell and Cole 1990; Shy 2007). Following similar logic, in 2003 the IOC adopted the Stockholm Consensus, which allows trans-athletes to compete as the gender they identify as if they have undergone bodily modifications that "minimize gender related advantages" (Ljungqvist and Genel 2005). According to the IOC Medical Commission (2003), the criteria for appropriate transgender bodies are:

> Surgical anatomical changes have been completed, including external genitalia changes and gonadectomy.
>
> Legal recognition of their assigned sex has been conferred by the appropriate official authorities.
>
> Hormonal therapy appropriate for the assigned sex has been administered in a verifiable manner and for a sufficient length of time to minimize gender-related advantages in sport competitions.

In June 2012, the IOC added an additional set of criteria, stating that athletes competing as women cannot have a testosterone level "within the male range" unless it "does not confer a competitive advantage because it is non-functional" (IOC Medical and Scientific Department 2012), thus minimizing what is viewed as an unfair hormonal advantage. These explicit criteria allow the IOC to incorporate trans and intersex athletes, and thus to validate the liberal moment of gender, without challenging the premise that modern competitive athletics rests on: the presumption that there are two genders and all athletes must be put into one of those two categories for competition.

These biology-based criteria quieted a slow-burning gender panic that resurfaced with each new case of a trans or intersex athlete (for discussion of intersex athletes, see Buzuvis 2010; Dreger 2010; Fausto-Sterling 2000; Nyong'o 2010). These cases raised questions about whether or not it is fair for cis- and trans-people to compete against one another (Cavanagh and Sykes 2006). The answer hinged on which gender ideology is given primacy (i.e., fair to whom?). While transwomen might self-identify as women, people who subscribed to biology-based ideologies of gender view these athletes as males who carry a size and strength advantage over females. The official goal of the IOC policies is to be fair to all athletes, which means that trans-athletes could compete as the gender with which they identify, but only if they met the aforementioned criteria. With such explicit criteria, cis-gender people could have confidence that only transwomen who were as "weak" as cis-women were able to compete, a move that diffused gender panic and upheld the logic of gender segregation in the arena of sports.

In the New York birth certificate case, a policy proposal intended to improve the lives of transgender people set off a rapid gender panic. Since many trans-people do not have genital surgery, they are often unable to have a sex marker that reflects their self-identity and gender presentation on their official documents (Currah and Moore 2009). In 2006, the City of New York proposed legislation that validated identity-based determination of gender by removing the genital surgical requirement for a change of sex marker on the birth certificate if applicants were over 18 years of age, had lived as their desired gender for at least two years, and had documentation from medical and mental health professionals stating that their transitions were intended to be permanent. Under this amendment, trans-people were still regulated by the medical institution but their genital configurations would not determine their gender. The New York City Board of Health worked closely with other officials and trans-rights advocates in writing the new policy, and politicians and transgender activists lauded the amendment, which was, by all accounts, expected to pass (Caruso 2006b; Cave 2006a).

Journalists initially presented the amendment in positive terms (e.g., Caruso 2006a; Colangelo 2006; Finn 2006). However, the proposed policy resulted in an intensely negative public reaction. The Board of Health was inundated with calls and emails from people asking how this policy change would affect access to gender-segregated spaces, such as restrooms, hospital rooms, and prison blocks (Currah and Moore 2009). To quell the panic, the Board of Health withdrew the proposal and quickly amended it to maintain emphasis on genitals as the criteria for determining gender. Transgender people in New York could change their sex marker, but like the requirement to compete in the Olympics, they would have to provide proof of genital surgery. In this way, the Board of Health attempted to balance biology-based and identity-based gender models that had come into collision, doing the gender naturalization work of symbolically restoring the primacy of bodies (here, genitals) for determining gender while still validating the possibility for gender transitions.

The "transgender rights" bills we analyzed also resulted in gender panics by embracing identity-based determination of gender. At both the federal and state level,

these bills typically offer protections for "gender identity and gender expression" or "transgender expression" in the realms of employment, housing, and public accommodations. In an attempt to make such protections widely inclusive, there is no definition of "expressions" or explicit bodily criteria for trans-people. The resulting gender panics center on this lack of definitional criteria. In response to the proposed bill in New Hampshire, some opponents worried that the bill "did not adequately define transgender individuals" (*The Lowell Sun* 2009). A similar argument was raised about the Massachusetts bill, with concerned citizens worrying that "transgender identity and expression" was too vague (Letter to the Editor 2009a) and created "dangerous ambiguity" over who was legally transgender (Prunier 2009) and therefore had access to men's or women's bathrooms. Highlighting this concern about bathroom access, one opponent in Massachusetts noted, "This bill opens the barn door to everybody. There is no way to know who of the opposite sex is using the [bathroom] facility for the right purposes" (Ring 2009). In these cases, what appears to critics as too much validation of identity-based determination of gender sets off panic, panic that is quelled if the bills do not pass into law. When the bills do pass, opponents continue to raise concerns about the potential for danger to women and children in public restrooms, a point we return to in the following sections.

By enforcing explicit bodily criteria for determining gender, the IOC and New York City policies shore up the fissures created in the strict two-category model of gender by the visibility of trans-people while also allowing for some degree of identity-based determination of gender. Similar to judicial rulings permitting name and sex marker changes on government documents (Meyerowitz 2002), policies about birth certificates and athletes work to balance liberal values of autonomy with the belief that there are two genders and that all people (trans or cis) can be put into one category or the other. A lack of bodily criteria, in contrast, appears as a threat to the gender binary. An editorial opposing federal protections for trans-people highlights this fear clearly: "The Left seeks to obliterate the distinction between men and women. This distinction is considered to be a social construct.... For those of us who believe that the male-female distinction is vital to civilization, the Left's attempt to erase this distinction is worth fighting against" (Prager 2010). Similarly, Shannon McGinley, of the conservative Cornerstone Policy Research group, worried that the goal of transgender rights bills was "to create a genderless society" (Distaso 2009). These concerns illustrate our concept of "gender panic," as public debate centers on the necessity of culturally defending a rigid male–female binary that is simultaneously framed as stable and innate. These concerns further underscore the extensive naturalization work that goes into legitimating the current sex/gender/sexuality system. Yet, this work did not evenly center on gender-segregated spaces, or on all biological characteristics that could be used as criteria for determining gender. Rather, opposition gathered around "people with penises" in spaces designated as women-only.

Genitals = Gender: Determining Gender in Women-Only Spaces

In our three cases, concerned citizens and journalists posed many questions about what genitals would be allowed in which gender-segregated spaces. This overwhelming focus on genitalia as the determinant of gender is interesting when considered against other possible criteria. Within biology-based gender ideology, gender is determined at birth by doctors on the visible recognition of genitalia. However, such gender categorization is assumed by many to be the result of other, less visible, biological forces, namely, chromosomes and hormones. While genitalia and hormones can be modified, chromosomes are static—meaning, on some level, XY and XX could be the best criteria for maintaining a binary gender system. Within the transgender rights case, opponents to such bills occasionally drew on chromosomes to further their case for why such bills would be problematic. As one man wrote to a newspaper in Michigan: "Your DNA is proof of your genetic code and determines race [and] sex.... There is also one fact that transgender individuals cannot deny: your DNA proves if you are a man or a woman. It does not matter what changes you have made to your sexual organs" (Letter to the Editor 2009b). Yet, such responses comprise a very small part of the discourse in our cases.

That less weight is given to chromosomes in these cases of gender determination is interesting. In everyday interactions, chromosomes are poor criteria for gender attribution, because they are not visible (Kessler and McKenna 1978). Athletes can be tested for chromosomal makeup. Yet, the IOC did not include chromosomes as part of the criteria for competition, as such a requirement would bar trans-athletes from competition. Similarly, our other cases do not use chromosomes as gender determination criteria, because such rigid genetic criteria would effectively invalidate the possibility of gender transitions. Where we saw a call for chromosomal criteria was in cis-people's imagined interactions with trans-people, scenarios that sought to delegitimize calls for identity-based determination of gender. That chromosomes did not figure widely in policy decisions, in contrast, suggests that identity-based gender ideologies have gained some degree of cultural legitimacy. To balance both ideologies,

institutions cannot use unchangeable criteria, such as chromosomes, to determine a person's gender.

Genitalia are the primary determiner of gender in all of our cases. Starting with the sports case, which has the most clearly defined criteria for determining gender, the IOC permits transwomen (who are assumed to have XY chromosomes) to compete as women as long as they undergo the removal of the testes and the penis.[4] While testes are a source of testosterone, which is a central concern in sports competition,[5] the IOC does not state why transwomen athletes must undergo a penectomy to compete as women, since penises themselves do not provide advantages in sports. Such a requirement may be partially due to deep cultural beliefs that a person with a penis cannot be a woman (Kessler and McKenna 1978), and so they cannot compete with women in athletics. Moreover, this requirement may be a result of a widely held belief that people with penises present a danger to women, a question we take up later in this article.

This emphasis on determining gender through hormone levels and genitalia is applied only to athletes attempting to compete as women. If an athlete competing as a woman has her gender called into question (usually for performing "too well" for a woman), her hormone levels are tested for "irregularities." In contrast, people who want to compete as men (cis or trans) are allowed to inject testosterone if their levels are seen as lower than "those naturally occurring in eugonadal men" (Gooren and Bunck 2004, 151). Thus, in this sex/gender/sexuality system, testosterone is a right of people claiming the category of "men." Further, while no athlete with a penis can compete as a woman, athletes are not required to have a penis to compete as men. Highlighting this point, "Will," an Australian transman who played football on a men's team, was required to undergo a hysterectomy in order to change his sex marker, but he was not required to have phalloplasty (Stark 2009). Moreover, his use of testosterone was not seen as an unfair advantage because his levels did not exceed those of an average cis-gender man.

The heightened attention to the presence or absence of a penis in spaces marked as "women only" was reflected in all of our cases. In news stories about the New York City birth certificate policy and the transgender rights bills, opponents frequently hinged their concerns on "male anatomies" (Cave 2006b) or "male genitalia" (Kwok 2006) in women's spaces. A common imagined interaction that generated gender panic was trans-women with "male anatomies" being housed with female prisoners (Cave 2006b; Staff 2006; Weiss 2006; Yoshino 2006), or transwomen "who still have male genitalia" using women's bathrooms (Kwok 2006; Yoshino 2006). While several articles included interviews with transmen activists who emphasized how hard it would be for them as people with facial hair to be forced to use a women's restroom on the basis of the sex marker on their birth certificates, only one opponent cited in the same articles used the example of transmen in the bathroom rather than transwoman.[6] Thus, biology-based gender ideologies were more likely to be deployed when debating transgender access to women's spaces. Those debates suggest that it is penises rather than other potential biological criteria that are the primary determiner of gender because male anatomies are framed as sexual threats toward women in gender-segregated spaces.

Separate and Unequal: Reproducing Gender Inequality in Gender-Segregated Spaces

Women-only spaces generate the most concern in these moments of gender ideology collision. In the resulting gender panics, ideas about "fairness" and "safety" work to naturalize gender difference and to maintain unequal gender relations. In these moments of ideological collision, two persistent ideologies about womanhood are deployed to counter identity-based determination of gender: Women are weaker than men, and, as a result, women are always at (hetero)sexual risk. This construction produces "woman" as a "vulnerable subjecthood" (Westbrook 2008), an idea that what it is to be part of the category of woman is to be always in danger and defenseless.[7] Conversely, men, or more specifically, penises, are imagined as sources of constant threat to women and children, an idea that reinforces a construction of heterosexual male desire as natural and uncontrollable. Women-only spaces, then, can be framed as androphobic and, as a result, heterophobic, due to the assumed inability of women to protect themselves from men combined with the assumption that all men are potential rapists. These ideas carry enough cultural power to temper institutional validation of identity-based determination of gender. What people are attempting to protect in these moments of ideological collision, we suggest, is not just women, but also the binary logic that gender-segregated spaces are predicated on and (re)produce.

Within the sports case, the IOC focused on the issue of fairness when determining when a transwoman can compete against cis-women. Attempting to maintain both the values of identity-based determination and the logic of gender difference that justifies gender-segregated athletic competitions, sports officials put transwomen athletes into a peculiar situation: In order to gain access to the chance to compete in tests of strength and endurance, they must first prove their weakness (Buzuvis 2010; Shy 2007). This equation of women with weakness also accounts for the regulation of women's, but not men's, sports: If women are inherently weak, they must be protected from competing with stronger bodies (e.g., men). Cis-men, in contrast, should not need such protection from people with XX chromosomes.

Gender panics around the issue of trans-athletes also focus on the question of safety. The United Kingdom's 2004 Gender Recognition Act, a law intended to grant more rights to transgender people, includes a provision that prohibits trans-athletes' competition in cases that endanger the "safety of competitors" (Cavanagh and Sykes 2006). Discussion of safety in this case revolved around regulating access to contact sports. Yet, during debate around this act, another meaning of safety surfaced. Lord Moynihan is reported as saying that "many people will be greatly concerned at the idea of themselves or their children being forced to share a changing room with a transsexual person" (Mcardle 2008, 46). The allusion is that transgender people present a sexual danger to vulnerable others, conflating transgenderism and sexual deviance.

This portrayal of transgender people as potential sexual dangers in gender-segregated spaces appeared repeatedly in our other two cases. People advocating biology-based determination of gender worried about protecting women and children, another group generally vested with vulnerable subjecthood, from sexual risk from people with penises who would, with the new policies, be legally able to enter women-only spaces. When opponents to the New York City birth certificate policy worried about "male anatomies" in women's prisons (Cave 2006b), they were hinting at the possibility that those "male anatomies" would sexually assault the women with whom they shared prison space. While most articles about the New York City proposal merely suggested this possibility, some were more explicit. An opinion piece argued that one of the dangers of the proposed law was "personal safety: Many communal spaces, like prison cells and public bathrooms, are segregated by sex to protect women, who are generally physically weaker than men, from assault or rape" (Yoshino 2006). Explaining his opposition to the transgender rights bill, New Hampshire Representative Robert Fesh similarly noted, "Parents are worried about their kids and sexual abuse" (Macarchuk 2009). In these imagined interactions, opponents to identity-based criteria for determining gender both rely upon and shore up an idea that women are uniquely susceptible to assault. Moreover, they position transwomen as dangerous, a perspective that is often used in other contexts to justify violence against them (Westbrook 2009).

Since the panics produced in these moments of ideology collision focus on the penis as uniquely terrifying, "gender panics" might more accurately be termed "penis panics." In these hypothetical interactions, opponents give penises the power to destroy the sanctity of women's spaces through their (presumed natural) propensity to rape. The imagined sexual threat takes three forms in the news stories we examined. Most commonly, the threat is stated in general terms, such as opponents claiming that passage of transgender rights bills in New Hampshire and Massachusetts would put "women and children at risk" (Love 2009) in public restrooms. Second, some opponents imagined cis-men pretending to be transwomen in order to gain access to women's restrooms for sexually nefarious purposes. Contesting the vague criteria of who counts as transgender, Representative Peyton Hinkle of New Hampshire stated his opposition to the bill by calling it an "invitation . . . to people with predatory tendencies to come and hide behind the fact that they are having a transgender experience" (Fahey 2009). A spokesperson for the Massachusetts Family Institute told a reporter that the anti-discrimination bill allowed sexual predators to enter women's restrooms under the "guise of gender confusion" (Nicas 2009). Finally, transwomen themselves (not cis-men pretending to be trans) are imagined as the potential threat. Dr. Paul McHugh, chair of the psychiatry department at Johns Hopkins University, is reported to have written an email protesting the proposed New York City policy that stated: "I've already heard of a 'transgendered' man who claimed at work to be 'a woman in a man's body but is a lesbian' and who had to be expelled from the ladies' restroom because he was propositioning women there" (Cave 2006b). In these imagined interactions, transwomen have legal permission to enter gender-segregated spaces without the proper biological credentials. As such, their presence transforms a nonsexual space into a dangerously (hetero) sexual one. Within this heteronormative logic, all bodies with male anatomies, regardless of gender identity, desire female bodies, and many of them (enough to elicit concern from the public) are willing to use force to get access to those bodies.[8]

That these imagined sexual assaults occur only in women-only spaces is worth further analysis, as women share space with men daily without similar concerns. We suggest that women-only spaces generate intense androphobia because, by definition, these spaces should not contain bodies with penises. If women are inherently unable to protect themselves, and men (or, more specifically, penises) are inherently dangerous (Hollander 2001), the entrance of a penis into women's space becomes terrifying because there are no other men there to protect the women. The "safe" (read: gender-segregated) space is transformed into a dangerous, sexual situation by

the entrance of an "improper body." These fears rely on and reproduce gender binarism, specifically the assumption of strong/weak difference in male/female bodies, as opponents assume that people who could be gaining access to women's space (people with penises) are inherently stronger than cis-women and easily able to overpower them.

This emphasis on the sexual threat of penises in women-only spaces shows that gender panics are not just about gender, but also about sexuality. In the sex/gender/sexuality system, all bodies are presumed heterosexual. This assumption makes gender-segregated spaces seem safe because they are then "sexuality-free zones." Because there are only two gender categories, gay men and lesbians must share gender-segregated spaces with heterosexual men and women, respectively, an entrance that is tolerated as long as such entrants demonstrate the appropriate visual cues for admittance and use the bathroom for the "right" purpose (waste elimination). The use of public restrooms for homosexual sex acts can, of course, create a panic (Cavanagh 2010). Gender-segregated spaces, then, can be conceived of as both homophobic and heterophobic, as the fear is about unwanted sexual acts in supposedly sex-neutral spaces. Unlike normative sexual interactions, where gender difference is required to make the interaction acceptable (Schilt and Westbrook 2009), in gender-segregated spaces, gender difference is a source of discomfort and potential sexual threat and danger. Rhetoric about women and children as inherently vulnerable to sexual threats taps into cultural anxieties about sexual predators and pedophiles, who are always imagined to be men (Levine 2002); such fears have been repeatedly successful in generating sex panics. Because unwanted sexual attention is seen as a danger to women and children, but rarely, if ever, as a danger to adult men (Vance 1984), men's spaces are not policed. This differential policing of gender-segregated spaces illustrates the cultural logics that uphold gender inequality and heteronormativity—two systems whose underlying logic necessitates male–female oppositeness.

Conclusion

In this article, we examine the process of determining gender. We argue that collisions of biology-based and identity-based ideologies in the liberal moment have produced a sex/gender/sexuality system where the criteria for determining gender vary across social spaces. Many people have long assumed that biological factors, such as chromosomes, are always the ultimate determiner of gender. Contrary to the dominant assumption, we suggest that the sex/gender/sexuality system is slowly changing.

As it has encountered liberal values of self-determinism, the criteria for determining gender have shifted away from pure biological determinism. In nonsexual gender-integrated spaces, identity can be used to determine gender, as long as that identity is as a man or a woman (Schilt and Westbrook 2009). By contrast, in gender-segregated spaces, a combination of identity and body-based criteria is used, allowing someone to receive cultural and institutional support for a change of gender only if they undergo genital surgery. Finally, in heterosexual interactions, biology-based criteria (particularly genitals) are used to determine gender (Schilt and Westbrook 2009).

While most cis-gender people keep the same classification in all spaces, transgender people may be given different gender classifications by social actors depending on the type of interaction occurring in the space. Thus, one could speak of a trans-person's "social gender," "sexual gender," and "sports (or other gender-segregated space) gender." To illustrate this point, Kye Allums, a trans-man who played college basketball on a woman's team, has a social gender of "man" and a sports gender of "woman." Within the criteria for trans-athletes, he can continue to play basketball with women as long as he does not take testosterone or have genital surgery (Thomas 2010), a modification that would change his sports gender from "woman" to "man." Another way to conceptualize this point is to say that access to gender-integrated social spaces is determined by identity while access to gender-segregated spaces is mostly determined by biology, a point we summarize in Table 1.

The criteria for gender determination vary across social spaces because of the different imagined purposes of interactions that should occur in these settings. Heterosexual encounters and gender-segregated spaces both justify and reproduce an idea of two opposite genders. In spaces in which a higher level of oppositeness is required

from participants, visual and behavioral gender cues often are not considered sufficient for determining gender and, instead, the participants must also demonstrate bodily oppositeness. Because heterosexual interactions and gender-segregated spaces rely on (and reproduce) gender binarism, it is these spaces where validation of identity-based determination of gender produces panics and biology-based gender ideologies reign. In contrast, validation of identity-based determination of gender is more likely to occur when it cannot be framed as endangering other people, particularly others seen as more worthy of protection than trans-people (cis-women and children). In gender-integrated workplaces, for example, coworkers may not feel endangered by working with a trans-man who has the "cultural genitals" to support his social identity as a man, such as facial hair, particularly if he identified himself as crossing from one side of the gender binary to the other (Schilt and Westbrook 2009). It is important to add, however, that, in these spaces, identity-based determination of gender is more likely to be accepted by others when the person in question is, in the social imagination, "penis free" (all trans-men as well as "post-op" trans-women), as the penis is culturally associated with power and danger. These attitudes have profound consequences for transgender rights.

The criteria for determining gender also differ for placement in the category of "man" or "woman." Here, we have focused on the criteria for accessing women-only spaces because it is those spaces that produced the most panic in our media sources and that have the clearest criteria for admission. This focus of cultural anxiety on trans-women is unsurprising. We have detailed how the mainstream media portrayed trans-women as dangerous to heterosexual men because they use their feminine appearance to trick men into homosexual encounters (Schilt and Westbrook 2009; Westbrook 2009). In these

Table 1 Criteria for Determining Gender across Contexts

	Nonsexual, Gender-Integrated	**Nonsexual, Gender-Segregated**	**Heterosexual**
Trans-men	Identity-based criteria determine gender.	Identity-based criteria determine gender.	Biology-based criteria determine gender.
	Changes to genitalia are not typically required to establish legitimacy of their gender.	Changes to genitalia are not typically required to gain access to men's spaces.	Changes to genitalia required. This criterion is not typically enforced in a violent way.
Trans-women	Identity-based criteria determine gender.	A combination of identity-based and biology-based criteria determine gender.	Biology-based criteria determine gender.
	Changes to genitalia are more typically required to establish legitimacy of their gender.	Changes to genitalia are required to gain access to women's spaces.	Changes to genitalia required. This criterion is often enforced in a violent way.

cases, it is again trans-women who are portrayed as dangerous, yet this time they are positioned as endangering women and children.

We do not take the lack of attention to trans-men in men-only spaces to mean that trans-men are more accepted by people who vocally oppose trans-women. In contrast, we suggest that trans-men and trans-women are policed differently. Transmen's perceived lack of a natural penis renders them, under the logic of vulnerable subjecthood, unable to be threatening (and, therefore, unlikely to generate public outcry). Cis-gender men, the group who would share a bathroom or locker room with trans-men, also are not seen in the public imagination as potential victims of sexual threat, as such an image is contradictory to cultural constructions of maleness and masculinity (Lucal 1995). Trans-men enter a liminal state, in some ways, as they cannot hurt men (making them women), but are not seen as needing protection from men (making them part of a "pariah femininity" [Schippers 2007] that no longer warrants protection). Thus, because of gender inequality, the criteria for the category "man" are much less strict than those for the category "woman," at least for access to gender-segregated spaces.

But why do genitals carry more weight in determining gender in these segregated spaces? Our research hints at three possible answers for further exploration. First, genitals are changeable criteria, unlike chromosomes, which allows for some validation of liberal values of self-determination. Second, male and female genitals are imagined to be opposite, so using them as the criteria for determining gender maintains a binaristic gender system. Finally, genitals play a central role in gender panics because gender and sexuality are inextricably intertwined. The social actors opposed to identity-based determination of gender assume that all bodies, regardless of gender identity, are heterosexual. Although genitals are not supposed to be used in interactions in gender-segregated spaces, a fear of their (mis)use drives the policing of bodies in those spaces, making sexuality a central force in deciding which criteria will be used to determine gender.

By using genitals as the criteria for determining gender, the sex/gender/sexuality system is able to adapt to new liberal ideals of self-determination and to withstand the threat that trans-people might pose to a rigid binary system of gender. Although the existence of transgender and genderqueer people is seen as capable of "undoing gender" (Deutsch 2007; Risman 2009), the binaristic gender system tends to adapt to and re-absorb trans-people (Schilt and Westbrook 2009; Westbrook 2010). Rather than being undone, gender is constantly "redone" (Connell 2010; West and Zimmerman 2009). Like all other norms and social systems, people create gender. Challenges to the gender system modify rather than break it. Gender crossing can receive some validation in the liberal moment, but only when a binary remains unquestioned. By providing criteria for who can transition and how they can do it, the sex/gender/sexuality system is both altered and maintained.

Notes

1. Following Kessler and McKenna (1978), we highlight the social construction of both "sex" and "gender" by using the term "gender" throughout this article, even in moments where most people use the term "sex" (e.g., "gender-segregated" rather than "sex-segregated"). We reserve "sex" for references to intercourse, unless using a specific term such as "sex marker".

2. We use the term "(hetero)sexuality" to highlight that when many social actors speak of "sexuality" they are inferring heterosexuality.

3. As sexuality and sexualization are social processes, it is difficult to draw a conceptual line between a sexual and nonsexual space. Workplaces, for example, can contain sexualized interactions, though the dominant understanding of a workplace might be nonsexual. We use this term to refer to settings in which the commonly agreed on purpose is nonsexual. Sexual interactions do, of course, occur in these settings, but many see such interactions as a violation of the expected purpose of these spaces.

4. It is notable that women athletes do not have to possess what would be considered female genitals in order to compete. The criteria for determining gender in sports are thus very similar to Kessler and McKenna's findings that "penis equals male but vagina does not equal female" (1978, 151) when determining gender.

5. This use of "sex hormones"—mainly the levels of testosterone—to determine gender emerged only in the sports case because of the belief that testosterone provides a competitive advantage.

6. The image of a trans-man in men-only spaces was referenced by opponents only once in our analysis. A conservative activist told a reporter that allowing "men" to go into women's bathrooms legally would create discomfort for women and put them at sexual risk. The reporter asked what bathroom transgender men should use, as their male appearance could also make cis-women uncomfortable in the bathroom. The activist replied, "They [trans-men] should use the women's bathroom, regardless of whom it makes uncomfortable because that's where they are supposed to go" (Ball 2009).

7. Often, it is actors with good intentions, such as antiviolence activists, who, in their attempt to protect a particular group, unintentionally (re)produce an idea that the group is constantly prone to attack and unable to protect themselves (Westbrook 2008).

8. The ability to harm others attributed to trans-people in these narratives should be problematized. The trans-people described by biological determiners function as monstrous specters, so there is often little nuance in these portrayals of trans lives. By contrast, arguments made for trans rights bills and for access to gender-segregated spaces often include descriptions of trans-people as victims of violence and harassment rather than as perpetrators.

References

Ball, Molly. 2009. Robocall distorts record. *Las Vegas Review-Journal*, 6 April.

Berns, Nancy. 2004. *Framing the victim: Domestic violence, media, and social problems.* Somerset, NJ: Transaction.

Best, Joel. 2008. *Social problems*, 1st edition. New York: Norton.

Birrell, Susan, and Cheryl L. Cole. 1990. Double fault: Renee Richards and the construction and naturalization of difference. *Sociology of Sport Journal* 7:1–21.

Buzuvis, Erin. 2010. Caster Semenya and the myth of a level playing field. *The Modern American* 6:36–42.

Caruso, David. 2006a. New York City to ease rules for records reflecting gender change. *The Associated Press*, 6 October.

Caruso, David. 2006b. New York City seeks to ease rules for official documents reflecting gender change. *The Associated Press*, 7 November.

Cavanagh, Sheila. 2010. *Queering bathrooms: Gender, sexuality, and the hygienic imagination.* Toronto, Ontario, Canada: University of Toronto Press.

Cavanagh, Sheila L., and Heather Sykes. 2006. Transsexual bodies at the Olympics: The International Olympic Committee's policy on transsexual athletes at the 2004 Athens Summer Games. *Body & Society* 12:75–102.

Cave, Damien. 2006a. New York plans to make gender personal choice. *The New York Times*, 7 November.

Cave, Damien. 2006b. No change in definition of gender. *The New York Times*, 6 December.

Colangelo, Lisa. 2006. Change of sex IDs on city docket. *New York Daily News*, 25 September.

Connell, Catherine. 2010. Doing, undoing, or redoing gender? Learning from the workplace experiences of trans-people. *Gender & Society* 24:31–55.

Connell, Raewyn. 1995. *Masculinities.* Berkeley: University of California Press.

Currah, Paisley, and Lisa Jean Moore. 2009. We won't know who you are: Contesting sex designations in New York City birth certificates. *Hypatia* 24:113–35.

Deutsch, Francine M. 2007. Undoing gender. *Gender & Society* 21:106–27.

Distaso, John. 2009. No to marriage, "bathroom bills." *New Hampshire Union Leader*, 24 April.

Dreger, Alice. 2010. Sex typing for sport. *Hastings Center Report* 40:22–24.

Fahey, Tom. 2009. Transgender rights in "bathroom bill." *New Hampshire Union Leader*, 15 March.

Fausto-Sterling, Anne. 2000. *Sexing the body: Gender politics and the construction of sexuality.* New York: Basic Books.

Finn, Robin. 2006. Battling for one's true sexual identity. *The New York Times*, 10 November.

Gamson, William A., David Croteau, William Hoynes, and Theodore Sasson. 1992. Media images and the social construction of reality. *Annual Review of Sociology* 18:373–93.

Goffman, Erving. 1977. The arrangement between the sexes. *Theory and Society* 4:301–31.

Gooren, Louis, and Mathijs Bunck. 2004. Transsexuals and competitive sports. *European Journal of Endocrinology* 151:425–29.

Hollander, Jocelyn A. 2001. Vulnerability and dangerousness: The construction of gender through conversation about violence. *Gender & Society* 15:83–109.

International Olympic Committee Medical Commission. 2003. Statement of the Stockholm Consensus on sex reassignment in sports. http://www.olympic.org/Assets/ImportedNews/Documents/en_report_905.pdf.

International Olympic Committee Medical and Scientific Department. 2012. IOC regulations on female hyperandrogenism. http://www.olympic.org/Documents/Commissions_PDFfiles/Medical_commission/2012-06-22-IOC-Regulations-on-Female-Hyperandrogenism-eng.pdf.

Jansen, Sue Curry. 2002. When the center no longer holds: Rupture and repair. In *Critical communication theory: Power, media, gender, and technology*, edited by Nick Couldry and James Curran. Lanham, MD: Rowman & Littlefield.

Kessler, Suzanne, and Wendy McKenna. 1978. *Gender: An ethnomethodological approach.* Chicago: University of Chicago Press.

Kwok, Stephan. 2006. N.Y. gender law not realistic. *Daily Trojan*, 10 November.

Letter to the Editor. 2009a. Seeking support against vaguely defined identities. *Sentinel & Enterprise*, 13 July.

Letter to the Editor. 2009b. Anti-discrimination ordinance would harm Kalamazoo County. *Kalamazoo Gazette*, 9 October.

Levine, Judith. 2002. *Harmful to minors.* Minneapolis: University of Minnesota Press.

Littleton v. Prange. 1999. No. 99-1214 (Tex. 18).

Ljungqvist, Arne, and Myron Genel. 2005. Transsexual athletes: When is competition fair? *Medicine and Sport* 366:S42–S43.

Lorber, Judith. 1993. Believing is seeing: Biology as ideology. *Gender & Society* 7:568–81.

Love, Norma. 2009. NH Senate committee rejects transgender plan. *The Associated Press*, 23 April.

Lowell Sun, The. 2009. Transgender rights bill passes in N.H. House. 8 April.

Lucal, Betsy. 1995. The problem with "battered husbands." *Deviant Behavior* 16:95–112.

Macarchuk, Alexis. 2009. N.H. transgender bill aims to extend protections. *University Wire*, 10 April.

Macdonald, Myra. 2003. *Exploring media discourse*. London: Arnold.

Mcardle, D. 2008. Swallows and amazons, or the sporting exception to the Gender Recognition Act. *Social & Legal Studies* 17:39–57.

Meadow, Tey. 2010. A rose is a rose: On producing legal gender classifications. *Gender & Society* 24:814–37.

Meyerowitz, Joanne. 2002. *How sex changed: A history of transsexuality in the United States*. Cambridge, MA: Harvard University Press.

Nicas, Jack. 2009. Downing backs transgender bill. *The Berkshire Eagle*, 20 February.

Nyong'o, Tavia. 2010. The unforgivable transgression of being Caster Semenya. *Women & Performance: A Journal of Feminist Theory* 20:95–100.

Prager, Dennis. 2010. Why activists connect men in dresses to same-sex marriage. *Creators Syndicate*, 31 May.

Prunier, Chanel. 2009. Transgender bill is misguided. *Telegram & Gazette*, 14 July.

Ring, Dan. 2009. Transgenders fighting for protection. *The Republican*, 15 July.

Risman, Barbara J. 2009. From doing to undoing: Gender as we know it. *Gender & Society* 23:81–84.

Schilt, Kristen. 2010. *Just one of the guys? Transgender men and the persistence of gender inequality*. Chicago: University of Chicago Press.

Schilt, Kristen, and Laurel Westbrook. 2009. Doing gender, doing heteronormativity: "Gender normals," transgender people, and the social maintenance of heterosexuality. *Gender & Society* 23:440–64.

Schippers, Mimi. 2007. Recovering the feminine other: Masculinity, femininity, and gender hegemony. *Theory & Society* 36:85–102.

Seidman, Steven. 1995. Deconstructing queer theory or the under-theorization of the social and the ethical. In *Social postmodernism: Beyond identity politics*, edited by Linda J. Nicholson and Steven Seidman. Cambridge, UK: Cambridge University Press.

Shy, Yael Lee Aura. 2007. Like any other girl: Male-to-female transsexuals and professional sports. *Sports Lawyers Journal* 14:95.

Staff. 2006. Facing facts Dec. 3–Dec. 9. *The New York Times*, 10 December.

Stark, Jill. 2009. I'm just an ordinary guy who wants to play footy. *Sunday Age*, 7 June.

Stryker, Susan. 2008. *Transgender history*. Seattle, WA: Seal Press.

Thomas, Katie. 2010. Transgender man is on women's team. *The New York Times*, 1 November.

Tucker, Ross, and Malcolm Collins. 2009. The science and management of sex verification in sport. *South African Journal of Sports Medicine* 21 (4): 147–50.

Vance, Carol. 1984. *Pleasure and danger: Exploring female sexuality*. New York: Routledge.

Weiss, Jillian Todd. 2006. NYC rejects birth certificate change regs. Transgender Workplace Diversity (blog), 5 December, 2006, http://transworkplace.blogspot.com.

West, Candace, and Don Zimmerman. 1987. Doing gender. *Gender & Society* 1:125–51.

West, Candace, and Don H. Zimmerman. 2009. Accounting for doing gender. *Gender & Society* 23:112–22.

Westbrook, Laurel. 2008. Vulnerable subjecthood: The risks and benefits of the struggle for hate crime legislation. *Berkeley Journal of Sociology* 52:3–24.

Westbrook, Laurel. 2009. Violence matters: Producing gender, violence, and identity through accounts of murder. Ph.D. diss., University of California, Berkeley, CA.

Westbrook, Laurel. 2010. Becoming knowably gendered: The production of transgender possibilities in the mass and alternative press. In *Transgender identities: Towards a social analysis of gender diversity*, edited by Sally Hines and Tam Sanger. London: Routledge.

Yoshino, Kenji. 2006. Sex and the city. *Slate Magazine*, 11 December.

Laurel Westbrook is an assistant professor of sociology at Grand Valley State University. Her research focuses on gendered violence, social movements, and the inner workings of the sex/gender/sexuality system. She is currently completing a book on what she terms "identity-based anti-violence activism."

Kristen Schilt is an assistant professor of sociology at the University of Chicago. She is the author of Just One of the Guys: Transgender Men and the Persistence of Gender Inequality *(University of Chicago Press, 2010). She is currently working on a second book project about major life changes.*

Feminism, Masculinity and Male Rape: Bringing Male Rape 'Out of the Closet'

Aliraza Javaid[*]

Department of Sociology, University of York, Heslington, York YO10 5DD, UK

Feminist research has played a pivotal role in uncovering the extent and nature of male violence against women and suggests that the main motivations for rape are the need for power, control and domination. This paper argues that, although feminist explanations of rape are robust and comprehensive, male victims of rape have largely been excluded from this field of research. While feminism has enabled the victimisation of women to be recognised, further understanding of the victimisation of men is required. Some feminist writers (such as hooks, 2000) have argued that men's emancipation is an essential part of feminism since men are equally harmed by gender role expectations and sexism. This paper makes a contribution to current knowledge through evaluating the social constructions, stigma and phenomenological realities associated with male rape (by both men and women), arguing that there has been neglect in this area that functions to support, maintain and reinforce patriarchal power relations and hegemonic masculinities.

Keywords: male rape; sexual violence; feminism; gender equality; gender expectations; masculinity

Introduction

Feminist theoretical research on sexual violence is extensive: it highlights the hidden figure of unreported rapes in official police statistics (Lees, 1997, 2002); examines police responses to rape and attempts to eliminate rape myths (Gregory & Lees, 1999). Feminist research also plays a pivotal role in uncovering the extent of male violence against women and reveals the effect rape has on female rape victims, but comparatively little research has provided for male rape victims.[1] To explore male rape, it is important to examine feminist theory because it seeks to emphasise the gendered nature of rape. Stanko (1990) argues that men rape other men for exactly the same reasons that they rape women: to exercise power and control over the victim. Feminism conceptualises rape as a violent act which, along with a consideration of hegemonic masculinity, may help us understand why male rape has been widely overlooked and discover whether social and gender expectations facilitate this neglect. How a man perceives himself as a man and in what ways masculinities are formed within a social and cultural setting are vital to understanding male rape. This is verified by Groth and Burgess (1980), Kelly (1988), Berrington and Jones (2002) and Lees (1997) who conclude that masculinity is a social concept.

Feminism and sexual violence

For over 30 years, feminist researchers and activists have framed sexual assault and rape as a 'women's issue'. It is important to closely dissect this to evaluate the extent to which feminism is fulfilling its aim of nourishing gender equality, and how broader feminist theory could facilitate the investigation of male rape.

Services for managing victims of rape have ameliorated over the past 10 years, for example, the emergence of 'rape suites', in the UK, designed to accommodate all rape victims, including male rape victims. This challenges Mezey and King (1989) who asserted that there are limited service provisions for male rape victims. The 'rape suites' include environments, often away from police stations, in which the victims of sexual assault can be interviewed and medically examined. In addition, the police attempt to supply specially trained police officers to deal with rape cases, the majority of whom are female. This is problematic since male rape victims may wish to speak to a trained officer who is also male. There is very little research regarding whether policing practice and policy have improved or exacerbated the situation for, and experience of, male rape victims.

In the past, it has been found that the Crown Prosecution Service has not pursued a high proportion of rape

---

[*] Email: ali_2p9@hotmail.co.uk

allegations or that the police classified them as 'no-crimes' (Gregory & Lees, 1999). Gregory and Lees (1999) also found that the police have tended to give their greatest attention to stranger rapes (where the victim does not know the attacker). Lees' (1997) research pointed to a criminal justice system and society that viewed stranger rape as 'true' rape, rather than acquaintance rape (a rape where the victim knows the attacker).

Gregory and Lees (1999) stressed that there was an urgent need for the police to take male rape more seriously, to keep victims informed throughout the legal process and for the police to respond efficiently to rape allegations, along with further training for the officials who deal with the victims of rape. Some feminist theory argues that it is not possible to utilise legal apparatus to challenge patriarchal oppression and domination when the procedures and language of these institutions and social processes are saturated with these same patriarchal structures and beliefs (see MacKinnon, 1989, 1991). One of these patriarchal beliefs is that a man cannot be raped; consequently, those men who report rape may be viewed, either by themselves or others, as not 'real men' for failing to fight off the perpetrator of the crime (Lees, 1997).

Documented research (Lees, 1997; Stanko, 1990) confirms that men do rape other men as a way to boost, preserve and execute 'hegemonic masculinity'; that is, the male sexual offender seeks power and control over their subordinate, powerless victim. For Groth and Burgess (1980), this enhances the sexual offender's masculinity by stripping away that of their victim. Ideas of power and control stem from areas of feminism, which place rape in an extensive social structure, wherein a hierarchy of patriarchal relations exists to enable men to exercise power and control over women (MacKinnon, 1991). Male rape, then, is conceptualised as an extension of male power and control over women where male offenders regard their male victims as inferior, weak and subordinate, revealing the intrinsic issue of domination that accompanies the hegemony (Stanko, 1990). Although feminism robustly accounts for rape, it does come with some limitations in the context of this paper, which are important to examine next.

How useful is feminism to the study of male rape?

Some theories on patriarchy are criticised for being too descriptive instead of analytical and as incapable of explaining the inception of male supremacy. Feminist theory has been criticised for not offering strategies for weakening male power structures (Bryson, 1992). Walby (1990) illustrates that the theoretical paradigm of patriarchy does not suggest that every single male person oppresses every single female person in society, but instead that patriarchal theory enables for a distinction between individual men on the one hand, and the structures of hegemony on the other. Therefore, the 'enemy' is male supremacy, which is perceived to be a social construction rather than an innate determination (Walby, 1990).

Further, much feminist theory has tended to concentrate on men as rape offenders and women as victims. Although the growth of feminism gave recognition to female rape victims, significantly less time has been expended on male victims of rape. Many examinations of rape were based on the assumption that men control and dominate women, and that sexual assault and other types of sexual violence carried out against females strengthen male primacy (Abdullah-Khan, 2008). This position overlooks that men do get raped and it has even been asserted that male rape victims may be perceived as a threat to support provision put in place for female rape victims:

> On the one hand, they [survivors organisations' spokespersons] acknowledge the contribution and work of feminist groups in putting men's violence, rape and sexual abuse on to the public agenda and the setting up of support services for women, while on the other hand, they repeatedly assert that RCC's [rape crisis centres] have been unhelpful, indeed hostile, to male survivors who have called telephone counselling lines for support. (Gillespie, 1996, p. 155)

Rape crisis centres in the UK have no systematic provision for male victims in place, even though the Ministry of Justice provides public funding so that such centres can give support to *all* victims of sexual violence. Male rape victims seeking help have been turned away from these centres within the UK (Cohen, 2014; Pitfield, 2013), leaving these men isolated and unable to obtain help (Donnelly & Kenyon, 1996). Donnelly and Kenyon (1996) argue that feminist-based rape crisis centres have been less ready to recognise and manage male rape victims, disbelieving that men can be raped. For example, they found that 'Many [rape crisis centres] believed that men couldn't be raped or that they were raped only because they "wanted to be"' (1996, p. 444). Consequently, they remark:

> Because they [male rape victims] are less likely to ask for assistance in dealing with their attacks, the consequences of sexual assault may be compounded and even more severe for males than for females. Thus responsive and understanding provision of services that make seeking and receiving attention less traumatic is vitally important for male victims. (Donnelly and Kenyon, 1996, p. 442)

Donnelly and Kenyon also state that, because of the fewer social, physical and cultural provisions available for men, men are reporting sexual assault at much lower rates. Similarly, Abdullah-Khan (2008) argues that this situation persists in the twenty-first century since there is still a considerable lack of services provision available to men, leaving male rape victims reluctant to report offences.

The main worry for feminist writers such as Gillespie (1996) appears to be the strain that male rape victims could place on resources for rape support services. She further argues that, while rape crisis centres can be forthcoming to the demand for survivor groups for male rape victims, resources available for the operation of women's support provision should not be reduced as a result:

> Developing services for men who need or want them should not be achieved at the expense of what is now 20 years of developing knowledge and expertise within the rape crisis movement. (Gillespie, 1996, p. 162)

Gillespie (1996) implies that there is no urgent need for rape crisis centres to include help for male rape victims since their number is small:

> Since the extensive media coverage of, albeit a small number, of male rape cases . . . it has become apparent that RCCs [rape crisis centres] are experiencing pressure to extend service provision to men, both from statutory services, who are also often funding bodies, and who may be on the management or executive committee of RCCs, and also from male survivors of sexual assault. While RCCs are generally supportive of the need for male rape survivor groups, they do not on the whole wish to divert hard won resources and to dissipate energies needed for running female support services in the pursuit of setting up separate services for men. Centres do not, in any case, receive many calls from genuine (male) rape survivors. (pp. 157–158)

Cohen (2014) states that feminist discourse has conceptualised particular ideas of victimisation as inherently female: rape and sexual violence are examples of these. It is therefore vital to highlight male victimisation in victimology,[2] not only to develop a greater understanding of it, but also to be alert researchers and funders to the relegation of male rape. The segregation of male rape can also create problems, although at least in this form it becomes visible. Cohen (2014) argues that much of feminist theory in the field of sexual violence has neglected male rape. Any neglect can only maintain

and reinforce patriarchal power relations and 'hegemonic masculinities'.

Walklate (2004) argues that much research, both empirically and conceptually, contributes to the marginalisation of male victims. Feminist activism and the feminist academy have highlighted awareness of a range of important issues: domestic violence, sexual violence, sexual assault and rape, but the rape of the male is underdiscussed and its taboo nature resounds of the shame historically attached to female rape victims (although this shame is of course still present today, it is at least tackled). Walklate (2004) states that it is vital to challenge approaches to the field of sexual violence that attempt to essentialise the differences between females and males.

Following Walklate, there is strong evidence that men can be, and are, raped by *women*. For example, in Weiss's (2010) recent study, it was found that 46% of men ($n = 94$) had been raped by women. This challenges historical and cultural stereotypes that present females as subordinate and passive, both sexually and physically, along with the idea that men are solely the offenders in sex crimes. Weiss further alerts us to the fact that men experience attempted forced sex, actual forced sex and other sex-related incidents a lot more commonly than we read/hear about. The view that men cannot be the victims of sexual violence by women is prevalent in many societies (and consequent law-making), but it does not resonate with lived social reality (Graham, 2006). According to Walklate (2004), sexual assault is not a gender-specific crime. While MacKinnon seeks to re-establish the sexual aspect of certain types of violence, she focuses solely on the extensive range of women's experiences over men's. She adds that 'Battery as violence denies its sex-specific nature . . . Not only in where it is done—over half the incidents are in the bedroom . . .' (1989, p. 92). A criticism of MacKinnon's argument is that she does not consider the possibility that women can perpetrate sexual violence and violence in general.

Abdullah-Khan (2008) and Weiss (2010) find evidence for sexual assault by women against men as well as men against men, while Walklate (2004) also alerts us to the possibility of sexual assault by lesbians and heterosexual women: '[T]his muting of women's voices and experiences as offenders within the criminal justice system is a feature they share with female professionals working within it' (p. 181).

Brownmiller's (1975, p. 292) influential text argues that male victims are not neglected or actively 'forgotten', but that female victims usurp them as the latter is *more* 'acceptable'. Neither, though, can we equate male victims with female victims and parallel the motivation for, and experience of, male rape with same as/more than/less than statements. Cohen (2014) warns us that comparing and contrasting male rape with female rape is deleterious because it fuels the continued polarisation of debate and limits the conceptualisation of harm, rendering male rape invisible or at least on the margins. Reductionist and essentialist conceptualisations of rape affect the recording, prosecution and reporting practices in sexual violence against men (Cohen, 2014).

Authors on the subject of male rape (excluding Abdullah-Khan, 2008; Cohen, 2014) are reluctant to 'blame feminism' for the neglect of male rape. Male rape is generally conceptualised in conventional frames rather than theorised as a topic in its own right (e.g., Groth & Burgess, 1980; Hodge & Canter 1998; Stermac, Sheridan, Davidson, & Dunn, 1996), which Cohen (2014) believes results in the subject of male rape being stymied. To tackle the marginalisation of male rape, a few studies argue that feminism has detracted from the subject of male rape (Abdullah-Khan, 2008; Cohen, 2014; Davies, 2002; Javaid, 2014a, 2014b). Such authors argue for feminism to re-consider its position on male rape. With this in mind, Cohen (2014) supports the view that feminism has rendered male rape 'invisible'. Mezey and King (1992/2000, p. vi) add:

> In becoming a 'women's issue' the debate about rape and sexual violence polarized women as victims and men as perpetrators ... in contrast, there has been no 'men's movement' to raise awareness of the plight of victims and demand effective services.

The concept of hegemonic masculinity may be useful in explaining why there is no men's movement *per se*; male rape victims may be reluctant to expose themselves to society as victims of a crime seen solely to affect the female population. In addition, many of these victims fear a negative reaction to them as the victim of such violence.

For many, male rape is just another aspect of men's violence against women:

> Rape law sets the boundaries within which it is acceptable for men to have sex. It is about men's not women's sexuality: men act, women are acted upon; men force, women succumb; men are the subjects, women are the objects. This is the case even where both the parties involved are men; as has frequently been observed, the raped man is culturally feminised by the act of rape. (AHRC, 2006)

Such myopic ideology, currently fairly widespread, needs challenging because while it persists, male rape victims will continue to suffer in silence (as many women still do of course). Even Abdullah-Khan (2008) can be

accused of keeping focus on the female victim of rape, segregating male rape. While Cohen's research (2014) lacks substantial empirical data, her work remains a vital touchstone within the debate on male rape.

Mezey and King (1992/2000) observe that the extensively dispersed statement that 'rape is a feminist issue' results in a dearth of research in male rape and service provision which overlooks male rape victims. In addition, the activity of 'fund-raising' for gendered issues is still very much an activity conducted by feminist groups; there are few male fund-raising groups by comparison. According to Graham, 'Male victims are largely neglected by a predominately feminist perspective that seeks to highlight the gendered nature of sexual assault as a social phenomenon' (2006, p. 187). Graham's study, however, adds little to contemporary understandings of how to create change and improve services for male rape victims. Nonetheless, these studies are valuable in putting male rape on the agenda since without them, the configuration of rape as something men do to dominate women leads to male rape victims being left behind. The reality is that male rape victims, and men who are victims of crime in general, remain *men* (Owen, 1995) with all that that entails. Accounts of sexual violence may then be partly attributed to the conception of ingrained social ideals and gender expectations, particularly of masculinity.

Hegemonic masculinity and its relevance to male rape

While social constructions of women as sexually vulnerable and physically weak fit a stereotyped view of the victims of sexual violence, expectations of what is required of men (tough, powerful, strong, invulnerable, impenetrable and self-sufficient) challenge perceptions of victimisation in general (Lees, 1997). While 'real' men are forced to take on a masculine role and avoid behaviours linked to femininity, male rape victims may be judged to have failed as men for not fighting off their aggressor (Lees, 1997). Feminising or gendering victimisation is mostly seen through the use of derogatory labels ascribed to men who have not achieved expectations of hegemonic masculinity[3] (Connell, 2005) and men who have been the victim of a sexual attack undermine the dominant, social ideal of masculinity (sexually dominant, powerful, potent and in control) (Weiss, 2010). Hegemonic masculinity, coupled with heterosexuality, has been presented by feminist theory as the dominant norm in which society intrinsically expects 'real' men to want, initiate and pursue sex only with women (Connell, 2005). In a culture that emphasises male superiority, power and control, subordination or powerlessness are unacceptable (Lees, 1997). Instead, men are seen to commit most conventional crimes and serious crime (including sexual violence; Connell & Messerschmidt, 2005); not suffer it. Men who report sexual violence appear to confirm that they have been powerless and contest codes of male (hetero)sexuality (Weiss, 2010). It is these assumptions that have been greatly neglected by criminology and victimology, and consequently these disciplines are accused of being 'gender-blind' (Walklate, 2004).

Societies' expectation that men must attain particular standards and norms of masculinity, together with a fear of being seen as homosexual or effeminate (Connell & Messerschmidt, 2005; Kimmel, 2009), dictates that men display the stereotypical behaviours associated with their gender as part of a procedure of impression management (Goffman, 1967). For example, by sexually 'hooking up' with a lot of women, men can confirm to others and even to themselves their heterosexuality and masculinity (Pascoe, 2005). According to Prohaska and Gailey, 'The key to hegemonic masculinity is power, whether over other men or women . . .' (2006, p. 15).

Both Carlson (2008) and Mullaney (2007) argue that, after a sexual assault, male victims may reaffirm their masculinity through carrying out risk-taking behaviour, physical violence and demonstrating an ability to care for themselves by not reporting the crime; all activities which aspire to re-establish or repair their 'broken' masculinity. However, men can move through multiple meanings of hegemonic masculinity according to their interactional needs, so can adopt hegemonic masculinity when it is desirable to do so, and simultaneously, strategically distance themselves from hegemonic masculinity at other times (Connell & Messerschmidt, 2005).

An example of masculine behaviour that might be perceived to facilitate the repair of masculinity in the midst of sexual victimisation is 'getting even' or 'fighting back'. The victim might display physical violence to prevent a perceived sexual threat or attack, proving their ability to take care of themselves (Weiss, 2010). This can reveal their victimisation without labelling themselves as 'feminine', passive or weak. Evidently, this process lessens feelings of emasculation and overcompensates through conforming to expectations of men as invulnerable and strong; characteristics that are conceptualised under the umbrella of hegemonic masculinity. Violent behaviour may mirror the anger that heterosexual men have displayed towards homosexual men who are perceived to threaten their sexuality and hegemonic masculinity (Nelson & Oliver, 1998). Analogously, although women making unwanted advances towards men or coercing them in some way may challenge masculinity, it contradictorily underpins it (Nelson & Oliver, 1998). In physically retaliating with violence to a male sexual offender, the male victim refutes that he is a homosexual (Weiss, 2010), but retaliating against a female abuser is problematic since the male victim may be perceived as failing in his heterosexuality (or as the aggressor himself).

'Taking care' of offenders and incidents themselves confirms to the male victims of sexual violence that they are competent and self-reliant; two further components of hegemonic masculinity (Lees, 1997). Maintaining their silence allows the male victim of a sexual attack to avoid the stigma and embarrassment that might be expected when reporting a sexual assault to the police (Abdullah-Khan, 2008; Carlson, 2008).

This shame, within the conception of hegemonic masculinity, may be used to explain why male rape victims are even more reluctant to report female-perpetrated incidents to the police than rapes committed by other men; although the assertion here is a theoretical, instead of an empirical, one and in need of testing. Social ideals of heterosexuality and masculinity dictate that men are the penetrator, not the penetrated, and pursuers of sex, rather than pursued (Weiss, 2010). In this conception of masculinities, it is women who are pursued and penetrated, so a man who discloses to the police that he did not want sex with a woman, but was forced to do so, challenges norms of masculinity and inverts heterosexual scripts (Weiss, 2010). Men are expected to neither complain about injury/pain nor be emotional (Weiss, 2010). Embarrassment in the victim can also be attributed to constructions of male sexuality that expects men to be virile and to satisfy women, a conception reinforced through contemporary pornography (Weiss, 2010).

According to Walklate (2004), while women are permitted to express emotion, this position is not available to men and the experience is often denied to them. For the functionalist sociologist Talcott Parsons (1937), gentleness and the expression of emotions are refused to men, as these are behaviours associated with femininity and men must seek masculine qualities, such as being tough and self-reliant. Men admitting that they have failed to achieve such masculine qualities may be viewed, or view themselves, as not 'real men' (Abdullah-Khan, 2008; Groth & Burgess, 1980; Hodge and Canter, 1998; Isely, 1991; Lees, 1997; Mezey & King, 1989).

While functionalism[4] has had some influence in criminology in order to account for the gendered nature of crime and victims, it fails to acknowledge social change and challenge unhelpful stereotypes. Parson's (1937) functionalist ideology is speculative in that it is theoretically imaginative, partial and without supporting data. Nonetheless, functionalism has been important in understanding the socialisation processes that define how men should behave. One aspect of this process is normative heterosexuality contrasted with homosexuality which threatens both heterosexuality and hegemonic masculinity (Nelson & Oliver, 1998). Walklate (2004) adds that normative heterosexuality is valued in all parts of social life, and by being so valued, defines both the form and the structure of the struggle of men to achieve the power and dominance. Simultaneously, normative heterosexuality structures the lives of men who choose not to, or fail to, engage in such a struggle (Walklate, 2004). For Goffman (1967), homosexual men often feel stigmatised by their sexual identity, and that there is an additional burden on the homosexual man to deal with the ramifications of 'discrediting' himself openly. On this basis, we might expect a gay male rape victim's reluctance to report to the police, or seek help from voluntary agencies, in the event of sexual violence (perpetrated by either a woman or a man).

By writing about the power of interpersonal interactions to formulate impressions, Goffman (1959) compares interaction to a dramaturgical performance with off-stage and on-stage behaviours. He stipulates that interacting is based on many factors such as other people's judgments of the person involved in the interaction. Male rape myths, for example that 'men cannot be raped' because of their masculinity (Abdullah-Khan, 2008), reinforce the blaming attitudes ingrained in societies whereby male rape victims are accused of inviting the rape (Hodge & Canter, 1998) and made to feel ashamed (Isely, 1991). According to Goffman '. . . unwarranted feelings of shame; ambivalence about oneself and one's audience . . . some of the dramaturgical elements of the human situation' (Goffman, 1959, p. 237) all contribute to our (mis)understanding of rape.

The work of Judith Butler (1993), regardless of the intricacy of her broader project, is useful in furthering our understanding of men as the victims of sexual assault and rape. Butler remarks that heterosexuality creates sexual differences, so that gendered subjectivities and heterosexual affiliations are comprehended with regards to *penetration*; heterosexuality is rooted in an understanding of whether bodies penetrate or are penetrated. Further, through the classification of anal penetration as 'unnatural' or 'abnormal', the credibility of male rape victims is further damaged. Butler's analysis suggests that the feminine is always the penetrated and the masculine is always the *impenetrable*. Research confirms that men suffer for failing societies' expectations that do not permit the male as victim (Abdullah-Khan, 2008; Carlson, 2008; Cohen, 2014; Connell, 2005; Groth & Burgess, 1980; Hodge & Canter, 1998; Isely, 1991; Javaid, 2014a, 2014b; Lees, 1997; Mezey & King, 1989; Nelson & Oliver, 1998; Pascoe, 2005; Weiss, 2010).

Male rape victims have reported feeling frightened, dehumanised and contaminated (Lees, 1997); all words used by the female victims of rape (Lees, 2002). The difference between male rape victims and female rape victims, though, is that the former tend to more widely report feeling angry when assaulted (Lees, 1997; though it is acknowledged that within the context of gendered expectation, women are rarely permitted to express or feel anger). Male rape victims equally report feeling powerless and vulnerable at the time of the attack (Groth & Burgess, 1980). Groth and Burgess's study is based on a small sample from therapeutic practice, limiting its scope for meaningful analysis; significantly more empirical research is the next step if we are to properly support the male victims of sexual assault.

The persistence of the myth of sexual assault as affecting the female population only does not resonate with our limited understanding of the social reality for male rape victims and is embedded in heterosexism (Connell, 2005). Challenging normative (hetero) sexuality can create a space for male rape victims, whether homosexual or heterosexual and whether sexually assaulted by a man or a woman. Stanko (1990) highlights men's reluctance to acknowledge or voice their fears, leading to male rape victims neither seeking help/treatment nor prosecution. To underline this, Stanko and Hobdell (1993, p. 400) state that 'Criminology's failure to explore men's experience of violence is often attributed to men's reluctance to report "weakness". This silence is, we are led to believe, a product of men's hesitation to disclose vulnerability'. To unquestioningly and uncritically accept that men—by virtue of being male—experience no fear or trauma is to reinforce the context in which men can too easily be the victims of unreported sexual violence. Stanko and Hobdell's research (1993) included in-depth interviews with male victims of different kinds of violence, suggesting that men connect with, what Connell (2005) describes as, hegemonic masculinity. The men in the study valued adventure, power and control and felt that they lost this when subjugated through assault. Walklate (2004) states that, while both excitement and thrill operate along with fear, danger and risk, and that these are usually discussed in male terms, they render men's victimisation 'invisible' and silence them.

Conclusion

Feminism has played a key role in uncovering the extent and nature of violence against women by men and it has also created frameworks for understanding the construction of hegemonic masculinity. What is lacking currently is an acknowledgement of these as a context in which the sexual assault of men is under-discussed, under-reported and under-resourced. Abdullah-Khan (2008) argues that male rape research demonstrates the main motivation for rape to be seeking power, control and domination; concepts first recognised by feminism to explain rape against women. Rape is used as a means to exert power and control and utilised to humiliate, degrade, destroy and hurt victims (Stanko, 1990). Some feminist writers (hooks, 2000) have argued that men's emancipation is an essential part of feminism since men are also harmed by gender roles and sexism. Social ideals regarding gender may be facilitating the neglect of male rape victims. For example, whilst social constructions of femininity (sexual vulnerability and physical weakness) fit the stereotypes for the female victims of sexual violence, they are even less helpful to the male victim than they have been to the female victim. Expectations from society of what is required of men (invulnerability, impenetrability and self-sufficiency) help to perpetuate the myth that 'men cannot be raped' (Lees, 1997). In a context where 'real' men are forced to take on their masculine role and avoid behaviours associated with femininity, male rape victims are judged, and judge themselves, to be failed men for not fighting off the perpetrator of a sexual assault (Lees, 1997). As explored here, men as the victims of sexual assault undermine the dominant, social ideals of masculinity, which in turn contributes to the neglect of male rape victims as a subject for empirical study.

Through critically evaluating the social constructions, stigma and phenomenological realities associated with the sexual assault of men (by women or men), this paper argues that the neglect of this field functions to maintain and reinforce patriarchal power relations and hegemonic masculinities. The project of gender equality is undermined by our failure to properly activate feminist theory in relation to this project.

Acknowledgements

I am very grateful to Dr Blu Tirohl for the helpful and insightful feedback and comments on an earlier version of this paper. I am also grateful to Dr Paul Johnson for his support and guidance. I would finally like to extend my gratitude to Dr Kaz Ali for inspiring me and for all his inspiring words throughout the time it took to complete this paper.

Notes

1. This paper will solely focus on adult male rape victims rather than male children who are raped, prison rape and

rapes that are also war crimes; these are very important areas for research that fall beyond the scope of this paper.
2. 'Victimology' is a branch of criminology, which essentially is the study of victims.
3. 'Hegemonic masculinities' refers to the culturally idealised patterns (practices, norms, and forms) of masculinity that perpetuate patriarchy. Essentially, the concept refers to the ideal or model of masculinity.
4. For functionalism, each aspect of society is interdependent and contributes to society's functioning and stability as a whole; in other words, society is held together by social consensus, wherein members of the society concur upon, and work collectively to achieve, stability and solidarity (see Merton, 1957).

Notes on contributor

Aliraza Javaid is a PhD student at the University of York, UK and he also teaches Sociology and Criminology at the University of York, Department of Sociology. He has an MRes in Social Sciences, an MSc in Clinical Criminology and a BSc (hons) Criminology. His research interests include gendered patterns in offending, risk behaviour and victimisation as well as the associated criminal/social justice and public policy.

References

Abdullah-Khan, N. (2008). *Male rape: The emergence of a social and legal issue*. Hampshire: Palgrave Macmillan.

AHRC. (2006). *Research centre for law, gender and sexuality*, Response to the Office for Criminal Justice Reform's Consultation Paper: 'Convicting rapists and protecting victims of rape—justice for victims of rape' Kent: CentreLGS.

Berrington, E., & Jones, H. (2002). Reality vs. myth: Constructions of women's insecurity. *Feminist Media Studies, 2*, 307–323.

Brownmiller, S. (1975). *Against our will: Men, women and rape*. London: Penguin.

Bryson, V. (1992). *Feminist political theory: An introduction*. London: MacMillan.

Butler, J. (1993). *Bodies that matter: On the discursive limits of sex*. New York, NY: Routledge.

Carlson, M. (2008). I'd rather go along and be considered a man: Masculinity and bystander intervention. *Journal of Men's Studies, 16*, 3–17.

Cohen, C. (2014). *Male rape is a feminist issue: Feminism, governmentality, and male rape*. Hampshire: Palgrave Macmillan.

Connell, R. W. (2005). *Masculinities* (2nd ed.). Berkeley: University of California Press.

Connell, R. W., & Messerschmidt, J. W. (2005). Hegemonic masculinity: Rethinking the concept. *Gender Society, 19*, 829–859.

Davies, M. (2002). Male sexual assault victims: A selective review of the literature and implications for support services. *Aggression and Violent Behavior, 7*, 203–214.

Donnelly, D. A., & Kenyon, S. (1996). Honey we don't do men: Gender stereotypes and the provision of services to sexually assaulted males. *Journal of Interpersonal Violence, 11*, 441–448.

Gillespie, T. (1996). Rape crisis centres and male rape: A face of the backlash. In M. Hester, L. Kelly, & J. Radford (Eds.), *Women violence and male power* (pp. 148–165). Buckingham: Open University Press.

Goffman, E. (1959). *The presentation of self in everyday life.* New York, NY: Doubleday.

Goffman, E. (1967). *Interactional ritual.* Chicago, IL: Aldine de Gruyter.

Graham, R. (2006). Male rape and the careful construction of the male victim. *Social Legal Studies, 15*, 187–208.

Gregory, J., & Lees, S. (1999). *Policing sexual assault.* London: Routledge.

Groth, A. N., & Burgess, A. W. (1980). Male rape: Offenders and victims. *American Journal of Psychiatry, 137*, 806–810.

Hodge, S., & Canter, D. (1998). Victims and perpetrators of male sexual assault. *Journal of Interpersonal Violence, 13*, 222–239.

hooks, B. (2000). *Feminism is for everybody: Passionate politics.* Cambridge, MA: South End Press.

Isely, P. J. (1991). Adult male sexual assault in the community: A literature review and group treatment model. In A. W. Burgess (Ed.), *Rape and sexual assault: A research handbook* (pp. 161–178). New York, NY: Garland.

Javaid, A. (2014a). Male rape: The 'invisible' male. *Internet Journal of Criminology.* Retrieved from http://www.internetjournalofcriminology.com/Javaid_Male_Rape_The_Invisible_Male_IJC_Jan_2014.pdf

Javaid, A. (2014b). Male rape: The unseen world of male rape. *Internet Journal of Criminology.* Retrieved from http://www.internetjournalofcriminology.com/Javaid_The_Unseen_World_of_Male_Rape_IJC_Jan_2014.pdf

Kelly, L. (1988). *Surviving sexual violence.* Cambridge: Polity Press.

Kimmel, M. S. (2009). Masculinity as homophobia: Fear, shame, and silence in the construction of gender identity. In A. L. Ferber, K. Holcomb, & T. Wentling (Eds.), *Sex, gender, and sexuality: The new basics* (pp. 58–70). New York, NY: Oxford University Press.

Lees, S. (1997). *Ruling passions. Sexual violence, reputation and the law.* Buckingham: Open University Press.

Lees, S. (2002). *Carnal knowledge. Rape on trial.* London: Women's Press.

MacKinnon, C. (1989). *Feminism unmodified.* Cambridge, MA: Harvard University Press.

MacKinnon, C. (1991). Reflections on sex equality under law. *The Yale Law Journal, 100*, 1281–1328.

Merton, R. (1957). *Social theory and social structure.* London: Free Press of Glencoe.

Mezey, G. C., & King, M. B. (1989). The effects of sexual assault on men: A survey of 22 victims. *Psychological Medicine, 19*, 205–209.

Mezey, G. C., & King, M. B. (Eds.). (1992/2000). *Male victims of sexual assault.* Oxford: Oxford University Press.

Mullaney, J. L. (2007). Telling it like a man: Masculinities and battering men's accounts of their violence. *Men and Masculinities, 10*, 222–247.

Nelson, A., & Oliver, P. (1998). Gender and the construction of consent in child-adult sexual contact: Beyond gender neutrality and male monopoly. *Gender and Society, 12*, 554–577.

Owen, J. (1995). Women-talk and men-talk: Defining and resisting victim status. In R. E. Dobash, R. P. Dobash, & L. Noaks (Eds.), *Just boys doing business: Men, masculinities and crime* (pp. 46–68). London: Routledge.

Parsons, T. (1937). *The structure of social action.* New York, NY: McGraw-Hill.

Pascoe, C. J. (2005). 'Dude, you're a fag': Adolescent masculinity and the fag discourse. *Sexualities, 8*, 329–346.

Pitfield, C. (2013). *Male survivors of sexual assault: To tell or not to tell?* Retrieved from http://webcache.googleusercontent.com/search?q=cache:BBMfwrMnd34J:roar.uel.ac.uk/3442/1/2013_DClinPsych_Pitfield.pdf+&cd=1&hl=en&ct=clnk&gl=uk&client=safari

Prohaska, A., & Gailey, J. A. (2006). Achieving masculinity through sexual predation: The case of hogging. *Journal of Gender Studies, 19*, 13–25.

Stanko, E. A. (1990). *Everyday violence: How women and men experience sexual and physical danger.* London: Harper Collins.

Stanko, E. A., & Hobdell, K. (1993). Assaults on men; masculinity and male violence. *British Journal of Criminology, 33*, 400–415.

Stermac, L., Sheridan, P. M., Davidson, A., & Dunn, S. (1996). Sexual assault of adult males. *Journal of Interpersonal Violence, 11*, 52–65.

Walby, S. (1990). *Theorising patriarchy.* Oxford: Basil Blackwell.

Walklate, S. (2004). *Gender, crime and criminal justice* (2nd ed.). Devon: Willan.

Weiss, K. G. (2010). Male sexual victimization: Examining men's experiences of rape and sexual assault. *Men and Masculinities, 12*, 275–298.

The Individual and Deviance: Deviant Compared to What?

Too sexy for my mustache. What, exactly, is deviant about this picture of a demonstrator at an Italian gay pride parade? He is dressed perfectly for the occasion.

Kids, do not try this at home or anywhere else, for that matter. It is deviant, criminal and individually destructive. Your social class might help you mitigate the harm for a while but there is no happy ending to this line.

What's the most deviant thing that you've ever done? Not necessarily "criminal," you understand. Just deviant. An action that you have performed that goes against the established norms; against what is expected from you in a specific context. All of us are deviants. I have been asking this question in my classes for many years now and I can tell you with great certainty that if you could anonymously report the most deviant thing that you have ever done, it could be categorized as having to do with "sex," "drugs," "theft," or "vandalism." While there might be one or two of you who once killed a man in Reno just to watch him die, you are in the extreme minority, thankfully. Most of us commit much more prosaic types of deviance. Deviance, after all, is normal.

The Hilton Hotel in Bangkok Thailand exhibits a mural depicting a Thai harem scene of 200 years ago. This might make a good topic for a contemporary reality show but it was normative back in the day among the 1%.

Sex workers carry a sign for their rights in the Pride Parade on August 26, 2012 in Ottawa, Ontario, Canada. Deviant compared to what?

What you will find in this week's readings is that deviance is universal but that there is no universal type of deviance. Much of deviance does not even depend on the act itself, but on the context in which the act is performed. Killing is wrong but if you wear a uniform and are authorized by the State to use force, or if you're defending yourself, killing is sometimes accepted as a "normal" reaction in a specific context. Similarly, we think of taking "drugs" as deviant, but not if you are 21 and the drug is alcohol; or if the doctor authorizes you to zone out on oxycodone. If you yell "go Marlins" during a Marlin game, you are not a deviant; if you yell it in Church, you are a deviant. In our culture, if you talk to God, you are praying; if God talks back, you are nuts.

There are laws that sanction this type of deviant activity. That's why it is called a crime.

Deviance is often in the eye of the beholder and the context in which an action is beheld. Can you think of a context in which this young man would be exhibiting normative behavior?

The study of deviance is an interesting field of Sociology. It is important because by studying deviance, we can see the boundaries that our society sets to acceptable behavior. The process of socialization that you studied a couple of weeks ago is the process though which we learn what is normal and deviant in our society. What is more important for our purposes, though, is to realize that what we consider deviant is relative; not all societies or groups consider the same actions deviant. Lately we have been hearing about polygamous marriages in the United States where men are wedded to numerous women. In our society, this is clearly a deviant from the norm and the legislations which have institutionalized the norm (it is also crazy). In other societies, most notably some Muslim cultures, polygamy is accepted and limited only by the ability of a man to economically support more than one wife.

Paint walls just anywhere in an urban center and you might be arrested for defacing public/private property. Do it in Wynwood, a neighborhood in Miami with a strong art culture, and you could become famous? Murals can be seen everywhere.

Wearing this jumpsuit outside of the jail house might be deviant, but what got him behind bars was a crime.

On the Sociology of Deviance

Kai T. Erikson

Human actors are sorted into various kinds of collectivity, ranging from relatively small units such as the nuclear family to relatively large ones such as a nation or culture. One of the most stubborn difficulties in the study of deviation is that the problem is defined differently at each one of these levels: behavior that is considered unseemly within the context of a single family may be entirely acceptable to the community in general, while behavior that attracts severe censure from the members of the community may go altogether unnoticed elsewhere in the culture. People in society, then, must learn to deal separately with deviance at each one of these levels and to distinguish among them in his own daily activity. A man may disinherit his son for conduct that violates old family traditions or ostracize a neighbor for conduct that violates some local custom, but he is not expected to employ either of these standards when he serves as a juror in a court of law. In each of the three situations he is required to use a different set of criteria to decide whether or not the behavior in question exceeds tolerable limits.

In the next few pages we shall be talking about deviant behavior in social units called "communities," but the use of this term does not mean that the argument applies only at that level of organization. In theory, at least, the argument being made here should fit all kinds of human collectivity—families as well as whole cultures, small groups as well as nations—and the term "community" is only being used in this context because it seems particularly convenient.[1]

The people of a community spend most of their lives in close contact with one another, sharing a common sphere of experience which makes them feel that they belong to a special "kind" and live in a special "place." In the formal language of sociology, this means that communities are boundary maintaining: each has a specific territory in the world as a whole, not only in the sense that it occupies a defined region of geographical space but also in the sense that it takes over a particular niche in what might be called cultural space and develops its own "ethos" or "way" within that compass. Both of these dimensions of group space, the geographical and the cultural, set the community apart as a special place and provide an important point of reference for its members.

When one describes any system as boundary maintaining, one is saying that it controls the fluctuation of its consistent parts so that the whole retains a limited range of activity, a given pattern of constancy and stability, within the larger environment. A human community can be said to maintain boundaries, then, in the sense that its members tend to confine themselves to a particular radius of activity and to regard any conduct which drifts outside that radius as somehow inappropriate or immoral. Thus the group retains a kind of cultural integrity, a voluntary restriction on its own potential for expansion, beyond that which is strictly required for accommodation to the environment. Human behavior can vary over an enormous range, but each community draws a symbolic set of parentheses around a certain segment of that range and limits its own activities within that narrower zone. These parentheses, so to speak, are the community's boundaries.

People who live together in communities cannot relate to one another in any coherent way or even acquire a sense of their own stature as group members unless they learn something about the boundaries of the territory they occupy in social space, if only because they need to sense what lies beyond the margins of the group before they can appreciate the special quality of the experience which takes place within it. Yet how do people learn about the boundaries of their community? And how do they convey this information to the generations which replace them?

To begin with, the only material found in a society for marking boundaries is the behavior of its members— or rather, the networks of interaction which link these members together in regular social relations. And the interactions which do the most effective job of locating and publicizing the group's outer edges would seem to be those which take place between deviant persons on the one side and official agents of the community on the other. The deviant is a person whose activities have moved outside the margins of the group, and when the community calls him to account for that vagrancy it is making a statement about the nature and placement of its boundaries. It is declaring how much variability and diversity can be tolerated within the group before it begins to lose its distinctive shape, its unique identity. Now there may be other moments in the life of the group which perform a similar service: wars, for instance, can publicize a group's boundaries by drawing attention to the line separating the group from an adversary, and certain kinds of religious ritual, dance ceremony, and other traditional pageantry can dramatize the difference between "we" and "they" by portraying a symbolic encounter between the two. But on the whole, members of a community inform one another about the placement of their boundaries by participating in the confrontations which occur when persons who venture out to the edges of the group are met by policing agents whose special business it is to guard the cultural integrity of the community. Whether these confrontations take the form of criminal trials, excommunication hearings, courts-martial, or even psychiatric case conferences, they act as boundary-maintaining devices in the sense that they demonstrate to whatever audience is concerned where the line is drawn between behavior that belongs in the special universe of the group and behavior that does not. In general, this kind of information is not easily relayed by the straightforward use of language. Most readers of this paragraph, for instance, have a fairly clear idea of the line separating theft from more legitimate forms of commerce, but few of them have ever seen a published statute describing these differences. More likely than not, our information on the subject has been drawn from publicized instances in which the relevant laws were applied—and for that matter, the law itself is largely a collection of past cases and decisions, a synthesis of the various confrontations which have occurred in the life of the legal order.

It may be important to note in this connection that confrontations between deviant offenders and the agents of control have always attracted a good deal of public attention. In our own past, the trial and punishment of offenders were staged in the market place and afforded the crowd a chance to participate in a direct, active way. Today, of course, we no longer parade deviants in the town square or expose them to the carnival atmosphere of Tyburn, but it is interesting that the "reform" which brought about this change in penal practice coincided almost exactly with the development of newspapers as a medium of mass information. Perhaps this is no more than an accident of history,

but it is nonetheless true that newspapers (and now radio and television) offer much the same kind of entertainment as public hangings or a Sunday visit to the local gaol. A considerable portion of what we call "news" is devoted to reports about deviant behavior and its consequences, and it is no simple matter to explain why these items should be considered newsworthy or why they should command the extraordinary attention they do. Perhaps they appeal to a number of psychological perversities among the mass audience, as commentators have suggested, but at the same time they constitute one of our main sources of information about the normative outlines of society. In a figurative sense, at least, morality and immorality meet at the public scaffold, and it is during this meeting that the line between them is drawn.

Boundaries are never a fixed property of any community. They are always shifting as the people of the group find new ways to define the outer limits of their universe, new ways to position themselves on the larger cultural map. Sometimes changes occur within the structure of the group which require its members to make a new survey of their territory—a change of leadership, a shift of mood. Sometimes changes occur in the surrounding environment, altering the background against which the people of the group have measured their own uniqueness. And always, new generations are moving in to take their turn guarding old institutions and need to be informed about the contours of the world they are inheriting. Thus single encounters between the deviant and his community are only fragments of an ongoing social process. Like an article of common law, boundaries remain a meaningful point of reference only so long as they are repeatedly tested by persons on the fringes of the group and repeatedly defended by persons chosen to represent the group's inner morality. Each time the community moves to censure some act of deviation, then, and convenes a formal ceremony to deal with the responsible offender, it sharpens the authority of the violated norm and restates where the boundaries of the group are located.

For these reasons, deviant behavior is not a simple kind of leakage which occurs when the machinery of society is in poor working order, but may be, in controlled quantities, an important condition for preserving the stability of social life. Deviant forms of behavior, by marking the outer edges of group life, give the inner structure its special character and thus supply the framework within which the people of the group develop an orderly sense of their own cultural identity. Perhaps this is what Aldous Huxley had in mind when he wrote:

> Now tidiness is undeniably good—but a good of
> which it is easily possible to have too much and at

too high a price. . . . The good life can only be lived in a society in which tidiness is preached and practiced, but not too fanatically, and where efficiency is always haloed, as it were, by a tolerated margin of mess.[2]

This raises a delicate theoretical issue. If we grant that human groups often derive benefit from deviant behavior, can we then assume that they are organized in such a way as to promote this resource? Can we assume, in other words, that forces operate in the social structure to recruit offenders and to commit them to long periods of service in the deviant ranks? This is not a question which can be answered with our present store of empirical data, but one observation can be made which gives the question an interesting perspective—namely, that deviant forms of conduct often seem to derive nourishment from the very agencies devised to inhibit them. Indeed, the agencies built by society for preventing deviance are often so poorly equipped for the task that we might well ask why this is regarded as their "real" function in the first place.

It is by now a thoroughly familiar argument that many of the institutions designed to discourage deviant behavior actually operate in such a way as to perpetuate it. For one thing, prisons, hospitals, and other similar agencies provide aid and shelter to large numbers of deviant persons, sometimes giving them a certain advantage in the competition for social resources. But beyond this, such institutions gather marginal people into tightly segregated groups, give them an opportunity to teach one another the skills and attitudes of a deviant career, and even provoke them into using these skills by reinforcing their sense of alienation from the rest of society.[3] Nor is this observation a modern one:

> The misery suffered in gaols is not half their evil; they are filled with every sort of corruption that poverty and wickedness can generate; with all the shameless and profligate enormities that can be produced by the impudence of ignominy, the range of want, and the malignity of despair. In a prison the check of the public eye is removed; and the power of the law is spent. There are few fears, there are no blushes. The lewd inflame the more modest; the audacious harden the timid. Everyone fortifies himself as he can against his own remaining sensibility; endeavoring to practice on others the arts that are practiced on himself; and to gain the applause of his worst associates by imitating their manners.[4]

These lines, written almost two centuries ago, are a harsh indictment of prisons, but many of the conditions they describe continue to be reported in even the most modern studies of prison life. Looking at the matter from a long-range historical perspective, it is fair to conclude that prisons have done a conspicuously poor job of reforming the convicts placed in their custody; but the very consistency of this failure may have a peculiar logic of its own. Perhaps we find it difficult to change the worst of our penal practices because we *expect* the prison to harden the inmate's commitment to deviant forms of behavior and draw him more deeply into the deviant ranks. On the whole, we are a people who do not really expect deviants to change very much as they are processed through the control agencies we provide for them, and we are often reluctant to devote much of the community's resources to the job of rehabilitation. In this sense, the prison which graduates long rows of accomplished criminals (or, for that matter, the state asylum which stores its most severe cases away in some back ward) may do serious violence to the aims of its founders; but it does very little violence to the expectations of the population it serves.

These expectations, moreover, are found in every corner of society and constitute an important part of the climate in which we deal with deviant forms of behavior.

To begin with, the community's decision to bring deviant sanctions against one of its members is not a simple act of censure. It is an intricate rite of transition, at once moving the individual out of his ordinary place in society and transferring him into a special deviant position.[5] The ceremonies which mark this change of status, generally, have a number of related phases. They supply a formal stage on which the deviant and his community can confront one another (as in the criminal trial); they make an announcement about the nature of his deviancy (a verdict or diagnosis, for example); and they place him in a particular role which is thought to neutralize the harmful effects of his misconduct (like the role of prisoner or patient). These commitment ceremonies tend to be occasions of wide public interest and ordinarily take place in a highly dramatic setting.[6] Perhaps the most obvious example of a commitment ceremony is the criminal trial, with its elaborate formality and exaggerated ritual, but more modest equivalents can be found wherever procedures are set up to judge whether or not someone is legitimately deviant.

An important feature of these ceremonies in our own culture is that they are almost irreversible. Most provisional roles conferred by society, those of the student or conscripted soldier, for example, include some kind of terminal ceremony to mark the individual's movement back out of the role once its temporary advantages have been exhausted. But the roles allotted the deviant seldom make allowance for this type of passage. He is ushered into the deviant position by a decisive and often dramatic ceremony, yet is retired from it with scarcely a word of public notice. And as a result, the deviant often returns home with no proper license to resume a normal life in the community. Nothing has happened to cancel out the stigmas imposed upon him by earlier commitment ceremonies; nothing has happened to revoke the verdict or diagnosis pronounced upon him at that time. It should not be surprising, then, that the people of the community are apt to greet the returning deviant with a considerable degree of apprehension and distrust, for in a very real sense they are not at all sure who he is.

A circularity is thus set into motion which has all the earmarks of a "self-fulfilling prophesy," to use Merton's fine phrase. On the one hand, it seems quite obvious that the community's apprehensions help reduce whatever chances the deviant might otherwise have had for a successful return home. Yet at the same time, everyday experience seems to show that these suspicions are wholly reasonable, for it is a well-known and highly publicized fact that many if not most ex-convicts return to crime after leaving prison and that large numbers of mental patients require further treatment after an initial hospitalization. The common feeling that deviant persons never really change, then, may derive from a faulty premise; but the feeling is expressed so frequently and with such conviction that it eventually creates the facts which later "prove" it to be correct. If the returning deviant encounters this circularity often enough, it is quite understandable that he, too, may begin to wonder whether he has fully graduated from the deviant role, and he may respond to the uncertainty by resuming some kind of deviant activity. In many respects, this may be the only way for the individual and his community to agree what kind of person he is.

Moreover this prophesy is found in the official policies of even the most responsible agencies of control. Police departments could not operate with any real effectiveness if they did not regard ex-convicts as a ready pool of suspects to be tapped in the event of trouble, and psychiatric clinics could not do a successful job in the community if they were not always alert to the possibility of former patients suffering relapses. Thus the prophesy gains currency at many levels within the social order, not only in the poorly informed attitudes of the community at large, but in the best informed theories of most control agencies as well.

In one form or another this problem has been recognized in the West for many hundreds of years, and this simple fact has a curious implication. For if our culture has supported a steady flow of deviation throughout long periods of historical change, the rules which apply to any kind of evolutionary thinking would suggest that strong forces must be at work to keep the flow intact—and this because it contributes in some important way to the survival of the culture as a whole. This does not furnish us with sufficient warrant to declare that deviance is "functional" (in any of the many senses of that term), but it should certainly make us wary of the assumption so often made in sociological circles that any well-structured society is somehow designed to prevent deviant behavior from occurring.[7]

It might be then argued that we need new metaphors to carry our thinking about deviance onto a different plane. On the whole, American sociologists have devoted most of their attention to those forces in society which seem to assert a centralizing influence on human behavior, gathering people together into tight clusters called "groups" and bringing them under the jurisdiction of governing principles called "norms" or "standards." The questions which sociologists have traditionally asked of their data, then, are addressed to the uniformities rather than the divergencies of social life; how is it that people learn to think in similar ways, to accept the same group moralities, to move by the same rhythms of behavior, to see life with the same eyes? How is it, in short, that cultures accomplish the incredible alchemy of making unity out of diversity, harmony out of conflict, order out of confusion? Somehow we often act as if the differences between people can be taken for granted, being too natural to require comment, but that the symmetry which human groups manage to achieve must be explained by referring to the molding influence of the social structure.

But variety, too, is a product of the social structure. It is certainly remarkable that members of a culture come to look so much alike; but it is also remarkable that out of all this sameness a people can develop a complex division of labor, move off into diverging career lines, scatter across the surface of the territory they share in common, and create so many differences of temper, ideology, fashion, and mood. Perhaps we can conclude, then, that two separate yet often competing currents are found in any society; those forces which promote a high degree of conformity among the people of the community so that they know what to expect from one another, and those forces which encourage a certain degree of diversity so that people can be deployed across the range of group space to survey its potential, measure its capacity, and, in the case of those we call deviants, patrol its boundaries. In such a scheme, the deviant would appear as a natural product of group differentiation. He is not a bit of debris spun out by faulty social machinery, but a relevant figure in the community's overall division of labor.

Notes

1. In fact, the first statement of the general notion presented here was concerned with the study of small groups. See Robert A. Dentler and Kai T. Erikson, "The Functions of Deviance in Groups," *Social Problems,* VII (Fall 1959), pp. 98–107.

2. Aldous Huxley, *Prisons: The "Carceri" Etchings by Piranesi* (London: The Trianon Press, 1949), p. 13.

3. For a good description of this process in the modern prison, see Gresham Sykes, *The Society of Captives* (Princeton, N.J.: Princeton University Press, 1958). For discussions of similar problems in two different kinds of mental hospital, see Erving Goffman, *Asylums* (New York: Bobbs-Merrill, 1962) and Kai T. Erikson, "Patient Role and Social Uncertainty: A Dilemma of the Mentally Ill," *Psychiatry,* XX (August 1957), pp. 263–274.

4. Written by "a celebrated" but not otherwise identified author (perhaps Henry Fielding) and quoted in John Howard, *The State of the Prisons,* London, 1777 (London: J. M. Dent and Sons, 1929), p. 10.

5. The classic description of this process as it applies to the medical patient is found in Talcott Parsons, *The Social System* (Glencoe, Ill.: The Free Press, 1951).

6. See Harold Garfinkel, "Successful Degradation Ceremonies," *American Journal of Sociology,* LXI (January 1956), pp. 420–424.

7. Albert K. Cohen, for example, speaking for a dominant strain in sociological thinking, takes the question quite for granted: "It would seem that the control of deviant behavior is, by definition, a culture goal." See "The Study of Social Disorganization and Deviant Behavior" in Merton et al., *Sociology Today* (New York: Basic Books, 1959), p. 465.

Anomie, Deviance, and the Religious Factor: Data from 104 NFL Players

Eric M. Carter[1] & Michael V. Carter[2]

Abstract

The proliferation of deviant and criminal behavior among National Football League (NFL) players has garnered unprecedented attention over the past decade. Why *are* many of these wealthy and famous athletes engaged in deviant and illegal behavior? And more importantly, can this bad behavior be mitigating and deterred via a form of social support? This paper examines the hypothesis that the religious factor (as a form of social support) acts as a deterrent to deviant/illegal behavior and as a key buffer between anomie and deviance (arrests). These relationships are examined in a snowball sample of 104 NFL players. It was found that religiosity reduces personal anomie among players in the study group by enhancing positive group integration and support. Religiosity, also, appears to have a deterrent effect on deviance/illegal behavior as well as a buffering effect between anomie and deviance, as the multiplicative term suggests there is an interaction effect.

Keywords: religion; social support; anomie; deviance; professional athletes

Introduction and Background

The fall of 2014 has been consumed by questions and conversation regarding the deviance and illegal behavior of many NFL (National Football League) players. There have been a host of these high profile athletes engaged in deviant and unlawful behaviors ranging from substance abuse to domestic violence to child abuse. Aside from the dialogue surrounding why these athletes are committing these acts, which is certainly important, there are increasing conversations about what might deter these bad behaviors. Might the religious factor be a deterrent for professional football players?

From Durkheim ([1912] 1965) to Merton (1938, 1957) and beyond, social theorists have argued that religion is a key form of social integration and regulation. For Glock and Stark (1965), "one of the abiding general propositions of sociology is that religion serves the central and crucial function in society of supporting . . . social integration" (p. 170). From this standpoint, the religious factor should reduce levels of personal anomie among anomic individuals (for this study, professional football players), and as a result lower the probability of deviant and criminal behavior, by providing social integration, regulation, and support. Thus, individuals who are integrated into a religious community should be less likely to engage in deviant and unlawful behavior.

However, research on the impact of religion on deviance has long been controversial among social scientists. Hirschi and Stark's (1969) classic research, "Hellfire and Delinquency," cited that religion had no real deterrent effect on deviant, delinquent behavior. Since then, a number of other researchers (Rhodes and Reiss, 1970; Burkett and White, 1974; Albrecht, Chadwick and Alcorn, 1977; Higgins and Albrecht, 1977; Jenson and Erickson, 1979; Tittle and Welch, 1983; Hadaway, Elifson and Petersen, 1984; Brownfield and Sorenson, 1991; Cochran, Beeghley and Wilbur, 1992; Bainbridge, 1992; Benson, 1992; Benda and Corwyn, 1997; Lee, Rice and Gillespie, 1997; Johnson et al., 2000; Baier and Wright, 2001; Johnson, 2003) have found religious influence to have moderate to significant deterrent effects on deviant and criminal behavior. Thus, the perspective that religion reduces deviance and crime is not "without empirical foundation" or, for that matter, the need for more research (Dilulio Jr., 2009, p. 115).

With the range of findings over the past fifty years in mind, this research reconsiders the relation between the religious factor and deviance using data from 104 NFL

[1] PhD, Department of Sociology, Georgetown College, 400 E. College St., Georgetown, KY 40324, USA. Phone: 502-863-7968, Email: eric_carter@georgetowncollege.edu.

[2] PhD, Office of the President; Campbellsville University, Campbellsville, KY, USA (Michael Carter, President of the University and Professor of Sociology)

From *Journal of Sociology and Social Work, Vol 2, No 2, December 2014* by Eric M. Carter and Michael V. Carter. Copyright © 2014 by American Research Institute for Policy Development. Reprinted by permission.

(National Football League) players. As a way to get at this relationship between religion and deviance, we first investigate the impact of religion on personal anomie. If professional football players are anomic, in many cases, they are more likely to commit deviant acts (Carter, 2009). So, can religion, while mitigating their personal anomie, also buffer acts of deviance and unlawful behavior?

Hypotheses

With the growing concern over the deviant and illegal behaviors of many NFL players (Benedict, 1997; Benedict andYaeger, 1998; Blumstein and Benedict, 1999; Carter, 2009; Eitzen and Sage, 2009) and prior empirical evidence showing the importance of integration and social support in relation to anomie and deviance (Carter, 2009), three core hypotheses emerged.

The first hypothesis is that religiosity reduces personal anomie among players in the study group. The second hypothesis is that religiosity has a deterrent effect on deviance/illegal behavior. The third hypothesis is that

religiosity acts as a key buffer between players' personal anomie and their illegal behavior.

Research Methodology

Data for this study were taken from 104 current and former NFL players from the 2001–2006 time-period[3]. Data were collected from these players in six states via the use of a survey instrument composed of 60 total variables. Types of variables range from socio-demographic to Likert-type attitudinal concerning a variety of topics thought to be important in assessing anomie, religiosity, and unlawful behavior. While the larger study (Carter, 2009) encompassed a wide range of variables, the focus of this analysis is on religiosity as a possible buffer between anomie and illegal behavior and whether or not the religious factor has a deterrent effect on anomie and deviance/criminal behavior.

The sample is a non-probability snowball sample (Berg, 2007). Random or other probability formats were not available due to the extremely difficult nature of

Table 1 Summary of Descriptive Statistics for the Study Group (N = 104)

Characteristic		Sample Data	Frequency
Age:	Mean	30.10	
	Standard Deviation	4.028	
	Range	22–39	
Race:	Percent White	38.5%	40
	Percent Black	61.5%	64
Player Status:	Percent Current	42.3%	45
	Percent Former/Retired	56.7%	59
Years Played:	Mean	4.52	
	Standard Deviation	2.014	
	Range	1–11	
Marital Status:	Percent Married	48.1%	50
	Percent Not Married	51.9%	54
Education:	Percent Graduated College	35.6%	37
	Percent Not Graduated College	64.6%	67
Income:	Percent Earning $0–$500,000	39.4%	41
	Percent Earning $500,001 and above	60.6%	63
Family Structure:	Percent Raised in 2 Parent Home	36.5%	38
	Percent Raised in Single Parent Home	63.5%	66
Location:	Percent Raised in Rural Location	37.5%	39
	Percent Raised in Urban Location	62.5%	65
Social Class:	Percent Raised Middle Class and Above	40.4%	42
	Percent Raised Lower Class/Poor	59.6%	62

Altruism:	Percent Willing to Donate (Time/Money)	77.9%	81
	Percent Not Willing to Donate	22.1%	23
Happiness Level:	Percent Happy	55.8%	58
	Percent Unhappy	44.2%	46
Arrests:	Percent Arrested	31.7%	33
	Percent Not Arrested	68.3%	71

Table 2   Means, Standard Deviations, and Factor Loadings for Responses to the Anomie Scale (N = 104)

Item	Mean	SD	Factor Loading
1. In spite of what people say, the lot of the average man is getting worse.	1.58	.844	.790
2. It's hardly fair to bring children into the world with the way things look for the future.	1.53	.737	.681
3. Nowadays a person has to live pretty much for today and let tomorrow take care of itself.	1.83	.853	.754
4. These days a person doesn't know who he can count on.	1.83	.794	.730
5. There's little use writing to public officials because they aren't really interested in the problems of the average man.	1.74	.547	.618
6. More and more I feel helpless in the face of what's happening in the world today.	1.39	.730	.687
7. There is too much drinking of alcoholic beverages today.	1.54	.880	.802
8. people should never smoke marijuana because it leads to a life of drugs.	1.33	.999	.844
9. Almost everyone finds leisure time more satisfying than work.	1.81	.801	.721
10. Today's sexual morality seems to be, "anything goes."	2.48	.668	.772

Reliability Coefficient (alpha) = .933
Eigenvalue = 7.53; Percent of Variance = 53.77

access to this highly guarded social group. Contacts were made through an intricate network of friendships from two initial informants (former NFL players).

The sample is composed of 45 (42.3%) current NFL players and 59 (56.7%) retired players. The mean age of the participants is 30.10 and ranges from 22–39. There were 40 (38.5%) white respondents and 64 (61.5%) black respondents.

The range for years played in the NFL is 1-11, with 4.52 being the average number of years played for players in this study group. See Table 1 for other descriptive statistics.

Measures

The less social integration and support (via religion), it is hypothesized, the greater should be the anomic effects (illegal behavior). In Table 1, illegal behavior was operationalized as a dichotomous variable. It should be noted that illegal behavior referred to those who had been arrested after they entered the NFL. Approximately one-third of the study group reported being involved in illegal behavior with 33 (31.7%) players being arrested after entering the NFL.

The literature on NFL players and crime (Benedict and Yaeger, 1998; Blumstein and Benedict, 1999) suggests that approximately 20% of NFL players have committed illegal acts. Our study group had a rate of illegal behavior higher than other sampled groups.

Anomie is measured by the five item Srole (1956) scale, one item from the Neal and Seeman (1964) powerlessness scale, and four items from the Abrahamson (1980) gratification scale. Conceptually, these items should be closely related with attitudes that accompany what Durkheim ([1897] 1951) conceived as anomie. See Table 2 for the anomie scale.

Religiosity is measured through the development of an index comprised of three items. See Table 3 for the religiosity index. This index focuses on religiosity as a key form of social integration and support, which has been noted to reduce personal feelings of anomie (Kanagy, Willits, and Crider, 1990).

In order to construct composite measures of anomie and religiosity, a considerable number of items presumably relating to each attribute were subjected to factor analysis, correlational analysis, and the computation of

Table 3 Means, Standard Deviations, and Factor Loadings for Responses to the Religiosity Index (N = 104)

Item	Mean	SD	Factor Loading
1. I believe there is a living God/Higher Power.	2.33	1.05	−.840
2. I have a personal relationship with my God/HP	1.90	1.26	−.929
3. I pray to my God/HP.	1.65	1.33	−.907

Reliability Coefficient (alpha) = .919
Eigenvalue = 1.53; Percent of Variance = 11.70

Table 4 Correlation Matrix for Arrests, Anomie, and Religiosity for NFL Players (N = 104)

	Arrests	Anomie	Relig.	Age	Race	Yrs. Play	Mar. St	Edu.	Income	Fam. St	Loc.	Soc. Cla	Altru.	Lev. H
Arrests	1.00													
Anomie	.503	1.00												
Relig.	−.399	−.562	1.00											
Age	−.449	−.540	.439	1.00										
Race	.284	.407	−.226	−.277	1.00									
Yrs. Played	.019*	.006*	.012*	.179*	.042*	1.00								
Mar. Stat.	−.367	−.515	.398	.375	−.347	.106*	1.00							
Edu.	−.463	−.634	.448	.453	−.445	.008*	.531	1.00						
Income	.170*	.528	−.325	−.476	.131*	−.154*	−.248	−.387	1.00					
Fam. Struc.	.303	.519	−.239	_.201	.385	.027*	−.269	−.479	.287	1.00				
Loc.	.315	.640	−.368	−.274	.449	−.047*	−.407	−.545	.472	.567	1.00			
Soc. Class	.182*	.163*	−.249	−.244	.034*	−.090*	.149*	−.207	.178*	.014*	.132*	1.00		
Altru.	−.284	−.403	.353	.244	.136*	−.058*	.281	.299	−.240	.116*	−.269	.155*	1.00	
Lev. Hap.	−.433	−.639	.383	.384	−.346	.009*	.392	.500	−.401	−.555	−.570	−.260	.318	1.00

* Not Significant at the 0.05 Level

Chronbach's alpha. Those items that overlapped each dimension were systematically taken out until items relating to each of the constructs were finally distinct. The anomie scale and religiosity index were each found to have an acceptable degree of reliability. The reliability coefficient for the anomie scale is 0.933, while the reliability coefficient for the religiosity index is 0.919.

Single items were also included in the survey to measure (and control for): (a) age, (b) race, (c), years played in the NFL, (d) marital status, (e) education, (f) income, (g) family structure, (h) location, (i) social class, (j) altruism, and (k) level of happiness. See Table 1 for descriptive statistics.

Analyses

Before analyzing whether religiosity acts as a buffer between anomie and illegal behavior and is a deterrent to deviance/arrests among NFL players in the study group, some background information is needed. First, the results of the correlation analysis reveal that anomie is positively correlated to illegal behavior (r = .503), religiosity is negatively correlated to anomie (r = −.562), and religiosity is negatively correlated to illegal behavior (r = −.399). All are significant correlations. See Table 4 for correlation matrix.

Second, using multiple regression analysis, five variables were shown to be significant in reducing the unexplained variance in the dependent variable (anomie). The five variable model explained 64.9% of the variance in the anomie scale.

The five variables included in the model are: (a) location, (b) age, (c) level of happiness, (d) religiosity, and (e) education. Most importantly, this analysis reveals that high levels of religiosity are associated with low levels of anomie. See Table 5 for regression model (anomie).

Third, logistic regression analysis with illegal behavior (arrests) being the dependent variable resulted in the development of an equation in which two variables made significant contributions to the predictive power: (a) anomie, and (b) religiosity. The two variable model

Table 5 Step-Wise Regression for Anomie with NFL Players Presented in Standardized Regression Coefficient Form (N = 104)

Step	Loc.	Age	Lev. of Hap.	Relig.	Edu.	Adjusted R^2	F Ratio or Entering Variable	Level of Significance
1	.640					.404	70.92	.001
2	.533	−.394				.545	62.63	.001
3	.383	−.320	−.299			.597	51.87	.001
4	.338	−.245	−.265	−.228		.632	45.30	.001
5	.277	−.203	−.235	−.198	−.185	.649	39.09	.001

Variables not entering: Arrests, Race, Years Played, Marital Status, Income, Family Structure, Social Class, Altruism

Table 6 Step-Wise Regression for Criminal Activity (Arrests) with NFL Players in Unstandardiz Regression Coefficient Form (N = 104)

Step	Anomie	Religiosity	R^2	Wald	Level of Sig.
1	2.44		.363	19.77	.001
2	1.77	−2.37	.433	8.56	.01

Variables not entering: Age, Race, Years Played, Marital Status, Education, Income, Family Structure, Social Class, Altruism, Level of Happiness

Table 7 Logistic Regression for Criminal Activity (Arrests) Including Interaction Term with NFL Players in Unstandardized Regression Coefficient Form (N = 104)

Independent Variable	B	S.E.	Wald
Anomie	2.39*	1.90	1.57
Religiosity	−2.63*	.113	5.43
Interaction Term (Anomie by Religion)	−.668	.742	.811
Age	1.19	1.59	.559
Race	−.605	.786	.592
Years Played	−.056	.170	.106
Marital Status	.015	.725	.000
Education	−2.25*	1.25	3.25
Income	1.77*	.904	3.85
Family Structure	−.527	.981	.288
Location	.557	1.11	.252
Social Class	−.332	.650	.262
Altruism	.452	.671	.453
Level of Happiness	.994	.786	1.60
Chi-Square for Model	51.94*		
R^2	.551		

*$p < .05$ level

explained 43.3% of the variance in the dichotomous variable, illegal behavior.

In essence, respondents appear to have a higher probability of engaging in illegal behavior if they are anomic and less religious. See Table 6 for regression model (criminal activity).

Congruent with prior research (Carter, 2009), these analyses reveal important associations among key variables. Anomie, illegal behavior, and religiosity, as a form of social integration and support, all appear to be significantly related. Then, is religiosity a buffer between the personal anomie of players in the study group and their illegal behavior?

An additional logistic regression analysis was performed to test for an interaction effect between anomie and religiosity. The multiplicative term (B = −.668) suggests that there is an interaction effect. This further analysis reveals that religiosity is an underlying factor in illegal behavior. The multiplicative term implies that as the level of religiosity goes up, the effect of anomie goes down in relation to illegal behavior. This additional analysis appears to confirm the theoretical propositions, and is consistent with, and supports, the analyses. Indeed, for this study group, religiosity appears to be an important buffer between anomie and illegal behavior. See Table 7 for regression model (criminal activity with interaction term).

Conclusion

While this research does not allow us to make generalizations about the impact of religion on the entire population of professional football players, it does show some interesting relationships between 104 players' religiosity, personal anomie, and deviance. For this study group, the religious factor appears to act as a buffer between players' personal anomie and deviance/criminal behavior. Not only does religion act as a mitigating factor, it more importantly appears to reduce the likelihood of deviance and arrests for these 104 NFL players. For these players, we argue that religion furnishes integrative and social support in an anxious and uncertain professional and social environment. Put simply, it appears to be a positive and supportive influence in their lives. With these findings alongside current patterns of bad behavior among NFL players and a spirited public debate about this behavior and what can be done about it, future research is warranted.

Notes

1. PhD, Department of Sociology, Georgetown College, 400 E. College St., Georgetown, KY 40324, USA. Phone: 502-863-7968, Email: eric_carter@georgetown college.edu
2. PhD, Office of the President; Campbellsville University, Campbellsville, KY, USA (Michael Carter, President of the University and Professor of Sociology)
3. Qualitative data (Carter, 2009) from the 2001-2006 time-period along with new qualitative data (up to present) support the quantitative data and findings in this research note.

References

Abrahamson, M. (1980). Sudden wealth, gratification and attainment: durkheim's anomie of affluence reconsidered. American Sociological Review, 45, 49–57.

Albrecht, S.L., Chadwick, B.A., & Alcorn, D.S. (1977). Religiosity and deviance: application of an attitude-behavior contingent consistency model. Journal for the Scientific Study of Religion, 16, 263–274.

Baier, C., & Wright, B. (2001). "If you love me: keep my commandments": a meta-analysis of the effect of religion on crime. Journal of Research in Crime and Delinquency, 38, 3–21.

Bainbridge, W.S. (1992). Crime, delinquency and religion. In J.F. Schumaker (Ed.), Religion and mental health (pp. 199–210). New York: Oxford University Press.

Benda, B., & Corwin, R. (1997). Religion and delinquency. Journal for the Scientific Study of Religion, 36, 81–92.

Benedict, J. (1997). Public heroes, private felons. Boston: Northeastern University Press.

Benedict, J., & Yaeger, D. (1998). Pros and cons: the criminals who play in the nfl. New York: Warner Books.

Benson, P.L. (1992). Religion and substance abuse. In J.F. Schumaker (Ed.), Religion and mental health (pp. 211–220). New York: Oxford University Press.

Berg, B. (2007). Qualitative research methods for the social sciences. Boston: Pearson.

Blumstein, A., & Benedict, J. (1999). Criminal violence of nfl players compared to the general population. Chance, 12, 12–15.

Brownfield, D., & Sorenson, A. (1991). Religion and drug use among adolescents: a social support conceptualization and interpretation. Deviant Behavior, 12, 259–276.

Burkett, S., & White, M. (1974). Hellfire and delinquency: another look. Journal for the Scientific Study of Religion, 13, 455–462.

Carter, E. (2009). Boys gone wild: fame, fortune, and deviance among professional football Players. Lanham, MD: University Press of America.

Cochran, J., Beeghley, L, & Bock, W.E. (1992). The influence of religious stability and homogamy on the relationship between religiosity and alcohol use among protestants. Journal for the Scientific Study of Religion, 31, 441–456.

Dilulio Jr., J. (2009). More religion, less crime? science, felonies, and the three faith factors. Annual Review of Law and Social Sciences, 5, 115-133.

Durkheim, E. ([1897] 1951). Suicide. New York: Free Press.

Durkheim, E. ([1912] 1965). The elementary forms of religious life. New York: Free Press.

Eitzen, D.S., & Sage, G.H. (2009). Sociology of north american sport. Boulder, CO: Paradigm Publishers.

Glock, C., & Stark, R. (1965). Religion and society in tension. Chicago: Rand McNally.

Hadaway, K.C., Elifson, K.W., & Peterson, D.M. (1984). Religious involvement and drug use among urban adolescents. Journal for the Scientific Study of Religion, 23, 109–128.

Higgins, P.C., & Albrecht G.L. (1977). Hellfire and delinquency revisited. Social Forces, 55, 452–458.

Hirschi, T., & Stark, R. (1969). Hellfire and delinquency. Social Problems, 17, 202–213.

Jenson, G., & Erickson, M.L. (1979). The religious factor and delinquency: another look at the hellfire hypothesis. In R. Wuthnow (Ed.), the religious dimension (pp. 157–177). New York: Academic Press.

Johnson, B. (2003). The role of african-american churches in reducing crime among black youth. (pp. 1–8). Center for Research on Religion and Urban Civil Society: Philadelphia.

Johnson, B., Larson, D., De Li, S., & Joon Jang, S. (2000). Escaping from the crime of inner cities: church attendance and religious salience among disadvantaged youth. Justice Quarterly, 17, 377–391.

Kanagy, C.L., Willits, F.K., & Crider, D.M. (1990). Anomia and religiosity: data from a panel study of middle-aged subjects. Journal for the Scientific Study of Religion, 29, 226–235.

Lee, J., Rice, G., & Gillespie, B.V. (1997). Family worship patterns and their correlation with adolescent behavior and beliefs. Journal for the Scientific Study of Religion, 36, 372–381.

Merton, R. (1938). Social structure and anomie. American Sociological Review, 3, 672–682.

Merton, R. (1957). Social theory and social structure. Glencoe, IL: Free Press.

Neal, A.G., & Seeman, M. (1964). Organizations and powerlessness. American Sociological Review, 29, 216–226.

Rhodes, A.L., & Reiss, A.J. (1970). The "religious factor" and delinquent behavior. Journal of Research in Crime and Delinquency, 7, 83–89.

Srole, L. (1956). Social integration and certain corollaries: an exploratory study. American Sociological Review, 21, 709–716.

Tittle, C.R., & Welch, M.R. (1983). Religiosity and deviance: toward a contingency theory of constraining effects. Social Forces, 61, 653–682.

BDSM Disclosure and Stigma Management: Identifying Opportunities for Sex Education

Tanya Bezreh
Emerson College, Boston, MA, USA

Thomas S. Weinberg
Buffalo State College, Buffalo, NY, USA

Timothy Edgar
Emerson College, Boston, MA, USA

While participation in the activities like bondage, domination, submission/sadism, masochism that fall under the umbrella term BDSM is widespread, stigma surrounding BDSM poses risks to practitioners who wish to disclose their interest. We examined risk factors involved with disclosure to posit how sex education might diffuse stigma and warn of risks. Semi-structured interviews asked 20 adults reporting an interest in BDSM about their disclosure experiences. Most respondents reported their BDSM interests starting before age 15, sometimes creating a phase of anxiety and shame in the absence of reassuring information. As adults, respondents often considered BDSM central to their sexuality, thus disclosure was integral to dating. Disclosure decisions in nondating situations were often complex considerations balancing desire for appropriateness with a desire for connection and honesty. Some respondents wondered whether their interests being found out would jeopardize their jobs. Experiences with stigma varied widely.

KEYWORDS Disclosure, coming out, stigma, sexual minority resources, sexuality education, BDSM, sadism, masochism, sadomasochism

Study Aims

The topic of disclosure of an interest in BDSM (an umbrella term for sexual interests including bondage, domination, submission/sadism, and masochism) remains largely unaddressed in current resources. There is evidence that interest in BDSM is common (Renaud & Byers, 1999), often stigmatized, and that people hesitate to disclose it (Wright, 2006).

We do not assume that disclosure of BDSM interests is analogous to "coming out" about homosexuality, nor that all people interested in BDSM want to or "should" disclose. Rather, we are inspired by the myriad resources available for helping lesbian, gay, and bisexual (LGB) individuals navigate disclosure, stigma, and shame. Many foci of LGB outreach, such as assuring people that they are not alone in their sexual inclinations, helping people deal with shame that may be associated with feeling "different," helping people cope with stigma, and warning people of the potential dangers of disclosure, translate readily to the arena of BDSM. This project did exploratory research into the disclosure experiences of people interested in BDSM to identify potential areas of support that can be integrated into sex education.

What Is Bdsm?

This project mainly uses the term BDSM to indicate an inclusive concern for people interested in bondage (B), domination (D), submission (S), sadism (the same "S") and masochism (M). When citing research that uses the term SM (alternately "S/M" and "S&M"), we keep the term. Sometimes BDSM is referred to as "kink" by practitioners. An early study concluded that because of such varied activities as spanking, bondage, and role play, sadomasochists "do not make up a homogenous enough group to warrant classification as a unity" (Stoller, 1991, p. 9). Weinberg (1987) suggests that SM could be defined by the "frame" with which people distinguish their pretend play from actual violence or domination; this frame hinges

[1]This project originated as a Master's thesis in health communication, which proposed delivery mechanisms for this outreach and information. Also, we would like to thank Jim Dattolo, Theodore Dubro, and Greg Howard.

[2]Address correspondence to Tanya Bezreh. E-mail: tanya@tanyabezreh.com

on the BDSM credo, "safe, sane, and consensual." Another commonality is the recurring elements that are "played with," including "power (exchanging it, taking it, and/or giving it up), the mind (psychology), and sensations (using or depriving use of the senses and working with the chemicals released by the body when pain and/or intense sensation are experienced)" (Pawlowski, 2009).[1]

Background

The prevalence of BDSM in the United States is not precisely known, but a Google search of "BDSM" in 2010 returned 28 million Web pages. Janus and Janus (1993) found that up to 14% of American males and 11% of American females have engaged in some form of SM. A study of Canadian university students found that 65% have fantasies of being tied up, and 62% have fantasies of tying up a partner (Renaud & Byers, 1999).

The first empirical research on a large sample of SM-identified subjects was conducted in 1977, and the sociological and social-psychological research which followed was primarily descriptive of behaviors and did not focus on the psychosocial factors, etiology, or acquisition of SM identity or interest (Weinberg, 1987). From research in other sexual minorities, it is known that constructing a sexual identity may be a complicated process that evolves over time (Maguen, Floyd, Bakeman, & Armistead, 2002; Rust, 1993). Weinberg (1978) pointed out that a key component of a man identifying as gay involves converting "doing" into "being," that is, seeing behaviors and feelings as standing for who he essentially *is*. Whether this process is analogous to people identifying with BDSM is not known. Kolmes, Stock, and Moser (2006) noticed variation in respondents they surveyed: for some people who engage in BDSM it is an alternative sexual identity, and for others "'sexual orientation' does not seem an appropriate descriptor" (p. 304).

An interest in SM can appear at an early age and usually appears by the time individuals are in their twenties (Breslow, Evans, & Langley, 1985). Moser and Levitt (1987) found that 10% of an SM support group they studied "came out" between the ages of 11 and 16; 26% reported a first SM experience by age 16; and 26% of those surveyed "came out" into SM before having their first SM experience. A study by Sandnabba, Santtila, and Nordling (1999) surveyed members of SM clubs in Finland and found that 9.3% had awareness of their sadomasochistic inclinations before the age of 10.

There is little research about the ways stigma affects SM-identified individuals, but there is much evidence that SM is stigmatized. Wright (2006) documented cases of discrimination against individuals, parents, private parties, and organized SM community events, demonstrating that SM-identified individuals may suffer discrimination, become targets of violence, and lose security clearances, inheritances, jobs, and custody of children. According to Link and Phelan (2001), stigma reduces a person's status in the eyes of society and "marks the boundaries a society creates between 'normals' and 'outsiders'" (p. 377). Goffman (1963) noted that stigmatized groups are imbued with a wide range of negative traits, leading to discomfort in the interactions between stigmatized and nonstigmatized individuals. The interactions are worse when the stigmatized condition is perceived to be voluntary, for example, when homosexuality is seen as a choice. According to Goffman, individuals reshape their identity to include societal judgments, leading to shame, guilt, self-labeling, and self-hatred.

Sadism and masochism have a history of being stigmatized medically. The *Diagnostic Statistical Manual (DSM)* first classified them as a "sexual deviation" (APA, 1952, 1968) and later "sexual disorders" (APA, 1980). In response to lobbying on the part of BDSM groups who pointed to the absence of evidence supporting the pathologization of sadism and masochism, the APA took a step toward demedicalizing SM (Moser & Kleinplatz, 2005). The current definition in the *DSM-IV-TR* hinges the classification of "disorder" on the presence of distress or nonconsensual behaviors[2] (APA, 2000). Drafts of the forthcoming *DSM* available on the Web emphasize that paraphilias (a broad term that includes SM interests) "are not *ipso facto* psychiatric disorders" (APA, 2010).

Demedicalization removes a major barrier to the creation of outreach, education, anti-stigma campaigns and human services. In 1973, the *DSM* changed its classification of homosexuality, which had also been categorized as a "sexual disorder," and much de-stigmatization followed in the wake of that decision (Kilgore et al., 2005). With demedicalization, sex educators can adopt reassuring and demedicalizing language about SM, and outreach efforts are better able to address stigma in society at large.

Only a few passages in extant research touch on what it may be like to disclose an interest in BDSM. A National Coalition of Sexual Freedom survey of adult SM group members found that 70% "were at least partially closeted" (Wright, 2006). Breslow (1986) found that the majority of an SM-identified sample had revealed their interests to significant others. Kamel (1983) outlined the stages of emerging sadomasochistic desires and integration into community for leathermen (i.e., gay men who wear leather to indicate interest in BDSM). He described phases of disenchantment, depression, and "a second 'closet'" but provided no data. Moser and Levitt (1987) found a positive association between the level of well-being and the degree of integration into SM sub-cultures. Kolmes et al. (2006) found that disclosing an interest in SM to therapists can be dangerous. The 175 BDSM-inclined therapy patients surveyed in their study had experienced 118 incidents of biased care including therapists considering BDSM to be unhealthy, confusing BDSM with abuse, and assuming that BDSM interests are indicative of past family/spousal abuse (Kolmes et al.).

Meanwhile, BDSM imagery is proliferating across the American pop cultural landscape, a fact first noted in the scientific literature by Falk and Weinberg (1983). In April 2011 the number-one song on the Billboard "Radio Songs" and "Pop Songs" charts was "S&M" by pop star Rihanna (Billboard, 2011). A 1997 *Newsweek* brief article commenting on "the mainstreaming of S&M" in advertising proclaimed that "S&M has become so common-place, so banal, that it can safely be used to sell beer" (Marin, 1997, p. 85).

Weiss (2006), however, cautions against assuming the proliferation of BDSM imagery itself automatically leads to acceptance. She sees BDSM often represented as "an abnormal, damaged type" (p. 111) and of more normative representations (what she calls "acceptance via normalization") she questions whether something need be common to be acceptable. Weiss sees both approaches as reinforcing "boundaries between normal, protected, and privileged sexuality, and abnormal, policed, and pathological sexuality" (p. 111). When considering how to frame sex education that includes BDSM, educators have a choice of advocating for acceptance of BDSM behaviors specifically or educating about sexual diversity in general. In a theoretical discussion of the politics of SM, Macnair argues that the end of oppression of sexual minorities comes ultimately with "the end of distinct groups as such" (Macnair, 1989, pp. 151–152).

A "coming out" model of BDSM disclosure may inadvertently and inaccurately distinguish certain sexual behaviors as different from "normal" sexual behaviors. Pawlowski (2009) outlines the ways that various BDSM behaviors fall on a continuum from mild to extreme, where the mild version may not even be identified as BDSM, and concludes that BDSM behaviors are "nothing more than the extreme end of 'normal,' 'ordinary,' 'conventional' behaviors" (p. 74). Macnair also concludes that "in general" SM activities share much in common with non-SM behaviors (Macnair, 1989). Elements of SM, such as exploration of pleasure/pain thresholds, teasing, role playing, and power exchange, are present in many sexual behaviors to varying degrees. Kinsey data from the 1960s, for example, showed that 50% of respondents overall were aroused by being bitten (Gebhard, 1969). Highlighting the variability of human sexual behaviors and fantasies in general may be the best way to allow an individual to find themselves reflected in the information presented.

Existing Resources Informing BDSM Disclosure Decisions are Sparse

The most comprehensive treatment of disclosure as related to BDSM is a book called *When Someone You Love Is Kinky*. Designed to be given to someone who has questions or misgivings about learning that their loved one is kinky, it explains kink and why feeling seen or "coming out" might be important (Easton & Liszt, 2000). *Healthcare Without Shame* by Charles Moser is a handbook for people who want to disclose their sexuality to their doctors and gives guidance to caregivers on how to respond (Moser, 1999). Moser advocates for disclosing an interest in BDSM before suspicion of abuse triggers mandatory reporting. *The Kinky Girl's Guide to Dating* by Luna Grey offers about seven pages of assurance and warnings about coming out and tips such as using a pseudonym and discretion when joining mailing lists (Grey, 2004).

Online resources are sparse. The Web page *Coming Out into SM: Our Stories* offers 12 brief accounts of people identifying an interest in SM (Coming out into SM, 1996). Some BDSM social groups try to allay newcomers' fears with a few words on the topic of "coming out" or attending a first meeting (e.g., Kay, n.d., ¶ 1; Mitzi & Thomas, 2006). Searching online for "coming out in SM" shows a Web site for a group therapy practice in New Jersey which warns that mental health professionals can be called upon to testify in domestic violence and divorce/child custody proceedings: "Your mental health records may be subpoenaed . . . You are literally unsafe if you see a mainstream psychotherapist (IPG, n.d, ¶ 5)."

These resources create a contradictory landscape, some encouraging disclosure, others making it sound dangerous. Meanwhile, BDSM appeared for the first time in a mainstream teen sex ed book: *S.E.X.* includes a discussion on role play, bondage, D/S, and "edge play" as well as a caution against using BDSM play as a way to deny abuse (Corinna, 2007). There is no discussion of identity construction or disclosure, but it is an excellent resource for educators seeking an overview of BDSM (Corinna, p. 171). It also marks a "coming out" as it were of BDSM into teen sexuality education.

Disclosure as a Way of Connecting

In psychology, appropriate self-disclosure is a key ingredient in building intimacy and positive regard, but evaluating the appropriateness of self-disclosure is a complex operation pitting individual factors (personality, gender) and situation (timing, setting, type of relationship) against social norms, which may vary depending on upbringing, culture of origin, and so on (Derlega & Grzelak, 1979). Inappropriate disclosure can be perceived as "weird" (Goffman, 1967).

Disclosure of sexual orientation has generally been correlated with positive health and psychological outcomes, bolstering outreach that supports or encourages disclosure of homosexuality. Lesbian and gay youths, for example, who disclose their sexual orientation have been found to feel less loneliness and guilt, greater comfort, wholeness, psychological adjustment, self-esteem, a feeling of authenticity, a sense of being loved and accepted for who one is, and greater access to supportive communities (Savin-Williams, 2001). By contrast, hiding is stressful. Smart and Wegner (2000) described the cognitive burden associated with the constant preoccupation with hiding one's homosexuality as a "private hell." In a study about homosexuality and attempted suicide, Cato and Canetto (2003) reveal that "the experiences associated with being a stigmatized sexual minority while young and vulnerable are likely components of [suicide] risk. Coming to terms with one's sexual minority status can be psychologically challenging" (p. 497).

While we cannot assume these findings translate into the arena of BDSM disclosure, we are inspired by the compassion demonstrated in LGB awareness campaigns that combat isolation and shame. A recent campaign reassuring LGB young people who are bullied or feel different featured contributors such as President Obama:

> I . . . know what it's like to grow up feeling that sometimes you don't belong. It's tough. And for a lot of kids, the sense of being alone or apart—I know can just wear on you . . . But what I want to say is this. You are not alone. You didn't do anything wrong . . . with time you're going to see that your differences are a source of pride and a source of strength. (Obama, 2011, pp. 9–10)

What can be done to begin to express this type of reassurance to young people who may feel "alone or apart" because of their BDSM interests? To inform this question, we were curious how disclosure of an interest in BDSM is currently being considered. The following questions guided the research:

1. What motivates people to identify with BDSM?
2. What concerns do people have about disclosing an interest in BDSM?
3. What experiences have people had disclosing an interest in BDSM?
4. What sex education and outreach needs and wishes do BDSM-identified people have?

Methods

A study was designed to collect qualitative data in order to form a general descriptive and exploratory picture. As the disclosure decision-making process of this population is largely unstudied, it is appropriate to begin with qualitative methods. IRB approval was obtained from the respective institutions of the authors. Respondents were recruited online via postings on an SM listserv, FetLife.com, craigslist.org, social networking sites, and snowball sampling among those who had already been interviewed. Recruitment text asked people to share experiences about "coming out into SM." After 15 interviews had been processed, new recruitment was done targeting people who practice these behaviors but do not participate in the SM "scene" or do not disclose. Only individuals 18 or older were included in the study. Participants gave verbal consent at the beginning of telephone interviews.

The interview protocol was semi-structured with an interview schedule of open-ended questions about respondents' experiences with identifying and disclosing their interest in SM. Questions fell into three broad categories: *development of self-identity* ("How old were you when you first had the feelings or fantasies that you later learned were part of SM? When did you learn these feelings were sadomasochistic? How did you learn this? How did you feel about all of this at that time?"), *disclosure* ("Have you told other people who are not into SM about your feelings/ fantasies/ behavior/ desires? What is the relationship of these people to you? Why did you tell them? How did they respond to what you told them? How did you feel about their responses?"), and *larger theoretical constructs about SM* ("How do you describe yourself and your interests? What is your definition of SM? How do you conceptualize your SM interests within the framework of other sexual minority identifications?"). We also asked demographic questions and Kinsey scales on hetero/homosexuality, submissive/dominant role, and added a scale on monogamy/ polyamory.

Interviews lasted between 1.5 and 2 hours. Interviews were professionally transcribed and verified by the researchers. All identifying characteristics were removed from the data. Transcripts were analyzed in Word using color coding, memos, and manual sorting. Categories emerged inductively.

Results

Of 20 respondents, 9 were in their twenties, 5 in their thirties, 3 in their forties, and 3 in their fifties. Thirteen

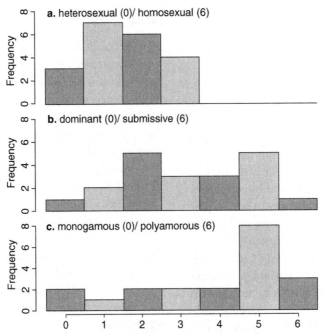

FIGURE 1 The Kinsey scales. Respondents rated themselves on scales from 0–6, where zero meant exclusively heterosexual, dominant, and monogamous, and six meant exclusively homosexual, submissive, and polyamorous. The y-axis shows the frequency of each answer.

were male (one of whom identified as gender bending) and 7 were female (one of whom identified as trans). Five had graduate degrees, 10 had college degrees, and 2 were in college. As seen in Figure 1, scale questions about sexual orientation, role preference of dominant or submissive, and relationship preference of monogamous or polyamorous revealed a diverse sample, though none of the respondents identified as "predominantly homosexual, but incidentally heterosexual" or "exclusively homosexual with no heterosexual." Most respondents reported being highly identified with SM, one liked some of the behaviors but did not identify with words such as "kink" or "SM," and several hesitated to adopt a general label such as "SM" to describe their specific interests.

Overall, respondents born in the 1940s, 1950s, and 1960s reported more shame and stigma experiences than respondents born in the 1970s and 1980s. Many of the older respondents discovered their sexual interests in total isolation, not knowing whether anyone else shared their interests. In contrast, by the time they were teenagers, all but one of the younger people knew about some forms of sexual behavior that gave them a context for their interests, even if they did not know about BDSM specifically, or did not know about whether others shared their specific interests.

Interest in BDSM can Develop in Childhood

As shown in Figure 2, 13 respondents reported that by age 15 they were aware of fantasies or feelings which they later identified as SM-related. Seven respondents reported that awareness by age 10. These respondents characterized their childhood SM interests as preceding sexual fantasy or as their earliest sexual fantasies. None of the respondents mentioned their interest to their parents when they were children. Several, however, reported a time of childhood innocence characterized by an unabashed ability to express their interests to peers. One male recalls:

> I was somewhere around 6 or 7. I had my 1-year-older sister drag me into field with a bunch of the local boys where they broke some switches and proceeded to switch me. And I ran off screaming and in tears once I broke loose. I got back to the house, sat on the stone steps on the porch and began to feel the welts and became aware that I was . . . juvenilely aroused. And I spent the day watching with regret while the welts faded. And then the next day I asked them to do it again.

On the other hand, one female respondent recalled misgivings about early play:

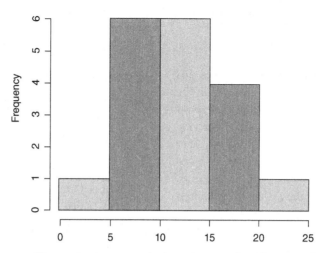

Age at first awareness (n=18)

FIGURE 2   Age at first awareness. Respondents were asked at what age they first experienced fantasies or feelings that the later realized were related to BDSM. This frequency chart shows the number of responses for age categories 0–5, 6–10, 11–15, 16–20, and 21–25. Two respondents are not included because they did not feel the question applied to them, having discovered BDSM for reasons other than intrinsic fantasies.

When I was probably 8 or so I remember one summer playing Roman master and slave with my brother . . . I only remember playing it once, actually. I think I was really getting into it and sort of scared myself. Because, you know, slaves and masters are very, very bad things and I was really enjoying being the master and that . . . started to bother me.

Levels of Identification Can Vary

One respondent characterized SM as "sort of a sexual orientation," and many respondents described BDSM as central to their sexual arousal. Others became interested in BDSM gradually through dating someone, trying and liking an activity, or reading about it. Respondents reported many reasons for finding BDSM appealing, including creativity, pageantry, exploration, play, rush, friendliness of the scene, emphasis on consent and communication, physical release, self-exploration, spiritual experiences, emphasis on non-genital sex, and acquisition of skills and knowledge of how the body works.

Relationships to the BDSM "scene" ranged from those who attended "play parties" to those who preferred private settings. Incongruities between one's own values and those perceived in the BDSM "scene" impeded respondents' identification with BDSM. For example, one respondent who hesitated to identify himself as "kinky" argued that "this whole dominatrix stuff, where a person is all dressed up in leather with a whip and everything,

that's not attractive to me . . ." Several felt "scene" behaviors and fashions were too prescriptive or homogenous. One respondent balked at too big a deal being made of his interest: "Just because I'm into SM activity doesn't mean . . . that's the focus of my time or energy."

It Can be Dangerous when people do not Have Good Information about BDSM

An interest in BDSM can exist without knowing about BDSM. One respondent explored BDSM behaviors extensively in high school without terminology or safety precautions:

We knew what we liked . . ., but we didn't know words for it . . . Thinking about it now when we were doing . . . pretty major DS scenes all without a safe word I'm like: oh my God it's amazing we didn't kill ourselves.

Dangerous play is one consequence of not being taught about BDSM in a comprehensive and accepting way, but another is the risk of learning about BDSM in a negative frame. One respondent with a childhood interest in bondage remembered being in "seventh or eighth grade," hearing the term "dominatrix," and asking her father's friend, "What's a dominatrix?" She received an answer about torture and how "crazy guys get off on it." She recalled:

It made me feel even more ashamed. I'm like: *Oh my God! I'm like a female Attila the Hun . . . Men wouldn't be my sexual partners, they'd be my POWs. Oh my God. I'm a horrible person.* It made me feel just so bad.

Lack of reassurance and visibility of BDSM created distress and shame for several respondents. Unaware in the 1950s that there was such a thing as BDSM, one respondent kept his interests a secret, describing an "underlying feeling of like: *God, there's something horribly wrong with me*, that if anybody knew about it . . . they'd be gone." Even after learning that there was a name for their interests, several reported distress reconciling their BDSM interests with their understandings of pacifism and feminism.

Whether to Disclose is a Complex Consideration

Respondents varied in their choice to disclose. Some had disclosed to no one at all or only to lovers, while others had disclosed to friends, parents, or society at large. A sense of integrity was one motivator: "Being myself and exploring myself without shame and encouraging others to do likewise," "Life is easier and there's less angst because you don't have to worry about keeping it secret." Others disclosed for reasons such as being asked directly, to share honestly with friends, to be able to talk about a relationship with friend, or as political activism.

Respondents commonly worried that unwanted or inappropriate disclosure would be burdensome to the recipient of the information: "If I want to be good friends with somebody, I want them to have a good sense of who I am, but I don't want to dump things in their laps unnecessarily or make them uncomfortable." One respondent felt he needed to protect his parents even though they are aware of his interest:

> I've been going to this club for a while. I know my mom knows that it's a BDSM club and I'm pretty sure my dad does. Usually when I say I'm going, I just say I'm going like "into DC" or "the club in DC," so they don't have to think about it.

Many respondents expressed resignation to the norm of not talking about BDSM, and some merely understood it as a silence norm they experienced in other areas of sexuality: "I don't bring up my lifestyle in contexts where it's not appropriate."

Respondents assessed the safety of disclosure based on overall evaluation of a person; being seen as judgmental or narrow was sometimes disqualifying. Not surprisingly, someone else admitting an interest in BDSM functioned as an invitation to disclosure. After hearing a

friend say she enjoyed being tied up during sex, one respondent was able to admit her fantasies for the first time, saying, "She was . . . the first person I really confessed to . . ."

Parents Might Need Help Understanding When Their Children Disclose

Many respondents did not feel a need or desire to "come out" to their parents about their BDSM interests. One deemed homosexuality a worthy thing to "come out" about whereas BDSM, for her, was not. Five respondents had disclosed to their parents. Three disclosed on principle, one was directly asked, and another respondent had reason to believe her mother knew but was not certain. At first, this last respondent considered not disclosing: "I started out thinking, well I don't know why anybody would come out to their parents who's kinky. It certainly is none of my parent's business what I do and what an awkward conversation to have!" But the respondent moved forward with telling her mom to allay potential fears. "I actually did come out as kinky to her . . . because I knew that she had very negative associations with BDSM . . . and I wanted her to know that it was safe and caring."

Three parent reactions were described as cautious and focusing on safety. One mother was baffled. A male respondent recalled:

> . . . she's like, "uh, I don't understand. I don't have a context to put this in. I kinda understand what you're talking about. Did I fail somewhere in raising you?" Jestingly. And, then I said, "No. But, you know, right now it seems that I'm enjoying this and, you know, it's really doing something for me." So . . . she's like, "Have a good time, be careful."

Another respondent invited a conversation through passive disclosure by not hiding the BDSM book he was reading. He was surprised that his mom responded with concern:

> So my mom came up to me sometime later, and was like, "[Name], are you into S&M?" And I was like, "Yes." And she was like, "Oh," which was sort of a worried mom thing that she does. And I was actually surprised, because my introduction to [SM] was in an environment where it was so normal. And my parents are generally such open-minded people that I didn't actually expect her to even have that response. I think that she's still weirded out by it.

This respondent followed the conversation with some online information: "And we talked about it and she was like, 'Make sure everything is safe and stuff.' And I was like, 'Yes, mom. They do focus on that a lot.'" This focus on safety and the assumption that his interests were unsafe seemed to disappoint this respondent, who was eager to engage in a much richer discussion.

Some respondents reported overtly negative parental reactions. One respondent born in 1986 was "outed" when she was 11 by the counselor she was seeing because of her parents' divorce:

> I confessed to her that I liked the idea of somebody tying me up. And I liked the idea of tying somebody else up . . . I talked to her about it and then regretted it because I came back and I went into my room and a lot of the pictures [for example of pop star Trent Reznor of the band Nine Inch Nails in bondage] were taken off the wall. And I turned to my dad, like, "Where did a lot of my posters go?" And he goes, "You know why you can't have them. And I'm not going to explain it to you." And I asked, "Did she say something to you, or did you guys talk about me?" Which makes me still feel very uncomfortable to this day. Because she had no right; what I told her was in confidence.

The respondent describes how she "got the message" from her father's reaction, and thereafter took pains to prevent her mother from also finding out.

> I felt really ashamed . . . so when I was with my mom, I discussed nothing of the kind with her. I was so scared that he was going to say something to her. So I just tried to be the good girl. You know? Good daughter. 'Hey, let's go get coffee. Let's paint our nails!' Because I was always so scared.

The same respondent described a process of writing and then burning her writing:

> . . . stuff that I wrote, some of it I thought was just way too dangerous and, as soon as I got done writing it . . ., I'd burn it in the wood stove . . . Or . . . I'd always go to another dumpster, of another apartment complex. Just in case, you know, in my horrible, pre-teen sitcom mind that somebody is going to find it and recognize my handwriting. I was always so paranoid.

Disclosure in Dating Can be Fraught with Stigma

Disclosing one's interests to partners met outside of a BDSM context created anxiety for many of the respondents. Some respondents attempted to make the process less awkward by disclosing over the computer, via humor, or sneaking BDSM into sex playfully. A number of people described being rejected by potential partners who refused to participate or learn about BDSM. Refusing partners were worried that the BDSM interest would supersede other sexual activities, were "appalled" by hearing about activities at an SM nightclub, or judged BDSM (in this case, using Velcro wrist restraints) as oppositional to a loving relationship. After her suggestion to try these restraints on her boyfriend, one respondent offered, "How about if you tied me up. Would that make you comfortable?" to which the boyfriend replied, "No that would make me extremely uncomfortable and there's a lot of things wrong with this." Another respondent to the study who worked as a "master" to paying clients reported having some clients with "enormous psychological issues" because they've been told they were "sick" or "depraved," who then never mentioned their interests again.

Several respondents dated solely within BDSM-identified circles, describing a preference for disclosing their interests up front as a pragmatic component of finding a compatible partner. Some used Internet dating sites that cater to specific kinks or sites that allow users to specify their interests through a searchable interface. However, this foregrounding of sexual information did not appeal to everyone: "I don't look for the sexual practices, because that's not the primary element of the relationship that I'm interested in." However, falling in love with a person who does not share one's kinks presented difficulties. One respondent considered "toning down" her kinks to make a relationship work, but another regretted not taking the kink mismatch more seriously before he got married:

> I wish I had known enough to say maybe this isn't the right long term relationship for me. I still thought I could sort of suppress everything and, you know, make it to the grave without having to confront these difficult things; that I'd just keep them all buried and let it be.

Disclosure in dating can have big implications for someone trying to keep an interest in BDSM a secret, as was the case for one of the older respondents who married someone he did not even want to be dating anymore, thinking, "I can't break up with her now because I just told her my secret. And if I broke up she might start telling everybody."

Notably, respondents were happy about situations where they got to explore their interests: "I was so happy to be with someone else who was also kinky, whose sexuality complemented mine and who I could play around with and explore these things with."

A Positive and Accepting Experience is Possible

Not all respondents reported difficulty with identity formation in their developmental years; some experienced accepting and encouraging environments. The younger respondents described attending a boarding school with a kinky goth-identified subgroup, attending a liberal college with openly kink-identified students, or coincidentally developing friendship with another kinky person:

> I had a kinky friend . . . starting in middle school. And then in high school I had a kinky boyfriend, and that created a very positive . . . environment where I was free to explore being kinky without fear of rejection.

One respondent described SM becoming normalized for him:

> The more that I experience it, the more it's like anything else that I do. It's just a thing that I do . . . some people do it and some people don't. And it moves me further and further away from being able to see why some people are so threatened by it.

Several respondents remembered their sense of astonishment at discovering they were not alone in their desires and that there were social support organizations. This was especially true of the older respondents who experienced long periods of not knowing whether anyone shared their interests:

> When I first went to that nightclub . . . I felt like I was at home . . . All of my life I've had to hide sexuality desires and like wow, here's a place where you don't have to hide.

Many of the young respondents gravitated toward BDSM social groups called "TNGs" that limit their membership to ages 19–35. Some respondents deeply connected with these groups: "I just really felt that I had this sense of belonging . . . It was wonderful." Here, too, there was a disclosure element to attending a first meeting:

> I had a sense of vulnerability of exposing a part of myself that I had always found very difficult and complicated to expose and to share with people. I wasn't sure how people would take it, whether I would be rejected or . . . people would think I was out there or what have you.

People Wonder Whether it is Necessary to Hide at Work

Most respondents had not disclosed at work. Even two of the respondents who insisted they were completely "out" about their interest in SM put a caveat around being "out"

at work. One respondent was actively deciding whether to choose a career path where he envisioned his interests being accepted versus a more high-power one where he imagined hiding might be required. The question on several respondents' minds was whether disclosure needs to be actively avoided to protect one's job security:

> I have security clearance that I have to maintain. So, there's some vague concern there in the sense that I wouldn't necessarily want my personal business coming out at work, because it could potentially jeopardize my career. But I'm not really sure that it could or not. It's not really something you can go ask.

A respondent who had been a politician concluded: "Being visible in the political world did mean the kinky stuff had to be very, very much under the radar." For another respondent, the fear of being judged for BDSM themes in her master's thesis was stalling her degree completion.

Mainly, people craved information about whether they had any protection from discrimination. Assuming secrecy would be a problem, not the behaviors in question, one respondent volunteered her interests during the background investigation for her overseas government job, writing, "I participate in consensual sadomasochistic activity. This is not a secret. It is not blackmail material."

People are Aware of Stigma

All respondents were aware of stigma against SM. The main stigma reported was a taboo against discussing the topic ("There's no socially accepted way to express ourselves . . ."), which made open communication difficult and rare. The taboo frustrated one respondent who found deep meaning and beauty in her BDSM experiences: "It's completely outrageous that we can't even talk about the greatest, most powerful mystery of our beings." The stigma landscape was articulated by one respondent as:

> The vast majority of people still think that SM has to do with either Torquemada or Heliogabalus . . . and not the 37% that the Durex survey showed used gags and blindfolds in their adult sex.[3]

This respondent posits a cyclical relationship between stigma and disclosure, saying that these misperceptions persist "because we're not out about who we are." Many respondents were indeed circumspect about their disclosures, citing real risk: "I personally know someone who spent three years in prison for assault in a consensual scene. Handled it with aplomb, but they sent him to jail. And he was a Bay area guy . . . This was not Kansas. So it's real." Another respondent reported a neighbor notifying social services about his BDSM activities and consequently having to explain and disclose to his son.

Basic Sex Education Needs are Unmet

Respondents were asked what they would wish for from social services or sex education. Visibility of BDSM in general and specific kinks in particular was a common desire. Some expressed frustration about not knowing anyone who admitted these desires; the prevalence of SM pornography was the only way they knew others had these interests. Those whose interests appeared early in life expressed a need for reification, communication ("if somebody would have come to me and talked straight with me"), understanding, and reassurance ("if somebody just told me that 'there's nothing wrong with you' . . . I think I would have felt a lot better."). Asked what the ideal message of reassurance might be, one respondent offered:

> that whatever it is, if you're dominant or submissive . . . that it's okay to express these things . . . They've been shown in paintings. They've been in literature. They've been with civilization . . . since the beginning of time.

Many respondents wished specifically for greater ease in talking about SM, hoping for skills or an "acceptable way" to broach the subject. One respondent wished for education of society at-large about consent, concluding that, "If people understood consent, then explaining how it makes the whole world of kinky behavior safe and responsible becomes trivia." Respondents wished for more media and court engagement with the human rights issues involved in BDSM. One concluded, "I wish people were more out. I really do. I wish people weren't so afraid and so intimidated . . ." One respondent saw the interview process as an exemplary solution, suggesting simply talking "about real sex . . . seems to be what society might need to just get over . . . the taboo nature of it all." Many of the study respondents ended the interview with expressions of gratitude for being offered an opportunity to talk openly about this topic.

Discussion

The results from this study and literature review demonstrate that there are many stigma and disclosure issues in BDSM which sexuality education and other social services could address.

While individual experiences varied widely, the data show the stigma around BDSM manifesting in negative framing of BDSM, invisibility and marginalization of BDSM, and taboos regarding speaking about BDSM. Many respondents reported initial childhood ease around fantasies turning to self-judgment or shame as they struggled to reconcile their interests with negative cues from their environments. Many reclaimed their fantasies and reported feeling good about their interests in the present, but even when personal acceptance was achieved, disclosure necessitated continuing consideration of stigma. Evidence of isolation was found in respondents not revealing their interests to spouses, lovers, or friends. Evidence of stress was found, both in planning and enacting disclosure as well as in preventing unwanted disclosure, for example, as in fear of BDSM interests being inadvertently revealed at work. Respondents universally reported awareness of a norm of silence surrounding disclosure of an interest in BDSM, which they variously chose either to respect or disregard.

When thinking about disclosure resources, a useful distinction can be drawn between disclosure to a lover or spouse and disclosure to a family member, roommate, or friend. The motivations, risks, and "appropriateness" calculations vary greatly between these two areas. In considering disclosure to family and friends, the most common concern was that disclosure be appropriate and not burden the recipient of the disclosure. Respondents were torn between the desire for sharing and integrity and a desire to act appropriately. The data revealed complex considerations of personal variables and fluctuating social norms in deciding the appropriateness of disclosing an interest in BDSM, suggesting it can be a challenging and confusing task.

For the development of resources, individuals have vastly different levels of identification with these fantasies or behaviors. Some wanted to disclose to society at-large, for others there was no interest in disclosure at all. Stigma experiences varied from people who were explicitly judged upon disclosure to people who were integrated into accepting environments where the behaviors were not taboo and disclosure seemed unnecessary.

Subpopulations of those interested in BDSM may have different sexuality education needs. For example, children and young people who have fantasies that they later realize are related to BDSM might benefit from parent education about compassionate responses to human sexual variation. people who consider their BDSM interests a core component of their sexual identities or are involved in BDSM activism might benefit greatly from "coming out" language and concepts. However, people who see BDSM as a private sexual activity may not relate to framing disclosure as "coming out" and benefit from reassuring education about human sexual variation or highly private access to compassionate support about the trials of dating.

Sex educators need to be aware that some young people are already experiencing accepting environments, either socially, via media, or via books like *s.e.x.* (Corinna, 2007). It cannot be assumed that everyone experiences all kinds of stigma, and education about risk would ideally be designed not to induce fear and stigma.

Limitations

This study has several limitations. The sample size is small and probably biased toward people who have strong SM interests and who have disclosed their interests, as much study recruiting was done via SM organization mailing lists. The sample did not include any respondents who identified as purely homosexual. Fourteen respondents lived in major cities on the East Coast; this underrepresents rural areas, conservative areas, and sexually progressive cities such as San Francisco. Given the wide variation among respondents, it is possible that subgroups within these populations have specific and distinct experiences of disclosure and stigma not brought to light here. This study is formative qualitative research and cannot be generalized.

Suggestions for Further Research

Studies of subsets of this population might reveal variations in stigma and disclosure experiences: How do they vary by demographic, psychosocial variables, or by specific fantasy or interest? In-depth study of disclosure within sexual relationships might reveal best practices and help people prepare for common difficulties. The appearance of these interests in childhood and teen years invites work on parent education. Studying how (and whether) these topics appear in sex education classrooms today could help support sex educators.

Implications

While future research may broaden the scope of knowledge on this topic, we proceeded to synthesize our findings with the literature review to posit how one might address the known disclosure concerns at our current state of knowledge. Testing these and other messages and developing materials for this population present a unique opportunity for sex education and health communication research because this population has not ever been targeted by campaigns or outreach.

That said, we are not naïve to the struggle often surrounding even basic sex education in America, and we imagine that parents, teachers, and administrators will have concerns about this topic. Outreach to this population may begin in specialized, niche, online, or progressive efforts. Furthermore, a separate research focus is needed to address safety and behavior education. Our emphasis is on helping young people form healthy self-concepts by reassuring them about common sexual variations and helping them navigate stigma and disclosure. Some suggestions for developing such resources are:

- *Reflect the research that we do know.* There is enough scientific evidence to support much general education about BDSM. For example, an interest in BDSM can begin in childhood; BDSM activities are wide ranging; there is evidence that participation in them is common; the activities may or may not involve pain. Some people do "kinky" things without calling it BDSM; kinkiness is hard to define.
- *Have the destigmatizing facts on hand.* Be prepared to explain that research does not support past stigmatization and that current APA pronouncements do not see an interest in sadism or masochism as a problem unless they lead to clinically significant distress or to nonconsensual behaviors.
- *Know the biology.* Explaining how assorted variations of human sexuality are pleasurable (e.g., the endorphin rush of heavy sensation, or the relaxation effect of surrender) might validate people's fantasies.
- *Teach about consent.* Teaching people about consent in general, or teaching BDSM safety fundamentals such as "safe, sane, and consensual" and "safe words," may allay ethical concerns and elucidate the dissimilarity of BDSM and abuse.
- *Adapt existing disclosure advice.* The existing body of literature pertaining to "coming out" could be adapted for disclosure of an interest in BDSM. Educators could address that disclosure can be stressful, that there are ways of assessing the safety and timing of disclosure, and that one can anticipate reactions, especially questions about safety. Educators could validate the complexity of the decision about whether to disclose.
- *Validate disclosure as well as nondisclosure.* At this point, there is not enough research to conclusively advocate for or against disclosure of BDSM interest from a health point of view. Educators can use the existing knowledge of disclosure benefits and motivations in general and warn of the risks of BDSM disclosure in hopes of supporting informed decision making.
- *Invite dialogue.* Since people are reluctant to disclose in order not to burden their friends and family, and to comply with local norms the onus may be on

friends and family to invite the conversation. Society at large, and caretakers, medical providers, and human services providers in particular, might be educated on how to invite disclosure, or present accepting attitudes.

- *Coping with stigma.* Sexuality education might include strategies on how to cope with rejection or negative judgments that may be encountered. To deal with internalized stigma, educational materials could address self-doubt and self-judgment, and build self-esteem.
- *Create resources.* Resources could be developed such as hotlines, safe places to discuss disclosure, advice columns, and so forth.
- *Inform about resources.* people can be informed about the National Coalition of Sexual Freedom and its database of "Kink Aware Professionals" and the books *When Someone You Love is Kinky* and *Healthcare Without Shame.*

It is Difficult to Know How Much to Say About the Risks of Disclosure

While there have been cases of BDSM being stigmatized, risk is difficult to quantify. Paradoxically, addressing the current stigma environment might codify and reinforce stigma. Some known risks of disclosure in the current climate are:

- When disclosing to a therapist, there is a risk of being told one is "sick" and being "treated" for an interest in SM. There is also the risk of therapy records being subpoenaed and used against people. Despite the proposed clarification in the *DSM*, actions of individual therapists and legal precedents are unpredictable.
- When disclosing in a dating situation, there is risk of rejection and judgment, as well as potential for frustration and romantic distress.
- When disclosing in nondating situations, there is risk of stigma such as being judged negatively by friends, relations, or employers.
- Some BDSM behaviors might be criminalized even where there is consent. In some cases this may be relevant to a disclosure decision.

Is it possible to warn people of these risks and still present a neutral, welcoming attitude toward sexual diversity? The answer may vary across regions, educators, and target groups. Rather than reinforce a stigma, a legitimate ethical choice for sex educators might be to remain silent on certain dimensions of this topic. Risk might be reduced by nondiscrimination legislation and more social services helping those who experience

discrimination or stigma. As things stand, members of this sexual minority may have to fight like members of the LGB "coming out" movement did, voluntarily incurring personal risk and stigma in the name of pioneering disclosure of BDSM.

Conclusion

Addressing stigma and disclosure in this population is a relatively new area offering many opportunities for research and resource development. Young people whose sexualities involve BDSM interests currently do not receive many of the reassurances or support offered to other sexual minorities. If they learn about BDSM via a stigmatizing environment, they are at risk of developing shame and isolation. If they learn about it through pop culture, it may be a shallow or stigmatizing understanding. If they act on certain interests without good information, they may be doing dangerous things without proper safety precautions. Once they identify with BDSM, they are confronted with myriad disclosure decisions, each fraught with potential for connection and each with a potential of judgment and stigma. We identified some ways sex education might begin to address some of these concerns. More research on the population and testing of specific education strategies are needed, but we are confident that addressing marginalization and stigma and supporting the decision-making process surrounding disclosure of an interest in BDSM is a worthy new direction for sexuality education.

Notes

1. For help understanding how intense sensation can be pleasurable, we recommend *Speaking the Unspeakable: S/M and the Eroticisation of Pain* (Landridge, 2009).
2. Educators may find an essay "Is SM Pathological?" (Kleinplatz & Moser, 2007) helpful to navigating the *DSM* diagnostic criteria.
3. The statistic about gags and blindfolds could not be verified, but a Durex survey did find that 23% of British people surveyed had tried bondage, 41% spanking, 42% role play, and 37% owned handcuffs (Durex, 2009).

References

American Psychiatric Association. (1952). *Diagnostic and statistical manual of mental disorders* (1st ed.). Washington, DC: Author.

American Psychiatric Association. (1968). *Diagnostic and statistical manual of mental disorders* (2nd ed.). Washington, DC: Author.

American Psychiatric Association. (1980). *Diagnostic and statistical manual of mental disorders* (3rd ed.). Washington, DC: Author.

American Psychiatric Association. (2000). *Diagnostic and statistical manual of mental disorders* (4th ed., text rev.). Washington, DC: Author.

American Psychiatric Association. (2010). *Proposed draft revisions to DSM disorders and criteria.* Retrieved from http://www.dsm5.org/ProposedRevisions/Pages/proposedrevision.aspx?rid=188#

Billboard. (2011, week of April 23). S&M-Rihanna: Currently charting. Retrieved from http://www.billboard.com/features/rihanna-the-billboard-cover-story1004120008.story#/song/rihanna/ s-m/23241718

Breslow, N. (1986). Comparisons among heterosexual, bisexual, and homosexual male sadomasochists. *Journal of Homosexuality, 13*(1), 83–107.

Breslow, N., Evans, L., & Langley, J. (1985). On the prevalence and roles of females in the sadomasochistic subculture: Report on an empirical study. *Archives of Sexual Behavior, 14,* 303–317.

Cato, J. E., & Canetto, S. S. (2003). Attitudes and beliefs about suicidal behavior when coming out is the precipitant of the suicidal behavior. *Sex Roles, 49*(9), 497–505.

Coming out into SM: Our Stories (1996). Retrieved from http://www.black-rose.com/cuiru/archive/2-6/come-out.html

Corinna, H. (2007). *s.e.x.* New York, NY: Marlowe & Company.

Derlega, V. J., & Grzelak, J. (1979). Appropriateness of self-disclosure. In G. J. Chelune (Ed.), *Self-disclosure: Origins, patterns, and implications of openness in interpersonal relationships* (pp. 151–176). San Francisco, CA: Jossey-Bass.

Durex. (2009). The British sex survey 2009. Retrieved from http://www.durex.com/en-GB/SexualWellbeingSurvey/Pages/British-Sex-Survey-2009-Results.aspx

Easton, D., & Liszt, C. A. (2000). *When someone you love is kinky.* Oakland, CA: Greenery Press.

Falk, G., & Weinberg, T. S. (1983). Sadomasochism and popular Western culture. In T. Weinberg & G. W. L. Kamel (Eds.), *S and M: Studies in sadomasochism* (pp. 137–144). Buffalo, NY: Prometheus Books.

Gebhard, P. (1969). Fetishism and sadomasochism. In J. H. Masserman (Ed.), *Dynamics of deviant sexuality* (pp. 71–80). New York, NY: Grune & Stratton.

Goffman, E. (1963). *Stigma, notes on the management of spoiled identity.* Englewood Cliffs, NJ: Prentice Hall.

Goffman, E. (1967). *Interaction ritual.* Chicago, IL: Aldine.

Grey, L. (2004). *The kinky girl's guide to dating.* Oakland, CA: Greenery Press.

Institute for Personal Growth (IPG). (n.d.). Other sexual minorities. Retrieved from http://www.ipgcounseling.com/other_services.html

Janus, S., & Janus, C. (1993). *The Janus report on sexual behavior.* New York, NY: John Wiley & Sons.

Kamel, G. W. L. (1983). *The leather career: On becoming a sadomasochist.* In T. Weinberg & G. W. L. Kamel (Eds.), *S and M: Studies in sadomasochism* (pp. 73–79) Buffalo, NY: Prometheus Books.

Kay, T. (n.d.). Coming out and getting in. Retrieved from http://www.rcdc.org/articles/tamar-comingout.html

Kilgore, H., Sideman, L., Amin, K., Baca, L., & Bohanske, B. (2005). Psychologists' attitudes and therapeutic approaches toward gay, lesbian, and bisexual issues continue to improve: An update. *Psychotherapy: Theory, Research, Practice, Training, 42*(3), 395–400.

Kleinplatz, P., & Moser, C. (2007). Is SM pathological? In D. Langdridge & M. Barker (Eds.), *Safe, sane and consensual: Contemporary perspectives on sadomasochism* (pp. 55–62). New York, NY: Palgrave MacMillan. (Reprinted from *Lesbian & Gay Psychology Review, 6*(3), 255–260, 2005)

Kolmes, K., Stock, W., & Moser, C. (2006). Investigating bias in psychotherapy with BDSM clients. *Journal of Homosexuality, 50*(2), 301–324.

Langdridge, D. (2007). Speaking the unspeakable: S/M and the eroticisation of pain. In D. Langdridge & M. Barker (Eds.), *Safe, sane and consensual: Contemporary perspectives on sadomasochism* (pp. 85–97). New York, NY: Palgrave MacMillan.

Link, B. G., & Phelan, J. C. (2001). Conceptualizing stigma. *Annual Review of Sociology, 27,* 363–385.

Macnair, M. (1989). The contradictory politics of SM. In S. Shepherd & M. Wallis (Eds.), *Coming on strong: Gay politics and culture* (pp. 147–162). London, England: Unwin Hyman.

Maguen, S., Floyd, F. J., Bakeman, R., & Armistead, L. (2002). Developmental milestones and disclosure of sexual orientation among gay, lesbian, and bisexual youths. *Applied Developmental Psychology, 23,* 219–233.

Marin, C. (1997, December 29–January 5). "Lick me, flog me, buy me! The main-streaming of S&M has turned us into a jaded culture of kink." *Newsweek, 131,* 85.

Mitzi & Thomas. (2006, October 25). Your first black rose gateway meeting. Retrieved from http://www.br.org/blackrose/index.php?option=com_content&task=view&id=46&Itemid=46

Moser, C., & Levitt, E. E. (1987). An exploratory-descriptive study of a sadomasochistically oriented sample. *Journal of Sex Research, 23,* 322–337.

Moser, C. (1999). *Health care without shame.* San Francisco, CA: Greenery Press.

Moser, C., & Kleinplatz, P. J. (2005). DSM-IV-TR and the paraphilias: An argument for removal. *Journal of Psychology & Human Sexuality, 17*(3/4), 91–109.

Obama, B. (2011). President Obama shares his message of hope and support for LGBT youth who are struggling with being bullied. In D. Savage & T. Miller (Eds.), *It gets better: Coming out, overcoming bullying, and creating a life worth living* (pp. 9–10). New York, NY: Penguin Group.

Pawlowski, W. (2009). BDSM: The ultimate expression of healthy sexuality. In W.J. Taverner & R. W. McKee (Ed.), *Taking sides: Clashing views in human sexuality* (11th ed., pp. 70–75). New York, NY: McGraw-Hill.

Renaud, C. A., & Byers, E. S. (1999). Exploring the frequency, diversity and content of university students' positive and negative sexual cognitions. *Canadian Journal of Human Sexuality, 8*(1), 17–30.

Rust, P. C. (1993, March). "Coming out" in the age of social constructionism: Sexual identity formation among lesbian and bisexual women. *Gender and Society, 7*(1), 50–77.

Sandnabba, N. K., Santtila, P., & Nordling, N. (1999). Sexual behavior and social adaptation among sadomasochistically oriented males. *The Journal of Sex Research, 36*(3), 273.

Savin-Williams, R. C. (2001). *Mom, dad, I'm gay: How families negotiate coming out.* Washington, DC: American Psychological Association.

Smart, L., & Wegner, D. M. (2000). The hidden costs of stigma. In T. F. Heatherton, R. E. Kleck, M. R. Hebl, & J. G. Hull (Eds.), *The social psychology of stigma* (pp. 220–242). New York, NY: Guilford Press.

Stoller, R. (1991). *Pain and passion.* New York, NY: Plenum.

Weinberg, T. S. (1978). On 'doing' and 'being' gay: Sexual behavior and homosexual self-identity. *Journal of Homosexuality, 4*, 143–156.

Weinberg, T. S. (1987). Sadomasochism in the United States: A review of recent sociological literature. *The Journal of Sex Research, 23*(1), 50–69.

Weiss, M. D. (2006). Mainstreaming kink: The politics of BDSM representation in U.S. popular media. *Journal of Homosexuality, 50*(2), 103–132.

Wright, S. (2006). Discrimination of SM-identified individuals. *Journal of Homosexuality, 50*(2), 217–231.

Abuse of a Corpse: A Brief History and Re-theorization of Necrophilia Laws in the USA

John Troyer

Department of Comparative Studies, The Ohio State University, Columbus, USA

Abstract In September 2006, Wisconsin police discovered Nicholas Grunke, Alexander Grunke, and Dustin Radtke digging into the grave of a recently deceased woman. Upon questioning by police, Alexander Grunke explained that the three men wanted to exhume the body for sexual intercourse. In the Wisconsin state court system, the three men were charged with attempted third-degree sexual assault and attempted theft. None of the men could be charged with attempted necrophilia, since the state of Wisconsin has no law making necrophilia illegal. What the Wisconsin case exposed was the following gap in US jurisprudence: many states have no law prohibiting necrophilia. This article on US necrophilia laws argues that human corpses and the laws that govern the use of dead bodies are uniquely positioned to cause precisely these legal discrepancies since the dead body is a quasi-subject before the law. This examination also presents an argument about one of the fundamental reasons that this gap in US law exists. Specifically, it is argued that the ambiguous juridical standing of the human corpse in necrophilia cases compounds the sexual monstrousness of the necrophiliac and of necrophilic acts. This article is the first part of a much larger study on the dead body and the law.

KEYWORDS: necrophilia; corpse; sexuality; deviancy; death; law

Introduction

On September 2, 2006, at approximately 11 pm, the sheriff's office in Grant County, Wisconsin, Grant County Sheriff's Department (2006) dispatched officers to investigate an "unoccupied, suspicious vehicle" (p. 2)[1] near the St. Charles Cemetery. Police officers from the city of Cassville, Wisconsin, as well as Deputies from the Grant County Sheriff's office, discovered that 20-year-old twin brothers Nicholas and Alexander Grunke and their friend Dustin Radtke, also 20 years old, had been digging into the grave of the recently deceased Laura J. Tennessen. Ms. Tennessen, age 20, had died a week earlier in a motorcycle accident. Upon questioning by police, Alexander Grunke explained that the three men wanted to exhume the body so that Nicholas Grunke "could have sexual

intercourse with her [at] a pre-selected location behind his house" (p. 3). Nicholas Grunke and Dustin Radtke fled from the cemetery while Alexander Grunke was being

questioned and the two were later apprehended walking along a county road. Before going to the St. Charles cemetery that night, the men stopped at a nearby Wal-Mart store and purchased condoms "because Nick wanted to use them when he had sex with the corpse" (p. 3).[2]

All three men were charged with damage to cemetery property, attempted criminal damage to private property, and attempted third-degree sexual assault. Ms. Tennessen's corpse was never actually removed from its grave since the casket was inside a burial vault and the vault's locked lid stopped the trio from retrieving the body. When the case went to trial in mid-September 2006, the presiding judge, the Honorable George S. Curry, was presented with an intriguing argument by each of the three men's personal legal counsel.[3] Neither Nicholas Grunke nor the other two men could be charged with attempted third-degree sexual assault or any other necrophilic related crime because the laws in the state of Wisconsin do not criminalize sexual acts with dead bodies. The lawyers for the three men presented this argument, even though Wisconsin statute 940.225(7), the section of Wisconsin law that defines sexual assault crimes, applies: "whether a victim is dead or alive at the time of the sexual contact or sexual intercourse" (Wisconsin Statutes, 2006).[4]

* Correspondence: John Troyer, PhD, Visiting Assistant Professor, Department of Comparative Studies, The Ohio State University, 451 Hagerty Hall, 1775 College Road, Columbus, OH 43210 1340, USA. Tel: 6123106872. E-mail: troy0005@tc.umn.edu

John Troyer, *Mortality, Vol. 13, No. 2, May 2008*, Copyright © 2008 by Taylor & Francis, Ltd. Reprinted by permission of Taylor & Francis, Ltd., http://www.tandfonline.com

In what seems a true bit of counterintuitive logic, Judge Curry faced the following dilemma. Since Laura Tennessen was already dead at the time of the alleged crime and therefore no longer a *person* before the law, her body was legally recognized as human remains and not as a *victim*. Had Laura Tennessen died while the crime was being committed, then the attempted sexual assault charges could stand and the three men could have been charged with a Class G felony, which entailed "a fine not to exceed US$25,000 or imprisonment not to exceed 10 years, or both" (Wisconsin Statutes, 2006).[5] Judge Curry made a ruling from the bench and removed the attempted sexual assault charges. Nicholas Grunke, Alexander Grunke, and Dustin Radtke were then charged with the remaining illegal acts, namely, damage to cemetery property and attempted theft of movable property, a category that included Laura Tennessen's corpse. What shocked many of the case's observers was that even if the three men had actually succeeded in taking the body from the grave, they could have only been charged with theft of private property since Tennessen's post-mortem body belonged to her parents. After Judge Curry's ruling,[6] Wisconsin State Senator Dale Schultz became a vocal advocate for changing the law, in large part because the cemetery involved is in his legislative district. Senator Schultz released a press statement after the initial court ruling that summed up many state legislators' sentiments: "You'd think a state which unfortunately has seen the likes of Ed Gein and Jeffery Dahmer would have addressed this issue long ago" (Schultz, 2006).[7]

What this particular Wisconsin[8] case helps to illustrate is a surprising gap in US jurisprudence, namely, that many US states have no laws that specifically outlaw necrophilia.[9] Further, the state laws that do exist are sometimes extremely vague in their wording and can be easily circumvented by legal counsel. In addition, the states that actually possess necrophilia laws vary widely as to how sexual acts with dead bodies are defined and what kind of penalty should be administered for committing necrophilic acts. In this paper on necrophilia laws in the USA, the apparent inconsistency in US laws will be examined by presenting the three main kinds of laws that encompass sexual activity with human corpses. This examination also presents an argument about one of the fundamental reasons that this gap in US law exists. Specifically, it is argued that the ambiguous juridical standing of the human corpse in necrophilia cases compounds the sexual monstrousness of the necrophiliac and of necrophilic acts. The ambiguous legal space occupied by the dead body, then, also produces a human monstrousness for the corpse, although a dead human monster that is different from the necrophiliac. Toward the end of advancing this argument, this paper examines Michel Foucault's analysis of the human monster and the social degenerate from his 1974–1975 lectures on the abnormal individual.[10]

In the USA, both of these human bodies, the necrophiliac and the corpse, function outside the law, and the legal statutes of US states must be revised to somehow re-absorb these bodies back into the larger social order. The problem that repeatedly arises in these kinds of legal cases is not exclusively the question of how the law should (or *must*) define the necrophiliac. To be sure, this is a problem for a prosecutor when the law does not criminalize, let alone even mention, necrophilia. More often than not, the problem is how the law should *legally* recognize the human corpse. The monstrous qualities of the necrophiliac and the human corpse are quite specific in their own rights and my use of the term "monster" does not suggest a strict homology between the two. It is a situation, as suggested by Foucault (2003), where the ". . . frame of reference of the human monster is, of course, law" (p. 55). Without question, it is quite easy to recognize the necrophiliac as a legally defined monster but the challenge taken up by this article is to articulate how the human corpse takes on monstrous qualities amidst discussions of necrophilia laws.

Three General Kinds of US Laws

Approximately 40 of the 50 US states have some version of a law that defines illegal actions with human corpses. The inappropriate handling of corpses is sometimes defined as sexual but often includes other acts. This full array of inappropriate behaviors ranges from acts of grave desecration to tampering with the dead body at a crime scene. Only four states (Arizona, Georgia, Hawaii, and Rhode Island) explicitly use the word "necrophilia" in the respective state's statutory code. Hawaii's law explains, for example, that ". . . this section prohibits any sort of outrageous treatment of a human corpse, including sexual contact (necrophilia) and physical abuse" (Hawaii, 2006).[11] The remaining 36 states have an assortment of laws that encompass a penumbra of sexual acts: in Massachusetts there are "Crimes Against Chastity, Morality, Decency and Good Order," (Massachusetts, 2006)[12] and in Mississippi the law bars "Unnatural Intercourse" (Mississippi, 2006).[13] These laws often apply to deviant sexual behavior that may or may not include necrophilia. Nine US states (Illinois, Kansas, Louisiana, Nebraska, New Mexico, North Carolina, Oklahoma, Vermont, and Wisconsin) have no laws that address necrophilia.

Through examining the laws (or absence of laws) in all 50 states, three general kinds of statute become identifiable. These three kinds of laws are best described as (1) abuse of a corpse laws, (2) necrophilia laws that explicitly prohibit sexual activity with a dead body, and (3) unnatural acts or crimes against nature laws. (See Table I for a state by state listing of these laws and their potential penalties.)

Abuse of a Corpse Laws

The abuse of a corpse laws make reference to acts committed by a person that he or she "knows would outrage reasonable family sensibilities" or "would outrage reasonable community sensibilities."[14] Most of these laws do not make explicit reference to human sexual activity and/or specific sex acts. What constitutes the *outrage* against family or community sensibilities will of course be the key legal question in such a case. Some of these laws will also include language that provides safe harbor for individuals who work with dead bodies, i.e., funeral directors and medical examiners, so that a specific occupation is not prevented from doing its job. Contemporary examples of the abuse of a corpse law exist in approximately 14 states. Here is the law in the state of Ohio (2006):

> Ohio:[15]
> 2927.01 Abuse of a corpse.
> (A) No person, except as authorized by law, shall treat a human corpse in a way that the person knows would outrage reasonable family sensibilities.
> (B) No person, except as authorized by law, shall treat a human corpse in a way that would outrage reasonable community sensibilities.
> (C) Whoever violates division (A) of this section is guilty of abuse of a corpse, a misdemeanor of the second degree. Whoever violates division (B) of this section is guilty of gross abuse of a corpse, a felony of the fifth degree.
> Effective Date: 07-01-1996[16]

The abuse of a corpse statutes emerged historically, in part, from the writings of Dr. Richard Freiherr von Krafft-Ebing and his book *Psychopathia sexualis* (1933). The text was first published in Germany in 1882 and subsequently translated into English for publication in the USA. One hundred twenty-five years later, English translations of the *Psychopathia sexualis* remain in print, albeit as cultural artifacts and not a diagnostic manual. The relationship between the US abuse of a corpse laws and the book itself is not one of pure cause and effect; rather, Krafft-Ebing is one of the first medical authorities to articulate necrophilia as a sexual pathology. By defining the pathology, it became a human act that could be recognized in the law as criminal. Krafft-Ebing devotes a

number of pages in his book to what he terms "Mutilation of Corpses" and examines some infamous cases in European history. What Krafft-Ebing created with the *Psychopathia sexualis* was an index of reported sexual abuses of human corpses and the remedies sought by local legal authorities. He also medically defined the notion of human sexual desire towards dead bodies. As Krafft-Ebing (1933) explained, "It is possible that the corpse—a human form absolutely without will—satisfies an abnormal desire, in that the object of desire is seen to be capable of absolute subjugation, without possibility of resistance" (p. 100).[17] Krafft-Ebing also notes that ". . . this horrible kind of sexual indulgence is so monstrous that the presumption of a psychopathic state is, under all circumstances, justified . . ." (p. 611). These laws work by using extremely broad language to suggest socially taboo acts involving dead bodies without any explicit definition of what the "abuse" entails.

Necrophilia Laws

The necrophilia laws, as opposed to corpse abuse statutes, are far more explicit at criminalizing sexual activities with corpses. In many instances, the necrophilia laws are in fact older abuse of a corpse law with new and improved references to specific human sex acts. These laws may in fact still bear the title "Abuse of a Corpse," minus the sweeping generalities of their progenitors. The statutory language used can be both general in the description of human sexuality as well as extremely specific. Here are two quite different examples of necrophilia laws.[18] The first is from the state of Minnesota (2006):

> Minnesota:[19]
> 609.294 BESTIALITY.
> Whoever carnally knows a dead body or an animal or bird is guilty of bestiality, which is a misdemeanor. If knowingly done in the presence of another the person may be sentenced to imprisonment for not more than one year or to payment of a fine of not more than US$3,000 or both.
> History: 1967 c 507 s 5; 1971 c 23 s 42; 1984 c 628 art 3 s 11; 1986 c 444

The second law is from the state of Nevada (2006):

> Nevada:[20]
> SEXUAL PENETRATION OF DEAD HUMAN BODY
> 201.450 Unlawful act; penalty.
> 1. A person who commits a sexual penetration on the dead body of a human being is guilty of a category A felony and shall be punished by imprisonment

Table I.   Index of American abuse of a corpse, necrophilia, and crimes against nature laws.

State	Legal code	Title of law	Type of law	Potential penalty
Alabama	Section 13A-11-13	Abuse of Corpse	Abuse of Corpse	Class C felony: Up to 10 years in prison; not more than US$15,000 fine
Alaska	Section 11.61.130	Misconduct Involving a Corpse	Necrophilia	Class A misdemeanor: Not more than 1 year imprisonment; US$10,000 fine
Arizona	32-1364	Crimes against the Dead	Necrophilia	Class 4 felony: 2 1/2 years in prison; an amount fixed by the court not more than US$150,000 fine
Arkansas	5-60-101	Abuse of a Corpse	Abuse of a Corpse	Class D felony: Sentence shall not exceed 6 years in prison; fine not exceeding US$10,000
California	Section 7052 of the Health and Safety Code	Human Remains: Sexual Contact	Necrophilia	Felony: Up to 8 years in prison; no apparent fine
Colorado	18-13-101	Abuse of a Corpse	Abuse of a Corpse	Class 2 misdemeanor: Maximum 12 months imprisonment; US$1,000 fine, or both
Connecticut	Section 53a-73a	Sexual assault in the fourth degree	Necrophilia	Class D felony: Prison term not less than 1 year nor more than 5 years; fine not to exceed US$5,000 or Class A misdemeanor: Prison term not to exceed 1 year; a fine not to exceed US$2,000
Delaware	Statute 1332	Abusing a Corpse	Abuse of a Corpse	Class A misdemeanor: Up to 1 year incarceration; fine up to US$2,300; restitution or other conditions as the court deems appropriate
Florida	872.06	Abuse of a Dead Human Body	Necrophilia	Second Degree felony: Imprisonment not exceeding 15 years; US$10,000 fine
Georgia	Statute 16-6-7	Necrophilia	Necrophilia	Imprisonment not less than 1 year and not more than 10 years
Hawaii	Statute 711-1108	Abuse of a Corpse	Necrophilia	Misdemeanor: Imprisonment for a maximum of 1 year; no fine
Idaho	18-6605	Crime Against Nature	Crimes Against Nature	Prison sentence of not less that 5 years in the state prison; no fine
Illinois	No Law	No Law	No Law	Special Note: Sex with Dead Animals is against the law
Indiana	Indiana Code 35-45-11-2	Abuse of Corpse	Necrophilia	Class D felony: 6 months in prison; not more than US$10,000 fine
Iowa	709.18	Abuse of a Corpse	Necrophilia	Class D felony: No more than 5 years confinement; at least US$500 and no more than US$7,500 fine
Kansas	No Law	No Law	No Law	No Law

continued

Table I. Continued

State	Legal code	Title of law	Type of law	Potential penalty
Kentucky	Kentucky Revised Statute 525.12	Abuse of Corpse	Necrophilia	Class D felony: At least 1 year but not more than 5 years in state prison; not less than US$1,000 and not greater than US$10,000 fine
Louisiana	No Law	No Law	No Law	No Law
Maine	Statute 508	Abuse of Corpse [sexual acts not included]	Abuse of a Corpse	Class D crime: Less than 1 year in county jail; US$2,000 fine
Maryland	Statute 3-322	Unnatural or Perverted Sexual Practice	Crimes Against Nature	Misdemeanor: Imprisonment not longer than 10 years; fine not exceeding US$1,000
Massachusetts	Part IV: Chapter 272	Crimes Against Chastity, Morality, Decency, and Good Order		
	Chapter 272: Section 34	Crime Against Nature [may or may not include necrophilia]	Crimes Against Nature	Imprisonment in the state prison for 20 years; no fine
Michigan	Section 750.160	Disinterment, Mutilation, Defacement, or Carrying Away of Human Body	No Law [against necrophilia]	Felony: Imprisonment for not more than 10 years; fine of not more than US$5,000
Minnesota	Minnesota Statute 609.294	Bestiality	Necrophilia ["carnally know"]	Misdemeanor: Imprisonment for not more than 1 year and/or US$3,000 fine
Mississippi	Statute 97-29-19	Dead Bodies: Disinterment for Sale or Wantonness	Imprisonment in the state penitentiary not more than 5 years or in the county jail not more than 1 year and/or not be fined more than US$500	
Missouri	Statute 566.070	Deviate Sexual Assault [dead body is not stipulated]	No Law	No Law
Montana	Part 4. Provisions Relating to Corpses, Section 44-3-404	Criminal Penalty [individual "purposely touches, removes or disturbs" the corpse]	Abuse of a Corpse	Misdemeanor: Imprisonment in the county jail for not more than 1 year and/or not more than US$500 fine
Nebraska	No Law	No Law	No Law	No Law
Nevada	Nevada Revised Statute: 201.450	Sexual Penetration of Dead Human Body	Necrophilia	Category A felony: Imprisonment in the state prison for life with the possibility of parole after a minimum of 5 years served; not more than a US$20,000 fine

Table I. Continued

State	Legal code	Title of law	Type of law	Potential penalty
New Hampshire	Section 644:7	Abuse of a Corpse	Abuse of a Corpse	Misdemeanor: Potential prison term for 1 year; fine ranging from US$1,000 to US$1,200
New Jersey	Statute 2C:22-1	Disturbing, Desecrating Human Remains	Necrophilia	Crime of the Second Degree: Imprisonment for 3 years; fine not to exceed US$1,000
New Mexico	No Law	No Law	No Law	No Law
New York	Statute 130.20	Sexual Misconduct	Necrophilia	Class A Misdemeanor: A term fixed by the court that does not exceed 1 year; amount fixed by the court that does not exceed US$1,000
North Carolina	No Law	No Law	No Law	No Law
North Dakota	Chapter 12.1-20-12	Deviate Sexual Act	Necrophilia	Class A Misdemeanor: Maximum of 1 year in prison and/or US$2,000 fine
Ohio	2927.01	Abuse of a Corpse	Abuse of a Corpse	2nd Degree Misdemeanor (division A): Not more than 90 days in jail; Not more than US$750 fine
				5th Degree Felony (division B): 6, 7, 8, 9, 10, 11, or 12 month prison term; fine not more than US$2,500
Oklahoma	No Law	No Law	No Law	No Law
Oregon	Chapter 166.087	Abuse of Corpse in the First Degree	Necrophilia	Class B Felony: Maximum 10 years in prison; a fine fixed by the court that does not exceed US$250,000
Pennsylvania	Statute 5510	Abuse of Corpse	Abuse of Corpse	2nd Degree Misdemeanor: Imprisonment for not more than 2 years; fine not exceeding US$5,000
Rhode Island	Section 11-20-1.2	Necrophilia	Necrophilia	Imprisonment for not less than 1 year or more than 10 years; potential fine not to exceed US$10,000
South Carolina	Section 16-17-600	Destruction or Desecration of Human Remains or Repositories Thereof	Abuse of a Corpse	Felony: Imprisonment for not less than 1 year or more than 10 years and/or fined US$5,000
South Dakota	34-27-19	Removing dead body maliciously or with intent to sell or dissect as misdemeanor	Crime Against Nature (Wantonness)	Class 1 Misdemeanor: 1 year imprisonment in a county jail and/or US$2,000 fine
Tennessee	39-17-312	Abuse of Corpse	Abuse of Corpse	Class E Felony: Prison for not less than 1 year nor more than 6 years; fine not to exceed US$3,000
Texas	Statute 42.08	Abuse of Corpse	Abuse of Corpse	Class A Misdemeanor: Confinement in jail not to exceed 1 year and/or a fine not to exceed US$4,000

continued

Table I.   Continued

State	Legal code	Title of law	Type of law	Potential penalty
Utah	79-9-704	Abuse or Desecration of a Dead Human Body	Necrophilia	3rd Degree Felony: Prison term not to exceed 5 years; fine not exceeding US$5,000
Vermont	No Law	No Law	No Law	No Law
Virginia	Statute 18.2-126	Violation of Sepulture; Defilement of a Dead Human Body	Necrophilia [willfully and intentionally defiles]	Class 6 Felony: Imprisonment of not less than 1 year but no more than 5 years and/or a fine of not more than US$2,500
Washington	Revised Code of Washington 9A.44.105	Sexually Violating Human Remains	Necrophilia	Class C Felony: Confinement in a state correctional institution for 5 years and/or a US$10,000 fine
West Virginia	Statute 61-8-14	Disinterment or Displacement of Dead Body or Part Thereof	Abuse of a Corpse	Misdemeanor: Not more that 1 year in jail and/or fined not more than US$2,000
Wisconsin	No Law	No Law	No Law	No Law
Wyoming	Title 6-4-501	Opening Graves and Removing Bodies	Abuse of a Corpse	Misdemeanor: Fine of not more than US$750
	Title 6-4-502	Mutilation of Dead Human Bodies	Abuse of a Corpse	Felony: Imprisonment for not more than 3 years and/or a fine of not more than US$5,000

in the state prison for life with the possibility of parole, with eligibility for parole beginning when a minimum of 5 years has been served, and shall be further punished by a fine of not more than US$20,000.

2. For the purposes of this section, "sexual penetration" means cunnilingus, fellatio or any intrusion, however slight, of any part of a person's body or any object manipulated or inserted by a person into the genital or anal openings of the body of another, including, without limitation, sexual intercourse in what would be its ordinary meaning if practiced upon the living.

(Added to Nevada Revised Statutes by 1983, 344; A 1991, 1010; 1995, 1204; 1997, 2503, 3190; 2005, 2878)

What these two examples highlight are the obviously different approaches that separate states have taken when outlawing necrophilia. The penalties for the crimes vary widely and, in the case of the Minnesota law, the language suggests that the necrophilic act is an act of bestiality, i.e., that the human corpse is a beast not unlike an animal or a bird, and is an act that must be committed in the presence of another person in order for their to be a crime. The conflation of bestiality laws with necrophilia laws is not exclusive to the Minnesota statute. More often

than not, either a bestiality law or a necrophilia law was already part of a state's legal code and the missing sex act was added to the preexisting statute.

The Minnesota law is also part of another historical trend in US necrophilia statutes, where "prior to 1967, Minnesota defined 'sodomy' to include 'sexual intercourse with a dead body.' In that year, however, Minnesota removed necrophilia and bestiality from the definition of sodomy and enacted a new section combining the two and reducing the penalty for both offenses" (Ochoa & Newman Jones, 1997, pp. 556–557). The prosecution of sodomy, vis-à-vis laws similar to the old Minnesota statute, would have included any and all deviant sexual activity. As states began to liberalize their sodomy laws to avoid prosecuting heterosexual and homosexual sex acts, the prosecution of necrophilia crimes also declined. Nevada's law is one of the most comprehensive necrophilia statutes in the USA, although (and interestingly enough) the word "necrophilia" never appears in the law itself,[21] and has some of the strictest penalties.

Unnatural Acts or Crimes Against Nature Laws

The third group of laws is by far the most juridically ambiguous. The language is at times very vague and tends towards the supposed absolutization of a common, social understanding of perversity or "unnatural sexual acts." As a result of this ambiguity, these laws are the most problematic for states that want to prosecute an individual who is caught having sex with a dead body but the law does not explicitly state that necrophilic sex acts are illegal. Whereas in the past simply using the term "sodomy" would have sufficed, that particular legal route is no longer sufficient. What becomes important in this last grouping of laws is how a judge would understand state laws to apply to unnatural human acts, crimes against nature, and/or perverse sexual practices, etc. Many of the laws in this group could be used in a number of different situations that extend beyond necrophilia, including but not limited to socially accepted homosexual and heterosexual sex acts. The fundamental problem with these laws is whether or not the legal difference between a living body and dead body is stipulated. One example of this third category of law comes from the state of Idaho (2006):

> Idaho:[22]
> TITLE 18
> CRIMES AND PUNISHMENTS
> CHAPTER 66
> SEX CRIMES
> 18-6605. CRIME AGAINST NATURE—PUNISHMENT.
> Every person who is guilty of the infamous crime against nature, committed with mankind or with any animal, is punishable by imprisonment in the state prison not less than 5 years.

One question that arises with the Idaho statute is whether or not necrophilia would constitute a crime against nature. If it did qualify as a crime against nature, then does "mankind" include dead bodies? Or does mankind connote only living bodies and not include corpses? If that is the case, then Idaho effectively has no law outlawing necrophilia.

UK Necrophilia Law

While it is beyond the scope of this article to fully examine US and European necrophilia laws, other countries' statutes do provide interesting insights into these legal questions. That kind of international comparative study is an article unto itself. As a small gesture towards a broader, international comparison, here is the necrophilia law for the UK as taken from the 2003 Sexual Offences Act (United Kingdom, 2003a):

> United Kingdom Sexual Offences Act 2003[23]
> [Section] 70 Sexual penetration of a corpse
> (1) A person commits an offence if—
> (a) he intentionally performs an act of penetration with a part of his body or anything else,

> (b) what is penetrated is a part of the body of a dead person,
> (c) he knows that, or is reckless as to whether, that is what is penetrated, and
> (d) the penetration is sexual.
> (2) A person guilty of an offence under this section is liable—
> (a) on summary conviction, to imprisonment for a term not exceeding 6 months or a fine not exceeding the statutory maximum or both;
> (b) on conviction on indictment, to imprisonment for a term not exceeding 2 years.

In the *Explanatory Notes* attached to the 2003 Sexual Offences Act, various scenarios involving the necrophilia law are presented. It should be noted that, "these explanatory notes . . . have been prepared by the Home Office in order to assist the reader in understanding the Act. They do not form part of the Act and have not been endorsed by Parliament."[24]

> Section 70: Sexual penetration of a corpse
> 133. Section 70 makes it an offence for a person (A) intentionally to penetrate any part of the body of a dead person (B) with his penis, any other body part (for example his finger), or any other object, where that penetration is sexual. The offence is committed when A knows or is reckless as to whether he is penetrating any part of a dead body. This is intended to cover when A knows he is penetrating a dead body, for example in a mortuary, or where A is reckless as to whether B is alive or dead. It will not cover situations where A penetrates B fully believing B to be alive, but in fact B is dead, or where B unexpectedly dies during intercourse. The penetration must be sexual. A definition of sexual is given in section 78. This is to exclude legitimate penetration of corpses, for example that which occurs during an autopsy (p. 21).

What is most striking about the UK law is the insistence on *sexual penetration* for a crime to have occurred. The UK law seems to preclude other sexual acts from being considered criminal, such as masturbating onto or next to a corpse. It is entirely unclear whether or not non-penetration related sex acts could evade prosecution. While the Nevada law also lists penetration, that particular statute provides an additional list of illegal sex acts (cunnilingus, fellatio, etc.) that encompass a plurality of human sexual practices. While the UK law and the Explanatory Notes are more explicit than many US laws, the insistence on penetration restricts the very same law in a number of ways.[25]

The Corpse and the Necrophiliac

Most academic, medical, and/or legal discussions of necrophilia cases focus on the *living individuals* that commit or have allegedly committed necrophilic acts.[26] The logic behind this discursive focus makes sense, since it is difficult to ignore the spectacular quality of individuals committing sex acts with dead bodies. Necrophilia is that rare kind of sexual deviancy that truly captures public attention with its abject perversity and titillating, lascivious details. Rosman and Resnick (1989) note, "Necrophilia, a sexual attraction to corpses, is a rare disorder that has been known since ancient times. According to Herodotus, the ancient Egyptians took precautions against necrophilia by prohibiting corpses of the wives of men of rank from being delivered immediately to the embalmers, for fear that the embalmers would violate them" (p. 153). Ochoa and Newman Jones (1997) articulate modern US disgust with necrophilia this way: "Our own culture has rules governing the treatment of corpses, including many enforced by law, which are based primarily on widespread horror at corpse desecration . . . Unlike other deviant sexual behaviors, however, necrophilia also violates other cultural norms . . . such as requiring consent, protecting ownership of personal property, and protecting public health and safety" (pp. 542–543). What is often left out of these academic, medical, and legal discussions, however, is the dead body itself. This is not to suggest that human corpses should be granted some form of *agency* during acts of necrophilia, since the fundamental reason that most necrophiliacs seek out dead bodies for sexual gratification, as suggested by Krafft-Ebing and reiterated by Rosman and Resnick (1989, pp. 158–159), is the total absence of resistance from that body. Yet, by focusing largely on the necrophilic perpetrator and the pathology's etiology, as well as the legal requirements for punishment, the corpse is left out of the discussion. What role, then, does the corpse play in understanding necrophilia laws? More importantly, what are the gaps in the laws defining the corpse's involvement?

In "Defiling the Dead: Necrophilia and the Law," Ochoa and Newman Jones (1997)[27] present an intriguing argument about the dead body's legal status in US necrophilia cases. Their analysis delves into the problems faced by language and the law when discussions turn towards defined legal rights for dead bodies. These rights go beyond the dead body itself and involve claims made on behalf of the corpse by either the next of kin or the state. A key problem highlighted in the article, for example, is that states such as California which have tried to use rape laws to prosecute necrophiliacs have failed. The problems arose because "rape requires a live victim"

(Ochoa & Newman Jones, 1997, p. 547). As in the Wisconsin case, the term "victim" requires a living person and, unless the language used to write a law makes these qualitative distinctions clear, prosecutors are left with few options.

A handful of legal cases in different states have focused more specifically on the alleged necrophiliac's intent.[28] The courts reviewed a series of cases that included the following scenarios: an individual commits a sex act with an already dead body (e.g., in a morgue or funeral home), an individual kills a person for the expressed purposes of committing a sex act, or a person is killed as part of a crime and the killer then decides to have sex with the corpse. The last two scenarios clearly fall under murder provisions within the law but the final example begs the question: was a necrophilic crime also committed? Was the crime a true act of necrophilia or a spontaneous act committed without premeditation? The Nevada Supreme Court issued the following ruling on these questions with regards to its own state law:

> We also do not believe that NRS 201.450—which is popularly known as the "necrophilia" statute . . . is intended only to apply to medically classifiable "necrophiles." The plain meaning of the statute is to punish the act of sexual penetration of a dead human body, regardless of motive (Ochoa & Newman Jones, 1997, p. 565).

The predictable problem is that even if the necrophilic intent of a defendant can be authoritatively determined (as in the Wisconsin case) the sexual abuse of a corpse may itself not be illegal. Ochoa and Newman Jones (1997) discuss a 1994 Washington state case; as often happens, the necrophilia case caused the enactment of a new law prohibiting necrophilic acts:

> In State v. Ryan, the defendant broke into the same funeral home twice within six days and damaged property, stole items, and made sexual contact with several corpses. He was convicted of two counts of second degree burglary and one count of first degree malicious mischief. The court found that the second break-in was sexually motivated and imposed an exceptional sentence of 120 months for each burglary count. The Washington Court of Appeal upheld the trial court's imposition of an exceptional sentence, despite the defendant's argument that the sentencing court improperly considered his sexual contact with the corpses. Ryan could not, however, be charged with necrophilia because "Ryan's contact with the corpses was apparently not a crime at the time he broke into the funeral home." Shortly after Ryan's initial arrest, a bill was introduced in the state legislature making necrophilia illegal (pp. 562–563).

Two Kinds of Bodies

What many state laws (and the legislators that write the laws) seem to miss is that necrophilia statutes necessarily produce a legal space that encompasses two *separate* and two *very different* kinds of human bodies. One of the bodies is a sexual deviant and the actions of his/her body represent either real or imagined transgressive acts. Yet, the necrophiliac is a unique kind of deviant whose pathology seeks out a specific and legally ambiguous kind of human body. Indeed, a corpse is a particular kind of human body that simultaneously remains outside legal scrutiny and represents enormous legal obstacles once it is scrutinized, for it cannot testify in court, be a witness, be held in contempt, or be cross-examined; in short, it cannot *do* anything. It is these legal obstacles that lead me to the following point: dead bodies are uniquely positioned within the law to cause precisely these kinds of legal dilemmas, especially when necrophilia is involved.

One of the fundamental issues at hand is that a dead body is a quasi-subject before the law. When a person dies in the USA, the corpse retains some, but certainly not all, of the rights of a living individual. T. Scott Gilligan and Thomas F. H. Stueve (1995), in their book *Mortuary law*, explain the quasi-subject status of the dead body this way:

> It is not property in the commercial sense, but the law does provide a bundle of rights to the next of kin in relation to that body. The survivor is given the right to take the body for purposes of disposition, to allow body parts to be used within the confines of the law, to exclude others from possession of the body, and to dispose of the body. This bundle of rights renders the dead body the quasi-property of the surviving family member (p. 6).[29]

Under US law, then, some other person or institution needs to do something with the dead body because it has become both the property and responsibility of an external agent. This legal reasoning makes clear that the human corpse requires external intervention, a requirement that leads me to my next point: dead human bodies, for the most part, do not follow human law. This is not to suggest that dead bodies necessarily break the law, rather that the law is not something dead bodies have the ability to follow. In a sense, the human corpse exists outside the absolute control of human law, which becomes problematic when state authorities try to manage the living and the dead population vis-à-vis the law. Human corpses function as biological bodies *in defiance* of the law and the state can do little about it. What little can be done involves turning the corpse into property, disposing of the corpse, and/or waiting for the legal problems to go away.

The human corpse exists, then, as a body outside the law and upon which no coercive, legal action can be taken to correct that fact. No law, it bears stating, will ever successfully reverse the dead body's post-mortem state. As a result of this legal defiance, the corpse occupies a juridical space in which conditions of possibility exist to potentially transform the dead body into a kind of biological monster once it becomes used for sexual purposes. The formulation of the monster in this argument diverges from those commonly used in many historical accounts of the monster. In those accounts, the monster is the lurking beast, coming from foreign lands and/or a creature of unknown origin. Instead, Michel Foucault's articulation of the "human monster" in his lectures on the abnormal individual are found more useful when discussing the dead body. In those lectures, Foucault (2003) argues that:

> The frame of reference of the human monster is, of course, law. The notion of the monster is essentially a legal notion, in a broad sense, of course, since what defines the monster is the fact that its existence and form is not only a violation of the laws of society but also a violation of the laws of nature. Its very existence is a breach of the law at both levels. The field in which the monster appears can thus be called a "juridico-biological" domain. However, the monster emerges within this space as both an extreme and an extremely rare phenomenon. The monster is the limit, both the point at which law is overturned and the exception that is found is only in extreme cases. The monster combines the impossible and the forbidden (pp. 55–56).[30]

The *juridico-biological space* that Foucault describes is the conceptual site in which this paper positions dead bodies. That legal space is the location within necrophilia laws where the monstrous activities of the necrophiliac and the monstrous legal status of the human corpse collide. The monstrous legal status of the human corpse should be understood in this argument as denoting a body beyond the total control of the law and a monstrous condition explicitly produced by the necrophiliac's violation of the dead body. The human corpse is always a potential monster but a monster that the law continually tries to control. Once a necrophiliac violates a human corpse, that particular dead body becomes an extreme affront to the state's control of both societal and natural law. A human corpse used by a necrophiliac for sexual pleasure is a rare and, for lack of a better term, out-of-control body.

Undeniably, the human corpse is most certainly a common body in the USA and it would seem counterintuitive to even suggest (as Foucault does about the monster) that the dead body is "an extremely rare phenomenon." Indeed, approximately 6,500[31] newly dead bodies can be found in the USA on any given day but these same corpses are not a visible kind of body. Nor are these same dead bodies described as being sexual objects, let alone sexually acted upon bodies. Despite the success of US television programs that create simulacrums of dead bodies, the organically authentic and unmediated human corpse is almost entirely out of public view. This simultaneous postmortem presence and absence is precisely the paradox that necrophilic acts expose and transgress. When the law responds to the necrophilic transgression, it produces a space that makes the necrophilia-violated dead body both highly visible and undeniably present in a situation that defies public disregard. Indeed, it would seem many US necrophilia cases attract almost limitless levels of fascination. The legal space that encompasses necrophilia produces a dead body that is suddenly so visible that it becomes a monster of extreme proportions.

In Conclusion—Dual Monsters: The Corpse and the Necrophiliac

Necrophilia's abject qualities combine, as Foucault suggests, supposedly impossible acts and forbidden desires. This notion of the *impossible* connotes actions not supposed to happen and entities not supposed to exist within a society governed by law. Yet, the impossible act always holds the potential of occurring and the monster's actions make those impossibilities all too real. Necrophiliacs commit acts that instantly propel them outside the law and into the extra-juridical land of human monsters. The corpse, as it exists within US statutes, is both an exceptional and exceptionally ignored juridico-biological monster, a monster of both nature (its decomposing realities) and of people (the law). It is a human body that is everywhere present and nowhere visible except for select constituencies. As a result, the law is presented with two kinds of monstrous bodies: the necrophiliac-violated corpse and the necrophiliac. The two single bodies require each other, and only each other, to produce a sexual act that truly embodies abject, deviant human behavior.

Adding to the extremity of the situation is the fact that one of the monsters is unimaginably active during the forbidden sex act while the other is disturbingly passive, offering no resistance to the socially abject qualities of the sex. Furthermore, when individuals such as the young men in Wisconsin are caught while attempting to commit a sexual act with a dead body, and the law is not prepared to prosecute the attempted act (which is not criminal if there is no law against it) then what kind of new and supposedly impossible legal limit has been reached? The law is exposed as able to define the sexual monster but not offer any protection from its reach. More to the point, the most severe charge that Nicholas Grunke, Alexander Grunke, and Dustin Radtke faced was attempted property theft, a situation that re-focused attention on the attempted necrophilic act. This re-focusing exposed an even more complicated situation; namely, the only way state authorities could protect Laura Tennessen's corpse was by making it property. As a result of this legal maneuvering, the human corpse can be socially rehabilitated, but only as a quasi-subject owned by another. This then makes the dead body's defiance a problem for someone else, the recognized rehabilitator of the monster.

In its most troubling sense, what necrophilia produces are these two distinct kinds of human monsters. One of the monsters, the necrophiliac, must always be an extremely rare case because if he or she is not *only* an extreme case, then it suggests a level of human sexual activity that far exceeds the bounds of normalized behavior. The law works to expel the necrophiliac monster since he or she exists within the living population and is potentially dangerous. Yet dangerous to whom, the question should be asked, since dead bodies will never be conscious of physical danger. The other monster, the corpse, is a different kind of abnormal creature but a monstrous body all the same. It is a decomposing, quasi-subject that living humans create laws to control and protect even though that protection does nothing to change the postmortem status of the dead body. The corpse monster seems to always represent that monstrous body which holds the possible possibility of being brought back into the human fold through legal strictures. The law works, in this situation, to try and re-admit dead bodies back into the living population but with limitations. A dead body can only be given another chance, so to speak, by literally being owned.

In the end, the necrophiliac and the human corpse are monsters that truly confront the social order with a kind of degeneracy that suggests that no law is adequate. As Foucault (2003) explains, ". . . the degenerate is someone who is a danger. The degenerate is someone who cannot be reached by any kind of penalty. The degenerate is someone who, at all events, cannot be cured" (pp. 317–318). Such a definition clearly applies to necrophiliacs, individuals who break taboos at the mere utterance of their pathology. Yet, the necrophiliac exposes the US social order, as Ochoa and Newman Jones (1997) suggest, to another degenerate body, one that also fits the definition: the human corpse. A different kind of degenerate than the necrophiliac, the corpse that has garnered the attention of a necrophiliac is a legally problematic body all the same. Both of these monsters evade the law but perhaps the corpse does it best by physically degenerating, through decomposition.

Critics will of course say that this kind of semantic word play is disingenuous, given the lack of life in a dead body. Yet it seems to me that the dangerous, penalty immune, incurable body described by Foucault fits the human corpse and its legal pitfalls. Maybe what the necrophiliac really exposes is not loopholes in the law but a deeper US pathology *for the living* when it becomes necessary to see dead bodies as dead. More than just dead, a human corpse in the USA must remain asexual and inert. If the dead body can be sexually violated and understood to have been abused in the ways living bodies are, then maybe he/she/it is somehow *still alive* and something more than just property. Yet since current US law is unable to transform a corpse into more than property, necrophiliacs violate not a person but an inanimate object that looks far too human to be owned and simply vandalized.

In the case of the necrophiliac, the laws of nature and the laws of humans are entangled in a struggle to define the appropriate boundaries for social necro-degeneracy. US legal statutes are expected to automatically recognize the illegality of corpse abuse and, as a result, state authorities often assume that the law will make necrophilia a crime. That is, of course, until someone is caught having sex with a dead body and the law has nothing to say about it.

Postscript

On March 5, 2008, the state of Wisconsin Supreme Court heard oral arguments in state V. Alexander Caleb Grunke et al. on whether existing Wisconsin statutes criminalize sexual contact or intercourse with a deceased victim. The court's decision is expected in the early summer. The oral arguments can be listened to here: http://www.wicourts. gov/supreme/scoa.jsp?docketnumber= &begindate=&e nddate=&partyname=Grunke&sortby=date

Notes

1. From the Grant County Sheriff's Department criminal complaint filed on September 5, 2006, in the *State of Wisconsin vs. Alexander Caleb Grunke, Nicholas Owen Grunke, Dustin Blake Radtke*. DA Case No.: 2006GT001256. Available on the Smoking Gun website at www.thesmokinggun.com

2. Statement of Dustin Radtke during a tape-recorded interview with Grant County Sergeant Detective James E. Kopp.

3. For video of the case's court proceedings see: Reading of the Criminal Complaint at http://video.google.com/videoplay?docid=1935403243530201584 September 15, 2007, Preliminary Court Hearing (where the sexual assault charges are dropped) at http://video.google.com/videoplay?docid=-4548876004565391259

4. See Wisconsin statute *940.225(7) Death of victim*. Available at http://www.legis.state.wi.us

5. See Wisconsin Statute *939.50 Classification of felonies*. Available at http://www.legis.state.wi.us

6. Judge Curry's decision to remove the attempted sexual assault charges was appealed by the State of Wisconsin and in July 2007 the Wisconsin Court of Appeals for the Fourth District affirmed Judge Curry's decision that the current law does not cover sexual acts with dead bodies. The written decision by the Wisconsin Court of Appeals contains the following explanation: "While sexual intercourse with a corpse unquestionably presents a case of sexual immorality, the relevant question is whether sexual intercourse with a corpse, unrelated to the individual's death, is an activity the legislature intended to proscribe in a statute geared toward protecting bodily security" (p. 7). The Court of Appeals found that the State of Wisconsin Legislature did not state that necrophilia was part of the original statute. To read the entire Court of Appeals decision see http://www.wicourts.gov/ca/opinion/DisplayDocument.html? content=html&seqNo=29824

   The State of Wisconsin appealed the July 2007 decision to the Wisconsin State Supreme Court. On November 5, 2007, the Wisconsin State Supreme Court agreed to review the case. No date has yet been set for the oral arguments.

7. Taken from the September 6, 2006, Press Release: "Schultz to Sponsor Bill Punishing Heinous Act of Sex with Corpse." See Senator Schultz's official website for more information: http://www.legis.wi.gov/senate/sen17/news

   Senator Schultz has co-sponsored legislation that would make sex acts with a human corpse illegal. The proposed legislation, Senate Bill 247, reads as follows: "SEXUAL ASSAULT OF A CORPSE. Whoever has sexual contact or sexual intercourse with a corpse is guilty of a Class G felony. For the purpose of this subsection, a 'corpse' is the body of a human being who, at the time of the sexual intercourse or sexual contact, had been declared dead by a physician, coroner, or medical examiner." To read the legislative history for this bill see http://www.legis.state.wi.us/2007/data/SB247hst.html

8. Ironically, the state of Wisconsin does have a law that encompasses necrophilia but it only involves *representations* of necrophilia. Wisconsin statute *944.21 Obscene material or performance* states: "The legislature intends that the authority to prosecute violations of this section shall be used primarily to combat the obscenity industry and

shall never be used for harassment or censorship purposes against materials or performances having serious artistic, literary, political, educational or scientific value. The legislature further intends that the enforcement of this section shall be consistent with the first amendment to the US constitution, article I, section 3, of the Wisconsin constitution and the compelling state interest in protecting the free flow of ideas." See http://www.legis.state.wi.us.

As result of this law, any obscene material that contains "sexual conduct" includes: *944.21(2)(e)* "*Sexual conduct*" means the commission of any of the following: sexual intercourse, sodomy, bestiality, necrophilia, human excretion, masturbation, sadism, masochism, fellatio, cunnilingus or lewd exhibition of human genitals." See http://www.legis.state.wi.us

Had Nicholas Grunke, Alexander Grunke, and Dustin Radtke created a representation of necrophilia (a photo, a video, a painting, etc.) and then publicly displayed it they could have been charged with an obscenity crime. The punishment for this initial offense would have required them to forfeit the representation to State of Wisconsin authorities. In the event they would have used Laura Tennessen's corpse in the representation then an obscenity charge of *representing necrophilia* might have been possible.

9. A constant question that comes up is how many documented cases of necrophilia have actually occurred either globally or in the USA. The research into this question is quite thin and one of the only recent studies to examine necrophilia cases was done in 1989. Jonathan P. Rosman and Phillip J. Resnick published their study, "Sexual Attraction to Corpses: A Psychiatric Review of Necrophilia" in *The Bulletin of the American Academy of Psychiatry and the Law*. The study examines 122 cases of necrophilia, either reported and/or confirmed from all over the world. A. A. Brill also comments on the frequency of necrophilia cases in a 1941 article, appropriately entitled "Necrophilia." Brill states: "I said in starting that necrophilic acts were known as a sporadic occurrence from the beginning of history. From my own investigation I dare say they happen more frequently than is known. That we hear so little about them is due to the abhorrent nature of the perversion. people dislike to report them. In discussing this problem recently with Inspector John J. O'Connell of the New York City Police Academy, he told me of two cases that came to his knowledge within the last few months, but which were never reported. Now and then, the situation is of such a nature that it cannot be kept from the public" (Brill, 1941, pp. 69–70).

10. Foucault, 2003.
11. Hawaii Statute *711–1108 Abuse of a corpse*. Available at http://www.capitol.hawaii.gov
12. Massachusetts, 2006.
13. Mississippi, 2006.
14. This is common wording for many of the Abuse of a Corpse laws and is not taken from any one specific law.

15. See http://www.ohio.gov
16. The use of the abuse of a corpse law, with its broad and ambiguous language, can turn in many directions. A recent use of the Ohio law, in a non-sex related case, came in October 2001. The case centered on Cincinnati, Ohio photographer Thomas Condon, who was charged with multiple counts of *gross abuse of a corpse* after he took pictures of bodies in an Ohio county morgue. Condon had permission from local authorities to take the photographs but did not have the families' permissions. Most of the photographs were close-up shots of bodily appendages (a hand, a leg, etc.) and not easily identifiable body parts, such as a face. He also placed objects, such as a doll, in the hand of one body. Condon intended to digitally alter the photographs before putting them on display in a planned gallery exhibition, making sure that any identifiable marks (tattoos, obvious scars, etc.) on the bodies were removed. Cincinnati police arrested Condon after he dropped the film off for developing and the employees of the photo developer handed the photos over to the authorities. Condon was sentenced to 2½ years in the state penitentiary and served a year before being released. For more information on the Thomas Condon case see the following at http://citybeat.com/2002-04-18/cover.shtml and a segment on the National Public Radio Program Radio 360 at http://www.studio360.org/yore/show112004.html
17. Krafft-Ebing, 1933.
18. Many thanks to Mary Roach, who in her book *Stiff: The curious lives of human cadavers* (2003) briefly mentioned both the Minnesota and Nevada laws (p. 43).
19. See http://www.state.mn.us
20. See http://www.leg.state.nv.us
21. Ochoa & Newman Jones, 1997, p. 565.
22. See http://www.state.id.us
23. For more information see UK Office of Public Sector Information at http://www.opsi.gov.uk
24. Full a complete listing of the *Explanatory Notes* see www.opsi.gov.uk/acts/en2003/ukpgaen_20030042_en.pdf
25. A 2007 murder trial in the UK involved a case of necrophilia. In December 2007, Craig Bidgway was convicted for the murder of his wife Danielle Birda and the attempted murder of their son William. Bidgway confessed during a police interview to murdering his wife and to then having sex with Danielle Birda's dead body. His taped confession was played for a jury during the trial in the Cardiff Crown Court. On the tapes, Bidgway explained that, "She was dead and I made love to her . . . I wanted to show her how much I loved her." Interestingly enough, only The Sun and the Daily Telegraph reported the sexual offense committed by Bidgway. Most other UK publications only discussed the murder and attempted murder. It does not appear that prosecutors used the Sexual Offences Act for this case. For articles discussing the necrophilic aspects of the crime see http://thesun.co.uk/sol/homepage/news/article558982.ece and http://www.telegraph.co.uk/news/main.jhtml?xml=/news/2007/12/05/nstrangle105.xml

26. See the following articles listed in the References: Brill (1941), Brownlie (1963), Ehrlich et al. (2000), Klaf & Brown (1958), Price (1963), and Rosman & Resnick (1989).
27. Ochoa & Newman Jones, 1997.
28. Ochoa & Newman Jones, 1997, pp. 543–566.
29. Gilligan & Stueve, 1995.
30. Foucault, 2003.
31. The most recent and complete set of mortality statistics for the USA come from 2004. During that year, 2,397,615 individuals were reported dead. That means roughly 6,568 dead bodies were present on any given day across the USA in 2004. These numbers can be found at the National Center for Health Stastistics at http://www.cdc.gov/nchs/fastats/deaths.htm

References

Brill, A. A. (1941). Necrophilia. *Journal of Criminal Psychopathology, 2*, 433–443 & *3*, 50–73.

Brownlie, A. R. (1963). Necrophilia: Need the parliament trouble? *Medicine, Science and the Law, 3*, 313–315.

Ehrlich, E., Rothschild, M. A., Pluisch, F., & Schneider, V. (2000). An extreme case of necrophilia. *Legal Medicine, 2*, 224–226.

Foucault, M. (2003). *Abnormal: lectures at the Collège de France, 1974–1975* (GRAHAM BURCHELL, Trans.). New York: Picador.

Gilligan, T. S., & Stueve, T. F. H. (1995) *Mortuary law* (9th ed.). Cincinnati, OH: The Cincinnati Foundation for Mortuary Education.

Hawaii. (2006). Hawaii Revised Statutes. Hawaii Statute *711-1108 Abuse of a corpse.* Retrieved December 23, 2007, from http://www.capitol.hawaii.gov

Idaho. (2006). Idaho Code. Idaho Statute *18-6605 Crime Against Nature.* Retrieved December 23, 2007, from http://www.state.id.us

Klaf, F., & Brown, W. (1958). Necrophilia, brief review and case report. *The Psychiatric Quarterly, 32*, 645–652.

Krafft-Ebing, R. v. F. (1933) *Psychopathia sexualis* (F. J. REBAMN, Trans., 12th ed.). Brooklyn, New York: Physicians and Surgeons Book Company.

Massachusetts. (2006). The General Laws of Massachusetts. Massachusetts Statute *Chapter 272 Crimes Against Chastity, Morality, Decency and Good Order.* Retrieved December 23, 2007, from http://www.mass.gov

Minnesota. (2006). Minnesota Statutes. Minnesota Statute *609.294 Bestiality.* Retrieved December 23, 2007, from http://www.state.mn.us

Mississippi. (2006). Mississippi Code. Mississippi Statute *97-29-59. Unnatural intercourse.* Retrieved December 23, 2007, from http://www.mississippi.gov

Nevada. (2006). Nevada Revised Statutes. Nevada Statute *201.45 Sexual Penetration of Dead Human Body.* Retrieved December 23, 2007, from http://www.leg.state.nv.us

Ochoa, T. T., & Newman Jones, C. (1997). Defiling the dead: Necrophilia and the law. *Whittier Law Review* (Spring), *18*, 539–578.

Ohio. (2006). Ohio Revised Code. Ohio Statute *2927.01 Abuse of a corpse.* Retrieved December 23, 2007, from http://www.ohio.gov

Price, D. E. (1963). Necrophilia complicating a case of homicide. *Medicine, Science and the Law, 3*, 121–131.

Roach, M. (2003). *Stiff: the curious lives of human cadavers.* New York: W.W. Norton & Company.

Rosman, J. P., & Resnick, P. J. (1989). Sexual attraction to corpses: A psychiatric review of necrophilia. *The Bulletin of the American Academy of Psychiatry and the Law, 17*, 153–163.

Schultz, D. (2006). *Schultz to sponsor bill punishing heinous act of sex with corpse.* Retrieved June 27, 2006, from http://www.legis.wi.gov/senate/sen17/news

United Kingdom. (2003a). United Kingdom Office of Public Sector Information. *Explanatory Notes.* Retrieved December 23, 2007, from http://www.opsi.gov.uk/acts/en2003/ukpgaen_20030042_en.pdf

United Kingdom. (2003b). United Kingdom Office of Public Sector Information. *United Kingdom Sexual Offences Act.* Retrieved December 23, 2007, from http://www.opsi.gov.uk

Wisconsin. (2006). Wisconsin Statutes. Wisconsin Statute *939.50 Classification of felonies.* Retrieved December 23, 2007, from http://www.legis.state.wi.us

Wisconsin Statutes. (2006). Wisconsin Statute *940.225(7) Death of victim.* Retrieved December 23, 2007, from http://www.legis.state.wi.us

Wisconsin, Grant County Sheriff's Department. (2006). *Criminal complaint state of Wisconsin vs. Alexander Caleb Grunke, Nicholas Owen Grunke, Dustin Blake Radtke* (DA Case No.: 2006GT001256). Retrieved December 23, 2007, from http://www.thesmokinggun.com/archive/0906061grave2.html

Biographical Note

John Troyer is Visiting Assistant Professor, Department of Comparative Studies, The Ohio State University, where he teaches the cultural studies of science and technology. His PhD dissertation "Technologies of the Human Corpse" was nominated for the 2007 National Council of Graduate Schools Distinguished Dissertation in the Arts and Humanities.

Relationships and the Individual

Marriage is an arrangement that we all think we recognize. It is the legal bond which allows two people, usually a male and a female, previously unrelated, to become a family, right? Most of us come from family structures and marriage is the necessary step that individuals take to pair up and start a family of their own, right? Well, yes. But let's break this down. Let's start by examining the meaning of "family." "What is family, anyway?" asked William Sayres in his 1992 article exploring the comparative meaning of family across cultures. In the United States, people tend to view marriage as a choice between two people, based on mutual feelings of love. In other nations and in other times, marriages have been arranged through an intricate process of interviews and negotiations between entire families, or in other cases, through a direct system such as a "mail order bride." To someone raised in New York City, the marriage customs of a family from Nigeria may seem strange, or even wrong. Conversely, someone from a traditional Kolkata family might be perplexed with the idea of romantic love as the foundation for marriage lifelong commitment. In other words, the way in which people view marriage depends largely on what they have been taught.

Families seem to be cultural universals. That is, every human group organizes members into kinship groups. Yet, the term "family" is very difficult to define. We, in the West, regard a family to have the basic building block of a husband, a wife and their children. In polygamous cultures men have more than one wife. Cultures where women have more than one husband are called polyandrous. We tend to encourage marriage before children are born to the couple. Yet the Banaro of New Guinea requires that a woman give birth before she can marry and she cannot marry the father of her child.

The traditional family at sunset. Maybe literally.

Given this diversity in the composition of the "family," any definition has to be broad. A family is a relationship established by people who consider themselves related by blood, marriage, or adoption. Families can be classified as nuclear (husband, wife, and children) and extended (including grandparents, aunts, uncles and cousins, e.g., , in addition to the nuclear unit). The family of orientation is the family in which we develop into adults and the family of procreation is the family that is formed when an adult couple has its first child.

So if a family is so multidimensional and variable across cultures, what is marriage? Marriage is equally complex. The sex of the bride and groom used to be taken for granted. Now, many European countries and several U.S. States have legalized same sex marriage, and in 2015, the Supreme Court ruled that the U.S. Constitution guarantees a right to same sex marriage. While many people might consider this to be a strange deviation from traditional Western concepts of marriage, other societies have practices that highlight the malleability of the concept. Still, we can define marriage as a group's approved mating arrangement, usually marked by a ritual of union designed to indicate the couple's new status.

Some societies prefer that an individual chose a partner from within the group (endogamy), others encourage that individuals marry outside their group (exogamy). In the United States, for example, most African-Americans marry African-Americans, "whites" marry "whites." This is an example of an endogamous marriage practice. Simultaneously, we encourage the exogamous practice of marrying outside of the kinship group. We discourage incestuous marriages.

So we pair up in a variety of ways around the globe to keep the species alive through socially acceptable methods. Species reproduction is a biological process, yes. But societies establish the parameters that individuals must follow for the society to reproduce.

Love has many faces. Should the government decide who has the right kind of love?

Sexual Hookup Culture: A Review

Justin R. Garcia[1]
Chris Reiber[2], Sean G. Massey[2], and Ann M. Merriwether[2]

"Hookups," or uncommitted sexual encounters, are becoming progressively more engrained in popular culture, reflecting both evolved sexual predilections and changing social and sexual scripts. Hook-up activities may include a wide range of sexual behaviors, such as kissing, oral sex, and penetrative intercourse. However, these encounters often transpire without any promise of, or desire for, a more traditional romantic relationship. A review of the literature suggests that these encounters are becoming increasingly normative among adolescents and young adults in North America, representing a marked shift in openness and acceptance of uncommitted sex. We reviewed the current literature on sexual hookups and considered the multiple forces influencing hookup culture, using examples from popular culture to place hooking up in context. We argue that contemporary hookup culture is best understood as the convergence of evolutionary and social forces during the developmental period of emerging adulthood. We suggest that researchers must consider both evolutionary mechanisms and social processes, and be considerate of the contemporary popular cultural climate in which hookups occur, in order to provide a comprehensive and synergistic biopsychosocial view of "casual sex" among emerging adults today.

Keywords

Casual sex, hookup, hooking up, human sexuality, sexual behavior, mating strategies, sexual scripts

> There's a stranger in my bed
> There's a pounding in my head
> Glitter all over the room
> Pink flamingos in the pool
> I smell like a minibar
> DJ's passed out in the yard
> Barbies on the barbeque
> Is this a hickey or a bruise
> —*Last Friday Night (T.G.I.F.)*
> (Perry, Gottwald, Martin, & McKee, 2011)

Justin R. Garcia, The Kinsey Institute for Research in Sex, Gender, and Reproduction, Indiana University, Bloomington; Chris Reiber, Graduate Program in Biomedical Anthropology, Department of Anthropology, Binghamton University; Sean G. Massey, Women's Studies Program, Binghamton University; and Ann M. Merriwether, Departments of Psychology and Human Development, Binghamton University.

JRG is supported in part by the National Institute of Child Health and Human Development, National Institutes of Health (Grant T32HD049336). We thank Melanie Hill for valuable discussion and feedback on an earlier draft of this review. We also thank Maryanne Fisher and Catherine Salmon for helpful editorial feedback.

Correspondence concerning this article should be addressed to Justin R. Garcia, The Kinsey Institute for Research in Sex, Gender, and Reproduction, Indiana University, 1165 East Third Street, Morrison Hall 313, Bloomington, IN 47405. E-mail: justin.r.garcia@gmail.com

[1] The Kinsey Institute, Indiana University, Bloomington
[2] Binghamton University

Popular media representations of sexuality demonstrate the pervasiveness of a sexual hookup culture among emerging adults. The themes of books, plots of movies and television shows, and lyrics of numerous songs all demonstrate a permissive sexuality among consumers. As an example, the lyrics above, from the chart-topping pop song *Last Friday Night (T.G.I.F.)* by singer–songwriter Katy Perry highlight someone's Friday night partying, presumably including casual sex, alcohol, and a piecemeal memory of the nights events. Research on media portrayals of sexual behavior has documented this pattern as well. In a 2005 *Kaiser Family Foundation* report about sex on television, media was highlighted as the primary basis for emerging adults' opinions about sex, consistent with their result of 77% of prime-time television programs containing some sexual content (Kunkel, Eyal, Finnerty, Biely, & Donnerstein, 2005). In terms of a more permissive uncommitted sexual content, 20% of sexual intercourse cases involved characters who knew each other but were not in a relationship, and another 15% involved characters having sex after just meeting (Kunkel et al., 2005). Other studies have shown that college students believe their peers are substantially more sexually permissive than was actually the case (Chia & Gunther, 2006; Reiber & Garcia, 2010). These incorrect beliefs of peer sexual norms are in part influenced by students' perceptions of media and the influence of media on peers (Chia & Gunther, 2006). Popular culture is simultaneously representing *aspects* of actual contemporary sexual behavior and providing sexual scripts for emerging adults. In the current review, we examine and explore these patterns in sexual hookups.

Hooking up—brief uncommitted sexual encounters among individuals who are not romantic partners or dating each other—has taken root within the sociocultural milieu of adolescents, emerging adults, and men and women throughout the Western world. Over the past 60 years, the prioritization of traditional forms of courting and pursuing romantic relationships has shifted to more casual "hookups" (Bogle, 2007, 2008). Among heterosexual emerging adults of both sexes, hookups have become culturally normative. Dating for courting purposes has decreased (but certainly not disappeared) and sexual behavior outside of traditional committed romantic pair-bonds has become increasingly typical and socially acceptable (Bogle, 2007, 2008). In one sample of undergraduate college students, both men and women had nearly double the number of hookups compared to first dates (Bradshaw, Kahn, & Saville, 2010). Most notably, individuals of both sexes are willing to openly discuss the topic and advertise their acceptance and experiences of hooking up.

Sexual hookups are most comprehensively understood in an interdisciplinary framework that combines multiple levels of analyses. In this review, we consider how aspects of sexual popular culture reflect both the biological reproductive motive, social–sexual scripts, and how individuals adaptively, facultatively, respond to their environment. The evolutionary biological and sociocultural paradigms produce parallel, sometimes interacting, and sometimes contradictory, patterns of explanation. The emergence of sexual hookup culture provides a case of human social behavior through which to explore the relationship and possible interaction between evolved mating psychology and cultural context.

Cultural Shifts in Dating

Hookup culture has emerged from more general social shifts taking place during the last century. As early as the 1920s, with the rise of automobile use and novel entertainment venues throughout North America, traditional models of courting under parental supervision began to fade (Bailey, 1988; Stinson, 2010). An increase in "dating" during this period gave way to a more permissive peer-influenced social–sexual script (Bailey, 1988; Stinson, 2010). With the invention of visual media, images of erotic sex began finding their way into popular culture (Black, 1994; Doherty, 1999). In opposition to this, censorship laws established during the 1930s and lasting until the late 1960s limited depictions of erotic life in film, including depictions of uncommitted sex (Herbert & McKernan, 1996; Robertson, 2001; Vieira, 1999). Young

adults became even more sexually liberated in the 1960s, with the rise of feminism, growth of college party events, widespread availability of birth control (condoms and oral contraceptives), and deposing of parental expectations as central to mating and marriage (Laumann, Gagnon, Michael, & Michaels, 1994; Stinson, 2010). Again in opposition, many health care providers in the 1960s denied oral contraceptives to single, unmarried, women (Coontz, 2005). Throughout American history, young adults were told, and at least publicly endorsed, that sexual behavior should only occur in the context of a marital union.

Representation of Hookups in Popular Culture

Contemporary popular culture is now ripe with examples that depict and often encourage sexual behavior, including premarital and uncommitted sex. Popular media, including television, has become a source of sex education, filled with (inaccurate) portrayals of sexuality (Kunkel et al., 2005; Strasburger, 2005; Ward, 2003). Many popular representations suggest uncommitted sex, or hookups, can be both biophysically and emotionally enjoyable and occur without "strings." Recent entertainment media have highlighted uncommitted sexual encounters and the more-common-than-not experimentation with this type of behavior. The film *Hooking Up*, released in 2009, details the chaotic romantic and sexual lives of adolescent characters. The film *No Strings Attached*, released in 2011 and staring Natalie Portman and Ashton Kutcher, features the uncommitted element of uncommitted sex, as two friends attempt to negotiate a sexual, yet nonromantic, component of their relationship. Popular television shows often portray hooking up as acceptable, entertaining, and perfectly sensible. The hit British series *Skins*, which began in 2007, and was remade in North America in 2011, often highlights the uncommitted sexual exploits of adolescents. The popular reality show *Jersey Shore*, which started its run in 2009, glorifies hookups among strangers, acquaintances, friends, and former partners. Popular pro-hookup same-sex representations have also emerged in television series like *Queer as Folk* and *The L-Word*. Several popular books on hookups have hit the shelves, with unscientific yet racy claims. These include, *The Happy Hook-Up: A Single Girl's Guide to Casual Sex* (Sherman & Tocantins, 2004), *The Hookup Handbook: A Single Girl's Guide to Living It Up* (Rozler & Lavinthal, 2005), *Hooking Up: A Girl's All-Out Guide to Sex and Sexuality* (Madison, 2006), *Making the Hook-Up: Edgy Sex With Soul* (Riley, 2010), and *11 Points Guide to Hooking Up: Lists and Advice About First Dates,*

Hotties, Scandals, Pickups, Threesomes, and Booty Calls (Greenspan, 2011).

Operationalizing "Hookups"

Hookups may include any sexual behavior in a seemingly uncommitted context. Nearly all hookups involve kissing; 98% of undergraduate respondents in one study reported kissing within a hookup (Fielder & Carey, 2010a). Other behaviors are less ubiquitous. In another study, a combined 81% of undergraduate respondents engaged in some form of hookup behavior, with 58% having engaged in sexual touching above the waist and 53% below the waist, 36% performed oral sex, 35% received oral sex, and 34% engaged in sexual intercourse in the context of a hookup (Reiber & Garcia, 2010). Research has found minimal gender differences in terms of hookup behaviors. The term *hookup* focuses on the uncommitted nature of a sexual encounter rather than focus on what behaviors "count." The ambiguity of this term may allow individuals to adaptively manipulate others' perceptions of their sexual behavior.

Operational definitions of hookups differ among researchers. Hookups may be characterized as a form of "casual sex" or "uncommitted sexual encounter." Hatfield, Hutchison, Bensman, Young, and Rapson (in press) define casual sex as "outside of a 'formal' relationship (dating, marriage, etc.), without a 'traditional' reason (such as love, procreation, or commitment) for doing so" (p. 3). Paul, McManus, and Hayes (2000) omitted the possibility of hooking up with previous partners or friends, by defining a hookup as "a sexual encounter, usually only lasting one night, between two people who are strangers or brief acquaintances. Some physical interaction is typical but may or may not include sexual intercourse" (p. 79). Using a broad situational definition, Garcia and Reiber (2008) told participants "a hook-up is a sexual encounter between people who are not dating or in a relationship, and where a more traditional romantic relationship is NOT an explicit condition of the encounter" (p. 196). Lewis, Granato, Blayney, Lostutter, and Kilmer (2011) used a more behaviorally specific definition, in which hooking up was defined as a "event where you were physically intimate (any of the following: kissing, touching, oral sex, vaginal sex, anal sex) with someone whom you were not dating or in a romantic relationship with at the time and in which you understood there was no mutual expectation of a romantic commitment" (p. 4). Glenn and Marquardt (2001) used an explicitly heteronormative definition for participants: a hook-up is "when a girl and a guy get together for a physical encounter and don't necessarily expect anything further" (p. 82).

Friends With Benefits

On the surface, hookups are slightly different from more protracted mutual exchange arrangements for uncommitted sex, like those often referred to with colloquialisms such as "friends with benefits" (FWBs), "booty calls," or "fuck-buddies" (Jonason, Li, & Richardson, 2011). In terms of popular public discourse, *Urban Dictionary* defines FWBs as "two friends who have a sexual relationship without being emotionally involved. Typically two good friends who have casual sex without a monogamous relationship or any kind of commitment" (Friends with benefits, 2003) and also "a safe relationship, that mimics a real partnership but is void or greatly lacking jealousy and other such emotions that come with a serious relationship" (Friends with benefits, 2005). Yet, popular culture representations (e.g., The film *Friends with Benefits*, released in 2011 staring Mila Kunis and Justin Timberlake) suggest FWB partnerships may not truly be void of romantic elements.

FWB relationships represent a unique variation of hooking up worthy of more research attention, which it is beginning to generate. In one study, 60% of 125 undergraduates reported having a FWB relationship at some point in their lives (Bisson & Levine, 2009). Of those who had engaged in a FWB experience, 98.7% were with an opposite sex partner and 1.3% with a same-sex partner. Much like in the movie of the same name, a common concern of participants describing their FWB relationships was the potential formation of unanticipated romantic feelings. At the time of the survey, 35.8% stayed friends but stopped having sex with their most recent FWB partner, 28.3% were maintaining an FWB relationship, 25.9% ended their relationship or friendship, and 9.8% initiated a romantic relationship (Bisson & Levine, 2009). Because these situations represent a greater entanglement of friendship, trust, and emotional comfort, FWBs are distinct from notions of hooking up in some aspects. Namely, hookup scenarios do not implicitly include a friendship relationship component as a condition.

Hooking Up as Contemporary Casual Sex

There are also a large number of colloquial expressions used to describe uncommitted sexual behavior, including labels like "no strings attached" (NSA) sex, "casual encounters," and "one-night stands." It is important to explore whether, and in what context, these phrases (e.g., NSA) are really interchangeable with "hookups." Hookups are different from infidelity situations (extrapair copulations), in which an individual engages in sex with an extrarelational partner, but is still functionally committed to the relationship partner. However, some sexual subcultures with open relationships actually allow extrarelationship casual sex without considering it to be a betrayal. For instance, the frequency of open relationships among gay men, where extrarelational casual sex is permissible, has been estimated as high as 60% (Hoff & Beougher, 2010). In a sample of 2027 gay men from Australia, although 15% had no sexual relationship at time of the survey, 30% of men had a "regular" monogamous relationship partner, 23% had a casual sex partner, and 32% had both a regular (open relationship) partner and casual sex (Zablotska, Frankland, Prestage, Down, & Ryan, 2008). In these cases, some extrapair encounters may constitute uncommitted hookups, albeit not among "singles."

Across gender, ethnicity, or sexual orientation, nearly all adult Americans experience sexual activity, including sex beyond the context of a marital union (Finer, 2007; Garcia & Kruger, 2010; Herbenick et al., 2010). It is important to note that uncommitted sex and one-night stands have been studied outside the current "hookup culture" frame (Boswell & Spade, 1996; Cates, 1991; Hatfield et al., in press; Maticka-Tyndale, 1991). Uncommitted sexual encounters became a topic of particular scientific interest beginning in the mid 20th century (Ellis, 1958; Kinsey, Pomeroy, & Martin, 1948; Kinsey, Pomeroy, Martin, & Gebhard, 1953), and especially during the sexual liberation period of the 1960s and 1970s (Altman, 1971, 1982). Attention to causal sexual encounters among men who have sex with men also emerged as an area of study during the AIDS epidemic in the 1980s until today. Yet, this larger casual sex literature has remained largely disjointed from investigations of "hookups." Research (especially from a public health perspective) on brief uncommitted sexual behaviors outside of traditional relationships extends well beyond heterosexual collegiate populations, including same-sex sexual behaviors among men who have sex with men. These complementary literatures and approaches should be integrated into the future study of hookup behavior, because the study of human sexuality must consider the vast range of variation and potential in human sexual behaviors.

A case in point, findings from the National Survey of Sexual Health and Behavior identified a much higher rate of American men and women who had ever engaged in same-sex sexual behavior compared to those who identify with a homosexual orientation (see Herbenick et al., 2010, for a detailed account of same-sex and opposite sex sexual behavior in the United States by age group). This raises an important, but as of yet unanswered, question: If a proportion of *heterosexual* Americans have at some point engaged in at least one same-sex sexual encounter,

is the context of such a scenario a hookup? Although speculative, it seems most probable that many such encounters are sexual experiments and uncommitted, but investigations of how this relates to the larger hookup culture are sorely lacking.

Frequency of Hooking Up

A vast majority of today's young adults, from a wide range of college student populations studied so far, report some personal "casual" sexual experience (Bogle, 2008; England, Shafer, & Fogarty, 2007; Fielder & Carey, 2010a; Fisher, Worth, Garcia, & Meredith, 2012; Garcia & Reiber, 2008; Welsh, Grello, & Harper, 2006; Gute & Eshbaugh, 2008; Hatfield et al., in press; Lambert, Kahn, & Apple, 2003; Lewis et al., 2011; Paul et al., 2000). The most recent data suggest that between 60% and 80% of North American college students have had some sort of hookup experience. This is consistent with the view of emerging adulthood (typical college age) as a period of developmental transition (Arnett, 2000), exploring and internalizing sexuality and romantic intimacy, now including hookups (Stinson, 2010).

Although much of the current research has been done on college campuses, among younger adolescents, 70% of sexually active 12–21 year olds reported having had uncommitted sex within the last year (Grello, Welsh, Harper, & Dickson, 2003). Similarly, in a sample of seventh, ninth, and 11th graders, 32% of participants had experienced sexual intercourse and 61% of sexually experienced teenagers reported a sexual encounter outside the context of a dating relationship; this represents approximately one fifth of the entire sample (Manning, Giordano, & Longmore, 2006).

Hookup Venues

Among college students, hookups have been reported in a variety of college settings. One study of students' perceptions of hookups reported that 67% occur at parties, 57% at dormitories or fraternity houses, 10% at bars and clubs, 4% in cars, and 35% at any unspecified available place (Paul & Hayes, 2002). In addition to college campus locations, spring break and holidays have been a time many individuals, particularly emerging adults, will purposely plan to experiment or engage in uncommitted sexual activity and other high-risk behaviors (Josiam, Hobson, Dietrich, & Smeaton, 1998). In a study of Canadian college students on spring break, of those explicitly planning to participate in casual sex, 61% of men and 34% of women engaged in intercourse within a day of meeting a partner (Maticka-Tyndale, Herold, & Mewhinney, 1998). This is echoed in another more recent report, where regardless of relationship status, approximately 30% of participants had sex with someone they met on spring break (Sönmez et al., 2006). Such settings may help facilitate a preexisting desire for hookups (i.e., playful atmosphere and presence of alcohol).

More generally, in a sample of sexually experienced men and women, participants indicated a variety of settings where they met someone with whom they had casual sex: 70% at a party, 56% at a singles bar, 43% while away on vacation, 28% at a dance, 7% while away on business, and 5% on a blind date (Herold & Mewhinney, 1993). In addition to sharing common social venues with heterosexuals, gay men and other men who have sex with men have an expanded array of venues in which hookups may occur. Research specifically sampling gay men and other men who have sex with men have similarly found bars to be common places for gay men to meet, socialize, and find others for casual sexual encounters (Mustanski, Lyons, & Garcia, 2011). Although uncommitted sex among gay men occurs in a variety of locations, antigay prejudice and structural heterosexism can limit the availability of supportive and safe options for connecting with other men (Harper, 2007). Consequently, more anonymous, sometimes public, spaces have been an alternative for some gay men. In a sample of 508 gay and bisexual men in college (all under the age of 30), nearly one third admitted to meeting partners in anonymous places (i.e., bathhouses, restrooms, gyms, bookstores, movies, parks, the street, or other public places) (Seage et al., 1997). Public cruising areas, Internet cruising networks, and bathhouses are somewhat popular venues (although by no means archetypal) for explicitly initiating uncommitted sex among men who have sex with men (Binson et al., 2001). These are not findings that seem to be prevalent among lesbians and women who have sex with women or among heterosexual hookups.

Theoretical Frameworks for Hookup Research

An interdisciplinary biopsychosocial model can synthesize traditionally disconnected theoretical perspectives and provide a more holistic understanding of hookup culture. Hatfield et al. (in press) state that

> while many scholars emphasize cultural factors and others emphasize evolutionary factors, increasingly most take a cultural and biopsychosocial approach—pointing out that it is the interaction of culture, social context, personal experience, and biological factors that shape young people's attitudes and willingness to participate in casual sexual encounters. Which of

these factors prove to be most important depends on culture, personality, gender, and social context. (pp. 3–4)

Some empirical studies of hookup behavior have also advocated multifactorial approaches (Eshbaugh & Gute, 2008; Garcia & Reiber, 2008).

Evolutionary and social models often generate parallel hypotheses about uncommitted sex, although "each addresses a different level of analysis" (Fisher et al., 2012, p. 47). Using two midlevel theories, Fisher et al. (2012) explained that "parental investment theory is an example of an ultimate level of explanation, while social role theory is an example of a proximate level, although each leads to the same prediction" (p. 47). They argued that evolution may be most helpful in exploring the reproductive motive, and sexual scripts may be useful in exploring the cultural discourse agenda. That is, evolutionary biology influences *why* emerging adults engage in uncommitted sex and the way young men and women react to these encounters (ultimate level explanations). At the same time, social roles and sexual scripts influence *how* emerging adults navigate their desires in a particular socio-cultural context (proximate level explanations). For instance, that religiosity (religious feelings and attendance at religious services) was related to lower frequency of engaging in intercourse during a hookup encounter (Penhollow, Young, & Bailey, 2007) may be envisioned as an adaptive sociocultural constraint. Or, that high degrees of closeness to peer social networks and peer communication about hookups was associated with more sexual hookups (Holman & Sillars, 2012) may be considered as a facultative response to adaptively react to peer expectations and local norms.

It is important to point out that many sociocultural theorists disagree with the idea that culture offers only a proximate level explanation for human sexual behavior. However, it is not the goal of this review to resolve this debate. Instead, we attempt to articulate better the multitude of factors that shape the rich variety of human sexuality to enhance understanding of uncommitted sex among emerging adults. In the next two sections, we will introduce both evolutionary and social script views of uncommitted sex, to simultaneously consider the influence of each on hookup culture.

Evolution and "Short-Term" Sexual Behavior

Human evolutionary behavioral studies attempts to explain sexual behavior by understanding our evolutionary history and how this may influence behavioral patterns in a given environment. There are several *different* midlevel evolutionary or biological theories about the nature of human sexual behavior. These theories seek to understand the way evolutionary pressures influence human sexual propensities, variation, and, in some cases, sex differences. This logic is based on the premise that, compared to asexual reproduction, sexual reproduction is quite costly. Sexually reproducing organisms pay many costs, including the time, energy, and resources spent in finding and attracting mates—tasks that are unnecessary for asexual reproducers (Daly, 1978). Offsetting the costs of sexual reproduction in large-bodied organisms is the benefit sexual reproduction provides against easy colonization by parasites and pathogens (Van Valen, 1973). Sexual reproduction scrambles up genes, creating genotypes that are novel environments and forcing the parasites and pathogens to begin anew in their quest to exploit the host. Thus, large-bodied organisms with long lifespans generally benefit evolutionarily from sexual reproduction despite its substantial costs.

Sexual reproduction is characterized by sexes—generally male and female—whose evolutionary best interests differ because their potential reproductive rates differ (Clutton-Brock & Parker, 1992). In humans, producing a viable offspring, from gestation through lactation, takes females longer than it takes males. The sex with the faster potential reproductive rate—generally males—can benefit by attempting to co-opt the reproductive effort of multiple members of the opposite sex. However, the sex with the slower potential reproductive rate—generally females—will be operationally in short supply relative to the sex with the faster potential reproductive rate, simply because it takes them longer to complete a reproductive venture.

According to evolutionary theorists, this discrepancy in reproductive rate between the sexes sets up general predictions about sex-specific mating behaviors (Bateman, 1948; Clutton-Brock & Parker, 1992; Trivers, 1972). Males are predicted to compete for access to the reproductive potential of the slower sex; this generates expectations of psychological and physical adaptations in males that enhance their chances of success, including aggression and an array of physical features (e.g., large size, musculature, physical weaponry like antlers) that would assist them in competing with other males for access to females. Females are predicted to be choosy concerning their mates because they invest more in each offspring, and they stand to lose more if they make a poor reproductive choice. Relative parental investment costs are thought to be the arbiters of mating behaviors (Trivers, 1972). Thus in sex role reversed species where males provide a majority of parental support, it is females that are then expected to compete more for mates and

be more indiscriminate in their mating (Alcock, 2005). Generally, females choose mates on the basis of whatever is most important to the success of the reproductive venture—at the least, good genes for the offspring, but often for particular resources with which to provision offspring, protection, and/or apparent willingness to assist in parenting. Because females choose males on the basis of critical features and resources, males are expected to compete with other males to acquire and display these features and resources. This provides a basic framework with which to begin, and in humans we expect complex cognitive processes to be overlaid on it.

In terms of applying this logic to human sexual behavior and in particular sexual hookups, uncommitted sex has most often been interpreted in evolutionary terms as a fitness-enhancing short-term mating strategy (Buss, 1998; Buss & Schmitt, 1993). In this view—sexual strategies theory—men prefer as many mates as possible, including short-term sexual encounters that can potentially maximize reproductive output. Men will attempt to mate with a maximum number of partners (sexual variety), consent to sex more quickly than women, and provide minimal resources to any but long-term partners, only conceding to a long-term relationship for the purposes of enhancing offspring vitality (Symons, 1979; Buss, 1998). Also in this view, women are expected to prefer long-term relationships to extract a maximum amount of resources from mates. Women will engage in short-term sex when it is typically viewed as an infidelity to obtain better quality genes for offspring (Gangestad & Thornhill, 1997). That is, sexual strategies theory (a midlevel theory within the larger evolutionary metatheoretical framework) does allow for *both* men and women to engage in long-term and short-term sexual behaviors, but for sex-specific evolutionary reasons (Buss & Schmitt, 1993; Schmitt et al., 2003). In Petersen and Hyde's (2010) thorough meta-analytic review of gender differences in sexuality research (834 individual studies and 7 national data sets, across 87 countries), men and women are more similar than different in a majority of sexual behaviors. The exceptions, yielding the greatest effect sizes, included men's greater permissiveness toward casual sex behavior and casual sex attitudes. This mirrors an earlier review finding that gender differences in attitudes toward casual sex were some of the most pronounced differences of all sexual behaviors (Oliver & Hyde, 1993).

In measuring propensities for nonrelational sex, a variety of studies conducted within North America have demonstrated that men consistently have higher sociosexuality scores than women (Schmitt, 2005). Research on sociosexuality has suggested individual differences in disposition toward engaging in sexual behavior and exhibitionism, with some individuals more permissive (unrestricted) and some nonpermissive (restricted) about sexual frequency (Simpson & Gangestad, 1992). Individuals with more permissive sociosexuality rate physical attraction as more important than other characteristics in a potential partner (Simpson & Gangestad, 1992). Several scholars have argued that the degree to which evolution shapes mating behaviors, including sociosexuality, will be contingent on particular environmental conditions (Frayser, 1985; Low, 2000; Schmitt, 2005). To support the idea that sociosexuality is likely a combination of evolved sex-specific mating strategies and social structural factors, in a study of over 200,000 participants from 53 nations, Lippa (2009) demonstrated that although consistent sex differences emerged, gender equality and economic development tended to predict the magnitude of sex differences in sociosexuality (more permissive). Similarly, Wood and Eagly (2002) have endorsed a biosocial model for understanding sex differences cross-culturally that takes into account multiple levels of analyses, including biological constraints alongside social and economic constraints.

In support of evolved sexual strategies, in a cross-cultural study of 16,288 individuals across 52 nations, Schmitt et al. (2003) showed that on average men self-report a greater desire for sexual partner variety than women, regardless of relationship status (married or single) or sexual orientation (heterosexual or homosexual). Using the short-term seeking measure (asking participants on a 7-point scale whether they are actively seeking a short-term mate), they reported that, in North America, relatively more men (65.2%) than women (45.4%) fall into the category of seeking short-term mates *in any way* (any score above 1 on the scale). Of note, using the cross-cultural responses of those who are single (excluding those currently involved in a relationship), 79.3% of men and 64.0% of women reported seeking a short-term mate in some way. Evolutionary-inclined researchers have often used these findings to point to the adaptive nature of sex-specific mating strategies (see Schmitt, 2005). These data demonstrate fairly modest relative sex differences in propensities toward sex beyond a committed relationship—which are indeed important to document. Yet, a cross-cultural sex difference of 15.3% in number of single men and single women interested in seeking a short-term mate does not necessarily reveal discreet sex-specific (short-term) mating strategies per se. This is especially true considering that, compared to males, the relative risks of sexual behavior are higher for females: unintended pregnancy, increased transmission of disease, and greater susceptibility to sexual violence.

Although there is a reasonable proportional difference between sexes, there are still nearly two thirds of unpartnered women interested in uncommitted sex and over one fifth of unpartnered men who are not interested in this activity. In short, there is significant overlap between the sexes and significant variation within the sexes. All things considered, the simplest expectation is that evolutionary processes will result in both men and women desiring both sex and pair-bonding. Extrarelational sex is part of the human mating repertoire, as is pair-bonding. Individuals have competing sexual and relational motivations at any given time, which should be expected to go in one direction or the other, depending on an individual's environmental context.

The popularity of hooking up among *both* men and women presents a problem for approaching human sexuality purely from the perspective of sexual strategies theory. That both men and women are engaging in this behavior at such high rates is not consistent with the model. Homosexual relationships also presents a quandary for sexual strategies theory. Although the proportion of gay men in open relationships seems to support the theory (i.e., males are more sexually eager), the expectation that males should mate-guard their partners to prevent sexual infidelity cannot simultaneously coexist with such prevalence of open relationships among gay men.

Several evolutionary scholars have started to question the ability of sexual strategies theory to accurately reflect patterns of short-term sex in a shifting ecological context, and they have proposed alternative evolutionary approaches (Gangestad & Simpson, 2000; Li & Kenrick, 2006; Garcia & Reiber, 2008; Fisher, 2011; Pedersen, Putcha-Bhagavatula, & Miller, 2011). For instance, Li and Kenrick (2006) have pointed to the benefits of using an evolutionary economic model of tradeoffs to understand sex differences in willingness to engage in short-term sex, and sex similarities in prioritization of short-term partners. Using biological and cross-cultural evidence, Fisher (1992, 2011) has argued human possess a dual reproductive strategy of social monogamy (serial or long-term) and clandestine adultery. Pedersen et al. (2011) applied attachment fertility theory and demonstrated relatively few sex differences, arguing that predictions from sexual strategies theory are not consistent with their data. In their comparison of theoretical models, they found that attachment fertility theory

> posits that short-term mating and other forms of mating outside of pair-bonds *are natural byproducts* of a suite of attachment and care-giving mechanisms . . . selected for in human evolutionary history to

ultimately enable men and women to seek, select, create, and maintain a pair-bond . . . pointing to an increasingly coherent picture of the underlying biological and chemical systems involved . . . that generally operate similarly for men and women. (Pedersen et al., 2011, p. 639)

If humans possess a fairly flexible sexual repertoire, yet pair-bonding is essential, this sets the stage for a conflict between competing motivational drives that are fine tuned to particular environments.

In accordance with an evolutionary model, the simplest, most general prediction is that men will be relatively more competitive and sexually eager, and that women will be relatively choosier. Further, in accordance with an evolutionary model emphasizing pair-bonding, *both* men and women will have competing motivational drives for sexual engagement and pair-bond formation. This might assume that penetrative sexual intercourse between fertile men and women entails a sizable risk of reproduction for females—an assumption that simply no longer applies to humans in the 21st century. In contemporary industrialized cultures, pleasurable sexual behaviors can be divorced from reproduction and used for other purposes, including social standing and simple enjoyment, among others. Contraception and reproductive technologies allow women greater control over reproduction, but this should not be enough to *completely* overwrite millions of years of evolutionary pressure to shape certain aspects of mating psychology. Rather, in these contemporary conditions, those who use contraception to optimize their reproductive output may well be evolutionarily favored. Women could, for example, use contraception to control the timing of pregnancies in ways that maximize the chance of success, or ensure parentage by favored males over lesser-quality mates. And males too may be able to control siring a child and the cross-culture expectation of fatherhood (see Gray & Anderson, 2010, for a review on evolution and fatherhood). Thus, contraception is simply an additional feature of the environment of reproduction, and males and females are expected to attempt to manipulate it in their own favor. Psychological adaptations that support the "choosy female" strategy are still evident, even when individuals choose to engage in nonreproductive sexual behavior. However, the ability to divorce sex from reproduction should allow for less discrepancy between males and females in willingness to engage in uncommitted sex and negotiations of both sexual and romantic desires. Clearly, the evolved reproductive motive involves both sexes desiring sex and desiring pair-bonds, but having different ways of obtaining each and different prioritizations for each.

Sexual Scripts and Uncommitted Sex

Sexual script theory suggests that our sexual behaviors are dictated by a set of "scripts" that are used to organize and interpret sexual encounters into understandable conventions (Simon & Gagnon, 1986). Scripts, particularly gender-normative ones, dictate behaviors, such as who does what and when in context (e.g., men ask women on a date, men pay the bill on a first date, men initiate sex after date). The most widely produced and promoted cultural sexual scripts are heterosexual in nature and include those focused on male roles (Kim et al., 2007; Tolman, 2006; Ward, 1995). For men, sex is portrayed as central to male identity, men prefer nonrelational sex, and men are active sexual agents. Women are portrayed as sexual objects, sexually passive compared to men, and women act as sexual gatekeepers. Sexual script theory is generally vague when it comes to origins, focusing more on descriptions of scripts. Wiederman (2005), Phillips (2000), and Jhally (2007) have argued that scripts are not only sexualized but also gendered, with underlying sexual messages being noticeably different for men and women. Many researchers (Jhally, 2007; Kim et al., 2007; Phillips, 2000; Ward, 1995) have favored culture and subculture environment elements such as popular media (i.e., television, films, magazines) as the origin of gendered sexual scripts. But this does little to explain why the media industry produces these scripts in the first place. It is not by accident that consumer behavior can be well-explained by those products most salient to human survival and reproduction, and why messages of love and sex are among the most producible (Saad, 2007). But, on their own, both the evolutionary perspective and the social scripts perspective have thus far been inadequate in fully unpacking the origin of sexual messages, their propagation, and their social retention. Without identifying a primary, hierarchal, origin, it is likely that media is reflecting actual behavioral change in a circular way—media is a reflection of our evolutionary penchants, further exaggerated and supported by the presumption that it is popular.

Images of a polymorphous sexuality that decenters the reproductive motive and focuses instead on sexual pleasure are consistently appearing in popular media. In music lyrics, for example, although opera arias and art songs have contained messages about reproduction and mating for more than 400 years, it is contemporary music lyrics where an erotic uncommitted sexuality has predominated (Hobbs & Gallup, 2011). Some popular portrayals go against the popular trend, such as *American Idol* star Kelly Clarkson's Billboard Hot 100 song "I Do Not Hook Up," released in 2009, cowritten and covered under the title "Hook Up" by American singer–songwriter Katy Perry. Other representations celebrate sexual liberation, such as Kylie Minogue's "All the Lovers" and Madonna's frequent reversal of male sexual dominance (Guilbert, 2002). Hobbs and Gallup (2011) performed a content analysis of song lyrics from Billboard's Top Ten charts for Country, Pop, and R&B. They found that of 174 different songs in the Top Ten lists from 2009, 92% contained messages about reproduction or mating, with the best-selling songs containing more such messages than less-successful songs: "the ubiquitous presence of these reproductive themes is a reflection of evolved properties in the human psyche, where people are voting with their pocket books and listener preferences are driving the lyrics" (Hobbs & Gallup, 2011, p. 404). It seems plausible that sexual scripts in popular entertainment media are exaggerated examples of behaviors that are taken to an extreme for the purposes of media sensationalism and activation of core guttural interests.

Conflicting gendered scripts may contribute to mixed perceptions and expectations of hookups. In a detailed qualitative study of girls' first sexual experiences, Phillips (2000) made the case that conflicting media discourse messages make it difficult for women to navigate sexual initiation. The first sexual experiences described by the 30 participants were almost all quite negative (and, in some cases, horrific). Girls receive conflicting messages about being a "good girl" and a "pleasing woman," but also a "together woman." A "together woman" is agentic and experienced, such as the character Samantha from *Sex in the City*, who is sexually assertive and displays a strong, almost stereotypically masculine desire discourse. Many women find the discrepant messages difficult to navigate: to be a good girl, to be a "Samantha," or to try and be both. Messages often portray the sexually assertive woman as a woman who has extreme difficulty in being genuine and having a meaningful romantic relationship. Psychoanalytic analysis views this conflict as the Madonna–whore dichotomy, where women face challenges in being viewed as both a sexually expressive being and a maternal committed being, and at the same time their romantic or sexual partners face challenges with categorizing women as one or the other (Welldon, 1988). Presumably, these same conflicting discourse messages can make it difficult for individuals to psychologically navigate hookups, including sexual decision-making.

There seems to be inconsistency in the scripts pertaining to the casualness and emotional investment in causal sexual encounters. An example of this disconnect is presented by Backstrom, Armstrong, and Puentes (2012), whose study examined the responses of 43 college women who described their difficulties in their negotiations of cunnilingus, such as desiring it in a hookup or not desiring it in a relationship. As another example, a qualitative study of men's hookup scripts also displayed inconsistency in casualness (Epstein, Calzo, Smiler, & Ward, 2009). Men easily described stereotypic hookups and FWBs as nonrelational and noncommitted, and in an oppositional fashion compared to romantic committed "dating-esque" relationships. Yet, in interviews, participants also expressed distinct discomfort with these extrarelational scripts. Men voiced alternative definitions that highlighted emotional connection and the potential for committed romantic relationships.

While contrary to no-strings attached hookup discourse, these alternative romance and commitment-oriented scripts are not surprising. Similar discourse messages are present in other aspects of popular media. This is consistent with Phillips's (2000) conclusion that media messages are contradictory. In addition to media focused on casual sex, emerging adults have simultaneously been fed a Disney film diet with romantic relational scripts in which men and women live happily ever after, as heterosexual love conquers all (Tanner, Haddock, Zimmerman, & Lund, 2003). It is curious that, although purporting to regale the audience with nonrelational sex, the previously mentioned films *Friends with Benefits* and *No Strings Attached* also highlight this; in the end, couples in both movies actually end up in seemingly monogamous romantic relationships. Although the evolutionary reproductive motives produce contradictory motivations, for both short-term sex and long-term commitment, some media scripts apparently do the same.

Hookups as More Than "Just Sex"

Despite the high prevalence of uncommitted sexual behavior, emerging adults often have competing nonsexual interests. In a study of 681 emerging adults, 63% of college-aged men and 83% of college-aged women preferred, at their current stage of life or development, a traditional romantic relationship as opposed to an uncommitted sexual relationship (Garcia, Reiber, Merriwether, Heywood, & Fisher, 2010). Although there is a proportional sex difference, note that a substantial majority of both sexes would prefer a romantic relationship, despite their particular developmental stage of emerging adulthood. In another survey of 500 students who all had experiences with hookups, 65% of women and 45% of men reported that they hoped their hookup encounter would become a committed relationship, with 51% of women and 42% of men reporting that they tried to discuss the possibility of starting a relationship with their hookup partner (Owen & Fincham, 2011). The gender differences observed are modest, and point to the convergence of gender roles in hookup culture; even though there are some gender differences, it should not be ignored that the curves overlap significantly.

Just as the discourse of hooking up is often in conflict with itself, individuals often self-identify a variety of motivations for hooking up. In one investigation of the concomitant motivations for hookups, Garcia and Reiber (2008) found that while 89% of young men and women reported that physical gratification was important, 54% reported emotional gratification and 51% reported a desire to initiate a romantic relationship; there were no sex differences in the responses. That a substantial portion of individuals reported emotional and romantic motivations appears to be in apparent conflict with the sexual strategies framework discussed earlier, which predicts significant sex differences. However, this is not in conflict with an evolutionary pair-bond hypothesis, which suggests that humans desire both sex and romantic intimacy (Garcia & Reiber, 2008). Indeed, some hookups turn into romantic relationships. Paik (2010a) found that individuals in relationships that start as hookups or FWBs report lower average relationship satisfaction. However, this varied as a function of whether the participants initially wanted a relationship. If individuals were open to a serious committed relationship initially, relationship satisfaction was just as high as those who did not engage in (initially) uncommitted sexual activity prior to starting a relationship (Paik, 2010a). The entanglement of more intimate and emotional aspects with sex is something the romantic comedy movies mentioned earlier highlight.

Again in seeming contrast to the sex-specific mating strategies, contemporary hookup behavior involves a high degree of female sexual assertiveness for sexual desire and pleasure. In another study of self-reported motivations for hooking up, which included 118 female first-semester students, 80% indicated sexual desire, 58% spontaneous urge, 56% perceived attractiveness of the partner, 51% intoxication, 33% willingness of the partner, and 29% desire to feel attractive or desirable (Fielder & Carey, 2010a). Contrary to some media messages, individuals do not appear to be engaging in truly no-strings attached sex. Competing interests at multiple levels result in young adults having to negotiate multiple desires, and multiple social pressures. Again, the most fruitful explanation is that both men and women have competing sexual and romantic interests, with tremendous individual differences in such desires.

Not all sexual subcultures necessarily experience casual sex in the same "singles" context. As such, the simultaneous motivations for sex and romance may appear

different. Beyond heterosexual hookups, casual sex (not necessarily referred to as "hookups") has been reported to be a normative sexual script among men who have sex with men. Despite the existence of casual sex and open relationships among gay men, there is also a strong desire for romantic and companionate attachment (Clarke & Nichols, 1972). Early ethnography by Cory (1951; also known as Edward Sagarin) described sections of gay culture as being "brought together, driven by the sensual impulse, seeking new forms and new partners for the love of the flesh, hoping to find excitement and satisfaction . . ." (p. 115). The origins of these pro-sex scripts have been theorized to be due to a subculture focused on male sexuality (Mealey, 2000). Another explanation is the social relegation of gay men to the status of "deviant," limiting access to socially sanctioned relationship scripts. However, discourse surrounding monogamy in gay relationships does demonstrate simultaneous desires for sexual variety and commitment, representing a kaleidoscope of issues about trust, love, and sexual behavior (Worth, Reid, & McMillan, 2002). Because same-sex relationships are naturally removed from the reproductive motive, it may be possible that part of the larger hookup culture is borrowed from sexual subcultures involving greater emphasis on the positive erotic.

Hookup Culture and Sexual Risk

The negative consequences of hookups can include emotional and psychological injury, sexual violence, sexually transmitted infections, and/or unintended pregnancy. Despite various health risks, in a qualitative study of 71 college students (39 women and 32 men), nearly half of participants were unconcerned with contracting a sexually transmitted infection from penetrative intercourse during a hookup, and a majority were unconcerned about diseases in hookups that included fellatio or cunnilingus (Downing-Matibag & Geisinger, 2009). Most students reported not considering or realizing their own health risks during hookups, particularly those that occurred within their own community such as with someone else on their own college campus. Compounding disease risks, individuals involved in hookups are more likely to have concurrent sexual partners (Paik, 2010b). In a sample of 1,468 college students, among the 429 students who had engaged in oral sex, anal sex, or vaginal intercourse in their most recent hookup, only 46.6% reported using a condom (Lewis et al., 2011). Although, in Paul et al.'s (2000) study, conducted nearly a decade earlier, of those hookups that included sexual intercourse, a higher, yet still too low, 81% of participants reported using a condom. Among women in their first semester of college, Fielder and Carey (2010a) reported that condoms were used for 0% of oral sex hookups, and only 69% of vaginal sex hookups. Health-based hookup research like this may lead to programs for correcting misperceptions of sexual risk and sexual norms to ultimately restore individual locus of control over sexual behavior, reproductive rights, and healthy personal decision-making.

Prevalence of Alcohol and Drugs

In addition to sexual risk-taking, in terms of low condom use, another issue of concern involving hookups is the high comorbidity with substance use. As part of a larger study, in a sample of several thousand individuals aged 15–25, men and women who had used marijuana or cocaine in the last 12 months were also more likely than nonusers to have had nonmonogamous sex in the past 12 months (van Gelder, Reefhuis, Herron, Williams, & Roeleveld, 2011)—although an operational definition for these presumably uncommitted partnerships was not discussed. More specifically, in one study of undergraduate students, 33% of those reporting uncommitted sex indicated their motivation was "unintentional," likely due to alcohol and other drugs (Garcia & Reiber, 2008). In Fielder and Carey's (2010a) study among 118 first-semester female college students, participants reported that 64% of uncommitted sexual encounters follow alcohol use, with a median consumption of 3 alcoholic drinks. Similarly, another study employing a web-based survey found that nearly 61% of undergraduate students used alcohol, with an average of 3.3 alcoholic drinks, during their most recent hookup (Lewis et al., 2011). Further, in a study based on 71 interviews with college students, nearly 80% indicated that alcohol was involved in initiating their most recent hookup, with 64% attributing the progression and extent of the hookup to alcohol (Downing-Matibag & Geisinger, 2009). Alcohol use has also been associated with type of hookup: greatest alcohol use was associated with penetrative sexual hookups, less alcohol use with nonpenetrative hookups, and least amount of alcohol use among those who did not hookup (Owen, Fincham, & Moore, 2011). In one study of men and women who had engaged in an uncommitted sexual encounter that included vaginal, anal, or oral sex, participants reported their intoxication levels: 35% were very intoxicated, 27% were mildly intoxicated, 27% were sober, and 9% were extremely intoxicated (Fisher et al., 2012). Alcohol and drug use drastically increases the overall risks of sexual activity (Abbey, Ross, McDuffie, & McAuslan, 1996). Alcohol may also serve as an excuse, purposely consumed as a strategy to protect the self from having to justify hookup behavior later (Paul, 2006). This paints a picture very different from popular representations of alcohol and substance use in hookups,

which are often handled with a detached air of humor. For instance, the interactive book *Hookups & Hangovers: A Journal* (Chronicle Books, 2011) is playfully described by the publisher: "here to help piece together all the hilarious and humiliating details of last night's party. Playful prompts—including 'Where did I wake up?' and 'So drunk, I can't believe I . . .' as well as space to rate your hookups and hangovers—make this guided journal the perfect accessory for the morning after." These findings raise several concerns about the occurrence of hookups and the psychological impact such behaviors have on the individuals involved.

Although alcohol and drugs are likely a strong factor, it is still largely unclear what role individual differences play in shaping decisions to engage in hookups. In a sample of 394 young adults, the strongest predictor of hookup behavior was having previously hooked up—those who engaged in penetrative sex hookups were approximately 600% more likely than others to repeat this over the course of a university semester (Owen et al., 2011). Other factors may include media consumption, personality, and biological predispositions. Garcia, MacKillop, et al. (2010) demonstrated an association between the dopamine D4 receptor gene polymorphism (DRD4 VNTR) and uncommitted sexual activity among 181 young men and young women. Although genotypic groups in this study did not vary in terms of overall number of sexual partners, individuals with a particular "risk-taking" variant of the dopamine receptor D4 gene (DRD4 VNTR; also associated with substance abuse) were shown to have a higher likelihood of having uncommitted sexual encounters (including infidelity and one-night stands)—however, no sex differences were observed. This suggests that biological factors that contribute to motivating the different *contexts* of sexual behavior for *both* men and women may be fairly sexually monomorphic (Garcia, Reiber, et al., 2010). This may, in some cases, point to fairly stable individual differences.

Hookup Culture and Psychological Well-Being

The discrepancy between behaviors and desires, particularly with respect to social–sexual relationships, has dramatic implications for physical and mental health. Despite widespread allure, uncommitted sexual behavior has been shown to elicit a pluralistic ignorance response promoting individuals to engage in behaviors regardless of privately feeling uncomfortable with doing so (Lambert et al., 2003; Reiber & Garcia, 2010). Individuals overestimate others' comfort with hookups and assign variable meanings to those behaviors (Lambert et al., 2003; Reiber & Garcia, 2010). Misperception of sexual norms is one potential driver for people to behave in ways they do not personally endorse. In a replication and extension of Lambert et al.'s study (2003), Reiber and Garcia (2010) found that 78% of individuals overestimated others' comfort with many different sexual behaviors, with men particularly overestimating women's actual comfort with a variety of sexual behaviors in hookups.

Hookup scenarios may include feelings of pressure and performance anxiety. In Paul et al.'s (2000) study on hookups, 16% of participants felt pressured during their typical hookup. In this sample, 12% of participants felt out of control when penetrative intercourse was not involved while 22% percent felt out of control when sexual intercourse took place. Note that this study asked participants about typical hookups, and although this was informative for general patterns, it does not capture specific factors influencing specific individual scenarios. That is, it is unclear how one might rate a "typical" hookup if, for instance, one instance involved sexual coercion and regret while other hookup experiences before and/or after such an event were consenting and more enjoyable. In a multiethnic sample of 109 women, hookup scripts were compared to rape scripts, and, even though hookup scripts contained psychological consequences such as shame, a majority did not presume sexual assault (Littleton, Tabernik, Canales, & Backstrom, 2009). Further, in a qualitative study that asked 187 participants to report their feelings after a typical hookup, 35% reported feeling regretful or disappointed, 27% good or happy, 20% satisfied, 11% confused, 9% proud, 7% excited or nervous, 5% uncomfortable, and 2% desirable or wanted (Paul & Hayes, 2002). However, this same study found that feelings differed during compared to after hookups: during a typical hookup, 65% of participants reported feeling good, aroused, or excited, 17% desirable or wanted, 17% nothing in particular or were focused on the hookup, 8% embarrassed or regretful, 7% nervous or scared, 6% confused, and 5% proud (Paul & Hayes, 2002). Just as multiple motivations can be in conflict, and multiple discourse messages can be in conflict, individuals' affective reactions during and after a hookup can be in conflict.

An individual history of hookup behavior has been associated with a variety of mental health factors. In a recent study of 394 young adults followed across a university semester, those participants with more depressive symptoms and greater feelings of loneliness who engaged in penetrative sex hookups subsequently reported a reduction in both depressive symptoms and feelings of loneliness (Owen et al., 2011). At the same time, those participants who reported less depressive symptoms and fewer feelings of loneliness who engaged in penetrative sex hookups subsequently reported an increase in both

depressive symptoms and feelings of loneliness (Owen et al., 2011). In another study, among 291 sexually experienced individuals, those who had the most regret after uncommitted sex also had more symptoms of depression than those who had no regret (Welsh et al., 2006). However, in the same sample, women's but not men's degree of depressive symptoms increased with number of previous sex partners within the last year (Welsh et al., 2006). In the first study to investigate the issue of self-esteem and hookups, *both* men and women who had ever engaged in an uncommitted sexual encounter had lower overall self-esteem scores compared to those without uncommitted sexual experiences (Paul et al., 2000). The potential causal direction of the relationship between self-esteem and uncommitted sex is yet unclear (Paul et al., 2000; Fielder & Carey, 2010b).

Hookups can result in guilt and negative feelings. In a study of 169 sexually experienced men and women surveyed in singles bars, when presented with the question "I feel guilty or would feel guilty about having sexual intercourse with someone I had just met," 32% of men and 72% of women agreed with the statement (Herold & Mewhinney, 1993). The percentage of women expressing guilt was more than twice that of men. This is consistent with a classic study by Clark and Hatfield (1989), which demonstrated that men are much more likely than women to accept casual sex offers from attractive confederates. Conley (2011) replicated and extended this finding, demonstrating that, under certain conditions of perceived comfort, the gender differences in acceptance of casual sex is diminished. In a study of 333 men and 363 women on a college campus, in deliberate hookup situations women had more thoughts of worry and vulnerability than men (Townsend & Wasserman, 2011). Moreover, as number of sex partners increased, marital thoughts decreased, for both sexes (Townsend & Wasserman, 2011).

Qualitative descriptions of hookups reveal relative gender differences in terms of feelings afterward, with women displaying more negative reactions than men (Paul & Hayes, 2002). This is also consistent with earlier work demonstrating a gender difference, with women generally identifying more emotional involvement in seemingly "low investment" (i.e., uncommitted) sexual encounters than men (Townsend, 1995). Moreover, in a study of 140 (109 female, 31 male) first-semester undergraduates, women, but not men, who had engaged in penetrative intercourse during a hookup showed higher rates of mental distress (Fielder & Carey, 2010b). Possibly contributing to findings on gender differences in thoughts of worry, in a sample of 507 undergraduate students, more women than men leaned toward a relationship outcome following a hookup. Only 4.4% of men and 8.2% of women (6.45% of participants) expected a traditional romantic relationship as an outcome, while 29% of men and 42.9% of women (36.57% of participants) ideally wanted such an outcome (Garcia & Reiber, 2008). It is possible that regret and negative consequences result from individuals attempting to negotiate multiple desires. It is likely that a substantial portion of emerging adults today are compelled to publicly engage in hookups while desiring both immediate sexual gratification and more stable romantic attachments.

Not all hookup encounters are necessarily wanted or consensual. Individuals occasionally consent to engage in a sexual act but do not necessarily want sex (Peterson & Muehlenhard, 2007). In a sample of 178 college students, participants noted that a majority of their unwanted sex occurred in the context of hookups: 77.8% during a hookup, 13.9% in an ongoing relationship, and 8.3% on a date (Flack et al., 2007). Similarly, in a sample of 761 women students, approximately 50% of women reported at least one experience of unwanted sex (Hill, Garcia, & Geher, 2012). Of those women, 70% experienced unwanted sex in the context of a hookup and 57% in the context of a committed romantic relationship (Hill et al., 2012). Even more worrisome, a proportion of hookups also involve nonconsensual sex. In a study by Lewis et al. (2011), 86.3% of participants portrayed their most recent hookup experience as one they wanted to have, while 7.6% indicated that their most recent hookup was an experience they did not want to have or to which they were unable to give consent. Unwanted and nonconsensual sexual encounters are more likely occurring alongside alcohol and substance use.

Hookup Regret

A number of studies have included measures of regret with respect to hookups, and these studies have documented the negative feelings men and women may feel after hookups. In a large web-based study of 1,468 undergraduate students, participants reported a variety of consequences: 27.1% felt embarrassed, 24.7% reported emotional difficulties, 20.8% experienced loss of respect, and 10% reported difficulties with a steady partner (Lewis et al., 2011). In another recent study conducted on a sample of 200 undergraduate students in Canada, 78% of women and 72% of men who had uncommitted sex (including vaginal, anal, and/or oral sex) reported a history of experiencing regret following such an encounter (Fisher et al., 2012). A vast majority of both sexes indicated having *ever* experienced regret. There were few sex differences in reasons for regret, and better quality sex reduced the degree of regret reported (Fisher et al., 2012). It appears the method of asking participants whether and when they had experienced regret (i.e., ever, last hookup, or typical hookup) produces a sex difference, but in terms of categorical presence, it is most emerging adults who have experienced a kaleidoscope of reactions. This is consistent with Stinson's (2010) message of sexual development requiring experimentation, including trial and error, and good feelings and bad feelings.

On average, both men and women appear to have higher positive affect than negative affect following a hookup. Those with positive attitudes toward hookups and approval of sexual activity show the greatest positive affect (Lewis et al., 2011). However, there are also negative consequences experienced by *both* sexes. In a study of 270 sexually active college-aged students, 72% regretted at least one instance of previous sexual activity (Oswalt, Cameron, & Koob, 2005). In a report of 152 female undergraduate students, 74% of women had either a few or some regrets from uncommitted sex: 61% had a few regrets, 23% had no regrets, 13% had some regrets, and 3% had many regrets (Eshbaugh & Gute, 2008). Further, categorical presence of uncommitted sex in a female's sexual history was related to higher overall regret scores from sexual activity, although regret due to lack of commitment was not specifically addressed. Two types of sexual encounters were particularly predictive of sexual regret: engaging in penetrative intercourse with someone known less than 24 hours and engaging in penetrative intercourse with someone only once. Among a sample of 1,743 individuals who had experienced a previous one-night stand, Campbell (2008) showed that most men and women have combinations of both positive and negative affective reactions following this event. Using evolutionary theory to predict responses of regret, Campbell (2008) showed that men had stronger feelings of being "sorry because they felt they used another person" whereas women had stronger feelings of "regret because they felt used." Again, both men and women had experienced some sexual regret, but the frequency and intensity of negative reactions appeared to vary by sex, with women more negatively impacted from some hookup experiences.

There are substantial individual differences in reactions to hookups not accounted for by gender alone. Among a subsample of 311 young adults with hookup experience, when asked to generally characterize the morning after a hookup encounter, 82% of men and 57% of women were generally glad they had done it (Garcia & Reiber, 2008). The gap between men and women is notable, and demonstrates an average sex difference in affective reactions. Yet, this finding also conflicts with a strict sexual strategies model because more than half of women were glad they engaged in a hookup (and they were not in the context of commandeering extrapartner genes for offspring). With respect to scripts, although presumably being sexually agentic (e.g., the "Samantha"), only slightly more than half of women were actually generally glad they had hooked up, suggesting these encounters may not truly be pleasurable for all. Similarly, in a study of 832 college students, 26% of women and 50% of men reported a positive emotional reaction following a hookup, and 49% of women and 26% of men reported a negative reaction (the remainders for each sex had a mix of both positive and negative reactions; Owen et al., 2010). These findings accord with the social sexual double standard creating greater pressure for women (Crawford & Popp, 2003; Fisher et al., 2012). Although the direction of the sex differences is in agreement with the evolutionary model, that nearly a quarter of women report primarily positive reactions is inconsistent with a truly sex-specific short-term mating psychology and with discourse messages of uncommitted sex being simply pleasurable. Also inconsistent with both of these theoretical models is that a quarter of men experience negative reactions. Taken alone, neither a biological nor social model is sufficient to explain these individual differences.

Some research has considered the interactions of sex and individual differences in predicting hookup behavior. The Mating Intelligence Scale, designed to measure an individual's cognitive abilities in the evolutionary domain of mating (see Geher & Kaufman, 2011), was used to assess hookup behavior in a sample of 132 college students. Young men higher in mating intelligence were more likely than others to have hooked up with strangers, acquaintances, and friends; while young women higher in mating intelligence were only more likely than others to have had more hookup experiences with acquaintances (O'Brien, Geher, Gallup, Garcia, & Kaufman, 2009). The authors proposed that given the potential risks and costs of sex to females, sex with strangers would be disadvantageous; and because women do not generally report having sexual motives toward opposite sex friends (Bleske-Rechek & Buss, 2001), women with high mating intelligence were likely striking the optimal balance, whereas men high in mating intelligence were obtaining maximum sexual encounters (O'Brien et al., 2009). In this regard, there are sex differences in cognitive processes, but one cannot necessarily presume that the sexes vary fundamentally in their behavioral potentials; rather, they vary in their decision-making, consistent with other evolutionary models.

It is still unclear the degree to which hookups may result in positive reactions, and whether young men and young women are sexually satisfied in these encounters.

Fine (1988) has argued that sex negativity is even more pronounced for women and the possibility of desire seems to be missing from the sexual education of young women. Armstrong, England, and Fogarty (2009) addressed sexual satisfaction in a large study of online survey responses from 12,295 undergraduates from 17 different colleges. Because cunnilingus often facilitates women's orgasm, participants were asked about oral sex rates and orgasm in their most recent hookup and most recent relationship sexual event. In this study, men reported receiving oral sex both in hookups and in relationships much more than women. In first-time hookups, 55% included only men receiving oral sex, 19% only women receiving oral sex, and 27% both mutually receiving; in last relationship sexual activity, 32% included only men receiving oral sex, 16% included only women receiving oral sex, and 52% included both mutually receiving. In both contexts, men also reached orgasm more often than women. In first time hookups, 31% of men and 10% of women reached orgasm; in last relationship sexual activity, 85% of men and 68% of women reached orgasm. Armstrong et al. (2009) concluded with an important message:

> A challenge to the contemporary sexual double standard would mean defending the position that young women and men are equally entitled to sexual activity, sexual pleasure, and sexual respect in hookups as well as relationships. To achieve this, the attitudes and practices of both men and women need to be confronted. Men should be challenged to treat even first hookup partners as generously as the women they hook up with treat them. (p. 377)

Taken together, this points to a need for further and more diverse attention to the impact of hookups on the physical and mental health of individuals, as recommended by Heldman and Wade (2010). Further, more attention is needed on potential positive aspects of hooking up, such as promoting sexual satisfaction and mutual comfort and enjoyment (see Armstrong et al., 2009).

Conclusion

Hookups are part of a popular cultural shift that has infiltrated the lives of emerging adults throughout the Westernized world. The past decade has witnessed an explosion in interest in the topic of hookups, both scientifically and in the popular media. Research on hookups is not seated within a singular disciplinary sphere; it sits at the crossroads of theoretical and empirical ideas drawn from a diverse range of fields, including psychology, anthropology, sociology, biology, medicine, and public health. The growth of our understanding of the hookup phenomenon is likely predicated on our ability to integrate these theoretical and empirical ideas into a unified whole that is capable of explaining the tremendous variety in human sexual expression.

Both evolutionary and social forces are likely facilitating hookup behavior, and together may help explain the rates of hookups, motivations for hooking up, perceptions of hookup culture, and the conflicting presence and lack of sex differences observed in various studies. Several scholars have suggested that shifting life-history patterns may be influential in shaping hookup patterns. In the United States, age at first marriage and first reproduction has been pushed back dramatically, while at the same time age at puberty has dropped dramatically, resulting in a historically unprecedented time gap where young adults are physiologically able to reproduce but not psychologically or socially ready to "settle down" and begin a family and child rearing (Bogle, 2007; Garcia & Reiber, 2008).

Together, the research reviewed here can help us better understand the nature of uncommitted sex today. It is worth noting, however, that several shortcomings in our knowledge continue to impede the understanding of hookup behavior. Both the historical transformations that have resulted in the reordering of sexual scripts and the demise of romantic courting among emerging adults remain mysterious (Bogle, 2007; Heldman & Wade, 2010). Second, recall bias may affect individuals' reports of previous romantic and sexual engagements; previous partners may be viewed as less desirable when individuals perceive their current partner as superior, thus creating a dissonance effect (see Geher et al., 2005). Much of the research asking participants about previous hookup relationships may therefore be biased due to recall. Third, there exists a vast and rich literature on men who have sex with men (MSM), specifically addressing casual sex and cruising among this population, and typically focused on sexual health and HIV prevention (see van Kesteren, Hospers, & Kok, 2007). The literature reviewed here primarily focuses on heterosexual hookups among emerging adults, with some researchers not controlling for sexual orientation (some purposefully) and others restricting to exclusively heterosexual samples. Future hookup research should venture into the MSM literature to explore patterns of casual sex among these populations to understand other sexual subcultures where uncommitted sexual behavior is prevalent. Moreover, there exists little published literature on the hookup patterns among lesbians and women who have sex with women. Last, the cross-cultural data provide a unique understanding of sexual behavior and romantic attachments; some societies engage in sex for pleasure and others for procreation (see Hatfield & Rapson, 2005; Gray & Garcia, 2013). Westernized culture often views sex as something for pleasure and fun (despite the frequency of behavioral patterns such as using the sexual "missionary" position and reduced female sexual stimulation), which dramatically influences our sexual perceptions, purposes, and pleasures (Hatfield & Rapson, 2005; Gray & Garcia, 2013).

Understanding hookups during the critical stage of late adolescent development and young adulthood is paramount for protecting and promoting healthy sexuality and healthy decision-making among emerging adults. Of the varied experiences and health risks young men and young women will experience, perhaps none are as pervasive and widely experienced as engagement in and desire for romantic attachments and experiences with sexual activity. Indeed, cross-cultural anthropological literature suggests men and women will go to extreme lengths for love and sex (Fisher, 1992; Hatfield & Rapson, 2005; Jankowiak & Paladino, 2008).

This review suggests that uncommitted sex, now being explored from a variety of disciplinary and theoretical perspectives, is best understood from a biopsychosocial perspective that incorporates recent research trends in human biology, reproductive and mental health, and sexuality studies. Both popular scripts and predictions from evolutionary theory suggest that a reproductive motive may influence some sexual patterns, such as motivation and regret following uncommitted sex. However, patterns of casual sex among gay men highlight inadequacies of the reproductive motive and suggest that further theorizing is necessary before a satisfactory evolutionarily informed theory can be established. Further, the findings that a majority of both men and women are motivated to engage in hookups, but often desire a more romantic relationship, is also consistent with a more nuanced evolutionary biopsychosocial perspective that takes into account social context and the cross-cultural and biological centrality of the pair-bond (Fisher, 1992; Jankowiak & Fischer, 1992; Pedersen et al., 2011; Gray & Garcia, 2013). Hookups, although increasingly socially acceptable, may leave more "strings" than public discourse would suggest.

References

Abbey, A., Ross, L. T., McDuffie, D., & McAuslan, P. (1996). Alcohol and dating risk factors for sexual assault among college women. *Psychology of Women Quarterly, 20,* 147–169. doi:10.1111/j.1471-6402.1996.tb00669.x

Alcock, J. (2005). *Animal behavior: An evolutionary approach* (8th ed.). Sunderland, MA: Sinauer Associates.

Altman, D. (1971). *Homosexual: Oppression and liberation.* New York, NY: Outerbridge & Dienstfrey.

Altman, D. (1982). *The homosexualization of America: The Americanization of the homosexual.* New York, NY: St Martin's.

Armstrong, E. A., England, P., & Fogarty, A. C. K. (2009). Orgasm in college hookups and relationships. In B. J. Risman (Ed.), *Families as they really are* (pp. 362–377). New York, NY: Norton.

Arnett, J. J. (2000). Emerging adulthood: A theory of development from the late teens through the twenties. *American Psychologist, 55,* 469–480. doi:10.1037/0003-066X.55.5.469

Backstrom, L., Armstrong, E. A., & Puentes, J. (2012). Women's negotiations of cunnilingus in college hookups and relationships. *Journal of Sex Research, 49,* 1–12. doi:10.1080/00224499.2011.585523

Bailey, B. L. (1988). *From front porch to back seat: Courtship in twentieth century America.* Baltimore, MD: Johns Hopkins University Press.

Bateman, A. J. (1948). Intra-sexual selection in *Drosophila. Heredity, 2,* 349–368. doi:10.1038/hdy.1948.21

Binson, D., Woods, W. J., Pollack, L., Paul, J., Stall, R., & Catania, J. A. (2001). Differential HIV risk in bathhouses and public cruising areas. *American Journal of Public Health, 91,* 1482–1486. doi:10.2105/AJPH.91.9.1482

Bisson, M. A., & Levine, T. R. (2009). Negotiating a friends with benefits relationship. *Archives of Sexual Behavior, 38,* 66–73. doi:10.1007/s10508-007-9211-2

Black, G. D. (1994). *Hollywood censored.* Cambridge, MA: Cambridge University Press.

Bleske-Rechek, A. L., & Buss, D. M. (2001). Opposite-sex friendship: Sex differences and similarities in initiation, selection, and dissolution. *Personality and Social Psychology Bulletin, 27,* 1310–1323. doi:10.1177/01461672012710007

Bogle, K. A. (2007). The shift from dating to hooking up in college: What scholars have missed. *Sociology Compass, 1/2,* 775–788.

Bogle, K. A. (2008). *Hooking up: Sex, dating, and relationships on campus.* New York, NY: New York University Press.

Boswell, A. A., & Spade, J. Z. (1996). Fraternities and collegiate rape culture: Why are some fraternities more dangerous places for women? *Gender & Society, 10,* 133–147. doi:10.1177/089124396010002003

Bradshaw, C., Kahn, A. S., & Saville, B. K. (2010). To hook up or date: Which gender benefits? *Sex Roles, 62,* 661–669. doi:10.1007/s11199-010-9765-7

Buss, D. M. (1998). Sexual strategies theory: Historical origins and current status. *Journal of Sex Research, 35,* 19–31. doi:10.1080/00224499809551914

Buss, D. M., & Schmitt, D. P. (1993). Sexual strategies theory: An evolutionary perspective on human mating. *Psychological Review, 100,* 204–232. doi:10.1037/0033-295X.100.2.204

Campbell, A. (2008). The morning after the night before: Affective reactions to one-night stands among mated and unmated women and men. *Human Nature, 19,* 157–173. doi:10.1007/s12110-008-9036-2

Cates, W. (1991). Teenagers and sexual risk taking: The best of times and the worst of times. *Journal of Adolescent Health, 12,* 84–94. doi: 10.1016/0197-0070(91)90449-V

Chia, S. C., & Gunther, A. C. (2006). How media contribute to misperceptions of social norms about sex. *Mass Communication & Society, 9,* 301–320. doi:10.1207/s15327825mcs0903_3

Chronicle Books. (2011). *Hook-ups & hangovers: A journal.* San Francisco, CA: Chronicle Books.

Clark, R. D., & Hatfield, E. (1989). Gender differences in receptivity to sexual offers. *Journal of Psychology & Human Sexuality, 2,* 39–55. doi:10.1300/J056v02n01_04

Clarke, L., & Nichols, J. (1972). *I have more fun with you than anybody.* New York, NY: St. Martin's.

Clutton-Brock, T. H., & Parker, G. A. (1992). Potential reproductive rates and the operation of sexual selection. *Quarterly Review of Biology, 67,* 437–456. doi:10.1086/417793

Conley, T. D. (2011). Perceived proposer personality characteristics and gender differences in acceptance of casual sex offers. *Journal of Personality and Social Psychology, 100,* 309–329. doi:10.1037/a0022152

Coontz, S. (2005). *Marriage, a history: How love conquered marriage.* New York, NY: Penguin Books.

Cory, D. W. (1951). *The homosexual in America.* New York, NY: Greenberg.

Crawford, M., & Popp, D. (2003). Sexual double standards: A review and methodological critique of two decades of research. *Journal of Sex Research, 40,* 13–26. doi:10.1080/00224490309552163

Daly, M. (1978). The cost of mating. *American Naturalist, 112,* 771–774. doi:10.1086/283319

Doherty, T. (1999). *Pre-code Hollywood.* New York, NY: Columbia University Press.

Downing-Matibag, T. M., & Geisinger, B. (2009). Hooking up and sexual risk taking among college students: A health belief model perspective. *Qualitative Health Research, 19,* 1196–1209. doi:10.1177/1049732309344206

Eliot, J., & Stilwell, M. (2010). *All the Lovers* [Recorded by Kylie Minogue]. On *Aphrodite* [CD]. Parlophone.

Ellis, A. (1958). *Sex without guilt.* New York, NY: Lyle Stuart.

England, P., Shafer, E. F., & Fogarty, A. C. K. (2007). Hooking up and forming romantic relationships on today's college campuses. In M. S. Kimmel & A. Aronson (Eds.), *The gendered society reader* (3rd ed., pp. 531–547). New York, NY: Oxford University Press.

Epstein, M., Calzo, J. P., Smiler, A. P., & Ward, L. M. (2009). "Anything from making out to having sex": Men's negotiations of hooking up and friends with benefits scripts. *Journal of Sex Research, 46,* 414–424. doi:10.1080/00224490902775801

Eshbaugh, E. M., & Gute, G. (2008). Hookups and sexual regret among college women. *The Journal of Social Psychology, 148,* 77–89. doi: 10.3200/SOCP.148.1.77-90

Fielder, R. L., & Carey, M. P. (2010a). Prevalence and characteristics of sexual hookups among first-semester female college students. *Journal of Sex & Marital Therapy, 36,* 346–359. doi:10.1080/0092623X.2010.488118

Fielder, R. L., & Carey, M. P. (2010b). Predictors and consequences of sexual "hookups" among college students: A short-term prospective study. *Archives of Sexual Behavior, 39,* 1105–1119. doi:10.1007/s10508-008-9448-4

Fine, M. (1988). Sexuality, schooling and adolescent females: The missing discourse of desire. *Harvard Educational Review, 58,* 29–53.

Finer, L. B. (2007). Trends in premarital sex in the United States, 1954–2003. *Public Health Reports, 122,* 73–78.

Fisher, H. E. (1992). *Anatomy of love: The natural history of monogamy, adultery, and divorce.* New York, NY: W. W. Norton & Company.

Fisher, H. E. (2011). Serial monogamy and clandestine adultery: Evolution and consequences of the dual human reproductive strategy. In S. C. Roberts (Ed.), *Applied Evolutionary Psychology.* New York, NY: Oxford University Press. doi:10.1093/acprof:oso/9780199586073.001.0001

Fisher, M. L., Worth, K., Garcia, J. R., & Meredith, T. (2012). Feelings of regret following uncommitted sexual encounters in Canadian university students. *Culture, Health & Sexuality, 14,* 45–57. doi:10.1080/13691058.2011.619579

Flack, W. F., Daubman, K. A., Caron, M. L., Asadorian, J. A., D'Aureli, N. R., Gigliotti, S. N., . . . Stine, E. R. (2007). Risk factors and consequences of unwanted sex among university students: Hooking up, alcohol, and stress response. *Journal of Interpersonal Violence, 22,* 139–157. doi:10.1177/0886260506295354

Frayser, S. G. (1985). *Varieties of sexual experience: An anthropological perspective on human sexuality.* New Haven, CT: HRAF Press.

Friends with benefits. (2003). In *Urbandictionary.com.* Retrieved from http://www.urbandictionary.com/define.php?term=friends%20with%20benefits

Friends with benefits. (2005). In *Urbandictionary.com.* Retrieved from http://www.urbandictionary.com/define.php?term=friends%20with%20benefits

Gangestad, S. W., & Simpson, J. A. (2000). The evolution of human mating: Trade-offs and strategic pluralism. *Behavioral and Brain Sciences, 23,* 573–587. doi:10.1017/S0140525X0000337X

Gangestad, S. W., & Thornhill, R. (1997). The evolutionary psychology of extra-pair sex: The role of fluctuating asymmetry. *Evolution and Human Behavior, 18,* 69–88. doi:10.1016/S1090-5138(97)00003-2

Garcia, J. R., & Kruger, D. J. (2010). Unbuckling in the Bible Belt: Conservative sexual norms lower age at marriage. *The Journal of Social, Evolutionary, and Cultural Psychology, 4,* 206–214.

Garcia, J. R., MacKillop, J., Aller, E. L., Merriwether, A. M., Wilson, D. S., & Lum, J. K. (2010). Associations between dopamine D4 receptor gene variation with both infidelity and sexual promiscuity. *PLoS ONE, 5,* e14162. doi:10.1371/journal.pone.0014162

Garcia, J. R., & Reiber, C. (2008). Hook-up behavior: A biopsychosocial perspective. *The Journal of Social, Evolutionary, and Cultural Psychology, 2,* 192–208.

Garcia, J. R., Reiber, C., Merriwether, A. M., Heywood, L. L., & Fisher, H. E. (2010a, March). *Touch me in the morning: Intimately affiliative gestures in uncommitted and romantic relationships.* Paper presented at the Annual Conference of the NorthEastern Evolutionary Psychology Society, New Paltz, NY.

Geher, G., Bloodworth, R., Mason, J., Stoaks, C., Downey, H. J., Renstrom, K. L., & Romero, J. F. (2005). Motivational underpinnings of romantic partner perceptions: Psychological and physiological evidence. *Journal of Personal and Social Relationships, 22,* 255–281. doi:10.1177/0265407505050953

Geher, G., & Kaufman, S. B. (2011). Mating intelligence. In R. J. Sternberg & S. B. Kaufman (Eds.), *The Cambridge handbook of intelligence* (pp. 603–620). Cambridge, England: Cambridge University Press.

Glenn, N., & Marquardt, E. (2001). *Hooking up, hanging out, and hoping for Mr. Right: College women on dating and mating today.* New York, NY: Institute for American Values.

Gray, P. B., & Anderson, K. G. (2010). *Fatherhood: Evolution and human paternal behavior.* Cambridge, MA: Harvard University Press.

Gray, P. B., & Garcia, J. R. (2013). *Darwin's bedroom: Evolution and human sexual behavior.* Manuscript submitted for publication.

Greenspan, S. (2011). *11 points guide to hooking up: Lists and advice about first dates, hotties, scandals, pickups, threesomes, and booty calls.* New York, NY: Skyhorse Publishing.

Grello, C. M., Welsh, D. P., Harper, M. S., & Dickson, J. W. (2003). Dating and sexual relationship trajectories and adolescent functioning. *Adolescent & Family Health, 3,* 103–112.

Guilbert, G.-C. (2002). *Madonna as Postmodern Myth: How One Star's Self-Construction Rewrites Sex, Gender, Hollywood and the American Dream.* Jefferson, NC: McFarland.

Gute, G., & Eshbaugh, E. M. (2008). Personality as a predictor of hooking up among college students. *Journal of Community Health Nursing, 25,* 26–43. doi:10.1080/07370010701836385

Harper, G. W. (2007). Sex isn't that simple: Culture and context in HIV prevention interventions for gay and bisexual male adolescents. *American Psychologist, 62,* 803–819. doi:10.1037/0003-066X.62.8.806

Hatfield, E., Hutchison, E. S. S., Bensman, L., Young, D. M., & Rapson, R. L. (in press). Cultural, social, and gender influences on casual sex: New developments. In Jan M. Turner & Andrew D. Mitchell (Eds.), *Social psychology: New developments.* Hauppauge, NY: Nova Science.

Hatfield, E., & Rapson, R. L. (2005). *Love and sex: Cross-cultural perspectives.* Lanham, MD: University Press of America.

Heldman, C., & Wade, L. (2010). Hook-up culture: Setting a new research agenda. *Sexuality Research and Social Policy, 7,* 323–333. doi:10.1007/s13178-010-0024-z

Herbenick, D., Reece, M., Schick, V., Sanders, S. A., Dodge, B., & Fortenberry, J. D. (2010). Sexual behavior in the United States: Results from a national probability sample of men and women ages 14–94. *Journal of Sexual Medicine, 7,* 255–265. doi:10.1111/j.1743-6109.2010.02012.x

Herbert, S., & McKernan, L. (1996). *Who's who of Victorian cinema.* London, England: British Film Institute.

Herold, E. S., & Mewhinney, D. K. (1993). Gender differences in casual sex in AIDS prevention: A survey of dating bars. *Journal of Sex Research, 15,* 502–516.

Hill, M., Garcia, J. R., & Geher, G. (2012). *Women having sex when they don't want to: Exploring the occurrence of unwanted sex in the context of hook-ups.* Manuscript submitted for publication.

Hobbs, D. R., & Gallup, G. G. (2011). Song as a medium for embedded reproductive messages. *Evolutionary Psychology, 9,* 390–416.

Hoff, C. C., & Beougher, S. C. (2010). Sexual agreements among gay male couples. *Archives of Sexual Behavior, 39,* 774–787. doi:10.1007/s10508-008-9393-2

Holman, A., & Sillars, A. (2012). Talk about "hooking up": The influence of college student social networks on non-relationship sex. *Health Communication, 27,* 205–216. doi:10.1080/10410236.2011.575540

Jankowiak, W. R., & Fischer, E. F. (1992). A cross-cultural perspective on romantic love. *Ethnology, 31,* 149–155. doi:10.2307/3773618

Jankowiak, W. R., & Paladino, T. (2008). Desiring sex, longing for love: A tripartite conundrum. In W. R. Jankowiak (Ed.), *Intimacies: Love and sex across cultures* (pp. 1–36). New York, NY: Columbia University Press.

Jhally, S. (2007). *Dreamworlds 3: Desire, sex & power in music video* [DVD]. Northampton, MA: Media Education Foundation.

Jonason, P. K., Li, N. P., & Richardson, J. (2011). Positioning the booty-call relationship on the spectrum of relationships: Sexual but more emotional than one-night stands. *Journal of Sex Research, 48,* 486–495. doi:10.1080/00224499.2010.497984

Josiam, B. M., Hobson, J. S. P., Dietrich, U. C., & Smeaton, G. (1998). An analysis of the sexual, alcohol and drug related behavioural patterns of students on spring break. *Tourism Management, 19,* 501–513. doi: 10.1016/S0261-5177(98)00052-1

Kim, J. L., Sorsoli, C. L., Collins, K., Zylbergold, B. A., Schooler, D., & Tolman, D. L. (2007). From sex to sexuality: Exposing the heterosexual script on primetime network television. *Journal of Sex Research, 44,* 145–157. doi:10.1080/00224490701263660

Kinsey, A. C., Pomeroy, W. B., & Martin, C. E. (1948). *Sexual behavior in the human male.* Philadelphia, PA: W. B. Saunders.

Kinsey, A. C., Pomeroy, W. B., Martin, C. E., & Gebhard, P. H. (1953). *Sexual behavior in the human female.* Philadelphia, PA: W. B. Saunders.

Kunkel, D., Eyal, K., Finnerty, K., Biely, E., & Donnerstein, E. (2005). *Sex on TV 4.* Menlo Park, CA: Henry J. Kaiser Family Foundation.

Lambert, T. A., Kahn, A. S., & Apple, K. J. (2003). Pluralistic ignorance and hooking up. *Journal of Sex Research, 40,* 129–133. doi:10.1080/00224490309552174

Laumann, E., Gagnon, J. H., Michael, R. T., & Michaels, S. (1994). *The social organization of sexuality: Sexual practices in the United States.* Chicago, IL: University of Chicago Press.

Lewis, M. A., Granato, H., Blayney, J. A., Lostutter, T. W., & Kilmer, J. R. (2011). Predictors of hooking up sexual behavior and emotional reactions among U.S. college students. *Archives of Sexual Behavior,* doi: 10.1007/s10508-011-9817-2

Li, N. P., & Kenrick, D. T. (2006). Sex similarities and differences in preferences for short-term mates: What, whether, and why. *Journal of Personality and Social Psychology, 90,* 468–489. doi:10.1037/0022-3514.90.3.468

Lippa, R. A. (2009). Sex differences in sex drive, sociosexuality, and height across 53 nations: testing evolutionary and social structural theories. *Archives of Sexual Behavior, 38,* 631–651.

Littleton, H., Tabernik, H., Canales, E. J., & Backstrom, T. (2009). Risky situation or harmless fun? A qualitative examination of college women's bad hook-up and rape scripts. *Sex Roles, 60,* 793–804. doi:10.1007/s11199-009-9586-8

Low, B. S. (2000). *Why sex matters.* Princeton, NJ: Princeton University Press.

Madison, A. (2006). *Hooking up: A girl's all-out guide to sex and sexuality.* New York, NY: Prometheus Books.

Manning, W. S., Giordano, P. C., & Longmore, M. A. (2006). Hooking up: The relationship contexts of "nonrelationship" sex. *Journal of Adolescent Research, 21,* 459–483. doi:10.1177/0743558406291692

Maticka-Tyndale, E. (1991). Sexual scripts and AIDS prevention: Variations in adherence to safer-sex guidelines by heterosexual adolescents. *Journal of Sex Research, 28,* 45–66. doi:10.1080/00224499109551594

Maticka-Tyndale, E., Herold, E. S., & Mewhinney, D. M. (1998). Casual sex on spring break: Intentions and behaviors of Canadian students. *Journal of Sex Research, 35,* 254–264. doi:10.1080/00224499809551941

Mealey, L. (2000). *Sex differences: Developmental and evolutionary strategies.* London, England: Academic Press.

Mustanski, B., Lyons, T., & Garcia, S. C. (2011). Internet use and sexual health of young men who have sex with men: A mixed-methods study. *Archives of Sexual Behavior, 40,* 289–300. doi:10.1007/s10508-009-9596-1

O'Brien, D. T., Geher, G., Gallup, A. C., Garcia, J. R., & Kaufman, S. B. (2009). Self-perceived Mating Intelligence predicts sexual behavior in college students: Empirical validation of a theoretical construct. *Imagination, Cognition and Personality, 29,* 341–362. doi:10.2190/IC.29.4.e

Oliver, M. B., & Hyde, J. S. (1993). Gender differences in sexuality: A meta-analysis. *Psychological Bulletin, 114,* 29–51. doi:10.1037/0033-2909.114.1.29

Oswalt, S. B., Cameron, K. A., & Koob, J. J. (2005). Sexual regret in college students. *Archives of Sexual Behavior, 34,* 663–669. doi: 10.1007/s10508-005-7920-y

Owen, J., & Fincham, F. D. (2011). Young adults' emotional reactions after hooking up encounters. *Archives of Sexual Behavior, 40,* 321–330. doi:10.1007/s10508-010-9652-x

Owen, J., Fincham, F. D., & Moore, J. (2011). Short-term prospective study of hooking up among college students. *Archives of Sexual Behavior, 40,* 331–341. doi:10.1007/s10508-010-9697-x

Owen, J. J., Rhoades, G. K., Stanley, S. M., & Fincham, F. D. (2010). "Hooking up" among college students: Demographic and psychosocial correlates. *Archives of Sexual Behavior, 39,* 653–663. doi:10.1007/s10508-008-9414-1

Paik, A. (2010a). "Hookups," dating, and relationship quality: Does the type of sexual involvement matter? *Social Science Research, 39,* 739–753. doi:10.1016/j.ssresearch.2010.03.011

Paik, A. (2010b). The contexts of sexual involvement and concurrent sexual partnerships. *Perspectives on Sexual and Reproductive Health, 42,* 33–42. doi:10.1363/4203310

Paul, E. L. (2006). Beer goggles, catching feelings, and the walk of shame: The myths and realities of the hookup experience. In D. C. Kirkpatrick, S. Duck, & M. K. Foley (Eds.), *Relating difficulty: The processes of constructing and managing difficult interaction* (pp. 141–160). Mahwah, NJ: Lawrence Erlbaum Associates.

Paul, E. L., & Hayes, K. A. (2002). The casualties of "casual" sex: A qualitative exploration of the phenomenology of college students' hookups. *Journal of Social and Personal Relationships, 19,* 639–661. doi: 10.1177/0265407502195006

Paul, E. L., McManus, B., & Hayes, A. (2000). "Hook-ups": Characteristics and correlates of college students' spontaneous and anonymous sexual experiences. *Journal of Sex Research, 37,* 76–88. doi:10.1080/00224490009552023

Pedersen, W. C., Putcha-Bhagavatula, A., & Miller, L. C. (2011). Are men and women really that different? Examining some of sexual strategies theory (SST)'s key assumptions about sex-distinct mating mechanisms. *Sex Roles, 64,* 629–643. doi:10.1007/s11199-010-9811-5

Penhollow, T., Young, M., & Bailey, W. (2007). Relationship between religiosity and "hooking up" behavior. *American Journal of Health Education, 38,* 338–345.

Perry, K., Gottwald, L., Martin, M., & McKee, B. (2011). Last Friday night (T.G.I.F.) [Recorded by K. Perry]. On *Teenage dream* [CD]. New York, NY: Capitol Records. (2010).

Petersen, J. L., & Hyde, J. S. (2010). A meta-analytic review of research on gender differences in sexuality, 1993–2007. *Psychological Bulletin, 136,* 21–38. doi:10.1037/a0017504

Peterson, Z. D., & Muehlenhard, C. L. (2007). Conceptualizing the "wantedness" of women's consensual and nonconsensual sexual experiences: Implications for how women label their experiences with rape. *Journal of Sex Research, 44,* 72–88.

Phillips, L. M. (2000). *Flirting with danger.* New York, NY: New York University Press.

Reiber, C., & Garcia, J. R. (2010). Hooking up: Gender differences, evolution, and pluralistic ignorance. *Evolutionary Psychology, 8,* 390–404.

Reitman, I., Medjuck, J., Clifford, J. (Producers), & Reitman, I. (Director). *No Strings Attached* [Motion picture]. United States: Paramount Pictures.

Riley, C. (Ed.). (2010). *Making the hook-up: Edgy sex with soul.* Berkeley, CA: Cleis Press.

Robertson, P. (2001). *Film facts.* New York, NY: Billboard Books.

Rozler, J., & Lavinthal, A. (2005). *The hookup handbook: A single girl's guide to living it up.* New York, NY: Simon Spotlight Entertainment.

Saad, G. (2007). *The evolutionary bases of consumption.* Mahwah, NJ: Lawrence Erlbaum Associates.

Schmitt, D. P. (2005). Sociosexuality from Argentina to Zimbabwe: A 48-nation study of sex, culture, and strategies of human mating. *Behavioral and Brain Sciences, 28,* 247–275. doi:10.1017/S0140525X05000051

Schmitt, D. P., Alcalay, L., Allik, J., Ault, L., Austers, I., Bennett, K. L., . . . Zupanèiè, A. (2003). Universal sex differences in the desire for sexual variety: Tests from 52 nations, 6 continents, and 13 islands. *Journal of Personality and Social Psychology, 85,* 85–104. doi:10.1037/0022-3514.85.1.85

Seage, G. R., Mayer, K. H., Lenderking, W. R., Wold, C., Gross, M., Goldstein, R., . . . Holmberg, S. (1997). HIV and hepatitis B infection and risk behavior in young gay and bisexual men. *Public Health Reports, 112,* 158–167.

Shafer, M., Glotzer, L., Zucker, J., Gluck, W. (Producers), & Gluck, W. (Director). *Friends with Benefits* [Motion picture]. United States: Sony Pictures.

Sherman, A. J., & Tocantins, N. (2004). *The happy hook-up: A single girl's guide to casual sex.* Berkeley, CA: Ten Speed Press.

Siegel, J., Rowland, M., Scordia, V. (Producers), & Scordia, V. (Director). (2009). *Hooking Up* [Motion picture]. United States: Morbid Mind Productions.

Simon, W., & Gagnon, J. H. (1986). Sexual scripts: Permanence and change. *Archives of Sexual Behavior, 15,* 97–120. doi:10.1007/BF01542219

Simpson, J. A., & Gangestad, S. W. (1992). Sociosexuality and romantic partner choice. *Journal of Personality, 60,* 31–51. doi:10.1111/j.1467-6494.1992.tb00264.x

Sönmez, S., Apostolopoulos, Y., Yu, C. H., Yang, S., Mattila, A. S., & Yu, L. C. (2006). Binge drinking and casual sex on spring-break. *Annals of Tourism Research, 33,* 895–917. doi:10.1016/j.annals.2006.06.005

Stinson, R. D. (2010). Hooking up in young adulthood: A review of factors influencing the sexual behavior of college students. *Journal of College Student Psychotherapy, 24,* 98–115. doi:10.1080/87568220903558596

Strasburger, V. C. (2005). Adolescents, sex, and the media: Ooooo, baby, baby—A Q&A. *Adolescent Medicine Clinics, 16,* 269–288. doi: 10.1016/j.admecli.2005.02.009

Symons, D. (1979). *The evolution of human sexuality.* New York, NY: Oxford University Press.

Tanner, L. R., Haddock, S. A., Zimmerman, T. S., & Lund, L. K. (2003). Images of couples and families in Disney feature-length animated films. *American Journal of Family Therapy, 31,* 355–373. doi:10.1080/01926180390223987

Tolman, D. L. (2006). In a different position: Conceptualizing female adolescent sexuality development within compulsory heterosexuality. *New Directions for Child and Adolescent Development, 112,* 71–89. doi:10.1002/cd.163

Townsend, J. M. (1995). Sex without emotional involvement: An evolutionary interpretation of sex differences. *Archives of Sexual Behavior, 24,* 173–206. doi:10.1007/BF01541580

Townsend, J. M., & Wasserman, T. H. (2011). Sexual hookups among college students: Sex differences in emotional reactions. *Archives of Sexual Behavior, 40,* 1173–1181. doi:10.1007/s10508-011-9841-2

Trivers, R. (1972). Parental investment and sexual selection. In B. Campbell (Ed.), *Sexual selection and the descent of man: 1871–1971* (pp. 136–179). Chicago, IL: Aldine Press.

van Gelder, M. M. H. J., Reefhuis, J., Herron, A. M., Williams, M. L., & Roeleveld, N. (2011). Reproductive health characteristics of marijuana and cocaine users: Results from the 2002 National Survey of Family Growth. *Perspectives on Sexual and Reproductive Health, 43,* 164–172. doi:10.1363/4316411

van Kesteren, N. M. C., Hospers, H. J., & Kok, G. (2007). Sexual risk behavior in HIV-positive men who have sex with men: A literature review. *Patient Education and Counseling, 65,* 5–20. doi:10.1016/j.pec.2006.09.003

Van Valen, L. (1973). A new evolutionary law. *Evolutionary Theory, 1,* 1–30.

Vieira, M. (1999). *Sin in soft focus.* New York, NY: Harry Abrams.

Ward, L. M. (1995). Talking about sex: Common themes about sexuality in the prime-time television programs children and adolescents view most. *Journal of Youth and Adolescence, 24,* 595–615. doi:10.1007/BF01537058

Ward, L. M. (2003). Understanding the role of entertainment media in the sexual socialization of American youth: A review of empirical research. *Developmental Review, 23,* 347–388. doi:10.1016/S0273-2297(03)00013-3

Welldon, E. V. (1988). *Mother, Madonna, whore: The idealization and denigration of motherhood.* London, England: Free Association Books.

Wells, G., Perry, K., & DioGuardi, K. (2009). *I Do Not Hook Up* [Recorded by Kelly Clarkson]. On *All I Ever Wanted* [CD]. RCA.

Welsh, D. P., Grello, C. M., & Harper, M. S. (2006). No strings attached: The nature of casual sex in college students. *Journal of Sex Research, 43,* 255–267. doi:10.1080/00224490609552324

Wiederman, M. W. (2005). The gendered nature of sexual scripts. *The Family Journal, 13,* 496–502. doi:10.1177/1066480705278729

Wood, W., & Eagly, A. H. (2002). A cross-cultural analysis of the behavior of women and men: Implications for the origins of sex differences. *Psychological Bulletin, 128,* 699–727. doi:10.1037/0033-2909.128.5.699

Worth, H., Reid, A., & McMillan, K. (2002). Somewhere over the rainbow: Love, trust and monogamy in gay relationships. *Journal of Sociology, 38,* 237–253. doi:10.1177/1440783021287566

Zablotska, I., Frankland, A., Prestage, G., Down, I., & Ryan, D. (2008). *Gay Community Periodic Survey: Sydney February 2008.* Sydney, Australia: National Centre in HIV Social Research, The University of New South Wales.

Received February 11, 2012
Revision received February 11, 2012
Accepted February 22, 2012 ∎

Positive Effects of Parental Divorce on Undergraduates

Caitlin Halligan[1]

I. Joyce Chang[2]

David Knox[3]

Three hundred and thirty-six undergraduates from two large universities in the Southeast and Midwest completed a 31-item Internet questionnaire revealing their (mostly white and ages 18–23) reaction to the divorce of their parents. Perceived positive effects included a happier mother (57%); happier father (43%); closer relationships with mother, father, or siblings (45%, 29%, 36%, respectively); less parental conflict (35%); and greater appreciation for one's siblings (40%). Significant differences between women and men included that females were closer with their mother ($p < .05$), males had a better relationship with their stepsiblings ($p < .05$) and females were more likely to agree that they were slow to express their feelings in a relationship ($p < .05$). Symbolic interaction was used as the theoretical framework to interpret the data. Implications and limitations are suggested.

KEYWORDS

Adult children, divorce, family relations, marriage and remarriage

Divorce rates in the United States continue to be among the highest in the world. Over a million divorces occur each year in the United States, with 60% including children. The stigma of divorce remains. The uncoupling process is difficult for spouses and children alike and involves stress for spouses and their children. Although the stereotypical cultural printout is that divorce is "bad" and that children of divorce are from a "broken home," this research emphasizes the silver lining. Even in the worst of divorces, there are positive outcomes. We asked 336 undergraduates whose parents were divorced to identify positive outcomes. Indeed, we found that something good often comes out of something bad.

Address correspondence to David Knox, Department of Sociology, East Carolina University, A-416 Brewster Building, East Carolina University, 10th St., Greenville, NC 27858, USA. E-mail: knoxd@ecu.edu

[1] Undergraduate, East Carolina University, Greenville, North Carolina, USA

[2] Department of Educational Leadership and Development, University of Central Missouri, Warrensburg, Missouri, USA

[3] Department of Sociology, East Carolina University, Greenville, North Carolina, USA

Background

Researchers have studied various aspects of divorce, particularly its outcome for children. Negative outcomes include depression and anxiety (Gähler & Garriga, 2012), altered relationships with peers (Gähler & Garriga, 2012), and lower academic performance (McGuinness, 2006). Other researchers have found increased risks of early and out-of-wedlock parenthood, lower academic levels, psychological maladjustment in children, economic problems, and future divorces among young adults with divorced parents (Furstenburg & Kiernan, 2001; Gähler & Garriga, 2012). In a study in the Netherlands, the researchers focused on the family obligations after divorce and noted that the respondents tended to express stronger norms of family obligation (Wijckmans & Bavel, 2013). Although these researchers emphasized that divorce need not always have a negative outcome, they did not reveal how stronger norms of family obligation develop. Researchers have also identified the negative outcomes of children who have experienced multiple parental divorces (Lambert, 2013) but have failed to identify any positive outcomes from any party of the divorce.

Exceptions to focusing on negative outcomes of divorce include the research of McGuinness (2006) and Wallerstein, Lewis, and Blakeslee (2000). McGuinness (2006) found that children undergo emotional pain but divorce can lead to a healthy lifestyle for the child depending on the family process and functional family

Caitlin Halligan, I. Joyce Chang, David Knox, *Journal of Divorce & Remarriage*, Vol. 55, No 7. Copyright © 2014 by Taylor & Francis, Ltd. Reprinted by permission of Taylor & Francis, Ltd., http://www.tandfonline.com

relationships. Wallerstein et al. (2000) found that a third of the children in their study were doing well and had great relationships with their parents in the short term but later most of these children were depressed, suffered from insomnia, had unrealistic hopes (e.g., parents would get back together and everything would return to normal), had lower rates of educational success, and had higher rates of alcohol and drug abuse. Hence, although there were positive divorce outcomes, they did not last.

Another exception is research in Israel on the positive consequences of parental divorce among Israeli young adults. The researchers found that less than a quarter of the respondents thought that the divorce had more negative than positive outcomes. Indeed, these young adults whose parents had divorced reported increased awareness of the complexity of marriage and relationships and had more realistic expectations of marriage and relationships than young adults whose parents were still married (Sever, Guttman, & Lazar, 2007).

More recently, Mohi (2014) surveyed a sample of 233 University of Southern Florida undergraduates from divorced and intact families with the goal of identifying positive outcomes. Fourteen percent of the respondents reported feeling relieved, relaxed, or happy at the time of their parents' divorce. Ten face-to-face interviews were also conducted. The most common response to the question of impact was that the participant would strive to perform better than their parents in their own relationships by learning from their parents' mistakes rather than repeat them. One of the respondents illustrates this point:

> I think when I was younger it did [have an impact on me], but growing up and getting into my second and third relationships it was more of, um, I guess like I saw what they had and what they did wrong and I didn't wanna do that. So then, you know, I looked at it more as like a positive effect, I would guess, on my relationship and I wanted it to last longer so I kept communicating. (Mohi, 2014, p. 25)

Hypotheses, Methods, and Participants

Additional positive outcomes from divorce might include escaping from an abusive parent, escape from a home riddled with arguing parents who never show affection or love, and an improved relationship with one or both parents. These and other positive outcomes (e.g., happier parents, more quality time with parents, new stepparent, new siblings, moving to new place, less time with parent that one doesn't like or has a negative relationship with, new stepparent might have resources—a place at the beach—or

a valued characteristic—airline pilot [can get free tickets], and avoiding chronic exposure to conflict between parents at war in the house) are the focus of this study.

Hypotheses

In addition to identifying positive outcomes of the divorce of one's parents, several hypotheses included assessing significant differences between women and men in regard to perception of less parental conflict; feeling closer to one's mother, father, or siblings; perception of one's mother or father being happier since the divorce; respondent's report of enjoying spending more time alone with one's mother or father since the divorce; closer relationship with one's grandparents; relying less on one's parents for making one's decisions; being more compassionate for people going through a difficult time; greater exposure to different values, traditions, or lifestyles; greater tolerance for different points of view; growing closer to one's friends; growing closer to one's boyfriend or girlfriend; parents being more supportive of respondent's interests; perception that mother or father made greater effort to spend quality time with respondent since the divorce; respondent seeking counseling; respondent's standard of living improved; parents more civil to each other; desire that parents were still married; and improved relationship with mother or father.

Methods

The data were analyzed by SPSS (version 13) statistical software.

Participants

The participants in this study consisted of 336 volunteers (85% female, 14.7% male) who had experienced parental divorce. Over half (62%) were either first- or second-year undergraduates with 88% between the ages of 18 and 23. The sample was predominantly White (79.6%), followed by African American (9.9%) and Hispanics or Latino American (4.5%). The majority of participants self-reported an exclusively heterosexual orientation (83.8%), with 12.3% identifying as predominantly heterosexual, and 2.1% exclusively homosexual. As for their current relationship, 44% were not married and not in a relationship and 42% were never married and in a committed relationship (2% were engaged and 7% married). In regard to their longest relationship, 41% reported 1 to 3 years and 25% reported 3 years or longer.

About one in five (19%) of the respondents was an only child. Of those who had siblings, 28% reported that they were the oldest child, 32% the youngest, and 22% the middle child. As for half-siblings, 42% reported have half-siblings, with 28% having stepsiblings. Over a quarter (28%) reported that one parent had remarried (20% reported that both parents had remarried). Aside from their parent's remarriage, 15% reported that one parent was in a serious relationship (10% reported that both parents were in a serious relationship). Fifteen percent reported that their divorced parents were single (and presumably not seeing anyone). Twelve percent did not fit any of these categories.

The primary postdivorce living arrangement for the respondent was living with mother (48.7%), followed by mother with stepfather (18%), with father (6%), and with father and stepmom (5%). Fifteen percent reported living with mother and father equally. As for age of the respondent at the time of the divorce of her or his parents, 20% were between 1 and 3 years old, 28% between 4 and 8 years old, and 25% between 9 and 13 years old. Fifteen percent reported that they were between 14 and 18 (5% were 19 or older and 6% were 1 year or younger). In regard to the importance of religion, over two thirds (69%) agreed that religion was "somewhat to very important."

A 31-item (many with multiple questions) questionnaire on "Effects of Divorce" was posted on the Internet. E-mails were sent to undergraduate students in entry-level sociology classes from two universities (one in the Southeast and one in the Midwest) about this research project. The survey link was available for 3 weeks in the spring semester of 2013. The online survey consisted of questions on respondents' demographic information and perception and attitudes toward parental divorce, stepfamilies, and relationships. Demographic questions included gender, year in school, relationship status, religion, number of serious relationships, and so on. Five-point Likert-type items were used for questions concerning perception of parental divorce (e.g., "I could have saved my parents' marriage"), postdivorce parent–child relationship (e.g., "I have a good relationship with my biological mother"), benefits of divorce (e.g., "My parents are more civil to each other since the divorce"), and benefits of stepfamilies (e.g., "I can turn to my stepsiblings for support")

Findings and Discussion

A primary goal of the study was to identify whether there were any positive effects of parental divorce. Results revealed that respondents did, indeed, identify positive outcomes of their parents' divorce. The majority of the respondents agreed or strongly agreed with being more compassionate (65.63%), having a greater tolerance for different viewpoints (63.16%), and enjoying spending time alone with mother (57.71%). A majority also reported being more independent and less reliant on

parents (53.51%). In regard to whether their parents have a "good divorce," 34.35% agreed or strongly agreed and 38.79% disagreed or strongly disagreed.

Table 1 provides the percentage of respondents who agreed or strongly agreed on the positive effects questionnaire items, thus confirming positive outcomes of their parents' divorce.

Gender Differences

In addition to identifying positive outcomes of divorce, there were significant differences between women and men experiencing these positive outcomes. These included the following (see Table 2):

1. Female undergraduates reported having a better relationship (following their parents' divorce) with their biological mothers than did male students, $t(206) = 3.13$, $p < .01$ (Question: "I have a good relationship with my biological mother"). One explanation for a closer daughter–mother bond is related to the fact that almost half (49%) of the respondents (mostly female) reported that they lived with their mother following the divorce. Only 6% of the respondents reported living with their dad (15% reported an equal amount of time living with both partners).

2. Compared to male students, female students also reported perceiving that their mothers were happier following divorce, $t(204) = 2.46$, $p < .05$ (Question: "My mother is happier since the divorce"). Divorced mothers might have reason to rejoice: Their husband (with whom they had an aversive relationship) is gone, they are more likely to remain in the family home, they have their children, and they have money from the ex (e.g., child support). It is the father who typically moves out of the house, only sees his children every other weekend, and pays child support.

3. Female undergraduates when compared to male undergraduates reported an average higher score on the item "I liked spending time alone with my mother since my parents' divorce," $t(202) = 2.49$, $p < .05$. Consistent with the previous finding, because most ex-wives end up with custody of the children, their daughters had increased opportunities to be alone with their mothers, in some cases to be a companion through the divorce, sharing some enjoyable times together.

4. Female undergraduates when compared to male undergraduates reported an average higher score on the item concerning greater tolerance for people with different viewpoints, $t(205) = 2.46$, $p < .05$

Table 1 Positive Effect of Divorce: Percentage of Respondents Agreement

	%
Since my parents' divorce, I am more compassionate for people who are going through a difficult time.	65.63%
I have greater tolerance for people with different viewpoints since my parents' divorce.	63.16%
Since my parents' divorce, I have been exposed to different family values, tradition, and lifestyles.	60.01%
I have liked spending time alone with my mother since my parents' divorce.	57.71%
My mother is happier since the divorce.	57.20%
I rely less on my parents for making decisions since my parents' divorce.	53.51%
I have liked spending time alone with my father since my parents' divorce.	45.61%
My mother has made a greater effort to spend quality time with me since the divorce.	45.61%
I can spend more time with the parent I prefer since my parents' divorce.	45.37%
Since my parents' divorce, I have felt closer to my mother.	44.98%
My relationship with my mother has improved since my parents' divorce.	44.74%
My father is happier since the divorce.	43.85%
My parents' divorce has made me closer to my friends.	42.54%
Since my parents' divorce, I have greater appreciation for my siblings.	40.78%
My father has made a greater effort to spend quality time with me since the divorce.	38.60%
Since my parents' divorce, I felt closer to my siblings.	35.96%
After my biological parents' divorce, I noticed that I was exposed to less conflict between my parents on a daily basis.	34.93%
My relationship with my father has improved since my parents' divorce.	34.65%
I think my parents have a "good" divorce.	34.35%
My parents are more civil to each other since the divorce.	34.21%
My parents' divorce has resulted in a closer relationship with my grandparents.	32.20%
My standard of living improved since my parents' divorce.	30.70%
Since my parents' divorce, I have felt closer to my father.	30.13%
My parents' divorce has made me close to my boyfriend or girlfriend.	28.95%
My parent(s) tried to be more supportive of my interests since the divorce.	28.95%
I wish my parents were still married to each other.	28.80%
After my parents' divorce, I saw a counselor to help me.	24.23%

Note. Agreement response included those who answered "agree" or "strongly agree" on the questionnaire.

Divorce is an experience that removes one from the traditional innocent belief that all issues are clear cut. Because the child of divorce might feel stigmatized as no longer having a "real" (e.g., intact) family, they might feel more tolerant for others and their viewpoints who are out of the mainstream.

5. Compared to male students, female students reported an improved standard of living, $t(198) = 2.69$, $p < .01$. Although divorce is typically associated with lower income, 79.2% of respondents had parents who were divorced more than 6 years (58.8% 10 years or more), thus permitting them time to recover from the divorce economically.

Additional Observations

Not everyone in our sample escaped the divorce of the parents unscathed. One fourth of the respondents reported that their experience of their parents' divorce was very difficult. However, this difficulty did not deter the interest of the respondent in getting married, as 81.7% reported that they plan to get married in the future. Furthermore, the respondents are determined to avoid divorce in their own marriage, as 66% reported that they would do "anything" to stay married.

The respondents also confirmed a clear understanding that they could not have "saved" (94.6%) their parents' marriage. Another finding from the data was that,

Table 2   Means for Males and Females on Positive Effects of Divorce

| | Gender | | | | | |
| | Males | | Females | | | |
	M	*SD*	*M*	*SD*	*t*	*df*
I think my parents have a "good" divorce.	3.00	1.34	2.89	1.42	.43	214
After my biological parents' divorce, I noticed that I was exposed to less conflict between my parents on a daily basis.	2.83	1.42	3.17	1.31	1.28	186
Since my parents' divorce, I have felt closer to my mother.	2.55	1.33	3.45	1.34	3.13**	206
Since my parents' divorce, I have felt closer to my father.	2.81	1.22	2.78	1.40	0.98	202
Since my parents' divorce, I have felt closer to my siblings.	3.35	1.20	3.51	1.23	.01	202
Since my parents' divorce, I have had a greater appreciation for my siblings.	3.61	1.24	3.70	1.16	.33	160
My mother is happier since the divorce.	3.27	1.01	3.82	1.66	2.46*	204
My father is happier since the divorce.	3.18	1.04	3.41	1.21	1.03	195
I have liked spending time alone with my mother since my parents' divorce.	3.29	0.82	3.84	1.80	2.49*	202
I have liked spending time alone with my father since my parents' divorce.	3.48	0.91	3.25	1.35	.81	202
My parents' divorce has resulted in a closer relationship with my grandparents.	3.25	1.37	3.20	1.31	.19	183
I can spend more time with the parent I prefer since my parents' divorce.	3.18	1.31	3.58	1.19	1.64	191
I rely less on my parents for making decisions since my parents' divorce.	3.91	1.09	3.64	1.21	1.16	202
Since my parents' divorce, I am more compassionate for people who are going through a difficult time.	3.78	1.07	3.96	1.05	.88	206
Since my parents' divorce, I have been exposed to different family values, tradition, and lifestyles.	3.78	1.04	3.82	1.11	.22	203
I have greater tolerance for people with different viewpoints since my parents' divorce.	3.53	1.05	3.97	0.91	2.46*	205
My parents' divorce has made me closer to my friends.	3.47	1.32	3.38	1.10	.41	201
My parents' divorce has made me close to my boyfriend or girlfriend.	3.24	1.41	3.27	1.22	1.12	149
My parent(s) tried to be more supportive of my interests since the divorce.	2.94	1.22	3.15	1.01	1.60	193
My mother has made a greater effort to spend quality time with me since the divorce.	3.00	1.22	3.42	1.25	1.7	195
After my parents' divorce, I saw a counselor to help me.	2.28	1.31	2.44	1.49	.55	175
My standard of living improved since my parents' divorce.	2.53	1.19	3.16	1.22	2.69**	198
My parents are more civil to each other since the divorce.	2.78	1.45	2.95	1.40	.61	198
My father has made a greater effort to spend quality time with me since the divorce.	3.19	1.20	2.94	1.48	.89	200
I wish my parents were still married to each other.	2.59	1.54	2.15	1.42	1.59	206
My relationship with my mother has improved since my parents' divorce.	2.82	1.02	3.48	1.28	2.61**	197
My relationship with my father has improved since my parents' divorce.	3.06	1.06	2.94	1.43	.46	197

*$p < .05$. **$p < .01$. ***$p < .001$.

compared to undergraduate males, undergraduate females showed more hesitation to express their true inner feelings, $t(222) = 2.45$, $p < .05$ (Question: "I hesitate to express my true feelings because I might get hurt"). One reaction to divorce could be that females with divorced parents might view the divorce of their mother as very painful to their mother and seek to avoid such relationships, which could eventuate in pain in their own life by guarding their emotions and feelings and not expressing one's true feelings.

Male students compared to female students reported a better relationship with their stepsiblings, $t(230) = 2.05$,

$p < .05$ (Question: "I have a good relationship with my stepsiblings"). The fact that females reported a stronger bond with their mother might put emotional pressure on the female not to develop strong ties with their father's new partner's children. Because males are less bonded with their mothers following divorce (translate: less socially controlled) they are freer to establish close relationships with their father's new wife and her children.

A theoretical framework might be helpful in viewing the various findings already presented. We suggest such a framework in the next section.

Theoretical Framework

Symbolic interaction theory, developed by Max Weber (1864–1920), George Simmel (1858–1918), and Charles Horton Cooley (1864–1929), focuses on how meanings, labels, and definitions are learned through interaction with others. Using symbolic interaction to view divorce, individuals respond to their definitions of situations rather than to objective situations themselves. For example, children of divorced parents typically respond to the cultural meanings of divorce: Divorce is a disaster, my parents should stay together, and my life will be ruined. They do not consider alternative perspectives: Divorce can free them from being exposed to the relentless conflict of their parents, divorce can mean a closer relationship with each parent, and divorce can mean new stepsiblings and family members for life. Only when children of divorce are asked to articulate the positives of divorce do they consider the positives. Outcome is socially constructed and this is no more evident than finding positives in a one's parental divorce.

Implications

There are three implications for the data. First, the data provide empirical evidence that, although divorce does have its emotional and financial downside, it is not without benefits to the mother, father, children, and stepchildren.

Second, the fact that one outcome of divorce is a stronger emotional bond between daughter and mother suggests that structure might be operative, because women are more often granted custody. Were more men seeking custody, granted custody, and staying in the lives of their children, equal bonding with both parents would be more likely and less often would one parent be in a position to prejudice the child against the other parent; hence children could end up closer to both parents following divorce.

Third, were both parents to remain equally in the lives of their children following divorce each child might feel free to embrace the new stepfamily of both their mother and father. The finding that only males were closer to their stepsiblings reflects that daughters who are closer with their mothers following divorce might feel that they are betraying their mother if they establish close emotional bonds with their stepsiblings. Hence these daughters do not benefit from the new family system that could embrace them. Given that everyone can benefit from nurturing family members, regardless of whether biological or not, striving toward this end is a worthy goal.

We have experienced divorce firsthand: The parents of the first and second authors divorced; the third author experienced a traditional (and adversarial) divorce when his children were 9 and 13. Divorce can be an emotional and financial disaster, but it is not always, as these data reveal. Indeed, there is a silver lining of divorce.

Limitations

There are several limitations of this study. First, the data should be interpreted cautiously in that they are skewed toward females (85%), whites (80%) and freshmen and sophomores (62%). Second, the convenience sample of 336 undergraduates is hardly representative of the 19.8 million college students throughout the United States (U.S. Census Bureau, 2013).

Third, the data are quantitative, with no qualitative interviews to provide insights on the raw statistics. Subsequent research might include interviews with students who are asked open-ended questions about their feelings and reactions to their parents' divorce.

Fourth, missing data is a common issue in many online surveys. Although 336 undergraduates participated in this survey, not all questions were answered. Hence, there might be a strong self-selection bias.

Finally, this study focused on micro positive aspects of divorce. Subsequent research might take a macro view and seek to identify the positive functions of divorce for society. Gans (1972) identified the positive functions of poverty for society. A similar view might be explored in regard to the positive outcomes of divorce for society.

References

Furstenburg, F., & Kiernan, K. (2001). Delayed parental divorce: How much do children benefit? *Journal of Marriage and Family, 63,* 446–457.

Gähler, M., & Garriga, A. (2012). Has the association between parental divorce and young adults' psychological problems changed over time? Evidence from Sweden, 1968–2000. *Journal of Family Issues, 34,* 784–803.

Gans, H. J. (1972). The positive functions of poverty. *American Journal of Sociology, 78*, 275–289.

Lambert, A. (2013). Perceptions of romantic relationships in adult children of divorce. *Journal of Divorce & Remarriage, 54*, 126–141.

McGuinness, T. (2006). Marriage, divorce, and children. *Journal of Psychosocial Nursing, 44*(2), 17–20.

Mohi, G. W. (2014). *Positive outcomes of divorce: A multi-method study on the effects of parental divorce on children* (Honors thesis). College of Sciences and the Burnett Honors College, University of Central Florida, Orlando, FL.

Sever, I., Guttman, J., & Lazar, A. (2007). Positive consequences of parental divorce among Israeli young adults. *Marriage and Family Review, 42*(2), 7–28.

U.S. Census Bureau. (2013). *Statistical abstract of the United States, 2012–2013* (131st ed.). Washington, DC: Author.

Wallerstein, J., Lewis, J., & Blakeslee, S. (2000). *The unexpected legacy of divorce: A 25 year landmark study.* New York, NY: Hyperion.

Wijckmans, B., & Bavel, J. V. (2013). Divorce and adult children's perceptions of family obligations. *Journal of Comparative Family Studies, 44*, 292–307.

Modern Prejudice and Same-Sex Parenting: Shifting Judgments in Positive and Negative Parenting Situations

Sean G. Massey[1] Ann M. Merriwether[1]
Justin R. Garcia[2]

The current study compares the effects of traditional and modern antihomosexual prejudice on evaluations of parenting practices of same-sex and opposite-sex couples. Undergraduate university student participants (N = 436) completed measures of traditional and modern antihomosexual prejudice and responded to a vignette describing a restaurant scene in which parents react to their child's undesirable behavior. The parents' sexual orientation and the quality of their parenting (positive or negative quality) were randomly varied. It was predicted that participants who score higher in modern prejudice would rate the negative parenting behaviors of same-sex parents more negatively than similar behaviors in opposite-sex parents. It was also predicted that this modern prejudice effect would be most pronounced for male participants. Both hypotheses were supported.

KEYWORDS

Attitudes, heterosexism, modern prejudice, same-sex parenting, vignettes

Introduction

My partner and I [two women] were attending a parent teacher conference, and my son (he's 6), his homeroom teacher kept suggesting that strong male role models in his life might help with his recent behavioral problems. (A lesbian mom)

When my boys run wild in the grocery store, I keep wondering if people notice that we're a gay couple. (A gay dad)

At the 2011 LGBTQ Families Conference in Rochester, New York, a group of lesbian, gay, and bisexual parents came together to discuss the challenges their families confront when they are interacting as same-sex parents in a public setting. This "public parenting" discussion led to a number of examples on the part of the participants (two examples open this article). Many participants felt there were few differences between their family and the heterosexual families they knew, and that the interactions they had with their children's teachers, pediatricians, and other parents were often without incident. If something did go wrong during any of these interactions, it was understood as something that could have happened to any family, regardless of the parents' sexual orientation. In some cases, however, these parents encountered situations in which a question was asked or a decision was made that suggested others' attitudes toward them as gay-, lesbian-, or bisexual-headed families were less favorable, and potentially due to antigay/antilesbian bias.

This process of sorting through ambiguous attributions (Crocker & Major, 1989) and deciding what is and is not prejudice has been described as a kind of microaggression (Massey, 2007; Sue et al., 2007). Such microaggressions have been found to take a psychological toll on their victims, including increased self-doubt, frustration, isolation, and emotional turmoil (Chakraborty & McKenzie, 2002; Clark, Anderson, Clark, & Williams, 1999; Solorzano, Ceja, & Yosso, 2000; Steele, Spencer, & Aronson, 2002). The aggressed are often left to sort out whether an aggression has actually occurred, and what an appropriate response might be, all while weighing up the consequences of taking action or suppressing their frustration.

This research was supported in part by the Interdisciplinary Research Group for the Study of Sexuality at Binghamton University, State University of New York. J.R.G. is supported in part by National Institutes of Health NICHD grant T32HD049336. Address correspondence to Dr. Sean G. Massey, Women, Gender & Sexuality Studies, Binghamton University, P.O. Box 6000, Binghamton, NY 13902-6000, USA. E-mail: smassey@binghamton.edu.
[1] Binghamton University, Binghamton, New York, USA
[2] The Kinsey Institute, Indiana University, Bloomington, Indiana, USA

One aspect of these stories that we wish to further explore is the relationship between overt and subtle manifestations of antigay/antilesbian prejudice. Specifically, the current study examines how antihomosexual prejudice affects the evaluations of the parenting practices of gay and lesbian parents as compared to heterosexual parents.

Same-Sex-Headed Households

The number of same-sex-headed households in the United States has grown steadily over the past 20 years. The 2010 U.S. Census puts the number of same-sex couples who are living together at 646,464 (131,729 same-sex married couple households and 514,735 same-sex unmarried couple households). According to the 2000 U.S. Census, approximately 163,879 households with children were headed by same-sex couples (Paige, 2005). Lesbian and bisexual women were more likely to be parents than gay or bisexual men, with 33% of female same-sex-couple households and 22% of male same-sex-couple households reporting having a child under the age of 18 living with them (Gates, 2011; Paige, 2005). According to results from the 2008 general social survey, 19% of gay and bisexual men and 49% of lesbians and bisexual women are parents to children (Gates, 2011).

As the number of same-sex couples and, as a result, same-sex parenting overall has increased, attitudes toward same-sex parenting have improved. From 2007 to 2011, public condemnation of same-sex parenting in the United States dropped from 50% to 35%, while acceptance has remained relatively stable (Pew Research Center, 2011). Attitudes, however, reflect a strong partisan bias, with 53% of Republicans still saying same-sex parenting is bad for society while only 28% of Democrats expressed these same negative attitudes. To complicate matters more, Gates (2011) found that the percentage of same-sex couples raising children was higher in more conservative parts of the country. This complex array of factors impacting attitudes toward same-sex parents has resulted in a confusing landscape of limitations and prohibitions, as well as protections and antidiscrimination laws related to same-sex parenting.

Attitudes toward Same-Sex Parenting

A large body of psychometric research on antihomosexual prejudice has developed over the past 50-plus years (see Massey, 2009). Since the 1970s, questions about same-sex parenting have been included in many of the measures of antihomosexual prejudice (e.g., Herek, 1984; MacDonald, Huggins, Young, & Swanson, 1973). These scales have included items such as "homosexuals should not be allowed to raise children" and "male homosexual couples should be allowed to adopt children the

same as heterosexual couples." However, these measures primarily have assessed approval or disapproval, and have not included evaluations of actual parenting behaviors or skills (c.f., Massey, 2007).

Only recently have researchers begun focusing on how antihomosexual attitudes might affect evaluations of the quality of same-sex parenting. Meanwhile, another body of literature has focused on dispelling the myths about the negative effects of same-sex parenting on children (Patterson, 2009).

In a special issue of *Journal of GLBT Family Studies* focusing on the future directions of same-sex parenting research, Morse, McLaren, and McLachlan (2007) used vignettes to explore attitudes toward same-sex parenting among Australian heterosexuals. The vignettes used described a family situation in which the sexual orientation of the parents varied. The researchers found that overall participants believed that, compared to heterosexual parents, gay and lesbian parents were less emotionally stable, responsible, competent, sensitive, and nurturing parents. In addition, participants' levels of antihomosexual prejudice were a strong predictor of believing that same-sex parenting was tied to more negative outcomes (Morse et al., 2007).

In the same volume, Massey (2007) reported similar results among U.S. participants. In this study participants responded to a vignette describing a scene at a restaurant in which a 4-year-old boy misbehaved and one of his two parents intervened. The sexual orientation of the parents and the gender of the intervening parent were randomly assigned and participants were asked to evaluate the parenting skills of the intervening parent. Higher levels of traditional heterosexism predicted more negative evaluations of gay and lesbian parents. In addition, modern antihomosexual prejudice (Massey, 2009), measured as the denial of the existence of antigay/antilesbian discrimination, predicted more negative evaluations. It was suggested that future research should explore the effect of modern antihomosexual prejudice in parenting situations in which the appropriateness of the parenting behaviors was more ambiguous (Massey, 2007).

Modern Prejudice and Antigay/Antilesbian Attitudes

The modern prejudice framework, introduced in late 1980s and originally applied to race (McConahay, 1986; Sears, 1988), has suggested that as people become less willing to overtly display racial prejudice, this prejudice goes "underground" and is expressed in more subtle, indirect ways. Pearson, Dovidio, and Gaertner (2009) have explained that these new forms of racism can be seen in white people who express egalitarian views and who actually regard themselves as not being prejudiced. However, in ambiguous situations, where negative attitudes can be attributed to a non-prejudiced cause, these same people were more likely to discriminate. These subtle forms of prejudice have been found to influence hiring decisions, college admissions decisions, helping behavior, and legal decisions (see Pearson et al.,2009). Recent research has extended the idea of modern prejudice beyond race, to include gender and sexual minorities (Anderson & Kanner, 2011; LaMar & Kite, 1998; Massey, 2009; Raja & Stokes, 1998).

Massey (2009) introduced a multidimensional measure that included a modern antihomosexual prejudice scale. This measure has included sub-scales for both traditional "old- fashioned" heterosexism and modern antihomosexual prejudice. Modern antihomosexual prejudice was assessed using items that revealed participants' likelihood to deny that antihomosexual discrimination was still a problem in society. This *Denial of Discrimination* measure was found to correlate modestly ($r = .45$) with *Traditional Heterosexism*, with men reporting higher levels of both traditional and modern prejudice than women. In addition, modern antigay/antilesbian prejudice was found to be a stronger predictor of negative evaluations of same-sex parenting than was traditional heterosexism (Massey, 2007).

Current Study

The current study aimed to explore the impact of modern prejudice on evaluations of same-sex parents. Results from the modern racism literature suggest that although overt prejudice may have diminished or become more subtle, it has not disappeared altogether (Gaertner & Dovidio, 1986; Katz & Hass, 1988; McConahay, 1986; Sears, 1988). In ambiguous situations, or situations in which an alternative explanation for negative judgment can be found, people will express their prejudice. The current study has built upon the same-sex parenting vignettes of previous research (Massey, 2007; Morse et al., 2007), but has provided both positive and negative parenting scenarios. By varying the sexual orientation and gender of parents, as well as the relative positive/negative parenting scenario, the effects of persistent but subtle modern prejudice can be assessed. Although traditional antigay/antilesbian attitudes were not expected to have vanished altogether, it was believed that modern prejudice would also have an impact on heterosexual participants' responses to scenarios involving same-sex couples.

Hypothesis 1

Past research on antihomosexual prejudice has suggested that gay and lesbian parents will be evaluated more negatively than heterosexual parents (Massey, 2007).

Consistent with these findings, participants with higher levels of traditional ("old-fashioned") antihomosexual prejudice are expected to evaluate same-sex parents more negatively than opposite-sex parents. This difference was not expected for those with lower levels of traditional antihomosexual prejudice.

Hypothesis 2

Although overt, traditional, antihomosexual prejudice may be declining, it has been demonstrated that it is not disappearing altogether, and is instead becoming more subtle, manifesting in situations where it can be attributed to a non-prejudiced cause. The second hypothesis, therefore, was that modern antihomosexual prejudice will moderate the evaluation of the parenting practices of same-sex parents relative to opposite-sex parents, but only in negative parenting situations, where doing so would not suggest overtly antigay/antilesbian attitudes. When evaluating identical negative parenting behaviors, the behaviors of same-sex parents will be viewed as more negative than those of opposite-sex parents. Modern antihomosexual prejudice will not be expected to have an impact on participants' evaluations of positive parenting behaviors.

Hypothesis 3

A robust literature has demonstrated that men have consistently more negative attitudes toward homosexuality than do women (Herek, 2000a; Kite & Whitley, 1996; Ratcliff, Lassiter, Markman, & Snyder, 2006). This gender difference also has been found in modern forms of antihomosexual prejudice (Massey, 2009). Our third hypothesis, therefore, was that participant gender will interact with modern antihomosexual prejudice and its effect on evaluations of negative parenting behaviors. Male participants who are high in modern antihomosexual prejudice are expected to evaluate the negative parenting behaviors of same-sex couples more negatively than similar behaviors in opposite-sex couples. Modern antihomosexual prejudice will not be expected to have an effect on female participants' evaluations of negative parenting behaviors, and participant gender is not expected to interact with modern antihomosexual prejudice in evaluations of positive parenting behaviors.

Methods

Participants

Participants were undergraduate students attending a midsized state university in northeastern United States. Participants were recruited through the Department of Psychology human subject pool, as well as other introductory survey courses. Participants received course credit for their participation. Because this study explored heterosexuals' attitudes toward same-sex parents, only participants who identified as heterosexual were included in the analyses. Cases with incomplete or missing data were removed from the current sample.

Four hundred thirty-six (436) participants completed the online survey (36.7% male and 63.0% female). Ninety-five percent (94.7%) of participants were between 18 and 21 years old, 4.8% were between 22 and 25, and only .2% were between 31 and 40. Participants identified as white (71.4%), Asian/Pacific Islander (19.2%), African-American (4.6%), and Caribbean-American (4.8%). Fourteen percent (13.8%) identified as Hispanic or Latino.

Questionnaire

The questionnaire was administered electronically via Qualtrics (www.qualtrics.com), a Web-based survey provider. The questionnaire consisted of sociodemographic questions, several attitude measures, and participants' evaluations of parenting practices after reading a parenting vignette. Potential participants were notified that the study was completely anonymous and that they could skip any question(s) they did not wish to answer. To protect potential participants and maintain complete anonymity, no identifying information was collected. All aspects of the current study were approved by a university institutional review board.

Attitudes toward Gay Men and Lesbian Women

Two subscales were taken from Massey's (2009) multidimensional measure of heterosexuals' attitudes toward lesbian women and gay men. The first, *traditional heterosexism*, was adapted from Herek (1984). This scale assesses overt, traditional (or "old-fashioned") antigay/antilesbian attitudes that claim that homosexuality is immoral, unnatural, and perverted and that, therefore, certain rights and privileges can and should be denied to homosexuals. This measure includes items such as "female homosexuality is a sin," "homosexuality is just as moral a way of life as heterosexuality," and "it is important for gay and lesbian people to be true to their feelings and desires."

The second measure, *denial of discrimination*, was modeled after McConahay's (1986) measure of modern or subtle racism. This scale assesses a more subtle and modern form of antihomosexual prejudice that is demonstrated through the denial of ongoing discrimination, the belief that gay people and straight people have equal opportunities for advancement, and that gay people's complaints about discrimination are unwarranted. This measure includes items such as "on average people in

our society treat gay people and straight people equally," "most lesbians and gay men are no longer discriminated against," and "discrimination against gay men and lesbians is no longer a problem in the United States."

Responses on both subscales were measured on a 5-point Likert scale, from 1 = strongly disagree to 5 = strongly agree. Both scales were found to be both reliable (Traditional Heterosexism, alpha = .93; Denial of Discrimination, alpha = .87) and valid.

Parenting Vignettes

Each participant was presented with a vignette (see Appendix). Participants were asked to read the vignette, and then evaluate the quality of parenting. The presentation of vignettes was randomized to prevent any survey ordering effects.

Of the four vignettes in each category, the sex of the adult parents in the vignette was randomized. Vignettes either had two men (Steve and Mark), two women (Beth and Mary), or a man and a woman (Steve and Beth). In the case of opposite-sex parents (Steve and Beth), the role of active parent was varied. This results in a total of eight vignettes created, with four vignette types for each of the two thematic story lines (positive context or negative context): same-sex male parents, where one male responds to the child; same-sex female parents, where one female responds to the child; opposite-sex parents, where the male responds to the child; opposite-sex parents, where the female responds to the child.

Two vignettes were created, one illustrating a positive parenting situation and the other a negative parenting situation (see Appendix). The positive parenting vignette was adapted from an earlier study by Massey (2007). In the positive vignette, a family of two adults and a child are eating at a restaurant. During the meal the child gets upset and one of the parents responds by calmly engaging with the child. The child eventually calms down and continues eating. An additional, negative, parenting vignette was created for this study. In the negative vignette, a similar situation is described. Two parents and a child are eating at a restaurant. The child gets upset and one of the parents responds. In this negative scenario, however, the parent who engages with the child gets frustrated and eventually angrily strikes the child on the hand. The scene resolves similarly to the positive vignette with the child eventually calming down and eating.

In both the positive and negative scenarios, the gender of the (active) parent who interacts with the child and the sexual orientation of the couple are varied while the rest of the story remains constant. Three variables— parenting behavior (positive/negative), gender of active parent (male/female), and sexual orientation of parents (heterosexual/ homosexual)—result in a total of eight possible vignettes.

Parenting Evaluation Questions

Participants completed a panel of questions (adapted from Massey, 2007) evaluating the quality of parenting demonstrated in the vignettes: "How would you rate [Mark]'s parenting skills?," "How well did [Mark] handle the situation?," and "How appropriate is [Mark]'s response to the child's behavior?" The name of the actor in the question matched the name used in the randomized vignette. Responses were measured on a 7-point Likert scale (alpha = .80), and ranged from 1 = very unskilled/inappropriate/badly to 7 = very skilled/appropriate/well.

Results

Participants were randomly assigned to one of eight possible vignettes (positive/negative parenting, same-sex/opposite-sex couple, and male/female active parent). As shown in Table 1, random assignment and missing data correction resulted in between 50 (11.5%) and 59 (13.5%) cases for each vignette condition.

Traditional heterosexism, denial of discrimination, and overall parenting evaluation measures were calculated by averaging the corresponding items after adjusting for those that required reverse coding. As shown in Table 2, all measures were found to be internally consistent.

As shown in Table 3, higher levels of traditional heterosexism were moderately correlated with higher levels of denial of discrimination. In addition, a small and negative correlation was found between traditional heterosexism and overall parenting evaluation of same-sex couples

Table 1 Frequencies for Vignette Conditions

Vignette Condition	N	%
Negative – Gay – Man	58	13.3
Negative – Lesbian – Woman	50	11.5
Negative – Straight – Woman	58	13.3
Negative – Straight – Man	59	13.5
Positive – Gay – Man	50	11.5
Positive – Lesbian – Woman	58	13.3
Positive – Straight – Woman	50	11.5
Positive – Straight – Man	53	12.2
Total	436	100

across parenting condition. As traditional heterosexism increased, evaluations of the parenting of same-sex couples decreased. No correlation was found between denial of discrimination and overall parenting evaluation of same-sex couples.

Traditional Heterosexism (Old-Fashioned Prejudice)

Hypothesis 1 predicted that higher levels of traditional heterosexism would result in more negative evaluations of same-sex couples in both positive and negative parenting conditions. In order to compare those higher and lower in traditional heterosexism, a variable was created using a mean split of traditional heterosexism (M = 1.89, SD = 0.90). A three-way univariate ANOVA was conducted to investigate differences in overall parenting evaluation for parenting condition, sexual orientation of couple, and levels of traditional heterosexism.

In order to test Hypothesis 1, it was necessary to first determine whether the experimental manipulation of positive and negative parenting condition had an effect on the parenting evaluation. As shown in Table 4, the ANOVA revealed a main effect for parenting condition $F(1, 404) = 174.85, p < .001$, indicating the manipulation was indeed successful. In addition, the main effect for traditional heterosexism was also significant $F(1, 404) = 5.87, p < .016$, supporting Hypothesis 1. No main effect was found for sexual orientation of the couple.

Table 2 Descriptives for Independent and Dependent Variables

Variable	N	M	SD	Cronbach's Alpha
Parenting Evaluation	434	3.84	1.59	.932
Traditional Heterosexism	414	1.89	0.90	.960
Denial of Discrimination	423	2.12	0.66	.833

Note. Parenting Evaluation ranges from 1 = bad to 7 = good; Traditional Heterosexism and Denial of Discrimination both range from 1 = low to 5 = high.

TABLE 3 Correlations among Measures for Same-Sex Parents Condition

Measure	1	2	3
1. Parenting Evaluation	—	−.157*	−0.111
2. Traditional Heterosexism		—	.530**
3. Denial of Discrimination			—

*$p < .05$. **$p < .01$.

Table 4 Three-Way Univariate ANOVA for Overall Parenting Evaluation by Parenting Condition, Traditional Heterosexism, and Sexual Orientation of Parents

Source	df	F	p
(A) Parenting Condition	1	174.85	.001
(B) Traditional Heterosexism	1	5.87	.016
(C) Sexual Orientation of Parents	1	0.79	.376
A × B × C (interaction)	1	1.39	.239
Error (within group)	404		

Denial of Discrimination (Modern Antihomosexual Prejudice)

Hypothesis 2 predicted that modern antihomosexual prejudice—assessed using the denial of discrimination scale—would moderate the relationship among the sexual orientation of the couple, parenting condition, and evaluation of parenting. Although higher levels of denial of discrimination were not expected to negatively affect the evaluation of same-sex parents in the positive parenting condition, they were expected to do so in the negative parenting condition. Similar to the analysis for Traditional Heterosexism, a variable was created using a mean split of denial discrimination ($M = 2.12$, $SD = .658$). Three-way univariate ANOVA was conducted to investigate differences in overall parenting evaluation for parenting condition, sexual orientation of couple, and levels of modern antihomosexual prejudice (see Table 5).

As shown in Table 5, the ANOVA assessing denial of discrimination revealed a main effect for parenting conditions $F(1, 414) = 195.05$, $p < .001$, but not for denial of discrimination $F(1, 414) = 1.49$, $p < .223$ or the sexual orientation of the couple $F(1, 414) = 1.35$, $p < .246$. As predicted, however, a significant three-way interaction was found among denial of discrimination, the sexual orientation of the couple, and the parenting condition $F(1, 414) = 4.22$, $p < .040$.

Table 5 Three-Way Univariate ANOVA for Overall Parenting Evaluation by Parenting Condition, Denial of Discrimination, and Sexual Orientation or Parents

Source	df	F	p
(A) Parenting Condition	1	195.05	.001
(B) Denial of Discrimination	1	1.49	.223
(C) Sexual Orientation of Parents	1	1.35	.246
A × B × C (interaction)	1	4.22	.040
Error (within group)	414		

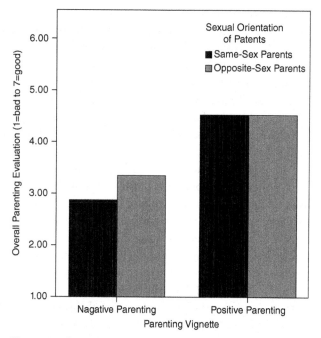

Figure 1 Overall evaluation of parenting by sexual orientation of parents and parenting condition for participants scoring above average in denial of discrimination.

As shown in Figure 1, when evaluating a negative parenting situation, participants scoring above the mean on denial of discrimination rated same-sex parents more negatively ($M = 2.86$, $SD = 1.27$) than opposite-sex parents ($M = 3.35$, $SD = 1.38$). However, when evaluating a positive parenting situation, participants scoring above the mean on denial of discrimination evaluated same-sex and opposite-sex parents similarly ($M = 4.55$, $SD = 1.35$ and $M = 4.53$, $SD = 1.17$, respectively).

Separate Tukey-Kramer post hoc analyses were conducted for the positive and negative conditions to explore the three-way interaction and verify which conditions resulted in significant differences in parenting evaluations. Although the omnibus ANOVA revealed a significant three-way interaction, and the graphed mean differences appear in the predicted direction, the post hoc tests failed to reveal significant differences in the evaluation of the parenting of same- and opposite-sex couples in the negative parenting conditions.

Interaction among Denial of Discrimination, Parenting Condition, Sexual Orientation, and Participant Gender

Hypothesis 3 predicted that participants' gender would moderate the relationship among parenting condition, denial of discrimination, sexual orientation of the couple, and evaluation of parenting. Male participants with higher levels of denial of discrimination were expected to be more negative when evaluating same-sex parents in negative parenting condition than female participants. A four-way univariate ANOVA was conducted to investigate differences in overall parenting evaluation for participant gender, parenting condition, sexual orientation of couple, and levels of denial of discrimination. As shown in Table 6, the four-way interaction was significant $F(11, 403) = 1.98, p = .029$.

In order to investigate the differences that contributed to this interaction, the split file option in SPSS was used to conduct separate two-way univariate ANOVAS holding parenting condition and participant gender constant. As shown in Table 7, a significant interaction was found between sexual orientation of parents and denial of discrimination for male participants in negative parenting conditions $F(1, 75) = 6.19, p = .015$. No other significant interactions were found for any other conditions.

Tukey-Kramer post hoc tests were then conducted to explore the significant interaction between sexual orientation of the parents and denial of discrimination for male participants in the negative parenting condition and determine which mean differences in parenting evaluation were significant.

Table 6 Four-Way Univariate ANOVA for Overall Parenting Evaluation by Parenting Condition, Denial of Discrimination, Sexual Orientation of Parents, and Participant Gender

Source	df	F	p
(A) Parenting Condition	1	167.53	.001
(B) Denial of Discrimination	1	2.92	.088
(C) Sexual Orientation of Parents	1	1.38	.242
(D) Participant Gender	2	1.41	.245
A × B × C × D (interaction)	11	1.98	.029
Error (within group)			

Table 7 Two-Way Univariate ANOVA for Overall Parenting Evaluation by Denial of Discrimination and Sexual Orientation of Parents (for Male Participants in Negative Parenting Condition Only)

Source	df	F	p
(A) Denial of Discrimination	1	1.62	.207
(B) Sexual Orientation of Parents	1	0.83	.365
A × B (interaction)	1	6.19	.015
Error (between group)	75		

In negative parenting situations, male participants scoring above the mean on denial of discrimination were significantly more negative ($p < .05$) in their evaluation of same-sex parents ($M = 2.47, SD = 1.11$) than were those scoring below the mean ($M = 3.53, SD = 1.08$). In addition, as shown in Figure 2, male participants scoring above the mean on denial of discrimination were significantly ($p < .01$) more negative in their evaluation of same-sex parents in negative parenting situations ($M = 2.47, SD = 1.11$) than in their evaluation of opposite-sex parents ($M = 3.43, SD = 1.41$). None of the other post hoc tests were significant.

Discussion

The current study explored how heterosexual participants' attitudes toward gay men and lesbians affect their relative evaluation of the parenting practices and skill of same-sex versus opposite-sex couples. Overall, participants' evaluation of parenting was not directly affected by the sexual orientation of the parents being evaluated. This finding was consistent with public opinion data, which has suggested that, in general, attitudes toward gay men and lesbians have been improving, and that attitudes toward same-sex parenting are also improving (Gates, 2011; Massey, 2010; Pew Research Center, 2011).

However, as predicted, traditional (or "old-fashioned") heterosexism continues to negatively influence heterosexuals' judgments of same-sex parents.

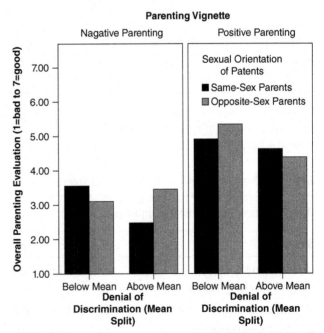

Figure 2 Male participants' overall parenting evaluation by denial of discrimination, parenting condition, and sexual orientation.

Participants with higher levels of traditional heterosexism were found to evaluate the parenting behaviors of same-sex parents more negatively than the very same parenting behaviors of opposite-sex parents.

It was also predicted that as antihomosexual prejudice has become less socially acceptable, instead of disappearing altogether, it would become more subtle and manifest in situations in which it could be attributed to a non-prejudiced cause. Consequently, modern antihomosexual prejudice (measured as denial of discrimination) would interact significantly with the sexual orientation of the couple and the parenting condition, affecting participants' evaluations of the parenting behavior. This prediction was also supported. Participants who scored higher in modern antihomosexual prejudice were more critical of the negative parenting behaviors of same-sex parents than the very same behaviors among opposite-sex parents. However, this difference was not found in positive parenting situations.

Finally, because past research has demonstrated that males have tended to express more antihomosexual prejudice than females, it was predicted that the modern prejudice effect, described previously, would be more robust for male participants than for females. This prediction was also supported. When participant gender was added to the model, a significant four-way interaction was revealed. Post hoc tests showed that when evaluating a negative parenting situation, male participants with higher levels of denial of discrimination will evaluate same-sex parents significantly lower than opposite-sex parents. These differences were not found among female participants or in positive parenting situations.

One explanation for these findings is that the persistence of antihomosexual prejudice may be at odds with more widespread positive shifts in attitudes toward gay men and lesbians and same-sex parenting. Consequently, the expression of these attitudes is becoming more subtle. When called on to evaluate the positive parenting of same-sex parents, the pressures to conform to increasingly gay- and lesbian-affirmative societal expectations will lead those higher in modern antihomosexual prejudice to express more favorable judgments. However, when evaluating less than desirable parenting behaviors among same-sex parents, when a negative judgment is likely to be attributed to negative parenting behaviors, those higher in modern prejudice will make more negative judgments, and these judgments will be more negative than the judgments made for heterosexual parents engaging in similar negative parenting behaviors.

In addition, the relationship between antihomosexual prejudice and the male gender role has been well established (Kimmel, 2004; Herek, 1986). Because antihomosexual prejudice is particularly persistent among males, the need to channel this prejudice into a more subtle and relatively socially acceptable outlet is likely to be more pronounced for males.

Implications for Same-Sex Parenting

The past decade has seen some dramatic improvements in the rights of gay men, lesbians, and bisexuals in the United States: the dismantling of Don't Ask, Don't Tell, which prohibited gay men and lesbians from serving openly in the military; the U.S. Supreme Court's *Lawrence v. Texas* decision, which overturned sodomy laws across the country; and the successes of the marriage equality movement (although this progress has been met by resistance—e.g., the recent passage of an amendment by voters in North Carolina that alters their state constitution to outlaw same-sex marriage, stating "marriage between one man and one woman is the only domestic legal union that shall be valid or recognized [in the state]"), to name only a few. These changes echo the continuing improvements demonstrated in public opinion research related to gay and lesbian rights.

Gay men and lesbians represent a ready and willing pool of prospective parents, and research has demonstrated them to be as capable and as beneficial as opposite-sex parents (Patterson, 2009). This may be particularly promising, given the great deal of progress still needed within the child welfare system. Reports from child welfare agencies across the United States reveal large numbers of children in need of permanent families. In 2010, more than 400,000 children were in foster care and 115,000 children were waiting to be adopted (U.S. Department of Health and Human Services, 2012). However, the number of families who have actually taken steps to adopt has been decreasing since 1995 (Jones, 2008). One particularly relevant application of this research, therefore, is in considering the impact modern antihomosexual prejudice may have in the evaluation of same-sex couples as potential foster and adoptive parents.

Subjective evaluations are a core part of foster and adoption processes and take place during initial orientations, foster/adoption trainings, home studies, and staffing team meetings, among other encounters. However, these evaluations also provide opportunities for the displacement of antihomosexual prejudice onto other decisions not directly related to the sexual orientation of the parents. Same-sex couples that are considering becoming parents, and who are scrutinized by adoption caseworkers, court-appointed special advocates, and family court judges among others, could become victims of modern antihomosexual prejudice. Studying the relationship between modern antihomosexual prejudice and evaluations of same-sex parenting is important, therefore, because it can reveal attitudes and subsequent behavioral patterns that individuals are not aware they possess. Raising awareness of these attitudes is vital to improving the lives of gay and lesbian people, but it is also a critical step in being able to utilize a potentially valuable pool of prospective adoptive and foster parents.

As stated earlier, trends in old-fashioned or traditional heterosexism are moving in a favorable direction. This study, however, suggests that overt old-fashioned prejudice is not the only type of prejudice affecting the lives of gay-, lesbian-, and bisexual-headed families. Although researchers have developed tools to measure modern antihomosexual prejudice, similar public opinion data assessing modern prejudice has not yet become available. These data will need to be collected in order to properly assess the prevalence of this more subtle, but insidious, form of prejudice. As this literature grows so will the practical information available to gay, lesbian, and bisexual parents and prospective parents, as well as practitioners in child welfare.

Finally, it is also important to remember that the values and ideological assumptions that are influencing prejudice, as well as the functions it serves, may be multiple (Herek, 2000b; Biernat, Vescio, & Theno, 1996). Modern racism, for example, has been found to be related to beliefs about affirmative action, economic competition, or reverse discrimination in employment (McConahay, 1986; Sears, 1988). Modern antigay/antilesbian prejudice may also be associated with numerous values, beliefs, and concerns, including changing representations of the family and changing gender role expectations, shifting social values (i.e., marriage equality and attitudes about sex), and the increasing openness and influence of gay people worldwide. Although the current study explored the influence of a particular set of values and beliefs in a particular context, future research should explore other ways that modern prejudice is influencing heterosexuals' attitudes toward gay, lesbian, and bisexual parents and their families.

Limitations

One challenge of using factorial ANOVA to explore these questions was that post hoc interpretations of three-way and four-way interactions are challenging. Even when significant interactions have been found in the omnibus ANOVA, finding significant differences among particular interactions is frequently limited by increasingly small cell sizes and extremely conservative critical tests of significance. Although Rosenthal and Rosnow (1985) have suggested that the situation can be improved by focusing post hoc tests on theory-driven comparisons only, this greater complexity would necessitate more variables, and more variables are still best met with larger samples.

While larger sample sizes would be informative, so too would participant pools with wider sociodemographic variation. Participants in the current study were all university students. While this is consistent with much of the existing literature, the current sample did not allow for analyses across age groups, educational attainment, and many other sociodemographic characteristics.

Another possible limitation of the current study may have been the vignettes used. Teasing apart positive and negative condition can be difficult, given all the factors that go into one's assessment of expected and acceptable parenting behavior. More subtle variation in the positive and negative conditions would help inform the consistency of these patterns; although, this would require substantial sample sizes. Moreover, extending these vignettes beyond readable text, to include audiovisual stimuli of scenarios, would be interesting and informative. Future research should continue to extend the parenting scenarios for testing heteronormative prejudice.

Future Research

This study represents only a small part of a program of research that attempts to address and expand what is known about how same-sex parents navigate a world in which modern prejudice operates. A wide range of questions still remain regarding the influence of modern antihomosexual prejudice.

Gender of Active Parent

Previous studies of antihomosexual prejudice have suggested that gay men are evaluated more negatively than lesbians and that this difference is due primarily to the attitudes of heterosexual males toward gay men (Herek, 2002). In addition, many believe that women make better parents than men (Deutsch & Saxon, 1998). Although this study explored the influence of gender of participant, the sample size did not allow an investigation of the influence of the gender of the target (parent). It is likely that the gender of the evaluator and gender of the target will interact to influence evaluations of same-sex parenting practices.

Gender of Child

Future research should continue to explore the various ways that gender interacts with antigay/antilesbian prejudice. The current study examined the interaction of gender of evaluator, gender of target, and modern prejudice in terms of their impact on the evaluation of parenting a male child. It is likely that the gender of the child will also affect both traditional and modern antigay/antilesbian prejudice. In addition, the gender role of the evaluator is also an important factor. In what ways might gender role traditionalism influence participants' judgments of same-sex and opposite-sex parenting?

Interpersonal Contact

The significant influence of interpersonal contact on attitudes toward gay men and lesbians has been well documented (Herek & Capitanio, 1996). Massey (2010) reported a relationship between amount of contact and both old-fashioned and modern antihomosexual prejudice. However, these findings were preliminary and did not explore the type and context of the contact and how it may interact with gender of evaluator and gender of target. Contact has been shown to have a greater effect on attitudes when the contact is in the context of equal status interactions (Allport, 1954; Herek & Capitanio, 1996). Public parenting may provide such a context; being a parent often creates opportunities for interaction with other parents. Future research should explore the effect of interpersonal contact, in the context of public parenting, on attitudes toward same-sex parenting. However, given the complex relationship between aversion and contact (Gaertner & Dovidio, 1986), it is also important to be aware of the influence modern antihomosexual prejudice may have on the frequency of interaction between heterosexuals and homosexuals and their families.

Public Parenting

This study has only explored the attitudes and judgments of heterosexuals toward gay men and lesbians. It is also necessary to explore how aware same-sex parents and their families are of these judgments, how important the attitudes of others are in their lives, and how (if at all) these families react to these potential judgments. What are the consequences of the possible microaggressions on the physical and mental health of same-sex parents and their families? In what ways, if at all, do same-sex parents change their parenting practices to accommodate the judgments of a condemning public?

Modern Antihomosexual Prejudice in Other Contexts

As Sears (1988) has pointed out, modern forms of prejudice are made manifest in symbolic ways. Just as modern racism was found to influence positions taken on government policies such as busing and affirmative action, modern antihomosexual prejudice may influence how people understand the "definition" of marriage, what is in the "best interest of the child," and threats to "unit cohesiveness."

The values that collude with modern prejudice may extend beyond same-sex parenting and influence evaluations and decision making in domains such as teaching, counseling, and law enforcement, among others. In these situations, the salience of antigay/antilesbian stereotypes (i.e., sexually predatory, overly sensitive, not masculine/feminine "enough", etc.) may be of particular concern. For instance, in two polls by the Gallup News Service (Newport, 2001), respondents' views on employment protections for homosexuals varied considerably for different occupations. In a 2002 poll only 11% supported antigay discrimination in employment (Newport, 2003). When asked about particular occupations, however, the responses varied. Whereas only 6% were opposed to the occupations of salesman, the percentage was significantly higher for high school teacher (33%), clergy (39%), or elementary school teacher (40%). Better tools are needed to explore how and when subtle prejudice continues to influence intergroup relations in a variety of socially and politically important situations. Future research should explore how modern prejudice has influenced these judgments and the experiences of gay men, lesbians, and bisexuals who occupy these roles.

Conclusion

The parents who shared their experiences during the 2011 LGBTQ Families Conference in Rochester, New York, described at the start of this article, reported public parenting experiences that were both positive and negative. The current study has echoed the ambivalence of these experiences, demonstrating (albeit among undergraduate college students) tentative progress that may also guide the evaluations of practitioners, service providers, and the general public in terms of improving attitudes toward same-sex parenting. Although overt and hostile prejudice may indeed be diminishing, modern, subtle prejudice continues to affect the lives of lesbians, gay men, and their families. Prejudicial judgments, however subtle, that serve to limit access of these families to potential support and resources, ultimately harm today's youths. Scholars must continue to explore the impact this subtle but pernicious prejudice has on the well-being of same-sex families, and how best to reduce its presence.

Appendix: Vignettes
Positive Parenting

You are sitting in a restaurant eating dinner. Across the room are [two women] sitting together with what looks to be a four-year-old boy. You notice that the two are holding hands. [One woman, Mary], places [her] arm around [the other, Beth], and leans over and kisses [her] on the cheek. Then they both take turns talking to the child.

When their dinner arrives [Beth] puts some food in a small colorful bowl and places it in front of the child. The child looks at it and frowns. All of a sudden he picks up his bowl of food, throws it on the floor, and starts screaming. Other people in the restaurant turn to look at them. [Beth] picks the child up and tries to get him to calm down. The child pushes away, yelling, "No! No! No!" It takes [Beth] several minutes to calm the child down and get him to sit back down in his highchair. [Mary] places a new bowl of food in front of the child. Eventually the child begins eating on his own.

Negative Parenting

You are sitting in a restaurant eating dinner. Across the room are [a man and a woman] sitting together with what looks to be a four-year-old boy. You notice that the two are holding hands. [The man, Steve], places his arm around [the woman, Beth], and leans over and kisses [her] on the cheek. Then they both take turns talking to the child.

When their dinner arrives [Steve] puts some food in a small colorful bowl and places it in front of the child. The child looks at it and frowns. All of a sudden he picks up his bowl of food, throws it on the floor, and starts screaming. Other people in the restaurant turn to look at them.

[Steve] grabs the bowl off the floor and in an angry, raised voice tells the child to be quiet and eat his dinner. The child picks up the bowl and starts to throw it. [Steve] smacks the child's hand and yells at him to "put that down!" The child starts to cry. It takes [Steve] several minutes to calm the child down. It is clear [Steve] is getting more and more frustrated by the child's behavior. But eventually [he] gets him to sit back down at the table. [Beth] places a new bowl of food in front of the child. Eventually the child begins eating on his own.

Note: Bracketed text varies by sexual orientation of the couple and the gender of active parent. Brackets did not appear in versions provided to participants.

References

Allport, G. (1954). *The nature of prejudice.* New York, NY: Addison Wesley.

Anderson, K. J., & Kanner, M. (2011). Inventing a gay agenda: Students' perceptions of lesbian and gay professors. *Journal of Applied Social Psychology, 41,* 1538–1564.

Biernat, M., Vescio, T. K., & Theno, S. A. (1996). Violating American values: A 'value congruence' approach to understanding outgroup attitudes. *Journal of Experimental Social Psychology, 32,* 387–410.

Chakraborty, A., & McKenzie, K. (2002). Does racial discrimination cause mental illness? *British Journal of Psychiatry, 180,* 475–477.

Clark, R., Anderson, N. B., Clark, V. R., & Williams, D. R. (1999). Racism as a stressor for African Americans. *American Psychologist, 54,* 805–816.

Crocker, J., & Major, B. (1989). Social stigma and self-esteem: The self-protective properties of stigma. *Psychological Review, 96,* 608–630.

Deutsch, F. M., & Saxon, S. E. (1998). The double standard of praise and criticism for mothers and fathers. *Psychology of Women Quarterly, 22,* 665–683.

Gaertner, S. L., & Dovidio, J. F. (1986). The aversive form of racism. In J. F. Dovidio & S. L. Gaertner (Eds.), *Prejudice, discrimination, and racism* (pp. 61–89). Orlando, FL: Academic Press.

Gates, G. J. (2011, winter). Family formation and raising children among same-sex couples. National Council on Family Relations, FF51. Retrieved from http://williamsinstitute.law.ucla.edu/wp-content/uploads/Gates-Badgett-NCFR-LGBT-Families-December-2011.pdf

Herek, G. M. (1984). Attitudes toward lesbians and gay men: A factor analytic study. *Journal of Homosexuality, 10*(1–2), 39–51.

Herek, G. M. (1986). On heterosexual masculinity: Some psychical consequences of the social construction of gender and sexuality. *American Behavioral Scientist, 29*(5), 563–577.

Herek, G. M. (2000a). Sexual prejudice and gender: Do heterosexuals' attitudes toward lesbians and gay men differ? *Journal of Social Issues, 56*(2), 251–266.

Herek, G. M. (2000b). The social construction of attitudes: Functional consensus and divergence in the US public's reactions to AIDS. In G. Maio & J. Olson (Eds.), *Why we evaluate: Functions of attitudes* (pp. 325–364). Mahwah, NJ: Lawrence Erlbaum.

Herek, G. M. (2002). Gender gaps in public opinion about lesbians and gay men. *Public Opinion Quarterly, 66*(1), 40–66.

Herek, G. M., & Capitanio, J. P. (1996). "Some of my best friends": Intergroup contact, concealable stigma, and heterosexuals' attitudes toward gay men and lesbians. *Personality and Social Psychology Bulletin, 22*(4), 412–424.

Jones, J. (2008). Adoption experiences of women and men and demand for children to adopt by women 18–44 years of age in the United States, 2002. *Vital and Health Statistics, 23*(27). Hyattsville, MD: National Center for Health Statistics, U.S. Department of Health and Human Services.

Katz, I., & Hass, R. G. (1988). Racial ambivalence and American value conflict: Correlational and priming studies of dual cognitive structures. *Journal of Personality and Social Psychology, 55,* 893–905.

Kimmel, M. S. (2004). Masculinity as homophobia: Fear, shame, and silence in the construction of gender identity. In P. F. Murphy (Ed.), *Feminism and masculinities* (pp. 182–199). New York, NY: Oxford University Press.

Kite, M. E., & Whitley, B. E. (1996). Sex differences in attitudes toward homosexual persons, behaviors, and civil rights: A meta-analysis. *Personality and Social Psychology Bulletin, 22*(4), 336–353.

LaMar, L., & Kite, M. (1998). Sex differences in attitudes toward gay men and lesbians: A multidimensional perspective. *Journal of Sex Research, 35*(2), 189–196.

MacDonald, A. P., Huggins, J., Young, S., & Swanson, R. A. (1973). Attitudes toward homosexuality: Preservation of sex morality or the double standard? *Journal of Consulting and Clinical Psychology, 40*(1), 161.

Massey, S. G. (2007). Sexism, heterosexism, and attributions about undesirable behavior in children of gay, lesbian, and heterosexual parents. *Journal of GLBT Family Studies, 3*(4), 457–483.

Massey, S. G. (2009). Polymorphous prejudice: Liberating the measurement of heterosexuals' attitudes toward lesbians and gay men. *Journal of Homosexuality, 56*(2), 147–172.

Massey, S. G. (2010). Valued differences or benevolent stereotypes? Exploring the influence of positive beliefs on anti-gay and anti-lesbian attitudes. *Psychology & Sexuality, 1*(2), 115–130.

McConahay, J. B. (1986). Modern racism, ambivalence, and the modern racism scale. In J. F. Dovidio & S. L. Gaertner (Eds.), *Prejudice, discrimination, and racism* (pp. 91–125). San Diego, CA: Academic Press.

Morse, C. N., McLaren, S., & McLachlan, A. J. (2007). The attitudes of Australian heterosexuals toward same-sex parenting. *Journal of GLBT Family Studies, 3*, 425–455.

Newport, F. (2001). American attitudes toward homosexuality continue to become more tolerant. Princeton, NJ: Gallup News Service. Retrieved from http://www.gallup.com/poll/4432/american-attitudes-toward-homosexuality-continue-to-become-more-tolerant.aspx

Newport, F. (2003). Public shifts to more conservative stance on gay rights. Princeton, NJ: Gallup News Service. Retrieved from http://www.gallup.com/poll/8956/public-shifts-more-conservative-stance-gay-rights.aspx

Paige, R. U. (2005). Proceedings of the American Psychological Association, Incorporated, for the legislative year 2004. Minutes of the meeting of the Council of Representatives July 28 & 30, 2004, Honolulu, HI. Retrieved from http://www.apa.org/governance/ (To be published in Volume 60, Issue Number 5 of the *American Psychologist.*)

Patterson, C. J. (2009). Children of lesbian and gay parents: Psychology, law, and policy. *American Psychologist, 64*, 727–736.

Pearson, A. R., Dovidio, J. F., & Gaertner, S. L. (2009). The nature of contemporary prejudice: Insights from aversive racism. *Social and Personality Psychology Compass, 3*(3), 314–338.

Pew Research Center. (2011). Most say homosexuality should be accepted by society. Retrieved from http://pewresearch.org/pubs/1994/poll-support-for-acceptance-of-homosexuality-gay-parenting-marriage

Raja, S., & Stokes, J. P. (1998). Assessing attitudes toward lesbians and gay men: The modern homophobia scale. *Journal of Gay, Lesbian, and Bisexual Identity, 3*(2), 113–134.

Ratcliff, J. J., Lassiter, G. D., Markman, K. D., & Snyder, C. J. (2006). Gender differences in attitudes toward gay men and lesbians: The role of motivations to respond without prejudice. *Personality and Social Psychology Bulletin, 32*(10), 1325–1338.

Rosenthal, R., & Rosnow, R. L. (1985). *Contrast analysis: Focused comparisons in the analysis of variance.* New York, NY: Cambridge University Press.

Sears, D. O. (1988). Symbolic racism. In I. Katz and S. Taylor (Eds.), *Eliminating racism: Profiles in controversy* (pp. 53–84). New York, NY: Plenum Press.

Solorzano, D., Ceja, M., & Yosso, T. (2000). Critical race theory, racial microaggressions, and campus racial climate: The experiences of African American college students. *Journal of Negro Education, 69*, 60–73.

Steele, C. M., Spencer, S. J., & Aronson, J. (2002). Contending with group image: The psychology of stereotype and social identity threat. In M. Zanna (Ed.), *Advances in experimental social psychology* (vol. 23, pp. 379–440). New York, NY: Academic Press.

Sue, D. W., Capodilupo, C. M., Torino, G. C., Bucceri, J. M., Holder, A. M. B., Nadal, K. L., & Esquilin, M. (2007). Racial microaggressions in everyday life: Implications for clinical practice. *American Psychologist, 62*(4), 271–286.

U.S. Department of Health and Human Services. (2012). The AFCARS Report: Preliminary FY 2010 estimates as of June 2011. Retrieved from http://www.acf.hhs.gov/programs/cb/stats_research/ afcars/tar/report18.pdf

Module 10
Prejudice and the Individual

Prejudice refers to beliefs, thoughts, feelings, and attitudes that someone holds about a group. A prejudice is not based on experience; instead, it is a prejudgment, originating outside of actual experience. Racism is a type of prejudice that is used to justify the belief that one racial category is somehow superior or inferior to others. The Ku Klux Klan is an example of a racist organization; its members' belief in white supremacy has encouraged over a century of hate crime and hate speech.

People joined the 50th Martin Luther King Memorial March, on January 20, 2014 in Raleigh, USA. The 50th March in memory of Dr. Martin Luther King's birthday.

While prejudice refers to biased *thinking*, **discrimination** consists of *actions* against a group of people. Discrimination can be based on age, religion, health, and other indicators. Prejudice and discrimination can overlap and intersect in many ways. Here are four examples of how prejudice and discrimination can occur. *Unprejudiced nondiscriminators* are openminded, tolerant, and accepting individuals. *Unprejudiced discriminators* might be those who, unthinkingly, practice sexism in their workplace by not considering females for certain positions that have traditionally been held by men. *Prejudiced nondiscriminators* are those who hold racist beliefs but do not act on them, such as a racist store owner who serves minority customers. *Prejudiced discriminators* include those who actively make disparaging remarks about others or who perpetuate hate crimes.

303

Acts of discrimination and ideas of prejudice are directed at various target types. Have you ever been a target of discrimination or prejudice? How can you tell?

Institutional discrimination is when a societal system has developed with an embedded disenfranchisement of a group, such as the U.S. military's historical nonacceptance of minority sexualities as recently experienced surrounding the "do not ask, do not tell" policy. Institutional discrimination can also involve the promotion of a group's status, such as occurs with white privilege. While most white people are willing to admit that non-white people live with a set of disadvantages due to the color of their skin, very few white people are willing to acknowledge the benefits they receive simply by being white. **White privilege** refers to the fact that dominant groups often accept their experience as the normative (and hence, superior) experience. Feminist sociologist Peggy McIntosh (1988) described several examples of "white privilege." For instance, white women can easily find makeup that matches their skin tone. White people can be assured that, most of the time, they will be dealing with authority figures of their own race. How many other examples of white privilege can you think of?

A black man sits on a bench in a park reserved for whites. This was common place during the apartheid years in South Africa and similar warnings appeared at water fountains and entrances to restaurants in the United States up until the 1960s.

Group pride can often turn into a world view based on lack of information about other groups. **Ethnocentrism** and **xenophobia** are reflections, at a cultural level, of the same in-group versus out-group dynamics explored in Social Identity Theory.

Ethnocentrism, as sociologist William Graham Sumner (1906) described the term, involves a belief or attitude that one's own culture is better than all others. Almost everyone is a little bit ethnocentric. And a high level of appreciation for one's own culture can be healthy; a shared sense of community pride, for example, connects people in a society. But ethnocentrism can lead to disdain or dislike for other cultures, causing misunderstanding and conflict.

Ethnocentrism can be so strong that when confronted with all the differences of a new culture, one may experience disorientation and frustration. In sociology, we call this **culture shock**. A traveler from Miami might find the nightly silence of rural Montana unsettling, not peaceful. An exchange student from China might be annoyed by the constant interruptions in class as other students ask questions—a practice that is considered rude in China. Perhaps the Miami traveler was initially captivated with Montana's quiet beauty and the Chinese student was originally excited to see an American-style classroom first hand. But as they experience unanticipated differences from their own culture, their excitement gives way to discomfort and doubts about how to behave appropriately in the new situation. Eventually, as people learn more about a culture, they recover from culture shock.

Does it look like she is being accepted by the group behind her? Why would this be? Who are your "others?" What kind of people considers you the "other?"

Cultural relativism is the practice of assessing a culture by its own standards rather than viewing it through the lens of one's own culture. Practicing cultural relativism requires an open mind and a willingness to consider, and even adapt to, new values and norms. However, embracing everything about a new culture is not always possible. Even the most culturally relativist people from societies in which women have political rights and control over their own bodies would question whether the widespread practice of female genital mutilation in countries such as Ethiopia and Sudan should be accepted as a part of cultural tradition. Sociologists attempting to engage in cultural relativism may struggle to reconcile aspects of their own culture with aspects of a culture they are studying.

If you were to write a play featuring this woman, what role would she play?

Sometimes when people attempt to rectify feelings of ethnocentrism and develop cultural relativism, they swing too far to the other end of the spectrum. **Xenocentrism** is the opposite of ethnocentrism, and refers to the belief that another culture is superior to one's own. (The Greek root word *xeno*, pronounced "ZEE-no," means "stranger" or "foreign guest.") An exchange student who goes home after a semester abroad may find it difficult to associate with the values of their own culture after having experienced what they deem a more upright or nobler way of living.

A modern devout Muslim woman. What do you think she is typing on her laptop?

Xenophobia is a fear or contempt of that which is foreign or unknown, especially of strangers or foreign people. It comes from the Greek words (*xenos*), meaning "foreigner," "stranger," and (*phobos*), meaning "fear." The term is typically used to describe a fear or dislike of foreigners or of people significantly different from oneself.

Perhaps the greatest challenge for sociologists studying different cultures is the matter of keeping a perspective. It is impossible for anyone to keep all cultural biases at bay; the best we can do is strive to be aware of them.

Memorial for the ancient slave trade, Stone Town, Zanzibar, Tanzania, Africa.

Unseen Injustice: Incivility as Modern Discrimination in Organizations

Lilia M. Cortina
University of Michigan

This article advances a theory of incivility as a veiled manifestation of sexism and racism in organizations. To support this argument, I draw from social psychological research on modern discrimination. The result is a multilevel model of *selective incivility,* with determinants at the level of the person, organization, and society. Selective incivility could be one mechanism by which gender and racial disparities persist in American organizations, despite concerted efforts to eradicate bias. I discuss scientific and practical implications.

Recent years have seen increasing scholarship on subtle, nonphysical manifestations of interpersonal mistreatment in the workplace, including *general incivility.* This term encompasses low-intensity conduct that lacks a clear intent to harm but nevertheless violates social norms and injures targeted employees (Andersson & Pearson, 1999; Cortina, Magley, Williams, & Langhout, 2001). In this paper I extend the notion of incivility by examining it through lenses of gender and race. The central argument is that incivility, in some cases, is not "general" at all but instead represents contemporary manifestations of gender and racial bias in the workplace. That is, with the rise of taboos, policies, and laws prohibiting discrimination against specific social groups, blatant intentions and efforts to alienate women and minorities from organizational life are no longer tolerated. However, one can mask discrimination (even without realizing it) behind everyday acts of incivility and still maintain an unbiased image. This would be consistent with research demonstrating that prejudices persist in covert forms within society in general (e.g., Dovidio & Gaertner, 1998) and within organizations in particular (e.g., Brief, Dietz, Cohen, Pugh, & Vaslow, 2000).

I begin the article with a recap of theory and findings from research on workplace incivility. Next is an in-depth review of theories of modern discrimination, focusing on

cognitive, affective, social, and organizational antecedents. An integration of these two bodies of literature then supports the proposition that incivility can constitute a particularly insidious, behavioral manifestation of modern/contemporary/covert sexism and racism. The result is a multilevel model of incivility as modern discrimination in organizations. In the latter half of the paper, I address implications of this "selective incivility" model for research, policy, and practice in organizations. The following definition of workplace discrimination frames this work: "Unfair employment discrimination [occurs] when persons in a 'social category' . . . are put at a disadvantage in the workplace relative to other groups with comparable potential or proven success" (Dipboye & Halverson, 2004: 131).

This article's novel contributions are fourfold. First, by building bridges with social psychological scholarship on discrimination, I extend the organizational literature on antisocial work behavior to address issues of *race and gender.* Most studies of workplace aggression, deviance, bullying, and so forth to date have focused almost exclusively on "general" conduct irrespective of social categories, without recognizing that antisocial work behavior may often reflect bias against members of undervalued social groups. A second contribution of the present work is to the social psychology literature. A common criticism of social psychology (e.g., Fiske, 2000) is that research on "discrimination" and "intergroup conflict" has addressed attitudes and affect in great detail, often to the neglect of action. Attitudes, stereotypes, and ideologies are certainly important, but a complete understanding of intergroup relations requires attention to intergroup *behavior.* The current article does just that by bringing to light the specific behavioral experience of selective

Portions of this paper were presented in April 2004 at the annual meeting of the Society for Industrial-Organizational Psychology, Chicago. Many thanks to Kim Lonsway, Abby Stewart, and Arzu Wasti for their valuable comments on earlier versions.

incivility. The few psychologists who have looked at actual discriminatory conduct have generally focused on "formal discrimination"—for example, unfair selection decisions (e.g., Brief et al., 2000; Dovidio & Gaertner, 2000). In contrast, I take an in-depth look at a form of "interpersonal discrimination," which Hebl, Foster, Mannix, and Dovidio define as "nonverbal, paraverbal, and . . . verbal behaviors that occur in social interactions" (2002: 816); this represents a third contribution of the present article. Finally, I integrate concepts from organizational and social psychology, management science, and the law to propose fruitful new directions for research and practice in cases of selective incivility in the workplace.

Workplace Incivility: Definition, Incidence, and Impact

Andersson and Pearson define *workplace incivility* as "low intensity deviant behavior with ambiguous intent to harm the target, in violation of workplace norms for mutual respect. Uncivil behaviors are characteristically rude and discourteous, displaying a lack of regard for others" (1999: 457). They conceptualize this as a specific form of *employee deviance* (Robinson & Bennett, 1995), which, in turn, represents a subset of *antisocial employee behavior* (Giacolone & Greenberg, 1997). When unambiguous intentions and expectations to harm the target or organization are present, definitions of incivility overlap with *psychological aggression* (e.g., Baron, 2004; Neuman, 2004). However, incivility differs from psychological aggression when behaviors lack clear, conscious intentionality. That is, although incivility may occasionally have visibly injurious objectives, it can often be attributed to other factors, such as the instigator's ignorance, oversight, or personality; intent, whether present or not, is ambiguous to one or more of the parties involved (Andersson & Pearson, 1999; Pearson, Andersson, & Wegner, 2001). However, workplace incivility, by definition, is completely distinct from *physical aggression* and *violence* (e.g., VandenBos & Bulatao, 1996).

Incivility is perhaps one of the most pervasive forms of antisocial behavior in the workplace. To assess incivility prevalence, my colleagues and I surveyed employees in a range of work settings; the incidence rates we uncovered illustrate the ubiquity of this phenomenon. For example, 71 percent of a court employee sample (Cortina et al., 2001), 75 percent of a university employee sample (Cortina & Magley, 2007), and 79 percent of a law enforcement sample (Cortina, Lonsway, & Magley, 2004) reported that they had encountered some form of uncivil conduct at work in recent years. Other researchers have

reported similarly high rates of related workplace behaviors: for example, "generalized harassment"—75 percent (Einarsen & Raknes, 1997); "generalized workplace harassment"—64 percent (Rospenda, 2002); and "rude or disrespectful treatment"—67 percent (Neuman, 2004).

The proliferation of incivility in the workplace has very real, very negative consequences for employees, workgroups, and organizations. Barling and colleagues (Barling et al., 1996; Barling, Rogers, & Kelloway, 2001) have theorized that experiences of abusive behaviors at work lead to negative mood, cognitive distraction, fear, and perceived injustice. Others (e.g., Andersson & Pearson, 1999; Cortina et al., 2001; Miner-Rubino & Cortina, 2004) have added damaged social identity and anger to this list. These cognitive and affective reactions, in turn, adversely influence targets' occupational, psychological, and physical health. Some have proposed that these negative consequences extend beyond the targeted employee to affect bystanders, workgroups, and whole organizations (Andersson & Pearson, 1999; Miner-Rubino & Cortina, 2004).

Data are emerging to support theories that although incivility may be subtle, its effects are not. Empirical research suggests that employees targeted with uncivil behavior experience greater job stress and dissatisfaction, lower creativity, cognitive distraction, and psychological distress. Possibly in an attempt to dampen the increased stressfulness of work, targets also use more substances. Moreover, incivility disrupts employee relationships and derails cooperation, rending the social fabric of the workgroup. Personnel targeted with pervasive incivility ultimately lose commitment to their organizations and exit at higher rates (Cortina et al., 2001, 2002; Lim & Cortina, 2004; Pearson, Andersson, & Porath, 2000; Pearson et al., 2001; Pearson & Porath, 2004; Richman et al., 1999; Rospenda, 2002). Even employees who merely *observe* uncivil treatment (e.g., toward colleagues) show lower job satisfaction and commitment and greater job burnout and turnover intentions; such observer effects emerge even while controlling for negative affectivity, so they cannot be attributed to a negative dispositional stance making observers more attuned to negative stimuli in their environments (Miner-Rubino & Cortina, 2006). These adverse individual and collective consequences have financial implications for employers, who must absorb the costs of employee distraction and discontentment, job accidents, substance abuse, sick leave, work team conflict, productivity decline, and turnover.

Explaining how such a "low-grade" phenomenon as incivility can have such widespread consequences, my colleagues and I (Cortina & Magley, 2004; Cortina et al., 2001) have asserted that many uncivil work behaviors fall into the category of *daily hassles*—that is, routine nuisances of everyday life (e.g., Lazarus, 1999; Lazarus & Folkman, 1984). Daily hassles lack the drama and intensity of *major life events*. Nevertheless, chronic, low-key stressors that repeat over time can "wear down" an individual, both psychologically and physically (e.g., Wheaton, 1997). Moreover, targeted employees may have difficulty developing effective means of coping with and controlling such ambiguous phenomena. Hopelessness and resignation may result (Deitch et al., 2004). Following Richman and colleagues' (1996; Rospenda, 2002) reasoning, personnel might also find interpersonal hostility highly unexpected and unnecessary in the work environment (in contrast to task-based stressors, which might seem more routine and therefore more tolerable in that context). For all of these reasons, daily interpersonal stressors at work can accumulate to have a greater impact on psychological and health outcomes than major time-limited disturbances (e.g., Cortina & Magley, 2004; Cortina et al., 2001; Deitch et al., 2004; Lazarus, 1999; Lazarus & Folkman, 1984).

In sum, prior research has laid important foundations in defining incivility, delineating its impact, and articulating its relationship to other categories of *generalized* hostility in the workplace. Questions remain about how incivility relates to *specific* forms of workplace mistreatment, such as that based on sex and race.[1] Incivility, sexual harassment, and racial harassment share certain features, all entailing behaving in an antisocial way; degrading, offending, or intimidating targets; and violating standards of interpersonal respect. In addition, similar motivations may drive these different forms of abuse, such as instigators' pursuit of social power/dominance, disregard for authority and norms, desire for valued resources, self-presentational goals, and value differences with the target (Andersson & Pearson, 1999; Buchanan, 2005; Cleveland & Kerst, 1993; Deitch et al., 2004; James, Lovato, & Khoo, 1994; Lim & Cortina, 2005; O'Leary-Kelly, Paetzold, & Griffin, 2000; Pearson & Porath, 2004; Sanchez & Brock, 1996; Schneider, Hitlan, & Radhakrishnan, 2000; Thacker & Ferris, 1991).

In addition, perhaps incivility, sexual harassment, and racial harassment are, at times, one and the same. This may seem illogical, given that incivility is facially neutral by definition. That is, "generally" uncivil behaviors have no overt reference to gender, race, or other social category. This nevertheless does not rule out the possibility that incivility sometimes represents *covert* manifestations of gender and racial bias in the workplace. The theory advanced in this article will elucidate this possibility. Such *selective incivility* could be one mechanism by which gender and racial disparities persist in organizations, despite concerted legislative, judicial, and organizational efforts to eradicate bias.

Contemporary Perspectives On Discrimination

The last four decades have seen sweeping changes in antidiscrimination laws, practices, and ideologies in the United States. Owing to Title VII of the Civil Rights Act of 1964 and related reforms, blatant employment discrimination based on gender and race (among other factors) has become illegal. Women and people of color now enjoy much greater access to occupational and economic opportunities than in the past. Along with these tangible changes, attitudes toward women's paid employment, and white attitudes toward ethnic minorities, have become more positive, tolerant, and accepting. Public expression of sexist and racist beliefs has undergone a radical decline (Benokraitis, 1997; Brief & Barsky, 2000; Brief et al., 1997, 2000; Brief & Hayes, 1997; Dipboye & Halverson, 2004; Dovidio & Gaertner, 1998; Dovidio, Gaertner, & Bachman, 2001; Operario & Fiske, 1998; Swim, Aikin, Hall, & Hunter, 1995; Tougas, Brown, Beaton, & Joly, 1995). The importance of these changes cannot be overstated.

In spite of progress, gender and racial disparities endure in American organizations, particularly at the highest levels, where power is most concentrated (e.g., Benokraitis, 1997; Brief et al., 1997; Brief & Hayes, 1997; Pettigrew & Martin, 1987; Valian, 1998). This is true across a range of industries, from the military to the federal government to the Fortune 500 (Dovidio, Gaertner, & Bachman, 2001). According to Census and Department of Labor statistics, women and ethnic/racial minorities still receive less pay, face greater unemployment, and work in lower-status jobs than their white male counterparts; this remains true even after controlling for education, experience, and skill level (Brief et al., 1997; Dipboye & Halverson, 2004). In 2002 the Equal Employment Opportunity Commission (EEOC) received 84,442 complaints of employment discrimination; two out of every three allegations were based on either gender or race (U.S. Equal Employment Opportunity Commission, 2003). Illustrating the striking persistence of these forms of bias, Benokraitis (1997) noted that, in the mid 1990s, white men constituted one-third of the U.S. population. At the same time, they made up "85% of tenured professors, 85% of partners in law firms, 80% of the U.S. House of Representatives, 90% of the U.S. Senate, 95% of Fortune 500 CEOs . . . and 100% of all US presidents" (1997: 5).

One might wonder how discrimination could be so robust against several decades of legal, organizational, and attitudinal reform. Some suggest that these changes may have been effective in reducing blatant or "old-fashioned" discrimination, but *subtle* discrimination lives on in the world of work (e.g., Benokraitis, 1997; Brief & Barsky, 2000; Brief, Buttram, Elliott, Reizenstein, & McCline, 1995; Deitch et al., 2004; Dipboye & Halverson, 2004). In fact, contemporary antifemale and antiminority bias is sometimes so ambiguous that instigators are unaware of its discriminatory nature, and they typically have rational, nondiscriminatory explanations for their conduct. As Dipboye and Halverson explain, "Much of today's discrimination takes a more subtle form and has slipped out of the light into the dark side of the organization" (2004: 132).

The ambiguity inherent in subtle discrimination makes it particularly difficult for targets and managers to recognize, much less control. Meyerson and Fletcher compellingly summarize this situation as it relates to gender:

> As we enter the year 2000, the glass ceiling remains. What will it take to finally shatter it? Not a revolution . . . the women's movement [once] used radical rhetoric and legal action to drive out overt discrimination, but most of the barriers that persist today are insidious—a revolution couldn't find them to blast away. Rather, gender discrimination now is so deeply embedded in organizational life as to be virtually indiscernible. Even the women who feel its impact are often hard-pressed to know what hit them (2000: 127).

Similar arguments can be made for persistent but subtle racial bias in the workplace. The glass ceiling holds strong in contemporary organizations, impeding women and employees of color from advancing to the same levels and at the same rates as their white male contemporaries. Moreover, "glass walls" keep women and minorities confined to certain occupational categories (Brief & Barsky, 2000; Rowe, 1990). These concealed barriers likely take many forms, one of which may be selective incivility. Theories of *modern discrimination* explain how and why this might be the case.

To account for persistent gender and racial inequalities in the United States, social psychologists have identified various forms of modern discrimination. In the realm of race relations, these concepts include *aversive racism* (Dovidio & Gaertner, 1998; Gaertner & Dovidio, 1986), *symbolic racism* (Sears, 1988, 1998), and *modern racism* (Brief et al., 2000; McConahay, 1986; McConahay & Hough, 1976). The gender bias literature refers to similar phenomena, such as *modern sexism* (Swim, Scott, Sechrist, Campbell, & Stangor, 1995), *neosexism* (Tougas et al., 1995), and *contemporary sexism* (Jackson, Esses, & Burris, 2001). Although each conceptualization

of contemporary discrimination is slightly different, the mythologies behind the behaviors are well-represented by McConahay's depiction of modern racism against blacks:

> The principal tenets of modern racism are these: (1) Discrimination is a thing of the past because Blacks now have the freedom to compete in the marketplace and to enjoy those things they can afford. (2) Blacks are pushing too hard, too fast, and into places where they are not wanted. (3) These tactics and demands are unfair. (4) Therefore, recent gains are undeserved and the prestige granting institutions of society are giving Blacks more attention and the concomitant status than they deserve (1986: 92–93).

Modern racists see these views as empirical fact rather than opinion or racist ideology. In fact, they ostensibly endorse egalitarian values, publicly condemn racism, and strongly identify themselves as nonprejudiced. This explicit rejection of overt bias—combined with implicit antiminority (or antifemale) beliefs—yields subtle, often unintentional and unconscious forms of discrimination. However, to maintain an egalitarian identity, modern racists only engage in discrimination when there is a plausible, non-racial (or nongendered) explanation for the differential treatment—for instance, a business justification. Absent a reasonable, nonprejudiced rationale for disparate conduct, discrimination does not manifest (Brief et al., 1995, 1997, 2000; James, Brief, Dietz, & Cohen, 2001; McConahay, 1986; McConahay & Hough, 1976). This allows the would-be instigators to protect themselves from charges of racism.

Contemporary forms of bias are distinct from "old-fashioned" sexism and racism, characterized by blatant antipathy, beliefs that women and people of color are inherently inferior, endorsement of pejorative stereotypes, and support for open acts of discrimination. Such antiquated beliefs and overtly discriminatory conduct are becoming less and less common (Brief et al., 1997; Dovidio & Gaertner, 1998; McConahay, 1986; McConahay & Hough, 1976; Sears, 1988, 1998; Swim et al., 1995; Tougas et al., 1995). For this reason, scholars are beginning to recognize that

> singular attention to major discriminatory acts in the workplace is insufficient for explaining the experience of discrimination many minority members experience on the job, and may be an increasingly inadequate research focus in the future as the social and political landscape shifts toward newer forms of racism and discrimination (Deitch et al., 2003: 1300–1301).

Different theories have emerged about the developmental history of modern discrimination. One is that this "second-generation" form of bias has recently arisen to replace old-fashioned sexism and racism, now deemed undesirable and, at times, unlawful (Benokraitis & Feagin, 1995; Brief et al., 1997; Forbes, Adams-Curtis, & White, 2004; Pettigrew & Martin, 1987; Tougas et al., 1995). A second argument is that prejudice has had a long history in our society, persisting over time in different manifestations, as affected by each sociohistorical moment. An elaborated version of this hypothesis is that negative attitudes toward women and ethnic minorities have continued despite social pressure to renounce prejudice; rather than going away, the negative attitudes become stored in memory and change from explicit to implicit (Dovidio, Gaertner, Kawakami, & Hodson, 2002). A final possibility is that subtle, unintentional, unconscious forms of discrimination are not new; what may be new is their visibility, now that blatant discrimination no longer overshadows them. Regardless of their developmental trajectory, prejudice and discrimination seem to be alive and well in the contemporary American workplace.

Research has identified various factors that fuel discrimination, including cognition, affect, and the organizational and societal context. Some of these same driving forces could also underlie discriminatory forms of workplace incivility, so here I highlight studies of each category of antecedent. The resulting model follows recent multilevel trends in the organizational sciences (e.g., Klein & Kozlowski, 2000), attending to influences at the level of the individual, the organization, and society. The review below is intended to be illustrative rather than exhaustive—to demonstrate how scholarship on bias and discrimination can inform science and practice related to incivility in organizations. Figure 1 displays a conceptual model of the ideas that follow.

Person-Level Explanations

Research on modern discrimination has primarily attended to intraindividual cognitive and affective events that drive a person to discriminate.

Cognition

Theories of social cognition lie at the heart of the literature on modern discrimination, which focuses in particular on categorization and stereotyping. *Social categorization* refers to the cognitive process by which our minds place people into social categories based on salient cues, such as gender, race, and age. This is argued to be a natural, automatic, and often unconscious process. This process has various benefits: easing the cognitive burden, simplifying perception and judgment, and helping us make sense of an intricate social environment. Without social categorization, the complexity of person perception would be overwhelming (e.g., Devine & Monteith, 1999; Dovidio, Gaertner, & Bachman, 2001; Fiske, 2000; Jones, 2002; Operario & Fiske, 1998; Stone, Stone, & Dipboye, 1992).

Categorization of a person into a particular group often triggers *stereotypes*—that is, prevalent and overgeneralized knowledge, beliefs, and expectancies about members of that social category (e.g., Hilton & von Hipple, 1996; Jones, 2002; Miller & Turnbull, 1986; Stone et al., 1992). In short, stereotypes are the "cultural baggage" that social categories carry (Operario & Fiske,

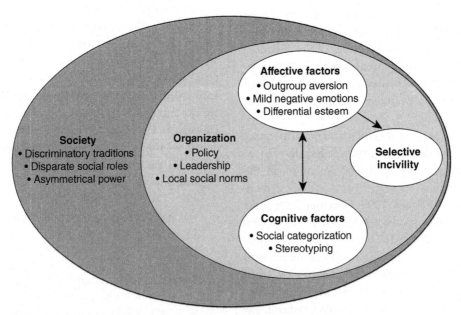

Figure 1 Integrated Model of Incivility As Modern Discrimination in Organizations.

1998: 40). They allow perceivers to understand (often inaccurately) and make predictions about others, averting the onerous task of learning in-depth details about each individual encountered. Indeed, we tend not to seek further personal information after placing someone into a social category, instead basing impression formation largely on stereotypes associated with that category (e.g., Operario & Fiske, 1998; Stone et al., 1992).

Stereotypes come in explicit and implicit varieties. *Explicit* stereotypes operate at the conscious level and occur with intention, effort, awareness, and control. Attitudes and stereotypes can also be *implicit*, however, occurring unintentionally, unconsciously, and effortlessly (e.g., Banaji & Dasgupta, 1998; Baron & Banaji, 2006; Devine, 1989; Devine & Monteith, 1999; Greenwald & Banaji, 1995; Jones, 2002; Valian, 1998). The implicit variant of stereotyping is particularly implicated in modern discrimination. That is, a modern sexist or racist unknowingly applies negative stereotypes to women and people of color, which can lead the stereotyper to mistreat members of these social groups. However, the mistreatment only arises in situations when there is a plausible, nonprejudiced explanation for the behavior so that the instigator can maintain a nondiscriminatory self-image.

Stereotypes of outgroup members can also be "ambivalent," containing both positive and negative elements. That is, they need not reflect uniform antipathy or contempt. Across years of stereotyping research (e.g., Allport, 1954; Fiske, Cuddy, Glick, & Xu, 2002; Glick & Fiske, 1999, 2001), scholars have identified two core stereotype dimensions: warmth and competence. Some groups are the object of benevolent or paternalistic stereotypes, being perceived as warm but generally incompetent; these include housewives, the elderly, and the disabled. Others, in contrast, are seen as low in warmth but (overly) high in competence, so they are targeted with a more hostile, envious stereotype; these groups include black professionals, career women, and Asians. Hostility toward these "envied" outgroups becomes amplified when they achieve success, status, and power, posing a competitive threat to the ingroup.

Affect

Some scholars claim that, compared to stereotypic cognition, prejudice is the better predictor of discriminatory behavior (Fiske, 2000). Prejudice refers specifically to an affective reaction to people solely because of their membership in a specific social category. Particularly relevant are the categories of ingroup and out-group. That is, social categorization processes lead all people to categorize others as "one of us" versus "one of them." This gives rise to positive affective biases toward ingroup members, coupled with negative feelings toward individuals in the outgroup (Fiske, 2002; Jones, 2002; Operario & Fiske, 1998).

The negative affect toward the outgroup can take different forms, not simply amounting to a homogeneous feeling of contempt. For example, research by Fiske and colleagues (2002) has shown that people tend to feel "paternalistic prejudice" toward groups stereotyped as warm but incompetent; this prejudice entails a strong sense of pity, without admiration or envy. Groups stereotyped as cold but competent conjure up the opposite emotional profile: envy and admiration, but little pity. Regarding these latter findings, Fiske et al. wrote that "admiration for high-competence out-groups ... coexisted with envy, suggesting a volatile mix of emotions that could create hostility when groups feel threatened" (2002: 897).

Diffuse, unconscious antifemale and antiminority feelings are thought to underlie modern discrimination (McConahay, 1986; McConahay & Hough, 1976; Sears, 1988, 1998; Swim et al., 1995; Tougas et al., 1995). Dovidio, Gaertner, and Bachman (2001) have emphasized the subtlety of these negative emotions in aversive racists, who experience mild fear, disgust, uneasiness, and indifference when they encounter ethnic minorities. This contrasts with "the open flame of racial hatred" that fuels traditional racism (2001: 419). In addition, Jackson and colleagues (2001: 49) have shown that an important component of contemporary sexism is greater feelings of esteem (i.e., respect) for men than women—a differential, affective "gut reaction" to social groups. Because this visceral response toward members of particular social groups is outside conscious awareness and control, modern sexists and racists can maintain a nonprejudiced self-concept.

Situational Explanations

A complete understanding of workplace discrimination requires attention to the surrounding context—at the level of both the immediate organization and the larger society. These contexts provide the proximal and distal backdrops of discriminatory cognitions, emotions, and behaviors in the workplace. The shaded, concentric ovals surrounding the model in Figure 1 convey the pervasive influence of context on all aspects of this process. In social psychological research on modern discrimination, scholars have, to some extent, discussed the societal context, so this review of situational factors begins there. Next will come the workplace context, which is discussed more in the organizational sciences.

Societal context

All organizations operate within a larger society/culture, which certainly affects the unfolding of discrimination.

Historically speaking, racism and sexism have a long tradition in American history, and people tend to internalize the values and beliefs of their culture. Not long ago in this country, women were denied the right to vote, own property, and matriculate in many institutions of higher education; employers could openly fire or refuse to hire women solely on the basis of their gender. Likewise, "the periods of slavery and Jim Crow forced African Americans, unlike any other ethnic group, into a legalized second-class citizenship for over 300 years" (Sears, 1998: 79). Other U.S. ethnic minority groups have also encountered oppression in policies of mass internment, forced expulsion from their homelands, discriminatory immigration practices, and antimiscege-nation laws (Operario & Fiske, 1998).

Although many of these overt discriminatory practices have since been abandoned, the structure of society remains such that men and whites tend to occupy different social roles than women (Eagly & Steffen, 1984; Eagly & Wood, 1999) and ethnic minorities (Dovidio, Gaertner, & Bachman, 2001; Sears, 1998), which helps to sustain stereotypes. Moreover, people growing up in the United States still encounter stereotypic imagery in cartoons, books, films, and other cultural media (Brief & Barsky, 2000; Fiske, 2002; Operario & Fiske, 1998). This social heritage maintains prejudice against women and people of color. It also follows individuals into their places of work: "Employees come to the organization with heavy cultural and social baggage obtained from interactions in other social contexts" (Scott, 1992: 20).

The structure of society also perpetuates unequal distributions of power, and asymmetrical power combined with prejudice sets the stage for oppression. Powerful people often seek to preserve the status quo in order to bolster their own status, maintain access to valued resources, and increase personal and collective self-esteem (Dovidio, Gaertner, & Bachman, 2001; Fiske, 1993, 2000, 2001, 2002; Jones, 2002; Operario & Fiske, 1998; Tajfel & Turner, 1986). Power also gives individuals at the top of the social structure the tools to translate their biases into discriminatory conduct. With respect to race, Operario and Fiske argue that "prejudice alone does not determine racism; everyone has prejudices, because all people prefer their group over others. History and society confer power to certain groups, granting them excessive ability to exercise their prejudice" (1998: 49). In contrast, powerlessness necessitates dependence on and acquiescence to the demands of the powerful (Fiske, 1993; Jones, 2002; Operario & Fiske, 1998). These social structural forces provide prime conditions for discrimination to thrive, in ways both blatant and subtle.

Organizational context

Turning now to the more immediate context, the organizational environment should play an important role in either enabling or inhibiting discrimination. It is also a level of context that seems particularly malleable—more so than the social structural context, given the difficulties inherent in effecting change at the broad societal level. However, social psychologists have largely ignored the workplace in studies of modern discrimination. The focus of this review therefore now switches to field research in organizational psychology. This literature suggests that several features of the work environment are especially relevant to discrimination: policy, leadership, and group norms.

Many U.S. organizations presently have policies that reflect Title VII of the Civil Rights Act of 1964—protecting certain classes of employees (including women and personnel of color) from discrimination or harassment based on social category membership. Numerous scholars, however, emphasize that a good policy is necessary but not sufficient to inhibit discriminatory and antisocial work behavior; consistent *enforcement* of that policy is paramount (e.g., O'Leary-Kelly et al., 2000; Riger, 1991; Williams, Fitzgerald, & Drasgow, 1999). To implement policies effectively, strong leaders must be present.

Leaders set the tone for the entire organization, and employees look to them for cues about what constitutes acceptable conduct. Organizations tend to have fewer problems with (blatant) discrimination when their authority figures establish clear expectations for respectful behavior, model nondiscriminatory values and conduct, take discrimination complaints seriously, and sanction those who discriminate. Arguments and evidence supporting this claim have emerged particularly in studies of sexual harassment (e.g., Fitzgerald, Drasgow, Hulin, Gelfand, & Magley, 1997; Hulin, Fitzgerald, & Drasgow, 1996; O'Leary-Kelly et al., 2000; Pryor, Giedd, & Williams, 1995; Williams et al., 1999). In a similar vein, organizational authorities can send messages to employees that either promote or inhibit racial discrimination (Brief et al., 1995, 1997, 2000).

Another feature of the organizational context that can influence discrimination is its local social norms (Dipboye & Halverson, 2004). The need for belonging and acceptance by ingroup members is a powerful motivator for human behavior (e.g., Baumeister & Leary, 1995; Fiske, 2000), including organizational behavior (Williams, 1998; Williams & Sommer, 1997). In fact, personnel often work in groups or teams, facing pressure to conform to group norms. Even without a formal "team" structure, many organizations foster a psychological sense of community, and informal social norms arise (Heller, 1989; Pretty & MacCarthy, 1991; Sarason,

1974). Group norms "not only define reality for group members but also communicate how members can obtain the approval and avoid the criticisms of fellow group members" (Dipboye & Halverson, 2004: 145). As a result of these group processes, people adapt their cognitions, emotions, and behaviors to fit better into the social world of work. Thus, when coworkers convey expectations for or model biased behavior, an employee is more likely to follow suit and engage in discrimination (Brief et al., 2000; Robinson & O'Leary-Kelly, 1998).

Person-Situation Interactional Explanations

With a few exceptions, the organizational context literature reviewed above focuses primarily on overt discrimination. Drawing on Dipboye and Halverson's (2004) reasoning, we find that the picture becomes more complicated when we consider how the organizational environment might influence *covert* discrimination. The organization's implicit or explicit support for discrimination (as indicated by lax enforcement or absence of a nondiscrimination policy, permissive leader behavior, and sexist or racist norms) could create an immediate social context that promotes discriminatory conduct. However, employees bring their own personal convictions and affective tendencies to that context. The result is a person-by-situation interaction that determines whether or not discriminatory behavior occurs and, if it does, whether it is overt versus covert and implicit versus explicit. Figure 2 summarizes how person and situation factors jointly influence discriminatory behavior.

As Figure 2 demonstrates, when we cross the organizational context and individual tendencies, (at least) four different behavioral possibilities emerge. The lower left quadrant represents the ideal situation: a nonbiased individual works for an organization that, likewise, does not permit biased conduct; that employee will likely not discriminate against women and minorities. Even if the employee unconsciously endorses negative beliefs or feelings toward female or minority coworkers, a strong anti-discriminatory context should prevent that person from acting on his or her implicit biases (Brief et al., 2000).

The opposite situation appears in the upper right quadrant: when a biased employee works for a bias-tolerant company, the likelihood of overt discrimination (e.g., sexual and racial harassment) is high. This employee may be fully aware of and open about the biased nature of his or her conduct, and the organization does not motivate the individual to restrain his or her prejudices.

Note that in both of these situations the individual's approach (pro or con) to bias is in line with that of the organizational environment. A different picture emerges in the case of individuals whose feelings and beliefs about discrimination are in conflict with those advanced by the organization (Dipboye & Halverson, 2004). This disconnect fosters ideal conditions for covert discrimination.

The lower right quadrant of Figure 2 portrays a situation in which a biased employee works for an organization that deters discriminatory conduct. Motivation to avoid sanctions, to remain in the organization, and to fit in with the workgroup could inhibit the employee from expressing visible bias (i.e., no blatant sexual or racial harassment). However, these organizational influences might only drive discrimination "underground." In other words, in lieu of open, overt acts of hostility, the employee may express personal biases against female coworkers and colleagues of color covertly (Dipboye & Halverson, 2004). Concealing discrimination in this way could be a conscious choice on the part of the employee.

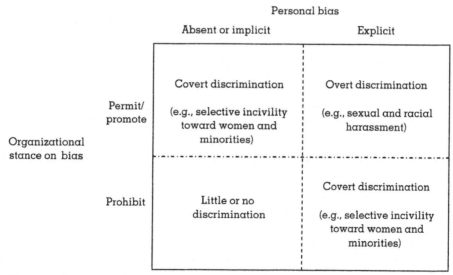

Figure 2 Person-by-Organization Influences on Discriminatory Behavior.

The upper left quadrant applies to two different types of employees, although the behavioral outcome is the same. In one situation an employee with no implicit or explicit biases against women and minorities works for an organization in which there is pressure (e.g., from peers) to engage in sexist or racist behavior. Assuming that the employee is motivated to remain with the organization (e.g., for financial or professional reasons), the conflict between the individual and the immediate context may yield discrimination that is quite subtle. That is, the person is ideologically opposed to sexism and racism and therefore unlikely to engage knowingly in overtly discriminatory behavior. This person, however, spends forty (or more) hours per week working in an antifemale and/or anti-minority climate. His or her fundamental need for belonging, acceptance, and security could foster covert discrimination against women and/or colleagues of color, as a means of "fitting in" in the discriminatory environment. The biased conduct would need to be subtle and rationalizable, and perhaps even unconscious, for the employee to maintain an unbiased self-image.

A second possibility for the upper left quadrant is that an employee self-identifies as non-prejudiced but implicitly harbors negative thoughts and feelings toward women or people of color. This person also works in a context that is in some way antifemale or antiminority. This environment permits and perhaps even encourages the employee to act on implicit biases, but explicit discrimination (e.g., sexual or racial harassment) would be aversive to his or her egalitarian identity. Instead of overtly discriminating against undervalued social groups, the employee could disproportionately target them with negative behavior that is too subtle and facially neutral to appear biased. This antisocial conduct would be a concealed, unintentional, unconscious form of discrimination (Dipboye & Halverson, 2004).

Workplace Incivility As Modern Discrimination

How might social psychological concepts of modern/covert/aversive discrimination inform our understanding of incivility in the workplace? These theories suggest different paths to selective incivility. In one case reasonable, forward-thinking, tolerant employees unknowingly target women and minorities with disproportionate incivility, despite being explicitly opposed to sexism and racism. That is, the employees' *implicitly* stereotypic attitudes, preference for ingroup members, motivation to maintain social power, and so forth could give rise to subtle biases against the outgroup. Lax antidiscrimination policies,

permissive leadership behavior, and antisocial models in the workplace could set the stage for employees to act on those biases. Cultural traditions of sexism, racism, and asymmetrical power compound the situation. These instigators might have plausible, nonracial, and nongendered explanations for the uncivil conduct (e.g., "I didn't see you," "I'm having a bad day," "I thought you were done speaking")—explanations that they themselves believe.

In other cases selective incivility might not be so innocent, because "some people may be particularly motivated to think in stereotypic ways and may use controlled processing to promote stereotype use" (Devine & Monteith, 1999: 356, note 1). For example, an employee may consciously experience blatant antipathy toward women and minorities and make no attempt to prevent it from influencing his or her behavior toward coworkers, but may hide prejudice behind the guise of "general" incivility. This attempt at concealment may be particularly likely if a biased employee works in an organization with strong nondiscrimination policies and norms, enforced by strong leaders. Overt disrespect (e.g., harassment) of women and minorities would not be tolerated in such a context, so the employee must find more discreet and rationalizable methods of expressing bias; selective incivility is one means toward this end. That is, bias may emerge in the form of low-level deviance that, absent any overtly sexist or racist content, can be attributed to something less objectionable than prejudice (e.g., instigator oversight, personality, work overload). In this example the employee can explain the conduct in a way that has nothing to do with gender or race, but this would be a deceitful "cover-up" for bias.

A third scenario could be that an employee has strong egalitarian values, both explicit and implicit, but works alongside coworkers who express sexism and racism on a regular basis. The employee is caught in a quandary: not going along with the biased conduct could lead to ostracism from the peer group, which constitutes a significant part of the employee's social world, but participating in blatantly biased behavior would be antithetical to the employee's values and, thus, highly aversive. One means of solving this dilemma would be to target women and people of color with subtle disrespect—that is, incivility. The discriminatory nature of this conduct would fit in with group norms, and the low-level (possibly unconscious) nature of the deviance might be tolerable for the instigator, who prides him or herself on being nonsexist and nonracist.

Given the theories and scenarios reviewed above, I propose that incivility is not always an "equal opportunity" form of antisocial work behavior. Specifically, in many organizations women and ethnic minority employees likely experience more uncivil treatment than men and whites. This should be especially true for organizations that lack strong nondiscrimination policies, have leaders who turn a blind eye to (or even model) antifemale and antiminority conduct, and employ individuals who openly express bias.

In many cases disproportionate incivility toward women and people of color would likely comprise the most ambiguous forms of disrespectful conduct (e.g., interrupting an employee, failing to include an employee in professional camaraderie, ignoring an employee). These subtle behaviors could be attributed to many factors other than race or gender (e.g., instigator oversight, target hypersensitivity), making it particularly difficult to label them as discriminatory. They are thus means by which personnel can mistreat women and people of color while maintaining a nonprejudiced image to themselves and others. The apparent neutrality of this behavior could avert disciplinary actions related to Title VII violation.

It could be, however, that more transparent forms of incivility (e.g., rumor spreading, accusations of incompetence, anger outbursts) would *not* show intergroup differences. These behaviors, when targeted at female and minority employees disproportionately, might be perceived as sexist or racist, which would be aversive to the instigator's egalitarian self-concept. This might also trigger organizational or legal sanctions. Therefore, it makes sense that many instigators (those who want to avoid penalties or labels as sexist/racist) would refrain from blatant forms of discriminatory disrespect.

This profile of findings would be highly consistent with modern understandings of discrimination. For example, *aversive racism theory* (e.g., Dovidio & Gaertner, 1998; Dovidio, Gaertner, & Bachman, 2001; Dovidio, Gaertner, Niemann, & Snider, 2001) suggests that discrimination will not emerge in situations where the discriminatory nature of the conduct is apparent, either to the instigator or others. This is because "aversive racists" consciously endorse values of egalitarianism and justice and condemn prejudice both internally and externally. However, these same individuals implicitly harbor negative emotions and cognitions toward minorities, driving them to discriminate in subtle or rationalizable ways. That is, they discriminate (1) when the biased nature of the behavior is not obvious or (2) when a negative response can be attributed to something other than race. Both of these descriptions fit many manifestations of workplace incivility.

From the target's perspective, who would be most at risk for selective incivility? According to theories of ambivalent stereotyping (e.g., Fiske et al., 2002; Glick & Fiske, 1999, 2001) and intergroup competition (e.g., Jackman, 1994), the most vulnerable might be professionally and economically successful women and minorities—those who are perceived as highly competent and advancing in ways that threaten the dominant majority. This is based on research showing that successful outgroups, such as black professionals, Asians, career women, business women, and feminists, are often stereotyped as (too) competent, ambitious, and hardworking and, at the same time, interpersonally unpleasant and cold. This can trigger admiration to some extent, but also envy and hostile competition from the dominant majority. Again, though, to avoid appearances of racism and sexism, the hostility may often take a disguised form, such as selective incivility.

Evidence From The Target's Perspective

The theories reviewed above explain forces that may promote incivility as a covert form of modern discrimination against undervalued social groups. But is there any empirical evidence to this effect? With workplace incivility being a new area of inquiry, the empirical record on this topic remains limited. Several studies do, however, suggest that gender bias may underlie some manifestations of incivility. Fewer data are available on race and incivility, but findings from one study do suggest potential racial bias.

Starting first with incivility as subtle sexism, qualitative data suggest that incivility and gender bias are often one and the same. Specifically, my colleagues and I (Cortina et al., 2002) examined the interpersonal experiences of 4,608 attorneys practicing in the federal courts. Respondents who had indicated any recent encounter with workplace incivility were asked to provide brief descriptions of the uncivil conduct that had had the greatest impact on them. Many women detailed experiences of incivility that they attributed to gender, despite the mistreatment not being explicitly gendered on its face. Some of the behaviors described represented more overt, active, direct forms of disrespect:

> Male judges and attorneys tend to cut short, ignore, or exclude female attorneys.
>
> There is still a big gap in how women attorneys are treated by male attorneys: extremely aggressive behavior in depositions; failure to listen; repeated interruptions in all contexts.
>
> A court clerk apparently did not believe that I was an attorney even though I had been sitting at counsel table for two weeks of the trial. He treated me rudely and kept me from getting exhibits in order in a document-intensive case. I believe this occurred because I am a young-looking female.

More often, though, the disproportionately uncivil treatment of women was more subtle, indirect, and perhaps unintentional and unconscious:

> I was plaintiff's counsel on a motion, but the magistrate spoke exclusively to the male defense counsel and deferred to him throughout the in-chamber hearing. Magistrate treated me like I wasn't in the room.
>
> The person in charge of the settlement program . . . refused to speak to me in that conference, and would only address my male co-counsel, even though I had identified myself as lead counsel.
>
> The bankruptcy bar . . . is rather small and exclusive. To be young and female is to be discounted and ignored and makes it very difficult to establish yourself. I hated my first 5 years of practice because of it. Good thing I'm tough.

These previously unpublished quotes illustrate how incivility can represent gender discrimination (and sometimes age discrimination) of a less blatant type. The last examples are consistent with the form of bias that Fiske (2002: 125) calls "cool neglect," or withholding "basic liking and respect" rather than being openly hostile.

The Cortina et al. (2002) study is particularly well-suited to testing the theory articulated above. The participants were female attorneys, who would elicit the "career woman" (and sometimes "feminist") stereotype, which includes high competence but low warmth (e.g., Fiske et al., 2002; Glick & Fiske, 1999, 2001). These women are making inroads into a prestigious profession that was once exclusively the province of men. Men, as members of the dominant majority,[2] may feel a sense of threat, competition, and hostility toward these outgroup members who are "encroaching" on their terrain. In some cases men could justify uncivil behavior as part of their job, which mandates "zealous advocacy" for clients. Note, however, that opposing counsel were not the only instigators of incivility in these narratives, since the rude behavior also came from judges, court clerks, and other court personnel. Behavior from these various sources cannot be attributed to trial strategy or the adversarial model of justice.

Corroborating these qualitative findings, quantitative research also suggests gender differences in the experience of incivility. Specifically, the Cortina et al. (2002) attorney study also included a survey, in which more women (65 percent) than men (47 percent) described recent experiences of "general incivility" in the context of their work. This gender difference echoes the results of Björkqvist, Österman, and Hjelt-Bäck (1994), who reported that 55 percent of female compared to 30 percent

of male university employees had faced "work harassment" during the previous six months. Likewise, in a survey (Cortina et al., 2001) of 1,180 court employees, women described greater frequencies of incivility than did their male colleagues.

The gender differences just reported were based on composite measures of workplace incivility, making it difficult to pinpoint which types of incivility are more prone to being discriminatory. Extending these findings, my colleagues and I (Cortina et al., 2004) have provided in-depth evidence of both gender- and race-based disparities in the experience of specific uncivil behaviors. Our results were based on survey data from two organizations: (1) a city government in which women have a strong presence and (2) a law enforcement agency that employs sizable numbers of ethnic minorities. With some exceptions, women and ethnic minorities reported more frequent encounters with specific uncivil behaviors at work, compared respectively to men and whites. Gender and racial differences were particularly large for the most *ambiguous* behaviors (e.g., "ignored you or failed to speak to you [e.g., 'the silent treatment']," "doubted your judgment on a matter over which you had responsibility," "withheld information that you needed to do your job correctly," "failed to give you an award or recognition you deserved"). Many of these ambiguous and "withholding" behaviors could be attributed to instigator oversight or target hypersensitivity, making it difficult to label them as prejudiced. These behaviors are thus means by which employees may disproportionately target women and minorities with disrespect while maintaining a nonprejudiced self-image.

In contrast, we (Cortina et al., 2004) did not find gender or racial differences in the experience of more *blatant* or overtly disrespectful behavior (e.g., "made jokes at your expense," "refused to work with you," "targeted you with anger outbursts or 'tempter tantrums'"). These behaviors, when targeted disproportionately at women and minorities, could be attributed to prejudice more readily, which could threaten instigators' self-concept and trigger sanctions from the employer or court system. Modern racists and sexists would likely want to avoid such outcomes.

New Directions For Research

These empirical studies support the theory of selective incivility advanced in this article. The findings are preliminary, however, elucidating only half of the incivility equation (the target's perspective) and rarely addressing issues of race. Thus, this theory and this evidence raise intriguing possibilities, to be addressed in future research on workplace intersections of incivility, sexism, and racism.

Generally speaking, research related to workplace incivility could benefit from stronger alliances with social psychology, and vice versa. Given the richness of social and organizational scholarship on discrimination, the independence of these two bodies of literature is striking. Both arenas offer novel concepts that could be mutually informative. They also tend to favor different paradigms: lab experiments dominate social psychological research, whereas surveys are more typical in the organizational sciences. Research informed by multiple conceptual traditions, diverse methodologies, and questions of both basic and applied significance could take studies of workplace incivility (and other discriminatory behaviors) down interesting new paths.

A second recommendation is that organizational researchers of antisocial work behaviors follow the model set by social, feminist, and cultural psychology and routinely engage issues of gender and race. This includes studies of not only incivility but also other forms of "general" interpersonal mistreatment: bullying (Hoel, Rayner, & Cooper, 1999), aggression (Baron, 2004; Neuman, 2004), interpersonal deviance (Robinson & Bennett, 1995), petty tyranny (Ashforth, 1994), social undermining (Duffy, Ganster, & Pagon, 2002), organizational retaliation behavior (Skarlicki & Folger, 1997), and counterproductive work behavior (Spector & Fox, 2002). To date, gender and race (and other social identities) have been largely absent from this literature. A few studies, reviewed above, have addressed gender and incivility, but there has been little discussion of incivility and *race*. Indeed, the neglect of race in the burgeoning literature on antisocial work behavior has persisted for much too long, perhaps owing to the fact that "it has become somewhat taboo to recognize the role of racism in contemporary American work organizations" (Brief & Hayes, 1997: 100). Importantly, this research should not require targets to have insight into the discriminatory nature of the conduct they face, owing to the inherent ambiguity of uncivil situations (Andersson & Pearson, 1999) and to employees' reluctance to identify as victims of prejudice (Magley, Hulin, Fitzgerald, & DeNardo, 1999).

Beyond targets, the perspective of instigators also deserves further scholarly attention. In fact, tests of the theory summarized in Figure 1 necessarily imply an instigator focus. This work will require innovative methods to avoid problems of socially desirable responding. In particular, research on aversive racism, neosexism, and so on shows that individuals responsible for these "modern" forms of discrimination strongly identify as nonprejudiced. In other words, they see their own behavior as reasonable, fair, and unbiased, so they would not openly admit to disproportionately targeting female and minority employees with uncivil conduct. It is therefore critical that we develop unobtrusive techniques for assessing selective incivility.

On another front, social psychologists interested in modern discrimination should consider the negative interpersonal behaviors discussed in the organizational literature (e.g., incivility, aggression, bullying, etc.) as potential behavioral vehicles for subtle sexism and racism. All of these actions appear, at face value, to have nothing to do with social categories, stereotypes, or prejudices. However, as this article illustrates, seemingly neutral insensitivity or aggression toward persons could, in many cases, serve as a convenient mask for unfair discrimination against *socially undervalued* persons. Studies of this possibility would help address a deficit that is often lamented in social psychology: little research in the bias literature directly assesses discriminatory behavior. This is a major problem, because "thoughts and feelings do not exclude, oppress, and kill people; behavior does" (Fiske, 2000: 312). Selective incivility is a specific behavior that could be the focus of novel social psychological research.

Questions may arise as to what methods may be most appropriate to launch this line of inquiry. Scholars interested in the antecedents of incivility could use the social psychological experiment as one research tool, pinpointing the personal and social conditions under which individuals are most likely to disrespect others—particularly women and people of color. Techniques developed by organizational psychologists could also benefit social research on modern discrimination. Particularly promising for this purpose are new survey methods for assessing implicit motivation and cognition, such as the "conditional reasoning" paradigm (e.g., James, 1998; James & Mazerolle, 2003). In addition, organizational and social psychologists could collaboratively translate stereotype-control strategies developed in the laboratory into respectful-workplace initiatives, followed by evaluation of those initiatives in actual organizations. Finally, despite some discussion of societal influences on modern discrimination, empirical attention to this topic has been sparse. Cross-cultural methods of studying organizational behavior (e.g., Gelfand, Raver, & Ehrhart, 2002; Schaffer & Riordan, 2003) could allow us to understand how social structural forces impinge on bias in multinational organizations. These are just a few examples of how social and organizational psychologists—and management scholars from other disciplines—could pool their ideas and methodologies to advance research on incivility and discrimination in the modern workplace.

Implications For Policy and Practice

Nonspecific workplace mistreatment—in the absence of overtly sexual, sexist, or racist conduct—is not typically regarded as a Title VII violation. However, in this article I propose that employees may at times be differentially targeted with incivility *on the basis of their sex or race,* potentially creating disparate work environments across social groups. At the very least, this could interfere with the recruitment and retention of a diverse workforce; at worst, pervasive patterns of incivility toward protected classes of employees could expose the organization to legal liability. For these reasons it is critical that organizations and policy makers develop effective strategies for managing this disguised form of workplace discrimination.

Referring again to Figure 1, interventions are possible for every factor that fuels selective incivility, at the level of both person and context. Indeed, it is important that both levels be targeted, as Figure 2 illustrates. If explicit, internal bias persists in an individual working in a non-discriminatory context, the person may simply transmute the bias into covert, rationalizable forms of discrimination. Likewise, an employee who fundamentally opposes gender and race bias, but who works in discriminatory organizations, may give in to social pressures and discriminate covertly. Given that selective incivility has antecedents at multiple levels, it seems only logical that attempts to manage it also take a multilevel approach. Below is a discussion of person-level interventions, followed by societal and organizational actions.

Person-Level Interventions

To reduce the incidence of selective incivility, some might assume that interventions should primarily target the organizational context, with less hope for intrapersonal reform. However, the social psychology literature is replete with ideas on how to do both: modify the environment so as to influence individual cognition and affect, which could ultimately inhibit discriminatory behavior. These techniques could potentially be applied to the management of workplace incivility. A complete review of this literature is beyond the scope of this article, but I highlight several segments as an illustration.

The emphasis in stereotype scholarship on unconscious cognitive processes, unintentionality, and automaticity may give the false impression that organizational attempts at influencing social thought and emotion would be pointless. On the contrary, research shows that it is possible to intervene at the outset of these internal processes, manipulating perceivers' cognitive representations of their social worlds. Social categorization may be automatic, but social category boundaries—and the dimensions around which they organize—are far from fixed. Thus, it is possible to broaden peoples' conceptions of who belongs to their ingroup. This can foster more positive, respectful attitudes and behavior toward individuals formerly perceived as out-group members.

To give a concrete example of this, Gaertner and Dovidio (2000) developed the *common ingroup identity model.* This intervention shifts conceptions of social group membership from many separate groups to a more inclusive, superordinate group. Experimental and field studies support the model, with the superordinate identity created using a range of strategies (e.g., spatially integrating people, creating a common group name, implementing joint evaluation and reward systems) in a range of settings. The common group identity cultivates greater interdependence, cooperation, and respect among individuals who were formerly members of separate groups (e.g., Dovidio, Gaertner, & Bachman, 2001; Dovidio, Gaertner, Niemann, & Snider, 2001; Dovidio, Kawakami, & Gaertner, 2000; Gaertner & Dovidio, 2000).

Even when gender- or race-based social categorization occurs, it does not always yield stereotypic thought, emotion, and behavior. Despite being natural and automatic, stereotyping is not inevitable—it *can* occur automatically but does not *always* occur. For instance, people apparently do not engage in negative stereotypic thinking when they are motivated to endorse a positive judgment of the target. To demonstrate this, research shows that when an employee receives a positive evaluation by a member of a stereotyped group, the employee is motivated by self-interest to respect that person's opinion; stereotype activation does not occur (e.g., Devine & Monteith, 1999; Erber & Fiske, 1984; Neuberg & Fiske, 1987).

Moreover, when it does occur, stereotype *activation* does not unavoidably lead to stereotype *application.* Although a social perceiver may initially categorize a person and trigger a stereotype, the perceiver can be motivated to replace this automatic categorical processing with more controlled, intentional, individuated processing, and this can prevent a discriminatory behavioral response. For example, situations that involve high stakes, emphasize the need for accuracy, hold people accountable for their judgments, relax undue time pressures, or require cooperation to work toward shared goals give rise to individuated processing in lieu of stereotyping (e.g., Devine & Monteith, 1999; Dipboye & Halverson, 2004; Fiske, 2000, 2001, 2002; Greenwald & Banaji, 1995; Valian, 1998). In addition, learning and self-regulation processes can help individuals self-monitor and recognize situations in which they are susceptible to stereotyped responding; they can then interrupt stereotypic thinking, even if it is activated, and generate nondiscriminatory behavior (Brief & Barsky, 2000; Monteith, 1993). To quote Gordon Allport, social perceivers can sometimes "put the brakes on prejudice" (1954: 332).

Situational Interventions

Societal context. Legal frameworks make up an important piece of the fabric that holds civil society together. However, one might wonder whether existing law is relevant to uncivil work behavior: because a defining feature of incivility is that intentionality is ambiguous, does the absence of clear discriminatory intent remove legal liability? The issue of intent factors into some, but not all, legal definitions of discrimination. For example, in *McDonnel Douglas Corp. v. Green* (1973), the U.S. Supreme Court ruled that proof of intent to discriminate must be present before a behavior can be considered unlawful *intentional discrimination* or *disparate treatment.* However, in *Griggs v. Duke Power Co.* (1971), the Supreme Court also ruled that *unintentional discrimination* or *adverse impact* is also unlawful. In other words, if an organizational practice has differential, adverse effects on protected classes of employees, then that practice may be illegal, even if the effects are unintentional. Likewise, the U.S. Equal Employment Opportunity Commission (1993) has stated that practices that have the *effect* of interfering with work or creating a hostile work environment for women and racial minorities constitute unlawful sexual and racial harassment, respectively, regardless of the employer's intent. Thus, when workplace incivility is disproportionately targeted at women and minorities and interferes with their work and/or contributes to a hostile environment, this situation may violate law.

Despite potential legal implications, it is unclear whether legal grievance mechanisms present effective solutions to the problem of selective incivility. These mechanisms require the target to formally complain about the behavior, which may not be a realistic expectation. Employees generally have high thresholds for whistle-blowing (Miceli & Near, 1992), and isolated acts of subtle discrimination may not seem "severe" enough to warrant complaint (Dipboye & Halverson, 2004; Rowe, 1990). As Neuman notes, "How (and to whom) do you report having had your feelings hurt, and what reporting system captures the time you spend ruminating about the perceived mistreatment? Furthermore, would you believe that such an incident is serious enough to merit a formal report?" (2004: 74). Moreover, individual instances of misconduct may not appear discriminatory unless considered in the aggregate (Crosby, 1984; Crosby, Iyer, Clayton, & Downing, 2003; O'Leary-Kelly

et al., 2000), particularly compared to conduct targeted at men and whites.

Further reducing complaint likelihood, targets may experience attributional uncertainty about incivility—a low-level behavior that lacks clear intent (Andersson & Pearson, 1999) and has no overtly gendered or racial content (Lim & Cortina, 2005). They may have difficulty deciding whether they are experiencing general incivility or, rather, discrimination based on their social category membership (Cortina et al., 2002; Schneider et al., 2000). Even if they do suspect differential negative treatment, targets may still hesitate to label their instigators' behavior as discriminatory. This would imply that the instigators are prejudiced, which is generally seen as immoral or evil in the current political climate of this country. Thus, accusations of prejudice could embroil targets in emotionally charged, painful situations, which they would likely prefer to avoid (Monin & Miller, 2001; Swim et al., 2003). Given the subtlety and attributional uncertainty inherent in these situations, it is even less likely that incivility targets would file discrimination complaints with management.

In the rare cases when employees do come forward with reports of selective incivility, managers (or judges and juries) might not find such "minor," seemingly neutral misconduct worthy of reprimand. This may be especially true when instigators can provide a plausible, nonracial, nongendered account for their behavior. To make matters worse, some research suggests that people who merely *observe* one social group (e.g., women) treated less favorably than another (men) are less likely to perceive the treatment as discriminatory, compared with perceptions of the individuals who *are the direct targets* of the disparate treatment (Swim et al., 2003). Managers are even further removed from potentially discriminatory situations—only *hearing reports* about them—so they may be even less likely to believe that discrimination has taken place. Moreover, it is difficult to discern discrimination in individual cases; patterns of discrimination often emerge only with the aggregation of multiple incidents across persons, places, or time (Crosby, 1984; Crosby et al., 2003; O'Leary-Kelly et al., 2000). For all of these reasons, traditional, reactive, and legalistic approaches to combating blatant discrimination may not be effective for managing subtle biases in the form of selective incivility.

Organizational context. To create respectful, incivility-free work environments, it would behoove organizations to look beyond traditional methods of achieving and managing diversity; in particular, the reactive complaint mechanism may have limited utility. Proactive, preventative, and educational approaches seem more promising instead. For example, in the interest of incivility prevention, senior management can model appropriate, respectful workplace behavior and clearly state expectations of civility in mission statements or policy manuals. Reference checks for prospective employees can include questions about interpersonal behavior. All new employees should receive education about civility expectations, and employees at all levels could undergo interpersonal skills training. When incivilities do arise, instigators should be sanctioned swiftly, justly, and consistently (Pearson et al., 2000; Pearson & Porath, 2004).

Given the links to gender and race theorized in this article, I would also recommend that efforts to prevent incivility dovetail with those addressing overt discrimination (e.g., sexual and racial harassment). For example, organizational procedures, policies, and practices to set norms of civility could explicitly discuss equitable respect toward women and men and members of different ethnic groups (as well as employees who are young and old, gay and straight, etc.). Leaders should emphasize that unacceptable discrimination includes not just overt acts of misoygyny and bigotry but also subtle devaluation and exclusion of social minorities. The intended effect should be a broadening of employees' construals of what it means to be non-prejudiced (Brief & Barsky, 2000). Organizational interventions should also incorporate solutions from the social psychology literature on stereotyping and prejudice, detailed above. This sort of combined strategy would provide a more efficient and effective means of combating antisocial work behavior, which has many behavioral faces (general, gendered, raced, etc.). Related training programs might then attract broader audiences, being relevant to all employees (regardless of gender or ethnicity) and avoiding resistance met by interventions that exclusively target gender discrimination, racial discrimination, and so forth (Cortina et al., 2002; Lim & Cortina, 2005; Podgor, 1996). As Brief et al. note, "The forces driving discrimination in the workplace are many, and any legitimate attempt to combat discrimination must be multifaceted" (1997: 68).

Conclusion

This article integrates the literature on workplace incivility with that addressing modern sexism and racism. The resulting concept—selective incivility—is almost certainly more pervasive than blatant discrimination and harassment in the workplace. Incivility is also, by definition, more insidious, taking hold in such an ambiguous and stealthy manner that it is difficult to identify, manage, and prevent. This speaks to the need for particular vigilance about issues of "general" incivility, which may not be so

general after all. More research on the nature, causes, and consequences of this workplace phenomenon will bring us closer to being able to combat it effectively. And, to the delight of many, perhaps this ongoing work will ultimately add a crack to the proverbial glass ceiling.

Notes

1. Of course, workplace mistreatment can be based on other social dimensions as well, such as sexual orientation, age, disability status, and so on. The theory elaborated in this paper focuses primarily on gender and race; however, similar arguments could be developed for other characteristics that divide and stigmatize individuals.
2. In the year before my colleagues and I (Cortina et al., 2002) collected our data, only 23 percent of all lawyers nationwide were women (Eighth Circuit Gender Fairness Task Force, 1997). Thus, in this profession men clearly remain the dominant majority.

References

Allport, G. W. 1954. *The nature of prejudice.* Reading, MA: Addison-Wesley.

Andersson, L. M., & Pearson, C. M. 1999. Tit for tat? The spiraling effect of incivility in the workplace. *Academy of Management Review,* 24: 452–471.

Ashforth, B. 1994. Petty tyranny in organizations. *Human Relations,* 47: 755–778.

Banaji, M. R., & Dasgupta, N. 1998. The consciousness of social beliefs: A program of research on stereotyping and prejudice. In V. Y. Yzerbt, G. Lories, & B. Dardenne (Eds.), *Metacognition: Cognitive and social dimensions:* 157–170. Thousand Oaks, CA: Sage.

Barling, J., Dekker, I., Loughlin, C., Kelloway, E., Fullagar, C., & Johnson, D. 1996. Prediction and replication of the organizational and personal consequences of workplace sexual harassment. *Journal of Managerial Psychology,* 11: 4–25.

Barling, J., Rogers, A., & Kelloway, E. 2001. Behind closed doors: In-home workers' experience of sexual harassment and workplace violence. *Journal of Occupational Health Psychology,* 6: 255–269.

Baron, R. A. 2004. Workplace aggression and violence: Insights from basic research. In R. W. Griffin & A. M. O'Leary-Kelly (Eds.), *The dark side of organizational behavior:* 23–61. San Francisco: Jossey-Bass.

Baron, S. B., & Banaji, M. R. 2006. The development of implicit attitudes: Evidence of race evaluations from ages 6 and 10 and adulthood. *Psychological Science,* 17: 53–58.

Baumeister, R. F., & Leary, M. R. 1995. The need to belong: Desire for interpersonal attachments as a fundamental human motivation. *Psychological Bulletin,* 117: 497–529.

Benokraitis, N. V. 1997. Sex discrimination in the 21st century. In N. V. Benokraitis (Ed.), *Subtle sexism: Current practice and prospects for change:* 5–33. Thousand Oaks, CA: Sage.

Benokraitis, N. V., & Feagin, J. R. 1995. *Modern sexism* (2nd ed.). Engelwood Cliffs, NJ: Prentice Hall.

Björkqvist, K., Österman, K., & Hjelt-Bäck, M. 1994. Aggression among university employees. *Aggressive Behavior,* 20: 173–184.

Brief, A. P., & Barsky, A. 2000. Establishing a climate for diversity: The inhibition of prejudiced reactions in the workplace. *Research in Personnel and Human Resources Management,* 19: 91–129.

Brief, A. P., Buttram, R. T., Elliott, J. D., Reizenstein, R. M., & McCline, R. L. 1995. Releasing the beast: A study of compliance with orders to use race as a selection criterion. *Journal of Social Issues,* 51: 177–193.

Brief, A. P., Buttram, R. T., Reizenstein, R. M., Pugh, S. D., Callahan, J. D., McCline, R. L., & Vaslow, J. B. 1997. Beyond good intentions: The next steps toward racial equality in the American workplace. *Academy of Management Executive,* 11(4): 59–72.

Brief, A. P., Dietz, J., Cohen, R. R., Pugh, S. D., & Vaslow, J. B. 2000. Just doing business: Modern racism and obedience to authority as explanations for employment discrimination. *Organizational Behavior and Human Decision Processes,* 81: 72–97.

Brief, A. P., & Hayes, E. L. 1997. The continuing "American dilemma": Studying racism in organizations. *Trends in Organizational Behavior,* 4: 89–105.

Buchanan, N. T. 2005. The nexus of race and gender domination: The racialized sexual harassment of African American women. In P. Morgan & J. Gruber (Eds.), *In the company of men: Re-discovering the links between sexual harassment and male domination:* 294–320. Boston: Northeastern University Press.

Cleveland, J., & Kerst, M. 1993. Sexual harassment and perceptions of power: An underarticulated relationship. *Journal of Vocational Behavior,* 42: 49–67.

Cortina, L. M., Lonsway, K. A., & Magley, V. J. 2004. *Reconceptualizing workplace incivility through the lenses of gender and race.* Paper presented at the annual meeting of the Society for Industrial-Organizational Psychology, Chicago.

Cortina, L. M., Lonsway, K. L., Magley, V. J., Freeman, L. V., Collinsworth, L. L., Hunter, M., & Fitzgerald, L. F. 2002. What's gender got to do with it? Incivility in the federal courts. *Law and Social Inquiry,* 27: 235–270.

Cortina, L. M., & Magley, V. J. 2007. *Patterns and profiles of response to incivility in organizations.* Working paper, University of Michigan, Ann Arbor.

Cortina, L. M., Magley, V. J., Williams, J. H., & Langhout, R. D. 2001. Incivility in the workplace: Incidence and impact. *Journal of Occupational Health Psychology,* 6: 64–80.

Crosby, F. J. 1984. The denial of personal discrimination. *American Behavioral Scientist,* 27: 371–386.

Crosby, F. J., Iyer, A., Clayton, S., & Downing, R. A. 2003. Affirmative action: Psychological data and the policy debates. *American Psychologist,* 58: 93–115.

Deitch, E. A., Barsky, A., Butz, R. M., Brief, A. P., Chan, S., & Bradley, J. C. 2003. Subtle yet significant: The existence and impact of everyday racial discrimination in the workplace. *Human Relations,* 56: 1299–1324.

Devine, P. G. 1989. Stereotypes and prejudice: The automatic and controlled components. *Journal of Personality and Social Psychology,* 56: 5–18.

Devine, P. G., & Monteith, M. J. 1999. Automaticity and control in stereotyping. In S. Chaiken & Y. Trope (Eds.), *Dual-process theories in social psychology;* 339–360. New York: Guilford Press.

Dipboye, R. L., & Halverson, S. K. 2004. Subtle (and not so subtle) discrimination in organizations. In R. W. Griffin & A. M. O'Leary-Kelly (Eds.), *The dark side of organizational behavior:* 131–158. San Francisco: Jossey-Bass.

Dovidio, J. F., & Gaertner, S. L. 1998. On the nature of contemporary prejudice: The causes, consequences, and challenges of aversive racism. In J. L. Eberhardt & S. T. Fiske (Eds.), *Confronting racism: The problem and the response:* 3–32. Thousand Oaks, CA: Sage.

Dovidio, J. F., & Gaertner, S. L. 2000. Aversive racism and selection decisions: 1989 and 1999. *Psychological Science,* 11: 315–319.

Dovidio, J. F., Gaertner, S. L., & Bachman, B. A. 2001. Racial bias in organizations: The role of group processes and its causes and cures. In M. E. Turner (Ed.), *Groups at work: Theory and research:* 415–444. Mahwah, NJ: Lawrence Erlbaum Associates.

Dovidio, J. F., Gaertner, S. L., Kawakami, K., & Hodson, G. 2002. Why can't we just get along? Interpersonal biases and interracial distrust. *Cultural Diversity and Ethnic Minority Psychology,* 8(2): 88–102.

Dovidio, J. F., Gaertner, S. L., Niemann, Y. F., & Snider, K. 2001. Racial, ethnic, and cultural differences in responding to distinctiveness and discrimination on campus: Stigma and common group identity. *Journal of Social Issues,* 57: 167–188.

Dovidio, J. F., Kawakami, K., & Gaertner, S. L. 2000. Reducing contemporary prejudice: Combating explicit and implicit bias at the individual and intergroup level. In S. Oskamp (Ed.), *Reducing prejudice and discrimination:* 137–163. Mahwah, NJ: Lawrence Erlbaum Associates.

Duffy, M. K., Ganster, D. C., & Pagon, M. 2002. Social undermining in the workplace. *Academy of Management Journal,* 45: 331–351.

Eagly, A. H., & Steffen, V. J. 1984. Gender stereotypes stem from the distribution of women and men into social roles. *Journal of Personality and Social Psychology,* 46: 735–754.

Eagly, A. H., & Wood, W. 1999. The origins of sex differences in human behavior: Evolved dispositions versus social roles. *American Psychologist,* 54: 408–423.

Eighth Circuit Gender Fairness Task Force. 1997. Final report and recommendations of the Eighth Circuit Gender Fairness Task Force. *Creighton Law Review,* 31(1): 1–181.

Einarsen, S., & Raknes, B. I. 1997. Harassment in the workplace and the victimization of men. *Violence and Victims,* 12: 247–263.

Erber, R., & Fiske, S. T. 1984. Outcome dependency and attention to inconsistent information. *Journal of Personality and Social Psychology,* 47: 709–726.

Fiske, S. T. 1993. Controlling other people: The impact of power on stereotyping. *American Psychologist,* 48: 621–628.

Fiske, S. T. 2000. Stereotyping, prejudice, and discrimination at the seam between the centuries: Evolution, culture, mind, and brain. *European Journal of Social Psychology,* 30: 299–322.

Fiske, S. T. 2001. Effects of power on bias: Power explains and maintains individual, group, and societal disparities. In A. Y. Lee-Chai & J. A. Bargh (Eds.), *Use and abuse of power: Multiple perspectives on the causes of corruption:* 181–193. Philadelphia: Psychology Press.

Fiske, S. T. 2002. What we know now about bias and intergroup conflict, the problem of the century. *Current Directions in Psychological Science,* 11: 123–128.

Fiske, S. T., Cuddy, A. M. C., Glick, P., & Xu, J. 2002. A model of (often mixed) stereotype content: Competence and warmth respectively follow from perceived status and competition. *Journal of Personality and Social Psychology,* 82: 878–902.

Fitzgerald, L. F., Drasgow, F., Hulin, C. L., Gelfand, M. J., & Magley, V. J. 1997. The antecedents and consequences of sexual harassment in organizations: A test of an integrated model. *Journal of Applied Psychology,* 82: 578–589.

Forbes, G. B., Adams-Curtis, L. E., & White, K. B. 2004. First-and second-generation measures of sexism, rape myths and related beliefs, and hostility toward women. *Violence Against Women,* 10: 236–261.

Gaertner, S. L., & Dovidio, J. F. 1986. The aversive form of racism. In J. F. Dovidio & S. L. Gaertner (Eds.), *Prejudice, discrimination, and racism:* 61–89. Orlando, FL: Academic Press.

Gaertner, S. L., & Dovidio, J. F. 2000. *Reducing intergroup bias: The common ingroup identity model.* Philadelphia: Psychology Press.

Gelfand, M. J., Raver, J. L., & Ehrhart, K. H. 2002. Methodological issues in cross-cultural organizational research. In S. G. Rogelberg (Ed.), *Handbook of research methods in industrial and organizational psychology:* 216–246. Malden, MA: Blackwell.

Giacalone, R. A., & Greenberg, J. 1997. *Antisocial behavior in organizations.* Thousand Oaks, CA: Sage.

Glick, P., & Fiske, S. T. 1999. Sexism and other "isms": Interdependence, status, and the ambivalent content of stereotypes. In W. B. Swann, Jr., J. H. Langlois, & L. A. Gilbert (Eds.), *Sexism and stereotypes in modern society: The gender science of Janet Taylor Spence:* 192–221. Washington, DC: American Psychological Association.

Glick, P., & Fiske, S. T. 2001. An ambivalent alliance: Hostile and benevolent sexism as contemporary justifications for gender inequality. *American Psychologist,* 56: 109–118.

Greenwald, A. G., & Banaji, M. R. 1995. Implicit social cognition: Attitudes, self-esteeem, and stereotypes. *Psychological Review,* 102: 4–27.

Griggs v. Duke Power Company, 401, U.S. 424 (1971).

Hebl, M. R., Foster, J. B., Mannix, L. M., & Dovidio, J. F. 2002. Formal and interpersonal discrimination: A field study of bias toward homosexual applicants. *Personality and Social Psychology Bulletin,* 28: 815–825.

Heller, K. 1989. The return to community. *American Journal of Community Psychology,* 17: 1–16.

Hilton, J. L., & von Hipple, W. 1996. Stereotypes. *Annual Review of Psychology,* 47: 237–271.

Hoel, H., Rayner, C., & Cooper, C. L. 1999. Workplace bullying. *International Review of Industrial and Organizational Psychology,* 14: 195–223.

Hulin, C. L., Fitzgerald, L. F., & Drasgow, F. 1996. Organizational influences on sexual harassment. In M. Stockdale (Ed.), *Sexual harassment in the workplace: Perspectives, frontiers, and response strategies:* 127–150. Thousand Oaks, CA: Sage.

Jackman, M. R. 1994. *Paternalism and conflict in gender, class, and race relations.* Berkeley: University of California Press.

Jackson, L. M., Esses, V. M., & Burris, C. T. 2001. Contemporary sexism and discrimination: The importance of respect for men and women. *Personality and Social Psychology Bulletin,* 27: 48–61.

James, E. H., Brief, A. P., Dietz, J., & Cohen, R. R. 2001. Prejudice matters: Understanding the reaction of whites to affirmative action programs targeted to benefit blacks. *Journal of Applied Psychology,* 86: 1120–1128.

James, K., Lovato, C., & Khoo, G. 1994. Social identity correlates of minority workers' health. *Academy of Management Journal,* 37: 383–396.

James, L. R. 1998. Measurement of personality via conditional reasoning. *Organizational Research Methods,* 1: 131–163.

James, L. R., & Mazerolle, M. D. 2003. *Personality in work organizations.* Thousand Oaks, CA: Sage.

Jones, M. 2002. *Social psychology of prejudice.* Upper Saddle River, NJ: Prentice-Hall.

Klein, K. J., & Kozlowski, S. W. J. 2000. *Multilevel theory, research, and methods in organizations: Foundations, extensions, and new directions.* San Francisco: Jossey-Bass.

Lazarus, R. S. 1999. *Stress and emotion: A new synthesis.* New York: Springer.

Lazarus, R. S., & Folkman, S. 1984. *Stress, appraisal, and coping.* New York: Springer.

Lim, S., & Cortina, L. M. 2004. *A multi-level model of incivility in the workplace.* Paper presented at the annual meeting of the Academy of Management, New Orleans.

Lim, S., & Cortina, L. M. 2005. Interpersonal mistreatment in the workplace: The interface and outcomes of general incivility and sexual harassment. *Journal of Applied Psychology,* 90: 483–496.

Magley, V. J., Hulin, C. L., Fitzgerald, L. F., & DeNardo, M. 1999. The outcomes of self-labeling sexual harassment. *Journal of Applied Psychology,* 84: 390–402.

McConahay, J. B. 1986. Modern racism, ambivalence, and the modern racism scale. In J. F. Dovidio & S. L. Gaertner (Eds.), *Prejudice, discrimination, and racism:* 91–125. Orlando, FL: Academic Press.

McConahay, J. B., & Hough, J. C. 1976. Symbolic racism. *Journal of Social Issues*, 32: 23–45.

McDonnel Douglas Corp. v. Green, 411 U.S. 792 (1973).

Meyerson, D. E., & Fletcher, J. K. 2000. A modest manifesto for shattering the glass ceiling. *Harvard Business Review*, 78(1): 127–136.

Miceli, M. P., & Near, J. P. 1992. *Blowing the whistle: The organizational and legal implications for companies and employees.* New York: Lexington Books.

Miller, D. T., & Turnbull, W. 1986. Expectancies and interpersonal processes. *Annual Review of Psychology*, 37: 233–256.

Miner-Rubino, K., & Cortina, L. M. 2004. Working in a context of hostility toward women: Implications for employees' well-being. *Journal of Occupational Health Psychology*, 9: 107–122.

Miner-Rubino, K., & Cortina, L. M. 2006. *Observed incivility toward women at work: The role of organizational justice.* Paper presented at the APA/NIOSH Work, Stress and Health Conference, Miami.

Monin, B., & Miller, D. T. 2001. Moral credentials and the expression of prejudice. *Journal of Personality and Social Psychology*, 81: 33–43.

Monteith, M. J. 1993. Self-regulation of prejudiced responses: Implications for progress in prejudice reduction efforts. *Journal of Personality and Social Psychology*, 65: 469–485.

Neuberg, S. L., & Fiske, S. T. 1987. Motivational influences on impression formation: Outcome dependency, accuracy-driven attention, and individuating processes. *Journal of Personality and Social Psychology*, 53: 431–444.

Neuman, J. H. 2004. Injustice, stress, and aggression in organizations. In R. W. Griffin & A. M. O'Leary-Kelly (Eds.), *The dark side of organizational behavior*: 62–102. San Francisco: Jossey-Bass.

O'Leary-Kelly, A. M., Paetzold, R. L., & Griffin, R. W. 2000. Sexual harassment as aggressive behavior: An actor-based perspective. *Academy of Management Review*, 25: 372–388.

Operario, D., & Fiske, S. T. 1998. Racism equals power plus prejudice: A social psychological equation for racial oppression. In J. L. Eberhardt & S. T. Fiske (Eds.), *Confronting racism: The problem and the response*: 33–53. Thousand Oaks, CA: Sage.

Pearson, C. M., Andersson, L. M., & Porath, C. L. 2000. Assessing and attacking workplace incivility. *Organizational Dynamics*, 29(2): 123–137.

Pearson, C. M., Andersson, L. M., & Wegner, J. W. 2001. When workers flout convention: A study of workplace incivility. *Human Relations*, 54: 1387–1419.

Pearson, C. M., & Porath, C. L. 2004. On incivility, its impact, and directions for future research. In R. W. Griffin & A. M. O'Leary-Kelly (Eds.), *The dark side of organizational behavior*: 403–425. San Francisco: Jossey-Bass.

Pettigrew, T. F., & Martin, J. 1987. Shaping the organizational context for black American inclusion. *Journal of Social Issues*, 43: 41–78.

Podgor, E. 1996. Lawyer professionalism in a gendered society. *South Carolina Law Review*, 47: 323–348.

Pretty, G. H., & McCarthy, M. 1991. Exploring psychological sense of community among women and men of the corporation. *Journal of Community Psychology*, 19: 1351–1361.

Pryor, J. B., Giedd, J. L., & Williams, K. B. 1995. A social psychological model for predicting sexual harassment. *Journal of Social Issues*, 51: 69–84.

Richman, J. A., Rospenda, K. M., Nawyn, S. J., Flaherty, J. A., Fendrich, M., Drum, M., & Johnson, T. P. 1999. Sexual harassment and generalized workplace abuse: Prevalence and mental health correlates. *American Journal of Public Health*, 89: 358–363.

Riger, S. 1991. Gender dilemmas in sexual harassment policies and procedures. *American Psychologist*, 46: 497–505.

Robinson, S. L., & Bennett, R. J. 1995. A typology of deviant workplace behaviors: A multidimensional scaling study. *Academy of Management Journal*, 38: 555–572.

Robinson, S. L., & O'Leary-Kelly, A. M. 1998. Monkey see, monkey do: The influence of work groups on the antisocial behavior of employees. *Academy of Management Journal*, 41: 658–672.

Rospenda, K. 2002. Workplace harassment, services utilization, and drinking outcomes. *Journal of Occupational Health Psychology*, 7: 141–155.

Rowe, M. P. 1990. Barriers to equality: The power of subtle discrimination to maintain unequal opportunity. *Employee Responsibility and Rights Journal*, 3: 153–163.

Sanchez, J. I., & Brock, P. 1996. Outcomes of perceived discrimination among Hispanic employees: Is diversity management a luxury or a necessity? *Academy of Management Journal*, 39: 704–719.

Sarason, S. B. 1974. *The psychological sense of community: Prospects for a community psychology.* Cambridge, MA: Brookline Books.

Schaffer, B. S., & Riordan, C. M. 2003. A review of cross-cultural methodologies for organizational research. *Organizational Research Methods*, 6: 169–215.

Schneider, K. T., Hitlan, R. T., & Radhakrishnan, P. 2000. An examination of the nature and correlates of ethnic harassment experiences in multiple contexts. *Journal of Applied Psychology*, 85: 3–12.

Scott, W. R. 1992. *Organizations: Rational, natural, and open systems.* Upper Saddle River, NJ: Prentice-Hall.

Sears, D. O. 1988. Symbolic racism. In P. A. Katz & D. A. Taylor (Eds.), *Eliminating racism: Profiles in controversy*: 53–84. New York: Plenum Press.

Sears, D. O. 1988. Racism and politics in the United States. In J. L. Eberhardt & S. T. Fiske (Eds.), *Confronting racism: The problem and the response*: 76–100. Thousand Oaks, CA: Sage.

Skarlicki, D. P., & Folger, R. 1997. Retaliation in the workplace: The roles of distributive, procedural, and interactional justice. *Journal of Applied Psychology*, 82: 434–443.

Spector, P. E., & Fox, S. 2002. An emotion-centered model of voluntary work behavior: Some parallels between counterproductive work behavior and organizational citizenship behavior. *Human Resource Management Review,* 12: 269–292.

Stone, E. F., Stone, D. L., & Dipboye, R. L. 1992. Stigmas in organizations: Race, handicaps, and physical unattractiveness. In K. Kelley (Ed.), *Issues, theory, and research in industrial/organizational psychology:* 385–457. Oxford: North-Holland.

Swim, J. K., Aikin, K. J., Hall, W. S., & Hunter, B. A. 1995. Sexism and racism: Old-fashioned and modern prejudices. *Journal of Personality and Social Psychology,* 68: 199–214.

Swim, J. K., Scott, E. D., Sechrist, G. B., Campbell, B., & Stangor, C. 2003. The role of intent and harm in judgments of prejudice and discrimination. *Journal of Personality and Social Psychology,* 84: 944–959.

Tajfel, H., & Turner, J. C. 1986. The social identity theory of intergroup behavior. In S. Worchel & W. G. Austin (Eds.), *Psychology of intergroup relations:* 7–24. Chicago: Nelson-Hall.

Thacker, R. A., & Ferris, G. R. 1991. Understanding sexual harassment in the workplace: The influence of power and politics within the dyadic interaction of harasser and target. *Human Resource Management Review,* 1: 23–37.

Tougas, F., Brown, R., Beaton, A. M., & Joly, S. 1995. Neosexism: Plus ça change, plus c'est pareil. *Personality and Social Psychology Bulletin,* 21: 842–849.

U.S. Equal Employment Opportunity Commission. *Guidelines on harassment based on race, color, religion, gender, national origin, age, or disability.* 58 Fed. Reg. 51,266. Washington, DC: U.S. Equal Employment Opportunity Commission.

U.S. Equal Employment Opportunity Commission. 2003. *Charge statistics FY 1992 through FY 2002.* Washington, DC: U.S. Equal Employment Opportunity Commission.

Valian, V. 1998. *Why so slow? The advancement of women.* Cambridge, MA: MIT Press.

VandenBos, G. R., & Bulatao, E. Q. 1996. *Violence on the job: Identifying risks and developing solutions.* Washington, DC: American Psychological Association.

Wheaton, B. 1997. The nature of chronic stress. In B. H. Gottlieb (Ed.), *Coping with chronic stress:* 43–74. New York: Plenum Press.

Williams, J. H., Fitzgerald, L. F., & Drasgow, F. 1999. The effects of organizational practices on sexual harassment and individual outcomes in the military. *Military Psychology,* 11: 303–328.

Williams, K. D. 1998. Social exclusion. In R. M. Kowalski (Ed.), *Aversive interpersonal behaviors:* 133–170. New York: Plenum Press.

Williams, K. D., & Sommer, K. L. 1997. Social exclusion by coworkers: Does rejection lead to loafing or compensation? *Personality and Social Psychology Bulletin,* 23: 693–706.

Lilia M. Cortina (lilia@umich.edu) is an associate professor of psychology and women's studies at the University of Michigan. She received her Ph.D. in psychology from the University of Illinois at Urbana-Champaign. Her research addresses victimization and gender in organizations, focusing in particular on employee experiences of incivility and sexual harassment.

Racial Microaggressions and the Asian American Experience

Derald Wing Sue, Jennifer Bucceri, Annie I. Lin, Kevin L. Nadal, and Gina C. Torino
Teachers College, Columbia University

Racial microaggressions were examined through a focus group analysis of 10 self-identified Asian American participants using a semistructured interview and brief demographic questionnaire. Results identified 8 major microaggressive themes directed toward this group: (a) alien in own land, (b) ascription of intelligence, (c) exoticization of Asian women, (d) invalidation of interethnic differences, (e) denial of racial reality, (f) pathologizing cultural values/communication styles, (g) second class citizenship, and (h) invisibility. A ninth category, "undeveloped incidents/responses" was used to categorize microaggressions that were mentioned by only a few members. There were strong indications that the types of subtle racism directed at Asian Americans may be qualitatively and quantitatively different from other marginalized groups. Implications are discussed.

Keywords: Asian American experience, racial microaggressions, microinsult, microinvalidation

It is well documented that racism has been a constant, continuing, and embedded part of American history and society (Jones, 1997; Smedley & Smedley, 2005). Many Americans still cling to the belief, however, that the civil rights movement eliminated racism in our nation and created equality between Whites and people of color (Thompson & Neville, 1999). Although the civil rights movement had a significant impact on changing racial attitudes and overt prejudicial behaviors, racism is far from eradicated and continues to plague the nation (President's Initiative on Race, 1998; Sue, 2003). Instead of overt expressions of White racial superiority, research supports the contention that racism has evolved into more subtle, ambiguous, and unintentional manifestations in American social, political, and economic life (Sue, 2003; Dovidio, Gaertner, Kawakami, & Hodson, 2002). The "old fashioned" type where racial hatred was overt, direct, and often intentional, has increasingly morphed into a contemporary form that is subtle, indirect, and often disguised. Studies on the existence of implicit stereotyping suggest that the new form of racism is most likely to be evident in well-intentioned White Americans who

are unaware they hold beliefs and attitudes that are detrimental to people of color (Banaji, 2001; Banaji, Hardin, & Rothman, 1993; DeVos & Banaji, 2005). The "new" manifestation of racism has been likened to carbon monoxide, invisible, but potentially lethal (D. W. Sue & D. Sue, 2003; Tinsley-Jones, 2003). Some researchers prefer to use the term "racial microaggression" to describe this form of racism which occurs in the daily lives of people of color. They are so common and innocuous that they are often overlooked and unacknowledged (Solorzano, Ceja, & Yosso, 2000). Sue et al. (2006) define microaggressions as "brief and commonplace daily verbal, behavioral and environmental indignities, whether intentional or unintentional, that communicate hostile, derogatory or negative racial slights and insults that potentially have harmful or unpleasant psychological impact on the target person or group." Simply stated, microaggressions are brief, everyday exchanges that send denigrating messages to people of color because they belong to a racial minority group. These exchanges are so pervasive and automatic in daily interactions that they are often dismissed and glossed over as being innocuous. What constitutes racial microaggressions, how they impact people of color and the strategies used to deal with them have not been well conceptualized or researched (Sue et al., 2006).

Although it is generally accepted that African Americans and Latino/Hispanic Americans experience both overt and covert forms of prejudice and discrimination, Asian Americans are frequently viewed as a model

Derald Wing Sue, Jennifer Bucceri, Annie I. Lin, Kevin L. Nadal, and Gina C. Torino, Department of Counseling and Clinical Psychology, Teachers College, Columbia University.

Correspondence concerning this article should be addressed to Derald Wing Sue, Teachers College, Columbia University, Department of Counseling and Clinical Psychology, Box 36, 525 West 120th Street, New York, NY 10027. E-mail: dw2020@columbia.edu minority who have made it in this society and experience little in the form of racism (Wong & Halgin, 2006). Despite the long documented history of racism toward Asian Americans, there has been a lack of attention paid to prejudice and discrimination directed against them (D. W. Sue & D. Sue, 2003). One reason may be that many White Americans tend to dichotomize racial issues in Black and White terms (Liang, Li, & Kim et al., 2004). As a result, the psychological needs of Asian Americans arising from racism are often overshadowed by the experiences of Whites and Blacks, and research findings for these racial groups are often assumed to speak to the experiences of Asian Americans as well.

Despite the belief that Asian Americans have somehow "made it" in our society and are "immune" to racism, widespread prejudice and discrimination continue to take a toll on their standard of living, self-esteem, and psychological well being (Wong & Halgin, 2006). Indeed, the study of Asians in America is the study of widespread prejudice and discrimination leveled at this group. Denied the rights of citizenship, forbidden to own land, and incarcerated in internment camps, this group has been the target of large-scale governmental actions to deny them basic civil and human rights (D. W. Sue & D. Sue, 2003).

Research reveals that overt racial discrimination is identified as one of the potential social risk factors of mental illness, is related to physical and psychological well-being, and contributes to stress, depression, and anger in its victims (Chakraborty & McKenzie, 2002; Kim, 2002). For example, in a survey of studies examining racism, mental health researchers found that higher levels of discrimination were associated with lower levels of happiness, life satisfaction, self-esteem, and mastery or control (Williams, Neighbors, & Jackson, 2003). However, many of the existing studies examining the relationship between racist events and mental health typically have not included the experiences of Asian Americans (Liang et al., 2004). As a result, these findings may not accurately describe the Asian American experience of racism and high levels of discrimination.

An interesting and valuable means of studying the manifestation and impact of racism upon Asian Americans is through the concept of racial microaggressions. Microaggressions have been described as subtle, stunning, often automatic exchanges which are "put downs" (Pierce, Carew, Pierce-Gonzalez, & Willis, 1978, p. 66). People of color experience them as subtle insults directed toward them, often automatically and unconsciously (Solorzano et al., 2000). Social psychologists have outlined the many ways contemporary racism can be expressed resulting in harm and disadvantage to the target person or group

(Jones, 1997; Dovidio et al., 2002). Some examples of racial microaggressions include (a) teachers who ignore students of color, (b) taxi drivers who fail to pick up passengers of color, or (c) airport security personnel screening passengers of color with greater frequency and care. Because microaggressions often occur outside the level of conscious awareness, well-intentioned individuals can engage in these biased acts without guilt or knowledge of their discriminatory actions (Sue, 2003). Despite the intentions of the perpetrator, these acts of discrimination can significantly harm the victims (Delucchi & Do, 1996; Sue, 2003). Racial microaggressions can also take form as verbal statements such as, "You speak such good English," "But you speak without an accent," and "So where are you really from?" (Solorzano et al., 2000). Asian Americans and Latino/Hispanic Americans indicate that they perceive these statements as invalidating and insulting because they reflect a worldview that racial/ethnic minorities are aliens in their own country (DeVos & Banaji, 2005; D. W. Sue & D. Sue, 2003). Unfortunately, through selective perception, many Whites are unlikely to hear the inadvertent racial slights that are made in their presence (Lawrence, 1987). As a result, White individuals may unconsciously perpetuate Eurocentric attitudes of White supremacy and in effect cause individuals of color to feel invalidated or inferior.

Ever since the civil rights movement, critical race theory has provided a means for challenging Eurocentric epistemologies and dominant ideologies such as beliefs in objectivity and meritocracy that has masked the operation of racism, especially as they relate to groups like Asian Americans (Matsuda, Lawrence, Delgado, & Crenshaw, 1993; Sleeter & Bernal, 2004). Although not referred to as microaggressions, Asian American Studies has used counter-storytelling, media/film analyses, and narrative critiques to elucidate the Asian American experience of both overt and covert forms of racism (Hu-DeHart, 1995; Hyun, 2005; Nakanishi, 1995). Although the Ethnic and Asian American Studies literature lend support to the existence of racial microaggressions, there is a paucity of psychological studies on their effects for all racial groups (Delgado & Stefancic, 1992; Johnson, 1988; Lawrence, 1987). A review of that literature reveals only one study on African-Americans that focuses specifically on microaggressions (Solorzano et al., 2000). The investigators reported that microaggressions resulted in a negative racial climate for Blacks, and often fostered emotions of self-doubt, frustration, and isolation on the part of the victims (Solorzano et al., 2000). They concluded that the cumulative effects of racial microaggressions can be quite devastating. Sue (2003) believes that "this contemporary form of racism is many times over more problematic, damaging, and injurious to persons of color than overt racist acts" (p. 48). It has been noted that the collective effects of racial microaggressions may theoretically result in "diminished mortality, augmented morbidity and flattened confidence" (Pierce, 1995, p. 281). Without documentation and analysis to help better understand microaggressions, the threats that they pose and the assaults they justify can easily be ignored or downplayed (Solorzano et al., 2000).

Sue et al. (2006) have proposed a taxonomy of racial microaggressions that classifies them under three forms: microassault, microinsult, and microinvalidation. Microassaults are defined as explicit racial derogations that are verbal (i.e., racial epithets), nonverbal (behavioral discrimination), or environmental (offensive visual displays) attacks meant to hurt the person of color. It is generally deliberate and conscious. Calling someone a "Chink" or "Jap," White parents discouraging a son or daughter from dating Asian Americans, or displaying Asian caricatures of exaggerated slanted eyes and large buck teeth are examples. Microassaults are most similar to old fashioned forms of racism in that they are deliberate and conscious acts by the aggressor (Dovidio & Gaertner, 2000).

The two other forms (microinsults and microinvalidations), however, tend to operate unconsciously, are unintentional, and generally outside the level of conscious awareness. They are seemingly consistent with the research literature on the power of implicit racist attitudes and beliefs (Banaji, 2001; DeVos & Banaji, 2005). These microaggressions are not consciously intended by the perpetrator, but from the perspective of the recipient, they represent a negative experience. A microinsult is a behavioral action or verbal remark that conveys rudeness, insensitivity, or demeans a person's racial identity or heritage. A White manager who states to a prospective applicant of color that "the most qualified person should get the job" may be perceived as implying that people of color are not qualified. Microinvalidations are actions that exclude, negate or nullify the psychological thoughts, feelings or experiential reality of a person of color. When an Asian American is complimented for speaking good English or when Blacks are warned not to be so oversensitive, the underlying messages may be that Asians are perpetual foreigners in their own country and that the experiential reality of racism for African Americans is not real.

Because Sue et al. (2006) were more concerned with the unintentional and automatic expressions of microaggressions, they chose to concentrate on the latter two rather than microassaults. They created a taxonomy of microaggressions and proposed categories of each with their own distinct themes: (a) microinsult (*ascription of intelligence*—assigning high or low intelligence to a racial group, *second class citizenship*—treated as a lesser being or group, *pathologizing values/communications*—notion that values and/or communication styles of people of color are abnormal, and *assumption of criminal status*—presumed to be a criminal, dangerous or deviant based on race) and (b) microinvalidation (*alien in own land*—assumption that racial minority citizens are foreigners, *color blindness*—denial or pretense that one does not see color, *myth of meritocracy*—success in life is due to individual effort and not race, and *denial of individual racism*—denial that personal racism or one's role in its perpetuation). A ninth category, environmental invalidation was identified, but it appears to be more of a mechanism for delivering microaggressions (verbal, behavioral and environmental) instead of a free standing and distinct expression.

Although there is considerable conceptual and anecdotal support for the researchers' taxonomy and classification scheme (American Counseling Association, 1999; Banaji, 2001; Dovidio et al., 2002), its recent formulation has not been adequately researched. Studies examining the deleterious effects of "old fashioned" or overt forms of racism are plentiful, but few have examined the more covert forms as manifested in microaggressions. Further, the above taxonomy was derived from considering microaggressions across several racial/ethnic minority groups (African Americans, Asian Americans, and Latino/Hispanic Americans), and there is an underlying assumption that they apply equally to all groups of color. Although many social scientists have suggested that racism and stereotyping operate under similar principles for all marginalized groups (Bienat, 2003; Jones, 1997), some have hypothesized that there may be qualitative differences of how racism is expressed against Asian Americans as opposed to African Americans or Latino/Hispanic Americans (Liang et al., 2004; Yoo & Lee, 2005). Understanding the manifestations of racism is critical to designing effective interventions to counter the negative effects of racial oppression (Thompson & Neville, 1999), especially as it affects Asian Americans (Noh, Beiser, Kaspar, Hou, & Rummens, 1999). The current study was conducted in order to qualitatively explore the experience of racial microaggressions among Asian Americans and to identify typical microaggressive themes. By exploring the types of microaggressions Asian Americans experience, messages being conveyed, reactions to these experiences, and how individuals deal with the effects of these encounters, we hope to increase understanding of the dynamics of subtle racism directed at Asian Americans.

Method

The present study utilized a qualitative method to identify microaggressions directed at Asian Americans, explored the various forms they take, studied their impact upon recipients, and determined the means used to cope with their impact. Focus groups were used as a method to capture the richness of the participants' experiences by allowing the social group interactions to facilitate the development of meaning (Krueger, 1998). Focus groups have been found to be an effective means of obtaining in-depth information about a relatively unexplored concept (Seal, Bogart & Ehrhardt, 1998; Krueger, 1994) and used successfully to explore racial perceptions on a number of topics (Saint-Germain, Bassford & Montano, 1993; Solorzano et al., 2000; Thompson, Bazile, & Akbar, 2004). In this case, we were interested in understanding social interactions and events related to experiences of subtle racism directed toward Asian Americans by describing, comparing, contrasting, cataloguing, and classifying microaggressions.

Participants

The ideal number for effective focus group analysis ranges from 4-12 people (Seal, Bogart, & Ehrhardt, 1998). Participants were selected based on purposive criterion with the aim of choosing a sample that typifies the phenomenon under investigation (Patton, 1990). All participants in the two focus groups had to self identify with being Asian American, were born and raised in the United States, and agree that racism and discrimination against people of color (particularly Asian Americans) exist in the United States. These three criteria were essential to insure that the phenomena under investigation would be present in the discussions. A total of 10 self-identified Asian Americans participated in the study: 1 male and 9 female; 4 Chinese Americans, 2 Filipino Americans, 1 Korean American, 1 Japanese/German American, and 1 Asian Indian/European American. Eight were students, two were working professionals, and all were in their mid-20s with only one in her early 40s. Two focus groups of five were formed from the volunteers.

Researchers

The researchers for the study consisted of 5 doctoral and 5 masters' students in counseling psychology taking a graduate research seminar in racism and antiracism taught by the senior author at a private Eastern University. Because qualitative research places the role of the researcher as the central means of data collection, identification of personal values, assumptions and biases are required at the initial onset of the study (Fassinger, 2005). This allows us to account for potential biases and assures that the contributions to the research setting, methodology, analysis, and interpretation can be useful rather than detrimental (Krueger, 1998; Polkinghorne, 2005). All students taking the course did so voluntarily because of their strong interest in the topic of racism. The team consisted of three African Americans, three Asian Americans (including the senior author), two Latinos, and three White Americans. The instructor (senior author) has over 30 years of research related to topics of diversity, multiculturalism, racism, and antiracism. As this was a two-year seminar, considerable time was spent in the study of racism directed toward Asian Americans which allowed for the informed formulation of the study. It is also clear that team members bring certain biases to the study. Team members believe, for example, that subtle racism exists, that it occurs against Asian Americans, that it possesses detrimental psychological consequences, and that it may be ethnic group specific. Further, all were members of a research seminar that might inadvertently influence their work on the project (pleasing the instructor). As a result, every effort was made to ensure objectivity, but it is acknowledged that these biases may shape the way data are collected, viewed, and interpreted.

Measure

Two formal means of collecting data were used: (a) a brief demographic questionnaire aimed at obtaining basic information related to Asian ethnicity, gender, age, occupation, and education, and (b) a semistructured interview protocol. The protocol was developed from a review of the literature on microaggressions (Pierce et al., 1978; Solorzano et al., 2000; Sue, 2003), research related to implicit and explicit stereotyping (Banaji, 2001; Banaji, Hardin, & Roth, 1993), aversive racism (Dovidio et al., 2002; Jones, 1997), and Asian American experiences of racism (Kim, 2002; Liang et al., 2004; Wong & Halgin, 2006). As we wanted to allow the participants considerable freedom in responding to the questions and prompts, all questions were open-ended, and generally aimed at eliciting real life examples that they experienced. In general, the eight questions were intended to generate a variety of microaggressive examples, explore the impact they had on participants, construe meaning from the interaction, and outline how participants responded. Transition and ending questions were also developed to aid in moving from one topic to another and to bring closure to the focus group activity. A copy of the interview protocol is found in the Appendix.

Procedures

Participants were solicited throughout the local university community (campus and neighborhood) through posted flyers, word of mouth, classroom invitations, and a website asking for volunteers. Asian American participants who volunteered were placed in one of two focus groups. No financial compensation was offered. Each focus group lasted for 2 hours and was conducted by a two-person team: the facilitator and observer. Both the facilitator and observer were Asian Americans and part of the research team. As the topic dealt with subtle racism against Asian Americans, it was believed that facilitators of the same race would minimize any hesitancy or reluctance to disclose negative sentiment about interactions with those outside of their own group. The role of the facilitator was to lead the discussion while the observer noted nonverbal behaviors and group dynamics (Krueger, 1998). Prior to the interview, both researchers went through a brief behavioral rehearsal related to moderating the focus group discussion, and anticipating and overcoming possible resistances to the flow of the discussion. Immediately after the interview and after the focus group was dismissed, a debriefing session was held between the two researchers related to their own reactions, observations about the group, major themes that arose, climate in the room, and discussion of problematic issues. The focus group discussions took place in an enclosed private room at Teachers College, Columbia University. All participants were asked to sign a consent form that included permission to audiotape the entire session. The debriefing between the two researchers was also audiotaped. The tapes were transcribed verbatim making sure that the identities of participants were removed. Tapes were destroyed after transcription. The transcript was subsequently checked for accuracy by the two facilitators before they were presented to the team for qualitative analysis.

A four-person research team, which included the facilitator and observer, went over the entire transcript to record responses or situations illustrating microaggressions generated in the focus groups and the content of responses from the group participants were analyzed qualitatively. The team task was to look at what types of microaggressions Asian Americans experience, the messages that are being conveyed via these microaggressions, and the type of reactions (i.e., behavioral, cognitive, and/or affective) Asian Americans have in response to these microaggressions. In keeping with focus group analysis (Seal et al., 1998; Krueger, 1998; Miles & Huberman, 1994), each member of the research team individually identified topic areas or domains used to conceptually organize the overwhelming amount of data generated from the group discussion. The narratives and descriptions from the group participants were analyzed qualitatively along the following domains: (a) identifying microaggressions from the perspective of the participant, (b) producing illustrative critical incidents, (c) analyzing the unintentional/intentional themes, (d) categorizing their impact, and (e) describing typical responses to microaggressions.

The preliminary analysis was then presented to the senior author and other seminar members who acted as auditors in reviewing and providing feedback to the team in order to reach consensus that approximate the "truth." The procedure used in the consensual process was similar to the one described in consensual qualitative research (CQR) (Hill, Thompson, & Williams, 1997; Hill et al., 2005), although the unit of study was a focus group rather than an individual. Because of member interactions in the two groups, using CQR to analyze general, typical, or variant themes independently among individuals was compromised. Rather, transcripts were analyzed according to the degree of uniform consensus reached by each group during a discussion of the microaggressive episode. As qualitative research is ultimately about the study of experience or experiences, using a modified CQR procedure to arrive at consensus was considered an appropriate methodology (Polkinghorne, 2005). Once consensus was reached in the large group, the team members were asked to individually extract core ideas from the domains. Core ideas are defined as a summary or abstract derived from the domains that integrate the data in a holistic fashion linked to the context of the phenomenon under study. Once accomplished, the members of the team presented their individual analysis to one another, reached consensus about their contributions in a group meeting, and presented it to the auditors. The roles of the auditors, as prescribed in CQR were threefold: (a) compare and contrast the work of the independent team members, (b) minimize the effects of groupthink by encouraging divergent perspectives, and (c) help finalize the themes in a group working session. The results of both focus groups were then combined.

Results

The following section will provide examples of the themes gleaned from the combined focus group transcripts. In addition, the messages conveyed by each microaggression to the recipient and the intent of the aggressor will be explicated to reach a deeper understanding of their meanings. Eight microaggressive themes were identified. There were, however, several microaggressive incidents that could not be classified under any of these themes and/or did not receive group consensus to develop an additional category. Thus, we used the category "undeveloped incidents/responses" to include these incidents.

Theme 1: Alien in Own Land

This theme emerges from both focus groups and can be described as a microaggression which embodies the assumption that all Asian Americans are foreigners or foreign-born. An example of this theme was universally voiced by Asian Americans of all ethnicities and manifested in questions or remarks like "Where are you from?" "Where were you born?" or "You speak good English." The participants were often torn between whether the comments were well intentioned expressions of interest in them or perceptions that they were foreigners and did not belong in America. Furthermore, the meaning construed by recipients is that they were different, less than, and could not possibly be "real" Americans. That this phenomenon has empirical reality was a finding that White Americans, on an implicit level, equated "White" and "American" with one another while Asian and African Americans were less likely associated with the term "American" (DeVos & Banaji, 2005).

On the whole, the participants did not see the questions or "compliments" as benign and curious, but disturbing and uncomfortable. One Chinese American participant shared that while she was working in a restaurant, a White customer came in and attempted to converse with her in Japanese. She interpreted the behavior as the person perceiving her as a foreigner and not fluent in English. Worse yet, the person could not distinguish between Chinese and Japanese Americans. The focus group members did not perceive the intent of the questions to be overtly malevolent. They believed the person might have been attempting to establish a relationship with the Chinese American and might have wanted to indicate that he was not like other White Americans and could speak an Asian language.

Theme 2: Ascription of Intelligence

This theme also emerges from both focus groups. It is described as a microaggression that occurs when a degree of intelligence is assigned to an Asian American based on his/her race. Many of the participants describe teachers and fellow students making statements such as "You are really good at math," "You people always do well in school," or "If I see lots of Asian students in my class, I know it's going to be a hard class." The message conveyed

is that all Asians are bright and smart, especially in math and science. Interestingly, the work on stereotype threat suggests that this belief is shared by many Whites, and that it may actually depress academic performance among them when in the presence of Asian Americans (Steele, 1997; Steele & Aronson, 1995).

The participants believed that the conscious intent of these statements was to compliment Asian Americans, since being good at math was perceived by aggressors as a positive quality. However, the impact of assuming Asian Americans are good at math can be harmful. Participants describe feeling pressured to conform to a stereotype that they did not endorse, particularly if they were not good at math or did not enjoy it. In essence, they expressed feelings of being trapped. One Korean woman, for example, describes her coworkers bringing every math question for her to solve. Not only did it seem to operate from a stereotype, but it added pressure to help them, and resulted in a heavier workload for the woman. She also expressed discomfort at another major side effect: Asian Americans were viewed as intelligent while other people of color were perceived as less intelligent. It created tensions between her and other Black and Latino coworkers.

Theme 3: Denial of Racial Reality

Participants of all Asian ethnic backgrounds share that many microaggressions invalidate their experiences of discrimination. In one case, a Vietnamese American male was told that "Asians are the new Whites." The participant in the study indicated that the remark dismissed his experiences of racism, indicated that Asians experience no discrimination, suggested inequities do not exist for Asians, and that they have made it in society. In other words, the Vietnamese male felt that the perpetrator saw Asians as a model minority, similar to Whites and experience minimal socioeconomic or educational disadvantages. While the intent of the aggressor may be to compliment the Asian American individual by saying that Asians are more successful than other people of color, the negating message is that Asians do not experience racism—denying their experiential reality of bias and discrimination.

Theme 4: Exoticization of Asian American Women

A fourth theme found in both focus groups is exoticization of Asian American women who are relegated to an exotic category. One Chinese American women stated, "White men believe that Asian women are great girlfriends, wait hand and foot on men, and don't back-talk or give them shit. Asian women have beautiful skin and are just sexy and have silky hair." One Korean American woman indicated that she is frequently approached by White men who are very forthcoming with their "Asian fetishes" of subservience and pleasing them sexually. Nearly all members of the focus groups interpreted these microaggressions as indicating that Asian women are only needed for the physical needs of White men and nothing more. Again, participants felt that the intent of the aggressor in these situations may be to praise Asian women for their ability to take care of a man's every need. One participant was quite vocal in stating that the continual subjugation of Asian American women to roles of sexual objects, domestic servants, and exotic images of Geishas, ultimately "equates our identities to that of passive companions to White men." Many of the participants also suggested that the exotic image of Asian American women also serves as an unconscious backlash to feminist values and that it potentially creates antagonism with White women as well.

Theme 5: Invalidation of Interethnic Differences

This theme is most closely associated with the statement: "All Asians look alike." One Filipino American woman states, "I am always asked are you Chinese?" Another example of this is conveyed by a Chinese American who stated that new acquaintances oftentimes make statements like, "Oh, my ex-girlfriend was Chinese, or my neighbor was Japanese." These microaggressions tend to minimize or deny differences that may exist between interethnic groups or the existence of other Asian American groups. Participants believed the microaggression suggests that all Asian Americans are alike and that differences between groups do not exist and/or do not matter. The intent of the aggressor in this situation is to express that they are familiar with Asians, but instead the message received is that the aggressor assumes that all Asians are Chinese or Japanese. Moreover, it is assumed by the aggressor that most Asians are familiar with each other, regardless of their Asian ethnic background.

Theme 6: Pathologizing Cultural Values/ Communication Styles

Another microaggression theme involves the perception of cultural values and communication styles other than that of the White majority as being less desirable or indicators of deficits. One Chinese American woman expressed exasperation at how class participation (usually verbal) is valued strongly in academic settings and that grades are often based upon it. Because of Asian cultural values that emphasize the value of silence, less verbal Asians are often perceived as lacking in interest, disengaged, or inattentive by the teacher. Many of the participants felt disadvantaged, for example, when verbal participation in class was graded. They felt forced to conform to Western norms and values ("talking more") when such behavior violated their cultural upbringing. Although the Asian participants could see that educators might be attempting to enforce an objective grading standard, they unintentionally negated traditional Asian cultural values and penalized their Asian American students. Another example was relayed by a Vietnamese American male who describes being derided and teased by friends for using chopsticks as a utensil. He stated that the message was quite clear; eating with forks, knives, and spoons is the right/correct way to eat and "the American way."

Theme 7: Second Class Citizenship

Being treated as a lesser being or second class citizen was another common experience. A number of Asian Americans relayed similar stories of Whites being given preferential treatment as consumers over Asian American customers. A typical story involved a Korean American female who told of dining with White friends. Although she frequently ordered the wine, it is usually her friends who are asked to taste and approve the wine selection. She would often feel snubbed because Whites were believed to more knowledgeable about wine, and their opinions were more important. Another Asian American woman described how her eight family members were taken to a table to the back of the restaurant, even though there were available tables elsewhere. She interpreted the action to mean that they were lesser customers and did not deserve a table in the front of the restaurant. The message, they believed was that Asian Americans are not deserving of good service and are lesser than their White counterparts.

Theme 8: Invisibility

This theme is used to label incidents that involve the experience of being overlooked without the conscious intention of the aggressor. Experiences with the theme of invisibility are commonplace among Asian American individuals of all ethnic groups who share that they were often left out whenever issues of race were discussed or acknowledged. One Chinese American female stated, "Like even most race dialogues are like very Black and White...like sometimes I feel like there's a lot of talk about Black and White, and there's a huge Asian population here and where do we fit into that?" Another example involved an Asian American appointed to a committee and having someone suggest that they needed "to appoint a person of color" to the group as well. The messages being conveyed were that Asians are not an ethnic minority group, experience little or no discrimination, and that their racial concerns are unimportant. In addition, the Asian participants felt trapped in that when issues of race are discussed, they were considered like Whites, but never fully accepted by their White peers.

Theme 9: Undeveloped Incidents/ Responses

There were a number of stories told by participants that could not be categorized easily. The eight themes identified above seemed universally endorsed by the informants. Some of the incidents, however, were mentioned by one or two individuals in the group and it was difficult to determine the degree of consensus. It is believed that with more time and probing, it might have been possible to more clearly identify a particular theme. For example, one Chinese American woman describes an experience she had while she was driving her mother's car, with her Chinese name and last name on the license plate. She recalls being pulled over despite the fact that she was in the middle of two cars, and they were all going relatively the same speed. The stereotype operating here was that Asians are poor drivers, and therefore, she was singled out. Another example of the stereotype theme occurs when a gay Vietnamese male shared that an online dating site posted a statement that read, "No Asians, real men only." The message being conveyed in this situation is that Asian men do not fit the masculine qualities of Whites and therefore are not deemed as "real" men.

Discussion

The primary purpose of this study was to identify the types and dynamics of racial microaggressions experienced by Asian Americans. Although the eight racial microaggression themes seemed to be universally endorsed by Asian Americans in both focus groups, caution must be exercised in generalizing these findings to all Asian American groups. Our study consisted of only 10 participants, did not include all Asian ethnicities, and was not gender balanced. There was only one male participant, for example, which may make these themes gender specific. Although such an argument can be made, especially with respect to the exoticization of Asian women, sufficient anecdotal and scholarly literature suggests that the other seven are commonly mentioned by Asian Americans of both genders (Yoo & Lee, 2005; Wong & Halgin, 2006). Nevertheless, future studies might explore how gender may potentially interact with race and influence the types of microaggressions likely to be experienced by both women and men.

It could also be argued that the theme "second class citizenship," arose from our interview questions which used the phrase and may have artificially created the category. Although we were cognizant of this potential problem, we also defined the category as "inferior treatment of Asian Americans in preference to others over them." Thus, we believe that the commonalities of these microaggressive incidents are more important than the categorical name as the theme "inferior/lesser treatment" could have been used instead. In addition, a reanalysis of our transcripts revealed that an overwhelming number of microaggressive incidents classified under this theme arose from the previous six questions, prior to using the term "second class citizen."

Our study provides strong support that microaggressions are not minimally harmful and possess detrimental consequences for the recipients. Most participants described strong and lasting negative reactions to the constant racial microaggressions they experienced from well intentioned friends, neighbors, teachers, co-workers, and colleagues. They described feelings of belittlement, anger, rage, frustration, alienation, and of constantly being invalidated. Common comments from the groups were they felt trapped, invisible, and unrecognized. Although we wanted to more clearly identify how the Asian American participants behaviorally responded to what they perceived as a racial microaggression, the strategies they used to deal with it, and the impact it had on them, the focus group members spent the majority of time (a) describing microaggressive events, (b) interpreting what the message meant to them, and (c) talking about the intent of the perpetrator.

Interestingly, most of the participants acknowledged that the majority of those who engaged in microaggressions did so unintentionally, and the perpetrators often perceived their own remarks or actions in a positive light (interest in the Asian American person: "Where were you born?"). Nevertheless, most of the Asian American participants were clear that the remarks reflected a biased worldview that tended to communicate something negative and disrespectful about their group. In general, it appears that most of the Asian American participants experienced psychological conflict and distress because of several dilemmas they faced.

First, they remarked that it was often difficult to determine whether a microaggression occurred. Were they being oversensitive or misreading the remarks or questions? They described spending considerable psychic energy trying to discern the motives of the person and/ or dealing with inner turmoil and agitation caused by the event. A few stated that it was often easier to deal with a clearly overt act of bias than microaggressions that often created a "guessing game."

Second, most of the racial microaggressions that occurred came from peers, neighbors, friends or authority figures. It disturbed them that personal or respected acquaintances could make such insensitive or hurtful remarks. What bothered them most, however, was their occasional tendency to "make excuses" for friends by rationalizing away their biases and by denying their own racial reality. Although we did not specifically explore the differential impact of microaggressions from acquaintances versus strangers, it appears that some of the participants felt that microaggressive behaviors were easier to handle and less problematic when they came from strangers.

Third, many expressed severe conflict about whether to respond to microaggressions given that most were unintentional and outside the level of awareness of the perpetrator. Pointing out a microaggression to a friend, for example, generally resulted in denial, defensiveness, and a negative outcome for the relationship. A few shared that they simply were at a loss of how to respond, or that the incident occurred so quickly a chance for some sort of intervention had long passed. They described being angered and upset without any recourse other than to "stew on it." Some indicated being especially angry at themselves when they finally thought of what they could have said or done ("Damn it, that's what I should have said.") Again, we did not explore this aspect of the participants' inner turmoil; blaming themselves for not having a "comeback" and having to deal with the agitation for a prolonged period of time. We can only conclude that the emotional turmoil could be long lasting and take a psychological toll on the recipient.

Last, deciding to respond also had major consequences. Some of the informants stated that responding with anger, striking back, or confronting the person generally did no good. It only served to make the victim appear "paranoid" or suggest that the responder had some major personal problem. Unfortunately, our study did not explore the adaptive strategies used effectively by Asian American participants. In a future study it would be important to explore more deeply the psychological impact microaggressions had on the recipients, how they handled the situation, what outcome resulted, and what they would have done differently upon reflection.

Our study also points out that microaggressions often play a role in denying the racial reality of Asian Americans and strongly perpetuate the "model minority" myth. As mentioned previously, there is a strong belief that they are somehow immune to the effects of racism (Liang

et al., 2004; Wong & Halgin, 2006). Testimony from Asian Americans indicates that racial microaggressions are very hurtful and distressing to them. Besides the individual pain suffered by Asians in America, the belief that they fare better than other minority groups in achieving success in education and employment have major social implications. First, when the model minority myth is endorsed, it can become a justifiable reason to ignore the problem of discrimination against Asian Americans and be used as a convenient rationale to neglect them in research and intervention programs (Miller, 1992; Wong & Halgin, 2006). Second, it is often used by some to reaffirm the belief in a democratic society in which any group can be successful if they work hard enough or possess the right values. The result is to minimize racism or societal oppression as important forces in how minority groups do in America (D.W. Sue & D. Sue, 2003). Third, it can foster hard feelings and interethnic conflicts between Asian Americans and other groups of color. This was constantly mentioned in the themes above. Thus, it is important for social scientists and the general public to possess a realistic picture of Asian Americans and to understand the many overt and covert manifestations of racism directed at them.

Our study also potentially adds meaning to the original taxonomy of microaggressions proposed by Sue et al. (2006). Four of eight themes were similar and/or overlapping: alien in own land, ascription of intelligence, pathologizing cultural values/communication styles, and second class citizen. The four other themes color blindness, criminality/assumption of criminal status, denial of individual racism, and myth of meritocracy did not arise from our focus groups. It is important to note that the current study also identified four themes not originally proposed in the Sue et al. (2006) taxonomy: denial of racial reality, exoticization of Asian American women, invalidation of interethnic differences, and invisibility.

One major explanation is the strong possibility that different racial groups may be more likely to experience certain classes of microaggressions than others. Asian Americans, for example, may be more likely to experience microaggressions with themes that revolve around "alien in own land," "invisibility," and "invalidation of interethnic differences" than African Americans. This statement is not meant to suggest that Blacks may not also be victim to these racial microaggression themes, but they may be more prone to experience racial microaggressions around other themes like "assumption of criminal status" and "color blindness" than Asian Americans. Further, the form that microaggressions take in a similar category may be quite different between two racial groups. The theme "ascription of intelligence" for Asian Americans (intelligent and good in math and science) is contrasted to that of African Americans (intellectually inferior). In addition, a closer analysis of the total of twelve themes derived from both studies (collapsing the four common ones) reveal the possibility of further coalition into a higher order category. For example, the theme "denial of racial reality" is very similar in its effects to "color blindness." It is clear that further research regarding taxonomy of microaggressions and their culture specific manifestations would be valuable in clarifying these issues.

Although the qualitative method used in this study was rich and informative, it would be helpful to begin developing survey scales or instruments that allow for and supplement the qualitative findings on Asian American racial microaggressions. Fortunately, there has been an increasing number of studies addressing the issue of perceived discrimination against Asian Americans (Noh et al., 1999; Barry & Grillo, 2003), quantification of coping strategies (Yoo & Lee, 2005), and the development of inventories to measure race-related stress among Asian Americans (Liang et al., 2004). Indeed, the latter researchers have developed the Asian American Racism-Related Stress Inventory (AARRSI), a 29-item Likert scale consisting of three subscales: general racism, socio-historical and perpetual foreigner. Although reliability and validity appear good, it is the specific items that seem very consistent with our qualitative findings. For example, the AASRRSI contains items such as: "At a restaurant you notice that a White couple who came in after you is served first," "You are asked where you are really from," and "Someone you do not know asks you to help him/her fix his/her computer."

The experiential reality of Asian Americans has continued to indicate the existence of racial microaggressions, but their ambiguous and subtle nature makes them difficult to identify and quantify (Sue et al., 2006). Sue (2003) has often stated that the task in the study of subtle and implicit racism is "to make the invisible, visible." Using the categories developed in this study and combining them with the conceptual items of the AARRSI may prove fruitful as a guide to developing items that allow for their measurement and ultimate unmasking of Asian American microaggressions.

Appendix I: Script for Asian American Facilitator

Hi, my name is "facilitator." Thank you for coming here today to participate in this focus group. The purpose of this group is to gain a better understanding of day-to-day discrimination and experiences of subtle racism. I am sure that you are familiar with overt forms of discrimination such as racial slurs or hate crimes. However, today we are interested in hearing about your experiences of subtle acts of being discriminated against because of your race. These experiences may have occurred in any setting or at anytime in your life. We will be asking you some questions that we encourage you to answer to the best of your ability and we recognize that many of you will have unique experiences of being subtly discriminated against. There are no wrong answers.

At this time, I'd like to introduce "observer," who will be a nonparticipating member of our group today. He/She is here to record our conversation so that I can be involved in the group without having to take too many notes.

Okay, so, I am going to give everyone a form now which basically states that your participation in this group is entirely voluntary and that you may decline to participate and leave the group at any time. Please read this sheet carefully before signing it. It discusses potential risks to you as members of this group as well as the use of audiotaping during this session. I'd like to give everyone the opportunity to ask any questions they may have before we begin the group. *Question/Answer...*

Statement of Confidentiality

We will be audiotaping this session in an effort to maintain the integrity of your dialogue. However, your identities will not be revealed to anyone, and only the researchers will have access to this tape. This discussion is to be considered confidential, and we would hope that you will all respect each other rights to privacy by not repeating any portion of this discussion outside of this session.

Opening Question

At this time we would like for each of you to say your first name, your occupation and why you are interested in participating in this study.

General Question

Asian Americans often have experiences in which they are subtly, invalidated, discriminated against, and made to feel uncomfortable because of their race. In thinking about your daily experiences, could you describe a situation in which you witnessed or were personally subtly discriminated against because of your race?

Interview Questions

- What are some subtle ways that people treat you differently because of your race?

- Describe a situation in which you felt uncomfortable, insulted, or disrespected by a comment that had racial overtones.
- Think of some of the stereotypes that exist about your racial group. How have others subtly expressed their stereotypical beliefs about you?
- In what ways have others made you feel "put down" because of your cultural values or communication style?
- In what ways have people subtly expressed that "the White way is the right way"?
- In what subtle ways have others expressed that they think you're a second-class citizen or inferior to them?
- How have people suggested that you do not belong here because of your race?
- What have people done or said to invalidate your experiences of being discriminated against?

Transition Questions

- What are some of the ways that you dealt with these experiences?
- What do you think the overall impact of your experiences has been on your lives?

Ending Questions

So today you shared several experiences of subtle discrimination. Some of you said. . .

There were several themes that were consistent across many of your experiences. These themes include. . .

Does that sound correct? If not, what themes might you add?

References

American Counseling Association. (1999). *Racism: Healing its effects*. Alexandria, VA: American Counseling Association.

Banaji, M. R. (2001). Implicit attitudes can be measured. In H. L. Roediger, III, J. S. Nairne, I. Neath, & A. Surprenant (Eds.), *The nature of remembering: Essays in honor of Robert G. Crowder* (pp. 117–150). Washington, DC: American Psychological Association.

Banaji, M. R., Hardin, C., & Rothman, A. J. (1993). Implicit stereotyping in person judgment. *Journal of Personality and Social Psychology, 65*, 272–281.

Barry, D. T., & Grillo, C. M. (2003). Cultural, self-esteem, and demographic correlates of perception of personal and group discrimination among East Asian immigrants. *American Journal of Orthopsychiatry, 73*, 223–229.

Biernat, M. (2003). Toward a broader view of social stereotyping. *American Psychologist, 58*, 1019–1027.

Chakraborty, A., & McKenzie, K. (2002). Does racial discrimination cause mental illness? *British Journal of Psychiatry, 180*, 475–477.

Delgado, R., & Stefancic, J. (1992). Images of the outsider in American law and culture: Can free expression remedy systemic social ills? *Cornell Law Review, 77*, 1258–1297.

Delucchi, M., & Do, H. D. (1996). The model minority myth and perceptions of Asian-Americans as victims of racial harassment. *College Student Journal, 30*, 411–414.

DeVos, T., & Banaji, M. R. (2005). American = White? *Journal of Personality and Social Psychology, 88*, 447–466.

Dovidio, J. F., & Gaertner, S. L. (2000). Aversive racism and selection decisions: 1989 and 1999. *Psychological Science, 11*, 315–319.

Dovidio, J. F., Gaertner, S. L., Kawakami, K., & Hodson, G. (2002). Why can't we all just get along? Interpersonal biases and interracial distrust. *Cultural Diversity and Ethnicity Minority Psychology, 8*, 88–102.

Fassinger, R. E. (2005). Paradigms, praxis, problems, and promise: Grounded theory in counseling psychology research. *Journal of Counseling Psychology, 52*, 156–166.

Hill, C. E., Thompson, B. J., Hess, S. A., Knox, S., Williams, E. N., & Ladany, N. (2005). Consensual qualitative research: An update. *The Journal of Counseling Psychology, 52*, 196–205.

Hill, C. E., Thompson, B. J., & Williams, E. N. (1997). A guide to conducting consensual qualitative research. *The Counseling Psychologist, 25*, 517–572.

Hu-DeHart, E. (1995). Ethnic studies in U.S. higher education: History, development, and goals. In J.A. Banks & C.A.M. Banks (Eds.). *Handbook of research on multicultural education*. (pp. 696–707). New York: Macmillan Publishing.

Hyun, J. (2005). *Breaking the bamboo ceiling*. New York: HarperCollins Publisher.

Johnson, S. (1988). Unconscious racism and the criminal law. *Cornell Law Review, 73*, 1016–1037.

Jones, J. M. (1997). *Prejudice and racism* (2nd ed.). Washington, DC: McGraw-Hill.

Kim, J. G. S. (2002). Racial perceptions and psychological well being in Asian and Hispanic Americans. *Dissertation Abstracts International, 63*(2-B), 1033B.

Krueger, R. A. (1994). *Focus groups: A practical guide for applied research* (2nd ed.). Thousand Oaks, CA: Sage.

Krueger, R. A. (1998). *Analyzing & reporting focus group results*. Thousand Oaks, CA: Sage.

Lawrence, C. (1987). The id, the ego, and equal protection: Reckoning with unconscious racism. *Stanford Law Review, 39*, 317–388.

Liang, C. T. H., Li, L. C., & Kim, B. S. K. (2004). The Asian American Racism-Related Stress Inventory: Development, factor analysis, reliability, and validity. *Journal of Counseling Psychology, 51*, 103–114.

Matsuda, M., Lawrence, C., Delgado, R., & Crenshaw, K. (Eds.). (1993). *Words that wound: Critical race theory, assaultive speech, and the first amendment*. Boulder, CO: Westview Press.

Miles, M. B., & Huberman, A. M. (1994). *Qualitative data analysis: An expanded sourcebook.* (2nd edition). Thousand Oaks, CA: Sage.

Miller, S. K. (1992, November 13). Asian Americans bump against glass ceilings. *Science, 258,* 1224–1226.

Nakanishi, D. T. (1995). Asian Pacific Americans and colleges and universities. In J.A. Banks & C.A.M. Banks (Eds.). *Handbook of research on multicultural education* (pp. 683–695). New York: Macmillan Publishing.

Noh, S., Beiser, M., Kaspar, V., Hou, F., & Rummens, J. (1990). Perceived racial discrimination, depression and coping: A study of Southeast Asian Refugees in Canada. *Journal of Health and Social Behavior, 40,* 13–207.

Patton, M. Q. (1990). *Qualitative evaluation and research methods.* Thousand Oaks, CA: Sage.

Pierce, C. (1995). Stress analogs of racism and sexism: Terrorism, torture, and disaster. In C. Willie, P. Rieker, B. Kramer, & B. Brown (Eds.), *Mental health, racism, and sexism* (pp. 277–293). Pittsburgh: University of Pittsburgh Press.

Pierce, C., Carew, J., Pierce-Gonzalez, D., & Willis, D. (1978). An experiment in racism: TV commercials. In C. Pierce (Ed.), *Television and education* (pp. 62–88). Beverly Hills, CA: Sage.

Polkinghorne, D. E. (2005). Language and meaning: Data collection in qualitative research. *Journal of Counseling Psychology, 52,* 137–145.

President's Initiative on Race (1998). *One America in the Twenty-First Century.* Washington, DC: U.S. Government Printing Office.

Saint-Germain, M. A., Bassford, T. L., & Montano, G. (1993). Surveys and focus groups in health research with older Hispanic women. *Qualitative Health Research, 3,* 341–367.

Seal, D. W., Bogart, L. M., & Ehrhardt, A. A. (1998). Small group dynamics: The utility of focus group discussions as a research method. *Group Dynamics: Theory, Research, and Practice, 2,* 253–266.

Sleeter, C. E., & Bernal, D. D. (2004). Critical pedagogy, critical race theory, and antiracist education. In Banks, J. A. & Banks, C. A. M. (Eds.). *Handbook of research on multicultural education.* (pp. 240–258). San Francisco: Jossey Bass.

Smedley, A., & Smedley, B. D. (2005). Race as biology is fiction, racism as a social problem is real. *American Psychologist, 60,* 16–26.

Solorzano, D., Ceja, M., & Yosso, T. (2000). Critical race theory, racial microaggressions, and campus racial climate: The experiences of African American college students. *The Journal of Negro Education, 69,* 60–73.

Steele, C. M. (1997). A threat in the air: How stereotypes shape intellectual identity and performance. *American Psychologist, 52,* 613–629.

Steele, C. M., & Aronson, J. (1995). Stereotype threat and the intellectual test performance of African Americans. *Journal of Personality and social Psychology, 69,* 797–811.

Sue, D. W. (2003). Overcoming our racism: The journey to liberation. CA: Jossey-Bass.

Sue, D. W., Capodilupo, C. M., Torino, G. C. Bucceri, J. M., Holder, A. M. B., Esquilin, M. E., et al. (2006). *Racial microaggressions in everyday life: Implications for counseling.* Manuscript submitted for publication.

Sue, D. W., & Sue, D. (2003). Counseling the culturally diverse: Theory and practice. New York, NY: John Wiley & Sons, Inc.

Thompson, C. E., & Neville, H. A. (1999). Racism, mental health, and mental health practice. *The Counseling Psychologist, 27,* 155–223.

Thompson, V. L. S., Bazile, A., & Akbar, M. (2004). African Americans' perceptions of psychotherapy and psychotherapists. *Professional Psychology: Research & Practice, 35,* 19–26.

Tinsley-Jones, H. (2003). Racism: Calling a spade a spade. *Psychotherapy: Theory, Research, Practice, Training, 40,* 179–186.

Williams, D. R., Neighbors, H. W., & Jackson, J. S. (2003). Racial/ethnic discrimination and health: Findings from community studies. *American Journal of Public Health, 93,* 200–208.

Wong, F., & Halgin, R. (2006). The "Model Minority", bane or blessing for Asian Americans? *Journal of Multicultural Counseling and Development, 34,* 38–49.

Yoo, H. C., & Lee, R. M. (2005). Ethnic identity and approach-type coping as moderators of the racial discrimination/well-being relation in Asian Americans. *Journal of Counseling Psychology, 52,* 497–506.

Overcoming Ethnocentrism through Developing Intercultural Communication Sensitivity and Multiculturalism

Qingwen Dong, Kenneth D. Day & Christine M. Collarço

Introduction

The United States is a country of immigrants and it is critical for the country to promote cultural diversity and appreciate different cultural heritages (Dong, 1995). Ethnocentrism is viewed as lacking acceptance of cultural diversity and intolerance for outgroups (Berry & Kalin, 1995). This lack of acceptance of cultural diversity has a strong tendency to lead to negative stereotypes toward other cultural/ethnic groups, negative prejudice and negative behaviors against these group members. As the world becomes a global village and more and more people with diverse cultural backgrounds interact with each other constantly, it is imperative to investigate what factors could help overcome ethnocentrism. This study, by examining two of these factors, hopes to identify a better route to look for ways and means to overcome people's ethnocentrism. Reducing ethnocentrism would greatly facilitate accommodating diversity in the United States, making it a model country for diversity, equality and democracy.

In this study, the authors focus on three constructs: ethnocentrism, intercultural communication sensitivity, and multiculturalism. Research has shown that ethnocentrism tends to be negatively correlated with intercultural communication sensitivity and cultural diversity. In order to explore ways to overcome ethnocentrism, the study has three major objectives. First, it examines the impact of intercultural communication sensitivity on overcoming ethnocentrism. Second it investigates the impact of multiculturalism on overcoming ethnocentrism. Third, it proposes some measures for researchers, policy makers, and educators to use in overcoming ethnocentrism.

Literature Review

Ethnocentrism

The theoretical concept of ethnocentrism, as developed by Sumner (1906), suggested that in most intergroup contexts, one's own group is the center of everything, and all other things are related to or dependent on it. Berry and Kalin (1995) pointed out that the ethnocentrism concept tends to be viewed as "the synonym for general antipathy towards all outgroups" (p. 303). The two Canadian scholars conducted numerous studies on this topic and observed that ethnocentrism shows that "a lack of acceptance of cultural diversity, a general intolerance for outgroups and a relative preference for one's ingroup over most outgroups" (p. 303).

Neuliep and McCroskey (1997) developed a generalized ethnocentrism scale (GENE) to assess how individuals feel regarding their own culture. The scale was modified and adapted for examining people's ethnocentric views by a number of communication researchers. The GENE is a valid measurement of ethnocentrism that may be experienced by anyone, regardless of culture.

Ethnocentrism has been described as an individual psychological disposition which has both positive and negative outcome (Neuliep & McCroskey, 1997). On the one hand, ethnocentrism serves as an antecedent towards "patriotism and willingness to sacrifice for one's central group" (Neuliep & McCroskey, 1997, p. 389) and helps in constructing and maintaining one's cultural identity (Chen & Starosta, 2004). On the other hand, ethnocentrism leads to misunderstandings (Neuliep & McCroskey, 1997) and reduced levels of intercultural-willingness-to-communicate (Lin & Rancer, 2003).

Studies have also shown that ethnocentrism may be mediated by culture. Lin, Rancer, and Trimbitas (2005) found that Romanian students were more ethnocentric than American students. The authors proposed that these results may result from Romania's history of conflict with the Hungarians and being a polarized country. Neuliep, Chaudoir, and McCroskey (2001) found that Japanese students scored higher on the GENE than their American counterparts. They noted that Japan's 'parochial' psychology, that serves as the foundation for modern Japanese thinking and their homogenous culture,

"Overcoming Ethnocentrism through Developing Intercultural Communication Sensitivity and Multiculturalism" by Qingwen Dong, Kenneth D. Day and Christine M Collaco, *Human Communication*, Volume 11, Issue 1, pp. 27–38. Reprinted by permission of Qingwen Dong, Ph.D.

may account for these results. In Japan, the term "gaijin" is used to describe "people from the outside" (p. 140). In both studies, men scored higher than women (Lin et al., 2005), suggesting that socialization accounts for this difference (Neuliep et al., 2001).

Ethnocentrism is also highly related to individuals' identity formation. Kim, Kim, and Choe (2006) reviewed identity's link to ethnocentrism as it relates to multicultural issues. Kim et al. found that Koreans were more ethnocentric in comparison to Japanese and native English speakers. Koreans also scored highest in identity measurement.

According to Chen and Starosta (2000) intercultural communication sensitivity is a prerequisite for intercultural communication competence. As one's intercultural communication sensitivity increases, one's competence in intercultural communication increases. Hence, ethnocentrism can be viewed as "an obstacle to intercultural communication competence" (Neuliep & McCroskey, 1997, p. 389).

Intercultural communication sensitivity

It is crucial for individuals to develop intercultural communication competence today due to the fact that almost all of us are dealing with intercultural situations every day and everywhere. According to Chen and Starosta (2000), intercultural communication competence has two prerequisites: intercultural communication awareness and intercultural communication sensitivity. Although intercultural communication sensitivity may be related to many cognitive, affective and behavioral aspects of our interactions with others, it focuses primarily on individuals' affective abilities, such as managing and regulating emotions. Cultural awareness provides the foundation for intercultural communication sensitivity, which in turn, leads to intercultural communication competence (Chen & Starosta, 2000).

Research suggested that individuals with higher intercultural communication sensitivity tend to do well in intercultural communication settings (Peng, 2006). Bennett (1993) proposed a Developmental Model of Intercultural Sensitivity (DMIS), which suggests that individuals with intercultural sensitivity tend to transform themselves from the ethnocentric stage to the ethno-relative stage. This model includes six developmental stages (Bennett & Bennett, 2004). The first three stages of denial, defense and minimization are viewed as "ethnocentric." Individuals view their own culture as central to reality, and individuals act by "avoiding cultural differences through denying its existence, raising defense against the differences and minimizing its importance" (Bennett & Bennett, 2004, p.153). The next three stages (acceptance, adaptation, and integration) are viewed as "ethno-relative." During these stages, people experience the culture in the context of other cultures, and can be construed as "seeking cultural difference through accepting its importance, adapting a perspective to take it into account, or by integrating the whole concept into a definition of identity" (Bennett & Bennett, 2004, p.153).

The intercultural sensitivity model suggests that as one's experience of cultural difference increases, one's competence in intercultural situations goes up (Greenholtz, 2000). Olsen and Kroeger (2001) discovered that university staff and faculty members who were highly proficient in a language other than English and who had diverse cultural experience would have greater likelihood of possessing higher intercultural communication skills. One study showed that students who studied abroad developed a much higher average increase in terms of ethno-relativism than students who did not (Williams, 2005). This study indicated that in order to receive the gains of increased intercultural communication skills, individuals must interact in the culture. Another study found that employing analysis and evaluation of cultural difference in general education curriculum is more effective in improving students' levels of intercultural communication sensitivity (Mahoney & Schamber, 2004).

Multiculturalism

"Immigration has been one of the most persistent and pervasive influences of the United States" (Dong, 1995, p. 9). Due to immigration, globalization and ethnic diversification, multiculturalism is a pronounced characteristic of the United States. Multicultural ideology refers to "overall evaluation of the majority group addressing the degree to which they possess positive attitudes toward immigrants and cultural diversity" (Arends-Toth & Van de Vijver, 2002, p. 252). When individuals hold a positive overall evaluation, they tend to appreciate cultural diversity and cultural maintenance of ethnic groups.

Arends-Toth and Van de Vijver (2002) suggested that one main principle of multiculturalism is to focus on cultural diversity which, however, is perceived differently by majority and minority group members. People in minority groups, such as those in new immigrant groups, tend to promote multiculturalism, believing that multiculturalism helps them protect their cultures, self, and identity. On the other hand, people in the majority groups tend to have a mixed view of multiculturalism. On the positive side, they believe multiculturalism brings diverse views and stronger economic forces to the country. On the negative side, they view multiculturalism as a desire of immigrant groups to maintain their own culture and challenge the superior cultural and social status (Arends-Toth & Van de Vijver, 2002).

Multiculturalism is viewed as a "paradox in dealing with the question of how to construct a society that accommodates universal rights with the rights of minority groups" (Bailey & Harindranath, 2006, p. 304). Over the past five decades, the viewpoint of multiculturalism has been clearly becoming more and more visible and a popular perspective across the Western societies according to Bailey and Harindranath. In their study, the two authors argued that alternative media help produce a forum of cultural expression, "enabling a dialogue across and within cultures-both minority and majorities on what constitutes such shared values and rights, and for the redefinition of the identities of multicultural nations in the West" (p. 299). They suggested that alternative media provide a means of engaging ethnic minorities in political discourse to help address issues of marginalization of minority cultures.

One of the most prominent areas in promoting multiculturalism is the field of education. Statistics showed that most hate crimes occurring in schools or colleges are related to racial bias, religious bias, and bias against victims' ethnicity or national origins (Arizaga, Bauman, Waldo, & Castellanos, 2005). Therefore, teachers play an important role in helping students develop a multicultural perspective to appreciate cultural diversity and other perspectives. Efforts have been made to educate teachers in multicultural issues to increase their knowledge about cultural similarities and differences (Arizaga et al, 2005). In addition, teachers are required to attend education programs to develop a better understanding of diverse population to overcome prejudice.

In summary, the review of literature shows that it is potentially fruitful for communication researchers to examine the factors which can help reduce individuals' ethnocentrism in Western democratic society like the United States. Berry and Kalin (1995) defined ethnocentrism as "a lack of acceptance of cultural diversity, a general intolerance for outgroups, and a relative preference for one's ingroup over most outgroups." The literature suggests that ethnocentrism has the potential to lead to negative stereotypes, negative prejudices, and negative behaviors against minority or ethnic group members. Chen and Starosta (2004) suggested that intercultural communication sensitivity may help promote an individual's ability to respect cultural differences, foster multiple cultural identities, and maintain multicultural coexistence. Furthermore, they suggested that a multicultural mindset may enable individuals to be successful in the diverse cultural environment like the United States. The review of the literature suggests that both intercultural communication sensitivity (Chen & Starosta, 2004) and multiculturalism (Berry & Kalin, 1995) promote cultural diversity and appreciation of cultural maintenance of different cultural groups, thus, motivating people to overcome ethnocentrism. In

order to explore these relationships in terms of empirical evidence, this study proposes two hypotheses:

H1: Those who have a higher level of intercultural communication sensitivity tend to have a lower level of ethnocentrism.

H2: Those who have a higher level of multiculturalism tend to have a lower level of ethnocentrism.

Method

Sample

Participants were 419 undergraduate college students from two universities located in the western United States. The sample for the study included 248 (59%) undergraduates from a small, private university and 171 (41%) from a large, state university. The participants ranged in age from 17 to 51, with a mean of 20.6 years. In the sample, 138 (33%) were male participants while 276 (66%) were female respondents. Not including ten respondents who did not indicate their race/ethnicity, the racial/ethnic composition of the sample was 50% Caucasian, 33% Asian American, 5.5% African American, 7.2% Hispanic, and 2.4% selecting Others.

Procedures

A self-administered questionnaire was distributed to subjects during class sessions. The five-page questionnaire contained seven sections including instruments to measure intercultural communication sensitivity, multiculturalism, and ethnocentrism. The participants were told that the purpose for conducting the study was to investigate communication behaviors. Every participant was informed that the survey was voluntary and the information was completely confidential and anonymous. The survey took 10–15 minutes for the participants to complete.

Measurement

Intercultural Sensitivity Scale. The Intercultural Communication Sensitivity items were those of Chen and Starosta's (2000) Intercultural Sensitivity Scale. This scale contains 24 five-point Likert items with nine items reversed scored. The ICS scale is intended to measure individuals' feelings about interacting with people who have different cultural backgrounds. The scale includes five sub-scales, interaction engagement, respect for cultural differences, interaction confidence, interaction enjoyment, and interaction attentiveness. The 24 statements include "I enjoy interacting with people from different cultures," "I respect the values of people from different cultures," and "I am open-minded to people from different cultures." The alpha reliability coefficient of the scale is 0.88.

Multiculturalism scale. Berry and Kalin (1995) developed the multiculturalism ideology scale to assess support for having a culturally diverse society in Canada. This measurement consists of 10 five-point Likert-scale items with a high score to indicate a stronger support for cultural diversity and appreciation of maintenance of different cultural groups. These ten statements include "You can learn a lot from cultural groups," "Cultural groups should mix as much as possible," and "The more cultural groups there are, the better it is for society." The alpha reliability coefficient of the scale is 0.79.

Ethnocentrism Scale. Neuliep and McCroskey (1997) developed a revised Generalized Ethnocentrism Scale (GENE) that was adopted for the study. This scale is designed to assess people's feelings regarding their culture. The 22 five-point Likert scale statements include "Most other cultures are backward compared to my culture," "My culture should be the role model for other cultures," and "Other cultures should try to be more like my culture." The alpha reliability coefficient of the scale is 0.89.

Results

The means for the three variables were 3.9 for intercultural communication sensitivity, 3.5 for multiculturalism, and 2.6 for ethnocentrism. Standard deviations for the three variables were 0.4 for intercultural communication sensitivity, 0.5 for multiculturalism, and 0.4 for ethnocentrism, suggesting considerable variability on all three across respondents.

Correlation analysis was also performed. As predicted, there were significant negative correlations between ethnocentrism and both intercultural communication sensitivity and multiculturalism. As Table 8.1 indicates, the more an individual exhibited intercultural communication sensitivity, the less the individual scored on ethnocentrism ($r = -0.42$; $p < 0.01$). Similarly, the higher an individual scored multiculturalism, the lower the individual scored on ethnocentrism ($r = -0.37$; $p < 0.01$).

Table 8.1 Correlation Analysis of Three Key Factors

Variables	1	2	3
Ethnocentrism	1		
Intercultural Communication Sensitivity	−0.42**	1	
Multiculturalism	−0.37**	0.45**	1

Note: ** Correlation is significant at the 0.01 level (2-tailed).

A stepwise regression analysis (see Table 8.2 for details) explored the relative contribution of each variable. The results suggests that intercultural communication sensitivity plays a stronger role in overcoming individuals' ethnocentrism since it was entered as the variable explaining the greatest amount of variance in the dependent variable, ethnocentrism (Beta $= -0.32$, $p < 0.01$). Multiculturalism was found to explain additional variance unexplained by intercultural communication sensitivity (Beta $= -.23$; $p < 0.01$). If these results are taken as evidence of causal effects, then both intercultural communication sensitivity and multiculturalism make unique contributions to the reduction of ethnocentrism. Thus, both hypotheses were supported.

Discussion

The findings of the study suggest that additional attention should be given to potential factors that may reduce ethnocentrism. As a number of studies have shown, ethnocentrism has the potential to lead to negative stereotypes, negative prejudice, and negative behaviors against ethnic/minority group members. Therefore, it is possible for researchers to make a significant contribution to the reduction of ethnocentrism. Currently, there are very few empirical studies in this area examining which specific factors help reduce ethnocentrism. This study focused on two likely potential factors related to ethnocentrism, and the results indicated that both intercultural

Table 8.2 Hypothesis testing (Stepwise Regression Analysis) Summary of Regression Analysis for Variables Predicting Ethnocentrism (N=419)

(Dependent variable = Ethnocentrism)

Variables	B	SE	t	Beta
Intercultural Comm Sensitivity	−0.27	0.04	6.48	−0.32**
Multiculturalism	0.17	0.04	4.63	−0.23**

**$p < 0.01$

communication sensitivity and multiculturalism are significant predictors of ethnocentrism.

The major significance of this study is that it provides empirical evidence that higher levels of intercultural communication sensitivity and multiculturalism may lead to reduced ethnocentrism. These findings provide useful evidence to researchers, politicians, educators, and students. Researchers will continue to explore this highly social impact area to develop theories as well as practical solutions to deal with intergroup communication patterns and issues. Politicians should consider this issue and how this issue affects the diversity, equality, and democracy in our society. The United States is a leading country in the world in terms of democracy, equality, and freedom. If it has a high level of ethnocentrism, it will be very hard for people to enjoy democracy, equality and freedom. Educators and students are the two sides of the coin. Ethnocentrism tends to affect students more, and educators should play a crucial role in educating students to develop an open mindedness, appreciating cultural diversity and respect different cultural values, attitudes and ideals.

This study suggests that practitioners should promote intercultural communication sensitivity and multiculturalism at schools, in neighborhoods, communities, and other locations to educate people to "be sensitive" to others' cultures and "be appreciative of" others' cultures. This sensitivity and appreciation will greatly help us develop ethno-relative mindsets and move away from ethnocentrism mindsets. How they can effectively do this, however, is not quite so clear. Day (1998), in reviewing approaches to increasing respect for other cultures, has suggested that lectures advocating positions that would encourage decreased ethnocentrism and prejudice are less likely to be effective than first-hand, one-on-one encounters with members of other cultures.

The study has three major limitations commonly seen in studies. First, the sample was selected from college students at the university setting. The homogeneous population might limit the generalizability of results. People's differences in age, social economic status, and other demographics may affect people's attitudes towards the concept of ethnocentrism.

Secondly, the current study only focused on two possible predictors: intercultural communication sensitivity and multiculturalism. These two key factors are important but there must be additional factors that deserve further investigation.

Finally, although the survey is a powerful method to generate perception information about individuals, other research methods including experiments, field research, focus group and personal interviews should be explored

to investigate ethnocentrism to generate rich data to the timely issue facing communication researchers.

There are additionally a number of caveats specific to this study. First, the greater strength of intercultural communication sensitivity as a predictor of ethnocentrism may in fact be an artifact of measurement. The lower reliability of multiculturalism is likely to result in an underestimation of its effect on ethnocentrism, thus suggesting the need to exercise caution in attributing a greater influence to intercultural communication sensitivity.

Second, all three variables in this study are constructs in part shaped by measures. The sets of attitudinal statements or self-reported behaviors may overlap in ways which result in correlations being found not because one variable influences the other but because the constructs in part measure the same underlying factor.

Finally, exploring the causal connections between these three variables will be challenging because neither intercultural communication sensitivity nor multiculturalism can be manipulated as a treatment to see how they affect ethnocentrism. If these two variables are seen as "causes" of ethnocentrism, then interventions which are expected to affect these variables would need to be applied in a causal model which sees these variables as mediating variables. Evidence for the plausibility of this model would need to look at goodness of fit statistics comparing this mediating effect model with alternative ones.

In terms of suggestions for future research, the authors would like to see large cross-sectional surveys conducted, including different ethnicity, ages, social economic status and education backgrounds. Additionally, as noted above, longitudinal or experimental studies that track how these variables change in relationship to each other would be insightful in better developing a causal model of the inter-relationships among these variables. Future research would also benefit from other paradigms and methodologies which look for the best solutions to deal with this timely and highly critical issue and problem.

References

Arends-Toth, J., & Van de Vijver, F. J. R.(2003). Multiculturalism and acculturation: Views of Dutch and Turkish-Dutch. *European Journal of Social Psychology, 33,* 249–266.

Arizaga, M., Bauman, S., Waldo, M., & Castellanos, L. P. (2005). Multicultural sensitivity and interpersonal skills training for preservice teachers. *Journal of Humanistic Counseling, Education and Development, 44,* 198–208.

Bailey, O. G., & Harindranath, R. (2006). Ethnic minorities, cultural difference and the cultural politics of communication. *International Journal of Media and Cultural Politics, 2,* 299–316.

Bennett, J. M. (1993). Cultural marginality: Identity issues in intercultural training. In R. M. Paige (Ed.), *Education for the intercultural experience* (2nd ed., pp. 109–135). Yarmouth, ME: Intercultural Press.

Bennett, J. M., & Bennett, M. J. (2004). Developing intercultural sensitivity: An Integrative approach to global and domestic diversity. In D. Landis, J. M. Bennett, & M. J. Bennett (Eds.), *Handbook of intercultural training* (pp. 147–165). Thousand Oaks, CA: Sage.

Berry, J. W., & Kalin, R. (1995). Multicultural and ethnic attitudes in Canada: An Overview of the 1991 national survey. *Canadian Journal of Behavioral Science, 27,* 301–320.

Chen, G. M., & Starosta, W. J. (2000). The development and validation of the international communication sensitivity scale. *Human Communication, 3,* 2–14.

Chen, G. M., & Starosta, W. J. (2000). Intercultural Sensitivity. In L. A. Samovar & R. E. Porter (Eds.) *Intercultural Communication: A reader* (pp. 406–413). Belmont, CA: Wadsworth Publishing Company.

Chen, G.. M., & Starosta, W. J. (2004). Communication among cultural diversities: A Dialogue. *International and Intercultural Communication Annual, 27,* 3–16.

Day, K. D. (1998). Fostering respect for other cultures in teaching intercultural communication. In K. S. Sitaram, & M. H. Prosser (Eds.), *Civic discourse: Multiculturalism, cultural diversity, and global communication* (pp. 131–142). Stamford, CT: Ablex Publishing. Dong, Q. (1995). Self, identity, media use and socialization: A student of adolescent Asian immigrants to the United States. *Unpublished doctoral dissertation,* Washington State University, Pullman, Washington.

Greenholtz, J. (2000). Accessing cross-cultural competence in transnational education: The intercultural development inventory. *Higher Education in Europe, 25(3),* 411–416.

Kim, S., Kim, H, & Choe, Y. (2006). An exploratory study on cultural differences between Koreans, Japanese, and Native speakers of English. *Human Communication, 9,* 57–70.

Lin, Y., & Rancer, A. S. (2003). Ethnocentrism, intercultural communication apprehension, intercultural willingness-to-communicate, and intentions to participate in an intercultural dialogue program: Testing a proposed model. *Communication Research Reports, 20,* 62–72.

Lin, Y., Rancer, A. S. & Trimbitas, O. (2005). Ethnocentrism and intercultural-willingness-to-communicate: A cross-cultural comparison between Romanian and US American college students. *Journal of Intercultural Communication, 34,* 138–151. Mahoney, S. L. & Schamber, J. F. (2004). Exploring the application of a developmental model of intercultural sensitivity to a general education curriculum on diversity. *JGE: The Journal of General Education, 53, 311–334.*

McCroskey, J. C. (2006). The role of culture in a communibiological approach to communication. *Human Communication, 9,* 31–35.

Neuliep, J. W. & McCroskey, J. C. (1997). Development of a US and generalized ethnocentrism scale. *Communication Research Reports, 14,* 385–398.

Neuliep, J.W., Chaudoir, M., & McCroskey, J.C. (2001). A cross-cultural comparison of ethnocentrism among Japanese and United States college students. *Communication Research Reports, 18(2),* 137–146.

Olson, C. L., & Kroeger, K. R. (2001). Global competency and intercultural sensitivity. *Journal of Studies in International Education, 5(2), 116–137.*

Peng, S. (2006). A comparative perspective of intercultural sensitivity between college students and multinational employees in China. *Multicultural Perspectives,* 8(3), 38–45.

Williams, T. R. (2005). Exploring the impact of study abroad on students' intercultural communication skills: Adaptability and sensitivity. *Journal of Studies in International Education, 9(4),* 356–371.

Sumner, W. G. (1906). *Folkways.* Boston, MA: Ginn.

Module 11

Inequality and the Individual

The questions of what it means to be an American is not an idle one. Every day immigrants flood to this country to become part of its social, political, economic and cultural fiber. They might be coming primarily for jobs but once here, they try the best they can to integrate into the society. Many come from countries that hold different "values" than we claim to hold in the United States. Yet, over time, socialization does its work and we all, or our children, learn the rules of the society. What exactly ARE the values of this society? Why are so many Americans so SURE that this is the best society in the world? How can an individual even believe that without having visited every society in the world?

Hundreds of thousands of immigrants participate in March protesting against immigration restrictions proposed by U.S. Congress, Los Angeles, CA, May 1, 2006.

Once, early in my career, I had a foreign student in one of my classes from Sweden. She was going to do a presentation on a certain day and the night before she had seen Ronald Reagan speak to the American people. In that speech, Reagan referred to the U.S. as the "greatest country on earth" and to Americans as the "greatest people on earth." These phrases caught the attention of my student and during her presentation she digressed to express how amazed she was to hear the President of the United States speak in such a manner. "If our president were to make such assertions," she said, "to say that Sweden was the greatest country or the Swedes the greatest people, he would be laugh at. He would have no credibility." Her comments stuck with me because here in the U.S. such assertions are the norm, not the exception. It is accepted to believe that "we are the greatest." Indeed, one of our values is to think of ourselves as the greatest. What does it mean to be an American?

One characteristic of being an American is living in a very stratified society. **Social stratification** refers to a society's categorization of its people into rankings of socioeconomic tiers based on factors like wealth, income, race, education, and power. In geology, stratification refers to the distinct vertical layers found in rock. This is a good way to visualize social structure. Society's layers are made of people, and society's resources are distributed unevenly throughout the layers. The people who have more resources represent the top layer of the social structure of stratification. Other groups of people, with fewer resources, represent the lower layers of our society. In the United States, people like to believe everyone has an equal chance at success. This emphasis on self-effort perpetuates the belief that people control their own social standing. However, social scientists recognize that social stratification is a society-wide system that makes inequalities apparent.

Poverty is not a new condition in the United States but the reasons for poverty have changed since the shift to a service economy began in the 1970s. Now, the term "working poor" is not an oxymoron. Low wage employment, even with several jobs, often does not provide a worker with the basics of life. Combine that with the rising cost of housing and cuts in mental health services and some of the reasons why poverty is linked to homelessness are understood.

No individual, rich or poor, can be blamed for social inequalities. A person's social standing is affected by the structure of society. Although individuals may support or fight inequalities, social stratification is created and supported by society as a whole.

Factors that define stratification vary in different societies. In most societies, stratification is an economic system, based on **wealth**, the net value of money and assets a person has, and **income**, a person's wages or investment dividends. While people are regularly categorized based on how rich or poor they are, other important factors influence social standing. For example, in some cultures, wisdom and charisma are valued, and people who have them are revered more than those who do not. In some cultures, the elderly are esteemed; in others, the elderly are disparaged or overlooked. Societies' cultural beliefs often reinforce the inequalities of stratification.

Sociologists distinguish between two types of systems of stratification. Closed systems accommodate little change in social position. They do not allow people to shift levels and do not permit social relations between levels. Open systems, which are based on achievement, allow movement and interaction between layers and classes. Different systems reflect, emphasize, and foster certain cultural values, and shape individual beliefs. Stratification systems include class systems and caste systems, as well as meritocracy. A **caste system** is one in which people are born into their social standing and will remain in it their whole lives. People are assigned occupations regardless of their talents, interests, or potential. There are virtually no opportunities to improve one's social position. A **class system** is based on both social factors and individual achievement. A **class** consists of a set of people who share similar status with regard to factors like wealth, income, education, and occupation. Unlike caste systems, class systems are open. People are free to gain a different level of education or employment than their parents. **Meritocracy** is another system of social stratification in which personal effort—or merit—determines social standing. High levels of effort will lead to a high social position, and vice versa. The concept of meritocracy is an ideal—that is, a society has never existed where social rank was based purely on merit.

In our individualistic society, the ability to become rich or poor is often presented as a personal choice; like deciding which road to take or which key to hit on our keyboard. We can, after all, be whatever we want to be, right? And if we are not, it is our fault, right?

Social Stratification in the United States

Many people think of the United States as a "middle-class society." They think a few people are rich, a few are poor, and most are pretty well off, existing in the middle of the social strata. But a Federal Reserve Bank study in 2009 showed that a mere one percent of the population holds one third of our nation's wealth. This shows that there is not an even distribution of wealth. Millions of women and men struggle to pay rent, buy food, find work, and afford basic medical care. In the United States, as in most high-income nations, social stratifications and standards of living are in part based on occupation.

The upper class is considered America's top, and only the powerful elite get to see the view from there. In the United States, people with extreme wealth make up one percent of the population, and they own one-third of the country's wealth. Money provides not just access to material goods, but also access to power. America's upper class wields a lot of power.

The 1% has nowhere left to climb?

Many people call themselves **middle class**, but there are differing ideas about what that means. People with annual incomes of $150,000 call themselves middle class, as do people who annually earn $30,000. In the United States, the middle class is broken into upper and lower subcategories.

Upper-middle-class people tend to hold bachelor's and postgraduate degrees. They have studied subjects such as business, management, law, or medicine. Comfort is a key concept to the middle class. Upper-middle-class people tend to pursue careers that earn comfortable incomes.

Lower-middle-class members hold bachelor's degrees or associate's degrees from two-year community or technical colleges. In the lower middle class, people hold jobs supervised by members of the upper middle class. They fill technical, lower-level management, or administrative support positions. Compared to lower-class work, lower-middle-class jobs carry more prestige and come with slightly higher paychecks.

The **lower class** is also referred to as the **working class**. Just like the middle and upper classes, the lower class can be divided into subsets: the working class, the working poor, and the underclass. Compared to the lower middle class, lower-class people have less of an educational background and earn smaller incomes. They work jobs that require little prior skill or experience, often doing routine tasks under close supervision.

Working-class people, the highest subcategory of the lower class, often land decent jobs in fields like custodial or food service. The work is hands-on and often physically demanding, such as landscaping, cooking, cleaning, or building. Beneath the working class is the working poor. Like the working class, they have unskilled, low-paying employment. However, their jobs rarely offer benefits such as healthcare or retirement planning, and their positions are often seasonal or temporary. They work as sharecroppers, migrant farm workers, housecleaners, and day laborers.

The **underclass** is America's lowest tier. Members of the underclass live mainly in inner cities. Many are unemployed or underemployed. Those who do hold jobs typically perform menial tasks for littlepay. Some of the underclass are homeless. For many, welfare systems provide much-needed support through food assistance, medical care, housing, and the like.

Social mobility refers to the ability to change positions within a social stratification system. **Upward mobility** refers to an increase—or upward shift—in social class. **Downward mobility** indicates a lowering of one's social class. **Intergenerational mobility** explains a difference in social class between different generations of a family. **Intragenerational mobility** describes a difference in social class that between different members of the same generation. For example, the wealth and prestige experienced by one person may be quite different from that of his or her siblings. **Structural mobility** happens when societal changes enable a whole group of people to move up or down the social class ladder. Structural mobility is attributable to changes in society as a whole, not individual change. In the first half of the 20th century, industrialization expanded the U.S. economy, raising the standard of living and leading to upward structural mobility.

Children are particularly vulnerable to poverty. More than 16 million children in the United States—22% of all children—live in families with incomes below the federal poverty level—$23,550 a year for a family of four.

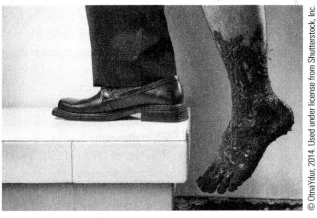

Social mobility. Myth and reality?

When analyzing the trends and movements in social mobility, sociologists consider all modes of mobility. Scholars recognize that mobility is not as common or easy to achieve as many people think. In fact, some consider social mobility a myth.

Inequality Regimes
Gender, Class, and Race in Organizations[1]

Joan Acker
University of Oregon

In this article, the author addresses two feminist issues: first, how to conceptualize intersectionality, the mutual reproduction of class, gender, and racial relations of inequality, and second, how to identify barriers to creating equality in work organizations. She develops one answer to both issues, suggesting the idea of "inequality regimes" as an analytic approach to understanding the creation of inequalities in work organizations. Inequality regimes are the interlocked practices and processes that result in continuing inequalities in all work organizations. Work organizations are critical locations for the investigation of the continuous creation of complex inequalities because much societal inequality originates in such organizations. Work organizations are also the target for many attempts to alter patterns of inequality: The study of change efforts and the oppositions they engender are often opportunities to observe frequently invisible aspects of the reproduction of inequalities. The concept of inequality regimes may be useful in analyzing organizational change projects to better understand why these projects so often fail and why they succeed when this occurs.

Keywords: gender; class; race; intersectionality; organizations

Much of the social and economic inequality in the United States and other industrial countries is created in organizations, in the daily activities of working and organizing the work. Union activists have grounded their demands in this understanding, as have feminist and civil rights reformers. Class analyses, at least since Harry Braverman's 1974 dissection of *Labor and Monopoly Capital* have often examined the doing of work, the labor process, to understand how class inequalities are produced and perpetuated (Burawoy 1979). Feminists have looked at the gendering of organizations and organizational practices to comprehend how inequalities between women and men continue in the face of numerous attempts to erase such inequalities (Acker 1990; Collinson and Hearn 1996; Ferguson 1984; Kanter 1977). Scholars working on race inequality have examined the production in work organizations of racial disparities that contribute to society-wide racial discrimination and disadvantage (Brown et al. 2003; Royster 2003).

Most studies of the production of class, gender, and racial inequalities in organizations have focused on one or another of these categories, rarely attempting to study them as complex, mutually reinforcing or contradicting processes.[2] But focusing on one category almost inevitably obscures and oversimplifies other interpenetrating realities. Feminist scholars of color have argued for 30 years, with the agreement of most white feminist scholars, that much feminist scholarship was actually about white middle-class women, ignoring the reality that the category gender is fundamentally complicated by class, race/ethnicity, and other differences (Davis 1981; hooks 1984; Joseph 1981). Similar criticisms can be made of much theory and research on race and class questions: "race," even when paired with "ethnicity," encapsulates multiple social realities always inflected through gender and class differences. "Class" is also complicated by multiple gendered and racialized differences. The conclusion to this line of thinking—theory and research on inequality, dominance, and oppression must pay attention to the intersections of, at least, race/ethnicity, gender, and class.

The need for intersectional analyses has been, for the past 15 years at least, widely accepted among feminist scholars (Collins 1995; Crenshaw 1995; Fenstermaker and West 2002; Weber 2001). How to develop this insight

AUTHOR'S NOTE: I want to thank Don Van Houten with whom I did the research that inspired this analysis, Barbara Czarniawska who helped me to rewrite the article to make it more comprehensible, Sandi Morgen who has been an invaluable research partner, and all the many other feminist scholars whose work has made mine possible.

into clear conceptions of how dimensions of difference or simultaneous inequality-producing processes actually work has been difficult and is an ongoing project (Holvino 2001; Knapp 2005; McCall 2005; Weber 2001). Different approaches provide complementary views of these complex processes. For example, Leslie McCall (2001, 2005), using large data sets, shows how patterns of gender, race, and class inequality vary with the composition of economic activity in various areas of the United States. The analysis I suggest contrasts with McCall's approach, as I propose looking at specific organizations and the local, ongoing practical activities of organizing work that, at the same time, reproduce complex inequalities. The organizing processes that constitute inequality regimes are, of course, related to the economic decision making that results in dramatically different local and regional configurations of inequality across the United States. Exploring the connections between specific inequality regimes and the various economic decisions that affect local economies would be still another approach to these complex interrelations. Here, my goal is limited—to develop the analysis of organizational inequality regimes.

I base this analysis on the voluminous research, including some of my own (Acker 1989, 1991, 1994; Acker and Van Houten 1974), on the organization of work and power relations in organizations. This analysis has its origins in my earlier arguments about the gendering of organizations, reconceptualizing that approach to add class and race and extending the discussion in various ways (Acker 1990, 1992).[3]

Inequality Regimes

All organizations have inequality regimes, defined as loosely interrelated practices, processes, actions, and meanings that result in and maintain class, gender, and racial inequalities within particular organizations. The ubiquity of inequality is obvious: Managers, executives, leaders, and department heads have much more power and higher pay than secretaries, production workers, students, or even professors. Even organizations that have explicit egalitarian goals develop inequality regimes over time, as considerable research on egalitarian feminist organizations has shown (Ferree and Martin 1995; Scott 2000).

I define inequality in organizations as systematic disparities between participants in power and control over goals, resources, and outcomes; workplace decisions such as how to organize work; opportunities for promotion and interesting work; security in employment and benefits; pay and other monetary rewards; respect; and pleasures in work and work relations. Organizations vary in the degree to which these disparities are present and in

how severe they are. Equality rarely exists in control over goals and resources, while pay and other monetary rewards are usually unequal. Other disparities may be less evident, or a high degree of equality might exist in particular areas, such as employment security and benefits.

Inequality regimes are highly various in other ways; they also tend to be fluid and changing. These regimes are linked to inequality in the surrounding society, its politics, history, and culture. Particular practices and interpretations develop in different organizations and subunits. One example is from my study of Swedish banks in the late 1980s (Acker 1994). My Swedish colleague and I looked at gender and work processes in six local bank branches. We were investigating the degree to which the branches had adopted a reorganization plan and a more equitable distribution of work tasks and decision-making responsibilities that had been agreed to by both management and the union.[4] We found differences on some dimensions of inequality. One office had almost all women employees and few status and power differences. Most tasks were rotated or shared, and the supervision by the male manager was seen by all working in the branch as supportive and benign. The other offices had clear gender segregation, with men handling the lucrative business accounts and women handling the everyday, private customers. In these offices, very little power and decision making were shared, although there were differences in the degrees to which the employees saw their workplaces as undemocratic. The one branch office that was most successful in redistributing tasks and decision making was the one with women employees and a preexisting participatory ethos.

In the following sections, I discuss in some detail the varying characteristics of inequality regimes, including the bases of inequality, the shape and degree of inequality, organizing processes that create and recreate inequalities, the invisibility of inequalities, the legitimacy of inequalities, and the controls that prevent protest against inequalities. I also discuss efforts to reduce inequality in organizations, including consideration of what elements in inequality regimes impede and/or further change. Finally, I speculate about changes in inequality regimes that are emerging as a consequence of globalizing processes.

What Varies? The Components of Inequality Regimes
The Bases of Inequality

The bases for inequality in organizations vary, although class, gender, and race processes are usually present. "Class," as I use the term, refers to enduring and systematic differences in access to and control over resources for provisioning and survival (Acker 2006; Nelson 1993). Those resources are primarily monetary in wealthy industrial societies. Some class practices take place as employment occurs and wages are paid. Thus, class is intrinsic to employment and to most organizations. In large organizations, hierarchical positions are congruent with class processes in the wider society. The CEO of the large corporation operates at the top of the national and often global society. In smaller organizations, the class structure may not be so congruent with society-wide class relations, but the owner or the boss still has class power in relations with employees. "Class" is defined by inequality; thus, "class equality" is an oxymoron (Ferguson 1984).

Gender, as socially constructed differences between men and women and the beliefs and identities that support difference and inequality, is also present in all organizations. Gender was, in the not too distant past, almost completely integrated with class in many organizations. That is, managers were almost always men; the lower-level white-collar workers were always women. Class relations in the workplace, such as supervisory practices or wage-setting processes, were shaped by gendered and sexualized attitudes and assumptions. The managerial ranks now contain women in many organizations, but secretaries, clerks, servers, and care providers are still primarily women. Women are beginning to be distributed in organizational class structures in ways that are similar to the distribution of men. Gender and class are no longer so perfectly integrated, but gendered and sexualized assumptions still shape the class situations of women and men in different ways.[5]

"Race" refers to socially defined differences based on physical characteristics, culture, and historical domination and oppression, justified by entrenched beliefs. Ethnicity may accompany race, or stand alone, as a basis for inequality. Race, too, has often been integrated into class hierarchies, but in different patterns than gender. Historically, in the United States, women and men of color were confined to the lowest-level jobs or excluded from all but certain organizations. People of color were totally excluded from the most powerful (white, male) organizations that were central in shaping the racialized and gendered class structure of the larger society. For example, the twentieth-century U.S. military was, until after World War II, a racially segregated organization dominated by white men. Other examples are the elite universities such as Harvard and Yale.

Other differences are sometimes bases for inequality in organizations. The most important, I believe, is sexuality. Heterosexuality is assumed in many organizing processes and in the interactions necessary to these processes. The secretary is or was the "office wife" (Kanter

1977). Homosexuality is disruptive of organizing processes because it flouts the assumptions of heterosexuality. It still carries a stigma that produces disadvantages for lesbians and gays. Other bases of inequality are religion, age, and physical disability. Again, in the not too distant past, having the wrong religion such as being a Jew or a Catholic could activate discriminatory practices. Today, having a Middle Eastern origin or being a Muslim may have similar consequences. Currently, age seems to be a significant basis for inequality, as are certain physical inabilities. I believe that although these other differences are important, they are not, at this time, as thoroughly embedded in organizing processes as are gender, race, and class.

Shape and Degree of Inequality

The steepness of hierarchy is one dimension of variation in the shape and degree of inequality. The steepest hierarchies are found in traditional bureaucracies in contrast to the idealized flat organizations with team structures, in which most, or at least some, responsibilities and decision-making authority are distributed among participants. Between these polar types are organizations with varying degrees of hierarchy and shared decision making. Hierarchies are usually gendered and racialized, especially at the top. Top hierarchical class positions are almost always occupied by white men in the United States and European countries. This is particularly true in large and influential organizations.[6] The image of the successful organization and the image of the successful leader share many of the same characteristics, such as strength, aggressiveness, and competitiveness. Some research shows that flat team structures provide professional women more equality and opportunity than hierarchical bureaucracies, but only if the women function like men. One study of engineers in Norway (Kvande and Rasmussen 1994) found that women in a small, collegial engineering firm gained recognition and advancement more easily than in an engineering department in a big bureaucracy. However, the women in the small firm were expected to put in the same long hours as their male colleagues and to put their work first, before family responsibilities. Masculine-stereotyped patterns of on-the-job behavior in team-organized work may mean that women must make adaptations to expectations that interfere with family responsibilities and with which they are uncomfortable. In a study of high-level professional women in a computer development firm, Joanne Martin and Debra Meyerson (1998) found that the women saw the culture of their work group as highly masculine, aggressive, competitive, and self-promoting. The women had invented ways to cope with this work culture, but they felt that they were partly outsiders who did not belong.

Other research (Barker 1993) suggests that team-organized work may not reduce gender inequality. Racial inequality may also be maintained as teams are introduced in the workplace (Vallas 2003). While the organization of teams is often accompanied by drastic reductions of supervisors' roles, the power of higher managerial levels is usually not changed: Class inequalities are only slightly reduced (Morgen, Acker, and Weigt n.d.).

The degree and pattern of segregation by race and gender is another aspect of inequality that varies considerably between organizations. Gender and race segregation of jobs is complex because segregation is hierarchical across jobs at different class levels of an organization, across jobs at the same level, and within jobs (Charles and Grusky 2004). Occupations should be distinguished from jobs: An occupation is a type of work; a job is a particular cluster of tasks in a particular work organization. For example, emergency room nurse is an occupation; an emergency room nurse at San Francisco General Hospital is a job. More statistical data are available about occupations than about jobs, although "job" is the relevant unit for examining segregation in organizations. We know that within the broad level of professional and managerial occupations, there is less gender segregation than 30 years ago, as I have already noted. Desegregation has not progressed so far in other occupations. However, research indicates that "sex segregation at the job level is more extensive than sex segregation at the level of occupations" (Wharton 2005, 97). In addition, even when women and men "are members of the same occupation, they are likely to work in different jobs and firms" (Wharton 2005, 97). Racial segregation also persists, is also complex, and varies by gender.

Jobs and occupations may be internally segregated by both gender and race: What appears to be a reduction in segregation may only be its reconfiguration. Reconfiguration and differentiation have occurred as women have entered previously male-dominated occupations. For example, women doctors are likely to specialize in pediatrics, not surgery, which is still largely a male domain. I found a particularly striking example of the internal gender segregation of a job category in my research on Swedish banks (Acker 1991). Swedish banks all had a single job classification for beginning bank workers: They were called "aspiranter," or those aspiring to a career in banking. This job classification had one description; it was used in banking industry statistics to indicate that this was one job that was not gender segregated. However, in bank branches, young women aspiranters had different tasks than young men. Men's tasks were varied and brought them into contact with different aspects of the business. Men were groomed for managerial jobs. The women worked as tellers or answered telephone inquiries. They had contact only with their immediate supervisors and coworkers in the branch. They were not being groomed for promotion. This was one job with two realities based on gender.

The size of wage differences in organizations also varies. Wage differences often vary with the height of the hierarchy: It is the CEOs of the largest corporations whose salaries far outstrip those of everyone else. In the United States in 2003, the average CEO earned 185 times the earnings of the average worker; the average earnings of CEOs of big corporations were more than 300 times the earnings of the average worker (Mishel, Bernstein, and Boushey 2003). White men tend to earn more than any other gender/race category, although even for white men, the wages of the bottom 60 percent are stagnant. Within most service-sector organizations, both white women and women of color are at the bottom of the wage hierarchy.

The severity of power differences varies. Power differences are fundamental to class, of course, and are linked to hierarchy. Labor unions and professional associations can act to reduce power differences across class hierarchies.[7] However, these organizations have historically been dominated by white men with the consequence that white women and people of color have not had increases in organizational power equal to those of white men. Gender and race are important in determining power differences within organizational class levels. For example, managers are not always equal. In some organizations, women managers work quietly to do the organizational housekeeping, to keep things running, while men managers rise to heroic heights to solve spectacular problems (Ely and Meyerson 2000). In other organizations, women and men manage in the same ways (Wacjman 1998). Women managers and professionals often face gendered contradictions when they attempt to use organizational power in actions similar to those of men. Women enacting power violate conventions of relative subordination to men, risking the label of "witches" or "bitches."

Organizing Processes that Produce Inequality

Organizations vary in the practices and processes that are used to achieve their goals; these practices and processes also produce class, gender, and racial inequalities. Considerable research exists exploring how class or gender inequalities are produced, both formally and informally, as work processes are carried out (Acker 1989, 1990; Burawoy 1979; Cockburn 1985; Willis 1977).

Some research also examines the processes that result in continuing racial inequalities. These practices are often guided by textual materials supplied by consultants or developed by managers influenced by information and/ or demands from outside the organization. To understand exactly how inequalities are reproduced, it is necessary to examine the details of these textually informed practices.

Organizing the general requirements of work

The general requirements of work in organizations vary among organizations and among organizational levels. In general, work is organized on the image of a white man who is totally dedicated to the work and who has no responsibilities for children or family demands other than earning a living. Eight hours of continuous work away from the living space, arrival on time, total attention to the work, and long hours if requested are all expectations that incorporate the image of the unencumbered worker. Flexibility to bend these expectations is more available to high-level managers, predominantly men, than to lower-level managers (Jacobs and Gerson 2004). Some professionals, such as college professors, seem to have considerable flexibility, although they also work long hours. Lower-level jobs have, on the whole, little flexibility. Some work is organized as part-time, which may help women to combine work and family obligations, but in the United States, such work usually has no benefits such as health care and often has lower pay than full-time work (Mishel, Bernstein, and Boushey 2003). Because women have more obligations outside of work than do men, this gendered organization of work is important in maintaining gender inequality in organizations and, thus, the unequal distribution of women and men in organizational class hierarchies. Thus, gender, race, and class inequalities are simultaneously created in the fundamental construction of the working day and of work obligations.

Organizing class hierarchies

Techniques also vary for organizing class hierarchies inside work organizations. Bureaucratic, textual techniques for ordering positions and people are constructed to reproduce existing class, gender, and racial inequalities (Acker 1989). I have been unable to find much research on these techniques, but I do have my own observations of such techniques in one large job classification system from my study of comparable worth (Acker 1989). Job classification systems describe job tasks and responsibilities and rank jobs hierarchically. Jobs are then assigned to wage categories with jobs of similar rank in the same wage category. Our study found that the bulk of sex-typed women's jobs, which were in the clerical/secretarial area

and included thousands of women workers, were described less clearly and with less specificity than the bulk of sex-typed men's jobs, which were spread over a wide range of areas and levels in the organization. The women's jobs were grouped into four large categories at the bottom of the ranking, assigned to the lowest wage ranges; the men's jobs were in many more categories extending over a much wider range of wage levels. Our new evaluation of the clerical/secretarial categories showed that many different jobs with different tasks and responsibilities, some highly skilled and responsible, had been lumped together. The result was, we argued, an unjustified gender wage gap: Although women's wages were in general lower than those of men, women's skilled jobs were paid much less than men's skilled jobs, reducing even further the average pay for women when compared with the average pay for men. Another component in the reproduction of hierarchy was revealed in discussions with representatives of Hay Associates, the large consulting firm that provided the job evaluation system we used in the comparable worth study. These representatives would not let the job evaluation committees alter the system to compare the responsibilities of managers' jobs with the responsibilities of the jobs of their secretarial assistants. Often, we observed, managers were credited with responsibility for tasks done by their assistants. The assistants did not get credit for these tasks in the job evaluation system, and this contributed to their relatively low wages. But if managers' and assistants' jobs could never be compared, no adjustments for inequities could ever be made. The hierarchy was inviolate in this system.

In the past 30 years, many organizations have removed some layers of middle management and relocated some decision making to lower organizational levels. These changes have been described as getting rid of the inefficiencies of old bureaucracies, reducing hierarchy and inequality, and empowering lower-level employees. This happened in two of the organizations I have studied—Swedish banks in the late 1980s (Acker 1991), discussed above, and the Oregon Department of Adult and Family Services, responsible for administration of Temporary Assistance to Needy Families and welfare reform (Morgen, Acker, and Weigt n.d.). In both cases, the decision-making responsibilities of frontline workers were greatly increased, and their jobs became more demanding and more interesting. In the welfare agency, ordinary workers had increased participation in decisions about their local operations. But the larger hierarchy did not change in either case. The frontline employees were still on the bottom; they had more responsibility, but not higher salaries. And they had no increased control over their job security. In both cases, the workers liked the changes in the content of their jobs, but the hierarchy was still inviolate.

In sum, class hierarchies in organizations, with their embedded gender and racial patterns, are constantly created and renewed through organizing practices. Gender and sometimes race, in the form of restricted opportunities and particular expectations for behavior, are reproduced as different degrees of organizational class hierarchy and are also reproduced in everyday interactions and bureaucratic decision making.

Recruitment and hiring

Recruitment and hiring is a process of finding the worker most suited for a particular position. From the perspectives of employers, the gender and race of existing jobholders at least partially define who is suitable, although prospective coworkers may also do such defining (Enarson 1984). Images of appropriate gendered and racialized bodies influence perceptions and hiring. White bodies are often preferred, as a great deal of research shows (Royster 2003). Female bodies are appropriate for some jobs; male bodies for other jobs.

A distinction should be made between the gendered organization of work and the gender and racial characteristics of the ideal worker. Although work is organized on the model of the unencumbered (white) man, and both women and men are expected to perform according to this model, men are not necessarily the ideal workers for all jobs. The ideal worker for many jobs is a woman, particularly a woman who, employers believe, is compliant, who will accept orders and low wages (Salzinger 2003). This is often a woman of color; immigrant women are sometimes even more desirable (Hossfeld 1994).

Hiring through social networks is one of the ways in which gender and racial inequalities are maintained in organizations. Affirmative action programs altered hiring practices in many organizations, requiring open advertising for positions and selection based on gender- and race-neutral criteria of competence, rather than selection based on an old boy (white) network. These changes in hiring practices contributed to the increasing proportions of white women and people of color in a variety of occupations. However, criteria of competence do not automatically translate into gender- and race-neutral selection decisions. "Competence" involves judgment: The race and gender of both the applicant and the decision makers can affect that judgment, resulting in decisions that white males are the more competent, more suited to the job than are others. Thus, gender and race as a basis for hiring or a basis for exclusion have not been eliminated in many organizations, as continuing patterns of segregation attest.

Wage setting and supervisory practices

Wage setting and supervision are class practices. They determine the division of surplus between workers and management and control the work process and workers. Gender and race affect assumptions about skill, responsibility, and a fair wage for jobs and workers, helping to produce wage differences (Figart, Mutari, and Power 2002).

Wage setting is often a bureaucratic organizational process, integrated into the processes of creating hierarchy, as I described above. Many different wage-setting systems exist, many of them producing gender and race differences in pay. Differential gender-based evaluations may be embedded in even the most egalitarian-appearing systems. For example, in my study of Swedish banks in the 1980s, a pay gap between women and men was increasing within job categories in spite of gender equality in wage agreements between the union and employers (Acker 1991). Our research revealed that the gap was increasing because the wage agreement allowed a small proportion of negotiated increases to be allocated by local managers to reward particularly high-performing workers. These small increments went primarily to men; over time, the increases produced a growing gender gap. In interviews we learned that male employees were more visible to male managers than were female employees. I suspected that the male managers also felt that a fair wage for men was actually higher than a fair wage for women. I drew two implications from these findings: first, that individualized wage-setting produces inequality, and second, that to understand wage inequality it is necessary to delve into the details of wage-setting systems.

Supervisory practices also vary across organizations. Supervisory relations may be affected by the gender and race of both supervisor and subordinate, in some cases preserving or reproducing gender or race inequalities. For example, above I described how women and men in the same aspiranter job classification in Swedish banks were assigned to different duties by their supervisors. Supervisors probably shape their behaviors with subordinates in terms of race and gender in many other work situations, influencing in subtle ways the existing patterns of inequality. Much of this can be observed in the informal interactions of workplaces.

Informal interactions while "doing the work"

A large literature exists on the reproduction of gender in interactions in organizations (Reskin 2003; Ridgeway 1997). The production of racial inequalities in workplace interactions has not been studied so frequently (Vallas 2003), while the reproduction of class relations in the daily life of organizations has been studied in the labor process tradition, as I noted above. The informal interactions and practices in which class, race, and gender inequalities are created in mutually reinforcing processes have not so often been documented, although class processes are usually implicit in studies of gendered or racialized inequalities.

As women and men go about their everyday work, they routinely use gender-, race-, and class-based assumptions about those with whom they interact, as I briefly noted above in regard to wage setting. Body differences provide clues to the appropriate assumptions, followed by appropriate behaviors. What is appropriate varies, of course, in relation to the situation, the organizational culture and history, and the standpoints of the people judging appropriateness. For example, managers may expect a certain class deference or respect for authority that varies with the race and gender of the subordinate; subordinates may assume that their positions require deference and respect but also find these demands demeaning or oppressive. Jennifer Pierce (1995), in a study of two law firms, showed how both gendered and racialized interactions shaped the organizations' class relations: Women paralegals were put in the role of supportive, mothering aides, while men paralegals were cast as junior partners in the firms' business. African American employees, primarily women in secretarial positions, were acutely aware of the ways in which they were routinely categorized and subordinated in interactions with both paralegals and attorneys. The interaction practices that re-create gender and racial inequalities are often subtle and unspoken, thus difficult to document. White men may devalue and exclude white women and people of color by not listening to them in meetings, by not inviting them to join a group going out for a drink after work, by not seeking their opinions on workplace problems. Other practices, such as sexual harassment, are open and obvious to the victim, but not so obvious to others. In some organizations, such as those in the travel and hospitality industry, assumptions about good job performance may be sexualized: Women employees may be expected to behave and dress as sexually attractive women, particularly with male customers (Adkins 1995).

The Visibility of Inequalities

Visibility of inequality, defined as the degree of awareness of inequalities, varies in different organizations. Lack of awareness may be intentional or unintentional. Managers may intentionally hide some forms of inequality, as in the Swedish banks I studied (Acker 1991). Bank workers said that they had been told not to discuss their wages with their coworkers. Most seem to have complied, partly because they had strong feelings that their pay was part of their identity, reflecting their essential worth. Some said

they would rather talk about the details of their sex lives than talk about their pay.

Visibility varies with the position of the beholder: "One privilege of the privileged is not to see their privilege." Men tend not to see their gender privilege; whites tend not to see their race privilege; ruling class members tend not to see their class privilege (McIntosh 1995). People in dominant groups generally see inequality as existing somewhere else, not where they are. However, patterns of invisibility/visibility in organizations vary with the basis for the inequality. Gender and gender inequality tend to disappear in organizations or are seen as something that is beside the point of the organization. Researchers examining gender inequality have sometimes experienced this disappearance as they have discussed with managers and workers the ways that organizing practices are gendered (Ely and Meyerson 2000; Korvajärvi 2003). Other research suggests that practices that generate gender inequality are sometimes so fleeting or so minor that they are difficult to see.

Class also tends to be invisible. It is hidden by talk of management, leadership, or supervision among managers and those who write and teach about organizations from a management perspective. Workers in lower-level, nonmanagement positions may be very conscious of inequalities, although they might not identify these inequities as related to class. Race is usually evident, visible, but segregated, denied, and avoided. In two of my organization studies, we have asked questions about race issues in the workplace (Morgen, Acker, and Weigt n.d.). In both of these studies, white workers on the whole could see no problems with race or racism, while workers of color had very different views. The one exception was in an office with a very diverse workforce, located in an area with many minority residents and high poverty rates. Here, jobs were segregated by race, tensions were high, and both white and Black workers were well aware of racial incidents. Another basis of inequality, sexuality, is almost always invisible to the majority who are heterosexual. Heterosexuality is simply assumed, not questioned.

The Legitimacy of Inequalities

The legitimacy of inequalities also varies between organizations. Some organizations, such as cooperatives, professional organizations, or voluntary organizations with democratic goals, may find inequality illegitimate and try to minimize it. In other organizations, such as rigid bureaucracies, inequalities are highly legitimate. Legitimacy of inequality also varies with political and economic conditions. For example, in the United States in the 1960s and 1970s, the civil rights and the women's movements challenged the legitimacy of racial and gender inequalities, sometimes also challenging class inequality. These challenges spurred legislation and social programs to reduce inequality, stimulating a decline in the legitimacy of inequality in many aspects of U.S. life, including work organizations. Organizations became vulnerable to lawsuits for discrimination and took defensive measures that included changes in hiring procedures and education about the illegitimacy of inequality. Inequality remained legitimate in many ways, but that entrenched legitimacy was shaken, I believe, during this period.

Both differences and similarities exist among class, race, and gender processes and among the ways in which they are legitimized. Class is fundamentally about economic inequality. Both gender and race are also defined by inequalities of various kinds, but I believe that gender and racial differences could still conceivably exist without inequality. This is, of course, a debatable question. Class is highly legitimate in U.S. organizations, as class practices, such as paying wages and maintaining supervisory oversight, are basic to organizing work in capitalist economies. Class may be seen as legitimate because it is seen as inevitable at the present time. This has not always been the case for all people in the United States; there have been periods, such as during the depression of the 1930s and during the social movements of the 1960s, when large numbers of people questioned the legitimacy of class subordination.

Gender and race inequality are less legitimate than class. Antidiscrimination and civil rights laws limiting certain gender and race discriminatory practices have existed since the 1950s. Organizations claim to be following those laws in hiring, promotion, and pay. Many organizations have diversity initiatives to attract workforces that reflect their customer publics. No such laws or voluntary measures exist to question the basic legitimacy of class practices, although measures such as the Fair Labor Standards Act could be interpreted as mitigating the most severe damages from those practices. In spite of antidiscrimination and affirmative action laws, gender and race inequalities continue in work organizations. These inequalities are often legitimated through arguments that naturalize the inequality (Glenn 2002). For example, some employers still see women as more suited to child care and less suited to demanding careers than men. Beliefs in biological differences between genders[8] and between racial/ethnic groups, in racial inferiority, and in the superiority of certain masculine traits all legitimate inequality. Belief in market competition and the natural superiority of those who succeed in the contest also naturalizes inequality.

Gender and race processes are more legitimate when embedded in legitimate class processes. For example, the low pay and low status of clerical work is historically and currently produced as both a class and a gender inequality. Most people take this for granted as just part of the way in which work is organized. Legitimacy, along with visibility, may vary with the situation of the observer: Some clerical workers do not see the status and pay of their jobs as fair, while their bosses would find such an assessment bizarre.[9] The advantaged often think their advantage is richly deserved. They see visible inequalities as perfectly legitimate.

High visibility and low legitimacy of inequalities may enhance the possibilities for change. Social movements may contribute to both high visibility and low legitimacy while agitating for change toward greater equality, as I argued above. Labor unions may also be more successful when visibility is high and legitimacy of inequalities is low.

Control and Compliance

Organizational controls are, in the first instance, class controls, directed at maintaining the power of managers, ensuring that employees act to further the organization's goals, and getting workers to accept the system of inequality. Gendered and racialized assumptions and expectations are embedded in the form and content of controls and in the ways in which they are implemented. Controls are made possible by hierarchical organizational power, but they also draw on power derived from hierarchical gender and race relations. They are diverse and complex, and they impede changes in inequality regimes.

Mechanisms for exerting control and achieving compliance with inequality vary. Organization theorists have identified many types of control, including direct controls, unobtrusive or indirect controls, and internalized controls. Direct controls include bureaucratic rules and various punishments for breaking the rules. Rewards are also direct controls. Wages, because they are essential for survival in completely monetized economies, are a powerful form of control (Perrow 2002). Coercion and physical and verbal violence are also direct controls often used in organizations (Hearn and Parkin 2001). Unobtrusive and indirect controls include control through technologies, such as monitoring telephone calls or time spent online or restricting information flows. Selective recruitment of relatively powerless workers can be a form of control (Acker and Van Houten 1974). Recruitment of illegal immigrants who are vulnerable to discovery and deportation and recruitment of women of color who have few employment opportunities and thus will accept low wages are examples of this kind of control, which preserves inequality.

Internalized controls include belief in the legitimacy of bureaucratic structures and rules as well as belief in the legitimacy of male and white privilege. Organizing relations, such as those between a manager and subordinates, may be legitimate, taken for granted as the way things naturally and normally are. Similarly, a belief that there is no point in challenging the fundamental gender, race, and class nature of things is a form of control. These are internalized, often invisible controls.[10] Pleasure in the work is another internalized control, as are fear and self-interest. Interests can be categorized as economic, status, and identity interests, all of which may be produced as organizing takes place. Identities, constituted through gendered and racialized images and experiences, are mutually reproduced along with differences in status and economic advantage. Those with the most powerful and affluent combination of interests are apt to be able to control others with the aim of preserving these interests. But their self-interest becomes a control on their own behavior.

Can Inequality Regimes Change?

Inequality regimes can be challenged and changed. However, change is difficult and change efforts often fail. One reason is that owner and managerial class interests and the power those interests can mobilize usually outweigh the class, gender, and race interests of those who suffer inequality. Even where no obvious economic interests are threatened by changes, men managers and lower-level employees often insist on maintaining ongoing organizing patterns that perpetuate inequalities. For example, white masculine identity may be tied to small relative advantages in workplace power and income. Advantage is hard to give up: Increasing equality with devalued groups can be seen and felt as an assault on dignity and masculinity. Several studies have shown that these complicated motives on the part of white men, in particular, can scuttle efforts at organizational change, even when top management is supporting such change. For example, Cynthia Cockburn (1991) analyzed the multiple ways that men resisted equality efforts in four British organizations in spite of top-level support for these efforts. In the Oregon pay equity project (Acker 1989), some male unionists could not believe that women's work might be as skilled as theirs and thus deserve higher pay. The men maintained this objection even though their own wages would not be lowered if the women's wages were increased. It was as though their masculine self-respect depended, to a degree, on the differences in pay between women and men, not the actual level of pay.

Successful change projects seem to have had a number of common characteristics. First, change efforts that target a limited set of inequality-producing mechanisms seem to be the most successful. In addition, successful efforts appear to have combined social movement and legislative support outside the organization with active support from insiders. In addition, successful efforts often involve coercion or threat of loss. Both affirmative action and pay equity campaigns had these characteristics. Affirmative action programs sought to increase the employment opportunities for women of all races and men of color in organizations and jobs in which they had very low representation. The federal legislation required such programs, and similar equality efforts, in organizations that received government funds. Employers who did not follow the law were vulnerable to loss of funds. Pay equity projects, intended to erase wage inequality between women-predominant jobs and men-predominant jobs of equal value, were authorized primarily by state and local legislation and took place primarily in public-sector organizations. In both types of efforts, the mobilization of civil rights and women's movement groups was essential to success.

When the political climate changed, beginning in the 1980s, pressures against such equality-producing initiatives grew.[11] By 2006, affirmative action programs had become mere bureaucratic paper shuffling in most organizations, undermined by a lack of outside enforcement and inside activism and by legal attacks by white men claiming reverse discrimination.[12] Pay equity efforts were undermined by industrial restructuring, attacks on labor unions, delegitimation of the public sector, and legal attacks.[13] Industrial restructuring began to undermine blue-collar, well-paid, male employment and to turn unions away from pay equity to the problems of their white male members and the defense of unions themselves against employer attacks. Unions had been prime actors in the pay equity movement; their relative weakening undermined the movement. Furthermore, government organizations came under attack in the era of private-sector, free market celebration, and funds for various programs including wage reforms were cut. When pay equity campaigns succeeded, wage gains were often modest, as, for example, the Oregon case showed (Acker 1989). The modest gains that did occur resulted from political compromise to keep costs down: The potential costs of raising clerical and other service workers' pay to comparable levels with skilled blue-collar workers or the pay of female-typed professions to the pay of male-typed professions were enormous. These potential costs were, I believe, the underlying reasons for legal challenges to pay equity (Nelson and Bridges 1999). Real pay equity extending into the private sector would have imposed huge increases in labor costs at the very time that employers were cutting their workforces, turning to temporary workers, outsourcing, and off-shoring jobs to save on labor costs.

The history of pay equity projects reveals a fundamental contradiction facing many efforts to reform inequality regimes: The goals of inequality reduction or elimination are the opposite of some of the goals of employing organizations, particularly in the United States at the beginning of the twenty-first century. In the private sector, management wants to reduce costs, increase profit, and distribute as much as possible of the profit to top management and shareholders. In the public sector, management wants to reduce costs and minimize taxes. Reducing costs involves reducing wages, not raising them, as pay equity would require. While wage inequality is not the only form of inequality, eliminating that inequality may be basic to dealing with other forms as well.

Another lesson of this history is that a focus on delimited areas of inequality, such as gender and racial imbalance in job categories or pay gaps between female and male jobs of equal value, do nothing to address underlying organizational class inequality. Both of these models of intervention work within the organizational class structure: Affirmative action intends to remove racial and gender barriers to entry into existing hierarchical positions; pay equity efforts compare male and female jobs and sometimes white predominant jobs and other-than-white predominant jobs within organizational class levels, not across those levels.[14]

These interventions also fail to address other underlying processes of inequality regimes: the male model of organizing or the persistent gendering and racialization of interactions in the workplace. Family-friendly policies provide only temporary relief for some people from the male model of organizing. The use of family-friendly policies, primarily by women when they have young children, or the use of part-time work, again primarily involving women, may increase gender inequalities in organizations (Glass 2004). Such measures may reinforce, not undermine, the male model of organizing by defining those who conform to it as serious, committed workers and those who do not as rather peripheral and probably unworthy of promotions and pay increases (Hochschild 1997).

Diversity programs and policies seem to be often aimed at some of the more subtle discriminatory processes dividing organizational participants along lines of race/ethnicity and sometimes gender through education and consciousness raising. Diversity programs replaced, in many organizations, the affirmative action programs that came under attack. As Kelly and Dobbin (1998) point out, diversity programs lack the timetables, goals, and other proactive measures of affirmative action and ·may be more acceptable to management for that reason.

But that may also be a reason that diversity training will not basically alter assumptions and actions that are rooted in the legitimation of systems of organizational power and reward that favor whites, particularly white men. The legitimacy of inequality, fear of retaliation, and cynicism limit support for change. The invisibility of inequality to those with privilege does not give way easily to entreaties to see what is going on. The intimate entwining of privilege with gendered and racialized identity makes privilege particularly difficult to unsettle.

Change projects focused on gendered behaviors that are dysfunctional for the organization provide examples of the almost unshakable fusion of gendered identities and workplace organizing practices. For example, Robin Ely and Debra Meyerson (2000) describe a change project aimed at discovering why a company had difficulty retaining high-level women managers and difficulty increasing the proportion of women in upper management. The researcher/change agents documented a culture and organizing practices at the executive level that rewarded stereotypical "heroic" male problem-solving behaviors, tended to denigrate women who attempted to be heroes, and failed to reward the mundane organization building most often done by women. Although members of the management group could see that these ways of behaving were dysfunctional for the organization, they did not make the links between these organizing practices, gender, and the underrepresentation of women. In their eyes, the low representation of women in top jobs was still due to the failure of individual women, not to system processes.

Globalization, Restructuring, and Change in Inequality Regimes

Organizational restructuring of the past 30 years has contributed to increasing variation in inequality regimes. Restructuring, new technology, and the globalization of production contribute to rising competitive pressures in private-sector organizations and budget woes in public-sector organizations, making challenges to inequality regimes less likely to be undertaken than during the 1960s to the 1980s. The following are some of the ways in which variations in U.S. inequality regimes seem to have increased. These are speculations because, in my view, there is not yet sufficient evidence as to how general or how lasting these changes might be.

The shape and degree of inequality seem to have become more varied. Old, traditional bureaucracies with career ladders still exist. Relatively new organizations, such as Wal-Mart, also have such hierarchical structures.

At the same time, in many organizations, certain inequalities are externalized in new segmented organizing forms as both production and services are carried out in other, low-wage countries, often in organizations that are in a formal, legal sense separate organizations. If these production units are seen as part of the core organizations, earnings inequalities are increasing rapidly in many different organizations. But wage inequalities are also increasing within core U.S.-based sectors of organizations.

White working- and middle-class men, as well as white women and all people of color, have been affected by restructuring, downsizing, and the export of jobs to low-wage countries. White men's advantage seems threatened by these changes, but at least one study shows that white men find new employment after layoffs and downsizing more rapidly than people in other gender/race categories and that they find better jobs (Spalter-Roth and Deitch 1999). And a substantial wage gap still exists between women and men. Moreover, white men still dominate local and global organizations. In other words, inequality regimes still seem to place white men in advantaged positions in spite of the erosion of advantages for middle-and lower-level men workers.

Inequalities of power within organizations, particularly in the United States, also seem to be increasing with the present dominance of global corporations and their free market ideology, the decline in the size and influence of labor unions, and the increase in job insecurity as downsizing and reorganization continue. The increase in contingent and temporary workers who have less participation in decisions and less security than regular workers also increases power inequality. Unions still exercise some power, but they exist in only a very small minority of private-sector organizations and a somewhat larger minority of public-sector unions.

Organizing processes that create and re-create inequalities may have become more subtle, but in some cases, they have become more difficult to challenge. For example, the unencumbered male worker as the model for the organization of daily work and the model of the excellent employee seems to have been strengthened. Professionals and managers, in particular, work long hours and often are evaluated on their "face time" at work and their willingness to put work and the organization before family and friends (Hochschild 1997; Jacobs and Gerson 2004). New technology makes it possible to do some jobs anywhere and to be in touch with colleagues and managers at all hours of day and night. Other workers lower in organizational hierarchies are expected to work as the employer demands, overtime or at odd hours. Such often excessive or unpredictable demands are easier to meet for those without daily family responsibilities. Other gendered aspects of organizing processes may be less obvious than before sex and racial discrimination emerged as legal issues. For example, employers can no longer legally exclude young women on the grounds that they may have babies and leave the job, nor can they openly exclude consideration of people of color. But informal exclusion and unspoken denigration are still widespread and still difficult to document and to confront.

The visibility of inequality to those in positions of power does not seem to have changed. However, the legitimacy of inequality in the eyes of those with money and power does seem to have changed: Inequality is more legitimate. In a culture that glorifies individual material success and applauds extreme competitive behavior in pursuit of success, inequality becomes a sign of success for those who win.

Controls that ensure compliance with inequality regimes have also become more effective and perhaps more various. With threats of downsizing and off-shoring, decreasing availability of well-paying jobs for clerical, service, and manual workers, and undermining of union strength and welfare state supports, protections against the loss of a living wage are eroded and employees become more vulnerable to the control of the wage system itself. That is, fear of loss of livelihood controls those who might challenge inequality.

Conclusion

I had two goals in writing this article. The first was to develop a conceptual strategy for analyzing the mutual production of gender, race, and class inequalities in work organizations. I have suggested the idea of inequality regimes, interlinked organizing processes that produce patterns of complex inequalities. These processes and patterns vary in different organizations; the severity of inequalities, their visibility and legitimacy, and the possibilities for change toward less inequality also vary from organization to organization. In the United States at the present time, almost all organizations have two characteristics that rarely vary: Class inequality, inflected through gendered and racialized beliefs and practices, is the normal and natural bedrock of organizing, and white men are the normal and natural top leaders.

My second goal was to better understand why so many organizational equality projects have had only modest success or have failed altogether. Looking at organizations as inequality regimes may give some clues about why change projects designed to increase equality are so often less than successful. Change toward greater equality is possible, but difficult, because of entrenched economic (class) interests, the legitimacy of class interests, and allegiances to gendered and racialized identities and advantages. When class identities and interests are integrated with gender and racial identities and interests, opposition may be most virulent to any moves to alter the combined advantages. However, top male executives who are secure in their multiple advantages and privileges may be more supportive of reducing inequalities than male middle managers who may lose proportionately more through equality organizing.

Greater equality inside organizations is difficult to achieve during a period, such as the early years of the twenty-first century, in which employers are pushing for more inequality in pay, medical care, and retirement benefits and are using various tactics, such as downsizing and outsourcing, to reduce labor costs. Another major impediment to change within inequality regimes is the absence of broad social movements outside organizations agitating for such changes. In spite of all these difficulties, efforts at reducing inequality continue. Government regulatory agencies, the Equal Employment Opportunity Commission in particular, are still enforcing antidiscrimination laws that prohibit discrimination against specific individuals (see www.eeoc.gov/stats/). Resolutions of complaints through the courts may mandate some organizational policy changes, but these seem to be minimal. Campaigns to alter some inequality regimes are under way. For example, a class action lawsuit on behalf of Wal-Mart's 1.3 million women workers is making its way through the courts (Featherstone 2004). The visibility of inequality seems to be increasing, and its legitimacy decreasing. Perhaps this is the opening move in a much larger, energetic attack on inequality regimes.

Notes

1. Some of the analysis in this article is based on chapter 5 in my book *Class Questions: Feminist Answers* (Acker 2006). I began to develop the concept of inequality regimes in a series of papers beginning in 1999 (see Acker 2000).

2. An outstanding exception to this generalization is Cynthia Cockburn's (1991) *In the Way of Women: Men's Resistance to Sex Equality in Organizations*. Cockburn's study of gender equality programs in four large British organizations integrates understanding of class processes and racial discrimination in her analysis of efforts to achieve sex equality.

3. I base my analysis primarily on organizations in the United States. However, I also use research that I and others have done in Sweden, Norway, and Finland, where inequality issues in organizations are quite similar to those in the United States.

4. At that time, the employees of all banks in Sweden were organized by the same union, Svenskabankmannaforbundet. Thus, a union-management agreement applied to all banks, although they were separate enterprises. Also, at that time, the union cooperated with management on issues of organization of work. In our study, we did observations and interviews in branches of the two largest Swedish banks.

5. See Rosabeth Moss Kanter's (1977) *Men and Women of the Corporation* for an early analysis of the gendered realities faced by managerial women, realities of the workplace that made top jobs more difficult for women than for men. These gendered class realities still exist 30 years later, although they may not be as widespread as in 1977.

6. Women have never been more than a tiny fraction of the CEOs of *Fortune* 500 companies. In 2004, eight women were 1.6 percent of the CEOs of these companies (see http://www.catalyst.org/files/fact/COTE%20Fact sheet%202002updated.pdf).

7. In some European and Scandinavian countries in the 1970s and 1980s, there was a push for workplace democracy by social democratic parties and labor confederations that resulted in a number of innovations to give workers, usually through their unions, more voice in organizing decisions. In Sweden, for example, a codetermination law was passed in the late 1970s encouraging the signing of labor-management contracts on employee/union participation in many company and workplace issues (Forsebäck 1980). No such broad initiatives occurred in the United States.

8. An example of such naturalization of inequality occurred in 2005 when Lawrence Summers, then president of Harvard, explained the low representation of women in science by saying that women did not have the natural ability to do mathematics that men had. The local and national uproar over this explanation of inequality indicates how illegitimate such arguments have become.

9. The film *9 to 5* with Dolly Parton, Jane Fonda, and others captured this alternative view from below. Its great success suggests a wide and sympathetic audience that understood the critique of workplace relations.

10. Charles Perrow (1986) calls these "premise controls," the underlying assumptions about the way things are.

11. For a review and assessment of legislation and court antidiscrimination cases related to racial inequality, see Brown et al. (2003, chap. 5).

12. For an analysis of affirmative action and women's employment, see Reskin (1998).

13. Figart, Mutari, and Power (2002) discuss several reasons for the demise of comparable worth, including the privatization of many public services. See also Nelson and Bridges (1999) for a discussion that includes an analysis of court cases undermining pay equity.

14. Cynthia Cockburn (1991) also makes this point.

References

Acker, Joan. 1989. *Doing comparable worth: Gender, class and pay equity.* Philadelphia: Temple University Press.

———. 1990. Hierarchies, jobs, and bodies: A theory of gendered organizations. *Gender & Society* 4:139-58.

———. 1991. Thinking about wages: The gendered wage gap in Swedish banks. *Gender & Society* 5:390-407.

———. 1992. Gendering organizational theory. In *Gendering organizational theory,* edited by A. J. Mills and P. Tancred. Thousand Oaks, CA: Sage.

———. 1994. The gender regime of Swedish banks. *Scandinavian Journal of Management* 10:117-30.

———. 2000. Revisiting class: Thinking from gender, race and organizations. *Social Politics* (summer): 192-214.

———. 2006. *Class questions: Feminist answers.* Lanham, MD: Rowman & Littlefield.

Acker, Joan, and Donald Van Houten. 1974. Differential recruitment and control: The sex structuring of organizations. *Administrative Science Quarterly* 19:152-63.

Adkins, Lisa. 1995. *Gendered work.* Buckingham, UK: Open University Press.

Barker, James R. 1993. Tightening the iron cage: Concertive control in self-managing teams. *Administrative Science Quarterly* 38:408-37.

Brown, M. K., M. Carnoy, E. Currie, T. Duster, D. B. Oppenheimer, M. M. Shultz, and D. Wellman. 2003. *White-washing race: The myth of a color-blind society.* Berkeley: University of California Press.

Burawoy, Michael. 1979. *Manufacturing consent.* Chicago: University of Chicago Press.

Charles, Maria, and David B. Grusky. 2004. *Occupational ghettos: The worldwide segregation of women and men.* Stanford, CA: Stanford University Press.

Cockburn, Cynthia. 1985. *Machinery of dominance.* London: Pluto.

———. 1991. *In the way of women: Men's resistance to sex equality in organizations.* Ithaca, NY: ILR Press.

Collins, Patricia Hill. 1995. Comment on West and Fenstermaker. *Gender & Society* 9:491-94.

Collinson, David L., and Jeff Hearn, eds. 1996. *Men as managers, managers as men.* London: Sage.

Crenshaw, Kimberlé Williams. 1995. Mapping the margins: Intersectionality, identity politics, and violence against women of color. In *Critical race theory: The key writings that formed the movement,* edited by K. Crenshaw, N. Gotanda, G. Peller, and K. Thomas. New York: New Press.

Davis, Angela Y. 1981. *Women, race & class.* New York: Vintage.

Ely, Robin J., and Debra E. Meyerson. 2000. Advancing gender equity in organizations: The challenge and importance of maintaining a gender narrative. *Organization* 7:589-608.

Enarson, Elaine. 1984. *Woods-working women: Sexual integration in the U.S. Forest Service.* Tuscaloosa, AL: University of Alabama Press.

Featherstone, Liza. 2004. *Selling women short: The landmark battle for workers' rights at Wal-Mart.* New York: Basic Books.

Fenstermaker, Sarah, and Candace West, eds. 2002. *Doing gender, doing difference: Inequality, power, and institutional change.* New York: Routledge.

Ferguson, Kathy E. 1984. *The feminist case against bureaucracy.* Philadelphia: Temple University Press.

Ferree, Myra Max, and Patricia Yancey Martin, eds. 1995. *Feminist organizations.* Philadelphia: Temple University Press.

Figart, D. M., E. Mutari, and M. Power. 2002. *Living wages, equal wages.* London: Routledge.

Forsebäck, Lennart. 1980. *Industrial relations and employment in Sweden.* Uppsala, Sweden: Almqvist & Wiksell.

Glass, Jennifer. 2004. Blessing or curse? Work-family policies and mother's wage growth over time. *Work and Occupations* 31:367-94.

Glenn, Evelyn Nakano. 2002. *Unequal freedom: How race and gender shaped American citizenship and labor.* Cambridge, MA: Harvard University Press.

Hearn, Jeff, and Wendy Parkin. 2001. *Gender, sexuality and violence in organizations.* London: Sage.

Hochschild, Arlie Russell. 1997. *The time bind: When work becomes home & home becomes work.* New York: Metropolitan Books.

Holvino, Evangelina. 2001. Complicating gender: The simultaneity of race, gender, and class in organization change(ing). Working paper no. 14, Center for Gender in Organizations, Simmons Graduate School of Management, Boston.

hooks, bell. 1984. *Feminist theory: From margin to center.* Boston: South End.

Hossfeld, Karen J. 1994. Hiring immigrant women: Silicon Valley's "simple formula". In *Women of color in U.S. society,* edited by M. B. Zinn and B. T. Dill. Philadelphia: Temple University Press.

Jacobs, Jerry A., and Kathleen Gerson. 2004. *The time divide: Work, family, and gender inequality.* Cambridge, MA: Harvard University Press.

Joseph, Gloria. 1981. The incompatible ménage á trois: Marxism, feminism and racism. In *Women and revolution: The unhappy marriage of Marxism and feminism,* edited by L. Sargent. Boston: South End.

Kanter, Rosabeth Moss. 1977. *Men and women of the corporation.* New York: Basic Books.

Kelly, Erin, and Frank Dobbin. 1998. How affirmative action became diversity management: Employer response to antidiscrimination law, 1961 to 1996. *American Behavioral Scientist* 41:960-85.

Knapp, Gudrun-Axeli. 2005. Race, class, gender. *European Journal of Women's Studies* 12:249-65.

Korvajärvi, Päivi. 2003. "Doing gender"—Theoretical and methodological considerations. In *Where have all the structures gone? Doing gender in organisations, examples from Finland, Norway and Sweden,* edited by E. Gunnarsson, S. Andersson, A. V. Rosell, A. Lehto, and M. Salminen-Karlsson. Stockholm, Sweden: Center for Women's Studies, Stockholm University.

Kvande, Elin, and Bente Rasmussen. 1994. Men in male-dominated organizations and their encounter with women intruders. *Scandinavian Journal of Management* 10:163-74.

Martin, Joanne, and Debra Meyerson. 1998. Women and power: Conformity, resistance, and disorganized coaction. In *Power and influence in organizations*, edited by R. Kramer and M. Neale. Thousand Oaks, CA: Sage.

McCall, Leslie. 2001. *Complex inequality: Gender, class, and race in the new economy.* New York: Routledge.

———. 2005. The complexity of intersectionality. *Signs: Journal of Women in Culture and Society* 30:1771-1800.

McIntosh, Peggy. 1995. White privilege and male privilege: A personal account of coming to see correspondences through work in women's studies. In *Race, class, and gender: An anthology*, 2nd ed., edited by M. L. Andersen and P. H. Collins. Belmont, CA: Wadsworth.

Mishel, L., J. Bernstein, and H. Boushey. 2003. *The state of working America 2002/2003.* Ithaca, NY: Cornell University Press.

Morgen, S., J. Acker, and J. Weigt. n.d. *Neo-liberalism on the ground: Practising welfare reform.*

Nelson, Julie A. 1993. The study of choice or the study of provisioning? Gender and the definition of economics. In *Beyond economic man: Feminist theory and economics*, edited by M. A. Ferber and J. A. Nelson. Chicago: University of Chicago Press.

Nelson, Robert L., and William P. Bridges. 1999. *Legalizing gender inequality: Courts, markets, and unequal pay for women in America.* Cambridge, UK: Cambridge University Press.

Perrow, Charles. 1986. A society of organizations. *Theory and Society* 20:725-62.

———. 2002. *Organizing America.* Princeton, NJ: Princeton University Press.

Pierce, Jennifer L. 1995. *Gender trials: Emotional lives in contemporary law firms.* Berkeley: University of California Press.

Reskin, Barbara. 1998. *The realities of affirmative action in employment.* Washington, DC: American Sociological Association.

———. 2003. Including mechanisms in our models of ascriptive inequality. *American Sociological Review* 68:1-21.

Ridgeway, Cecilia. 1997. Interaction and the conservation of gender inequality. *American Sociological Review* 62:218-35.

Royster, Deirdre A. 2003. *Race and the invisible hand: How white networks exclude Black men from blue-collar jobs.* Berkeley: University of California Press.

Salzinger, Leslie. 2003. *Genders in production: Making workers in Mexico's global factories.* Berkeley: University of California Press.

Scott, Ellen. 2000. Everyone against racism: Agency and the production of meaning in the anti racism practices of two feminist organizations. *Theory and Society* 29:785-819.

Spalter-Roth, Roberta, and Cynthia Deitch. 1999. I don't feel right-sized; I feel out-of-work sized. *Work and Occupations* 26:446-82.

Vallas, Steven P. 2003. Why teamwork fails: Obstacles to workplace change in four manufacturing plants. *American Sociological Review* 68:223-50.

Wacjman, Judy. 1998. *Managing like a man.* Cambridge, UK: Polity.

Weber, Lynn. 2001. *Understanding race, class, gender, and sexuality.* Boston: McGraw-Hill.

Wharton, Amy S. 2005. *The sociology of gender.* Oxford, UK: Blackwell.

Willis, Paul. 1977. *Learning to labor.* Farnborough, UK: Saxon House.

Joan Acker is a professor emerita in the Department of Sociology, University of Oregon. She has written on class, women and work, gender and organizations, and feminist theory. She has been awarded the American Sociological Association (ASA) Career of Distinguished Scholarship Award and the ASA Jessie Bernard Award for feminist scholarship. Her new book is Class Questions: Feminist Answers *(2006, Rowman & Littlefield). Her most recent empirical research is a large, collaborative study of welfare reform in the state of Oregon,* Oregon Families Who Left Temporary Assistance to Needy Families or Food Stamps: A Study of Economic and Family Well-Being from 1998 to 2000.

Being Poor, Black, and American
The Impact of Political, Economic, and Cultural Forces

William Julius Wilson

Through the second half of the 1990s and into the early years of the 21st century, public attention to the plight of poor black Americans seemed to wane. There was scant media attention to the problem of concentrated urban poverty (neighborhoods in which a high percentage of the residents fall beneath the federally designated poverty line), little or no discussion of inner-city challenges by mainstream political leaders, and even an apparent quiescence on the part of ghetto residents themselves. This was dramatically different from the 1960s, when the transition from legal segregation to a more racially open society was punctuated by social unrest that sometimes expressed itself in violent terms, as seen in the riots that followed the assassination of Dr. Martin Luther King, Jr.

But in 2005, Hurricane Katrina exposed concentrated poverty in New Orleans. When television cameras focused on the flooding, the people trapped in houses and apartments, and the vast devastation, many Americans were shocked to see the squalid living conditions of the poor. Of course, the devastation of Katrina was broadly visited upon the residents of New Orleans, black and white, rich and poor, property owner and public housing tenant alike. But while many residents were able to flee, the very poor, lacking automobiles or money for transportation and lodging, stayed to wait out the storm with tragic results. And through Katrina, the nation's attention became riveted on these poor urban neighborhoods.

If television cameras had focused on the urban poor in New Orleans, or in any inner-city ghetto, before Katrina, I believe the initial reaction to descriptions of poverty and poverty concentration would have been unsympathetic. Public opinion polls in the United States routinely reflect the notion that people are poor and jobless because of their own shortcomings or inadequacies. In other words, few people would have reflected on how the larger forces in society—including segregation, discrimination, a lack of economic opportunity, and failing public schools—adversely affect the inner-city poor. However, because Katrina was clearly a natural disaster that was beyond

the control of the inner-city poor, Americans were much more sympathetic. In a sense, Katrina turned out to be something of a cruel natural experiment, wherein better-off Americans could readily see the effects of racial isolation and chronic economic subordination.

Despite the lack of national public awareness of the problems of the urban poor prior to Katrina, social scientists have rightly devoted considerable attention to concentrated poverty, because it magnifies the problems associated with poverty in general: joblessness, crime, delinquency, drug trafficking, broken families, and dysfunctional schools. Neighborhoods of highly concentrated poverty are seen as dangerous, and therefore they become isolated, socially and economically, as people go out of their way to avoid them.[1]

In this article, I provide a political, economic, and cultural framework for understanding the emergence and persistence of concentrated urban poverty. I pay particular attention to poor inner-city black neighborhoods, which have the highest levels of concentrated poverty. I conclude this article by suggesting a new agenda for America's ghetto poor, based on the analysis I put forth in the following sections.

Political Forces

Since 1934, with the establishment of the Federal Housing Administration (FHA), a program necessitated by the massive mortgage foreclosures during the Great Depression, the U.S. government has sought to enable citizens to become homeowners by underwriting mortgages. In the years following World War II, however, the federal government contributed to the early decay of inner-city neighborhoods by withholding mortgage capital and making it difficult for these areas to retain or attract families who were able to purchase their own homes. The FHA selectively administered the mortgage program by formalizing a process that excluded certain urban neighborhoods using empirical data that suggested a probable

"Being Poor, Black, and American: The Impact of Political, Economic, and Cultural Forces," by William Julius Wilson, *American Educator*, Spring 2011, pp. 10–25. Reprinted by permission of the author.

loss of investment in these areas. "Redlining," as it came to be known, was assessed largely on racial composition. Although many neighborhoods with a considerable number of European immigrants were redlined, virtually all black neighborhoods were excluded. Homebuyers hoping to purchase a home in a redlined neighborhood were universally denied mortgages, regardless of their financial qualifications. This severely restricted opportunities for building or even maintaining quality housing in the inner city, which in many ways set the stage for the urban blight that many Americans now associate with black neighborhoods. This action was clearly motivated by racial bias, and it was not until the 1960s that the FHA discontinued mortgage restrictions based on the racial composition of the neighborhood.[2]

Subsequent policy decisions worked to trap blacks in these increasingly unattractive inner cities. Beginning in the 1950s, the suburbanization of the middle class, already under way with government-subsidized loans to veterans, was aided further by federal transportation and highway policies that included the building of freeway networks through the hearts of many cities, which had a devastating impact on the neighborhoods of black Americans. These developments not only spurred relocation from the cities to the suburbs among better-off residents, the freeways themselves also "created barriers between the sections of the cities, walling off poor and minority neighborhoods from central business districts,"[3] For instance, a number of studies have revealed how Richard J. Daley, the former mayor of Chicago, used the Interstate Highway Act of 1956 to route expressways through impoverished African American neighborhoods, resulting in even greater segregation and isolation.[4] A lasting legacy of that policy is the 14-lane Dan Ryan Expressway, which created a barrier between black and white neighborhoods.[5]

Another particularly egregious example of the deleterious effects of highway construction is Birmingham, Alabama's interstate highway system, which curved and twisted to bisect several black neighborhoods rather than taking a more direct route through some predominantly white neighborhoods. The highway system essentially followed the boundaries that had been established in 1926 as part of the city's racial zoning law, although these boundaries were technically removed a few years before the highway construction began in 1956.[6]

At the same time, government policies such as mortgages for veterans and mortgage interest tax exemptions for developers enabled the quick, cheap production of massive amounts of tract housing[7] and drew middle-class whites into the suburbs.[8] A classic example of this effect of housing market incentives is the mass-produced suburban Levittown neighborhoods that were first erected in New York, and later in Pennsylvania, New Jersey, and Puerto Rico. The homes in these neighborhoods were manufactured on a large scale, using an assembly line model of production, and were arranged in carefully engineered suburban neighborhoods that included many public amenities, such as shopping centers and space for public schools. These neighborhoods represented an ideal alternative for people who were seeking to escape cramped city apartments, and were often touted as "utopian communities" that enabled people to live out the "suburban dream." Veterans were able to purchase a Levittown home for a few thousand dollars with no money down, financed with low-interest mortgages guaranteed by the Veterans Administration. However, the Levitts would not initially sell to African Americans. The first black family moved into Levittown, New York, in 1957, having purchased a home from a white family,[9] and they endured harassment, hate mail, and threats for several months after moving in. Levittown, New York, remains a predominantly white community today. Here, once again, we have a practice that denied African Americans the opportunity to move from segregated inner-city neighborhoods.

Explicit racial policies in the suburbs reinforced this segregation by allowing suburbs to separate their financial resources and municipal budgets from those of the cities. In the 19th and early 20th centuries, strong municipal services in cities were very attractive to residents of small towns and suburbs; as a result, cities tended to annex suburbs and surrounding areas. But the relations between cities and suburbs in the United States began to change following the Great Depression; the centurylong influx of poor migrants who required expensive services and paid relatively little in taxes could no longer be profitably absorbed into the city economy. Annexation largely ended in the mid-20th century as suburbs began to successfully resist incorporation. Suburban communities also drew tighter boundaries through the use of zoning laws, discriminatory land-use controls, and site selection practices that made it difficult for inner-city racial minorities to access these areas because these practices were effectively used to screen out residents on the basis of race.

As separate political jurisdictions, suburbs also exercised a great deal of autonomy through covenants and deed restrictions. In the face of mounting pressure for integration in the 1960s, "suburbs chose to diversify by race rather than class. They retained zoning and other restrictions that allowed only affluent blacks (and in some instances Jews) to enter, thereby intensifying the concentration and isolation of the urban poor."[10] Although these policies clearly had racial connotations, they also reflected class bias and helped reinforce the exodus of white working-class and middle-class families from urban neighborhoods and the growing segregation of low-income blacks in inner-city neighborhoods.

Federal public housing policy contributed to the gradual growth of segregated black ghettos as well. The federal public housing program's policies evolved in two stages that represented two distinct styles, The Wagner-Steagall Housing Act of 1937 initiated the first stage. Concerned that the construction of public housing might depress private rent levels, groups such as the U.S. Building and Loan League and the National Association of Real Estate Boards successfully lobbied Congress to require, by law, that for each new unit of public housing erected, one "unsafe or unsanitary" unit of public housing must be destroyed.

The early years of the public housing program produced positive results. Initially, the program mainly served intact families temporarily displaced by the Depression or in need of housing after the and of World War II. For many of these families, public housing was the first step on the road toward economic recovery. Their stays in the projects were relatively brief because they were able to accumulate sufficient economic resources to move on to private housing.

The passage of the Housing Act of 1949 marked the beginning of the second policy stage. It instituted and funded the urban renewal program, designed to eradicate urban slums, and therefore was seemingly nonracial. However, the public housing that it created "was now meant to collect the ghetto residents left homeless by the urban renewal bulldozers."[11] A new, lower income ceiling for public housing residency was established by the Federal Public Housing Authority, and families with incomes above that ceiling were evicted, thereby restricting access to public housing to only the most economically disadvantaged segments of the population.

This change in federal housing policy coincided with the Second Great Migration[*] of African Americans from the rural South to the cities of the Northeast and Midwest, which lasted 30 years—from 1940 to 1970. As the black urban population in the North grew, pressure mounted in white communities to keep blacks out. Suburban communities, with their restrictive covenants and special zoning laws, refused to permit the construction of public housing. And the federal government acquiesced to opposition to the construction of public housing in

the neighborhoods of organized white groups in the city. Thus, units were overwhelmingly concentrated in the overcrowded and deteriorating inner-city ghettos—the poorest and least-powerful sections of cities and metropolitan areas, In short, public housing became a federally funded institution that isolated families by race and class, resulting in high concentrations of poor black families in inner-city ghettos.[12]

In the last quarter of the 20th century, one of the most significant changes in these neighborhoods was the out-migration of middle-income blacks. Before the 1970s, African American families faced extremely strong barriers when they considered moving into white neighborhoods. Not only did many experience overt discrimination in the housing market, some were violently attacked, Although even today fair-housing audits continue to reveal the existence of discrimination in the housing market, fair-housing legislation has reduced the strength of these barriers. At the same time, middle-income African Americans have increased their efforts to move from areas with concentrated black poverty to more desirable neighborhoods throughout metropolitan areas, including white neighborhoods.[13]

In addition, beginning in 1980, when Ronald Reagan became president, sharp spending cuts in direct aid to cities dramatically reduced budgets for general reduced sharing (unrestricted funds that can be used for any purpose), urban mass transit, economic development assistance, urban development action grants, social service block grants, local public works, compensatory education, public service jobs, and job training. Many of these programs were designed to help disadvantaged individuals gain some traction in attaining financial security.[14] It is telling that the federal contribution was 17.5 percent of the total city budgets in 1977, but only 5.4 percent by 2000.[15] These cuts were particularly acute for older cities in the East and Midwest that largely depended on federal and state aid to fund social services for their poor population and to maintain aging infrastructure.

The decline in federal support for cities since 1980 coincided with an increase in the immigration of people from poorer countries—mainly low-skilled workers from Mexico—and whites steadily moving to the suburbs. With minorities displacing whites as a growing share of the population, the implications for the urban tax base were profound. According to the U.S. Census Bureau, in 2000, the median annual household income of Latinos was about $14,000 less than that of whites. With a declining tax base and the simultaneous loss of federal funds, municipalities had trouble raising enough revenue to cover basic services such as garbage collection, street

---

[*] This mass movement of African Americans was even larger and more sustained than the First Great Migration, which began at the turn of the 20th century and ended during the Great Depression, and had a more profound Impact on the transformation of the inner city.

cleaning, and police protection. Some even cut such services in order to avoid bankruptcy.[16]

This financial crisis left many cities ill-equipped to handle three devastating public health problems that emerged in the 1980s and disproportionately affected areas of concentrated poverty: first, the prevalence of drug trafficking and associated violent crime; second, the acquired immunodeficiency syndrome (AIDS) epidemic and its escalating public health costs; and third, the rise in the homeless population, including not only individuals, but entire families as well.[17] Although drug addiction, drug-related violence, AIDS, and homelessness are found in many American communities, their impact on the black ghetto is profound, A number of fiscally strapped cities have watched helplessly as these problems—aggravated by the reduction of citywide social services as well as high levels of neighborhood joblessness—have reinforced the perception that cities are dangerous places to live and have perpetuated the exodus of working-and middle-class residents. Thus, while poverty and joblessness, and the social problems they generate, remain prominent in ghetto neighborhoods, many cities have fewer and fewer resources with which to combat them.

Finally, policymakers have indirectly contributed to concentrated poverty in inner-city neighborhoods with decisions that have decreased the attractiveness of low-paying jobs and accelerated the relative decline in the wages of low-income workers. In particular, in the absence of an effective labor market policy, policymakers have tolerated industry practices that undermine worker security—including the erosion of benefits and the rise of involuntary part-time employment.

In sum, federal government policies, even those that are not explicitly racial, have had a profound impact on inner-city neighborhoods. These impacts have been felt in many cities across the country, but they perhaps have been felt more in the older central cities of the Midwest and Northeast—the traditional Rust Belt— where depopulated, high-poverty areas have experienced even greater problems.

Economic Forces

Older urban areas were once the hubs of economic growth and activity, and were therefore major destinations for people in search of economic opportunity. However, the economies of many of these cities have since been eroded by complex economic transformations and shifting patterns in metropolitan development. These economic forces are typically considered nonracial—in the sense that their origins are not the direct result of

actions, processes, or ideologies that explicitly reflect racial bias. Nevertheless, they have accelerated neighborhood decline in the inner city and widened gaps in race and income between cities and suburbs.[18]

Since the mid-20th century, the mode of production in the United States has shifted dramatically from manufacturing to one increasingly fueled by finance, services, and technology. This shift has accompanied the technological revolution, which has transformed traditional industries and brought about changes that range from streamlined information technology to biomedical engineering.[19]

In the last several decades, almost all improvements in productivity have been associated with technology and human capital, thereby drastically reducing the importance of physical capital.[20] With the increased globalization of economic activity, firms have spread their operations around the world, often relocating their production facilities to developing nations that have dramatically lower labor costs.[21]

These global economic transformations have adversely affected the competitive position of many U.S. Rust Belt cities. For example, Baltimore, Cleveland, Detroit, Philadelphia, and Pittsburgh perform poorly on employment growth, an important traditional measure of economic performance. Nationally, employment increased by 25 percent between 1991 and 2001, yet job growth in these older central cities did not exceed 3 percent.[22]

With the decline in manufacturing employment in many of the nation's central cities, most of the jobs for lower-skilled workers are now in retail and service industries (for example, store cashiers, customer service representatives, fast-food servers, and custodial work). Whereas jobs in manufacturing industries typically were unionized, relatively stable, and carried higher wages, those for workers with low to modest levels of education in the retail and service industries tend to provide lower wages, be unstable, and lack the benefits and worker protections—such as workers' health insurance, medical leave, retirement benefits, and paid vacations—typically offered through unionization. This means that workers relegated to low-wage service and retail firms are more likely to experience hardships as they struggle to make ends meet. In addition, the local economy suffers when residents have fewer dollars to spend in their neighborhoods.[23]

Beginning in the mid-1970s, the employment balance between central cities and suburbs shifted markedly to the suburbs. Since 1980, over two-thirds of employment growth has occurred outside the central city: manufacturing is now over 70 percent suburban, and wholesale and retail trade is just under 70 percent.[24] The suburbs of many central cities, developed originally as bedroom localities for commuters to the central business and manufacturing districts, have become employment centers in themselves. For example, in Baltimore, Detroit, and Philadelphia, less than 20 percent of the jobs are now located within three miles of the city center.[25]

Accompanying the rise of suburban and exurban economies has been a change in commuting patterns. Increasingly, workers completely bypass the central city by commuting from one suburb to another. "In the Cleveland region, for example, less than one-third of workers commute to a job in the central city and over half (55 percent) begin and end in the suburbs."[26]

Sprawl and economic stagnation reduce inner-city residents' access to meaningful economic opportunities and thereby fuel the economic decline of their neighborhoods. For example, in Cleveland, although entry-level workers are concentrated in inner-city neighborhoods, 80 percent of the entry-level jobs are located in the suburbs,[27] and there is little public transportation between these neighborhoods and jobs.

In addition to the challenges in learning about and reaching jobs, there is persistent racial discrimination in hiring practices, especially for younger and less-experienced minority workers.[28] This racial factor affects black males especially seriously. Today, most of the new jobs for workers with limited education and experience are in the service sector, which includes jobs that tend to be held by women, such as waitstaff, sales clerks, and nurse's aides. Indeed, "employment rates of young black women now exceed those of young black men, even though many of these women must also care for children."[29] The shift to service jobs has resulted in a greater demand for workers who can effectively serve and relate to the consumer. In an extensive study in Chicago that my colleagues and I conducted, many employers indicated they felt that, unlike women and immigrants (who have recently expanded the labor pool for service-sector jobs), inner-city black males lack these qualities.[30] Instead, low-skilled black males are perceived as dangerous or threatening. In the past, all black men had to demonstrate was a strong back and muscles for heavy lifting and physical labor in a factory, at a construction site, or on an assembly line. They did not have to interact with customers. Today, they have to search for work in the service sector, and employers are less likely to hire them because they have to come into contact with the public. Consequently, black male job-seekers face rising rates of rejection. This may well account for the higher dropout rate and lower academic achievement of black males in comparison with black females. Black males are far less likely than black females to see a strong relationship between their schooling and postschool employment.

With the departure of higher-income families, the least upwardly mobile in society—mainly low-income people of color—are left behind in neighborhoods with high concentrations of poverty and deteriorating physical conditions. These neighborhoods offer few jobs and typically lack basic services and amenities, such as banks, grocery stores and other retail establishments, parks, and quality transit.[31] Typically, these communities also suffer from substandard schools, many with rundown physical plants. Two of the most visible indicators of neighborhood decline are abandoned buildings and vacant lots. According to one recent report, there are 60,000 abandoned and vacant properties in Philadelphia, 40,000 in Detroit, and 26,000 in Baltimore.[32]

Cultural Forces

In addition to racial and nonracial political and economic forces, cultural forces may also contribute to or reinforce racial inequality. Two types of cultural forces are in play: (1) national views and beliefs on race, and (2) cultural traits—shared outlooks, modes of behavior, traditions, belief systems, worldviews, values, skills, preferences, styles of self-presentation, etiquette, and linguistic patterns—that emerge from patterns of intragroup interaction in settings created by discrimination and segregation and that reflect collective experiences within those settings.

Racism has historically been one of the most prominent American cultural frames and has played a major role in determining how whites perceive and act toward blacks. At its core, racism is an ideology of racial domination with two key features: (1) beliefs that one race is either biologically or culturally inferior to another, and (2) the use of such beliefs to rationalize or prescribe the way members of the "inferior" race should be treated as well as to explain their social position as a group and their collective accomplishments. Today, there is no question that the more categorical forms of racist ideology—in particular, those that assert the biogenetic inferiority of blacks—have declined significantly, even though they still may be embedded in institutional norms and practices. For example, school tracking, the practice of grouping students of similar capability for instruction, not only tends to segregate African American students but often results in placing some black students in lower-level classes, even though they have the cultural capital—requisite skills for learning—to compete with students in higher-level classes.[33]

However, there has emerged a form of what some scholars refer to as "laissez faire racism," a perception that blacks are responsible for their own economic predicament and therefore are undeserving of special government support.[34] The idea that the federal government "has a special obligation to help improve the living standards of blacks" because they "have been discriminated against for so long" was supported by only one in five whites in 2001, and has not exceeded support by more than one in four since 1975. Significantly, the lack of white support for this idea is not related to background factors such as level of education or age.

The vast majority of social scientists agree that as a national cultural frame, racism, in its various forms, has had harmful effects on African Americans as a group. Indeed, considerable research has been devoted to the effects of racism in American society. However, there is little research and far less awareness of the impact of emerging cultural frames in the inner city on the social and economic outcomes of poor blacks. Note that distinct cultural frames in the inner city have not only been shaped by race and poverty, but in turn often shape responses to poverty, including responses that may contribute to the perpetuation of poverty. Moreover, an important research question for social scientists is the following: how much of the framing of racial beliefs at the national level is based on the actual observed cultural traits among the inner-city poor and how much of it is the result of biased media reports and racial stereotypes?

In my own earlier work, I have discussed at length how several factors determine the extent to which communities, as areas bounded by place, differ in outlook and behavior.[35] These factors include the degree to which the community is socially isolated from the broader society; the material assets or resources controlled by members of the community; the benefits and privileges the community members derive from these resources; their accumulated cultural experiences from current as well as historical, political, and economic arrangements; and the influence members of the community wield because of these arrangements.

Culture is closely intertwined with social relations in the sense of providing tools (skills, habits, and styles) and creating constraints (restrictions on behavior or outlooks) in patterns of social interaction.[36] These constraints include cultural frames (shared visions of human behavior) developed over time through the processes of in-group meaning making (shared views on how the world works) and decision making (choices that reflect shared definitions of how the world works)—for example, in the inner-city ghetto cultural frames define issues of trust/street smarts and "acting black" or "acting white"—that lead to observable group characteristics.*

One of the effects of living in racially segregated neighborhoods is exposure to group-specific cultural traits (cultural frames, orientations, habits, and world-views as well as styles of behavior and particular skills) that emerged from patterns of racial exclusion and that may not be conducive to social mobility. For example, research has found that some groups in the inner city put a high value on "street smarts," the behaviors and actions that keep them safe in areas of high crime.[38] Street smarts may be an adaptation to living in unsafe neighborhoods. In this environment, it is wise to avoid eye contact with strangers and keep to yourself. This mindset may also lead someone to approach new situations with a certain level of skepticism or mistrust. Although such an approach is logical and smart in an unsafe neighborhood, the same behavior can be interpreted as antisocial in another setting. Moreover, this street-smart behavior may, in some cases, prevent individuals from performing well on a job interview, creating a perception that they are not desirable job candidates.

Other concrete examples from the writings of sociologists Elijah Anderson and Sudhir Venkatesh on ghetto experiences might prove to be even more illuminating.[39] Each author reveals the existence of informal rules in the inner-city ghetto that govern interactions and shape how people engage one another and make decisions. This decision making is influenced partly by how people come to view their world over time—what we call "meaning making." It is important to remember that the processes of meaning making and decision making evolve in situations imposed by poverty and racial segregation—situations that place severe constraints on social mobility. Over time, these processes lead to the development of informal codes that regulate behavior.

First of all, Anderson talks about the "code of the street," an informal but explicit set of rules developed to govern interpersonal public behavior and regulate

---

* There is mixed evidence for the outcomes of "acting white" as it applies to education. One of the most well-known studies of this concept was published by Signithia Fordham and John Ogbu in 1986. They studied African American students at a high school in Washington, DC, and concluded that the fear of acting white was one of the major factors undermining student achievement. In contrast, Prudence Carter's studies have not supported the idea that students who avoided "acting white" held lower educational aspirations. Roland Fryer presents yet another perspective. He found that a high grade point average (GPA) presents a social disadvantage for Hispanics and blacks in integrated schools and public schools, but he saw no such effect in schools that were segregated (80 percent or more black) or private. He also noticed a marked difference in this effect among black boys and black girls; black boys in public, integrated schools were particularly susceptible to social ostracism as their GPAs Increased, and were penalized seven times more than black students (including both genders) overall.[37]

violence in Philadelphia's inner-city ghetto neighborhoods, where crime is high and police protection is low. Anderson argues that the issue of respect is at the root of the code. In a context of limited opportunities for success, some individuals in the community, most notably young black males, devise alternative ways to gain respect that emphasize manly pride, ranging from simply wearing brand-name clothing, to having the "right look" and talking the right way, to developing a predatory attitude toward neighbors. Anderson points out, however, that no one residing in these troubled neighborhoods is unaffected by the code of the street—especially young people, who are drawn into this negative culture both on the streets and in the schools, as they must frequently adopt "street" behavior as a form of self-defense. As Anderson puts it, "the code of the street is actually a cultural adaptation to a profound lack of faith in the police and the judicial system—and in others who would champion one's personal security."[40]

A related informal but regulated pattern of behavior was described by Venkatesh in his study of the underground economy in ghetto neighborhoods. Venkatesh points out that "the underground arena is not simply a place to buy goods and services. It is also a field of social relationships that enable off-the-books trading to occur in an ordered and predictable manner."[41] This trading often results in disagreements or breaches because there are no laws on the books, but "in situations ostensibly criminal and often threatening to personal security, there is still a structure in place that shapes how people make decisions and engage one another."[42] In other words, informal rules actually govern what would appear on the surface to be random underground activity. These rules stipulate what is expected of those involved in these informal exchanges and where they should meet. Just as Anderson describes a "code of the street," Venkatesh talks about a "code of shady dealings."

Like Anderson in his effort to explain the emergence of the code of the street, Venkatesh argues that the code of shady dealings is a response to circumstances in inner-city ghetto neighborhoods, where joblessness is high and opportunities for advancement are severely limited. Furthermore, both Anderson and Venkatesh clearly argue that these cultural codes ultimately hinder integration into the boarder society and are therefore dysfunctional. In other words, they contribute to the perpetuation of poverty.

Anderson finds that for some young men, the draw of the street is so powerful that they cannot avail themselves of legitimate employment opportunities when they become available. Likewise, Venkatesh maintains that adherence to the code of shady dealings impedes social mobility. The "underground economy enables people to survive but can lead to alienation from the wider world," he states.[43] For example, none of the work experience accrued in the informal economy can be listed on a resume for job searches in the formal labor market, and time invested in underground work reduces time devoted to accumulating skills or contacts for legitimate employment.

However, many liberal scholars are reluctant to discuss or research the role that culture plays in the negative outcomes found in the inner city. It is possible that they fear being criticized for reinforcing the popular view that negative social outcomes—poverty, unemployment, drug addiction, crime—are due to the short-comings of the people themselves. Indeed, sociologist Orlando Patterson maintains that there is "a deep-seated dogma that has prevailed in social science and policy circles since the mid-1960s: the rejection of any explanation that invokes a group's cultural attributes—its distinctive attitudes, values and tendencies, and the resulting behavior of its members—and the relentless preference for relying on structural factors like low incomes, joblessness, poor schools and bad housing."[44]

Patterson claims that social scientists have shied away from cultural explanations of race and poverty because of the widespread belief that such explanations are tantamount to blaming the victim; that is, they support the conclusion that the poor themselves, and not the social environment, are responsible for their own poverty and negative social outcomes. He colorfully contends that it is "utterly bogus" to argue, as do by many academics, that cultural explanations necessarily blame the victim for poor social outcomes. To hold an individual responsible for his behavior is not to rule out any consideration of the environmental factors that may have evoked the questionable behavior to begin with. "Many victims of child abuse end up behaving in self-destructive ways," Patterson states. "To point out the link between their behavior and the destructive acts is in no way to deny the causal role of their earlier victimization and the need to address it."[45] Patterson also contends that a cultural explanation of human behavior not only examines the immediate relationship between attitudes and behavior but also looks at the past to investigate the origins and changing nature of these attitudes.

I agree with Patterson that cultural explanations should be part of any attempt to fully account for such behavior and outcomes. And I think it is equally important to acknowledge that recognizing the important role of cultural influences in creating different racial group outcomes does not require us to ignore or play down the much greater role of social, political, and economic forces that are clearly racial, as well as those that are ostensibly nonracial.

I also strongly agree with Patterson that an adequate explanation of cultural attributes in the black community must explore the origins and changing nature of attitudes and practices going back decades, even centuries. Unfortunately such analyses are complex and difficult.[46] For example, sociologist Kathryn Neckerman had to conduct years of research to provide the historical evidence to explain why so many black youngsters and their parents lose faith in the public schools. She shows in her book, *Schools Betrayed,* that a century ago, when African American children in most northern cities attended schools alongside white children, the problems commonly associated with inner-city schools—low achievement and dropping out—were not nearly as pervasive as they are today.[47]

Neckerman carefully documents how city officials responded to increases in the African American student population: by introducing and enforcing segregation between black and white children in the city schools. And she discusses at length how poor white immigrant children—whose family circumstances were at least as impoverished as their black counter-parts—received more and better resources for their education. "The roots of classroom alienation, antagonism, and disorder can be found in school policy decisions made long before the problems of inner-city schools attracted public attention," states Neckerman.[48] Clearly, we can more fully understand the frustration and current cultural dynamics in inner-city neighborhoods, in this case with reference to public schools, if we understand the history that work like Neckerman's uncovers.

Finally, although culture "partly determines behavior, it also enables people to change behavior."[49] Culture provides a frame for individuals to understand their world. By ignoring or only investigating culture at a superficial level, social scientists miss an opportunity to help people understand and then reframe attitudes in a way that promotes desirable behavior and outcomes.[50] However, attitudes must be reframed in conjunction with programs that address structural inequities.

For those committed to fighting inequality, especially those involved in multiracial coalition politics, the lesson from this discussion of key social, political, economic, and cultural forces is to fashion a new agenda that gives more scrutiny to both racial and nonracial policies. Given our devastating recent recession and slow, jobless recovery, it is especially important to scrutinize fiscal, monetary, and trade policies that may have long-term consequences for our national and regional economies. *We must ameliorate the primary problem feeding concentrated poverty: inner-city joblessness.* The ideal solution would be economic policies that produce a tight labor market—that is, one in which there are ample jobs for all applicants. More than any other group, low-skilled workers depend upon a strong economy, particularly a sustained tight labor market.

This new agenda should also include an even sharper focus on traditional efforts to fight poverty, to ensure that the benefits from any economic upturn are widely shared among the poor and that they become less vulnerable to downward swings in the economy. I refer especially to the following:

- combating racial discrimination in employment, which is especially devastating during slack labor markets;
- revitalizing poor urban neighborhoods, including eliminating abandoned buildings and vacant lots to make them more attractive for economic investment that would help improve the quality of life and create jobs in the neighborhood;
- promoting job training programs to enhance employment opportunities for ghetto residents;
- improving public education to prepare inner-city youngsters for higher-paying and stable jobs in the new economy; and
- strengthening unions to provide the higher wages, worker protections, and benefits typically absent from low-skilled jobs in retail and service industries.

In short, this new agenda would reflect a multi-pronged approach that attacks inner-city poverty on various levels, an approach that recognizes the complex array of factors that have contributed to the crystallization of concentrated urban poverty and limited the life chances of so many inner-city residents.

Notes

1. Paul A. Jargowsky, "Ghetto Poverty among Blacks in the 1980s," *Journal of Policy Analysis and Management* 13, no. 2 (Spring 1994): 288–310.
2. Michael B. Katz, "Reframing the 'Underclass' Debate," in *The "Underclass" Debate: Views from History,* ed. Michael B. Katz (Princeton, NJ: Princeton University Press, 1993), 440–478; David W. Bartelt, "Housing the 'Underclass,'" in *The "Underclass" Debate: Views from History,* ed, Michael B. Katz (Princeton, NJ: Princeton University Press, 1993), 118–157; Thomas J. Sugrue, "The Structure of Urban Poverty: The Reorganization of Space and Work in Three Periods of American History," in *The "Underclass" Debate: Views from History,* ed. Michael B. Katz (Princeton, NJ: Princeton University Press, 1993), 85–117; and Robin D. G. Kelley, "The Black Poor and the Politics of Opposition in a New South City, 1929–1970," in *The "Underclass"*

Debate: Views from History, ed. Michael B. Kate (Princeton, NJ: Princeton University Press, 1993), 293–333.

3. Katz, "Refraining the 'Underclass' Debate," 462. Also see Bartelt, "Housing the 'Underclass'"; Sugrue, "The Structure of Urban Poverty"; and Martin Anderson, *The Federal Bulldozer: A Critical Analysis of Urban Renewal, 1949–1962* (Cambridge, MA: MIT Press, 1964).

4. Raymond A. Mohl, "Planned Destruction: The Interstates and Central City Housing," In *From Tenements to the Taylor Homes: in Search of an Urban Housing Policy in Twentieth-Century America,* ed. John F. Bauman, Roger Blles, and Kristin M. Szylvlan (University Park, PA: Pennsylvania State University Press, 2000), 226–245; Adem Cohen and Elizabeth Taylor, *American Pharaoh: Mayor Richard J. Daley; His Battle for Chicago and the Nation* (Boston: Little, Brown, 2000); and Arnold R. Hirsch, *Making the Second Ghetto: Race and Housing in Chicago, 1940–1960* (Cambridge, MA: Cambridge University Press, 1983).

5. Cohen and Taylor, *American Pharaoh.*

6. Charles E. Connerly, "From Racial Zoning to Community Empowerment: The Interstate Highway System and the African American Community In Birmingham, Alabama," *Journal of Planning Education and Research* 22, no. 2 (December 2002): 99–114.

7. Robert J. Sampson and William Julius Wilson, "Toward a Theory of Race, Crime, and Urban Inequality," in *Crime and Inequality,* ed, John Hagan and Ruth D. Peterson (Stanford, CA: Stanford University Press, 1995), 37–54.

8. Katz, "Refraining the 'Underclass' Debate."

9. Rosalyn Baxandall and Elizabeth Ewen, *Picture Windows: How the Suburbs Happened* (New York: Basic Books, 1999).

10. Katz, "Reframing the 'Underclass' Debate," 461–462. On the history of suburbs in America, see Kenneth T. Jackson, *Crabgrass Frontier: The Suburbanization of the United States* (New York: Oxford University Press, 1985). For a good discussion of the effects of housing discrimination on the living conditions, education, and employment of urban minorities, see John Yinger, *Closed Doors, Opportunities Lost: The Continuing Costs of Housing Discrimination* (New York: Russell Sage Foundation, 1995).

11. Mark Condon, "Public Housing, Crime and the Urban Labor Market: A Study of Black Youth in Chicago," Working Paper Series (Cambridge, MA: Malcolm Wiener Center, John F. Kennedy School of Government, Harvard University, 1991), 4.

12. Sampson and Wilson, "Toward a Theory of Race," Also see Bartelt, "Housing the 'Underclass'"; Kelley, "The Black Poor and the Politics of Opposition"; Sugrue, "The Structure of Urban Poverty"; Hirsch, *Making the Second Ghetto*; and John F. Bauman, Norman P. Hummon, and Edward K. Muller, "Public Housing, Isolation, and the Urban Underclass," *Journal of Urban History* 17, no. 3 (May 1991): 264–292.

13. Lincoln Quillian, "Migration Patterns and the Growth of High-Poverty Neighborhoods, 1970–1990," *American Journal of Sociology* 105, no. 1 (July 1999): 1–37.

14. See Demetrios Caraley, "Washington Abandons the Cities," *Political Science Quarterly* 107, no. 1 (Spring 1992); 1–30.

15. Bruce A. Wallin, *Budgeting for Basks: The Changing Landscape of City Finances* (Washington, DC: Brookings Institution Metropolitan Policy Program, August 2005).

16. U.S. Department of Housing and Urban Development, *The State of the Cities, 1999* (Washington, DC: Government Printing Office, 1999).

17. Caraley, "Washington Abandons the Cities."

18. Radhika K. Fox and Sarah Treuhaft, *Shared Prosperity, Stronger Regions: An Agenda for Rebuilding America's Older Core Cities* (Oakland, CA: Pollcylink, 2005).

19. Fox and Treuhaft, *Shared Prosperity,* and Bill Joy, "Why the Future Doesn't Need Us," *Wired* (April 2000): 238–262.

20. William Julius Wilson, *When Work Disappears: The World of the New Urban Poor* (New York: Alfred A. Knopf, 1996).

21. Fox and Treuhaft, *Shared Prosperity.*

22. Fox and Treuhaft, *Shared Prosperity.*

23. Fox and Treuhaft, *Shared Prosperity,* and Wilson, *When Work Disappears.*

24. U.S. Department of Housing and Urban Development, *The State of the Cities.*

25. Fox and Treuhaft, *Shared Prosperity.*

26. Fox and Treuhaft, *Shared Prosperity,* 32.

27. Fox and Treuhaft, *Shared Prosperity.*

28. See, for example, Wilson, *When Work Disappears.* Joleen Kirschenman and Kathryn M. Neckerman, "'We'd Love to Hire Them, But. . .': The Meaning of Race for Employers," in *The Urban Underclass,* ed. Christopher Jencks and Paul E. Peterson (Washington, DC: Brookings Institution, 1991), 203–234; Kathryn M. Neckerman and Joleen Kirschenman, "Hiring Strategies, Racial Bias, and Inner-City Workers," *Social Problems* 38, no, 4 (November 1991); 433–447; and Harry J. Holzer, *What Employers Want: Job Prospects for Less-Educated Workers* (New York: Russell Sage, 1995).

29. Harry J. Holzer. Paul Offner, and Elaine Sorensen, "What Explains the Continuing Decline in Labor Force Activity among Young Black Men?" (paper presented for Color Lines Conference, Harvard University, August 30, 2003),

30. Wilson, *When Work Disappears.*

31. William Julius Wilson, *The Truly Disadvantaged: The Inner City, the Underclass, and Public Policy* (Chicago; University of Chicago Press, 1990); Wilson, *When Work Disappears*; and Fox and Treuhaft, *Shared Prosperity.*

32. Fox and Treuhaft, *Shared Prosperity.*

33. For a review of the literature on school tracking, see Janese Free, "Race and School Tracking: From a Social Psychological Perspective" (paper presented at the annual meeting of the American Sociological Association, San Francisco, CA, August 14, 2004).

34. Lawrence Bobo, James R. Kluegel, and Ryan A. Smith, "Laissez-Faire Racism: The Crystallization of a Kinder, Gentler, Antiblack Ideology." In *Racial Attitudes in the 1990s: Continuity and Change,* ed. Steven A. Tuch and Jack K. Martin (Westport, CT: Praeger, 1997), 15–44.

35. Wilson, *When Work Disappears.*

36. Charles Tilly, *Durable Inequality* (Berkeley, CA: University of California Press, 1998).

37. Signithia Fordham and John Ogbu, "Black Students' School Success: Coping with the Burden of 'Acting White,'" *Urban Journal* 18, no. 3 (1986): 176–206; Prudence L. Carter, "'Black' Cultural Capital, Status Positioning, and Schooling Conflicts for Low-Income African American Youth," *Social Problems* 50, no. 1 (2003): 136–155; Prudence L. Carter, *Keepin' It Real: School Success beyond Black and White* (New York: Oxford University Press, 2005); and Roland G. Fryer, "'Acting White': The Social Price Paid by the Best and Brightest Minority Students," *Education Next* 6, no. 1 (Winter 2006), 53–59.

38. Elijah Anderson, *Code of the Street: Decency, Violence, and the Moral Life of the Inner City* (New York: W. W. Norton, 1999).

39. Anderson, *Code of the Street*; and Sudhir Alladi Venkatesh, *Off the Books: The Underground Economy of the Urban Poor* (Cambridge, MA; Harvard University Press, 2006).

40. Anderson, *Code of the Street*, 34.

41. Venkatesh, *Off the Books*, 381.

42. Venkatesh, *Off the Books*, 377.

43. Venkatesh, *Off the Books*, 385. For another excellent study of how activities in the underground economy can adversely affect inner-city residents, see Loïc Wacquant, "Inside the Zone: The Art of the Hustler in the Black American Ghetto," *Theory Culture, and Society* 15, no. 2 (1998): 1–36.

44. Orlando Patterson, "A Poverty of the Mind," *New York Times*, March 26, 2006, section 4, page 13.

45. Patterson, "A Poverty of the Mind."

46. William Julius Wilson, *More Than Just Race: Being Black and Poor in the Inner City* (New York: W. W. Norton, 2009); and Orlando Patterson, "Taking Culture Seriously: A Framework and an Afro-American Illustration," In *Culture Matters: How Values Shape Human Progress*, ed. Lawrence E. Harrison and Samuel P. Huntington (New York: Basic Books, 2000), 202–218.

47. Kathryn M. Neckerman, *Schools Betrayed: Roots of Failure in Inner-City Education* (Chicago: University of Chicago Press, 2007).

48. Neckerman, *Schools Betrayed*, 174.

49. Patterson, "A Poverty of the Mind."

50. Patterson, "A Poverty of the Mind."

New Jobs, New Workers, and New Inequalities: Explaining Employers' Roles in Occupational Segregation by Nativity and Race

Jill Lindsey Harrison, *University of Colorado-Boulder*

Sarah E. Lloyd, *University of Wisconsin-Madison*

While sociologists have shown how employers contribute to occupational segregation along lines of race, gender, and nativity, little attention has been paid to unpacking why employers engage in those practices. We take on this gap through a case study of hired labor relations on Wisconsin dairy farms, which have become segregated along lines of nativity and race in recent years. We ask how these workplaces have become segregated, what employers' roles in this process have been, and why, in particular, employers have engaged in practices that contribute to workplace inequalities. We find that employers engage in practices that leave immigrant workers clustered in the low-end jobs for a complex array of reasons: to maintain profits within a changing industry context, meet their own middle-class aspirations, comply with their peers' middle-class lifestyle expectations, manage their own concerns about immigration policing, assert their own class identity, justify the privileges that they and their U.S.-born employees enjoy on the farm, and maintain the advantages they have gained. We argue that sociologists seeking to explain employers' roles in occupational segregation must examine not only the stories employers tell about different worker groups but also the stories they tell about themselves and the contexts that shape their aspirations and identities. Doing so provides more complete explanations for why occupational segregation occurs and does the important work of bringing whiteness into the spotlight and showing how privilege is quietly constructed and defended. Keywords: occupational segregation; workplace inequality; symbolic boundaries; immigrant workers; illegality.

Work in "America's Dairyland" is changing hands. Rural Wisconsin has long reflected the pastoral model of small-scale family farms established by German and Scandinavian immigrants in the 1800s (DuPuis 2002; Gilbert

Previous versions of this article were presented at the American Sociological Society annual meeting, the Rural Sociological Society annual meeting, and the Department of Sociology and Anthropology at North Carolina State University. The authors thank participants in these venues, as well as Jenn Bair, Sandy Brown, Jane Collins, Bill Friedland, Sanyu Mojola, Stef Mollborn, Isaac Reid, Laura Senier, Christi Sue, Amy Wilkins, six anonymous reviewers for the journal, and Editor Becky Pettit at *Social Problems*. Julia McReynolds, Trish O'Kane, and Brent Valentine helped with research design, data collection, and preliminary analysis. Data collection was supported by the Program on Agricultural Technology Studies (PATS) at UW-Madison, USDA Hatch Grant #WIS01272, and the Frederick H. Buttel Professorship funds. Direct correspondence to: Jill Harrison, Department of Sociology UCB 327, University of Colorado-Boulder, Boulder CO 80309. E-mail: jill.harrison@colorado.edu.

Social Problems, Vol. 60, Issue 3, pp. 281–301, ISSN 0037-7791, electronic ISSN 1533-8533. © 2013 by Society for the Study of Social Problems, Inc. All rights reserved. Please direct all requests for permission to photocopy or reproduce article content through the University of California Press's Rights and Permissions website at www.ucpressjournals.com/reprintinfo/asp. DOI: 10.1525/sp.2013.60.3.281.

and Akor 1988; Janus 2011). Yet our research shows that the state's dairy farms are expanding in size and increasingly hiring immigrants from Latin America, many lacking legal authorization to be in the United States, to do the low-level, arduous jobs of milking cows. Having hired these immigrant workers into nearly half of all dairy jobs over just the past 10 years, dairy farmers are thus playing an important role in rural Wisconsin's emergence as a new Latino immigrant destination (APL 2011).

In this article, we use this case as a timely opportunity to explain why employers organize workers in unequal ways. In so doing, we build upon scholarship that identifies how employers contribute to occupational segregation. Philip Moss and Chris Tilly (2001), Roger Waldinger and Michael I. Lichter (2003), and others using employer interviews and ethnographic observation have demonstrated that employers themselves engage in numerous practices that contribute to segregated workplaces, such as relying on racial and gender stereotypes in assessing workers, using those stereotypes to recruit workers thought to be most subservient, recruiting through specific worker networks, and telling stories about worker groups that naturalize unequal outcomes. These important contributions notwithstanding, the scholarship has provided few insights into *why* employers engage in those practices.

To provide a more complete explanation for why employers engage in practices that produce occupational segregation, we look not only at the stories employers tell about specific worker groups but also at the stories employers tell about themselves and the contexts within which they live. Through attending to Wisconsin dairy farmers' own biographies, identities, and aspirations, we glean a more thorough and nuanced explanation for why employers engage in practices that marginalize immigrant workers and naturalize that subordination. Namely, we find that employers organize workers in unequal ways not only because they succumb to stereotypes and greed but because the new and unequal organization of work and workers enables these employers to maintain profits within a changing industry context, meet their own middle-class aspirations, comply with their peers' middle-class lifestyle expectations, manage their own concerns about immigration policing, assert their own class identity, justify the privileges that they and their white, U.S.-born employees enjoy on the farm, and maintain the advantages they have gained.

Scholarship on Employers' Roles in Occupational Segregation

Considerable scholarship has documented occupational segregation by race and gender, showing persistent inequalities in terms of job placement, pay, promotion, authority, performance assessments, and treatment that further affect future job and career prospects. While neoclassical "supply side" perspectives attribute race- and gender-based inequalities to individual-level worker characteristics, sociologists using a wide range of methodological approaches and empirical contexts have demonstrated that workers' prospects in the job market are deeply shaped by race, gender, and other social structures independently of individual characteristics.

In this article, we build upon the body of occupational segregation scholarship concerned with employers' roles in such outcomes. Most such studies use in-depth interviews with employers and/or ethnographic observation in the workplace to identify the mechanisms through which employers organize work and workers in unequal ways. First, scholars have shown that employers attach meanings to race, nativity, and gender that make certain worker groups undesirable. Employers thus favor or discriminate against workers based on ascribed characteristics throughout the recruitment, interviewing, and position assignment processes; when evaluating the worth of skills; when allocating skills training opportunities; and when making promotions (Kanter 1977; Maldonado 2009; Matthews and Ruhs 2007; McDowell, Batnizky, and Dyer 2007; Moss and Tilly 2001; Neckerman and Kirschenman 1991; Reskin 1988; Steinberg 1990; Thomas 1985; Tomaskovic-Devey 1993; Waldinger and Lichter 2003; Zamudio and Lichter 2008).

Scholars have also shown that employers select for subordination. Employers seeking to fill low-end positions are principally concerned with maximizing worker compliance with the existing organization of work and otherwise maintaining control over the labor process. They use race, gender, and nativity as markers for such compliance and target groups deemed most likely to be compliant. The desired traits—willingness to take any job for any pay—are often coded as a "good attitude," "work ethic," and "soft skills" (Matthews and Ruhs 2007; Zamudio and Lichter 2008). Some scholars also emphasize that occupational segregation stems in part from the fact that employers have restructured work in ways that only the most subordinated workers would accept (Cranford 2005; Moss and Tilly 2001; Reskin 1998; Waldinger 1994).

Additionally, employers have been shown to reproduce segregation in the workplace by recruiting through existing workers' networks to staff low-end positions. Network recruitment facilitates restructuring, reduces hiring costs, gets workers to train and manage each other, reduces employee conflict, and enables employers to keep securing vulnerable workers (Cranford 2005; Granovetter 1995; Waldinger and Lichter 2003). Over time, those jobs become marked as "brown-collar jobs" or "women's jobs" and thus undesirable to other workers (Saucedo 2006; Tomaskovic-Devey 1993). In contrast to social capital scholarship that emphasizes the value of migrants' social networks for upward mobility, these studies instead find that "in some contexts immigrants may be piling up at the bottom rather than moving upwards" because of network recruitment (Cranford 2005:382).

Finally, these studies also demonstrate that employers use narrative devices to naturalize workplace inequalities. For example, many use racial or gender stereotypes to rationalize their statistical discrimination against certain worker groups or the clustering of particular groups of workers in low-end jobs (Holmes 2007; Kennelly 1999; Maldonado 2009; McDowell et al. 2007; Moss and Tilly 2001; Ruhs and Anderson 2007; Waldinger and Lichter 2003; Waldinger, Lim, and Cort 2007). At the same time, employers claim to be "colorblind" to deny their own culpability in racist practice and create an illusion of fairness (Maldonado 2009; Moss and Tilly 2001; Waldinger and

Lichter 2003). Employers explaining the clustering of immigrant workers in low-end jobs also often invoke a "dual frame of reference" narrative—comparing immigrant workers' low-end wages and positions to wages they might have earned "back home" as a way of justifying occupational segregation by nativity (Maldonado 2009; Matthews and Ruhs 2007; Piore 1979; Waldinger and Lichter 2003).

While scholars have illuminated *how* employers contribute to unequal outcomes in the workplace, relatively little attention has been paid to unpacking *why* employers engage in those practices. Certainly, studies invariably imply that employers are focused on maximizing profits and succumb to broader racial and gender stereotypes in assessing and managing workers. Yet sociology has long demonstrated that profit maximization is an incomplete explanation for human behavior. Additionally, the work of "symbolic boundaries" scholars indicates that we might be missing much of the explanation by only looking at employers' perceptions of, narratives about, and actions toward specific groups of workers. In her study of working class men, Michele Lamont (2000) showed that members of social groups define and defend themselves *in opposition to other groups*—"in an 'us' versus 'them' relational logic" (p. 57) of symbolic boundary making that reinforces material inequalities. This approach draws our attention not simply to the claims one group makes about another and the associated material consequences, but to the fact that such claims have a relational quality. Moreover, Lamont explains *why* people draw gendered, racial boundaries—not only to explain another group's position but also to justify their own position, define themselves, and assert their own identity. Such findings suggest that, to fully understand why employers engage in practices and narratives that help to produce and naturalize occupational segregation, we need to pay attention not only to employers' claims about specific worker groups but also their claims about themselves and to the broader contexts within which they build and defend their own identities and status.

In this article, we contribute to scholarship on occupational segregation by asking why employers engage in practices that contribute to workplace inequalities. We do so through a case study of hired labor relations on Wisconsin dairy farms, which have become segregated along lines of nativity and race in recent years. We ask the following questions: How have these workplaces become segregated by nativity and race? What roles have employers played in this process? Why, in particular, have employers engaged in those practices that contribute to workplace inequalities? In addition to identifying how employers perceive and react to broader structures such as industry restructuring and nativist immigration politics, we also look at employers' lives, the stories they tell about workers, and

the stories they tell about themselves. As we will demonstrate, employers engage in practices that leave immigrant workers clustered in the low-end jobs for a complex array of reasons: to maintain profits within a changing industry context, meet their own middle-class aspirations, comply with their peers' middle-class lifestyle expectations, manage their own concerns about immigration policing, assert their own class identity, justify the privileges that they and their U.S.-born employees enjoy on the farm, and maintain the privileges they have gained.

In the next section, we describe the patterns of occupational segregation on Wisconsin dairy farms. Then, we describe the research methods we used to analyze how and why those patterns of segregation emerged. Subsequently, we describe the process through which dairy farm workplaces have become segregated by race and nativity. This process includes four parts: employers create new, low-end jobs as part of industrializing their operations; hire immigrant workers into the new jobs; draw symbolic boundaries to explain the resultant inequalities; and use several measures to maintain the new, unequal organization of workers. Throughout our discussion, we draw on employers' own stories about their lives and secondary data about the broader political economic contexts to explain why they engage in practices that produce workplace inequalities.

Evidence of Occupational Segregation on Wisconsin Dairy Farms

Our 2008 survey of Wisconsin dairy farms found that most immigrant workers were located in entry-level dairy jobs—the "milker" category in Figure 1. We should note that on large farms this category includes "milkers" and "pushers," who work together, often as a team, to bring cows to the parlor, get them milked, and clean the manure from the parlor. For the sake of brevity, we have combined the three jobs, calling them "milkers." Most of those immigrant workers (89 percent) were from Mexico, and 8 percent were from elsewhere in Latin America. Milking jobs are largely deskilled, require working on the weekends, often require working night shifts, and receive the lowest wages on the farm ($9 per hour on average, with few nonwage benefits). Like most dairy jobs, these are year-round positions.

Dairy farm owners (not represented in Figure 1) do much of the nonmilking work themselves: negotiating with milk processors and input suppliers; monitoring feed rations, breeding, and calf care for the herd; and managing cropland, feed purchases, and employees. Most dairy farms have one to four owners who are

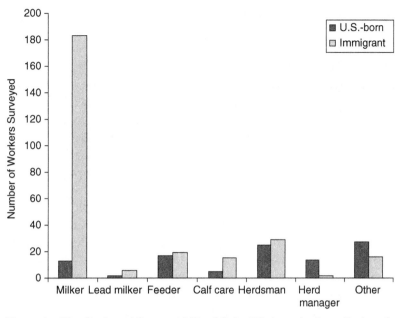

Figure 1 Distribution of Surveyed Hired Dairy Workers, by Farm Task and Worker Origin

Note: This figure includes full-time and part-time hired employees; co-owners are not included.

typically immediate kin. When farmers do need to hire employees to help conduct the nonmilking tasks, they often hire U.S.-born workers for those positions. Most U.S.-born dairy workers are located in nonmilking positions (as shown in Figure 1). All U.S.-born dairy workers in our survey were identified as white, and they have worked for their current employer for seven years on average. The nonmilking positions involve a greater variety of tasks, higher pay ($11 per hour on average), more decision-making authority, and more autonomy than the milking positions, as well as shifts that coincide closely with those of the traditional workweek. Wisconsin's dairy farms thus demonstrate clear patterns of occupation segregation by both nativity and race. The immigrant workers clustered in the low-end jobs are differentiated not only by their nonnative status but also because they are racially marked as "Mexican" or "Hispanic" by their employers and other residents of rural Wisconsin, while the U.S.-born workers clustered in the more desired positions are exclusively white.

On average, the immigrant workers we surveyed have lived in the United States for 7.5 years and have worked for their current employer for 2.5 years. Some of the immigrant workers first came to Wisconsin for jobs in other rural Wisconsin industries. Some worked in seasonal cannery jobs, where Mexicans and Mexican Americans have worked since the 1930s (Valdes 1991). Others worked in year-round meatpacking jobs, where Mexican immigrants have worked since meatpackers relocated out

urban areas across the United States to undermine the power of unionized workers starting in the 1980s (Kandel and Parrado 2005). Other immigrant dairy workers previously worked in agriculture, construction, manufacturing, and janitorial jobs elsewhere in the United States (mostly in California, Illinois, and Texas). Half had not worked in the United States prior to their current dairy job. As we will elaborate later, most immigrant dairy workers found their current jobs through kin and peer networks.

Data suggest that the majority of Wisconsin's immigrant dairy workers lack legal authorization to be in the United States. We refrained from asking any of our research participants about individual workers' legal status because we detected high levels of anxiety about immigration enforcement in the area at the time of our data collection and did not have time to establish significant rapport with the participants before meeting with them. However, other data provide insights into the legal status of these workers. Eight of the 12 immigrant workers with whom we conducted in-depth, confidential interviews voluntarily divulged their lack of legal status to us. All of the 20 farmers we interviewed expressed concerns about legal status issues, and most voluntarily divulged having employed unauthorized workers. The farmers in a series of exploratory focus groups we conducted in 2007 as the first stage in this project consistently directed conversation to legal status issues. The hired labor sessions at all major Wisconsin dairy industry meetings in the past several years have been dedicated to legal issues associated with hiring unauthorized workers. Additionally, other researchers find that approximately half of immigrant agricultural workers in the United States are unauthorized (e.g., U.S. Department of Labor 2005). We explain later in this article that employers manage their concerns about legal status issues by limiting immigrant workers' opportunities for promotion.

The majority of the hired workers on dairy farms were male (83 percent of the U.S.-born workers; 92 percent of immigrant workers). Our survey data suggest that gender and nativity intersect in the organization of hired dairy workers, as immigrant women were particularly clustered in milking positions. Only 1 of the 22 immigrant women in our survey held a nonmilking job, whereas 14 of the 18 U.S.-born women in our survey held nonmilking jobs. This finding merits further investigation; we will not parse it out here, as it did not emerge in our employer interviews.

Research Data and Methods

To understand employers' roles in the emergence of occupational segregation by nativity and race in dairy farm workplaces, we focus on 20 semistructured interviews we conducted with dairy farm owners and managers in 2010 and 2011. Employer interviews are a useful method for understanding why occupational segregation happens, as they help to illuminate how employers perceive the structural constraints within which they operate, how they organize work and workers to manage those constraining structures, why they find certain groups of workers useful for certain tasks, and how they justify inequalities among groups of workers.

Employer Interview Procedures

We recruited farmer interview participants from the participants of a survey we conducted in 2008 (see "supplementary data" below). We purposively sampled for variation in two factors that seemed likely to influence employers' labor management practices: farm size (our sample included seven from "small" farms with fewer than 300 cows; five from "medium" farms with 301 to 900 cows; and eight from "large" farms with more than 900 cows), and employee demographics (our sample included 3 with only U.S.-born employees; 5 with a mix of immigrant and U.S.-born employees; and 12 with only immigrant employees). Consistent with the broader population of dairy farmers, most (16) of the 20 interview participants were male; all were identified as white;

and most (19) were farm owners. All were from separate farms (i.e., none were co-owners).

Through open-ended questions, we asked our interview participants to describe and explain the organization of work and workers on their farms, describe their perceptions of and concerns about different groups of workers, and speculate about why dairy farms are largely segregated by nativity and race. The interviewer followed local parlance and referred to foreign-born workers as "immigrants" (while employers also used the terms "Mexicans," "Hispanics," and "Latinos") and U.S.-born workers as "locals" (while employers also used the terms "whites," "Caucasians," and "Americans"). The semistructured nature of the interviews allowed us to pursue certain themes of interest while also allowing the participants to narrate and interpret their experiences. This loosely structured approach also enabled us to develop the rapport necessary to discuss issues as sensitive as immigration enforcement and race. The interviews were conducted by one of the authors, a white woman familiar with dairy farming. Each interview took place at the participant's home or farm office, lasted one to two hours, and was recorded with the participant's consent. The interviewer recorded her observations and transcribed all of the interviews.

Employer Interview Analysis

Both authors read and coded several transcripts. Most of our coding themes emerged from the literature and original survey data that had prompted our interview questions (e.g., material motivations for expanding production and reorganizing work; mechanisms of reorganizing work and workers; perceptions of immigration enforcement; perspectives of different worker groups). Several themes emerged unexpectedly in the interviews (e.g., the rewards of the new industrial organization of work to employers, and the rewards of segregated workplaces to employers). Accordingly, drawing on the principles of grounded theory (Bryant and Charmaz 2007), we also coded for these emergent themes. We also identified the cases that did not seem to fit our emerging theories (namely, immigrant workers in nonmilking jobs) and used analytic induction to explain those deviant cases. Both authors then compared the coding schemes and discussed discrepancies, and subsequently developed one coding scheme. Then, one author coded the remaining transcripts. Later, after reviewers rightly noted that race, class, and gender norms appeared to intersect in motivating and shaping employers' labor management practices, we recoded the interviews accordingly and used an intersectional framework to help structure our discussion (Collins 1990).

Supplementary Data

Our descriptive data of dairy farm jobs come from a dairy farm survey we conducted in 2008. The farms surveyed were selected from a random sample of Wisconsin dairy farms thought large enough to have any employees (over 100 cows), and efforts were made to represent a variety of farm sizes and geographic regions. The survey participants included 83 farmers and all available employees (103 U.S.-born workers and 270 immigrant workers). The survey was administered on the farm by a bilingual, Latino researcher while the participants worked and took five to ten minutes to complete. The survey generated basic data about dairy farm labor force demographics, wages and other benefits, the organization of work, worker aspirations, and basic migration histories of immigrant workers.

To demonstrate how immigration enforcement shapes immigrant workers' experiences of illegality, we include here relevant key findings from 12 loosely structured interviews we conducted in 2008 with a subset of the immigrant dairy workers who had participated in our survey. All 12 were recruited at the time of the survey by the survey administrator. These interview participants included five women and seven men, and they represented a range of positions held on dairy farms (six milkers, two managers, and four feeders or other positions situated between milker and manager in the dairy farm workplace hierarchy). Two bilingual, white, female interviewers conducted these interviews with the workers in Spanish at a private setting of their choice, usually their homes. Each interview lasted one to two hours, and most consented to audio recordings. The interviewers recorded their observations and transcribed and translated all of the interviews.

Finally, to test the prevalence of the major employer narratives that emerged in our interviews among a broader population of farmers, we re-analyzed our notes from a series of five exploratory focus groups we conducted in 2007 with over 50 dairy and other farmers in Wisconsin. As the first stage in this research project, these loosely structured, unrecorded conversations were primarily designed to solicit farmers' major concerns about hired labor and recruit participants for subsequent interviews. Because we had not yet completed the survey at that point and thus were not aware of segregation by nativity and race on dairy farms, we did not ask about that pattern. However, re-analyzing the focus group notes enabled us to identify several themes that dominated focus group discussion, which turned out to be consistent with the themes that emerged in the farmer interviews. We also verified that none the focus group notes refuted

any of the patterns that emerged in the employer interviews. Note that the farmers we interviewed had not participated in the focus groups, so we could not ask them to comment on the focus group conversations.

Notes on Terminology

First, we refer to nonimmigrant workers as "U.S.-born" in this article but note throughout where respondents use different terminology. Second, we prefer to use the term "migrant" to describe foreign-born people living in the United States, because the term does not presume that the individual intends to reside in the United States permanently. However, because the workers we describe typically live and work at one place on a full-time, year-round basis, we use the term "immigrant" in this article to avoid the ways that "migrant farm worker" conjures up an image of a roving person who moves with the harvests. Throughout, we note where respondents use different terminology where appropriate. Third, we use the term "unauthorized" rather than "undocumented" to describe immigrants without legal status, as they commonly work and live with forged or stolen identification documents in order to appear "legal" and thus conduct basic activities such as acquiring a job, paying taxes, opening a bank account, and renting housing. Many immigrant workers believe that the paper trail of pay stubs and tax contributions may some day facilitate their bid for legal status. We avoid the common term "illegal," as it does not point to the specific legal infraction committed but instead portrays the immigrant as generally criminal in nature.

Occupational Segregation on Wisconsin Dairy Farms: How and Why Employers Contribute to Workplace Inequalities

We now explain how and why Wisconsin dairy farm workplaces have become segregated by nativity and race. We organize our narrative according to the process through which occupational segregation has emerged in this case and, throughout, we highlight why employers engage in practices that produce workplace inequalities. First, we describe how farmers industrialize their operations and create new, low-end jobs as part of that process. We explain that they do so to maintain profits and meet their own middle-class aspirations. Second, we describe how employers have hired a new group of workers to fill the new jobs and created new inequalities on the farm. We explain that these new inequalities enable farmers to comply with their peers' middle-class lifestyle expectations and manage their own concerns about immigration policing. Third, we show how farmers make sense of these inequalities through drawing symbolic boundaries between themselves and their different groups of workers. We explain that such narratives enable employers to assert their own class identity and justify the privileges that they and their U.S.-born employees enjoy on the farm. Finally, we describe the practices through which farmers maintain the new organization of work and workers, and we explain that they do so to secure the privileges they have acquired.

Industrializing the Farm and Creating New, Low-End Jobs for Hired Workers

Although Wisconsin dairy farms are still, on average, much smaller in scale than dairy farms in the western United States, the sector is industrializing in ways similar to other agricultural and non-agricultural industries and with the same goal of maximizing production (Barham, Foltz, and Aldana 2005; USDA 2011). In dairying, industrialization occurs on a wide spectrum of farm sizes and includes expanding the farm's herd size and upgrading the barns, milking parlors, tractors, and other equipment with the latest technologies. Industrial operations usually confine the cows indoors and feed them scientifically formulated feed rations tailored to each animal's life stage, rather than managing them on pasture. Some operations further boost production through using synthetic bovine growth hormone (Barham et al. 2005). Industrializing a dairy farm also usually includes intensifying production: shifting from milking cows twice per day in tie-stall stanchion barns to a system of milking the cows three times per day in machine-assisted milking parlors, which enable cows to be milked more expediently and reduce ergonomic strain for the worker. In many cases, expansion is the result of two existing farms joining together to increase efficiencies or to meet social obligations (e.g., so that children or other relatives can join and be supported by the business).

Dairy farmers manage farm expansion by hiring employees. As of 2006, at least 23 percent of all Wisconsin dairy farms hire some nonfamily labor, a percentage that increases quickly as herd size grows (Lloyd et al. 2006). The number of employees varies with farm size and family involvement. The highest number of employees recorded in our survey was 62; however, most dairy farms that hire any workers are still quite small and have only one or a few employees.

As dairy farmers expand their operations, they assign the vast majority of employees to one task: milking cows. Milkers work 8- to 12-hour shifts in a milking parlor that typically runs nearly 24 hours a day. In some cases, milkers work "split shifts," where they milk for approximately five hours in the morning and again in the evening. The milkers we interviewed have been at their current place of employment for several years on average and expressed appreciation for the fact that their jobs are full time and year-round, whereas most other entry-level agricultural jobs are seasonal. However, they also lamented that milking tends to be monotonous, dirty, and physically arduous, often requires working shifts that limit time with family and friends, and entails significant risks of ergonomic strain and injury from large animals. Indeed, many farmers we interviewed readily noted that they themselves despise milking cows:

> It gets kind of old to work holidays and every weekend . . . We milked like 80 cows, or 70 cows. You did every holiday and every weekend. You got bigger so you wouldn't have to do it—so you could have employees help do it.

Expanding production and hiring employees enabled these employers to focus on the tasks they find more personally fulfilling and to create time for other activities.

Maintaining Profits in a Changing Industry

To some extent, dairy farmers industrialize their operations and reorganize work in this way to maintain profits in a context of industry restructuring that squeezes farmers' profit margins. Rising land values, volatile feed prices, and consolidation among farm input manufacturers have increased production costs. At the same time, inadequate federal price supports (often set below the cost of production) and consolidation among milk processors and food retailers have lowered the prices dairy farmers receive for their milk and leave all but the largest farmers unable to dictate any of the terms of trade with milk buyers (USDA 2004). This combination of factors is faced by farmers in a wide variety of commodity sectors and shrinks farm profits, pressing farmers to leave the industry or find new sources of value (Heffernan 1998). The dominant advice given to farmers by university researchers and extension agents, dairy industry organizations, bankers, and policymakers is that the only sure way for farmers to survive this difficult "cost-price squeeze" is to expand production, industrialize operations, fund those changes with loans, and hire workers to do the routine work of milking cows (Buttel 1993; Fitzgerald 2003; Lobao and Meyer 2001). In some other sectors (notably, hogs and poultry), processors have used their market power to compel farmers to engage in contract relationships in which the processor determines prices, inputs, and production schedules, and even supplies worker crews to the farm (Heffernan 1998). While dairy farms do not engage in such contract relationships, they are price takers as much as farmers in other industries are. In this difficult economic context, dairy farmers expand and industrialize production to maintain profits.

Meeting Middle-Class Aspirations and Dominant Masculine Norms

Our interviews indicate that farmers are motivated to transition to industrialized dairying and create new milking jobs not only by shifts in their own individual work task preferences and shrinking profit margins. Rather, industrialization and the creation of deskilled jobs for hired workers together serves as a mechanism through which these farmers can meet their own middle-class aspirations and comply with the dominant masculine norms in rural Wisconsin. As the following statements from two farmer interviews illustrate, hiring workers to do the milking helps these employers take vacations, allow their children to participate in sports activities in the evenings and on weekends, and attend those events.

> When our four oldest children were all in high school, 1996, we did our farm expansion from 50 to 150 milk cows. Our children all helped on the farm every morning before school and every evening after school. My wife and I realized that we would need to hire some additional labor if we wanted to allow our children to be involved in some extra curricular activities.
>
> When our kids were older, we wanted it where we could both attend our kids' events and actually see them . . . Contrary to what some of the locals think—that it is all about money—it is really about lifestyle.

As these narratives illustrate, hiring workers to do the milking helps these employers meet their own middle-class lifestyle aspirations and to be better parents to their children.

The following narrative suggests that farmers' aspirations are framed not only in terms of lifestyle but also in terms of class identity.

> There was a point in my life where I was working hand-in-hand with my son and I said, "I'm a post-graduate degree person and you are going to go to college and be degreed, and here we are pushing and scraping manure around." I said, "I think there is a potential for us to do better than that." And that potential involved building a dairy and being more in management . . . I have a couple of engineering degrees and my son has an engineering degree and his wife is a graduate from Madison and my father

> graduated from Madison . . . We've always had a strong emphasis in my generation and prior generations back to my grandmother who was a college graduate at the turn of the last century.

That is, farmers can be motivated to expand their operations and hire workers to "push and scrape manure around" to comply with the scripts of a deeply rooted class identity that calls for managing others to do the mundane work.

Other farmers' statements reveal the gendered nature of these middle-class norms that valorize industrialization. For example, an owner of a large dairy farm described how, approximately ten years prior, he went to work on a very large dairy in another state for a summer, "just to see how the big boys did it, you know. And I was like, yes, I think I want to do this." This narrative reveals how expanding his operation enabled him to conform to dominant norms that define masculinity in terms of farm size and industrialization (see also Bell 2004).

Expanding production and creating milking jobs together constitute a way for farmers to respond to changing industry constraints, pursue their middle-class ambitions and identity, and comply with dominant masculine norms of rural Wisconsin. As will become clear in a later section, these farmers' identities are not just gendered and classed but implicitly raced as well, as farmers come to hire immigrant workers for these new jobs and view their nonwhite employees' aspirations and norms as very different from their own and those of their white employees.

Hiring New Workers and Creating New Inequalities

To fill these new milking jobs they have created, dairy farmers have had to find and retain workers who would accept those shifts and tasks. New workplace inequalities have emerged in the process of doing so, as new workers from abroad fill the milking positions while U.S.-born workers are clustered in the nonmilking positions.

The farmers we interviewed and those in our focus groups elaborated about the challenges in finding and retaining "U.S.-born" (or "white," "Caucasian," or "local") workers to fill the milking positions on their farms. The following statement from one farmer represents a typical narrative: that U.S.-born workers would insist upon only doing nonmilking tasks, refuse the shifts that were available, and quit coming to work after a week or two.

> When I moved home in '91, we started having more full-time employees, and that was the hell period . . . The white people [would last] six weeks, tops.

People not showing up, not coming to work . . . I was finding myself milking two or three times a day, and constantly. I was getting done at midnight and then getting up at four and trying to do field work.

In about 2000, Wisconsin dairy farmers started hiring immigrant workers for these milking positions. They reported that these immigrant workers have come to them—that carloads of immigrant workers comb the Wisconsin countryside looking for work, happy to take the milking jobs; accept the late-night, weekend, and swing shifts offered to them; stay in those positions for years; and are eager to work as many hours as possible. None claimed to have actively sought out immigrant workers, as employers in other industries have done (see Maldonado 2009:1018).

Dairy farmers all emphasized that immigrant workers expressed two key characteristics that solved the problems they experienced with U.S.-born workers: immigrant workers were committed to working long hours and compliant with the tasks and shifts offered to them. As one farmer explained:

They don't want to displease you . . . They are real defensive about losing their job. They want hours . . . They don't complain about the job or anything like that . . . And they will do it the way you tell them to . . . They will work as many hours as they can . . . They'll even hold down two jobs or something, just to get as much as they can.

In a public presentation in May 2007, one dairy farmer noted that his first immigrant employee worked 54 days in a row and summed up the experience by declaring, "It was too good to be true . . . I thought I'd died and gone to heaven." Another dairy farmer was quoted in a Wisconsin newspaper article as saying, "Hiring Hispanics was the best decision I ever made. I don't worry about them not showing up. I had to send one home once because he was trying to milk while throwing up" (Pabst 2009).

The new immigrant workers have not fully replaced U.S.-born workers. Rather, a new inequality has emerged in Wisconsin's dairy industry: the new immigrant workers are clustered in the milking jobs, while U.S.-born workers are clustered in the more desired, nonmilking jobs. Dairy farmers insisted that their workplaces are meritocratic (as others have found; see Maldonado 2009). As one farmer asserted, "We just want equal opportunity, give everyone the same chance no matter what." Claiming that everyone has an opportunity to earn promotions means that those in nonmilking positions (including the employers) have earned their privilege fairly. Yet, because of how dairy farmers have reconfigured their operations, what they really need and value are workers who will comply with milking positions for years on end—not employees who expect to be able to work their way up. Such claims also obscure the fact that race and nativity confer privileges to whites and systematically disadvantage immigrant workers as dairy farmers decide how to organize work and workers, as we explain below.

Managing White Peers' Middle-Class Expectations

The clustering of U.S.-born workers in the more desired positions on dairy farms stems in part from the fact that employers must manage those workers' own demands for schedules that coincide with a middle-class lifestyle. At times, employers fire workers who refuse the shifts and positions offered to them. Yet strong social ties in these rural communities compel employers to accommodate requests from kin and peers for the desired shifts and tasks.

Several stories from our focus groups illustrate this pressure. For example, one farmer noted that, after hiring a local high school student to help with the milking, the boy's parents called and told him: "We've got a good basketball team here. You can't make him work this weekend." Another focus group participant noted that U.S.-born workers' demands for normal workweek schedules conflicted with his own efforts to help his children pursue middle-class goals: "Three years ago I had three white people [working for me]. But they wanted our kids to come home from college on the weekends so they could have weekends off. We want our kids to be at college, not on the farm." Echoing a statement we heard from nearly all of our participants, one farmer noted in an interview that "white guys" "don't want to work weekends." Occupational segregation thus stems in part from the fact that employers manage their peers' middle-class expectations by channeling U.S.-born workers into the more desired shifts and tasks.

Managing the Threat of Immigration Policing

The clustering of immigrant workers in the low-end jobs is also driven by the ways in which immigrant workers and their employers manage the threat of immigration policing. As we will explain, immigrant workers navigate this threat by consenting to the jobs and shifts handed to them, and their employers capitalize on it by refraining from promoting their immigrant workers.

Susan Bibler Coutin (2000), Nicholas De Genova (2005), Martin Ruhs and Bridget Anderson (2007), and other "illegality" scholars emphasize that, to understand immigrants' experiences, we need to critically investigate what it means to be perceived and treated as "illegal" at any time and place. That is, one's experience of "illegality" and its consequences in the workplace are contingent on local politics, policing practices, and perceptions. Starting in the 1990s but gaining legitimacy and resources through the post-9/11 "war on terror," the United States has invested tremendous resources into hardening its border with Mexico and actively policing immigrants in the interior of the country through raids and apprehensions in workplaces, homes, and public spaces (Andreas 2001; Coleman 2007, 2009; Cornelius 2001; De Genova 2007; Golash-Boza 2012; Hernández 2008; Mendelson, Strom, and Wishnie 2009; Rosas 2006a, 2006b; Varsanyi 2008; Walker and Leitner 2011; Waslin 2009). Local law enforcement units, state governments, private militias, and nativist bureaucrats have joined the cause of surveilling and punishing immigrants. Much of this nativist politics has targeted those racially marked as Latino and presumed to be "illegal," such as the immigrant workers on Wisconsin dairy farms.

Although Wisconsin does not constitute a major focus of the federal and local immigration enforcement efforts, policing happens there in various sanctioned and informal ways. Federal police have raided workplaces and homes; many employers have received "no-match" letters from federal officials advising them that an employee did not report a valid social security number; immigrants we interviewed reported having been asked by neighbors and low-level bureaucrats if they are "legal"; and various municipalities have passed local anti-immigrant policies such as English-only laws (Walker and Leitner 2011). Indeed, in 2009, the Wisconsin Governor's Council on Migrant Labor initiated an investigation into the unsanctioned immigration policing practices conducted by Department of Transportation staff.[1] The immigrants we interviewed are acutely aware of such activity and regularly share relevant rumors and updates with each other.

As we have elaborated elsewhere, the immigrant dairy workers we interviewed emphasized that they live with memories of harrowing and expensive border crossings, under the weight of responsibilities to support their families and pay off debts, and fearful of being apprehended and deported (Harrison and Lloyd 2012; see also Stephen 2004). Thus they work long hours in the milking jobs (average of 57 per week), do not complain about their shifts or tasks, minimize their use of public space, and refrain from travelling home or otherwise taking vacations. For example, two immigrant workers explained to us that they work very long hours and refrain from taking days off because they need to pay off their debts to smugglers, who have been increasing their interest rates over time, and because the fear of encountering law enforcement makes them feel that they have nothing "safe" to do besides work: "You feel the weight of the

debt. I want to work more hours a day, two hours more. The more, the better. The debt you owe and the interest make you think." These two workers and several others noted that they leave their house only to go to work and, twice per month, to buy groceries. Dairy workers also refrain from traveling home for the same reasons, which is consistent with the broader pattern in which unauthorized immigrants have responded to U.S.-Mexico border intensification by "settling out" year-round in the United States rather than returning home seasonally to visit (Massey, Durand, and Malone 2003; Reyes 2004). Immigrant workers' sense of deportability and strategies for navigating the contours of the policing landscape thus coincide well with the ways employers have reorganized work in their expanded operations. Contemporary immigration enforcement channels immigrant workers into low-end jobs and disciplines them to stay there, much like others have found with education (Willis 1977) and contemporary welfare institutions (Peck 2001).

Employers, too, are concerned about the growing threat of immigration enforcement. Most of the farmers who participated in our interviews and focus groups stated that they knew or suspected that at least one of their current or past employees is not legally authorized. Some of our research participants have received "no-match" letters from the federal government advising them that an employee's reported social security number is invalid. Additionally, nearly all requested our advice about how to verify a worker's legal status, how carefully they should examine worker identification cards, or how to hire an immigration attorney. Fully aware that many unauthorized migrants carry forged or stolen identification, employers expressed a general sense of uncertainty about the legal status of immigrant workers.

Employers respond to their own fears of immigration enforcement in ways that contribute to occupational segregation by nativity and race, largely by limiting immigrant workers' chances for promotion. For example, some farmers reported to us that they refrain from training and granting responsibilities to presumed or actually unauthorized immigrant workers, as they would lose that "investment" if the workers were arrested for immigration violations. Several employers admitted that they were unwilling to promote immigrant workers into positions that require the use of tractors and other heavy machinery, as those require paperwork that might trigger an immigration-related investigation. Others noted that restricting immigrant workers to milking positions keeps them in the barn—out of sight—and thus partially hides employers' hiring practices from scrutiny by nativist neighbors and law enforcement (see also McCandless 2010). In other words, occupational segregation enables these employers to delicately balance the benefits of capitalizing on immigrants' presumed or actual tractability with the need to minimize the likelihood and consequences of drawing the attention of law enforcement.

We did encounter several immigrant workers who have been promoted into the more desired positions on dairy farms. To some extent, these exceptions further highlight the role of illegality in inhibiting immigrant workers' chances for promotion, as two of the three non-milker immigrant workers we interviewed have legal status. The third is not legally authorized but had experience working on large farms and completed a year of veterinary school, and his employer might believe that he has legal status. Additionally, an immigrant worker's chances for promotion appear also to be at least partially a function of farm size (as evident in Figure 2). Larger farms have sufficiently numerous jobs that the farm owner(s) cannot fill all of the nonmilking positions through their own networks and a have more complex structure of labor that allows for upward mobility. In contrast, small farms generally only hire milkers.

Drawing Symbolic Boundaries

As scholars have found in other contexts, dairy farmers have developed various ways to rationalize the fact that the valuable immigrant workers are overrepresented in entry-level jobs (Holmes 2007; Kennelly 1999; Maldonado 2009; McDowell et al. 2007; Moss and Tilly 2001; Ruhs and Anderson 2007; Waldinger and Lichter 2003; Waldinger et al. 2007). When asked to explain why dairy farms have become segregated by nativity and race in recent years, employers drew a complex set of symbolic boundaries (Lamont 2000) between themselves and

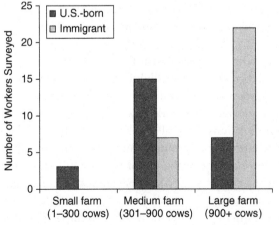

Figure 2 Herdsmen Surveyed, by Immigrant Status and Farm Size

Note: This figure includes full-time and part-time hired employees; co-owners are not included.

white workers, and between whites and immigrants. Although employers' stories often focused on their workers, the claims convey their own raced, gendered, and classed identity and show how employers define themselves in relation to their different worker groups. As we will demonstrate in this section, such boundaries enable employers to not only explain workplace inequalities, but also to express their own class identity and to justify the privileged positions of whites on dairy farms.

Asserting Class Identity

In expressing their frustrations with U.S.-born workers for rejecting milking jobs and demanding better ones, employers differentiated themselves from U.S.-born workers who refused the milking positions by using moral claims that differentiate employers (as hard working) from U.S.-born workers (as lazy, having a poor work ethic, and feeling unreasonably entitled to the best shifts and tasks). In doing so, they expressed their own class identity. The following is just one example of the extensive comments of this sort that dominated the interviews and focus groups:

> I think us Americans are all spoiled rotten little brats. I think the next generation, and I'm not sure why, but, they think everything should just be handed to them. And they shouldn't have to work. And they all think that they should start out three-quarters up the ladder, instead of starting on the bottom rung of the ladder and climbing.

By drawing boundaries between themselves and U.S.-born workers in this way, employers express their own class identity and assert that they have earned their middle-class status, whereas U.S.-born workers have not done so and are failing to comply with their class location.

Of course, disparaging U.S.-born workers for their "poor work ethic" dismisses those workers' motivations. As Margaret M. Zamudio and Michael I. Lichter (2008) suggest, U.S.-born workers' failure to show up for work and otherwise "lackluster performance" can be read as signs of resistance and agency—"an assertion of their right to work in a dignified manner"—rather than simply a character deficit, cultural problem, or indication of a disappearing "work ethic" (p. 587). At jobs in other sectors, workers can interact with their peers, stay cleaner, do varied tasks, work typical workweek hours, do work that is less physically demanding, have more opportunities to advance and take on responsibilities, receive overtime pay, earn nonwage benefits, have more flexibility with shifts, be covered by a union contract, and earn higher wages. Indeed, one farmer reflected upon the milking jobs on his farm by conceding, "I would not do that job."

Justifying White Privilege

Employers also drew racial boundaries between whites and immigrants along several lines to rationalize the clustering of immigrant workers in the milking positions. Doing so enabled employers to justify the privileged positions they and their U.S.-born employees enjoy on the farm.

Employers generously praised their immigrant workers for having a "good work ethic" and being "reliable" and "dependable" enough for milking jobs. Such praise dominated our employer interviews and focus groups and pivots around immigrant workers' purportedly cultural deference to authority and respect for working long hours:

> How they interpret somebody, a boss, an owner, is extremely respectful, compared to what American workers interpret . . . They very much have a hierarchy interpretation of society and what those expectations are.
>
> They are here to work. Their values are more similar to the farming community: . . . hard work, commitment, not scared of getting dirty.

Outside observers of the new labor relations on dairy farms also often hail immigrant dairy workers as "reliable." For example, in a 2009 *Wall Street Journal* article on the new role of immigrant workers on dairy farms nationwide, a university researcher was quoted as saying, "In the mid-'90s, I saw dairy managers who were afraid to expand their businesses because they couldn't find dependable help. Then, some dairies began to hire Latino immigrants, and found they were reliable and had a tremendous work ethic" (Jordan 2009). Framing immigrants as reliable rationalizes hiring them, and framing them as deferential rationalizes their overrepresentation in the low-end jobs.

Yet scholars have illustrated the need to critically evaluate the qualities that employers claim to find and value in various groups of workers. Waldinger and Lichter (2003) argue that "good attitude" is "the managerial euphemism for the proclivity to say 'yes' with no questions asked" (p. 225; see also Zamudio and Lichter 2008). Given that dairy farmers have the most difficult time getting U.S.-born workers to do the positions that immigrant workers have filled, immigrant workers' "reliability" should be understood as a rhetorical placeholder for compliance. These narratives about "reliability" and "strong work ethic" fetishize unauthorized immigrants' structurally produced propensities to self-exploit and be compliant; obscure the ways that they shoulder the burden of current U.S. immigration policies, law enforcement practices, international trade policies, and farm

restructuring; and depoliticize these consequences with claims of cultural difference.

This coding of compliance as "reliability" becomes clear when dairy farmers disparagingly characterize as "Americanized" those immigrants who reject or critique the terms and conditions handed to them (see also Maldonado 2009; Waldinger and Lichter 2003). One farmer explained this phenomenon among the "Mexicans" he has employed:

> Once they become Americanized they aren't worth a tinker's darn. They started doing the same thing that the American workers did. And usually after a year they would not show up, calling in and saying, "Hey, I can't make it." Or they would just not show up . . . It is about every year. I've had three crews and they usually last about a year and then they get Americanized.

Employers also drew racial boundaries between whites and immigrants along lines of ambition to do complex management jobs. Doing so enabled employers to rationalize the contradictory fact that the "reliable" and "respectful" immigrants were clustered in the low-end jobs and justify the privileges they and their U.S.-born employees enjoyed. Employers characterized U.S.-born workers as assertive and proudly described themselves as role models to their children, leaders among their peers, and advisors to their immigrant employees. In contrast, employers characterized immigrants as unambitious followers and claimed that the pooling of immigrant workers in entry-level positions on dairy farms is due to immigrants' shared, cultural lack of interest in moving up. The following statements exemplify this classic stereotype of immigrant workers as "'hardworking, but dumb' or 'dependable, but unambitious'" (Waldinger et al. 2007:6):

> The Veracruz people, they are only milking. They don't have a lot of ambition to do other things.
>
> What you find with the immigrant workers is they like a consistent job. They come in and they know what to do.
>
> Few of them are motivated for an advancement.
>
> I think with a lot of people that come from Mexico, they really aren't—their cultural background is not to seek promotion. Their cultural background is to stay in the soup.
>
> They don't want to tell other Hispanics what to do. That's what I've seen.

Others asserted that, unlike farmers and U.S.-born workers, immigrants are naturally proud of doing mundane, routine work. For example, one employer asserted that immigrant workers' perspective on milking is, "We can handle this. We can do this. This is our forte . . . That is just where their comfort zone is." Drawing boundaries between whites and immigrants along lines of ambition enables employers to justify their own privileged hours and tasks, naturalize the clustering of immigrants in the low-end positions, and explain why U.S.-born workers do not have to compete with immigrants for the better positions.

Some employers drew gendered boundaries between whites and immigrants along lines of preferences and interests in ways that imply that the two groups have distinct sets of masculine norms. For example, one employer we interviewed explained that U.S.-born workers dominated the higher-level positions on dairy farms (in this case, that of "feeder") because "Caucasian" or "American" men naturally *enjoy* working with trucks and other large equipment: "The feeder situation, I'd have to say, that has something to do with, we all like to drive trucks and tractors. It is never going to leave us. It is just the way it is." Another farmer asserted that, unlike U.S.-born men, "Mexican" men are naturally happy to milk cows and stay in entry-level positions:

> I've never had anybody that seemed to want to work and just milk cows and be satisfied with that, like the Mexicans do . . . They are just not as interested in being the top dog. They are happy to have a job, and milking cows is fairly easy . . . They don't have ambition to drive tractors like American guys, who want to be in the tractor all the time.

Such claims rationalize occupational segregation as an unproblematic consequence of racially differentiated masculine norms, where Mexican men purportedly enjoy different tasks than U.S.-born men. It is worth noting here that immigrants tell a different story. Nearly all of the immigrant workers we surveyed reported to us that they want to advance and learn new skills, especially in animal health care and machinery operation. Those we interviewed emphasized how monotonous the milking jobs were. As one stated, "Here is very monotonous. It is always the same, the same, the same, the same, the same . . ." Yet by drawing these boundaries in a context in which immigrant workers are afraid to complain, these employers naturalize the clustering of immigrants and justify the privileges that they and their U.S.-born workers enjoy in the workplace.

At other times, farmers justified U.S.-born workers' abilities to insist on better farm jobs by suggesting that whites and immigrants have different class norms in terms of different markers of success. For example, one farmer explained early in the interview why U.S.-born workers reject milking positions: "I'll be blunt. Milking is not a prestigious position." Later in the interview, this farmer explained that immigrant workers desire the milking jobs on his farm because "This is a prestigious position for them, I think."

Some employers attributed these racially differentiated definitions of prestige to poverty in immigrants' home communities. To legitimize the jobs to which immigrant workers are limited, a few farmers implied that coming from poor, Mexican households provides immigrant workers with a different set of class expectations than those of farmers or U.S.-born workers. For example, in the following statements, farmers identify immigrants' "dual frame of reference" (Matthews and Ruhs 2007; Piore 1979; Waldinger and Lichter 2003) as producing their "reliability":

> They are just happy to have a job period. Because where they come from they have seen a lot of people that don't have a job and don't have money and don't have anything . . . There just aren't any jobs. They are just real lucky to get a job and have a little money and be able to function in the economy. They are just tickled.
>
> What really makes them really reliable: all the ones I have are pretty much fresh out of Mexico . . . Those people grew up with nothing, and they appreciate what they get . . . They've got something. Where they come from they had nothing. They appreciate a job.

Asserting that immigrants and whites have different class norms, regardless of the reason, effectively justifies the privileged positions of employers and their U.S.-born employees.

Finally, some employers made racialized claims of different biological attributes between white and immigrant workers. Some arguments focused on physical characteristics. For example, one farmer hypothesized that few "Americans," "Caucasians," or "U.S.-born workers" are milkers because they "aren't able to move quite as fast as an immigrant worker" or don't have "the strength of being able to milk for 8 to 12 hours at a time." Another explained that immigrant workers are clustered in the milking positions because "it is a comfort zone for them. It is a job they can handle for their physical size." Others even made claims of groups' different intellectual capacities. For example, one farmer explained that "Mexicans" are not found in the advanced positions that require operating tractors because "they just conceptually don't get some of the same things" as "American" workers. Such boundary making enables employers to justify the privileged position of U.S.-born workers in the workplace relative to their immigrant counterparts and obscures employers' motivations for organizing their workers in unequal ways.

In sum, the employers we interviewed rationalized and thus reinforced workplace inequalities through drawing a complex set of boundaries between themselves, their U.S.-born workers, and their immigrant workers. In so doing, they asserted their own class identity and justified their own privilege and the relatively privileged positions of their U.S.-born employees. That is, occupational segregation and boundary making both help employers define who they are and who they want to be: ambitious, innovative leaders devoted to their kin and peers. Moreover, because their narratives focused on immigrants, whiteness and the privileges it entails remain largely obscured and unaccounted for.

Maintaining Unequal Workplaces and Securing Privilege

Employers engage in several practices that reproduce segregation on the farm: selecting for subordination, recruiting new milkers through existing immigrant workers' networks, and keeping the milking jobs as simplified as possible. As we explain below, doing so enables these employers to secure the privileges they have gained through the new, unequal organization of work and workers.

In interviews, employers describe how they actively select for subordinated workers who will comply with the terms handed to them. Dairy farmers reported that they seek workers who express subordination in several ways: working as many hours as possible, accepting any available shifts, not asking for days off, and willingly doing the same task, over and over, without complaint. As the following narrative illustrates, farmers actively search for and retain those employees who will stay in an entry-level position without complaint and lack the resources needed to demand otherwise:

> You have to find the right type of person . . . Mellow. More of a follower, not a leader . . . [Before we hire them,] we try to have an interview with them with our interpreter and we kind of ask them some questions, to give you some feedback. And if they start giving you feedback where they are telling you how good they are going to be and what they could do for the farm . . . sometimes we just don't hire that individual because we know that all of a sudden a month from now, two months from now, they are going to start to get a little antsy in their job. Because it is the same thing. Because they want to do more. They want to get out of the parlor. They want to do different things, and we are going to have issues. So we

> look for the type of person that is more mellow . . . You have to look for the right type of person that is going to stick with the job . . . You have to be like robot milkers . . . The ones that don't speak any English are easier to work with, because they can't talk back . . . They just come and do the job.

Doing so enables these employers to fill the essential milking positions that they, their kin, and their U.S.-born peers reject. Although several employers expressly noted that they appreciate workers who take the initiative to learn new skills and take on responsibilities, the primary labor challenge that all dairy farmers face is keeping the low-level milking positions filled. Thus, their primary labor management tasks are to select for the types of workers who they believe will stay in such positions without complaint, and to fire those who express too much ambition, autonomy, or frustration. Dairy farmers' practices thus illustrate what others have identified as the "inclusionary aspect of discrimination" (Saucedo 2006:976). Employers actively select for perceived or actually subordinated groups of workers to fill particularly onerous jobs in order to "maximize vulnerability and minimize resistance" (Zamudio and Lichter 2008:578). It is worth noting that some of the qualities that employers appreciate in their immigrant workers (such as not speaking English) also make those workers "unwelcomed guests" in the local community, as evident in the rash of "English-only" ordinances across the United States (Walker and Leitner 2011).

To further maintain the new workforce, dairy farmers recruit new workers for the low-end positions almost exclusively through current immigrant workers' personal networks. Many of our interview participants explained that they no longer consider hiring "local people," "whites," or "Caucasians" for milking positions, because recruiting through immigrant social networks enables them to find more workers willing to take the jobs that others reject. Additionally, as the following statement from one farmer illustrates, recruiting through immigrant networks can reduce employers' own labor management responsibilities:

> I don't even take job applications anymore . . . I haven't had a phone call for years. It's great. I just don't worry about it. I know there is going to be four people for every shift, seven days a week, and they are going to take care of stuff . . . If they want a day off, all they do is talk to one of the other ones and they figure it out.

Network recruitment thus helps these employers maintain certain advantages they have gained through the new organization of work and workers: more time for parenting, freedom from the mundane task of milking, and even freedom from managing the workers who do that task. The fact that dairy farmers have largely deskilled these milking positions surely enables them to view their employees as "interchangeable" as this farmer seems to do.

Of course, immigrant workers can capitalize on network recruitment. These networks constitute an important way in which marginalized worker groups gain some control over the labor process: they fulfill their own obligations to kin and peers in selecting new co-workers, cover shifts in case of illness or other obligations, maintain wages, and otherwise create some flexibility and intra-group autonomy in the workplace (see also Vallas 2003:385-86). This is especially true on larger dairy farms, whose bigger workforces facilitate such practices; smaller farms often have only one or two milkers. Yet network recruitment via current employees' networks for the lowest-level positions nonetheless tends to reproduce workplace inequality, as others have shown in other contexts (Cranford 2005; McDowell et al. 2007; Waldinger and Lichter 2003). As milking jobs are increasingly assigned to immigrants, they become marked as "brown-collar jobs" and thus undesirable to U.S.-born workers (Saucedo 2006; Tomaskovic-Devey 1993). Being hired into deskilled milking positions limits immigrant workers' opportunities for skill development that could help them attain better jobs. Working long hours in late shifts for low pay further reduces immigrant workers' abilities to attend English classes that might help them to attain better jobs, which is compounded by the fact that dairy farm jobs and workers' homes are often far from urban areas where such classes are offered.

Finally, employers further simplify the low-end jobs in order to maintain the current division of labor. By creating deskilled jobs, recruiting through immigrant networks, and selecting for subordination, these employers often end up hiring workers with few English language skills. Although a few farmers offer English classes on the farm for their immigrant workers, most immigrant dairy workers and their employers face an almost complete language barrier. One farmer explained that he has adjusted to relying on workers who cannot speak English (those with "a language scenario") for his milking jobs by keeping the jobs as simplified as possible: "You centralize and you can teach someone with a language scenario one task, and you can communicate on one task, and they didn't have to do multiple tasks." Continually simplifying the low-end work enables dairy farmers to manage communication problems and thus to maintain the profitability of hiring immigrant workers in the milking positions. Doing so also makes those jobs less attractive to workers

with other options, thus further solidifying occupational segregation on the farm.

Conclusions

Our analysis extends existing theories of occupational segregation by demonstrating *why* employers engage in practices that contribute to occupational segregation. The first part of the process by which occupational segregation on dairy farms emerges is the fact that employers industrialize their operations and create new, low-end jobs; they do so to maintain profits and meet their own middle-class aspirations. To fill those new jobs, they hire marginalized, immigrant workers; these new inequalities enable farmers to comply with their peers' middle-class lifestyle expectations and manage their own concerns about immigration policing. Dairy farmers make sense of these inequalities through drawing symbolic boundaries between themselves and their different groups of workers; such narratives enable employers to assert their own class identity and justify the privileges that they and their U.S.-born employees enjoy on the farm. Finally, farmers maintain the new organization of work and workers by selecting for subordination, recruiting new milkers through existing immigrant employees' networks, and keeping the milking jobs as simplified as possible; employers do so to secure the privileges they have acquired. In other words, Wisconsin dairy farmers contribute to occupational segregation through the same practices that scholars have observed in other industries; what this case illuminates is why they do so. Namely, employers organize work and workers in unequal ways not only because they succumb to racist stereotypes and seek to maximize their own income, but because these practices enable them to defend who they are and define and become who they aspire to be.

The consequences are clear. These employers' status mobility is built upon the status immobility of the immigrant workers they hire, who shoulder the burden of employers' moves. Employers effectively offload the tasks they resent to workers who have little ability to contest the organization of work and the wages received. Employers secure more time with their own children, but workers with the late shifts and long hours have little time to be parents themselves, especially when living far from home (see Parreñas 2001).

Our research demonstrates that sociologists working to fully understand how and why workplaces become segregated must attend not only to the stories employers tell about different groups of workers, but also to the stories they tell about themselves and the contexts within which they struggle to survive and thrive. Doing so produces more complete explanations for why they engage in practices that produce occupational segregation. It also does the important work of bringing whiteness into the spotlight, showing how privilege is quietly constructed and naturalized, and demonstrating how oppression is not accidental or merely unfortunate but serves productive, albeit unequal, purposes. Illuminating employers' own lives and identity work thus brings occupational segregation research into line with the broader trend in sociology to analyzing the relational, coconstitutive nature of privilege and oppression.

Note

1. From Harrison's personal observations at the meeting of the Governor's Council on Migrant labor, January 28, 2009.

References

Andreas, Peter. 2001. "The Transformation of Migrant Smuggling across the U.S.–Mexican Border." Pp. 107–25 in *Global Human Smuggling: Comparative Perspectives,* edited by D. Kyle and R. Koslowski. Baltimore, MD: Johns Hopkins. Applied Population Lab (APL). 2011. "A Look at the Demography and Geography of Wisconsin." Population Notes 19. Applied Population Lab, University of Wisconsin, Madison.

Barham, Bradford L., Jeremy Foltz, and Ursula Aldana. 2005. "Expansion, Modernization, and Specialization in the Wisconsin Dairy Industry." Research Report No. 7. Program on Agricultural Technology Studies, University of Wisconsin, Madison.

Bell, Michael Mayerfeld. 2004. *Farming for Us All: Practical Agriculture and the Cultivation of Sustainability.* University Park: Pennsylvania State University Press.

Bryant, Antony and Kathy Charmaz. 2007. *The Sage Handbook of Grounded Theory.* Los Angeles: Sage.

Buttel, Frederick H. 1993. "Ideology and Agricultural Technology in the Late Twentieth Century: Biotechnology As Symbol and Substance." *Agriculture and Human Values* 10(2):5–15.

Coleman, Mat. 2007. "Immigration Geopolitics beyond the Mexico–U.S. Border." *Antipode* 39(1):54–76.

———. 2009. "What Counts as the Politics and Practice of Security, and Where? Devolution and Immigrant Insecurity after 9/11." *Annals of the Association of American Geographers* 99(5):904–13.

Collins, Patricia Hill. 1990. *Black Feminist Thought: Knowledge, Consciousness, and the Politics of Empowerment.* Boston, MA: Unwin Hyman.

Cornelius, Wayne A. 2001. "Death at the Border: Efficacy and Unintended Consequences of U.S. Immigration Control Policy." *Population and Development Review* 27(4):661–85.

Coutin, Susan Bibler. 2000. *Legalizing Moves: Salvadoran Immigrants' Struggle for U.S. Residency.* Ann Arbor: University of Michigan Press.

Cranford, Cynthia J. 2005. "Networks of Exploitation: Immigrant Labor and the Restructuring of the Los Angeles Janitorial Industry." *Social Problems* 52(3):379–97.

De Genova, Nicholas. 2005. *Working the Boundaries: Race, Space, and "Illegality" in Mexican Chicago.* Durham, NC: Duke University Press.

———. 2007. "The Production of Culprits: From Deportability to Detainability in the Aftermath of 'Homeland Security.'" *Citizenship Studies* 11(5):421–48.

DuPuis, E. Melanie. 2002. *Nature's Perfect Food: How Milk Became America's Drink.* New York: New York University Press.

Fitzgerald, Deborah. 2003. *Every Farm a Factory: The Industrial Ideal in American Agriculture.* New Haven, CT: Yale University Press.

Gilbert, Jess and Raymond Akor. 1988. "Increasing Structural Divergence in U.S. Dairying: California and Wisconsin Since 1950." *Rural Sociology* 55(1):56–72.

Golash-Boza, Tanya. 2012. *Due Process Denied: Detentions and Deportations in the United States.* New York: Routledge.

Granovetter, Mark. 1995. *Getting a Job: A Study of Contacts and Careers.* Chicago: University of Chicago Press.

Harrison, Jill Lindsey and Sarah E. Lloyd. 2012. "Illegality at Work: Deportability and the Productive New Era of Immigration Enforcement." *Antipode* 44(2):365–85.

Heffernan, William. 1998. "Agriculture and Monopoly Capital." *The Monthly Review* 50(3):46–59.

Hernández, David Manuel. 2008. "Pursuant to Deportation: Latinos and Immigrant Detention." *Latino Studies* 6:35–63.

Holmes, Seth M. 2007. "'Oaxacans Like to Work Bent Over': The Naturalization of Social Suffering among Berry Farm Workers." *International Migration* 45(3):39–68.

Janus, Edward. 2011. *Creating Dairyland.* Madison: Wisconsin Historical Society Press.

Jordan, Miriam. 2009. "Got Workers? Dairy Farms Run Low on Labor." *Wall Street Journal,* July 30. Retrieved April 17, 2013 (http://online.wsj.com/article/SB124890678 343891639.html).

Kandel, William and Emilio A. Parrado. 2005. "Restructuring of the U.S. Meat Processing Industry and New Hispanic Migrant Destinations." *Population and Development Review* 31:447–71.

Kanter, Rosabeth Moss. 1977. *Men and Women of the Corporation.* New York: Basic Books.

Kennelly, Ivy. 1999. "'That Single-Mother Element': How White Employers Typify Black Women." *Gender and Society* 13(2):168–92.

Lamont, Michele. 2000. *The Dignity of Working Men: Morality and the Boundaries of Race, Class, and Immigration.* New York: Russell Sage Foundation.

Lloyd, Sarah, Michael M. Bell, Steve Stevenson, and Tom Kriegl. 2006. "Life Satisfaction and Dairy Farming Study." Center for Integrated Agricultural Systems, University of Wisconsin-Madison. Unpublished data.

Lobao, Linda and Katherine Meyer. 2001. "The Great Agricultural Transition: Crisis, Change and Social Consequences of Twentieth Century U.S. Farming." *Annual Review of Sociology* 27:103–24.

Maldonado, Marta Maria. 2009. "'It Is Their Nature to Do Menial Labour': The Racialization of 'Latino/a Workers' by Agricultural Employers." *Ethnic and Racial Studies* 32(6):1017–36.

Massey, Douglas S., Jorge Durand, and Nolan J. Malone. 2003. *Beyond Smoke and Mirrors: Mexican Immigration in an Era of Economic Integration.* New York: Russell Sage Foundation.

Matthews, Gareth and Martin Ruhs. 2007. "Are You Being Served? Employer Demand for Migrant Labor in the UK's Hospitality Sector." Working Paper No. 51. Center on Migration, Policy and Society, University of Oxford, Oxford, UK.

McCandless, Susannah. 2010. "Conserving the Landscapes of Vermont: Shifting Terms of Access and Visibility." Ph.D. Dissertation, School of Geography, Clark University, Worcester, MA.

McDowell, Linda, Adina Batnizky, and Sarah Dyer. 2007. "Division, Segmentation, and Interpellation: The Embodied Labors of Migrant Workers in a Greater London Hotel." *Economic Geography* 83(1):1–25.

Mendelson, Margot, Shayna Strom, and Michael Wishnie. 2009. "Collateral Damage: An Examination of ICE's Fugitive Operations Program." Washington, DC: Migration Policy Institute.

Moss, Philip and Chris Tilly. 2001. *Stories Employers Tell: Race, Skill, and Hiring in America.* New York: Russell Sage Foundation.

Neckerman, Kathryn and Joleen Kirschenman. 1991. "Hiring Strategies, Racial Bias, and Inner City Workers." *Social Problems* 38:433–47.

Pabst, Georgia. 2009. "Immigrants an Increasingly Important Labor Force in Wisconsin Dairy." *Milwaukee Journal Sentinel,* February 24. Retrieved April 17, 2013 (www.jsonline .com/news/wisconsin/40201192.html).

Parreñas, Rhacel Salazar. 2001. *Servants of Globalization: Women, Migration, and Domestic Work.* Palo Alto, CA: Stanford University Press.

Peck, Jamie. 2001. *Workfare States.* New York: Guilford.

Piore, Michael J. 1979. *Birds of Passage: Migrant Labor and Industrial Societies.* Cambridge, UK: Cambridge University Press.

Reskin, Barbara F. 1998. *The Realities of Affirmative Action in Employment.* Washington, DC: American Sociological Association.

Reyes, Belinda I. 2004. "Changes in Trip Duration for Mexican Immigrants to the United States." *Population Research and Policy Review* 23(3):235–57.

Rosas, Gilberto. 2006a. "The Managed Violences of the Borderlands: Treacherous Geographies, Policeability, and the Politics of Race." *Latino Studies* 4(4):401–18.

———. 2006b. "The Thickening Borderlands: Diffused Exceptionality and 'Immigrant' Social Struggles during the 'War on Terror.'" *Cultural Dynamics* 18(3):335–49.

Ruhs, Martin and Bridget Anderson. 2007. "The Origins and Functions of Illegality in Migrant Labor Markets: An Analysis of Migrants, Employers and the State in the UK." Center on Migration, Policy and Society (COMPAS), University of Oxford, Oxford, UK.

Saucedo, Leticia. 2006. "The Employer Preference for the Subservient Worker and the Making of the Brown Collar Workplace." *Ohio State Law Journal* 67(5):961–1021.

Steinberg, Ronnie J. 1990. "The Social Construction of Skill: Gender, Power, and Comparable Worth." *Work and Occupations* 17:449–82.

Stephen, Lynn. 2004. "The Gaze of Surveillance in the Lives of Mexican Immigrant Workers." *Development* 47(1):97–102.

Thomas, Robert J. 1985. *Citizenship, Gender, and Work: Social Organization of Industrial Agriculture.* Berkeley: University of California Press.

Tomaskovic-Devey, Donald. 1993. *Gender and Racial Inequality at Work: The Sources and Consequences of Job Segregation.* Ithaca, NY: ILR Press.

U.S. Department of Agriculture (USDA). 2004. "Economic Effects of U.S. Dairy Policy and Alternative Approaches to Milk Pricing." Report to Congress. United States Department of Agriculture, Washington, DC.

———. 2011. "Milk Production Report." National Agricultural Statistics Service, United States Department of Agriculture, February 18. Retrieved January 25, 2013 (http:// usda01.library.cornell.edu/usda/nass/MilkProd// 2010s/2011/MilkProd-02-18-2011.pdf).

U.S. Department of Labor. 2005. "Findings from the National Agricultural Workers Survey (NAWS) 2001–2002: A Demographic and Employment Profile of United States Farm Workers." Research Report No. 9. United States Department of Labor, Washington, DC.

Valdes, Dennis Nodin. 1991. *Al Norte: Agricultural Workers in the Great Lakes Region 1917–1970.* Austin: University of Texas Press.

Vallas, Steven P. 2003. "Rediscovering the Color Line within Work Organizations: The 'Knitting of Racial Groups' Revisited." *Work and Organizations* 30(4):379–400.

Varsanyi, Monica. 2008. "Immigration Policing through the Backdoor: City Ordinances, the 'Right to the City,' and the Exclusion of Undocumented Day Laborers. *Urban Geography* 29(1):29–52.

Waldinger, Roger. 1994. "The Making of an Immigrant Niche." *International Migration Review* 28(1):3–30.

Waldinger, Roger and Michael I. Lichter. 2003. *How the Other Half Works: Immigration and the Social Organization of Labor.* Berkeley: University of California Press.

Waldinger, Roger, Nelson Lim, and David Cort. 2007. "Bad Jobs, Good Jobs, No Jobs? The Employment Experience of the Mexican American Second Generation." *Journal of Ethnic and Migration Studies* 33(1):1–35.

Walker, Kyle E. and Helga Leitner. 2011. "The Variegated Landscape of Local Immigration Policies in the United States." *Urban Geography* 32(2):156–78.

Waslin, Michele. 2009. "Immigration Policy and the Latino Community Since 9/11." Pp. 39–51 in *Immigration Policy and Security: U.S., European, and Commonwealth Perspectives*, edited by T. E. Givens, G. P. Freeman, and D. L. Leal. New York: Taylor and Francis.

Willis, Paul. 1977. *Learning to Labor: How Working Class Kids Get Working Class Jobs.* New York: Columbia University Press.

Zamudio, Margaret M. and Michael I. Lichter. 2008. "Bad Attitudes and Good Soldiers: Soft Skills as a Code for Tractability in the Hiring of Immigrant Latina/os over Native Blacks in the Hotel Industry." *Social Problems* 55(4):573–89.

Global Forces and the Individual

Globalization refers to the process of integrating governments, cultures, and financial markets. Sometimes the efforts have obvious benefits, even for those who worry about cultural colonialism, such as campaigns to bring clean-water technology to rural areas without access to safe drinking water. Other globalization efforts, however, are more complex. Let us look, for example, at the free-trade agreement known as NAFTA (North American Free Trade Agreement). The agreement is among the countries of North America, including Canada, the United States, and Mexico, allowing much freer trade opportunities without the kind of tariffs (taxes) and import laws that restrict international trade. Such trade agreements can lead to both increases and decreases in job opportunities. As Americans import more goods from outside the country, jobs typically decrease, as more and more products are made overseas. This has a direct impact on an individual worker in the United States. Many prominent economists believed that when NAFTA was created in 1994 it would lead to major gains in jobs. But by 2010, the evidence showed an opposite impact; the data showed 682,900 U.S. jobs lost across all states. While NAFTA did increase the flow of goods and capital across the northern and southern U.S. borders, it also increased unemployment in Mexico, spurring greater amounts of illegal immigration motivated by a search for work. So we see how global forces work on many different dimensions that have an impact on the individual.

Money makes the world. Go around?

There are many forces driving globalization, including the global economy and multinational corporations that control assets, sales, production, and employment. Characteristics of multinational corporations include the following: A large share of their capital is collected from a variety of different nations, their business is conducted without regard to national borders, they concentrate wealth in the hands of core nations and already wealthy individuals, and they play a key role in the global economy.

Increased communications and air travel have further opened doors for international business relations, facilitating the flow not only of goods but of information and people as well. Today, many U.S. companies set up offices in other nations where the costs of resources and labor are cheaper. When a person in the United States calls to get information about banking, insurance, or computer services, the person taking that call may be working in India or Indonesia.

Alongside the process of globalization is **diffusion**, or, the spread of material and non-material culture. While globalization refers to the integration of markets, diffusion relates a similar process to the integration of international cultures. Middle-class Americans can fly overseas and return with a new appreciation of Thai noodles or Italian gelato. Access to television and the Internet has brought the lifestyles and values portrayed in American sitcoms into homes around the globe. Twitter feeds from public demonstrations in one nation have encouraged political protesters in other countries. When this kind of diffusion occurs, material objects and ideas from one culture are introduced into another.

Mom and her son in front of McDonald on July 3, 2012 in Xiang Yang. It took McDonald 19 years to reach 1,000 restaurants in China. In 2013 it reached 2,000 stores. They have to catch up to KFC, which has three times more stores in China than McDonalds. (KFC restaurant in Shanghai.)

Technological globalization is impacted in large part by **technological diffusion**, the spread of technology across borders. In the last two decades, there has been rapid improvement in the spread of technology to peripheral and semi-peripheral nations, and a 2008 World Bank report discusses both the benefits and ongoing challenges of this diffusion. In general, the report found that technological progress and economic growth rates were linked, and that the rise in technological progress has helped improve the situations of many living in absolute poverty. The report recognizes that rural and low-tech products such as corn can benefit from new technological innovations, and that, conversely, technologies like mobile banking can aid those whose rural existence consists of low-tech market vending. In addition, technological advances in areas like mobile phones can lead to competition, lowered prices, and concurrent improvements in related areas such as mobile banking and information sharing. However, the same patterns of social inequality that create a digital divide in the United States also create digital divides in peripheral and semi-peripheral nations. While the growth of technology use among countries has increased dramatically over the past several decades, the spread of technology within countries is significantly slower among peripheral and semi-peripheral nations. In these countries, far fewer people have the training and skills to take advantage of new technology, let alone access it. Technological access tends to be clustered around urban areas, leaving out vast swaths of peripheral-nation citizens. While the diffusion of information technologies has the potential to resolve many global social problems, it is often the population most in need that is most affected by the digital divide. For example, technology to purify water could save many lives, but the villages in peripheral nations most in need of water purification do not have access to the technology, the funds to purchase it, or the technological comfort level to introduce it as a solution.

Immigration

One of the greatest manifestations of globalizing forces is the increase in migration occurring throughout the world. The United States is a nation of immigrants and migrants continue to add to the global feel of American main streets.

Global forces drive migration and the United States is the country which receives the most immigrants. We are the world. How we treat our citizens is a reflection of how we view the world.

The Earliest Immigrants

The earliest immigrants to America arrived millennia before European immigrants. Dates of the migration are debated with estimates ranging from between 45,000 and 12,000 B.C.E. It is thought that early Indians migrated to this new land in search of big game to hunt, which they found in huge herds of grazing herbivores in the Americas. Over the centuries and then the millennia, Native American culture blossomed into an intricate web of hundreds of interconnected tribes, each with its own customs, traditions, languages, and religions. Today they are the exemplar minority group whose domination occurred through territorial conquest.

African Americans: Unwilling Migrants

If Native Americans are the only minority group whose subordinate status occurred by conquest, African Americans are the exemplar minority group in the United States whose ancestors did not come here by choice. A Dutch sea captain brought the first Africans to the Virginia colony of Jamestown in 1619 and sold them as indentured servants. This was not an uncommon practice for either blacks or whites, and indentured servants were in high demand. For the next century, black and white indentured servants worked side by side. But the growing agricultural economy demanded greater and cheaper labor, and by 1705, Virginia passed the slave codes declaring that any foreign-born non-Christian could be a slave, and that slaves were considered property.

The next 150 years saw the rise of American slavery, with black Africans being kidnapped from their own lands and shipped to the New World on the trans-Atlantic journey known as the Middle Passage. Once in the Americas; the black population grew until American-born blacks outnumbered those born in Africa. But colonial (and later, American) slave codes declared that the child of a slave was a slave, so the slave class was created. By 1869, the slave trade was internal in the United States, with slavesbeing bought and sold across state lines like livestock.

Asian Migration

The national and ethnic diversity of Asian American immigration history is reflected in the variety of their experiences in joining American society. Asian immigrants have come to the United States in waves, at different times, and for different reasons. The first Asian immigrants to come to the United States in the mid-19th century were Chinese. These immigrants were primarily men whose intention was to work for several years in order to earn incomes to support their families in China. Their main destination was the American West, where the Gold Rush was drawing people with its lure of abundant money. The construction of the Transcontinental Railroad was underway at this time, and the Central

Pacific section hired thousands of migrant Chinese men to complete the laying of rails across the rugged Sierra Nevada mountain range. Chinese men also engaged in other manual labor like mining and agricultural work. The work was grueling and under paid, but like many immigrants, they persevered.

Japanese immigration began in the 1880s, on the heels of the Chinese Exclusion Act of 1882. Many Japanese immigrants came to Hawaii to participate in the sugar industry; others came to the mainland, especially to California. Unlike the Chinese, however, the Japanese had a strong government that negotiated with the United States government to ensure the well-being of their immigrants. Japanese men were able to bring their wives and families to the United States, and were thus able to produce second- and third-generation Japanese Americans more quickly than their Chinese counterparts.

The most recent large-scale Asian immigration came from Korea and Vietnam and largely took place during the second half of the 20th century. While Korean immigration has been fairly gradual, Vietnamese immigration occurred primarily post-1975, after the fall of Saigon and the establishment of restrictive communist policies in Vietnam. Whereas many Asian immigrants came to the United States to seek better economic opportunities, Vietnamese immigrants came as political refugees, seeking asylum from harsh conditions in their homeland. The Refugee Act of 1980 helped them to find a place to settle in the United States.

Educated women pose a threat to traditional societies in many places around the globe. Should we understand the fear of educating women as a deep seated cultural tradition and accept it or should we try to encourage equal rights? Why?

Latino Migrations

Like the individuals comprising many "groups," Hispanic Americans have a wide range of backgrounds and nationalities. According to the 2010 U.S. Census, about 75 percent of the respondents who identify as Hispanic report being of Mexican, Puerto Rican, or Cuban origin. Of the total Hispanic group, 60 percent reported as Mexican, 44 percent reported as Cuban, and nine percent reported as Puerto Rican. Remember that the U.S. Census allows people to report as being more than one ethnicity.

Not only are there wide differences among the different origins that make up the Hispanic American population, there are also different names for the group itself. The 2010 U.S. Census states that "Hispanic" or "Latino" refers to a person of Cuban, Mexican, Puerto Rican, South or Central American, or other Spanish culture or origin regardless of race." There have been some disagreements over whether Hispanic or Latino is the correct term for a group this diverse, and whether it would be better for people to refer to themselves as being of their origin specifically, for example, Mexican American or Dominican American.

Mexican Americans form the largest Hispanic subgroup and also the oldest. Mexican migration to the United States started in the early 1900s in response to the need for cheap agricultural labor. Mexican migration was often circular; workers would stay for a few years, and then go back to Mexico with more money than they could have made in their country of origin. The length of Mexico's shared border with the United States has made immigration easier than for many other immigrant groups.

Cuban Americans are the second-largest Hispanic subgroup, and their history is quite different from that of Mexican Americans. The main wave of Cuban immigration to the United States started after Fidel Castro came to power in 1959 and reached its crest with the Mariel boatlift in 1980.

Arab Migrants

The first Arab immigrants came to this country in the late 19th and early 20th century. They were predominantly Syrian, Lebanese, and Jordanian Christians, and they came to escape persecution and to make a better life. These early immigrants and their descendants, who were more likely to think of themselves as Syrian or Lebanese than Arab, represent almost half of the Arab American population today (Myers, 2007). Restrictive immigration policies from the 1920s until 1965 curtailed all immigration, but Arab immigration since 1965 has been steady. Immigrants from this time period have been more likely to be Muslim and more highly educated, escaping political unrest and looking for better opportunities.

© Oleg Zabielin, 2014. Used under license from Shutterstock, Inc.

What does this image convey to you? Are these Kalashnikov wielding fighters a threat to our life style? Are we a threat to theirs? Maybe they are on our side?

Global Capitalism Theory and the Emergence of Transnational Elites

William I. Robinson[*]
January 2010

Abstract

The class and social structure of developing nations has undergone profound transformation in recent decades as each nation has incorporated into an increasingly integrated global production and financial system. National elites have experienced a new fractionation. Emergent transnationally-oriented elites grounded in globalized circuits of accumulation compete with older nationally-oriented elites grounded in more protected and often state-guided national and regional circuits. This essay focuses on structural analysis of the distinction between these two fractions of the elite and the implications for development. I suggest that nationally-oriented elites are often dependent on the social reproduction of at least a portion of the popular and working classes for the reproduction of their own status, and therefore on local development processes however so defined whereas transnationally-oriented elites are less dependent on such local social reproduction. The shift in dominant power relations from nationally- to transnationally-oriented elites is reflected in a concomitant shift to a discourse from one that defines development as national industrialization and expanded consumption to one that defines it in terms of global market integration.

Keywords: Elites, development, globalization, transnational, capitalism, crisis

JEL classification: F01, F54, F59, P16

[*] University of California-Santa Barbara, USA. E-mail: wirobins@soc.ucsb.edu

Copyright © UNU-WIDER 2009

This study has been prepared within the UNU-WIDER project on The Role of Elites in Economic Development.

UNU-WIDER acknowledges the financial contributions to the research programme by the governments of Denmark (Royal Ministry of Foreign Affairs), Finland (Ministry for Foreign Affairs), Norway (Royal Ministry of Foreign Affairs), Sweden (Swedish International Development Cooperation Agency—Sida) and the United Kingdom (Department for International Development).

ISSN 1798-7237
ISBN 978-92-9230-237-5

The World Institute for Development Economics Research (WIDER) was established by the United Nations University (UNU) as its first research and training centre and started work in Helsinki, Finland in 1985. The Institute undertakes applied research and policy analysis on structural changes affecting the developing and transitional economies, provides a forum for the advocacy of policies leading to robust, equitable and environmentally sustainable growth, and promotes capacity strengthening and training in the field of economic and social policy making. Work is carried out by staff researchers and visiting scholars in Helsinki and through networks of collaborating scholars and institutions around the world.

www.wider.unu.edu   publications@wider.unu.edu

Introduction

My objective here is to offer as theoretical reflection a 'big picture', that is, a macrostructural perspective through which to approach the theme of elites and development. A genealogy of inquiry into global inequalities and development in the modern era is a study in the original and evolution of the critique of capitalism and the distinct social forces and class agents that this system generates. Hence, how we conceptualize the role of elites in development will be tied to how we analyze capitalism as a world system and more specifically how we analyze its distinct social forces and class agents. In a nutshell, I suggest that globalization represents a new epoch in the ongoing evolution of world capitalism distinguished by the rise of a globally-integrated production and financial

UNU World Institute for Development Economics Research (UNU-WIDER) Katajanokanlaituri 6 B, 00160 Helsinki, Finland

Typescript prepared by Janis Vehmaan-Kreula at UNU-WIDER

The views expressed in this publication are those of the author(s). Publication does not imply endorsement by the Institute or the United Nations University, nor by the programme/project sponsors, of any of the views expressed.

system, an emergent transnational capitalist class, and incipient transnational state apparatuses. Structural changes in the world economy associated with globalization have contributed to a new fractionation among elites in the former Third World between nationally-oriented and transnationally-oriented groups. These two overlapping yet often competing sets of elites pursued distinct development strategies in the late twentieth and the early twenty-first centuries. The former sought to build national circuits of accumulation while the latter sought to integrate local circuits into new transnational circuits of accumulation. These contrasting strategies for development involved distinct sets of policies: the one, policies that would protect local agents from global competition; the other, policies that integrate local agents into emergent transnational circuits.

My propositions on globalization and in particular on national and transnational fractions of the elite are grounded in distinct strategies of accumulation and depart from conventional wisdom, yet they grow out of a rich history of intellectual and political debate. The theme of the role elites play in development is as old, or older, than the concept of development itself. Early enlightenment and bourgeois thinkers saw rising middle and commercial classes from whence many of them came as the agents of progress and modernization. Sociologists in the nineteenth and early twentieth centuries such as Compte, Spencer, and Weber, would develop these views into theoretical constructs. But as the middle classes of the early capitalist era achieved political power and became the new ruling groups, Marx and other nineteenth century radical thinkers critiqued the new order as generating the social conditions associated with underdevelopment. As Europe unleashed a new round of imperialist expansion in the late nineteenth and early twentieth centuries a new generation of Marxists thinkers, from Hilferding to Lenin, Bukharin, and Luxemburg identified the leading capitalist states as the agents behind the colonization and plunder of what would later be called the Third World. Among this generation, Leon Trotsky developed perhaps the most coherent theoretical explanation for inequalities between rich and poor countries in his theory of combined and uneven development.

In the wake of World War II and decolonization newly independent countries from Africa and Asia joined with their Latin American counterparts in shifting international political attention to global inequalities (see, inter-alia, Prashad 2007). How to account for this inequality and what to do about it became the focus of heated intellectual and ideological battles and formed the backdrop to the rise of development studies. United States president Harry Truman famously launched the 'era of development' in a 1949 speech, declaring that 'we must embark on a bold new program for making the benefits of our scientific advances and industrial progress available for the improvement and growth of underdeveloped areas' (Esteva 1991: 7). Behind the Truman declaration was the effort to open up the former colonial world to an expanding international capitalism. The story of the rise of modernization theory in the wake of the Truman declaration, largely in the US academy with ample support from the policymaking establishment, is now well known. The theme of enlightened elites leading societies into development and progress became a fundamental tenet of modernization and concomitant political development theories that dominated the social sciences from the 1950s into the 1970s. But alternative explanations for development and underdevelopment challenged the hegemony of modernization theory in the 1960s and on to the drumbeat of anti-colonial and revolutionary struggles across the Third World that challenged the very structures of the world capitalist system. From the perspective of new dependency, world-systems, and radical international political economy theories, elites in the Third World were largely seen as agents of a world capitalist system whose very constitution and reconstitution was founded on the unity and antagonism of core and peripheral or developed and underdeveloped regions of the world.

My own theory of global capitalism shares much with this radical intellectual tradition in development studies but also diverges on several key counts. I see globalization as a qualitatively new epoch in the ongoing evolution of world capitalism, characterized above all by the rise of truly transnational capital and the integration (or re-articulation) of most countries in the world into a new global production and financial system. The leading strata among national capitalist classes in both the North and the South have experienced ongoing integration across borders into an emergent transnational capitalist class (TCC) and at whose apex is a transnational managerial elite. The nation-state, while it does not disappear or even become 'less important', is undergoing transformation. The institutional apparatus of national states has become increasingly entangled in transnational institutional webs that bring them together with inter- and transnational institutions into what can be conceived as incipient transnational state apparatuses. During the 1980s and 1990s capitalists and elites around the world became fractionated along new lines: nationally-oriented and transnationally-oriented. Transnational fractions of local elites in competition with nationally-oriented fractions vied for, and in many countries around the world won state power. They utilized that power to push capitalist globalization, to restructure national productive apparatuses and integrate them into the new global production and financial system.

These are complex propositions that I have written about extensively elsewhere (see, in particular, Robinson 2003, 2004, 2008). Here I want to focus on the implications of this theory of global capitalism for elites and development. I want to suggest, in particular, that nationally-oriented elites who promoted developmentalist projects in the twentieth century often depended on the social reproduction of at least a portion of the popular and working classes for the reproduction of their own power and status, and therefore on local development processes, however so defined and however deficient. In distinction, transnationally-oriented elites who pushed restructuring and integration into global capitalism were less dependent on such local social reproduction. With the shift in elites came a shift in discourse from national industrialization and expanding internal markets to global market integration and macroeconomic, principally neo-liberal, policies that facilitated such integration.

There is little consensus on the appropriate terminology for inter-state and global inequalities. Here I will use interchangeably First and Third World, developed and developing/underdeveloped, core and periphery, and North and South, although I find *all* these terms problematic. Also, how to conceive elites is a contentious matter in political sociology that I cannot take up here. Suffice it to observe that much debate has centered on the relationship between classes and elites and whether or not these are commensurate analytical categories. By elites I refer to dominant political, socioeconomic and cultural strata, and in particular, to capitalists and landlords, along with top level managers and administrators of the state and other major social institutions and leadership positions in the political system. Capitalists are elites who own or manage means of production as capital. Elites who are not necessarily capitalists occupy key decision-making positions in institutions, whether in private corporations, the state, political parties or cultural industries. However, in my view the status of elites that are not capitalists proper is dependent on the reproduction of capital.

Nation-state capitalism and the turn to globalization

Diverse Fordist-Keynesian models of national corporate capitalism spread throughout the twentieth century from the cores of the world capitalist system to the former colonial domains in Latin America, Africa, and Asia. These countries tended to pursue a multiclass development model along radical Keynesian lines, often referred to as developmentalist, populist, or corporatist. Developmentalist capitalism took on a form distinct from its First World New Deal and social democratic variants, often involving a much greater role for the state and the public sector, mass social mobilizations growing out of anti-colonial, anti-dictatorial, and national-liberation movements, and populist or corporatist political projects. Both First and Third World models were predicated on a redistributive logic and on incorporation of labour and other popular classes into national historical blocs. The legitimacy of elites in the Third World may have been even more closely tied to the logic of this redistribution and the social reproduction of popular classes than their counterparts in the First World.

World capitalism developed in this period within the nation-state and through the interstate system. Nation-states were linked to each other through the international division of labour and through commercial and financial exchanges in an integrated international market regulated, at least in theory, by the Bretton Woods institutions. In this way the system provided for more insulated forms of national control over economic and social policy and greater autonomy in internal capitalist development, even as the international market disciplined countries into supporting the international rules of exchange rates and exchange and reproduced the world capitalist power structure. The world economy experienced a sustained period of growth in the quarter century after World War II – the so called 'golden age' of capitalism. But the illusion of prosperity burst with the world economic downturn that began in the 1970s and that threw national corporate capitalism into crisis.

The social origins of this crisis was to be found in the relative strength that working and popular classes won worldwide in relation to capital after many decades of class and social struggles in both the First and the Third World. Organized labour, increased taxes on profits and income, state regulation, revolutions in the Third World and the explosion of social movements and counter-hegemonic cultural practices everywhere constricted private capital's real or perceived capacity for accumulation. The expansion of collective rights, the institutionalization of Keynesian-Fordist class compromise, and the prevailing norms of a 'moral economy' that assumed capital and state reciprocities with labour and citizens and an ethnical obligation to minimal social reproduction – all this burdened capital with social rigidities that had to be reversed for a new phase of capitalist growth. Capital and its political representatives and organic intellectuals in the core countries organized a broad offensive – economic, political, ideological, military – that was symbolically spearheaded by the Reagan-Thatcher alliance. Emerging transnational elites from the centers of power in the world system launched a global counterrevolution that would be as much political and economic as social, cultural, and ideological, and that was still being fought out in manifold arenas in the twenty-first century.

In structural terms, this crisis was not merely cyclical. Cyclical crises eventually accumulate into more generalized crises involving social and political upheavals and ushering in periods of restructuring. *Restructuring crises* result in novel forms that replace historical patterns of capital accumulation and the institutional arrangements that facilitated them (see, inter-alia, Aglietta 1979; Kotz et al. 1994). The world capitalist crisis that began in the 1970s is generally identified as the turning point for globalization and in my view signaled the transition to a new transnational stage in the system. For much of the twentieth century First World Keynesian capitalism and Third World developmentalist capitalism shared two common features: state intervention in the economy and a redistributive logic. The crisis that began in the 1970s could not be resolved within the framework of these post-World War II social structures of accumulation. In the First World there was a progressive breakdown of the Keynesian-Fordist welfare states and in the Third World developmentalist projects became exhausted as manifest above all in economic contraction and the debt crisis of the 1980s.

Globalization became a viable strategy as capitalists and state managers searched for new modes of accumulation. 'Going global' allowed capital to shake off the constraints that nation-state capitalism had placed on accumulation; to break free of the class compromises and concessions that had been imposed by working and popular classes and by national governments in the preceding epoch. The decision by the US government to abandon the fixed exchange rate system in 1973 effectively did away with the Bretton Woods system and, together with deregulation, opened the floodgate to transnational capital movement and the meteoric spread of transnational corporations (TNCs). Capital achieved a newfound global mobility, or ability to operate across borders in new ways, which ushered in the era of global capitalism. The renewed power to discipline labour that this afforded transnational capital altered the worldwide correlation of class and social forces in its favour. What was international capital in the preceding epoch metamorphosized into transnational capital.

Emerging global elites and transnational capitalists set about to dismantle the distinct models associated with national corporate capitalism and to construct a new global 'flexible' regime of accumulation. In broad strokes, Keynesianism was replaced by monetarist policies, deregulation, and a 'supply side' approach that included regressive taxation and new incentives for capital. The Fordist class compromise was replaced by a new capital-labour relation based on deunionization, flexible workers and deregulated work conditions and the welfarist social contract was replaced by social austerity and the law of the market in social reproduction. More specifically, the prospects for capital to accumulate and make profits were restored during the 1980s and on and on by four key developments associated with capitalist globalization.

First was a new capital-labour relation based on the deregulation, informalization, and 'flexibilization' of labour. Second was a new round of *extensive* and *intensive* expansion. Extensively, the system expanded through the reincorporation of major areas of the former Third and Second worlds into the world capitalist economy, so that by the 1990s no region remained outside the system. Intensively, public and community spheres that formerly lay outside (or buffered from) the logic of market relations (profit making) were commodified and opened up to accumulation through privatization, state deregulation and reregulation, including the extension of intellectual property rights, and so on. Third, was the creation of a global legal and regulatory structure to facilitate what were emerging globalized circuits of accumulation, including the creation of the World Trade Organization. And fourth, was the imposition of the neo-liberal model on countries throughout the Third and the former Second worlds, involving structural adjustment programmes that created the conditions for the free operation of capital within and across borders and the harmonization of accumulation conditions worldwide. Through neo-liberalism the world has increasingly become a *single unified field for global capitalism*. Capital has come to achieve a newfound global mobility in a double sense, in that the material *and* the political obstacles to its unfettered movement around the world have dramatically come down. As capital became liberated from the nation-state and assumed new power relative to labour with the onset of globalization, states shifted from reproducing Keynesian social structures of accumulation to servicing the general needs of the new patterns of global accumulation.

A transnational production and financial system

Since the 1970s, the emergence of globally mobile transnational capital increasingly divorced from specific countries has facilitated the *globalization of production* (I include services here); the fragmentation and decentralization of complex production processes, the worldwide dispersal of the different segments in these chains, and their functional integration into vast global chains of production and distribution. World production is thus reorganized into new transnational, or global, circuits of accumulation through which values move instantaneously. National economies have been reorganized and reinserted as component elements of this new global production and financial system (on the anatomy of this system, see inter-alia, Dicken 2003; McMichael 1996), which is a qualitatively distinct world economic structure from that of previous epochs, when each country had a distinct national economy linked externally to one another through trade and financial flows. This is a shift from international market integration to global productive integration. I have referred to this distinction elsewhere as between a *world economy* – in which nation-states are linked to each other via trade and financial flows – to a *global economy* – in which the production process itself becomes globally integrated (Robinson 2003, 2004). At the same time an integrated global financial system has replaced the national bank-dominated financial systems of the earlier period. Global financial flows since the 1980s are qualitatively different from the international financial flows of the earlier period.

Globalization refers to a process characterized by relatively novel articulations of social power which were not available in earlier historic periods. The increasingly total mobility achieved by capital has allowed it to search out around the world the most favourable conditions for different phases of globalized production, including the cheapest labour, the most favourable institutional environment (e.g., low taxes) and regulatory conditions (e.g., lax environment and labour laws), a stable social environment, and so on. Transnational capital is the *hegemonic fraction* of capital on a world scale in the sense that it imposes its direction on the global economy and it shapes the character of production and social life everywhere. Although real power and control still remains rigidly hierarchal and has actually become more concentrated under globalization, the actual organizational form of economic activity is characterized by decentralized webs of horizontally interlocked networks in distinction to the old centralized hierarchies based on vertical integration. The rise of the global economy has been founded on the phenomenal spread since the late 1970s of diverse new economic arrangements associated with the transition from the Fordist regime of accumulation to new post-Fordist *flexible* regimes. Subcontracting and outsourcing have become a basic organizational feature

of economic activity worldwide. In the earlier epochs of capitalism firms tended to organize entire sequences of economic production, distribution, and service from within. The *maquiladora,* or offshore, factories that are the epitome of the 'global assembly line' are based on this type of subcontracting network, although the phenomenon has long since spread to just about all sectors of the world economy.

Subcontracting and outsourcing, along with a host of other new economic arrangements have resulted in the creation of vast transnational production chains and complex webs of vertical and horizontal integration patterns across the globe. The concepts of flexible accumulation and network structure capture the organizational form of globalized circuits (on this network structure, see, in particular, Castells 2000). Global production and service chains or networks are *global* in character, in that accumulation is embedded in *global* markets, involves *global* enterprise organization and sets of *global* capital-labour relations, especially deregulated and casualized labour pools worldwide. Transnational capital, as organized into the giant TNCs, coordinates these vast chains, incorporating numerous agents and social groups into complex global networks. Competition in the new global economy dictates that firms must establish global as opposed to national or regional markets, and that other economic agents must move beyond local markets if they are to remain viable.

Global capitalism and transnationally-oriented elites

Epochal changes in the system of world capitalism have had transformative effects on the world as a whole and on each region integrated in or rearticulated, to the system. Earlier epochs of world capitalism have had major implications for each country and region of the former Third World, which have gone through successive waves of ever-deeper integration into the system. With each new integration or reintegration there has been a corresponding fundamental change in social and class structures and the leading economic activities around which social classes and groups have exercised collective agency. The epoch of corporate capitalism that preceded globalization saw a deeper integration of Africa, Asia, and Latin America into world capitalism, including a major expansion of exports in most cases and the rise of new industrial, commercial, and financial elites and new middle and working classes. The groups came together in multi-class populist and corporatist projects that sought development through import-substitution industrialization and modernization. Each phase of historical change in the world capitalist system – builds on preceding ones and retains important elements from them. Global capitalism is now having a similar transformative effect on every country and region of the world. Developing countries have been experiencing a transition to a new model of economy and society as they become reinserted into the emerging global stage of world capitalism.

As transnational capital integrates the world into new globalized circuits of accumulation it has broken down national and regional autonomies, including the earlier pre-globalization models of capitalist development and the social forces that sustained these models. Through internal adjustment and rearticulation to the emerging global economy and society, local productive apparatuses and social structures in each region are transformed, and different regions acquire new profiles in the emerging global division of labour. Integration into the emergent global system is the causal structural dynamic that underlies the events we have witnessed in nations and regions all around the world over the past few decades. We want to pay particularly close attention to changes in the economic structure because they provide the material basis for related processes of change in practices and institutions, politics, class structure, and for inquiry into the theme of elites and development.

The remolding of each national and regional economy creates an array of contradictions between the old and new forms of accumulation. What sets a region off from other parts of the global economy in much of the development literature is uneven geographic development and distinct participation in an international division of labour. I suggest, however, that more determinant (of causal priority) in conceptualizing regions within the larger unity of the emerging global economy and society than uneven accumulation, while still important, is the distinct configurations of social forces and of institutions that arise from these configurations. If we are to properly understand the role of local and regional economies and social and class structures they must be studied from the perspective of their point of insertion into global accumulation rather than their relationship to a particular national market or state structure.

Transnational class formation in the developing countries is a major dimension of capitalist globalization. As global capitalism penetrates new spheres and subjects them to the logic of transnational accumulation, pre-globalization classes such as peasantries and artisans tend to disappear, replaced by new dominant and subordinate class groups linked to the global economy. We have generally seen in developing countries: the rise of new dominant groups and capitalist fractions tied to the global economy; the downward mobility – or proletarianization – of older middle classes and professional strata and the rise of new middle and professional strata; proletarianization of peasants and artisans and the rise of new urban and rural working classes linked to transnational production processes; the working class itself become flexibalized and informalized; the appearance of an expanding mass of supernumeraries or marginalized. A global working class has emerged that runs the factories, offices, and farms of the global economy, a stratified and heterogeneous class, to be sure, with numerous hierarchies and cleavages internal to it – gender, ethnicity, nationality, and so on.

Here I want to focus on elites. The TCC is comprised of the owners and managers of the TNCs and the private transnational financial institutions that drive the global economy (Sklair 2002; Robinson 2004). The TCC is a class group grounded in global markets and circuits of accumulation. The globally-integrated production and financial system underscores the increasing interpenetration on multiple levels of capital in all parts of the world, organized around transnational capital and the giant TNCs. It is increasingly difficult to separate local circuits of production and distribution from the globalized circuits that dictate the terms and patterns of accumulation worldwide, even when surface appearance gives the (misleading) impression that local capitals retain their autonomy. There are of course still local and national capitalists, and there will be for a long time to come. But they must 'de-localize' and link to transnational capital if they are to survive. Territorially restricted capital cannot compete with its transnationally mobile counterpart. As the global circuit of capital subsumes through numerous mechanisms and arrangements these local circuits, local capitalists who manage these circuits become swept up into the process of transnational class formation.

I have been writing about this process of transnational class formation and the rise of a TCC since the late 1990s (inter-alia, Robinson 1996, 2003, 2004). The topic has become part of a collective research agenda and the empirical evidence demonstrating the transnationalization of leading capitalist groups is now considerable (for a sampling, see, Sklair 2002; Kentor 2005). With the rise of transnational production chains and circuits of accumulation, transnationally-oriented capitalists in each country shift their horizons from national markets to global markets. Different phases of production, as they become broken down into component phases that are detachable and dispersed around the world, can be doled out to distinct economic agents through chains of subcontracting, outsourcing, and other forms of association. These agents become integrated organically into new globalized circuits, so that they are 'denationalized', in the material if not the cultural sense, and become transnational agents. The vast multilayered networks of outsourcing, subcontracting, collaboration, and so on, increasingly link local and national agents to global networks and structures. The TCC has increasingly exhibited a global political action capacity and placed itself on the world scene as a coherent actor. In the same way as business groups organize to orient national policy planning groups and lobby national governments, transnational business groups have become a powerful lobby in many countries around the world pushing for a shift in state policies toward promotion of the group interests of those integrated into transnational circuits.

The composition of capitalist classes and elites in developing countries is altered by capitalist globalization. The spread of transnational circuits of accumulation present elites in developing countries with new opportunities to pursue their class and group interests by reinserting local economic activity that they manage as segments of globalized circuits. Other groups whose reproduction was tied to domestic accumulation may lose out if they are unable to transnationalize their local activity. In my detailed case study on Central America (Robinson 2003) I have shown how local elites who previously strived to build up national circuits of accumulation were confronted from the 1980s and on with a situation in which these circuits were no longer viable *and* in which restructuring and integration into globalized circuits became a profitable option. Hence their class and group interests shifted from national development to participation in new global markets and production and service sequences. The restructuring and globalization of local production processes do bring about new opportunities for upward mobility among some sectors of the national population. But these benefits of global integration, as I shall argue below, do not constitute development in the traditional sense. As these processes have unfolded there have been ongoing struggles in recent decades between ascendant transnational and descendant national fractions of dominant groups and these struggles often form the backdrop to national political and ideological dynamics. Transnational fractions of local capitalist classes and bureaucratic elites vied for state power and in most countries won government in the 1980s and 1990s, or at least came to capture 'commanding heights' of state policymaking via key ministries such as foreign, finance, and central banks. In many developing countries transnational fractions utilized local states to latch their countries on to the train of capitalist globalization.

National and global accumulation and the State

Here there is a contradictory logic between national and global accumulation. On the one side are the only national fractions of dominant groups whose interests lie in national accumulation and traditional national regulatory and protectionist mechanisms. On the other are transnational groups tied to new globalized circuits of accumulation. Their interests lie in an expanding global economy. There is a tension between nation-centric class interests and those groups who develop new relationships linked to transnationalized accumulation. As conflicts arise between descending forms of national production and rising forms of globalized capital local and national struggles should be seen as simultaneously global and internal. Transnational fractions, as they have captured governments around the world, or come to positions in which they can influence and redirect state policies, have utilized national state apparatuses to advance globalization, pursue economic restructuring, and to dismantle the old nation-state social welfare and developmentalist projects. While pursuing the neo-liberal model at home they have also pursued world-wide market liberalization and projects of regional and global economic integration. They have promoted a supra-national infrastructure of the global economy.

Transnationally-oriented capitalists and state managers in developing countries have pursued a switch from 'inward oriented development', or accumulation around national markets such as the Import-Substitution Industrialization (ISI) models that predominated in many Third World regions in the middle part of the twentieth century, to 'outward-oriented development' involving export-promotion strategies and a deeper integration of national economies into the global economy. This switch involves the emergence of new economic activities and structures of production in each country and region integrating into the global economy (Robinson 2002; 2003). These new activities generally imply local participation in globalized circuits of accumulation, or in global production and service chains. As I have shown in great detail for Latin America (Robinson 2008), these activities include *maquiladora* assembly operations and other forms of transnational industrial subcontracting, transnational corporate agribusiness, transnational banking and other financial services, transnational services such as call centers, software production, data processing, tourism and leisure, and so forth, as well as, very importantly, the transnationalization of the retail sector, or what I call Walmartization, along with the supply systems that stock retail. The new dominant sectors of accumulation in the developing world are, in sum, increasingly integrated into global accumulation circuits in a myriad of ways.

It is important to explore the relationship between transnationally-oriented capitalist and business groups and elites in the state and the political system. As new transnational circuits of accumulation became dominant there were powerful pressures on state managers to promote these circuits locally – that is, promoting an environment friendly to transnational capital. Elites found that the reproduction of their status becomes linked to the new global accumulation strategy. Restructuring gave an immanent class bias to agents of the external sector. These agents tended to fuse with political managers of the neo-liberal state and in the latter decades of the twentieth century began to coalesce gradually, in a process checkered with contradictions and conflict, into a transnationalized fraction of the national elite that promote and manage new globalized circuits of accumulation. At the helm of transnational fractions of the elite we generally find a politicized leadership and a technocratic cadre steeped in neo-liberal ideology and economics and sharing a familiarity with the world of academic think tanks, world-class universities, and international financial institutions.

What were developmentalist states in the earlier epoch became neo-liberal states under globalization. These neo-liberal national states have functioned to serve *global* (over local) capital accumulation, including a shift in the subsidies that states provide, away from social reproduction and from internal economic agents and towards transnational capital. These neo-liberal states have performed three essential services: (1) adopt fiscal, monetary and trade policies that assure macro-economic stability and the free movement of capital; (2) provide the basic infrastructure necessary for global economic activity (air and sea ports, communications networks, educational systems, etc.), and; (3) provide social order, that is, stability, which requires sustaining instruments of social control, coercive and ideological apparatuses. When transnational elites speak of 'governance' they are referring to these functions and the capacity to fulfill them.

However, there are other conditions that transnational capitalists and elites require for the functioning and reproduction of global capitalism. National states are ill equipped to organize a supranational unification of macroeconomic policies, create a unified field for transnational capital to operate, impose transnational trade regimes, supranational 'transparency', and so forth. The construction of a supranational legal and regulator system for the global economy in recent years has been the task of sets of transnational institutions whose policy prescriptions and actions have been synchronized with

those of neo-liberal national state that have been captured by local transnationally-oriented forces. There is a new transnational institutionality, a new transnational configuration of power, but this is a very incomplete, contradictory, and open-ended process. A TNS apparatus is not the same as a 'global government', which does not exist. Transnational institutions attempt to coordinate global capitalism and impose capitalist domination beyond national borders. We can conceptualize a TNS apparatus as a loose network comprised of inter- and supranational political and economic institutions *together with* national state apparatuses that have been penetrated and transformed by transnational forces, and has not yet (and may never) acquired any centralized form. The TNS played a key role in imposing the neo-liberal model on the old Third World and therefore in reinforcing a new capital-labour relation. The IMF, for example, by conditioning its lending on a deregulation and flexibilization of local labour markets, as it has often done, is imposing the new capital-labour relation on the particular country and in the process fundamentally transforming local labour markets and class and power relations.

Transnational elites set about to penetrate and restructure national states, directly, through diverse political-diplomatic and other ties between national states and TNS apparatuses and functionaries, and indirectly, through the impositions of transnational capital via its institutional agents (IMF, World Bank, etc.) and the structural power that global capital exercises over nation-states. Local transnational nuclei, or pools, have liaised with the transnational elite as 'in-country' counterparts through a shared outlook and interest in new economic activities and through diverse external political, cultural, and ideological ties. These nuclei sought in recent decades to advance the transnational agenda by capturing key state apparatuses and ministries, by the hegemony they were expected to achieve in civil society, and by the power they wielded through their preponderance in the local economy and the material and ideological resources accrued through external linkages. Hence it is not that nation-states become irrelevant or powerless vis-à-vis transnational capital and its global institutions. Rather, power as the ability to issue commands and have them obeyed, or more precisely, the ability to shape social structures, shifts from social groups and classes with interests in national accumulation to those whose interests lie in new global circuits of accumulation.

Although they do not disappear, national states experience dramatic fracturing and restructuring. As globalization proceeds, internal social cohesion declines along with national economic integration. The neo-liberal state retains essential powers to facilitate globalization but it loses the ability to harmonize conflicting social interests within a country, to realize the historic function of sustaining the internal unity of nationally-conceived social formation, and to achieve legitimacy. Unable to resolve the contradictory problems of legitimacy and capital accumulation, local states opt simply for abandoning whole sectors of national populations. In many instances, they no longer bothered to try to attain legitimacy among the marginalized and supernumeraries, who are isolated and contained in new ways, or subject to repressive social control measures (such as, e.g., the mass incarceration of African Americans in the United States or 'social cleansing' in several Latin American countries). A fundamental contradiction in the global capitalist system is a globalizing economy within a nation-state based political system. A TNS apparatus is incipient and unable to regulate global capitalism or to ameliorate many of its crisis tendencies.

Power did shift in many countries from nationally-oriented dominant groups to these emerging transnationally-oriented groups. However, the crisis that exploded in 2008 with the collapse of the global financial system has exacerbated crises of legitimacy in many countries around the world and seriously undermined the ability of transnational elites to reproduce their authority. Global elites have been scrambling since the Asian crisis of 1997-8 to develop more effective transnational state apparatuses, or institutions and mechanisms that allow for transnational coordination and supervision. These efforts have intensified since the collapse of 2008. In March 2009, for instance, the Chinese government called for the creation of a new global reserve currency to replace the dominant dollar – a super-currency made up of a basket of national currencies and controlled by the IMF.

From a geographical to a social conception of development

As capitalism globalizes, the twenty-first century is witness to new forms of poverty and wealth, and new configurations of power and domination. Class, racial and gender inequalities have in many respects been aggravated by globalization and new social cleavages are emerging. One major new axis of inequality is between citizen and non-citizen in the face of a massive upsurge in transnational migration and the increasing use around the world of ethnic immigrant labour pools. Yet the dominant discourse on global inequality and development is still territorial, that is, inequality among nations in a world system. In the dominant development discourse what 'develops' is a nation-state. But global

society appears to be increasingly stratified less along national and territorial lines than across transnational social and class lines (Cox 1987; Hoogvelt 1997; Robinson 1998, 2002, 2003). Certain forms of conceptualizing the North-South divide obscure our view of social hierarchies and inequalities across nations and regions. Hurricane Katrina ravaged New Orleans in 2005, for instance, lifting the veil of race, class, poverty and inequality in the United States. The storm disproportionately devastated poor black communities who lacked the resources to take protection and whose Third World social conditions became apparent. A United Nations report released in the immediate aftermath of the hurricane observed that the infant mortality rate in the United States had been rising for the previous five years and was the same as for Malaysia, that black children were twice as likely as whites to die before their first birthday, and that blacks in Washington DC had a higher infant death rate than people in the Indian state of Kerala (UNDP 2005).

Clearly we need to rethink the categories of North and South and, indeed, the very concept of development. A sociology of national development is no longer tenable. In earlier epochs core and periphery referred to specific territories and the populations that resided therein. The center-periphery division of labour created by modern colonialism reflected a particular spatial configuration in the law of uneven development which is becoming transformed by globalization. The transnational geographic dispersal of the full range of world production processes suggests that core and peripheral production activities are less geographically bounded than previously, while new financial circuits allow wealth to be moved around the world instantaneously through cyberspace just as easily as it is generated, so that exactly *where* wealth is produced becomes less important for the issue of development.

While the global South is increasingly dispersed across the planet so too is the global North. Rapid economic growth in India and China have created hundreds of millions of new middle class consumers integrated into the global cornucopia even as it has thrown other hundreds of millions into destitution. Globalization fragments locally and integrates select strands of the population globally. The cohesive structures of nations and their civil societies disintegrates as populations become divided into 'core' and 'peripheral' labour pools and as local economic expansion results in the advancement of some (delocalized) groups and deepening poverty for others. We find an affluent 'developed' population, including a privileged sector among segmented labour markets linked to knowledge-intensive, professional and managerial activities and high consumption exists alongside a super-exploited secondary segment of flexibilized labour and a mass of supernumeraries constituting an 'underde-veloped' population within the same national borders. This social bifurcation seems to be a worldwide phenom-enon, explained in part by the inability of national states to capture and redirect surpluses through interventionist mechanisms that were viable in the nation-state phase of capitalism.

The great geographic core-periphery divide that gave rise to development studies is a product of the colonial and imperialist era in world capitalism and is gradually eroding, not because the periphery is 'catching up', but because of the shift from an international to a global divi-sion of labour and the tendency for a downward leveling of wages and the general conditions of labour. The inter-national division of labour has gone through successive transformations in the history of world capitalism. For many, the most recent permutation involves the shift in manufacturing from North to South, so that in the 'new international division of labor' (Frobel et al. 1980) the North specializes in high-skilled and better-paid labour supplying advanced services and technology to the world market while the South provides low-skilled and less paid labour for global manufacturing and primary commod-ity supply. But this analysis, as Freeman observes, has be-come increasingly obsolete

> due to the massive investments that the large popu-lous developing countries are making in human capital. China and India are producing millions of college graduates capable of doing the same work as the college graduates of the United States, Japan or Europe – at much lower pay.... The huge number of highly educated workers in India and China threat-ens to undo the traditional pattern of trade between advanced and less developed countries. Historically, advanced countries have innovated high-tech prod-ucts that require high-wage educated workers and extensive R&D, while developing countries spe-cialize in old manufacturing products. The reason for this was that the advanced countries had a near monopoly on scientists and engineers and other highly educated workers. As China, India and other developing countries have increased their number of university graduates, this monopoly on high-tech in-novative capacity has diminished. Today, most major multinationals have R&D centers in China or India, so that the locus of technological advance may shift (2005:3).

There remain very real regional distinctions in the form of productive participation in the global economy. But processes of uneven accumulation increasingly un-fold in accordance with a social and not a national logic. Different levels of social development adhere from the

very sites of social productive activity, that is, from *social*, not geographic, space. Moreover, privileged groups have an increasing ability to manipulate space so as to create enclaves and insulate themselves through novel mecha-nisms of social control and new technologies for the built environment. The persistence, and in fact *growth*, of the North-South divide remains important for its theoreti-cal and practical political implications. What is up for de-bate is whether the divide is something innate to world capitalism or a particular spatial configuration of uneven capitalist development during a particular historic phase of world capitalism, and whether tendencies towards the self-reproduction of this configuration are increasingly offset by countertendencies emanating from the nature and dynamic of global capital accumulation.

To explain the movement of values between differ-ent 'nodes' in globalized production, clearly we need to move beyond nation-state centric approaches and apply a theory of value to transformations in world spatial and institutional structures (the nation-state being the cen-tral spatial and institutional structure in the hitherto his-tory of world capitalism). The notion of net social gain or loss used by development economists has little mean-ing if measured, as it traditionally is, in national terms, or even in geographic terms. The distribution of social costs and gains must be conceived in transnational social terms, not in terms of the nation-state vis-à-vis the world economy, but transnationally as social groups vis-à-vis other social groups in a global society. Development should be reconceived not has a national phenomenon, in which what 'develops' is a nation, but in terms of de-veloped, underdeveloped, and intermediate population groups occupying contradictory or unstable locations in a transnational environment.

Conclusions: elites, development, and social reproduction in the globalization age

Under the emergent global social structure of accumu-lation the social reproduction of labour in each country becomes less important for accumulation as the output of each nation and region is exported to the global level. The transnational model of accumulation being imple-mented since the 1980s does not require an inclusionary social base and is inherently polarizing. Socioeconomic exclusion is immanent to the model since accumulation does not depend on a domestic market or internal social reproduction. To phrase it another way, there is a con-tradiction between the class function of the neo-liberal states and their legitimation function. For neo-liberal elites, successful integration into the global economy became predicated on the erosion of labour's income, the withdrawal of the social wage, the transfer of the costs of social reproduction from the public sector to individual families, a weakening of trade unions and workers movements, and the suppression of popular political demands. Hence, in the logic of global capitalism, the cheapening of labour and its social disenfranchisement by the neo-liberal state became conditions for 'development'. The very drive by local elites to create conditions to attract transnational capital has been what thrusts majorities into poverty and inequality.

At the core of what seemed to be an emerging global social structures of accumulation was a new deregulated capital-labour relation based on the casualization of labour associated with post-Fordist flexible accumulation, new systems of labour control and diverse contingent categories of labour. Workers in the global economy were themselves under these flexible arrangements increasingly treated as a subcontracted component rather than a fixture internal to employer organizations. In the Keynesian-Fordist order, the labour supply and the work force needed to be stable, which lent itself to more regulated and protected capital-labour relations, whereas in global capitalism labour is reduced to an input just as any other, meaning that it needs to be totally flexible, available in large numbers that can be tapped, added to the mix, shifted, and dispensed with at will. Labour is increasingly only a naked commodity, no longer embedded in relations of reciprocity rooted in social and political communities that were historically institutionalized in nation-states.

The decline of ISI industries and domestic market enterprises disorganized and reduced the old working class that tended to labour under Fordist arrangements, including unionization and corporatist relations with the state and employers. This fractionation often has political implications, as the declining group is more likely to belong to trade unions, to be influenced by a corporatist legacy, and to agitate for the preservation or restoration of the old labour regime and its benefits. It is also more likely to be male. The new workers faced a flexible and informalized labour regime. In many developing countries there has been a contraction of middle classes and professional strata that had developed through public sector employment and government civil service in the face of the dismantling of public sectors, privatizations, and the downsizing of states. At the same time, restructuring involves the rise of new middle and professional strata who may have the opportunity to participate in global consumption patterns, frequent modern shopping malls, communicate through cells phones, visit internet cafes, and so on. These strata may form a social base for neo-liberal regimes and become incorporated into the global capitalist bloc.

Added to income polarization is the dramatic deterioration in social conditions as a result of austerity measures that have drastically reduced and privatized health, education, and other social programmes. Popular classes whose social reproduction is dependent on a social wage (public sector) have faced a social crisis, while privileged middle and upper classes become exclusive consumers of social services channeled through private networks. Here we see the need to reconceive development in transnational social rather than geographic terms. The pattern under globalization is not merely 'growth without redistribution' but the simultaneous growth of wealth and of poverty as two sides of the same coin. Global capitalism generates downward mobility for most at the same time that it opens up new opportunities for some middle class and professional strata as the redistributive role of the nation-state recedes and global market forces become less mediated by state structures as they mold the prospects for downward and upward mobility.

In conclusion, the first few decades of globalization involved a change in the correlation of class forces worldwide away from nationally-organized popular classes and towards the transnational capitalist class and local economic and political elites tied to transnational capital. The elimination of the domestic market as a strategic factor in accumulation had important implications for class relations, social movements, and the struggle over development. By removing the domestic market and popular class consumption from the accumulation imperative, restructuring helped bring about the demise of the populist class alliances between broad majorities and nationally-based ruling classes that characterized the pre-globalization model of accumulation. Later on, popular classes – themselves caught up in a process of reconfiguration and transnationalization – stepped up their resistance and the hegemony of the transnational elite began to crack. The crisis that hit the global economy in 2008 with the collapse of the financial system had been building for some time and is rooted in the structural contradictions of global capitalism alluded to here.

Stepping back in perspective, the problematic of development in the South is ultimately the same as that of social polarization and overaccumulation in the global economy as a whole. Sustaining dynamic capitalist growth, beyond reining in global financial markets and shifting from speculative to productive investment, would require a redistribution of income and wealth to generate an expanding demand of the popular majority. This is a very old problem that has been debated for decades: how to create effective demand that could fuel capitalist growth. The ISI model was unable to achieve this on the basis of protected national and regional markets; the neo-liberal model has been unable to achieve this on the basis of insertion into global markets.

Seen from the logic of global capitalism the problem leads to political quagmire: how to bring about a renewed redistributive component without affecting the class interests of the dominant groups, or how to do so through the political apparatuses of national states whose direct power has diminished considerably relative to the structural power of transnational capital. This is a dilemma for the global system as a whole. The pressures to bring about a shift in the structure of distribution – both of income and of property – and the need for a more interventionist state to bring this about, is one side of the equation in the constellation of social and political forces that seemed to be coming together in the early twenty-first century to contest the neo-liberal order. Political, economic, and academic elites began to look for alternative formulas to address the global economic crisis and at the same time to prevent – or at least better manage – social and political unrest. In my own view, the struggle for development is a struggle for social justice and must involve a measure of transnational social governance over the process of global production and reproduction as the first step in effecting a radical worldwide redistribution of wealth and power downward to poor majorities.

References

Aglietta, M. (1979). *A Theory of Capitalist Regulation.* London: Verso.

Castells, M. (2000). *The Rise of the Network Society.* Vol. I, 2nd Edition. Oxford: Blackwell.

Cox, R. W. (1987). *Production, Power, and World Order: Social Forces in the Making of History.* New York: Columbia University Press.

Dicken, P. (2003). *Global Shift.* 4th Edition. London and New York: The Guilford Press.

Esteva, G. (1991). 'Development'. In W. Sachs, *The Development Dictionary: A Guide to Knowledge as Power.* London: Zed.

Freeman, R. (2005). 'China, India and the Doubling of the Global Labor Force: Who Pays the Price of Globalization'. *The Globalist,* 3 June, posted at *Japan Focus,* 26 August, and downloaded on 13 October from http://www.japanfocus.org/article.asp?id=377.

Frobel, F., J. Heinrichs, and O. Kreye (1980). [first published in German in 1977]. *The New International Division of Labour.* Cambridge: Cambridge University Press.

Hoogvelt, A. (1997). *Globalization and the Post-Colonial World: The New Political Economy of Development.* Baltimore: Johns Hopkins University Press.

Kentor, J. (2005). 'The Growth of Transnational Corporate Networks, 1962 to 1998'. *Journal of World-Systems Research,* 11 (2): 262–86.

Kotz, D. M., T. McDonough, and M. Reich (eds) (1994). *Social Structures of Accumulation: The Political Economy of Growth and Crisis.* Cambridge: Cambridge University Press.

McMichael, P. (1996). *Development and Social Change: A Global Perspective.* Thousand Oaks: Pine Forge.

Prashad, V. (2007). *The Darker Nations: A People's History of the Third World.* New York: New Press.

Robinson, W. I. (2008). *Latin America and Global Capitalism: A Critical Globalization Perspective.* Baltimore: Johns Hopkins University Press.

Robinson, W. I. (2004). *A Theory of Global Capitalism: Production, Class, and State in a Transnational World.* Baltimore: Johns Hopkins University Press.

Robinson, W. I. (2003). *Transnational Conflicts: Central America, Social Change, and Globalization.* London: Verso.

Robinson, W. I. (2002). 'Remapping Development in Light of Globalization: From a Territorial to a Social Cartography'. *Third World Quarterly,* 23 (6): 1047–71.

Robinson, W. I. (1998). 'Beyond Nation-State Paradigms: Globalization, Sociology, and the Challenge of Transnational Studies'. *Sociological Forum,* 13 (4): 561–94.

Robinson, W. I. (1996). *Promoting Polyarchy: Globalization, U.S. Intervention, and Hegemony.* Cambridge: Cambridge University Press.

Sklair, L. (2002). *Globalization: Capitalism and its Alternatives.* New York: Oxford University Press.

United Nations Development Program (UNDP) (2005). *Human Development Report.* New York: Oxford University Press/UNDP.

Globalization, Religious Fundamentalism and the Need for Meaning

Michael B. Salzman*

University of Hawaii at Manoa, 1776 University Avenue, Honolulu, HI 96822, United States

Keywords

Globalization
Religious fundamentalism
Need for meaning

Abstract

Globalization may well be the meta-context of our time. This paper seeks to enhance a theoretical understanding of the relationship between globalization and religious fundamentalism. Previous papers [Salzman, M. (2001). Globalization, culture & anxiety. *Journal of Social Distress and the Homeless, 10*(4): 337–352; Salzman, M. (2003). Existential anxiety, religious fundamentalism, the "clash of civilizations" and terror management theory. *Cross Cultural Psychology Bulletin, 37*(3): 10–16] utilized a Terror Management Theory perspective in the exploration of the interaction of globalization, culture, anxiety, fundamentalism and intercultural conflict. [Salzman, M. (2006). "Culture Wars" and intercultural conflict from three theoretical perspectives. *Paper presented at the XVIIIth international congress international association for cross-cultural psychology*] expanded this inquiry by looking at intercultural conflict through the theoretical perspectives of Social Identity Theory, Modernization Theory and Terror Management Theory. The purpose of this paper is to synthesize and extend this inquiry by specifically focusing on the phenomena of religious fundamentalism and its relationship to the processes and dynamics of globalization. This inquiry is anchored by the bedrock question of what human beings truly need and how they seek to address and satisfy real needs. This paper, then, examines the nature of religious fundamentalism, culture-threat, globalization and their interactions through multiple perspectives and considers their implications for conflict, terrorism, development and peace.

© 2008 Elsevier Ltd. All rights reserved.

Introduction

Globalization is, perhaps, the meta-context of our time. Human behavior cannot be accurately interpreted without a due attention to the context(s) within which that behavior is embedded and has been manifested. Attention to context is an act of intention. Such intention is required in order to comprehend the impact and likely consequences of the powerful forces unleashed by what has been called globalization. All human behavior may be analyzed in terms of person–context (environment–situation) interactions (Lewin, 1997).

A person brings an array of dispositional and acquired characteristics (i.e., traits and culture) to any situation or context. The characteristics of the person and the situation interact to produce behavior. This new context for human activity and experience has unleashed forces that overwhelm traditional sources of culturally derived meaning with its manic logic. It has its historical antecedents but is fueled by new and profound technological innovation. It has reshaped our world. It has been called a new revolution whose engine and executive power is finance capital. Its imperatives are the maximization of profit and the return on capital without regard to national identity, cultural or social consequences (Greider, 1997). Numerous writers have suggested that fundamentalism is a manifestation of resistance to globalization (e.g., Stevens, 2002). Fundamentalists tend to detest the homogenization of culture and the uprooting of traditional values and customs that anchor people in a meaningful and predictable world.

* Tel.: +1 808 956 3143.

E-mail address: msalzman@hawaii.edu.

0147-1767/$ – see front matter © 2008 Elsevier Ltd. All rights reserved.

doi:10.1016/j.ijintrel.2008.04.006

Article history:

Accepted 16 April 2008

Crime, violence, fundamentalism and xenophobia often come to the fore in societies where the traditional patterns of family and community have been disrupted. A hegemonic global capitalism and its cultural impositions produce such disruption. These problems are exacerbated by the sense of inferiority that arises in people who perceive themselves as not living up to the standards that define value in the new system while the forces of globalization threaten their faith in traditional sources of meaning and value that cultural values and religious belief systems provide. As economic globalization has accelerated in the post-Cold War era, new categories of winners and losers have been produced along with a rise in fundamentalism, hyper-ethnocentrism and the proliferation of neo-fascist and right-wing extremist organizations (Lee, 2000). In the late 19th and early 20th century such was the case when the technology-driven revolution unleashed by the industrial revolution physically and psychologically uprooted, dislocated and marginalized millions of people. Among its products were the rise of religious fundamentalism (i.e., Protestant fundamentalism in the U.S.), alternative worldviews, and political ideologies such as fascism and communism. These worldviews were attractive to millions because they addressed unmet human psychological needs as well as promising to alleviate material deprivation and offering psychological sustenance. These belief systems and ideologies offer psychological sustenance in the form of a meaning system and are therefore, a foundation for the construction of essential self-esteem.

What do human beings really need? Can we prevent human problems by addressing real human needs? Maslow (1968) proposed a hierarchy of human needs that included the need to feel a sense of belonging and self-esteem as well as basic physiological needs (air, food, water, etc.), safety and "self-actualization." He suggested that the higher order psychological needs (e.g., self-esteem and self-actualization) could not be realized until the lower order needs (physiological, safety and belonging) are satisfied. Becker (1971, 1973) and the empirically tested Terror Management Theory (TMT) he inspired suggest that self-esteem, a vital psychological resource, is a cultural construction. Self-esteem can only be achieved in a world of meaning.

Culture and religion infuse a persons' world with meaning. As cultures are shaken and millions are marginalized and alienated by the processes of globalization these human needs, physiological and psychological remain.

Culture and religion are related and influence each other bi-directionally. Both culture and religion provide individuals with the possibility of constructing meaning and in their lives (Becker, 1971; Greenberg, Solomon, & Pyszczynski, 1997; Hood, Hill, & Williamson, 2005). Self-esteem can only be constructed in a world of meaning

and religion and culture infuse the world with meaning. Self-esteem, then is a cultural construction, which may be defined as perceiving oneself as having value in a world of meaningful action (Becker, 1971). Self-esteem, as we shall see, serves as an essential defense against existential anxiety. Therefore, culture and religion serve essential psychological functions and address real existential human needs.

Is there a relationship between *globalization* and *religious fundamentalism*? If so, what might that relationship be? How can we make psychological sense of such a relationship? This inquiry is anchored by the bedrock question of what human beings need and how they seek to satisfy these physiological and psychological needs. The relationship and tensions among the needs for physiological sustenance, development, the motive to prosper as well as the psychological need for meaning (e.g., Yalom, 1980) and self-esteem are relevant and will serve to inform this inquiry. This paper will examine the nature of religious fundamentalism, culture-threat, globalization and their interactions through multiple perspectives and to consider the implications for conflict, terrorism, development, peace and theory building.

The Need for Meaning, Globalization and Religious Fundamentalism

Human Needs: The Need for Meaning

Hood et al. (2005) assert that the first basic question is "What do humans need (p. 12)." They provide an answer that is consistent with a central focus of this paper, "Beyond the basic needs dictated by our biological requirements like air, food, shelter humans need and seek meaning. Religion is a meaning system (p. 12)." People seek, construct and need meaning. Frankl (1963) wrote "Man's [Sic] search for meaning is a primary force in his [Sic] life not a 'secondary rationalization' of instinctual drives (p. 153)." According to his logotherapy "the striving to find meaning in life is the primary motivational force in man (p. 154)." He saw that humans are "able to live and die for the sake of his ideals and values! (p. 155)."

Baumeister (1991) identified four overlapping needs for meaning. The need for meaning includes the need for purpose (seeing one's life as oriented toward some imagined goal or state); value (seeing one's actions as right or justifiable); efficacy (having a sense of control over events); self-worth (seeing one's life as having positive value). Readers are invited to consider how religious fundamentalism may address these needs.

Becker (1971, 1973, 1975) offered a compelling analysis of culture and its psychological functions. He proposed that culture provides just those rules and customs, goals of conduct, that place right actions and ways of being at the individual's disposal facilitating the construction of self-esteem that may be achieved if the person has faith in the cultural worldview prescribing those standards and sees oneself as achieving those standards. He suggested that the function of self-esteem is to give the ego a steady buffer against anxiety. A crucial function of culture, then, is to make continued self-esteem possible. "Its task, in other words is to provide the individual with the conviction that he is an object of primary value in a world of meaningful action (p. 79)." He wrote that "One of the main reasons that cultures can be so directly undermining to one another is that, despite their many varieties they all ask and answer the same questions. So that when two different ways of life come into contact they clash on the same vital points (p. 113)." These few points are vital questions for anxiety-prone human animals to consider. His views on culture, intercultural conflict, the cultural construction of self-esteem, the anxiety-buffering characteristics of self-esteem and religion have informed the development of TMT and will illuminate this inquiry into the relationship between globalization and religious fundamentalism.

Becker (1971) cites Kluckhohn (1950) who identified six common human problems that cultures address in varying and often conflicting ways. These are: the relation of humans to nature, the innate, the types of personalities most valued, the ways humans should relate to each other, concepts of space and time, and the hierarchy of power in society and nature. These common problems are essential for human to consider. Cultures and religions address the crucial ontological questions of how to be and how to act in the world. The problem of knowing what is the hierarchy of power and determining one's place in it is critical not only for one's material well-being in social systems but it is ultimately a spiritual and religious issue. The ultimate power in the universe, for religious believers, is divine. Anxiety-prone humans seek to identify with the highest possible power because of the essential existential dilemma. Becker (1973, 1975) identified this dilemma as *Denial of Death*. He saw that humans, like all other life forms seek to live and continue existence. Humans, however, are cognitively capable of realizing that the primary biological motive to continue existence is impossible to satisfy because we face inevitable physical annihilation. We may believe that this is not final but on the observable level we are mortal and our existence is finite. Religion often promises literal immortality to believers.

Who adhere to its ontological prescriptions? Culture offers transcendence through its enduring symbols

of a larger meaningful entity that extends beyond one's finite life.

Becker (1975) thought that "culture itself is sacred, since it is the 'religion' that assures, in some way, the perpetuation of its members (p. 4)" either literally or symbolically. In this sense culture embodies the transcendence of death in some form or another. U.S. soldiers are told they are fighting to defend and perpetuate the "American Way" of life that will endure beyond the soldier's mortal life. Becker (1971) and others (e.g., TMT researchers Greenberg, Landau, Solomon, & Pyszczynski, in press) have concluded that virtually all cultures are fundamentally spiritual or religious in character. Both religion and culture, in this view, provide a pathway to a perception of literal or symbolic immortality and that in most contemporary cultures, religion plays a critical role in (existential) terror or anxiety management by providing standards of value to live up to and literal forms of death transcendence to those who do live up to them.

Becker (1973) explicitly argues that that even atheistic cultural worldviews are essentially religious. He proposed that all cultural worldviews are mythical hero systems that serve to provide a feeling of primary value or unshakeable meaning. Indeed, Becker (1975) named money the new universal immortality ideology. In an ascendant system of hegemonic global capitalism this immortality ideology becomes more compelling and at the same time more threatening to those belief systems that seek immortality from invisible, supernatural forces or secular ideological systems that promise an enduring place in the current of history. Post-Mao Chinese leadership, for example declared that to be rich is "glorious" which is a marked shift from "serve the people." Marxism and Maoism offered its believers the conviction that one is contributing to and part of the river of history that continues well beyond one's life. If money is the new immortality ideology defined by the cultural impositions (i.e., competition as a way of being) of a hegemonic global capitalist system one wonders if most people will see themselves as "losers" rather than "winners" in this system. What will they do with the resultant inferiority feelings that are produced by failing to live up to the cultural standards of value defined by globalization?

Inferiority feelings are intolerable and people are strongly motivated to relieve them and compensate for their corrosive effects. Alternative ideologies such as religious fundamentalism may provide for a pathway out of this aversive state. Even such staunch globalization proponents as Friedman (2000) acknowledge that "Although globalization has raised the absolute standard of living worldwide it has widened the gap between rich and poor (p. 39)" both within and among nations. The psychological sustenance obtained by the conviction that one is doing God's will must be compelling for those whose traditional sources of meaning and value have been overwhelmed by global capitalism and its cultural impositions.

Do humans require faith for good mental and physical health? Koenig, McCullough, & Larson (2001) reviewed 473 studies of the relationship between religiosity and health. Sixty-six percent of the studies reported a statistically significant relationship. Religious people had better health (e.g., less substance abuse), lived longer and received more social support. In general, they found that the more religious people had better physical and mental health than non-believers. In terms of the substance abuse as a health indicator one wonders if religion and faith in a worldview serves the same anxiety management function as the substances that many use for the self-medication of aversive affective states.

Humans transcend death by finding meaning for their lives, some kind of larger scheme into which one fits, something that endures such as God's will, duty to ancestors or an achievement that will enrich the world. Becker (1971) called religion the "Quest for the Ideal Heroism (p. 180)" because it purports to identify, and make accessible to believers, the highest levels of power and meaning. Religious fundamentalism directly addresses core human concerns.

Globalization and its Consequences

The overarching feature of globalization is integration and its driving motive is "free market capitalism" and its spread to "virtually every country in the world" (Pieterse, 2004, p. 9). Friedman (2000) defined globalization as "the inexorable integration of markets, nation-states and technologies to a degree never witnessed before–in a way that is enabling individuals, corporations and states to reach around the world farther, faster, deeper and cheaper than ever before (p. 9)." It is a global economic system driven and exported by the West along with its political institutions, technologies and culture with little regard to how these impositions may be received or to the reactions they may provoke (Stevens, 2002). The system is supported by an ideology, worldview and faith that Soros (1998) calls market fundamentalism. This ideology holds that markets are self-correcting and that the common interest is best served by allowing everyone to look out for his or her own interests. It assumes that any attempt to protect the common interest by collective decision-making distorts the market mechanism. In the nineteenth century it was called laissez-faire. Market fundamentalism has given supreme authority to capital and its imperatives. These imperatives are producing

wrenching and anxiety-generating social distress as well as changes in the politics of nations and cultures of the world's peoples. This description corresponds to what Marsella (2005a) considered to be the construction of a hegemonic global capitalist system and its attendant cultural impositions (i.e., individualism, competition, materialism and reductionism). This system, according to Marsella, is "hegemonic" because of "its control and dominance by powerful individual, national and multinational corporations whose policies, plans, and actions are threatening cultural and biological diversity and promoting the rise of global monoculturalism (p. 15)." The extent to which globalization dislocates individuals from their socio-cultural roots and creates psychosocial distress is reflected by the magnitude and intensity of resistance to globalization. Terrorism is a violent expression of resistance that uses the mechanisms and technologies (i.e., technologies and financial networks) of globalization itself to achieve its aims.

Friedman (2000) considered the effects of globalization on traditional cultures and the psychological sustenance that they provide. He uses the metaphor of the Lexus (forces of globalization) and the Olive Tree (traditional cultures). Friedman is an enthusiastic proponent of globalization but appears to recognize the intense dynamics between these two forces. He wrote that "olive trees" (traditional cultures) are important because they represent everything that roots, anchors, identifies and locates us in the world. They provide a profound sense of belonging to entities larger and more apparently enduring than ourselves whether it be family, community, tribe, nation or religion. He suggests that "We fight so intensely at times over our olive trees because, at their best they provide the feelings of *self-esteem* [emphasis added] and belonging that are as essential for human survival as is food in the belly (p. 31)." Globalization may address the age-old human aspiration for material betterment, development and prosperity for some or many but what of the psychological needs addressed by the "Olive Tree?" Friedman accurately predicted that the contradictions produced by these dynamics could produce a powerful backlash. In a sense, terrorism inspired by religious fundamentalism may be thought of as the revenge of the olive trees.

Pieterse (2004) proposed three paradigms that address the tension between globalization and culture. The first he named as the "Clash of Civilizations" paradigm that views cultural differences as immutable. The second is the "McDonaldization" thesis, which is a universalist notion where cultures become homogenized through the impact of multinational corporations and the global spread of capitalist relations. Third, he proposes globalization as a hybridization model where cultures mix and integrate and where there is no need to give up one's cultural identification. In this hybridization model "cohabitation is expected to yield new patterns of cross-cultural patterns of difference. This is a future of ongoing mixing, ever-generating new commonalities and new differences (p. 56)." Friedman (2000) adds that "Sustainable globalization requires a stable power structure, and no country is more essential for this than the United States (p. 464)." He favors a world stabilized by the U.S., which he considers to be a "benign superpower." Apparently, Mr. Friedman is not bothered by such imperial presumptions.

Religious Fundamentalism

"Inherent in my belief system is your wrongness" [Stephen Colbert, Colbert Report, May 1, 2007, Comedy Central].

Although the term "fundamentalist" was first used to describe a particular movement within American Protestantism in the early part of the 20th century, a period characterized by the dislocating power of industrialization and urbanization, it is now most commonly applied to Islam. As indicated by its defining characteristics, the fundamentalist phenomenon is not restricted to one particular religion. The consequences of the phenomenon may vary in destructiveness depending on the content of the worldview a particular religion espouses or, more likely, those aspects of the worldview made most salient at the time. Jewish fundamentalism has taken the form of religious Zionism such as that espoused by the Gush Emunim movement of settlers who see the settlement of biblical Israel as a divine promise (Hunter, 1990; Nielson, 1993). In Hinduism, perhaps the clearest case of fundamentalism is Rahitriya Swayamsevak Sangh (RSS) or the National Volunteer Society who propose that "Hindu society has degenerated because Hindus had not observed *Dharma* (Hunter, 1990, p. 61)." The *Dharma* is a code of conduct for various social categories, situations, and stages of life and its "degeneration" was held responsible for creating a vulnerability to foreign domination. The motive to recover the purity of antiquity, real or imagined, is again apparent. The search for "purity" seems related to the motive to purge the world of "evil." These impulses (i.e., seeking racial "purity") have visited great destruction on the world. The motive to recover or put (a sacred) history "right" seems common across various fundamentalisms as is its nature as a closed system. Indeed, Becker (1975), Fromm (1969), Rank (1958) and Lifton (1999) argued that the meaningfulness of one's life may be enhanced by worldviews depicting one's

group as engaged in a heroic struggle against evil and thus may be especially useful in warding off death anxiety.

Fundamentalism "is unusually capable of providing meaning through giving a sense of coherence to a fragmented world (Stevens, 2002, p. 34)" by providing a unifying philosophy of life and by meeting the human need for meaning. It is only in a meaningful world that anxiety-buffering self-esteem can be constructed (Salzman, 2003). A meaning system endows life with personal significance and allows an individual to see oneself as having significance and value. Hood et al. (2005), in their Intratextual model of fundamentalism, proposed that fundamentalism differs from other religious expressions in the elevation of a sacred text to a position of supreme authority. For fundamentalists the sacred text is the sole source of meaning. All concerns are subordinated to the ultimate concern of living according to divine will as indicated in the sacred text. Fundamentalists adhere to a literal interpretation of the sacred text. The sacred text (e.g., Bible, Qu'ran) subordinates all other potential sources of knowledge and meaning. They suggest that religious fundamentalism provides a "unifying philosophy of life within which personal meaning and purpose are embedded" (p. 15).

Hood et al. (2005) contrast this Intratextual model of fundamentalist thought with an Intertextual model for the structure of non-fundamentalist thought where, instead of a firm, bounded circle, there is a broken circle, indicating that very permeable boundaries exist in the thought processes of non-fundamentalists. This principle of intertextuality assumes that many texts may be authoritative and interrelated and may be consulted in the pursuit of truth. Indeed in the intertextual model of non-fundamentalist thought "truth is more properly understood as relative truth (p. 26)." In this model, not only do relative truths extend outward to peripheral beliefs but also peripheral beliefs may filter back into the interpretive process and exert continual influence on the understanding of texts and relative truths. Hence, no single sacred text is esteemed in a dynamic process. Instead, a multiplicity of authoritative texts suggests various relative truths, each tentatively held as long as the evidence is supportive.

Altemeyer and Hunsberger (1992) define fundamentalism as the belief that: there is one set of religious teachings that clearly contains the fundamental, basic, intrinsic, essential, inerrant truth about humanity and deity; that this essential truth is fundamentally opposed by forces of evil which must be vigorously fought; that this truth must be followed today according to the fundamental, unchangeable practices of the past; that those who believe and follow these fundamental teachings have a special relationship with the deity (pp. 118). "So fundamentalists of all types believe that they are opposed by forces of evil that must be confronted and defeated. As Becker (1975) noted that in order to avoid and defeat evil in the world "man is responsible for bringing more evil into the world than organisms could ever do merely by exercising their digestive tracts (p. 5)." He goes on to consider the destruction caused by the motive to purge "evil" from the world. He could be speaking of the destruction visited on the world by the various wars we have waged against what we label as evil whether it is witchcraft, communism, drugs or terrorism.

For fundamentalists, then, religion is a total and all encompassing way of life. It is a closed system. Fundamentalism provides certainty and clear and accessible standards to guide one through the confusion of modern life. The notion of multiple truths or relative truths may not be particularly comforting for people with certain dispositional characteristics under conditions of threat and fear. Fundamentalism addresses the core human concerns of meaning, personal significance and even offers a pathway to immortality. It is a blueprint for living. What may happen when such a belief system and the psychological functions its serves is threatened? Friedman and Rholes (in press), in a highly relevant recent study found that successfully challenging fundamentalist beliefs results in an increased awareness of mortality. This finding would seem to indicate the function of the belief.

Hood et al. (2005), citing Ammerman (1991) identified five central features of fundamentalism as the inerrancy of scripture, evangelism, premillenialism, separatism and biblical literalism. The authors suggest that evangelicals and fundamentalist agree on first three but vary more on separatism and biblical literalism. They assert that "confidence in the authoritative sacred text, held as objective truth, is applicable whether the text is the Bible, the Quran, the Vedas, the Torah or any other sacred text" is common across all fundamentalism. . .intratextualism is "essential to the understanding of the psychology of fundamentalism" (p. 22). The authors' (Hood et al., 2005) conclude that the primary psychological tenet of their book is that "fundamentalism provides a source of *meaning* [emphasis added] for its adherents (p. 29)." Fundamentalism, because it demands complete allegiance to a totally authoritative text that provides a unifying philosophy of life and a personal sense of coherence is a powerful meaning system for meaning seeking anxiety prone human beings. This allure of this characteristic, especially under conditions of threat, is illuminated by TMT (see Greenberg et al., 1997), as we shall see.

Fundamentalism and orthodoxy differ. Hunter (1990) proposed that fundamentalism is orthodoxy in confrontation with modernity. Modernity, as a construct, seems inextricably bound to westernization and hegemonic global capitalism. Orthodoxy, according to Hunter as a cultural system represents what could be called a consensus through time–more specifically, a consensus based upon the ancient rules and precepts derived from divine revelation. Its authority and legitimacy derive from an unfaltering continuity with truth as originally revealed truth in its primitive and purest expression. It is fair to say that fundamentalism is something else. The argument that fundamentalism emerges out of the defensive interplay between orthodoxy and modernity can be crystallized through three propositions and nearly everything else that distinguishes fundamentalism in its global contours derives from these three propositions: "All fundamentalist sects share the deep and worrisome belief that history has gone awry. What 'went wrong' with history is modernity in its various guises. The call of the fundamentalist, therefore is to make history right again (p. 58)." In practical terms, he asserts, this means that all fundamentalisms are characterized, to varying degrees, by a quality of organized anger.

Citing Iannaccone (1994), Hood et al. (2005) suggested that most successful religions, in terms of both growth and maintenance of membership, are those with absolute, unwavering, strict, and enforced normative standards for behavior.

Seeing one's life as having positive value (self-esteem or self-worth) is only possible in a world of meaning. Culture and religion infuse the world with meaning. Fundamentalist religion offer clear, unambiguous and achievable standards of value that allow for the construction of self-esteem. Fundamentalism is an extremely conservative ideology. It seeks the comfort of a return to a perceived, glorious historical past whether it be the return of the caliphate, a return to the "promised" land or a return to a pre-Darwinist understanding of the nature of life and the world. Threat provokes "conservative shifts" in ideologies as anxiety prone humans seek anxiety management and comfort in such motivated cognitions. Ideologies and other belief systems grow out of an attempt to satisfy the epistemic, existential and relational needs of our species. Therefore "ideology is a natural part of our psychological functioning and will always be present in one form or another . . . (Jost, 2006, p. 667)." Ideology, including religious and political (e.g., dogmatic Marxism) fundamentalisms, address core human needs and concerns which become compelling in the context of certain dispositional (relative closed-mindeness, authoritarianism and cognitive simplicity) and situational (i.e., system threat and mortality salience) antecedents (Jost, 2006). Stevens (2002) suggested that resistance to globalization becomes violent under certain conditions, that terrorist "sacrifice" may be seen as a "fit of anger over group insult and group frustration" (p. 10). Furthermore, the terrorist act is in service of a cause worth dying for. It is not abstract but personal. It emerges from a view of the world that makes sense of life and death (i.e., living according to God's will) and links the individual to "some form of immortality" (p. 12).

Globalization and Religious Fundamentalism: Theoretical Perspectives

Terror Management Theory

Terror Management Theory suggests that culture serves as a psychological defense against the terror inherent in human existence. This "terror" is identified as our awareness of our ultimate mortality and the precariousness of our existence. Furthermore, TMT theorists and researchers (Pyszczynski, Solomon, & Greenberg, 2003) inspired by Becker (1971, 1973, 1975) assert:

> From the perspective of TMT, the root cause of man's inhumanity to man is the existential contradiction into which we are all born: We are animals with an instinctive desire for life with enough intelligence to know that someday we will die. The potential for terror this knowledge creates lead us to seek shelter in the form of cultural worldviews that give life meaning and permanence, give us the opportunity to view ourselves as valuable, and provide some hope of transcending death. Whether these anxiety-buffering worldviews are religious or secular, they ultimately serve the same psychological function of protecting us from the "rumble of panic that lies beneath the surface and that energizes our quest for meaning in life and value in ourselves (pp. 148–149).

There is much empirical support for hypotheses generated by TMT. TMT proposes that cultures serve the vital psychological function of making anxiety-buffering self-esteem available to humans by providing worldviews and standards of value to achieve within that description of reality. Persons whose faith in that worldview is strong and who see themselves as living up to its standards of value achieve the anxiety-buffering effects of self-esteem needed in an existentially terrifying world. Self-esteem, then, is seen as a cultural construction. When faith in belief systems is shaken or threatened or if the standards of value prescribed by the believed (faith intact) worldview are not achieved or achievable the resultant unbuffered anxiety creates an aversive affective condition that requires "terror management" responses that may be quite destructive (i.e., the tendency to derogate, demonize, or

seek to harm the "other"). The "other" may be those who do not uphold one's worldview especially under conditions of threat. Religious fundamentalism offers very clear standards for the achievement of a sense of transcendent value and self-esteem but one must believe.

Over 350 empirical studies in fourteen countries have tested hypotheses generated by TMT. The first central hypothesis derived from TMT (the anxiety-buffer hypothesis) is that if a psychological structure provides protection against anxiety, then augmenting that structure should reduce anxiety in response to subsequent threats. Specifically since self-esteem serves as a buffer against anxiety strengthening self-esteem would be expected to reduce anxiety and anxiety-related behavior in response to threat (mortality salience). A large body of evidence is consistent with this idea (for a review, see Greenberg et al., 1997; Pyszczynski et al., 2003). The second central hypothesis (the mortality salience hypothesis) derived from TMT is that, if faith in the cultural worldview and self-esteem function to protect people from anxiety about death, then reminders of this primary fear should increase people's need for these psychological structures. The bulk of these studies have demonstrated that mortality salience increases positive reactions to those who uphold or validate the individual's worldview and negative reactions to those who violate or challenge the individual's worldview (Greenberg et al., 1990; Greenberg, Pyszczynski, Solomon, Simon, & Breus, 1994; Greenberg, Simon, Pyszczynski, Solomon, & Chatel, 1992; Ochsmann & Mathy, 1994; Rosenblatt, Greenberg, Solomon, Pyszczynski, & Lyon, 1989). Therefore, if one considers subjective culture ("the culture in our heads") to be a psychological structure (see Triandis, 1972), then the perception of threat would motivate people to defensively augment that structure (subjective culture) in response to threat. Fundamentalism may be such a defensive augmentation and our defenses against anxiety can be deadly.

The findings that conditions of mortality salience produce the tendency to distance, derogate or demonize those who do not support one's worldview (cultural and/or religious) was illustrated by the American reaction to France's opposition to the War on Iraq. Since 9/11 undoubtedly established the condition of mortality salience for Americans, France's refusal to support the American worldview that Iraq war was justified (because of 9/11) provoked an extremely negative reaction to France to the point of people pouring delicious French wine into the streets and the absurdity of renaming French Fries to "Freedom Fries."

Although this short summary of TMT findings illustrates that mortality salience affects a wide range of different areas in human life one should note that this only applies to worldview relevant domains. At least one study (McGregor et al., 1998) demonstrated mortality salience effects on subject's willingness to engage in direct aggression toward those who threaten important aspects of cultural worldviews. In this study moderately conservative and moderately liberal subjects were given the opportunity to allocate varying amounts of hot sauce that they believed would be consumed by subjects who strongly criticized either liberals or conservatives and who claimed not to like spicy foods. The results showed that mortality salient subjects (but not exam salient control subjects) administered substantially greater amount of hot sauce to subjects if the target criticized their preferred political position. This suggests that mortality salience effects on people's reactions to dissimilar others are not confined to derogation or physical distancing but may enhance the probability of pain inducing aggression.

The TMT findings cited support the proposition that culture serves as a psychological defense against the terror inherent in human existence and that cultures' varying answers to core existential concerns may provide for the potential for murderous intercultural conflict when mortality concerns are salient. Is there any reason for optimism? Can the shadow side of that great human adaptation called culture be managed? At least four studies suggest a way out of this dilemma. Mortality salience effects may be mediated by personality variables and primed cultural values. Greenberg et al. (1990) found that negative reactions to an attitudinally dissimilar other occurred only among high authoritarians. Low authoritarians did not exhibit the expected effects indicating that value systems that emphasize tolerance (as with low authoritarians) may be less likely to engender a negative reaction to dissimilar others and may actually encourage greater tolerance of difference. Greenberg et al. (1992) found that, under the mortality salience condition, subjects did not react negatively to the critic when the value of tolerance was primed and highly accessible. In sum (Jeff Greenberg, personal communication, June 21, 2002) "we know that high self-esteem, low authoritarianism and secure attachment style go along with resistance to negative effects of mortality salience (MS) whereas depression, low self-esteem and authoritarianism are associated with strong mortality salience effects such as the derogation of those who do not uphold the relevant cultural worldview." So there appears to be a significant interaction between dispositional and situational factors in the worldview defense response under conditions of the specific threat of mortality salience.

In the light of Vice President Cheney's 2007 saber rattling visit to a U.S. aircraft carrier in the Persian Gulf two recent TMT studies seem highly relevant. The studies were published under the interesting (in the light of Becker, 1975) title of "Mortality Salience, Martyrdom, and Military Might: The Great Satan versus the Axis of Evil." Becker (1975) wrote "the most violence perpetrated in history has been to eradicate evil. Evil then must be understood as a symbolic displacement rather that a rational process (p. 127)." Pyszczynski et al. (2006) investigated the effect of mortality salience on support for martyrdom attacks among Iranian college students. Participants were randomly assigned to answer questions about either their own death or an aversive topic (control condition) unrelated to death and then evaluated materials from fellow students who either supported or opposed martyrdom attacks against the United States. The control participants preferred the student who opposed martyrdom, the subjects who were reminded of death preferred the student who supported martyrdom and indicated they were more likely to consider such activities themselves. So much for the efficacy of saber rattling. Militaristic saber rattling and threat make mortality salient. Once blood begins to flow mortality salience conditions are manifest. Perhaps that is why wars are so easy to start and so difficult to stop. Once one sees the "other" as evil there would appear to be little room for peacemaking, empathy, compassion or compromise. Indeed, in their TMT analysis of the events of September 11th Pyszczynski et al. (2003) concluded, among other recommendations that that "we need to reduce the salience of mortality (p. 187)."

A second study examined the effect of MS on American college students' support for extreme military interventions by American forces that could kill thousands of people. Under the MS condition support for such measures increased among politically conservative but not politically liberal students. The events of 9/11 undoubtedly created the MS conditions for Americans and the American response to 9/11 certainly created MS conditions for the objects of the indiscriminate American military response. So it seems that the content of the existing worldview is bolstered under MS conditions. Herein lies some reason for optimism. The power of mortality salience to elicit destructive terror management defenses may be attenuated by priming the higher, more tolerant and more humane impulses and teachings resident in most, not all religious–cultural worldviews.

Greenberg et al. (1992) primed the value of tolerance for half the subjects under mortality-salient or control conditions for half the subjects (U.S. citizens). The subjects then evaluated a target person who criticized the United States under MS or control conditions. Under the mortality salience condition subjects did not react negatively to the critic when the value of tolerance was primed and highly accessible. In a recent yet unpublished study (Tom Pyszczynski, personal communication, May 15, 2007) the priming of compassionate values reverses the effect of mortality salience on support for extreme military tactics among Americans and eliminates the effect of mortality salience on anti-U.S. attitudes among Iranians. The U.S. study primed quotes from Jesus from the Bible or non-religious words of wisdom. In all conditions but one religious fundamentalism (Altemeyer scale) was associated with higher support for extreme militarism; but when reminded of death and Jesus's compassionate teachings, the relationship between religious fundamentalism reversed and became negative. In addition, in the mortality salience plus the "compassionate Jesus" led to decreased support for extreme militarism. In a follow-up study, mortality salience increased anti-U.S. attitudes when Iranians were primed with compassion in a secular way but mortality salience decreased anti-U.S. attitudes among Iranians primed with the value of compassion as teachings from the Quran.

Social Identity Theory

Another theoretical perspective offers insight into the dynamics of globalization and religious fundamentalism. Social Identity Theory (Tajfel & Turner, 1986) suggests that humans derived the vital psychological resource known as "self-esteem" through their identification with and belonging to groups. Although Social Identity Theory (SIT) does not seem to indicate why people seek and need self-esteem it acknowledges the centrality of the self-esteem motive. SIT holds that there is a strong tendency in people to divide the social world into "us" and "them." SIT proposes that individuals seek to enhance their self-esteem by identifying with specific social groups and that self-esteem is enhanced only to the extent that the persons involved perceive these groups as distinct and somehow superior to other competing groups. Therefore the homogenizing effects of globalization may threaten the distinctiveness of important groups (i.e., clan, tribe, nation, and religion) through which people seek to enhance the vital psychological resource known as self-esteem. When the distinctiveness and presumptive superiority of one's group is threatened a strong defensive reaction is likely. Humans apparently need something larger than self to belong to and identify with. Group identification, then, is both the foundation of intergroup conflict and a primary source of self-esteem. Although SIT recognizes the power of the self-esteem motive it does not seem to explain why we need this psychological resource whereas TMT demonstrates that self-esteem serves as a psychological defense

against the terror inherent in the human condition and clear implication is that, consistent with the mortality salience hypothesis, religious fundamentalism may represent the augmentation of cultural/religious worldviews under the condition of threat as represented by globalization and its homogenizing and dislocating effects.

Motivated Cognitions and Religious Fundamentalism

Jost (2006), based on his research, suggested that ideologies and other belief systems grow out of an "attempt to satisfy the epistemic, existential and relational needs of our species (p. 667). They are, then, motivated cognitions that are responses to real and perceived human needs. Therefore ideologies meet psychological needs. Ideology is related to meaning, religion and culture are related to meaning and fundamentalism is related to meaning. Humans need a world of meaning to act in order to construct the perception that one has value and one's life has value.

Bonanno and Jost (2006) found that heightened perceptions of uncertainty and threat in the aftermath of 9/11, generally increased the appeal of conservative leaders and opinions. Jost and colleagues found that predictors of conservatism were system threat and fear of death. Both of these predictors were elicited by the events of 9/11. Is fundamentalism a conservative response to system threat and/or fear of death? System threat has been identified as an antecedent condition for an ideological "conservative shift (Jost, 2006, p. 663)." SIT suggests, as previously indicated, that the homogenizing effects of globalization may threaten the distinctiveness of important groups (i.e., clan, tribe, nation and religion) through which people seek to enhance the vital psychological resource known as self-esteem. Globalization and its cultural impositions may represent a "system threat." That is, a threat to the system of meanings associated with culture and the psychological sustenance they provide. Gelfand, Nishi and Raver (2006) investigated "culture tightness and looseness." They defined this construct as consisting of two key components: the strength of social norms, or how clear and pervasive norms are within societies, and the strength of sanctions, or how much tolerance there is for deviance from norms within societies (p. 1227). "Citing McKelvey (1982) they suggest that, as a general rule, organizations in all societies that deal with conditions of great threat, danger, and vulnerability are expected to be tighter (stronger norms, less tolerance for deviance from norms) regardless of societal culture context. So it seems reasonable that, across cultures, environmental, systemic and mortal threat would motivate fundamentalism across cultures and religions. Religious fundamentalisms tend to have very strong norms, strict standards, and little tolerance for deviation from those norms. The culture-threat represented by globalization may well be a primary antecedent condition and motivation for a fundamentalist response.

Discussion and conclusions

What do we know or think we know about the relationship between globalization and religious fundamentalism and what are the implications?

Human beings are confronted with (at the core) common problems and needs. Humans seek for better or worse to address these problems and satisfy their needs. Cultures offer different solutions based on perception and ecologies to satisfy needs and solve problems. Marx (2000) may have been wrong about many things but this inquiry indicates that he was correct in his famous dictum "From each according to his abilities, to each according to his needs." Marx focused on economic needs and largely ignored human psychology and the psychological needs (i.e., the need for meaning and value) described in this paper. Religion and culture serve as primary resources enabling people to construct lives of meaning and value but they have a dark side. As noted by Marsella (2005b) and others, it is clear both from history and an analysis of our current realities that violence in the name of religion presents a grave threat to human survival.

So, this paper has been anchored by the question of what do humans truly need? What are the core needs, physiologically and psychologically, of this problematic species. Can human problems be prevented by adequately addressing and satisfying core human needs?

Clearly, globalization is a source of anxiety because it threatens traditional sources of meaning and value. Furthermore it has, for many serious analysts, now become a principle source of global injustice, inequity, corruption and violence (Nasser, 2005). Although one is ultimately responsible to construct a life of meaning and value, social and economic conditions may facilitate or impede this process. A globalization process that impoverishes and marginalizes masses of the world's people inhibits people's efforts to see their lives as having meaning and value. A globalization process that truly enhances development and opportunity would facilitate these efforts.

Human relations based on mutual respect for religious and cultural differences would not threaten existing religious and cultural worldviews and would not provoke anxiety and destructive anxiety reduction defenses. The Social Identity Theory perspective proposes that individuals derive self-esteem from groups they identify with or belong. Insult and disrespect that derogate the very sources of value (the religious and cultural groups) that people depend on for psychological sustenance provoke defensive response and our defenses can be dangerous and even result in a greater perception of threat. Human and intergroup relations based on mutual respect and social equality would serve to decrease destructive responses to the threat posed by the insults. Mutual respect can be a challenge when we viscerally disagree with particular decontextualized religious beliefs and cultural practices. Education may assist us in, at least understanding the context of such beliefs and practices and enhancing our understanding that all people are seeking to address their common human needs as best as they can in the circumstances and history such beliefs and practices are located. A healthy respect for diversity as well as an open exchange of information and possible solutions that varied cultures and religions bring to common human problems would benefit all because no people, culture or religion have all the ideas and solutions needed to address the complexities of human existence (Marsella, 2005b).

Fundamentalism is an anxiety driven response (Salzman, 2003). Religious fundamentalism, as an alternative ideology, may be seen as an anxiety driven response to find meaning and a sense of self-value in a worldview that offers people clear and accessible standards of value that if achieved provide an anxiety-buffer against the terror inherent in human existence. The religious martyr is promised literal heroic death transcendence, which may be a compelling motive for those experiencing humiliation and live lives devoid of accessible sources of the self-esteem.

Recall that a principle and well-tested hypothesis of TMT (anxiety buffer hypothesis) states that if a psychological structure provides protection against anxiety, then augmenting that structure should reduce anxiety in response to subsequent threats. Specifically since self-esteem serves as a buffer against anxiety then strengthening self-esteem would be expected to reduce anxiety and anxiety-related behavior in response to threat (mortality salience). When psychological resources provided by religion and culture is threatened by the forces of globalization and its cultural impositions people are motivated to both increase their faith in these worldviews and to seek clearer and more accessible standards of behavior and being that would enable them to see themselves as being of, in Becker's words (1971) of "primary value in a world of meaning (p. 79)." In TMT terms, faith in the religious and/or cultural worldview and the perception that one is living up to its prescribed standards of value are essential components of what we have called "self-esteem" which is constructed differently across cultures.

What to do? We can work to build just world based on a "just globalization" that would provide people with the possibility of meeting their physiological and psychological needs. We can work, in our communities, nations and world to construct and provide positive pathways to significance and to a "constructive heroism" because people strive for significance whether through altruism, providing for one's family, contributing to a better global future or suicide bombing. We can, through education and enlightened representatives of our diverse humanity, make salient the affirmative, humane values existent in all religions and cultural traditions. We can work to make salient the "higher angels of our nature." The affirmative and high values of mercy, justice, love, and compassion exist and find correspondence across belief systems. It is these we must make salient from the pulpit to the school. There is some evidence cited previously that when mortality is made salient it is the salient or primed values within the worldview that are activated and may attenuate destructive defensive responses. We can work to oppose, imperialism, militarism and saber rattling because they induce mortality salience and all of its negative effects. We can connect the "new" to existing structures in belief system thereby making the "new" (i.e., a "just" globalization) less threatening to existing systems. Although all cultures do not support materialistic, greedy, and competitive values it is most likely that all cultures place high value on supporting and providing for one's family. On this we agree.

We must beware of fear and its induction by demagogic leaders. Fear and threat produce cognitive simplicity, intolerance, derogation and demonization of the "different other" who adheres to a different belief system and worldview. We can teach children and ourselves to recognize and beware of fear mongers, suspect them of demagogic manipulation and learn how to deconstruct fear-inducing messages. We can work to base our relations, to the greatest degree possible, on the principles of mutual respect and social equality. If we really listen we will find that people, the world over are seeking respect and dignity as well as material sustenance.

Is there cause for optimism? Can we prime our higher natures and cultural values so that when such massive mortality salience producing events such as September 11th occur we will not descend to good and evil dichotomies that demonize the culturally and religiously different in order to assuage our existential dilemma. The theoretical perspectives and empirical findings presented in this paper clearly indicate that we have the power to nourish our higher natures if we possess the intention to do so.

This inquiry has identified substantial theoretical and experimental work that has indicated that culture, ideologies and religious belief systems serve as a psychological defense against the anxiety and terror inherent in the human condition. As such, this psychological defense must be addressed carefully and respectfully because of the anxiety and associated behavioral responses that may be aroused when threatened. Humans have a range of potentials from the murderous to the magnificent. This paper suggests that, with a full appreciation of the range of ontological prescriptions that exist within any cultural or religious belief system, we can prime the highest and least destructive elements of people's cultural and religious worldviews through education, religious institutions and media. By nourishing our higher potentials and natures and we make their expression more probable.

References

Altemeyer, B., & Hunsberger, B. (1992). Authoritarianism, religious fundamentalism, quest, and prejudice. *The International Journal for the Psychology of Religion, 2*, 113–133.

Baumeister, R. (1991). *Meanings of life*. New York: Guilford.

Becker, E. (1971). *The birth and death of meaning* (2nd ed.). New York: Free Press.

Becker, E. (1973). *The denial of death*. New York: Free Press.

Becker, E. (1975). *Escape from evil*. New York: Free Press.

Bonanno, G. A., & Jost, J. T. (2006). Conservative shift among high-exposure survivors of the September 11th terrorist attacks. *Basic and Applied Social Psychology, 28*, 311–323.

Frankl, V. (1963). *Man's search for meaning: An introduction to logotherapy*. New York: Washington Square Press Inc.

Friedman, M., & Rholes, W. S. (in press). Successfully challenging fundamentalist beliefs results in increased death awareness. *Journal of Experimental Social Psychology*.

Friedman, T. (2000). *Understanding globalization: The lexus and the olive tree*. New York: Anchor Books.

Fromm, E. (1969). *Escape from freedom*. New York: Henry Holt.

Gelfand, M. J., Nishii, L. H., & Raver, J. L. (2006). On the nature and importance of culture tightness-looseness. *Journal of Applied Psychology, 6*(91), 1225–1244.

Greenberg, J., Landau, M. J., Solomon, S., & Pyszczynski, T. (in press). The case for terror management as the primary psychological function of religion. In D. Wulff (Ed.), *Handbook of the Psychology of Religion*. London: Oxford University Press.

Greenberg, J., Pyszczynski, T., Solomon, S., Rosenblatt, A., Veeder, M., Kirkland, S., et al. (1990). Evidence for terror management theory. II. The effects of mortality salience reactions to those who threaten or bolster the cultural worldview. *Journal of Personality and Social Psychology, 58*, 308–318.

Greenberg, J., Pyszczynski, T., Solomon, S., Simon, L., & Breus, M. (1994). The role of consciousness and accessibility of death—related thoughts in mortality salience effects. *Journal of Personality and Social Psychology, 67*, 627–637.

Greenberg, J., Simon, L., Pyszczynski, T., Solomon, S., & Chatel, D. (1992). Terror management and tolerance: Does mortality salience always intensify negative reactions to others who threaten one's worldview? *Journal of Personality and Social Psychology, 63,* 212–220.

Greenberg, J., Solomon, S., & Pyszczynski, T. (1997). Terror management theory of self-esteem and cultural worldviews: Empirical assessments and conceptual refinements. In M. P. Zanna (Ed.), *Advances in experimental social psychology* (pp. 61–139). San Diego, CA: Academic Press, Inc.

Greider, W. (1997). *One world, ready or not: The manic logic of global capitalism.* New York: Simon & Shuster.

Hood, R. W., Hill, P. C., & Williamson, W. P. (2005). *The psychology of religious fundamentalism.* New York: Guilford.

Hunter, J. P. (1990). Fundamentalism in its global contours. In N. J. Cohen (Ed.), *The fundamentalist phenomena. Grand rapids* (pp. 56–72). Michigan: William B. Erdmans Publishing Company.

Jost, J. T. (2006). The end of the end of ideology. *American Psychologist, 61,* 651–670.

Koenig, H. G., McCullough, M. E., & Larson, D. B. (2001). *Handbook of religion and health.* New York: Oxford University Press.

Lee, M. A. (2000). *The beast reawakens.* New York: Routledge.

Lewin, K. (1997). *Resolving social conflicts and field theory in social science.* Washington, DC: American Psychological Association.

Lifton, R. J. (1999). *Destroying the world to save it: Aum Shinrikyo, apocalyptic violence, and the new global terrorism.* New York: Metropolitan Books.

Marsella, A. J. (2005a). Hegemonic globalization and cultural diversity: The risks of monoculturalism. *Australian Mosaic, 13*(11), 15–19.

Marsella, A. J. (2005b). Culture and conflict. Understanding, negotiating, and reconciling conflicting constructions of reality. *International Journal of Intercultural Relations, 29,* 651–673.

Marx, K. (2000). In D. McLennan (Ed.), *Critique of the gotha programme (1875)* (2nd ed.). Oxford: Oxford University Press.

McGregor, H. A., Lieberman, J. D., Greenberg, J., Solomon, S., Arndt, J., Simon, L., et al. (1998). Terror management and aggression: Evidence that mortality salience motivates aggression against worldview-threatening others, *Journal of Personality and Social Psychology, 74*(3), 590–605.

Maslow, A. H. (1968). *Toward a psychology of being.* Princeton, NJ: Van Nostrand.

Nasser, J. (2005). *Globalization and terrorism: The migration of dreams and nightmares.* New York: Rowman & Littlefield.

Nielson, N. C. (1993). *Fundamentalism, mythos and world religions.* Albany, NY: State University Press.

Ochsmann, R., & Mathy, M. (1994). *Depreciating of and distancing from foreigners: Effects of mortality salience.* Unpublished manuscript, Universitaet Mainz, Mainz, Germany.

Pieterse, J. N. (2004). *Globalization & culture.* Lanham, Maryland: Rowman & Littlefield.

Pyszczynski, T., Abdooahi, A., Solomon, S., Greenberg, J., Cohen, F., & Weise, D. (2006). Mortality salience, martyrdom, and military might: The great satan versus the axis of evil. *Personality and Social Psychology Bulletin, 32*(4), 525–537.

Pyszczynski, T., Solomon, S., & Greenberg, J. (2003). *In the wake of 9/11: The psychology of terror.* Washington, DC: American Psychological Association.

Rank, O. (1958). *Beyond psychology.* New York: Dover.

Rosenblatt, A., Greenberg, J., Solomon, S., Pyszczynski, T., & Lyon, D. (1989). Evidence for terror management theory I: The effects of mortality salience on reactions to those who violate or uphold cultural values. *Journal of Personality and Social Psychology, 57,* 681–690.

Salzman, M. (2001). Globalization, culture & anxiety. *Journal of Social Distress and the Homeless, 10*(4), 337–352.

Salzman, M. (2003). Existential anxiety, religious fundamentalism, the "clash of civilizations" and terror management theory. *Cross Cultural Psychology Bulletin, 37*(3), 10–16.

Salzman, M. (2006). "Culture Wars" and intercultural conflict from three theoretical perspectives. *Paper presented at the XVIIIth international congress international association for cross-cultural psychology.*

Soros, G. (1998). *The crisis of global capitalism.* New York: Public Affairs.

Stevens, M. J. (2002). The unanticipated consequences of globalization: Contextualizing terrorism. In Stout, C. E. (Ed.). *The psychology of terrorism.* 3 (pp. 31–56). London: Praeger.

Tajfel, H., & Turner, J. C. (1986). The social identity theory of inter-group behavior. In S. Worchel & L. W. Austin (Eds.), *Psychology of intergroup relations.* Chicago: Nelson-Hall.

Triandis, H. C. (1972). *The analysis of subjective culture.* New York: Wiley.

Yalom, I. (1980). *Existential psychotherapy.* New York: Basic Books.

Module 13

Collective Action and the Individual

Collective behavior is a non-institutionalized activity carried out by a group of people on a voluntary basis. Flash mobs are examples of collective behavior. Other examples of collective behavior can include anything from a group of commuters traveling home from work to the trend toward adopting the Justin Bieber hair flip. In short, it can be any group behavior that is not mandated or regulated by an institution.

There are four primary forms of collective behavior: the crowd, the mass, the public, and social movements. It takes a fairly large number of people in close proximity to form a crowd. Examples include a group of people attending a music concert, tailgating at a football game, or attending a worship service. Researchers have identified four types of crowds. Casual crowds consist of people who are in the same place at the same time, but who aren't really interacting, such as people standing in line at the post office. Conventional crowds are those who come together for a scheduled event occurring regularly, like a religious service. Expressive crowds are people who join together to express emotion, often at funerals, weddings, or the like. The final type, acting crowds, focus on a specific goal or action, such as a protest movement or riot.

TORONTO – JAN 26 : Elementary teachers protest Bill 115 on January 26 2013 in Toronto, Canada. An acting crowd that expresses the concerns of a social movement.

JOHANNESBURG, SOUTH AFRICA – AUGUST 21: The South African flag at the FNB Stadium in Soweto on August 21, 2010. The game set the record for the highest attendance at a South African Rugby match. A crowd or a mass?

A mass is a relatively large number of people with a common interest, though they may not be in close proximity, such as players of the popular game World of Warcraft. A public, on the other hand, is an unorganized, relatively diffused group of people who share ideas, such as the Libertarian political party. While these two types of crowds are similar, they are not the same. To distinguish between them, remember that members of a mass share interests whereas members of a public share ideas.

Social movements are purposeful, organized groups striving to work toward a common goal. These groups might be attempting to create change (Occupy Wall Street, Arab Spring), to resist change (anti-globalization movement), or to provide a political voice to specific groups that consider themselves disenfranchised (civil rights movements, Tea Party). Social movements, along with other social forces, create social change. Consider the effect of the 2010 BP oil spill in the Gulf of Mexico. This disaster exemplifies how a change in the environment, coupled with the use of technology to fix that change, combined with anti-oil sentiment in social movements and social institutions, led to changes in social institutions and social practices, from grassroots marketing campaigns that promote consumption of local seafood to municipal governments needing to coordinate with federal cleanups.

LOS ANGELES, CA APRIL 15, 2015: Two protestors hold signs advocating raising the minimum wage in front of a McDonald's restaurant during a demonstration in Los Angeles on April 15, 2015. Emotions of frustration and injustice are being expressed by participants of this expressive crowd.

We know that social movements can occur on the local, national, or even global stage. Some researchers have developed categories that distinguish among social movements based on what they want to change and how much change they want. Reform movements seek to change something specific about the social structure. Examples include anti-nuclear groups, Mothers Against Drunk Driving (MADD), and the Human Rights Campaign's advocacy for Marriage Equality. Revolutionary movements seek to completely change every aspect of society. These would include the 1960's counterculture movement, as well as anarchist collectives. Religious/Redemptive movements are "meaning seeking," and their goal is to provoke inner change or spiritual growth in individuals. Organizations pushing these movements might include Heaven's Gate or the Branch Davidians. Alternative movements are focused on self-improvement and limited, specific changes to individual beliefs and behavior. These include trends like transcendental meditation or a macrobiotic diet. Resistance movements seek to prevent or undo change to the social structure. The Ku Klux Klan and pro-life movements fall into this category. Social movements have, throughout history, influenced societal change.

TORONTO, ONTARIO/CANADA – 25th Tuesday November 2014 : Toronto's Black Community takes action in solidarity with Ferguson protesters in Toronto, Canada. Do the responses to Ferguson amount to a social movement?

Why Do People Engage In Collective Action?

Revisiting The Role of Perceived Effectiveness

Matthew J. Hornsey[1]*, Leda Blackwood[1], Winnifred Louis[1],
Kelly Fielding[1], Ken Mavor[2], Thomas Morton[3], Anne O'Brien[3],
Karl-Erik Paasonen[1], Joanne Smith[1], Katherine M. White[4],

Abstract

Research has shown only limited support for the notion that perceived effectiveness of collective action
is a predictor of people's intentions to engage in collective action. One reason for this may be that effectiveness has been defined rather narrowly in terms of
whether the action will influence key decision makers.
In addition to influencing decision makers, we argue
that the effectiveness of collective action might be
judged by other criteria, such as whether it is effective
in influencing third parties, building an oppositional
movement, and expressing values. Two hundred and
thirty one attendees at a rally filled out a questionnaire examining the perceived effectiveness of the rally
across the four hypothesized dimensions and their intentions to engage in future collective action. For those
participants who were not members of an organization,
future intentions were linked to the perceived effectiveness of the rally in expressing values and influencing the general public. For those who were members
of an organization, future intentions were linked only
to the perceived effectiveness of the rally in building
an oppositional movement. Perceptions of how effective the rally was in influencing decision makers were
not related to intentions for either members or non-
members. Implications for models of collective action
are discussed.

[1] University of Queensland

[2] Australian National University

[3] University of Exeter

[4] Queensland University of Technology

* Address correspondence to Dr Matthew Hornsey, School of
Psychology, University of Queensland, St Lucia 4072, Queensland,
Australia.

Fax: +61 7 3365 4466 Ph: +61 7 3365 6378 E-mail: m.hornsey@psy.
uq.edu.au

Why Do People Engage In Collective Action?

Revisiting The Role of Perceived Effectiveness

It is well documented that people's concerns about social
and economic issues do not necessarily translate into collective action (Klandermans, 2002; Olson, 1968). For example, a 1983 Gallup poll (cited in Fox & Schofield, 1989)
revealed that approximately 40% of people in the US believed it was likely that there would be nuclear war by 1998,
and 70% believed that they would not survive a nuclear
war. Despite this, surveys in the 1980s showed that only a
very small minority of people engaged in collective action
to try to prevent the proliferation of nuclear missiles (Hamilton, Knox, Keilin, & Chavez, 1987). This gulf between
perceived threat and collective action is apparent also in
laboratory studies in which participants are discriminated
against (e.g., Lalonde & Cameron, 1994; Lalonde & Silverman, 1994; Wright & Taylor, 1998; Wright, Taylor, &
Moghaddam, 1990). An unexpected but common finding
of these studies is that collective action is frequently nominated as a less attractive strategy than individual action or
even acceptance. This is despite the fact that collective action is traditionally considered to be a prerequisite for social
change (Hogg & Abrams, 1988; Tajfel & Turner, 1979).

Over the last 40 years, considerable attention has
been paid to this apparent paradox: Why are concerned
individuals so reluctant to engage in collective action?
One intuitive position is that people avoid collective action because they see it to be ineffective. In the case of
nuclear proliferation, for example, it could be that people feel as though they are powerless to stop the course
of events, and so they learn to stop trying. This is not
an irrational belief. In Australia in 2000, an estimated
1 million people (5% of the population) participated
in marches requesting that the government apologize
to indigenous Aborigines for aggressive assimilationist
policies implemented between the 1930s and 1960s. At

From *Journal of Applied Social Psychology, Vol. 36, No. 7, July 2006* by Hornsey, et al, Copyright © 2006 John Wiley and Sons. Reprinted
by permission.

the time of writing, the Australian government has not apologized. In 2003, millions of people in the US, England, and Australia protested against the declaration of war in Iraq, but these countries committed troops to the war regardless. When people make personal sacrifices to engage in collective action (in terms of time, money, and so forth) and then see an apparent indifference to this action on behalf of those in power, it is reasonable to expect that concerned individuals might eventually sink into a state of passivity and alienation (see Bynner & Ashford, 1994, for a broader discussion of political disaffection).

According to this argument, people should be more inclined to engage in collective action the more effective they feel this action would be in bringing about change (Abramson & Aldrich, 1982; Verba & Nie, 1972). Consistent with this notion, research has shown moderate but significant links between perceived effectiveness and intentions to engage in collective action. For example, an analysis of members of environmental organizations in the Netherlands revealed a positive relationship between perceptions of effectiveness and intentions to engage in collective action (Brunsting & Postmes, 2002). Similarly, moderate to high pairwise correlations have been found between measures of personal efficacy (i.e., judgements that one's personal actions can bring about desired change) and intentions to engage in collective action with regard to nuclear war (Tyler & McGraw, 1983; Wolf, Gregory, & Stephan, 1986). Smaller but significant relationships between efficacy and intentions have also emerged in research on willingness to attend union meetings (Flood, 1993) and willingness to engage in political action among African Americans (Berman & Wittig, 2004). Fox and Schofield (1989) found that those who scored highly on a measure of "nuclear efficacy" (e.g., "Nuclear war can be prevented through active citizen efforts to convince world powers to disarm") were more likely to sign a petition supporting bilateral disarmament than were those who scored low on this scale, although nuclear efficacy did not relate significantly to intentions to engage in collective action. Finally, Locatelli and Holt (1986) found that antinuclear activists who rated themselves as low on a global measure of "political powerlessness" (i.e., high on perceived efficacy) reported significantly stronger levels of antinuclear activism.

Despite these reasonably consistent results, other studies have shown that effectiveness perceptions tell only part of the story of why people engage in collective action. Klandermans and Oegema (1987), for example, interviewed 114 Dutch participants shortly before a major rally protesting against NATO's decision to deploy cruise missiles in Europe. Revealingly, the authors found that "None of the respondents was very optimistic about the effectiveness of the demonstration; those who intended to demonstrate were no exception. *None of them believed that the deployment of the cruise missiles could be stopped*" (p. 527, italics added). This disconnection between perceptions of effectiveness and intentions to engage in collective action was detected also by Schofield and Pavelchak (1989) who examined people's attitudes toward nuclear war before and after watching a movie depicting nuclear holocaust. After watching the movie, participants reported a decreased sense that they had the ability to prevent nuclear war, and at the same time an *increased* intention to engage in anti-nuclear activism.

More recent work on the role of identity in predicting intentions to engage in collective action has contributed to a de-emphasis on effectiveness considerations. In line with social identity theory (Tajfel, 1978; Tajfel & Turner, 1979), Simon and colleagues (1998) argued that a major contributor to whether people engage in collective action is the extent to which they internalize their identity as an activist. Simon and colleagues compared the predictive value of identity measures with cost-benefit analyses measured at the collective, social, and individual levels. The construct most relevant to the current analysis is the collective level, which was operationalized by identifying goals of the movement and measuring the extent to which participants (a) valued these goals and (b) expected that a sufficient number of people could be mobilized to achieve these goals. In line with Klandermans (1984) expectancy-value approach, the "collective motive" was calculated as a multiplicative function of these two considerations. The authors found that identification as an activist significantly predicted intentions to engage in collective action among members of the older people's movement in Germany (Study 1) and members of the gay movement in the US (Study 2). In contrast, the collective motive was a weaker predictor of intentions and was not significantly associated with past activist behaviours. The authors proposed that there are at least two independent pathways to willingness to engage in collective action; a pathway that involves the weighing up of costs and benefits associated with activism, and a second pathway derived from identity issues. According to the model, identification as an activist is associated directly with activism intentions independently of "rational" cost-benefit analyses considerations. Rather, high identifiers act out the behaviours associated with their activist identity without explicitly considering the costs and benefits of their actions (see also Kelly & Breinlinger, 1995a).

Subsequent research on the dual pathway model found robust support for the predictive value of activist identification, and weaker support for the role of effectiveness. Using a similar measure of the collective motive as Simon and colleagues (1998), Sturmer and Simon (2004) found that perceptions of collective effectiveness among members of the German gay movement did not predict participation in collective protest as measured 12 months later. Using a slightly different measure of the expectancy component of the collective motive (the extent to which the goals of the group could be achieved by participating in group activities), Sturmer, Simon, Loewy, and Jorger (2003) again found no relationship between expectancies and willingness to engage in future activities of the fat acceptance movement. In each case, identification with the social movement was a strong predictor, reinforcing the notion that collective action can be a direct expression of an identity rather than an outcome of cost-benefit analyses, including perceptions of effectiveness. This research broadly corresponds to earlier research by Kelly and Breinlinger (1995b), who showed that perceived group effectiveness positively predicted the extent to which women engaged in women's group activities in the ensuing 12 months. However, when identification as an activist was included as a predictor, effectiveness was not uniquely predictive of behaviors or intentions to engage in collective action. The fact that the predictive power of effectiveness dropped out when activist identification was included suggests that the relationship between perceptions of effectiveness and collective action is an artefact of high inter-correlations between effectiveness and activist identity, and that it is the latter construct that has the true explanatory power. This suggests that one needs to look sceptically at previously established links between effectiveness and intentions in which identity measures were not included as predictors (e.g., Flood, 1993; Tyler & McGraw, 1983; Wolf et al., 1986).

Reconceptualizing "Effectiveness"

In summary, despite the intuitive appeal of the notion that perceptions of effectiveness would be crucial in determining whether or not people engage in collective action, the evidence for such a relationship is mixed, and there is recent research to suggest that perceptions of collective effectiveness might play no role in predicting intentions over and above ratings of activist identification (Kelly & Breinlinger, 1995b; Sturmer et al., 2003; Sturmer & Simon, 2004). In this paper, we argue that the lack of support for the role of effectiveness might be partly a function of the fact that this construct has been defined in a relatively narrow manner, and that a more nuanced conceptualization of effectiveness might uncover relationships that have been obscured previously.

In the past literature on collective action, effectiveness has been operationalized in a number of different ways. Some researchers have measured it as a generalized sense that individuals can influence the political process (e.g., Locatelli & Holt, 1986), whereas others have measured it as a belief that the specific, material goals of the group can be achieved. Among those who operationalized it in terms of the specific goals of the group, effectiveness has been interpreted variously as the sense that the individual can contribute successfully to achieving the goals (Kelly & Breinlinger, 1995b; Schofield & Pavelchak, 1989; Sturmer et al., 2003; Wolf et al., 1986), the sense that enough people can be mobilized to achieve the goals (Berman & Wittig, 2004; Simon et al., 1998; Sturmer & Simon, 2004), or more directly as the sense that the group is capable of bringing about the desired change (Flood, 1993; Fox & Schofield, 1989; Tyler & McGraw, 1983). What unites all these conceptualizations is that they treat effectiveness strictly in terms of whether the collective action would influence decision makers and win the desired outcomes for the group. We argue, however, that people could use at least three other criteria for determining whether a particular piece of collective action might be perceived as effective. Specifically, we argue that in addition to conceptualizing effectiveness in terms of influencing key decision makers, collective actions may also vary in the extent to which they are seen to be effective in satisfying intragroup, broader societal, and individual motivations.[1] These criteria for effectiveness are discussed in more depth below.

In their analysis of politicized collective identity, Simon and Klandermans (2001) made the important point that much political activity involves an interaction between the ingroup (the protestors, or members of a social movement), the outgroup or opponent (e.g., government), and relevant third parties (e.g., the general public). In many cases, group members might seek to go beyond the power struggle between their group and the outgroup and to *convince third parties* that they are part of the broader societal power struggle (see Reicher & Hopkins, 1996, for a related argument). In this way, members of each group try to win support and alignments from the broader population. This, of course, has implications for what are considered to be effective strategies for collective action. If people stage a rally and march through the streets, it is likely that they do so with the hope that decision makers and policy makers will be either intimidated or persuaded by what the march represents. It is also possible, however, that the intended audience extends to third parties; those who are not engaged currently in collective action but are not aligned to the outgroup either, and who can be recruited to the cause. In this case, effectiveness might not be measured by how many concessions they obtain from the relevant outgroup (e.g., policy makers), but by the extent to which the rally shifts the sympathies and allegiances of neutral observers.

Alternatively, effectiveness may be judged not on the basis of perceived *influence* per se, but rather in terms of whether it is successful in strengthening solidarity and strategic connections within the group. Activists may be responding to the perception that increased cohesiveness and coordination is an ingredient in more effective social mobilization (Kinder, 1998). In other words, the intended audience might not be outsiders at all but rather the protestors themselves. This might particularly be the case when the movement is not defined by an organization but rather by a set of ideologies or principles. Protests against globalization or war, for example, can encompass a dizzyingly large number of individual organizations and entities who might normally have little to do with each other, but are bound together by a set of ideological perspectives and goals. A collective act such as a rally might be the only time that these groups are brought together. Fuelled by physical proximity and a shared voice, rallies can help knit splintered individuals and groups into a more coherent force, from which basis future collective action might be more influential. Rather than focusing on short-term influence, the aims of a piece of collective action might be to "rally the troops" in the hope of exerting change in the long-term. In these situations, effectiveness can be interpreted in terms of how successful the collective action is in *building an oppositional movement* (it should be noted that there are broad parallels between this process-oriented view of effectiveness and the tenets of resource mobilization theory; see Klandermans, 1984, for a review).

Finally, we argue that in some cases acts of collective action are not driven entirely by perceptions of influence or by the need to build an oppositional movement, but also by a simple need for *expression of values*. Expressing one's own values publicly might partially be motivated by the need to influence others, but public expression might also have a positive impact on the individual independent of instrumental considerations. Attitude theorists have long argued that attitudes have an expressive function in that they act as a marker of group membership and/or personal values (e.g., Anderson & Kristiansen, 1990; Herek, 1987; Katz, 1960). Furthermore, Tice (1992) argued that public acts of defiance help nourish and define one's sense of self, a motive that is independent of whether the act of defiance succeeds in initiating change. Consistent with this, Hornsey, Majkut, Terry, and McKimmie (2003) found that people with a strong moral basis for their attitude on a social issue were keener

to engage in public (but not private) collective action when they were led to believe they held a minority position than when they were led to believe that they held a majority position. This public act of counter-conformity was not driven by a desire to influence others or to recruit people to their position, suggesting that value expression was a valuable motive per se. Indeed, the mere expression of voice may be cathartic for people who feel they are subjected to unfair policies or procedures (Folger, 1977; Lind & Tyler, 1988; Lind, Kanfer, & Earley, 1990).

Collective actions are likely to vary considerably in the extent to which they are felt to be effective forums for expressing individual values. For example, people might feel that a rally misrepresents their values, whether because of the content of speeches, the content of placards, or the choice of protest strategy in which the group engages (e.g., peaceful protest as opposed to formal blockading; Polletta & Jasper, 2001). Indeed, if the attitudes and values expressed by a collective act misrepresent the attitudes and values of individual protestors, the level of frustration and threat could be considerable (Hornsey, Blackwood, & O'Brien, in press). It seems reasonable, then, that the likelihood of people engaging in collective action might vary as a function of the perceived effectiveness of the collective act in expressing their individual values.

In summary, we argue that there are at least four goals of collective action and, by extension, four criteria by which the effectiveness of collective action can be judged. These are (1) the extent to which the relevant outgroup (e.g., policy makers) would be influenced by the collective action (intergroup concerns), (2) the extent to which relevant third parties would be influenced by the collective action (broader societal concerns), (3) the extent to which the collective action would be successful in building an oppositional movement (intragroup concerns), and (4) the extent to which the collective action would be successful in expressing one's values (individual concerns). We examined the links between each of these perceptions of effectiveness and future intentions to engage in collective action, using an anti-globalization rally as the context.

The Current Study

In 2001, Brisbane, Australia was to be the venue for a Commonwealth Heads of Government Meeting (CHOGM), a reunion of heads of state of members of the Commonwealth (the former British Empire) with the goal of discussing cultural, economic, and political themes pertinent to member states. In the months leading up to the meeting, there was a well-publicized effort to organize blockades, sit-ins, and marches designed to disrupt CHOGM. Although there were a disparate number of groups planning to protest, and the content of people's concerns differed widely, the broad aims of the planned collective action was to protest against economic rationalism and globalization. This event was part of a series of high-profile anti-globalization protests that had taken place around the world since the late 1990s. With just weeks to go until the meeting was due to start, security fears regarding the planned protests increased to such a degree that CHOGM was cancelled. Regardless, on the date that the meeting was due to begin, a demonstration was organized around themes of global justice. A rally was held in the morning, consisting of an hour and a half of speeches and then an hour-long march through the city center. The march ended in a local park at which speeches, protest songs, and so forth continued for the afternoon. Approximately 2000 people attended the rally ("Protest March", 2001), and these people formed the population of interest for the current study.

A sample of protestors were given questionnaires in which we asked them the extent to which they identified as an activist, and the extent to which they felt the rally had been effective in achieving each of the goals described above. We then asked participants the extent to which they intended to attend future, related protests over the next six months. On the basis of Simon and colleagues' work on the dual pathway model (Simon et al., 1998; Sturmer et al., 2003; Sturmer & Simon, 2004), we expected that participants would express stronger intentions to engage in future collective action the more they identified as an activist. We also predicted that there would be a positive relationship between the four ratings of effectiveness and intentions, independent of activist identification. Given a paucity of previous research on the topic, we were not in a position to make strong predictions about whether some conceptualizations of effectiveness would be more predictive of intentions than others.

We did, however, expect that the various measures of effectiveness might be more predictive for some protestors than for others. Specifically, we distinguish between protestors who attended the rally as members of an organized activist group and those who attended as unaligned individuals. One possible difference between these sub-samples of the population is that group members have presumably internalized a need for organized protest and consolidated social movements to a greater extent than have non-members. With their greater focus on group agency, it seems reasonable to expect that ratings of the effectiveness of the rally in terms of intergroup considerations (influencing opposition groups) and intragroup considerations (building an oppositional movement) might be more strongly linked to intentions for members

than for non-members. In contrast, it could be that non-members will be more swayed by individual considerations (e.g., expressing values) than would members.

Method

Recruitment of Participants

Six recruiters identified by university name badges and clipboards approached protesters in the morning and afternoon during the speeches. Participants were given the questionnaire as they sat listening to the speeches. At the same time, participants were provided with an information sheet describing the nature of the study and the research team, and providing contact information through which participants could be informed of future results. Two hundred and thirty-one protesters participated in the survey. Given the rally was estimated to be 2000 people strong, this represents approximately 12% of all the people who attended across the three events. Respondents had a median age of 26 years, ranging from 11 to 70 years. Nine individuals did not note their sex; of the remaining, 42% were men ($n = 94$) and 58% women ($n = 128$).

Materials

The questionnaire consisted of a single page labeled "School of Psychology, University of Queensland". Participants first indicated their sex and age, and then indicated whether or not they were attending the rally as a member of an organization/collective. Ninety participants (39% of the sample) answered yes and 141 (61%) answered no. Those who answered yes were asked to indicate of which organization or collective they were members. Over 40 organizations were nominated, and no single organization was mentioned by more than 11 participants. The ratio of males to females in each sub-sample was roughly equivalent (60% members female, 56% non-members female). Members ($M = 28.44$) and non-members ($M = 29.88$) were also similar in age, $t(222) = 0.90, p = .37$.

Activist identification was measured using four items: "I identify as an activist," "I feel similar to activists," "I am a typical activist", and "Being an activist is an important part of who I am" (-3 = strongly disagree, 3 = strongly agree; $\alpha = .89$). To measure *effectiveness*, we asked participants to indicate the extent to which they thought the protests would be effective in "influencing government leaders and policy makers", "influencing public opinion", "building an oppositional movement", and "expressing certain values" that they hold. Participants responded on scales ranging from -3 ("counter productive") to 0 ("no impact") to $+3$ ("very effective"). These items were each designed to tap into the four dimensions of effectiveness defined earlier: influencing outgroups, influencing third parties, building an oppositional movement, and expressing values, respectively. The four effectiveness measures inter-correlated moderately (r ranging from .20 - .46; see Table 1 for a summary of inter-correlations among all measures). Finally, participants completed a three-item measure of *future protest intentions*. Participants indicated the likelihood that they would "attend next year's CHOGM protests", "attend protests on this theme in the next 6 months", and "attend protests in general in the next 6 months" (1 = very unlikely, 7 = very likely; α = .83).

Results

Examination of Means

The sample scored significantly above the mid-point of the scale in terms of activist identification, M = 0.70, SD = 1.50, $t(217)$ = 6.94, p < .001, and future intentions, M= 5.66, SD = 1.42, $t(216)$ = 17.24, p < .001. Participants were also relatively optimistic about the effectiveness of the rally in terms of influencing government leaders and policy makers (M = 0.66, SD = 1.21), influencing public opinion (M = 1.36, SD = 0.99), building an oppositional movement (M = 1.75, SD = 1.04), and expressing values (M = 2.07, SD = 0.93). In all cases, the ratings of effectiveness lay significantly above the mid-point of the scale (*ts* ranging from 8.28 to 33.56, *ps* < .001).

Before examining the relation between ratings of effectiveness and intentions, we first tested whether members and non-members differed on the key measures. Members and non-members did not differ in the extent to which they believed the rally would be effective in influencing government leaders and policy makers, $t(227)$ = −0.97, p = .34, or the extent to which they believed

it was effective in expressing values, $t(226)$ = −1.53, p = .13. Significant differences did emerge, though, on ratings of activist identification, $t(216)$ = −4.78, p < .001, perceived effectiveness in influencing public opinion, $t(227)$ = −3.96, p < .001, perceived effectiveness in building an oppositional movement, $t(226)$ = −2.34, p = .020, and future intentions, $t(215)$ = −5.02, p < .001. Members had stronger activist identities (M = 1.28), believed the rally would be more effective in influencing public opinion (M = 1.67), believed the rally would be more effective in building an oppositional movement (M = 1.94), and had stronger intentions to engage in collective action in the future (M = 6.23) than did non-members (M = 0.33, 1.16, 1.62, and 5.29 respectively).

Predicting Intentions

Hierarchical multiple regression was performed using participants' future intentions to engage in collective action as the criterion (see Table 2). In the first step, group membership (dummy coded such that 0 = non-members, 1 = members), activist identification, and the four measures of effectiveness were entered as predictors. These predictors accounted for a significant amount of variance, but only three variables contributed uniquely to the prediction of future intentions: group membership, activist identification, and perceived effectiveness in building an oppositional movement. As described above, the effect of group membership reflects the fact that members had stronger intentions to engage in collective action in the future than did non-members. Participants also had stronger intentions to engage in collective action the stronger their activist identity and the more they felt the rally was effective in building an oppositional movement.

In the second step of the analysis, five product terms were entered representing the interaction between group membership and each of the predictors used in the first step (in line with recommendations by Aiken & West, 1991, continuous variables were centered). The inclusion of the interaction terms resulted in a significant increase in variance explained. Three of the interaction terms contributed uniquely to the model, representing the interaction between group membership and, respectively, effectiveness in influencing public opinion, effectiveness in building an oppositional movement, and effectiveness in expressing values.

We analyzed simple slopes by performing regressions separately at each level of group membership (see Table 3 for a summary of results). Non-members expressed stronger intentions to engage in collective action the more they thought the rally was effective in influencing public opinion and the more they thought it was effective in expressing their values. Beliefs about how effective

Table 1 Intercorrelations Among Variables

	2	3	4	5	6
1. Activist Identification	.11	.34***	.53***	.29***	.63***
2. Influencing Government		.42***	.32***	.20**	.10
3. Influencing Public			.46***	.44***	.36***
4. Building Opposition				.41***	.48***
5. Expressing Values					.32***
6. Future Intentions					

Note. **p < .01; ***p < .001.

Table 2 Hierarchical Regression of Group, Activist Identification, and Effectiveness on Future Intentions

	Variable	β	SE	R²ch	Fch	df
Step 1	Group	.12*	.16	.46	29.00***	6, 207
	Activist Identification	.47***	.06			
	Influencing Government	−.06	.07			
	Influencing Public	.07	.09			
	Building Opposition	.16*	.09			
	Expressing Values	.08	.09			
Step 2	Group × Activist Identification	−.02	.12	.05	4.03**	5, 202
	Group × Influencing Government	.02	.14			
	Group × Influencing Public	−.22**	.19			
	Group × Building Opposition	.19*	.19			
	Group × Expressing Values	−.18*	.20			

*$p < .05$ **$p < .01$ ***$p < .001$

Table 3 Relationship Among Activist Identification, Effectiveness, and Future Intentions For Members and Non-Members

	Members β	Members SE	Non-Members β	Non-Members SE
Activist Identification	.52***	.08	.44***	.08
Influencing Government	−.12	.09	−.12	.10
Influencing Public	−.13	.12	.24*	.14
Building Opposition	.43***	.12	.06	.13
Expressing Values	−.15	.14	.17*	.11

*$p < .05$, ***$p < .001$

the rally was in influencing government and building an oppositional movement were not unique predictors of intentions for non-members. For members, the only effectiveness measure to influence their future intentions was the perceived effectiveness of the rally in building an oppositional movement. The more effective the rally was in building an oppositional movement, the more they intended to engage in future collective action in the future. Both members and non-members expressed stronger future intentions the stronger their identification as activists.

Discussion

Both qualitative (e.g., Klandermans & Oegema, 1987) and quantitative research (e.g., Fox & Schofield, 1989) suggest that perceptions of effectiveness might play only a limited role in explaining why people are or are not willing to engage in collective action. Indeed, recent evidence suggests that perceptions of effectiveness have no predictive power with regard to intentions to engage in collective action over and above people's identification as an activist (Kelly & Breinlinger, 1995b; Sturmer et al., 2003; Sturmer, & Simon, 2004). One possible reason for the limited support for the role of effectiveness is that effectiveness has been narrowly defined in terms of perceptions of influence over the relevant outgroups (e.g., government leaders, policy makers). We argue that a broader conceptualization of what an effective piece of collective action represents to people might help uncover relationships between collective action and willingness to engage in collective action. Specifically, we argue that there are at least four ways in which effectiveness can be conceptualized: in terms of influencing outgroups, influencing third parties, building an oppositional movement, and expressing values.

Data gathered among attendees at a rally lend support to the utility of a broad conceptualization of effectiveness. It is interesting to note that, if effectiveness had been measured in the spirit of the bulk of previous research – that is, in terms of whether the rally would be successful in influencing outgroups – no relationship would have emerged between effectiveness and intentions. On one hand, this result might seem surprising. The rally was organized in response to a planned meeting of heads of government, with the implicit (and at times explicit) agenda of pressuring heads of government to address social justice issues. One might think, then, that an important criterion for success might be the extent to which government leaders and policy makers would be influenced by the message and power that the collective action represented. However, the results suggest that this was not an important consideration when people were reporting whether they intended to engage in future collective action.

On the other hand, this result makes a degree of intuitive sense. When people rally against globalization, only the most optimistic of protestors would believe that their actions could reverse global macroeconomic policy, and to judge the success of a rally entirely on this basis would more often than not lead to disappointment. Similarly, when people protested against the impending war in Iraq, many would have done so with the knowledge that their actions would have very limited impact on whether or not the war commenced. Yet many people protested all the same, which suggests that the rallies were fulfilling functions other than influencing policy makers.

The current data suggest three alternative dimensions on which effectiveness might be judged, and provide evidence that each of these contributes in some way to influencing protestors' future intentions. For example, our sample expressed stronger intentions to participate in collective action the more they felt the current rally was effective in building an oppositional movement. Rather than focusing on whether the rally was effective in influencing outgroups, respondents seem to be focusing on the effectiveness of the rally in galvanizing a critical mass of opposition, a platform from which future influence attempts can be launched. In other words, rather than focusing on the short-term effects of the rally on external parties, people are motivated by the perceived success of the rally in consolidating the movement, with a view to implementing change in the medium to long term. This suggests that protestors themselves should be seen as potential targets of the rally, alongside outgroups and third parties, a phenomenon that has been obscured in the past by overly narrow or abstract definitions of effectiveness.

It should be noted, though, that the focus on building an oppositional movement was only predictive of intentions for a subset of our sample. For people who were members of an organization, effectiveness in terms of building an oppositional movement was a powerful predictor of intentions. Indeed, this construct was the *only* index of effectiveness that seemed to matter to members when it came to predicting future intentions. The effectiveness of the rally in influencing the general public or expressing values played no role at all when other factors were taken into account.

For non-members, a quite different pattern emerged in terms of what dimensions of effectiveness encourage people to engage in collective action in the future. In terms of predicting intentions, non-members were not influenced by whether the rally was effective in influencing government or building an oppositional movement. They were, however, more likely to engage in future collective action the more they felt the rally was effective in influencing the general public. As pointed out by Simon and Klandermans (2001), a mark of a politicized intergroup struggle is that protagonists try to enlist the sympathies of, and the support of, third parties. On the surface, this might be why rallies are often preceded by marches. Although the end point of a march might involve rallying around a symbolic hub of power (e.g., a government building), the march is designed to attract attention to the cause among neutral bystanders. Again, operationalizations of effectiveness that focus on influencing outgroups would not necessarily detect the importance of this process in predicting intentions.

Another factor that underpinned non-members' intentions was the extent to which the rally was effective in expressing their values. As has been pointed out by some attitude theorists (e.g., Anderson & Kristiansen, 1990; Herek, 1987; Katz, 1960), attitudes have an expressive function in that they act as a marker of group membership and/or personal values. When attitudes are expressed publicly, they might be especially nourishing in terms of defining who you are and what you stand for (Hornsey et al., 2003; Tice, 1992). Furthermore, when values are expressed en masse, it provides a voice for many people who otherwise might feel voiceless, and this might in itself be rewarding regardless of whether or not the voice influences others. To a degree, then, protestors are positioning themselves not just as *opponents* of the government, but also as *opposites*, providing a symbolic counterpoint to the status quo. Consistent with this notion, non-members reported stronger intentions to engage in future collective action the more effective the rally was seen to be in expressing their values, and this effect emerged over and above perceptions of influence.

One possible reason why our effects were moderated by group membership is that members and non-members have different psychological orientations when it comes to collective action. It could be that members are more focused on group agency than are non-members, and so judge effectiveness more in intragroup terms. Having already internalized the value of, and desire for, organized resistance, it is perhaps not surprising that members should view building an oppositional movement as a particularly powerful criterion for success. In contrast, it could be that non-members have less of a group orientation, leading them to focus more on broader societal concerns (e.g., influencing third parties) and individual concerns (e.g., value expression). It is important, however, not to automatically assume that this is explaining the observed pattern of results. An alternative explanation is that members of organized groups expect to engage in collective action over multiple future events and accordingly may be more focused on the long term effectiveness of the rally in building an oppositional movement. In contrast, unaligned individuals drawn to the rally (non-members) might be less mindful of the long term nature of intergroup struggle and so might be drawn to more immediate considerations such as influencing third parties or expressing values as key criteria for effectiveness. Further research and theory building is required to uncover the psychological underpinnings of why members and non-members appear to focus on different dimensions of effectiveness when determining future intentions.

It should be noted that, consistent with previous work (Kelly & Breinlinger, 1995b; Simon et al., 1998; Sturmer et al., 2003; Sturmer, & Simon, 2004), identification as an activist was by far the most powerful predictor of intentions. In line with the social identity perspective, this suggests that self-categorization processes and identity issues have a profound effect on people's behavioral expectations of themselves. But, unlike many previous studies (Kelly & Breinlinger, 1995b; Sturmer et al., 2003; Sturmer, & Simon, 2004), the effects of activist identification did not erase other more instrumental concerns regarding effectiveness. There is no support, then, for the notion that activists respond automatically to a behavioural script without reference to "rational" considerations; rather, it seems that identity considerations and effectiveness considerations contribute independently and uniquely to people's willingness to engage in collective action. Although this project was not designed as an explicit test of Simon and colleagues' dual pathway model of collective action (Simon et al., 1998), it is clear that the results provide support for this model.

On an applied level, the current data have implications for those attempting to recruit participants in collective action. Specifically, it suggests that organizers of collective action might benefit from tailoring their campaigns to suit their target audience. When recruiting from members of organized groups, organizers might be best advised to attend to the utility of the action in building an oppositional movement ("From little things big things grow"). When attempting to recruit from those who are not members of organized groups, organizers might attend to different outcomes such as influencing the general public ("send a message to all Australians") or expressing values ("have your say"). According to our data, attempts to recruit participants by focusing exclusively on influencing opposition groups ("Stop war"; "Ban nuclear weapons") might be less strategically effective in terms of attracting participants to collective action.

As in any study conducted in the field, however, a degree of common sense and caution should be exercised when attempting to generalize results from this study into other contexts. One notable feature of the rally in this study is that its themes – social justice and anti-globalization – were relatively diffuse and embraced a range of disparate issues. In these circumstances, it is possible that people would have been particularly attentive to whether the rally was effective in coalescing individual protestors into a coherent oppositional movement. If the collective action was engaged in by a group that already had well defined boundaries and was guided by a tight set of unifying principles, or was being conducted by a single organization, then the perceived utility of the action in terms of rallying internal support and building an oppositional movement might be less predictive of future intentions. Furthermore, the themes of the rally under investigation were so ambitious that it might not make much sense to think of effectiveness in terms of immediate influence over policy makers. In this case, we might see more of a focus on long-term goals (e.g., building an oppositional movement) or symbolic processes (e.g., expressing values) than if the goal of collective action was in immediate reach. If the collective action focused on a specific, concrete, and achievable aim (e.g., protesting against the building of a highway, or campaigning for a pay rise) then non-material benefits such as expression of values might become less important—and less predictive of intentions—than more immediate considerations such as whether the collective action would be effective in influencing the relevant outgroup.

This study carries with it some methodological limitations necessitated by the field context in which the research was conducted. For example, although protestors in the rally were approached at random, we have no way of knowing whether the respondents were representative of the broader population of protestors. Another limitation is that the measures of effectiveness were obtained using single items. Although this is not ideal, it should be noted that this limitation should have the effect of providing weaker support for the role of effectiveness relative to the multi-item measure of activist identification than one might expect if more sophisticated measurements were used. We acknowledge, however, that the relationship between indices of effectiveness and protest intentions reported here might fluctuate depending on how the relevant perceptions are operationalized. It can be argued that this is particularly the case with the "expressing values" item. Although this item was designed to refer to the expression of personal values – and thus was assumed to be acting in the service of an individual, intrapsychic need for self-expression - it is possible that the item could have been interpreted by some as referring to collective values. In future, it would be beneficial to see if the current findings can be replicated with less ambiguous multi-item scales. Finally, we acknowledge that although one's intention to engage in collective action represents a predictor of behavior, it is not a proxy for behavior. Future research is required to demonstrate that the role of effectiveness in predicting intentions translates into concrete action.

We also acknowledge that the dimensions of effectiveness described above are not exhaustive of the needs or goals that might be fulfilled by political protest and/or social movement participation. There may be other motivations that have yet to be discussed, including gaining social support and developing a sense of meaning. Theorizing about the definition of effectiveness in collective action is still in its infancy, and so we view this paper as a stimulus for further questioning and theorizing rather than a definitive summary.

Despite these limitations, the current data suggest that researchers can benefit from revisiting the role of effectiveness in explaining why people do or do not engage in collective action. With the literature increasingly emphasising the role of identity processes in collective action, the current data uncover rational bases for collective action that until now have been overlooked. By broadening our conceptualization of what criteria people use to judge effectiveness, it is hoped that fresh insights can be gained into what drives people to engage in collective action, even when the hopes of influencing key decision makers appear forlorn.

Note

1. Our argument here is analogous to work on the multiple functions of group membership (e.g., Deaux, Reid, Mizrahi, & Cotting, 1999), which argues that identification with groups not only serves a self-esteem function via intergroup comparisons, but also fulfils a range of other motivations, some of which are intragroup in nature.

References

Abramson, P. R., & Aldrich, J. H. (1982). The decline of electoral participation in America. *American Political Science Review, 76*, 502–521.

Aiken, L. S., & West, S. G. (1991). *Multiple regression: Testing and interpreting interactions.* London, UK: Sage Publications.

Anderson, D. S., & Kristiansen, C. M. (1990). Measuring attitude functions. *The Journal of Social Psychology, 130*, 419–421.

Berman, S. L., & Wittig, M. A. (2004). An intergroup theories approach to direct political action among African Americans. *Group Processes & Intergroup Relations, 7*, 19–34.

Brunsting, S., & Postmes, T. (2002). Social movement participation in the digital age: Predicting offline and online collective action. *Small Group Research, 33*, 525–554.

Bynner, J., & Ashford, S. (1994). Politics and participation: Some antecedents of young people's attitudes to the political system and political activity. *European Journal of Social Psychology, 24*, 223–236.

Deaux, K., Reid, A., Mizrahi, K., & Cotting, D. (1999). Connecting the person to the social: The functions of social identification. In T. R. Tyler, R. M. Kramer, & O. P. John (Eds.), *The psychology of the social self* (pp. 91–113). Mahwah, NJ: Lawrence Erlbaum.

Flood, P. (1993). An expectancy value analysis of the willingness to attend union meetings. *Journal of Occupational and Organizational Psychology, 66*, 213–223.

Folger, R. (1977). Distributive and procedural justice: Combined impact of voice and improvement on experienced inequity. *Journal of Personality and Social Psychology, 35*, 108–119.

Fox, D. L., & Schofield, J. W. (1989). Issue salience, perceived efficacy and perceived risk: A study of the origins of antinuclear war activity. *Journal of Applied Social Psychology, 19*, 805–827.

Hamilton, S. B., Knox, T. A., Keilin, W. G., & Chavez, E. L. (1987). In the eye of the beholder: Accounting for variability in attitudes and cognitive/affective reactions toward the threat of nuclear war. *Journal of Applied Social Psychology, 17*, 927–952.

Herek, G. M. (1987). Can functions be measured? A new perspective on the functional approach to attitudes. *Social Psychology Quarterly, 4*, 285–303.

Hogg, M. A., & Abrams, D. (1988). *Social identification: A social psychology of intergroup relations and group processes.* New York: Routledge.

Hornsey, M. J., Blackwood, L., & O'Brien, A. (in press). Speaking for others: The pros and cons of group advocates using collective language. *Group Processes & Intergroup Relations.*

Hornsey, M. J., Majkut, L., Terry, D. J., & McKimmie, B. M. (2003). On being loud and proud: Non-conformity and counter-conformity to group norms. British *Journal of Social Psychology, 42*, 319–335.

Katz, D. (1960). The functional approach to the study of attitudes. *Public Opinion Quarterly, 24*, 163–204.

Kelly, C., & Breinlinger, S. (1995a). Attitudes, intentions, and behavior: A study of women's participation in collective action. *Journal of Applied Social Psychology, 25*, 1430–1445.

Kelly, C., & Breinlinger, S. (1995b). Identity and injustice: Exploring women's participation in collective action. *Journal of Community and Applied Social Psychology, 5*, 41–57.

Kinder, D. R. (1998). Opinion and action in the realm of politics. In D. T. Gilbert, S. T. Fiske, and G. Lindzey (Eds.) The handbook of social psychology (4th ed., Vol. 2, pp. 778–867). New York: Oxford University Press.

Klandermans, B. (1984). Mobilization and participation: Social-psychological expansions of resource mobilization theory. *American Sociological Review, 49*, 583–600.

Klandermans, B. (1997). *The social psychology of protest*. Oxford, UK: Basil Blackwell.

Klandermans, B. (2002). How group identification helps to overcome the dilemma of collective action. *American Behavioral Scientist, 45*, 887–900.

Klandermans, B., & Oegema, D. (1987). Potentials, networks, motivations, and barriers: Steps towards participation in social movements. *American Sociological Review, 52*, 519–531.

Lalonde, R. N., & Cameron, J. E. (1994). Behavioral responses to discrimination: A focus on action. In M. P. Zanna & J. M. Olson (Eds.), *The psychology of prejudice: The Ontario symposium, Vol. 7* (pp. 257–288). Hillsdale, NJ: Lawrence Erlbaum.

Lalonde, R. N., & Silverman, R. A. (1994). Behavioral preferences in response to social injustice: The effects of group permeability and social identity salience. *Journal of Personality and Social Psychology, 66*, 78–85.

Lind, E. A., Kanfer, R., & Earley, P. C. (1990). Voice, control, and procedural justice: Instrumental and noninstrumental concerns in fairness judgments. *Journal of Personality and Social Psychology, 59*, 952–959.

Lind, E. A., & Tyler, T. R. (1988). *The social psychology of procedural justice*. NY: Plenum.

Locatelli, M. G., & Holt, R. R. (1986). Antinuclear activism, psychic numbing, and mental health. *International Journal of Mental Health, 15*, 143–161.

Olson, M. (1968). *The logic of collective action: Public goods and the theory of groups*. Cambridge, MA: Harvard University Press.

Polletta, F., & Jasper, J. M. (2001). Collective identity and social movements. *Annual Review of Sociology, 27*, 283–305.

Protest march for peace. (2001, October 7). *The Sunday Mail*, p. 15.

Reicher, S., & Hopkins, N. (1996). Seeking influence through characterizing self-categories: An analysis of anti-abortionist rhetoric. *British Journal of Social Psychology, 35*, 297–311.

Schofield, J. W., & Pavelchak, M. A. (1989). Fallout from The Day After: The impact of a TV film on attitudes related to nuclear war. *Journal of Applied Social Psychology, 19*, 433–448.

Simon, B., & Klandermans, B. (2001). Politicized collective identity: A social psychological analysis. *American Psychologist, 56*, 319–331.

Simon, B., Loewy, M., Sturmer, S., Weber, U., Freytag, P., Habig, C., Kampmeier, C., & Spahlinger, P. (1998). Collective identification and social movement participation. *Journal of Personality and Social Psychology, 74*, 646–658.

Sturmer, S., & Simon, B. (2004). The role of collective identification in social movement participations: A panel study in the context of the German gay movement. *Personality and Social Psychology Bulletin, 30*, 263–277.

Sturmer, S., Simon, B., Loewy, M., & Jorger, H. (2003). The dual-pathway model of social movement participation: The case of the fat acceptance movement. *Social Psychology Quarterly, 66*, 71–82.

Tajfel, H. (Ed.). (1978). *Differentiation between social groups: Studies in the social psychology of intergroup relations*. London, UK: Academic Press.

Tajfel, H., & Turner, J. C. (1979). An intergrative theory of intergroup conflict. In W. G. Austin & S. Worchel (Eds.), *The social psychology of intergroup relations* (pp. 33–48). Monterey, CA: Brooks/Cole.

Tice, D. M. (1992). Self-concept change and self-presentation: The looking glass self is also a magnifying glass. *Journal of Personality and Social Psychology, 63*, 435–451.

Tyler, T. R., & McGraw, K. M. (1983). The threat of nuclear war: Risk interpretation and behavioural response. *Journal of Social Issues, 39*, 25–40.

Veenstra, K., & Haslam, S. A. (2000). Willingness to participate in industrial protest: Exploring social identification in context. British *Journal of Social Psychology, 39*, 153–172.

Verba, S., & Nie, H. N. (1972). *Participation in America: Political democracy and social equality*. NY: Harper & Row.

Wolf, S., Gregory, W. L., & Stephan, W. G. (1986). Protection motivation theory: Prediction of intentions to engage in anti-nuclear war behaviours. *Journal of Applied Social Psychology, 16*, 310–321.

Wright, S. C., & Taylor, D. M. (1998). Responding to Tokenism: Individual action in the face of collective injustice. *European Journal of Social Psychology, 28*, 647–667.

Wright, S. C., Taylor, D. M., & Moghaddam, F. M. (1990). Responding to membership in a disadvantaged group: From acceptance to collective protest. *Journal of Personality and Social Psychology, 58*, 994–1003.

Technology and Collective Action: The Effect of Cell Phone Coverage on Political Violence in Africa

Jan H. Pierskalla[1] *Florian M. Hollenbach*[2]

The spread of cell phone technology across Africa has transforming effects on the economic and political sphere of the continent. In this paper, we investigate the impact of cell phone technology on violent collective action. We contend that the availability of cell phones as a communication technology allows political groups to overcome collective action problems more easily and improve in-group cooperation, and coordination. Utilizing novel, spatially disaggregated data on cell phone coverage and the location of organized violent events in Africa, we are able to show that the availability of cell phone coverage significantly and substantially increases the probability of violent conflict. Our findings hold across numerous different model specifications and robustness checks, including cross-sectional models, instrumental variable techniques, and panel data methods.

The mobile industry changed Africa. I must admit we were not smart enough to foresee that. What we saw was a real need for telecommunication in Africa, and that need had not been fulfilled. For me that was a business project." Mo Ibrahim, as quoted by Livingston (2011, 10).

This quote from Mo Ibrahim, a Sudanese-born cell phone magnate, exemplifies the increasing influence new media technologies have in Africa. During the recent events of the Arab Spring, cell phones and other new

media technologies have worked as catalysts for political collective action (Aday *et al.* 2012; Breuer, Landman, and Farquhar 2012). While many commentators describe the effect of modern communication technologies on political action, social scientific research is only slowly catching up (but see, for example, Aday *et al.* 2012; Breuer, Landman, and Farquhar 2012; Shirky 2008). In this article we ask whether modern communication technology has affected political collective action in Africa. Specifically we ask if the rapid spread of cell phone technology has increased *organized* and *violent* forms of collective action.

We focus on the connection between communication technology and violent, organized forms of collective action for several reasons. While scholars in economics and other fields have been concerned with the beneficial effects of cell phones for various development outcomes (Abraham 2007; Aker 2010; Aker, Ksoll, and Lybbert 2012; Aker and Mbiti 2010), the implications of increased cell phone communication are much less clear when it comes to politics.[1] The existing discussion in political science on new media and collective action is rather qualitative and lacks a specific focus on cell phones and their relationship to political violence.[2] Much of this literature stresses the possible positive effects of new media and technology for democracy, transparency, and accountability. While the quick and cheap spread of communication technology can improve political accountability through various mechanisms, private

[1] Jan H. Pierskalla is a Postdoctoral Fellow, German Institute of Global and Area Studies (GIGA), FSP 2, Neuer Jungfernstieg 21, 20354 Hamburg, Germany (jan.pierskalla@giga-hamburg.de).

[2] Florian M. Hollenbach is a Ph.D. candidate, Department of Political Science, Duke University, Perkins Library 326, Box 90204, Durham NC 27708, USA (florian.hollenbach@duke.edu).

Authors' names are listed in reverse alphabetical order; equal authorship is implied. This project was in part funded by the Program for the Study of Democracy, Institutions and Political Economy (DIPE) at Duke University. We thank Andreas Forø Tollefsen and colleagues for sharing the PRIO-GRID dataset with us. The availability of these data made life much easier on us. We are very grateful for comments and criticisms from four anonymous reviewers, the editors of the APSR, Cassy Dorff, Vincent Gawronski, Evan Lieberman, Nils W. Metternich, Brittany N. Perry, Audrey Sacks, Michael D. Ward, Erik Wibbels, and William Wittels. Their comments and suggestions helped to substantially improve our research and this paper. A previous version of this paper was presented at MPSA 2012 in Chicago. All remaining errors are our own. Data and replication files are available on the authors' dataverse subject to dissemination restrictions by the GSMA.

communication technology (and cell phones specifically) may also facilitate organized violence.

The vast literature on civil conflict onset and duration has explored structural determinants such as economic development, growth shocks, natural resources, elections, ethnic diversity, and political exclusion (see, for example, Cederman, Weidmann, and Gleditsch 2011; Collier and Hoeffler 2007; Collier et al. 2003; Fearon, Kasar, and Laitin 2007; Fearon and Laitin 2003; Metternich 2011; Ross 2006; Sambanis 2002; Weidmann 2009; Wucherpfennig et al. 2012). A smaller, but growing, body of research has investigated important factors at the individual and group level (Blattman 2009; Weinstein 2007; Wood 2003). On the other hand, little explicit attention has been given to the role of technology in facilitating violence. While some recent studies analyze the potential effects of mass media, like television and radio broadcasting (Warren 2013; Yanagizawa-Drott 2012), hardly any empirical research deals with individual-to-individual communication.[3]

We argue that private, mobile long-distance communication addresses crucial free-rider and coordination problems endemic to insurgent activity. Similar to other organizational technologies (Weinstein 2007), cell phones facilitate in-group organization and the implementation of insurgent activity against the greater power of the state. Given the motivation and opportunity for political violence through structural context conditions, cell phone coverage, *ceteris paribus*, should then increase the likelihood of violent collective action.

To test this proposition we use highly spatially disaggregated data on cell phone coverage and violent conflict in Africa. Today, Africa is the largest growing cell phone market in the world, with yearly growth rates of around 20% and an estimated 732 million subscribers in 2012 (The Economist 2012). What makes Africa special in this context is that cell phones not only provide a new way for communication, but in many areas are the only way for interpersonal, direct communication over distance. Many areas that are now covered by cell phone networks were never connected to land lines. At the same time, Africa is host to a large number of active or simmering civil conflicts (The World Bank 2011), often in areas with newly expanded access to cell phone technology. This directly poses the question: how does the introduction of easy interpersonal communication affect the incidence of organized violence on the continent?

We match proprietary data from the GSM Association (GSMA), an interest group of cell phone providers, on the spatial extent of GSM2 network coverage on the African continent and conflict events from the UCDP Georeferenced Event Dataset (Melander and Sundberg 2011; Sundberg, Lindgren, and Padskocimaite 2011) to

a lattice of 55 km × 55 km grid cells in Africa (PRIO-GRID), created by the Peace Research Institute Oslo (PRIO) (Tollefsen, Strand, and Buhaug 2012).

We then implement three complementary estimation strategies to assess the potential effect of cell phone coverage on violent collective action. First, we exploit spatial variation in conflict and cell phone coverage by estimating a series of statistical models and adjusting for important covariates using cross-sectional data. Second, to safeguard against reverse causality and to improve the identification of a causal effect, we rely on an instrumental variable strategy. Prior research on the spread of cell phone technology in Africa has established the importance of regulatory quality and competitive private markets (Buys, Dasgupta, and Thomas 2009), which we use as an instrument for the extent of cell phone coverage. Third, we expand our analysis to a three-year panel of grid cells to exploit variation in cell phone coverage over time, controlling for any grid-level time-invariant factors.

We are able to document a clear positive and statistically significant effect of cell phone coverage on violent collective action across all three approaches. In other words, modern means of private long-distance communication not only have economic benefits, but also facilitate overcoming collective action and coordination problems in the political realm. Under specific structural context conditions this translates to more organized violence.

This finding carries meaningful implications for research on civil conflict and collective action more generally. Our research indicates the importance of technological shifts for organized violence and calls for further research on the role of modern communication technology for both enabling and curbing violence. Echoing the findings of research on civil society (Berman 1997), we find that improvements in the ability to organize collective action do not automatically produce purely beneficial effects for overall society. Rather they empower political agents and groups more generally, which can raise the human costs of political struggles.

Cell Phones and Collective Action

Given the breathtaking spread of cell phone technology worldwide and the particularly fast expansion on the African continent, citizens across many regimes have vastly improved means for private, direct, and immediate long-distance communication. The availability of cell phone technology and networks to citizens in some of the poorest regions in the world has been lauded as an important transformative force for economic development. In particular, the decrease in communication costs associated with the rising availability of cell phones has been linked to a boost in labor and consumer market efficiency (Abraham 2007; Aker 2010; Aker and Mbiti 2010). This research emphasizes the diminishing effect of cell phone technology on information asymmetries between market participants. For example, in the case of Indian fishers, cell phone technology allowed for the monitoring of prices in nearby markets without the need to personally attend the market, while also giving fishers access to sell goods to markets at further distances (Abraham 2007). Similar developments have been noted for agricultural markets in Africa (Aker 2010; Aker and Mbiti 2010). In addition, African entrepreneurs are developing ways in which cell phones can be used to increase market efficiencies and deliver services to customers.[4] The increasing availability of cell phone coverage has gone hand in hand with the use of mobile money and mobile banking (Donner and Tellez 2008). In fact, the development to make payments and transfers via mobile money instead of cash or credit cards has proliferated widely in Africa and lowers transaction costs for many market participants and citizens.[5]

Interestingly, in Africa, this digital revolution is largely driven by private entrepreneurs, which have built up an extensive wireless infrastructure in a matter of years, often independent of governments or government-funded infrastructure.[6] Private cell phone providers have increased coverage at a vastly faster rate than landline providers. Today many areas that had never been connected to landline communication networks are covered by cell phone networks (Africa Partnership Program 2008; The World Bank 2010). One of the advantages of cell phone networks is that the expansion is much costly in terms of infrastructure investments and thus a more decentralized expansion is possible.

Existing economics research provides evidence of lower transaction costs through the provision of cell phones. While much of this work has emphasized the positive effects of this new technology on economic outcomes, research on the direct effects of cell phones in the political sphere is not quite as common. However, Aker, Collier, and Vincente (2011) show that in the case of Mozambique, cell phones can be used for voter education and can increase political participation in elections, as well as demands for accountability. The major takeaway is that cell phone usage, the availability of hotlines to voters, and text messaging can have positive effects on the political information available to voters as well as their political participation. In a similar vein Bailard (2009), using country level analysis as well as provincial data for Namibia, finds that the use of cell phones by citizens can decrease corruption. She argues that cell phones change the information environment, as they decentralize and increase the spread of information. In addition,

the proliferation of cell phones increases the probability of detection of corrupt officials and thus alters "the cost-benefit calculus of corrupt behavior by strengthening oversight and punishment mechanisms" (Bailard 2009, 337). Evidence further suggests that, through text messaging services, cell phones have been used to inform citizens of government wrongdoings, monitor elections, or report violence in many African states (Diamond 2012, 11).

More generally, observers of current events have linked cell phone technology to collective action, in particular peaceful protest, producing a new "protest culture" (Lapper 2010). In the context of authoritarian regimes, examples of cell phones aiding the organization of protests around the world are abundant, ranging from China in 1999, where Falun Gong was able to stage a large protest in a secure government complex, to Manila, Philippines in 2001 (Philippine Daily Inquirer 2001), or Kiev, Ukraine during the Orange Revolution (Diamond 2012, 12).[7]

Yet, cell phone technology does not only affect collective action in authoritarian governments. Protesters in Madrid, Spain in 2004 were able to organize quickly using text messaging (Shirky 2008, 180). The increased organization capabilities of protesters have been noted by the police in the riots in London in the summer of 2011, as well as protests over G20 summits (Bradshaw 2009; Sherwood 2011).

The link between political behavior and cell phone usage is also borne out in survey data. The 2008 wave of the Afrobarometer public opinion survey includes a question on the usage of mobile phone technology and protest behavior (Mattes *et al.* 2010). A simple regression of the protest item on cell phone usage, controlling for a number of socioeconomic factors, reveals a positive and highly statistically significant effect, i.e., cell phone users are more likely to participate in protests.[8]

While these observations and emerging scholarship highlight the positive effects of cell phone technology for peaceful forms of collective action, we argue that cell phones have another important effect: improved communication through cell phones can facilitate organization and coordination of groups for the purpose of *violent* collective action.

In a recent working paper, Shapiro and Weidmann (2012) pose a similar question about the spread of cell phone coverage and political violence in Iraq. The authors start from a theoretically ambiguous point. On the one hand, they emphasize that the availability of cell phones could lead to increased violence as it strengthens the position of insurgents against the coalition forces. On the other hand, cell phones could allow for better insurgent surveillance by U.S. and Iraqi forces, as well as lower the cost of whistle blowing on terrorists for the local population. Using district level data and a difference-in-difference design, the authors find that the expansion of the cell phone network in Iraq is associated with decreases in successful violent attacks by insurgent forces. Shapiro and Weidmann (2012) contend that this is due to the extensive use of cell phone surveillance by U.S. and Iraqi anti-insurgent forces as well as successful whistle-blower programs. Similarly, in the African context, Livingston (2011) argues, that while cell phones might empower rebel groups and produce more violence, there also exists the potential for a reduction in violence through improved monitoring for international peacekeeping or governmental forces, although such efforts have been rare so far.

While improved monitoring and well-organized counterinsurgency activities can leverage cell phone coverage to increase the capacity of the state to uphold the monopoly of violence, it is unclear how easily this can be achieved in the African context. Furthermore, there exist strong theoretical considerations that suggest the marginal benefits of improved communication technology are substantial for insurgent groups.

Organizing violence is fraught with challenges. Successful insurgent activity requires solving various collective action and coordination problems (Kalyvas and Kocher 2007; Wood 2003), such as the free-riding problem (Olson 1965). This is particularly true when it comes to the organization of political violence, where participation is risky and benefits are often unclear (Shadmehr and Bernhardt 2011). Free riding within groups arises because members of insurgent groups have to endure the high costs of engaging in violence, but the potential payoffs for toppling the government will accrue to the wider population. Hence, rebel leaders have to ensure that group members actively contribute continuously throughout the conflict. Collective action problems also arise in the support network of rebel groups. Effective insurgencies rely strongly on the tacit support of the local population (Kalyvas 2006). Here, insurgents have to convince supporters to offer material support or valuable information from local residents, who themselves have an incentive to free ride.

In addition, insurgent groups suffer from strong coordination problems. Even if rebel groups can convince members to actively fight and the local population offers tacit support, military action needs to be carefully coordinated to be successful. Warfare against state forces with superior military technology, firepower, and training relies on careful plotting of attacks, appropriate timing, coordination of group movements in target areas, and managing the retreat to safe havens. While organizing protests is often about getting the right people together at the right time and place, insurgent violence requires

the coordinated interplay of independent groups across distant geographic locations and time.

Recent work on mass media and violence has shown preliminary evidence on how radio and television can facilitate or block civil violence (Warren 2013; Yanagizawa-Drott 2012). Warren (2013) shows a reduction in militarized challenges to the state, if mass media access is widespread across its territory. The "soft power" of mass media enables the government to dissuade insurgent collective action through dissemination of progovernment propaganda. Observers of propaganda radio in Africa have highlighted the potential dangers for ethnic strife and violence (Livingston 2011). Going beyond qualitative accounts, Yanagizawa-Drott (2012) uses data on radio access in Rwandan villages to document the effects of "hate radio" on killings between Hutu and Tutsi during the genocide. Here, the use of mass media by one conflict faction shifted public perception and facilitated violent collective action. Both arguments emphasize the role of mass media in creating shared beliefs about the enemy and the convergence of privately held information. This can facilitate or hinder collective action and coordination. The formal literature on information and coordination problems in collective action against the government has also emphasized the importance of public (potentially government controlled) and private signals (Edmond 2012; Shadmehr and Bernhardt 2011).

We contend that, in contrast to mass media, access to individual communication technology like cell phones can undermine the effects of government propaganda and, more importantly, play an integral part in overcoming other specific collective action and coordination problems inherent in insurgent violence. Through improved communication and monitoring, cell phone technology aids overcoming internal collective action problems, allows the distribution of information to tacit supporters in the wider population, and, on an operational level, allows for real-time coordination of insurgent activity.

Several organizational technologies can be used to improve cooperation among group members when dealing with the free-riding dilemma. Selective incentives and external punishment can be used effectively by rebel leaders to elicit support from rank-and-file insurgents and civilian supporters. At the same time, free-riding behavior can also be curbed through repeated interaction, increased communication, and improvement in the monitoring of group member's actions. The cheap availability of cell phones naturally improves and increases the communication between group members and allows for the tightening of group networks. The interaction between group members becomes more likely as the provision of cell phones makes long distance communication easier, especially in the context of rural insurgencies in which factions operate apart from each other for longer periods of time. The reduction of transaction costs resulting from the access to cell phone technology is especially valuable in many infrastructure-poor African regions, where this development makes personal long-distance communication possible for the first time. It is important to note that this does not require each individual to own a cell phone device, as cell phones can be shared collectively between group members or villagers.

Enlarging the communication network of rebel groups as well as increasing the rate of communication by group members should raise in-group trust between individual participants. The possibility for fast and easy communication boosts the propensity and rate of information sharing within groups, creating a shared awareness among group members. As Shirky (2008, 51) writes, collective action is critically dependent on group cohesion. The expansion of within-group communication is likely to foster shared beliefs and awareness of groups, thus providing one channel of easing collective action. The higher rate of communication between individual group members also makes the transmission of messages and instructions from group leaders through the decentralized network more likely and efficient. Furthermore, the increase in two-way communication vastly raises opportunities for monitoring each other's behavior. Rebel leaders can exert better control over their rank and file and their wider support network, thus limiting free-riding behavior.

On a more general level, the spread of personal communication technology to the general population aids the flow of information and the coordination of beliefs not only within the particular groups, but also in the population. In instances when public or corporate private news sources are unavailable or pro-regime, the increased possibility of cell phone communication can aid the distribution of news. Anecdotal evidence suggests that cell phone communication can be useful as a substitute to traditional media, where the press is suppressed.[9] Indeed, tipping-point models of protest and popular support (Kuran 1991; Lohmann 1994) suggest that if citizens are able to communicate their privately held beliefs about the regime, without fear of reprisal, public support for the regime can quickly transform into widespread opposition. The spread of cell phones makes the transmission of news to citizens throughout the country more likely. The support for insurgent activity can increase in the general population when news about government wrongdoings are communicated through citizen communication. For example, when news about indiscriminate killings by the government are more likely

to travel through the population via cell phones, the general population may adjust the calculus of participation in nonviolent protests or even insurgent groups (Kalyvas and Kocher 2007). Reportedly, cell phones have been used effectively by Syrian rebels to spread information on government atrocities and rebel victories, greatly aiding insurgency efforts (Peterson 2012). The ability to spread information about government violence against civilians or other forms of repression through private communication networks should thus improve the position of the insurgents within the population.

Apart from affecting a group's ability to address collective action problems, the distribution of cell phones aids the coordination of actions, especially during asymmetric insurgent warfare. On a basic level, it allows insurgent commanders to better plan and implement operations. As noted above, successful insurgent warfare against the state requires high levels of coordination. The availability of cell phones can aid violent groups in the planning and execution of operations. Reportedly, Charles Taylor successfully utilized mobile phone technology to coordinate and control his rebel commanders in Liberia's civil conflict (Reno 2011, 4). Similarly, while Shapiro and Weidmann (2012) find a negative effect of cell phone availability on violence in Iraq, other research suggests that insurgents were aware and made use of the advantages of cell phones. One simple indication is that cell phone towers, in contrast to other infrastructure, were spared from insurgent attacks (Brand 2007). In addition, the use of cell phones to communicate enemy movements, scouting, and other intelligence has been emphasized (Cordesman 2005; Leahy 2005). Stroher (2007) highlights the use of cell phones by Iraqi insurgents as an organizational tool, for the spread of information, as well as to provide propaganda to group members and the population.

This also indicates that the gain of cell phone technology by rebels can possibly close the technological gap between government troops and the rebel movement. Prior to the availability of cell phone communication to private citizens, it is likely that the government had a significant advantage when it comes to in-group communication and group coordination. This likely affects combat strategies as well as, indirectly, the probability of winning for each side. The availability of cell phones may thus decrease or close the size of this gap. Common conflict models assume technology as an important factor in determining the probability of winning of the fighting parties (Blattman and Miguel 2010; Grossman 1991). Increasing the probability of winning by insurgents or rebels in turn should make the onset of conflict more likely.

While modern communication technology can play an important role for peaceful collective action in the form of protests, the marginal benefit of coordination is likely to be larger for organized violence. Protest in dense urban environments already enjoys several advantages for information sharing, monitoring, and coordination. Urban environments often offer other tools and opportunities to spread information and long-distance communication is less important in cities. Rural insurgents, on the other hand, can derive large benefits from private, mobile long-distance communication outside of major population settlements.

Empirical Implications

Given the logic laid out above we believe that, overall, the ability to communicate, monitor, coordinate, and spread information through private cell phone networks should improve the ability of rebel groups to organize political violence. Hence we contend that *local cell phone coverage will increase the probability of an occurrence of political violence.* We will test this proposition in the empirical section.

DATA

Testing the above specified argument requires a sample of cases in which violent collective action can conceivably be influenced by cell phone technology, as well as spatially disaggregated data on conflict and cell phone coverage. Given these requirements, focusing on the African continent offers several advantages over other world regions. The African continent has been, and still is, a major hotspot for organized violent conflict (The World Bank 2011), yet also exhibits strong temporal and spatial variation thereof. At the same time, cell phone technology has proliferated at a rapid pace across the continent in the last 15 to 20 years (Buys, Dasgupta, and Thomas 2009), including to regions with characteristics that make them more prone to hosting violent events (e.g., aggrieved populations, poverty, difficult terrain, etc.). Often cell phones are the first long-distance communication device available in those areas. This confluence of factors creates an ideal environment to assess the impact of modern communication technology on facilitating violent collective action. Most other world regions lack such a high level of variance in conflict and access to cell phone technology. In addition, high-quality georeferenced data on conflict events is scarce for most regions of the world. Fortunately, recent years have seen an increase in the number of available conflict datasets that provide this type of information, in particular, for Africa.

For our primary analysis, we rely on the recently updated conflict data provided in the UCDP Georeferenced Event Dataset (UCDP GED) (Melander and Sundberg 2011; Sundberg, Lindgren, and Padskocimaite 2011). The UCDP GED includes yearly event data on *organized* violence in Africa from 1989 up to 2010. Violent events are included in the data if the conflict with which the event is associated has totaled 25 or more deaths and the event itself led to at least one death.[10] We use data on organized forms of violent collective action, instead of data on protests, for two reasons: First, our theoretical argument is geared specifically to the effects of cell phone communication technology on organized and violent forms of collective action. Second, quality and coverage of georeferenced data on organized violent collective action in Africa is higher than for other, more spontaneous and nonviolent forms of collective action.

Each event in the conflict dataset is specified to a location through longitude and latitude coordinates and by a date. We can use these data to map violent events across Africa for a number of years.[11]

Importantly, since the event data are based on news reports, one might expect the danger of measurement bias, as cell phone coverage may affect the probability of reporting of events. This is a valid concern, but we believe it is mitigated through several factors. For one, the UCDP coding team relies on a large number of print, radio, and television news reports from regional newswires, major and local newspapers, secondary sources, and expert knowledge, attempting to cover events even in remote locations without access to cell phone coverage. Furthermore, the focus on events with at least one death increases the likelihood of better event coverage in comparison to more low intensity events like peaceful protests or strikes.[12] A quality comparison of the UCDP-GED and ACLED data by Eck (2012) concludes that the UCDP data have higher quality and report often dramatically more events in rural or remote areas compared to ACLED. In addition, we also control for a number of other factors that would account for measurement bias in the event count in our empirical models, such as distance to the capital, local GDP per capita, or population size. Conditional on these factors, it is unlikely that cell phone coverage will be associated with any further over-reporting of events.[13]

Data on cell phone coverage are provided through *Collins Coverage* by *Harper Collins* Publishers. The data are made available by cell phone companies via the *GSMA* or *Collins Bartholomew.*[14] The availability and extent of coverage is represented via spatial polygons. We received data on GSM 2G network coverage for the first quarter of 2007, 2008, and 2009.[15] Our data only indicate the availability of cell phone services, not network traffic and usage by citizens. Information on usage is simply not available and without further information on the number

Figure 1 Cell Phone Coverage 2007 (black) and Conflict Locations 2008 (gray) in Africa. Africa – Conflict Locations in 2008 – Cell Coverage 2007.

of subscribers might also be misleading with regard to the role of cell phone communication for collective action in the wider population. As noted above, the argument does not require the ownership of cell phones by each individual, as phones can be shared within groups and villages. More importantly, we believe assessing the effect of coverage is more relevant from a policy perspective. While individual use of cell phones is hard to measure and control, coverage is the first and most important step in extending access of cell phone technology to the wider population.

Figure 1 shows the distribution of conflictual events in Africa in 2008, as well as areas with available GSM 2G coverage in 2007. As one can easily see, cell phone coverage is most widely spread in South Africa, Namibia, Kenya, as well as in northern Africa (specifically Morocco, Tunisia, and Egypt). However, coverage has expanded massively in the past years and has become more and more available in other areas of the continent. While coverage is more likely in coastal areas, the map clearly shows that it has been expanded further into the continent and away from population centers. Areas with a clear overlap in cell coverage and conflict events are in Algeria, the DRC, Kenya, Nigeria, Uganda, and Zimbabwe.

To analyze the relationship between the local availability of cell phone coverage and the occurrence of violent events we follow Buhaug and Rød (2006) in relying on spatially disaggregated grid cells as our units of analysis. Our grid is partitioned into 0.5 × 0.5 decimal degree resolution cells, i.e., each grid cell is approximately 55 km × 55 km large. Using such high-resolution spatial units of

analysis allows us to avoid problems of data aggregation common in cross-national studies of violence. The grid was created by Tollefsen, Strand, and Buhaug (2012) at the Peace Research Institute Oslo (PRIO). The PRIO-Grid dataset provides grid cells and data for the whole world on a yearly basis from 1946 to 2008. Given our particular interest, we only use the data concerning Africa.

Using the grid provided in the PRIO-Grid dataset we create our dependent variables based on conflict locations in the UCDP GED dataset (Melander and Sundberg 2011; Sundberg, Lindgren, and Padskocimaite 2011). First, we generate a conflict indicator, a binary variable that takes the value of 1 in cases where one or more conflictual events were registered by UCDP GED in the given grid cell in 2008, and 0 otherwise. Our dataset consists of 10,674 cells, of which 3.3% experience violent conflict in 2008, thus conflict is quite rare. Second, for additional robustness checks we create a conflict count variable that counts the number of conflictual events in 2008 according to the UCDP GED data for each grid cell. Despite the increase in variation between grid cells, we use the count measure only as a secondary variable, because multiple counts within each grid-cell year are likely to be realizations of the same conflict process.

Our main independent variable of interest is generated in a similar manner. For each grid cell an indicator for cell phone coverage is created that takes the value of 1 if cell phone coverage existed in 2007 and 0 otherwise.[16] The distributions of cell phone coverage in 2007 and conflict locations in 2008 are presented in Figure 1. In

2007, cell phone coverage was available in 37% of grid cells; in 2008 this increased to 38%.

To identify a potential causal effect of cell phone coverage on violent conflict events we rely on three complementary strategies: First, we use a series of standard models on the cross-sectional data for 2008 and control for a number of potential confounding factors to approximate the potential causal effect of cell phone coverage. Second, we take the same cross-sectional data and implement an instrumental variable strategy that leverages exogenous variation in our main independent variable. Third, we use conflict data and lagged cell phone coverage for 2008, 2009, and 2010 to construct a short panel for African grid cells and implement a set of panel data approaches that exploit over-time variation.

Confounding Variables

A large literature on civil conflict has identified a collection of theoretically motivated factors that contribute to organized violence. It will be important to understand the effects of cell phone coverage in a context that provides motive and opportunity for violent collective action (Collier et al. 2003). The existing literature has emphasized structural factors that affect the motivation of parties potentially seeking violent conflict with the state, such as poverty, inequality, ethnic fractionalization, or ethnic exclusion. At the same time, other factors, for example mountainous terrain, forests, or natural resources, can impact the ability of groups to rebel and have also been identified as drivers of violence. For our first set of cross-sectional models it will be particularly important to control for other variables that contribute to conflict. It is reasonable that those variables which drive conflict are also likely to correlate with the availability of cell phone coverage and might thus induce omitted variable bias in our findings. The majority of control variables in our models are also provided in the PRIO-Grid dataset, but originally come from other sources. Time varying independent variables were lagged by one year (2007) to control for the possibility of reverse causality.

Our models include a measure of the distance to the capital as well as distance to the border for each grid cell, as certain conflicts are more likely to occur close to the capital or close to other countries (Buhaug and Rød 2006).[17] Similarly, conflict is more likely to occur in regions with larger populations (Fearon and Laitin 2003). Hence, an estimate of population size for each grid cell is included. These variables are particularly important since cell phone providers are most likely to build infrastructure around the capital and population centers. The data on capital and border distance are provided through the PRIO Grid, as are the population data, which originally

stem from CIESIN (2005).[18] We also include a variable measuring prior conflict levels for each grid cell, based on UCDP conflict events in each grid cell from 1989 to 2000.

In addition, we include controls for the percent of mountainous terrain, as this may be advantageous to guerrilla warfare and thus may make fighting more likely. It may also affect the likelihood of coverage availability.[19] This variable was originally collected by the UN Environment Programme (UNEP-WCMC World Conservation Monitoring Centre 2002), but is available in the PRIO GRID. In addition, we control for the percent of area in a grid cell that is equipped for irrigation.[20] This variable is again provided in the PRIO-Grid dataset, but was originally collected by Siebert et al. (2007).

Violent conflict is often thought to be more likely in poorer regions, where the substitution costs for engaging in violence are particularly low and grievances with the current government are high (Blattman and Miguel 2010; Collier and Hoeffler 2004; Fearon and Laitin 2003). Cell phone coverage, on the other hand, is more likely in richer areas of the continent. Thus controlling for income is highly warranted. Economic data are provided in the PRIO-Grid dataset as well, and originally stem from the G-Econ dataset by Nordhaus (2006). We use per capita GDP for 2000 calculated for each grid cell.[21]

For further robustness checks we control for potential ethnic grievances by including a variable on the exclusion of ethnicities. To do so we match data on the identity of ethnic groups in each grid cell with data on the political exclusion of ethnic groups in a given country, recording how many local ethnic groups are politically excluded. The spatial data on settlement patterns of ethnic groups originally stems from Weidmann, Rød, and Cederman (2010) and were merged with data on political exclusion by Cederman, Wimmer, and Min (2010).

Furthermore, we include data on the location of natural resources. This may be warranted as cell phone companies are likely to extend coverage to areas with important economic activity. In addition, as rebel groups try to capture natural resources, fighting in these areas is also more likely. We therefore include indicators for the location of diamond mines (Gilmore et al. 2005) as well as known gas and oil deposits (Lujala, Rød, and Thieme 2007). Summary statistics for all variables are included in the online Appendix.

Cross-Sectional Analysis

Using the data described in the prior section, we estimate a series of cross-sectional statistical models to evaluate our hypothesis. The main measure of conflict we use is the simple binary conflict indicator for each grid cell. Naturally, we utilize the generalized linear model framework to formulate our probability models. The dependent variable y_i for each grid cell i in 2008 is binary,

$$y_i = \begin{cases} 1 & \text{conflict,} \\ 0 & \text{otherwise,} \end{cases}$$

and is modeled as a binomial process. We link the response variable to observed covariates via a standard link function (i.e., logit) to the linear predictor η: $P(Y=y\,|\,X) = \mu = g(\eta)$. The linear predictor in turn is a function of control variables and our cell phone coverage indicator:

$$\eta_i = \mathbf{x}_i'\beta + c_i'\gamma,$$

where x_i is a vector of control variables and the intercept and C_i is the indicator of cell phone coverage. The parameter γ measures the impact of improved communication technology on violent collective action.

We consider five alternative estimation approaches. Each of these models has certain advantages and disadvantages. They address distinct issues present in our data and differ in the severity of assumptions needed to attribute causal effects to the estimated cell phone coverage parameter. Table 1 shows parameter estimates and z statistics for all models. The first column shows a baseline specification of only control variables, estimated with a standard logit model and robust standard errors to address issues of heteroskedasticity. The second column

Table 1   Binary DV Models

	Logit, Robust SE	Logit, Robust SE	Re-Logit, Robust SE	Mixed Effects Logit	Mixed Effects Logit	Fixed Effects OLS, Robust SE
(Intercept)	−3.814***	−4.020***	−4.020***	−4.020***	−3.340***	−0.014†
	(−20.178)	(−21.449)	(−21.422)	(−21.652)	(−16.490)	(−1.649)
Pre-2000 Conflict	0.020†	0.019†	0.019†	0.019***	0.021***	0.002**
	(1.861)	(1.850)	(1.834)	(5.680)	(6.192)	(3.040)
Border Distance	0.000	0.000	0.000	0.000	−0.000	−0.000**
	(0.450)	(0.884)	(0.922)	(0.941)	(−0.416)	(−2.701)
Capital Distance	0.000	0.000*	0.000*	0.000*	0.000	−0.000
	(1.629)	(2.264)	(2.270)	(2.327)	(1.604)	(−0.014)
Population	0.000*	0.000**	0.000**	0.000***	0.000***	0.000*
	(2.482)	(2.733)	(2.611)	(4.510)	(4.776)	(2.545)
Pct Mountainous	1.641***	1.578***	1.578***	1.578***	1.698***	0.056***
	(8.518)	(8.410)	(8.413)	(8.391)	(8.793)	(5.305)
Pct Irrigation	−0.027†	−0.031†	−0.031†	−0.031†	−0.046*	−0.001***
	(−1.663)	(−1.851)	(−1.651)	(−1.834)	(−2.456)	(−3.558)
GDP pc	−0.000***	−0.000***	−0.000***	−0.000***	−0.000***	−0.000
	(−3.589)	(−3.915)	(−3.881)	(−5.590)	(−3.924)	(−0.404)
Cell Phone Coverage		0.390**	0.390**	0.390**	1.112***	0.027***
		(2.798)	(2.798)	(2.836)	(7.319)	(5.824)
Mean Cell Coverage					−2.806***	
					(−8.505)	
Country Fixed Effects	**No**	**No**	**No**	**No**	**No**	**Yes**
AIC	2269.560	2263.781	2263.781	2222.052	2147.475	−7590.326
BIC	2326.699	2328.063	2328.063	2293.476	2226.041	−7211.780
Deviance	2253.560	2245.781	2245.781	2202.052	2125.475	240.027
Log-likelihood	−1126.780	−1122.891	−1122.891	−1101.026	−1062.737	3848.163
N	9343	9343	9343	9343	9343	9343

†$p = 0.1$. *$p = 0.05$. **$p = 0.01$. ***$p = 0.001$.

simply adds our cell phone coverage indicator as a covariate. The third column presents the results of a rare-events logistic regression to account for rare events bias (Tomz, King, and Zeng 2003). The fourth logit model includes country-level random effects to vary baseline levels of conflict across countries.[22] The standard random intercept model assumes zero correlation between the random effects and other covariates. To further control for potential omitted variable bias, we present in column 5 the results for a mixed effects logit model that also includes the country-level means of the cell phone coverage indicator. Including the country-level mean of the variable of interest allows for a correlation between the country random effect and the mean level of cell phone coverage (Gelman and Hill 2008, 506), removing the effects of country-level unobservables that affect cell phone coverage (Bell and Jones 2012). Last, we also include the estimates of a linear probability model estimated via OLS that allows the inclusion of country-level fixed effects to control for any unobserved time-invariant country characteristics that might bias our findings.[23]

The baseline specification in column 1 shows that a number of our control variables perform as expected. Prior levels of conflict have a statistically significant and positive effect on experiencing a conflict event in 2008. Similarly, population counts in the grid cell and mountainous terrain also increase the probability of conflict. On the other hand, in line with theoretical expectations and prior empirical findings the percentage of land with irrigation technology and GDP per capita reduce conflict (Buhaug and Rød 2006; Lujala, Buhaug, and Gates 2009; Buhaug *et al.* 2011; Fearon and Laitin 2003).

Across all models which include our measure of cell phone coverage, the cell phone coverage indicator is estimated to increase the probability of conflict and is precisely estimated—statistically significant below the 1% or even the 0.1% level. Even when controlling for the country level of cell phone coverage and only exploiting

within country variation, as in the mixed effects logit model, or including country fixed effects, we always find a clear positive effect. Given that we control for a sizable number of confounding variables, as well as unobserved country-level factors, the results in Table 1 offer a good first approximation of the effect of cell phone coverage on political violence. In addition, including the cell phone coverage variable improves model fit statistics. A likelihood ratio test between a model including cell phone coverage and the nested model results in a significant test statistic at the 1% level in favor of the model including our variable of interest. We implement further analyses of the model fit, amongst others using separation plots (Greenhill, Ward, and Sacks 2011); these are displayed in the online Appendix.

Substantive Effects

Before implementing further robustness checks, we evaluate the substantive effects of cell phone coverage. To evaluate the impact of access to cell phone technology we simulate first differences of predicted probabilities for the cell phone coverage indicator, setting all control variables at their respective means (King, Tomz, and Wittenberg 2000). Figure 2 plots the mean effects and 95% confidence intervals for each model. The baseline probability of conflict in a grid cell with all variables at their means, but with no cell phone coverage, is approximately 1%. A grid cell with the same configuration of control variables, but with access to cell phone coverage is expected to see an increase of roughly 0.5 percentage points. The estimated effect is even larger (one to three percentage points) in the models where we control for the mean level of coverage or include country fixed effects. Thus, holding everything constant and extending cell phone coverage to a grid cell is estimated to increase the probability of a conflict event occurring by 50% for the standard logit model and up to nearly 300% for the fixed effects model.

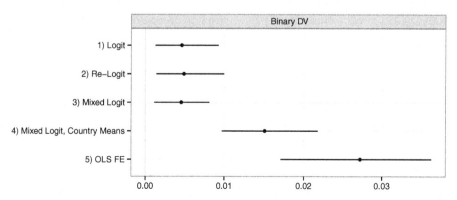

Figure 2 First Differences, With and Without Cell Phone Coverage, Binary Dependent Variable, Baseline $P(Y = 1|X) \approx 0.01$.

These results imply that cell phone coverage facilitates violent collective action. Whereas the probability of conflict is still very low, the marginal effect of cell phone provision holding all other variables constant is quite large. Compared to the baseline probability with no cell phone coverage, areas with cell phones are much more likely to experience violent events. This indicates that in areas with structural conditions that favor violence, cell phone coverage enables groups to overcome their collective action and coordination problems more easily, which translates to more organized conflict events.

Spatial Dependence

A common problem in the analysis of conflict, especially when using highly spatially disaggregated data, is spatial dependence between units of observation. The plot of conflict events in Figure 1 clearly shows a spatial clustering that suggests issues of nonindependence, i.e., a conflict event in one grid cell might increase the probability of a conflict event in a neighboring cell. Recently, the analysis of spatial dependence in comparative politics and international relations has gained increased attention (Beck, Gleditsch, and Beardsley 2006; Franzese and Hays 2008; Hays and Franzese 2007; Neumayer and Plümper 2012). Neglecting to account for spatial dependence in the data-generating process can lead to biased and inconsistent parameter estimates (LeSage and Pace 2009). A popular approach to modeling spatial dependence in the standard linear framework relies on the inclusion of a spatial lag. Usually a spatial lag represents the weighted average of the dependent variable in "neighboring" units. The neighborhood structure is defined through a spatial weights matrix and can be based on adjacency, nearest-neighbor, distance or other geographic or social connectivity concepts. The use of spatial lags for binary dependent variables or other distributions in the GLM setting has been employed in the analysis of conflict (Ward and Gleditsch 2002; Weidmann and Ward 2010) but presents formidable computational challenges (LeSage and Pace 2009). The correct estimation of parameters in the presence of the simultaneity between the dependent variable and the spatial lag becomes especially harrowing for large datasets.

Given that our African lattice has over 10,000 cells, computational hurdles become prohibitively high. Short of a correctly specified spatial lag model, many researchers rely on a simpler approach to avoid the computational issues of nonlinear spatial lag models. Any direct simultaneity can be avoided if the spatial lag is also temporally lagged. It is then only a standard covariate and can be included as such in the GLM specification. While not ideal, this approach is feasible and does capture some of the spatial dependence in the data. We calculate for our binary dependent variable a spatial conflict lag based on a six-nearest-neighbor spatial weights matrix in 2007. The online Appendix presents a table with the models from Table 1, including spatial lags. Across all models we find a statistically significant and positive effect of the spatial lag, suggesting that conflict in neighboring grids increases the likelihood of violence and underscores the presence of spatial dependence in the data. The cell phone coverage indicator is uniformly estimated to be positive, but just misses significance at the 10% level in the logit models. If we include country random effects and a control for the country mean of cell coverage to allow for correlated random effects or simply include country-level fixed effects, the effect is found to be significant below the 0.1% level.

Count Models

As an alternative to the indicator of conflict, we also employ the number of conflictual events in each grid cell as a dependent variable. The online Appendix shows parameter estimates and associated z statistics for a simple Poisson regression with robust standard errors, a negative binomial model to allow for overdispersion in the counts, and the same models with spatial lags. As with the binary dependent variable, the cell phone coverage indicator is estimated to have a positive effect on conflict counts and is statistically significant below the 0.1% level in the Poisson model and below the 10% level in the negative binomial model.

Alternative Measures, Natural Resources, and Ethnicity

One problem with using the UCDP conflict events as our dependent variable is potential measurement error in the conflict location. The UCDP data pinpoint latitude and longitude for each conflict event, but the accuracy of the location varies. For some events the exact location is identifiable, whereas for others, only the administrative unit or region is available. In the second case, UCDP uses the unit centroid as the location identifier. Fortunately, for each event the UCDP data record the quality of geographic information on a seven-point scale. We thus create a dependent binary and count variable that only considers events with fairly exact geographic information, to make sure our results are not biased by events where the exact location or spatial extent was unclear.[24]

In addition, we also consider the ACLED (Raleigh et al. 2010) conflict event data available for Africa from 1997 to 2010, which differs slightly in the definition of conflict events from UCDP. Importantly, ACLED also covers violent protests with death counts below the 25 person threshold. We repeat all analyses using binary and count dependent variables based on the alternative (*precise*) UCDP events and the ACLED events. Across both alternative measures, we obtain the same results in terms of substantive and statistical significance. For some models statistical significance even increases (all results are available in the online Appendix).

Our last alternative measure for the dependent variable takes advantage of new geo-coded data on social unrest in Africa (Salehyan *et al.* 2012). The "Social Conflict in Africa Database" (SCAD) codes news on a multitude of social conflict events, covering protests, riots, strikes, intercommunal conflict, and government violence against civilians, on the African continent from 1990 to 2011. Using this measure allows us to capture low intensity collective action that did not necessarily end in a large number of deaths. SCAD also provides the geographic coordinates of events. Identical to the previous analyses, we create an indicator and a count variable based on SCAD events for each grid cell. We use those observations that are geo-located with sufficient quality and are not already included in the ACLED database.[25] We run the same set of binary dependent variable models, count, and spatial lag models as before. While the results for our control variables change, reflecting the difference in processes between organized rebel violence and social unrest, for all models we still find a clear positive and highly statistically significant effect of cell phone coverage on the incidence of social conflict events (all results are available in the online Appendix).

Apart from considering alternative measures for the dependent variable, we also address two additional concerns of omitted variable bias. Recent studies on civil conflict and ethnicity have established a link between the political exclusion of ethnic minorities and the propensity for group conflict (Cederman and Girardin 2007; Cederman, Weidmann, and Gleditsch 2011; Cederman, Wimmer, and Min 2010). If politically excluded ethnic groups are more prone to engage in violent collective action and at the same time locations in which these groups are dominant are provided with less cell phone access, omitting information on ethnicity from our analysis might bias our estimates. To control for this possibility we utilize information on politically relevant local ethnic groups in each grid cell provided by the PRIO-GRID data, based on the Geo-referencing of Ethnic Groups (GREG) project (Weidmann, Rød, and Cederman 2010). Given the group identifier in each grid cell we join information on the status of political inclusion or exclusion at the national level in the Ethnic Power Relations Dataset for each group (Wucherpfennig *et al.* 2011). We

repeat the analysis for the binary and count models including a variable that measures the share of local ethnic groups that are politically excluded. For most models, we find that political exclusion of ethnic groups increases the probability of conflict, but has no effect on the direction or statistical significance of the cell phone coverage indicator (results are available in the online Appendix).

Similarly, as noted above, local natural resources might provide motives for local rebel groups to engage in extraction to secure access to economic rents (Collier and Hoeffler 2004; Lujala, Gleditsch, and Gilmore 2005). In addition, regions with lucrative petroleum or diamond deposits might receive better cell phone coverage as mining and oil companies can influence the construction of cell phone towers. To correct for potential omitted variable bias, we use information on the geographic location of diamond mines (Gilmore *et al.* 2005) and oil and gas deposits (Lujala, Rød, and Thieme 2007) and include an indicator variable for grid cells that cover a known resource deposit. As before, we re-estimate all models and find some evidence that petroleum increases the probability of conflict and diamond mines surprisingly reduce the incidence of violence. Though neither variable has any effect on the role of cell phone coverage, which stays consistently positive and statistically significant (results available in the online Appendix).

Matching

Alternative to the estimation of parametric models, we also explore the effect of cell phone coverage using matching methods. In particular, we rely on "Coarsened Exact Matching" (CEM) (Iacus, King, and Porro 2012). CEM bins observations into coarsened strata and matches based on the new groupings. This matching approach reduces imbalance in the sample based on all properties of the covariate distributions, not just differences of means or similar univariate statistics (Iacus, King, and Porro 2011). Details on the matching procedure are reported in the online Appendix. Overall, our matching-based estimates are very similar in magnitude to our original estimates and confirm the main finding.

Instrumental Variables

One important concern is the potential endogenity between conflict events and cell phone coverage in each grid cell. It is plausible that conflict destroys cell towers and reduces coverage, suggesting a potentially negative relationship in the data. Although we lag cell phone coverage by one year in our models to address causal ordering and the estimated positive effect suggests we might actually underestimate the true relationship, we aim to address fundamental endogeneity concerns with an explicit identification strategy relying on an instrumental variable.

Prior work on the spread of cell towers in Africa has identified a number of geographic characteristics that predict cell phone tower locations (Buys, Dasgupta, and Thomas 2009). However, in our case, for most of these variables the exclusion restriction of the instrumental variable estimator is likely to be violated since remoteness, difficult terrain, or population density have been found to predict conflict as well. Yet, in addition, Buys, Dasgupta, and Thomas (2009) identify the regulatory environment of African countries as an important predictor of cell phone coverage. A series of studies has found that healthy private competition in the cell phone market leads to better coverage and provision of cell phone services, in comparison to single-provider state-run systems (for references see Buys, Dasgupta, and Thomas (2009, 1495)). A World Bank study on telecommunications policy reform in 24 African economies finds important policy changes pertaining to privatization, increased competition, the formalization of regulations, and the creation of regulatory agencies, all contribute to improved coverage (The World Bank 2010). Buys, Dasgupta, and Thomas (2009) find the World Bank's Country Policy and Institutional Assessment (CPIA) measure of regulatory quality is an important variable that affects cell phone coverage, even for highly spatially disaggregated data. We argue that the CPIA regulatory coverage measure is a good instrument for our purposes, since it is a robust predictor of cell phone coverage, i.e., avoids "weak instrument" criticisms, and has a strong claim to justifying the exclusion restriction. While regulatory quality affects private market competitiveness and the extent of cell phone coverage, we believe it is unlikely that an alternative, unmeasured causal link to violence exists.[26]

A potential issue could be that poorer African countries were forced to introduce regulatory reform in light of budgetary pressures and demands by outside actors. However, we find no aggregate link between the level of development and a country's regulatory score, as measured by the World Bank data. Furthermore, the estimated models include a control for GDP per capita levels and hence any effects regulatory quality might exert on violent collective action through poverty is accounted for.

We use the average CPIA regulatory quality score from 2005 to 2007 as our instrument for cell phone coverage. Initially we estimate a simple linear probability model via two-stage least squares (2SLS) and robust standard errors, which generally does well in identifying marginal effects, even with binary dependent variables (Angrist and Pischke 2009, 197–205). We estimate models with and without the spatial conflict lag. For both models in the first stage regression of cell phone coverage on regulatory quality, our instrument, is highly statistically significant. The Kleibergen-Paap rk LM statistic and the Wald F statistic are very high and we are able to reject the null hypothesis of under-and weak identification. The results of the second stage are reported in Table 2, showing coefficient estimates and z statistics for the binary dependent variable models. Controls largely perform as expected, but more importantly the instrumented cell phone coverage variable is positive and highly statistically significant for both models. The exogenous variation in cell phone coverage induced by the regulatory quality increases the probability of local conflict events.[27]

Panel Data

Our last approach to estimate the effect of cell coverage on violent collective action exploits variation over time. Data on cell phone coverage is available for 2007, 2008, and 2009. We utilize these data to construct a short, three-year panel of our grid cells in 2008, 2009, and 2010. This offers us an additional opportunity to not only use geographic variation in coverage, but also changes over time. While in 2007 cell phone coverage existed in 36.9% of all grid cells, that value increased to 37.8% in 2008 and 42.5% in 2009. The expansion of cell phone coverage allows us to compare grid cells before and after the expansion. In a first step, we estimate OLS models for the binary and count dependent variable with country and year fixed effects and our standard set of controls, clustering standard errors at the country level. Again, we find a highly statistically significant and positive effect of cell phone coverage on violent conflict events (detailed results are presented in the online Appendix). More importantly, the panel structure allows us to now include grid-cell fixed effects. Here, we control for all observed and unobserved factors for each grid cell in the three-year period from 2008 to 2010. Since our standard control variables at the grid level are constant over time, we only include the cell phone coverage indicator as a predictor, apart from the grid cell and year effects. Table 3 shows the estimated coefficient for the cell phone coverage indicator for the binary and count measure.

For both models, the cell phone coverage variable is estimated to be positive and is statistically significant below the 5% and 1% level, respectively. The coefficient

Table 2 Instrumental Variable Models

	2SLS, Robust SE	2SLS, Robust SE
(Intercept)	−0.141***	−0.100***
	(−6.55)	(−5.42)
Spatial Lag		0.522***
		(9.91)
Pre-2000 Conflict	0.003***	0.001
	(3.98)	(2.28)
Border Distance	.0001***	.0001***
	(4.31)	(3.63)
Capital Distance	.0001***	.0001***
	(7.93)	(6.45)
Population	−0.000†	0.000
	(−1.88)	(−0.79)
Pct Mountainous	0.065***	0.033**
	(4.69)	(2.71)
Pct Irrigation	−0.004***	−0.022**
	(−4.31)	(−2.73)
GDP pc	0.000	0.000
	(0.57)	(1.14)
Cell Phone Coverage	0.289***	0.183***
	(6.33)	(4.62)
Kleibergen-Paap rk LM Statistic	108.698	110.235
Kleibergen-Paap rk Wald F Statistic	125.442	126.637
N	6598	6598

$^{\dagger}p = 0.1.$ $^{*}p = 0.05.$ $^{**}p = 0.01.$ $^{***}p = 0.001.$

Table 3. Panel Data

	(1) Binary DV, OLS, Clustered SE	(2) Count DV, OLS, Clustered SE
Cell Phone Coverage	0.0116*	0.0502**
	(0.00547)	(0.0158)
Cell & Year Effects	Yes	Yes
Observations	32022	32022
Adjusted R2	0.004	0.001
F	21.33	5.732

$^{*}p < 0.05.$ $^{**}p < 0.01.$
Clustered standard errors in parentheses.

size suggests an increase of one percentage point for the linear probability model and 0.05 events with the count dependent variable, very much in line with our prior estimates of the effect size. The results are substantively unchanged if we log-transform the count to make the distribution appear more normally distributed or alternatively estimate a Poisson fixed effects model. Again, this confirms our previous findings that the expansion of cell phone coverage in Africa facilitates violent conflict events.

Overall, our quantitative models demonstrate a clear positive association between cell phone coverage and the occurrence of violent organized collective action. This effect persists when controlling for a series of standard explanations of violence, as well as unobserved, time-invariant factors at the country and even grid level. Plainly, our results suggest that local cell phone coverage facilitates violent collective action on the African continent.

Conclusion

Whereas prior research has emphasized the positive consequences of expanding cell phone coverage across the African continent, this article is concerned with possible negative externalities. In general, increasing cell phone coverage in developing countries has been associated with higher levels of market efficiency, especially across labor markets and private goods markets. Cell phones decrease information asymmetries between market participants and facilitate economic exchange. However, few works have been concerned with the effect of new communication technologies in the political sphere. In particular, to our knowledge only Shapiro and Weidmann (2012) have examined how cell phone technology affects the propensity for political violence. Shapiro and Weidmann (2012) find that in the case of Iraq, the location of cell phone towers is negatively associated with violence.

In contrast, in this article we argue and provide evidence to show that cell phone technology can increase the ability of rebel groups to overcome collective action problems. In particular, cell phones lead to a boost in the capacity of rebels to communicate and monitor in-group behavior, thus increasing in-group cooperation. Furthermore, cell phones allow for coordination of insurgent activity across geographically distant locations.

We test the empirical relationship between cell phone coverage and the location of violent conflict across the African continent. To do so we utilize a grid of 55 km × 55 km cells across Africa. Using data on GSM2 coverage provided by the GSMA and georeferenced data on conflictual events by UCDP (Melander and Sundberg 2011; Sundberg, Lindgren, and Padskocimaite 2011), we create measures for each grid cell indicating whether cell phone coverage was available in 2007, as well as an indicator and count of conflictual events for 2008. In addition we include numerous other covariates to avoid potential omitted variable bias.

Across a wide range of empirical models, including various control variables and robustness checks, we find that cell phone coverage has a significant and substantive effect on the probability of conflict occurrence. When cell phone coverage is present, the likelihood of conflict occurrence is substantially higher than otherwise. We consistently find a relationship between cell phone coverage and violent conflict across standard logit models, models including controls for spatial correlation, random or fixed effects, as well as count models. In addition to traditional robustness checks, we furthermore include instrumental variable regressions to test for the possibility of endogeneity and panel data models.

The results in this article stand in contrast to the findings presented by Shapiro and Weidmann (2012) regarding the relationship between cell phones and violence in Iraq. However, we believe it is reasonable that the effects of cell phones are different across these cases. The context of political violence in African countries is much different from that in Iraq. The military capacity of the anti-insurgent forces is likely higher in the case of the U.S. military and government forces in Iraq. While government forces in Iraq have the ability to monitor cell phone activity of insurgents, this is much less likely for many African governments, especially with the more prominent role of private enterprises in spreading technology. In addition, explicit whistle blower programs have so far only been used rarely in Africa (Livingston 2011). Similarly, the technological and strategic capacity of anti-insurgency forces in Iraq is likely to be much higher than that of many African forces. Thus the expansion of cell phone coverage may be less advantageous to Iraqi insurgents, whereas in the right context, rebels can make great use of it. At a minimum our findings suggest that we need further research investigating the specific conditions under which modern technology plays a role in insurgent and counterinsurgency activities.

Numerous exciting avenues for future research exist. First, a better theoretical understanding on how communication technology can affect collective action is warranted. The underlying mechanism for our findings needs to be unpacked further. Distinguishing between collective action and coordination problems might be particularly important. Our results only imply an association at the aggregate level of the spatial unit and do not reveal the exact causal mechanism in operation or the role of individual-level behavior. Naturally, future research will have to engage these questions in more detail and bring different data to bear. We suspect that the use of communication technology varies across contexts, rebel and insurgent groups, as well as counterinsurgency strategies. Exploring potential interactions with country or group-level variables will further illuminate the effects of communication technology on violence. Prior research on internal rebel group organization and the use of violence has focused on the role of internal norms and discipline (Weinstein 2007). Similar to recruitment strategies and the use of violence against civilians, the adoption of technology and its effects on rebel group behavior appear as promising topics of research to complement our aggregate-level findings.

Second, cell phone coverage should similarly have an effect on other forms of collective action, such as nonviolent protests. We do present some auxiliary evidence on the link between cell phone coverage and protest behavior using aggregate data (SCAD), but more research is warranted. The marginal benefits of modern communication technology likely varies across violent and nonviolent activities, which could lead to important substitution effects.

We do not believe that the spread of cell phone technology has an overall negative effect on the African continent. The increase in violence induced by better communication might represent a short-term technological shock, while the positive effects of better communication networks on growth and political behavior may mitigate root causes of conflict in the long run.

If the economics literature is correct in assuming that cell phone technology increases the productivity of farmers or service-oriented industries, then the spread of cell phones throughout Africa increases the returns to productive economic activity in the long term. This implies that the opportunity costs to violence (i.e., lost wages) increase, reducing the incentive to fight. Several formal models have identified this potential link between violence and economic activity (Chas-sang and Padro-i-Miguel 2009; Dal Bó and Dal Bó 2011; Grossman 1991; Grossman and Kim 1995). Some empirical work has shown a link between increased returns to labor-intensive production and lower violence in Colombia (Dube and Vargas forthcoming), while another study on the link between unemployment and insurgent activity in Iraq and the Philippines finds the opposite effect (Berman, Felter, and Shapiro 2009). However, the effect of cell phones on incomes is likely to be a long-term process. If cell phone coverage increases economic activity and economic growth in the long run, it may indirectly lower political violence in the long term. However, we find that given contextual factors which make conflict likely, in the short run, cell phones increase the propensity for violent events.

Finally, the effect of communication technology on other aspects of the political arena is still quite unclear and has not been studied widely. More research is needed on whether the availability of widespread communication between citizens decreases the likelihood of electoral fraud or government repression, as, for example, found by Aker, Collier, and Vincente (2011) and Bailard

(2009). Can the possibility of private communication serve as a substitute for free and fair media and what are the effects across different political regimes? The increasing availability of spatially disaggregated data in combination with these data on cell phone coverage in Africa should allow us to answer a number of these questions in future projects.

Notes

1. However, recent research has tested the possible impact of mobile phones on voter information and participation, as well as its possible impact on fighting electoral fraud and corruption (Aker, Collier, and Vincente 2011; Bailard 2009).

2. See, for example, Earl and Kimport (2011) and Diamond and Plattner (2012).

3. To our knowledge, the only research that explicitly engages this question is a working paper by Shapiro and Weidmann (2012) on insurgent activity and cell phone towers in Iraq. The authors document a decrease in insurgent violence in areas with improved access to cell phone communication, which is attributed to the reduced cost of communicating information to counterinsurgency agents. We discuss their work in more detail further below.

4. A particular success story is a startup company named Esoko Ltd. from Ghana, which is active in 15 African countries and provides a mobile internet platform to share, collect, and analyze data regarding prices of agricultural goods (Mutua 2011).

5. The spread of this technology is exemplified by recent investments by Visa (Alliy 2011; Quandzie 2011). Further positive examples can be found in an OECD report on information technology and infrastructure in Africa (Africa Partnership Program 2008).

6. However, one should note that governments are always involved to some degree, even if it is only through granting permits and regulating the creation of cell phone networks.

7. More examples of protest mobilization via information technology in general and cell phones in particular can be found in Diamond (2012).

8. A detailed analysis of a simple cross-tab and the regression model can be found in the online Appendix (http://www.journals.cambridge.org/psr2013007).

9. For example, text messaging and cell phone communication is often used to relay newsworthy events and government repression to media sources outside the country when traditional reporting is impossible. As journalists are unable to work from within the country, let alone attend protest or other violent events, the communication of news is left to actors themselves or bystanders via text messaging (see, for example, Fowler 2007).

10. Violent events are defined by UCDP as the following: "The incidence of the use of armed force by an organised

actor against another organized actor, or against civilians, resulting in at least 1 direct death in either the best, low or high estimate categories at a specific location and for a specific temporal duration" (Sundberg, Lindgren, and Padskocimaite 2011, 5). The UCDP data combine information on state-based armed conflict, nonstate conflict, and one-sided violence. We believe our theoretical argument applies to some degree to all forms of violence, but in future research we hope to differentiate.

11. A number of robustness tests were performed by using the ACLED (Raleigh et al. 2010) conflictual event data as the dependent variable, as well as excluding those events with low precision on the conflict location. The results are presented in additional tables in the online Appendix.

12. Research in sociology and political science has evaluated the effect of "newsworthiness" on the likelihood of an event being reported in various news sources. The intensity or violence of an event is one of the important factors that often increases the chances of inclusion (Earl et al. 2004). Hence, by relying on UCDP-GED data, we maximize the chances that even events outside of areas with cell coverage are reported.

13. In addition, in our main empirical models we collapse the event counts to a simple binary dummy variable, which reduces the scope of potential measurement bias: the exact reporting of event counts might be influenced by the availability of modern communication technology, but an information on the mere presence of any violent events in a grid-cell year is much less likely affected by underreporting. We also tested for an interaction between capital distance and cell phone coverage. We find that the effect of cell phone coverage is weaker in areas far from the capital, which is the opposite of what one would expect if a positive association were solely driven by measurement bias. Last, we also visually compared maps of violence in Sierra Leone's civil war (1991–2002) based on the UCDP-GED data with a map based on household-level survey data collected by the World Bank. The map is provided by Sacks and Larizza (2012). The visual comparison reveals that the UCDP-GED data very clearly track patterns of self-reported violence in the 153 chieftains in Sierra Leone (see online Appendix). Importantly, UCDP GED constructed these event data based on news reports without local cell phone coverage (1991–2002), i.e. UCDP GED is able to report violent events of sufficient quality irrespective of modern communication technology.

14. GSMA website: http://www.gsma.com/home/; Collins Bartholomew website: http://www.bartholomewmaps.com/.

15. In addition we have data on the 3G network coverage. 3G coverage though is much smaller and concentrated in a few countries, e.g., South Africa. Since areas with 3G coverage are a strict subset of 2G coverage, i.e., any area with 3G coverage also has 2G coverage, but not vice versa, 3G networks are unlikely to have any appreciable effect on collective action above and beyond 2G technology.

16. While it would certainly be preferable to use the percentage of area covered by cell phone networks as our main independent variable, we are confident that given the size of the individual grid cells (55 km × 55 km) using an indicator variable should not affect our results substantively.

17. In addition this helps to control for under-reporting of events in remote areas.

18. As an alternative to using simple population counts, we also consider a log transformation. One issue for the transformation is the presence of grid cells with zero population. To address this issue (even if insufficiently), we add 1 to each population count to allow for the log transformation. Using log transformed population counts instead of the original counts has no implication for the effect of population on conflict, but does weaken our main findings for cell phone coverage somewhat. Importantly though, for our most conservative models and the instrumental variable estimation, all main findings are unaffected.

19. As an alternative measure we tested the share of forested land in each grid cell, which has no effect on our main results.

20. Unfortunately this measure is only available for the year 2000, however it should be highly correlated with later data.

21. Originally the GDP data are calculated for 1×1 decimal degree grid cells, thus each grid cell in the G-Econ dataset contains four grid cells of the PRIO-Grid dataset. We also consider a log transformation for the GDP variable, with no effect on the findings for GDP per capita or the cell phone coverage variable.

22. We estimate the mixed effects model using the lmer( ) function in R.

23. We present standard robust standard errors but the results are very similar with standard errors clustered at the country level.

24. Given the 55-km × 55-km grid size, we use all events that were coded 1–3 on the geographic location quality variable, i.e., observations with exact know locations, or where the limited area around an exact location or the district/municipality is known.

25. Specifically, we exclude events for which the geographic location was "nationwide" or "unknown."

26. More precisely, we assume that the instrument is independent of potential outcomes, that regulatory quality does not affect conflict other than through cell phone coverage, that the instrument is a good predictor of cell phone coverage, and, last, monotonicity in the first stage, which then identifies the local average treatment effect (LATE) (Angrist and Imbens 1994). The LATE here is the effect of cell phone coverage on violence in grid cells that received coverage due to regulatory effects, but not through other sources of cell phone service provision.

27. In addition, we obtain statistically positive results if conflict counts are the dependent variable. These results provide an important additional layer of confidence in our results. We also implement bivariate probit models with our regulatory quality score as a predictor in the equation for cell phone coverage. Using robust as well as clustered standard errors, we again find a clear positive and statistically significant effect of cell phone coverage on the probability of conflict (all results are available in the online Appendix).

References

Abraham, Reuben. 2007. "Mobile Phones and Economic Development: Evidence from the Fishing Industry in India." Information *Technologies and International Development* 4 (1): 5–17.

Aday, Sean, Farrell Henry, Lynch Marc, Sides John, and Deen Freelon. 2012. *Blogs and Bullets II: New Media and Conflict after the Arab Spring.* Tech. rept. United States Institute of Peace.

Africa Partnership Program. 2008. "ICT in Africa: Boosting Economic Growth and Poverty Reduction." Working Paper. 10th Meeting of the Africa Partnership Forum. http://www.oecd.org/dataoecd/46/51/40314752.pdf.

Aker, Jenny C. 2010. "Information from Markets Near and Far: Mobile Phones and Agricultural Markets in Niger." *American Economic Journal: Applied Economics* 2: 46–59.

Aker, Jenny C., Paul Collier, and Pedro C. Vincente. 2011. "Is Information Power? Using Cell Phones during an Election in Mozambique." Working Paper. http://www.pedrovicente.org/cell. pdf (Accessed April 22, 2012).

Aker, Jenny C., Christopher Ksoll, and Travis J. Lybbert. 2012. "Can Mobile Phones Improve Learning? Evidence from a Field Experiment in Niger." *American Economic Journal: Applied Economics* 4 (4): 94–120.

Aker, Jenny C., and Isaac M. Mbiti. 2010. "Mobile Phones and Economic Development in Africa." *Journal of Economic Perspectives* 24 (3): 207–32.

Alliy, Mbwana. 2011. *Visa Gets Serious: Let the Africa Mobile Payment Wars Begin.* Afrinnovator: Putting Africa on the Map. http://afrinnovator.com/blog/2011/11/20/visa-gets-serious-let-the-afric a-mobile-payments-wars-begin/ (Accessed March 22, 2011).

Angrist, Joshua D., and Guido Imbens. 1994. "Identification and Estimation of Local Average Treatment Effects." *Econometrica* 62 (2): 467–75.

Angrist, Joshua D., and Joern-Steffen Pischke. 2009. *Mostly Harmless Econometrics.* Princton, NJ: Princeton University Press.

Bailard, Catie Snow. 2009. "Mobile Phone Diffusion and Corruption in Africa." *Political Communication* 26 (3): 333–53.

Beck, Neal, Kristian Skrede Gleditsch, and Kyle Beardsley. 2006. "Space Is More than Geography: Using Spatial Econometrics in the Study of Political Economy." *International Studies Quarterly* 50 (1): 27–44.

Bell, Andrew, and Kelvyn Jones. 2012 (May). "Explaining Fixed Effects: Random Effects Modelling of Time-Series Cross-Sectional and Panel Data." Working Paper.

Berman, Sheri. 1997. "Civil Society and the Collapse of the Weimar Republic." *World Politics* 49 (3): 401–29.

Berman, Eli, Joseph Felter, and Jacob N. Shapiro. 2009. "Do Working Men Rebel? Insurgency and Unemployment in Iraq and the Philippines." NBER Working Paper.

Blattman, Christopher. 2009. "From Violence to Voting: War and Political Participation in Uganda." *American Political Science Review* 103 (2): 231–47.

Blattman, Christopher, and Edward Miguel. 2010. "Civil War." *Journal of Economic Literature* 48 (1): 3–57.

Bradshaw, Tim. 2009. "Twitter Used by Protest Groups to Galvanise Forces." *Financial Times*. http://search.proquest.com/docview/250171039?accountid=10598 (Accessed September 15, 2012).

Brand, Jon. 2007. "Iraqi Insurgents Target Water and Electricity, But Spare the Cell Phone." *PBS Online NewsHour.* http://www.pbs.org/newshour/extra/features/janjune07/infrastructure_1-29.html (Accessed October 13, 2012).

Breuer, Anita, Todd Landman, and Dorothea Farquhar. 2012. "Social Media and Protest Mobilization: Evidence from the Tunisian Revolution." Paper prepared for the 4th European Communication Conference for the Euopean Communication Research and Education Conference (ECREA) 2012.

Buhaug, Halvard, Kristian Skrede Gleditsch, Helge Holtermann, Gudrun Østby, and Andreas Forø. 2011. "It's the Local Economy, Stupid! Geographic Wealth Dispersion and Conflict Outbreak Location." *Journal of Conflict Resolution* 55 (5): 814–40.

Buhaug, Halvard, and Jan Ketil Rød. 2006. "Local Determinants of African Civil Wars, 1970–2001." *Political Geography* 25 (3): 315–35.

Buys, Piet, Susmita Dasgupta, and Timothy Thomas. 2009. "Determinants of a Digital Divide in Sub-Saharan Africa: A Spatial Econometric Analysis of Cell Phone Coverage." *World Development* 37 (9): 1494–505.

Cederman, Lars-Erik, and Luc Girardin. 2007. "Beyond Fractionalization: Mapping Ethnicity onto Nationalist Insurgencies." *American Political Science Review* 101 (1): 173–85.

Cederman, Lars-Erik, Nils B. Weidmann, and Kristian Skrede Gleditsch. 2011. "Horizontal Inequalities and Ethnonationalist Civil War: A Global Comparison." *American Political Science Review* 105 (3): 478–95.

Cederman, Lars-Erik, Andreas Wimmer, and Brian Min. 2010. "Why Do Ethnic Groups Rebel? New Data and Analysis." *World Politics* 62 (1): 87–119.

Chassang, Sylvain, and Gerard Padro-i-Miguel. 2009. "Economic Shocks and Civil War." *Quarterly Journal of Political Science* 4 (3): 211–28.

CIESIN. 2005. "Center for International Earth Science Information Network (CIESIN), Columbia University; and Centro Internacional de Agricultura Tropical (CIAT)." *Gridded Population of the World Version 3 (GPWv3): Population Density Grids*. Palisades, NY: Socioeconomic Data and Applications Center (SEDAC), Columbia University. http://sedac.ciesin.columbia.edu/gpw (Accessed June 20, 2011).

Collier, Paul, V. L. Elliott, Harvard Hegre, Anke Hoeffler, Marta Reynal-Querol, and Nicolas Sambanis. 2003. *Breaking the Conflict Trap. Civil War and Development Policy*. Washington, DC and New York, NY: World Bank and Oxford University Press.

Collier, Paul, and Anke Hoeffler. 2004. "Greed and Grievance in Civil War." *Oxford Economic Papers* 56 (4): 563–95.

Collier, Paul, and Anke Hoeffler. 2007. "Civil War." *Handbook of Defense Economics*, Vol. 2, eds. Sandler Todd, and Keith Hartley. New York, NY: Elsevier B.V., 712–738.

Cordesman, Anthony H. 2005. "Iraq's Evolving Insurgency." Working Paper. Center for Strategic and International Studies.

Dal Bó, Ernesto, and Pedro Dal Bó. 2011. "Workers, Warriors and Criminals: Social Conflict in General Equilibrium." *Journal of the European Economic Association* 9 (4): 646–77.

Diamond, Larry. 2012. "Liberation Technology." *Liberation Technology: Social Media and the Struggle for Democracy*, eds. Diamond Larry, and Marc F. Plattner. Baltimore, MD: The Johns Hopkins University Press, 3–17.

Diamond, Larry, and Marc F. Plattner, eds. 2012. *Liberation Technology: Social Media and the Struggle for Democracy*. Baltimore, MD: Johns Hopkins University Press.

Donner, Jonathan, and Camilo Andres Tellez. 2008. "Mobile Banking and Economic Development: Linking Adoption, Impact, and Use." *Asian Journal of Communication* 18 (4): 332.

Dube, Oeindrila, and Juan Vargas. "Commodity Price Shocks and Civil Conflict: Evidence from Colombia." *Review of Economic Studies*. Forthcoming.

Earl, Jennifer, and Katrina Kimport. 2011. *Digitally Enabled Social Change: Activism in the Internet Age*. Cambridge, MA: MIT Press.

Earl, Jennifer, Andrew Martin, John D. McCarthy, and Sarah A. Soule. 2004. "The Use of Newspaper Data in the Study of Collective Action." *Annual Review of Sociology* 30: 65–80.

Eck, Kristine. 2012. "In Data We Trust? A Comparison of UCDP GED and ACLED Conflict Events Datasets." *Cooperation and Conflict* 47 (1): 124–41.

Edmond, Chris. 2012. "Information Manipulation, Coordination, and Regime Change." Working Paper.

Fearon, James D., Kimuli Kasara, and David D. Laitin. 2007. "Ethnicity Minority Rule and Civil War Onset." *American Political Science Review* 101 (1): 187–93.

Fearon, James D., and David D. Laitin. 2003. "Ethnicity, Insurgency, and Civil War." *American Political Science Review* 97 (1): 75–88.

Foster, Vivien, and Cecilia Briceño Garmendia, eds. 2010. "Information and Communication Technologies: A Boost for Growth." *Africa's Infrastructure: A Time for Transformation*. Washington, DC: The International Bank for Reconstruction and Development/The World Bank, 165–180.

Fowler, Geoffrey A. 2007. "'Citizen Journalists' Evade Blackout on Myanmar News." *Wall Street Journal*. http://online.wsj.com/article/SB119090803430841433.html?mod=hps_us_page one (Accessed May 29, 2012).

Franzese, Robert J., and Jude C. Hays. 2008. "Interdependence in Comparative Politics: Substance, Theory, Empirics, Substance." *Comparative Political Studies* 41 (4/5): 742–80.

Gelman, Andrew, and Jennifer Hill. 2008. *Data Analysis Using Regression and Multilevel/Hierarchical Models*. New York, NY: Cambridge University Press.

Gilmore, Elisabeth, Nils Petter Gleditsch, Päivi Lujala, and Jan Ketil Rød. 2005. "Conflict Diamonds: A New Dataset." *Conflict Management and Peace Science* 22 (3): 257–92.

Greenhill, Brian, Michael D. Ward, and Audrey Sacks. 2011. "The Separation Plot: A New Visual Method for Evaluating the Fit of Binary Models." *American Journal of Political Science* 55 (4): 991–1002.

Grossman, Herschel I. 1991. "A General Equilirium Model of Insurrections." *American Economic Review* 81 (4): 912–21.

Grossman, Herschel I., and Minseong Kim. 1995. "Swords or Plowshares? A Theory of the Security of Claims to Property." *Journal of Political Economy* 103 (6): 1275–88.

Hays, Jude, and Robert Franzese. 2007. "Spatial-Econometric Models of Cross-Sectional Interdependence in Political Science Panel and TSCS Data." *Political Analysis* 15 (2): 140–64.

Iacus, Stefano M., Gary King, and Giuseppe Porro. 2011. "Multivariate Matching Methods that are Monotonic Imbalance Bounding." *Journal of the American Statistical Association* 106 (493): 345–361.

Iacus, Stefano M., Gary King, and Giuseppe Porro. 2012. "Causal Inference Without Balance Checking: Coarsened Exact Matching." *Political Analysis* 20 (1): 1–24.

Kalyvas, Stathis N. 2006. *The Logic of Violence in Civil Wars*. Cambridge, MA: Cambridge University Press.

Kalyvas, Stathis N., and Matthew Adam Kocher. 2007. "How 'Free' is Free Riding in Civil Wars? Violence, Insurgency, and the Collective Action Problem." *World Politics* 59 (2): 177–216.

King, Gary, Michael Tomz, and Jason Wittenberg. 2000. "Making the Most of Statistical Analyses: Improving Interpretation and Presentation." *American Journal of Political Science* 44 (2): 347–61.

Kuran, Timur. 1991. "Now Out of Never: The Element of Surprise in the East European Revolution of 1989." *World Politics* 44 (1): 7–48.

Lapper, Richard. 2010 (January 29). *Youthful Protesters Help Shape New Kind of Politics*. Financial Times. http://search.proquest.com/docview/250264463?accountid=10598 (Accessed May 29, 2012).

Leahy, Kevin C. 2005. "The Impact of Technology on the Command, Control, and Organizational Structure of Insurgent Groups." Masters thesis. U.S. Army Command and General Staff College.

LeSage, James, and R. Kelley Pace. 2009. *Introduction to Spatial Econometrics.* Boca Raton, FL: CRC Press.

Livingston, Steven. 2011. "Africa's Evolving Infosystems: A Pathway to Security and Stability." Africa Center for Strategic Studies Research Paper No. 2.

Lohmann, Susanne. 1994. "Dynamics of Informational Cascades: The Monday Demonstrations in Leipzig, East Germany, 1989-1991." *World Politics* 47: 42–101.

Lujala, Päivi, Halvard Buhaug, and Scott Gates. 2009. "Geography, Rebel Capability, and the Duration of Civil Conflict." *Journal of Conflict Resolution* 53 (4): 544–69.

Lujala, Päivi, Nils Petter Gleditsch, and Elisabeth Gilmore. 2005. "A Diamond Curse? Civil War and a Lootable Resource." *Journal of Conflict Resolution* 49 (4): 538–62.

Lujala, Päivi, Jan Ketil Rød, and Nadia Thieme. 2007. "Fighting Over Oil: Introducing a New Dataset." *Conflict Management and Peace Science* 24 (3): 239–56.

Mattes, Robert, Michael Bratton, Yul Derek Davids, and Cherrel Africa. 2010. *Afrobarometer: Round IV 2008.* Dataset.

Melander, Erik, and Ralph Sundberg. 2011. "Climate Change, Environmental Stress, and Violent Conflict—Test Introducing the UCDP Georeferenced Event Dataset." Paper presented at the International Studies Association, March 16–19, Montreal, Canada.

Metternich, Nils W. 2011. "Expecting Elections: Interventions, Ethnic Support, and the Duration of Civil Wars." *Journal of Conflict Resolution* 55 (6): 909–37.

Mutua, Will. 2011. "Startup Watch: Esoko Ltd: Powering an Agric Revolution." *Afrinnovator: Putting Africa on the Map.* http://afrinnovator.com/blog/2011/08/13/startup-watch-esoko-ltd-powerin g-an-agric-revolution/ (Accessed April 22, 2012).

Neumayer, Eric, and Thomas Plümper. 2012. "Conditional Spatial Policy Dependence: Theory and Model Specification." *Comparative Political Studies* 45 (7): 819–49.

Nordhaus, William D. 2006. "Geography and Macroeconomics: New Data and New Findings." *Proceedings of the National Academy of Sciences of the USA* 103 (10): 3510–17.

Olson, Mancur. 1965. *The Logic of Collective Action. Public Goods and the Theory of Groups.* Cambridge, MA: Harvard University Press.

Peterson, Scott. 2012. "Syria's iPhone Insurgency Makes for Smarter Rebellion." *The Christian Science Monitor.* http://www.csmonitor.com/World/Middle-East/2012/0801/Syria-s-iPhone-ins urgency-makes-for-smarter-rebellion (Accessed November 13, 2012).

Philippine Daily Inquirer. 2001. "Text Messages Bring Political Protests to Cyberspace." *Philippine Daily Inquirer* (January) http://news.google.com/newspapers?id=PX42AA AAIBAJ&sjid=hCUMAAAAIBAJ&dq=political 2012).

Quandzie, Ekow. 2011. "Africa Leads in Mobile Money Deployment as Users Hit Over 40 Million." *Ghana Business News.* http://www.ghanabusinessnews.com/2011/10/30/africa-leads-in-mobile-mone y-deployment-as-users-hits-over-40-million/ (Accessed April 22, 2012).

Raleigh, Clionadh, Andrew Linke, Havard Hegre, and Joakim Karlsen. 2010. "Introducing ACLED-Armed Conflict Location and Event Data." *Journal of Peace Research* 47 (5): 1–10.

Reno, William. 2011. *Warfare in Independent Africa.* Cambridge, UK: Cambridge University Press.

Ross, Michael L. 2006. "A Closer Look At Oil, Diamonds, and Civil War." *Annual Review of Political Science* 9: 265–300.

Sacks, Audrey, and Marco Larizza. 2012 (February). "Why Quality Matters: A Multi-Level Analysis of Decentralization, Local Government Performance and Trustworthy Government in Post-Conflict Sierra Leone." Working Paper.

Salehyan, Idean, Cullen S. Hendrix, Christina Case, Christopher Linebarger, Emily Stull, and Jennifer Williams. 2012. "The Social Conflict in Africa Database: New Data and Applications." *International Interactions* 38 (4): 503–11. www.scaddata.org (Accessed June 25, 2012).

Sambanis, Nicholas. 2002. "A Review of Recent Advances And Future Directions in the Quantitative Literature on Civil War." *Defence and Peace Economics* 13 (3): 215–43.

Shadmehr, Mehdi, and Dan Bernhardt. 2011. "Collective Action with Uncertain Payoffs: Coordination, Public Signals, and Punishment Dilemmas." *American Political Science Review* 105 (4): 829–51.

Shapiro, Jacob N., and Nils B. Weidmann. 2012. "Is the Phone Mightier than the Sword? Cell Phones and Insurgent Violence in Iraq." Working Paper. www.princeton.edu/~jns/papers/SW_2011_Cell_Phones_Insurgency_06SEP12.pdf (Accessed September 20, 2012).

Sherwood, Bob. 2011 (August 10). "Police Face Mobile Network Spreading its Angry Message." *Financial Times.* http://search.proquest.com/docview/882342765?acco untid=10598 (Accessed May 29, 2012).

Shirky, Clay. 2008. *Here Comes Everybody: The Power of Organizing Without Organizations.* London, UK: Allen Lane, Penguin Group.

Siebert, Stefan, Petra Döll, Jippe Hoogeveen, J-M Frenken, Karen Frenken, and Sebastian Feick. 2007. "Development and Validation of the Global Map of Irrigation Areas." *Hydrology and Earth System Sciences* 9 (5): 535–47.

Stroher, Tiffany. 2007. "Cell Phone Use by Insurgents in Iraq." Working Paper. Urban Warfare Analysis Center.

Sundberg, Ralph, Mathilda Lindgren, and Ausra Padskocimaite. 2011. *UCDP GED Codebook version 1.0-2011.* Code-book. Department of Peace and Conflict Research, Uppsala University. http://ucdp.uu.se/ged/data/ucdp_ged_v.1.0-codebook. pdf (Accessed January 20, 2012).

The Economist 2012. "Business this Week." *The Economist.* http://www.economist.com/node/21538210 (Accessed March 24, 2012).

The World Bank 2011. *The World Development Report 2011: Conflict, Security, and Development* Washington, DC: The World Bank Group.

Tollefsen, Andrea Forø, Havard Strand, and Halvard Buhaug. 2012. "PRIO-GRID: A Unified Spatial Data Structure." *Journal of Peace Research* 49 (2): 363–74.

Tomz, Mike, Gary King, and Langche Zeng. 2003. "ReLogit: Rare Events Logistic Regression." *Journal of Statistical Software* 8 (2): 246–47.

UNEP-WCMC World Conservation Monitoring Centre. 2002. *Mountain Watch 2002*. http://www.unep-wcmc.org/mountains/mountain_watch/pdfs/WholeReport.pdf (Accessed September 15, 2012).

Ward, Michael D., and Kristian Skrede Gleditsch. 2002. "Location, Location, Location: An MCMC Approach to Modeling the Spatial Context of War." *Political Analysis* 10 (3): 244–60.

Warren, T. Camber. 2013. "Not by the Sword Alone: Soft Power, Mass Media, and the Production of State Sovereignty." *International Organization*. Forthcoming.

Weidmann, Nils B. 2009. "Geography as Motivation and Opportunity: Group Concentration and Ethnic Conflict." *Journal of Conflict Resolution* 53 (4): 526–43.

Weidmann, Nils B., Jan Ketil Rød, and Lars-Erik Cederman. 2010. "Representing Ethnic Groups in Space: A New Dataset." *Journal of Peace Research* 47 (4): 491–99.

Weidmann, Nils B., and Michael D. Ward. 2010. "Predicting Conflict in Space and Time." *Journal of Conflict Resolution* 54 (6): 883–901.

Weinstein, Jeremy M. 2007. *Inside Rebellion: The Politics of Insurgent Violence*. New York: Cambridge University Press.

Wood, Elisabeth J. 2003. *Insurgent Collective Action and Civil War in El Salvador*. New York: Cambridge University Press.

Wucherpfennig, Julian, Nils W. Metternich, Lars-Erik Cederman, and Kristian Skrede Gleditsch. 2012. "Ethnicity, the State, and the Duration of Civil War." *World Politics* 64 (1): 79–115.

Wucherpfennig, Julian, Nils B. Weidmann, Luc Girardin, Lars-Erik Cederman, and Andreas Wimmer. 2011. "Politically Relevant Ethnic Groups Across Space and Time: Introducing the GeoEPR Dataset." *Conflict Management and Peace Science* 10 (10): 1–15.

Yanagizawa-Drott, David. 2012. "Propaganda and Conflict: Theory and Evidence From the Rwandan Genocide." Working Paper.

CPSIA information can be obtained at www.ICGtesting.com
Printed in the USA
LVOW02s0630240715

447093LV00004B/9/P